Scientific Foundations and Practical Applications of Periodization

G. Gregory Haff, PhD

Library of Congress Cataloging-in-Publication Data

Names: Haff, G. Gregory, 1969- author.
Title: Scientific foundations and practical applications of periodization /
  G. Gregory Haff, PhD.
Description: First edition. | Champaign, IL : Human Kinetics, [2025] |
  Includes bibliographical references and index.
Identifiers: LCCN 2023034531 (print) | LCCN 2023034532 (ebook) | ISBN
  9781492561675 (paperback) | ISBN 9781718217720 (epub) | ISBN
  9781492561682 (pdf)
Subjects: LCSH: Periodization training. | Coaching (Athletics) |
  Athletes--Training of. | Sports science. | BISAC: SPORTS & RECREATION /
  Bodybuilding & Weightlifting
Classification: LCC GV546 .H32 2025 (print) | LCC GV546 (ebook) | DDC
  613.7--dc23/eng/20230830
LC record available at https://lccn.loc.gov/2023034531
LC ebook record available at https://lccn.loc.gov/2023034532

ISBN: 978-1-4925-6167-5 (print)

Copyright © 2025 by G. Gregory Haff

Human Kinetics supports copyright. Copyright fuels scientific and artistic endeavor, encourages authors to create new works, and promotes free speech. Thank you for buying an authorized edition of this work and for complying with copyright laws by not reproducing, scanning, or distributing any part of it in any form without written permission from the publisher. You are supporting authors and allowing Human Kinetics to continue to publish works that increase the knowledge, enhance the performance, and improve the lives of people all over the world.

Notwithstanding the above notice, permission to reproduce the following material is granted to persons and agencies who have purchased this work: pp. 442-453.

The online learning content that accompanies this product is delivered on HK*Propel*, **HKPropel.HumanKinetics.com**. You agree that you will not use HK*Propel* if you do not accept the site's Privacy Policy and Terms and Conditions, which detail approved uses of the online content.

To report suspected copyright infringement of content published by Human Kinetics, contact us at **permissions@hkusa.com**. To request permission to legally reuse content published by Human Kinetics, please refer to the information at **https://us.humankinetics.com/pages/permissions-translations-faqs**.

The web addresses cited in this text were current as of February 2023, unless otherwise noted.

Senior Acquisitions Editor: Roger W. Earle; **Senior Developmental Editor:** Cynthia McEntire; **Managing Editor:** Hannah Werner; **Indexer:** Ferreira Indexing; **Permissions Manager:** Laurel Mitchell; **Graphic Designer:** Denise Lowry; **Cover Designer:** Keri Evans; **Cover Design Specialist:** Susan Rothermel Allen; **Cover Graphic:** Jason Marz/Moment/Getty Images; **Photographs:** Photo on page 3 © JONATHAN NACKSTRAND/AFP via Getty Images; Photo on page 25 © ODD ANDERSEN/AFP via Getty Images; Photo on page 51 © Toru Hanai/Getty Images; Photo on page 75 © Atsushi Tomura/Getty Images; Photo on page 105 © Paul Harding/Getty Images; Photo on page 127 © Chris Thelen/Getty Images; Photo on page 151 © Alain Grosclaude/Agence Zoom/Getty Images; Photo on page 177 © Laurence Griffiths/Getty Images; Photo on page 201 © Maddie Meyer/Getty Images; Photo on page 235 © FRANCK FIFE/AFP via Getty Images; Photo on page 267 © Kevin C. Cox/Getty Images; Photo on page 307 © LIONEL BONAVENTURE/AFP via Getty Images; Photo on page 335 © Chris Graythen/Getty Images; Photo on page 383 © Joel Auerbach/Getty Images; Photo on page 403 © Justin Casterline/Getty Images; All other photos © Human Kinetics, unless otherwise noted; **Photo Asset Manager:** Laura Fitch; **Photo Production Manager:** Jason Allen; **Senior Art Manager:** Kelly Hendren; **Illustrations:** © Human Kinetics, unless otherwise noted; **Printer:** Walsworth

Printed in the United States of America   10 9 8 7 6 5 4 3 2 1

The paper in this book was manufactured using responsible forestry methods.

Human Kinetics
1607 N. Market Street
Champaign, IL 61820
USA

United States and International
Website: **US.HumanKinetics.com**
Email: info@hkusa.com
Phone: 1-800-747-4457

Canada
Website: **Canada.HumanKinetics.com**
Email: info@hkcanada.com

This book is dedicated to all the sport scientists, coaches, athletes, and soldiers I have had the privilege to learn from, coach, and be inspired by, especially the men and women of the Australian Special Air Service Regiment (SASR).

A good plan violently executed now is better than a perfect plan next week.

>   General George S. Patton

We don't rise to the level of our expectations; we fall to the level of our training.

>   Archilochus (BC 680-645)

CONTENTS

Preface viii
Acknowledgments ix

PART I Foundations of Training Theory   1

1. The Training Process   3
2. Energetics and Training   25
3. Classification of Skills and Types of Training   51
4. Understanding Training Loads   75

PART II Fundamentals of Periodization   103

5. Periodization Theory   105
6. Multiyear and Annual Training Plans   127
7. Mesocycle and Microcycle Training Plans   151
8. Training Sessions and Days   177

PART III Advanced Periodization Topics 199

9 Fatigue, Recovery, and Periodization 201

10 Periodization of Nutrition 235

11 Integration of Monitoring Techniques Into Periodized Training Plans 267

12 Periodization Strategies for Optimal Competition Performance 307

PART IV Training Methods 333

13 Strength, Power, and Hypertrophy Training 335

14 High-Intensity Interval Training 383

15 Speed and Agility Development 403

Appendix 441
Glossary 454
References 465
Index 572
About the Author 589
Earn Continuing Education Credits/Units 590

PREFACE

The concept of systematically organizing the training practices of athletes is not new or novel; the precursors of periodized training date back more than 2,000 years. As one begins to reflect on the process of guiding the training practices of athletes, it becomes increasingly clear that the holistic development of an athlete encompasses more than their physical and tactical training. *Scientific Foundations and Practical Applications of Periodization* is designed to leverage the classic knowledge about periodization while integrating the ever-expanding body of scientific knowledge about human performance and the factors that optimize it.

A central theme of this text is that periodization is an integrated approach that exploits knowledge from many scientific disciplines to optimize the training process. The text is divided into four major content areas that are designed to provide the coach or sport scientist with a comprehensive understanding of how to create integrated periodized training plans. Part I provides the reader with a foundational understanding of the training process. The reader will first explore the training process (chapter 1) to develop a fundamental understanding of training. From there they will explore the key concepts of bioenergetics (chapter 2), which are necessary to understand how to train athletes most effectively. In chapter 3, the reader will be taught how to classify various skills and training activities. The final chapter in this part introduces the fundamental concepts associated with training loads and discusses how training is progressed over time.

Part II presents the fundamentals of periodization in four chapters. In chapter 5, the historical roots of periodization are presented and the differences between periodization, planning, and programming are explored. Additionally, various models of periodization are introduced and discussed. In chapter 6, the concepts of long-term training plans, specifically multiyear and annual training plans, are introduced and explained. In chapter 7, mesocycle and microcycle planning structures are discussed with a focus on developing an understanding of how these structures are interrelated. Finally, part II concludes with a detailed discussion about how training days and sessions are constructed to meet the goals of the macro-, meso-, and microcycle plans (chapter 8).

Part III introduces several advanced periodization topics. Chapter 9 discusses how fatigue and recovery are addressed within a periodized training plan. Chapter 10 presents a detailed discussion about nutritional periodization strategies. Chapter 11 discusses why and how monitoring is integrated into a periodized training plan. Finally, part III concludes with a detailed presentation about how to optimize performance when it most matters—during competition (chapter 12).

In part IV, various training methods are discussed including strength training (chapter 13), high-intensity interval training (chapter 14), and speed and agility development (chapter 15). These methods are included because the vast majority of individual and team sports integrate these training methods and performance targets into their periodized training plans.

Through HK*Propel*, instructors adopting *Scientific Foundations and Practical Applications of Periodization* have access to a presentation package with close to 800 slides. All readers can access a training session template, mesocycle training plan templates, and an annual training plan template plus directions for designing periodized programs through HK*Propel*. See the card at the front of the book for instructions on how to access the online content. These templates can be used to create periodized programs for athletes and teams. Eight templates appear in the appendix at the end of the book as well: a training session template (page 442), a mesocycle training plan template (page 443), and six examples of an annual training plan template (pages 444-453).

ACKNOWLEDGMENTS

In all our life's endeavors, we are a composite of the experiences we have and the people who are a part of our lives. This book has been one of the biggest challenges I have ever undertaken in my entire life and without the love and support of my wife, Erin, I would never have had the courage to even attempt to put my words to paper. Erin, you always challenge me to question my beliefs and see things from all sides. Your expertise as a "master coach" has forced me to challenge my beliefs in ways I had not considered. Over many years, you have moved our home to various places around the world, provided an environment for me to thrive, and held our family together while I jetted around the world or spent countless hours in the office or lab with my students. I can think of no one better to navigate the insanity of our world with, and I can honestly say without your love, support, trust, and belief in me I would never have survived the insanity of the world of academics. In many ways this book is a product of the long walks we have taken talking about training and how to better prepare athletes and the love and support you have given me.

With great pleasure and humility, I express my deepest gratitude to my mentor Professor Mike Stone. You are more than a mentor to me; you are one of my closest friends and confidants and the professional I model myself after. I have been blessed to work with you for almost 30 years and counting. If I can be half the sport scientist that you are, then I will have accomplished a lot in my career. I would also be remiss if I did not acknowledge Professor Andy Fry, the person who set me on this crazy adventure. After we first met at a weightlifting competition, where I did beat you handily, you have always been a close friend and confidant. I am always impressed by the quality of your research and your dedication to your craft and your family.

Over the years I have made many close friends in sport science, academia, and coaching. I thank my circle of friends who are always in the background encouraging me to be the best version of myself and who remind me to not be so hard on myself. I specifically want to thank Duncan French, the best applied sport scientist I know, for giving me a good kick in the butt when I needed a pep talk and for just being an amazing friend and someone I can count on when things get difficult. Additionally, I must acknowledge Professor Paul Comfort, the person my students refer to as British Greg, because I guess we are kindred spirits or versions of one another. Paul, you are an amazingly humble and gifted sport scientist. I am always amazed by how hard you work, and nothing inspires me more than coming to the University of Salford for research weeks with you, Dr. John McMahon, and Professor Jason Lake. Our epic burger runs are memories that I will always cherish.

Another person I must acknowledge is Professor Rhodri Lloyd. Rhodri, thank you so much for your unwavering friendship and support over the years. I have enjoyed all the moments we have shared. Whether a smoky bar in Croatia or a UKSCA or NSCA conference somewhere in the world, it is always memorable and interesting. Additionally, Professor Travis Triplett, you have truly been my friend since I first arrived in Boone, North Carolina, and over the last 30 years, I can say no matter where we are we somehow always end up enjoying our moments together. Remember, the next margarita is on me.

To my many students, you are the reason I do what I do. I am inspired by your enthusiasm and challenged by your questions. Your research has helped shape this book and our many conversations about training, science, and life have helped me crystalize my thoughts, which ultimately found their way into this book. While there are too many of you to list, I want you to know you are my family and when you are successful, I am overjoyed for you. I am always proud of who you have become, and I look forward to seeing your journey through this profession.

I would also like to acknowledge Roger Earle and the Human Kinetics team. Without Roger I would never have had the opportunity to write this book. Your friendship has been something I cherish and your unwavering support and belief in me during the process of putting my ideas to paper has been nothing short of amazing. I look forward to our next project together and I hope this book lives up to your expectations. To Cynthia McEntire, thank you for all your hard work to keep this book moving forward and dealing with all my peculiarities.

Finally, I must take a moment to remember my parents Guy and Sandy Haff. While I was unable to follow in my father's footsteps and serve my country as part of the U.S. Marine Corps, after spending time with the men and women of the Australian Special Air Service Regiment (SASR), I now understand what he was trying to get me to see and why he had me do all those crazy training activities growing up. Who would have thought all the strength training you had me do and the lessons you taught me would have resulted in this book. I wish you could see this one as I think you would be proud of the words I have written. Mom, thanks for believing that an unmotivated and dyslexic kid could accomplish anything he put his mind to and for forcing me to be a part of all those summer book clubs at the Randolph Public Library. Please know I am now a voracious reader who has a home library larger than I deserve. I miss you both very much and will come to Fort Jackson as soon as I can to visit you. Finally, to my sister Jennifer, while we live far apart and don't always see eye to eye, thanks for being who you are and loving and supporting me, even when I disappear for long periods.

PART I
FOUNDATIONS OF TRAINING THEORY

Training theory is an ever-evolving construct based on practical experience and scientific inquiry into how the body responds to various stimuli. As our understanding of how the body responds to these stimuli evolves, we can use this information to elevate and maximize performance via the manipulation of training loads. Therefore, when designing periodized training plans, it is critical that we completely understand the concept of training load.

Part I explores various concepts of training theory. The chapters are sequenced to develop a foundation from which training plans can be created. Chapter 1 defines training and explains how the body adapts to training stimuli. Chapter 2 examines the energetics that underpin the training process. Chapter 3 presents a method for classifying various skills and training activities that contribute to the training loads contained within training plans. Chapter 4 explores training load aftereffects, the modifiable factors that contribute to a training load, the need for individualization, methods of training load progression, and how to sequence training.

CHAPTER 1

The Training Process

The evolution of the training process is linked to our ever-increasing understanding of how the body adapts to different stimuli. Our understanding of these processes continues to increase as modern sport scientists examine the physiological, psychological, and performance effects of various training, recovery, and nutritional interventions. With an increased understanding of how the athlete's body responds and adapts to various training stimuli, more effective and efficient training programs can be developed to elevate overall athletic performance. This increased knowledge base has allowed modern coaches, sport scientists, and training theorists to expand their basic understanding of the training process and develop new training theories based on the evolution of this scientific evidence.

A central concept that underpins training theory is the belief that a structured, systematic, and focused system of training can be constructed to target the development of specific psychological, physiological, and performance characteristics that underpin an athlete's performance capacity. To accomplish this goal, it is important to understand how adaptations to training are stimulated and how the body responds to training stimuli. It is equally important to consider the athlete's psychological responses to various training and emotional stressors. Overall, understanding these concepts and how they relate to the development of sport performance allows for the development of more effective training programs.

Defining Training

Training is a term that is broadly used to represent an organized process of preparation designed to increase physical, psychological, intellectual, or mechanical performance (86, 88). In sport, training is considered a systematic process used to elevate an athlete's performance to the highest possible level. Training is very different from *exercising*, in which the main goal is to simply engage in physical activity rather than achieve the highest level of performance (196). Overall, an athlete's performance capacity is based on a complex blend of many factors (figure 1.1) that converge to mitigate the performance level achieved (124).

An athlete's genetic endowment is one of the major factors that affects their ability to achieve a high level of performance by establishing a genetic ceiling. The highest level of performance an athlete can achieve is highly individualized based on their genetic ceiling, and training can be considered a process for realizing genetic potential (205). Based on this premise, the training practices implemented by coaches and athletes should be designed to elevate performance levels to the athlete's genetic limits (37, 66, 196). Georgiades et al. (66) suggest that "truly elite level athletes are built—but only from those born with innate ability" (page 835). Based on this premise, it is clear that training has powerful effects on athletic performance (124, 205) because it can determine how close an athlete can get to their genetic ceiling.

In a broad sense, training comprises all the systematic, structured, and focused processes used by athletes to prepare for specific training goals (7). These processes are designed to prepare the athlete physically, technically, tactically, psychologically, and theoretically for their highest levels of performance (86, 88). Central to the ability of the training processes to prepare the athlete for the desired outcome is the use of scientific principles to exploit the body's ability to adapt to training activities and elevate performance levels. When coaches understand these scientific principles, they are better able to direct the athlete's training practices, increase the athlete's potential for achieving their performance goals, and elevate the athlete's performance closer to their genetic ceiling. Conversely, the coach who lacks an understanding of these principles will decrease the likelihood of guiding the athlete toward their performance goals.

Exploitation and Optimization of Training

The goal of the training process is to prepare the athlete for the highest possible performance (86, 88, 196). The achievement of this objective is largely related to the principles of **exploitation** and **optimization**.

Exploitation

The training process is exploitive, drawing on knowledge from a variety of scientific disciplines

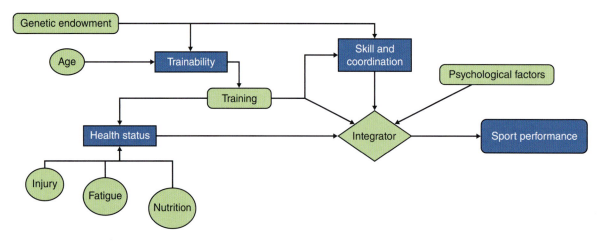

FIGURE 1.1 Interaction of factors affecting sport performance.

Adapted by permission from D. MacDougall and D. Sale, *The Physiology of Training for High Performance* (Oxford, United Kingdom: Oxford University Press, 2014), 4, reproduced with permission of the Licensor through PLSclear.

(figure 1.2) to stimulate a higher level of performance (7, 88, 196). For example, the coach who understands how to elevate an athlete's performance capacity via stimulating precise physiological adaptations is better able to design training interventions. The coach can exploit their knowledge about physiological principles to better match training interventions to the desired performance outcome and then target the specific physiological adaptations that underpin this outcome. Additionally, coaches who understand the interactions of physiological and psychological stress on the athlete's ability to adapt to the training practices will be able to enhance the athlete's training responsiveness and reduce the athlete's overall risk of injury (25, 109). Therefore, coaches who use scientific principles to guide their decision-making paradigm when constructing training plans are more likely to achieve successful performance outcomes. To effectively develop training interventions, the coach must understand how to exploit scientific principles and disciplines when training athletes to achieve high levels of performance.

Beyond exploiting known scientific principles, the coach and athlete also seek to exploit principles of training and performance (196). This allows the athlete to achieve the highest possible performance within the constraints of their unique characteristics. Therefore, each athlete requires a specific, individualized training plan to optimize

FIGURE 1.2 Scientific disciplines related to the training process.

their performance capacity. This requires the coach to understand how to adapt conventional training theory to better match the athlete's individual requirements and exploit scientific principles to optimize the training process.

Optimization

When examining the training process, it is clear that the goal is not simply to increase or decrease some performance characteristic (155) but to optimize the training process to achieve the ideal psychological state (109) and performance capacity (5, 49, 196). Central to the concept of training optimization is finding the balance between too little and too much **training load** (volume, intensity, frequency, etc.). Training loads that are too low increase injury risk and reduce performance potential due to poor fitness levels (56). Even though it is generally believed that increasing training loads, within reason, increases performance (33), there is compelling evidence that increasing training loads alone does not always result in higher levels of performance (155), depending on the athlete's ability to recover and adapt to the training stimulus. There are limits to the amount of training load that an athlete can tolerate (211) before injury and a reduction in performance occur (56). Based on this line of reasoning, it appears that there is a continuum of training loads ranging from ineffective loads that are too low to stimulate adaptation to excessive training loads that the athlete is not capable of adapting to (56). Somewhere in between these two extremes is what Gabbett (56) refers to as the "sweet spot" where injury risk is minimized and training adaptations are maximized.

Fundamentally, the proper balance in training load can be categorized as a dose–response relationship (169). The amount and type of training undertaken by the athlete is considered the dose, and how the athlete handles the training stressors is the response (169). The optimization of the training process involves finding the dosage of training that produces the desired psychological, physiological, and performance responses. Sands (169) suggests that this is what is called a Goldilocks problem: The training load should not be too little or too large but should be optimized (or "just right") to produce the most effective training stimulus. One could consider the training stimuli on a continuum from **undertraining** (i.e., too little training load) to **overtraining** (i.e., too much training load) on which a **zone of optimization** exists (figure 1.3). If the training load falls outside of this individualized zone of optimization, a reduction in performance capacity can occur, resulting in an increased risk of injury (56, 169) and a reduction in transference to performance gain. Note that the zone of optimization is not static, in that it can move depending on the athlete's psychological status, training status, training age, and other negative or positive factors. In fact, the zone of optimization is constantly in flux, moving in response to the training stimuli and the athlete's perception and response to those training stimuli.

The ability to optimize the training process is an individualized concept; many factors can affect an athlete's positive or negative response to the training stimulus. For example, the optimal training load for a novice athlete will be very different from that of an elite athlete (196). A training load that stimulates a training adaptation for a novice athlete will most likely result in a **detraining** response when applied to an elite athlete (222). Conversely, a training stimulus that would stimulate performance gain in an elite athlete will create an excessive loading scenario

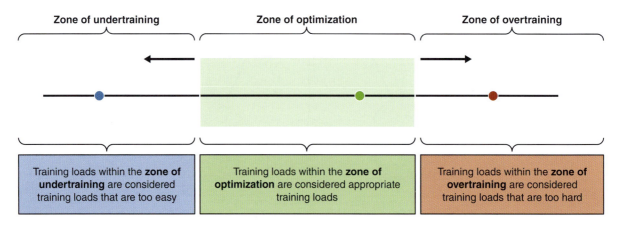

FIGURE 1.3 Zone of optimization.

Adapted by permission from W.A. Sands, "Monitoring the Elite Female Gymnast," *National Strength and Conditioning Journal* 13, no. 4 (1991): 66-71.

that will result in a reduced performance capacity and most certainly an increased risk of injury for the novice athlete. Additionally, if the athlete is in a period of high psychological stress, their ability to tolerate training loads can be impaired, resulting in a significantly increased risk of injury, a decreased performance capacity, and an impaired ability to recover from training (104, 197, 218). The athlete's current psychological and physiological states and training loads should be monitored so the coach can optimize the athlete's training loads to align with their individual needs, thus allowing them to more effectively progress (196).

Training Adaptation

In its most simplistic sense, **adaptation** is the process by which an organism adjusts to its environment (222). As the environment changes, the organism must adapt to survive. When extrapolated to the sporting environment, the athlete is exposed to constantly varying workloads from either training or competition that challenge their ability to adapt. If the athlete is unable to adapt to these workloads and the stressors they stimulate, they are at risk of excessive fatigue, overreaching, or overtraining (7). If these stressors are well-planned and varied appropriately, the athlete will be able to adapt and elevate their performance capacity.

Overall, the training loads imposed on the athlete provide powerful stimuli for adaptation (222). The greater the athlete's ability to adapt to the training stimuli, the greater the potential performance gains. The best method to manage these adaptations and improve sport performance is to use a well-organized periodized training plan that provides varying levels of stressors that align with the ever-changing psychological, physiological, and performance statuses of the athlete. The ability to induce adaptive responses is largely affected by key features of the adaptive process: overload, variation, specificity, reversibility, and individualization (37, 222).

Overload

For the athlete to increase performance capacity, they must be exposed to an exercise overload. An **overload** is a training load that is above that which the athlete typically encounters (37, 178). If the overload is applied correctly, the athlete will adapt to that training stimulus and achieve a performance gain as a result of breaking the current threshold of adaptation (figure 1.4).

The most common way to apply an overload is to manipulate the training load by increasing the **volume** or **intensity** of training, or some combination of alterations to both of these training variables (37, 79, 101). Training volume can be amplified by increasing the **frequency** of exposure (i.e., number of training sessions) or the **density** of exposure (i.e., frequency of training within a period of time) to the training load. The intensity of training can be augmented by increasing the resistance applied (i.e., absolute or relative intensity factors) (37) or the speed at which the activity is performed (38). Alternatively, the training load can be increased by changing the exercise to a novel activity (94, 101, 114, 196, 222) or to a different range of motion (37, 38) that provides the athlete with a stimulus that they are unaccustomed to in order to stimulate adaptation. If applied correctly,

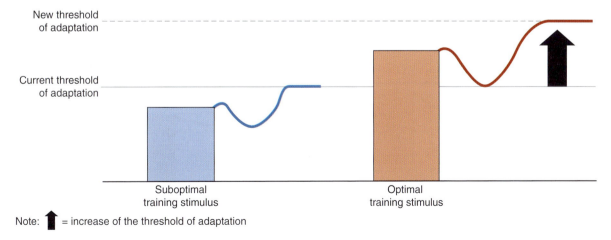

FIGURE 1.4 Relationship of training stimulus to the threshold of adaptation.

Adapted by permission from T.O. Bompa and G.G. Haff, *Periodization: Theory and Methodology of Training,* 5th ed., (Champaign, IL: Human Kinetics, 2009).

the increased training load stimulates adaptations that result in improved performance and a reduced risk of injury (figure 1.5).

If, however, the training load is always the same (i.e., monotonous), it will only provide an overload stimulus in the early stages of the training process, eventually resulting in a stagnation (i.e., plateau) of performance without stimulating any further performance improvements (figure 1.6) (188). To avoid this stagnation, the training load needs to be systematically varied to continually stimulate adaptation.

If, however, the training load is excessive or overly varied, a maladaptive response will manifest as a reduced performance capacity (excessive fatigue, overtraining, etc.) because the athlete is not able to adapt to the training loads that they are exposed to (figure 1.7). In these scenarios, injury is likely a result of the athlete's inability to adapt to or tolerate these training loads (42, 56, 213).

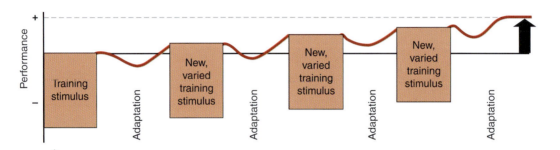

Note: ↑ = increase in performance; increasing training stimulus load ⇒ adaptation ⇒ performance improvement

FIGURE 1.5 Appropriate training stimulus and adaptations.

Adapted from Bompa and Haff (2009).

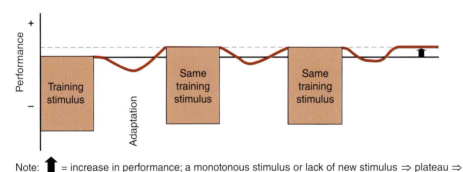

Note: ↑ = increase in performance; a monotonous stimulus or lack of new stimulus ⇒ plateau ⇒ lack of performance improvement over time

FIGURE 1.6 Monotonous training stimulus and adaptations.

Adapted from Bompa and Haff (2009).

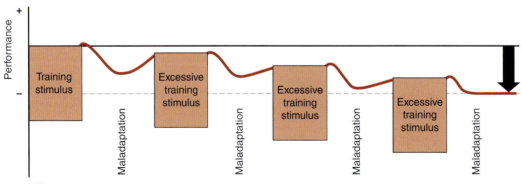

Note: ↓ = decrease in performance; excessive stimulus (load) ⇒ maladaptation ⇒ decrease in performance

FIGURE 1.7 Excessive training stimulus and adaptations.

Adapted from Bompa and Haff (2009).

Finally, if the load is too low, a detraining or **involution** effect will occur, causing a maladaptive response that results in a significant reduction in performance capacity. According to Viru (213), this is termed a *useless load* because it does not stimulate adaptation, maintain performance capacity, or induce recovery after a training load that provides an overload stimulus (30). In fact, compelling evidence in the scientific literature suggests that undertraining (i.e., very low training loads) can cause a significant injury risk as well as a reduced performance capacity in athletes (30, 36, 56, 58, 95). In order to create a protective effect against injury while improving performance, athletes must strive to not only train harder but also train smarter with more systematically structured and monitored training interventions (56).

Overall, it is important to note that the ability to adapt to a training load is highly individualized and is constantly in flux due to the dynamic nature of the athlete's adaptive responses and current psychological and physiological states. The dynamic nature of this process can be seen in the progression of training demands needed as part of an athlete's long-term athlete development plan (121).

For example, a load that stimulates adaptation for a novice athlete may only serve to maintain performance capacity for an intermediate athlete and will cause detraining effects for a more advanced athlete (222) (figure 1.8). Conversely, a training load that stimulates adaptations for a more advanced athlete will be excessive when applied to novice athletes and result in a significant increase in injury risk and occurrences of overtraining responses.

Ultimately, the primary objective of the training process is to systematically and progressively implement overload as part of the training process. This process is often referred to as **progressive overload**, in which the athlete is exposed to higher training loads to overcome the threshold of adaptation (figure 1.4). To be effective, these loads need to be implemented into the training plan in a progressive manner because significant increases or spikes in training have been associated with increased injury risk (57, 58, 183, 219). For example, Gabbett et al. (57) report that when workloads are sharply increased (i.e., >10%), there is an increased risk of injury. There are, however, scenarios in which a sharp spike in training, or what is termed **overreaching**, is warranted; if

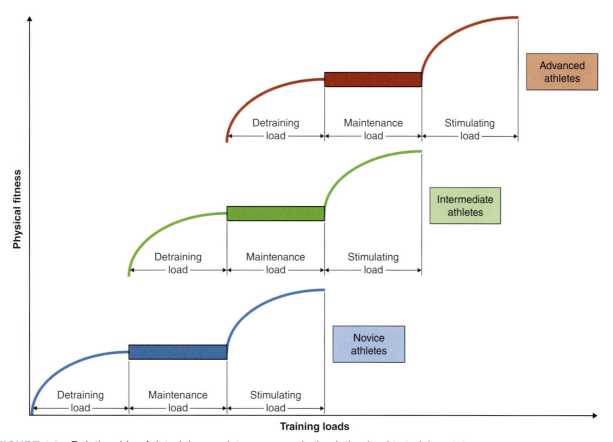

FIGURE 1.8 Relationship of detraining, maintenance, and stimulating load to training status.

programmed correctly, these increased periods of training can be powerful tools for inducing adaptation and performance gains in subsequent training periods (200). Based on these data, it is recommended that variations in training loads be carefully planned to minimize the risk of injuries associated with significant spikes in training loads.

As athletes become more trained, they require greater training stimuli to continue to adapt and elevate their performance capacity closer to their genetic ceilings. As an athlete progresses over time, there is a general increase in the athlete's ability to adapt to training loads (39, 171). Therefore, the athlete needs to be exposed to progressively increasing training loads in order to continue to stimulate adaptation and elevate performance (39, 141, 171). This is most evident in the progression of the athlete through their long-term athlete development plan (50, 122, 123), in which training focus and loads are varied to continue to stimulate adaptive responses and performance gains. It is important to note that there are no absolute guidelines that can be given, because the degree of progressive loading of training factors is highly individualized (39) and can be largely affected by the athlete's genetic makeup (66). For example, athletes who have the alpha-actinin-3 (ACTN3) R allele exhibit an enhanced response to resistance training, whereas those with the ACTN3 XX genotype display a reduced responsiveness to resistance training (163).

Variation

Variation in training stimulus is a core tenant of training theory (7) because it is directly linked to the stimulation of training adaptations (112, 187). If an athlete applies the same training load over time, there is a concomitant decrease in performance gain (222) as a result of the application of monotonous training loading structures (188). The monotonous implementation of training loads can stimulate plateauing or, in some cases, a reduction in performance capacity as a result of a reduced ability of the training load employed to induce adaptations that underpin performance gains (166, 188, 196). Stone and colleagues (188) have termed this reduction or stagnation of performance gains *monotonous program overtraining*. In fact, it has been reported that the degree of monotony within a training plan is significantly related to poor performance (154) and may also relate to an increased injury risk (51, 132, 144).

Ultimately, the periodization of training is a balancing act between the conflicting demands of training variation and the stability of training (7, 166, 222). It is commonly suggested that employing variation as part of the training plan is a key tenet of periodization (7, 101, 166, 211). The optimization of training adaptations is linked to systematic variations of the training load, which are continually fine-tuned to account for the athletes' ever-changing psychological and physiological states. Conceptually, one could link the concepts of overload and variation to account for the athlete's adaptation to the training process. By varying the training method, overload can be applied and further physiological and performance adaptations can be stimulated.

When constructing a periodized training plan, one can introduce variation into the training process by manipulating quantitative or qualitative training variables (222).

Quantitative Variation

Quantitative variation is the most commonly recognized form of employing training variation in the literature. It involves the manipulation of volume (i.e., frequency or density) and intensity (i.e., resistance, power output, or speed) of training.

The manipulation of training intensity is an important consideration when attempting to modulate the training stimulus to stimulate adaptation and/or induce recovery. For example, one could vary the amount of weight lifted within a resistance training program to balance the competing demands of stimulating adaptation and inducing recovery (78). Although the manipulation of training intensity is important, haphazard changes in intensity or the monotonous application of chronically high intensities can result in a reduction of effectiveness of the training plan (80). The manipulation of training intensity should be performed in an integrative manner that considers all training factors to best modulate adaptation and recovery from training.

When considering the volume of training, manipulation can be introduced within or between individual training weeks (**microcycles**) or blocks (**mesocycles**). This can be accomplished by increasing the number of training sessions per week (frequency of training) or the number of training sessions within a given training day (density of training). For example, the coach may vary the number of times per week a specific training focus is targeted to give the athlete more training stimulus (82). On some training days the athlete may train multiple times per day, whereas on other days they may complete one training session (7, 43, 100, 203). There is compelling evidence that undergoing multiple training sessions per day can induce greater physiological adaptations compared to once-a-day training (84,

100), resulting in a greater performance improvement (90). By dividing the daily training load across multiple training sessions the athlete will be better able to manage and recover from the training loads they are exposed to (203). When structuring training days with multiple sessions, the coach should not increase the total training load unless they are planning an overreaching training period. One of the bigger mistakes that young coaches and athletes make is to incrementally increase training load when training multiple times per day. As noted earlier in this chapter, this practice does not always result in improved performance, because it can create a scenario in which the athlete is exposed to an excessive training load that taxes their ability to recover and adapt, ultimately resulting in an increased injury risk. Therefore, when manipulating training frequency and density, consider the overall workload that the athlete will encounter and how the various workloads in the training plan interact.

Qualitative Variation

Qualitative variation is another important method for introducing variation into the training plan. This method involves changing exercises or focus to vary the training stimulus and enhance or direct the physiological and performance outcomes (37, 94, 212, 222). When systematically introducing, removing, and then reintroducing a training task, greater adaptation to the training stimulus can occur (94, 212). One example of how this can be accomplished is to introduce a novel or seminovel training exercise by periodically changing exercises that address a similar **biomotor ability** (7, 196). A greater rate of adaptation will occur when a training task is removed before adaptation is achieved and replaced with a task that addresses a similar biomotor ability (figure 1.9) (94).

For example, for a shot putter to develop upper-body strength and power, they may periodically shift their training exercises in a sequential pattern

	Exercise replacement and sequencing for the lower body							
Training block	**Block 1**				**Block 2**			
Exercises	Back squat	Back squat	Front squat	Front squat	Speed squat	Speed squat	Jump squat	Jump squat
	Quarter front squat	Quarter front squat	Quarter back squat	Quarter back squat	Back squat	Back squat	One-third back squat	One-third back squat
	Single-leg squat	Single-leg squat	Lunge	Lunge				
Week 1	1	2	3	4	5	6	7	8

a

	Exercise replacement and sequencing for weightlifting derivatives							
Training block	**Block 1**				**Block 2**			
Exercises	Hang power clean	Hang power snatch	Hang power snatch	Hang power clean	Power snatch	Power clean	Power snatch	Power clean
	Clean pull	Snatch pull	Snatch pull	Clean pull	Snatch pull (midthigh)	Clean pull (midthigh)	Snatch pull (midthigh)	Clean pull (midthigh)
	Clean grip RDL	Clean grip RDL	Snatch grip RDL	Snatch grip RDL	Clean grip RDL	Clean grip RDL	Snatch grip RDL	Snatch grip RDL
Week 1	1	2	3	4	5	6	7	8

■ = exercise replacement RDL: Romanian deadlift

b

FIGURE 1.9 Training variation via the introduction and reintroduction of exercises: *(a)* example of exercise replacement and sequencing for the lower body; *(b)* example of exercise replacement and sequencing for weightlifting derivatives.

between a focus on strength, strength–speed, and speed–strength development. In this scenario, the athlete may target strength development by using the military press during the general preparatory phase of training and replacing this exercise with the push press during the specific preparatory phase to change the training stimulus while still targeting the required movement pattern and muscle groups. As the athlete moves into the precompetitive or main competitive phase, they may shift toward the push jerk exercise to place a greater emphasis on power development. Thus, the exercise progression that is used in this scenario would be as follows:

military press → push press → push jerk

Another example of this concept can be seen in the preparation of speed skaters. During the general preparatory phase (i.e., off-season), speed skaters may undertake training modalities such as road or track cycling in order to maintain fitness and then return to on-ice training during the specific preparatory period of training (52). Similarly, a shot putter may compete in weightlifting during their general preparatory phase and return to event-specific training during the specific preparatory period. Based on the introduction–reintroduction paradigm, the speed skater would rapidly increase their skating performance because speed skating would be a seminovel training task. Similarly, when the shot putter returns to event-specific training, they would be exposed to a seminovel task and experience a greater gain in performance (7).

Specificity

It is well-noted within the scientific literature that training adaptations are highly specific to the training methods employed. When thinking of **specificity**, the most common discussion revolves around the SAID principle (specific adaptation to imposed demands). SAID suggests that training should closely relate to the performance target (164). In the most simplistic terms, the greater the specificity between the training activities and the sporting outcome, the greater the potential of training to affect performance. Conceptually, specificity can be considered an issue of transferability between the training activity and the performance outcome (61, 222). Ultimately, the greater the similarity between the training activities and the performance outcome, the greater the probability of a transfer of training effect (6, 7, 37, 61). The degree of transferability is largely affected by how similar the metabolic and mechanical characteristics of the training process are to the intended sporting outcome.

Metabolic Specificity

Metabolic specificity, also known as **bioenergetic specificity**, relates to how the energetic profile of the training activity relates to the profile of the targeted performance. Based on the targeted performance outcomes, the work-to-rest ratios and the intensities and durations of training can be systematically varied to engage specific energy systems during exercise, which stimulates specific adaptations that directly relate to the sport being trained for (165, 192). Therefore, prior to designing any periodized training program, a tactical evaluation of the specific sport must be completed (165). In their seminal paper on tactical metabolic training for team sports, Plisk and Gambetta (165) suggest there is a need to evaluate the competitive model, the nature and scope of tactics used, the work-to-relief pattern as well as the frequency distribution of efforts, and the core training drills that are available. By performing this type of analysis, the coach can better relate the metabolic demands of training to the attributes needed to enhance performance.

In addition to matching the energetic profile of the sport, there is also what might be considered a degree of training mode specificity (61). For example, a triathlete's cycling and running training does not directly translate to swimming performance, even though each activity has a similar bioenergetic profile (145). Using training exercises that simply match the bioenergetic or metabolic profile of the sport will not result in the optimal transfer of training effects to the competitive performance. Specifically, metabolic specificity must be considered in the construct of the mechanical demand of the sport.

Mechanical Specificity

Mechanical specificity is the relationship of the **kinetic profile** (i.e., force) and the **kinematic profile** (i.e., displacement, velocity, power, or rate of force development) of the training activities with the performance outcome (37, 191). In addition, movement patterns, such as the range of motion or acceleration patterns, can be considered in the context of mechanical specificity. Mechanical specificity considers not only the similarity of the external movement pattern but also the inherent neuromuscular factors that underpin the biomechanics of movement (21, 150). This concept is referred to as the ***principle of dynamic correspondence***, which is a foundational principle that must be considered when designing training programs (166). In this context, the degree of intra- and intermuscular task specificity needs to be considered (37, 195, 214). Intramuscular task specificity is related to how the motor cortex organizes motor unit activation, whereas intermuscular task specificity relates to the whole-muscle activation patterns (37, 195). Both intra- and intermuscular activation patterns can be altered in response to changes in movement pattern, muscle action, or the velocity of movement. Ultimately, the greater the similarity between the training activities and the actual physical performance, the greater the potential for a transfer of training effect.

Specificity and Transfer of Training Effect Paradox

From a theoretical perspective, the most specific form of training is to perform the sporting movement (179). This perspective is logical because it is well-established that the training modes and methods that are the most similar to the sport or activity result in the greatest transfer of training effects. However, this line of reasoning fails to consider the element of overload that is required to elicit specific physiological adaptations and the interplay of specific and nonspecific training methods required for the long-term enhancement of performance (61). This is where the specificity and transfer of training effect paradox manifests itself. Although short-term gains are most related to the training program's degree of specificity, it appears that task-specific training employed in isolation does not provide an appropriate stimulus for the development of the foundational qualities to achieve long-term performance gains (8). For example, it would seem logical that to improve sprinting performance, specific sprint training is required (167). However, to develop the muscular contractile characteristics and morphological characteristics necessary to maximize sprinting speed, nonspecific training such as heavy resistance training is required (61). Therefore, based on periodization theory, it is more logical to suggest that a holistic training approach in which periods of general and specific training are used may be the most effective methodology for maximizing performance outcomes (8, 75).

Reversibility

The principle of **reversibility** suggests that the adaptations that are achieved in response to a training stimulus can be lost if there is inadequate training stimuli to further develop or maintain the adaptations. If a training stimulus is completely removed or reduced below the level necessary to maintain the adaptation, a detraining or involution effect can occur. Ultimately, detraining can be considered a negative physiological adaptation or a maladaptation (7, 37) that can occur very rapidly if the training stimulus is significantly reduced or completely removed. For example, the complete removal of strength training from an athlete's concurrent training plan can result in a reduction of all performance capacities gained from training (e.g., 10 m sprint, 20 m sprint, countermovement jump, and maximal strength) in as little as 4 weeks (184). The overall degree of reduction will be affected by the duration of the removal of the specific training attribute.

Even if a training stimulus is being applied, there can be a diminished performance capacity in some scenarios (37). This is often referred to as involution, and it typically occurs in response to a monotonous training program that does not apply the appropriate degree of stimulus to stimulate adaptation and performance gains. Involution can also occur due to poor fatigue management. DeWeese et al. (37) suggest that involution is not uncommon after 12 to 16 weeks of training the same basic fitness characteristics.

Individualization

One of the key concepts that must always be considered when constructing training interventions is the **individualization** of training. In fact, the individualization of training is one of the central concepts that underpins modern training theories. As noted previously, the same training stimulus can induce variable adaptive responses in different athletes depending on their training status or history and their genetic makeup (164). Therefore, coaches need to tailor their training interventions to meet the individual athlete's needs. Regardless of the athlete's level of performance, it is important to consider the athlete's ability, potential, and learning characteristics and the demands of their sport. When individualizing an athlete's training program, several things should be considered: age and level of maturity, training age and training history, current psychological state, current work capacity, overall fitness level, injury status, and anthropometric characteristics.

Age and Level of Maturity

Many training programs that are effective for adults are not appropriate for youth or developmental athletes (77, 120). Lloyd et al. (120) clearly point out that the anatomy and physiology of children are different from those of adolescents, which are different from those of adults. Specifically, children express differences in muscle structure (113, 119), size (41, 119), activation patterns (40, 41, 156, 209), and function (44, 215) when compared to adults. Therefore, training programs designed for adults or advanced athletes should never be used or scaled for use with children, because these programs generally will not meet the needs of the growing and immature child (194). Additionally, children are not psychologically or physiologically able to tolerate these programs.

Training Age and Training History

The athlete's training age is the number of years the athlete has undertaken formalized training. Training age is important because some training modalities are only suitable for very experienced athletes (194). For example, when working with acrobatic sports, there is a long list of fundamental skills that must be mastered before advanced skills can be performed safely (194).

Training history is the athlete's training background, specifically the types of training they have undertaken. A coach should consider the athlete's training history and training age when making decisions about how best to guide the athlete's training.

Current Psychological State

Athletes are exposed to numerous psychological stressors that can affect their ability to adapt to and tolerate training stress (60, 134). Psychological stress is related not only to increased injury risk but also to reductions in performance adaptations (109). When the coach designs the athlete's training program, they must consider how psychological stressors outside the training process affect the athlete. For example, during periods of high academic stress, college football players have a greater risk of injury (134). During these periods, it is prudent for the coach to reduce training loads to ensure that athletes can tolerate the training process (109), thereby allowing the coach to better manage their overall injury risk (60). Due to the important links between psychological stress and the training process, evaluating athletes' levels of psychological stress is a key component of the wellness assessments implemented in many athlete-monitoring programs (138, 139).

Current Work Capacity

Athletes will vary in their ability to tolerate training loads, which can affect their overall durability and injury risk (194). The coach must consider the athlete's current training level and their ability to tolerate training loads to determine the optimal developmental path for the athlete. The coach should also consider the athlete's psychological response to training loads, which may affect their ability to recover from prescribed training loads.

Overall Fitness Level

Athletes who are highly trained and display high levels of fitness can tolerate higher training loads (194). Athletes who are not fit or who are returning from a period of inactivity are not able to tolerate higher training loads. When inappropriate training loads are applied to unfit athletes, there is an incremental increase in injury risk. Therefore, it is essential that the coach is aware of athletes' current fitness levels.

Injury Status

When examining an athlete's injury status, the coach must understand the various limitations the athlete may have. When athletes are injured or are recovering from injuries, modifications to the training program must be implemented to aid recovery. The coach needs to work closely with the medical support staff to ensure the athlete is able to transition through a return-to-play protocol and return to competition training.

Anthropometric Characteristics

An athlete's anthropometric characteristics can interact with training and performance (194). For example, taller athletes will generally perform better in basketball than shorter athletes, and smaller athletes tend to perform better in sports like gymnastics. Although there is little that can be done to alter an athlete's anthropometric characteristics, the coach can guide the athlete to appropriate sports for their size and shape to enhance their potential for success (194).

Generalized Theories of Training

The overall success of a training program is related to its ability to manage the adaptive and recovery responses to the systematically delivered training interventions (92). When considering the periodization of training, there are several generalized training theories that can help one better understand how athletes respond to training interventions: supercompensation, general adaptive syndrome, and the fitness–fatigue model.

Supercompensation

The supercompensation phenomenon, also known as *Weigert's law of supercompensation* (216), was first described by Folbrot in 1941 and later researched by Yakovlev (210). Sometimes this phenomenon is referred to as the *one-factor theory of supercompensation* (222) or the *stimulus-fatigue-recovery adaptation theory* (75, 80, 193).

Supercompensation is generally considered to be the relationship between work and restoration leading to an increase in physical adaptation (7) and an elevation in the athlete's level of preparedness (222). Fundamentally, preparedness can be classified by physical, psychological, intellectual, and mechanical means, which collectively represent the athlete's current performance capacity and how ready they are to train or compete. If preparedness is elevated, the athlete should demonstrate an increased performance capacity.

When undergoing training, athletes are exposed to a series of stimuli that alter their physiological and psychological states. These training-induced alterations can include acute metabolic (28, 45, 69-71, 160, 168, 202), hormonal (1, 59, 72, 111), inflammatory (1, 17, 182), cardiovascular (135), neuromuscular (64, 65, 133, 208), and cell-signaling (4, 22, 23, 220) responses to the training stimuli. The magnitude of the physiological response is dictated by the overall volume, intensity, or duration of training, with greater training loads stimulating greater physiological responses.

After a training session, the athlete's acute physiological responses will stimulate a state of **fatigue** (15, 129, 153), which can result in an inability to produce or maintain force production (64, 65, 107, 133, 143, 151) and a reduction in work capacity (47). Generally, two theories have been postulated as explanations for the accumulated fatigue associated with training: the peripheral (129) and central (153) governor models. The peripheral governor model suggests that fatigue is a result of an impairment of muscle function, whereas the central governor model suggests fatigue is related to a reduced capacity of the central nervous system to activate muscle (16). Both models give insight into factors that can contribute to fatigue (for more details, see chapter 9).

When fatigued, the athlete will have a reduced performance capacity that may be related to physiological responses seen during the postexercise period, such as reduced **phosphocreatine (PCr)** stores (69, 71), decreased levels of muscle **glycogen** (81, 157), increased **lactate** levels (70, 83), and elevated circulating **cortisol** levels (2, 74, 91, 152). Collectively, these responses create a temporary reduction in the athlete's performance capacity.

After a training session, the athlete must decrease the accumulated fatigue, restore muscle glycogen and PCr stores, reduce circulating cortisol levels, and deal with accumulated **lactic acid** (116). Recovery time after training is affected by many factors, including the volume and intensity of training (133, 148), the type of exercise performed (116), the type of muscle contraction performed (143), the speed of muscle contraction (99), the athlete's current training status (64), and potentially their genetic makeup. Recovery time can also be affected by the use of restoration techniques, the athlete's nutritional status (11), and the use of dietary supplements (34).

The supercompensation cycle is typically depicted as a four-stage process (figure 1.10). The initial response to an exercise bout or training session is the accumulation of fatigue (phase 1), which results in reduced functional capacity and overall level of preparedness. If adequate rest is provided after the completion of the exercise bout, the athlete progresses through a compensation phase (phase 2) in which the level of preparedness returns to baseline (i.e., homeostasis). Overall, the compensation phase is slow, progressive, and may require several hours to days to elevate preparedness (151). If sufficient time is allotted between training sessions, fatigue will dissipate, and energetic stores (especially glycogen) will be replenished. This allows the athlete to experience a rebound effect that includes an elevation in preparedness above baseline and results in what is termed *supercompensation* (phase 3). Fundamentally, the supercompensation response allows for the establishment of a new increased baseline in response to the positive effects of the training process. This elevation in preparedness serves as the foundation for a functional increase in athletic efficiency as the result of the body's adaptation to training. If, however, the resultant time between the initial training stimuli and the subsequent stimuli is too long, the effects of supercompensation will begin to dissipate; this leads to involution (phase 4), in which a reduction in preparedness occurs. These four phases of the supercompensation cycle (figure 1.11) are further described in the following sections.

Phase 1 (1 to 2 Hours)

Fatigue is a multidimensional phenomenon that will increase in response to an exercise bout. Exercise-induced fatigue is manifested via peripheral (16) and central (129) mechanisms and can have the following effects on the athlete:

• Exercise-induced peripheral fatigue can result from impairments in neuromuscular transmission and impulse propagation, impaired calcium (Ca^{2+}) handling by the **sarcoplasmic retic-**

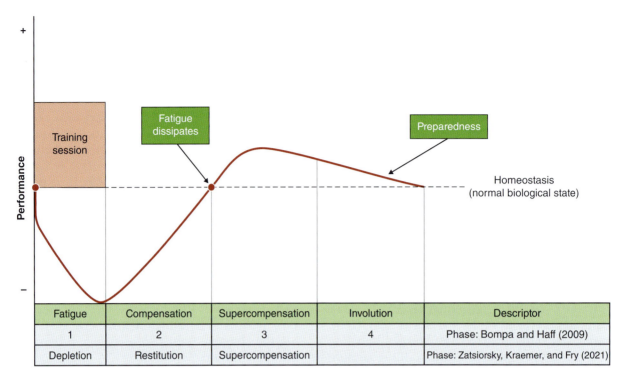

FIGURE 1.10 Supercompensation cycle of a training session (7, 223).

Adapted from T.O. Bompa and G.G. Haff, *Periodization: Theory and Methodology of Training,* 5th ed., (Champaign, IL: Human Kinetics, 2009). Adapted from V.M. Zatsiorsky, W.J. Kraemer, and A.C. Fry, *Science and Practice of Strength Training,* 3rd ed., (Champaign, IL: Human Kinetics, 2021).

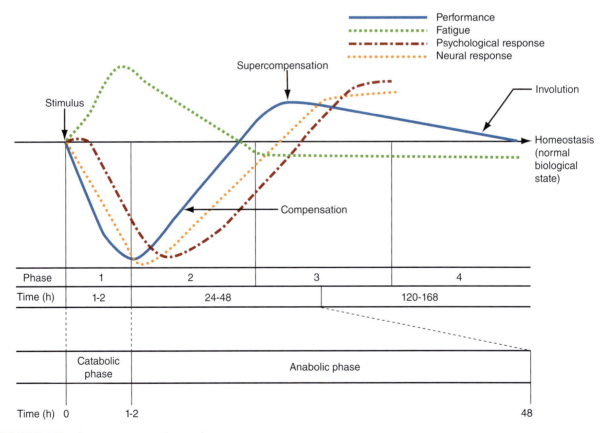

FIGURE 1.11 Supercompensation cycle.

Adapted by permission from T.O. Bompa and G.G. Haff, *Periodization: Theory and Methodology of Training,* 5th ed., (Champaign, IL: Human Kinetics, 2009), 16.

ulum, substrate depletion, and other factors that are associated with a disruption of the contractile process (129).

- The volume, intensity, and duration of the exercise bout results in reductions in several substrates. **Adenosine triphosphate (ATP)** stores can be reduced by 5% in as little as 15 seconds of exercise (71) but are never completely depleted because they are buffered by PCr and glycogen. PCr stores are significantly decreased within 5 to 30 seconds of exercise and are completely depleted after exhaustive exercise (69, 71, 93, 96, 105, 106). Glycogen stores can be significantly reduced in response to high-intensity interval exercise (10, 186), resistance training (81, 127, 128), and endurance training (3, 26, 29). When glycogen becomes significantly reduced, there is a concomitant reduction in the release of Ca^{2+} from the sarcoplasmic reticulum, which may contribute to the manifestation of fatigue (157).

- High levels of lactic acid were historically believed to result in a state of **acidosis** that altered the skeletal muscle contractile properties and caused a decrease in force-generating capacity (46, 217). More recently researchers have questioned the impact of lactic acid on fatigue, suggesting that the accumulation of inorganic phosphate (P_i), which is formed from the breakdown of PCr, is the major contributor to exercise-induced fatigue (85, 217). P_i appears to directly affect the handling of Ca^{2+} by the sarcoplasmic reticulum (201, 217) and decreases the myofibrillar Ca^{2+} sensitivity (48, 198), resulting in a reduction in crossbridge attachment force as a result of directly inhibiting crossbridge function (198).

- An increase in glucose uptake during exercise occurs despite a reduction in the amount of circulating insulin (110). This increased glucose uptake is facilitated during exercise as a result of contraction-induced **glucose transporter-4 (GLUT4)** translocation, which results in a greater sensitivity to circulating insulin and helps facilitate glucose uptake by the working tissue (149).

- Regardless of the exercise type, eccentric muscle actions can result in muscle damage (158). In particular, high-force eccentric muscle actions can result in ultrastructure muscular disruption (i.e., Z-line streaming and fiber degradation), **delayed onset muscle soreness (DOMS)**, decreased ranges of motion, and impaired force production capacities (98, 131, 158). The most common modes of exercise that stimulate these responses are resistance training (14), prolonged running (146), downhill running (18), high-intensity interval training (118), and team sport competition (115).

- After an exercise bout or a competitive engagement, there are impairments in technical performance capacities (180).

- As fatigue manifests itself, there can be a reduction in neural activation of the skeletal muscle, which is associated with central fatigue (65, 204). Exercise-induced central fatigue can also be associated with increases in mental fatigue that can occur in response to elevations in serotonin levels (35). Increases in mental fatigue can result in increases in the perception of effort, which result in a reduction in performance drive (170) and willingness to tolerate high levels of discomfort or pain that can be associated with training and competition.

Based on the various physiological responses to training that occur during this phase of the supercompensation cycle, this phase is sometimes referred to as the *catabolic phase*.

Phase 2 (24 to 48 Hours)

Phase 2 involves the initial stages of the recovery process. A variety of physiological responses can occur in this phase that are specifically related to the magnitude of the training stressors encountered (training volume, intensity, duration, etc.) and the types of exercise completed (resistance training, aerobic training, high-intensity interval training, etc.).

- Three to five minutes after the cessation of exercise, ATP stores are completely restored (89, 97), but it takes 8 minutes to completely restore skeletal muscle PCr (89). If, however, very high–intensity exercise is undertaken, the time for complete PCr recovery is extended to around 15 minutes (136).

- Within the first 30 minutes postexercise, there is a reduction in peak force-production capacity and the rate of torque development (24), which can remain suppressed for up to 96 hours postexercise (47).

- Within 1 to 2 hours after an exercise bout that contains many **stretch-shortening cycle (SSC)** actions (e.g., jumping, hopping), electromyographic (EMG) activity and **maximal voluntary contraction (MVC)** force output are restored (151). After this initial recovery, there is a secondary reduction in EMG activity and MVC force that can take several days to recover from depending on the intensity of the exercise bout. This bimodal recovery pattern seems to be associated with the length of time the athlete experiences muscle damage and soreness (151).

- Twenty to 24 hours after an intensive bout of exercise, glycogen stores will return to baseline based on the typical glycogen resynthesis rate (5-6 mmol · kg wet wt^{-1} · h^{-1}) (12). More time may be necessary for glycogen recovery if the exercise bout induces extensive muscle damage (27). Glycogen resynthesis rates are directly related to quantity and timing of carbohydrate consumption during the compensation phase of the supercompensation cycle (12).
- Muscle damage and the subsequent DOMS that can occur in response to an exercise bout can last up to 24 hours (62, 130) or can extend to 48 to 72 hours depending on the degree of muscle damage stimulated (147). One of the key aspects of the response to muscle damage is an inflammatory response, which plays a critical role in muscle repair (161).
- There is an increase in oxygen consumption postexercise that is referred to as the **excess postexercise oxygen consumption** (**EPOC**) (116, 137, 206). The type of exercise and the intensity of the exercise bout can directly affect the EPOC (206), which can remain elevated for 24 to 38 hours postexercise (13, 116, 140).
- Both resistance and endurance training can stimulate an elevation in resting energy metabolism that can last 15 to 48 hours postexercise depending on the magnitude of the exercise bout (103, 142, 185). Although the exact mechanism underpinning this elevation in energy metabolism is not fully understood, some authors suggest that increased protein synthesis (126, 181), increased thyroid hormone–induced thermogenesis (117), and increased sympathetic nervous system activity (165) all affect the postexercise energy expenditure.
- There is an increased muscle protein synthesis (MPS) rate after a bout of resistance training (19, 126). In most cases, MPS decreases to near-resting values by 24 hours postexercise (125), but it can remain elevated for up to 72 hours. As the athlete becomes more trained, the postexercise MPS rate becomes shorter (199).

Phase 3 (36 to 72 Hours)

The third phase of the supercompensation cycle is marked by performance and psychological factors returning to baseline or demonstrating a supercompensation response. Depending on the type of exercise and the magnitude of the physiological disturbances encountered, the following can occur:

- Psychological factors, such as perception of physical fitness (47), will return to baseline by 72 hours postexercise. By 96 hours postexercise, there is a potential for psychological supercompensation, which may be represented by an increase in confidence, positive thinking, motivation, and ability to cope and tolerate training (47).
- By 72 hours postexercise, the athlete's force-generating capacity may return to baseline and muscle soreness may dissipate (221).
- Running abilities are returned to baseline or supercompensate (i.e., increase above baseline values) by 72 hours postexercise (180).

Phase 4 (3 to 7 Days)

Phase 4 involves involution, or a detraining response, which occurs if the athlete is not exposed to a new training stimulus. When this occurs, the physiological responses stimulated by the supercompensation cycle will be decreased and the athlete will have a reduced performance capacity.

This simple description of the supercompensation cycle does not address all possible outcomes. Variations in the duration of the phases in the cycle will depend on the type and intensity of training undertaken by the athlete. For example, supercompensation may occur 6 to 8 hours after the completion of a training session containing medium-intensity aerobic endurance activities, but an intense session that places a high training stress on the central nervous system can require as much as 48 hours. In most instances, the recovery period after a training session, including supercompensation, will last about 24 hours. Conceptualizing the supercompensation cycle is an important part of understanding the training process.

It is well-documented that greater performance gains occur when more frequent training is undertaken by athletes (67, 73) (figure 1.12a), so it is unlikely that there will be 24 hours between training sessions. When there are longer intervals between training sessions, the athlete will experience smaller overall improvements in performance capacity (figure 1.12b) compared to more frequent training (67, 87, 162).

Although more frequent training sessions can result in greater performance gains, the coach must plan training so that intensities and volumes are varied to alter the energetic demands of the sessions contained in the microcycle. If the athlete is exposed to frequent training sessions that contain repetitive, high-intensity stimuli, the athlete's ability to adapt to the stimuli may be compromised and overtraining can result (53-55). When this

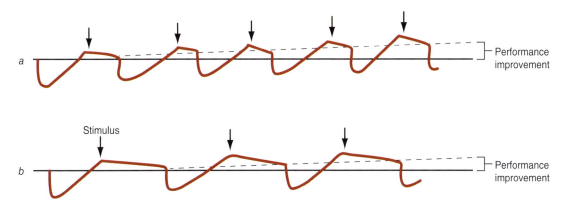

FIGURE 1.12 Summary of training effects: *(a)* short intervals between training and *(b)* long intervals between training.

Adapted by permission from D. Harre, D. Harre, and J. Barsch, "The Formation of the Standard of Athletic Performance," in *Principles of Sports Training: Introduction to the Theory and Methods of Training* (Michigan, U.S.A.: Ultimate Athlete Concepts, 2012), 70-112.

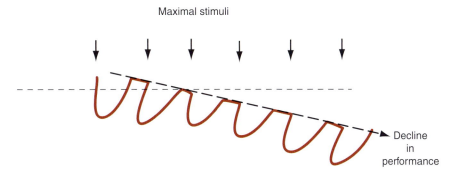

FIGURE 1.13 Effect of frequent high-intensity training on performance.

Adapted by permission from T.O. Bompa and G.G. Haff, *Periodization: Theory and Methodology of Training,* 5th ed., (Champaign, IL: Human Kinetics, 2009).

occurs, the athlete will experience a reduction in their performance capacity (figure 1.13).

Support for this contention can be found in research that has explored the training responses to resistance training (102, 162). When maximal attempts are undertaken too frequently, the athlete's ability to adapt to the training stress is impaired, performance gains are not optimized (162), and high-intensity overtraining occurs (53-55). When training to muscular failure is employed during resistance training, there is a lengthening of the time frame needed for recovery and supercompensation (68, 148, 159). It is clear from the scientific literature that training at high intensities too frequently does not maximize performance and can cause maladaptive responses. Despite this, many coaches and athletes still believe in training to exhaustion during every workout. When this practice is employed, the athlete never undergoes the compensation phase of the supercompensation process due to a lack of time to dissipate the high levels of accumulated fatigue. If the athlete is continually exposed to this type of stimuli, the overall level of fatigue continues to elevate and the time necessary to dissipate that fatigue is extended. A far better approach is to alternate the intensity of training so fatigue is better managed and supercompensation can occur.

One strategy that is often employed is to vary the rest between training sessions. An athlete may complete a series of training sessions between which the rest intervals are too short to allow for complete restoration, so fatigue accumulates (222). If a longer rest interval is provided prior to the next training session, there will be enough time for recovery and supercompensation in response to the first series of training (figure 1.14).

Modulating fatigue through the manipulation of training loads and rest intervals allows the time frames of supercompensation to be varied. Although the concept of supercompensation is generally accepted as a basic theory underpinning periodization, it may be too simplistic and should be considered in the context of other theories that explain responses to training stimuli.

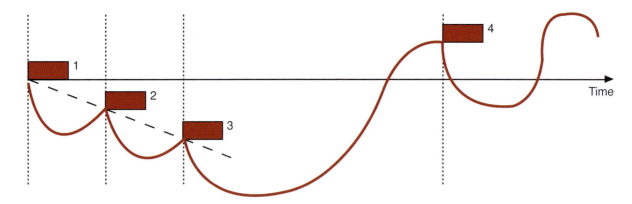

FIGURE 1.14 Example of varying recovery.

Reprinted by permission from V.M. Zatsiorsky, W.J. Kraemer, and A.C. Fry, "Basic Concepts of Training Theory," in *Science and Practice of Strength Training*, 3rd ed., (Champaign, IL: Human Kinetics, 2021).

General Adaptive Syndrome

General adaptive syndrome (figure 1.15) is a mechanistic model that describes the interplay between stress, adaptation, and recovery (32) and serves as the foundation for explaining adaptive responses to training stimuli (63, 75).

When a new training stimulus is introduced, fatigue, soreness, and stiffness accumulate and energy stores are reduced, which results in reduced performance capacity (20, 75). This initial response is the alarm phase. The alarm phase represents the initial stage of the adaptive process, which primarily occurs during the resistance phase. The ability of the athlete to adapt to training stressors is affected by many factors, including the structure of the training program, nutritional practices, psychological stressors, and genetics (32). If the athlete has excessive training loads, they are not likely to adapt to the cumulative stressors induced by training, which can ultimately converge to move the athlete into the overtraining phase (53). In this regard, it is important to remember that all stressors are additive and the cumulative effects of factors external to the training plan can affect the athlete's ability to adapt to the training plan. If, however, the training

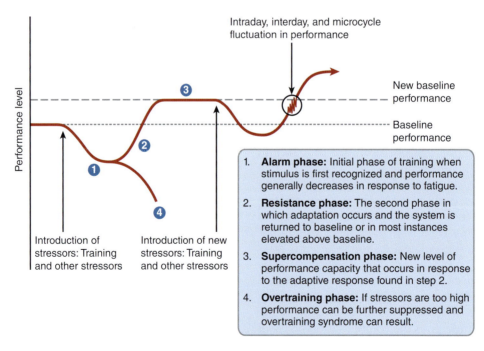

FIGURE 1.15 General adaptive syndrome and its application to periodization.

Reprinted by permission from G.G. Haff and E.E. Haff, "Training Integration and Periodization," in *NSCA's Guide to Program Design*, edited for the National Strength and Conditioning Association by J. Hoffman (Champaign, IL: Human Kinetics, 2012), 211.

plan is constructed correctly and the athlete can adapt to the training stimulus, their performance capacity will increase exponentially as a result of moving into the supercompensation phase.

Although general adaptive syndrome is generally accepted as a sound mechanistic theory underpinning periodization (7, 32, 75, 92, 193), several authors have begun to question its role (9, 108, 109). Kiely (108, 109) and Buckner et al. (9) have suggested that the application of the general adaptive syndrome to training theory and periodization is misguided and should no longer be considered as a conceptual framework for the training process. Although these authors' theories create debate and discussion, they appear to come from a narrow understanding of the work that underpins the theories of training and periodization (31, 32). Specifically, Kiely (108, 109) and Buckner et al. (9) suggest that general adaptive syndrome does not account for the effects of psychological and emotional states during the stress response. Although Selye's original concept of the stress response did not consider psychological or sociological implications over time, he later considered these additional factors and their relationship to the stress response (172-177). It is now clear that psychological stress affects recovery time (197), but, interestingly, a careful inspection of the work by Stults-Kolehmainen et al. (197) reveals that the basic pattern of recovery under varying degrees of psychological stress (figure 1.16) is very similar to the pattern presented by general adaptive syndrome (figure 1.15).

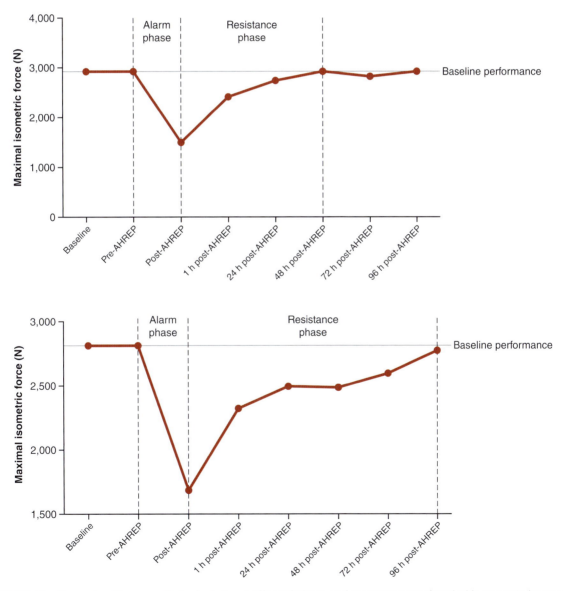

FIGURE 1.16 Example of how psychological stress affects fatigue and recovery associated with an acute heavy-resistance exercise protocol (AHREP) and its relationship to the general adaptive syndrome.

Based on this observation, the basic premise of the general adaptive syndrome stands up to scrutiny (32). The main point from this debate, however, is that the duration of the resistance phase is affected by training stressors and the compounded effects of external stressors (social, psychological, emotional, nutritional, etc.). Therefore, it is important to remember that all training stressors are additive and can affect the recovery adaptation process and performance capacity (figure 1.17).

Fitness-Fatigue Model

The **fitness–fatigue model**, also called the *two-factor theory*, considers that the athlete's level of preparedness is not static (222). Conceptually, **preparedness**, or the athlete's performance potential, should be considered the summation of the positive and negative effects of a training stimulus. The positive effect, or **fitness**, is a slow-changing **aftereffect**. The negative effect, or fatigue, is a fast-changing aftereffect. Zatsiorsky and colleagues (222) suggest that the fitness effect generally displays a moderate effect but is relatively long lasting. Conversely, the fatigue effect generally displays a greater magnitude and a relatively shorter duration. For example, at an average training load, it has been suggested that fatigue will dissipate three times faster than the fitness effect (222). Based on this gross estimation, Zatsiorsky and colleagues (222) suggest that the negative effects of fatigue may last 24 hours and the positive effects of fitness may last 72 hours. This example is a crude estimate; the magnitude and duration of the training stimulus will affect the time frames of fatigue dissipation and fitness retention. Still, it is widely accepted that fatigue dissipates at a more rapid rate than fitness, which then allows for elevated preparedness (20, 75, 222).

Remember that every training exercise, unit, bout, or cycle creates a fitness–fatigue response that modulates the overall state of preparedness (20, 75, 222). Classically, the fitness–fatigue paradigm is represented as a fitness, fatigue, and preparedness curve (figure 1.18) (20, 75, 222).

In reality, however, it is likely that training induces multiple fitness and fatigue aftereffects that are interdependent and exert a cumulative effect on the athlete's overall level of preparedness (figure 1.19) (20, 76, 80).

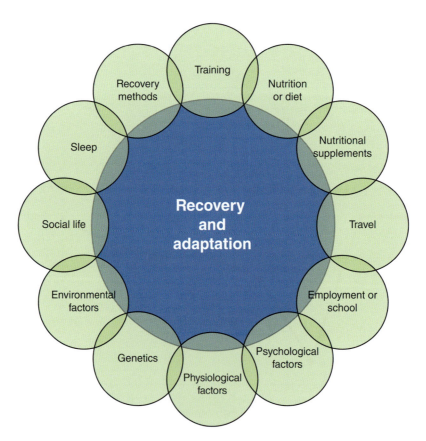

FIGURE 1.17 Factors that affect recovery and adaptation.

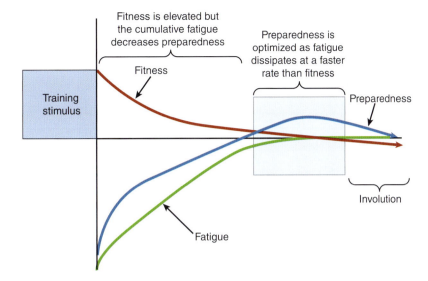

FIGURE 1.18 Fitness–fatigue paradigm.

Reprinted by permission from G.G. Haff and E.E. Haff, "Training Integration and Periodization," in *NSCA's Guide to Program Design*, edited for the National Strength and Conditioning Association by J. Hoffman (Champaign, IL: Human Kinetics, 2012), 219.

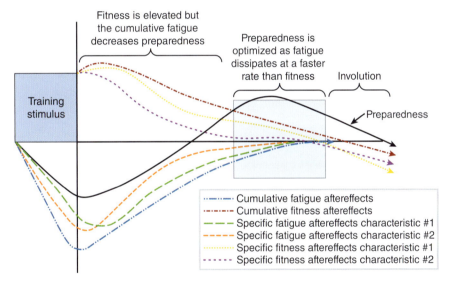

FIGURE 1.19 Modified fitness–fatigue paradigm depicting multiple training aftereffects.

Adapted by permission from G.G. Haff and E.E. Haff, "Training Integration and Periodization," in *NSCA's Guide to Program Design*, edited for the National Strength and Conditioning Association by J. Hoffman (Champaign, IL: Human Kinetics, 2012), 215.

It is also likely that the aftereffects of fatigue and fitness are exercise specific (193, 207, 223). In support of this, Stone and O'Bryant (189) suggest that the order of recovery from heavy loading (5 sets × 10 repetitions at 70% of one-repetition maximum [1RM]) is (a) upper body, (b) leg extensors, (c) lower back. Thus, various exercises that target different parts of the body during a training session have different effects on preparedness (figure 1.20).

The possibility of multiple fitness and fatigue aftereffects that occur simultaneously may partially explain why there are individual responses to variations in the training stimuli (76, 80). Therefore, one can conclude that there are different aftereffects for different training targets and that specific training interventions can modulate which aftereffects occur and how preparedness is affected (76).

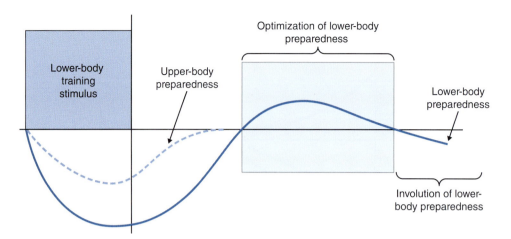

FIGURE 1.20 Effect of training focus on preparedness.

Adapted by permission from A. Turner and P. Comfort, "Periodisation," in *Advanced Strength and Conditioning: An Evidence-Based Approach,* edited by A. Turner and P. Comfort (London: Routledge Taylor Francis, 2018). Permission conveyed through Copyright Clearance Center, Inc.

Summary

Training is a structured process that is designed to enhance the athlete's physiological and psychological skills in order to improve their competitive performance. Athletes are not developed overnight, and the training process is a long-term endeavor. The coach must exploit scientific knowledge to optimize the overall implementation of the training plan. The training plan will evolve over time as the athlete adapts to the training loads. Understanding how the athlete responds to a training stimulus allows the coach to construct training interventions that increase the chance of improving performance while managing fatigue and reducing the risk of overtraining.

CHAPTER 2

Energetics and Training

The ability to transform food within the body into a biologically useable form of energy is essential for sustaining life and for performing the intense physical activities associated with sport performance and the training process. To sustain physical activity during training or competition, the body must have a continuous supply of energy. Coaches must have a comprehensive understanding of how the body meets these energetic demands so they can construct more effective training interventions.

A central component of the training process is the principle of specificity, which is best described by the acronym SAID: specific adaptation to imposed demands. This translates to the training process because the demands that the body is exposed to in the training process will dictate the training outcomes. A critical component of this process is **metabolic specificity**, or bioenergetic specificity, in which training interventions are designed to align with the energetic parameters associated with the sport or activity for which the athlete is training.

To effectively design physical training interventions that adhere to the principle of bioenergetic specificity, the coach must understand how the body supplies energy for physical activity. The coach must also understand how energy stores are replenished after the cessation of exercise. By understanding the time frame of restoration and the metabolic processes that facilitate the restoration of energetic stores, the coach will be able to construct training interventions that best align with the competitive goals of their athletes. Understanding the key principles associated with bioenergetics is necessary for designing and implementing periodized training plans.

Bioenergetics

Grasping the concept of exercise and training specificity requires a comprehensive understanding about how the body uses and produces **energy**, which is often referred to as *metabolic specificity* (89, 183). To effectively design and implement training programs, the coach must understand how energy is made available for specific types of exercise and how modifications to the training regime can affect the energetic demands of the training process. With a comprehensive understanding of these processes, the coach can construct more efficient and effective periodized training plans (183).

Bioenergetics, or the energetic flow in biological systems, involves the conversion of macronutrients, such as carbohydrates, proteins, and fats, into a usable form of chemical energy (89, 183). When the chemical bonds contained within these macronutrients are broken, energy is released to perform the required biological work. For example, during **catabolism**, energy is released from large molecules (i.e., food and energy substrates) when they are broken into smaller molecules, resulting in what is termed an *exergonic reaction* (183). Conversely, an **endergonic reaction** occurs during **anabolism** as energy is required to synthesize larger molecules from smaller molecules (89). The total of all the exergonic and endergonic reactions in a biological system is referred to as *metabolism*.

The energy that is derived from exergonic reactions is used to drive endergonic reactions through a high-energy molecule known as *adenosine triphosphate* (ATP) (figure 2.1). If there is an inadequate supply of ATP, it is not possible to undergo muscular activity or stimulate muscular growth (89). Due to the importance of ATP as an energy conveyor during muscular contraction, and therefore human movement, it is critical that the coach understands how training affects ATP hydrolysis (i.e., breakdown) and resynthesis (89, 183).

ATP, which is stored in limited amounts within the skeletal muscle, consists of one adenosine molecule and three phosphate molecules (figure 2.2a). The enzyme **adenosine triphosphatase (ATPase)** is required to catalyze the hydrolysis of ATP, as noted in the following equation:

$$ATP + H_2O \leftarrow ATPase \rightarrow ADP + P_i + H^+ + energy$$

Whenever ATP goes through hydrolysis, there is a removal of one **inorganic phosphate (P_i)**, thereby forming **adenosine diphosphate (ADP)** (figure 2.2b). This results in a release of energy that can be used to perform biological work, such as muscular contractions and tissue synthesis (126, 136). Further energy can be created by the

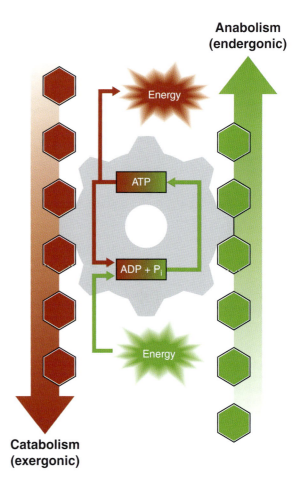

FIGURE 2.1 Overview of metabolism.

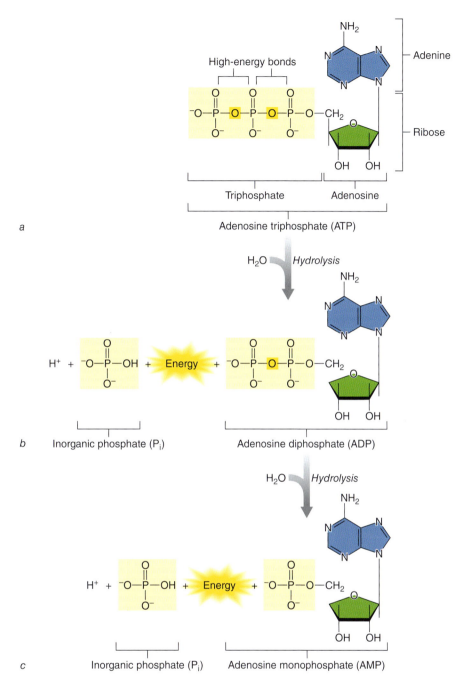

FIGURE 2.2 Adenosine triphosphate: *(a)* the chemical structure of an ATP molecule; *(b)* hydrolysis of ATP that leaves ADP, P_i, and H^+; and *(c)* hydrolysis of ADP that leaves AMP, P_i, and H^+.

Reprinted by permission from T.J. Herda and J.T. Cramer, "Bioenergetics of Exercise and Training," in *Essentials of Strength Training and Conditioning*, edited by G.G. Haff and N. Triplett (Champaign, IL: Human Kinetics, 2016), 45.

hydrolysis of ADP, resulting in the removal of a P_i and the formation of **adenosine monophosphate (AMP)** (figure 2.2c).

The body stores a limited amount of ATP within the skeletal muscle, and this amount provides energy for only about 20 seconds in the absence of any regeneration (8). Even though the body stores only a limited amount of ATP, it uses the various bioenergetic systems to ensure that ATP levels are never completely depleted (89, 183). ATP levels of skeletal muscle drop to only about 50% to 60% of their initial values (79, 100, 116, 185).

Typically, when an athlete is performing maximal exercise, muscular stores of ATP can supply energy for about 1 or 2 seconds before the body has to draw on the production of ATP from other sources (8, 126, 134, 136). During high-intensity exercise, such as an all-out sprint, ATP concentrations can decline significantly during the first 10 seconds of activity (134). This decline is most noted by the marked decreases in ATP contained within the fast-twitch (type II) muscle fibers. For example, after 10 seconds of maximal exercise there is a 40% decrease in type IIa ATP concentration and a 70% decrease in the ATP concentration of type IIx muscle fibers, but there are minimal reductions in the ATP concentrations in slow-twitch (type I) muscle fibers. If, however, exercise is extended from 10 to 25 seconds, there will be a 20% reduction in the ATP concentration of the type I muscle fibers and a less significant decline noted for the type II muscle fibers (134).

Energy Systems

A key aspect of muscles' ability to perform work for sustained periods is the continuous ability to regenerate ATP. For exercise-related bioenergetics, anaerobic and aerobic metabolism are often used (89). **Anaerobic** energy systems, such as the phosphagen and glycolytic systems, do not require the presence of oxygen and occur within the sarcoplasm of the muscle cell. The **aerobic** energy systems, such as the oxidative systems that include the **Krebs cycle** and electron transport, require the presence of oxygen and occur within the mitochondria (89).

Generally, the three major energy supply systems are active all the time and work simultaneously to replenish ATP (figure 2.3). The contributions of the phosphagen, glycolytic, and oxidative systems primarily depend on the activity's intensity and secondarily on its duration (53, 89).

The major difference between the primary energy systems is the rate at which they can deliver ATP (127). The most rapid supplier of ATP is the **phosphagen system** (also known as the *ATP-PC system*), followed by the fast glycolytic system, the slow glycolytic system, the oxidation of glycogen, and the oxidation of fats (127, 183). The enzymatic processes that activate and control each energy system work to ensure that a constant level of ATP is available.

During physical activity that requires a rapid rate of ATP usage (i.e., sprinting), rapid energy systems, such as the phosphagen and fast glycolytic systems, will be engaged to maintain ATP availability. When the rate of ATP use is relatively slow (i.e., distance running), ATP can be maintained with the primary use of the oxidative pathways.

Phosphagen System

The phosphagen system primarily provides energy for short-duration, high-intensity activities and is engaged at the initiation of all exercise regardless of intensity (183). This energetic system serves as the primary energy source for activities such as sprinting (e.g., 36 m and 100 m sprints), diving, weightlifting, powerlifting, American football, jumping, throwing events in athletics, vaulting in gymnastics, and ski jumping.

The phosphagen system is composed of three basic reactions that are used to produce ATP within skeletal muscle. In the first reaction, myosin ATPase is used to break down ATP into ADP and P_i, resulting in the release of energy. Because there are limited stores of ATP and there is four to six times more phosphocreatine (PCr) stored within the skeletal muscle, PCr can be used to quickly regenerate ATP (8, 138). This is accomplished with the second reaction, in which creatine kinase removes a phosphate from PCr and forms P_i, which is then added to ADP; this results in the formation of an ATP molecule and creatine (Cr), as shown in the following equation:

$$ADP + PCr \xrightleftharpoons{\text{creatine kinase}} ATP + Cr$$

Since significant reductions in ATP occur after as little as 10 seconds of high-intensity work (130), there is an increased reliance on PCr during this time. In fact, in as little as 10 seconds there can be a 50% to 70% decrease in PCr concentrations and a complete depletion in response to intensive exhaustive exercise that occurs to maintain ATP availability (95, 106, 107). Generally, the highest contribution of PCr to the buffering of ATP occurs within the first 2 seconds of the initiation of exercise. Within 5 seconds of exercise there can be a 50% reduction in the ability of PCr to buffer ATP, and within 30 seconds the contribution of PCr is

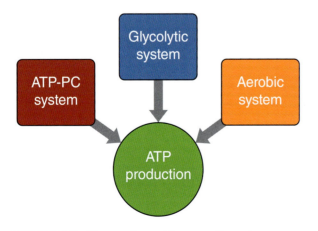

FIGURE 2.3 Three primary bioenergetic systems.

reduced by 70%. As PCr use increases, there is a concomitant increase in P_i concentration that stimulates an increased **glycolytic flux**, resulting in a shift from the use of PCr toward glycolysis as a means of buffering ATP (41, 169). Therefore, about 6 to 8 seconds after the initiation of exercise, there is an increase in the glycolytic energy system's contribution to the ATP supply that accounts for about 10% of ATP turnover (8, 67).

Another important enzymatic reaction used to maintain ATP availability is the myokinase reaction. This reaction removes a phosphate from ADP, resulting in the formation of AMP and P_i, after which the P_i is added to ADP to form an ATP, as shown in the following equation:

$$ADP + ADP \xrightleftharpoons{\text{myokinase}} ATP + AMP$$

Although this reaction is an important contributor to ATP production, it also serves a very important role in stimulating glycolysis (38).

Overall, the phosphagen system will supply energy until exercise ceases or the intensity decreases to a point where it does not result in PCr depletion and allows for the glycolytic or the oxidative system to become the primary supplier of ATP and creatine is rephosphorylated (89). When this occurs, the sarcoplasmic concentration of ATP will be maintained or will possibly increase, and the creatine kinase and myokinase reactions will slow or reverse.

Glycolytic System

Glycolysis occurs in the sarcoplasm and is considered the second anaerobic energy system. It serves as the primary energy supplier for activities that last from about 20 seconds to 2 minutes (130). The system breaks down carbohydrates, either blood glucose or muscle glycogen, to resynthesize ATP that can supply energy for biological work. However, even though the energy system can use both substrates, muscle glycogen is preferred (32). Due to requiring multiple enzymatic reactions to resynthesize ATP, the glycolytic system is markedly more complex than the single enzymatic processes of the phosphagen system (figure 2.4). As a result, this energetic pathway is not as rapid as the phosphagen system, but because there is a larger supply of blood glucose and muscle glycogen when compared to PCr, the system has a much greater capacity to supply energy.

The product of the glycolytic system is **pyruvate**, which can be converted into lactate in the sarcoplasm or shuttled into the **mitochondria**. Given its two endpoints, the glycolytic system is often referred to as either ***fast glycolysis*** or ***slow glycolysis***.

Fast Glycolysis

When pyruvate is converted to lactate, ATP is resynthesized at a faster rate but has a limited duration due to an increased production of H^+ and a concomitant reduction in cytosolic pH (89). In this scenario, the process is referred to as *fast glycolysis* because of the rapid nature of ATP resynthesis. Due to its ability to supply energy relatively quickly, the fast glycolytic system is particularly important for moderately high- to high-intensity exercise, such as resistance or sprint training, which has a high energetic demand (32, 183). However, as exercise intensity increases, the *glycolytic flux* (the rate of energy production by the fast glycolytic system) also increases, resulting in an accumulation of pyruvate, which is then converted to lactate (82, 175). Ultimately, when the rate of lactate production exceeds the rate of clearance, there will be an increased lactate accumulation (82).

Lactate Accumulation As the intensity of exercise increases, pyruvate accumulates in response to an increased glycolytic flux and the inability of the mitochondria to oxidize pyruvate fast enough (82). In this scenario, pyruvate is converted to lactate via the lactate dehydrogenase muscle reaction (190). This reaction is often falsely suggested to result in the production of lactic acid, which historically has been related to **metabolic acidosis** and fatigue (62). Due to the earlier steps in glycolysis that consume protons (165) and the physiological pH (i.e., about 7), lactate, not lactic acid, is the product of the lactate dehydrogenase reaction. Although high tissue concentrations of lactate are correlated with muscular fatigue during exercise, lactate is not the cause of fatigue (37, 82, 165). In fact, the lactate dehydrogenase reaction not only facilitates the ability of the glycolytic system to meet energy demands via the maintenance of cytosolic redox potential (oxidized nicotinamide adenine dinucleotide [NAD^+]/reduced NAD [NADH]) but also effectively buffers against acidosis because it consumes a proton (165).

Fatigue associated with metabolic acidosis is related to hydrogen proton (H^+) accumulation that results in a reduced intracellular pH. This accumulation of H^+ inhibits glycolytic reactions and impedes calcium (Ca^{2+}) binding with troponin C (65, 149) and can restrict crossbridge cycling (59, 90, 149, 186) and directly interfere with excitation–contraction coupling. Although metabolic acidosis has classically been associated with peripheral

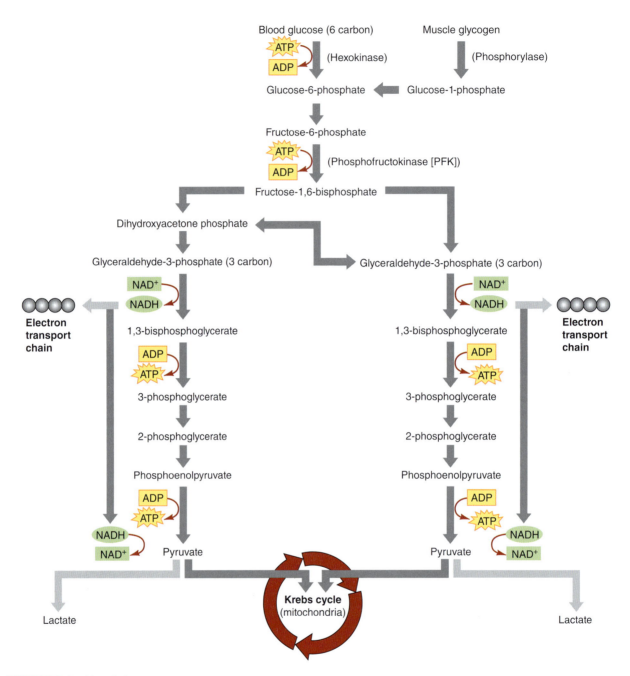

FIGURE 2.4 Glycolytic system.

Reprinted by permission from T.J. Herda and J.T. Cramer, "Bioenergetics of Exercise and Training," in *Essentials of Strength Training and Conditioning*, edited by G.G. Haff and N. Triplett (Champaign, IL: Human Kinetics, 2016), 47.

fatigue during exercise (165), evidence has made it clear that it is not directly related to lactic acid (82). Robergs, Ghiasvand, and Parker (165) have argued that although lactate is associated with H⁺ production, the actual source of metabolic fatigue is more likely a result of nonmitochondrial hydrolysis of ATP (165). Additionally, other factors, such as increased potassium (K^+) concentration and P_i, can impair Ca^{2+} release (16, 150), which also contributes to metabolic fatigue.

Lactate is not a waste product of glycolytic metabolism but rather an important fuel and a potential signaling molecule—a **lactormone**—that is continuously formed even in fully aerobic conditions (30). Under resting conditions, lactate concentrations in the blood and muscle are low. Typically, blood lactate levels range from 0.5 to 2.2 mmol · L⁻¹ at rest (74), whereas in muscle there is 0.5 to 2.2 mmol for each kilogram of wet muscle (muscle that has not been desiccated) (74). As exercise intensity increases, there is a concomitant increase in muscle fiber type lactate production (62, 74, 168). It is well-documented that type II (i.e., fast-twitch) muscle fibers have a significantly higher rate of lactate production when compared to type I (i.e., slow-twitch) muscle fibers (9, 54, 152). These higher rates of lactate production are reflective of the higher concentrations and activity of the glycolytic enzymes present in the type II muscle fibers when compared to type I fibers (9, 152).

The highest possible concentration of lactate accumulation is unknown (74). There are several reports that lactate concentrations can be elevated well above 20 mmol · L^{-1} (74, 91, 92). In fact, Hermansen and Stensvold (91) and Hermansen and Vaage (92) have reported lactate concentrations greater than 30 mmol · L^{-1} after multiple bouts of intense dynamic exercise. In addition to the effect of exercise intensity and muscle fiber type on lactate accumulation, the duration of exercise (74), initial glycogen levels (74), and the current state of training can all exert an influence on the degree of accumulation.

There is a greater degree of lactate accumulation after intermittent high-intensity activity, such as resistance training and sprinting, compared to continuous lower-intensity activity (91, 123, 192, 193). Additionally, the intensity of the intermittent activity will exert a significant effect on the amount of lactate accumulation. For example, Seiler and Sylta (173) had 62 highly trained cyclists perform three different **high-intensity interval training (HIIT)** sessions (4 sets of 16-minute, 4 sets of 8-minute, or 4 sets of 4-minute work bouts) separated by 2-minute recovery periods at 95±5%, 106±5%, and 117±6% of 40-minute time trial power, respectively. The blood lactate was highest in the 4 sets of 4-minute (12.7±2.7 mmol · L^{-1}) work bouts, followed by the 4 sets of 8-minute work bouts (9.2±2.4 mmol · L^{-1}) and the 4 sets of 16-minute work bouts (4.7±1.6 mmol · L^{-1}). Based on these data, it is clear that intensity and duration of the exercise activity influence which energy system primarily supplies energy, and this affects the overall lactate accumulation in response.

The state of training can also affect how much lactate is produced in response to a given workload (72, 183). Aerobically trained individuals are able to maintain lower lactate levels when performing exercise at submaximal power outputs when compared to untrained people (159, 183). This ability may largely be explained by aerobically trained individuals having increased mitochondrial activity (70, 71), increased capillary density (179), lower catecholamine responses, and a shift in isozyme patterns such as lactate dehydrogenase muscle to lactate dehydrogenase heart as a result of training (178). Additionally, when the same absolute submaximal resistance training workloads are performed, trained individuals produce less lactate than untrained individuals (157). Similar responses are also noted in response to short-term, high-intensity interval exercise (167).

When maximal exercise is performed, anaerobically trained athletes display significantly higher lactate concentrations when compared to untrained or aerobically trained athletes (100, 155). The ability to accumulate these higher lactate concentrations may be related to training-induced increases in anaerobic enzyme activities, changes in isozyme patterns, and increases in lactate buffering capacities, which allow for higher maximum intensities of exercise to be performed (155, 197). In fact, very high–intensity exercise performed for multiple bouts has been reported to result in concentrations of lactate greater than 20 mmol · L^{-1} (91, 92), with the highest lactate concentrations being reported in response to high-intensity exercise performed with short rest periods (21, 91, 112).

Lactate Usage The concentration of blood lactate reflects the balance between the production of lactate and its clearance. When lactate is produced, there are several pathways modulated by the monocarboxylate transporter proteins (MCT) (figure 2.5). Specifically, lactate can be transported via MCT into the mitochondria where it can be oxidized, or it can be transported to peroxisomes for coupled reoxidation of NADH, which is required for beta-oxidation (30, 82).

Another possible destination for lactate is to use an MCT to shuttle it out of the cell in conjunction with the extracellular transport of one H$^+$ (165). Once in the blood, lactate can be transported to, taken up by, and used as a fuel by adjacent skeletal muscle and other organs such at the brain, kidneys, heart, and liver (30, 190). During exercise, the oxidation of lactate is responsible for the removal of about 75% to 80% of the lactate produced, and the remainder is used for gluconeogenesis in the liver and kidneys (30). Additionally, research shows that lactate will work as a lactormone when it becomes elevated, resulting in a downregulation of other energy substrates, such as glucose and free fatty acids, which allows lactate to become a useful fuel source (165). Because lactate uptake depends on concentration gradients and there is a high capacity for lactate oxidation, lactate offers a fast and efficient fuel source (82, 165).

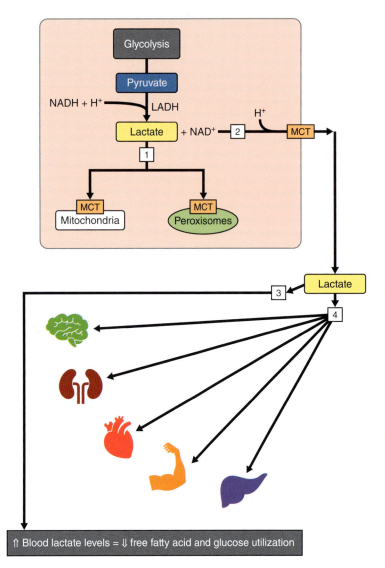

FIGURE 2.5 Fate of lactate: intracellular and cell–cell shuttle. (1) In intracellular lactate shuttle, an MCT transports lactate into the mitochondria or into the peroxisomes for coupled reoxidation of NADH. (2) An MCT is used for extracellular transport of lactate and one H⁺. (3) A signaling process is used to downregulate free fatty acid and glucose use in response to increases in lactate. (4) Lactate is used as an energy source (oxidized) by cells in the brain, kidneys, heart, liver, and muscles.

Adapted by permission from M.M. Hall, S. Rajasekaran, T.W. Thomsen, and A.R. Peterson, "Lactate: Friend or Foe," *PM&R: The Journal of Injury, Function, and Rehabilitation* 8, no. 3 (2016): S8-S15. Permission conveyed through Copyright Clearance Center, Inc.

Postexercise Lactate Removal The highest blood lactate levels tend to occur after repetitive bouts of high-intensity exercise (91), with peak lactate levels typically occurring between 5 to 7 minutes postexercise (73). This postexercise lag time is a result of the cellular transport mechanism for lactate (105, 183). As noted previously, MCT facilitates the entry of lactate into and out of the cell (20). There are several variants of the MCT found within different tissues in the body (26). MCT1 is responsible for lactate uptake, and MCT4 is responsible for facilitated lactate removal against a concentration gradient (26, 158). Both MCT1 and MCT4 appear sensitive to training, with endurance training enhancing the expression of MCT1 and anaerobic training enhancing the expression of MCT4 (20).

Although lactate is not directly associated with fatigue (82), its rate of removal may to some extent reflect the ability to recover (159). It can take up to 1 hour for blood lactate concentrations to return to baseline, but the rate of recovery is largely dictated by the muscle activity undertaken during the recovery period (73, 132). For example, if an athlete sits or lies down after a maximal intensity bout of exercise, lactate and H⁺ diffuse from the muscle (where concentrations are high) into the blood (where concentrations are lower) (132). Once it has entered circulation, lactate can be taken to the liver, where it undergoes **gluconeogenesis** (i.e., conversion into glucose), or it can be shuttled to active tissue, such as the heart, where it is converted to pyruvate by lactate dehydrogenase heart and used as a fuel for oxidative metabolism (132).

The recovery process can be enhanced if active recovery is employed. Active recovery that employs exercise with intensities of 50% to 70% of **maximal oxygen uptake ($\dot{V}O_2max$)** appears to optimize lactate clearance rates in endurance-trained athletes (64, 73, 95, 159). When active recovery is employed, lactate will be used as a fuel for producing energy via oxidative metabolism in the active muscles, such as the type I muscle fibers (132), instead of being shuttled to the liver.

Another factor related to the ability to deal with postexercise lactate is the training status of the athlete. Based on the available literature, both aerobically (73, 159) and anaerobically (142, 157, 194) trained athletes demonstrate enhanced lactate recovery rates (183).

Lactate Threshold and Onset of Blood Lactate
As exercise intensity increases, there are specific break points in the lactate accumulation curve (figure 2.6) (25, 48, 62, 110, 184) that correspond to a shift toward a greater reliance on anaerobic mechanisms of energy production as the intensity of exercise increases (89). The first break

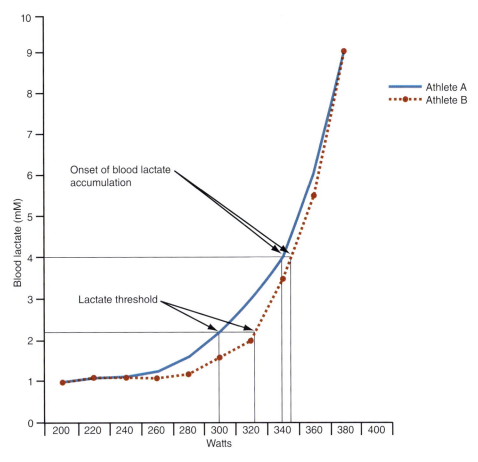

FIGURE 2.6 Lactate threshold and onset of blood lactate accumulation. Athlete A can produce 300 W at his lactate threshold, whereas athlete B can produce 320 W. Thus, athlete B can work at a 6.7% higher workload.

Reprinted by permission from T.O. Bompa and G.G. Haff, *Periodization: Theory and Methodology of Training,* 5th ed., (Champaign, IL: Human Kinetics, 2009), 294.

point is referred to as the **lactate threshold (LT)**. This represents the point at which blood lactate demonstrates an abrupt substantial increase above baseline levels in response to changes in exercise intensity (82, 184). Typically, the LT is best defined as a 1 mmol · L^{-1} increase in blood lactate concentration above resting levels in response to a grade increase in exercise intensity (figure 2.7) (46, 202).

In untrained individuals, the LT occurs between 50% and 60% of $\dot{V}O_2$max, whereas in trained individuals the LT can occur between 75% and 90% of $\dot{V}O_2$max (40, 104). Understanding the LT and the intensity (i.e., power of velocity) that can be maintained at this threshold is important, because it is a strong predictor of endurance performance (13, 56). Additionally, the heart rate at the LT has been found to be strongly correlated ($r = .78, p = .008$) to heart rate during a 60-minute time trial performed by trained cyclists (56). Taken collectively, it is clear that a large portion of the variance in time trial or endurance performance is explained by the speed of movement or power output at the LT (10, 60, 61).

Based on our current understanding, the LT can be related to heart rate and power output, and this break point may be an important minimal intensity when undertaking endurance training activities (82, 125). Although training at or around the LT can elevate the LT of sedentary individuals, higher-intensity training, such as that associated with the **onset of blood lactate accumulation (OBLA)**, is necessary to induce improvements in performance in well-conditioned athletes (82, 125).

The OBLA, which has been incorrectly referred to as the LT (139), represents the second break point on the lactate accumulation curve. This point is defined as the intensity of exercise where blood lactate reaches 4 mmol · L^{-1} during an incremental test (14, 86, 176, 177, 184). This criterion estimate of OBLA provides a very objective assessment of the anaerobic threshold, which represents a time point at which there is an incremental increase in net contribution from fast glycolytic means resulting in lactate formation (184). According to the scientific literature, the OBLA generally occurs somewhere

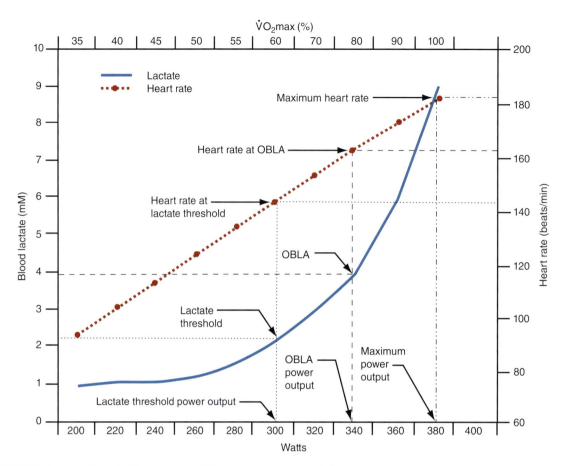

FIGURE 2.7 Lactate threshold and onset of blood lactate accumulation response to a graded cycle ergometer test.

Reprinted by permission from T.O. Bompa and G.G. Haff, *Periodization: Theory and Methodology of Training*, 5th ed., (Champaign, IL: Human Kinetics, 2009), 295.

between 90% to 93% of maximum heart rate in trained endurance athletes (56, 98, 153). Similar to the LT, the OBLA is a strong indicator of endurance performance capabilities (14, 56, 102). For example, Dumke et al. (56) report that 61% of the variance in a 60 km (37 mi) time-trial performance is explained by the heart rate corresponding to OBLA. It is important to note that exercise task specificity characterizes OBLA (138). When comparing bicycle, treadmill, and arm-crank exercise, the OBLA occurs at differing workloads (201). It is likely that variations in the amount of activated muscle mass partially explains these differences. For example, there is a higher metabolic rate for arm-crank and bicycling exercise when compared to treadmill exercise when performed at a given intensity or submaximal oxygen consumption (139, 201). Therefore, OBLA will occur sooner during bicycle and arm-crank exercise when compared to treadmill exercise (201). It is important to remember that if the OBLA is used to guide training, it must be determined during a graded exercise test of the mode being trained. If multiple modes of training are being used, then the OBLA must be determined during a graded exercise test for each mode of exercise.

Research suggests that the time points on the lactate accumulation curve associated with the LT and OBLA can be affected by the training stimulus the athlete undertakes (57, 104, 119, 122). For example, when endurance training is performed with intensities at or slightly above the LT, there will be a rightward shift of the lactate accumulation curve that alters the intensities associated with the LT and OBLA (39, 87, 103, 108, 177, 196). Researchers have also reported that the workloads at which the LT and OBLA occur are altered after periods of HIIT training (49, 57). For example, Esfarjani and Laursen (57) report that performing HIIT can shift the lactate accumulation curve to the right, elevating the intensity at which the LT occurs and significantly improving endurance performance. These responses are largely due to the fact that HIIT is performed at intensities substantially higher than the LT power, velocity, or heart rate (117). The effect of HIIT is related to the high-intensity efforts, which are undertaken for various durations (i.e., 30 s to 8 min) interspersed with lower-intensity recovery (i.e., 60 s to 4.5 min) (see chapter 14) (118, 121). One sport-specific variant of HIIT is a **small-sided game (SSG)**, which can be constructed in a manner that requires the athlete to train at intensities similar to more traditional HIIT methods (see chapter 14) and results in alterations to the LT while providing a time-efficient, sport-specific training stimulus for team sport athletes (113). The variety of training methodologies that can be used to alter the LT and OBLA allows the coach to choose training strategies that best align with the period and phases of the periodized training plan.

Maximal Lactate Steady State The **maximal lactate steady state (MLSS)** is the highest point of equilibrium between lactate production and clearance (20). It is often defined as the highest intensity of exercise at which blood lactate does not increase during exercise performed at a constant load (86, 184). Another way to look at the MLSS is to consider it as the highest blood lactate concentration ($MLSS_C$) and workload ($MLSS_W$) that can be maintained without continued lactate accumulation (20).

The $MLSS_W$ has often been used as an assessment of an athlete's endurance capacity (17, 18, 20, 154) and has been shown to elicit a blood lactate concentration of 4 mmol · L^{-1} (20). As a result, it has often been estimated with the quantification of the OBLA during an incremental test (86). The $MLSS_W$ has been correlated with performance, particularly the time sustained at a given speed (20). $MLSS_C$ is associated with blood lactate levels that range between 2 and 8 mmol · L^{-1} and has not been related to performance (12). The $MLSS_W$ delineates the low- to high-intensity exercise in which no $\dot{V}O_2$ steady state is observed and there is a shift away from fat toward carbohydrate fuel supply (19). When exercise intensity is above the MLSS, pyruvate production exceeds lactate clearance and blood pH decreases, resulting in the termination of exercise (20).

Slow Glycolysis

As the bout of exercise extends from 20 seconds toward the 2-minute mark, the intensity of exercise reduces, and the primary energy supplier shifts from fast to slow glycolysis. In this scenario, the need for rapid energetic supply is reduced and a slower rate of ATP resynthesis can meet the energetic demands. Instead of being converted into lactate, pyruvate is shuttled into the mitochondria, where it undergoes the Krebs cycle, resulting in a slower rate of ATP resynthesis that is directly related to an increased number of enzymatic reactions (89, 183). Even though slow glycolysis supplies energy at a slower rate, this system can be the primary supplier of energy for longer anaerobic bouts of exercise if the exercise intensity is low enough.

In summary, the intensity of the exercise bout dictates the rate of energetic demand, and this determines the fate of pyruvate. When energy demand is high and needs to be transferred quickly, pyruvate is primarily converted to lactate (fast glycolysis). Conversely, when energy demand is not as high and sufficient quantities of oxygen are present in the cell, pyruvate is shuttled into the mitochondria where it is oxidized (89, 183).

Oxidative System

The **oxidative system** is the most complex of the three energy systems (140) and is often referred to as the *aerobic energy system* (140). This system requires oxygen in order to resynthesize ATP within the mitochondria via mitochondrial respiration (6). The mitochondria are sometimes referred to as the *powerhouses* of the cell and can be found adjacent to myofibrils and scattered throughout the sarcoplasm (6, 140, 183).

The primary substrates used in the oxidative system are carbohydrates and fats (figure 2.8) (6, 69). For example, at rest, about 30% of the ATP produced is derived from carbohydrates and about 70% comes from fats (89, 183).

During exercise, the contribution of fat and carbohydrate oxidation to energy production is modulated by the intensity and duration of the exercise bout. As the intensity of exercise increases, the oxidation of carbohydrate (primarily muscle glycogen) will increase, and there is a progressive reduction in the oxidation of fat (126). When performing high-intensity exercise, nearly 100% of the energetic supply comes from the oxidation of muscle glycogen; the contribution from the oxidation of fats and proteins is minimal (89, 126). The advantage of this shift toward using muscle glycogen is that more ATP can be produced per unit of oxygen consumed (126). Additionally, the rate at which ATP can be resynthesized is greater than what can be achieved by a mixture of substrates.

Although carbohydrates are the primary fuel source during high-intensity exercise, during submaximal exercise performed for a continuous, prolonged period, such as marathon running or long-distance cycling, there is an increased reliance on fat oxidation and a reduced contribution

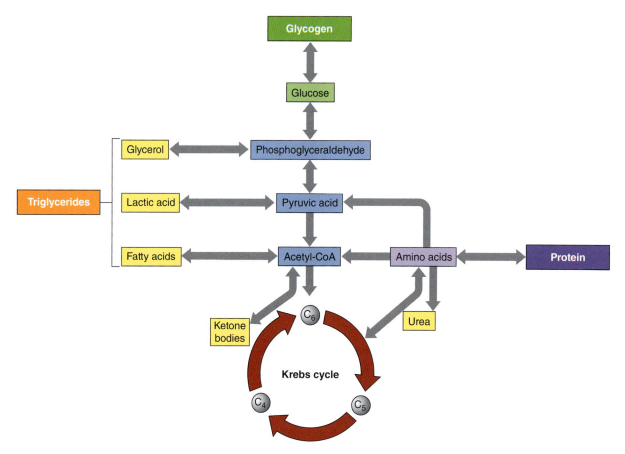

FIGURE 2.8 A simplified pathway for the metabolism of carbohydrates, fats, and protein.

Reprinted by permission from T.J. Herda and J.T. Cramer, "Bioenergetics of Exercise and Training," in *Essentials of Strength Training and Conditioning*, edited by G.G. Haff and N. Triplett (Champaign, IL: Human Kinetics, 2016), 54.

of carbohydrate oxidation (126). This shift can be partially explained by the reductions in muscle and liver glycogen that occur in response to this type of exercise. When there is a shift away from carbohydrate oxidation toward fat oxidation, the ability to maintain exercise intensity will be reduced (126).

Oxidation of Carbohydrates

The oxidation of glucose and glycogen begins with glycolysis. When the intensity of exercise is low enough and oxygen is available, the end product of glycolysis—pyruvate—is transported into the mitochondria and converted into acetyl coenzyme A (acetyl-CoA) where it enters the Krebs cycle (figure 2.9) (126, 183).

Specifically, for every molecule of glucose entering glycolysis, two molecules of pyruvate are formed and, in the presence of oxygen, are converted to two molecules of acetyl-CoA, resulting in two turns of the series of reactions contained within the Krebs cycle (161). For each turn of the Krebs cycle, one molecule of ATP is indirectly formed from guanine triphosphate (GTP) as a result of substrate level phosphorylation (89). Additionally, each turn results in the formation of a total of three molecules of NADH and one molecule of flavin adenine dinucleotide ($FADH_2$), which transport hydrogen atoms to the electron transport chain to be used to produce ATP from ADP (figure 2.10) (161).

The hydrogen atoms transported by NADH and $FADH_2$ are passed down the electron transport chain, which is a series of electron carriers known as *cytochromes*, to form a proton gradient that provides the energy for ATP production. Oxygen is the final electron acceptor, which results in the formation of water (89, 161). This process results in the production of ATP from oxidative phosphorylation, which accounts for over 90% of the ATP synthesis compared to substrate level phosphorylation (89). Ultimately, the oxidative system has a larger capacity to produce energy compared to the glycolytic system.

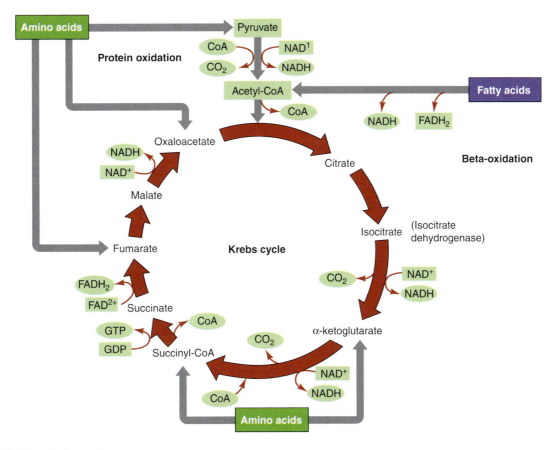

FIGURE 2.9 Krebs cycle.

Reprinted by permission from T.J. Herda and J.T. Cramer, "Bioenergetics of Exercise and Training," in *Essentials of Strength Training and Conditioning*, edited by G.G. Haff and N. Triplett (Champaign, IL: Human Kinetics, 2016), 52.

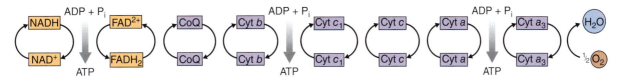

FIGURE 2.10 Electron transport chain. CoQ = coenzyme Q; Cyt = cytochrome.

Reprinted by permission from T.J. Herda and J.T. Cramer, "Bioenergetics of Exercise and Training," in *Essentials of Strength Training and Conditioning*, edited by G.G. Haff and N. Triplett (Champaign, IL: Human Kinetics, 2016), 52.

Oxidation of Fats

One important aspect of the oxidative energy system is that it has the capacity to use fat as a fuel (161). Fats, specifically triglycerides that are stored in fat cells, are broken down by the hormone-sensitive lipase enzyme into fatty acids and glycerol. Additionally, there are limited quantities of triglycerides and a form of hormone-sensitive lipase that breaks down triglycerides into free fatty acids and glycerol stored within the muscle (55, 89). For free fatty acids to be used as a fuel, they must enter the mitochondria and be converted to acetyl-CoA (89, 161). **Beta-oxidation** is a series of reactions that results in the formation of acetyl-CoA and H^+ (figure 2.9). Acetyl-CoA then enters the Krebs cycle, leading to the production of ATP via the electron transport chain (161). Ultimately, beta-oxidation has a larger capacity to produce ATP than either carbohydrate or protein oxidation (89).

Oxidation of Proteins

Although protein is not a major source of energy, it can be broken into its amino acid subunits and enter the bioenergetic pathways in a variety of places. Most amino acids can be converted to glucose (via gluconeogenesis), pyruvate, or various Krebs cycle intermediates in order to produce ATP (figure 2.9) (89, 161). Although amino acids contribute minimally to the production of ATP during short-duration exercise, it has been estimated that they can contribute between 3% and 18% of the fuel needed during prolonged exercise (29, 51, 124, 161, 180).

At least six amino acids—alanine, aspartate, glutamate, and the three branched-chain amino acids (BCAAs)—can be oxidized by skeletal muscle (78). Although these amino acids can contribute to fuel production, they do not all have the same metabolic potential. The BCAAs (valine, isoleucine, and leucine) appear to be the dominant amino acids oxidized by skeletal muscle (77, 78). The formation of urea and small amounts of ammonia is used to eliminate the metabolic waste products produced when amino acids are degraded (78, 89). The creation of ammonia is significant because it is toxic and is associated with central and peripheral fatigue (see chapter 9).

Energy Production Rate and Capacity

When looking at the bioenergetic processes, there are two inherent limits: the maximum rate (i.e., power) of ATP production and the amount of ATP (i.e., capacity) that can be produced (89, 133, 170, 183). The bioenergetic systems vary in the rate at which they can produce ATP and their capacity to meet the body's energy demands (table 2.1).

When considering intensity as a function of power output (111) or work performed per unit of time, there are clear differences in the ability of the bioenergetic systems to supply energy for specific activities (89, 133, 183). When conceptualizing the effect of intensity on energy supply, it is important to understand that even at $\dot{V}O_2max$, the intensity (i.e., power output) is 25% to 35% of the athlete's capacity to produce peak power outputs during a Wingate anaerobic cycle test (44). Based on these findings, aerobic exercise, even at $\dot{V}O_2max$, should not be classified as high-intensity exercise (44, 183).

Activities performed at maximum intensity demand a rapid rate of energy supply, which is met by the phosphagen system. Conversely, exercise performed at a low intensity but sustained for a long duration requires a prolonged supply of energy, which predominantly comes from the oxidative energy system (89, 183). For activities between these two extremes, the primary energy system will shift depending on the intensity and duration of the activity (table 2.2).

TABLE 2.1 Ranking the Energy Systems by Rate and Capacity of ATP Production

System	Rate of ATP production	Capacity of ATP production
Phosphagen	1	5
Fast glycolysis	2	4
Slow glycolysis	3	3
Oxidation of carbohydrates	4	2
Oxidation of fats and proteins	5	1

Note: 1 = fastest or greatest; 5 = slowest or least.

Reprinted by permission from T.J. Herda and J.T. Cramer, "Bioenergetics of Exercise and Training," in *Essentials of Strength Training and Conditioning*, edited by G.G. Haff and N. Triplett (Champaign, IL: Human Kinetics, 2016), 54.

TABLE 2.2 Effect of Duration and Intensity on the Primary Energy System Used

Duration of event	Intensity of event	Primary energy system
0-6 s	Extremely high	Phosphagen
6-30 s	Very high	Phosphagen and fast glycolysis
30 s-2 min	High	Fast and slow glycolysis
2-3 min	Moderate	Slow glycolysis and oxidative system
>3 min	Low	Oxidative system

Note: The relationships between duration, intensity, and primary energy systems used assume that the athlete strives to attain the best possible performance for a given event.

Adapted by permission from T.J. Herda and J.T. Cramer, "Bioenergetics of Exercise and Training," in *Essentials of Strength Training and Conditioning*, edited by G.G. Haff and N. Triplett (Champaign, IL: Human Kinetics, 2016), 54.

For example, short-duration, high-intensity activities, such as resistance or sprint training, have their energy needs met primarily by the phosphagen and fast glycolytic systems (89). As the intensity of the activity decreases and the total duration increases, there is a gradual shift toward slow glycolysis and the oxidative energy systems become the primary energy suppliers (52, 89, 170).

There is no time during exercise or rest when a single energy system provides all the necessary energy. During exercise, the contributions of the anaerobic and aerobic energy systems are primarily governed by the intensity of exercise and secondarily by the exercise duration (90, 166, 183, 186).

Substrate Depletion and Repletion

Depending on the intensity and duration of exercise, there can be selective depletion of energy substrates, which can be partially responsible for fatigue (89, 183). Specifically, the depletion of phosphagens (63, 73, 97, 170) and glycogen (31, 63, 109) are related to exercise-induced fatigue, but the depletion of other substrates, such as amino acids and fatty acids, do not typically occur to the extent that performance is impaired (89, 183). Due to the relationship between fatigue and the depletion of phosphagens and glycogen, the coach must understand the depletion and repletion patterns of these substrates when designing training interventions that align with the bioenergetics of the sport (160).

Phosphagens

Although fatigue during exercise is a complex phenomenon (see chapter 9), it can be partially explained by the decrease in ATP and PCr (i.e., the phosphagens) that occurs to meet the energetic demands of the exercise bout. The rate at which both ATP and PCr are depleted is significantly greater in response to high-intensity anaerobic exercise when compared to aerobic exercise (73, 97, 183). Although muscular stores of ATP can be reduced in response to high-intensity anaerobic exercise, they are never completely depleted. In fact, ATP stores tend to only decrease slightly in response to exercise (45, 183), and this decrease does not exceed 50% to 60% of preexercise values (185). On the other hand, PCr can be significantly reduced (50%-70% of baseline values) during the first moments (5-30 s) of high-intensity exercise and can be completely depleted in response to very intense, exhaustive exercise (95, 101, 141). The degree of PCr depletion is largely reflective of the important role that it plays in the maintenance of muscular stores of ATP during very intense anaerobic exercise. Additional ATP is supplied from the myokinase reaction and the oxidation of other energy sources such as glycogen and free fatty acids (89, 183).

The replenishment of ATP occurs rapidly, with 70% of ATP restored in about 30 seconds and complete restoration occurring within 3 to 5 minutes after the cessation of exercise (96). The restoration of PCr takes longer, with 50% restoration occurring in about 30 seconds (169), 84% occurring in about 2 minutes, 89% occurring in about 4 minutes, and complete restoration taking about 8 minutes (83, 96, 97). However, very high–intensity exercise can result in a slower PCr resynthesis rate that can last up to 15 minutes, likely as a result of increased H^+ concentration (137). Regardless, the overall repletion of the phosphagen pool occurs via aerobic metabolism (84), although the glycolytic system may also exert a large effect on recovery after high-intensity exercise (40, 50).

Glycogen

Relative to fat or protein stores, the body has limited glycogen stores, about 300 to 400 g of glycogen that are stored in skeletal muscle and 70 to 100 g that are stored in the liver that can be used when performing exercise (174). Both training and dietary factors have effects on the resting concentrations of both liver and muscle glycogen (147). For example, chronic anaerobic training, including both sprint and resistance training (27, 129), as well as typical aerobic training (71, 73) can stimulate an increase in resting muscle glycogen concentrations when aligned with appropriate nutritional interventions (85).

The rate of glycogen depletion is largely related to the intensity of the exercise being performed (174). During low-intensity exercise, liver glycogen appears to be more important, and its contribution to metabolic processes increases as the duration of exercise is extended (76). On the other hand, muscle glycogen is the more important energy supplier during moderate- and high-intensity exercise (146). For example, increases in relative intensity of 40%, 55%, and 75% of maximal workload (W_{max}) during cycling exercise result in increasing muscle **glycogenolysis** rates of 1.11, 1.53, and 3.00 g · min^{-1}, respectively (191). Similarly, there are increased muscle glycogenolysis rates of 0.7, 1.4, and 3.4 mmol · kg^{-1} · min^{-1} with relative increases in intensity of 50%, 75%, and 100% of $\dot{V}O_2$max, respectively (172). Generally, when relative intensities are above 60% of $\dot{V}O_2$max, muscle glycogen becomes an increasingly important energy substrate and, in some instances, can become completely depleted during exercise (171).

During low-intensity exercise (<50% of $\dot{V}O_2$max) there is typically a constant blood glucose concentration due to a lower rate of glucose uptake (89, 183). As exercise duration extends beyond 90 minutes, blood glucose levels will begin to fall as a result of reductions in liver glycogen availability (3, 89). Although these reductions in blood glucose rarely fall below 2.8 mmol · L^{-1} (3), some people will become hypoglycemic with exercise-induced blood glucose values less than 2.5 mmol · L^{-1} (4, 47). When liver glycogen stores are reduced and blood glucose levels are between 2.5 and 3.0 mmol · L^{-1}, there can be a reduced carbohydrate oxidation, which can eventually lead to exhaustion (42, 47, 89, 174, 183).

Intermittent exercise performed at very high intensities, such as resistance training, can result in a substantial depletion of 20% to 60% of pre-exercise glycogen levels in response to relatively low total workloads (i.e., few sets) (80, 115, 166, 186, 187). Although phosphagens are typically considered the primary bioenergetic limiter during resistance-training exercises with high intensities and few repetitions or sets, muscle glycogen can become increasingly important when higher total volumes of work are undertaken (166). In fact, the total volume of work seems to play a significant role in modulating the amount of glycogen used during a bout of high-intensity resistance training. For example, Roberts et al. (166) report that performing six sets of 12 repetitions with 35% of 1RM in the leg extension for a total volume of 25.2 arbitrary units (A.U.) (i.e., volume = sets × reps × % 1RM) results in a 38% reduction in muscle glycogen (figure 2.11).

When the same total volume was performed with six sets of six repetitions with 70% of 1RM, there was a 39% reduction in muscle glycogen. Interestingly, the higher-intensity exercise bout resulted in the same reduction in muscle glycogen, but the rate of glycogenolysis was significantly higher. Additionally, when repeated high-intensity exercise is performed, there is a selective increase in the rate of glycogen usage by the type II muscle fibers (128), which can result in reductions in high-intensity exercise performance (58, 166).

The ability to replenish glycogen postexercise is related to the amount of postexercise carbohydrate consumption (35). The highest rates of muscle glycogen replenishment occur in the first hour after the cessation of exercise (99) as a result of the

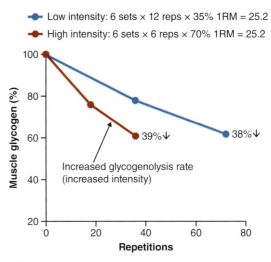

FIGURE 2.11 Example of muscle glycogen depletion during resistance training. Total volume = sets × reps × % 1RM; RM = repetition maximum.

Reprinted by permission from D. MacDougall and D. Sale, *The Physiology of Training for High Performance* (Oxford, United Kingdom: Oxford University Press, 2014), 187, reproduced with permission of the Licensor through PLSclear.

activation of glycogen synthase, which is upregulated in response to glycogen depletion (200), exercise-induced increases in insulin sensitivity (164), and the muscle's increased permeability to glucose (35). The consumption of carbohydrate immediately after exercise takes advantage of these effects and has resulted in significantly elevated glycogen storage in the first 2 hours of recovery after exercise (99). Burke, Kiens, and Ivy (35) highlight the importance of carbohydrate consumption postexercise as a useful strategy for starting the recovery process, which may be particularly important if 4 to 8 hours pass between exercise bouts (99). If there are longer periods of recovery between bouts of exercise, early carbohydrate consumption may not be as critical as long as there is adequate carbohydrate provided by the diet (156).

The general recommendation when glycogen storage needs to be maximized in the 6 hours postexercise is to consume 1 g carbohydrate· kg^{-1} · h^{-1} in small, frequent meals in order to enhance early postexercise recovery (see chapter 10) (36). Early postexercise carbohydrate consumption strategies are important if the athlete has shorter intervals between training, but if there are longer recovery periods between training (>6 h), muscle glycogen can be maintained as long as the athlete consumes adequate carbohydrate in their diet (36, 156). If the exercise bout has a high eccentric component, the rate of glycogen resynthesis can be reduced as a result of muscle damage (151, 203).

Bioenergetic Limiters of Performance

When designing training interventions, it is important to understand the various factors associated with the mechanisms of fatigue experienced during training and competition (chapter 9) (24, 183). Understanding bioenergetic limiters to performance is particularly important when trying to enhance performance and delay the onset of fatigue. Limiting factors can be classified in relation to the depletion of energy sources and increases in H^+ concentration, among other factors (89). Table 2.3 provides an example of how exercise type can be related to these limiting factors and their overall effect on performance (89, 183).

Explosive Events Lasting Less Than 2 Seconds

In activities such as field events (jumping, throwing), strength sports (weightlifting, powerlifting), or explosive movements in gymnastics where maximal efforts lasting less than 2 seconds are performed, energy supply predominantly comes from the resting stores of ATP and the hydrolysis of PCr (126). If the PCr reserves in the skeletal muscle were depleted or partially depleted prior to the performance of an explosive movement, PCr availability could be a performance limiter. This phenomenon can occur if explosive activities are performed in rapid succession or when they are combined with other sustained activities, such as those seen during periods of high-tempo performance in team sports or wrestling (126). In these scenarios, the time between bouts may not be adequate for PCr resynthesis and the increases in H^+ concentrations generated by fast glycolysis may result in the slowing of the creatine kinase reaction (144).

Maximal Efforts Lasting 12 to 15 Seconds

In activities such as sprinting, hurdling, racket sports, and most team sports where maximal efforts are performed for relatively short durations, energy is supplied by the phosphagen and fast glycolytic systems (126). With these types of efforts, the availability of PCr and the glycolytic flux, which dictates the maximal rate of muscle glycogen breakdown to lactate to produce ATP and H^+, are

TABLE 2.3 Bioenergetic Limiters of Performance

Exercise type	ATP and PCr	Muscle glycogen	Liver glycogen	Fat stores	H^+ concentration
Marathon	1	5	4-5	2-3	1
Triathlon	1-2	5	4-5	1-2	1-2
5,000 m run	1-2	3	3	1-2	1
1,500 m run	2-3	3-4	2	1-2	2-3
400 m swim	2-3	3-4	3	1	1-2
400 m run	3	3	1	1	4-5
100 m run	4	1-2	1	1	1-2
Discus	2-3	1	1	1	1
Snatch 1RM	2-3	1	1	1	1
Back squat 1RM	2-3	1	1	1	1
Five sets of 10RM leg press	4-5	4-5	1-2	1-2	4-5
Sets of 10 snatches at 60% of 1RM	4-5	4-5	1-2	1-2	4-5

Note: 1 = least probable limiter; 5 = most probable limiting factor; RM = repetition maximum; ATP = adenosine triphosphate; PCr = phosphocreatine; H^+ = hydrogen ion concentration.

Reprinted by permission from T.J. Herda and J.T. Cramer, "Bioenergetics of Exercise and Training," in *Essentials of Strength Training and Conditioning*, edited by G.G. Haff and N. Triplett (Champaign, IL: Human Kinetics, 2016), 57.

considered the primary bioenergetic limiters. The key regulators of glycolytic flux are the rate of the phosphorylase, phosphofructokinase (PFK), and lactate dehydrogenase enzymatic reactions (126).

When single maximal efforts are performed, the duration is short enough to allow the amount of H^+ produced to be buffered and not negatively affect the glycolytic enzymatic reaction rate (126). If these maximal efforts are repeated, which is typically seen in team sports, the time between efforts may be limited, resulting in a reduced removal of H^+ (120). When this occurs, it is possible the increased H^+ concentration may reduce glycolytic flux as a result of reducing the enzymatic rate of PFK (183). If multiple efforts combined with short rest intervals are continued, there would be a further increase in H^+ concentration, resulting in a further reduction in PFK activity, potential depletion of PCr, and significant reduction in muscle glycogen (1, 2).

When working with athletes who engage in this type of exercise, it is critical to prescribe appropriate training methods aligned with the bioenergetic demands of the sport to increase glycolytic enzyme concentrations and increase the athlete's ability to buffer H^+ (159, 160). In addition to these training-induced enzymatic adaptations, training can also stimulate an increased storage of muscle glycogen (1, 2). Having more muscle glycogen available or having more key glycolytic enzymes can result in a greater glycolytic flux, which will result in a more rapid energetic supply (126).

Maximal Efforts Lasting 15 to 60 Seconds

Intense activities such as the 200 m and 400 m track events, 40 m and 100 m swimming events, and those typically seen in team sports (e.g., soccer and ice hockey) can be sustained for durations of up to 60 seconds without slowing the tempo or stopping play (126, 183). By 60 seconds, the muscular stores of PCr will be almost completely depleted and muscle glycogen will become the major substrate used for the production of ATP (132). If, however, there is a greater amount of PCr stored in the skeletal muscle as a result of creatine supplementation, the effect of the phosphagen system can be extended, resulting in a concomitant improvement in high-intensity exercise performance during activities that last 15 to 60 seconds (7, 11). While the phosphagen system exerts an influence on performance in the 15- to 60-second time frame, the primary energy supplier is considered to be the fast glycolytic energy system, and performance is modulated by the maximal rate of glycolytic enzyme kinetics (anaerobic power) and the ability to buffer the H^+ that is generated by the production of lactate (anaerobic capacity) (126).

Remember that as the duration of exercise increases, the contribution of the aerobic system to energy supply also increases. When maximal exercise is performed for 60 seconds, it is estimated that 30% of the ATP used comes from the oxidation of muscle glycogen (figure 2.12) (126, 161). Therefore,

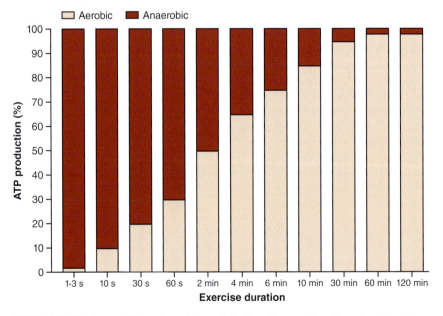

FIGURE 2.12 Anaerobic and aerobic contributions to exercise of varying durations.

Adapted by permission from S.K. Powers and E.T. Howley, *Exercise Physiology: Theory and Application to Fitness and Performance*, 5th ed., (New York, NY: McGraw Hill, 2004), 519. © McGraw-Hill Companies, Inc.

maximal power output in these types of events may also be affected by the kinetics of oxygen delivery and usage (126). Factors such as the athlete's $\dot{V}O_2$max can exert a significant effect on the resynthesis rates for PCr and the removal of lactate after the completion of intense exercise involving a large muscle mass. A higher $\dot{V}O_2$max has been associated with a superior recovery rate during repeated bouts of high-intensity intermittent exercise (188).

Maximal Efforts Lasting Up to 6 Minutes

With activities such as the 800 m and 1,500 m races in track and field; 200 m race in swimming; and speed skating, rowing, and paddling events, the primary energy supply comes from both anaerobic and aerobic metabolism (126). As the exercise bout progresses from 2 to 6 minutes, the aerobic system becomes the primary supplier of energy (figure 2.12), and the anaerobic system decreases its contribution to total energy supply (161).

During these high-intensity activities, the fast glycolytic system will produce lactate, which can accumulate within the skeletal muscle (where it is produced) or diffuse into the blood (132). Although blood lactate levels are interesting and are often measured to reflect what is going on in the skeletal muscle, the actual lactate concentration in the muscle is much more important (126, 132). The maximum accumulation of lactate occurs during intense exercise that lasts between 3 and 7 minutes (132). Along with this increased accumulation of lactate is an increased concentration of H^+, which results in a decreased pH and has been linked to fatigue (82). Elevations in H^+ concentrations can decrease energy supply capacity by interfering with the enzymatic processes of the fast glycolytic system and interfering with crossbridge cycling (i.e., contractile mechanism) (132).

Ultimately, the metabolic limitations of these types of exercise are primarily due to glycolytic enzyme kinetics (i.e., anaerobic power) and the tolerance (i.e., capacity) of H^+ accumulation (126, 132). Factors that limit oxygen availability and oxidative enzyme kinetics also can be considered metabolic limiters to the performance of these activities (126).

Endurance Events Lasting Up to 40 Minutes

Athletes who participate in endurance events, such as the 5,000 and 10,000 m running events, cross-country skiing, endurance cycling, and each stage of an Olympic triathlon, receive almost all of their ATP from the oxidative energy system (126). Therefore, an athlete's performance is largely affected by their $\dot{V}O_2$max, lactate threshold, and OBLA. With these types of events, the overall rate of ATP demand is lower than that typically seen with high-intensity exercise, so PCr, carbohydrates, and fats can all contribute to the production of ATP (132). These events are typically terminated before the complete depletion of muscle glycogen.

Due to the importance of glycogen as a fuel source during these events, the major metabolic limiting factors are the athlete's lactate threshold and OBLA (126). If exercise exceeds these break points, an accumulation of H^+ concentration can result in an inhibition of the mobilization and uptake of fatty acids and can stimulate pulmonary ventilation (126, 145).

Long-Distance Events Lasting Several Hours

Ninety-nine percent of the energy demand for long-distance events, such as marathons, road cycling, Ironman triathlons, and 50 km cross-country skiing, is met by aerobic energy supply via the oxidation of carbohydrates and fatty acids (126, 161). As the duration of the activity increases, there is a concomitant increase in fatty acid oxidation. For example, in a 2-hour, 20-minute marathon, 50% of the energy is supplied by the oxidation of fatty acids, whereas in a 5-hour cross-country ski race, the oxidation of fatty acids provides 70% of the energy required (126).

With long-distance events, the primary limiter of performance is the depletion of muscle and liver glycogen (126, 131). For example, as one progresses through a 2-hour, 20-minute marathon, there is a progressive reduction in muscle glycogen stores. After the first hour, muscle glycogen stores are decreased by about 55%; by the end of the second hour, they are decreased by 72%; and at the completion, they are decreased by 80% (126). As the duration of the activity extends, the ability to meet the ATP demand becomes compromised as both muscle and liver glycogen become depleted and fat oxidation is unable to increase sufficiently to offset this deficit. In fact, the oxidation of fat cannot meet the energetic demands of exercise intensities greater than 50% to 60% $\dot{V}O_2$max (131). It is not clear why fat oxidation cannot account for the depletion of glycogen stores. It is possible that the uptake of free fatty acids from the blood into the muscle or the transport of free fatty acids to the mitochondria may be the limiter in this process (131). Based on these data, having adequate glycogen stores is an important factor affecting the ability to compete in long-distance endurance events because fat oxidation does not allow the athlete to maintain a high-intensity performance.

Aerobic and Anaerobic Contributions to Exercise

Oxygen consumption is a measure of the respiratory system's ability to take in oxygen, the ability of the cardiovascular system to deliver oxygen to the working tissue, and the capacity of the working tissue to use oxygen, which all represent the athlete's ability to work aerobically (89, 135, 183). When low-intensity, steady-state exercise is undertaken, oxygen consumption will initially increase until oxygen demand equals oxygen consumption (figure 2.13) (89, 94, 135).

Regardless of the intensity of exercise when it is initiated, some of the energy must be supplied via anaerobic mechanisms due to the fact that the aerobic system is slow to respond to the initial demand for energy (89, 162). The **oxygen deficit** is the term used to describe this lag in oxygen uptake at the beginning of exercise (162). After the cessation of exercise, oxygen uptake remains elevated above preexercise levels for a variable amount of time depending on the intensity and duration of the exercise completed (89). This elevation in postexercise oxygen consumption has been referred to as the **oxygen debt** (66, 94) or the *excess postexercise oxygen consumption* (EPOC) (28, 66, 114, 189). Conceptually, the EPOC represents the oxygen uptake above resting used to restore the preexercise condition (182). Although there is a small to moderate relationship between the oxygen deficit and the EPOC (15, 88), they are not equal. During aerobic exercise, exercise intensities greater than 50% to 60% of $\dot{V}O_2$max exert the greatest effect on the EPOC (28). In addition to the intensity of exercise, the duration of the exercise bout can also exert an influence on the magnitude and the duration of the EPOC (89).

When exercise is performed above the athlete's $\dot{V}O_2$max, the anaerobic energy systems provide

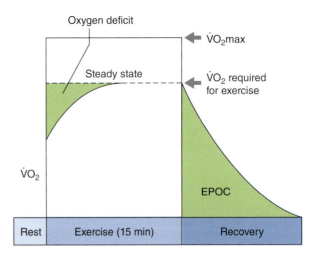

FIGURE 2.13 Low-intensity, steady-state exercise metabolism. Exercise is performed at 75% of maximal oxygen uptake ($\dot{V}O_2$max). EPOC = excess postexercise oxygen consumption; $\dot{V}O_2$ = oxygen uptake.

Reprinted by permission from T.J. Herda and J.T. Cramer, "Bioenergetics of Exercise and Training," in *Essentials of Strength Training and Conditioning,* edited by G.G. Haff and N. Triplett (Champaign, IL: Human Kinetics, 2016), 57.

the majority of the energy (figure 2.14) (89). As the intensity of the exercise bout increases, the contribution of the anaerobic energy systems increase and the duration of the exercise bout decreases (75, 195, 198). When examining the EPOC after anaerobic exercise, it appears that intensity exerts a significant influence. For example, with resistance training there is a more prolonged and substantial EPOC after more intense sessions when compared to lower-intensity bouts (28). Intensity is also an important factor modulating the magnitude of the EPOC during high-intensity intermittent bouts of supramaximal exercise (>100% $\dot{V}O_2$max). Specifically, these types of activities can significantly elevate the EPOC with lower total work than those performed with typical aerobic exercise. For example, supramaximal intermittent cycling bouts performed at 108% of $\dot{V}O_2$max stimulate an increased EPOC that can last up to 4 hours (5).

Regardless of the type of exercise performed, several factors contribute to the EPOC. In the period shortly after the cessation of exercise, the oxygen (O_2) consumed is used to resynthesize ATP and PCr (135) and replenish myoglobin and hemoglobin stores of O_2 (162). Additionally, lactate is oxidized to provide energy and is used as part of gluconeogenesis (135). The EPOC is also related to the thermogenic effects of hormones,

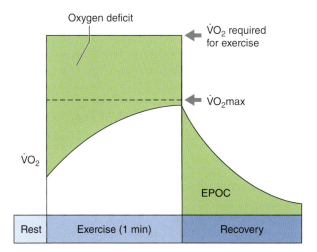

FIGURE 2.14 High-intensity, non-steady-state exercise metabolism. Exercise is performed at 80% of maximal power output. The required $\dot{V}O_2$ is the oxygen uptake required to sustain the exercise if such an uptake was possible to attain. EPOC = excess postexercise oxygen consumption; $\dot{V}O_2$ = oxygen uptake.

Reprinted by permission from T.J. Herda and J.T. Cramer, "Bioenergetics of Exercise and Training," in *Essentials of Strength Training and Conditioning*, edited by G.G. Haff and N. Triplett (Champaign, IL: Human Kinetics, 2016), 58.

Interrelationship of Energy Systems

The presentation of the various energy systems often implies that these systems operate in a quasi-sequential fashion; when one energy system becomes exhausted, another takes over (8). In reality, however, all components of the bioenergetic system (i.e., phosphagen, glycolytic, and oxidative) function in a complex, simultaneous manner. Thus, all three energy systems are always engaged, just with varying degrees of emphasis depending on the rate of energetic demand (figure 2.15).

Ultimately, the physiological demands associated with the exercise bout can be linked to a primary energy system (183). When very high–intensity exercise is completed, there is a significant reliance on the anaerobic energy systems to meet the demand for ATP (figure 2.16) (133). For example, a sprinter primarily draws on anaerobic energy supply to meet the energy demands of their event due to the requirement to produce very high power outputs in a very short time (133). Based on the times to complete the 100 m, 200 m, and 400 m sprints (figure 2.16a), it would be easy to assume that the energetic demands of these events are met exclusively with anaerobic means. This is not the case, however, because there is a degree of carbohydrate oxidation that contributes to ATP resynthesis during sprinting events. Therefore, there is an increasing aerobic contribution that coincides with a concomitant reduction in anaerobic energy

specifically the catecholamines (i.e., epinephrine and norepinephrine), and helps deal with the elevated body temperature postexercise (162). This period is also used to restore elevated heart rate, ventilation, and other physiological factors to baseline (135).

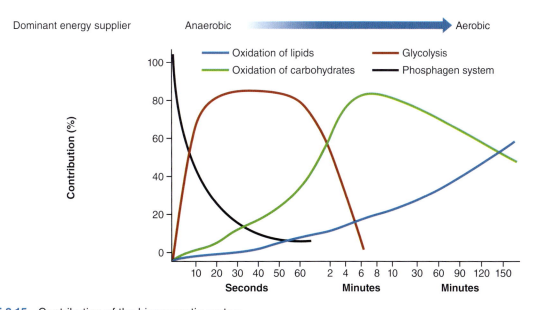

FIGURE 2.15 Contribution of the bioenergetic system.

Adapted from D. MacDougall and D. Sale, *The Physiology of Training for High Performance* (Oxford, United Kingdom: Oxford University Press, 2014), 11, reproduced with permission of the Licensor through PLSclear.

supply as the duration of the sprinting event is extended (figure 2.16b). For example, about 90% of the ATP required to run a 100 m sprint comes from the anaerobic energy systems, and only about 10% of the ATP comes from the aerobic system. As the distance is extended to 400 m, the anaerobic energy systems supply only about 70% of the ATP required to meet energy demands, and about 30% of the ATP comes from the aerobic system (133). If the duration of the activity is further extended and the intensity of the activity is reduced, the aerobic energy system's contribution to ATP production will continue to increase to better meet the activity's energy demands (figure 2.12). For example, about 50% of the ATP required to complete exercise bouts that last 2 minutes comes from the anaerobic systems, whereas about 85% of the ATP required for exercise bouts that last 10 minutes comes from the aerobic system (161). Ultimately, the contributions of the anaerobic and aerobic energy systems will vary depending on the sport (figures 2.17 and 2.18) and the types of engagements undertaken within those sports.

Ultimately, although all energy systems are simultaneously working, there will always be a primary energy system used to meet the activity's energy demands. As noted previously, the primary determinant of which energy system serves in this capacity is the intensity of the bout of exercise, and duration is the secondary determinant (24, 183). Due to this interaction and the need to align training factors with the energy profile of the targeted activity during the training process, the coach must understand these concepts to design appropriate training programs (160).

Bioenergetic Specificity of Training

When examining the various sports and their contrasting energy demands, it is clear that a range of strength, endurance, and metabolic combinations is required to optimize the athletic training process and ultimately improve performance capacity (117, 148). A key fundamental aspect of the training process is the principle of specificity, where the training response elicited by a given exercise or process is directly related to the physiological adaptive responses stimulated by the imposed training activities (68). In the context of bioenergetic specificity, or metabolic specificity, manipulating training intensities, rest intervals, and durations of activity allows the coach to design a training intervention that targets the development of a specific primary energy system during the athlete's training (table 2.4) (43, 68, 160, 183).

Understanding how the manipulation of these training factors modulates the development of specific energetic pathways will facilitate the coach's ability to align specific training interventions with

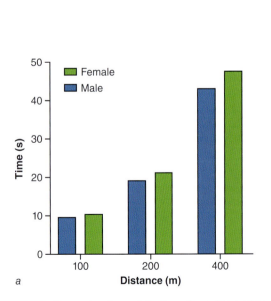
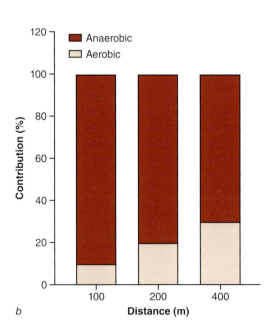

FIGURE 2.16 Approximate contribution of aerobic and anaerobic energy systems. *(a)* Exercise duration based on outdoor world records as of June 2020. *(b)* Contribution of anaerobic and aerobic energy systems.

Adapted from Maughan and Gleeson (2010).

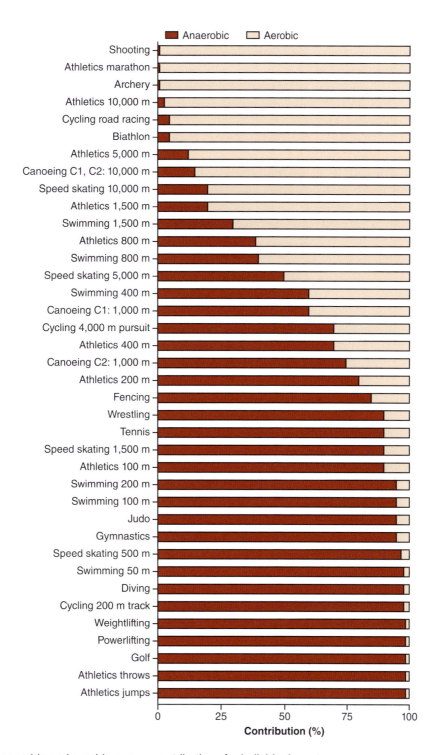

FIGURE 2.17 Anaerobic and aerobic energy contributions for individual sports.
Data from Bompa and Haff (2009).

the targeted outcomes. For example, to accomplish this goal in a team sport such as American football, Plisk and Gambetta (160) recommend creating a tactical model that outlines the work to relief pattern, frequency distribution, and central tenden-

cies of the targeted sporting activity. Although it is important to target bioenergetic factors as part of the training process, it is equally important to remember that training activities should combine metabolic, tactical, and technical tasks to comple-

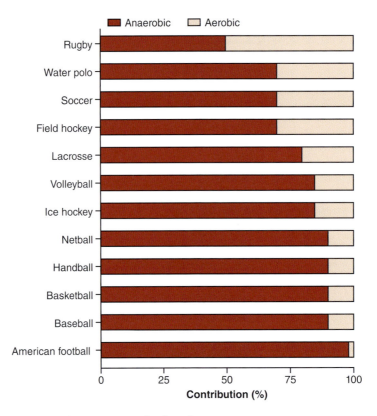

FIGURE 2.18 Anaerobic and aerobic energy contributions for team sports.
Data from Bompa and Haff (2009).

ment the strategic goals necessary for competitive success and create more time-efficient training interventions (160).

The metabolic profiles of most sports and training activities are similar to series of high-intensity, constant-effort, or near-constant-effort bouts of exercise that are interspersed with periods of rest (89). For example, resistance training is fundamentally a form of interval training that forms the foundation for many anaerobic sports, such as sprinting or football (183). Similarly, sports such as football, basketball, and hockey require high-intensity efforts interspersed with periods of lower-intensity efforts that serve as recovery periods. In these scenarios, the exercise intensity, or power output, that must be achieved is well above the maximal power output that can be sustained by solely using the aerobic energy system (89). In fact, trying to maximize aerobic power by focusing on aerobic endurance training at the cost of developing anaerobic power and capacity is of little benefit for most team sport athletes (93, 143). For example, it would make little sense for a basketball player to train with distance running instead of focusing on training that improves both anerobic power and capacity.

The use of aerobic endurance training is counterproductive when attempting to maximize the

TABLE 2.4 Bioenergetic Specificity and Work-to-Rest Intervals

Percentage of maximal power output	Targeted energy system	Average work time	Work-to-rest ratio (W:R)
90-100	Phosphagen	5-10 s	1:12 to 1:20
75-90	Fast glycolysis	15-30 s	1:3 to 1:5
30-75	Fast glycolysis, slow glycolysis, and oxidative system	30 s-3 min	1:3 to 1:4
20-35	Oxidative system	>3 min	1:1 to 1:3

energy adaptations necessary for most sporting activities (except pure endurance sports). A more appropriate strategy is the use of HIIT (see chapter 14), in which high-intensity exercise is interspersed with intermittent recovery to better modulate the bioenergetic factors associated with the training process. In fact, an appropriate HIIT program can elicit cardiopulmonary (33), metabolic, and neuromuscular (34) adaptations. Appropriately crafted HIIT programs can result in increased $\dot{V}O_2$max, buffering capacity, glycogen stores, anaerobic thresholds, and time to exhaustion (33). The beauty of HIIT is that it is a time-efficient training activity in which the major bioenergetic targets can be manipulated through altering factors such as the work-to-rest ratio (see chapter 14 for more information) (120).

Some coaches suggest that aerobic training is essential to enhance recovery in anaerobic sports. This premise is largely based on the fact that recovery after exercise is in large part an aerobic process (89) and is related to aerobic fitness (22, 23). In fact, there is ample evidence that even low-volume aerobic endurance training can negatively affect anaerobic performance capabilities, particularly in sports that rely on high-strength and high-power performances (81, 163, 181, 183, 199). Maximal aerobic capacity can be significantly enhanced with the use of specific anaerobic training, such as HIIT (see chapter 14), obviating the need to compromise anaerobic power and capacity by using aerobic endurance training to improve recovery. Based on this premise, a far better recommendation is to train for performance and not recovery. Implementing training interventions with the appropriate work-to-rest ratios and intensity profiles will maximize recovery.

Summary

Understanding the basic concepts associated with bioenergetics is central to developing training interventions that adhere to the principles of bioenergetic specificity. Three basic energy systems are used to maintain an available supply of ATP. These systems work simultaneously but have different rates and capacities, allowing energy consumption to be matched with energy production. Therefore, even though all energy systems operate simultaneously, a primary energy system can be associated with a given activity. Targeting the development of the primary energy system is a core concept that underpins the training process and should be considered as one of the more important aspects of the construction of appropriate training interventions. Fundamentally, the ability to modulate energy system selection via the manipulation of intensity, duration, and recovery intervals allows the coach to create more time-efficient training programs that can be used to optimize the training process.

CHAPTER 3

Classification of Skills and Types of Training

Coaches commonly classify sporting activities as individual (e.g., track and field, wrestling, mixed martial arts, weightlifting) or team (e.g., soccer, football, netball, basketball, volleyball, water polo) sports. Although there are clear differences in the training demands of individual and team sports that directly affect periodization and programming strategies, it is worthwhile to consider sport in more detailed ways.

One way is to classify sport as containing either open or closed skills (114). Open-skill sports (e.g., volleyball, netball, basketball) require the athlete to react to a constantly changing environment in which the athlete has to continually modify their movement patterns in response to externally paced stimuli. Conversely, closed-skill sports (e.g., running, swimming, weightlifting) have environments that are highly consistent and predictable, and the athletes' movements performed are clearly defined and tend to be self-paced (31).

Understanding the demands of the sporting environment is critical for the development of appropriate periodized programming interventions. For example, agility can be developed with either preplanned movement patterns (closed-skill movement pattern) or in response to external stimuli (open-skill movement pattern). Although both closed- and open-skill agility drills have benefits, these drills may be employed at different times in the annual training plan to enhance the transfer of training effect from the drill into the sporting environment.

Classification of Skills

Classifying the type of sport and the sporting skills used within a sport is a common practice among coaches. Classically sporting skills are classified as being either cyclic, acyclic, or acyclic combined (10, 13). Understanding these classifications allows the coach to align teaching methods with the type of skill being taught. For example, **acyclic skills** are likely more effectively taught by breaking the movement into smaller pieces, often referred to as *chunking*. Conversely, teaching **cyclic skills** as a whole appears to be a more effective strategy (10, 13). Ultimately, understanding these classifications affects how skills are taught to athletes and the programming strategies used when implementing periodized training plans.

Cyclic Skills

Sports such as walking, running, cross-country skiing, swimming, rowing, canoeing, and kayaking are traditionally considered cyclic skills. These sports contain repetitive movement patterns, which are considered hallmarks of cyclic skills (10, 13). For example, the running gait cycle has key phases that are continuously repeated: (a) braking, (b) propulsion, (c) recovery, and (d) preactivation (60). In most instances (with the exception of sprinting), cyclic sports are dominated by the endurance biomotor ability (9).

Acyclic Skills

Sports that contain a series of integrated functions performed in one action are classified as acyclic skills (10, 13). Sports such as weightlifting, shot putting, hammer throwing, most team sports, and combat sports (e.g., mixed martial arts, karate, boxing, judo) typically can be considered acyclic because, in these sports, a series of discrete movements are integrated into one action. In weightlifting, for example, the snatch is performed by incorporating five interlinked phases of movement (first pull, transition, second pull, catch, and recovery) into one fluid movement pattern. In many instances, acyclic skills are dominated by the strength and speed biomotor ability (i.e., power), but because of the complex nature of team sports, the endurance biomotor ability is also a contributor (9).

Acyclic Combined Skills

Acyclic combined skills are categorized by cyclical movement patterns that precede acyclic movements (10, 13). In sports classified as having acyclic combined skills, it is easy to distinguish between cyclic and acyclic movements. For example, sports such as pole vault and long jump contain a cyclic movement pattern during the run-up and then an acyclic movement pattern when the jumping movements are performed. Sports such as diving, figure skating, jumping events in track and field, and some elements of gymnastics (e.g., floor routine) are classified as acyclic combined (10, 13).

Classification of Biomotor Abilities

An alternative method for classifying sports and sporting skills is to consider their biomotor abilities (10, 13). In athletic performance, the basic constructs that underpin performance capacity require the athlete to express some combination of **strength, speed**, and **endurance**. Collectively, strength, speed, and endurance are classified as biomotor abilities, which display degrees of interaction with one another depending on the sport (figure 3.1).

Underpinning athletic performance capacity is the athlete's expression of the biomotor abilities of strength, speed, and endurance. Although there are always interactions between these biomotor abilities (figure 3.1), each sport is generally dominated by either strength, speed, or endurance (figure 3.2) (10, 12, 15, 40). For example, in a 100 m sprint, speed is the dominant biomotor ability for success.

Chapter 3 • Classification of Skills and Types of Training | 53

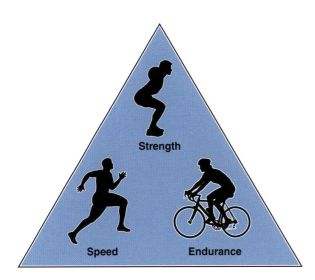

FIGURE 3.1 Biomotor abilities.

Conversely, the dominant motor ability for success in marathon running is endurance (figure 3.3).

Although every sport has a dominant biomotor ability, contemporary research indicates that many sports encompass several biomotor abilities (90). For example, long-distance cycling has endurance as its dominant biomotor ability, but cycling performance can be improved by increasing muscular strength, which highlights the importance of the strength biomotor ability (90). In fact, strength may be considered the critical or foundational biomotor ability, because it affects the other biomotor abilities and all facets of athletic performance (12, 15, 107). For example, strength is significantly related to sprint speed—the strongest athletes can sprint the fastest (2, 20, 25, 107)—and training-induced increases in lower-body strength translate into improvements in sprinting performance (98). In addition, integrating strength training into the training regimes of middle- and long-distance runners (5, 8, 63, 81), Nordic skiers (59, 80, 82), and cyclists (89, 91) results in enhanced performance compared to focusing on only the endurance biomotor ability. Ultimately, the scientific literature reveals that stronger, more powerful athletes perform better on a wide range of general and sport-specific skills (101, 102, 107) and reduce their overall injury risk (72, 107). Based on these data, it is apparent that there are many ways biomotor abilities integrate to underpin performance capacities.

There are also several sport-specific combinations of biomotor abilities (figure 3.4) that relate the biomotor abilities to various attributes of sport performance (figure 3.5). For example, the combination of speed and strength allows for the presentation of either **speed–strength** or **strength–speed**. When speed training is important but strength development is more important, one would target strength–speed development. When speed development against resistance is important but strength acquisition is less important, one would target speed–strength (111). Ultimately, speed–strength and strength–speed are related to power output (111) and the rate of force development (106).

Strength–endurance, also known as *muscular endurance*, is the ability to repetitively produce muscular force, which can be considered as either dynamic or isometric strength–endurance. Applications of considerable force in an uninterrupted manner (commonly associated with cyclic skills such as cycling, running, and rowing) or repeated applications of force with different short rest

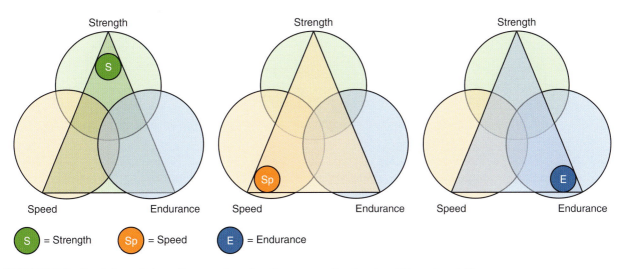

FIGURE 3.2 Depiction of strength, speed, and endurance as the dominant biomotor ability.

54 | Scientific Foundations and Practical Applications of Periodization

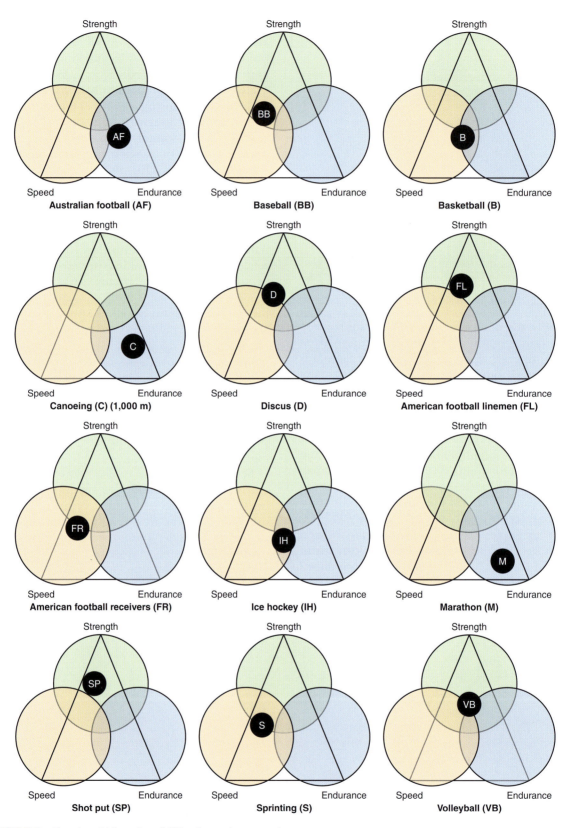

FIGURE 3.3 Dominant biomotor abilities for various sports.

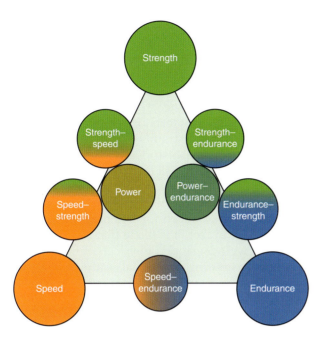

FIGURE 3.4 Sport-specific combinations of biomotor abilities.

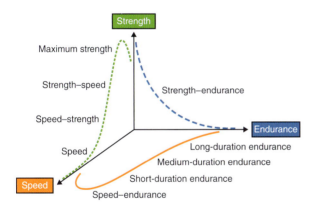

FIGURE 3.5 Interdependence of the biomotor abilities.
Adapted by permission from Y. Verkhoshansky and M.C. Siff, *Supertraining,* 6th ed., Expanded Version (Rome: Verkhoshansky, 2009), 152.

can work across a continuum from maximal speed through **speed–endurance** and endurance across increasing durations (figure 3.5). Speed–endurance is the ability to prolong the duration of motion at near maximal speed or the ability to repetitively produce maximal or near maximal speeds. These can be short-, medium-, and long-duration endurance activities. Ultimately, the relationship between speed and endurance is parabolic for endurance where speed is high and hyperbolic over the remainder of the range (113).

Taken collectively, the primary biomotor abilities provide insight into the main physical attributes that underpin sport performance, and the sport-specific combinations of biomotor abilities give insight into various sport-specific aspects of performance. Comprehension of these factors allows the coach to better understand the physical training requirements for a variety of sports.

Classification of Training

When constructing training programs, all coaches must address the physical, technical, tactical, and psychological aspects of the training process (14). These training factors are essential to the development of any training program. Although each is important, their emphasis should be varied depending on the athlete's training age, physical development, sport, level of development, and progress through the periodized training plan. Fundamentally, all training factors are interrelated, exert an influence on each other, and must be developed in a specific manner (14).

Physical Training

Physical training serves as the foundation from which all other training factors are developed (figure 3.6). In fact, a better developed physical foundation provides greater potential for the development of the athlete's technical, tactical, and psychological attributes.

Often it is easy for coaches, especially team sport coaches, to forget that technical abilities are underpinned by the athlete's physical capacities. If the physical foundation is not adequately developed, the athlete will often be unable to develop the technique necessary for successful sport performance. For example, the gymnastics skill known as the *still rings cross* (also called the *iron cross*) requires the athlete to have high levels of shoulder

intervals (commonly associated with acyclic skills such as repeated jumping activities) are representative of **dynamic strength–endurance** (112, 113). Activities that require the application of isometric tension of varying magnitudes and durations or the maintenance of a static posture are associated with **isometric strength–endurance** (113). Fundamentally, **global strength–endurance** can be classified in relation to the ability to repetitively produce force by many muscle groups, whereas **local strength–endurance** is associated with activities executed by a single muscle group (113).

When considering the relationships between the biomotor abilities of speed and endurance, one

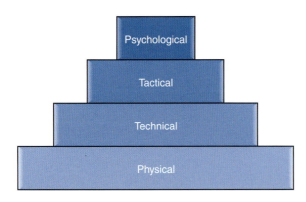

FIGURE 3.6 Pyramid of training factors.

Adapted by permission from T.O. Bompa and G.G. Haff, *Periodization: Theory and Methodology of Training,* 5th ed., (Champaign, IL: Human Kinetics, 2009), 57.

joint stability and astonishing upper-body strength for correct performance (93). A gymnast who does not possess the requisite levels of upper-body strength will not be able to effectively perform the techniques required to complete the still rings cross (35) or perform it at an appropriate level of proficiency (61). In this example, the inability of the athlete to effectively perform the still rings cross then limits the skills that can be employed in their competitive ring routine (i.e., tactics) and may also affect the athlete's overall competitive confidence (i.e., psychology). However, if appropriate training activities are used to develop the athlete's physical capacities (61) and strength (35), the technique necessary for competition can be further developed and mastered.

Inadequate physical foundation can also cause excessive fatigue, which can negatively affect the athlete's ability to develop other training factors. For example, if the athlete has not undertaken appropriate physical preparation and is easily fatigued during training, their ability to learn and master sport-specific skills (i.e., techniques) (1) and transfer these skills into competitive tactics (92) will be impaired. Additionally, in this scenario, the athlete may display impaired decision making, which can affect their overall tactical abilities (100). If, however, the athlete's physical capacities are improved with appropriate training interventions, the athlete will be able to master various technical skills and transfer these skills to tactical applications. The athlete will demonstrate increased self-confidence and other psychological factors (14).

Fundamentally, physical training stimulates the physiological adaptations that underpin sport performance (11, 77) and develops the fitness foundation necessary to maximize technical and tactical abilities while reducing the overall risk of injury. An athlete who lacks a strong physical foundation may not be able to tolerate training and maintain technical competency. Sport scientists have begun to explore the relationships between physical training loads and the athlete's risk of injury (45-47, 62). While undertaking sudden excessive amounts of physical training (e.g., overreaching or overtraining) has historically been associated with increased injury risk (45, 115), based on more recent research, there is also a significant increase in injury risk when training loads are inadequate or significantly reduced for extended periods of time (45, 62). In fact, it is likely that the establishment of a well-developed physical foundation via appropriate training stimuli (i.e., training smarter) serves to reduce injury risk (115) and increase performance capacity. In fact, Malone et al. (72) report that developing lower-body strength, sprinting speed, and repeated sprint ability (i.e., high-intensity endurance) in team sport athletes increases their ability to tolerate higher training loads while reducing overall injury risk. Athletes with poor levels of physical fitness experience higher levels of fatigue when exposed to intense training or competition loads. Fatigue serves as a **mediator** of injury risk and directly affects technical and tactical abilities. However, the athlete's overall physical fitness level serves as a **moderator** of the strong relationships among training load, fatigue, and injury risk or performance impairment (115). Based on this line of reasoning it is clear that physical training is an important part of the preparation of athletes.

Physical training can be conceptualized in two ways: It is used to increase the physiological adaptations that underpin sport-specific biomotor abilities, and it is used to translate those adaptations into a maximization of the sport-specific combinations of biomotor abilities. This is accomplished by designing a training intervention that is generally applied in a structured and sequential pattern (11, 14, 77, 97, 99) (figure 3.7).

Physical training can address two interdependent training targets: **general physical training (GPT)** and **sport-specific physical training (SSPT)**. Each of these targets are traditionally contained within the preparatory period of the annual training plan (see chapter 6) (14). GPT is the primary focus during the early portion of the preparatory period when the primary goal is to establish the athlete's physiological base. This base is generally established through high volumes of training performed with moderate intensities (11, 14). The time dedicated to GPT depends on many

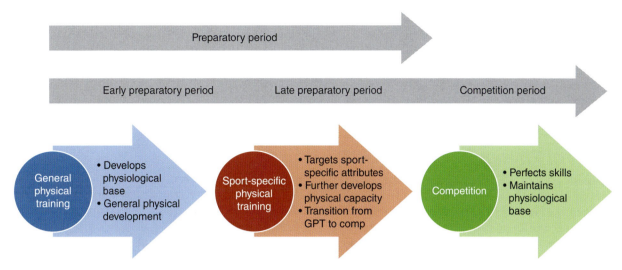

FIGURE 3.7 Application of a sequential approach to physical training.

factors, including the athlete's training age, chronological age, needs, current injury status, and sport.

As the athlete moves through the preparatory period, there is typically a shift toward SSPT (figure 3.8). The training base established as a result of the GPT prepares the athlete to tolerate the higher-intensity training loads associated with SSPT (11, 14). SSPT can be considered a transition between GPT and the competitive period of the training plan (77, 97). Ultimately, the physiological base established by the preparatory period serves as the foundation for the athlete's performance capacity during the competitive period.

During the competitive period, the primary objectives are to maximize sport performance and maintain the athlete's physiological base (77). In the best-case scenario, though, the athlete's sport-specific physical development would also increase (3). However, if training and competition are not appropriately sequenced or if adequate recovery is not applied, sport-specific physical development will deteriorate (11, 14, 77, 85).

An alternative approach to sequencing GPT and SSPT has been proposed by Anatoliy Bondarchuk (17, 19) to better address the needs of advanced athletes. Bondarchuk (18) suggests that although there is a basic sequence of general to specialized preparation, there are alternative approaches to applying exercises in GPT and SSPT. Specifically, he suggests that exercises typically associated

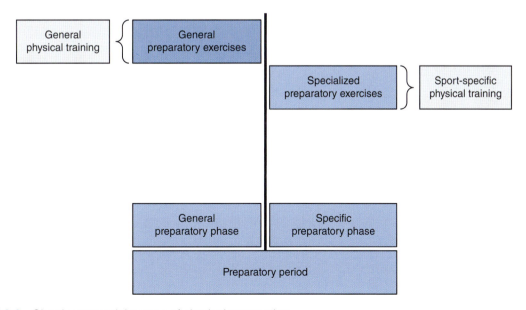

FIGURE 3.8 Classic sequential pattern of physical preparation.

with SSPT can be trained concurrently with those typically associated with GPT during the general preparation phase (figure 3.9). Bondarchuk proposes in his stage-complex model that the athlete engage with GPT and SSPT in the general preparatory phase and then shift their training focus to a variety of SSPT training exercises in the specific preparatory phase.

General Physical Training (GPT)

The main goal of GPT is to enhance the athlete's work capacity and stimulate the key physiological adaptations that underpin the athlete's ability to tolerate future workloads (16). The training interventions for this type of training are often employed to provide multilateral development of the key elements of physical fitness. This is most noted in the training practices of young athletes (69), in which a greater amount of time is dedicated to GPT during the general preparatory phase (figure 3.10). As the athlete becomes more developed, the amount of time spent targeting GPT is reduced due to the increasing demand for SSPT at the intermediate and advanced levels of performance. A variety of training methods can be employed during GPT, and the coach must consider the athlete's level of development and training needs based on the goals established for the phase of training.

The training exercises used during GPT are not sport specific and focus on the athlete's overall physical development (11, 14). They promote multilateral and holistic development and aim to develop not only the primary biomotor abilities of strength, speed, and endurance but also movement competency, which is largely affected by flexibility and mobility. This multilateral approach is suitable for laying a training foundation in the early preparatory period (11, 14) or for use with athletes who lack a sound physical training base. From a contemporary perspective, the use of multilateral training could be related to cross-training (83). For example, Paquette et al. (83) suggest that during early stages of the preparatory period, young distance runners can benefit from the use of cycling activities. This finding is not surprising because the vast majority of long-term athlete development models recommend the use of multilateral training and greater emphasis on the general preparatory period of training during the early stages of development (54).

Sport-Specific Physical Training (SSPT)

The physical capacities developed during GPT serve as the foundation for the activities in SSPT. SSPT is an important link between GPT and the competitive period of the periodized training plan (14, 77). The ability of SSPT to link to competition is grounded in the increased degree of specificity between the training exercises and the competitive performance. It is well-documented that targeting the physiological adaptations, movement patterns, metabolic characteristics, and performance characteristics that correspond to the specific sporting activity increases the transfer of training effects toward **sports form** (16) and maximizes competitive performance (38, 68, 84). The ability of SSPT to accomplish these end

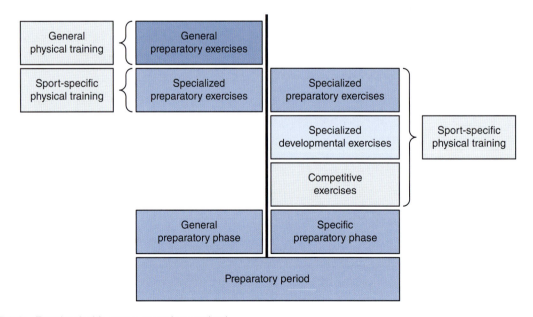

FIGURE 3.9 Bondarchuk's stage-complex method.

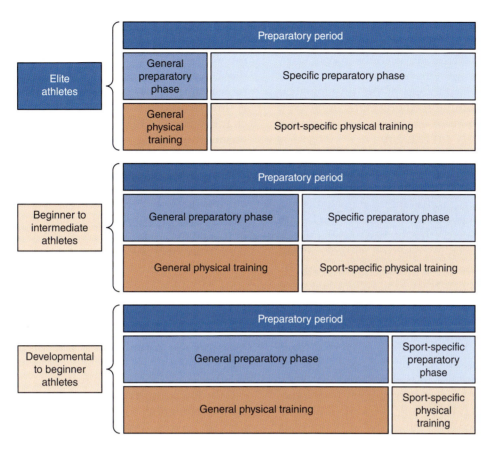

FIGURE 3.10 Example sequences of the preparatory period.

points requires training activities to be appropriately designed and implemented.

Implementation of General and Sport-Specific Physical Training

The effective implementation of GPT and SSPT requires a complete understanding of each as the incorrect implementation of these methods can result in a decrease in competitive performance (11, 14). GPT consists of exercises that typically do not target the competitive movements and skills and instead emphasizes athletes' overall work tolerance in a multilateral fashion (16). SSPT is designed to then translate the athletes' increased working capacity into improved sport form and performance. Bondarchuk (16) suggests that SSPT can be composed of two categories of exercises: **specialized preparatory exercises** and **specialized developmental exercises**.

Specialized preparatory exercises have a similar goal as those used during GPT but target muscle groups that contribute to the sporting movements being trained for. These exercises can be used in GPT or SSPT in either the preparatory or specific preparatory phases. When employed as part of the specific preparatory phase, these exercises would be targeted earlier in the phase.

Specialized developmental exercises typically engage part of the competitive movements and generally display the greatest specificity with the competitive movements (16). Ultimately, the transition from specialized preparatory exercises to specialized developmental exercises allows training to be delivered with increasing degrees of specificity between the training activities and the competitive movements or events.

Another way to understand the difference between GPT and SSPT is to examine training methods used to develop endurance capacity (11, 14). The classic approach to developing endurance is to engage in training that develops **low-intensity exercise endurance (LIEE)** (104). LIEE is typically developed with training that is performed below the lactate threshold. Many coaches believe that developing LIEE is essential for all sports, but this type of training has the potential to compromise performance in high-speed or strength- and power-based sports (48, 104). These types of sports call for **high-intensity exercise endurance (HIEE)** training (104), which requires the athlete to sustain activities for less than 2 minutes or to repetitively engage in high-intensity movements (104, 105). While the importance of HIEE is not a new concept, our understanding of the physiological responses and training methods that can be used to develop this type of endurance has expanded greatly (see chapter 14) (22, 23).

It is well-documented that HIEE training is best developed with the use of high-intensity interval training (HIIT), which Laursen and Buchheit (65) defined as "exercise consisting of repeated bouts of high-intensity work performed above the lactate threshold (a perceived effort of 'hard' or greater) or critical speed/power, interspersed with periods of low-intensity exercise or complete rest" (page 3). HIIT not only improves HIEE but can also result in enhanced abilities to engage in LIEE (22, 23) without the typical negative performance effects (104).

When constructing endurance training interventions during SSPT, a key strategy, referred to as *tactical modeling*, models the conditions that the athlete will experience in the sport (48, 84, 104). Tactical modeling is a central part of employing **tactical metabolic training** (48, 84), which includes conditioning activities based on the work intervals and work-to-rest ratios the athlete will experience in the competitive environment. This approach was first used with American football athletes to model the bioenergetic needs of competition during training (84), but it has become popular in many other team sports (109). Tactical modeling has become easier with the development of modern technology that can assist in quantifying competition demands, allowing coaches to develop and deliver more precise individualized training interventions that can address position requirements within a specific team sport (24, 44, 50).

Technical Training

Through the training process athletes continually strive to master specific techniques to achieve the most efficient movement patterns and optimize competitive performance. These techniques, or motor skills, encompass the movement patterns and skills required to perform the various activities associated with a given sport (11, 14). Ultimately the ability to perform at a high level depends on the development of proficient technique that allows the athlete to perform the required sporting movements efficiently and directly affects their level of performance and overall sporting outcome (14, 75).

To understand the importance of efficient technique, consider the concept of running economy (75). **Running economy** is often quantified based on the oxygen or energy cost of movement, which is considered a reliable predictor of running performance (43). Running economy's ability to predict performance is largely related to the fact that it is directly affected by both metabolic and biomechanical factors (108). The importance of running economy is highlighted by several researchers who have reported that it is one of the most important determining factors of running performance (28, 75, 96, 108). Environment, physiology, and anthropometry have all been proposed as factors that underpin running economy, but the ability to train and to modify running biomechanics (i.e., technique) is also important (75, 96). In fact, researchers suggest that endurance training, coupled with other training methods, has the ability to enhance running economy (96). There is strong evidence that the use of targeted physical training interventions, such as plyometric training (74, 96, 103), strength training (5-8), interval training that targets HIEE (7, 49, 74), and endurance training that targets LIEE (49), can increase running economy by lowering vertical oscillation, enhancing leg stiffness, aligning the ground reaction forces and leg axis vectors, increasing stride angles, lowering muscle activation during propulsion, and reducing antagonist–agonist coactivation (75).

After examining the running economy example, it is important to highlight that technique is largely affected by physical training, and athletes must have specific physical capacities to optimize technique. A great example of this is the still rings cross discussed earlier. A minimum level of strength is necessary to perform this skill (35), and as the gymnast's strength level increases, his proficiency in performing the skill increases. This highlights the importance of targeting basic technical skills that align with the novice athlete's physical capacities and shows why novice athletes often use different techniques than their elite counterparts. Additionally, as the athlete's physical capacities increase, the complexity of the technical skills practiced and used as part of the training process will also increase.

Aims of Technical Training

Dick (32) suggests that technical training has three general aims:

1. *Guiding the athlete's learning so they can perfect the techniques required by their sport.* To facilitate this goal, the coach must be educated about the technical demands required and must have a working knowledge of the teaching progressions and stages

of technical development required to guide the athlete toward a sound biomechanical model of technique (32).

2. *Stabilizing the performance of a given technique in the context of the sport.* The athlete must first master the given technique in a training environment designed to facilitate mastery. After mastering the technique under these conditions, the athlete then needs to be trained to perform the technique under conditions of fatigue and under conditions in which they are distracted by noise, weather, apparatus, simulated spectators, and other athletes (32).

3. *Using a given technique within a variable sporting environment.* The athlete must be exposed to training scenarios in which they are required to call on a variety of techniques to solve a specific performance problem (32). Exposing the athlete to these challenges will assist in the transference of training to competitive performance and provide a foundation for tactical strategies the coach can develop.

Deliberate Practice and Learning Technique

Understanding the athlete's level of development, current technical abilities, and areas of strength or deficiency is critical to technical training (14). Guadagnoli and Lee (51) suggest that it is important to understand the interaction between the athlete's level of skill and the relative difficulty of the skill that can be trained. This theory of skill development fits nicely with the theory of deliberate practice first suggested in the seminal work by Ericsson et al. (36). This work highlights the importance of increasing the amount of effortful practice over time. It also has been suggested that in order to maximize the effect of deliberate practice, there needs to be periodic rest and recovery (76). While there is some debate in the literature about aspects of the theory of deliberate practice (70), the need for increased focused, effortful training as the athlete develops is logical and aligns with the theories of periodization and long-term athlete development.

Technique Versus Style

Every sport has a technical model that is generally accepted as being the best or is considered the most efficient method of performance (14, 32). Generally, these models are based on biomechanical and physiological assessments and not on the techniques of elite or champion athletes, since their techniques may not be biomechanically or physiologically correct. Therefore, coaches and athletes should not attempt to duplicate the technical aspects displayed by champion athletes but rather should evaluate technique in alignment with accepted technical models.

Technical models should be used as points of comparison, but they should display a degree of plasticity to account for emerging evidence related to technical aspects of the sport. Ultimately, a technical model serves as a guide that the coach can refer to when constructing specific training interventions designed to address the athlete's technical deficiencies (32). Although technical models inform training, it is important to remember that athletes will tend to develop their own technical styles as they mature. Style does not reflect differences in the overall skill but rather in how that skill is performed (14).

Bompa and Haff (14) suggest that individual technical styles are simply adaptations of a generally accepted model of performance that reflect the individual athlete's needs. In weightlifting, for example, the object of the snatch is to move the barbell from the ground to an overhead position in one continuous movement. Historically, a common technique used to perform the snatch was referred to as the *split snatch*, which required the lifter to pull the barbell as high as possible then lower their body under the barbell into a split position. The modern technique for performing the snatch is referred to as the *squat snatch*, in which the barbell is pulled as high as possible and the athlete squats under the barbell while receiving the barbell on locked arms overhead. Both the split snatch and squat snatch move the barbell from the floor to a position overhead, but biomechanical analyses reveal that the squat snatch is a more effective technique (53, 66).

Periodization of Learning Technique

There is limited research on the integration of skill acquisition into a periodization framework that specifically targets the development of techniques used in high-performance sport (76). Overall, technique development is typically given a simple time allocation.

Farrow and Robertson (39) suggest that longitudinal skill development in athletes can benefit from the application of a periodized training process. Based on the periodization literature, Farrow and Robertson (39) developed a technical skill–based periodization framework that can be used with athletes. Specifically, the framework included aspects of specificity, progression, overload, reversibility, and tedium (referred to by the acronym SPORT). Although this framework offers an initial construct from which to contextualize the periodization of technical training, significant research is still needed to better understand how to optimize an athlete's technical development.

Specificity The concept of specificity is commonly discussed within the periodization literature, but it is not often considered in the technical skills development literature. When considering technical training, specificity should be considered in the context of how closely the training reflects the techniques used in the competitive environment (39, 76).

Progression In technical training, progression can be considered in multiple ways. For example, progression can be considered in the context of how much the athlete improves their individual technical skills or the ability of the athlete to complete and tolerate an increased technical training load (39, 76). Based on these two aspects of progression, the coach can better plan the athlete's technical training pathway and ensure that it integrates with the other aspects of the periodized training plan.

Overload The concept of training load can be extended to technical training to include the aspects of cognitive effort needed when learning or practicing technical skills (76). Cognitive effort is the mental work required to make the decisions that underscore movement (67), to solve technical issues related to skill execution or information processing, or to guide decision making in complex sporting environments such as those seen in many team sports (39). Extended periods of high cognitive effort can result in mental fatigue, which can lead to reduced physical performance capacity (73). Therefore, when constructing technical training interventions, much like physical training, the coach must consider the cognitive demand when making decisions about the volume of technical training and be aware of the overall accumulated cognitive load (39).

When constructing technical training interventions, the athlete should be exposed to sufficient overload to stimulate improvements in skills performance (39). A key consideration is that the training load associated with the early development of the skill will be affected by the cognitive load of learning the skill. As the skill is mastered and stabilized and the athlete demonstrates a degree of consistency, there will be a reduction in the overall contribution of the cognitive load to the overall training load.

When this occurs the coach will need to change the technical training program to increase the training load (i.e., overload) and in some instances increase the cognitive load associated with the training process. The concept of introducing overload into technical training is similar to what is typically done when programming physical training (39). Overall, the coach must consider the interactions of the cognitive load created by the technical training and the training load of the physical training activities when considering the construction of the athlete's periodized training plan.

Reversibility The principle of reversibility suggests that athletes will lose the gains achieved from training when the training stimulus is reduced or when training stops (39). When examined in the context of skills acquisition (i.e., technical training), the concept of reversibility sheds light on the importance of quantifying the degree of learning achieved at various stages of development and of considering how reversible the development of this skill is. A key aspect of understanding reversibility is the quantification of the degree of learning achieved or how long the skill remains without training before the effects of reversibility occur. The ultimate test of the transfer of technical training is the actual competition and the ability to employ the trained skills in a competition. As such the coach can evaluate the athlete's ability to maintain the capacity to perform the skill in competition, where the highest cognitive loads are experienced (39). If a reduction in technical training results in reversal of technical skill proficiency within the competitive environment, the coach can schedule further technical training that systematically reintroduces the athlete to technical loads designed to improve the deficient technical skill (39).

Tedium A key aspect of periodization is the importance of structured or planned variation (55). **Tedium** is a state of training monotony that can induce training boredom and hinder technical development (39). Alterations in one or more programming variables should be introduced into the training plan to reduce tedium.

Farrow and Robertson (39) highlight the importance of reducing tedium in technical training by introducing practice variability into the athlete's technical training program. Technical training can be varied in multiple ways, including introducing changes within a single training session or sequencing specific training progressions across a series of training periods (i.e., block periodization). Another way to create variation is to introduce different skill-specific drills or require the athlete to perform skills in variable environments (e.g., wet, cold, hot). When considered in team sport environments, variability can be introduced by providing contextual interference (39).

Tactical Training

Competitive tactics and strategies are central concepts associated with successful coaching and competition results. A key aspect of tactical training is allowing technical skills to transfer to competitive performance. Typically, physical development and the mastery of technical skills provide the foundation for the tactics used within competition (14). Because tactics involve application of a series of technical skills it is easy to see that technical skills competency and tactics are intimately related (110). Therefore, once technical skills are developed, they can be integrated into the tactical training process, and once the tactic is mastered, implemented in competition.

Tactical training should be aligned with competitive performance by

- developing a thorough understanding of the sport rules and regulations,
- understanding the central tactical strategies typically employed in the sport,
- evaluating the tactical strategies and trends used by opponents,
- examining the athlete's strengths and weaknesses and how they relate to tactical trends, and
- deconstructing the tactical model used in a variety of competitive environments and developing contingency plans.

Based on careful inspection of the competitive environment and critical appraisal of the athlete's physical and technical capacities, the coach can construct the tactical training interventions.

The ability to effectively analyze tactical aspects of sport has increased dramatically due to the development of sport-specific observation instruments (79) and the advancement of technological systems (e.g., global positioning system [GPS], Prozone-STATS, OPTA, microsensors) (95) that allow for the development of tactical metrics that can guide physical preparation, tactical training, and tactical strategies (26). For example, the use of GPS and microsensor technologies, such as built-in inertial measurement units (IMUs), has increased in many team sports (e.g., Australian rules football, soccer, American football, and rugby) (57, 71, 94). Data collected by these devices yield detailed information about positional demands during match play. This information can be used to modify physical training practices and to better understand the tactical demands of the competitive environment (94). Additionally, these devices yield data about the number of collisions and impacts within a match (57), which can be used to better match the physical and tactical aspects of training to the demands of the competitive environment (21). For example, data collected with GPS and IMUs can guide the construction of small-sided games that target the physical demands of a soccer match while facilitating tactical development (78). Ultimately, it is important to realize that tactical training is fluid, and information collected on competition and training performance should be used to develop training interventions that affect performance (21).

Development of the Tactical Plan

A key job of a coach, or the coaching staff, is developing the tactical game plan (figure 3.11) (14). This plan is constructed based on very detailed analyses of several key factors about the team and

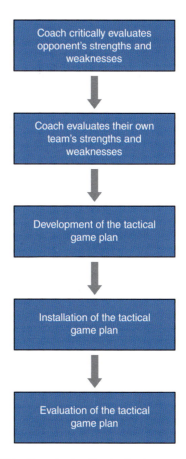

FIGURE 3.11 Developing the tactical game plan.

their opponent, including historical competition data, external parameters, and individual athlete parameters (figure 3.12) (86). For example, the coach needs to consider the team's competitive history against the opponent when working on the tactical game plan. The coach can use considerations about the competitive schedule and location to make training decisions (87, 88) and construct tactical strategies to optimize competitive success. As part of this analysis, the coach must consider the opponent's tactical trends and the opponent's strengths and weaknesses (as a team and for individual players). During this process, it is also important for the coach to critically evaluate their own team's strengths and weaknesses and determine where critical opportunities exist to design tactics to capitalize on them.

An emerging trend in high-performance sport is the use of **machine learning** algorithms based on game position data to translate tactical aspects of sports (such as soccer) into tactical models that can be used to guide coaching decisions (86). For example, across an entire season of the English Premier League, an expectation maximization algorithm was used to automatically identify team formations. These data were implemented as part of tactical planning. To accomplish this, Rein and Memmert (86) proposed the application of a "big data technological stack" for the tactical analysis of soccer (figure 3.13).

As part of this process, a tactical model is developed through machine learning to analyze numerous inputs. In soccer, for example, the inputs could be psychological data, tracking data, physiological data, health and injury data, coaching data, scouting data, historical data, and crowd data. To implement a big data technological stack process, it is necessary to build an appropriate infrastructure to collect and efficiently store data so they are easily accessible and analyzable (86). Typically, physiological and tracking data (e.g., monitoring data from GPS) and relevant video and

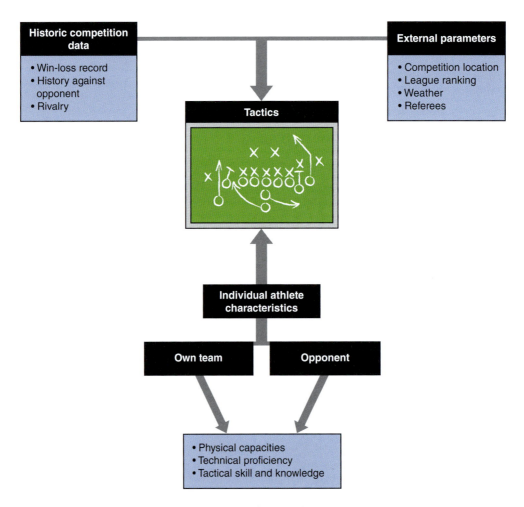

FIGURE 3.12 Factors to consider when creating a tactical game plan.

Chapter 3 • Classification of Skills and Types of Training | 65

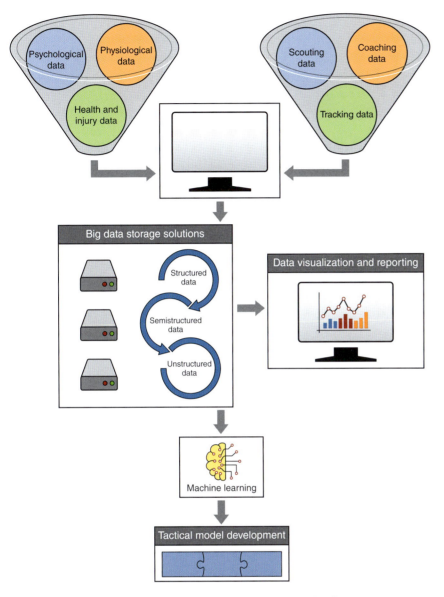

FIGURE 3.13 An example of a big data technological stack in elite sport.

In 2007, Kelly and Coutts (64) presented a systematic approach to establishing the tactical training plan prior to a team sport in-season competition (figure 3.14). This model follows a four-step process:

1. Predict a match difficulty score based on collected data.
2. Plan weekly training interventions based on data analysis.
3. Monitor weekly training to fine-tune future match difficulty scores.
4. Review all data and initiate step 1 of the process.

The following data need to be collected prior to initiating the development of the tactical plan: information about the level of competition, the number of training days between competitions, the location of the competition, and training load (64).

Kelly and Coutts (64) suggested that the level of competition exerts the greatest effect on the calculated match difficulty score, followed by the time frame between multiple competitions. When the coach considers the level of competition, they must rank the strongest to weakest team in their competitive schedule, including their own team. During the competitive phase of the annual training plan, this ranking is constantly recalculated to reflect the current level of competition. For example, if we examine the National Football League (NFL), a ranking scoring system can be developed (table 3.1) and used to rank the 32 teams from week to week based on the NFL power rankings.

observational data are collected and stored for comprehensive analysis. A processing pipeline, which includes the implementation of machine learning, is used to extract relevant information from the data to build an explanatory or predictive model that can inform training and competitive tactics (30). One thing to consider is the ability to extract and visualize relevant information from the data collected and integrate these data with the coach's experiential knowledge of the sport-specific, ecologically relevant problems (30). This information is then translated into a tactical model that informs the coach's development of the tactical training plan and the tactical game plan used during competition.

To evaluate the training days between competitions, a scoring system is established: shorter durations between competitions receive higher scores and longer durations receive lower scores (table 3.1). In addition, the location of travel can be factored into the predicted match difficulty score (table 3.1). Once the scores for each factor are established for each opponent, the coach can use this information to project how difficult the competition will be and thus better guide their physical, technical, and tactical training. Remember that this scoring criteria needs to be recalculated at the beginning of each new training week (64).

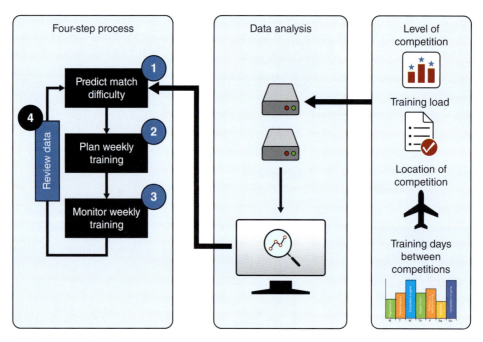

FIGURE 3.14 Basic process for informing in-season training.

Table 3.2 shows a ranking matrix for the first 4 weeks of the 2018 NFL season; to obtain the ranking score, each team's power index rating (i.e., NFL.com power rankings) was used to calculate a ranking based off the method presented in table 3.1. Specifically, the score was calculated based on the team's ranking, the number of days between competitions, and the location of the next competition.

Based on the competitive schedule, we can see that out of 32 teams in the NFL (table 3.2), the New York Giants' average power index ranking ranged between 14 and 26 during the first 4 weeks. When the team's competitive schedule is examined, we can determine the predicted difficulty score for each week's opponent (table 3.3). We use the NFL power rankings to calculate a ranking score and then determine the travel and days between com-

TABLE 3.1 Categories and Scoring for Level of Opposition for a 32-Team League

Ranking and scoring for 32-team league		Scoring for days between competitions		Scoring for match location	
Ranking	Score	Days	Score	Location	Score
1-4	35-32	4	20	Away with travel	3
5-8	31-28	5	18	Away without travel	2
9-12	27-24	6	16	Home	1
13-16	23-20	7	14		
17-20	19-16	8	12		
21-24	15-12	9	10		
25-28	11-8	10	8		
29-32	7-4	11	6		
		12	4		
		13	2		
		14	1		

Data from Kelly and Coutts (2007).

TABLE 3.2 Ranking Matrix for the First 4 Weeks of the 2018 NFL Season

Teams	Weekly power index ranking from NFL.com				Ranking score			
	Week 1	Week 2	Week 3	Week 4	Week 1 score	Week 2 score	Week 3 score	Week 4 score
Atlanta Falcons	8	7	9	14	28	29	27	22
Carolina Panthers	11	8	10	5	25	28	26	31
Chicago Bears	15	16	14	17	21	20	22	19
Dallas Cowboys	22	25	19	24	14	11	17	12
Houston Texans	12	13	23	28	24	23	13	8
Indianapolis Colts	32	30	22	26	4	6	14	10
Jacksonville Jaguars	6	5	2	4	30	31	34	32
New Orleans Saints	3	12	12	6	33	24	24	30
New York Giants	14	15	26	25	22	21	10	11
Philadelphia Eagles	1	1	8	3	35	35	28	33
San Francisco 49ers	19	22	20	31	17	14	16	5
Tampa Bay Buccaneers	28	19	7	8	8	17	29	28
Tennessee Titans	13	24	21	19	23	12	15	17
Washington Redskins	26	17	24	18	10	19	12	18

petitions scores (table 3.2). Once this is done, the predicted difficulty score can be determined for the opponent, in this case the Jacksonville Jaguars for week 1 (table 3.3). The predicted difficulty score for the Jaguars was 32, but the Giants' score was 29. Therefore, the Jaguars would be considered a somewhat difficult opponent for the Giants, and the Giants must consider revisions to their microcycle to address this.

This concept has been expanded by Robertson and Joyce (88) to better inform the training practices during the week leading into a rugby competition. Their model examined the use of match location, days between matches, number of time zones crossed, and the ranking of the opponent (previous year and current year). Ultimately, they determined that this model was able to correctly predict the competition outcome 66.2% of the time. In a follow-up study, Robertson and Joyce (87) expanded on their model to include fixed factors available to the team prior to the commencement of the competitive season and dynamic factors during the season. Two interesting findings were that the previous season's ranking was the strongest indicator of competitive difficulty and that the effect of travel to away games became a stronger mediator of competitive performance later in the season. Analyses like these give the coach insight into how to manipulate physical, technical, and tactical training to optimize performance in team sports.

Development and Implementation of the Tactical Game Plan

Once the coach has systematically analyzed the opponent and determined the match difficulty score, they can develop the preliminary game plan. Based on the data analyzed and their own experience, the coach will structure objectives designed to address the tactical challenges revealed in the analysis. This will result in group tactical strategies as well as individual tactical objectives that are assigned to individual players based on their strengths and weaknesses. The tactical objectives are then integrated into the tactical training plan.

During the time leading up to the competition, the coach will install the tactical game plan. Aspects of this plan will be installed in stages, allowing the athletes to practice and perfect the various aspects of the plan. This process requires the coach to use structured practice sessions that allow for the development of good technique and tactical performance. A key aspect of this process is ensuring that some of the training sessions mirror the competitive model. As the athletes move

TABLE 3.3 New York Giants' Predicted Competition Difficulty Score for the First 4 Weeks of the 2018 NFL Season

Week	Giants' opponent	Giants' location	Days between competition		Difficulty scoring		Travel score		Days between competitions score		Predicted difficulty score		Final score	
			Giants	Opponent	Giants	Opponent	Giants	Opponent	Giants	Opponent	Giants	Opponent	Giants	Opponent
1	Jacksonville Jaguars	Home	>14	>14	25	30	1	3	1	1	29	32	15	20
2	Dallas Cowboys	Away	7	7	22	14	3	1	14	14	37	31	13	20
3	Houston Texans	Away	6	7	21	23	3	1	16	14	36	42	27	22
4	New Orleans Saints	Home	7	7	10	24	1	1	14	14	27	39	18	33

Note: ☐ = Favors opponent ☐ = Favors New York Giants.

through the training week toward competition, the coach should reinforce key aspects of the tactical plan and make modifications as needed in response to evaluations of the athletes' progress in the plan. In some situations, the coach may choose to add additional tactical elements or simplify tactics if athletes are not responding well to the training. The coach must ensure enough flexibility in the tactical plan that the athletes are able to respond to the ever-changing environment of competition.

After the tactical game plan has been installed, the next stage of the process is the implementation of the plan in the actual competition. During the early stages of the competition, the main tactical strategies are tested. A key strategy that coaches strive to apply during this portion of the competition is revealing the opponent's tactical game plan while concealing many aspects of their own. If the coach has prepared their athletes well, the athletes should be able to analyze and comprehend the ever-changing tactical situations that arise during the competition and choose appropriate strategies to counteract the opponent's tactics. Ultimately, a key part of tactical training is developing each athlete's ability to instantaneously recognize and solve tactical problems during competition. This ability is developed in training and is based on the athlete's cumulative tactical knowledge and experience, team dynamics, and overall tactical preparation. In team sports, a central factor of tactical plan success is individual athletes' decision-making processes being aligned with the team's collective decision-making dynamics. The coordinated efforts of each athlete allow for rapid, rational, creative, and efficient solutions to the ever-changing tactical challenges that occur during the competition.

After the competition, the coach needs to perform a detailed analysis of the tactical game plan and the effectiveness of the plan. As part of this process, the coach should closely examine how the tactical plan was implemented and examine the team's ability to apply the plan. A comprehensive analysis of this process and the competitive outcome will reveal the strengths and weaknesses of the plan and guide the coach's future tactical planning. The most appropriate time to analyze the outcome of the tactical plan is often dictated by the outcome of the competition. If the outcome is favorable, the analysis and dissemination of information to athletes can occur during the first practice session after the competition. If the outcome is not favorable, the analysis may take more time, and dissemination of information to the athletes may not occur until 2 or 3 days after the competition. In the latter scenario, the delay in providing this information can allow time for psychological wounds to heal and foster a more rational discussion about the performance. When addressing the team and individual athletes about the analysis of the plan, the coach must highlight any positives about the performance but also be clear and reasonable about the key areas where more work is needed. It is also essential that the coach project confidence and optimism and provide strategies to employ as the team moves forward.

Psychological Training

When following a holistic approach to training, a key aspect of the athlete's progression is developing psychological factors that underpin successful performance. Many coaches and athletes suggest that the ability to perform at a high level is often related to the athlete's motivation, self-confidence, effective focus, and cognitive flexibility (76). Successful athletes display strong interpersonal skills that allow them to be good teammates and team leaders. Successful athletes also need to be able to regulate their physical and emotional intensity (76).

A key attribute that appears to determine the probability of success (when talent is equal) is referred to as *grit* (34). Grit has been defined as a "sustained and focused application of talent over time" (34, page 1087) and "the tenacious pursuit of a dominant superordinate goal despite setbacks" (33, page 319). Duckworth et al. (34) also suggest that "grit entails working strenuously toward challenges, maintaining effort and interest over years despite failure, adversity, and plateaus in progress" (pages 1087-1088). Ultimately, qualities associated with grit are courage, conscientiousness, long-term goals, resilience, and excellence (figure 3.15) (34). If coaches were asked what characteristics underpin successful athletic performance, they would provide similar lists of attributes.

Courage

Courage is the ability to manage the fear of failure and is an important predictor of success (34). In this context, athletes who demonstrate high levels of grit are not afraid to fail and embrace failure as part of the training process (76). These athletes realize that a lot can be learned from failure and that perseverance is an important part of high-level performance.

Conscientiousness

Athletes who have high levels of grit tend to be conscientious and are achievement-oriented. They tirelessly work to do a good job and complete the

FIGURE 3.15 Qualities associated with grit.

tasks in front of them. The conscientious athlete also knows that it is more important to commit to training goals than it is to just show up for practice (33, 76).

Long-Term Goals

A central part of success in sport is the ability to set and work toward long-term goals. Long-term goals provide the context and framework that guide the athlete and help cultivate the athlete's drive, sustainability, stamina, and passion for the training process. Athletes who have high levels of grit are better able to set long-term goals and endure the process of accomplishing those goals (33, 76).

Resilience

Resilience is an important aspect of grit. Attributes such as optimism, confidence, and creativity allow the athlete to persevere no matter what obstacles appear in front of them. Athletes who have high levels of grit will stay the course when they experience disappointment or boredom. Individuals with low levels of grit tend to cut their losses and change their trajectory (34), which often results in them opting out of a sport. Ultimately, grittier athletes are less likely to drop out when things get tough compared to those who display less grit (33, 37).

Excellence Versus Perfectionism

Successful athletes with grit tend to be on a quest to achieve excellence. Excellence should be considered an attitude. The pursuit of excellence is far more forgiving than the pursuit of perfection because it allows for continual improvement and prioritizes progress (33, 76).

If coaches are queried about what characteristics underpin successful athletic performance, they would provide a list of attributes that mirror those presented by Duckworth et al. (33, 34). Coaches might use different words, but the fundamental concepts would be aligned.

Hardy et al. (56) lent evidence to the concept of grit, suggesting that perseverance over time and resilience to setbacks are two of the primary attributes displayed by superelite athletes. One of the most interesting findings of their research suggests that superelite athletes tend to become more motivated as a result of setbacks (56, 58). Gulbin et al. (52) also found that Australian Olympic athletes consistently demonstrate greater determination and perseverance when facing obstacles and setbacks. These data highlight the importance of motivational concepts, such as grit, that drive superelite athletes to overcome adversity in their quest to attain high levels of sporting success (27, 58).

Superelite athletes are also more likely to engage in higher quality practice as a result of their higher focus on task mastery (29, 42). A major factor that affects the quality of practice is the creation of what Hodges et al. (58) call a *deliberate environment* that helps foster high levels of sporting success. In a deliberate environment, the athlete's decisions and behaviors are guided by their goals and align with the ultimate goal of improvement (41, 42). Hodges et al. (58) suggest that superelite athletes' grit and their need to achieve facilitate sustained high-performance lifestyles, commitment to high-quality training, and high levels of achievement. While grit is only one aspect of the psychological attributes that underpin performance, it does provide a strong rationale for the importance of developing the athletes' psychological capabilities.

Integrating Psychological Training

Part of the training process is to help create an environment in which athletes develop the psychological attributes required for sporting success. Balague (4) suggests that psychological and mental training are important parts of periodized training and need to be incorporated into the training process. However, Mujika et al. (76) suggest there is limited information looking at how psychological skills should be incorporated into the athlete's periodized training plan.

One important aspect of psychological training is that it can be used to develop an athlete's self-confidence, especially in those who are recovering from injury or progressing to higher levels of competition that challenge their abilities. Psychological training, much like physical training, is very individualized, and often it is important to determine which specific psychological skills are needed (76). Additionally, the psychological demands of the sport are an important factor to understand when developing an athlete's psychological training plan (4). Depending on the sport and the athlete's psychological needs, psychological training activities such as goal setting, relaxation techniques, visualization, and mental rehearsal can be integrated into the athlete's annual training plan (4). Although there are no agreed-on periodization models that specifically target psychological training, Mujika et al. (76) suggest ways of integrating psychological training into the periodization plans for athletes competing in team (table 3.4) or individual (table 3.5) sports.

Balague (4) presents another potential model (figure 3.16) that integrates psychological interventions into a periodized training plan for horizontal jumps. In this example, the psychological requirements of the sport are aligned with the various periods and phases of training. Based on these demands, specific psychological training interventions are presented.

Mujika et al. (76), however, suggest that it may be impossible to provide a specific sequence for psychological skills training for sport performance enhancement in elite athletes. They also say that psychological skills are not universally accepted as being essential or trainable. They suggest that to implement psychological training, one should consider the athlete's existing psychological skills and level of development and then determine the connection between the required psychological skills and the demands of training in the various periods and phases of the athlete's annual training plan (76).

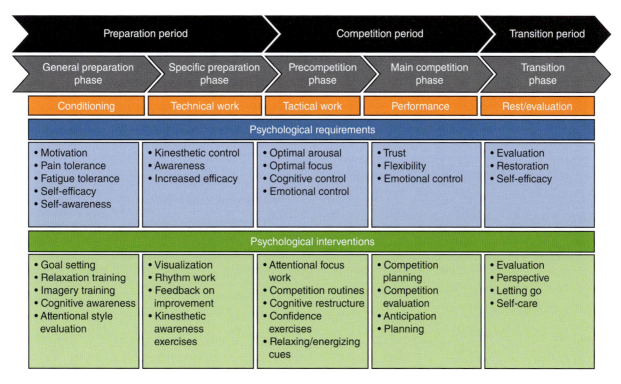

FIGURE 3.16 Example of the integration of psychological training into a periodized training plan.

TABLE 3.4 Example Integration of Psychological Training Into the Periodized Plan for Team Sport Athletes

Period	Macrocycle				Transition period
	Preparation period		Competitive period		
			Main competitive phase		
Phases	General preparation phase	Specific preparation phase	Main season	Playoffs	Transition phase
Psychological training activities	Motivation, pain and fatigue management	Kinesthetic awareness and control	Optimal arousal, effective focus, self-management	Trust, flexibility, confidence	Effective evaluation of self-care and restoration
	Development of self-awareness	Increased self-efficacy, emotional management, learning style awareness	Competition routines, attentional focus, relaxing and energizing cues	Competition plan, cognitive restructuring tools, tolerance of ambiguity, team confidence	Self-identity development
	Goal setting for practice, imagery, relaxation and activation techniques	Use of video, improvements log	Promoting uniformity, togetherness, group initiative, collaboration activities	Mindfulness, interpersonal trust	New goal setting
	Individual engagement	Promoting contact among players, group discussions		Empowering team decision making, creative use of talents	
	Team communication				

Adapted from Mujika, Halson, Burke, et al. (2018).

TABLE 3.5 Example Integration of Psychological Training Into the Periodized Plan for Individual Sport Athletes

Period	Macrocycle				Transition period
	Preparation period		Competitive period		
			Main competitive phase		
Phases	General preparation phase	Specific preparation phase	Main season	Playoffs	Transition phase
Psychological training activities	Motivation, pain and fatigue management	Kinesthetic awareness and control	Optimal arousal, effective focus, self-management	Trust, flexibility, confidence	Effective evaluation of self-care and restoration
	Development of self-awareness	Increased self-efficacy, emotional management, learning style awareness	Competition routines, attentional focus, relaxing and energizing cues	Competition plan, cognitive restructuring tools, tolerance of ambiguity	Self-identity development
	Goal setting for practice, imagery, relaxation and activation techniques	Use of video, improvements log, rhythm work		Mindfulness	New goal setting

Adapted from Mujika, Halson, Burke, et al. (2018).

Summary

When preparing athletes, the ability to classify the various skills and types of training is necessary to better align training and competition. Generally, all sport performance is dictated by some combination of strength, speed, and endurance abilities. Classifying dominant biomotor abilities for individual sports can guide the coach's training decisions. Regardless of the sport, training is generally divided into physical, technical, tactical, and psychological categories. In many ways, physical training is strongly linked to technical, tactical, and psychological skills, and it is often considered the foundation of training. If the athlete's physical capacities are not adequately developed, their ability to develop technical and tactical skills will be impaired, which can exert a negative effect on their psychological state.

Technique, tactics, and psychological abilities are also affected by fatigue, so it is essential that the athlete's physical capacities are optimized with appropriate physical training.

Throughout the training process, the athlete strives to perfect their technical skills and optimally apply them to tactical situations. The athlete's technical proficiency will influence how complex the coach's tactical competition plans can be. Novice or developing athletes must continually strive to refine their technical skills to provide the coach with more tactical options.

The process of developing tactical training interventions is based on systematic analyses of a variety of factors, including the strengths and weaknesses of the opponent and the coach's own team. More detailed analyses can be used to develop metrics that guide training decisions and aid in the installation of the tactical training plan.

CHAPTER 4

Understanding Training Loads

A key factor that affects the physiological and performance responses to a training plan is how training loads are applied and manipulated. Our understanding of how training loads affect the athlete's physiological and performance responses continues to evolve as new research is completed, and we therefore continue to refine our training practices and more effectively craft training plans that maximize athlete performance capacity.

To effectively prescribe training, the coach must understand the various factors that contribute to training load and how these factors affect the athlete's performance capacities. Central to this understanding is the realization that how an athlete responds to the prescribed training load is highly individualized. Basic training load progressions serve as templates for designing custom training load prescriptions. Coaches who understand these basic training load progressions can use them to best meet their athletes' needs.

Defining Training Load

Training load is the quantitative determination of the amount of training work completed (206). Central to the periodization paradigm is the ability to prescribe appropriate training loads that are balanced with sufficient recovery to promote favorable performance outcomes and minimize the risk of illness, injury, and maladaptive responses (27, 55). The ability of the training process to accomplish these goals is largely determined by the training load and how the athlete responds to it.

The application of training load is largely dictated by the periodization models chosen for the athlete (80); this represents a dose–response relationship between the applied training stimulus and the resultant athlete response (6, 14, 55). The applied training stimulus is typically referred to as the ***external load*** and represents the physical work performed by the athlete (55). In team sports, these loads are often represented by objective measures such as the number of sprints, accelerations, jumps, collisions, or distances covered (27, 66). In the weight room, the volume load (i.e., reps × weight lifted), velocity of movement, power, repetitions completed, and load lifted are often quantified when determining the external load. **Internal load** represents the athlete's physiological and psychological responses to the physical stimuli (66, 80). The internal load is most often quantified using heart rate or perceptual measures (55, 66), but it can also be evaluated by measuring hormonal (e.g., testosterone, cortisol) or metabolic (e.g., lactate, energy expenditure) responses to the external load.

Although the external load is the primary determinant of the internal load, other factors can exert significant effects on the athlete's response (figure 4.1) (110). For example, the athlete's genetic makeup can dictate their response to various types

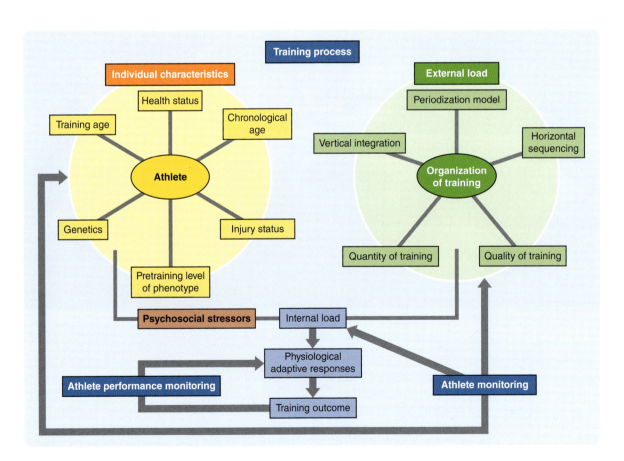

FIGURE 4.1 Training process and the interaction of the internal and external load.

Adapted by permission from G.G. Haff, "Periodization for Tactical Populations," in *NSCA's Essentials of Tactical Strength and Conditioning,* edited for the National Strength and Conditioning Association by B.A. Alvar, K. Sell, and P.A. Deuster (Champaign, IL: Human Kinetics, 2017).

of training (15, 152, 153). Athletes with the alpha-actinin-3 (ACTN3) XX allele are more susceptible to strenuous exercise compared to those with RR or RX homozygote profiles (45). In fact, Pickering and Kiely (152) suggest that athletes with the ACTN3 XX homozygote profile exhibit a reduced responsiveness to resistance training, increased post-eccentric-exercise muscle damage, and an increased injury risk. Additionally, Pickering et al. (154) report that those who have a high aerobic genotype score, based on five single nucleotide polymorphisms (VEGF rs2010963, ADRB2 rs1042713 and rs1042714, CRP rs1205, and PPARGC1Ars 8192678), display a greater responsiveness to 8 weeks of aerobic training.

Other factors also exert a significant influence on the athlete's response to training. Impellizzeri, Rampinini, and Marcora (110) suggest that an athlete's pretraining level of phenotype—the athlete's fitness level at the start of the training intervention—can also influence the internal load. This level is affected by the athlete's training history, injury and health status, chronological age, and psychological state (34, 80, 117). Collectively, these factors are considered to be individual athlete characteristics, which directly affect the athlete's **adaptive potential**. The interaction of the athlete's adaptive potential with the applied external load can positively or negatively affect the athlete's internal load, which regulates the athlete's physiological adaptive responses that lead to training or performance outcomes (80).

Ultimately, the periodized training plan stimulates the appropriate physiological adaptive responses and enhances the targeted training outcomes. If the periodized plan is correctly constructed and effectively monitored (see chapter 11), the coach can ensure a balance between the external and internal training loads (i.e., adaptive stimulus and recovery) and performance can be maximized (80).

Training Load and Its Effects

An athlete who encounters a training load exhibits numerous physiological responses that can result in acute and chronic performance responses. These responses make up the **training effect**, which is typically classified into the following categories: acute, immediate, cumulative, delayed, and residual.

Acute Training Effects

Acute training effects are the athlete's physiological and performance responses that occur during a single exercise or a series of exercises (115, 212). For example, an athlete performing a tempo run would show alterations in heart rate and respiration that reflect the intensity of the run. Another example of an acute training effect is the decline in movement velocity that occurs across a set of squats (199, 200), which can be considered a marker of fatigue (72, 73). Additionally, from a biochemical perspective, the reductions in adenosine triphosphate (ATP) and phosphocreatine (PCr) that occur during this set would be considered an acute training effect (72, 73).

Immediate Training Effects

Immediate training effects occur in response to an individual training session and manifest soon after the completion of the workout (figure 4.2) (115, 212). For example, immediately after performing a resistance-training session containing the bench press and the back squat, there are marked reductions in mechanical muscle function (i.e., countermovement jump height and velocity against a given load) and alterations to the athlete's biochemical profile (i.e., testosterone, cortisol, growth hormone, creatine kinase) (150) and bioenergetic substrate availability (72, 73). Factors that contribute to the immediate training effects are related to programming constructs such as the exercises, intensity, volume, and workloads used to construct the session, as well as the total duration of the session.

Cumulative Training Effects

Cumulative training effects represent the physiological and motor or technical responses to a series of training sessions or a specific training program (20, 22, 115, 212). This represents the body's progressive adaptation to training and is typically monitored over months to years (48). The changes in body state and level of motor or technical ability that occur in response to a series of training bouts ultimately determine the direction of the athlete's performance (114).

Delayed Training Effects

Delayed training effects are the longer-term responses to a training session or period of training (20, 22, 212). The immediate response to a training

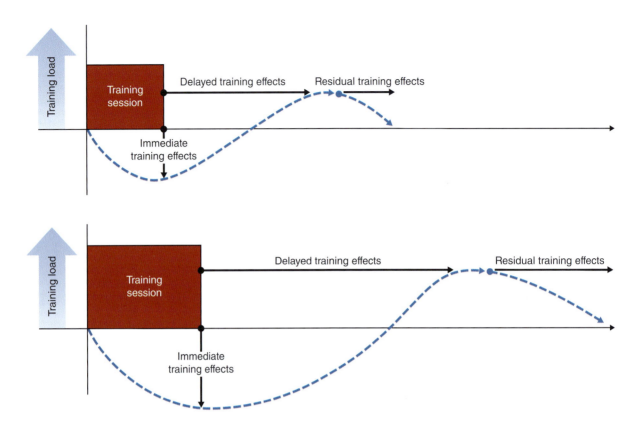

FIGURE 4.2 Depiction of training effects.

program is typically considered a fatigue response, while the delayed training effects represent the positive training responses that occur once fatigue has dissipated (20, 22). The onset of the delayed training effects is directly affected by the contents of the training session or training period. Specifically, the more intense or the greater the training workload, the longer the time frame before the performance gains are realized (figure 4.2).

Residual Training Effects

Residual training effects represent the body's recovery and preparation response (48). When the athlete ceases training, the developed adaptive responses begin to dissipate. The time frame in which the training effect dissipates effectively represents the ability to retain the training effect; this is the residual training effect (114, 212). Conceptually, the three broad categories of residual training effects include short-term, medium-term, and long-term residuals (114).

Short-Term Residuals

Short-term residual training effects are training factors that are retained for a few days to a number of weeks (114). For example, within 2 weeks after the cessation of a resistance training program, there can be a 9% to 11.5% reduction in maximal force development capacity (7, 91). This decline would represent the short-term residuals for strength.

Medium-Term Residuals

Medium-term residual training effects are training adaptations that can be retained for several months. For example, 2 months after the cessation of soccer training, an athlete will show a significant reduction in numerous cardiovascular adaptations, including peak oxygen uptake ($\dot{V}O_2$peak) (mL · kg^{-1} · min^{-1}), peak ventilation rate (L · min^{-1}), and running speed (km · h^{-1}) (134).

Long-Term Residuals

Long-term residual training effects are training adaptations that can be maintained for years or potentially remain as permanent adaptations (114), such as mastering specific motor skills or other longer-term physiological and performance adaptations.

These various training effects are generally interrelated and can be conceptualized by the following sequence (114) (figure 4.3):

1. The acute training effects within a training session contribute to the immediate training effects.
2. The immediate training effects from several training sessions directly affect the cumulative training effects.
3. The cumulative training effects directly affect the athlete's preparedness and athletic performance capacity and can be related to the delayed and residual training effects.

Appropriate periodized training models consider the interplay of the various training effects to capitalize on the ability to vertically integrate and horizontally sequence training interventions. **Vertical integration** of training involves designing training programs that integrate complementary training factors at key time points, whereas **horizontal sequencing** involves planning training to capitalize on the duration of residual training effects to better guide training practices.

Factors Contributing to Training Load

Three global factors—loading factors, contents, and organization of training—influence the training load experienced by the athlete (figure 4.4). These factors are largely interrelated and can influence each other. For example, the volume of training affects the intensity of the training activity, with higher-volume training requiring lower intensities. Additionally, the sequence of training can be affected by the modes or methods selected as part of the training program. To truly understand training load, the coach must recognize the factors that can contribute to and affect training load.

Volume of Training

The volume of training is central to the training process. In its most simplistic form, volume is the total quantity of the activity performed (24, 207) or the total amount of work accomplished (24).

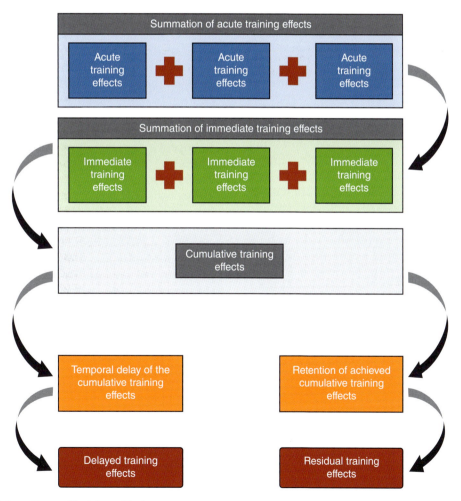

FIGURE 4.3 Interactions of training effects.

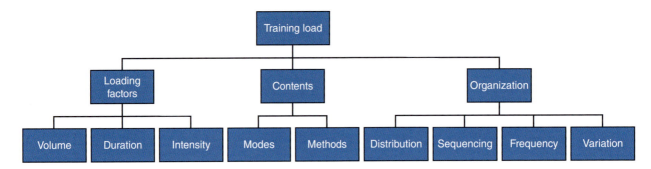

FIGURE 4.4 Factors that typically contribute to the training load.

Depending on the sport or the type of activity being quantified, the volume of training can be described in a variety of ways:

- Time or duration of training
- Distance covered
- Number of repetitions completed for an exercise or series of technical elements
- Total amount of work completed (e.g., in resistance training, the volume load = sets × repetitions × resistance in kg)

Regardless of how it is defined, training volume exerts an important effect on the athlete's long-term adaptations to the training process (207). The quantification of training volume is typically a key part of any athlete monitoring program (chapter 11).

Given its importance, volume must be accurately assessed. When examining endurance sports such as cycling, running, and cross-country skiing, it is appropriate to measure training volume as the distance covered (50) or as the time allotted to the training target (44, 112, 163, 197, 198). For example, Rønnestad and Hansen (161) presented an annual training plan for an elite cyclist where the volume of training was represented as the total hours of training, which was further subdivided into the number of hours allotted for several targeted training activities (i.e., strength training, high-intensity training, moderate-intensity training, and low-intensity training). Although quantifying training time is useful, a more informative approach is to depict training volume using time and distance (e.g., cycling 200 m in 15.4 s) (44) or time allocated to a specific training zone (141).

In sports such as baseball (124), softball (12), and the throwing events in track and field (13, 125), the volume of training is often represented as the number of **repetitions** (in this case, throws) completed. However, counting repetitions is generally considered a poor method for quantifying volume in resistance training, weightlifting, and powerlifting (77). In these scenarios, determination of volume load (77, 108, 109, 155, 204), which is expressed as kilograms (sets × repetitions × resistance in kilograms) or metric tons of training (24, 77) (chapter 13), is the preferred method for quantifying training volume (77).

Modern technologies can provide accurate assessments of training volume (41). For example, global positioning systems (GPS) can accurately quantify the distance covered during training and competition, the volume of high-speed engagements, and changes of direction during team sport technical and tactical training (41, 191). In resistance training, technologies can accurately measure the displacement of movement, which may be used to better determine the volume load (108) (see chapter 11). As more technologies evolve, the ability to quantify training volume will continue to improve, thereby allowing for the optimization of training prescription as well as enhancing the ability to monitor the progress of training.

Regardless of how training volume is quantified it is well-documented that the volume of training will increase as the athlete becomes more developed (76, 148). Younger or less-developed athletes typically require less training volume to stimulate physiological and performance adaptations than their more experienced counterparts. The progression of increasing training volume can be seen in the work of Gullich and Emrich (76), who report that a young athlete progressing through their athletic career will increase the number of training sessions they complete over time. This results in an increase in the overall training volume in the athlete's annual training plan (figure 4.5). The ability to increase training volume is important because it enables the athlete to further develop technical and tactical abilities, which typically require increased repetitions as the athlete develops.

In modern sports, there has been an increase in the total amount of time dedicated to training (53). For example, between 1970 and 2001, the volume

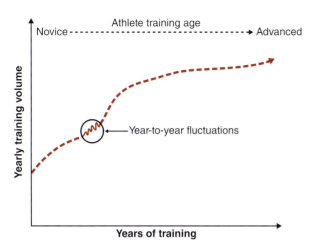

FIGURE 4.5 Theoretical relationship of the volume of training over time.

of training undertaken by international-class Norwegian rowers increased from 924 to 1,128 hours per year (an increase of about 20%) (53). With the overall increase in time dedicated to training it is now common for distance runners to undertake 500 hours of training per year (18, 19, 111, 193, 194) or for rowers, swimmers, cyclists, and triathlon athletes to complete more than 1,000 hours of training per year (53, 68, 75, 139, 143, 166, 168, 211) to maximize their performance capacities. Although the volume of training undertaken by an athlete is individualized and dictated by numerous factors (such as training age, genetics, and tolerance to training), as an athlete becomes more developed, more training is necessary to increase performance capacity.

Coaches use three common methods to target an increase in training volume (24):

1. Increase the volume of training within a given session.
2. Increase the frequency of training.
3. Increase both of these.

A key consideration when increasing an athlete's training volume is their ability to recover from the programmed training interventions. An athlete who has a lower training age generally is not able to tolerate the same amount of training volume as a more advanced athlete (67). As training age increases, the athlete has increased work capacity and ability to recover from specific training interventions, which enables them to benefit from higher volumes of training (155). Although it is well-established that increasing training volume can improve performance, the coach must be cognizant of the athlete's current training status and not increase training volume too quickly (65), because rapid spikes in training volume can significantly increase injury risk (67) and may be counterproductive to long-term training goals.

Frequency of Training

The number of training sessions in a given period, such as a day or week, is often referred to as the ***frequency of training*** (24, 47). It is generally accepted that increasing the frequency of training results in a greater volume of training that can translate into greater performance gains (70, 74, 92, 171, 198). For example, when examining the training practices of elite cross-country skiers and biathletes between 1985 and 2011, Tønnessen et al. (198) reported that these athletes completed about 500 training sessions per year totaling about 800 hours each year. Most interesting was the finding that during this time, there was a positive relationship ($r = .59$, $p = .055$) between total training volume and championship title performance. In addition, it was noted that the increase in training volume was largely related to an increase in training frequency, but the duration of the individual training sessions remained relatively constant (1.7 ± 0.2 h). It is not uncommon for elite athletes to complete between 4 and 12 training sessions per week (1-4, 123, 197, 198).

Although frequency is one of the main mechanisms for altering the training process, often it is a forgotten modifiable factor when designing training programs (42). Remember that the training frequency an athlete undertakes is based on a relationship between work capacity and recoverability. Specifically, the athlete's ability to recover from the training process is a critical consideration when determining the overall programmed training frequency.

As an athlete's training age increases, they are generally able to tolerate greater training volumes, which are typically divided into more frequent training sessions (9, 42). The ability to increase training frequency is affected by the athlete's current training status (212) and overall level of development (171). Smith (171) reports that it is not uncommon for athletes to engage in 5 to 14 training sessions per week depending on their level of development and the phase of their periodized training plan. Nutritional (33, 43, 137, 157, 158, 172) and other recovery interventions (135, 144, 157, 160) are often used to help the athlete recover from more frequent training (chapter 9). These practices allow the athlete to better tolerate higher training loads.

It is difficult to determine the amount of recovery time needed between high-frequency training periods (i.e., within a given training day or microcycle) because many factors can affect recovery. The greater the workload (i.e., intensity and volume) of a training session, the more time the athlete will need for recovery of preparedness and performance capacity (113, 155, 205, 212). Although the training workload exerts a significant effect on the duration of recovery after a training session, remember that complete recovery is not required prior to the next training session (62). A common strategy to facilitate more frequent training and recovery is to create training sessions with varying workloads within the training day or microcycle (47, 155). This practice is extremely effective for modulating training stimuli and balancing workload demands with recovery requirements while allowing for increased training frequency. Ultimately, the ability to engage in more frequent training has the potential to increase adaptation (165) and performance (70, 146). In addition, modulating the frequency of training gives the coach flexibility in how training is delivered (47) and increases the quality of individual training sessions by making session workloads more manageable.

Density of Training

The frequency or distribution of training is often referred to as the ***density of training*** (47). Conceptually, the density of training represents the balance between the time allocated to work and recovery. Shorter time frames between bouts of work are associated with a greater density of training. For example, if two training days were constructed with an equal total training volume but the first training day contains three training sessions and the second contains one, the first day would have a greater training density (47). If constructed correctly, training days with higher densities allow the intensities of training during each smaller session to be maintained at a higher level compared to a single training session of an equal training volume (92). Training density also can be conceptualized as a method for varying training volume between individual training weeks (47). For example, the number of training sessions within a week of training can be manipulated to either create a functional overreaching (see chapter 9) or tapering (see chapter 12) period of training (11). During a period of planned overreaching, the volume of training can be increased by increasing the density of training (i.e., increasing the number of training sessions) within a predetermined period, such as 2 weeks, and then reducing the density (i.e., reducing the number of training sessions) within the subsequent training period to increase recovery (97). When constructing training programs, the coach should consider work and recovery and modulate training density to better guide training outcomes.

The density of training can be examined as **relative density** or **absolute density**. The relative density is the percentage of work volume the athlete performs compared with the total volume accomplished within a training session (24). In the following equation for determining relative density, the **absolute volume** is the total volume of work completed within a given session, and the **relative volume** is the duration of the training session:

$$\text{relative density (\%)} = \frac{\text{absolute volume}}{\text{relative volume}} \times 100$$

For example, if the athlete completes 90 minutes of work during a training session that takes 120 minutes to complete, the relative density of the training session would be calculated as follows:

$$\text{relative density (\%)} = \frac{90}{120} \times 100 = 75\%$$

Based on these calculations, the athlete worked 75% of the time during this training session.

Although relative density is useful, absolute density, or the ratio of effective work to absolute volume of work in the training session, is considered a more important metric to calculate (24). The following equation can be used to determine the absolute density of training:

$$\text{absolute density (\%)} = \frac{(\text{absolute volume} - \text{volume of rest intervals})}{\text{absolute volume}} \times 100$$

For example, if during a 110-minute training session the athlete accumulated an absolute volume of 90 minutes of which rest intervals accounted for 20 minutes, the absolute density would be calculated as follows:

$$\text{absolute density (\%)} = \frac{(90 - 20)}{90} \times 100 = 77.8\%$$

Based on these calculations, the absolute density is 77.8%. Conceptually, the absolute density can be considered a factor of intensity.

Intensity of Training

The intensity of training is the amount of energy expended or work performed per given unit of time, the amount of sustained isometric force produced, or the velocity of progression (119, 120, 209). Fundamentally, the more work an athlete completes per unit of time, the greater the intensity (38) and the greater the neuromuscular activation that occurs to meet the performance requirement (88). The overall pattern of neuromuscular activation will be affected by the external load (170), the speed of movement (49), the level of fatigue (170), and the exercise performed (49, 88). An additional factor that can affect the intensity of an exercise is the athlete's degree of psychological stress (186, 187). When an athlete is under psychological stress, they tend to reduce their intensity but perceive their exercise as being more intense (186). Because of these relationships, the coach should always monitor the athlete's current level of psychological stress as this provides the coach with information about the athletes' ability to tolerate prescribed training loads.

Fundamentally, intensity should be thought of as the rate of doing work, and it should be considered in the context of the primary energy system used during the activity (29, 38, 105, 173, 208). From a bioenergetic perspective, there are generally six intensity zones that are used to relate intensity, duration of effort, and bioenergetic contributions (table 4.1).

Intensity Zone 1 In this intensity zone, the bioenergetic supply comes almost exclusively from anaerobic metabolism and lasts for up to 6 seconds. This zone is classified as the maximal intensity level because it is marked by the highest power outputs (38, 105, 181). The intensity of work undertaken in this zone is significantly higher than the athlete's $\dot{V}O_2$max, thus requiring the energy supply to come primarily from anaerobic means. For activities performed in this intensity zone, most of the energy is supplied by the phosphagen (ATP-PC) system. As noted in chapter 2, this energy system is capable of supplying energy for only a short time because it relies almost exclusively on muscular stores of adenosine triphosphate (ATP) and phosphocreatine (PCr) (105, 181). Due to the rapid demand for energy when undertaking exercise in this intensity zone, an oxygen deficit results because oxidative (aerobic) metabolism cannot meet the energy demands (29, 105, 181). After the completion of the exercise bout, there is excess postexercise oxygen consumption (EPOC). The rise in oxygen consumption replenishes both ATP and PCr stores. Ultimately, ATP and PCr serve as the primary limiters to short-duration, high-intensity performance (181).

Intensity Zone 2 Due to the rapid demands for energy that occur during very high–intensity exercise that is performed for 6 to 30 seconds, the anaerobic energy systems are the primary energy supplier for intensity zone 2. To meet this demand for energy, the ATP-PC and the fast glycolytic energy systems are engaged (105, 181), but due to the rapid reductions of the muscular stores of ATP that occur during these activities, the muscular stores of PCr are used to maintain the supply of energy. When the duration of very high–intensity exercise surpasses 10 seconds, the amount of PCr available to ensure ATP demand is met decreases by 50%, and by 30 seconds very little PCr is available to maintain ATP supply (129). Thus, as the duration of exercise extends from 10 to 30 seconds, there is an increasing reliance on the fast glycolytic energy system, which uses blood glucose and muscular stores of glycogen (129, 181). As a result, there is typically increased lactate accumulation depending on the intensity and duration of the exercise bout (105, 129, 181). Due to the increased lactate accumulation, there is a significant increase in the EPOC when very high–intensity exercise is completed (see chapter 2) (26).

TABLE 4.1 Intensity Zones and Bioenergetics

Intensity zone	Event duration (s)	Intensity level	Primary energy system	Bioenergetic contribution	
				Anaerobic (%)	Aerobic (%)
1	<6	Maximal	ATP-PC	100-95	0-5
2	6-30	Very high	ATP-PC and fast glycolysis	95-80	5-20
3	31-120	High	Fast and slow glycolysis	80-50	20-50
4	121-180	Moderate	Slow glycolysis and oxidative	50-40	50-60
5	181-1,800	Low	Oxidative	40-5	60-95
6	>1,800	Very low	Oxidative	5-2	95-98

Note: ATP-PC = adenosine triphosphate-phosphocreatine.

Intensity Zone 3 Activities performed within intensity zone 3 typically last from 31 to 120 seconds (e.g., 400 m run, 100-200 m freestyle swim) and are classified as high-intensity activities. The breakdown of muscle glycogen stores (via the fast and slow glycolytic systems) is the primary energy supplier to meet the majority of the energy demands (105, 129). As the duration of the activity extends from 31 seconds toward 120 seconds, the contribution of the fast glycolytic energy system decreases and the contribution of the slow glycolytic energy system increases (105, 181). When the fast glycolytic system predominates, the rapid breakdown of muscle glycogen can result in the formation of lactic acid, which is quickly converted to lactate. Although not solely responsible for the fatigue responses to intense exercise, the accumulation of lactate and hydrogen can exert some negative effects on exercise performance (51). Ultimately, the primary limiter to performance in this intensity zone is the muscular stores of ATP, PCr, and muscle glycogen (see chapter 2).

Intensity Zone 4 Moderate-intensity activities performed in zone 4 rely on an equal energy contribution from both anaerobic and aerobic energetic systems (105, 181). The exercises within this zone are classified as moderate-intensity activities because energetic demand is met by contributions from both the slow glycolytic and aerobic energetic systems. Activities within this zone last between 121 and 180 seconds (2 to 3 min), and the primary limiter to performance in this zone is muscle and liver glycogen stores (181).

Intensity Zone 5 Activities within intensity zone 5 typically last between 181 and 1,800 seconds (3-30 min) and predominantly rely on the aerobic energy system to meet the activity's energy demands. A strong cardiovascular system is an important factor for determining success in these activities because the availability of oxygen plays a critical role in the function of the oxidative pathway's ability to meet the energy demands (105, 181). Although the primary limiter to performance is the supply of energy (e.g., muscle and liver glycogen and fat stores), performance in zone 5 is also affected by pacing strategies that can be used to modulate energy expenditure (169).

Intensity Zone 6 Activities in intensity zone 6 (e.g., marathon, triathlon, road racing in cycling, race walking) generally rely on oxidative metabolism and are considered low intensity based on work per unit of time (i.e., power output) (24, 39, 181). The power output at $\dot{V}O_2max$ is about 25% to 35% of the peak power output achieved during maximal anaerobic exercise (39). The main limiter to performance in zone 6 is the ability to meet the energy demands (181). Specifically, as the duration of the activity increases, there is a progressive reduction in the availability of muscle glycogen, which results in decreased ability to maintain exercise intensity (128). During endurance activities that last more than 60 minutes, it is generally recommended that the athlete ingest carbohydrates to maintain performance capacities (128, 181).

Although exercise intensity can be broadly quantified within these six zones, it is important to consider that the intensity of training is a function of the activities performed during a given period and varies depending on the sport (23). In resistance training, for example, the intensity of exercise is often quantified in kilograms, the percentage of maximum performance (37, 77) (table 4.2), or as a function of movement velocity ($m \cdot s^{-1}$).

In these scenarios, the athlete's training plan can be quantified as a percentage of the athlete's best performance (83). For example, if the athlete's 1RM in the back squat is 120 kg (265 lb), then 96 kg (212 lb) would be a moderate intensity. Training loads also can be determined from a percentage of a given RM load. For example, if the athlete's 10RM is 100 kg (220 lb) and the coach intends to prescribe a moderate-intensity day, then a load of 80 kg (176 lb) could be prescribed for sets of 10. Ultimately, there are several ways to prescribe resistance training loads, and this will be described in more detail in chapter 13.

When examining the loads presented in table 4.2, any resistance training exercise performed with loads greater than 100% of the athlete's maximal capacity are considered supramaximal efforts that can only be performed with eccentric or isometric muscle actions. Although typically used to describe resistance training intensities, table 4.2 can also be used to describe intensity based on the velocity of movements in activities such as sprinting. For example, if a sprinter can run 100 m in 9.8 seconds, which results in a movement speed of 10.2 $m \cdot s^{-1}$, the speed of movement could then be quantified in relation to various levels of intensity. If this athlete can move at a higher speed across a shorter distance (e.g., 60 m in 5.4 seconds = 11.1 $m \cdot s^{-1}$), the intensity would be supramaximal because the speed is greater than 100% of the athlete's maximal velocity in the 100 m.

Another example of how velocity and intensity can be related is seen in the relationship between the velocity achieved at $\dot{V}O_2max$ and the athlete's

TABLE 4.2 Intensities for Speed and Strength Exercises

Intensity zone	Maximum performance (%)	Intensity
10	>100	Supramaximal
9	100	Maximal
8	95-99	Very heavy
7	90-94	Heavy
6	85-89	Moderately heavy
5	80-84	Moderate
4	75-79	Moderately light
3	70-74	Light
2	65-69	Very light
1	<65	Extremely light

maximal sprinting speed (31). The difference between these velocities is referred to as the **anaerobic speed reserve**. Movement speeds undertaken within this zone are considered higher-intensity activities, which must be undertaken for shorter distances. The use of these metrics is common in track and field (i.e., running), where athletes train at faster speeds for shorter distances or slower speeds for longer distances than what they perform in competition to target different aspects of their physiological and performance development. For example, a 200 m runner may perform short sprints at much faster speeds or longer sprints at slower speeds. Based on this construct, the coach can use the combination of velocity and distance to provide training stimuli of varying intensities.

In team sports, GPS technology can be used to establish acceleration (≥ 2.78 m · s^{-1}), high-speed running (>4.17 m · s^{-1}), and sprinting (>7.00 m · s^{-1}) (203) thresholds. The intensity of training or competition can be quantified based on the time spent within these predetermined thresholds (104, 189). Additionally, during contact sports such as rugby, player load (i.e., combined vectors of anterior–posterior, mediolateral, and longitudinal accelerometer load), 2D player load (i.e., acceleration in the mediolateral and anterior–posterior planes), and player load slow (i.e., all accelerations from triaxial accelerometers that occur at speeds less than 2.0 m · s^{-1}) can be quantified using GPS to indicate the number of collisions and repeated high-intensity efforts (64). Although GPS-based methods for monitoring training load are becoming increasingly popular, there is a lack of uniformity in how these metrics are classified, and there is limited information on the most appropriate zones for women's sports (156).

Another common method for quantifying intensity in team sports is the use of heart rate monitoring (16, 63, 104, 164, 175). The athlete's internal load can be classified as low, medium, or high intensity depending on the time spent within predetermined heart rate zones that are related to the athlete's maximal heart rate (55, 71). For example, Stanula et al. (174) established three position-specific heart rate zones that can be used to quantify intensity during ice hockey games. For forwards, heart rate–based intensity zones were defined as low (75.2%-79.5%), moderate (80%-92.4%), and high (92.9%-100%) intensity based on percentage of maximal heart rate. Heart rate–based intensity zones for defensemen were defined as low (69.4%-75.8%), moderate (76.4%-89%), and high (89.5%-100%) intensity. Based on these data, it is evident that when using heart rate zones to quantify intensity during team sports, these zones may need to be position specific and must be individually determined.

Due to the well-documented linear relationship between heart rate and workload, graded exercise tests are typically used to establish an athlete's maximal heart rate (82), anaerobic or lactate threshold, and $\dot{V}O_2$max. This information allows for the optimal implementation of heart rate–based training (24). Although graded exercise tests are the gold standard for establishing maximal heart rate, an age-predicted maximal heart rate also can be established (159) using the following equation:

maximal heart rate (beats · min^{-1}) = 220 – age in years

Although this equation can predict maximal heart rate within ±12 beats per minute, a newer equation has been proposed (190):

$$\text{maximal heart rate (beats} \cdot \text{min}^{-1}) = 208 - (0.7 \times \text{age in years})$$

The newer equation appears to better represent the actual maximal heart rate and accounts for the noted overestimation of maximal heart rate that occurs with individuals under the age of 40 with the classic equation (190). Based on maximal heart rate, specific training zones for sports like cycling can be established to align training goals, heart rate zones, and intended performance outcomes (table 4.3) (69).

Although the athlete's maximal heart rate is a useful metric, the athlete's individual anaerobic threshold (IAS) can be used to determine basic training ranges or establish evolution training zones. For example, for an athlete with a heart rate of 180 beats per minute at the IAS, their basic training intensities would range between 130 to 150 beats per minute (low end = heart rate (IAS) − 50 beats per minute; high end = heart rate (IAS) − 30 beats per minute). This heart rate range is used to develop aerobic adaptations generally used in training sessions that last 2 to 7 hours (50). After completing basic training, training focus shifts to evolution training, which is designed to enhance lactate tolerance. Typically, this type of training is used as the athlete shifts toward a competition focus. This type of training employs intervals with and without full recovery and is typically performed for 3 to 15 minutes. The intensities used in the evolution training zone are established by subtracting 5 beats per minute from the athlete's heart rate at IAS and adding 5 beats per minute to the heart rate at IAS, which, when based on the same athlete with a heart rate of 180 beats per minute at the IAS, this range is between 175 to 185 beats per minute (50).

Heart rate is an effective tool for guiding training intensities in some instances, but in endurance sports such as cycling, technological advances have allowed for the quantification of power, which can be used to better monitor and guide training (8, 118, 151). The power-based measurement devices (i.e., SRM, PowerTap, Ergomo, Quarq, power meters) used in cycling require a system that quantifies power-based training zones (table 4.4) (8).

To establish power-based training zones, the athlete must first determine their **functional threshold power**, which is established by taking 95% of the average wattage achieved during a 20-minute, all-out time trial on a flat surface (8). For example, if the cyclist achieved an average power output of 300 W during the 20-minute time trial, the functional threshold power would be 285 W. Once the threshold power is identified, the seven power-based training zones (table 4.4) can be used to construct a periodized training plan.

Regardless of how it is quantified, intensity is one of the fundamental factors that affects performance outcomes and it is a key factor to manipulate in all periodized training plans. Based on observations of the training process (17, 60, 182, 201), the average training intensity is inversely related to how long the improvement in performance can be maintained, the magnitude of the performance gain, and the rate of detraining (figure 4.6) (201). Zatsiorsky and colleagues (213) use the analogy "soon ripe, soon rotten" to describe this relationship between the intensity of training and the duration and magnitude of performance gain.

TABLE 4.3 Aerobic Training Zones Established From Performance Testing of High-Performance Cyclists

Zone number	Descriptor	Heart rate (% maximum)	Duration of effort (min)	Blood lactate (mmol · L⁻¹)	Power output (% maximum)*	Perceived exertion
0	Recovery	<65			40-50	Recovery
1	Aerobic	65-75	>240	<1.5	50-65	Easy
2	Extensive endurance	75-80	90-240	1.5-3.5	65-72.5	Comfortable
3	Intensive endurance	80-85	15-90	3.3-3.6	72.5-80	Comfortable to uncomfortable
4	Threshold	85-92	15-60	3.5-6.0	80-90	Uncomfortable
5	$\dot{V}O_2$max	92-100	3-7	>6.0	90-100	Stressful

*Percentage of 4-minute max or maximal aerobic power.

Adapted by permission from L.A. Garvican, T.R. Ebert, M.J. Quod, et al., "High-Performance Cyclists," in *Physiology Tests for Elite Athletes*, edited by R.K. Tanner and C.J. Gore (Champaign, IL: Human Kinetics Publishers, 2013).

TABLE 4.4 Power-Based Training Zones for Cycling

Training zone		Percentage			Example calculations[b]	
Zone number	Name or purpose	Power threshold[a]	Heart rate threshold[a]	Perceived exertion	Average power (W)	Average heart rate (beats · min^{-1})
1	Active recovery	≤55	≤68	<2	≤157	≤122
2	Endurance	56-75	69-83	3	160-214	124-149
3	Tempo	76-90	84-94	4	217-257	151-169
4	Lactate threshold	91-105	95-105	5	259-299	171-189
5	V̇O$_2$max	106-120	≥106	6	302-342	≥191
6	Anaerobic capacity	121-150		>7	345-428	
7	Neuromuscular power			Max		

[a]Based on the functional threshold power achieved during a 20-minute time trial.
[b]Based on a functional threshold power of 285 W and a threshold heart rate of 180 beats · min^{-1}.
Adapted from H. Allen and A. Coggan, *Training and Racing with a Power Meter*, 2nd ed., (Boulder, CO: VeloPress, 2010), 49.

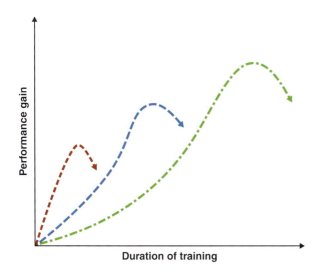

FIGURE 4.6 Theoretical rates of performance gain.
Adapted by permission from M.H. Stone, M.E. Stone, and W.A. Sands, "The Concept of Periodization," in *Principles and Practice of Resistance Training* (Champaign, IL: Human Kinetics, 2007), 261.

Interaction of Training Volume and Intensity

A fundamental aspect of the training process is the trade-off that exists between training volume and intensity (23). A central construct of periodized training is the manipulation of these variables to target specific physiological and performance outcomes (182, 201). Generally, there is an inverse relationship between training volume and intensity. For example, when training volume is high, intensity is generally low, while higher intensities are typically associated with lower volumes (24). Varying the intensity and volume of training stimulates different physiological adaptations and performance outcomes. Thus, a comprehensive understanding of the physiological adaptive responses to the volume and intensity of training is central to constructing an effective periodized training plan.

Although the intensity and volume of training are often considered as isolated constructs, training is a balancing act between the quality and quantity of the applied training process, which is probably best understood in the context of the workload accomplished (182), which is a metric that is affected by both the volume and intensity of training. For example, when training intensity is increased and is performed for longer durations, the overall workload increases, which significantly increases the physiological stress on the athlete. This greater physiological stress creates a greater energy demand (i.e., reductions in PCr and muscle glycogen) (101, 102) and causes increased hormonal disturbances (121) and greater neuromuscular fatigue (122).

In a training year, the volume and intensity of training will vary according to the periods and phases of the periodized training plan and the targeted outcomes (figures 4.7 and 4.8). Classically, an athlete in the early stages of preparation focuses more on general preparation, which is used to establish a physiological base that prepares the athlete for higher-intensity training (79, 182). To accomplish this goal, the athlete undertakes higher workloads via higher-volume, lower-intensity training. This type of training enhances endurance and work capacity and establishes the physiological foundation that supports more sport-specific training in the preparation and competitive periods of the annual training plan (24, 182). Due to the high levels of fatigue associated with higher volumes of training, the athlete's overall preparedness for competition during this phase is reduced (155, 171, 182, 213). Bondarchuk (25) referred to this phe-

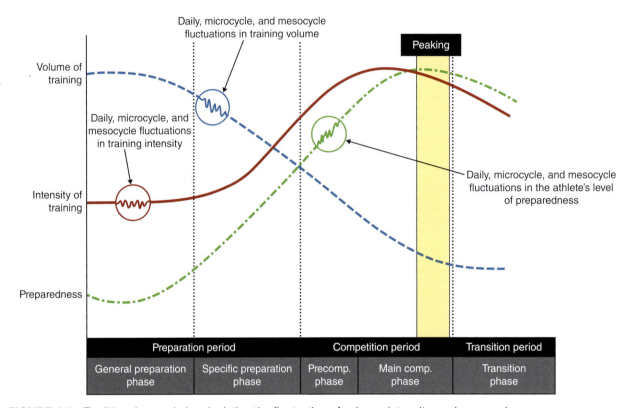

FIGURE 4.7 Traditional annual plan depicting the fluctuation of volume, intensity, and preparedness.

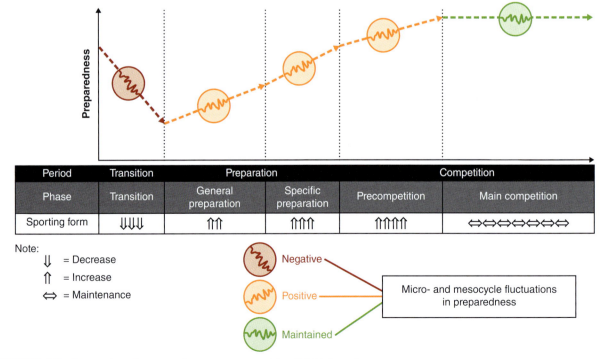

FIGURE 4.8 Dynamics of preparedness across an annual training plan.

nomenon as a *reduction in sporting form*, which translates to a reduction in preparedness and is associated with periods of training with higher volumes of nonspecific training. Although high volumes of training are important for establishing fitness during the general preparation phase, initial elevation in **sporting form** and preparedness may reverse through continued exposure to high volumes of these two training factors and ultimately compromise the athlete's development (25).

As the athlete transitions into the specific preparatory period, a decrease in the volume of work coincides with an increase in training intensity coupled with more focused, sport-specific training. This phase of training further increases sporting form and preparedness, but the volume of work in this phase can create accumulated fatigue that does not allow for the optimization of these two factors (25). Therefore, to continue to elevate these factors, volume is typically further reduced, intensity is elevated, and more sport-specific (i.e., technical) training is undertaken. Continued elevation in sporting form and preparedness will occur during the precompetitive phase because of modifications to the volume and intensity of training. During the main competitive phase, fluctuations in the volume and intensity of training are employed to ensure the maintenance of sporting form and overall preparedness to maximize the potential for competitive success.

Fluctuations in both sporting form and preparedness occur at the micro- and mesocycle levels because of programming decisions that are used to alter training volume and intensity. Thus, when constructing a periodized training plan that considers programming structures implemented at various times of the year, the coach must consider the relationships between volume and intensity and how these modifiable training factors affect the athlete's preparedness (23).

Variation of Training Load

A central theme related to the periodization of training load is the removal of training monotony. Stone and colleagues (177) suggest that monotonous training occurs from programming that uses the same type of exercise and loading within a prescribed training period. The application of a monotonous training load results in plateauing or performance reduction in response to a lack of novel training stimuli (23). O'Toole (145) suggests that the degree of monotony is related to the occurrence of poor performance, which could be considered a form of overtraining (see chapter 9) (177). In addition to overtraining, athletes who undertake long periods of monotonous training at high intensities are at a greater risk of experiencing injuries (149) or illness (131).

Varying the training loads not only reduces the risk of injury, illness, or overtraining, it also stimulates physiological adaptations (36) and performance gains (106). When athletes are exposed to unfamiliar training stimuli, the exercise-specific cell-signaling responses are magnified when compared to responses to familiar training interventions (36). Due to the importance of cell-signaling responses in the adaptive process, the ability to create physiological disturbances over time is particularly important (35). For example, Coffey and Hawley (35) suggest that as athletes become more trained, variations in how training stimuli are applied are required to further stimulate adaptive responses that underpin performance. In addition to these adaptive responses, the introduction of novel training stimuli creates a rapid improvement in skill acquisition and performance. If the training stimuli are not altered, the rate of adaptation will begin to slow over time (28, 106). Mujika et al. (140) suggest that a state of tedium occurs when training is monotonous and the ability to enhance skill development is reduced.

Overall, the appropriate variation of training load is one of the most important factors to consider when constructing periodized training plans (23, 155). The degree of training variation is affected by numerous factors, including the athlete's training age and level of development, the structure of the training (i.e., session, microcycle, and mesocycle) implemented, and the overall structure of the annual training plan. Generally, an increasing need for training load variation occurs as the athlete progresses from novice to intermediate to advanced status (35, 155). The lowest degree of training load variation is applied to the novice athlete and the application of sophisticated loading strategies too early in the athlete's development can have negative consequences on their overall development. Coaches working with these athletes must consider that relatively simple loading strategies may be more effective than more sophisticated training methods, which should be reserved for more advanced athletes (155). Conceptually, the coach should consider that all athletes exist on a developmental continuum ranging from novice to advanced and that every athlete should strive to progress toward an advanced status (155), but not every athlete will achieve an advanced status

(47). Understanding where the athlete is on this developmental continuum is an important consideration when planning training loads as attempting to apply advanced training loading strategies too early in the athlete's overall development can have a negative impact on their overall development.

Regardless of the athlete's level, variations in training load can be introduced within or between microcycles. For example, variations to the training load within a microcycle can be achieved by alternating the training intensity across the microcycle (i.e., day-to-day variation) to have periods that stimulate adaptations and lower training loads to stimulate recovery. This type of load application has been shown to stimulate the greatest physiological adaptations (182) and has been successfully employed with both endurance (145) and strength and power athletes (182). This type of training load variation can be implemented on a session-by-session basis with more advanced athletes who may train multiple times per day. In this scenario, the morning session may contain a high training load, whereas the afternoon session is performed at a lower intensity. To create contrast between microcycles, workload can be increased by adding or decreased by reducing the number of training sessions between weeks of training or manipulating the volume or intensity of each training session (155).

Training load must be individualized, and appropriate loading progressions must be applied. Effective implementation of training load variation relies on understanding how the athlete is developing and how they are responding to the imposed training load. Implementing athlete monitoring programs (see chapter 11) allows the coach to more effectively individualize the training load.

Individualization of Training Load

When designing periodized training plans, one of the worst strategies a coach can employ is simply mimicking the programs of elite athletes (182) or programs that proliferate on social media or the Internet. This practice does not take into consideration the athlete's individual capacities and training history or their chronological, biological, or training ages, which can all affect how an athlete responds to a prescribed training load (23). Coaches should also consider the athlete's current health status and their level of stress outside of the training environment, because stressors are additive and can influence how an athlete responds (see chapter 1).

Individualizing the training process is a key component of the application of a periodized training plan (46, 100) because the ability to prescribe training loads according to the athlete's individual needs increases the overall effectiveness of the training process (100). As noted in chapter 1, the coach's ability to tailor training interventions, including training loads, is essential to address the athlete's individual needs. Central to the ability to individualize the training process is testing the athlete's capacities through an ongoing monitoring process, which provides data that can be used to guide the coach's decisions about the effective application of training load (81).

The need for a precise individualized training program is not as critical for novice athletes as it is for advanced athletes (184). For novice athletes, the key is the careful management of training loads, because they have a lower training age and training tolerance. This does not mean the coach should not consider individualization at this level, but less individualization may be warranted (184). As the athlete progresses toward an advanced training status, there is an increasing demand for more individualization of the training process and the application of precise variations in training load. This is where performance testing and monitoring become increasingly important parts of constructing training interventions. In elite sports, sport scientists provide coaches with critical information from which training decisions can be made (figure 4.9) (81).

Central to this process is the collection of data that reveals the athlete's current health status, performance deficits, and performance capacity. These data are then contextualized and used by the coach, with assistance from the sport scientist, to project a performance progression based on the athlete's historic training data. From here, the coach constructs a personalized training plan that addresses the athlete's needs. As the athlete moves through the training process, the monitoring program (see chapter 11) provides detailed information the coach can then use to further refine the training process (81). Ultimately, training load tolerance is an individualized construct affected by the athlete's genetics and lifestyle decisions (e.g., social life, work life, nutrition). The integration of a structured monitoring process can help the coach understand how the athlete is responding to the training load and better prescribe training to maximize physiological adaptation and performance gain.

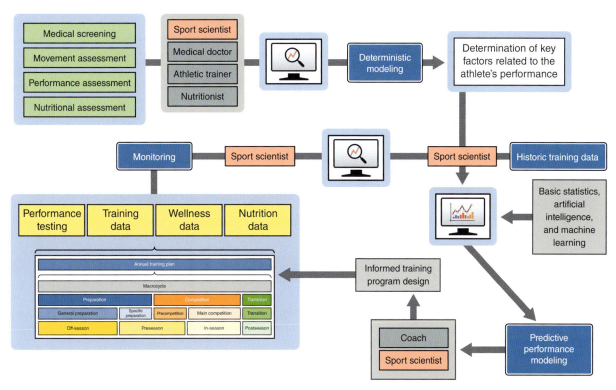

FIGURE 4.9 Theoretical model of the sport scientist's role in the individualization of the periodization process.

Reprinted by permission from G.G. Haff, "Periodization and Programming of Individual Sports," in *NSCA'S Essentials of Sport Science*, edited for the National Strength and Conditioning Association by D. French and L. Torres Ronda (Champaign, IL: Human Kinetics, 2022).

Training Load Progressions

Training loads are broadly classified into three basic categories (212): stimulating, retaining, and detraining. A **stimulating load** provides overload and results in positive adaptations that elevate preparedness. A **retaining load** maintains the athlete's current level of preparedness but does not provide enough overload to stimulate positive adaptations. If the training load is reduced too much, the athlete will be exposed to what is often referred to as a **detraining load** and they will experience a reduction in overall preparedness and performance capacity. Although all of these loads are used in periodized training plans, how an athlete responds to them is highly individualized and is related to their level of development. For example, stimulating loads that are effective with novice athletes would be largely ineffective when applied to advanced athletes, because they would be far below those required to stimulate physiological and performance adaptations (212). As the athlete becomes more trained, the loads that once were stimulating loads will become maintaining or detraining loads, supporting the need for progressive overload to ensure continued development of physiological and performance outcomes. Continued systematic implementation of progressive overload over time is critically important as athletes become more trained. Greater training loads must be employed to stimulate positive physiological adaptations and advance performance development.

As the athlete becomes more trained and adapts to the training load, an increase in training load will continue to stimulate increased positive physiological and performance adaptations. This is typically accomplished via the use of progressive loading strategies, which allow the athlete to be exposed to increasing training loads that align with their current capacities. The athlete's response to the applied training load is extremely complex and depends on numerous factors (figure 4.10).

Conceptually, the training load (figure 4.10, subsystem A) is designed to address the needs of the athlete, and the loading properties employed affect the athlete's responsiveness to the training process. The athlete's ability to tolerate the applied training load is directly related to the athlete's current fitness levels (figure 4.10, subsystem B), which are regulated by the effects of the training load and by factors external to training (such as psychological stress) to stimulate a specific training response. The

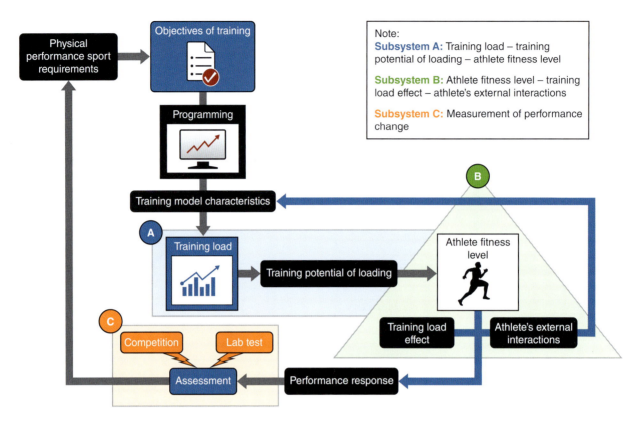

FIGURE 4.10 Training load and the athlete.

resultant performance response can be monitored (figure 4.10, subsystem C) via laboratory testing or, more importantly, by direct assessment of competitive outcomes. Data garnered from this process are used to inform subsequent training objects and provides the coach with a dynamic, systematic approach for informing programming decisions. Ultimately, the prescription of training loads is a fluid construct that is modifiable based on the athlete's response to the training load; therefore, the coach must pay careful attention to how the periodized training program is constructed and informed by the integrated monitoring activities and continually fine-tune the athlete's training process (46).

When training loads are applied appropriately, the athlete experiences positive adaptations that result in performance improvements. Central to the ability of training loads to stimulate positive adaptations is the ability to provide overload, which develops physiological adaptations and enhances performance capacities. If training overload is applied in a systematic manner, the athlete's performance capacity will increase. If, however, there is a sudden increase in training load, more time may be required before physiological adaptations and performance gains are realized (115, 212). In these situations, the coach must be aware that there may be an increased risk of maladaptive responses or injury (21). Overall, it is important to remember that the time required for recovery after exposure to a training load is directly proportional to the magnitude of the training load and that systematic and monitoring-informed loading progressions allow the coach to better manage recovery, adaptation, and direct performance gains.

Central to the appropriate application of training loads is a well-crafted and informed periodized training program that allows for the systematic manipulation of training load across the levels of the training process. Although the appropriate sequencing of a training program is directly related to improvements in performance capacity, there are infinite ways to apply training loads. The training capacities of the athletes are central to the effective implementation of the training process. Although there are numerous methods for prescribing training workloads (especially as they relate to specific sports), there are several loading schemes that are commonly used within periodized training plans.

Standard Loading

Standard loading involves using similar training loads and methodologies of applying those loads across the preparatory period of training, resulting in improvements in the early portion of the period (23). As the athlete shifts into the competitive period, training load is reduced but training targets remain constant, resulting in a performance plateau. This plateau occurs in response to an overall reduction in training variation, which is necessary to induce physiological and performance adaptations. If this form of loading is undertaken for too long during the competitive period, it is very likely that there will be an involution of performance capacity that occurs in the later stages of the competitive period (107).

With this model, it is critical that overall training load is increased from year to year. The effective time period for this loading model only occurs at the initiation of each training year when a novel training stimulus is delivered to the athlete (23). Ultimately, this model of loading is suboptimal and is not as effective at stimulating long-term training adaptations as step loading, summated microcycles, wave loading, or conjugated sequencing (23, 155, 185).

Linear Loading

Although there are many references in the literature to the linear application of training loads within a periodized training plan, the application of linear loading schemes violates one of the major tenants of periodization: the removal of training linearity (78, 155, 179, 185). In his seminal text, Matveyev (127) suggests that there is a lack of linearity within periodized training models, stating that "wave oscillations characterize load dynamics both in relatively small and more prolonged phases (stages, periods) of the training process" (page 81). Additionally, Berger, Harre, and Ritter (17) clearly state that "individual performance cannot be developed in a linear manner" (page 123), and Nádori (142) says "the changes between one training period and the subsequent one are not linear but saltatoric in nature" (page 25).

Even though there is strong evidence (17) that linear loading does not optimize sporting performance, this paradigm remains popular in some circles (32, 98). Proponents of linear loading models suggest that they will continue to stimulate performance gains as long as the athlete trains at their maximal capacity and is exposed to progressively increasing training loads (10, 32, 103, 214). In fact, Buckner et al. (32) suggested that as long as a linear progressive overload is applied, performance gains will continue and other periodized loading models are not necessary. If this is true, one would expect to see continuous physiological

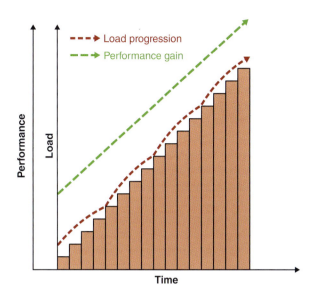

FIGURE 4.11 Theoretical increases in performance in response to linear application of progressive overload.

adaptation and improved performance as training load is increased over time (figure 4.11).

Although all loading models require the longitudinal application of progressive overload, the linear application of loading is only beneficial during short periods (40, 56, 57, 59, 214). In fact, Zourdos et al. (214) suggest that this model of loading may be best suited for a single block (mesocycle) of training and should not be employed year-round. If extended for long periods and undertaken without time for recovery and unloading, overtraining is very likely to occur as a result of a high-intensity, monotonous training stimulus (see chapter 9) (145, 177). Ultimately, the application of linear loading progressions is a suboptimal loading strategy except when it is employed during very short periods, due to the inability of the athlete to recover from the ever-increasing training stimuli.

Flat Loading

Flat loading models employ the continuous application of the same training load across a given period (21, 162). Based on mathematical modeling, the application of a flat loading paradigm for 30 days (i.e., one mesocycle) results in a significantly lower rate of performance gain when compared to the application of a step loading model. These findings are not unexpected, as it is well-documented that the constant application of one training load results in a diminished performance enhancement because the training load is unable to stimulate the physiological adaptations that underpin performance gains (17).

Due to the limitations of flat loading models, Bompa and Buzzichelli (21) suggest that their application should be limited to two microcycles (figure 4.12a) that introduce a large workload, which results in a high physiological demand. They also suggest that only one recovery or unloading microcycle is required to dissipate the accumulated fatigue from the first two microcycles (21). However, research from Halson et al. (97) reveals that after two microcycles of intensified training, it takes two microcycles with reduced loading to stimulate performance restoration. It is likely that the magnitude of the workload employed during the two flat loaded microcycles will dictate the number of microcycles needed to restore performance capacity.

Flat loading models can also be used to construct recovery or unloading microcycles (figure 4.12b). For example, after a particularly stressful series of microcycles, multiple regeneration or unloading microcycles with the same workload may be employed, which could be considered a flat loading model (62, 147).

Prior to the integration of flat loading models, the athlete generally completes a preparation phase in which step loading models are used to progressively increase work capacity (21, 142). For example, Nádori (142) employed flat loaded recovery microcycles after intensive microcycles that were step loaded or flat loaded in the precompetition and main competition phases of the annual training plan of a modern pentathlete. Another recommendation for the application of flat loading models is to place them within the specific preparation phase and the competitive period of the annual training plan (21). Regardless of how flat loading models are applied, it is important to consider the magnitude of the loading employed and how this relates to the amount of recovery required to restore or enhance preparedness and performance.

Step Loading

One of the classic methods for implementing progressive overload within a periodized training plan is to use step loading models (62, 155, 171). The basic format used with these models is to structure a series of increasing workload microcycles followed by an unloading microcycle that is designed to stimulate physical and psychological regeneration as well as greater physiological adaptation that translates into performance gains (23). There are numerous step loading models (figure 4.13) that can be constructed, but the most common are based on 3- to 6-week blocks of training (17, 147, 162, 213), with the most common duration being 4 weeks (23, 84, 155, 162, 213).

A common practice is to use a 3:1 loading paradigm (figure 4.13b) in which training load is increased in the first three microcycles and then reduced in the fourth microcycle to induce recovery (62). The training load increases over the first three microcycles are accomplished by altering the training volume, intensity, density, or some combination of these factors (84). The third microcycle of this series is the most intense; it is thought to provide a powerful stimulus for adaptation and creates the highest levels of fatigue (62, 84). Due to the accumulated fatigue that occurs across the loading microcycles, the unloading microcycles are strategically placed following the most intense microcycle. Unloading microcycles allow for reductions in fatigue, elevations in preparedness (86, 87), and enhanced physiological adaptations, which are all necessary for the next block of training (180). Some coaches recommend testing during the last days of this microcycle (and prior to initiating the next block of training) because fatigue is reduced and performance tends to be elevated (62).

The greater the number of progressively loaded steps there are within the training block, the longer the period of unloading needs to be to manage the accumulated fatigue (23, 97). For example, if two or three loading steps are contained within a block

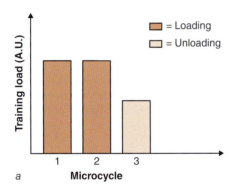

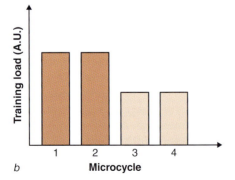

FIGURE 4.12 Example flat loading models: *(a)* classic flat loading model; *(b)* flat loading–flat unloading model.

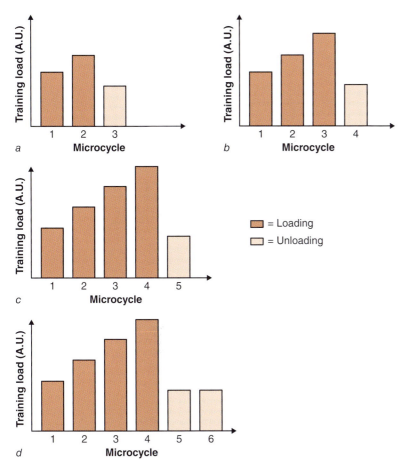

FIGURE 4.13 Four step loading structures: *(a)* 2:1 (loading:unloading); *(b)* 3:1 (loading:unloading); *(c)* 4:1 (loading:unloading); *(d)* 4:2 (loading:unloading).

of training, a 1-week unloading microcycle may suffice (figure 4.13*a*). However, four progressively increasing workload microcycles may require two unloading microcycles to manage fatigue, as presented in Nádori's (142) 4:2 step loading paradigm (figure 4.13*d*). In addition to the length, one must also consider the magnitude of the training loads used prior to the implementation of the unloading microcycles. For example, if the magnitude of the loading across three microcycles is very high, an unloading period of two microcycles may be warranted to better manage fatigue and avoid maladaptive training responses.

The strength of the step loading model is that it allows for progressive overload to be applied, which helps develop a foundation for successive training blocks. This type of loading is also excellent for novice athletes or those who are not accustomed to high-intensity training (23, 155). To enhance the effectiveness of step loading models, several authors have suggested that greater intermicrocycle variation needs to be implemented (23, 62, 155). For example, Fry, Morton, and Keast (62) suggest that higher volumes and intensities of training be integrated into the progressive loading portion of the training block to magnify adaptive responses. It has also been suggested that periodic alterations in loading within each microcycle improves adaptive responses and translate to greater performance gains (23, 62, 155, 188). Support for including greater variations within (e.g., light and heavy days of training) and between microcycles can be found in human (54, 99, 195, 196) and animal (30) studies. Based on these data, incorporating low to high variations in training loads at the microcycle and mesocycle levels is an essential aspect of effectively employing step loading models.

One strategy that can be used to enhance the effectiveness of step loading is structuring a **summated microcycle** (23, 155, 182). This loading strategy provides inter- and intramesocycle variation that allows for an increased potential of training effects that converge at the appropriate time, thereby minimizing the potential for involution (i.e., detraining) effects and stimulating long-term training adaptations (61, 62, 155, 162). In this paradigm, each block of training progresses from an extensive to an intensive workload and is followed by a brief period of restitution (155). When looking at this from a strength-training perspective, each microcycle would be allocated to a specific targeted outcome, such as strength–endurance, maximal strength, or speed–strength. The first three microcycles of the 3:1 model have increases in training volumes or intensities followed by an unloading microcycle, then the basic pattern is repeated (155). A strength of this model is that it allows for large contrasts between the training in each microcycle and the ability to reintroduce training factors in a cyclic manner that prevents large reductions in the aftereffects (or residual training effects) associated with the training factors targeted in each microcycle (155). Due to the increased training variables in the summated microcycle model, it is ideally suited for intermediate and advanced athletes (23, 155, 182).

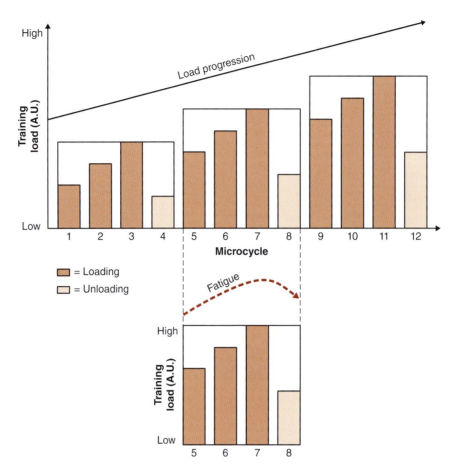

FIGURE 4.14 Connected step loaded training blocks. As fatigue increases across the four microcycles, the unloading cycle is used to stimulate recovery. At the end of the unloading microcycle, testing can be performed.

When building a periodized training plan, a series of step loaded training blocks can be connected to create a longitudinal progression of loading across several mesocycles, while allowing for wavelike fluctuations in training load at the microcycle level as well as across several mesocycles (figure 4.14) (62, 178, 213).

Concentrated Loading

Concentrated loading is the application of short bouts of significantly increased workload (79, 182, 205); this is also called *workload accumulation* (116, 155) or *planned overreaching* (52, 126, 192). This advanced loading strategy is applied as a steep increase in workload marked by intensified training that has the potential to result in enhanced physiological adaptations that can underpin significant performance gains after a period of recovery (62, 205). The duration of recovery required in response to this loading structure is largely dictated by the magnitude and duration of the concentrated loading phase (figure 4.15) (79, 84, 178).

When an appropriate recovery period is implemented, the accumulated fatigue will dissipate resulting in an elevation in preparedness that translates into a supercompensation of performance capacity (79, 93, 182, 205). If the workload employed in the concentrated loading period is relatively small, the time frame needed to induce supercompensation will be relatively short (figure 4.15a), but the magnitude of the performance gain will be smaller. If the magnitude of the concentrated load is high, greater fatigue is created and the time frame needed to induce supercompensation will be longer (figure 4.15b), but the gain in performance will be substantially greater (84).

In the literature, durations ranging from one to four microcycles of concentrated loading have been integrated into annual training plans (116, 155, 182, 205). A common approach for employing this model is to construct a concentrated loading block of training (e.g., 4 microcycles) followed by a block of training (e.g., 4 microcycles) that returns to normal levels (i.e., reduced workload compared to the concentrated loading block) (figure 4.16a)

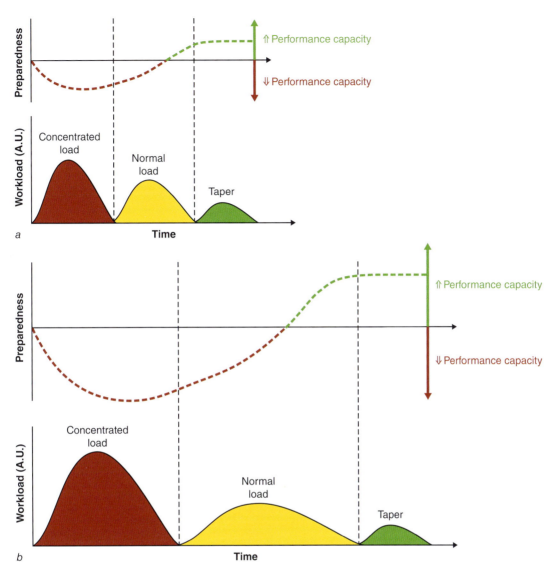

FIGURE 4.15 Example concentrated loading restitution patterns: *(a)* example short-duration concentrated loading period; *(b)* example long-duration concentrated loading period.

(84). After completing these two blocks of training, a two-microcycle recovery block is employed to facilitate recovery and elevate preparedness and performance capacity. This basic structure is commonly used in block periodization training models (see chapter 5) (84).

Another strategy is to use shorter concentrated loading periods, specifically a 1-week microcycle, followed by a return to normal training loads for two microcycles (figure 4.16b). Next, training loads are further reduced for 1 week to create a recovery microcycle (84, 155). If training is sequenced in this manner, a supercompensation effect occurs at the end of the 4-week block in response to a reduction in fatigue and the convergence of the delayed (84, 155) or residual training effects (114)

that elevate overall preparedness and performance capacity.

Support for using concentrated loading strategies is found in studies that have explored the endocrine responses to prolonged (≥3 week) increases in training load (89, 93, 94, 96, 133, 155). When examining these intensified training periods, testosterone levels, cortisol levels, and the **testosterone:cortisol (T:C) ratio** are used as indices of the anabolic–catabolic balance as well as physiological training stress (155). Haff et al. (85) demonstrated that there was an inverse relationship between the training load (i.e., volume load) and the T:C ratio of elite female weightlifters. When training load was increased, there was a concomitant reduction in the T:C ratio, which was reversed after a period

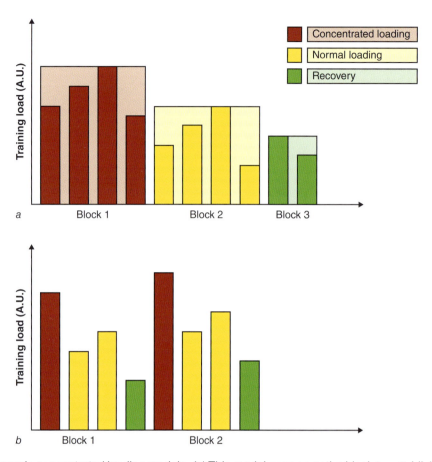

FIGURE 4.16 Example concentrated loading models. *(a)* This model uses an entire block to establish the concentrated load, followed by a normal training block and then a recovery block. *(b)* This model uses an individual concentrated loading microcycle, followed by two microcycles of normal loading and then one recovery microcycle.

of reduced training stress. Performance capacity mirrored the T:C ratio response to fluctuations in training load, which lends support for the use of the T:C ratio as an indicator of preparedness.

Although the T:C ratio is related to preparedness (130, 155, 182), it is not a measure of overtraining (chapter 9). A high T:C ratio is indicative of an anabolic status and a high level of preparedness, whereas a reduction in the T:C ratio indicates an elevated catabolic state and a low level of preparedness (130, 202). When athletes undertake periods of concentrated loading, there is a reduction of testosterone and an elevation in cortisol, which results in a reduction in the T:C ratio (155, 202) and in overall preparedness. A T:C ratio reduction of greater than 30% is considered the critical cutoff where significant reductions in preparedness exist (5, 85, 130).

Testosterone and the T:C ratio become suppressed (89, 94, 96, 133, 155, 182) after prolonged periods (≥3 weeks) of increased training load, but after a return to normal training, they become elevated above the levels achieved before the concentrated loading period (i.e., supercompensation) (85). Additionally, after recovery from short periods (e.g., 1 microcycle) of overreaching, there is a significant elevation in the T:C ratio, which corresponds to an increased level of preparedness (58, 176). Of additional interest is that athletes who have prior exposure to short periods of overreaching appear to be able to better tolerate these loading periods and tend to have greater performance gains when using these loading strategies (58, 59).

Sequencing of Training Load

When constructing periodized training plans, one of the most important factors to consider is how the training loads employed are sequenced. Appropriate sequencing allows for load progression across various blocks of training and facilitates phase potentiation as the athlete moves through the training plan. **Phase potentiation** occurs when the delayed training effects from a previous training block enhance the outcomes stimulated by the current training block (99, 155). Harris et al. (99) present a good example of the benefits of phase potentiation when applied to the strength-training practice of NCAA Division I American football players. Based on their data, optimal strength and power gains occur after the completion of a period of maximal strength development. These findings align with the work of Zamparo et al. (210), Minetti (136), and Haff (79), who all suggest that when targeting the maximization of power development, training loads should be sequenced across several periods of training in the following order:

hypertrophy → maximal strength → power optimization

Concentrated loading would be used with the hypertrophy block of training. This is followed by a reduction in overall training load as the athlete shifts toward maximal strength development. A further reduction in training load is then employed when targeting the optimization of power development (figure 4.17).

Similarly, Verkhoshansky and Siff (205) suggest that a sequential approach can be used to develop speed–strength capacity:

general physical preparation → strength → technique and speed

In this example, after the athlete uses general methods to establish a fitness base with aerobic training means, the athlete shifts their focus toward strength loading while maintaining some emphasis on general physical preparation (figure 4.18). As the focus shifts from general physical preparation to strength loading, technique and speed development training is introduced. The focus on this attribute will gradually increase as strength loading is reduced, resulting in a unidimensional focus on speed development. Although there will be a point at which strength loading is completely removed, it cannot be removed indefinitely because maximal strength is a critical biomotor ability that underpins speed (167). Generally, the period without strength loading should not exceed 2 to 3 weeks (90, 91, 95, 113, 132, 138).

Ultimately, there are numerous ways to sequence the loading paradigms discussed in this chapter

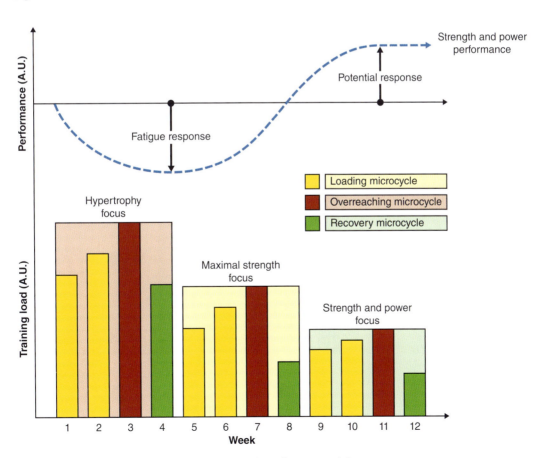

FIGURE 4.17 Example of phase potentiation in strength and power training.

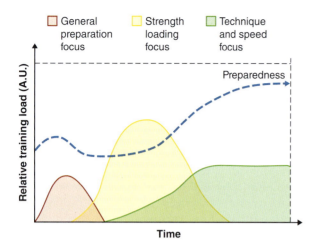

FIGURE 4.18 Sequential model for developing speed–strength.

(23, 155, 182, 183). In fact, many of the basic loading strategies can be integrated into a training plan at different times throughout the training year (figure 4.19). For example, if the athlete is in the preparatory period, a step loading model can be used to increase the athlete's work capacity and prepare them for more intensive training in subsequent periods. This practice is commonly employed early in the strength-training process in which a 3:1 step loading paradigm is used in conjunction with a strength–endurance or hypertrophy focus (i.e., higher-volume training) to establish a foundation for higher-intensity work (23, 182, 183).

Due to the high volumes of training, increased fatigue and reduced preparedness occur during this block of training. Therefore, this period of training is classified as a concentrated loading block. As the athlete shifts into the second block of training, there will be a reduction in training volume, which creates a recovery block to capitalize on the delayed training effects established in the concentrated loading block. At this time, there is generally a shift toward maximal strength development and a continued use of the 3:1 step loading model (182). The next three blocks of training shift the focus toward the maximization of strength and power development. Each block will begin with a 1-week concentrated loading microcycle followed by a 2-week microcycle of normal training and one unloading microcycle. At the end of these three blocks of training, a flat loading block of training might be employed, resulting in further elevation

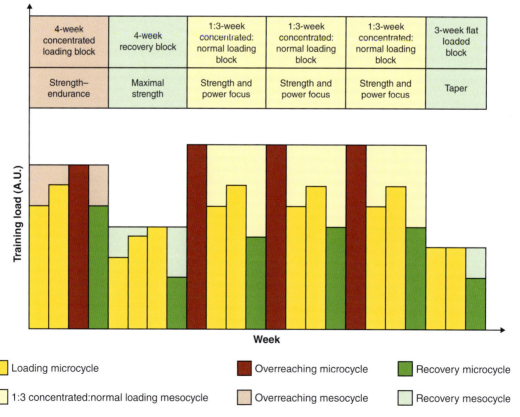

FIGURE 4.19 Example integration of multiple loading paradigms into a training cycle to emphasize power.

in preparedness and supercompensation of the desired performance outcome. Although this example is typically used in strength and conditioning, training load sequences should be designed to meet the individual athlete's needs by considering their training status, current health and injury status, time available for training, training goals, and the overall physiological and performance outcomes targeted (23).

Summary

How training loads are integrated into periodized training plans influences the training outcomes. The coach must understand how the applied training loads (i.e., external loads) affect the athletes (i.e., internal loads) and how these loads relate to one another and modulate preparedness and performance. Based on this understanding, the coach also needs to consider the factors that can be manipulated to regulate the training load implemented within the periodized training plan. Athletes are not the same, and prescribing training loads is a highly individualized process. As athletes become more developed, greater individualization of training loads is required. Regardless of the level of athlete, the overall progression of training loads is an important consideration. As training age increases, athletes undertake larger training loads to further stimulate performance gains. Ultimately, there are numerous ways a coach can sequence training loads within a periodized training plan. The coach's experience coupled with data collected about an athlete's response to the training process can heavily influence decisions made about the application and manipulation of the training loads.

PART II
FUNDAMENTALS OF PERIODIZATION

Periodization is a critical aspect of the training process. Understanding the main constructs that underpin this paradigm is an essential part of the development of athletes. As there is a lot of confusion about periodization within the contemporary scientific and applied literature, it is important that coaches develop a comprehensive understanding of what periodization is and how to navigate the key levels of the process of designing periodized training plans. Part II outlines the key aspects of a periodized training plan, starting with explaining the theory of periodization in chapter 5. Chapter 6 discusses the importance of constructing multiyear and annual training plans to establish the scaffolding from which other layers of the periodization process are designed. Chapter 7 explores the meso- and microcycles constructed to achieve the goals established in the annual training plan. Chapter 8 examines the structure of individual training days and how to classify and structure each training session to optimize the training process.

CHAPTER 5

Periodization Theory

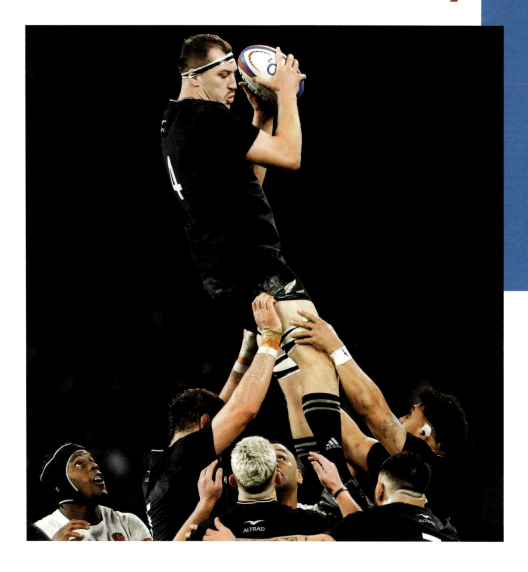

When thinking about how to guide the training practices of an athlete, coaches often immediately focus on the athlete's physical training (1, 97, 104) without considering the other factors needed to prepare for competition (59). Fundamentally, the periodization of training extends far beyond simply programming physical training to include all activities the athlete undertakes to optimize performance (59). These planning considerations include periodizing skill acquisition, psychological development, dietary practices, and recovery strategies to optimize the athlete's overall performance capacity (104). These must be included in the overall periodization plan to optimize the training process (14).

The ultimate goal of an athlete's training plan is to modulate physiological adaptations, enhance technical mastery, develop tactical capacity, and enhance psychological factors associated with high levels of performance (17, 59). Managing this process requires an overbridging system to organize the various factors to be considered when planning the athlete's training. Periodization offers coaches and sport scientists an organizational framework from which training can be structured and delivered to athletes.

To effectively employ periodization strategies, one must understand the history of periodization and how it is defined. Additionally, one must understand how periodization differs from the **planning** and **programming** of training as well as the goals of periodization before examining the various models used to guide the training process and make informed decisions about when certain models are most appropriate.

A Brief History of Periodization

The construct of periodization has been scrutinized by several modern sport scientists and coaches (1, 2, 29, 33, 83-85, 97). This is largely due to misinformation about the history of periodization and lack of understanding of the differences between periodization and programming. This is most noted in the work of Buckner et al. (29), who suggested that "periodization was created to help manage the stress of sport with the stress of lifting weights" (page 646). If we examine the history of periodization, it is evident that this statement is wildly inaccurate and does not reflect the rich history of periodization and the training process.

Although the origins of periodization are unknown, historic evidence dating back more than 2,000 years reveals precursors of periodization being discussed by ancient thinkers such as Claudius Aelius Galenus (Galen) (AD 129-216) and Philostratus (AD 170-245) (17, 73, 76). In his treatise "On the Preservation of Health" (*De sanitate tuenda*), Galen proposed a categorization and sequencing of exercises that could be considered precursors to modern periodization of strength training (49, 73, 76, 127). He also appears to focus on the need for recovery by referencing the need to bathe, relax, and practice good nutrition after training (16). Another example of periodization in the ancient literature can be found in Philostratus' essay "Gymnasticus," in which he describes a compulsory 10-month training camp followed by a 1-month centralized preparation in the city of Elis prior to the Olympic Games (38, 49, 76).

With the advent of the modern Olympic era, there was an increased interest in training for sport performance (73). In *Olympic Sport*, one of the first monographs dedicated to high-performance sport, Boris Kotov (86) introduced the three original stages of preparation: general fitness preparation, more specialized training, and specific preparation for competition (73). In 1930, Lauri Pihkala (118) proposed dividing the annual training plan into preparatory, spring, and summer phases followed by active rest after the completion of the season. Additionally, he conceptualized the idea of sequencing training from extensive to intensive workloads and highlighted the importance of balancing the work-to-rest ratio in the training process (73, 118). In the 1930s, German coaches reportedly devised the first long-term training plans when they created quadrennial training plans to prepare athletes for the 1936 Olympic Games (16). Ideas generated in the 1930s served as a foundation for several texts published in the Soviet Union about the preparation of athletes for a variety of sports (73).

Probably the most noted moment in the history of periodization is a book published by Soviet sport scientist Leonid P. Matveyev (98), in which he presented a model of training based on a questionnaire that asked Russian athletes how they trained for the 1952 Olympic Games. The model contained phases, subphases, and training cycles that were similar to the annual training plans developed by German coaches (16). Because of his work, Matveyev is often considered the founder of the traditional model of periodization (76) and is often the focus of modern sport scientists and coaches who are critical of the periodization construct (29, 84, 97). Although Matveyev did make a huge contribution to the development of periodization theory, it is important to remember that other sport scientists and coaches from Russia (Bondarchuk, Ozolin, Verkhoshansky, Zatsiorsky), Russia/Israel (Issurin), Germany (Harre), Romania/Canada (Bompa), Estonia (Viru), Hungary (Nádori), Ukraine (Plantonov), and the United States (Stone, O'Bryant, Garhammer, Plisk, Counsilman, Kraemer, Fleck) have all contributed to the evolution of the periodization process (8-13, 19, 22, 24, 26, 34, 41, 63-65, 67, 70, 74, 76, 98, 107-110, 114, 119, 120, 122, 139, 140, 154-162, 166, 171).

Defining Periodization

Although periodization is widely considered a critical tool for managing an athlete's training, to date there is no universally accepted definition of the concept within the coaching or scientific literature (30, 35, 36, 59, 84). It is likely that the lack of a universal definition contributes to a lot of the confusion about what periodization is within the contemporary literature (55, 152). The most simplistic definition is that periodization is planned training variation (29, 41-43, 47, 87, 88, 145). Although training variation is a key component of a periodized training plan, periodization also serves as a directional template that systematically guides the methodological decisions about the prescribed training activities, and this should be considered when defining the construct (59, 111).

Based on the continued reference to the sequencing of training within the classic periodization literature, some authors suggest that periodization is simply a tool for sequencing the variation of training units (i.e., training cycles) in mutually dependent periods to guide the athlete's state of preparedness and optimize performance at some predetermined time (e.g., a key competition) (16, 59, 76, 113, 122). Several authors have latched onto the continued reference to the sequential aspect of periodization in the classic literature to falsely suggest that the construct is overly rigid and is disconnected from how athletes actually adapt or respond to training (33, 59, 84, 97). The propagation of this misguided interpretation of the periodization literature has even led some authors to suggest that periodization is no longer a useful tool for managing the training practices of the modern athlete (29, 33, 84, 97, 111). In reality, periodization should not be considered a rigid or unmodifiable planning strategy but instead it should be considered a scaffolding framework around which training is planned and programming decisions are made to address the athlete's specific needs and situations (59, 104, 111).

When contemplating periodization as a scaffolding framework, one could consider it is "a cyclical approach to training in which periodic changes in training parameters (volume, intensity, loading, exercise selection, etc.) are planned so that the athlete achieves optimal performance at the appropriate time" (page 53) (62). Verkhoshansky and Verkhoshansky (152) suggest that this is the best general definition of periodization offered in the Western literature because it attempts to link the *how* and *why* of the training process. Plisk and Stone (122) add to this definition by relating periodization to the constructs of game theory: "In terms of game theory, periodization is the use of planned unpredictability to manipulate or outmaneuver another player. The other player in this case is the body's adaptive mechanism" (page 21). When taking these two definitions together with the work of Verkhoshansky and Verkhoshansky (152), it is clear that periodization is not a rigid construct but rather a method of organizing, planning, and delivering modifiable training activities that are guided by the athlete's responses to the applied training stimuli.

In this text, **periodization** is defined as a cyclical training approach in which the logical integration and sequencing of modifiable training parameters (i.e., volume, intensity, training density, training frequency, exercise selection, and mode) are planned to optimize the athlete's performance outcomes at appropriate times.

Periodization, Planning, and Programming

Another factor that has increased the confusion about periodization is the misuse of the term (16). The scientific and coaching literature references numerous types of periodization models—traditional (4, 92), linear (51, 123), nonlinear (89), undulating (5, 6, 51), flexible (32, 99, 100), and tactical (125, 126)—but these are actually planning or programming structures. Careful inspection of these models suggests extensive confusion among the concepts of periodization, planning, and programming. Though these terms are interrelated, they are not interchangeable and should not be considered as such (figure 5.1).

To untangle this confusion, one must first consider that periodization is a scaffolding framework that serves as a macromanagement strategy and provides a blueprint from which training can be guided (figure 5.2) (35, 59, 61). This blueprint is used to forecast and assign periods of time allocated to the development of specific fitness attributes, physical skills, or performance targets (35, 59, 61, 104). The process of forecasting is simply establishing key training objectives, based on the athlete's needs, and aligning development with specific training cycles (e.g., multiyear; annual; macro-, meso-, and microcycles) (59, 111).

108 | Scientific Foundations and Practical Applications of Periodization

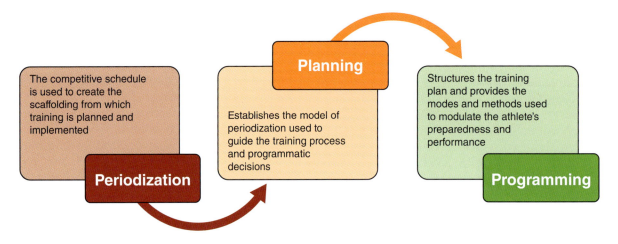

FIGURE 5.1 Periodization, planning, and programming.

Adapted by permission from G.G. Haff and K. Kendall, "Strength and Conditioning," in *Coaching for Sports Performance*, edited by T. Baghurst (England: Routledge, 2019), 337. Reproduced by permission of Taylor and Francis Group, LLC, a division of Informa plc.

Once the global blueprint of training is established, the coach can plan the training models that will be used to direct the loading patterns the athlete will be exposed to (59, 61). Based on the macromanagement decisions made at the periodization level and the loading progressions determined at the planning level, the coach constructs a training program. At the programming level, the modes and methods of training are prescribed to deliver the training stimulus to the athlete (35, 59, 61). Fundamentally, programming involves the micromanagement of training and heavily relies on

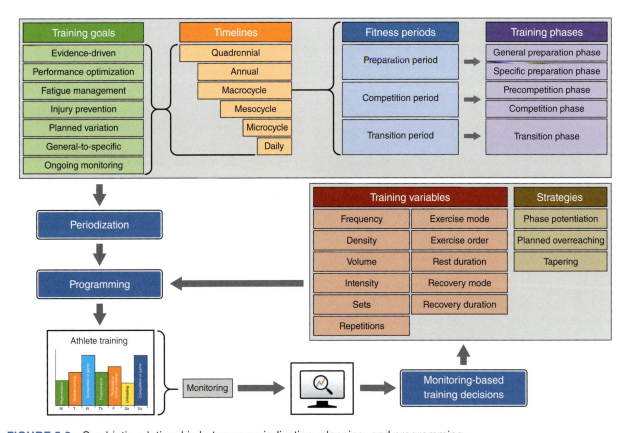

FIGURE 5.2 Symbiotic relationship between periodization, planning, and programming.

Reprinted by permission from G.G. Haff, "Periodization and Programming of Individual Sports," in *NSCA's Essentials of Sport Science*, edited for the National Strength and Conditioning Association by D. French and L. Torres Ronda (Champaign, IL: Human Kinetics, 2022).

a structured monitoring program to inform strategic decisions about how training stimuli are delivered to the athlete (36, 59, 61, 122). In fact, DeWeese et al. (36) suggest that the integration of a monitoring program into the training process is one of the most critical considerations underpinning the training process because it allows the coach to determine whether the athlete is responding as planned to the prescribed training interventions. Information garnered from the monitoring program informs the strategic decisions made around the training process and allows for this process to be fine-tuned. Ultimately, the greatest degree of flexibility can be found at the programming level, where there is the greatest ability to modify or adapt the training prescription to meet the athlete's current level of preparedness (i.e., sporting form). Modifications to the daily training plan can be made based on objective and subjective data on the athlete's current training state and overall level of preparedness. It is, however, important to remember the goals of the training period and to contextualize any modifications made to the daily training environment so they are in alignment with those goals.

When developing the actual training program, the coach should program one mesocycle (i.e., 2- to 6-week training period) at a time so the next mesocycle can be adapted to better match the athlete's responsiveness to the training process and be aligned with the directional aspects established by the periodization process. It would be unwise to construct every training intervention that the athlete would be exposed to for the entire annual training plan at one time, because it would be impossible to gauge how the athlete will progress through the training process.

Goals of Periodization

Generally, four interrelated goals are targeted by the periodization of training (56). The first goal is organizing the training process to elevate performance at predetermined times or to maintain performance for the duration of a competitive sport season (54-56). The ability to elevate performance is influenced by the second goal, which focuses on stimulating the physiological adaptations that underpin the targeted performance outcome. These adaptations are largely affected by the multidimensional application of specific training interventions implemented as part of planning and programming. Specifically, this goal focuses on modulating training stressors to balance the adaptive and restorative processes (55, 57). The ability to achieve this goal allows for the third goal to be achieved, which is reducing the potential for overtraining or training monotony while maximizing training adaptive responses (56, 57). The final goal of periodization is developing long-term athletic abilities (57). Since periodized training plans are typically sequenced over time, they are ideally suited for the long-term development of athletes (52-55, 60, 134). This is accomplished by planning variations in the training interventions so they align with the athlete's level of development and provide progressive development of key training targets over the course of the athlete's athletic career (57).

One of the key factors that affects the ability to accomplish these goals is the application of training variation at the planning and programming levels of the process (37, 55). Although there are infinite ways that variation can be introduced into the overall periodized training plan, training variation should not be randomly or excessively introduced to the training process because this can reduce performance and significantly increase injury risk (37, 55, 117).

Ultimately, planning and programming of training variation must be applied in a logical and systematic manner so the main goals of the periodization process are accomplished (60). The implementation of a variety of training models can provide direction for the training process and help guide the programming decisions the coach makes when constructing the overall periodized training plan.

Hierarchical Structures of Periodization

When designing a periodized training plan, several interrelated levels are used to guide the training process. These levels of organization span from global or long-term structures, such as multiyear training plans, to smaller structures, such as individual training sessions (figure 5.3) (55). The long-term training configurations are generally considered to be macromanagement structures used to establish the global goals and timelines that constrain the training process. For example, a multiyear training plan establishes the long-term progression of the developmental goals during the given time frame (e.g., 4 years) (55). These goals are directly targeted with the use of annual training plans that are interlinked and constructed based on the athlete's level of development (17, 55, 76), the targeted training goals established in the multiyear training plan

(7, 80, 112), and the demands of the competitive schedule (17, 45). Each annual training plan is composed of one or more macrocycles, depending on the established competitive demands. In a team sport, for example, the annual training plan would typically contain one macrocycle because there is only one competitive season (55); however, for an individual sport, the plan would require more than one macrocycle because the sport has multiple major competitions in a year (45). Macrocycles generally last several months to 1 year depending on the sport's competitive schedule.

Each macrocycle is further subdivided into preparation, competitive, and transition periods used to inform the programming of training at the mesocycle level. The mesocycle, which is sometimes referred to as a *medium-duration training structure* (56, 70, 71, 172), is where the programming of training begins. When constructing periodized training plans, coaches typically design training interventions one mesocycle at a time so the next mesocycle is prescribed based on the athlete's progress. Mesocycles are also called *blocks of training* (55, 56); these serve as the foundation of the **block periodization** training model (70, 71). Each mesocycle typically contains two to six microcycles, which typically last 7 days.

Microcycles are sometimes referred to as *short-duration training structures*. Haff (55) suggests that the microcycle is the most important level of the periodization of training because it is where the programming decisions are made. There is a large degree of flexibility in how training interventions are implemented at this level. Based on data

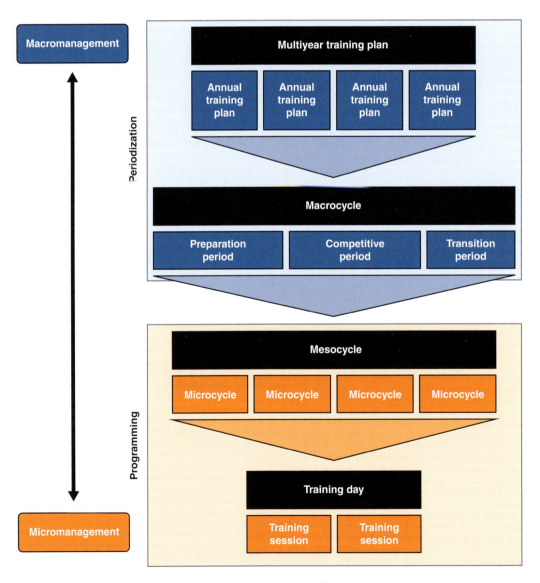

FIGURE 5.3 Hierarchical levels used in periodization and programming.

garnered from an integrated monitoring program (see chapter 11), the coach can modify the training program as warranted. Structurally, the location of the microcycle within the annual training plan and its relationship to the meso- and macrocycles dictate the actual makeup of the training activities programmed (55).

Each microcycle is further subdivided into training days. The structure of the **training day** is based on the goals of the microcycle and is aligned with the goals targeted by the prescribed mesocycle. Each training day will have one or more training sessions. The number of training sessions prescribed depends on the athlete's level of development and ability to tolerate training, the amount of time available for training, and the established training objectives and goals (55). Each training session contains specific training units that outline the activities to be undertaken as part of the training process.

Training Models Used in Periodization

The scientific and coaching literature provides numerous training models that can be placed on a continuum from multilateral to unilateral (106, 149, 172). Generally, these models are classified into one of three basic categories: parallel, sequential, or emphasis (figure 5.4) (56, 59, 106).

Parallel Training Models

In **parallel training models**, multiple training factors or biomotor abilities are simultaneously trained with the same focus. Parallel training models are considered multilateral training (56, 150, 151). With this approach, all targeted factors are trained concurrently within a training session, training day, series of training days, or within a micro- or mesocycle. The concept of parallel models can be extended to specific training targets such as physical, technical, tactical, and psychological training. For example, all these factors would be trained with equal focus during a block of training (figure 5.5*a*), across a week of training (figure 5.5*b*), or over another defined phase of training.

Conceptually, parallel training models are thought to be ideal for developing multifaceted fitness because all training factors are developed (150). There are numerous examples of the use of parallel models in the literature, including **complex training models** and **variational training models**.

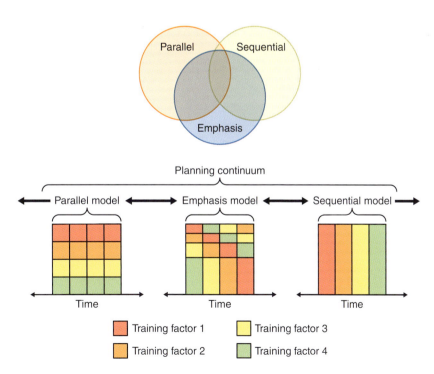

FIGURE 5.4 Three basic categories of planning: parallel, sequential, and emphasis models. Parallel models are multifactorial and sequential models are unidirectional. Emphasis models contain aspects of parallel and sequential models; they are multifactorial, but they have varying degrees of focus and contain sequenced training to allow training to be focused on fewer targets.

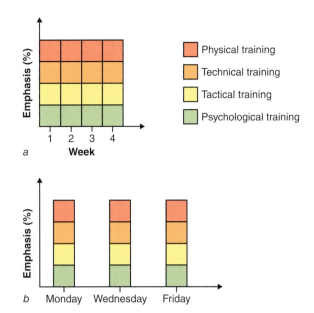

FIGURE 5.5 Parallel training models: *(a)* mesocycle (block) parallel training example; *(b)* microcycle (week) parallel training example.

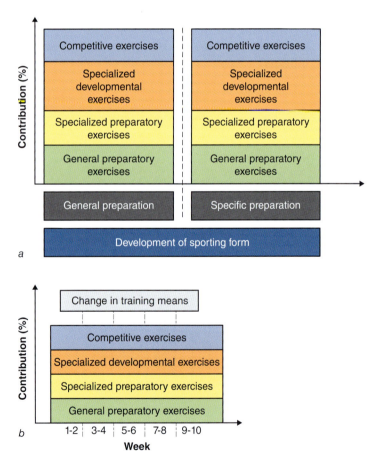

FIGURE 5.6 Bondarchuk's *(a)* complex and *(b)* complex variational models of training.
Adapted from Bondarchuk (2010).

Complex Training Models

In complex training, several factors are trained concurrently (15, 150). This model uses a diverse series of training means to simultaneously develop several fitness factors. For example, Verkhoshansky and Siff (150) suggest that a complex training session might contain resistance training, plyometric training, and sprint training and put the same degree of emphasis on each training factor. This could be extended to a microcycle (i.e., a week of training), during which these training means are dispersed across the training week.

Bondarchuk (25) presents a base complex model in which several exercise types are trained simultaneously in a training block as the athlete develops sporting form (figure 5.6*a*). The model contains **general preparatory exercises**, specialized preparatory exercises, specialized developmental exercises, and **competitive exercises** (table 5.1).

In this parallel training model, the exercise targets and the means of training (i.e., specific exercises, programmatic factors) are held constant as the athlete develops their sporting form. This model typically is used in periods of the annual training plan where the athlete has yet to elevate preparedness to a competition level. The means of training employed with this model depend on the athlete's level of development and individual developmental needs and the performance requirements.

Variational Training Models

An alternative to the complex training model is the **complex variational training model** in which the targeted exercise groupings are held constant and the means of training are altered every 2 to 6 weeks (figure 5.6*b*) (25). These alterations often align with the various periods of training and result in an elevation of preparedness to competition level. With this model, continuity between the exercises that are employed in each mesocycle is important.

The decision to use a parallel model of periodization is largely dictated by the developmental level of the athlete, the targeted training objectives, and what period of training is being undertaken (150). Parallel models appear to work well with youth, novice, or developmental athletes because the training loads required to stimulate adaptations are not as high (56) and

TABLE 5.1 Bondarchuk Exercise Classifications

Exercises	Description
General preparatory exercises	General exercises that do not repeat the competitive movement or parts of the movement or activate the muscle groups used in these movements. These are used for general physical development and increasing overall work capacity.
Specialized preparatory exercises	These exercises do not replicate the competitive movements or parts of the movement, but they do engage the muscle groups used in these movements.
Specialized developmental exercises	These are used to repeat parts of the competitive movements. They have the greatest similarity to the competitive activity and are used to transition toward the development of sporting form.
Competitive exercises	These are the competitive movements, or the sport event, that the athlete competes in. Exercises in this category are used in training and competition.

Adapted from Bondarchuk (2010).

fall well below these athletes' training tolerance (figure 5.7).

As the athlete progresses, there is a need to increase the overall training load because a stimulating load for a novice athlete does not provide enough training load to stimulate adaptations for an intermediate or advanced athlete (see figure 1.8, page 9) (170). Using this model, the workload of all factors is typically increased to address the need for greater training load to induce adaptation. Initially, an increase in the number of training days can facilitate the increase in overall workload (figure 5.8). As the athlete becomes more trained, it might be warranted to separate the training factors and not train them all on the same day. This might require the athlete to target specific training factors on a given training day and spread the total workload across multiple training days (figure 5.8) (81) or sessions within the training week.

As the workload is increased for each training factor, the total workload the athlete is exposed

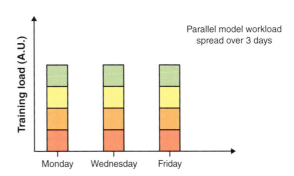

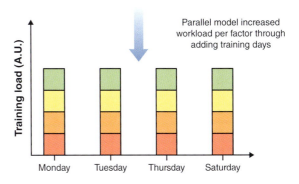

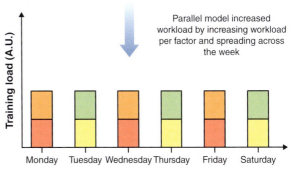

FIGURE 5.8 Examples of workload increase in parallel models.

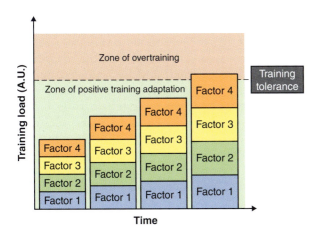

FIGURE 5.7 Relationship between training load and tolerance in parallel models.

to can approach or exceed the athlete's workload tolerance (figure 5.7). If the athlete is exposed to too much load, there is an increased risk of overtraining and injury (101, 133, 135, 138). To address the increased workload requirement, more advanced strategies for organizing training are required. Specifically, the use of sequential models that have more unilateral foci may be required to provide enough training stimulus to induce adaptations (81).

Sequential Training Models

Sequential training models are alternatives to parallel models and are used to arrange individual or a limited number of training factors into logical, sequential patterns that target a specific outcome (15, 56, 59, 77, 147, 165). These models were created to address many of the drawbacks of parallel training models, such as restrictions in the ability to simultaneously develop multiple motor and technical abilities, excessively long preparation periods, and an inability to prepare athletes for more dense competitive schedules (77).

Sequential training models are ideally suited for intermediate to advanced athletes who require greater training stimuli than those provided by parallel training models (149, 165). Conceptually, sequential training models allow the athlete's training to be saturated with a focused training stimulus while minimizing the risk of the athlete approaching their maximal level of training tolerance (figure 5.9).

There are several examples of the use of sequential models in the scientific and coaching literature (56, 146, 153, 167, 169). For example, when examining strength-training practices for developing power, there is strong evidential support for using sequential models in which training that targets the development of hypertrophy is followed by maximal strength development and culminates with the elevation of power-generating capacity (figure 5.10a) (56, 169). Additionally, the use of sequential training models has also been shown to be an ideal model for the optimization of endurance performance (figure 5.10b) (146, 153, 167). When focusing on endurance performance, local muscular endurance is targeted first, followed by an emphasis on increasing prolonged work capacity at specific speeds and culminating with targeting the enhancement of maximal speed at the competitive distance (146).

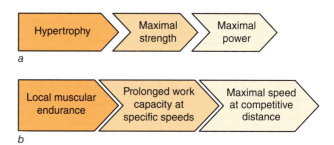

FIGURE 5.10 Sequential models for (a) power development and (b) endurance performance.

Central to the effectiveness of sequential training models is the employment of **concentrated loading** or **accentuated loading** blocks that provide a unidirectional training stimulus followed by periods of restitution that culminate with supercompensation of preparedness and performance (see chapter 4) (153). Verkhoshansky and Siff (149) suggest that training volume that is 23% to 25% higher than the general annual training volume constitutes a concentrated loading period. It is recommended that these periods last between three and six microcycles, depending on the magnitude of the loading applied, and be followed by two microcycles focused on restoration (figure 5.11) (165). Even though concentrated loading blocks focus on a primary targeted attribute, technical training is never totally removed from the training process (149).

Variants of sequential training models are commonly used in individual sports such as weightlifting (142), cross-country skiing (136), cycling (40, 129, 131), track and field (115, 116), judo (96), and other endurance sports (78). Although they are more commonly used in individual sports, variants of the sequential model have also been success-

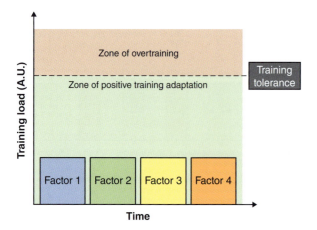

FIGURE 5.9 Relationship between training load and tolerance in sequential models.

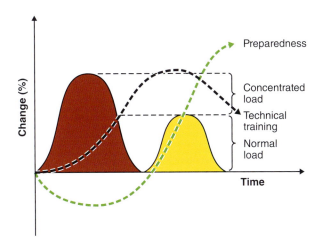

FIGURE 5.11 Sequential training models and concentrated loading.

fully employed with team sports such as American football (50, 66), basketball (121), ice hockey (131), and team handball (95).

The constructs that underpin the basic principles of sequential training have made these models very popular methods for preparing modern athletes. They serve as the foundation for **block training** and **conjugated sequential loading models**.

Block Training Models

In the 1980s, the concept of the training block became widely used by coaches to construct training interventions (70, 71). The **training block** is a training cycle that contains concentrated specialized workloads followed by periods of restitution. Issurin (70) suggests that there are four considerations when conceptualizing the training block:

1. It is not possible to develop multiple training attributes with concentrated workloads, so the number of targeted attributes must be reduced.
2. The optimal development of multiple training attributes with highly concentrated training can only be accomplished with consecutively linked training blocks.
3. The sequence of training blocks is critical; while one training factor is being emphasized with concentrated loading strategies the other training factors will decline.
4. Physiological and performance adaptations require 2 to 6 weeks to develop, which corresponds to a mesocycle of training.

Based on these four premises, blocks of training that focus on a limited number of training targets that are sequentially constructed are used to guide the training process when employing the use of the block periodization training model.

The roots of block periodization can be traced to the work of Yuri Verkhoshansky, a professor who developed the **concentrated unidirectional training model** (149, 164). This model uses concentrated workloads followed by periods of restitution (69). Central to this model are **long-lasting delayed training effects (LDTE)** (149), which are revealed under these conditions. When an athlete is exposed to a concentrated load, there is a reduction in performance capacity, which gradually elevates and then supercompensates after the completion of a period of training with reduced loading (153). Verkhoshansky and Verkhoshansky (153) said that these effects could best be developed with three specialized training blocks that were used to produce the desired training responses and stimulate a substantial increase in a sport-specific performance (figure 5.12).

In the basic example presented in figure 5.12, block 1 contains concentrated strength loads based on higher-volume, lower-intensity training associated with reductions in preparedness. As the athlete moves through block 2, the LDTE underpin the performance gains that occur when training volume is reduced and training intensity is elevated, resulting in a rise in overall preparedness. As the athlete moves into block 3, there is a further reduction in training volume, an elevation in training intensity, and an increase in preparedness. Across the three blocks of this example, the power output or event-specific performance elevates (149). Verkhoshansky and Verkhoshansky (153) suggest that block periodization models should only be used with high-level athletes who no longer adapt to more traditional training models and who have developed a high level of technical mastery. The basic principles of the three-block model can be adapted to a variety of sports and the preparation means used for those sports.

Another example of the use of block models can be seen in the numerous works of Dr. Anatoliy Bondarchuk (20, 22, 23, 25). Bondarchuk (24, 26) was one of the most successful coaches to employ a mesocycle block–based training system that allowed him to achieve the landmark accomplishment of being the coach of all medal winners in the hammer throw in three successive, nonboycotted Olympic Games. Bondarchuk (22) established three specialized mesocycle blocks that were referred to as *developmental, retention,* and *restorative* blocks of training. The developmental mesocycle uses increasing workloads and serves as a

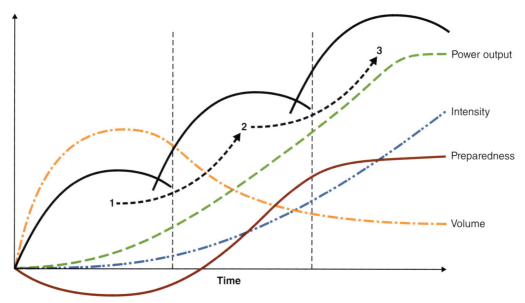

FIGURE 5.12 Basics of Verkhoshansky's block periodization model.

Adapted by permission from Y. Verkhoshansky and N. Verkhoshansky, "Organization of Special Strength Training in the Training Process and the Block Training System," in *Special Strength Training Manual for Coaches* (Rome: Verkhoshansky, SSTM, 2011).

concentrated load. The retention mesocycle stabilizes training loads and increases focus on competitive performance. The restorative mesocycle prepares the athlete for the next developmental mesocycle. Typically, the developmental and retention mesocycles are four microcycles long, and the restorative mesocycle is shortened to two microcycles. Ultimately, the timing of these mesocycles is dictated by the athlete's responses to the training process and the competitive schedule (21, 22, 70). Two example mesocycle block models are presented in figure 5.13.

The block complex model (figure 5.13*a*) is designed to employ general development exercises and specialized preparatory exercises in the general preparation phase. The specific preparation period uses specialized developmental and competitive exercises. The block complex variational model (figure 5.13*b*) has the same progression of exercises, but the training means change every 2 to 4 weeks (25).

This basic approach was also used by world-renowned swimming coach Gennadi Touretski, who subdivided the annual plan into stages lasting 6 to 12 weeks (76, 124, 143). He used the following sequence of training blocks: preparation, general, specific, and competitive (124). As his block structures evolved, he modified them to include general, specific, and competition blocks. The general block focused on aerobic and complementary workloads, and the specific block focused on the development of event-specific energetics and competitive swimming speed. The competitive block aligned with what is typically referred to as a *taper* (see chapter 12) (143). Touretski also used a short recovery cycle to link these 6- to 12-week stages (76, 124, 143).

The most noted advocate for the block periodization model is Dr. Vladimir Issurin (70, 77). His block model was first proposed and implemented with elite canoe-kayak athletes (75) to reduce training workloads and attain a high level of success in the 1988 Seoul Olympic Games (82). The basic structure employed was to divide the annual training plan into five to six stages. The last stage led into the season's most important competition (70). Each stage was subdivided into three types of mesocycle training blocks with the following guidelines and goals (70, 76):

1. Accumulation (14-42 days): improves overall aerobic endurance, muscular strength, and basic technical ability with a long-term training adaptation retention effect
2. Transmutation (14-28 days): focuses on sport- and event-specific outcomes and abilities with notable training responses but also accrued fatigue
3. Realization (8-25 days): models competition demands (e.g., maximal speed) while lessening training stress to prioritize recovery and diminish accrued fatigue

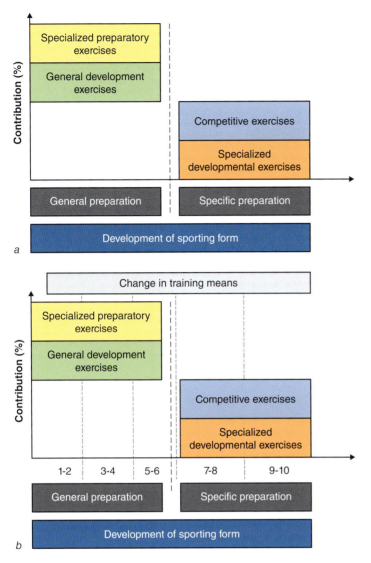

FIGURE 5.13 Bondarchuk's *(a)* block complex and *(b)* block complex variational models of training.

Adapted from Bondarchuk (2010).

Accumulation Mesocycle Block The **accumulation block** has several names, including the concentrated loading block (62, 122, 141), the overreaching block (55, 122), and the developmental block (22, 23) (figure 5.14). Regardless of the terminology used, the focus of this block of training is developing a general physical base via the use of substantial workloads that target a specific ability, such as muscular strength, anaerobic endurance, or aerobic endurance (70, 161). The length of an accumulation block is typically 2 to 6 weeks (55), but this depends on the time necessary to establish the targeted training effect, the rate of involution, and the competitive schedule (60).

Ultimately, the training effect established by completing an accumulation block is affected by the duration of the training contained in the block (60, 141, 161) and the duration the residual training effects can be maintained (60, 122, 141). The longer the accumulation block is, the longer the residual training effects can be maintained (60, 70) and the longer the time before supercompensation occurs (60, 141, 161). Ultimately, when accumulation blocks are structured correctly, they establish a training base for subsequent training blocks. As such, these should be considered foundational training blocks (60).

Transmutation Mesocycle Block A **transmutation block** (60, 70, 161), or normal training block (122, 141), is used after the completion of an accumulation block to transition toward the development of more sport-specific training (70, 76) (figure 5.14). Conceptually, the main goal of this block of training is to take the attributes established in the accumulation block and translate them into an increase in overall preparedness (60, 161). This goal is accomplished by targeting more sport-specific training, focusing on that which underpins competitive performances, and employing higher intensities of training that can create significant fatigue (60, 70, 76). For example, if an athlete undertook strength–endurance training in the accumulation block, they would shift their training focus toward maximal strength in the transmutation block (60). The fitness established in the accumulation block would increase the work capacity of the athlete and allow them to better tolerate the transmutation block's main focus of increasing maximal strength.

The length of time dedicated to the transmutation block is based on the time course associated with involution (i.e., rate of decay) of the training effects established by the accumulation block, the fatigue generated in the current training block, and the amount of time necessary for adaptive responses and elevations in preparedness to occur (60). If the transmutation block is extended beyond 6 weeks, there will be a greater chance that the residual training effects established in the accumulation block will be reduced, resulting in a reduction in the ability to supercompensate preparedness and performance in the realization block (60, 70, 76, 161).

Realization Mesocycle Block The realization mesocycle is similar to the tapering strategy discussed in the literature (27, 103, 105) because its main goals are to reduce accumulated fatigue and

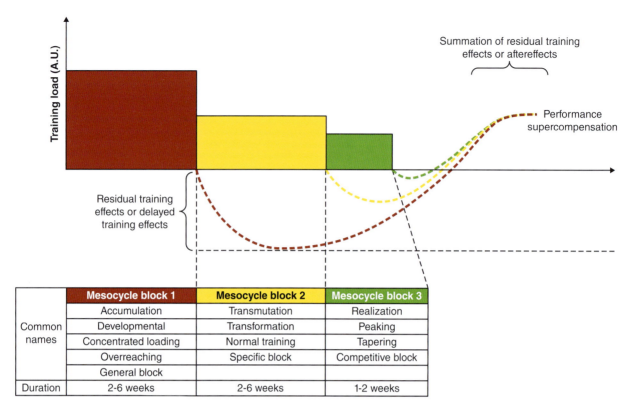

FIGURE 5.14 Basic block model structure.

elevate the athlete's level of preparedness and performance capacity (60). The **realization block** should last 1 to 2 weeks (55, 58, 60), which has been shown to be the optimal length for most tapering strategies (see chapter 12) (27, 103, 105). The key to effectively constructing a realization mesocycle is creating a scenario that allows for the training residuals created in response to the accumulation and transmutation mesocycles to converge to elevate preparedness, maximize sport-specific abilities, and optimize performance capacity (60, 70, 76, 161). The realization mesocycle typically leads into a competition.

The progressive sequencing of accumulation, transmutation, and realization mesocycles serves as the foundation for block periodization training models. The duration of each mesocycle is largely predicated by the needs of the athlete, the density of the competition schedule, and the overall structure of the macrocycle and annual training plan (60).

A significant amount of research supports the use of block training models with canoe-kayak athletes (48, 82), alpine skiers (28), soccer players (93, 94), ice hockey players (131), track and field athletes (116, 117), cyclists (128, 129), and cross-country skiers (130, 136). When structured correctly, block models can be very useful, but one must consider how the blocks of training are sequenced and the interplay between the involution of training effects and the durations used for each block of training.

Conjugated Sequential Loading Models

Sequencing training loads so overreaching or concentrated loadings are followed by periods of recovery can be accomplished by using conjugated sequential loading models; also referred to as the ***coupled successive system*** (69, 122, 148, 149, 163). This advanced system of organizing training introduces unidirectional training targets that provide a progressively stronger training effect and allow for the coupling of the training residuals to facilitate a positive cumulative performance effect at the end of the sequence (148). This method can be very useful when working with advanced athletes because sequencing specific training targets allows for a large degree of variation between the different periods of the sequence.

Plisk and Stone (122) suggest that this model allows for the saturation of a specific training factor, such as strength development, which creates fatigue and decrements in some performance variables. As the athlete shifts to the next period of training, the emphasis on strength development is reduced and focus shifts to another training factor, such as speed development (figure 5.15). After completing this block of training, the athlete can undertake another series of blocks that are performed at a progressively higher intensity or volume. Ultimately, if structured correctly, a conjugated sequential pattern of training results in a supercompensation response.

Several advantages to this type of loading paradigm are presented in the literature (122, 132, 137, 144, 148, 168). For example, Verkhoshansky and Siff (148) suggest this system is efficient because it allows for up to a 20% reduction in the overall training volume that the athlete needs to induce training adaptations. The use of the conjugated sequential model can elevate performance to a greater extent than traditional loading patterns (46). Because this model relies on the exploitation of delayed training effects (see chapter 4), periods of reduced training must be programmed after periods of concentrated loading, which allows for recovery and elevations of preparedness (148). During the concentrated loading block, there will be significant amounts of fatigue, so the model is best applied with advanced athletes who have the training base to tolerate this type of loading (122). For athletes who have the appropriate training history, this loading model allows for better fatigue management, because the unidirectional focus allows for a reduction in overall fatigue when compared to parallel or complex training models in which all training factors are given equal focus (56).

A central concept of the conjugated sequential model is the ability to sequence training in a manner that elevates preparedness and performance at a specific time (18). For example, if speed–endurance is the targeted attribute for the sequence of training, four blocks of training can be constructed to maximize this attribute (figure 5.16). One example sequence for the development of speed–endurance would be to move the training load targets from general preparation, to strength development, to speed enhancement, and finally to speed–endurance loading (148). As the athlete moves through this sequence, the delayed training effects from each concentrated load converge to help enhance the development of the targeted outcome. As the athlete moves toward the end of the sequence, there is a reduction in the volume of loading to provide the recovery necessary to elevate preparedness and enhance the targeted outcome.

Another example of a conjugated sequence model is presented in Plisk and Stone's (122) seminal article on periodization, which presents a preseason that employs periods of concentrated loading and recovery (figure 5.17). In this example, 3-week blocks of concentrated loading are interspersed with 4-week blocks of recovery. By manipulating training density, different training loads can be used without affecting the basic volume and intensity of training (122). Greater reductions in the density of training during the recovery blocks can provide even greater contrast between training blocks, allowing for greater recovery. Additionally, conjugated sequential models allow for development of a greater and more stable work capacity. This model also allows for a high degree of functional effectiveness (148).

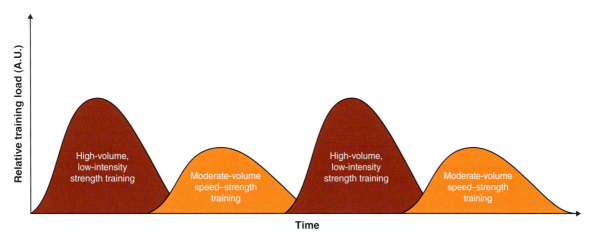

FIGURE 5.15 Basic conjugated sequence model applied to resistance training targeting speed–strength development.

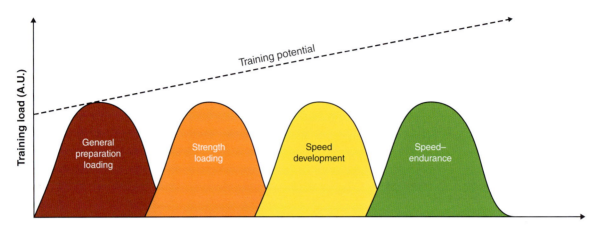

FIGURE 5.16 Example conjugated sequence model for the development of speed–endurance.

Conjugated sequential model of training															
Training variables		**Training block**													
		Concentrated loading block 1			Recovery block 1				Concentrated loading block 2			Recovery block 2			
	Week	1	2	3	4	5	6	7	8	9	10	11	12	13	14
Strength and power training	Total sessions	12			12				12			12			
	Days/week	4	4	4	3	3	3	3	4	4	4	3	3	3	3
Speed, agility, and conditioning training	Total sessions	6			12				6			12			
	Days/week	2	2	2	3	3	3	3	2	2	2	3	3	3	3
Modified conjugated sequential model of training															
Training variables		**Training block**													
		Concentrated loading block 1			Recovery block 1				Concentrated loading block 2			Recovery block 2			
	Week	1	2	3	4	5	6	7	8	9	10	11	12	13	14
Strength and power training	Total sessions	12			8				12			8			
	Days/week	4	4	4	2	2	2	2	4	4	4	2	2	2	2
Speed, agility, and conditioning training	Total sessions	6			12				6			12			
	Days/week	2	2	2	3	3	3	3	2	2	2	3	3	3	3

FIGURE 5.17 Example of preseason applications of a conjugated sequential model of training. Reducing the number of strength and power sessions in the modified model gives greater contrast between blocks of training.

Adapted by permission from T.O. Bompa and G.G. Haff, "Principles of Training," in *Periodization: Theory and Methodology of Training* (Champaign, IL: Human Kinetics Publishers, 2009), 51. Adapted from Plisk and Stone (2003).

Emphasis Training Models

An alternative approach to planning training is the **emphasis training model**, or pendulum model, which incorporates aspects of the parallel and sequential models (figure 5.4) (56, 59). With this model, several key training factors are trained simultaneously with varying degrees of focus that shift over time to align with the demands of the periodized training plan (56, 59, 172). When this training model is performed, the training emphasis is typically rotated every 2 weeks to optimize performance capacity (172). Zatsiorsky and colleagues (172) suggest that by varying the degrees of emphasis, one can have some training factors that are trained with loads that stimulate an adaptive response, while other training factors can be undertaken with loads that maintain the athlete's current state (figure 5.18). Additionally, some training factors would receive a minimal training emphasis and would undergo a detraining response because of this loading decision.

Due to the complexity of this model, it is ideally suited for intermediate to advanced athletes who have congested competition schedules, such as team sport athletes (59, 131). This model is also useful for individual sport athletes, such as those in track cycling (106), sprinting (44), and mixed martial arts.

Chapter 5 • Periodization Theory | **121**

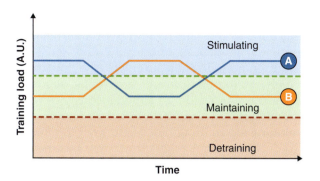

FIGURE 5.18 Sample emphasis model. When training factor A is in the stimulating zone, factor B is in the maintaining zone, and vice versa.

Adapted by permission from V.M. Zatsiorsky, W.J. Kraemer, and A.C. Fry, *Science and Practice of Strength Training,* 3rd ed. (Champaign, IL: Human Kinetics, 2021).

parallel-emphasis model and block-emphasis model that exist on the continuum (figure 5.19). With parallel-emphasis models, multiple training factors are trained simultaneously, but with varying degrees of emphasis. One example of a parallel-emphasis model is the vertical integration model (44). On the other end of the continuum is the block-emphasis model, which is best represented by the multitarget block model (68, 69).

Vertical Integration Model

The **vertical integration model** was designed by legendary track coach Charlie Francis to be used when training sprinters. In this model the emphasis on several individual training components was manipulated to balance the intensity and volume of training targeted at these components: strength training, plyometric training, speed work, tempo work, core conditioning, and electromyostimulation (44). Fundamentally, this is an example of a parallel-emphasis model because six different training objectives are trained simultaneously with various degrees of emphasis during a given period. Specifically, the volume of training allocated to strength training, plyometric training,

Globally we can consider a continuum of loading models that range between parallel and sequential models (figure 5.4) with emphasis models containing aspects of both of these models (56, 59). If emphasis models are thought of in the context of this continuum, one could consider the variety of emphasis models that include various forms of the

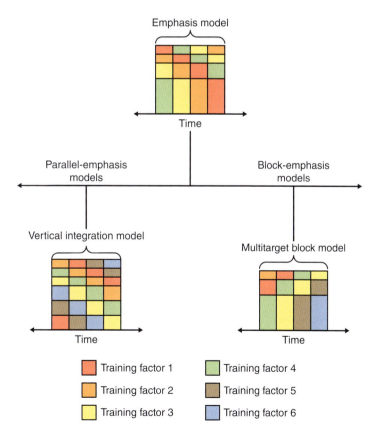

FIGURE 5.19 Example types of emphasis models: vertical integration and multitarget block modeling.

speed work, tempo work, core conditioning, and electromyostimulation are varied so that different training factors are emphasized at different times (44). For example, when maximum strength is the training focus, there is a concomitant reduction in the volume of plyometric and speed training. If there is an emphasis on speed work, there is a significant reduction in how much emphasis is placed on strength training.

Proponents of the vertical integration model suggest that the true strength of the model is that it ensures that there is a reduction in the involution effects that are typically seen with more traditional sequential models when specific training targets (i.e., strength training, plyometric training, speed work, tempo work, and core conditioning) are not consistently trained. For example, in classic sequential periodization models, the sprinter would undertake several mesocycles of lower-intensity work to build a fitness base, followed by a series of mesocycles where maximal strength is developed, and then culminating with several mesocycles that target high-speed sprinting work. When examining this sequence, there is a reduction in the training volume undertaken, and reductions in fitness and strength would be expected by the time the athlete undertakes significant speed work, which would reduce the athlete's ability to tolerate this work for more than two microcycles (44). Additionally, Francis suggested that opportunities for mastering sprinting technique are reduced because high-intensity speed work is performed for short periods (44). Conceptually, the vertical integration model accounts for these issues because the six key factors associated with preparing sprinters are consistently trained throughout the duration of the annual plan, just with varying degrees of focus.

Block-Emphasis Model

The block-emphasis model is necessary for sports that require the development of several abilities to achieve competitive success. This type of development is often necessary for team, combat, aesthetic, and some endurance (e.g., triathlon, duathlon) sports, in which athletes need to develop strength, speed, explosiveness, aerobic and anaerobic endurance, and technical and tactical abilities to achieve competitive success (69). Due to limitations of the amount of concentrated training within the classic parallel model and the inability of the sequential model to allow for the simultaneous development of multiple training targets, an alternative approach is needed for these athletes.

The block-emphasis model is one potential solution for the shortcomings of parallel and sequential models of training (55, 60, 69). This model of periodization leverages the constructs of vertical integration and horizontal sequencing of training factors to simultaneously develop several targeted capacities (55, 56). Specifically, multitargeted training blocks are used to develop two or three complementary training factors (i.e., vertical integration) (table 5.2) and then sequence the development of other training factors over time (i.e., horizontal sequencing) (72).

Issurin (72) recommends that these multitargeted training blocks be used to sequence the development of one primary and one compatible training modality along with tactical and technical training. In this scenario, 65% to 70% of the total workload would target the primary and compatible training factors, with the remaining workload being used to target tactical and technical training (30%-35%). Key to this example is that technical and tactical training receive a constant focus that is important for many sports, such as team sports, while key physical capacities are developed or maintained.

Similarly, a training plan could be developed that allocates physical training to two or three complementary training factors in addition to allocating time to technical and tactical training. In this case, the technical and tactical training could still be allocated about 30% of the total workload, with the rest of the workload being subdivided between the primary (30%), secondary (25%), and tertiary (15%) physical training targets. In this scenario, a horizontal sequence will be used to plan the progression of the training targets, and although accentuated loading will be used for the primary training target, the other two factors will be allocated maintenance loadings. For example, if the development of speed and agility is the target of the training plan, three blocks could be constructed (figure 5.20): the first targeting maximal strength, the second focusing on muscular power, and the third emphasizing speed and agility development.

The training workloads allocated to each of these blocks would be modulated depending on their emphasis while maintaining a focus on tactical and technical training. The key to constructing and sequencing the emphasis in each training block is to determine the end goal of the periodized training plan. Once this is accomplished, the primary emphasis of each training block is established and then matched with the

TABLE 5.2 Complementary Training Factors

Dominant (primary) training emphasis	Complementary training factors
Aerobic endurance	Strength–endurance training
	Maximal strength training
	Anaerobic endurance training
	Technical and tactical training (if done first)
Anaerobic endurance	Strength–endurance training
	Aerobic–anaerobic mixed endurance training
	Power endurance training
	Sprint training
	Agility training
	Explosive strength training and power training
	Muscular strength training
	Technical and tactical training (if done first)
Sprint ability	Maximal strength training
	Plyometric training
	Explosive strength training and power training
	Agility training
	Technical and tactical training (if done first)
Maximal strength	Sprint training
	Agility training
	Explosive strength training and power training
	Anaerobic endurance training
	Technical and tactical training (if done first)
Explosive strength training and power training	Sprint training
	Agility training
	Maximal strength training
	Plyometric training
	Technical and tactical training (if done first)
Technical training	Any emphasis as long as it is performed before other training factors
Tactical training	Any emphasis as long as it is performed before other training factors

Adapted by permission from G.G. Haff and E.E. Haff, "Training Integration and Periodization," in *NSCA's Guide to Program Design*, edited for the National Strength and Conditioning Association by J. Hoffman (Champaign, IL: Human Kinetics, 2012), 235; Adapted from Issurin (2008).

appropriate complementary training factors (table 5.2). For example, if maximal strength is the primary emphasis of the training block, then the primary complementary training factors would be sprinting, agility, and power training. In the example presented in figure 5.20, the complementary training factors are prescribed at a reduced workload in the maximal strength block. As the athlete moves into the block of training that primarily emphasizes muscular power development, maximal strength becomes a tertiary emphasis and speed and agility training are elevated to a secondary emphasis. Once this block of training is completed, the athlete transitions into a block of training that has a primary emphasis on speed and agility training, a secondary emphasis on power training, and a tertiary emphasis on maximal strength development.

The block-emphasis model is useful for team and combat sports because technical and tactical training must be continuously trained throughout the periodized training plan. Generally, when

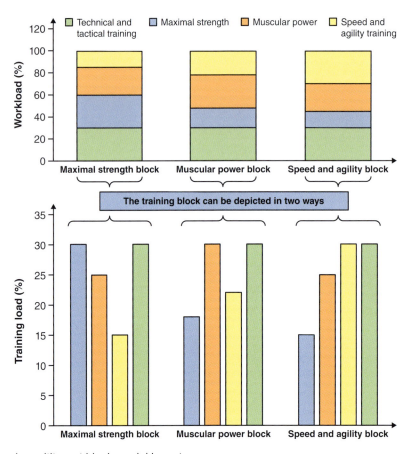

FIGURE 5.20   Example multitarget block model layout.

this model is employed, each block lasts 2 to 6 weeks, depending on where the block sits within the periodized plan and the sequence of training needed to elevate preparedness and performance.

Selecting Appropriate Periodization Models

When considering the selection of a periodization model, remember that parallel, emphasis, and sequential models are all useful. Numerous factors need to be considered when deciding which training model to employ, including the type of sport (i.e., individual versus team), the length of the competitive season, the density of the competitive schedule, the athlete's training history, and the athlete's level of development. Careful thought can help inform selection of a periodization model.

When considering **long-term athlete development (LTAD)**, it is well-documented that multilateral training is a central part of the early stages of the athlete's development (57, 90, 91). Due to the need to develop multiple training factors during this period, the parallel model of periodization would be a logical choice. As the athlete becomes more trained and progresses through the various stages of the LTAD pathway, they will move toward employing emphasis or sequential periodization models.

Support for progressing from multilateral (i.e., parallel) models toward unilateral (i.e., sequential) models can be found in the multilateral training literature (31). Coffey and Hawley (31) suggest that during the early phases of development, the skeletal muscles' adaptive responses are similar between single mode (i.e., unilateral) and concurrent (i.e., multilateral) training. As the athlete develops, divergent exercise stimuli start to stimulate exercise-specific adaptations that initiate transformation of the skeletal muscle phenotype. This coincides with an increasing need for greater training loads to stimulate a disruption in homeostasis and further stimulate adaptive responses, which results in an increased occurrence of the interference effect. Specifically, as the athlete becomes more trained, there is a muted adaptive response and performance gain with concurrent training models when compared to models that employ a single mode of training (31). When contextualized with the periodization literature, there is a clear need to undertake greater training loads to continue to stimulate physiological adaptations and performance gains as one becomes more trained. As noted earlier in this chapter, using concentrated loading blocks (i.e., accentuated loading) and sequential models of periodization (55, 153) is recommended to increase adaptive responses as athletes become more trained because higher training loads can be employed.

When the parallel, emphasis, and sequential models of periodization (59) are aligned with the hypothetical time frame of skeletal muscle adaptation (31), the untrained or novice athlete would generally employ a parallel model of periodization (figure 5.21). As the athlete progresses to a moderately trained state, there will be a need for greater training loads, which can be addressed with the application of emphasis models of periodization (59). Once the athlete becomes highly trained, sequential models may be required to stimulate the physiological adaptations necessary to further increase performance capacity. Ultimately, the need to move away from parallel periodization models becomes increasingly important as the athlete's training history lengthens.

Another factor to consider when deciding which periodization model to use is the type of sport. Although it is often thought that parallel models are necessary for team sports, the increased density and length of the competitive schedule present in modern sports (3, 39) makes the management of training loads too difficult with this periodization model. Therefore, the emphasis model of periodization is recommended for modern team sport athletes who do not have long off-seasons and are required to participate in congested competitive schedules. The plasticity of the model allows for the training emphasis to shift based on travel distance, opponent strength, and the training period or phase alignment within the season (125, 126).

Emphasis models may be useful for individual sports that require the development of multiple training targets, such as combat sports. Success in a sport such as mixed martial arts requires a variety of technical skills (i.e., fighting styles) and a diverse array of physical performance capacities (79, 102). The emphasis model is a viable method for organizing the training for these athletes. The emphasis model is also useful for tactical athletes (e.g., military, fire, police) who must maintain a high state of readiness across a vast array of physical and performance capacities and for whom there is no competitive season. By organizing training with an emphasis model and cycling through the targeted emphasis every 2 to 4 weeks, tactical athletes are better able to maintain their state of preparedness and be physically ready for unforeseen engagements.

Although the three main periodization models are often thought of in isolation, there are situations in which multiple models could be used within an annual training plan. For example, early in the training year, after time away from training (i.e., transition phase), it may be warranted to use a parallel model to develop a balanced fitness base. After completing this period of training, key

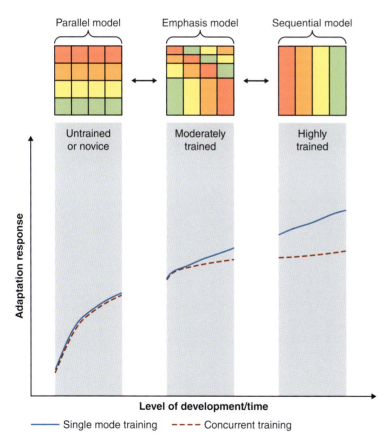

FIGURE 5.21 Hypothetical alignment of the time frame of skeletal muscle functional adaptations from concurrent training with periodization models and levels of development.

Adapted from Coffey and Hawley (2017).

training attributes, such as maximal strength or power, could be developed with sequential models prior to the initiation of the competitive season. Once in the competitive season, an emphasis model could be employed in conjunction with a monitoring program that guides the progression of the emphasized training attributes.

Summary

Periodization of the training process is a critical part of athlete development. It serves as a scaffolding framework around which training models and specific training programs are formulated to address the individual needs of the athlete or team. Although periodization provides the timelines (i.e., scaffolding) for the training process, the planning level determines the model of training (parallel, sequential, or emphasis) used to guide the training process. Classically, the parallel model of training was prescribed for all athletes, but these models appear to be most beneficial for novice or developmental athletes. As athletes become more trained, they require a greater training stimulus to continue to make physiological adaptations. To meet these requirements, sequential models of periodization (e.g., block periodization, conjugated sequential models) were developed. These models provide powerful stimuli for adaptation and have been found to be very effective, but because of their sequential nature, they may not be ideal for team or combat sport athletes. In these instances, an emphasis model (e.g., parallel emphasis or block emphasis) would allow for the development of multiple training targets and for maintaining technical and tactical training. Regardless of which periodization model is selected, all programming decisions are made based on the timelines established within the periodized plan, the training model chosen to deliver a training stimulus, and the information garnered from an integrated monitoring program.

CHAPTER 6

Multiyear and Annual Training Plans

Elite athlete performance development is based on a long-term, focused training process that engages the athlete in deliberate practice. Central to the ability to guide an athlete's development is the construction of a long-term athlete development model composed of several multiyear training plans. This developmental framework guides the athlete's training process and allows them to accumulate deliberate practice over time (55). Once the developmental framework is established, each multiyear training plan is subdivided into a series of annual training plans used to guide the athlete's development over time (29).

Conceptually, the annual training plan is foundational because it outlines the key activities that will be targeted throughout a year of training (30).

The coach's greatest challenge is to craft a plan that stimulates both physiological and psychological adaptations while managing fatigue and recovery, allowing for performance optimization at key points within the year (12). When working with less-developed athletes, the coach will establish the targeted training outcomes and construct and implement this training plan with little or no input from the athlete. As the athlete becomes more developed, the coach will consult the athlete when establishing the annual training plan objectives and structure (12). It is well-documented that when the coach engages the athlete in this key step of planning, the athlete has a sense of ownership over their training, and the collaboration serves as a motivational tool (50, 51).

Understanding long-term planning strategies and implementing them into the athlete's training process is an important part of guiding the athlete's development. As such, coaches must understand the importance of multiyear and annual training plans.

Multiyear Training Plans

Training is a long-term process that requires sustained dedication and focus. This process can take as many as 15 years and is typically broken into manageable parts to provide a clear outline of the proposed direction for the training process (38, 73). The longest planning structure used in the periodization process is the **multiyear training plan**, which contains a series of annual training plans linked together to guide the athlete's training toward specific developmental and performance outcomes (20, 27, 29, 44, 46, 64, 71, 73, 87). Traditionally, multiyear training plans are comprised of two to four interlinked annual training plans, with the quadrennial training plan being used most often to structure the training process between two successive Olympic Games (27, 46, 71, 87). In North America, quadrennial training plans also have been used with high-school (46) and collegiate athletes (27) due to their alignment with the academic calendar.

Regardless of the length of the multiyear training plan, it serves as a directional guide but does not provide a finite description of the programming strategies employed (64). Olbrect (64) suggests that long-term competition goals (e.g., achieve a top 3 placing in 2 years), motivational goals (e.g., national team selection), and technical goals and conditioning objectives should be included in the multiyear training plan. The multiyear training plan has been presented as a performance pathway, where the athlete's development from identification toward elite performance is outlined.

A good example of the application of a multiyear training plan is provided by Jeffreys (46), who outlines a quadrennial training plan for a high-school soccer player (figure 6.1). In this 4-year plan, each year targets different objectives, which are sequenced so optimal performance is achieved in the last year of the plan. The first year of the multiyear plan targets foundational development, or general preparation; the second year focuses on continued development; the third year shifts toward performance development (i.e., sport-specific preparation); and the fourth year targets performance optimization (i.e., competition). As the athlete progresses through each year of the plan, training is expanded to focus on more soccer-specific outcomes. This progression aligns

Goals

Year 1 (freshman): to develop key generic movement patterns associated with soccer
Year 2 (sophomore): to develop key combinations of movements associated with soccer
Year 3 (junior): to develop key movement patterns associated with soccer, along with the ability to read and react to soccer-specific stimuli
Year 4 (senior): to optimize movement ability in soccer-specific situations

FIGURE 6.1 Example multiyear training plan for a high-school soccer player.
Adapted from Jeffreys (2008).

with the development model presented by Balyi (5), in which the training focus shifts and the level of training increases in each year of the quadrennial training plan.

Regardless of how it is organized, a multiyear training plan provides an overview of the athlete's intended developmental pathway (29). The direction of this pathway is based on forecasting the athlete's development and can be modified to meet the athlete's rate of technical development or maturation at each stage of the plan (29). Ultimately, a series of multiyear plans can be used to organize the athlete's career (83) and should be considered in the context of a long-term athlete development (LTAD) model or performance pathway (29).

Long-Term Athlete Development Models

A LTAD model is a series of multiyear training plans that is used to chart the athlete's development toward elite performance (6-8, 17, 29). Ford et al. (17) present various periods of development, and Haff (29) proposed that these can serve as foundations for syncing LTAD with the periodization of training. Haff (29) proposed a LTAD model that integrates the athlete's **chronological age**, **general training age**, and **specific training age** with various developmental targets (figure 6.2). While the model by Haff (29) presents a basic framework for integrating periodization and LTAD, some youth athletes will be *early maturers* and others may be *late maturers* and the time frames presented in figure 6.2 may be modified depending on the athlete's maturation rate.

The basic model presented in figure 6.2 contains five multiyear training plans that align with various levels of development. Starting with the onset of training, the primary emphasis in the first multiyear training plan is to establish basic movement literacy, often referred to as **FUNdamental training**, and deemphasize competition (6-8, 17, 29). This multiyear plan contains four annual training plans for boys and three for girls. Each successive annual training plan within the first

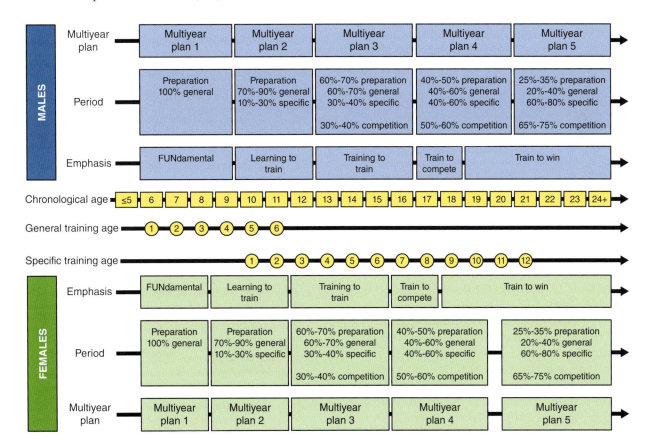

FIGURE 6.2 Haff's model for integrating periodization modeling and long-term athlete development.

Adapted by permission from G.G. Haff, "Periodization Strategies for Youth Development," in *Strength and Conditioning for the Young Athlete: Science and Application,* edited by R. Lloyd and J.L. Oliver (London, England: Routledge, 2019), permission conveyed through Copyright Clearance Center, Inc.

multiyear plan is structured based on the principles of motor learning to advance the developmental process (29).

The movement literacy or basic movement competency developed in the first multiyear training plan serves as the foundation for the subsequent multiyear training plan and influences the decisions made when determining the direction of the athlete's progression. In the second multiyear training plan, more sport-specific training is incorporated through technical skill development and developmental competitions (29). The ratio of the percentage of time spent focused on training to time spent focused on competition will vary across the multiyear plan, starting at 90:10 the first year, 80:20 the second year, and 70:30 in the third and fourth years (29). These ratios are guidelines; the exact ratio will depend on the athlete's sport, training experience, technical competency, and stage of maturation. Regardless, it is important to remember that practice (i.e., training) is the primary goal of the second multiyear training plan.

As the athlete moves into the third multiyear training plan, competition becomes increasingly important. However, planning too many competitions will reduce the amount of time dedicated to training, which can negatively affect the athlete's overall development (8, 29). During this period, about 60% of the athlete's time should be spent on training and 40% should be spent on competition. Remember that during this multiyear training plan the athlete's development is still a priority, and competitive success is not the primary goal (29).

At the onset of the fourth multiyear training plan, there is a major shift toward achieving competitive success. This plan emphasizes sport-specific fitness, skill development, and technical and tactical development (8). Generally, the ratio of the percentage of time dedicated to training and competition will vary between 40:60 and 60:40 so the athlete can develop the requisite physiological adaptations and physical skills necessary to optimize competitive performance (29).

After completing the fourth multiyear training plan, the athlete will continue to engage in multiyear training plans for the duration of their participation in sport. At this stage, the athlete spends 25% to 35% of their time on training and 65% to 75% on competition (29), but this ratio is likely to vary depending on the athlete's ever-changing physical status and their competitive schedule.

Although figure 6.2 presents a viable model for syncing LTAD with multiyear periodization models, it does not provide the modes and methods of training that should be used with the athlete (29). The success of any LTAD plan is based on the individualization of the coaching process. Therefore, the multiyear training plan must be constantly reevaluated and optimized to meet the athlete's specific needs and rate of development.

Annual Training Plan Structures

The **annual training plan** is an important level of planning used to guide the athlete's training across 1 year (12, 19). Although it is typically aligned with the calendar year, this may not always be the case. For example, the annual training plan for a youth athlete who participates in school-based sports may be established based on their academic schedule (29, 46). However, the most influential factor for the timeline of any annual training plan is the athlete's competitive schedule (12, 19).

Fundamentally, an annual training plan is subdivided into smaller, more manageable periods (71) to allow better management of the training process (12). Based on the competitive schedule, the annual training plan is divided into a macrocycle or series of macrocycles, which will be further divided into periods and phases that align with specific times and types of training.

The Macrocycle

While the **macrocycle,** when it contains one competitive season, is synonymous with the annual training plan (30, 60, 63), it is plausible that some athletes will engage in multiple competitive seasons within their annual training plans (30, 32). To account for this possibility, Haff (30, 32) suggests that it is more appropriate to consider the macrocycle in the context of preparing for and participating in a competitive season when determining how many macrocycles are contained within the annual training plan.

Macrocycles are generally divided into distinct **periods** and **phases** that are structured and sequenced to guide the training process (30, 32, 55). Traditionally, there are three periods—preparation, competition, and transition—which can be further subdivided into phases. As the athlete progresses through each period in the macrocycle, specific adaptations are targeted by manipulating specific training activities to align with the changing focus of each phase of the training period (30).

Preparation Period

The **preparation period** (or preparatory period) is one of the most important parts of the annual training plan because it lays the foundation for successful competitive performance (12, 29, 71). Specifically, this time is used to develop the athlete's physiological, psychological, technical, and tactical abilities. A hallmark of this period is higher volumes and lower intensities of training performed with nonspecific training methods that build the athlete's work capacity, thereby allowing them to better handle higher-intensity training and competitions later in the annual training plan. If inadequate emphasis is placed on the preparation period, the athlete will not develop the required training base to handle higher-intensity training, which increases their injury risk (23) and reduces their potential to maximize performance capacity (12).

Depending on the structure of the annual plan (e.g., mono-cycle, bi-cycle, tri-cycle, or multipeak), the preparation period lasts 3 to 6 months (11, 12). This period is generally two times as long as the competitive period with individual sports (e.g., cycling, weightlifting, speed skating). It is shorter, but not less than 2 to 3 months, for team sports (e.g., soccer, American football, hockey, volleyball). The length and structure of the preparation period are highly specific to each sport, and this period will be further subdivided into general preparation and specific preparation phases.

General Preparation Phase Characteristically, the **general preparation phase** has the highest volume of training performed with lower intensity to develop general motor abilities and skills through diverse training means (12, 29, 34, 43, 60). The key focus of this phase is to increase work capacity and general physical preparation (12) with the use of general physical training (GPT) (see chapter 3). Due to the larger training loads in this phase, one of the main outcomes is establishing a high level of physical conditioning, which improves the athlete's physiological and psychological capacities to undertake and tolerate training and competition.

As the athlete progresses through this phase, there is an increase in the workload to increase working capacity. The intensity of training is also important, but it is not a primary emphasis (12). Bompa and Haff (12) suggest that the amount of time dedicated to intense training should not exceed 40% of the total training time during this phase of training, especially with novice or developmental athletes. Although this general recommendation is useful, the actual amount of intense training in this phase is largely dictated by the athlete's overall level of development and ability to tolerate training.

Regardless of the athlete's level of development, this phase of training results in marked increases in fatigue due to elevated workloads. As fatigue increases, the athlete's level of preparedness will decrease, resulting in suppressed performance capacity and a potential increase in risk of injury (2, 67, 72). Due to the negative effect of high fatigue on technical performance capacity, the athlete's ability to perform complex technical skills will be reduced and relatively unstable (12). As a result, competitions should not be undertaken during this phase and focus should be on developing the physiological foundation and establishing a high work capacity, which will be leveraged in later periods of training.

Specific Preparation Phase The second phase of the preparation period is the **specific preparation phase**, which is designed to capitalize on the physiological and psychological attributes established during the general preparation phase (12, 29). As with the general preparation phase, there is a focus on continuing to increase the athlete's working capacity to further enhance the foundation for the competitive period. Central to this phase is sport-specific physical training (SSPT) (see chapter 3), in which the athlete focuses on sport-specific motor and technical abilities and develops sport-performance preparedness prior to the competitive period (34). There is still an emphasis on high workloads, but the activities in those workloads shift to include more sport-specific training methods and an increased emphasis on sport-specific skills and techniques (12). Specific exercises are integrated into this training phase to target the bioenergetics, prime movers, movement patterns, and technical requirements of the sport. Conceptually, these exercises link the physical capacities developed in the general preparation phase and the physical, technical, and tactical attributes that underpin the performances required in the competitive period (12).

There must be some continued focus on GPT to cultivate and maintain the general physical attributes established during the general preparation phase. As the athlete progresses through this phase, there is a concomitant increase in the amount of specialized training, which translates into progressive increases in performance capacities and overall preparedness and elevations in actual athletic performance. Although competition is not a focus during this phase, exhibitions or "friendlies" (i.e., inter-team scrimmages) can be integrated into the later stages of the phase to provide a means for evaluating the athlete's technical and tactical preparation prior to the competitive period. Data garnered from these events should be used to modify and fine-tune the training process to better prepare the athlete for the competitive period.

The typical sequence of phases within the preparation period is shown in figure 6.3 (34). The time dedicated to each phase largely depends on the athlete's overall level of development and the number of macrocycles in the annual training plan. It is widely accepted that there is an inverse relationship between the amount of time spent targeting general preparation and the athlete's level of development (figure 6.4) (43). For example, a youth athlete in the early stages of their long-term athlete development plan would dedicate more training time to the general preparation phase (29). Conversely, more-developed athletes will reduce the time they spend in the general preparation phase and dedicate more time to the specific preparation phase (29, 43).

Although the classic preparation period sequence of general to specific preparation phases is commonly used, especially with novice and beginner athletes, an alternative approach to structuring the preparation period is to simultaneously undertake GPT and SSPT by targeting exercises associated with both the general and specific preparation phases. In this scenario, as the athlete moves through the preparation period, there can be a progressive increase in the amount of time

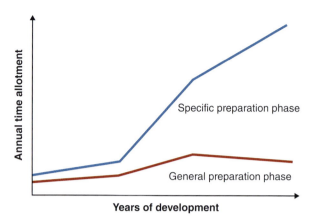

FIGURE 6.4 Relationship between the general and sport-specific preparation phases and the time in the annual training plan dedicated to each phase.

Adapted by permission from V. Issurin, *Block Periodization 2: Fundamental Concepts and Training Design* (Michigan, USA: Ultimate Athlete Concepts, 2013).

dedicated to SSPT and a progressive decrease in the amount of time dedicated to GPT as the athlete progresses through the preparation period (figure 6.5).

A novice athlete could dedicate 70% to 75% of their training time to general training exercises during the general preparation phase and reduce the time allotted to this training to 30% to 40% during the sport-specific phase (54). Conversely, an advanced athlete could spend 40% to 50% of their training time during the general preparation phase on general training exercises and reduce this to 30% to 40% during the sport-specific phase (54). Regardless of how these phases are sequenced, the goal of the preparation period is to set the

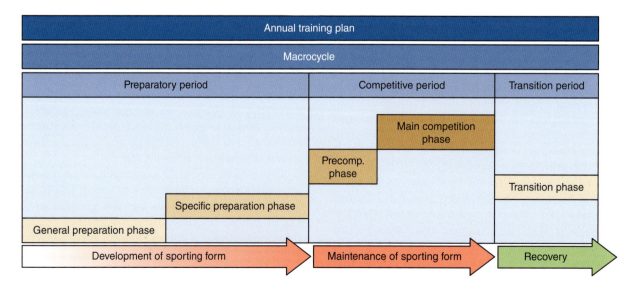

FIGURE 6.3 Sequence of the periods and phases in the annual training plan.

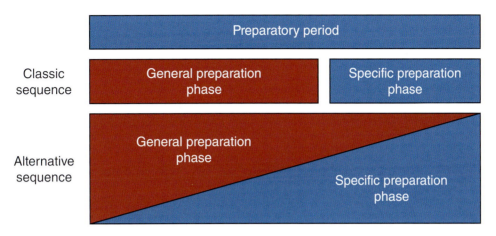

FIGURE 6.5 Sequence of general and specific preparatory phases.

foundation for the competition period in which competitive success becomes the primary focus.

Competition Period

In the **competition period** (or competitive period), the hard work undertaken during the preparation period is translated into competitive performance. This period contains the targeted competitions and requires the athlete to continue to elevate or maintain their sport-specific fitness, enhance the psychological traits that underpin performance, perfect and consolidate technique, and perfect tactical maneuvers (4, 12).

As the athlete progresses through this period, training intensity increases while volume decreases (12). In strength–power or speed-based sports (e.g., sprinting, sprint cycling, weightlifting, throwing, powerlifting), training intensity can increase dramatically while training volume is progressively decreased compared to the preparation period. With endurance sports (e.g., running, cycling, swimming, cross-country skiing, rowing), training volume can be maintained or slightly reduced compared to the preparation period. During the competitive microcycle (i.e., the week of competition), intensity and volume will be manipulated according to contemporary tapering strategies to reduce fatigue and elevate performance (see chapter 12). For team sports that do not target a true peak during the bulk of the competition period, the optimization of performance will be targeted by manipulating training volume and intensity to ensure that physical attributes are maintained and fatigue is reduced prior to each competition. The ultimate peak will be reserved for the championship match at the end of the season.

Across the competitive period, two of the main goals are to elevate the athlete's preparedness and increase their performance capacity. The ability to effectively manage training during the competitive period is largely linked to an effective monitoring program (see chapter 11), which is used to inform the programming decisions and ensure that the athlete is optimally prepared for each competition (24, 68, 69). If the training plan is appropriately monitored and individualized, the athlete will optimize their performance at the appropriate time. A central concern during this period is the removal of too much training load, which can result in reduced performance capacity. This is particularly concerning as it is difficult to restore performance capacity as sudden increases in training volume and intensity can result in significant amounts of fatigue that negatively affect performance capacity. Additionally, if training loads are reduced too significantly during the competition period, there can also be a significant increase in injury risk (24, 25). Although historically the ability to modulate training load and performance has been considered an art form based on science (12), recent technological advances in athlete monitoring have allowed coaches to make more informed decisions about the training process and better manage training loads.

The overall length of the competitive season is sport dependent. Long seasons are typically seen in team sports for which leagues establish the length of the competitive period. For example, in the Union of European Football Associations, the competitive season runs from July through May of the next year (11 months), leaving only 1 month for the off-season and preparation period (85). Super Rugby requires teams to contest 16 games (exclusive of finals) between February and July or August (i.e., 6-7 months) (68, 69). Individual sports, on the other hand, provide the coach with a bit more freedom to determine the length of the competitive period and which competitions are targeted (12). For example, a weightlifting coach could strategically select four competitions from all of the available competitions in a calendar year (10, 48, 74). In this scenario the coach will target one or two priority competitions, such as a national championship and world championship, within the annual training plan and two minor competitions that serve as performance checks and are interspersed between these two competitions (48). With strategic thinking the coach can select these minor competitions so that they can individualize the lengths of the various training periods in each macrocycle, thus increasing the chances of optimal performances at the major competitions (48).

While individual sports often allow the coach greater freedom in selecting competitions, higher-level athletes may be required to participate in specific qualifying events to compete in the Olympic Games. For example, in Olympic combat sports, such as taekwondo, required competitions are undertaken during various periods within the annual training plan when seeking to qualify for the Olympic Games. French (22) reports that between 2011 and 2012, the British taekwondo athletes had four competitive periods leading into preselected major competitions (i.e., British Open, French Open, German and Dutch Open, and European Championships) before specific preparation for the London Olympic Games. In addition to these main competitive tournaments, several other tournaments were used as part of the lead-up to the targeted competition.

All competition periods are based on the start date of the season and should be constructed based on these considerations:

- The overall length of the competition period
- The number of competitions in the period
- The time intervals between each competition
- The travel requirements of each competition (e.g., Do you have to fly or travel long distances?)
- The qualifying criteria, which may dictate which competitions are required and the locations of the competitions
- The time required for specialized preparation before the targeted competition
- The time needed for recovery and regeneration

Once these factors are considered, the competitive period is generally divided into the precompetition and main competition phases (12).

Precompetition Phase The **precompetition phase** links the specific preparation phase and the main competition phase. It generally contains exhibitions or friendlies in which technical and tactical aspects that underpin competitive success are trialed. For example, this may be a time when an athlete tests a new nutritional strategy or weight-cutting method to determine how this affects their performance. In team sports, the coach may shift the competitive lineup to trial new combinations to determine which athletes work best together with certain tactical plans. Ultimately, this phase of training uses competition as a training tool; competitive success is not the primary targeted outcome. This phase provides the coach with objective feedback about the athlete's training level and state of preparedness for the main competitive phase of the annual training plan (12). These competitions should be integrated into the training process, do not require alterations to the training plan to maximize performance, and are simply used to fine-tune training to prepare for the main competition phase.

Main Competition Phase The primary goal of the **main competition phase** is to maximize preparedness at key times to optimize competitive performance. This phase of the annual training plan contains all the competitive engagements the athlete is required to contest. In team sports, the actual structure of each microcycle contained within this phase largely depends on the time between competitions as well as league requirements for the allocation of days off from training. For individual sports, the structure is somewhat easier to construct due to the ability to target fewer competitions or design shorter competitive periods. Regardless, sport-specific training methods are the central component of the training interventions in this phase of the annual training plan. In addition, the athlete's physical performance characteristics are maintained or, ideally, elevated across this phase (4).

Typically, the training volume contained in this phase will be 50% to 75% lower than in the preparation period for sports that require speed, strength, power, or technical mastery (12). In concert with a decreasing training volume throughout the phase, there is a gradual increase in the intensity of training, which usually reaches its highest level 2 to 3 weeks prior to the main competition. Due to the higher intensities of training and the stress of competition, the athlete's stress levels will generally be elevated during this phase (11, 12). Although stress levels generally increase across the phase, they tend to fluctuate in response to stressful activities, such as competition; intense training; and short periods of unloading or recovery. Therefore, when constructing the main competition phase, it is important to ensure that recovery and unloading are strategically aligned with these periods of higher stress. Additionally, if a comprehensive monitoring program is integrated into the training process, modifications to the planned training loads can be made to ensure that the athlete's stress levels are well managed.

The coach should strive to arrange the athlete's competitive schedule based on an increasing level of importance leading into the targeted competition (12). For example, a coach for an Australian national-class weightlifter might have their athlete target the Australian Open in March, the state championship in July, and the Australian National Championships in September. Structuring the competitive season is relatively easy for individual sport athletes, but it is much more challenging with team sport athletes for which the team's league establishes the overall competition schedule. Another strategy that can be employed is to intersperse higher-level competitions with lower-level competitions to allow the athlete to train through (i.e., continue to train without alteration) some competitions and focus their efforts on the main targeted competitions. This strategy is commonly used by Division I football programs in the United States in which lower-level competitions are strategically placed throughout the competitive season.

One of the most important considerations in the competitive period is that the athlete cannot be taken to a true peak for every competition. A true peak can be held for only 8 to 14 days (see chapter 12), and although performance is elevated during this time, the athlete does lose fitness as a result of the reduced training load associated with the tapering process (31). Typically, after a true peak is achieved, the athlete must return to a new preparation period to rebuild their fitness and work capacity. With many sports, especially team sports, a peak is planned only for the main targeted competitions (e.g., championship, Olympics). For all other competitions, the athlete will continue to maintain their training and the coach will manipulate key training variables to modulate the athlete's preparedness in accordance with several key factors, including the level of competition, location of the competition, days between competitions, and number of time zones crossed (68, 69).

Transition Period

The **transition period** is a bridge between macrocycles, annual training plans, or multiyear training structures (12, 15, 29, 60, 71). This important period is used to reduce physiological and psychological fatigue and prepare the athlete for subsequent training periods. Dick (15) suggests that when used to link between annual training plans, this period of regeneration should be constructed to recharge the athlete so that they are prepared for the subsequent training period. Generally, this period is recommended to last between 2 to 6 weeks (15, 54), and under normal circumstances it will not extend beyond this time frame (12). Generally, there are three basic approaches to constructing the transition period: employment of passive rest, employment of active rest, or some combination of passive and active rest (12).

Passive Rest Some athletes and coaches believe that the transition period should be a time where there is a complete cessation in training (i.e., passive rest) so that the athlete can mentally and physically recover from the training that occurred prior to the transition period (65, 75). While there may be some instances where the complete cessation of training during the transition period is warranted, such as major injury, this practice is generally discouraged because of the significant maladaptive responses associated with suddenly ceasing training (9, 11, 15).

A complete cessation of training (i.e., passive rest) during the transition period can cause significant detraining effects during the 2 to 6 weeks typically employed during this period (61, 62). When highly trained athletes who are used to frequent training with large training loads abruptly reduce or completely cease training, they may experience **detraining syndrome** (82), which is sometimes referred to as Entlastungssyndrom by German scientists (39, 42) or as *exercise abstinence syndrome* or *exercise dependency syndrome* (3, 53, 80). This type of detraining can occur when an athlete intentionally ceases training (e.g., in retirement) or has to stop training due to a major injury (53). The following are symptoms of detraining syndrome (12):

- Gastric disturbances
- Headaches
- Insomnia
- Dizziness and fainting
- Anxiety and depression

- Sensation or occurrence of cardiac arrhythmia
- Loss of appetite
- Nonsystematic precordial disturbances
- Extrasystolia and palpitations
- Profuse sweating

These maladaptive responses are not considered pathological and are reversible if training is resumed within 2 weeks of the cessation of training. If, however, the time frame without training is extended to greater than 2 weeks, these maladaptive responses will persist for longer durations. While these responses often occur with the cessation of training, the severity of these responses will be highly specific to the individual athlete (12).

Active Rest The second strategy for constructing the transition period is active rest, in which training volume and workloads are reduced to induce physical and psychological recovery and restoration while maintaining a minimum training stimulus. Typically, this strategy contains low-level physical activities that ensure the athlete is ready for subsequent training periods (21, 49, 60). Even though the athlete is continuing to train, the reduced training loads will not provide enough training stimulus to maintain the physiological adaptations and the level of performance established prior to the initiation of the transition period (12, 49). Therefore, it is critical that a retraining period follows all transition periods to restore the athlete's physical performance capacities. Generally, it is recommended that the duration of the retraining period is similar to or slightly longer than the transition period (49). Typically, the longer the transition period, the greater the emphasis will be on the general preparation phase in the subsequent preparation period.

Detraining and the Transition Period Whether passive or active rest strategies are used in the transition period, a degree of detraining will occur. The magnitude of detraining will be affected by the duration of the transition period. Short-term detraining, which typically lasts less than 4 weeks, can result in significant reductions in cardiorespiratory (61, 76), neuromuscular (61, 76, 77), and metabolic (61) capacities, which can affect the athlete's performance capabilities. As the detraining period extends beyond 4 weeks, the negative effects of detraining increase because there is a greater loss of the physiological adaptations that underpin performance (table 6.1) (61, 62, 75).

In short-term detraining, endurance athletes generally display a 4% to 25% reduction in time to exhaustion and endurance performance (61, 62). These reductions appear to be related to a rapid decline in cardiorespiratory fitness (41) or maximal aerobic capacity (14, 16, 61, 84). In fact, within 4 days of detraining, maximal aerobic capacity can be reduced by 4% (16, 84), by 3 weeks of detraining it can be reduced by 7% (14), and by 4 weeks of detraining it can be reduced by 14% (61). If the detraining period extends to 8 weeks, the athlete's maximal aerobic capacity can be decreased by as much as 20% of pretraining values (62). These reductions in maximal aerobic capacity are likely related to reductions in blood volume, stroke volume, and maximal cardiac output (table 6.1). Bompa and Haff (12) suggest that the physiological responses to detraining are proportional to the athlete's training status, with highly trained endurance athletes demonstrating greater maladaptive response to detraining. Additionally, these maladaptive responses seem to progressively increase as the duration of the detraining period is extended.

The athlete's ability to express high levels of strength and power can also be negatively affected by periods of short- and long-term detraining. When detraining lasts 3 weeks or less, there are small reductions in upper-body (decrease of 0.5%-2.0%) and lower-body (decrease of 0.9%-1.6%) strength (26, 40). If the duration of detraining is extended to 4 weeks, there can be a 6% to 10% reduction in maximal strength (36, 45) and a 14% to 17% reduction in the ability to express maximal power outputs (36). If the duration of detraining is extended to 8 weeks, there will be a continued reduction in performance (additional decrease of 11%-12%) (36, 61, 62). Overall, the reductions in strength and power performance may be related to preferential atrophy of the type II muscle fibers (40, 78) and a reduced neural drive (1, 35-37).

It appears that training status exerts an influence on the magnitude of the performance decline associated with detraining (12). Highly trained individuals demonstrate a greater rate and magnitude of strength loss when compared to lesser-trained individuals. Lesser-trained individuals appear to be able to maintain their strength and power performance capacities for 2 to 3 weeks of detraining, whereas highly trained individuals appear to exhibit significant reductions in strength and power performance in this same period (40, 52, 59).

In some instances, short-term detraining is something that cannot be avoided. For example, in professional sports, short periods (≤2 weeks) away from competition are mandated due to collective

TABLE 6.1 Effects of Short-Term and Long-Term Detraining

Physiological and performance factors	Detraining characteristics	Duration of detraining	
		Less than 4 weeks	More than 4 weeks
Cardiorespiratory	Blood volume	↓	↓
	Maximal cardiac output	↓	↓
	Maximal heart rate	↑	↑
	Maximal oxygen uptake	↓	↓
	Maximal ventilatory volume	↓	↓
	Mean blood pressure	↑	↑
	Oxygen pulse	↓	↓
	Stroke volume during exercise	↓	↓
	Submaximal heart rate	↑	↑
	Ventilatory equivalent	↑	↑
	Ventricular dimension/mass	↓	↓
Skeletal muscle	Arterial-venous oxygen differences	⇔	↓
	Capillary density	↓	↓
	EMG activity	↓	↓
	Fiber type distribution	Altered	Altered
	Glycogen synthase activity	↓	↓
	Mean fiber cross-sectional area	↓	↓
	Mitochondrial ATP production	↓	n/a
	Oxidative enzyme activities	↓	↓
	Type II:I area ratio	↓	↓
Metabolic characteristics	Adrenaline-stimulated lipolysis	↓	↓
	Bicarbonate level	↓	↓
	High-density lipoprotein cholesterol	↓	↓
	Insulin-mediated glucose uptake	↓	↓
	Lactate threshold	↓	↓
	Low-density lipoprotein cholesterol	↑	↑
	Maximal respiratory exchange ratio	↑	↑
	Muscle GLUT4 protein content	↓	↓
	Muscle glycogen level	↓	↓
	Muscle lipoprotein lipase activity	↓	↓
	Postprandial lipemia	↑	n/a
	Submaximal blood lactate	↑	↑
	Submaximal respiratory exchange ratio	↑	↑
Performance	Endurance performance	↓	↓
	Strength and power performance	↓	↓
	Sprint time (10, 15, and 20 m)	↑	↑
	Sprint interval performance time	↑⇔	↑
	Change of direction time	↑⇔	↑
	Body mass	↑⇔	↑
	Body fat	↑⇔	↑
	Lean body mass	↓⇔	↓

Notes: ↑ = increased, ↓ = decreased, ⇔ = no change; n/a = no data available; EMG = electromyographic; ATP = adenosine triphosphate; GLUT4 = glucose transporter-4.

Adapted by permission from T.O. Bompa and G.G. Haff, *Periodization: Theory and Methodology of Training* (Champaign, IL: Human Kinetics, 2009), 159.

bargaining agreements, and in team sports, such as soccer (70) or Australian football (13), short detraining periods (≤2 weeks) often occur around holidays. Depending on the magnitude and intensity of the training that occurs prior to the detraining period, there can be a significant reduction in repeated sprint ability, which can significantly decrease performance capacity (70). If, however, the training prior to this short period of detraining is significant, the magnitude of the maladaptive response will be markedly less (13).

The coach must carefully consider where the transition period will occur. Transition periods typically occur after the completion of a main competitive phase, and ideally should last 2 to 6 weeks (12). Passive rest may be employed during the first week, especially if the athlete has injuries. Active rest should be implemented in the second week and progressively increased across the transition period. During the active rest phase of the transition period, the athlete can participate in activities that are not typically used in their training at low volumes and intensities. For example, a basketball player might use volleyball as a transition activity, or a runner might use cycling. An alternative approach would be to gradually shift toward the athlete's typical training modes across these weeks and slowly increase the volume and intensity of training to prepare the athlete for the subsequent preparation period.

Although the transition period is often thought of as a recovery and regeneration period, it is also a time during which the coach can plan. For example, this time can be used to critically analyze the previous macrocycle or annual training plan and benchmark the performance and developmental goals against those outlined in the multiyear training plan. In addition, the coach and the athlete should meet to discuss the athlete's goals and training objectives for the next macrocycle of the annual training plan and discuss any additional items related to the athlete's training process.

Seasons Although period (i.e., *preparation period, competition period,* and *transition period*) and phase (i.e., *general preparation phase, specific preparation phase, precompetition phase, and main competition phase*) terminology is common in the periodization literature, most coaches use terms such as *off-season, preseason, in-season,* and *postseason* to delineate the key parts of the annual training plan (28, 29). Figure 6.6 aligns various phrases with the terminology commonly used within collegiate and professional sports.

For example, the general preparation phase aligns with the off-season, while the specific preparation phase aligns with the preseason. The competitive period aligns with the in-season, and the transition phase aligns with the postseason. Regardless of the terminology used to subdivide the annual plan, it is important the annual plan's structure is well thought out and designed to maximize or optimize performance at key times.

Classification of Annual Training Plans

Although numerous items can be included in the annual training plan, a basic template might include

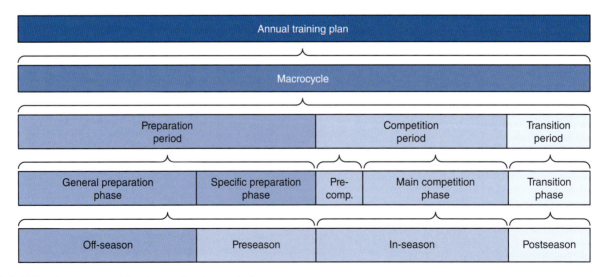

FIGURE 6.6 Relationship of periodization periods to seasons.

Adapted by permission from G.G. Haff, "Periodization Strategies for Youth Development," in *Strength and Conditioning for the Young Athlete: Science and Application*, edited by R. Lloyd and J.L. Oliver (London, England: Routledge, 2019), permission conveyed through Copyright Clearance Center, Inc.

only the competitive calendar and a breakdown of the various periods and phases. A more extensive annual training plan includes a detailed competitive calendar and defined periods and phases of training aligned with training factor emphasis, nutritional goals, psychological training, recovery strategies, medical screenings, performance testing, peaking index, and the holiday schedule. Regardless of the level of detail, the annual training plan should be used to create a visual guide of the athlete's training across the training year.

Even though an annual training plan can be structured multiple ways, the number of competitive seasons will largely dictate the number of macrocycles in the annual training plan. The structure of the annual training plan also takes into consideration the athlete's level of development and individual needs and the requirements of the targeted sport. These considerations affect the overall time frames dedicated to the various periods in the annual training plan. Traditionally, the three most common structures are mono-, bi-, or tri-cycle annual training plans.

Mono-Cycle Annual Training Plans

Matveyev presented a basic annual training plan designed to target one major competitive period (34, 57, 79) (figure 6.7). An annual training plan that employs a single macrocycle to target performance during one major competitive period is typically referred to as a ***mono-cycle annual training plan*** (12). Mono-cycle annual training plans are often seen in seasonal sports, such as cycling, triathlon, and most team sports. The mono-cycle is subdivided into preparation, competitive, and transition periods (figure 6.8) based on the competitive period and the individual competitions therein. The annual training plan will be further subdivided into five phases: general preparation, specific preparation, precompetition, main competition, and transition (figure 6.9). When looking at this figure, note that as the focus on the general preparation phase decreases, there is a concomitant increase in the focus on specific preparation.

The time dedicated to the general preparation phase is predicated by numerous factors, including how long the transition period was in the previous annual training plan, the overall training age of the athlete, and the targeted sport (12). For example, a very short general preparation phase may be integrated into a soccer player's annual training plan (56), and in some instances this phase may be completely removed (11).

After the specific preparation phase, the athlete transitions into the precompetition phase in which there is an increased emphasis on sport-specific preparation for competition. This is accomplished by shifting training toward sport-specific activities and exhibition matches or friendlies. These events prepare the athlete for the main competition phase,

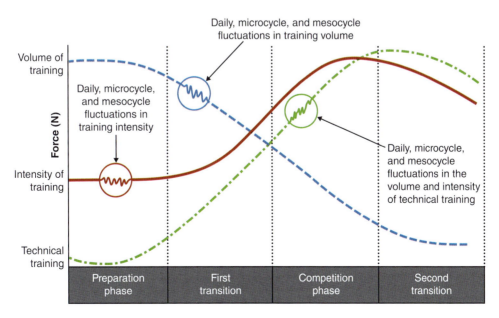

FIGURE 6.7 Matveyev's classic model of an annual training plan.

Adapted by permission from G.G. Haff and E.E. Haff, "Training Integration and Periodization," in *NSCA's Guide to Program Design,* edited for the National Strength and Conditioning Association by J. Hoffman (Champaign, IL: Human Kinetics, 2012), 223. Adapted from M.H. Stone and H. St. O'Bryant, *Weight Training: A Scientific Approach,* 2nd ed., copyright © 1987 by Burgess.

Example mono-cycle annual training plans

Model		Month 1	2	3	4	5	6	7	8	9	10	11	12
M1	Period	Preparation						Competition					Transition
	Phase	General preparation				Specific preparation		Precompetition		Main competition			Transition
M2	Period	Preparation							Competition				Transition
	Phase	General preparation					Specific preparation		Precompetition		Main competition		Transition
M3	Period	Preparation						Competition					Transition
	Phase	General preparation					Specific preparation			Precompetition	Main competition		Transition

Example bi-cycle annual training plans

Model		Month 1	2	3	4	5	6	7	8	9	10	11	12
B1	Period	Preparation				Competition		Transition	Preparation	Competition			Transition
	Phase	General preparation		Specific preparation		Precompetition	Main competition	Transition	Specific preparation	Pre-competition	Main competition		Transition
B2	Period	Preparation	Competition			Preparation				Competition		Transition	
	Phase	Specific preparation	Pre-competition	Main competition		General preparation		Specific preparation		Main competition		Transition	

Example tri-cycle annual training plans

Model		Month 1	2	3	4	5	6	7	8	9	10	11	12
T1	Period	Preparation	Competition		Transition	Preparation	Competition	Transition	Preparation	Competition		Transition	
	Phase	General preparation	Pre-competition	Main competition	Transition	Specific preparation	Main competition	Transition	Specific preparation	Main competition		Transition	
T2	Period	Preparation		Competition		Preparation		Competition	Transition	Preparation	Competition		Transition
	Phase	General preparation	Specific preparation	Main competition		General preparation	Specific preparation	Main competition	Transition	Specific preparation	Main competition		Transition

FIGURE 6.8 Mono-, bi-, and tri-cycle annual training plan structures. There are infinite sequential structures that can be used to craft an annual training plan; the models presented here are only examples. All annual training plans must be dictated by the individual athlete's level of development and training needs.

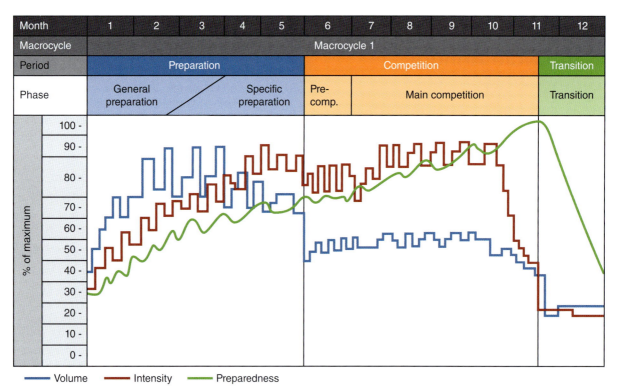

FIGURE 6.9 Example of a basic mono-cycle annual training plan.

in which competitive performance becomes the primary emphasis of training. Prior to the most important competition of the year (usually the championship match), there will typically be a 2-week tapering period in which there is a reduction in training volume and a maintenance of training intensity (see chapter 12). The goal of the taper is to remove fatigue and elevate preparedness to stimulate a performance supercompensation at the key competitive engagement (12). After the completion of a taper, a transition period is often undertaken prior to refocusing training on a preparation period.

The coach can use a template to organize a mono-cycle annual training plan. Figure 6.10 is an example of an annual plan for a high-school or collegiate American football team. The top part of the template notes the months and the days. Unlike traditional annual training plans that list only the week-ending date (11), the template in figure 6.10 allows for the exact day of the competition to be highlighted and color coded to indicate a home game (green) or an away game (red). Another color (black) can be used for school holidays and another for other important events (purple).

Once the key competition and holiday dates are highlighted on the annual training plan template, the individual macrocycle can be defined. There is only one competitive season, so only one macrocycle is presented. Once the macrocycle duration is defined, the annual training plan can be subdivided into periods and phases.

In North America, high-school and collegiate football is typically played between August and December. Therefore, the first 31 weeks of this annual training plan are designated as the preparation period. The preparation period is further subdivided into the general and specific preparation phases. The first 11 weeks (January 14 to March 31) are dedicated to the general preparation phase, establishing a solid physical foundation from which sport-specific performance is developed. During this phase, strength training focuses on work capacity development (i.e., strength endurance), and acceleration is the targeted speed attribute (66). Additionally, plyometric progressions for jumping and tossing are targeted, and posture, balance, stability, and mobility progressions that underpin agility are integrated into the training plan (66).

The next 4 weeks (April 1 to 28) are dedicated to the specific preparation phase, in which the strength-training focus shifts toward the development of maximal strength, and activities that enhance speed development are integrated. The complexity and intensity of plyometric training increases, and speed and power cutting drills are added. At the end of the specific preparation phase, the athlete will participate in a team scrimmage.

The remaining 16 weeks of the preparation period are subdivided into an 8-week general preparation phase (April 29 to June 23) and an 8-week specific preparation period (June 24 to August 18). These phases are critical to establishing the physical foundation necessary for the rigors of the competitive season. The various levels of training are modulated to ensure the progressive development of strength, explosiveness, speed, and agility (66). Due to league rules, no formal technical or tactical training is undertaken during this period, but athletes are encouraged to undertake technical training with teammates or on their own. During the later stages of this preparation period, a training camp (August 5 to September 1) is typically planned leading into the competition period.

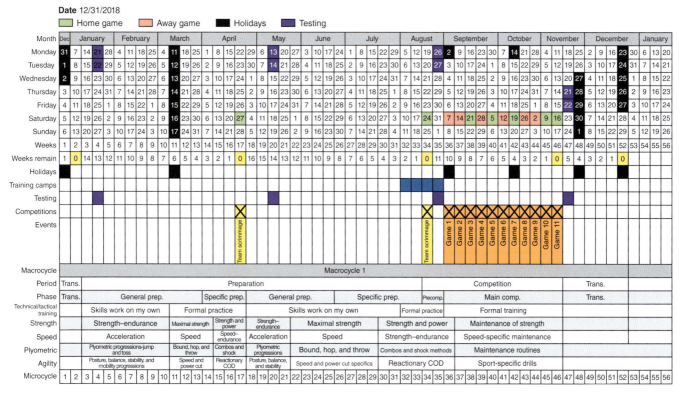

FIGURE 6.10 Mono-cycle annual training plan for a high-school or collegiate American football team.

The competitive period starts the week of August 19 and lasts until November 17, when the last competition of the season is contested. The first 2 weeks of the competitive season are considered the precompetition phase, and an intersquad scrimmage is planned on August 24. The main competitive phase lasts from September 2 until November 17. After the completion of the main competition phase, a 5- to 6-week transition period is planned to accommodate the athletes' academic and holiday schedules.

Figure 6.10 is merely an example of how a mono-cycle annual training plan can be constructed. Ultimately, there are several ways a mono-cycle annual training plan can be outlined (figure 6.8), and coaches should use these basic concepts when constructing annual training plans that meet the specific needs of their athletes and sports.

Bi-Cycle Annual Training Plans

The **bi-cycle annual training plan** is useful for sports that have two competition periods, such as spring club soccer and fall school soccer, or for athletes who compete in two different sports across the annual training plan (e.g., a high-school athlete who plays volleyball in the fall and competes in track and field in the spring). The bi-cycle plan has two macrocycles to guide the athlete to two distinct competitive periods (12). Although there are numerous ways a bi-cycle annual training plan can be constructed (figure 6.8), the duration of each macrocycle is structured according to the duration of each competitive period. Figure 6.11 gives a basic example of an annual training plan that uses a bi-cycle structure in which the two competitive seasons are represented as two distinct macrocycles.

The first macrocycle lasts 5.5 months and contains a 2.5-month preparation period (preparation 1) that is subdivided into general and specific preparation phases. As the athlete moves through this period, the proportion of training dedicated to general preparation progressively decreases as the amount of training that targets specific preparation increases. As the athlete moves through the preparation period, their preparedness is elevated. During the 2.5-month competition period (competition 1), training volume and intensity will fluctuate according to the competitive demands but will generally be higher than in preparation 1.

After macrocycle 1, a 1- to 2-week transition period is scheduled, after which a second prepa-

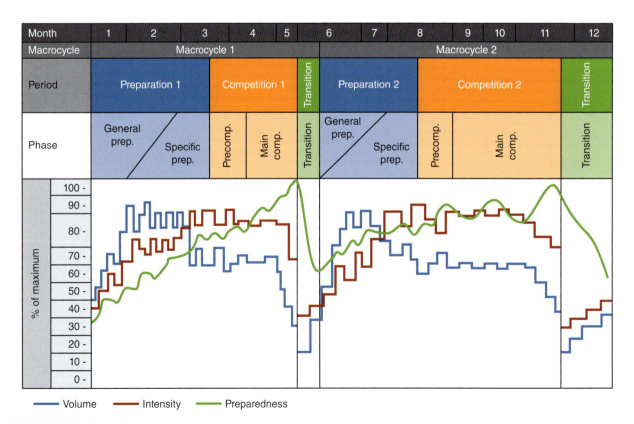

FIGURE 6.11 Basic bi-cycle annual training plan.

ration period (preparation 2) that lasts approximately 2 months is planned. Less overall time will be dedicated to general preparation during this period, and a greater amount of time will be dedicated to specific preparation. As the athlete transitions into the 3.5-month competition period, the intensity of training will be elevated, and the volume of training will be progressively decreased to elevate preparedness. After competition period 2, the athlete will undertake a 6-week transition period that links to the next annual training plan.

As shown in figure 6.12, a bi-cycle annual training plan could be used with a high-school athlete who competes in cross country and outdoor track and field. Two macrocycles are shown in the figure; the first corresponds with the cross country season, and the second is structured to optimize performance in the outdoor track and field season.

Macrocycle 1

The first macrocycle lasts 21 weeks and is subdivided into the following periods:

- *Preparation period 1*: The first preparation period lasts 10 weeks and contains a 6-week general preparation phase (July 6 to August 16) and a 4-week specific preparation phase (August 17 to September 13). The goal of this preparation period is to elevate the athlete's overall preparedness for the first competition period.
- *Competition period 1:* The first competition period lasts 9 weeks (September 14 to November 15) and is subdivided into a 3-week precompetition phase (September 14 to October 4) and a 6-week main competition phase (October 5 to November 15). The main goal of the competition period is to capitalize on the foundation established in the first preparation period and to increase performance capacity to ensure competitive success at specific events.
- *Transition period 1:* After the first competition period, a 2-week transition period (November 16 to 29) links to the next macrocycle. During this period, the primary focus is recovery from the previous macrocycle. The coach and athlete can reflect on how the athlete is progressing toward the overall goals established for the annual training plan and make modifications to the next macrocycle plan.

Macrocycle 2

The second macrocycle lasts 31 weeks and is subdivided into the following periods:

- *Preparation period 2*: The second preparation period lasts 13 weeks (November 30 to February 28), which is notably longer than the first preparation period (10 weeks). The first 5 weeks of this period (November 30 to January 3) are dedicated to general preparation, and the remaining 8 weeks (January 4 to February 28) focus on specific preparation. Due to the longer preparation period and the increased emphasis on the specific preparation phase, a much larger training base can be established to provide a foundation for the longer outdoor track and field season.
- *Competition period 2:* The second competitive period lasts 13 weeks (March 1 to May 30). This period contains a 3-week precompetition

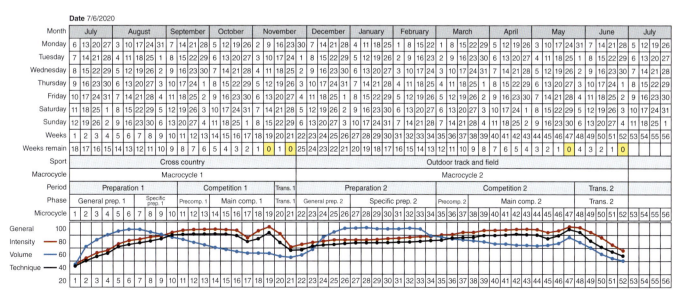

FIGURE 6.12 Example bi-cycle annual training plan for cross country and outdoor track and field.

phase (March 1 to March 21) and a 10-week main competitive phase (March 22 to May 30).

- *Transition period 2:* This 5-week period (May 31 to July 4) is designed to focus on recovery from the competition period and link to the next annual training plan. During this time, the coach and athlete should reflect on the training and competitive performances of the past year and begin the process of planning the next annual training plan.

Tri-Cycle Annual Training Plans

When an athlete has three major competitive seasons in their annual training plan, it is structured as a **tri-cycle annual training plan** to optimize performance at three distinct times (12). For example, a tri-cycle annual training plan would be ideal for a high-school distance runner who competes in cross country running in the fall, indoor track and field in the winter, and outdoor track and field in the spring. In this scenario, the annual training plan would have three macrocycles that each target a major competition (such as the state championship). The tri-cycle annual training plan also would be ideal for a high-school athlete who competes in three sports, such as football in the fall, basketball in the winter, and track and field in the spring. In this example, each macrocycle would prepare the athlete for the specific sport being contested and target the key competition for that sport.

A tri-cycle annual training plan also can be used to target three major competitions (e.g., qualifying competition, national championship, and world championship). In this case, the most important competition is targeted in the last macrocycle (12). In this scenario, the longest preparation period occurs in the first macrocycle, when the athlete builds their physical, technical, and tactical foundation for the entire annual training plan. When these plans are used with elite or developed athletes, the general preparation phase occurs only in the first macrocycle; all subsequent macrocycles have only specific preparation phases (12).

As with mono- and bi-cycle plans, each macrocycle is initiated with higher volumes of training performed at lower intensities. As the athlete moves through the annual training plan, the volume gradually decreases, and the intensity increases so preparedness can be optimized at the appropriate time. A basic example of a tri-cycle annual training plan is presented in figure 6.13. This plan

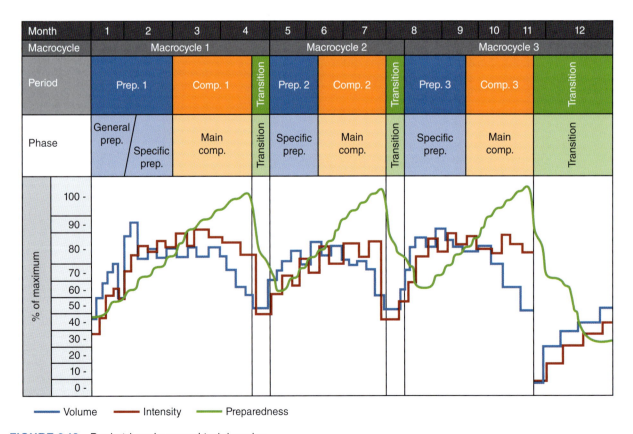

FIGURE 6.13 Basic tri-cycle annual training plan.

incorporates three macrocycles in which the major competitions are 3 to 4 months apart.

Macrocycle 1

The first macrocycle lasts approximately 16 weeks and is subdivided into the following periods:

- *Preparation period 1*: This is the longest preparation period of the annual training plan. This 8-week period is subdivided into general and specific preparation phases. This period contains the longest general preparation phase because it lays the foundation for the annual training plan. There is a nonlinear increase in training volume and intensity throughout the general preparation phase. As the athlete moves into the specific preparation phase, the volume undulates, and the intensity continues to increase in a nonlinear manner.
- *Competition period 1*: At only 6 weeks, the first competition period is the shortest of the three competition periods. This period is marked by maintaining training intensity, which is varied to modulate preparedness while managing fatigue. The volume of training is gradually decreased.
- *Transition period 1*: This period lasts 1 week and serves as a link between competition period 1 and preparation period 2. This period is marked by a reduction in training load (i.e., volume and intensity), which provides time for the athlete to recover.

Macrocycle 2

The second macrocycle lasts approximately 14 weeks and is subdivided into the following periods:

- *Preparation period 2*: This is shorter than the first preparation period and lasts about 6 weeks. There is only a specific preparation phase. As with all preparation periods, there is a gradual increase in volume and intensity to provide the foundation for the subsequent competition period.
- *Competition period 2*: The second competition period is longer than the first and lasts approximately 7 weeks. This period is marked by an overall optimization of preparedness, which is accomplished through modulating the volume and intensity of training.
- *Transition period 2*: This transition period is only 1 week, and it allows the athlete to focus on recovery and prepare for the final macrocycle.

Macrocycle 3

The third macrocycle lasts approximately 19 weeks and is subdivided into the following periods:

- *Preparation period 3*: The final preparation period is the shortest, lasting 5 weeks. Due to the length of this period, there is only a specific preparation phase to prepare the athlete for the subsequent competition period.
- *Competition period 3*: The last competition period is the longest, lasting about 8 weeks. Because this macrocycle leads into the most important competition of the annual training plan, the volume and intensity of training are modulated to optimally elevate preparedness and optimize performance at the competition.
- *Transition period 3*: After the last competition period, there is a longer transition period of about 6 weeks. This gives the athlete time to recover physically and psychologically from the rigors of the annual training plan prior to initiating the next annual training plan.

Peaking Index and Preparedness

The **peaking index**, or **preparedness index**, is used to rank an athlete's readiness to compete and reflects the physiological, technical, and psychological status of the athlete. Conceptually, preparedness indicates the athlete's performance potential, which is in constant flux depending on the training activities undertaken (86). As training factors are manipulated, they have the potential to increase fatigue and reduce preparedness or decrease fatigue and increase preparedness. For example, during the general preparation phase of the annual training plan, the volumes of training are the highest, resulting in a large amount of accumulated fatigue and a concomitant reduction in preparedness. Conversely, during the competition period leading into a major competition, there will be a reduction of the total volume of training (i.e., tapering) that results in a reduction in fatigue, an elevation in preparedness, and an optimization of performance capacity, if timed correctly (see chapter 12). Although this basic example demonstrates the relationship between preparedness and fatigue, remember that preparedness is related to both fitness and fatigue (see chapter 1). If training loads are removed too often or for extended periods, there will be a reduction in fatigue, but preparedness will not elevate because fitness levels will be decreased due to a lack of training stimulus (12). This is increasingly important when planning competitive schedules because it is impossible to reach peak performance for every competition (i.e., remove all fatigue). Therefore, when outlining the competitive schedule, the coach must determine when high-priority competitions occur and deliberately manipulate training loads (i.e., volume and intensity) to optimize preparedness at the level assigned to each competition (68, 69).

One way to represent the level of preparedness for the annual plan is to use a numerical indicator referred to as the *peaking index* (11, 12). According to Bompa and Buzzichelli (11), the peaking index is represented on a numerical scale from 1 (100% preparedness) to 5 (≤50% preparedness) (table 6.2). This scale is typically used to indicate the targeted level of preparedness for individual microcycles and mesocycles within the annual training plan. Although the 5-point peaking index scale has historically been used as part of the construction of the annual training plan, some coaches find it difficult to use because it has limited utility for describing preparedness during individual microcycles in the competitive period.

An alternative approach is to use a 10-point peaking scale that aligns with the session rating of perceived exertion (sRPE) scale. The sRPE scale has historically been used to answer the question, "How was your workout?" (58), with the following options: 0 = rest/no training; 1 = very, very easy; 2 = easy; 3 = moderate; 4 = somewhat hard; 5-6 = hard; 7-9 = very hard; and 10 = maximal (18, 58). Although typically used as a monitoring tool, the sRPE scale can serve as a foundation for the development of a peaking index that can align the planning and monitoring process (see chapter 11 for more on sRPE).

A 10-point peaking index (table 6.2) provides expanded options for describing the projected level of preparedness during the individual microcycles contained within the annual plan. Because it is impossible to peak for every competition, it is critical to prioritize competitions and accept that some competitions will be contested without complete recovery or peak preparedness. By assigning a level of preparedness (based on the 10-point peaking index) to each microcycle in the annual training plan, the coach can provide a framework from which training decisions are made during the planning process.

When using the 10-point peaking index, the coach should align the projected index score with the various periods, phases, and competitions. For example, during the preparation period, specifically the general preparation phase, the highest cumulative workloads (i.e., volume load) are typically encountered as the athlete targets the development of a baseline fitness. During this time, the athlete will display significant levels of fatigue, which will reduce overall preparedness. When planning, the coach may suggest that the athlete's level of preparedness (i.e., peaking index) should be between 7 and 10 for the microcycles in the general preparation phase. As the athlete moves into the specific preparation phase, the level of preparedness would be expected to elevate due to the incorporation of more sport-specific training activities. Thus, a peak index of between 4 and 7

TABLE 6.2 Peaking Indexes

Classic 5-point peaking index		New 10-point peaking index	
Peaking index	Level of preparedness	Peaking index	Level of preparedness
1	100%	1	100%
2	90%	2	90%
3	70%-80%	3	80%
4	60%	4	70%
5	≤50%	5	60%
		6	50%
		7	40%
		8	30%
		9	20%
		10	≤10%

Note: The peaking index is modulated by training load and is related to the athlete's overall preparedness. There is a reduced level of preparedness when there are high levels of fatigue and an increased level of preparedness when there are low levels of fatigue.

Adapted from Bompa and Haff (2009).

might be planned. As the athlete moves into the competitive period, the athlete's training activities will be modulated between a peaking index of 1 and 4 based on the competitive schedule and other factors such as travel.

An example of how the peaking index can be incorporated into the annual training plan is shown in figure 6.14. In this example, peaking indexes of between 7 and 10 are presented for the general preparation phase, and the specific preparation phase is aligned with peaking indexes between 5 and 7. Most of the competition period has a peaking index between 2 and 4, and a peaking index of 1 is reserved for the most important competition in the annual training plan. The exact peaking index that the coach projects should be aligned with the strength of the opponent, account for travel, and give an estimate of the balance between fitness and fatigue (i.e., preparedness). When higher-level competitions are scheduled, the peaking index will move to 2. If the competition is relatively weak, the peaking index is generally set at 4. A peaking index of 4 or 5 is also often used for bye weeks where higher volumes of training may be introduced to increase the athlete's physical capacities.

Practical Steps for Constructing Multiyear Training Plans

A basic five-step approach can be used to create and organize a multiyear training plan (table 6.3). Step 1 is to evaluate the athlete's level of development and performance abilities to establish a

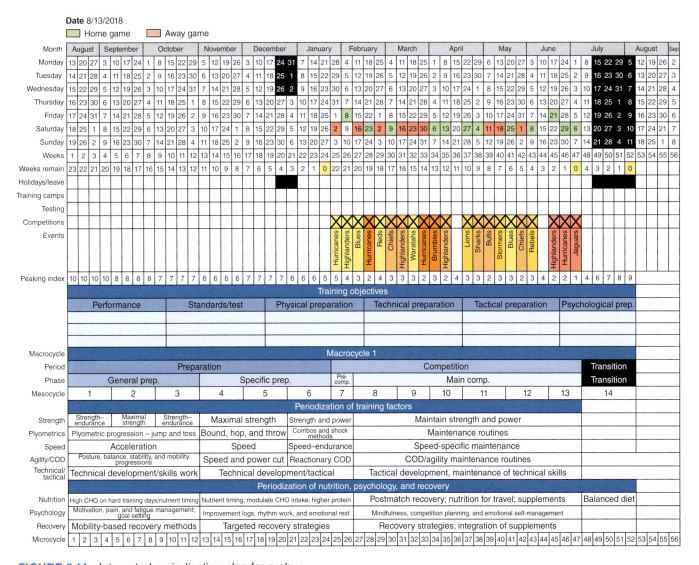

FIGURE 6.14 Integrated periodization plan for rugby.

TABLE 6.3 Practical Steps for Developing a Multiyear Training Plan

Step	Action
1	The coach evaluates the athlete's current level of development and overall performance abilities. This evaluation should consider physical, technical, tactical, and psychological developments and how these relate to long-term success in the targeted sport.
2	The coach will project the athlete's rate of progress based on the athlete's current level of development, overall performance abilities, and developmental data related to their sport.
3	The coach and athlete should develop realistic long-term goals that align with the athlete's projected rate of progress.
4	The coach establishes the sequential developmental pattern across the multiyear training plan.
5	After each annual training plan contained in the multiyear training plan, the coach will reevaluate the athlete's progress and make modifications to the multiyear training plan where needed.

Adapted from Haff (2016).

baseline from which to project the athlete's development (27, 29). When performing this evaluation, the coach should consider the athlete's physical and psychological development and their technical and tactical abilities to create a developmental pathway that leads to long-term success in the targeted sport. For example, youth athletes will require greater emphasis on general fitness (27) and developing physical literacy during the early stages of their development (29), whereas advanced athletes will spend less time on general physical preparation and dedicate more time to developing sport-specific training outcomes to optimize competitive performance (27).

Step 2 is to project the athlete's rate of development across the duration of the plan (27). This projection is based on the athlete's current level of development and performance capacity and data on typical progression rates for the targeted sport. For example, for a 12-year-old male sprinter, the coach would expect a 1.04 second decrease in 60 m sprint time between the ages of 12 and 16 (81). Based on these data, the coach projects where they expect the athlete to be in 4 years.

Step 3 is to establish realistic long-term training and performance goals (27) based on the earlier projections and the athlete's level of development, and step 4 is to establish a logical sequential progression toward these goals from which each annual training plan in the multiyear training plan is developed. It is helpful to consider the multiyear training plan as a guide or template around which each annual training plan is constructed (27).

The multiyear training plan is a principal guide for the training process and is not cast in stone. Depending on the athlete's rate of progress, the goals in the multiyear training plan may shift to align with the athlete's changing abilities (27).

Therefore, step 5 of the planning process is to reevaluate the athlete's progress and adjust the multiyear training plan as needed.

Practical Steps for Constructing Annual Training Plans

Once the multiyear training plan is constructed, the coach can begin to work on the individual annual training plans. It is illogical to outline every annual training plan in a multiyear training plan at once, so focusing on only one annual training plan at a time is key to the process. If the athlete is new to training, the first annual training plan will be developed based on the coach's experience and will align with the early stages of an established LTAD model for the targeted sport (29). Otherwise, the coach will base the subsequent annual training plan on the annual plan that the athlete is currently completing (30).

Typically, the coach will lay out the next year's annual training plan during the transition period at the end of the current annual training plan (12, 27). Step 1 in designing the annual training plan is reflecting on the previous year's training and the athlete's performance results and testing data (table 6.4). During this process, the coach can determine whether the athlete's progress aligns with what was established in the multiyear training plan.

Step 2 in the planning process is determining what training activities or other factors did not go according to plan (27). Typically, the coach will examine these factors to determine why these adverse events happened and how to mitigate them in the future. Step 3 looks at the previous

TABLE 6.4 Practical Steps for Designing an Annual Training Plan

Step	Action
1	The coach critically evaluates the performance results and tests data from the previous annual training plan to gauge the athlete's rate of progress.
2	The coach examines the previous annual training plan to determine which training activities or other factors were not successful or did not go according to plan.
3	The coach inspects the previous annual training plan to determine which training activities or cycles were successful.
4	The coach consults with the athlete to get their feedback on the overall plan and talk about their goals.
5	The coach aligns the annual training plan goals with those established within the multiyear training plan and those established for the annual plan being constructed.
6	The coach designs an annual training plan template to meet the athlete's or sport's needs.
7	The coach notes all planned holidays, stressful time periods (e.g., exam periods for student–athletes), and training camps on the annual training plan.
8	The coach collects information about the number of competitive seasons and competitions, the locations of competitions, and the length of the competitive season, and adds this information to the annual training plan template.
9	The coach determines the number of seasons in the annual training plan and subdivides the annual training plan into macrocycles.
10	The coach determines the location of the preparatory, competition, and transition periods in the annual training plan and adds them to the annual training plan template.
11	The coach establishes the lengths of the general preparation, specific preparation, precompetition, main competition, and transition phases and outlines them on the annual training plan template.
12	The coach establishes where performance is to be optimized and uses the peaking index to define this on the annual training plan template.
13	The coach notes when medical and performance testing will be conducted within the annual plan.

Adapted from Haff (2016).

annual training plan to determine which training activities, cycles, or competition strategies were particularly successful. The coach should also look at what training activities preceded these successful strategies.

In step 4, the coach engages the athlete to get their feedback on the previous annual training plan. This is critical because it allows the athlete to express their feelings about how things went, which helps create an effective learning environment (47). Engaging athletes in this manner allows them to contribute to the planning process, which increases the likelihood that they will be more invested in and engaged with the training process (47).

In step 5, the coach aligns the annual training plan goals with those established in the multiyear training plan and those discussed with the athlete. This step is critical because it helps guide the decisions made in the annual training plan and serves as the overarching goals for the coming year of training.

In step 6, the coach can begin designing the overall annual training plan using an annual training plan template (see the appendix or HK*Propel*) (12, 27, 34). Step 7 involves noting planned holidays, stressful times of the year (e.g., exam periods for student–athletes), and training camps. Step 8 involves collecting information about the number of competitions and the overall length of the competitive season. The coach also should determine where the most important competitions will take place (33). Additionally, it is important for the coach to be familiar with the rules of the league or the union rules established by their league (if working with professional athletes). For example, the National Collegiate Athletics Association limits the number of training hours allowed during parts of the year; the coach must know this so they can plan accordingly. The coach also needs to note whether the athlete competes in multiple sports or in multiple seasons, because this will affect the number of macrocycles outlined in the next step.

In step 9, the coach divides the annual training plan into macrocycles (27, 33). Once this is completed, they can further subdivide the macrocycles into preparation, competition, and transition periods (step 10). Based on how the coach decides to subdivide the macrocycles, they can further subdivide the periods into general preparation, specific preparation, precompetition, main competition, and transition phases (step 11). Once all of this is completed, the coach can place a numeric indicator for the peaking index on the template to align with the targeted level of preparedness (step 12). In the last step, step 13, the coach should note on the annual training plan template when medical and performance testing will be conducted (12).

Summary

Developing elite performance is based on dedicated and focused training undertaken over time. Multiyear and annual training plans are considered the cornerstones of the periodization process and are used to organize the long-term development of athletes. Several interlinked multiyear training plans are considered an athlete's developmental plan, which guides training from the initiation of the athlete's career until the achievement of elite performance. A coach's ability to develop an individualized, multiyear training plan that guides the athlete's development relies on forecasting a progression rate for the athlete and constructing training processes that guide training in alignment with the forecasted goals. This multiyear plan can be adjusted based on the actual rate of progress through each annual plan.

The annual training plan organizes the direction of training across one calendar or academic year. Based on the number of competitive seasons targeted, the annual training plan is divided into macrocycles that define the timelines for the preparation, competition, and transition periods of training. These periods are further subdivided into general preparation, specific preparation, precompetition, main competition, and transition phases that provide the framework from which detailed training programs are developed. The individualized annual training plan defines the times when performance must be optimized or brought to a peak.

A coach's ability to develop annual training plans is based on a good understanding of the periodization process. The annual training plan is organized using a template (see the appendix or HK*Propel*) that provides an overview of the various key points in the annual plan and includes factors such as training focus, nutritional interventions, psychological training, recovery methodologies, performance testing, and medical screenings.

Based on the annual training plan, the coach will craft training programs designed to achieve specific performance, training, and testing goals. As the athlete progresses through the annual training plan, the coach uses an integrated monitoring program, testing data, and performance trajectories to inform their training decisions. The coach can adjust the forecasted path of development in accordance with the goals set forth for the annual training plan.

CHAPTER 7

Mesocycle and Microcycle Training Plans

When conceptualizing the periodization process, the multiyear training plan provides the long-term developmental direction for training. Based on this direction, the individual annual training plans are broken into one or more macrocycles that establish the preparation, competition, and transition periods. From here, the coach divides these periods into specific phases of development: general and specific preparation, precompetition, main competition, and transition phases. After establishing these phases, the coach begins the actual programming process.

The first stage of the programming process is to determine the sequence and duration of the individual mesocycles used to create the athlete's training plan. This process allows the coach to ensure alignment between the targeted goals outlined in the annual training plan and the development of sporting form or level of preparedness. Once this has been completed, the coach can outline the structure of each *microcycle* in the *mesocycle*. To construct flexible and responsive training interventions, the coach generally designs the microcycles and programming interventions for one mesocycle at a time. The coach can make modifications to the training process based on the athlete's actual rate of progress from one mesocycle to the next and not be arbitrarily bound by predetermined training structures. These modifications to the training process are guided by an integrated monitoring program as well as the coach's experience.

To effectively design and implement micro- and mesocycles, the coach must understand the types, sequences, loading patterns, and methods used to integrate various training factors into each type of training cycle. When constructing a periodized training plan the coach should work from the mesocycle to the microcycle.

Mesocycle

The mesocycle is a medium-duration training cycle, sometimes referred to as a *block* of training, which serves as a key level of the programming process (22, 24, 28). Although mesocycles are typically 2 to 6 weeks long, the most commonly used mesocycle duration is 4 weeks due to the potential for asymptotic training effects that can occur if training interventions are not varied after 4 weeks (22, 35). Typically associated with the early stages of involution, these asymptotic training effects can manifest as either a stagnation or a decline in the physiological or performance gains associated with the training process (22, 40). However, if the mesocycle focus is altered and the training stimulus is changed after 4 weeks, these asymptotic effects can be offset and there can be continued progress toward the targeted training goals.

The annual training plan provides the coach with a blueprint from which decisions can be made about the sequence and duration of the individual mesocycles in the athlete's training program (7). Based on the intended direction of the training process, the coach can align the objectives targeted by each mesocycle with the periods and phases contained within the annual training plan. As part of this process, mesocycles are sequenced to guide the training process and provide the basic framework from which the microcycle can be constructed.

Types of Mesocycles

Different types of mesocycles can be constructed by manipulating the contents and training structures of each microcycle in the planned mesocycle. Once structured, mesocycles can be aligned with the periods and phases outlined by the periodization model (figure 7.1). The classic periodization literature (1, 7, 22, 46) provides several classifications of mesocycles that target specific objectives and contain characteristics that dictate the progression of the training process (table 7.1) (22). For example, mesocycles associated with the preparation period typically are used to develop or elevate basic or sport-specific fitness while enhancing technical skills that will be required during the competition period (22). The mesocycles used within the competitive period are structured to increase performance capacity, maximize competitive success, and modulate training stress to manage cumulative fatigue prior to competition (25).

Although various mesocycles are aligned with the periods and phases that they are placed under, note that not all mesocycle types are used within a given preparation or competition period. In some instances, two mesocycles of the same type can be sequenced as long as the targeted emphasis is stressed in a different way (1). Regardless of how one conceptualizes the mesocycle, individual mesocycles are sequenced and interlinked to guide the training process.

In the early 1980s, high-performance coaches began using the term *training block* to describe mesocycles that contained highly specialized workloads focused on a minimal number of training targets and performed with increased training volumes (28, 31, 32). The training blocks serve as the foundation for the block periodization model, which is an alternative to traditional multitargeted training models (31). In this context, training blocks, or mesocycles, are used to plan training with specific targeted blocks to create concentrated unidirectional (i.e., sequential) or multitargeted (i.e., emphasis) block periodization models (32).

With the advent of the training block concept, several new mesocycle taxonomies were created (table 7.2). For example, when working with hammer throwers, Bondarchuk (4) simplified the mesocycle taxonomy to three basic structures: the developmental, retention, and restorative blocks of training. Similarly, Touretski, who worked with

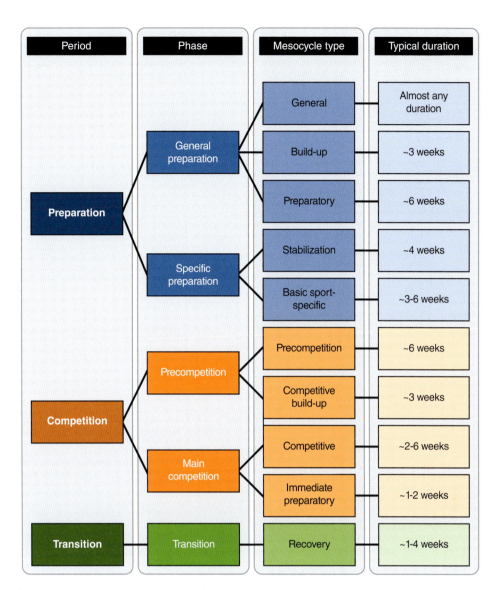

FIGURE 7.1 Classic mesocycles and their association with periods and phases of planning.

swimmers, reduced the mesocycle taxonomy to four basic structures: the general, specific, competition, and recovery blocks of training (31, 42, 49). When working with canoe-kayak athletes, Issurin (28, 31) and Issurin and Kaverin (30) reduced the mesocycle taxonomy to three types: the **accumulation mesocycle**, **transmutation mesocycle**, and **realization mesocycle**.

When these works are synthesized into a common set of principles, the following conclusions can be made:

- Blocks of training, or mesocycles, can be developed with workloads that focus on a minimal number of training targets to create more-targeted training interventions (4, 21, 29, 31).

- Three or four basic mesocycle types can be created based on the 9 to 10 different mesocycle variants used in the classic periodization literature (1, 7, 9, 22, 27, 31, 35).

- A mesocycle should last 2 to 6 weeks, depending on the goal of the block (31), to allow for positive adaptations without the accumulation of excessive fatigue (4, 27, 31) or the occurrence of asymptotic training effects (22, 40).

- The appropriate sequencing of mesocycles is used to guide the training process and allow for enhanced competitive performance at key predetermined periods (4, 9, 21, 31).

Based on these conclusions, the most common mesocycle taxonomy in the sporting world includes

TABLE 7.1 Objectives and Characteristics of the Classic Mesocycle Types

Type	Objectives	Characteristics
General	Develop characteristics of basic fitness	Uses high-volume, low-load activities Emphasis on multilateral training
Build-up	Elevate foundational fitness or skills during long preparation periods	Incorporates progressively increased training loads
Preparatory	Develop general fitness characteristics that serve as the foundation for skills development	Training moves from extensive to intensive Emphasis on multilateral training
Stabilization	Develop sport-specific fitness Refine and master technical skills	Focused on sport-specific conditioning Emphasis on technical skills mastery
Basic sport-specific	Enhance sport-specific preparation Elevate sport-specific skill sets Increase sport-specific fitness	Major emphasis on sport-specific skills development
Precompetitive	Increase competitive performance capacity Prepare for competitive peak	Focus on sport-specific training activities
Competitive build-up	Establish or reestablish foundational skills or fitness	Increased workloads targeting sport-specific fitness
Competitive	Establish the highest competitive performance possible	Specific emphasis on the competitions contained within the mesocycle
Immediate preparatory	Optimize competitive abilities prior to a competition Reduce cumulative fatigue	Precedes a specific competition or testing period
Recovery	Stimulate restoration Prepare athlete for subsequent training cycle	Has a significant reduction in training load (i.e., volume, intensity, and structure) Can be used after a series of competitions or to link macrocycles and annual plans

TABLE 7.2 Alternative Mesocycle Taxonomies

Author	Sport	Type	Characteristics
Bondarchuk (4)	Hammer throw	Developmental	Increased workloads that serve as a concentrated load
		Retention	Stabilized training loads, increased focus on competitive performance
		Restorative	Altered training designed to induce recovery and prepare for the next developmental mesocycle
Touretski (49)	Swimming	General	Training focused on aerobic and complementary workloads
		Specific	Training focused on event-specific energetics and competitive models
		Competition	Training is altered to maximize performance with the use of reduced training loads, often associated with a taper.
		Recovery	Altered training designed to induce recovery and prepare for the next developmental mesocycle
Issurin and Kaverin (30)	Canoe-kayak	Accumulation	Concentrated loading mesocycle that focuses on the development of general physical training preparation
		Transmutation	Reduced training workload with more sport-specific training at higher intensities
		Realization	Reduced training loads that are used as a taper and to elevate performance at a competition

the accumulation, transmutation, and realization mesocycles (table 7.3). As noted previously, this taxonomy is a central construct that underpins the structure of the block periodization models presented in chapter 5.

Sequencing of Mesocycles

Many factors affect decisions about the mesocycle sequence used to guide the programming strategies incorporated into the athlete's periodized training plan. Ultimately, the structure of the macrocycle and the sequence of the periods and phases determined when conceptualizing the annual training plan allow the coach to choose and sequence a series of mesocycles that guide construction of the training program. For example, if a 20-week macrocycle is planned (figure 7.2) and the coach has allocated 12 weeks to the preparation period, they might employ a 6-week preparatory mesocycle during the general preparation phase and a 6-week basic sport-specific mesocycle during the specific preparation phase. In this example, the competition period is 6 weeks, which allows the coach to plan a 4-week competitive mesocycle followed by a 2-week immediate preparatory mesocycle that leads into the targeted competition. After the major competition, a 2-week transition period might be planned in which a recovery mesocycle is scheduled.

In another example, an endurance athlete may undertake a preparation period in which a series of eight mesocycles of varying durations are sequenced to prepare for a competition period (figure 7.3). After a transition period in which very little training is completed, the athlete would not have an acceptable level of fitness and would require a gradual introduction to the training process to increase their work capacity so they can handle more-intensive training in subsequent mesocycles. In this case, the athlete might initiate the preparation period with the use of an introductory mesocycle to gradually increase their fitness and work capacity (33). From there, the athlete would engage in a series of mesocycle blocks that transition from general to precompetitive targets to prepare for competition (33).

A variety of mesocycle sequences can guide the training process during the competition period, and these are largely dictated by the demands of the sport. If the competition period is short (i.e., <2 months), two or three competition mesocycles can be used with each mesocycle containing precompetition, competition, and recovery microcycles (33). If the competition period lasts 3 or 4 months, the basic sport-specific, precompetition, and recovery mesocycles could be employed depending on the spacing of the competitive engagements. The basic sport-specific mesocycle can be used to restore sport-specific fitness while offsetting the

TABLE 7.3 A Simplified Mesocycle Taxonomy

Mesocycle classification	Alternative names found in the literature	Duration	Characteristics
Accumulation block	Concentrated loading block	2-6 weeks	Contain high training volumes that result in the longest training residuals and the highest levels of fatigue Elevate general fitness and provide a foundation for subsequent mesocycle blocks of training
	Developmental block		
	General block		
	Overreaching block		
	Planned overreaching block		
Transmutation block	Normal training block	2-4 weeks	Reduced total training workload compared to the accumulation block and used to elevate the athlete's level of preparedness Contain higher training intensities that can result in cumulative fatigue and produce shorter residual training effects
	Phase-potentiation block		
	Retention block		
	Specific block		
	Transformation block		
Realization block	Competitive block	8-14 days	Reduced training loads to induce recovery, amplify preparedness, and maximize performance Facilitate the convergence of the training residuals created by the previous two blocks of training
	Peaking block		
	Restoration block		
	Taper block		

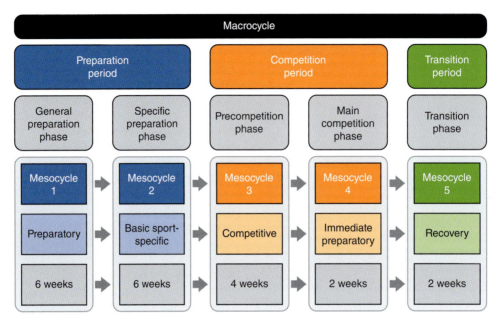

FIGURE 7.2 Example mesocycle sequences based on classic mesocycle taxonomy.

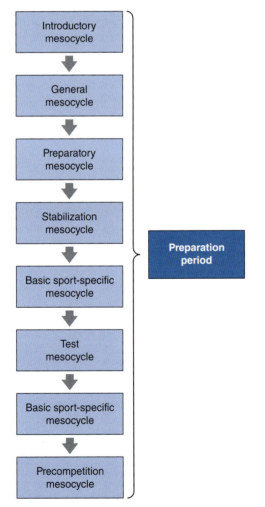

FIGURE 7.3 Example arrangement of mesocycles used in the preparation period of an endurance athlete.

Data from Coutts, Hocking, and Bilsborough (2019).

monotony of repeated competition loads and the potential declines in fitness that can occur across long competitive periods (33). Ultimately, how the mesocycles are arranged and sequenced is predicated by the length of the preparation and competition periods and the distribution of important or critical competitions (33).

Mesocycle Loading Patterns

Although there are numerous ways to define the progression of training load across a series of mesocycles, loading is always dictated by the athlete's level of development, current fitness state, and the placement of the mesocycle within the annual training plan. It is important to carefully control the monotony and strain that the athlete is exposed to in each microcycle. Through appropriate implementation of training load variation, the coach can ensure that the athlete is exposed to training stimuli that maximize adaptive responses and minimize injury risk.

As noted in chapter 4, the most common way to progress the total training load across a series of microcycles contained within a mesocycle is to use a step loaded progression (figure 4.13, page 95). Within each step loaded mesocycle, a series of microcycles is used to modulate the training load across the mesocycle (figure 7.4) and a series of three build-up mesocycles can be sequenced to progressively increase the athlete's training load. After this is completed, a recovery mesocycle can be implemented. In each of the build-up mesocycles, the microcycles could be sequenced as follows:

introductory (7 days) → ordinary (7 days) → shock (7 days) → recovery (7 days)

During the third build-up mesocycle, the athlete will be exposed to the highest overall training loads in this series, and this mesocycle might be considered an overreaching or accumulation mesocycle. Therefore, the loads in the shock microcycle within the mesocycle will be significantly higher than those in the first two mesocycles.

Although step loaded mesocycles are common in the periodization and programming literature (18, 23, 39, 40, 44), there are numerous other ways to structure the loading parameters in a mesocycle. For example, an accentuated loading mesocycle can be created in which two shock microcycles are separated by one ordinary microcycle and followed by a recovery microcycle (figure 7.5). The second mesocycle would contain reduced training loads but would be initiated with one shock microcycle followed by two ordinary microcycles and a recovery microcycle (51).

The ultimate goal when constructing mesocycle sequences is to place them in an order that directs the training process in accordance with the annual training plan. Nádori (39), in his seminal paper, presents an example annual training plan for a modern pentathlete (figure 7.6) that uses a series of 13 mesocycles in which summated microcycles are planned to induce a training effect during the preparation period (referred to as foundation in the figure). During this period, various mesocycle work-to-rest ratios (3:1, 4:1, or 4:2) are used to elevate the athlete's sporting form and prepare them for the competition period. During the preseason (i.e., precompetition phase), the mesocycle is structured to further elevate the athlete's sporting form prior to initiating the competition period. Once the competition period is initiated, the mesocycle work-to-rest ratios (1:1, 3:2, 3:1, or 3:2) oscillate based on the placement of the competitions in this period.

It is, however, important to note that the example presented by Nádori (39) is a classic example

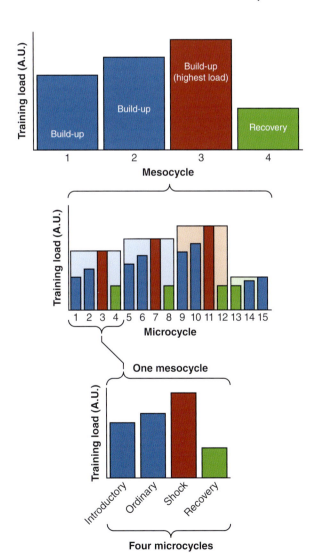

FIGURE 7.4 Example step loaded mesocycle broken into microcycles.

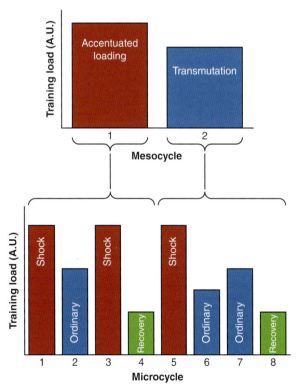

FIGURE 7.5 Example mesocycle loading pattern incorporating several shock microcycles.

of how mesocycles can be sequenced as part of an annual training plan and may not easily translate to some modern sporting situations. An alternative methodology for sequencing the mesocycles in the annual training plan can be centered on the use of accumulation, transmutation, and realization mesocycles (figure 7.7). With this strategy, the amount of time dedicated to each mesocycle type depends on the location of the training in the annual plan and the time

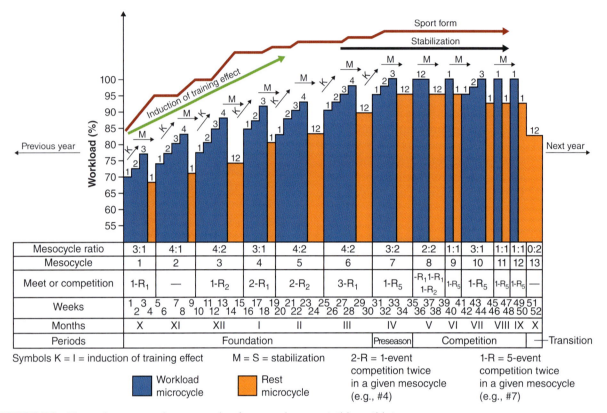

FIGURE 7.6 Example mesocycle sequencing for a modern pentathlon athlete.

Adapted by permission from L. Nádori, "Theoretical and Methodological Basis of Training Planning," in *Theoretical and Methodological Basis of Training Planning with Special Considerations Within a Microcycle,* edited for the National Strength and Conditioning Association by L. Nádori and I. Granek (Lincoln, NE: NSCA, 1989), 16.

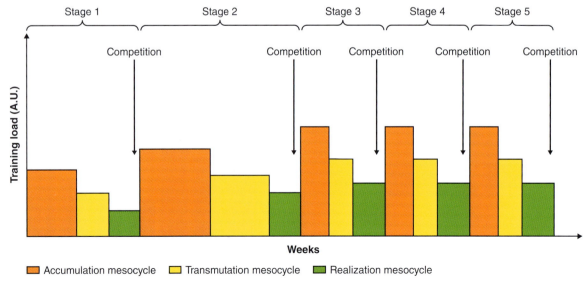

FIGURE 7.7 Example annual training plan using accumulation, transmutation, and realization mesocycle structures.

until the planned competition. When more time is available, longer accumulation and transmutation mesocycles can be planned (figure 7.7, stages 1-2). Conversely, when there is a greater density of competitions (figure 7.7, stages 3-5), short accumulation and transmutation mesocycles are used. This strategy has become popular in the modern sporting context due to the ability to maximize performance in less time compared to classic mesocycle sequencing models.

Regardless of which mesocycle sequence and loading patterns are used, the actual loading sequence depends on many factors. For example, when structuring the loading contained within the mesocycle the coach needs to consider the athlete's current level of development, training age, training status, and the structure of their competitive calendar. Additionally, the athlete's progress toward the goals established in the annual training plan must be considered.

Integration of Training Factors

Mesocycles typically present a summation of the total training load during a given time. The composition of the training load in each mesocycle can be represented by various combinations of training factors depending on the periodization model (i.e., parallel, sequential, or emphasis) being implemented (figure 7.8).

If a sequential model is used, the mesocycle would be representative of the total workload and would be composed of a series of individual or minimal training factors. Conversely, if a parallel or emphasis periodization model is planned, the mesocycle would target multiple training factors, and the total training load presented in the mesocycle would represent a summation of the total training loads established for each microcycle. Although sequential training models are used for some training activities, such as resistance training or conditioning, the training programs of most athletes, especially team sport athletes, will often include mesocycles that contain multiple training activities, including physical, tactical, and technical training. For example, Hamilton (26) presented an example series of mesocycles for an international field hockey team in which the total mesocycle training load was comprised of training loads associated with hockey training, strength training, conditioning, robustness training, and speed and agility training (figure 7.9). In each mesocycle, the contributions of these training factors to the

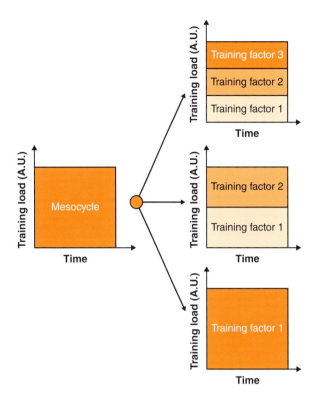

FIGURE 7.8 Example mesocycle training load contributions.

total training load vary, which is reflected in the individual microcycles. This example illustrates the total training load of the mesocycle as a composite of the training activities undertaken in the microcycles. Depending on the period of training, the contribution of the various training factors will be modulated, and the total training load will vary according to where the mesocycle is in the annual training plan.

When working with an individual sport, such as orienteering, the total training load is typically the lowest during the transition phase and then increases across the general preparation phase. As the athlete transitions into the specific preparation phase, the total training load is reduced, and it continues to be reduced as the athlete moves into the competitive phase (47, 48). Tønnessen et al. (47) present annual training plan data for eight world champions in orienteering that contains transition, general preparation, specific preparation, and competition phases (figure 7.10). In this example, 12 mesocycles are presented in which the total training load is distributed between strength training and three zones of conditioning. As the athlete progresses through the various mesocycles, the time allocated to each training target is modulated to guide the athlete toward the main

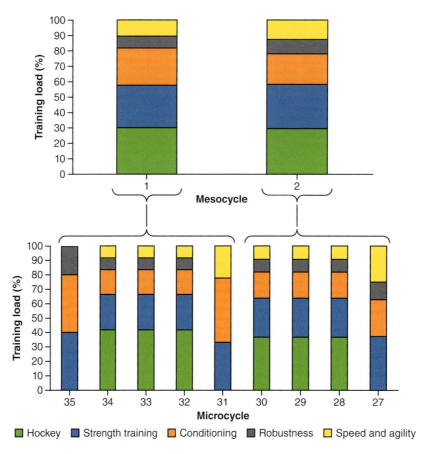

FIGURE 7.9 Example integrated mesocycle structure for an international field hockey team.
Data from Hamilton (2019).

competition in the last mesocycle of the annual training plan.

Guidelines for Constructing Mesocycles

The mesocycle is one of the more important planning structures used to guide the athlete's development in accordance with the goals and timelines established by the annual training plan. It is flexible and can be revised based on information garnered from an integrated monitoring program (see chapter 11) to adjust the training process to align with the athlete's changing levels of development. Mesocycles are also used to characterize the progress of intensity and the extent of loading while guiding the rhythmic fluctuations between periods of high loading and shorter periods of unloading (10).

When constructing mesocycles, the coach must consider the following important factors:

- The amount of time that the athlete has available to train and how this time is allotted to the various training units the athlete needs to complete.
- The distribution between the various training targets. As part of an integrated training plan, the coach must consider, for example, how much training time is allotted for strength training, conditioning, and technical and tactical training. The amount of time allotted is largely predicated upon the goals of the mesocycle and how it contributes to the overall sequence of the training process.
- The overall load progression used in the mesocycle and how each training factor relates to this progression. Remember that the load progression within the mesocycle is linked to the loading strategies in the microcycle and should be carefully examined during the planning process because it can be modified in response to an integrated monitoring plan.
- The loading progression and intertraining unit load fluctuations used at the microcycle level and how these relate to the planned mesocycle load progression and ratio of loading to recovery.

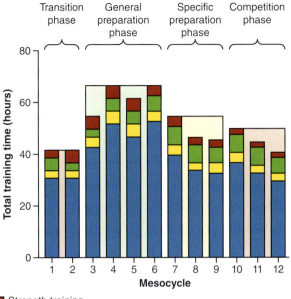

FIGURE 7.10 Example integration of training factors for an endurance sport athlete.

Adapted from Tønnessen, Svendsen, Ronnestad, et al. (2015).

- The location of external stressors that could negatively affect the athlete's ability to tolerate the prescribed training load. For example, during periods of high academic stress in Division I college football, there is an increased risk of injury; therefore, coaches should consider reducing physical training loads to help athletes better manage overall training load (34).

Guided by the goals established by the various phases and periods of the annual training plan, the coach can choose which mesocycle loading, sequencing, and integration strategies they will employ. When constructing a mesocycle, remember that it is used to guide the training decisions made when programming the microcycles within it and the training decisions made at the microcycle level contribute to the overall mesocycle structure. Remember that the mesocycle is a guide for the training process and is not set in stone; it can be modified based on the information collected as part of a comprehensive monitoring plan. However, the monitoring program should never dictate the mesocycle or microcycle plans but should be used to inform the coach's programming decisions.

Microcycles

The microcycle is probably the most important planning level used to construct a periodized training program. It is a critical part of the programming process because it contains very specific training objectives guided by the overarching goals set forth by the mesocycle (40, 46). The basic structure of a microcycle tends to span 2 to 14 days (3, 33); its length depends on the period of training in which it appears (33). For example, in a preparatory period, the most common microcycle duration is 7 days (1, 29), but it could be extended up to 14 days depending on the requirements of the athlete and the structure of the training plan (25). During the competition period, the microcycle can last 3 to 14 days, accounting for the density of the competitive schedule and alterations to the athlete's level of preparedness or sporting form (33). Although the 7-day microcycle is often used for sports with one major competition each week, such as U.S. college football, the duration of the microcycle will be altered when more-dense competitive periods are scheduled. Conversely, in sports such as U.S. college volleyball, a 3- to 4-day microcycle could be employed to better account for the occurrence of multiple competitions in close proximity (25).

The periodization model (i.e., parallel, sequential, or emphasis), along with factors such as the specific requirements of the sport, the athlete's ability to tolerate training stress, and the amount of time allocated for training, will influence what type of microcycle is constructed and how it is structured and employed within the training program. Ultimately, the type of microcycle developed is dictated by the period and phase in which it appears (figures 7.11 and 7.12) and the goal established for the mesocycle (22).

Types of Microcycles

Although there are infinite ways to construct microcycles to address an athlete's needs, several standard microcycle formats have been defined within the periodization literature (22, 35). Generally, the two global categories are the preparatory and competitive microcycles (22). During the general preparation phase of the annual training plan, general preparatory microcycles are used to develop basic fitness (46). During the specific preparation phase of the annual training plan, sport-specific preparatory microcycles are used to develop sport-specific fitness and technical skills (25, 46). These two global microcycle types are further subdivided into introductory, ordinary, shock,

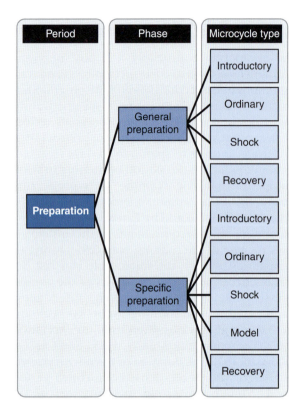

FIGURE 7.11 Classifications of microcycles used in preparatory periods.
Adapted from Haff (2016).

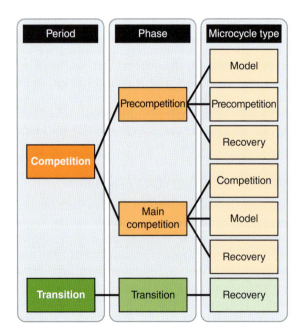

FIGURE 7.12 Classifications of microcycles used in competition and transition periods.
Adapted from Haff (2016).

recovery, precompetitive, model, and competition microcycles (25, 33, 46, 50).

Introductory Microcycle

The **introductory microcycle** is used to introduce new skills and training activities while elevating performance capacity (22). During general preparation phases, it establishes or reestablishes general athletic abilities; during specific preparation phases, it establishes sport-specific skills (22). Generally, introductory microcycles are used only in the preparation period of the annual training plan.

Ordinary Microcycle

The **ordinary microcycle** can be used during any phase of the annual training plan and contains activities performed at submaximal intensities with lower training loads (25, 50). When ordinary microcycles are grouped together, training loads are gradually and uniformly increased across a series of successive microcycles. This type of microcycle can also be grouped with other types of microcycles, and training loads will be altered depending on the goal established for the subsequent microcycle.

Shock Microcycle

A **shock microcycle**, sometimes referred to as a *concentrated loading* or *overreaching microcycle* (25), is noted by a sudden dramatic increase in training load designed to saturate the athlete with a training stimulus and bring them out of a state of stagnation (46, 50). The overall training loads employed in a shock microcycle can be more than double those seen in the ordinary microcycles that typically precede them (33). When a shock microcycle is correctly integrated into a mesocycle, delayed training effects can occur after the fatigue associated with the microcycle is dissipated (11).

Due to the high levels of fatigue, these microcycles are typically used only with advanced athletes during the preparation period, but they can also be used during the competition period if there is an extended break from competition. Shock microcycles need to be used with caution and only with highly trained athletes (25). After the completion of a shock microcycle, a lower-intensity microcycle, such as an ordinary or recovery microcycle, is typically employed. However, in some instances two successive shock microcycles, often referred to as a **double-shock microcycle**, can be employed with highly trained, elite athletes (25, 50). Verkhoshansky and Siff (50) suggest that it is inadvisable to use more than four shock microcycles or more than one double-shock microcycle in a given annual training plan due to increased risk of injury or potential overtraining.

Recovery Microcycle

A **recovery microcycle**, sometimes referred to as a *restorative microcycle* (33), contains reduced training loads marked by reductions in the intensity and volume of training to allow the athlete to rest, heal, and prepare for the next microcycle or block of training (25). Recovery microcycles are commonly placed after microcycles with high training loads, such as shock microcycles. For example, the training load planned for the recovery microcycle should be one-quarter, one-third, or one-half of the training load of the shock microcycle (33). The degree of training load reduction within the recovery microcycle is largely predicated by the magnitude of the loads employed within the microcycle that precedes it (33). As a rule, the greater the loads in the microcycle that precedes the recovery microcycle, the greater the reduction in training load employed in the recovery microcycle.

Precompetitive Microcycle

The **precompetitive microcycle** is used to elevate the athlete's performance in preparation for competition and serves as a transition into competitive microcycles (25). The actual structure of the microcycle largely depends on the athlete's overall fitness level, which dictates which training methods are used (33). Traditionally, the overall volume of training during this type of microcycle is relatively low but emphasizes sport-specific activities to elevate performance (25). In some instances, training sessions with large training loads may be performed during the beginning or in the middle of this microcycle (33). This microcycle type may be considered as part of the early portion of a precompetition taper (see chapter 12) (25).

Model Microcycle

A **model microcycle** is used to reproduce or represent the distribution of work and rest in a competition microcycle. Specifically, this microcycle is structured to mirror the placement of competition events as well as the number of days between competitive engagements to prepare the athlete for the competition microcycle (33). For example, if competitions are on Wednesday and Saturday during a competitive microcycle, the structure of the model microcycle would model the training sequences used in the competition microcycle and aligns two hard training sessions where the competitions occur. Although the model microcycle is most often used within the competition period of the annual training plan, it can also be used during the sport-specific preparation phase to familiarize the athlete with the flow of the competition microcycle (33). Generally, the magnitude of the training load planned for this type of microcycle will dictate the density of training and the duration of the cycle. Specifically, the higher the training load planned, the shorter the microcycle and the fewer training sessions it has (33).

Competition Microcycle

The **competition microcycle** covers the time period prior to and including the competition (50). This microcycle typically includes the training prior to the competition, the travel to the competition, activities related to the actual competition (e.g., warm-up, walk-through), and the recovery activities after the competition (25).

Microcycles should be considered interchangeable structures grouped together to create the mesocycles of training that guide the training process. Microcycles are selected and sequenced based on the targeted training objectives established by the mesocycle, and are designed to guide the training process in accordance with the progression established by the annual training plan (22, 25).

Sequencing Microcycles

There are numerous ways to sequence the microcycles in a mesocycle. By modulating various microcycle sequential patterns, specific training stimuli can be incorporated into the mesocycle to target desired physiological and performance adaptations (22). The most common microcycle sequences are the following:

ordinary (7 days) → ordinary (7 days) → ordinary (7 days) → recovery (7 days)

introductory (7 days) → ordinary (7 days) → ordinary (7 days) → recovery (7 days)

If the athlete's training stagnates, one of the following 4-week sequences could be implemented:

shock (7 days) → ordinary (7 days) → ordinary (7 days) → recovery (7 days)

shock (7 days) → ordinary (7 days) → shock (7 days) → recovery (7 days)

shock (7 days) → recovery (7 days) →
shock (7 days) → recovery (7 days)

If the athlete is in a competition period, the microcycle sequence could be as follows:

ordinary (7 days) → precompetition (7 days) →
competition (7 days) → recovery (7 days)

model (7 days) → precompetition (7 days) →
competition (7 days) → recovery (7 days)

The key to successfully crafting effective training plans is to consider the microcycle in the context of the athlete's needs, the period and phase of training, and the overarching goals established by the annual training plan (22). As part of the training process, the individual training sessions in each microcycle can be modified depending on the athlete's current training state (see chapter 11) while staying consistent with the individual microcycle goals (22, 25).

Structuring Microcycles

There are unlimited possible microcycle structures that can be created to guide the athlete's training process. The overall structure of each microcycle is guided by the targeted training goals and loading patterns established by the mesocycle and the athlete's level of development and overall training capacity. For example, an advanced athlete would be expected to have a higher training tolerance and capacity compared to a novice athlete. Therefore, microcycles with more frequent training performed at higher intensities and greater contrasts in intensity and volume would be prescribed for the advanced athlete compared to the novice athlete (3).

It may not always be possible to individualize the microcycle, especially within team-based sports in which individual athletes might have different training capacities and levels of development. League or union rules may place constraints on the amount of time an athlete can engage in training activities or the number of rest days allocated within the microcycle. For example, in the United States, the NCAA limits the number of contact hours available for training collegiate athletes during the off- and in-season periods. These limits affect how many training sessions are in each microcycle and the overall structure of the microcycle. In these scenarios, the microcycle structure must be carefully considered.

One possible consideration is the number of training sessions in the microcycle (3). The number of training sessions is dictated by the athlete's training capacity, ability to recover from training, and level of development. Additionally, the frequency of training is affected by the allocated time for training and the athlete's participation in training camps (3). To address these factors, there are numerous possible microcycles the coach could prescribe.

Microcycles can be structured with a variety of training frequencies that include single or multiple training sessions per training day (3). For example, microcycles can contain 3 to 6 training days per week with one session allocated to each training day (figure 7.13). For athletes who have a higher level of development and a greater training capacity and can accommodate the additional training time, microcycles with a greater density or frequency of training can be constructed. The most common method used to increase training frequency is programming microcycles that intersperse training days with multiple training sessions with days with no training (figure 7.14).

Another programming strategy is to increase the number of sessions within a microcycle by planning some days with multiple training sessions and some days with single sessions (figure 7.15). For example, in a 3 + 1 microcycle, there are 3 successive half days of training and 1 half day of rest. This pattern is then completed two times resulting in a total of 9 training sessions, and the only day with no training session scheduled is the last day of the microcycle (figure 7.15*a*). If the athlete requires a greater density of training, this basic pattern can be modified to create a 5 + 1 (five sessions plus a half day of rest) microcycle. This structure includes two training sessions on the first and second days and one session on the third day. This pattern is repeated, and then the last day of the microcycle has no training sessions (figure 7.15*b*). If needed, a training session can be added to the last day to create the 5 + 1 + 1 (five training sessions plus a half day of rest and an additional half day of training) microcycle (figure 7.15*c*). Note that the 5 + 1 and 5 + 1 + 1 microcycles are intensive microcycles that should be reserved for athletes with well-developed training capacities (3).

When visualizing the microcycle, all aspects of the athlete's training need to be presented. Although most coaches focus on the physical training (e.g., strength training, conditioning), the coach should also indicate where tactical and technical training occur within each microcycle. For example, French (17) presented an

(a) Three sessions per week

Day	Monday	Tuesday	Wednesday	Thursday	Friday	Saturday	Sunday
Morning or afternoon	Training		Training		Training		

Day	Monday	Tuesday	Wednesday	Thursday	Friday	Saturday	Sunday
Morning or afternoon		Training		Training		Training	

(b) Four sessions per week

Day	Monday	Tuesday	Wednesday	Thursday	Friday	Saturday	Sunday
Morning or afternoon	Training	Training		Training		Training	

Day	Monday	Tuesday	Wednesday	Thursday	Friday	Saturday	Sunday
Morning or afternoon	Training	Training		Training	Training		

(c) Five sessions per week

Day	Monday	Tuesday	Wednesday	Thursday	Friday	Saturday	Sunday
Morning or afternoon	Training	Training	Training		Training	Training	

Day	Monday	Tuesday	Wednesday	Thursday	Friday	Saturday	Sunday
Morning or afternoon	Training	Training	Training	Training	Training		

(d) Six sessions per week

Day	Monday	Tuesday	Wednesday	Thursday	Friday	Saturday	Sunday
Morning or afternoon	Training	Training	Training	Training	Training	Training	

Day	Monday	Tuesday	Wednesday	Thursday	Friday	Saturday	Sunday
Morning or afternoon		Training	Training	Training	Training	Training	Training

FIGURE 7.13 Example microcycle structures with one training session per day: *(a)* three sessions per week; *(b)* four sessions per week; *(c)* five sessions per week; *(d)* six sessions per week.

example preparatory period microcycle for an Olympic taekwondo athlete in which 14 sessions are planned (figure 7.16*a*). In this example, three training sessions are planned for Monday, Tuesday, and Friday. On Wednesday and Thursday, only two sessions are planned, and Saturday has only one training session. When looking at the various training activities, note that 21.4% of the sessions are allotted for strength training, 14.3% of the sessions are designated for conditioning, and 64.3% of the sessions are focused on taekwondo-specific training (figure 7.16*b*).

In addition to presenting training sessions, the coach may also indicate where other activities are placed within the microcycle. For example, the coach may indicate where recovery sessions are delivered or when rehabilitation sessions are scheduled. Additionally, activities such as team or individual meetings could also be integrated into the microcycle structure.

Microcycle Loading Patterns

When constructing microcycles, remember that the structure of the loading should change across the cycle, and the degree to which the load is altered within each training session should be related to the athlete's individual ability to tolerate training and to recover from the imposed training demands (1). Although it is important to have hard training sessions interspersed within the microcycle (14),

a

Day	Monday	Tuesday	Wednesday	Thursday	Friday	Saturday	Sunday
Morning	Training		Training		Training		
Afternoon	Training		Training		Training		

Day	Monday	Tuesday	Wednesday	Thursday	Friday	Saturday	Sunday
Morning		Training		Training		Training	
Afternoon		Training		Training		Training	

b

Day	Monday	Tuesday	Wednesday	Thursday	Friday	Saturday	Sunday
Morning	Training		Training		Training	Training	
Afternoon	Training		Training		Training	Training	

Day	Monday	Tuesday	Wednesday	Thursday	Friday	Saturday	Sunday
Morning	Training	Training		Training		Training	
Afternoon	Training	Training		Training		Training	

c

Day	Monday	Tuesday	Wednesday	Thursday	Friday	Saturday	Sunday
Morning	Training	Training	Training		Training	Training	
Afternoon	Training	Training	Training		Training	Training	

Day	Monday	Tuesday	Wednesday	Thursday	Friday	Saturday	Sunday
Morning	Training	Training		Training	Training	Training	
Afternoon	Training	Training		Training	Training	Training	

FIGURE 7.14 Example microcycle structures with two training sessions per day: *(a)* 3 days per week; *(b)* 4 days per week; *(c)* 5 days per week.

it is equally important to include training days with lower loads to reduce training monotony and strain and enhance recovery (5, 6, 13). It is well-documented that elevated training monotony and strain increase the risk of injury and negative training outcomes, such as performance plateauing and overtraining (13, 37, 52). Interestingly, when comparing a microcycle with 6 loaded training days and 1 day of rest to a microcycle with 4 hard days of training, 2 easier days of training, and 1 day of rest, the same total training load can be accomplished while manipulating levels of monotony and strain (figure 7.17). This mix of heavier and lighter training days in the microcycle increases training variability, which results in a lower overall monotony and strain (figure 7.17a) compared to 6 training days in the week with loaded training sessions (figure 7.17b) (13).

The actual structure of the microcycle can vary significantly depending on the type of microcycle planned, the available time for training, and the athlete's needs. The training load in the microcycle is related to the training demand, which can be classified as a percentage (3, 10), a general categorization (e.g., high, medium, and low) (29), or using zones (table 7.4) (29, 53).

Chapter 7 • Mesocycle and Microcycle Training Plans | **167**

Day	Monday	Tuesday	Wednesday	Thursday	Friday	Saturday	Sunday
Morning	Training	Training	Training	Training	Training	Training	
Afternoon	Training		Training		Training		

a

Day	Monday	Tuesday	Wednesday	Thursday	Friday	Saturday	Sunday
Morning	Training	Training	Training	Training	Training	Training	
Afternoon	Training	Training		Training	Training		

b

Day	Monday	Tuesday	Wednesday	Thursday	Friday	Saturday	Sunday
Morning	Training	Training	Training	Training	Training	Training	Training
Afternoon	Training	Training		Training	Training		

c

FIGURE 7.15 Example microcycles with multiple and single training sessions: *(a)* 3 + 1 microcycle structure; *(b)* 5 + 1 microcycle structure; *(c)* 5 + 1 + 1 microcycle structure.

One common approach to determine the training load is the **session rating of perceived exertion (sRPE) scale** (12), in which training is rated as follows: 10 = maximal; 7-9 = very hard; 5-6 = hard; 4 = somewhat hard; 3 = moderate; 2 = easy; 1 = very, very easy; and 0 = rest (36). To estimate the session load, the sRPE is multiplied by the duration of the whole training session, including warm-up, main training session, cool-down, and recovery intervals (14, 15):

session load (arbitrary units) = duration (min) × sRPE

The main benefit of this method is that loads for all types of training can be calculated on the same scale, allowing the coach to estimate the training loads for individual sessions and across the microcycle.

Microcycles are generally classified into three basic categories: one-, two-, and three-peak microcycle designs (3, 29). There are various ways to construct a one-peak microcycle in which concentrated loading can be used to provide a substantial training response (figure 7.18). For example, a sharp increase in training demand can be planned for the second day of the microcycle followed by reducing training demand across 4 training days to induce recovery (figure 7.18*a*). Alternatively, training demand can be increased across 3 training days and then maximized on the fourth day (figure 7.18*b*). The day with the highest training demand should be followed by 2 days with reduced training demand.

It is more common to use two-peak microcycle designs because they expose the athlete to relatively large amounts of total training demand while reducing overall fatigue (29). By incorporating days with reduced training demand (figure 7.19), the monotony and strain associated with the microcycle can be significantly reduced, which allows the athlete to better recover between sessions. For example, two miniblocks with high- to very high–demand training days that are separated by reduced training demand days designed to enhance recovery can be integrated into a microcycle (figure 7.19*a*). Additionally, in high-demand microcycles, a wave loading structure can be used to create two miniblocks of training that employ 3 training days with increasing training demand (figure 7.19*b*).

Another potential two-peak microcycle strategy can be used during the competitive period (figure 7.20); in this case, a high-demand training day is planned during the early to middle portion of the microcycle and the last day of the microcycle is a competition (figure 7.20*a*). If the last two days of the microcycle contain two competitions, such as in a weekend tournament, two successive days of high-demand training can be planned (figure 7.20*b*).

a

Day	Monday	Tuesday	Wednesday	Thursday	Friday	Saturday	Sunday
Morning	Session	Session	Session		Session	Session	
Middle of the day	Session	Session	Session	Session	Session		
Evening	Session	Session		Session	Session		

b

	Monday	Tuesday	Wednesday	Thursday	Friday	Saturday	Sunday
0700							
0730							
0800		Conditioning long intervals	TKD high-volume striking			Conditioning repeat sprint intervals	
0830							
0900	TKD technical drilling and technique				TKD technical drilling and technique		
0930							
1000							
1030							
1100							
1130		TKD technical training	Strength training	TKD movement and agility			
1200							
1230							
1300							
1330							
1400	TKD speed/high-tempo striking				TKD speed/high-tempo striking		Rest
1430							
1500							
1530							
1600							
1630				TKD sparring			
1700							
1730		TKD technical training					
1800	Strength training				Strength training		
1830							
1900							
1930							
2000							

FIGURE 7.16 Example preseason microcycle for an elite Olympic taekwondo athlete: *(a)* microcycle broken down by session; *(b)* example microcycle session content.

Adapted from French (2019).

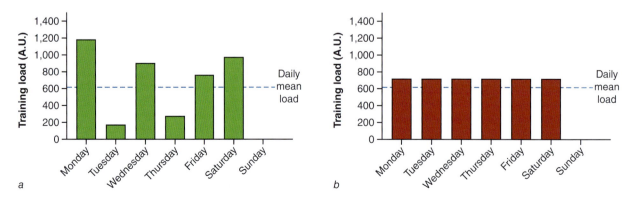

FIGURE 7.17 Microcycle structure's effect on monotony and strain: *(a)* 4 heavy days + 2 light days + 1 recovery day microcycle; *(b)* 6 loaded days + 1 recovery day microcycle.

Chapter 7 • Mesocycle and Microcycle Training Plans | 169

TABLE 7.4 Training Demand, Intensity, and Intensity Zone

Training demand	Intensity	Intensity zone	Percentage of maximum
Very high	Maximum	5	90-100
High	Heavy	4	80-90
Moderate	Medium	3	70-80
Low	Low	2	60-70
Very low	Very low	1	50-60
None (recovery)	Recovery	0	<50

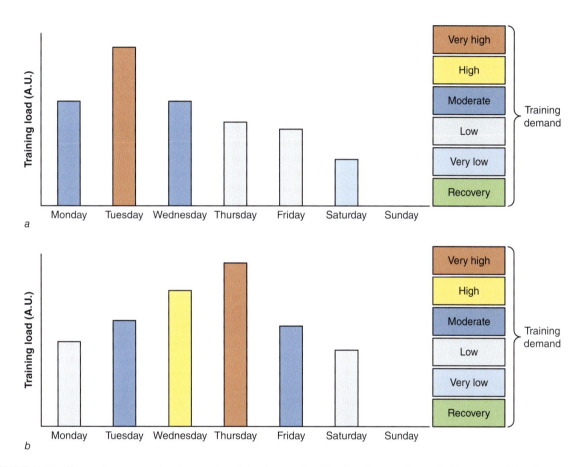

FIGURE 7.18 Example one-peak microcycles: *(a)* microcycle with high demand early in the cycle; *(b)* microcycle with high demand later in the cycle.

Three-peak microcycles are also commonly used when implementing high workloads, such as in shock microcycles (29). With three-peak microcycles, it is important to intersperse high-demand training days with lower-demand days to decrease monotony and allow the athlete to recover (figure 7.21) (13).

Figures 7.18 to 7.21 show the summation of all training factors undertaken on a given training day. The coach must consider the integration of training factors within the microcycle and how the training demand associated with each training factor is sequenced across the microcycle.

Integration of Microcycles

When constructing microcycles, a variety of training means likely will be employed and contribute to the total training demands. Whether the microcycle is for a team or individual sport athlete, the coach must consider how the technical, tactical, and physical training are integrated into the microcycle

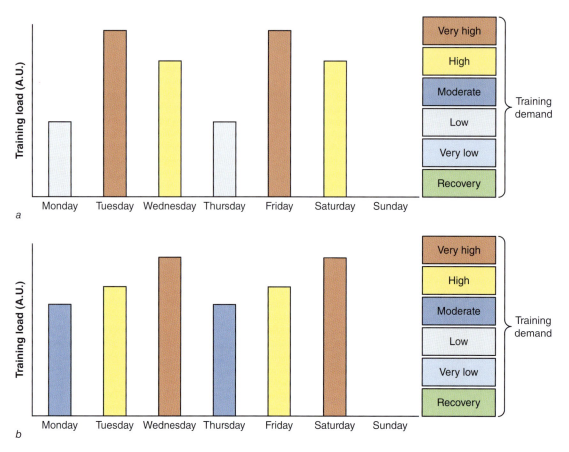

FIGURE 7.19 Example two-peak microcycles: *(a)* microcycle with two high-demand training days in the cycle; *(b)* microcycle with two ascending-demand training days.

to optimize the development of the athlete's performance capacities. In support of this, figure 7.22 presents a two-peak microcycle for an international field hockey team in which 50% of the training time is allotted to hockey-specific training, 25% is allotted to strength training, and 25% is allotted to conditioning. Varying degrees of training demand were planned for each training factor and on each training day.

Similarly, when working with individual sport athletes, such as a mixed martial arts athlete, the coach must balance technical, tactical, and physical training by employing a variety of training factors including strength and conditioning (resistance training), Brazilian Jujitsu or grappling, striking, and wrestling must be incorporated into the microcycle (figure 7.23) (17). For example, figure 7.23 presents a two-peak microcycle in which training demand is allocated as follows: 30% Brazilian Jujitsu or grappling, 30% striking, 20% wrestling, and 20% resistance training.

To offset negative load interactions that can lead to injury or overtraining, not all training targets should receive the same degree of emphasis or stimulate the same degree of training demand (16). This is particularly important during the competition period (i.e., in-season), in which competitions occur at various times within the microcycle. It is important to intersperse targeted recovery sessions into the overall microcycle structure to manage the fatigue generated as a result of the competition (see chapter 9). For example, an in-season, two-peak microcycle for an Australian rules football team might be structured so the early part of the microcycle is a postmatch miniblock dedicated to recovery, which is followed by a miniblock of loading and a miniblock dedicated to unloading prior to the next competition (figure 7.24). In this scenario, the main training sessions are on Tuesday and Thursday. Training sessions in the morning target warm-up, activation, speed work, and skills training. Later in the day, resistance training and physiotherapy treatments are completed. The day before the next match is dedicated to unloading; the athlete performs warm-up, activation, and speed work followed by low-intensity captain runs (8).

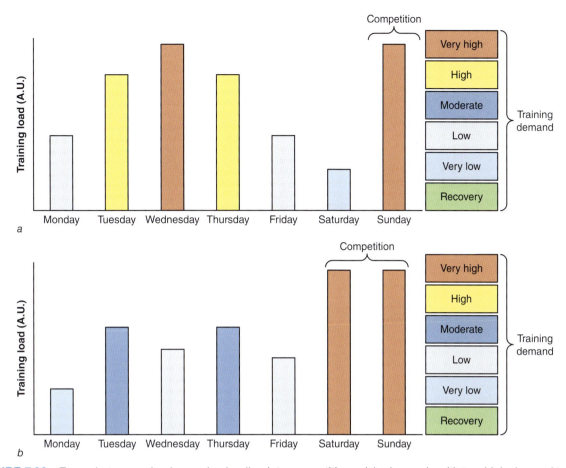

FIGURE 7.20 Example two-peak microcycles leading into competitions: *(a)* microcycle with two high-demand training days, with the second being a competition; *(b)* microcycle with two adjacent high-demand competition days.

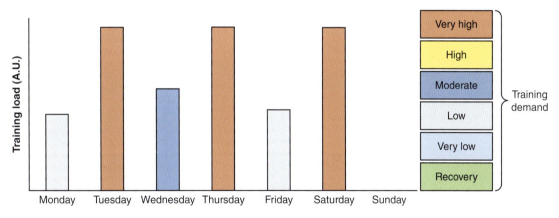

FIGURE 7.21 Example three-peak microcycle.

Although this basic microcycle design can be used in most situations, travel requirements may significantly affect the structure of the miniblocks used to construct the competition microcycle. For example, if a rugby sevens team arrives at the location of a weekend tournament on a Monday, the first day of the microcycle is dedicated to travel, recovery, and mobility sessions designed to help the athletes deal with the stressors associated with travel (41) (figure 7.25). The next 2 days of the microcycle serve as the miniblock of loading. Tuesday's morning session is focused on warm-up and mobility work, high-intensity interval training (HIIT), and light skills work. The afternoon features

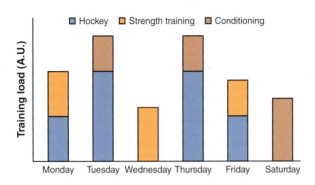

FIGURE 7.22 Example microcycle for an international field hockey team.

Data from Hamilton (2019).

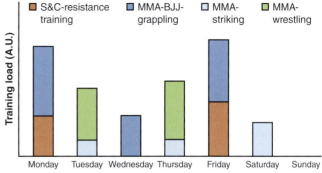

FIGURE 7.23 Example microcycle for a professional mixed martial arts athlete.

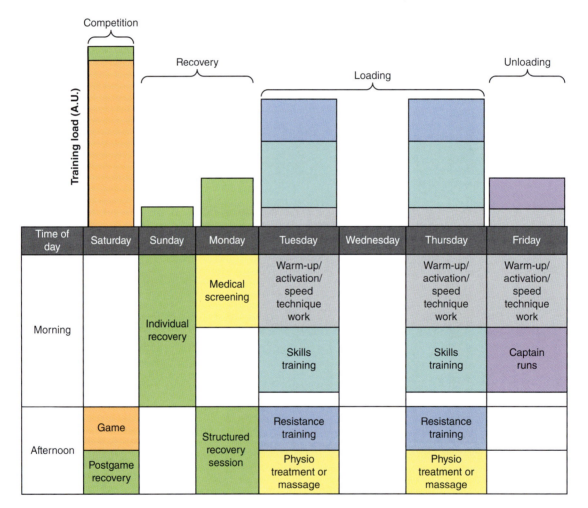

FIGURE 7.24 Example in-season microcycle for an Australian rules football team.

Data from Coutts, Hocking, and Bilsborough (2019).

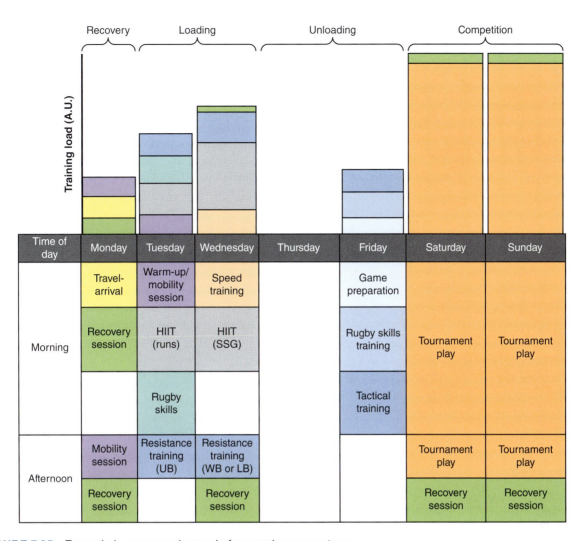

FIGURE 7.25 Example in-season microcycle for a rugby sevens team.

an upper-body resistance training session. On Wednesday, the athletes start the day with speed training and small-sided games (i.e., HIIT). In the evening, the athletes perform a higher-intensity, whole-body (weightlifting derivatives) or lower-body (squats and deadlifts) resistance training session followed by a targeted recovery intervention. No training is conducted on Thursday, and Friday morning is used for game preparation, some light skills work, and some tactical training. Finally, the tournament is conducted across both Saturday and Sunday with multiple competitions undertaken during this time. The end of each day includes targeted recovery strategies (41).

Guidelines for Constructing Microcycles

When building microcycles, remember that they are part of the bigger training picture and need to align with the overall mesocycle training goals. Each microcycle serves as a piece of the mesocycle and integrates physical, technical, and tactical training activities and recovery, nutrition, and psychological interventions (38). The athlete's capacity to manage the various components of an integrated microcycle is based on the coach's ability to design microcycles that modulate the training stimulus and minimize the negative load interactions often associated with fatigue. This balancing act is most evident when concurrent training methods are incorporated into the microcycles of team sport athletes. In these situations, it is often recommended to limit neuromuscular fatigue prior to performing strength training by completing it before engaging in HIIT or to place a minimum of 6 hours between each training factor (2, 20). Additionally, Fyfe, Buchheit, and Laursen (20) recommend that if HIIT is performed within 24 hours of a strength-training session, HIIT activities with lower absolute or relative loads should be used. Based on these recommendations, a basic integrated microcycle can be constructed to modulate neuromuscular fatigue and minimize the interference effects typically associated with concurrent training in team sports (figure 7.26).

It is advisable not to use microcycle structures found in books or on social media. Instead, the coach should design integrated microcycles that address the needs of their athletes and the sports they coach. When crafting effective microcycles, the coach must consider the following (10):

- The magnitude and intensity of loading across the microcycle must be precisely constructed to manage the overall training load and the pattern of loading prescribed for the athlete. Consider the cumulative level of demand on each training day and ensure that the monotony and strain in the microcycle are carefully managed (14).

- Specific units of physical, tactical, and technical training must be employed to achieve a specific training objective. The structure and placement of these units must be carefully considered to ensure variability in the intraday and interday application of the prescribed training units. This is critical to ensure balance between the stimulus and recovery within each microcycle. Although complete recovery is not necessary between training units (18, 19), varying the training load (i.e., reducing training monotony) is an essential aspect of the microcycle. In fact, inserting sessions with lower training loads into the microcycle can accelerate the recovery process due to an enhancement of active recovery (1).

- The time frame between training units should be carefully managed. For example, it is generally recommended that units with a high neuromuscular load, such as strength training, be performed at least 6 hours prior to engaging in conditioning activities, such as HIIT, when these units are planned on the same training day (20). Alternatively, a microcycle sequencing in which concurrent training activities, such as strength training and conditioning, are placed on alternate days results in the greatest strength gains when compared to when both activities are conducted in the same session (43, 45).

- Technical, speed, and speed–strength development should be conducted on training days when the athlete is the most recovered. These activities should not immediately follow training sessions that contained extensive conditioning (i.e., endurance training) demands (1). If scheduling requires that technical, speed, and speed–strength training be completed on the same day as conditioning, conditioning must be performed after these activities. Dick (10) suggests that speed, elastic strength, and maximum strength training should never be performed following days of high demand, especially training days that target anaerobic endurance training.

- For competitive microcycles, the competition must occur 2 to 3 days after a higher load training day to capitalize on the supercompensation effect (1).

Although these basic guidelines apply in most situations, different types of microcycles require different structures and different ratios of work and recovery (19). Regardless of the type of microcycle, the ability to construct and arrange microcycles with a variety of training means a flexible programming framework is central to the art of coaching (10).

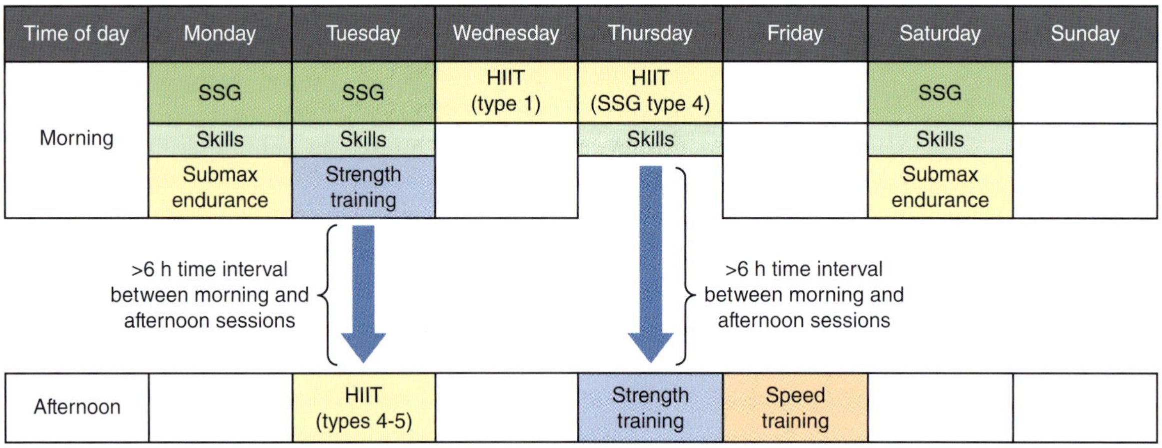

Time of day	Monday	Tuesday	Wednesday	Thursday	Friday	Saturday	Sunday
Morning	SSG	SSG	HIIT (type 1)	HIIT (SSG type 4)		SSG	
	Skills	Skills		Skills		Skills	
	Submax endurance	Strength training				Submax endurance	
Afternoon		HIIT (types 4-5)		Strength training	Speed training		

>6 h time interval between morning and afternoon sessions

>6 h time interval between morning and afternoon sessions

FIGURE 7.26 Example integrated microcycle for team sports.
Data from Fyfe et al. (2019).

Summary

The mesocycle structure is a critical part of the programming and periodization process. Classically, various categories of mesocycles were sequenced and integrated to guide the training process. More recently, the use of the block concept has resulted in a streamlined mesocycle taxonomy, producing three common mesocycles: accumulation, transmutation, and realization. Regardless of the mesocycle taxonomy used, the overall training load is progressively increased across the preparation period as the athlete's work capacity is increased. As the athlete transitions into the competition period, the mesocycle structure and progression are dictated by the competitive schedule. Although the most common mesocycle is 4 weeks long, the mesocycle can be reduced to as little as 2 weeks or extended to 6 weeks depending on how the coach plans the training process. The actual makeup of the mesocycle is based on the loading patterns presented in each microcycle within it.

When building each mesocycle, the coach must ensure that each microcycle is designed to minimize monotony and strain while ensuring that the training load between microcycles is modulated in accordance with the work-to-rest ratio planned for the mesocycle. To accomplish this, the total training load within each training day must be varied to create light and heavy training days. Depending on the breakdown of each microcycle, various strategies can be used to modulate training loads by increasing or decreasing the number of high training load days within the microcycle. When entering the competitive period, the placement of high training load days is related to the time frame between competitions. Although the most common microcycle lasts 7 days, the placement of competitions may require the microcycle to be shortened to as few as 2 days or extended to 14 days (when longer times between competitions are available). Regardless of the duration of the microcycle, the composition of each training session in a training day is used to create the training loads represented in the microcycle plan. Structuring loads that vary by day and session is critically important when designing effective microcycles and, by extension, mesocycles.

CHAPTER 8

Training Sessions and Days

The coach's ability to design and organize individual training sessions for each training day in a series of microcycles is a critical aspect of the programming level of the periodization process. This ability allows the coach to develop training programs that guide the athlete's training activities in accordance with the goals of the period and phase of training. **Training sessions**, or workouts, are generally composed of several **training units** that target the development of specific biomotor abilities, physical attributes, or technical and tactical abilities. Depending on the athlete's level of development, time available for training, and the period or phase of training, the coach may have the athlete undertake single or multiple training sessions in a training day. Manipulating the number of training sessions in a training day allows the coach to introduce further variation into the training process.

When the sessions for each training day are integrated and sequenced, the coach must consider the fatigue associated with each session and the athlete's ability to recover between sessions. By varying the type of training session or the training load in each session, the training stimulus can be manipulated to maximize the athlete's ability to adapt to the training process. Based on the type of training session, the coach selects, integrates, and sequences specific training units to create the structure of the training session. Ultimately, the quality of the training session is dictated by the integration and sequencing of the training units used to create the session.

To effectively structure each training day, the coach must understand the various types of training sessions that can be programmed. The basic structure of a training session must also be considered because certain activities are germane to all training sessions. Therefore, it is important for the coach to develop a comprehensive understanding of the key structures used in each training session and how to integrate them into the training day and microcycle.

Training Session Types

There are many ways to classify training sessions, or workouts. The most common method of classification is based on the session organization and the tasks and loads in the session (66, 67).

Training Session Organization

One method of defining the training session is based on its organizational structure, typically categorized as group, individual, or mixed training sessions (figure 8.1) (20, 21, 66, 67).

Group Training Sessions

The most common method of structuring a training session, especially in team sports and in centralized training systems in which a group of high-level athletes train together (66), is the group training session (21). Group training sessions may not include every member of a team and may be subdivided into disciplines or specialties within the team. In American football, for example, group sessions are structured to address the needs of the offensive and defensive players. Further subdivisions of the defensive playing group are often made to provide more position-specific training (e.g., for linemen,

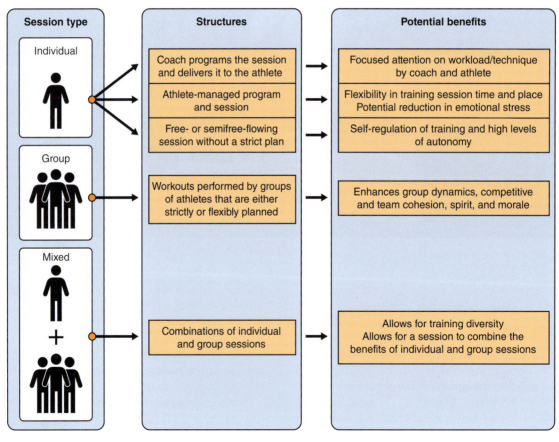

FIGURE 8.1 Workouts classified by organizational structure.

linebackers, defensive backs). After the subgroup training sessions, the coach can bring the defensive group back together to integrate each group's individual techniques into a larger defensive tactical strategy. Although subdividing the group allows for more individualized work, these sessions are not ideally suited for addressing an individual athlete's specific deficiencies, which are better addressed with targeted individual or mixed sessions (21, 66, 67). The main benefits of group training sessions are that they allow the coach to control the structure and form of the training session to develop key aspects of the team's development, such as team tactics and the development of team spirit and morale.

Individual Training Sessions

In individual training sessions, the coach can provide the athlete with more focused attention by working one-on-one with them. In these sessions, the coach can more easily target the athlete's individual physical, technical, or psychological deficiencies. Since the coach can provide more attention to an individual athlete, they are better able to provide coaching feedback to the athlete and more effectively adjust the training session to align with the athlete's specific needs. These sessions are common in individual sports such as track and field (i.e., athletics) since an athlete may have a personal coach who monitors and guides each training session.

Individual training sessions can also be undertaken virtually with (8, 9) or without the coach being physically present (23). Using a smartphone or tablet and a video conferencing application (e.g., Zoom, FaceTime, Microsoft Teams), the athlete can stream the session, allowing the coach to work with them in real time or record the session for the coach to review at a later time. This type of coaching, often referred to as the *video coach* or the **remote coach** (8, 9, 23), has become increasingly popular, and was especially valuable during the COVID-19 pandemic when social distancing was necessary.

Although the remote coach model can increase athlete compliance with the training process (23), there are limitations to its effectiveness (8). Due to camera angle limitations, potential technical issues, and possible delays between training and feedback, this type of coaching is not as effective as in-person coaching (9). It is, however, more effective than having no coach present, so it should be considered only when in-person coaching is not an option.

While it is generally accepted that having a coach present during training will improve the development of the athlete, there is also value in scheduling individual training sessions in which the coach is not present and the athlete is in charge of managing and delivering the session to themselves (20, 21). These sessions help engage the athlete in the training process by providing them some autonomy and control over what they are doing (20, 21). Additionally, these training sessions are more flexible and allow the athlete to determine when in the training day the sessions are completed. Although they are useful in developing the athlete's ability to self-regulate their training, these sessions should be reserved for elite and developed athletes who have the physical and psychological skills to handle them. Additionally, these types of sessions should not make up the majority of the athlete's training; face-to-face coaching is critical to overall development.

Mixed Training Sessions

Mixed training sessions have individual and group components (66, 67). For example, the entire team might engage in a group warm-up, divide into individual training sessions, come back together for a group training session, and finish with a group cool-down (20, 21). Mixed sessions can be used in team and individual sports depending on the coach's plan and the individual athletes' needs. For example, a U.S. college Division I basketball team may start with a group warm-up where the coach outlines the goals for the session after which the athletes are given time to work individually on their free throw shooting. After completing this individual technical work, the athletes reconvene and work on various offensive and defensive strategies and other technical and tactical skills. Following the technical and tactical training activities the athletes may undertake a high-intensity interval training session (HIIT), followed by a group cool-down.

When constructing a mixed training session, the coach can use various combinations of individual and group training activities to create creative and engaging sessions. Which activities are chosen is largely dictated by the athlete's training age or level of development and their ability to effectively complete the required training activities.

Training Task Classification

Another way to classify the training session is based on the prevalent tasks in the session (20, 21, 66, 67). Currently there is no consensus in the literature about how to define the tasks in a training session, but Bompa and Haff (21), Bompa and Buzzichelli (20), and Issurin (66, 67) have each offered their own task classifications. Even though these authors have offered several classification options, there are additional task categories that have not been included in these classifications. Based on the available literature we can consider six types of sessions: physical training, technical, tactical or techno-tactical, combined, assessment, and recovery sessions.

Physical Training Sessions

Physical training sessions develop various physical qualities. For example, these sessions can be constructed to target strength training, speed and agility, metabolic conditioning, endurance, and flexibility or mobility. In some instances, these sessions also contain technical tasks. For example, including small-sided games is a common HIIT strategy for team sports, such as soccer (31, 58), in which tactical and physical conditioning are undertaken in a session. From a planning perspective, considering the types of physical training in the session provides the coach with a more informative way to define this type of training session. Without the watchful eye of the coach during these sessions, the athlete might develop poor technical movement patterns that are very difficult to correct once ingrained.

Technical Sessions

The technical session introduces new technical skills and provides opportunities to perfect them. A key aspect of a technical session is the coach's real-time evaluation and immediate correction of the athlete's technical deficiencies to prevent bad techniques from becoming ingrained (66, 67).

Tactical or Techno-Tactical Sessions

The tactical or techno-tactical session translates the skills mastered in technical sessions into tactical skills. In these sessions, athletes develop, practice, and perfect individual or team tactics through physical and mental exercises and theoretical training sessions in which tactical strategies are discussed (66, 67). These sessions need to be carefully planned so sport-specific activities are performed in situations that mirror the stressful situations the athlete will encounter during competition (66, 67).

Combined Sessions

Combined sessions develop more than one target ability (66, 67). For example, the first part of a training session can be designed to develop technical skills, and the later portion of the session can be used for conditioning. Freeman (44) presents a four-step progression for combined training sessions:

1. Learning or perfecting technique or tactics
2. Developing speed or coordination
3. Strength training
4. Training for general and specific endurance

Although this progression suggests practicing techniques and tactics first when the athlete is fresh so fatigue will not interfere with learning, this strategy may not always be prudent (44). For example, speed and coordination exercises should be performed before technical work if technique is practiced under heavy loaded conditions, such as in weightlifting or throwing. Additionally, if maximal speed development is the primary target of the session, speed training should immediately follow the warm-up (44).

Issurin (67, 69) suggests that an alternative strategy for constructing the training session is to create conjugate exercises in which there is a simultaneous development of sport-specific motor abilities and technical skills development. Speed-assisted or speed-resisted exercises are common strategies for constructing conjugate exercises.

Assessment Sessions

Assessment sessions are periodically undertaken to monitor an athlete's progress (21) and evaluate the athlete's physical and technical abilities (66, 67). These sessions can be used to evaluate physiological, mechanical, or physical performance capacities with tests that serve as surrogates for actual competitions (27, 95). Assessment sessions should be carefully planned because specific equipment and conditions are required. Alternatively, these sessions can be structured to contain exhibition or practice competitions to gauge an athlete's level of development and preparedness for competition (21). Because maximal effort is required in these sessions, it is important to consider the placement of these sessions within the microcycle.

Recovery Sessions

Recovery sessions are an important part of the overall periodized training plan (105). In these sessions, water immersion protocols, massage, meditation, or other forms of recovery can be integrated into the athlete's program (118). Recovery sessions can be used to prepare for specific training sessions, stimulate acute recovery during the competitive phase, or decrease physiological stress related to travel. For example, after long-haul travel a training session of active or passive recovery techniques (see chapter 9) will facilitate recovery (114). Recovery sessions also can be strategically placed around competitions.

Training Load Classification

Another way to classify training sessions is to use load classifications to differentiate sessions (66, 67). Issurin (66) suggests three basic training session types: developmental, retention, and restorative. Conceptually, all training programs are created from various combinations of these three training session types. The coach can classify various training sessions using a training load classification system like the one presented in figure 8.2, where the training session type can be aligned with a loading scale (i.e., sRPE) (66) and the time to completely recover (146).

Although classifying sessions by training load can be useful when planning the loading progressions and variations in the training program, the main limitation of this session classification system relates to how these strategies relate to psychological and neurophysiological effort (66). This session classification approach may work well for strength, power, endurance, or speed training, but may not align well with training sessions with high neuroemotional stress (67).

Another strategy to address some of these limitations is to multiply the session rating of perceived exertion (sRPE) by the duration of the training session to yield the session training load (41, 96). The main benefit of this method is that it allows the training load for all types of training to be determined on the same scale (see chapter 11). This allows the coach to better understand the load requirements during individual training days and across a microcycle.

Defining a Training Session

The training session, or workout, is a critical component of the training day within the microcycle used to create the mesocycle. When joined together and properly sequenced, each training session serves as an individual building block that contributes to the overall training process (66, 67). Each training session generally lasts approximately 2 hours, but, depending on the sport and the phase of the annual training plan, it can be extended up to 5 hours (21).

Training sessions may be defined based on duration, falling into one of three categories:

1. Short-duration training session: 30 to 90 minutes
2. Moderate-duration training session: 2 to 3 hours
3. Long-duration training session: more than 3 hours (21)

The coach plans the duration of the training session based on the athlete's current level of physical preparedness, the training units incorporated into the session, and how the session fits into the training day, microcycles, and mesocycles within the training period. For example, during an in-season period, a cyclist may train 5 to 6 hours during an individual training session, while an American football player may train only 1.5 to 2 hours. Different sports require different training

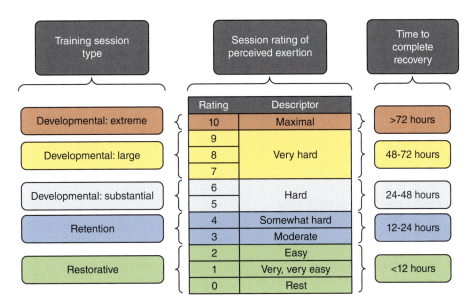

FIGURE 8.2 Defining training sessions by training load.

durations, which can be additionally affected by the athlete's individual needs.

Depending on the athlete's level of development, each training day will contain single or multiple training sessions composed of a variety of training units (52, 54). Typically, a single training session is defined as having less than 40 minutes of rest between the training units contained in the session (52, 65). When training contains more than 40 minutes between training units, it is likely that the total time allocated to the training session will be greater depending on how the training units are integrated into the session.

Constructing Training Sessions

A properly designed training session is made of various training units sequenced to address the athlete's individual needs (20, 21, 86). Bompa and Buzzichelli (20) suggest that a training session generally contains three or four main structural components, or training units. The three-component training session generally contains a warm-up, the body of the training session, and a cool-down. The four-component training session also includes an introduction prior to the warm-up. Bompa and Buzzichelli (20) suggest that three-component training sessions are generally used with advanced athletes because they require less explanation and motivation than athletes with lower levels of development. Although it seems logical to use a three-component training session with advanced athletes and a four-component training session with developing athletes, it is more appropriate to consider using a five-component training session structure with all athletes (86). This session adds a closing summary after the cool-down. The inclusion of the introduction and closing summary allows the coach to highlight the key training goals for the session and provide the athlete with feedback at the end of the session. These important communication points help the coach and athlete develop and strengthen communication to ensure everyone is on the same page.

Organizing Training Sessions

The organization of a training session is much like a lesson plan because it guides the direction of the training process (86). The training session is subdivided into several key tasks that provide structure and guide the athlete through the session.

Introduction

The training session begins by convening the athletes for a 5- to 10-minute meeting used to take care of housekeeping items prior to initiating the training session (70, 80). During this time, the coach makes announcements, goes through the future schedule, shares recognitions, provides a schedule of meetings or training, and provides information about the goals and objectives for the training session (21, 80). For team sports, after the coach gives the general training objectives, it may be warranted to break the team into smaller groups so coaches can discuss specific individual or positional goals and objectives (21). The coach should also use the introduction as a time to motivate the athlete for successful training (80).

To effectively deliver an introduction, the coach must be prepared and organized so they can clearly and concisely communicate the important facts that need to be conveyed. In some instances, they might use audiovisual aids or handouts to strengthen their message. Handouts are extensions of the athlete's training program and provide specific goals or objectives the athlete needs to focus on during the training session (21). The athlete should receive their training program in advance of the training session so that they can familiarize themselves with it and mentally prepare for the session. This may be facilitated with the use of modern programming technologies (e.g., Visualcoaching Pro, TeamBuildr, BridgeAthletic, TrainHeroic) that deliver training programs directly to the athlete's smartphone or tablet. An additional benefit of providing the program prior to the session is it allows the athlete to bring questions that can be addressed during the session introduction.

Warm-Up

The warm-up is an integral part of all training sessions or competitions (12, 13) and prepares the athlete both physically and mentally (71, 132). Warm-up techniques can be broadly classified as either passive or active (12, 21). **Passive warm-up** techniques involve external methods, such as saunas, hot showers, hot baths, heating pads, or diathermy, to increase muscle and core temperature without depleting energy substrates (12). Although passive warm-up techniques can enhance performance (42), they are not practical for most athletes. More frequently, **active warm-up** techniques, such as jogging, calisthenics, cycling, or rowing, are used to increase muscle and core temperature prior to training or competition (13). These techniques tend to create greater metabolic and cardiovascular changes than passive warm-ups.

A well-crafted, active warm-up can stimulate several temperature-related and non-temperature-related physiological responses (figure 8.3) and may potentially increase subsequent performance (71). Temperature-related effects include elevations in muscle and core temperature (12, 13), which are likely to increase nerve conduction rate, the speed of metabolic reactions, and the speed and force of muscle contractions and to reduce reaction time (12, 13, 142). Additionally, the amount of oxygen delivered to the working muscle (5) increases as a result of increased vasodilation and blood flow (142) and an increased release of oxygen from **hemoglobin** and **myoglobin** (5, 6, 12, 13).

While many of the benefits of the warm-up are temperature related, additional benefits are non-temperature related (12, 13). Non-temperature-related effects include increased muscle blood flow, elevations in baseline oxygen consumption, positive psychological effects, and postactivation potentiation performance enhancement effects (12).

From a psychological perspective, the warm-up provides valuable time for athletes to prepare for training or competition (12). Support for this can be seen in research that shows that when athletes imagine a warm-up, there is enhanced physiological performance (91). Due to the psychological responses associated with a warm-up, it may be better to consider the warm-up as a key part of a preperformance routine when the athlete is attempting to optimize their level of activation (12, 108). In this regard, the warm-up may also provide the athlete with time to concentrate and focus on the tasks ahead, ultimately resulting in an increased level of preparedness.

The most noted performance effect of a warm-up is related to **postactivation performance enhancement (PAPE).** PAPE is represented as an enhanced muscle function after acute muscle activity (17, 115). In the classic literature, this is referred to as **postactivation potentiation (PAP)** (122), in which the main mechanisms underpinning the response have been related to myosin regulatory light chain phosphorylation (50, 62) or an elevation in calcium (Ca^{2+}) in the cytosol (2). More recently, however, the use of the PAP terminology has come under question, and the PAPE taxonomy has become more popular when talking about the effect of a conditioning stimulus (i.e., warm-up) on a performance outcome (17, 115). The PAPE response has been suggested to be a result of changes in muscle temperature, muscle and muscle fiber water content, and muscle activation that occur in response to the warm-up (17). The PAPE response appears to be most prevalent in strength and power performance (126, 128, 129) and seems to be greater in stronger athletes (128, 130). Although the PAPE response is well-documented, much more research is required to understand how to optimally use various warm-up strategies to maximize the performance enhancement.

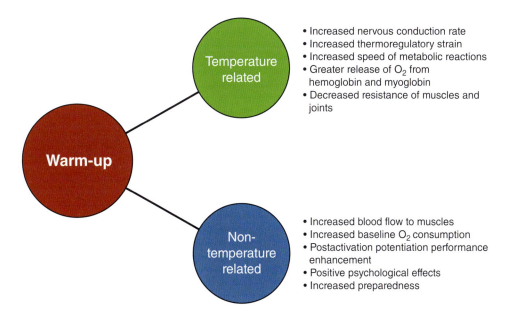

FIGURE 8.3 Possible warm-up effects.

Regardless of how a warm-up is conceptualized, the goal of enhancing performance and reducing overall risk of injury remains the same. Although a lot of research explores the performance benefits of a warm-up, much less directly links the warm-up to a reduction in injury risk. The current belief is that a well-structured dynamic warm-up can reduce the overall risk of injury during training and competition (142). For example, a structured warm-up after halftime during a football game has been shown to reduce the number of musculotendinous injuries (i.e., sprains and strains) per game (16). It is likely that the main injury-reduction benefit of the warm-up is related to the increase in body temperature as a result of the activities performed (78).

Components of a Warm-Up

The classic approach to building a warm-up divides the time into two phases: a **general warm-up** followed by a **specific warm-up** (78). Classically, the general warm-up consists of slow aerobic activity (such as jogging, cycling, or skipping) that increases heart rate, blood flow, muscle temperature, and respiration rate while reducing the viscosity of the joint fluids (71). This phase is followed by a period of general stretching that replicates the ranges of motion required for the upcoming event (71, 78). The athlete then transitions to a specific warm-up that contains sport-specific movement patterns that serve as a rehearsal of the skills that will be performed in the training session (144).

Although **static stretching**, a form of slow constant stretching in which the stretch is held for 15 to 30 seconds, has been recommended as a key part of the warm-up by some coaches (20) and researchers (83), it is clear based on contemporary research that a **dynamic warm-up** that uses **dynamic stretching** or mobility drills is a superior method for preparing the athlete for training or competition. In fact, static stretching has been shown to reduce performance capacity in all types of activities, most notably during strength- and power-based activities (26, 43, 131, 141). Bompa and Buzzichelli (20) suggest that the negative effects of static stretching can be reduced by placing it after the general warm-up. However, ample research suggests that no matter where static stretching is in the warm-up, it results in performance decrements compared to using a dynamic warm-up (26, 131, 139, 145). For example, Young and Behm (145) reported that a combination of general (i.e., running) and specific (i.e., jumping) warm-up activities exerted a positive performance-enhancement effect, and static stretching, no matter where it was in the warm-up period, resulted in negative effects on performance. Based on this research, it is recommended that static stretching is not included in the warm-up phase of a training session. Attempts to increase flexibility through static stretching should be reserved for the cool-down or targeted training sessions where this modality of training is the primary focus.

The structure of the warm-up should allow for elevation of the muscle and core temperatures without reducing energy stores (71). Typically, the total warm-up will last 20 to 45 minutes, with 5 minutes dedicated to the general warm-up and at least 15 minutes dedicated to the specific warm-up (figure 8.4) (21, 63, 71, 86).

Although these general warm-up guidelines work in most instances, as the complexity of the sport increases, so does the duration of the warm-up. The athlete may need to extend the specific warm-up to 20 to 40 minutes. Additionally, the ideal duration of the warm-up is very individualized and should be modified based on the athlete's specific requirements and preferences (21).

Although the classic methods of coupling a general and specific warm-up have existed for some time, the efficacy of these methods has been questioned, and alternative warm-up methods have been proposed (71, 78). Jeffreys (71) suggests that classic warm-up models do not always consider the overall development of the athlete and may not be designed as well as the body of a training session. The warm-up is a critical part of the athlete's overall development, and the construction of each warm-up requires the coach to consider short-, medium-, and long-term planning strategies (i.e.,

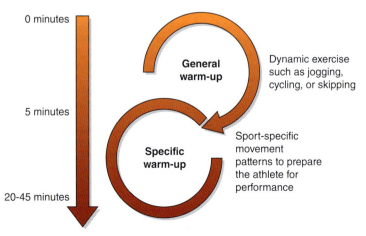

FIGURE 8.4 Classic warm-up breakdown.

periodization strategies) (72). Thus, the warm-up needs to be crafted in a periodized manner and incorporate progressions of development. A relatively new strategy to accomplish this goal is to use the **raise, activate and mobilize, and potentiate (RAMP)** protocol developed by Professor Ian Jeffreys (figure 8.5) (71, 72, 78).

Similar to the general warm-up, the main aim of the raise phase is to use carefully crafted strategies to raise body temperature and increase muscle elasticity, muscle contraction rates, and oxygen delivery and uptake and to divert blood flow (72). The end goals of the raise phase are similar to those of the classic general warm-up, but they are achieved with different methods. Although the general warm-up tends to use arbitrary activities such as cycling, rowing, or jogging to increase muscle and body temperature, activities included in the raise phase are carefully selected, highly specific to the athlete's needs, and programmed in a periodized manner to optimize long-term skill development and movement competency (71, 72). Typically, this is accomplished through the use of locomotor movements, the development of skills, or a combination of both (72). Incorporating movement-competency activities into the warm-up allows for a high density of skills application in a given period. The types of skills used in the raise phase vary depending on the context and the sport or activity the warm-up is targeting. In a team sport context, a multisport setup in which basic sport skills such as kicking, catching, hitting, swinging, and jumping can all be integrated into the raise phase of the warm-up (72, 76).

The raise phase progresses from low- to moderate-intensity activities, simple to complex movements, and low to high cognitive challenges (76).

It's easy to regulate intensity in the raise phase because intensity directly relates to the speed at which the activities are performed. Modulating the complexity and cognitive challenge requires more thought and careful planning. The complexity of the movements increases from single movement patterns into combinations of movements. For example, simple movements, such as side shuffling, backpedaling, or linear running, can be performed as discrete activities or can be combined to create more complex movement challenges (76). Cognitive challenge can be increased by adding decision-making tasks or degrees of freedom within a given movement into the warm-up. Ultimately, the coach should consider the raise phase of the warm-up as more than just a way to increase muscle and body temperature; it is a valuable time that can be used to improve movement competencies.

The activate and mobilize phase is analogous with the dynamic stretching component of classic warm-up strategies (71, 72). During this phase, movement patterns such as squatting, lunging, and crawling are used develop **mobility**, or movement through a range of motion, with activities that integrate motor control, stability, and flexibility (69). The dynamic activities in this phase should be designed to prepare the athlete for the pending session and enhance the athlete's overall movement literacy (71). Through appropriate exercises, key movement patterns can develop motor control and mobility during the warm-up. Coaches can leverage an infinite number of possible exercises to construct the activate and mobilize phase of the warm-up (71). Generally, these exercises fall into one of five categories: squat, lunge, stepping single-leg stance, brace, and reach movement pattern groups (72). Using exercises from each movement

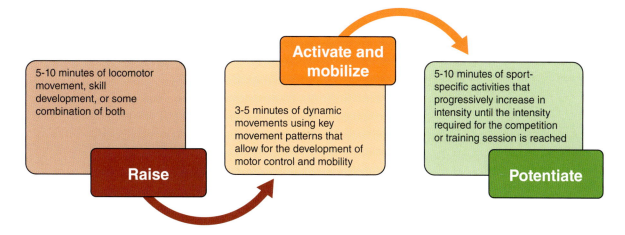

FIGURE 8.5 The raise, activate and mobilize, and potentiate (RAMP) warm-up protocol.

pattern group allows the athlete to practice specific movement patterns while mobilizing discrete areas of the body to better prepare for the main training session. Once the athlete masters a movement pattern, the coach can implement a progressive sequence to increase the physical challenge. For example, once a static lunge pattern is mastered, the athlete could progress to a series of different lunging strategies that increase in complexity (72):

static lunge → walking lunge → lunge with varied directional reach → lunge with different degrees of rotation

A key benefit of this strategy is that multiplanar movements integrate multiple joints into a single dynamic stretch to better prepare the athlete for their sport (71). Ultimately, activation and mobilization exercises provide a time-efficient way to warm up and to continue to develop movement literacy, which should be continually reinforced (71-73).

The potentiate phase serves as a bridge between the activate and mobilize phase and the body of the training session (75). This phase of the warm-up prepares the athlete for subsequent performance, especially in activities that require high levels of speed, strength, and power. Although often considered analogous to the specific warm-up, the potentiate phase differs in that it requires a progressive increase in intensity as the athlete moves through the phase (71). When used to prepare for a training session, the athlete uses a progressive sequence of activities to maximize performance in the session and develop specific skills and abilities to optimize performance in the short, medium, and long term (72). This is very different from traditional warm-up strategies because this phase is not solely focused on short-term goals and may incorporate activities used for long-term athlete development and provide significant intensity to optimize performance in the subsequent session (75). Alternatively, when used as part of the competition warm-up, the potentiate phase will include a progression of sport-specific activities that maximize the athlete's physiological and psychological performance capacities and prime them for the subsequent sport performance (71).

Jeffreys (71, 72, 75) suggests that the potentiate phase of the warm-up, if structured correctly, can serve as a discrete session or a progressive series of exercises to develop a specific capacity while physiologically and psychologically preparing the athlete to undertake the main training session. Discrete activities do not need to be related to the main session but are structured to focus on the development of a key capacity (72). For example, prior to performing a technical session, the potentiate phase could include maximal speed development activities to address a long-term development target. Alternatively, if a progressive series of activities is used, the potentiate phase of the warm-up could use a wide range of skills, such as jockeying and acceleration, which are related to defensive capabilities in team sports. These activities can be structured as a progression from basic to more sport-specific activities (72). The activities used in the potentiate phase of the warm-up must be carefully structured to provide a time-efficient way to incorporate more developmental training into the athlete's training session.

Overall, the RAMP warm-up methodology is a way to more effectively use the time dedicated to the warm-up. The warm-up can last 13 to 45 minutes; duration depends on the structure of the potentiate phase and the athlete's needs. For example, an athlete preparing for a running activity could move through a series of ankle drills, low-amplitude skips, A drills, and form runs as part of the raise phase of the warm-up. From there the athlete could perform a series of dynamic stretches to activate and mobilize the body before undertaking more intensive warm-up activities. In the potentiate phase, the athlete could perform 60 m acceleration runs and ins and outs prior to beginning the running session (table 8.1). More complex warm-up structures can also be created to incorporate more drills and activities that prepare the team sport athlete for training or competition (table 8.2).

For more information on how to optimally construct warm-ups, see Ian Jeffreys' text *The Warm-Up: Maximise Performance and Improve Long-Term Athlete Development* (77).

Body of the Training Session

The body of the training session targets the development of very specific training objectives. The athlete is introduced to and practices new skills and tactical maneuvers, goes through structured training activities to improve specific biomotor abilities, and enhances psychological abilities (21). Issurin (66, 67) refers to this portion of the training session as the *loading phase* due to the concentration of specific training tasks selected to address some targeted outcome. The content of this portion of the training session depends on many factors, including the athlete's level of development, sex, and age; the sport being trained for; and where the session falls in the annual training plan (21). This portion of the session can be created to

TABLE 8.1 RAMP Warm-Up for Running

Duration (min)	Phase	Setup	Activity
5-10	Raise	Lines set 20 m (66 ft) apart	2 × ankle drills
			Low-amplitude skips
			4 × A drill (single exchange)
			5 × form runs
3-5	Activate and mobilize	Lines set 15 m (49 ft) apart	Calf walks with rotation
			Single-leg knee flexion
			Reverse lunge
			Single-leg Romanian deadlift
			Squat and reach
			Mountain climber
5-10	Potentiate	70-80 m (230-262 ft) straight line running	6 × 60 m (197 ft) acceleration runs
			3 × 60 m (197 ft) ins and outs

Adapted by permission from I. Jeffreys, *The Warm-Up: Maximize Performance and Improve Long-Term Athlete Development* (Champaign, IL: Human Kinetics, 2019), 175.

TABLE 8.2 RAMP Warm-Up for Rugby

Duration (min)	Phase	Setup	Activity
10	Raise	Lines set 20 m (66 ft) apart	2 × walking
			2 × lunging
			2 × skipping
			2 × shuffling
			2 × carioca
			2 × backward skipping
5	Activate and mobilize	Lines set 15 m (49 ft) apart	Calf walk with shoulder rotation
			Speed-skater lunge
			Mountain climber
			Inchworm
			Squat with lateral shift
			Single-leg Romanian deadlift
10-15	Potentiate	50 m (164 ft) sprint	5 × 20 m (66 ft) rolling starts
			4 each side shuffle and stick
			4 each side adjustment and cut
			4 each side acceleration to day light
			6 × feint cut and drive

guide training in a uniform or integrated complex manner. A uniform session is structured to focus only on strength training, metabolic conditioning, or technical training. Conversely, an integrated complex session might contain several segments that target different training factors. For example, a training session for a hammer thrower may have three distinct training segments that focus on technical, strength, and sprint training (22). As a general rule, no more than three training factors should be targeted within an individual training session (21). If too many factors are targeted, it is likely that the athlete's overall rate of improvement will be impaired, and depending on how the loading is structured, there could be an increased risk of overtraining if this practice occurs frequently. For novice to intermediate athletes, the body of the training session would be structured to target technical and tactical development and mastery, speed and agility development, strength development, and endurance development.

Technical and Tactical Development and Mastery

New technical skills or tactical elements should be addressed earlier in the training session when the athlete is less fatigued (21). If the athlete is fatigued when attempting to learn and develop new motor skills, it is very likely nonoptimal and nonspecific coordination strategies will be learned, thereby impairing long-term development (4, 99, 120). Therefore, best practice is to structure the training session so that the athlete learns and develops technical and tactical skills under minimal fatigue. Once these skills are mastered, they can then be applied under conditions of fatigue to better align with the competitive environment.

Speed and Agility Development

Training that targets speed or agility development should occur when the athlete is in a nonfatigued state. Ideally, this training is performed at the start of (74) or early in the training session (21) prior to strength or endurance training (21). If, however, the focus of the training session is primarily the development of speed, all speed-based training activities should follow the warm-up. Similarly, when coordination or agility is the major focus of the training session, this training is performed immediately after the warm-up because fatigue can significantly affect the athlete's ability to perform complex motor skills (4, 99, 120).

Strength Development

Classically, strength development is placed after technical and tactical and speed and agility development in a training session (21). Although this is the most common practice, in some situations strength and speed activities can be coupled to take advantage of the PAPE effect (127, 128). This allows for the creation of a **strength–power potentiation complex (SPPC)** (134) or a **complex pair** (62) that is used to acutely increase performance. Briefly, SPPC involves the performance of a high-force (51) or high-power (3, 116) movement that induces a PAPE response during the subsequent performance of a high-power or high-velocity movement. For example, performing heavy-loaded strength training (i.e., 70%-90% 1RM) before sprint activities has been shown to be very effective at acutely increasing sprint performance (7, 94, 143). Similarly, coupling heavy-loaded strength-training activities (i.e., 70%-90% 1RM) with plyometric activities has been shown to result in the enhancement of horizontal (121) and vertical (125) plyometric performance. These acute performance effects are most noted when employed with highly trained athletes (29) who have higher levels of strength (i.e., back squat >2 times body mass) (121, 126).

Endurance Development

Exercises that develop general and specific endurance are generally placed at the end of the main body of the training session (21, 86) when the athlete is better able to acquire or perfect movements and tactics, develop speed and agility, and maximize the development of strength without the negative effects of the fatigue generated by these types of activities. Ideally, these types of activities should be performed in sessions separated by a minimum of 6 to 24 hours (14), although it is not always feasible to do so. If a separate endurance session isn't possible, the next best-case scenario is to place endurance development activities at the end of the training session (21).

Although this is a common sequence, remember that after technical and tactical skills are mastered, the coach may choose to test the athlete's technical and tactical skills under fatigue. In these situations, endurance activities may be used to create the residual fatigue under which techniques and tactics are tested.

Ultimately, the coach uses the training session objectives to guide decisions about the structure of the session. Each training session is then structured as either a single- or multitask session. Single-task sessions are more frequently associated with speed–strength sports, such as weightlifting, and cyclic sports, such as cycling, running, swimming, and rowing (86). Multitask training sessions are more often associated with combined events, such as gymnastics and decathlon, combat sports, and team sports, due to the greater demands placed on these athletes. However, as athletes advance in their sports, there is a general trend to implement more frequent training sessions and target single tasks in those sessions so the athlete can focus more energy and effort on the prescribed training factors.

Cool-Down

After the body of the training session, the athlete should perform a structured cool-down to begin the recovery process and return to homeostasis (21). The cool-down allows the body to begin to remove waste products, replenish energy stores, and initiate tissue repair (68). When carefully planned and implemented, the cool-down can maximize recovery from the training session (21, 32), which can take up to 72 hours, depending on the intensity and volume of the session (15, 84, 87, 97).

A survey of collegiate athletic trainers in the United States revealed that 89% recommend a structured cool-down, and 53% of those recommend an active cool-down (113). For the 11% of trainers who did not recommend a structured cool-down, the most common reason was a lack of time (67), which highlights the importance of educating coaches, trainers, and athletes about the importance of this key part of the training session so that time can be allocated to ensure its inclusion.

The cool-down typically lasts 10 to 40 minutes (21, 32, 67) and can be broken into active recovery exercises, breathing and relaxation exercises, and static stretching and foam rolling exercises (figure 8.6) (67).

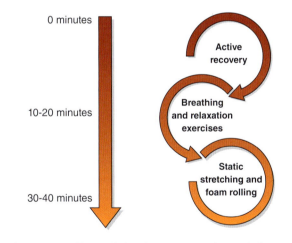

FIGURE 8.6 Example basic structure of a cool-down.

Active Recovery Exercises

The first stage of the cool-down contains active recovery strategies performed at a low intensity for 10 to 20 minutes, depending on the sport (see chapter 9 for more details) (21). Although there is ample evidence that active recovery strategies provide significant benefits compared to passive recovery strategies (19, 79, 100, 103), some studies question their use after training and competition (137, 138). However, most coaches and trainers still consider it best practice to include active recovery (113).

Kurz (86) suggests that walking is a great active recovery modality, especially when the main body of the training session contains nonheterolateral movement, such as homolateral gait, cycling, rowing, and weightlifting. Although walking is a great active recovery strategy, the most commonly recommended recovery activity is low-intensity jogging, with 53% of trainers recommending it (113). Alternatively, in cycling, it is generally recommended to perform a low- to moderate-intensity, active, cycle-based recovery session that lasts no more than 30 minutes (118, 138). A shorter strategy, lasting 10 to 15 minutes, targets low-intensity spinning with a light gear on rollers, which is recommended when working with track cycling (118). Regardless of the sport or type of training session, the active recovery portion of the cool-down should not significantly tax the athlete.

Breathing and Relaxation Exercises

Sport is highly demanding both physically and cognitively, and each type of stress needs to be addressed with specific recovery strategies (111). Some authors have recommended breathing and relaxation exercises during the second stage of the cool-down (66, 67). Although there is limited research into the effects of psychological relaxation techniques in the cool-down, there is support for using systematic breathing techniques as possible tools to induce relaxation (111). Their inclusion can be enhanced by coupling them with the static stretching activities in the third stage of the cool-down (38). Much more research is needed to understand the value of incorporating these techniques into the cool-down.

Static Stretching and Foam Rolling Exercises

The third stage of the cool-down should focus on stretching undertaken for 10 to 20 minutes (21). Static stretching can improve range of motion (i.e., flexibility) without compromising performance. These improvements appear to be enhanced by the increased muscle temperatures stimulated by the training session (46, 71). Adding static stretching to the cool-down can significantly enhance recovery rates from both training and competition stress (117).

Historically, it has been proposed that when static stretching is included in a cool-down, it can enhance recovery through the dispersal of edema that may accumulate in response to tissue damage (18). Reducing edema may play a role in reducing the onset of muscle soreness associated with a training session (28). Research has begun to question the use of postexercise static stretching as a method for inducing recovery (39, 112). Dupuy et al. (39) report that static stretching did not have a positive effect on delayed-onset muscle soreness. Similarly, Pooley et al. (112) report that static stretching does not result in significant reductions in muscle soreness postexercise. Based on this emerging data, the primary reason for including static stretching in the cool-down is to positively affect range of motion rather than to reduce muscle soreness.

Recently, foam rolling has become a popular technique used as part of a cool-down. The athlete uses their body mass on a foam roller to apply pressure to the soft tissue (88, 89), facilitating myofascial release. This technique has been shown to expedite recovery in athletes after demanding bouts of exercise (34) and may help improve passive and dynamic ranges of motion (88, 89). Mohr et al. (102) reported that combining foam rolling with a static stretching program resulted in the greatest improvement in range of motion. Foam rolling may also exert a positive effect on posttraining or competition muscle soreness and fatigue (124). Although the combination of static stretching and foam rolling as part of a cool-down appears to be a worthwhile practice (102), further research is needed to understand the overall benefit and the mechanism associated with these benefits.

Overall, the cool-down is a critical part of the training session and should be well-thought-out and properly structured to address the athlete's needs. The coach needs to consistently reinforce the importance of the cool-down and hold athletes accountable to ensure that this part of the training session is completed with the focus and dedication seen during the main body of the session.

Duration of the Training Session

Training session duration can be short (30-90 min), moderate (2-3 h), or long (>3 h) (21). When designing a training session, the coach can manipulate the duration of the warm-up, the body of the session, and the cool-down to alter the duration of the overall training session (table 8.3).

Many factors can affect the duration of the session, including the athlete's level of development, the type of training session, the characteristics of the sport, and the period or phase of training in which the session occurs. For example, a novice or developmental athlete may not have the fitness to tolerate a moderate- or long-duration training session, so the coach might implement a short-duration session and manipulate the amount of time dedicated to each training unit. Ultimately, the duration of the session will affect the fatigue generated, and this should be considered when designing the individual training days.

Fatigue is a multifactorial response to training or competition (64, 101) and can manifest itself as an inability to sustain further exercise (40) or as an impaired ability to produce maximal force (90) or to control motor function that results in an acute deterioration in exercise performance (24, 64, 90). Generally, fatigue can be considered to be of peripheral (i.e., muscular) or central (i.e., neural) origins.

Peripheral fatigue is related to impairments in neuromuscular transmission and impulse propagation, impairment of Ca^{2+} handling by the sarcoplasmic reticulum, substrate depletion, and various other metabolic factors that can disrupt energy production and muscular contractions (36, 109). Very

TABLE 8.3 Example Short, Moderate, and Long Training Session Durations

Short session (90 min)		Moderate session (120 min)		Long session (190 min)	
Time (min)	Training session activity	Time (min)	Training session activity	Time (min)	Training session activity
5	Introduction	5	Introduction	5	Introduction
20	RAMP warm-up	20	RAMP warm-up	35	RAMP warm-up
45	Main body of session	70	Main body of session	120	Main body of session
20	Cool-down	25	Cool-down	30	Cool-down

intense exercise bouts (61, 119) or long bouts of exercise (30, 61) can compromise the availability of glycogen, resulting in decreased performance (56).

Central fatigue is often associated with a failure of the central nervous system to recruit skeletal muscle (48, 98, 107). Alterations in the ability of the neural impulse to activate skeletal muscle may be related to fatigue-induced alterations in neurotransmitters such as dopamine, serotonin, and possibly acetylcholine (107, 136). Historically, the investigation of central fatigue was centered on motor system performance and less on the cognitive aspects of fatigue (98, 136). However, exercise-induced elevations in serotonin can lead to central fatigue and mental fatigue (37), which can also result in impaired performance (123). Schiphof-Godart et al. (123) demonstrated that mental fatigue can increase the perception of effort and reduce the voluntary drive and willingness to perform physical activity. Additionally, mental fatigue can negatively affect motivation by decreasing the perceived value of the task (123). Ultimately, the coach must know that both peripheral and central fatigue can accumulate in response to training and competition.

Coaches have many strategies to deal with fatigue, such as altering the structure of the training session (55), employing dietary supplement strategies to offset reductions in energy substrates (56, 110), and incorporating targeted recovery strategies (see chapter 9) (92). When considered in the context of programming and the design of the training session, the coach should consider the effect of the program structure on fatigue and the effect of fatigue on the training process. For example, if the major objective of the training session is to learn new technical skills, this activity should be undertaken when the athlete is least fatigued (21) and possibly interspersed with intermittent rest periods. Additionally, the coach must consider that high levels of mental fatigue can also be associated with a reduced ability to train and perform the activities planned for a given training session. Therefore, the coach must look at the cognitive load of the planned training session and consider the effect of mental fatigue on the training process.

Additionally, the coach must consider the intensity of the various training units in the session and within the training day to ensure appropriate variation to better manage fatigue. For example, if the planned training session requires the athlete to engage in high-intensity efforts, such as speed and agility work, the coach should consider reducing the number of training units in the session and shortening the duration of the session (21). Conversely, if lower-intensity training units are planned, more training units can be programmed and undertaken for a longer duration.

When planning the training session, the coach must consider the athlete's current training status. The athlete's ability to dissipate fatigue and recover from a training session, training day, or microcycle can be affected by numerous factors. One of the most important is the athlete's current training age and physical status (21). For example, athletes who have developed higher levels of physical fitness will be better able to tolerate higher levels of fatigue and will tend to recover more quickly from these sessions (81). Conversely, athletes who have lower fitness levels will experience higher levels of fatigue and may not be able to tolerate the planned training stress. In these instances, the coach should modify the training session to accommodate the athletes' levels of fitness (21). The coach may also need to consider implementing greater variation in intensity and volume within the training plan to better manage fatigue.

Ultimately, the degree of physiological disturbance stimulated by a training session is proportional to the rate of recovery, with training sessions that contain greater intensities and volumes of training stimulating greater accumulated fatigue and thus requiring more time for recovery and preparedness (21). When designing any training program, the coach must consider the structures of each training session and training day in the context of how fatigue and recovery are related to the planned sessions.

Training Session Blueprint

When constructing a training session, the coach should create a session blueprint that defines the structure of the training program to be delivered during the session. This can be done on paper or by using the digital delivery applications mentioned earlier (e.g., Visualcoaching Pro, TeamBuildr, BridgeAthletic, TrainHeroic). The training session plan should contain all the pertinent information necessary to complete the session and be easily understood. Ideally the training session plan should be provided to the athlete prior to the session to allow them to better prepare mentally and physically. Additionally, where appropriate, the coach should post the session plan in a defined location so that the athlete can refer to it throughout the session.

There are many ways a training session can be constructed and presented to the athlete. Each session should contain several basic elements that guide the athlete through a session (figure 8.7). The training session blueprint should indicate the date, time, and location of the session and list any specialized equipment needed. The blueprint must also include the session objectives, which help the athlete better understand what is expected of them. Based on these objectives, the coach should provide a training prescription of specific exercises, drills, and activities that the athlete will undertake during the session. These activities should be clearly described, and there should be a detailed description of the workload (e.g., repetitions, sets, duration), intensity (e.g., percentage of repetition maximum, speed, power, heart rate), and rest intervals for all activities in the session. It is also important to note any specific items that the athlete needs to focus on when performing the prescribed drills and exercises. These notations can be specific to each athlete or global to the needs of a group of athletes. All items should be easy to understand.

A completed training session template is presented in figure 8.8. In this example of a discus training session, the main objective is to work on throwing technique. This four-part session includes an introduction, a warm-up, the main body of the session, and a cool-down. The warm-up is based on the RAMP protocol and provides an opportunity for the athlete to work on overall movement competency. The main body of the session contains specific drills to improve key technical skills necessary for successful throwing. The active cool-down includes sport-specific stretching.

Classically, paper copies of each training session were given to each athlete. More recently, the increased availability of coaching software allows coaches to deliver electronic versions of the training program that an athlete can access on their smartphone, tablet, or computer. These applications also allow athletes to link video and notes to the training session and provide direct feedback to the coach, which can be integrated into a comprehensive monitoring program (see chapter 11) and provide the coach with information that they can use to fine-tune the athlete's training.

Training Day Structure and Timing

The training day consists of one or more interconnected training sessions (52-54) designed to meet the training objectives established for the micro- and mesocycles in which they are contained. These objectives are typically addressed by manipulating the density of training (i.e., number of training sessions) via the employment of one or more interrelated training sessions. Ultimately, the number of training sessions in a training day is dictated by time available for training, the athlete's level of development, league rules, and the overall objectives and goals established for the period or phase of training (49, 54).

FIGURE 8.7 Factors typically contained in a training session template.

Athlete:	Chris Brooks		
Training session:	149	Session start time (HR:MIN)	15:00
		Session stop time (HR:MIN)	
Date (month/day/year):	05/20/2021		
Location:	Eiler-Martin Stadium	**Equipment needed** Discus (2 kg): 10	
Objective:	Work on technique		

Element	Duration	Activities		Notes
Introduction	3 min	1. Describe the objectives of the session 2. Stress what the athlete should focus on during the session		
Warm-up	20 min	**Activity**	**Dosage**	**Notes**
		Jogging	400 m	
		Walking quad stretch	60 m	
		Walking hamstring stretch	60 m	
		Walking lunges	60 m	
		Walking forward lunge with a twist	2 x 60 m	
		Jogging carioca	2 x 60 m	
		Jogging high knees	60 m	
		Jogging butt kicks	60 m	
		Explosive skip for height	60 m	Drive vertically
		Explosive skip for distance	2 x 60 m	
		Dynamic build-up acceleration runs	2 x 60 m	
Main body	90 min	**Activity**	**Dosage**	**Notes**
		Flip drill	2 sets of 10 throws	Maintain upright posture
		Standing throw	2 sets of 10 throws	Focus on foot position
		South African drill	2 sets of 6-10	Focus on getting discus up
		Full throws	3 sets of 10 throws with submax effort	Focus on slow to fast rhythm
		Full throws	10 maximal efforts	
Cool-down	16 min	**Activity**	**Dosage**	**Notes**
		Slow jogging	400 m	
		Chest stretch	2 x 30 sec hold	
		Upper-back stretch	2 x 30 sec hold	
		Shoulder stretch	2 x 30 sec hold	Both shoulders
		Hamstring stretch	2 x 30 sec hold	Both legs
		Hip and thigh stretch	2 x 30 sec hold	Both sides
		Calf stretch	2 x 30 sec hold	Both legs
		Groin stretch	2 x 30 sec hold	
		Iliotibial band stretch	2 x 30 sec hold	Both legs
		Quadriceps stretch	2 x 30 sec hold	Both legs
Session notes	Remember 2 x = two sets			

FIGURE 8.8 Example template for a training session for a thrower.

Training Sessions on Non-Competition Training Days

When designing a training day, the coach must consider how each training day in the microcycle interrelates with the other training days to accomplish the goals of the microcycle. Additionally, the coach must consider the interplay of the structure of each training day because a single training session or multiple interrelated training sessions can be planned (53).

Single-Session Training Days

When designing single-session training days, the coach must consider how the various components of the session will interact and affect fatigue and training capacity. If a multitargeted training session is designed, the main body of the session should contain no more than three training targets (21). The coach must carefully consider where in the training session to target each specific training factor. For example, if the session targets both strength and endurance development, the coach must carefully consider the order of training. It is recommended to target strength development first and endurance training or HIIT second (47, 106), because performing endurance training or HIIT prior to strength training can impede strength development (33, 106) as a result of a compromised ability to produce the force necessary to induce positive adaptive responses (82). However, in this scenario the strength-training portion of the session can induce neuromuscular fatigue that can affect performance during HIIT and potentially increase injury risk if the HIIT portion of the session is not structured correctly (47). The coach must decide the priority of the training session and adjust it accordingly. For example, the coach might consider having the athlete perform upper-body resistance training prior to HIIT that taxes the lower body (82). If, however, the session targets lower-body or whole-body resistance training, the subsequent intensity of the HIIT session should be reduced to accommodate the increased neuromuscular fatigue associated with the strength-training portion of the session (47). Although multitarget training sessions can be constructed and provide the athlete with appropriate training stimuli, if time is available the coach might consider placing training factors such as strength training and HIIT or endurance training into separate training sessions within the training day or on different training days.

Multiple-Session Training Days

Whenever possible, the coach should consider planning multiple training sessions throughout the day. Ample evidence suggests that superior training adaptations occur when the training day is structured in this manner (1, 35, 53, 54, 57, 135). For example, Häkkinen and Kallinen (57) report that when female strength athletes split their daily training volume into two shorter sessions, greater gains in strength occur compared to completing the same training volume in one daily training session. These enhanced strength gains are associated with significantly greater increases in muscle cross-sectional area and maximal voluntary neural activation. Similarly, Viru (140) reports that when male strength athletes divide their daily training volume into two sessions, they are exposed to more effective training stimuli that enhance strength development. Based on these findings, the division of the daily training load into multiple training sessions should be considered as a way to increase the quality of training (67).

Increasing the density of training (i.e., sessions per day) is not only important for increasing training quality but also a way to increase the daily training load (140). In fact, it is not uncommon for elite athletes to undergo three or more training sessions per day as a way to manage overall training stress and enhance the physiological, psychological, and performance adaptations required to improve competitive performance (67).

The coach can also manipulate the number of daily training sessions to create intermicrocycle variation that can be sequenced into a series of mesocycles and allow for the modulation of the supercompensation response associated with the training progression (25). If multiple training sessions are employed, the coach needs to modulate the training loads planned for each session to account for accumulated fatigue across the training day and between training days. For example, neuromuscular fatigue tends to persist for at least 6 to 8 hours after strenuous endurance exercise, including HIIT, and it may take up to 24 hours for complete recovery to occur (10, 11, 82, 133). Therefore, the coach should plan a minimum 6- to 8-hour recovery period after this type of training (14, 47).

Although the 6- to 8-hour recovery window between training modes is widely implemented by coaches, it is likely the length of the recovery window will be affected by the type of exercise performed and the training status of the athlete (47,

82). Intersession recovery strategies may also affect the duration of the recovery window. Therefore, the coach should consider the effect of the training session on the athlete's recovery rate and then consider what recovery strategies best align with the overall training goals established for the training day. Based on these factors, the coach can provide recovery strategies that help the athlete better manage the day's training stress (see chapter 9).

Training Sessions on Competition Days

Recently, there has been much discussion about using targeted training strategies on the day of competition to enhance performance (93, 104). Based on the available scientific evidence, **priming exercises**, such as resistance training, can be employed 4 to 12 hours prior to competition to enhance an athlete's preparedness for and performance in competition (figure 8.9) (45, 59, 60, 85, 93).

Priming sessions have been a popular topic of discussion for the last 30 years or so. Fry et al. (45) reported that some weightlifters demonstrate significantly greater competitive performance if a low-volume, moderate-intensity training session is performed 5 to 6 hours prior to competition. More recently, Harrison et al. (59) reported an enhanced performance capacity 6 to 24 hours after the completion of a session that includes low-volume, high-intensity resistance training or low-load ballistic exercises. Priming sessions have been proposed as a strategy for individual and team sports (93).

Harrison et al. (60) reported that coaches believe priming sessions that contain resistance training translate into improvements in speed and power (96% of coaches), strength (54% of coaches), and agility (51% of coaches). Of the coaches surveyed, 51% reported that they were currently using priming sessions, and 30% reported that they had previously used this strategy but were not currently using it. Coaches reported prescribing a large variety of exercises in a priming session, with unloaded jumps (87%), loaded jumps (60%), and the bench press (54%) being the most commonly used (figure 8.10) (60).

Coaches also indicated that their priming sessions typically contained two or three lower-body exercises and two or three upper-body exercises. Generally, low numbers of sets (2.8 ± 0.9) and repetitions (3.8 ± 1.3) were prescribed, and loading schemes ranged from unloaded to heavy loaded (≥85% of 1RM) (figure 8.11). Most coaches surveyed stated that their priming sessions lasted less than 30 minutes (<15 minutes = 34%; 15-30 minutes = 59%) and were performed within 16 hours of competition (0-8 hours = 59%; 9-16 hours = 11%).

Based on the available evidence, coaches should consider programming a **priming session** on the day of competition. By manipulating the intensity and volume of the priming session, the coach elevates the athlete's preparedness and performance capacity so they are maximized during the window of optimal performance enhancement (figure 8.9). Because this window generally lasts 6 to 12 hours, most priming sessions are planned for the morning prior to an evening competition. While priming sessions appear to be a valuable tool for enhancing competitive performance, much more research is needed to determine the optimal structure and placement of these sessions.

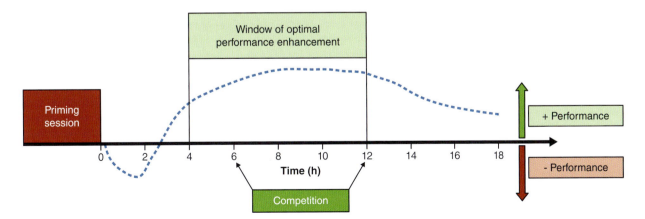

FIGURE 8.9 Theoretical window of enhanced performance post priming session.
Adapted from Harrison, James, McGuigan, et al. (2020).

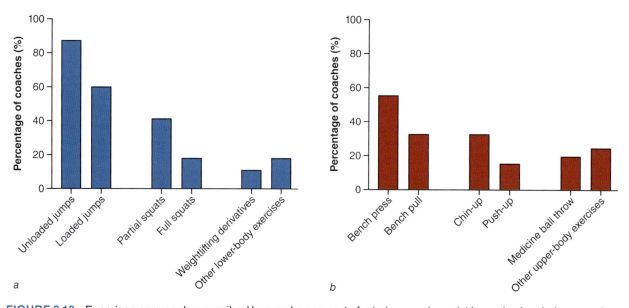

FIGURE 8.10 Exercises commonly prescribed by coaches as part of priming sessions: *(a)* lower-body priming exercises; *(b)* upper-body priming exercises.

Adapted from Harrison, James, McGuigan, et al. (2020).

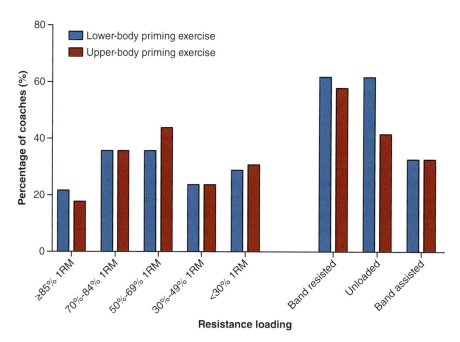

FIGURE 8.11 Training load commonly prescribed as part of priming exercise.

Adapted from Harrison, James, McGuigan, et al. (2020).

Summary

The coach's ability to design and implement structured training sessions that guide the training process is one of the fundamental aspects of programming. Training sessions can be constructed to train groups of athletes or individual athletes or to provide both group and individual training activities. While there are infinite types of training sessions, all training sessions fall into one of six types of sessions: physical training, technical, tactical or techno-tactical, combined, assessment, or recovery sessions. Sessions are typically considered to be short duration (30-90 min), moderate duration (2-3 h), or long duration (>3 h).

Understanding the athlete's physiological responses to training and the fatigue arising from training helps inform the coach's decisions about the structure of each training day. When single-session training days that contain multiple training factors are programmed, the coach must consider the order of targeted training activities so fatigue can be managed and the targeted attribute can be more effectively trained. Ideally, wherever possible, the coach should plan multiple training sessions within the training day and provide 6 to 8 hours of recovery between divergent training sessions, such as resistance training and HIIT.

Each training session should contain several key units sequenced to create the session. The warm-up, which is often overlooked or poorly planned, is an important training unit that should be designed based on the principles of the RAMP warm-up protocol. This warm-up protocol provides a time-efficient method for enhancing movement competency, optimally preparing the athlete for the main body of the training session. For the main body of the training session, coaches must consider the physical and cognitive load the athlete experiences when determining the optimal duration for this part of the training session. All training sessions should conclude with a structured cool-down, which should never be cut short or removed from the athlete's training session. The cool-down often contains key training units, such as stretching or mobility training, used to improve the athlete's range of motion within key movement patterns.

PART III

ADVANCED PERIODIZATION TOPICS

Once the basic concepts of periodization are mastered, the coach must develop an understanding of several advanced concepts that can help further elevate the athlete's performance capacity. Conceptually, periodization is a system of structuring training to help manage the two competing factors of fatigue and recovery. Throughout part III, coaches will develop an understanding of fatigue, explore how nutrition can enhance recovery and adaptation, examine the key concepts of monitoring, and learn how to peak or optimize performance. In chapter 9, a detailed exploration of the mechanisms of fatigue and ways to amplify recovery are contextualized in alignment with periodized training plans. Following this discussion, a deep dive into the emerging area of the periodization of nutrition (chapter 10) is presented. From there, chapter 11 moves into key aspects of athlete monitoring and ways to integrate monitoring into a periodized training plan. Part III culminates with a detailed exploration of how periodization strategies can be used to optimize competition performance within the annual training plan (chapter 12).

CHAPTER 9

Fatigue, Recovery, and Periodization

A central goal of the training process is to provide the athlete with training loads that stimulate physiological and psychological adaptations that ultimately translate into improved performance. A central component of this process is that the athlete must be exposed to intensified training, often referred to as *overload* (184), to enhance performance capacity (182, 184). When overload is applied, the athlete will experience acute feelings of fatigue and reductions in preparedness and performance capacity. If adequate rest follows the session or period of training, the athlete's level of fatigue will dissipate relatively quickly and there will be a concomitant elevation in both preparedness and performance, often referred to as *supercompensation* (figure 9.1) (141, 182).

When there is an imbalance between training stress and recovery, maladaptive responses can manifest as longer-term reductions in preparedness and performance (184). Compounding this problem is that preparedness and performance are also affected by stressors from sources other than training, such as psychosocial or life stressors (e.g., work, school, relationships) (figure 9.2).

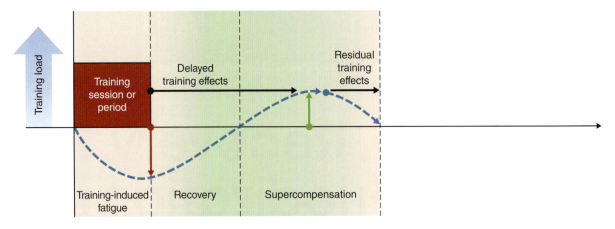

FIGURE 9.1 Supercompensation.

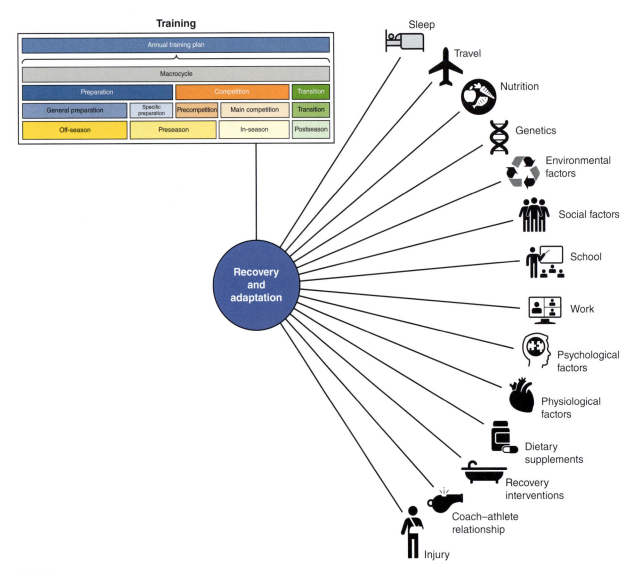

FIGURE 9.2 Factors that affect recovery and adaptation.
Adapted from Stone, Stone, and Sands (2007).

Although the coach can help the athlete learn to manage stressors outside the training environment, how they manage the training process will have the most effect on the athlete's stress levels. Ultimately, the biggest tool the coach can use to affect recovery and adaptation is a properly designed periodized training program that leverages an integrated monitoring program to avoid excessive monotony and strain and to balance training overload and recovery (24, 197). To augment the athlete's ability to deal with the fatigue from training and modulate the recovery process, the coach should consider integrating select recovery strategies into the periodized training plan (14, 197). To do this, the coach must understand fatigue and how it manifests in response to various training activities and how increasing levels of fatigue can result in overreaching or overtraining. The coach also must be familiar with the various recovery strategies and know how and when to integrate them into the periodized training plan.

Fatigue

Fatigue is common in sport and in life. This must be considered when constructing an athlete's periodized training plan. Fatigue can be defined in many ways; for example, a biomechanist might consider fatigue to be a decrement in muscle force output (189, 329), a physiologist might consider fatigue to be a failure of a specific physiological system (99), and a psychologist might consider fatigue to be a sensation of tiredness (139). If we combine these perspectives into one holistic definition, fatigue can be defined as sensations of tiredness and associated decrements in muscular performance and function (1, 99, 138, 269). Based on this definition, fatigue can be considered in the context of performance fatigability and perceived fatigability (72, 149). **Performance fatigability** is the decline of an objective measure of performance over a specific period. It depends on the capacity of the nervous system to provide adequate activation from the descending commands and afferent feedback for the targeted task and the contractile capacities of the muscle involved in that task (72). **Perceived fatigability** is attributed to psychological factors, such as arousal, motivation, mood, and pain, which can be modulated by factors such as core temperature and hydration status (72). By considering fatigue in the context of these two aspects of fatigability, the level of fatigue reported by an individual can be normalized to the demands of the task that stimulated it.

Since exercise is terminated at exhaustion and not at a point of fatigue (137, 138), the latter is often considered to be a safety mechanism that prevents injury during exercise (137, 203, 209). Since some degree of fatigue is an inevitable negative consequence of physical training, there has been significant scientific inquiry into the various mechanisms that underpin it and its impact on exercise performance. Fatigue can occur in response to impaired muscle function, which is called *peripheral fatigue*, and in response to a reduction in the capacity of the central nervous system to activate muscle, which is called *central fatigue* (45, 313).

Peripheral Fatigue

Peripheral fatigue is often marked by reductions in force and power production due to factors within the motor unit (i.e., the motor neuron and the muscle it innervates [71, 73]) that can exert a direct influence on performance (44, 317). This type of fatigue occurs when the regulatory or support systems are unable to maintain muscle contractility or the bioenergetic energy supply and waste removal necessary to preserve physical activity (146). Ultimately, peripheral fatigue results in an attenuation of crossbridge function (i.e., muscle contraction) within the skeletal muscle (81). Factors that potentially mediate the peripheral fatigue response include impairments to excitation–contraction coupling and crossbridge dysfunction, with synergistic effects stimulated by elevated concentrations of inorganic phosphate (P_i), adenosine diphosphate (ADP), and hydrogen ions (H^+) (6, 80, 146). In addition, low levels of glycogen, especially intramyofibrillar glycogen, negatively affect the release of calcium (Ca^{2+}) from the sarcoplasmic reticulum and can significantly affect the fatigue response to exercise (79, 205). It is generally believed that peripheral fatigue develops prior to central fatigue during maximal (65) and submaximal (168) exercise and that peripheral fatigue dominates when exercise is performed within the severe intensity domain (i.e., maximal or supramaximal) (11).

Central Fatigue

Central fatigue is the inability of the central nervous system to activate or maintain activation of skeletal muscle (95). Fundamentally, central fatigue occurs due to a decreased neural drive to the skeletal muscle, resulting in a diminished voluntary activation and subsequent decline in force output, thereby compromising performance

(11, 95, 250, 284). Reductions in neural drive can occur due to alterations to the premotor region of the brain (281) and within the motor cortex and spinal motoneurons (312). Although central fatigue plays a role in limiting performance, the general consensus is that it plays only a minor role in highly trained athletes (74, 79, 80, 95).

Historically, research examining central fatigue focused on the performance of the motor system (285), but more recently there is an increased interest in the cognitive aspects of fatigue (181). Specifically, it appears that central fatigue may be heavily influenced by psychological factors such as motivation (181, 237, 285) and the presence of competitors (268). There appears to be a neural component to an athlete's ability to tolerate the sensations of fatigue, and psychological factors may significantly affect exercise termination (211). Robertson and Marino (237) suggest that during self-paced or exhaustive incremental exercise, the athlete decides whether to stop or how to regulate pace to complete the bout without catastrophic failure or a meaningful reduction in performance. Theoretically, the lateral prefrontal cortex allows the integration of afferent signals combined with motivational and emotional context provided by the anterior cingulate cortex and the orbitofrontal cortex (237). Athletes make decisions about the most relevant task response necessary for the current situation based on the integration of these signals. Robertson and Marino (237) suggest that depending on the mode of exercise, the task response, which is carried out via the premotor area and the basal ganglia, can vary from acting to modify the pace of exercise (i.e., speeding up, slowing down) to termination of the activity.

The magnitude of fatigue associated with a given exercise task generally depends on its duration and intensity (313). Shorter, more intense bouts of exercise (i.e., above the critical power in the severe intensity domain) are often associated with a consistent magnitude of peripheral fatigue, and longer-duration, steady-state exercise in the heavy domain is associated with greater central fatigue (287). However, it has been suggested that the amount of fatigue after exercise is independent of the duration of exercise when exercise is performed with severe intensities that result in task failure (i.e., 3-minute and 12-minute cycling to task failure) (250). Regardless, when exhaustive, whole-body exercise is performed, there is a 25% to 45% reduction in quadriceps twitch force (i.e., peripheral fatigue) and a 5% to 12% reduction in voluntary muscle activation (i.e., central fatigue) (313), which can significantly compromise whole-body exercise performance capacity (7).

Fatigue is a complex phenomenon with a range of physiological and psychological mediators. Repeated maximal efforts can elicit a high degree of central and peripheral fatigue, possibly requiring a prolonged recovery period (286). Thomas and colleagues (286) assessed the etiology and recovery of fatigue after heavy resistance training (10 sets of 5 repetitions of back squats at 80% of one-repetition maximum [1RM]), plyometric exercise (10 sets of 5 jump squats), and maximal sprinting (15 sets of 30 m sprints). Interestingly, this study demonstrated that training methods that require repeated maximal-intensity efforts elicited marked neuromuscular fatigue that may require up to 72 hours before full recovery. The fatigue noted after each activity was determined to be of both central and peripheral origins, with central fatigue recovering at a more rapid rate than peripheral fatigue. Based on these findings, Thomas and colleagues (286) suggested that maximal efforts should be separated by at least 48 hours to allow the athlete to recover from the residual fatigue. Additionally, these authors suggested that the root cause of this fatigue is multifactorial, and it is important that appropriate monitoring and recovery strategies are employed to facilitate the removal of this fatigue.

Interrelationships of Stress, Fatigue, and Recovery

When looking at the interrelationships of stress states, accumulated fatigue, and recovery demands, the basic assumption that can be made is that as stress increases there is a concomitant increase in fatigue that results in an increased recovery demand (141). When resources (such as time) are limited, the recovery demand is further exasperated, resulting in an increased level of stress and fatigue and creating a vicious cycle of compounding stress, fatigue, and reduced recovery. One method of representing the interrelationship among stress, fatigue, and recovery is the scissors model, which is based on the assumption that an increase in stress produces fatigue and an increased recovery demand (141). A simplistic form of this model shows a symmetrical increase in stress or fatigue and recovery demands that drift apart as stress levels or fatigue elevate (i.e., scissors function). As shown in figure 9.3, this is depicted by the two axes drifting apart as stress levels are elevated.

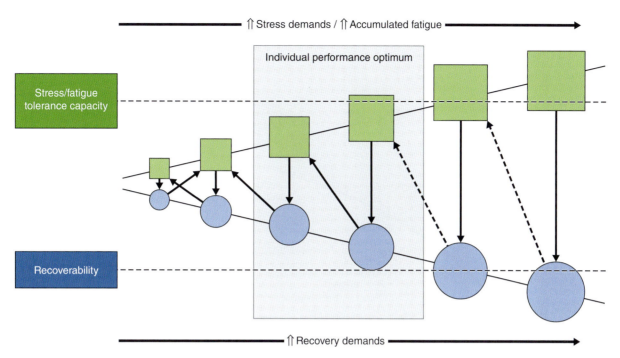

FIGURE 9.3 Scissors model for explaining stress, fatigue, and recovery.

Adapted by permission from K.W. Kallus and M. Kellmann, "Burnout in Athletes and Coaches," in *Emotions in Sport*, edited by Y.L. Hanin (Champaign, IL: Human Kinetics, 2009), 212.

When intermediate levels of stress are encountered and adequate recovery (solid arrows in figure 9.3) is available, the athlete can find their zone of optimum performance. Beyond this zone, however, the athlete cannot meet the stress demands placed on them and will be at increased risk for *overreaching* or *overtraining* due to impaired recovery (dashed arrows in figure 9.3) without additional recovery activities.

Overreaching and Overtraining

When performance plateaus or decreases in response to training and nontraining stress, coaches and athletes often call this *burn out, overwork, excessive fatigue, staleness,* or *underrecovery* (202, 331). Fundamentally, Zatsiorsky and colleagues (331) suggest that these terms have been used synonymously with the term *overtraining*. Although overtraining is widely discussed by coaches and athletes, there exists some confusion about what it is, what we know about it, and what we need to learn. To address this confusion, a joint task force consisting of several prominent international sport and exercise science organizations came together in 2006 and again in 2013 to present a common definition for overtraining, establish the current state of understanding about the concept, and provide direction for further inquiry (184, 185). As part of these seminal papers, a continuum was established that linked acute fatigue, overreaching, and overtraining (figure 9.4).

Based on this continuum, an athlete undergoing physical training is exposed to an overload that initially stimulates a fatigue response that is dissipated relatively quickly as the athlete recovers, resulting in improvements in performance (184). As training continues, or if the coach deliberately increases training load for a short time (i.e., overreaching), the athlete may experience short-term reductions in performance. If the increased training load is balanced with appropriate recovery, the athlete will eventually display a performance supercompensation. If, however, there is an imbalance between training load and recovery, signs and symptoms of prolonged training distress (i.e., overtraining) will occur and the athlete may need months to recover.

Chapter 1 introduced the general adaptive syndrome (figure 1.15, page 20) as a basic framework for understanding the interplay of training stress, fatigue, adaptation, and recovery (61). Zatsiorsky and colleagues (331) adapted this seminal construct and related it to the overtraining continuum (figure 9.5). This adapted depiction of the general adaptive syndrome presents several levels of training stress and responses.

206 | Scientific Foundations and Practical Applications of Periodization

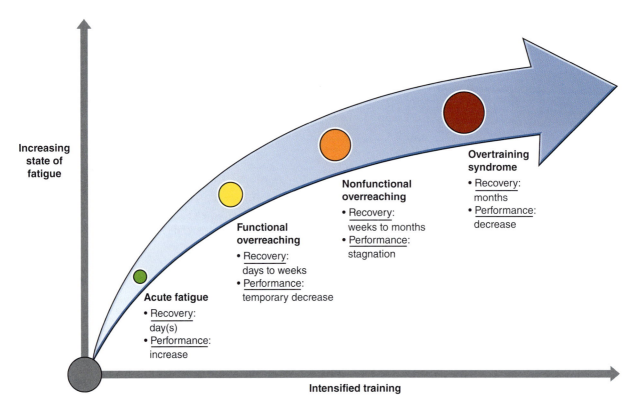

FIGURE 9.4 Continuum of overtraining.
Adapted from Meeusen, Duclos, Foster, et al. (2013).

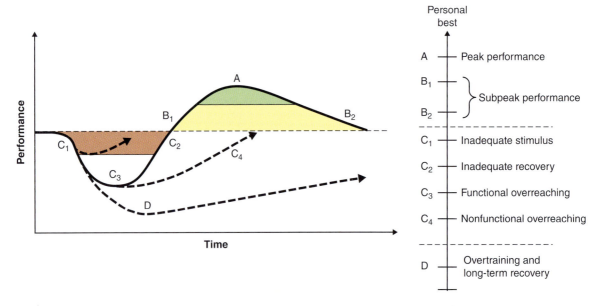

FIGURE 9.5 Relationship between the general adaptive syndrome and various levels of training stress.
Reprinted by permission from V.M. Zatsiorsky, W.J. Kraemer, and A.C. Fry, *Science and Practice of Strength Training,* 3rd ed. (Champaign, IL: Human Kinetics, 2021), 180.

One of the unique aspects of this adaptation is that in addition to depicting how properly designed periodized training programs result in the optimization of performance, it illustrates how excessive overload coupled with inadequate recovery can lead to **overtraining syndrome (OTS)** (331). Additionally, this figure illustrates how suboptimal performance may not be related to overtraining but instead may result from a poorly timed or integrated periodized training program. If, for example, the applied training load provides an inadequate training stimulus (C_1) or inadequate recovery (C_2), performance will not result in a supercompensation response (figure 9.5). In addition to presenting the effect of excessive overload on overreaching (C_3 and C_4) and overtraining (D), this figure also depicts the effect of a mistimed training program (B_1 and B_2).

Overreaching

Overreaching can occur when an athlete's training program does not provide an appropriate training stimulus and recovery is suboptimal (184). Overreaching is an accumulation of fatigue that occurs in response to training or nontraining stress and results in short-term decrements in performance (40, 183, 184). These performance decrements can appear with or without the physiological and psychological maladaptive symptoms typically associated with overtraining. Typically, restoration of performance occurs within several days to weeks after overreaching if appropriate programming strategies are integrated into the athlete's periodized training plan (183, 184, 331).

Overreaching, or supercompensation, training (202) is a programming strategy in which the coach introduces planned periods of intensive training (16, 274) to elevate the athlete's level of performance (202). Intentional overreaching strategies do not always result in performance supercompensation, so a coach must understand the differences between functional overreaching and nonfunctional overreaching.

Functional Overreaching

Functional overreaching (FOR) typically occurs when a short period of intense training is followed by reduced training loads that facilitate recovery and stimulate elevations in both preparedness and performance (figure 9.6) (183, 184, 191, 331). The use of FOR strategies is common in the programs for intermediate to elite athletes (212). In fact, Plisk and Stone (212) suggest that correctly programmed FOR, or concentrated loading, strategies are an effective method for maximizing the development of strength, speed, and power. Conceptually, the sequential block model of periodization leverages the benefits of FOR via the sequencing of accumulation, transmutation, and realization mesocycles to stimulate a performance supercompensation after the completion of the sequence (128, 212, 297).

When overreaching strategies are integrated into the training process, there is a time lag before increased performance or performance supercompensation occurs. In chapter 4, this is referred to as a *delayed training effect*. The magnitude of the training load applied during the overreaching period directly affects the duration before supercompensation and the magnitude of the gain in performance (figure 4.2, page 78). In most instances, supercompensation occurs within 2 to 5 weeks of reducing training loads (109, 212, 307). However, if the overreaching period is extended or includes excessively high training loads, supercompensation will be delayed because more recovery time is required to dissipate the accumulated fatigue.

Nonfunctional Overreaching

An imbalance between training and recovery may lead the athlete to experience **nonfunctional overreaching (NFOR)** (183). The first signs and symptoms of prolonged training distress are per-

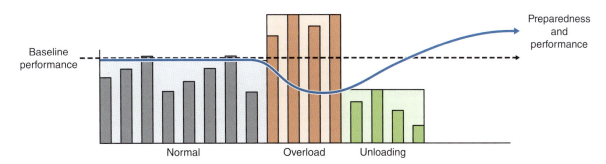

FIGURE 9.6 Graphic depiction of functional overreaching.

formance stagnation or decreases in performance (figure 9.7), psychological disturbances (i.e., decreased vigor, increased fatigue), and hormonal disruptions. Depending on the magnitude of these maladaptive responses, it may be weeks to months before the athlete completely recovers (184).

Several additional factors, such as inadequate nutrition (i.e., inadequate caloric intake or carbohydrate consumption), illness, psychosocial stress, and sleep disorders, can also occur with NFOR (183, 184). At this point, it can be difficult to distinguish between NFOR and OTS, depending on the tools used to diagnose OTS.

NFOR is representative of the mismanagement of the training process via poor programmatic decisions or inadequate attention to recovery. For example, if the overload training period lacks appropriate training variation, performance will not progress as expected and will hit what many coaches refer to as a *plateau* (191, 274, 331). Zatsiorsky and colleagues (331) suggest that this often occurs as a result of poorly designed training plans and on-the-fly programming modifications that lack context within the overall training plan. Compounding this maladaptive response is a failure to consider the caloric requirements associated with the training loads planned in the overreaching period (143). In their seminal paper, Costill and colleagues (54) reported that during periods of intense training like that experienced during planned overreaching, a failure to consume sufficient amounts of carbohydrate to meet the energetic demands of the training period can result in chronic muscular fatigue. In their study, athletes who displayed symptoms of NFOR consumed around 1,000 kcals · day^{-1} less than their estimated energetic requirements and consumed less carbohydrate than those who displayed FOR responses. Ultimately, the importance of integrating nutritional strategies that align with training loads, support recovery, and facilitate specific physiological adaptive responses cannot be understated (197). The coach should integrate nutritional (see chapter 10) and recovery periodization strategies into the periodized training plan to ensure the athlete optimizes the performance gains achieved from overreaching strategies and reduces the risk of developing NFOR and OTS (184).

Overtraining

The difference between NFOR and overtraining is subtle, and it is often difficult to differentiate between these two maladaptive responses to the training process (183, 184). As with NFOR, overtraining is characterized by reductions in performance, but it is also associated with maladaptive psychological and physiological responses to the training load (111, 276). The main difference between NFOR and overtraining is that overtraining is related to a prolonged maladaptation as indicated by decreases in performance and alterations to several psychological, biological, neurochemical, and hormonal factors (184).

Classically, overtraining has been divided into two subtypes—sympathetic and parasympathetic—based on the origins of maladaptive symptoms (157, 202, 274). The symptoms associated with **sympathetic overtraining** are generally representative of a prolonged stress response (274). This form of overtraining generally relates to increases in sympathetic nervous system activity at rest, such as an increased resting heart rate, which may translate into restlessness and excitation (91, 157). **Parasympathetic overtraining** has been suggested to be representative of an advanced stage of overtraining in which parasympathetic activity dominates at rest and during exercise and there is sympathetic inhibition (157). With this form of overtraining, there is a predominance of vagal tone and adrenal insufficiency plus reduced heart rate at rest and during exercise related to inhibition and depression (91, 157). Ultimately, it is difficult to differentiate between the symptoms

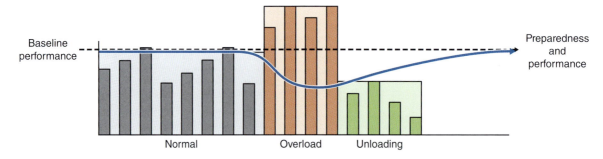

FIGURE 9.7 Graphic depiction of nonfunctional overreaching.

of sympathetic and parasympathetic overtraining, because many of them overlap (table 9.1). Although the classic literature talks about sympathetic and parasympathetic overtraining (157, 202, 274), the continuous nature of overtraining makes it difficult to isolate symptoms to differentiate between these overtraining subtypes.

As with NFOR, overtraining is fundamentally a mismanagement of the training process that results in maladaptive responses due to the athlete's inability to tolerate the programmed training loads (i.e., volume and intensity). This mismanagement can result in high-volume overtraining or high-intensity overtraining (83).

High-Volume Overtraining

As noted previously, increasing training volume is an important programming strategy that increases training loads over time. Although it is inevitable that training volumes need to be increased, remember that more training volume is not always better and that simply increasing training volume does not always translate to better performance (83). Significantly increasing training volume for an extended time increases the risk of overtraining; this is referred to as ***high-volume overtraining***. This risk is most noted in endurance athletes who are often exposed to high volumes of training (i.e., km per week) for long periods (165, 166). Endurance athletes may be at a greater risk of developing high-volume overtraining (83), while strength–power athletes can also be at an increased risk of high-volume overtraining if their overall volume of training is significantly increased (i.e., increased sets × reps, number of exercises, or total training sessions) for long periods (84, 273).

The potential risk of high-volume overtraining can apply to military personnel as well. During training exercises, military personnel are often placed under high volumes of training coupled with high levels of cognitive stress, lack of sleep, and limited food availability, putting them at an increased risk of overtraining (306). This risk is magnified with special forces operators who often

TABLE 9.1 Classic Signs and Symptoms of Sympathetic and Parasympathetic Overtraining

	Sympathetic	**Parasympathetic**
Sports	Team sports	Endurance sports
	Strength and power sports	
Performance	↓ ↔ performance	↓ ↔ performance
Psychological factors	↓ motivation	↑ listlessness
	↑ irritability	↑ depression
	↑ depression	↑ sleep
Appetite	↓ appetite	↔ appetite
Cardiovascular parameters	↑ resting, exercise, and recovery heart rate	↑ resting bradycardia
	↑ resting, exercise, and recovery blood pressure	↓ ↔ exercise heart rate
	↑ ECG abnormalities	↓ ↔ postexercise heart rate recovery
		↓ ↔ blood pressure response to exercise
Endocrine system	↑ cortisol concentration	↓ responsiveness to stressors
	↑ catecholamine concentration	
	↑ postexercise hormonal recovery time	
	↓ testosterone concentration	
	↓ testosterone:cortisol ratio	
Miscellaneous	↓ muscle and liver glycogen stores	↑ hypoglycemia during exercise
	Variable exercise-induced lactate responses	↓ exercise and postexercise lactate concentrations

Note: ↑ = increased, ↓ = decreased, ↔ = no change; ECG = electrocardiogram.

engage in training practices that expose them to excessive training loads that push them well beyond their capabilities (47).

Ultimately, the most effective strategy for managing high-volume overtraining risk is using logical periodization strategies that progressively increase training loads and leverage structured monitoring strategies to guide the training process. Although the coach must be mindful of the risks of high-volume overtraining, this doesn't mean they will never expose athletes to high volumes of training. As noted previously, exposing athletes to higher volumes of training is an important programming strategy that can result in FOR, but when poorly programmed and not correctly monitored, the athlete will be at an increased risk of becoming overtrained. This risk is magnified if the coach has not appropriately periodized the athlete's training program.

High-Intensity Overtraining

Although high-volume overtraining is more typically discussed within the scientific literature, overtraining that occurs in response to repeated exposure to very high–intensity training has also received significant attention. This type of overtraining is typically referred to as **high-intensity overtraining** (83). High-intensity overtraining is most commonly associated with resistance training (85, 97) in which the athlete performs training activities with repeated maximal loading, such as performing training with RM loads in every training session (85). Every athlete has a maximal-resistance training capacity that is largely a function of the volume and intensity of training performed (figure 9.8). When this capacity is exceeded by excessive

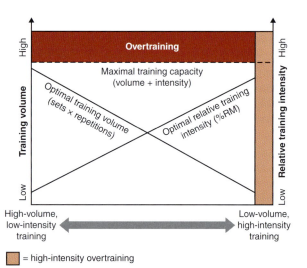

FIGURE 9.8 Resistance-training overtraining: the interplay between volume and intensity. Note the interrelationships of training volume (sets × reps), relative intensity (%RM), and overtraining. Maximal-resistance training capacity is a function of the combination of training volume and relative intensity. Training that exceeds the maximal training capacity can increase the risk of overtraining.

Reprinted by permission from A.C. Fry, "The Role of Training Intensity in Resistance Exercise Overtraining and Overreaching," in *Overtraining in Sport*, edited by R.B. Kreider, A.C. Fry, and M.L. O'Toole (Champaign, IL: Human Kinetics Publishers, 1998), 111.

amounts of either high-volume, low-intensity or low-volume, high-intensity resistance training, overtraining can occur (85). Conceptually, training programs that employ high-volume, high-intensity training and combinations of high-volume and high-intensity training have the potential to contribute to overtraining (figure 9.9).

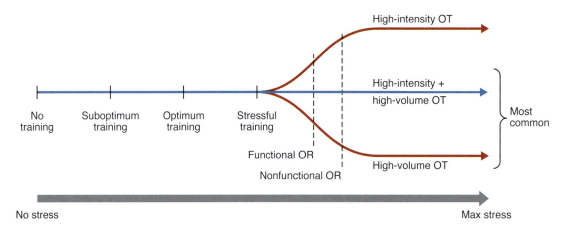

FIGURE 9.9 Resistance-training stress continuum leading to overtraining syndrome. Note: An understanding of the responses and adaptations to the entire continuum of training is necessary to understand the causes and the development of overtraining in the weight room.

Reprinted by permission from V.M. Zatsiorsky, W.J. Kraemer, and A.C. Fry, *Science and Practice of Strength Training*, 3rd ed., (Champaign, IL: Human Kinetics, 2021), 179.

Overtraining occurs more often due to frequent high volumes of high-intensity training or high volumes of monotonous training (97, 331). Due to the link between poor programming strategies and the mismanagement of the training process with overtraining risk, the coach should pay attention to the balance between the volume and intensity of the programs they create and ensure that an integrated monitoring program (see chapter 11) guides the training process to avoid overtraining.

Monitoring and Preventing Overtraining

It is difficult to determine the prevalence of NFOR or OTS because many factors contribute to an inability to tolerate training. Based on survey research, about 10% (range, 7%-21%) of collegiate swimmers and other endurance athletes report experiencing NFOR or OTS (219). Meeusen and colleagues (184) suggest that the risk of experiencing NFOR or OTS increases over the course of the athlete's career. Based on survey research, 60% of female and 64% of male elite runners report at least one occurrence of OTS, and nonelite adult runners report a career OTS occurrence rate of 33% (193, 195). Similarly, when examining 272 Swedish high-school junior national athletes from 16 different sports, there was a 37% OTS occurrence rate (144). Additionally, 29% of British age-group swimmers have developed NFOR or OTS at least once, and higher-skilled swimmers are at a greater risk (178). These data show that the risk of NFOR and OTS occurring is not solely limited to elite athletes but can occur in nonelite and youth athletes. It is critical that coaches and athletes of all levels take steps to prevent NFOR and OTS.

The best method for preventing overtraining is an integrated periodized training plan that leverages a comprehensive monitoring program to guide the coach's programming decisions (67). Because there is a lack of definitive criteria for diagnosing OTS, a reliable marker to determine OTS should meet several key criteria. Meeusen and De Pauw (183) suggest that the marker should

- be sensitive to changes in the training load;
- be unaffected by other factors, such as nutrition or chronobiological rhythms;
- display changes prior to the occurrence of OTS;
- be sensitive enough to distinguish between acute and chronic changes;
- be relatively easy to measure, not too invasive, and provide rapid results;
- be inexpensive;
- be derived at rest from submaximal or standardized exercise of relatively short duration; and,
- not interfere with the training process.

Although these criteria set a framework for monitoring overtraining, at this time no known test for OTS satisfies all of these criteria (183).

A comprehensive discussion about the integration of monitoring strategies into a periodized training plan is presented in chapter 11. For now, consider monitoring several factors specifically related to overtraining: performance, psychology, hormones, and immunology (183).

Performance

A central feature of overtraining is the inability to sustain intense exercise, which can manifest as decreased sport-specific performance when training load is maintained or increased (186). Meeusen and colleagues (184) suggest athletes who have transitioned into OTS are able to start a normal training sequence or competition but are unable to complete the prescribed training load or race at their normal level. Fundamentally, the key indicator of OTS is an unexplained decrease in performance (184), making performance testing an essential part of the diagnosis of OTS (35, 290).

Meeusen and De Pauw (183) suggest that the type of performance test and the intensity or duration of the test are essential when determining performance changes associated with OTS. Halson and Jeukendrup (111) suggested that time-to-fatigue tests likely show greater declines in performance and may be the most diagnostic of overreaching or OTS. Additionally, these tests can be useful for assessing substrate kinetics and hormonal responses to exercise (183). Although these tests are useful, it is likely that sport-specific performance tests are more appropriate.

When considering the implementation of a performance testing battery to monitor for potential risk of overtraining, the coach needs to consider tests that are sensitive to fatigue, minimally invasive, and not time-consuming. If the athlete can easily perform the selected tests without negatively affecting the programmed training, the coach can use the data collected to monitor changes that could be indicative of the onset of NFOR or OTS. Although there are numerous factors to consider when performing diagnostic performance testing to detect the progression of NFOR to OTS, it is important that the test employed give maximal amounts of information with a minimal amount of effort. Commonly tested factors include assessments of the rate of force development, speed and velocity of movement, vertical jump performance, and strength.

Rate of Force Development

With the emergence of the isometric midthigh pull (IMTP) (103) test as a methodology for monitoring changes in the isometric force–time curve (275), it has been hypothesized that this test may be diagnostic of symptoms of overtraining (331). Specifically, the **rate of force development (RFD)** appears to be extremely sensitive to changes in training volume (102, 124, 277). When training volume (i.e., sets × reps × kg [lb] lifted) is the highest, the amount of accumulated fatigue increases, resulting in a depressed RFD. Conversely, when training volume is reduced (e.g., during a taper), there is a reduction in accumulated fatigue that translates into an increase in the RFD (277). Additionally, since time-dependent RFD bands (i.e., 0-50 ms, 0-100 ms, 0-150 ms, 0-200 ms, and 0-250 ms) and the peak RFD can be quantified, the accumulation of fatigue might alter the force–time curve in different ways. For example, Suarez and colleagues (277) report that after the completion of a strength–endurance mesocycle, there are reductions in each RFD band that increase after a subsequent strength–power block in which the overall training volume is reduced (figure 9.10). Ultimately, it appears that the assessment of the RFD with the IMTP may be useful for monitoring performance changes that could be indicative of the early stages of overtraining (331).

Zatsiorsky and colleagues (331) have proposed that changes in the slope of the force–time curve (i.e., RFD) may be indicative of the early stages of overtraining (figure 9.11), but this has not been specifically investigated in relation to overtraining. As an overtraining monitoring tool, a rightward shift of the force–time curve would be indicative of a reduced RFD. Conversely, an increased RFD would be indicated by a leftward shift of the force–time curve. Importantly, based on the available literature, peak force would not be expected to change in response to overtraining (331).

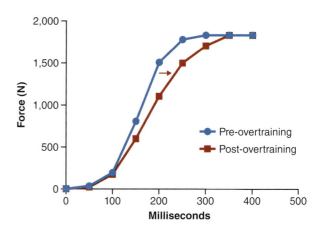

FIGURE 9.11 Theoretical isometric force–time curve response to overtraining. Note: The rate of force development shifts to the right and peak force is unaltered. Various RFD bands likely respond differently to overtraining.

Adapted from Zatsiorsky, Kraemer, and Fry (2021).

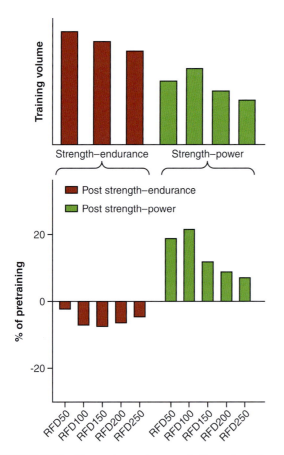

FIGURE 9.10 Percentage changes in the rate of force development in response to different mesocycle targets.

Adapted from Suarez, Mizuguchi, Hornsby, et al. (2019).

Speed and Velocity of Movement

Zatsiorsky and colleagues (331) have suggested that speed or velocity of movement is highly sensitive to overreaching and overtraining. For example, Fry and colleagues (86) reported that an athlete who is overreached or overtrained shows significant reductions in sprinting speed. Ultimately, the ability to sprint or move quickly is very sensitive to fatigue. Research suggests velocity loss may be an indicator of neuromuscular fatigue during resistance training (246), suggesting that the athlete's ability to rapidly create force declines as they become fatigued. Based on this concept, Vernon and colleagues (298) present compelling data that the load-velocity profile is very sensitive to fatigue. Specifically, it was noted that back squat velocity remains depressed for up to 72 hours after a training session focused on maximal strength development. Although these data provide a theoretical foundation for possibly using resistance-training velocity as a potential marker of fatigue and the early stages of the progression toward overtraining, more research needs to be completed to truly understand how the load-velocity profile responds to overreaching and overtraining.

Vertical Jump Performance

The vertical jump is one the most common tests athletes perform. When the test is employed as an overtraining monitoring tool, vertical jump height is not as sensitive to the progression of fatigue toward overtraining. It appears that changes to vertical jump kinetics are more diagnostic (331).

The increased availability of force-plate technologies provides coaches the ability to more comprehensively examine the force–time curve during the performance of unloaded and loaded vertical jumps (15). Several aspects of a vertical jump force–time curve may be useful when monitoring athletes for overtraining. For example, Cormack and colleagues (53) have clearly demonstrated that the flight time to contraction time ratio (FT:CT) is an effective tool for measuring neuromuscular fatigue (figure 9.12). In fact, when the FT:CT and the external training load are measured across a season in Division I basketball, the FT:CT ratio appears to decrease in response to increases in external training loads (115). However, at this time the FT:CT ratio has only been examined to determine athlete preparedness; further research is warranted to determine whether this metric is useful as an OTS monitoring tool.

Zatsiorsky and colleagues (331) have suggested that calculating the eccentric RFD from a countermovement vertical jump may be useful in monitoring for OTS. As noted earlier, the RFD is very sensitive to fatigue, and it is possible that eccentric RFD will be reduced when the athlete is experiencing highly fatiguing training that increases their risk of becoming overreached or overtrained.

Many other variables can be examined based on the vertical jump force–time curve, including the reactive strength index modified (RSImod) (115) and impulse (51), which may also be sensitive to

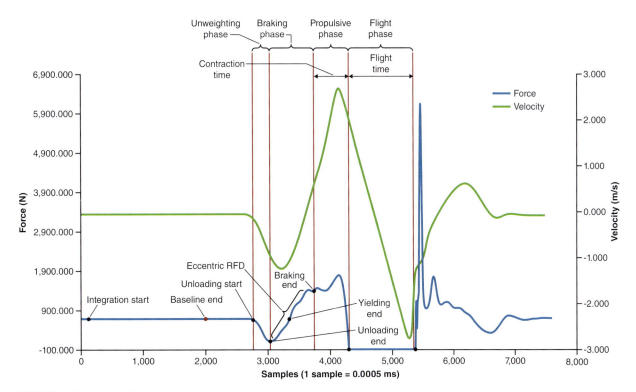

FIGURE 9.12 Vertical jump force–time curve measures.

overtraining. Although the RSImod and impulse appear to be sensitive to fatigue, there is no known research exploring the relationship between these variables and the progression toward overreaching and overtraining. However, due to the ease of quantifying these variables, many coaches have incorporated them into their monitoring programs.

Strength Testing

Although it may seem logical that increases in fatigue will result in decreases in maximal strength, the reality is that strength remains relatively stable (86, 298, 331). For example, Vernon and colleagues (298) reported that maximal strength (1RM) is not altered at 24, 48, 72, and 96 hours after a strength- or power-training session. Similarly, if maximal loads are used within a 2-week overtraining phase, maximal strength appears to be maintained longer than other performance measures, such as the velocity of movement (331). If, however, extreme loading (e.g., 10 sets of 1RM) is performed daily for 2 weeks, maximal strength may decrease (85), but this is unlikely in normal training scenarios and is an extremely poor way to implement resistance training. Therefore, Zatsiorsky and colleagues (331) suggest that maximal strength may be one of the last performance measures to display a decline when the athlete is progressing into a state of overtraining.

When considering athlete monitoring and the occurrence of overtraining, note that there may be a sequential pattern in the occurrence of the signs and symptoms that can be detected by a comprehensive monitoring program (figure 9.13). For example, psychological disturbances, such as mood, would be considered one of the earliest signs of an imbalance between stress and recovery. As this imbalance becomes greater, the athlete will display alterations to their RFD, which will then lead to reductions in their ability to perform high-speed movements. Ultimately, as the athlete moves toward a state of overtraining, strength is one of the last physical performance factors to display a decline (331). Ideally, the coach could use the items presented in figure 9.13 as part of their monitoring program to detect early signs of impending issues and align them with the expected responses to the planned training period. If, for example, the coach plans a short period of intensive training, they would expect psychological disturbances, impairments in the RFD, and decreases in speed performance. Conversely, if these symptoms occur unexpectedly, the coach should investigate further to determine why the athlete is not recovering from training and make appropriate changes to the athlete's program.

Psychology

It is well-documented that OTS, historically referred to as *staleness*, is associated with psychological symptoms (183, 193, 194, 331). These relationships were first reported in 1987 in the seminal paper presented by Morgan and colleagues (194). These authors reported that mood state dis-

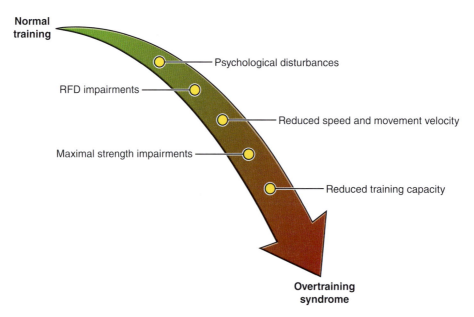

FIGURE 9.13 Theoretical sequence of signs of overtraining.

Adapted from Zatsiorsky, Kraemer, and Fry (2021).

turbances increased in a dose–response-dependent manner as swimmers' training load was increased and that these disturbances returned to normal when training load was decreased. To assess an athlete's mood, the **Profile of Mood States (POMS)** questionnaire can be used as a monitoring tool to evaluate general and specific moods. When athletes are exposed to intense training periods, this monitoring tool typically indicates increases in markers of the athlete's negative mood (e.g., tension, depression, anger, fatigue, and confusion) and decreases in markers of positive mood or vigor (183). Based on the available research, these disturbances tend to increase in a stepwise manner as the volume or intensity of training increases, with the highest training loads and greatest mood disturbances coinciding (183). Conversely, when the athlete undergoes a taper (see chapter 12), there is a reduction in negative mood states and an increase in vigor (i.e., positive mood state). At the end of the taper, the athlete will typically display a positive mood state pattern similar to what is observed at the beginning of the training period (193, 194).

In addition to the POMS, alternative questionnaires, such as the **Recovery–Stress Questionnaire for Athletes (RESTQ-Sport)** (140), **Daily Analysis of Life Demands for Athletes (DALDA)** questionnaire (109), and the self-condition scale (291), have been developed to monitor an athlete's psychological response to training. The most extensively studied of these is the RESTQ-Sport, which is a 76-question test used to evaluate 19 separate factors that assess OTS and recovery responses (183, 184). This questionnaire has a possible advantage of detecting an imbalance between stress and recovery before symptoms of OTS (e.g., apathy, drowsiness, fatigue, irritability) are apparent (183).

Although psychological monitoring is important, these tests can be biased or rendered invalid if the athlete does not answer the questions honestly or if the tools are overused (183). Therefore, the coach must take time to explain the values of these measures with their athletes and stress the importance of honest answers. Additionally, the coach must also remember that stressors are additive and stressors outside of training can influence an athlete's responses on psychological assessments (183).

Hormones

The endocrine system is often evaluated to determine how an athlete responds to acute stress and adapts to chronic stress (39). Although it has been suggested that many hormones are related to OTS, testosterone, cortisol, and the testosterone:cortisol (T:C) ratio are the most studied (3, 331). It has been hypothesized that the T:C ratio represents the anabolic or catabolic status of the athlete and that testosterone and cortisol affect many other body systems in an attempt to counteract the effects of overtraining (331).

The importance of the T:C ratio as an overtraining diagnostic tool was originally presented by Adlercreutz and colleagues (3), who defined cutoff changes in the T:C ratio that could be used to monitor for overtraining. In particular, they suggested that if the T:C ratio decreases by more than 30% or below 0.35×10^{-3}, an athlete could be at risk for overtraining (3). Even though the theoretical concepts that underpin the theories of Adlercreutz and colleagues (3) make sense, changes in this ratio do not always align with overtraining (331). For example, overtraining stimulated by high-volume training almost always results in a reduction in the T:C ratio, whereas high-intensity overtraining seems to exert only a minimal effect on this ratio (331). Therefore, it is evident that this ratio is indicative of the physiological strain of training and is generally not recommended as a tool for diagnosing overreaching or overtraining (184).

It is, however, important to note that the T:C ratio changes in response to alterations in training load that occur during a properly periodized training plan (102, 125, 302). Vervoorn and colleagues (302) report that the T:C ratio varies in response to the changes in training load that occur within a season of elite rowing training. Specifically, athletes who participated in a period of significantly increased training load showed a concomitant decrease in the T:C ratio (i.e., favors catabolism). Conversely, during periods of reduced training load, the T:C ratio increases (i.e., favors anabolism). Similarly, Haff and colleagues (102) report that when there are significant increases in weightlifting volume load, such as during shock microcycles, there are reductions in the T:C ratio, and when volume load is reduced (i.e., unloading or recovery weeks), the T:C ratio tends to rebound. Although historically the T:C ratio was suggested to be an indicator of OTS, it is generally accepted that this ratio cannot be used as a sole indicator of overreaching or overtraining (331) but should be considered a marker of preparedness (102, 304).

It is possible that other hormones such as leptin, adiponectin, and ghrelin may be related to training stress and possibly overreaching and overtraining (136). Jurimae and colleagues (136) suggest that basal and postexercise measurements of these parameters may provide information about energetic regulatory mechanisms that may change in response

Immunology

Athletes undergo systematic training that creates adaptive microtrauma, stimulates an acute local inflammatory response, and promotes the healing process that ultimately leads to positive adaptations (262, 263). This process is largely enhanced with appropriately periodized training plans that modulate training loads to facilitate recovery and adaptation. If, however, the athlete is exposed to inappropriately planned training that contains high volumes of high-intensity training coupled with limited rest, a state of chronic local inflammation can occur, resulting in the release of cytokines that activate monocytes (IL-1β, IL-6, TNF-α) (262). When this occurs, large quantities of proinflammatory cytokines (IL-1β, TNF-α) are released and systematic inflammation can occur, which may contribute to the occurrence of OTS.

This basic paradigm was first proposed by Professor Lucille Smith (262, 263) and is often referred to as the **cytokine theory of overtraining**. Based on this theory, it is believed that the production of large quantities of proinflammatory cytokines, as well as additional cytokines, is associated with the various signs and symptoms of overtraining as a consequence of systemic inflammation. Interestingly, Smith also proposes that there may be a link between these immunological responses and the common psychobehavioral changes that typically accompany overtraining (262, 263). A growing body of evidence suggests that elevated levels of the proinflammatory cytokines (IL-1β, IL-6, TNF-α) can communicate with the brain and induce behavioral changes that may be representative of a "sickness behavior" (62). Based on this line of reasoning, cytokines may represent a link between the body (i.e., circulation) and the brain (169), stimulating behavioral changes during overtraining similar to those seen during injury and sickness (62, 69). For example, cytokines may interact with the hypothalamus, producing the following mood and behavioral changes that have been associated with OTS (263):

- Constant fatigue
- Decreased appetite
- Changes in sleep patterns (hypersomnia or hyposomnia)
- Increased risk of depression
- Increased apathy
- Reduced self-esteem
- Emotional instability
- Fear of competition
- Becoming easily distracted
- Lowered resilience

Ultimately, it appears that the elevations in cytokines stimulated by tissue trauma and chronic inflammation may partially explain the changes in mood, behavior, or cognitive function associated with OTS (263).

In addition to affecting behavior, cytokines can inhibit the release of certain hormones in the hypothalamus (173) that are required to release testosterone from the periphery of the body. Thus, it is possible that cytokines play a regulatory role that partially explains why testosterone is suppressed when an athlete is overtrained (84, 263, 273, 292). Additionally, cytokines appear to increase circulating levels of other hormones, such as cortisol (253, 273), which is typically elevated when an athlete is overtrained (84, 263, 273, 292). It is also likely that alterations in the circulating levels of both testosterone and cortisol can influence mood and behavior, which are changes associated with overtraining (273).

Smith also proposes that athletes suffering from tissue trauma and chronic inflammation may experience an upregulation of humoral immunity and a suppression of cell-mediated immunity, which may partially explain why overtrained athletes are more at risk for various illnesses, including colds and upper respiratory tract infections (263). When humoral immunity is upregulated, a specific cytokine response is produced (IL-6, IL-4, and IL-10). Cell-mediated immunity is downregulated, presenting a different cytokine patten (i.e., IL-12 and interferon-γ) (70, 192, 239). Ultimately, athletes exposed to excessive training may experience chronic injuries that can upregulate the humoral arm of the adaptive immune system while suppressing cell-mediated immunity. The overtrained athlete is at an increased risk of infection and illness (263).

Recovery Theory

Recovery is a multifaceted process that can significantly affect how the athlete responds to the training process. Coaches need to understand how to optimize the training process and incorporate recovery methodologies and techniques. The coach must consider three discrete recovery time periods (296, 327): interexercise recovery, postexercise recovery, and delayed recovery.

Interexercise Recovery

Interexercise recovery is generally related to the bioenergetic activity that occurs during a training bout to ensure the availability of energy substrates. Fatigue during this period is partially related to the availability of phosphagens and the ability of the bioenergetic pathways to meet energy demands (21, 24). In this regard, the speed of recovery during an exercise bout is affected by muscular stores of adenosine triphosphate (ATP), phosphocreatine (PCr), and glycogen. Periodized nutrition and supplementation strategies may be necessary to maximize the availability of energy stores (see chapter 10). This may include creatine monohydrate supplementation to maximize PCr stores (155) or the implementation of strategic consumption of carbohydrate during a training session to optimally support the body's demand for energy (36).

Postexercise Recovery

After the completion of a training session, metabolic byproducts are removed, energy stores are replenished, and tissue repair is initiated (129, 145, 296). These **postexercise recovery** effects do not result in an instantaneous return to a resting state. As discussed in chapter 2, there is an elevation in oxygen consumption in the time immediately postexercise, which is often referred to as *excess postexercise oxygen consumption* (EPOC) (29, 94, 160, 289). The degree of the physiological disturbance (i.e., intensity, volume, or a combination thereof) imparted by the exercise bout will largely mediate the magnitude and duration of the EPOC. Ultimately, this time is used to resynthesize ATP and PCr (179), replenish myoglobin and hemoglobin stores of oxygen (217), oxidize lactate to provide energy as part of gluconeogenesis (179), deal with elevated body temperature (217), and restore other physiological factors (179).

During the postexercise period, the restoration of muscle glycogen is often of particular interest to coaches and athletes, especially those who are engaging in multiple training sessions per day and are attempting to maximize performance during training. After the cessation of exercise, the rate at which glycogen is restored is directly related to the amount of carbohydrate consumed (56). If the athlete's diet does not contain adequate amounts of carbohydrate, they will have a muted ability to recover from intensive training sessions that results in declining performance capacities and, potentially, overtraining (266). Typically, if adequate carbohydrate is consumed, muscular stores of glycogen can be restored within 20 to 24 hours of recovery (58). If, however, the diet has an inadequate amount of carbohydrate or training causes excessive amounts of muscle damage, there may be a delay in the glycogen resynthesis rate, resulting in an extended recovery time (55, 56). In most situations, athletes do not have 24 hours before their next training session, competition, or physical activity, so nutritional periodization strategies become essential to modulate the resynthesis of glycogen in ways that align with the targeted outcomes of the training plan (see chapter 10).

Delayed Recovery

Delayed recovery, or long-term recovery (24), is often related to the supercompensation effects stimulated by a well-designed periodized training plan. When structured correctly, a periodized training plan employs strategic training load manipulations that facilitate the reduction of fatigue while maintaining fitness to elevate preparedness and stimulate supercompensation (24). As noted in chapter 4, the greater the magnitude and duration of the training load, the greater the accumulated fatigue and the longer the duration necessary to remove fatigue, elevate preparedness, and stimulate supercompensation (figure 4.2, page 78). The fundamentals of delayed recovery underpin many sequential models of periodization, such as block periodization, where periods of concentrated loading (i.e., accumulation) are followed by periods of lower loads that are designed to elevate preparedness and performance (figure 9.14). Conceptually, the coach can consider delayed recovery to be synonymous with delayed training effects or a supercompensation response to the imposed training stimulus.

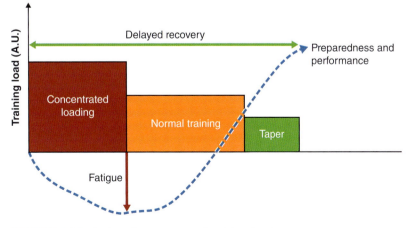

FIGURE 9.14 Delayed recovery and training load.

Factors Affecting Recovery

An athlete's ability to recover from training is affected by numerous controllable and uncontrollable factors (figure 9.2, page 202). One of the most important factors to consider is the structure of the periodized training plan. The coach should consider the effect of the athlete's age and training status, as well as how nutrition (see chapter 10) affects the recovery process. Additionally, due to the increased amount of travel during competition periods, the coach must also consider how travel, fatigue, and recovery are related.

Age

An athlete's age influences their ability to adapt to the training process (89, 238). It is widely believed that older athletes require longer recovery periods after training than their younger counterparts. Support for this belief can be partially explained by the slower rate of recovery of older athletes after exercise that contains large amounts of eccentric muscle actions (66, 161) that stimulate greater amounts of muscle damage (161, 242). In fact, older athletes tend to have longer recovery times after eccentric exercise (66, 242). These delays can be manifested as a longer time period before neuromuscular performance recovers (27), which may increase their overall risk of injury. Overall, older athletes appear to be at a greater risk of sustaining an injury than their younger counterparts (238). In addition to these slower recovery rates, older athletes also display an increased perception of muscle soreness and fatigue, which can affect their willingness to train (27).

Older athletes take longer to recover from intense exercise than younger athletes (204). For example, Taylor and colleagues (283) report that children require about half the recovery time of adults. Similarly, Ratel and colleagues (221) report that during 10 consecutive maximal cycle sprints, children can maintain power output with 30-second recovery intervals, whereas adults required 5-minute intervals. Based on these data, age does affect recovery rates. Therefore, when constructing training interventions, the coach must consider the age of their athletes and how age affects the athlete's ability to recover from the prescribed training. This consideration is simply another logical step in the individualization of training at the center of training theory.

Training Status

It is important to consider the athlete's training status when examining how rapidly an athlete recovers from training. As noted in chapter 1 (figure 1.8, page 9), training loads that are effective for novice athletes would result in detraining if they were applied to advanced athletes (330). As athletes become more trained, they require greater training loads and variation in training stimulus to increase performance. Therefore, the coach must introduce unloading periods to induce recovery from particularly hard training sessions, microcycles, or mesocycles. Additionally, it may be warranted to align specific recovery interventions during periods of intensive training.

One factor often overlooked is the effect of muscular strength on an athlete's ability to recover from training and competition. Athletes exposed to spikes in training load, often as part of a shock microcycle or session, have an increased risk of sustaining an injury (92). Interestingly, this increased risk is significantly reduced when stronger athletes are exposed to these types of microcycles or sessions (170). In addition to strength, well-developed physical capacities also seem to reduce injury risk (90). One reason for these findings is that stronger, more physically fit athletes generally display a faster rate of recovery from high-intensity training sessions when compared to weaker athletes (132, 255). Incorporating training activities that enhance maximal strength and overall fitness is essential for enhancing the athlete's ability to recover from training and competition stressors.

Travel Considerations

Travel is common in many athletes' annual training plans (110). In fact, athletes often undertake long-haul, transmeridian travel to compete in world championships, the Olympic Games, and league or tournament play (110, 130). Athletes are at risk of **travel fatigue** when exposed to frequent travel (130). If the athlete's travel requires them to cross multiple time zones, a desynchronization between the body's circadian rhythms and the external 24-hour light–dark cycle can occur (110), resulting in **jet lag** (245).

The magnitude of jet lag is largely affected by the number of time zones crossed and the direction of travel (50). Symptoms of jet lag, such as disturbed sleep patterns, daytime fatigue, reduced alertness, decreased mental and physical performance capacity, gastrointestinal disruptions, and headaches can occur when an athlete undertakes travel across multiple time zones (>3) (50, 130). Many of these symptoms can be resolved at a rate of 1 day per time zone crossed (245), but in some instances if the change in time zone is greater than 8 hours, these symptoms can persist for as long as 1 week (50). Additionally, eastward travel tends to result in a greater degree of jet lag, which extends recovery time compared to westward travel. Although the effect of jet lag is episodic, frequent exposure to jet lag during a competitive season can result in travel fatigue (50, 245). Samuels (245) proposed a conceptual model that differentiates between jet lag and travel fatigue, taking into account travel direction, number of time zones crossed, travel frequency, and the length of the athlete's competitive season (figure 9.15).

In this model, the concept of the time-zone differential, which accounts for circadian factors related to time of day and circadian resynchronization (264, 265), was introduced to explain how the effects of travel direction and distance translate into the episodic occurrences of jet lag (245). Additionally, the model also introduced the concept of travel fatigue and how it is affected by the recovery window, which accounts for the available recovery time and modulates the effects of travel distance and frequency and their effect on cumulative fatigue across a competitive season (245).

The athlete's response to travel is highly individualized and can be affected by several additional factors (310). For example, younger and fitter individuals who have flexible sleeping habits seem to better handle travel difficulties (310). Additionally, an individual's chronotype seems to affect how they handle travel. For example, morning types (i.e., larks) are better able to adjust to eastward travel when compared to evening types (i.e., owls) (310) who are better able to handle westward travel.

Many strategies can be employed to help the athlete cope with travel (figure 9.16). Generally, these strategies are broken into three phases: pretravel, during travel, and posttravel (245).

Pretravel

If the athlete's competition schedule allows, they can begin implementing pretravel strategies about 7 days prior to departure. For example, a team can adjust its training schedule to facilitate recovery prior to travel. If traveling eastward, plan an evening flight. If travel requires going across 10 or more time zones, schedule layovers (227, 245, 310). Another strategy is to preadjust to the time zone to be visited by going to bed 1 hour earlier each night before traveling east or 1 hour later each night before traveling west.

During Travel

When flying, the athlete should employ strategies that facilitate recovery and help them tolerate the process of traveling. One strategy often recommended is to have the athlete adjust their watch or smartphone to the layover or destination time zone as soon as they get on the plane (245). To facilitate rest and relaxation, the athlete should consider bringing eye shades and ear plugs or noise-cancelling listening devices to decrease overstimulation (245). While traveling, the athlete should avoid large meals,

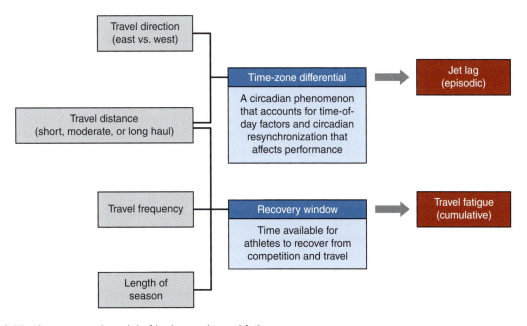

FIGURE 9.15 A conceptual model of jet lag and travel fatigue.

Adapted from Samuels (2012).

FIGURE 9.16 Coping with travel.

caffeine, and alcohol (110). Athletes should focus on maintaining hydration via water consumption and avoid boredom eating (110, 245). Finally, sleep should be aligned with the destination schedule (245).

Posttravel

The posttravel period lasts 2 to 4 days after arrival (245). During this time, the coach must strategically plan meals, sleep, rest, recovery, and training to accommodate a rapid adjustment of the circadian rhythms to the destination's time zone. Athletes should avoid alcohol consumption and long naps and strive to create regular sleep and eating schedules. When necessary, athletes can take short power naps of less than 20 minutes (24).

Psychological Aspects of Recovery

Modern athletes are under a unique array of stressors, ranging from the physical stress of training and competition to the psychological stressors associated with increased public scrutiny (i.e., mainstream and social media), group dynamics if in a team sport, recovery from injury, potential lack of a support network (e.g., if located far from family), and the overall length of the competitive season (197, 232). Additionally, a congested competitive schedule may provide insufficient time to psychologically recover between competitions (224), which can lead to a lack of motivation, impaired concentration and cognitive performance, and reduced volition (142, 200). Mental fatigue and altered mood states can be further affected by the outcomes of competitive engagements (199). Furthermore, overreaching and overtraining have been linked to psychological disturbances such as negative mental feelings and depression (234). Because of the effects of these psychological stressors on injury risk and performance, a coach must consider psychological recovery strategies as part of an integrated periodization plan.

A coach who designs recovery strategies must remember that *recovery* is an umbrella term that includes both physiological and psychological aspects (142, 260). As the coach designs the periodized recovery plan, they should consider individualized targeted psychological recovery strategies and the psychological effects of more traditional recovery interventions, such as massage and hydrotherapy. Conceptually, psychological training can target the development of volitional skills, which help the athlete overcome pain and fatigue, and recovery skills, which help the athlete cope with the demands of training and competition (20). Targeted psychological strategies can include imagery, relaxation techniques, mindfulness training, and cognitive self-regulation (43, 142), all of which can be strategically placed in the athlete's periodized training plan. Although the implementation of these strategies has become increasingly popular, much more research is required to determine the efficacy of these methods.

Recovery Modalities

Coaches and athletes can integrate a large array of recovery modalities into their periodized training plans to enhance athlete tolerance to training and competition workloads. The coach can consider a plethora of modalities for the athlete's periodized training plan. Although a simple search of social media sites and the Internet can reveal many fantastical and non-evidence-based recovery methodologies, it is important that the coach only consider methods that have been scientifically scrutinized and have strong evidence to support their efficacy. Although an extensive exploration of recovery methods is outside the scope of this chapter, it is important to classify potential recovery methods, highlight some of the available recovery methods, and show how they can be used within training plans.

Classification of Recovery Methods

Recovery methods can be classified as either passive or active.

Passive Recovery

One of the most important passive recovery methods is sleep. In one study from the Australian Institute of Sport, coaches and athletes indicated that inadequate sleep was one of the most prominent problems affecting fatigue and tiredness (77). Additionally, sleep is increasingly being recognized as an essential contributor to an athlete's overall health and well-being, and it exerts a significant influence on performance (107). Fundamentally, the recuperative outcomes of sleep are largely affected by three key factors: the duration (i.e., total sleep time), quality, and phase (i.e., circadian timing) of sleep (101, 244). Although the vast majority of the research looking at sleep has focused on the duration of sleep and sleep–wake patterns (106), there has been increasing interest in examining how sleep quality is related to sport performance (101).

Research shows that many athletes have poor sleep quantity or quality (107, 151). In fact, many athletes do not achieve the general 8 hours of sleep recommended for nonathletes (162). Research from the Australian Institute of Sport reveals that athletes average about 6.8 hours of sleep per night. An average of 86% of the time they spend in bed they are asleep, which is referred to as sleep efficiency (162). Athletes in individual sports tend to get less sleep (about 6.5 h) and have poorer sleep efficiency (85.9%) when compared to team sport athletes (7 hours, 86.4% sleep efficiency) (42, 162). It has been suggested that differences in the sleep patterns between individual and team sport athletes are a result of individual sport athletes having early morning training sessions that reduce their overall time in bed (162). Additionally, alterations to an athlete's sleep patterns are affected by their demanding training schedules and frequent travel, coupled with the physical and psychological stresses of being an athlete (133). Many factors can negatively affect an athlete's sleep patterns (figure 9.17).

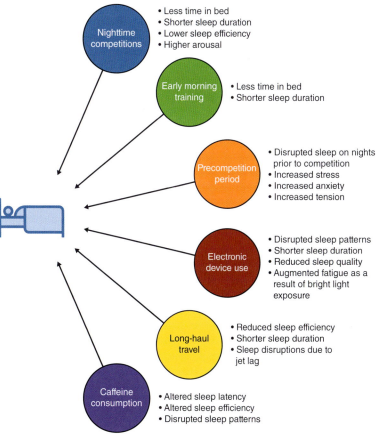

FIGURE 9.17 Common factors affecting sleep patterns.
Data from Caia et al. (2018).

Competition and training session schedules have been highlighted as potential factors that affect sleep. For example, increased nighttime competitions and multifaceted postmatch requirements (e.g., media commitments, medical treatments, recovery interventions) can alter when the athlete is able to go to bed and their sleep patterns (42). Early morning training can also significantly affect an athlete's amount of sleep. During the lead-up to the 2008 Olympic Games, the sleep patterns of seven swimmers were monitored; it was noted that training between 6:00 and 8:00 a.m. resulted in athletes waking about 4 hours earlier than nontraining days (249). When this research was replicated with a range of individual and team sport athletes, it was determined that when athletes were required to initiate training between 5:00 and 6:00 a.m., they tended to get less than 5 hours of sleep. Conversely, when training began between 7:00 and 10:00 a.m., the amount of sleep athletes got was increased to 6 to 7 hours. Finally, if training began between 10:00 and 11:00 a.m., athletes tended to get more than 7 hours of sleep (249).

One emerging problem is the use of smartphones and other electronic devices around bedtime, which has been linked to reduced sleep quality, decreased sleep efficiency, sleep loss, and increased daytime fatigue (76, 220, 240). Reductions in sleep time are often a result of using these devices without a predetermined beginning or end and can be exacerbated if the athlete engages with stimulating and interactive platforms, such as social media (42).

It is generally recommended that athletes strive to develop good sleep hygiene practices, such as establishing a regular bedtime routine, sticking to consistent waking times, and avoiding the use of technology (e.g., smartphone, tablet, computer) prior to sleeping (87, 305). Athletes should strive to get 9 to 10 hours of sleep per day, with 80% to 90% of this sleep occurring at night. The remaining 10% to 20% of the sleep requirement can be made up through naps.

If the athlete develops a sleep debt, naps (309) or sleep extension strategies (87) can be used. When the athlete is experiencing sleep deprivation, a 30-minute afternoon nap can enhance the athlete's performance capacity (309). Similarly, if the athlete extends their sleep during normal sleep times, they can enhance physiological and cognitive performance normally associated with sleep loss (87).

Active Recovery

A cool-down (discussed in chapter 8) that contains light exercise provides an enhanced postexercise recovery rate compared to passive recovery strategies, such as sitting quietly (190). Generally, active recovery activities that are performed at less than 50% of $\dot{V}O_2max$ are associated with more rapid lactate clearance rates (176, 190, 225, 282, 311), a more efficient body temperature decline (222), greater reductions in central nervous system activity (225), and decreased exercise-induced muscle soreness (226).

Active recovery strategies have the potential to offset the typical performance deficits associated with exercise-induced fatigue (188, 190, 226). When evaluating the recovery from a 5 km (0.62 mi) cycle time trial, the implementation of a low-intensity (50% of $\dot{V}O_2max$) active recovery protocol resulted in significantly less performance decline during a subsequent 5 km (0.62 mi) time trial compared with a passive recovery strategy (190). Additionally, when 5 minutes of light cycling with minimal resistance is performed after an acute bout of exercise, there is a more rapid restoration of maximal force-generating capacity when compared to passive recovery strategies (188).

When employed after a training session or competition, active recovery has the potential to speed up the 3-day course of recovery (226). Reilly and Rigby (226) reported that an active recovery consisting of 12 minutes of light jogging and stretching after a soccer match induced a significantly faster rate of performance recovery and significantly decreased muscle soreness compared to passive recovery (226).

Although active recovery is one of the most effective postexercise interventions, it does have some drawbacks. Specifically, some researchers suggest the metabolic cost associated with active recovery could impede muscle glycogen resynthesis (49) and result in significant reductions in PCr stores (267). Even when postexercise carbohydrate supplements are coupled with an active recovery, muscle glycogen resynthesis rates can be slightly impaired (26) when compared to a passive recovery that is coupled with carbohydrate consumption.

Active recovery strategies have great potential to positively affect the course of postexercise recovery. Although to date there is no consensus on the optimal duration or intensity of an active recovery regime, it appears that low-intensity active recovery activities (<50% of $\dot{V}O_2max$ or <50% of maximum heart rate) followed by 10 to 20 minutes of static stretching is prudent (24).

Methods Used to Enhance Recovery

Numerous potential recovery strategies can be integrated into an athlete's periodized training plan. Several commonly employed methodologies are discussed here.

Massage

Massage has been used as a rehabilitation and relaxation-inducing tool for thousands of years (315) and is frequently used by athletes to facilitate recovery (214). The most common form of massage used by athletes is the classic Western or Swedish massage (172, 214, 315). With this type of massage, techniques such as effleurage (gliding movements), petrissage (tissue kneading or pressing), friction (application of pressure), or tapotement (rapid striking) are used for 10 to 30 minutes (41).

Most athletes and coaches believe that massage improves performance (64, 214) and can provide several benefits, such as relieving muscle tension, reducing muscle pain, improving flexibility and range of motion, increasing blood flow, and enhancing the clearance of substances, such as lactate or creatine kinase (17). However, there is limited empirical data supporting these potential benefits, and much more research is required to truly understand the benefits of massage as a recovery intervention.

A meta-analysis by Davis and colleagues (64) highlights the difficulties in defining the benefits of massage. Most of the current body of scientific evidence uses small numbers of participants, and the effects of massage may be muted due to the individual variability in the responses to these interventions. Additionally, it has been reported that the vast array of massage techniques made it difficult to define the effect of these recovery strategies. Ultimately, based on the available literature, it was determined that there was no evidence that massage improved performance measures (e.g., strength, jump, sprint, or endurance performance) (64). However, it was determined that massage significantly improved flexibility and reduced pain and delayed onset muscle soreness by up to 13%.

Although limited evidence supports the positive effect of a recovery massage, some evidence suggests the main benefits of massage are related to an improved psychological response, which leads to an enhanced sense of relaxation (315). Massage is linked to reductions in anxiety (167, 316, 332), tension (316), stress (228), and depression (134); improved mood (316); and increased relaxation (316), sense of well-being (19), and perception of recovery (116, 117). Ultimately, these significant psychological responses to massage may be of particular benefit to the athlete during recovery even without strong supporting research.

When implemented as part of a periodized recovery plan, a massage after training or competition may benefit the athlete (8, 159, 172, 315). This type of massage is generally initiated 20 to 30 minutes after completion of the training session or competition and can last 7 to 12 minutes (24). If the massage takes place 1 to 2 hours after a highly fatiguing bout of training, it should last 15 to 20 minutes (159). If the exercise bout stimulates greater fatigue, the duration of the massage can be extended to 40 to 50 minutes (325) and repeated several times a day (159).

Self-Massage

Self-massage using **rolling devices**, in which a targeted muscle is rolled and compressed using a **foam roller** or massage bar or stick, has gained popularity among athletes and coaches (207). When using a foam roller, the athlete uses their body weight to apply pressure to the soft tissues using a rolling motion (46, 320). When using a massage stick, the athlete uses the upper body to apply pressure to the soft tissue using a rolling motion (46). This type of self-massage has largely increased in popularity because it is an affordable, easy-to-perform, and time-efficient method that is widely believed to enhance performance and facilitate recovery (46). However, there is no consensus on the benefits of its use as a recovery tool (46, 208, 320).

When compared to passive recovery, foam rolling has been shown to help people recover more quickly from exercise-induced decreases in sprint and strength performance (320). In fact, based on effect sizes determined by their meta-analysis, Wiewelhove and colleagues (320) report that the use of foam rolling as a recovery tool will result in 62% of the population experiencing an accelerated recovery of sprint performance and 58% of the population experiencing an accelerated recovery of strength performance. In another study, Rey and colleagues (230) reported that a 20-minute foam roller session enhanced the recovery of agility performance to a greater extent than a passive recovery session. Although these findings are promising, they are based on a limited body of research; therefore, much more research exploring the recovery benefits of postexercise foam rolling is warranted.

Similar to traditional massage methods, foam rolling may exert its greatest influence on psychological factors. Postexercise foam rolling has been found to alleviate perceived muscle pain (320). Based on the effect sizes reported by Wiewelhove and colleagues (320), 66% of the population will experience reductions in muscle pain with the use of postexercise foam rolling. This finding is important because muscle soreness has been linked to reduced sprint, jump, and strength performance (38). Additionally, altered muscle function may result in a decrease in the intensity of training (208, 320).

One question that could be asked is which is more effective: foam rolling or roller massages performed with a roller massage bar or stick? Based on a meta-analysis by Wiewelhove and colleagues (320), it appears that foam rollers are more effective as a postexercise recovery tool when compared to rolling performed with a roller massage bar or stick. However, it is important to note that these findings are based on a limited number of studies and much more research is warranted.

Based on the available evidence, the use of a foam roller as a posttraining recovery tool may be warranted. A structured foam roller recovery session lasting 15 to 20 minutes that contains at least two 45-second bouts of rolling performed on a series of targeted muscle groups is recommended (230).

Cryotherapy

The cooling of the body for therapeutic or recovery purposes is often referred to as *cryotherapy* (12, 156) and can include the use of cooling garments, ice massages, cold drinks, and **cold water immersion (CWI)** at temperatures between 10 and 20 °C (50 and 68 °F) (113, 156). More recently, an additional cryotherapy known as *cryostimulation*, in which the athlete is exposed to very cold air or gas (–100 to –160°C [–148 to –256 °F]) for brief periods (2-5 min), has become popular among athletes (22, 278).

The effects of cryotherapy are partially a product of cold temperatures reducing the neuronal transmission rates, resulting in a downregulation of the perception of pain to the central nervous system and reducing the potential for muscle spasm (308, 322). Although the cryotherapy-induced reductions in pain may be beneficial, the reduction of neural transmission rates may also result in short-term declines in athletic performance via a decrease in muscular contractile speed or force-generating capacity (243, 326). As a result of these effects, it is likely that there will be acute impairments in performance after a cryotherapy treatment (59, 252). For example, Didehdar and Sobhani (68) have reported that vertical jump performance is impaired for up to 10 minutes after CWI (15 min at 5 °C [41 °F]), and 36.6 m sprint performance is impaired for 20 minutes post CWI. Additionally, Crowe and colleagues (59) have reported that sprint cycling performance can be significantly reduced for up to 1 hour after CWI (15 min at 13-14 °C [55-57 °F]).

Based on these data, care must be taken when implementing cryotherapy-based recovery methods. Specifically, the coach must consider the time between training sessions. If there is less than 30 minutes between training sessions or competitive engagements, cryotherapy methods should be avoided.

Even though cryotherapy can promote muscle relaxation and reduce creatine kinase levels (75, 218) and, depending on timing, improve performance recovery (218), it is possible that chronic use of this recovery method can reduce endurance and resistance-training adaptive responses (82, 201, 215, 236, 324). Although some studies suggest that the chronic use of cryotherapies after training results in muted performance gains, this may not always be the case (108). For example, Halson and colleagues (108) report that the implementation of CWI (15 min at 15 °C [59 °F]) four times per week did not negatively hinder training adaptations and may in fact improve a number of aspects of performance. Additionally, Horgan and colleagues (122) report that the implementation of CWI (15 min at 15 °C [59 °F]) two times per week resulted in trivial improvements in squat jump performance. Although there is no current consensus on the effect of the chronic use of cryotherapy recovery techniques, Mujika and colleagues (197) suggest that coaches who wish to take a conservative approach could consider periodizing the implementation of cryotherapies so that during certain times of the annual training plan cryotherapies are withheld (i.e., general preparation phase) or implemented (i.e., main competition phase), depending on the goal of the phase. In addition, to implement cryotherapies as a recovery method, the coach must understand the indications and contraindications associated with each technique.

Cryostimulation Cryostimulation (CRY) is a relatively new form of cryotherapy that has become popular as a recovery method (12, 131, 241). It has two forms: whole body or partial body (114, 278). The main differences between these two forms are temperature, head exposure, and source of cold stimulation. Specifically, whole-body CRY uses a –110 °C (–166 °F) temperature, the head is exposed, and a compressor is used to apply the cold stimulation. Partial body CRY uses a –160 °C (–256 °F) temperature, the head is not exposed, and nitrogen gas is used to apply the cold stimulation (114).

Although some studies show improvements in performance (156), there is limited research that CRY benefits functional recovery (210). For example, Piras and colleagues (210) report that 3 minutes of partial-body CRY performed at –160

°C (−256 °F) enhanced recovery during the time between a strength training and an interval training session. Based on these findings, it appears that partial-body CRY may be useful when athletes are required to perform multiple training sessions in a condensed period.

CRY may exert its greatest effect on subjective recovery and muscle soreness when applied after intensive training (22). The analgesic effects of the cold temperatures used with CRY have been shown to affect the athlete's sense of well-being (279), perception of fatigue (206), and awareness of soreness (5, 206); to increase concentrations of anti-inflammatory cytokine IL-10; and to decrease proinflammatory cytokine IL-2 and chemokine IL-8 (12). Additionally, CRY decreased circulating creatine kinase by 40% when applied on alternating days during a typical microcycle performed by professional rugby players (13). Although some research supports the use of whole-body and partial-body CRY to enhance functional and subjective recovery, much more research is needed to optimize the use of this novel cryotherapy methodology.

Ice Massage Ice massage is often used as a method for treating postexercise muscle soreness (2, 100, 126). This type of massage is performed for 7 to 10 minutes and repeated every 20 minutes. Ice is applied to exposed skin with circular or longitudinal strokes, with each stroke overlapping the previous stroke (98). Ice massage has been shown to decrease temperature faster than applying an ice bag (332). Overall, this recovery method has a minimal frostbite risk, but the application may need to be modified for diabetic athletes.

Ice Bags or Cold Packs Another form of cryotherapy is the use of ice bags or cold packs to enhance postexercise recovery (197). Although some evidence indicates this recovery method may decrease both proinflammatory and anti-inflammatory cytokines and depress anabolic hormonal responses (201), there are very few studies that look at the efficacy of this recovery method. When the application of cold packs is compared to CWI or cryostimulation, it appears that cold packs are less effective at inducing recovery (213). Although more research is warranted, the use of ice bags or cold packs is still common practice. Typically ice bags or cold packs are used for 2 hours in a repeating pattern of a 20-minute cold application followed by a 20-minute removal period.

Thermotherapy

Various techniques, such as warm water immersion, saunas, steam baths, warm whirlpools, hydrocollator packs (hot packs), paraffin baths, and infrared lamps, are considered forms of thermotherapy (24). Thermotherapies increase cardiac output and lower peripheral resistance, facilitating increased subcutaneous and cutaneous blood flow (25, 318, 319). Increases in blood flow allow for elevated cellular, lymphatic, and capillary permeability, which can increase metabolism, nutrient delivery, and waste removal from the cells (57, 180). Although it is unlikely that the application of some thermotherapies will reach the deep tissue, there is a lot of anecdotal information about the proposed benefits of this recovery method.

Research from animal studies reveals that thermotherapy can expedite muscle repair following injury and restore muscle mass following immobilization (180, 256, 280). However, thermotherapy studies on humans have produced mixed results (122, 180). Therefore, more systematic studies that explore the effects of temperature and the timing of these techniques is warranted to determine how or if these techniques should be used as part of a recovery strategy.

Thermotherapy does have some contraindications, with the most obvious being that high temperatures can result in burns. There is some evidence that the application of heat can increase the inflammatory response, swelling, and edema (321). Additionally, when some individuals are exposed to hot water immersion, ectopic beats, hypotension, heat syncope, excessive tachycardia, and, in rare instances, death can occur (321). Additionally, if an athlete has an open wound, a skin condition, peripheral vascular disease, impaired circulation, or acute musculoskeletal injuries, care must be taken if thermotherapy techniques are used (321).

Hot water immersions (HWI) and saunas are often used as part of periodized recovery plans. Although the use of a sauna is often considered by coaches and athletes to be an important recovery intervention (261), there is limited research exploring its efficacy (254, 261). Sauna bathing is a form of passive heat therapy characterized by exposure to high temperatures for a brief time (163) and is commonly used as a recovery intervention by athletes during periods of intensive training (261). The Finnish sauna, which is marked by dry air (humidity of 10%-20%) and relatively high temperatures between 80 and 100 °C [176 and 212 °F] (163), is considered by some sport scientists to be one of the most important recovery interventions for athletes (261).

It has been hypothesized that the temperatures used in a Finnish sauna relax muscles, nerves, and blood vessels, resulting in an overall state of relaxation and well-being (187, 235, 261). Research from Rissanen and colleagues (235) suggests that a high-temperature sauna bath lasting 30 minutes seems to magnify the fatigue response associated with neuromuscular performance. Therefore, the coach should ensure that when a sauna bath is used after a strength session, there is at least 24 hours before the next training session. This effect does not appear to occur after endurance or concurrent (i.e., strength and endurance) training. For example, Mero and colleagues (187) report that a 30-minute far-infrared sauna bath at a temperature of 35 to 50 °C [95-122 °F] with a humidity of 25% to 35% enhances neuromuscular recovery after the performance of a 34- to 40-minute maximal endurance training session.

Although it appears that acute sauna use does not enhance recovery, it is possible that chronic use may have some benefits. Scoon and colleagues (254) report that when endurance athletes sat in a humid sauna for 30 minutes after each training session for 3 weeks, they experienced an enhanced recovery after the training period. Specifically, run time to exhaustion was enhanced by 32%, and 5K time-trial performance was improved by 1.9%. The authors suggested that one possible explanation for this enhanced performance might be related to an increase in blood volume. Support for this hypothesis can be found in the work of Stanley and colleagues (271), who reported that 30 minutes of sauna bathing (87 °C [189 °F], 11% humidity) following normal training for 10 days resulted in moderate to large plasma volume expansion in well-trained cyclists. Based on these studies, it seems that the use of sauna bathing is of benefit for endurance athletes. However, much more research is needed to determine how to optimally integrate sauna bathing into the recovery practices of athletes.

Classically, when employed as a recovery technique, the sauna should be undertaken for 5 to 30 minutes at temperatures of 70 to 100 °C (158-212 °F) with a humidity level of 10% to 20% (187, 235, 261). There are large individual differences in the ability to tolerate sauna bathing, so if this recovery method is used, the protocol must be designed to meet the individual athlete's needs.

Contrast Therapy

Contrast therapy is the alternation of thermotherapy and cryotherapy techniques (119). This practice is generally believed to enhance recovery after training and competition (52, 60, 301). Although the most common form of contrast therapy is the combination of HWI and CWI (14), other combinations of thermotherapy and cryotherapy techniques can be employed as part of a recovery plan (135). For example, a hot–cold contrast can be created by combining sauna bathing (70-100 °C [158-200 °F]) with CWI (15 °C [59 °F]) or a cold shower (18 °C [64 °F]) (24). Additionally, hot (32°C [90 °F]) and cold showers (18 °C [64 °F]) can be combined to create a contrast therapy protocol (135). Although there are mixed results on the effectiveness of contrast therapies on performance (9, 52, 60, 135), there are positive psychological benefits to employing this recovery technique (135).

Contrast therapies result in what is often called a *muscle pumping action,* which occurs in response to alternating between thermotherapy, which stimulates vasodilation, and cryotherapy, which stimulates vasoconstriction (52, 78, 119). For example, Fiscus and colleagues (78) provide compelling evidence that when a hot–cold contrast (4:1) is applied for 20 minutes, there is significant fluctuation in blood flow, with increased arterial blood flow noted during the hot condition and reduced arterial blood flow noted during the cold condition. This pumping action, or blood flow fluctuation, likely increases blood flow and metabolite removal and enhances recovery (5, 52). Contrast therapy has been shown to relieve stiffness (158, 295), increase the removal of creatine kinase (i.e., marker of muscle damage) (96), increase lactate removal (52, 196), and reduce sympathetic activity, resulting in improvements in neurological recovery of the peripheral nervous system (52, 104). In addition to the scientific evidence supporting the use of contrast therapy, empirical reports (198) also support its use as a recovery methodology. Generally, contrast therapy can be performed using 1 to 2 minutes of thermotherapy followed by 1 minute of cryotherapy and repeating these two treatments for a total of 6 to 15 minutes of treatment (18, 135, 301).

Hydrotherapy

Water immersion as a method for inducing recovery between successive training sessions or competitions is of particular interest to coaches and athletes because it is easy to employ and has been extensively researched (301, 321). For thermoneutral water immersion (20-36 °C [68-97 °F]), the only things required are water and a container, bath, or pool the athlete can immerse in. When the athlete is immersed in water, they are exposed to a compressive force referred to as **hydrostatic pressure** (24, 301, 321). The increase in hydrostatic pressure during water immersion stimulates the displacement of fluids from the extremities toward the central cavity of the body (321). Additionally, increased cardiac output increases blood flow that, when coupled with an increased diffusion gradient, results in an augmented rate of substrate delivery and waste clearance (93, 147, 258), which may translate into an enhanced recovery rate (321, 322). In addition to these physiological responses, there can be positive psychological responses to this recovery methodology, such as lowering perceptions of fatigue (24). Based on the available evidence, water immersion protocols seem to exert both physiological and psychological responses that could enhance recovery.

There are various recommendations about how best to apply thermoneutral hydrotherapy techniques to stimulate a hydrostatic pressure-induced movement of interstitial fluids. Generally, thermoneutral water immersion strategies should

- be employed within 30 minutes after the cessation of exercise,
- use water temperatures between 20 and 36 °C [68-97 °F],
- last for 15 to 20 minutes, and
- use greater immersion depths (301, 321, 322).

Although these general recommendations have been investigated, more research is warranted to determine the optimal water immersion duration necessary to optimize or maximize restoration.

Hydrotherapy can also be implemented using CWI (≤20 °C [68 °F]), HWI (≥36 °C [97 °F]), and contrast water therapy (CWT) (301).

Cold Water Immersion   CWI is one of the main recovery methods used by athletes to expedite the recovery of performance during intense training or competition (171, 197). There has been a significant increase in research exploring the acute responses to CWI and the long-term effect of frequent use of CWI as a recovery strategy (88, 108, 122, 123, 288). To understand these responses, it is important that the coach be familiar with the mechanisms that explain how CWI affects recovery (197). The primary mechanisms associated with CWI include increases in hydrostatic pressure; decreases in tissue temperature; increases in buoyancy; decreases in muscle perfusion; decreases in nerve conduction velocity; and decreases in the permeability of cellular, lymphatic, and capillary vessels (197, 288). These mechanisms can stimulate anti-inflammatory effects, decrease perceptions of fatigue, increase the removal of metabolic waste products, reduce secondary tissue damage, increase reabsorption of interstitial fluids, and reduce recovery time (for extensive review, see Tipton et al. [288]). Ultimately, both acute and chronic recovery will be influenced by these effects (197).

Several meta-analytic studies (164, 213) have revealed that when CWI is employed after strenuous exercise, there are generally positive effects on performance recovery. Versey and colleagues (301) have reported that CWI protocols that require the athlete to be immersed for 5 to 15 minutes in water between 10 and 15 °C (50-59 °F) appears to result in the greatest performance gain. However, the responses to CWI protocols are highly individualized (272) and can be affected by the athlete's body surface area, body mass, body composition, and perception (123, 272, 334). Body composition is probably one of the more important factors mediating the effect of CWI on performance. In fact, the differences in body composition between athletes of different ages, genders, and ethnicities partially explain the different recovery responses to CWI (272). Coaches may need to consider CWI protocols that are specifically designed to address the individual needs of their athletes.

Although there is ample evidence that CWI can affect acute recovery responses, there is currently much debate about the efficacy of chronic use (31, 88, 108, 122, 236, 288). The main theory presented against its use centers on the blunting of specific molecular mechanisms that underpin exercise-induced adaptations (32, 88). The negative effects of CWI seem to be most noted when regularly used in conjunction with a resistance-training program (171). Malta and colleagues (171) reported in their meta-analysis that the regular use of CWI in conjunction with exercise programs has a deleterious effect on resistance-training adaptations (i.e., hypertrophy and strength) but exerts no effect on aerobic exercise performance. Based on these findings, a conservative recovery approach would be to withhold CWI after resistance-training sessions (197).

Although the debate about the efficacy of long-term use of CWI has recently received a lot of attention, the idea of periodically withholding recovery strategies or periodizing them to align with targeted training goals is not a new or novel idea. In their seminal text *Supertraining*, Siff and Verkhoshansky (259) stated that, "if certain recovery methods are employed after a workout, then the positive aftereffects (or training effects) stimulated by the workout tend to be negated and the overall training effect can be significantly diminished.

Thus, the unskilled use of recovery methods can markedly increase the amount of training work and yet not provide a corresponding training effect" (page 438). Based on these statements and emerging research, the coach should strategically implement CWI strategies in accordance with the targeted outcomes of the period or phase of the periodized training plan. It may be recommended to withhold CWI during the general preparation phase to maximize adaptations to training, because fatigue appears to exert a major effect on training adaptations. Conversely, during the main competition phase, CWI recovery strategies can be employed to maximize recovery (197).

When used as a postexercise recovery method, CWI can be employed for 10 to 20 minutes at temperatures between 12 and 18 °C (54-64 °F) (24). Although these recommendations have classically been used with all athletes, emerging evidence suggests that CWI recovery strategies need to be individualized (251, 272, 328). For example, depending on the subject's physical characteristics (e.g., body fat, muscle mass) and beliefs about CWI recovery methods, the immersion protocol could be undertaken for 10 to 17 minutes at 12 °C (54 °F) or for 10 minutes at 15 °C (59 °F). Ideally, much more research is needed to understand how to individualize CWI as a recovery method.

Hot Water Immersion HWI is typically performed with water temperatures greater than 36 °C (97 °F), with immersion times lasting between 10 and 24 minutes (158, 216, 293, 294, 301, 303). HWI protocols require the use of heated pools, spas, or baths large enough for the athlete to immerse an extremity or their entire body. It is believed that the increase in core temperature and the increased hydrostatic pressure associated with water immersion cause a cascade of physiological effects that assist with recovery (24). There is conflicting research on the efficacy of HWI as a recovery tool. Some studies suggest that this hydrotherapy method enhances recovery (127, 294), and other studies suggest it is not effective (158, 293, 303).

For example, Vaile and colleagues (293) reported that when HWI (14 min and 38 °C [100 °F]) was used daily after training, there was no significant benefit on subsequent cycling sprint or time-trial performance compared to CWI or CWT. Similarly, Hung and colleagues (127) report that using a HWI protocol (30 min at 40 °C [104 °F]) every third day for 2 weeks resulted in impaired shooting performance in archery.

Although there has been some promising evidence of HWI after exercise or injury in animal models, the results of studies examining these responses in humans are mixed (180). There is a need for more research to establish the efficacy of HWI and to determine whether this method should be used as a part of a postexercise recovery methodology. Due to the current lack of evidence, HWI is generally not recommended as a recovery method (301).

Contrast Water Therapy The most common recommendations for implementing contrast hydrotherapy protocols suggest that **contrast water therapy (CWT)** should alternate between three to seven times between 1 minute of CWI and 1 to 2 minutes of HWI to accumulate 6 to 15 minutes of immersion (301). CWT typically uses HWI at temperatures above 36 °C (97 °F) and CWI at temperatures between 7 and 20 °C (45-68 °F) (119, 198). There is no consensus on the order of the rotations; some studies suggest that CWT should finish with HWI, and others suggest it should end with CWI (301). Of the studies that demonstrated positive benefits for CWT, four finished in hot water (120, 148, 295, 314) and seven finished in cold water (5, 34, 270, 293, 294, 299, 300). Based on the available evidence, it is recommended that the CWT begin with HWI and end with CWI to minimize the possibility of swelling and to allow for a pain-free range of motion (198). For example, an athlete could undertake a 6- to 15-minute recovery protocol of two to five rotations of 2 minutes of HWI (38 °C [100 °F]) coupled with 1 minute of CWI (18 °C [64 °F]) (figure 9.18).

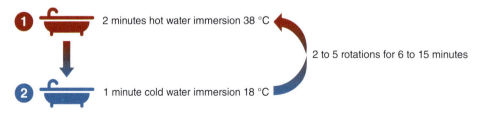

FIGURE 9.18 Example contrast water therapy protocol.

Compression

Compression garments are popular tools used by athletes to aid recovery after strenuous exercise. This recovery method has its origins in clinical settings in which limb compression is used to treat a range of inflammatory conditions (30), deep-vein thrombosis (37), and chronic venous insufficiency (4). When applied as a recovery tool, it is believed that the use of compression allows for the creation of an external pressure, similar to what is experienced with water immersion protocols, to heighten venous return after exercise and enhance the removal of metabolic waste products that accumulate in response to exercise (10, 63). Furthermore, the elevation of external pressure stimulated by compression garments may also reduce the intramuscular space available for swelling, attenuating the inflammatory response and reducing muscle soreness (10, 23, 63).

A growing body of evidence suggests that compression garments do speed recovery after exercise that induces muscle damage, such as resistance training (121, 174), which appears to result in an enhanced performance capacity (10, 33, 118, 323). Generally, athletes who wear compression garments after resistance training experience enhanced strength recovery within 2 to 8 hours and after 24 hours of completing the training session (33). It has been hypothesized that these improvements are a result of compressive garments ameliorating swelling and reducing the progression of muscle damage (33, 152-154).

The use of this recovery method after metabolic exercise appears to offer varying degrees of benefit depending on the time frame examined (33). Brown and colleagues (33) report a limited short-term recovery benefit (0-2 hours after exercise), but there are large, very likely beneficial effects of their use 24 hours after metabolic exercise or prior to endurance performance. The finding that compression garments were not effective at enhancing recovery during limited short-term recovery periods is somewhat surprising considering this recovery method has been reported to be effective for enhancing repeated cycle sprint ability when a short recovery period of 20 minutes is used (10). It is likely that variations in the application of compression may differ between studies and be a result of the highly individualized response to recovery methods.

Another promising application of compression garments is to have the athlete wear them overnight while sleeping (257). Shimokochi and colleagues (257) have reported that after an intensive training session consisting of 10 sets of 10 repetitions of maximal isokinetic eccentric and concentric knee extensor contractions with 30 seconds between sets, participants experience a faster rate of recovery if compression garments are worn overnight. Specifically, 24 hours after the first bout, maximal force-production capacity is 10% greater after wearing compression garments while sleeping when compared to sleeping without compression garments. Although much more research is needed to validate these findings, these results may offer the athlete a way to enhance the recovery benefits of sleep.

Based on the available evidence, coaches should consider integrating compression garments into a periodized recovery plan. This recovery method may be of particular use after activities such as resistance training (33) and the training practices associated with team sports (229, 231).

External Pneumatic Compression

The use of external pneumatic compression is a recovery method that is gaining in popularity (112, 247). Dynamic external pneumatic compression differs from static compression in that it uses whole-leg or whole-arm sleeves that inflate and deflate through a series of zones using modest inflation pressures that range between about 20 and 100 mmHg (112). This type of compressive treatment appears to enhance flexibility (248), reduce muscle soreness (247), lessen muscle swelling (48), and decrease lymphedema (150). External pneumatic compression also appears to enhance the recovery rate between successive bouts of exercise, resulting in enhanced performance (333) and maintained performance during periods of overreaching (112).

An additional benefit of external pneumatic compression is that it appears to increase mRNA expression of genes related to skeletal muscle hypertrophy (i.e., MHY2m, IGFBP5, MYOM1) and oxidative stress resilience (i.e., CAT, SUOX) (175). When used in conjunction with high-intensity interval training, this recovery method appears to reduce markers of proteolysis.

When examined collectively, 15 to 20 minutes of dynamic external pneumatic compression appears to be an effective recovery method that can be used within any period of the athlete's annual training plan. However, much more research is needed to determine the optimal method for applying this recovery methodology.

Combining Recovery Strategies

The coach can integrate many recovery strategies into the athlete's periodized training plan (14). To optimize recovery, it may be warranted to use protocols that leverage several different recovery strategies simultaneously (190, 233). For example, Monedero and Donne (190) designed a recovery intervention that used 3.75 minutes of active recovery (cycling at 50% of $\dot{V}O_2$max) followed by 8.5 minutes of massage, resulting in significantly greater improvements in 5 km (3 mi) time-trial performance when compared to either active recovery or massage alone. In another study, Viitasalo and colleagues (303) created a recovery session that lasted 20 minutes and used warm water immersion (36.7-37.2 °C [98-98.9 °F]) combined with underwater jet massage to stimulate an enhanced rate of recovery. Reilly and colleagues (223) designed a recovery intervention that employed deep-water running, a combination of active recovery and hydrotherapy, to stimulate a decrease in muscle soreness and maintain range of motion. Finally, Martinez-Guardado and colleagues (177) reported that when athletes are competing within a congested time period (i.e., tournament), the combination of intermittent pneumatic compression and CWI maintained muscle mechanical properties and enhanced perceived recovery.

Ultimately, infinite combinations of recovery methods can be constructed to meet an athlete's specific needs. When deciding which combination of recovery methods to employ, the coach must consider how each method affects recovery and adaptation and then align those with the goals of the phase of the periodized training plan.

Periodization of Recovery Methods

The integration of recovery methods into the periodized annual training plan is an important consideration for athletes and coaches (197). Two opposing theories are often presented when considering whether to use recovery methods (197). The first theory centers on the idea that structured recovery methods allow the athlete to recover more efficiently from each training session, thereby allowing them to train harder more frequently, which translates into improved performance over the long term (197, 296). The second theory suggests that postexercise fatigue and inflammation are necessary to stimulate training-induced adaptations that translate to improved performance (296). Based on the second theory, it may be prudent to withhold recovery methods to ensure the anticipated training benefits are not dampened (105, 197).

The scientific literature provides ample evidence that many proactive recovery strategies (e.g., hydrotherapy, whole-body cryotherapy, massage, compression garments) can improve the rate of recovery after an acute bout of intensive training (28, 105, 113, 121, 164, 213, 214). Much less research directly investigates the effects of chronic exposure to recovery methods on training-induced adaptive responses (82, 88, 105, 215, 236). At this time, no consensus exists on the effect of chronic exposure to recovery methods; some studies suggest that recovery methods, such as CWI, dampen the adaptive response to resistance training (171, 215), but others suggest no negative effects on adaptive responses to resistance training (122, 123) or aerobic training (215) and no negative effects on sprint cycling performance (105). A conservative approach to implementing a recovery plan could systematically withhold certain recovery methods, such as CWI, after some resistance-training sessions during key parts of the preparatory period of the annual training plan.

Conceptually, the coach should consider integrating specific recovery methods into their periodized training plan. As with physical training, if recovery methods are implemented in a haphazard and unplanned manner with a lack of variation, the effectiveness of these methods will be muted. Therefore, the coach must consider the acute and chronic effects of the various recovery methods that they integrate into the athlete's periodized training plan. Based on the work of Mujika and colleagues (197), there are five basic recovery intervention strategies that the coach should consider:

1. Withholding recovery at certain times to maximize training-induced physiological adaptations (chronic recovery)
2. Using recovery methodologies to prepare for a certain training session or microcycle (acute recovery)
3. Using recovery methodologies to manage competition-induced fatigue (acute recovery)
4. Employing recovery strategies during periods of intensive travel to manage fatigue

and psychological stress (acute and chronic recovery)

5. Employing recovery strategies after an injury to enhance recovery and reduce the risk of injury

Based on these considerations, the coach can decide which recovery strategies to withhold or include depending on the periods and phases of training in the athlete's periodized training plan (figure 9.19). For example, during the general preparatory phase, the primary goal is to induce training adaptations, so recovery strategies that employ cryotherapy methods, such as CWI, might be withheld, and emphasis on recovery methods that might enhance adaptations, such as HWI, nutritional strategies, and external pneumatic compression, could be preferentially targeted.

Conversely, during the competition period, the primary goal is to enhance the recovery process after intense training sessions or competitions and not stimulate adaptive responses. In this instance, recovery strategies such as CWI, targeted nutritional strategies, massage, and mindfulness training may be helpful, especially when the competition schedule becomes congested. For example, when competitions are 7 days apart, two hydrotherapy strategies could be integrated into the competition microcycle (figure 9.20).

In this scenario, 10 total minutes of CWI immersion (two immersions at 15 °C [59 °F] × 5 min) are scheduled after the first competition and on the day prior to the next competition. CWT is scheduled for the third and fifth days after the competition; the athlete performs three rotations of 2 minutes of HWI (38 °C [100 °F]) and 1 minute of CWI (15°C [59 °F]).

Alternatively, several recovery methods could be integrated into the competition microcycle (figure 9.21). In this example, the postcompetition recovery plan includes foam rolling (5-10 min) followed by a CWI protocol (two immersions at 15 °C [59 °F] × 5 min) and the consumption of a carbohydrate and protein beverage. One and two days after the match (game + 1 and game + 2), active recovery, such as stretching (5-20 min) and foam rolling (5-10 min), could be used. After the two hardest training sessions (game + 3 and game + 4), the athlete performs foam rolling (5-10 min) and then wears compression garments for 24 hours after the completion of their last training session of the day. In the first unloading session (game + 5), the athlete uses CWT (2 min HWI at 38 °C [100 °F] and 1 minute CWI at 15 °C [59 °F]), then after the last

Period	Phase	Recovery recommendations
Preparation	General preparation	• Withhold some strategies to maximize adaptation • Use strategies that maximize training adaptations and align with the goals of the period
Preparation	Specific preparation	• Specific recovery after specific sessions, particularly those that require high levels of skill and/or high-quality training sessions • Use strategies to reduce fatigue and soreness prior to key training sessions
Competition	Main competition	• Use recovery strategies to minimize fatigue and maximize performance capacity • Use recovery strategies to manage travel and jet lag–based fatigue • Use strategies based on availability
Competition	Taper	• Use recovery strategies to minimize fatigue • Use recovery strategies to maintain high-intensity training while reducing the time required to taper

FIGURE 9.19 Recovery recommendation alignments with the periods and phases of a periodized training plan.
Adapted from Mujika, Halson, Burke, et al. (2018).

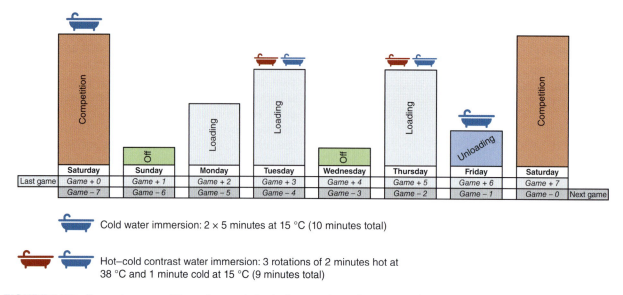

FIGURE 9.20 Example competition microcycle hydrotherapy-based recovery plan.

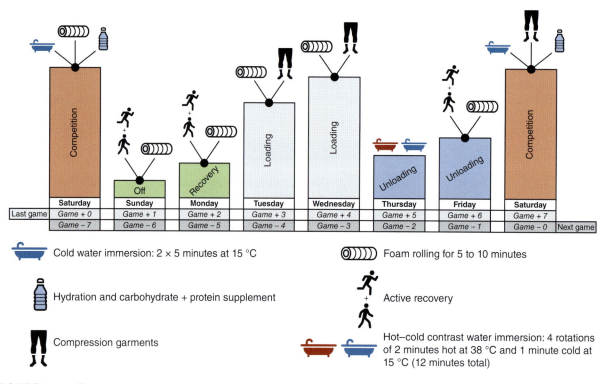

FIGURE 9.21 Example competition microcycle recovery plan using multiple recovery strategies.

training session (game + 6) of the microcycle, the athlete performs active recovery, such as stretching (5-20 min) and foam rolling (5-10 min). Ultimately, there are numerous ways to integrate recovery sessions into the competition microcycle depending on what is available and the time the athlete can dedicate to recovery.

Summary

The most effective way to ensure recovery and maximize training adaptations is to have a well-thought-out periodized training plan that leverages a structured athlete monitoring system. As part of the periodized training plan, it is important that recovery methods are not haphazardly implemented but instead are carefully considered and aligned with the goals of each phase of the annual training plan. As part of the athlete's periodized recovery plan, the coach should consider the acute and chronic effects of the chosen recovery methods and determine how best to combine various methods to maximize recovery and minimize the risk of overtraining. As with training, it is important to apply the principle of variation to the structure of the athlete's recovery plan. Ultimately, the coach must also remember that all the best recovery methods will never overcome a poorly conceived periodized training program.

CHAPTER 10

Periodization of Nutrition

The coaching and scientific communities generally recognize the importance of periodizing physical training (83, 84, 217) but, historically, less emphasis has been placed on the organization of athletes' nutritional practices (134, 193, 259). Due to the numerous interactions among physical training, nutrition, and long-term physiological and performance adaptations, contemporary coaches and sport scientists have increasingly become interested in what is commonly referred to as *nutritional periodization* (134).

Although there is no single unified definition of **nutritional periodization**, it typically refers to the planned, structured, and strategic manipulation of nutritional interventions to enhance the adaptive responses to the training process to optimize long-term performance capacity. Although the concepts associated with nutritional periodization are not new, the first theoretical guidelines for periodizing nutritional practices were presented in the 2007 International Association of Athletics Federations Nutrition Consensus Statement (257, 259). In this statement, several suggestions were made about how to approximate energetic demands of different periods and phases within an athlete's periodized annual training plan and how nutritional strategies can be manipulated to enhance the adaptive responses to training (257, 259).

Conceptually, the periodization of nutrition can be considered using several strategies (193):

- Manipulating nutritional intake to align with the needs and goals of training and competition
- Manipulating nutritional strategies to increase capacity for fuel use from specific substrates (e.g., fat versus carbohydrate) with the goal of increasing performance capacity
- Alternating between nutritional strategies to either enhance physiological adaptations or to optimize performance
- Organizing nutritional interventions throughout the day to maximize the interactions between exercise and nutritional intake

These strategies need to be contextualized with the periods and phases in an athlete's annual training plan. Based on an understanding of how manipulating nutritional strategies can affect adaptation and recovery or enhance performance, strategic decisions can be made to align specific nutritional interventions with the training process at the macro-, meso-, and microcycle levels of the overall periodized training plan (259). Ultimately, to effectively integrate nutritional and supplementation strategies into an athlete's overall periodized training plan, the nutritional support staff and coach must work together to ensure the targeted goals at each level of the periodized training plan align with the nutrition, supplementation, and programming strategies. To facilitate this collaboration, this chapter presents information about nutrition and how the manipulation of nutritional strategies affects physiological and performance outcomes. Based on this information, key concepts related to the periodization of nutrition will be presented along with information about how these strategies can amplify the training-induced performance adaptations associated with periodized training models.

Macronutrients

Macronutrients—carbohydrate, protein, and fat—are essential components of the diet that maintain the body's structural and functional integrity (114). To understand how nutritional interventions can be manipulated or periodized to maximize physiological adaptations and optimize performance, the coach must understand how the body uses carbohydrate, protein, and fat to provide energy for physical performance (see chapter 2). Additionally, the coach should understand some basic facts about each of these macronutrients.

Carbohydrates

Carbohydrates are composed of carbon-, hydrogen-, and oxygen-based molecules. Generally, carbohydrates are categorized based on the number of sugar (saccharide) units they contain: monosaccharides, oligosaccharides, and polysaccharides (92, 114, 250).

Monosaccharides

The simplest carbohydrate molecule is the **monosaccharide**, a single-sugar molecule often referred to as *simple sugar*. The three most important monosaccharides from a nutritional standpoint are **glucose**, **fructose**, and **galactose** (92). Glucose, sometimes called *blood sugar*, is the most common form of carbohydrate transported in the body. Glucose is formed as an end product of the breakdown of more complex carbohydrates (i.e., oligosaccharides or polysaccharides) but also naturally occurs in food. Additionally, small amounts of glucose can be synthesized in the liver from amino acids, glycerol, pyruvate, and lactate through a process called *gluconeogenesis* (92). Overall, the body can very easily break down glucose to be used as a fuel substrate to supply energy, to be stored as glycogen in the muscle and liver, or to be converted to triglyceride and stored for later use (92).

From a nutritional standpoint, the second most important monosaccharide is fructose, sometimes referred to as *levulose* (92). Fructose can be found in fruits, vegetables, and honey and accounts for the sweet taste associated with these foods. When these foods are consumed, fructose is taken into the bloodstream from the digestive tract and converted to glucose in the liver (127).

The final nutritionally important monosaccharide is galactose. Although not found in large quantities in nature, galactose generally combines with glucose to form the disaccharide lactose, often referred to as *milk sugar* (92). The galactose that is free in nature is absorbed into the body and taken to the liver where it is converted into glucose, which is then used as a fuel, stored as glycogen, or converted to triglyceride and stored for later (92).

Oligosaccharides

When monosaccharides are bound together, they form complex carbohydrates such as **oligosaccharides**. The most common oligosaccharides are the disaccharides, sometimes referred to as *double sugars* (92). Common disaccharides, such as sucrose (i.e., glucose + fructose), lactose (i.e., glucose + galactose), and maltose (i.e., glucose + glucose) are formed when glucose is bound to additional glucose molecules or to other monosaccharides.

The most common naturally occurring disaccharide is sucrose, a combination of glucose and fructose. Sucrose is found in most fruits and is often crystallized from the syrup of sugarcane and sugar beets (92, 250). It is purified and crystalized to make the brown, white, and powdered sugars that are sold in grocery stores (92, 250).

The second most common disaccharide is lactose, which is found only in the milk of lactating animals (92). In some instances, lactose can be difficult to digest, resulting in excessive fluid and gas buildup in the bowels that leads to bloating and cramping (169, 241, 261). Lactose intolerance is common and generally occurs as a result of a deficiency in the lactose-digesting enzyme lactase (261). Individuals who are lactase enzyme deficient need to avoid milk products and be conscious of hidden sources of lactose (e.g., trace amounts in baked goods, cereals, and salad dressings) (261).

The final common disaccharide is maltose, which is formed from the combination of two molecules of glucose (92). Sometimes referred to as *malt sugar*, maltose is produced when seeds sprout. The sprouting process can be altered by the addition of heat through malting, which is the first step in the production of alcoholic beverages such as beer. Malting results in the formation of α-amylase and maltase (148), which degrade starch into maltose and other simple sugars (92). Once the malt is formed, it is manipulated to create what is referred to as *wort* and is then combined with yeast to initiate the fermentation process during which most of the carbohydrate is converted to ethanol and carbon dioxide (148). Very few food products or beverages other than alcohol contain maltose. It can, however, be produced in the small intestine from the digestion of starches (92).

Polysaccharides

Complex carbohydrates, or **polysaccharides**, are composed of more than 10 monosaccharides that have been bound together (92). When the polysaccharide is composed of one type of monosaccharide, it is called a **homopolysaccharide**, and when two or more different monosaccharides are combined, it is called a **heteropolysaccharide** (160). Ultimately, polysaccharides can come from either plant sources (i.e., starch or fiber) or animal sources (i.e., glycogen) (92).

Plant Polysaccharides   Starch and fiber are the two most common plant polysaccharides. Specifically, starch is a storage form of glucose that exists in two forms, amylose and amylopectin, which can be found in grains, legumes, and vegetables (92). Foods that contain a high level of amylopectin tend to have a higher glycemic index, which is associated with a rapid increase in blood glucose (99, 139).

Fiber, a nonstarch structural polysaccharide, is one of the most abundant molecules on Earth and is primarily comprised of cellulose, hemicelluloses, pectins, gums, and mucilages (92). These structural components are found only in plants and cannot be digested by the human stomach or small intestine (16).

Animal Polysaccharides   The primary animal polysaccharide is glycogen, which is a homopolysaccharide composed of subunits of glucose that are stored in the liver or skeletal muscle (92). The synthesis of glycogen occurs from the addition of glucose units to an existing glycogen chain. One of the unique aspects of glycogen is that it contains extensive branching, which generally occurs on about every 8 to 13 glucose residues on the glycogen molecule (92, 140). The overall branching of glycogen is important because this structure facilitates the rapid breakdown of the molecule into its individual glucose units. The process of breaking down glycogen is referred to as *glycogenolysis*, which occurs because many enzymes are working on the glycogen unit at one time (160). Importantly, the more extensively branched the glycogen molecule is, the greater its ability to supply energy.

Generally, the total amount of glycogen stored in the body is relatively small, with a maximum of about 100 g being stored in the liver and 400 to 500 g being stored in the muscle (175), providing about 2,400 kcals of energy (4 kcals · g carbohydrate^{-1}). The total amount of glycogen stored in the body is affected by the athlete's body size and diet and will be reduced in response to fasting and exercise (175). Ultimately, the primary supplier of energy during most forms of exercise is carbohydrate, particularly in the form of glycogen (61, 95).

Glycemic Index

The **glycemic index (GI)** is a numerical ranking system used to compare the acute glycemic response of foods (128). Foods classified as having a high GI ranking are quickly digested and appear rapidly in the bloodstream as glucose (92). Conversely, foods that are slowly digested and absorbed into the bloodstream have a lower GI ranking (92). The GI ranking is based on glucose or white bread, which is given a reference value of 100 (13, 58, 92). Based on this reference, foods are classified as high GI (HGI ≥70), moderate GI (MGI = 56-69), or low GI (LGI ≤55) (table 10.1) (13, 58).

The GI for a particular food is primarily influenced by the rate at which the carbohydrate is digested (165). Factors such as the type of carbohydrate (166), the fiber content, the portion size, and the fat or protein content of the food (281) can all affect the rate of digestion and, by extension, the GI.

Close and colleagues (58) suggest that it is essential that sport nutritionists understand the GI of carbohydrate food sources because this can influence the postprandial responses to feeding and affect substrate oxidation (75). Based on the available evidence, the consumption of LGI carbohydrate foods in the hours prior to exercise results in a lower insulin response in the postprandial period compared to the consumption of HGI carbohydrate foods. As a result of a lower insulin response, there is an increased free fatty acid availability and lipid oxidation during exercise and a more stable plasma glucose concentration, potentially resulting in a sparing of muscle glycogen (204).

When considering the effect of GI on exercise performance, the picture is not as clear. Although some research has indicated that the consumption of LGI carbohydrate foods prior to exercise can result in enhanced performance via glycogen sparing (201), more recent systematic reviews and meta-analyses provide evidence that there is likely no difference in the effect of GI on performance (79, 110). Although this emerging evidence is compelling, additional research linking GI and performance is required.

During the postexercise period, the ability of MGI and HGI carbohydrate foods to increase plasma glucose levels and enhance the uptake of glucose by the skeletal muscle may be a particularly important consideration when attempting to maximize the rate of glycogen resynthesis and enhance the rate of recovery (41, 42). Specifically, the consumption of HGI carbohydrate foods immediately postexercise may be particularly beneficial for increasing muscle glycogen storage if the recovery time between exercise sessions is 6 hours or less (31, 145, 201).

Carbohydrate Requirements for Athletes

Carbohydrates in the form of muscle glycogen and plasma glucose are effective and dominant fuels for a variety of athletic events (107), including endurance (38), strength–power (95), and team (225) sports. As a result of the importance of muscle glycogen to performance in many sporting activities, early nutritional guidelines recommended high-carbohydrate diets for all athletes (62), regardless of the total energy demand or needs of the athlete. More recently, these recommendations have shifted to consider the energetic costs of the training process and the alignment of the daily carbohydrate intake with the actual needs of the athlete (265, 266). Based on these recommendations, carbohydrate intake can be considered on a continuum; in some situations, high carbohydrate availability meets the demands of the training plan, and in other situations there is low carbohydrate availability and endogenous or exogenous carbohydrate availability are well below the demand of the physical activity (193, 206, 259). For example, Close and colleagues (58) suggest that on days of low energy expenditure, an athlete may need to consume only 2 to 4 g · kg body mass^{-1} · day^{-1} of carbohydrate, but on days with a high energy cost, the athlete should increase carbohydrate consumption to 6 to 8 g · kg body mass^{-1} · day^{-1} (table 10.2). Although these targets are set to ensure that carbohydrate needs are met, there may be situations in which reducing carbohydrate intake below what is required to meet energy demands is warranted to stimulate specific physiological adaptations (265, 266).

Protein

Although most people think of protein in the context of skeletal muscle, protein also has a role in a variety of key functions in the human body (58, 250). The human body contains structural proteins (e.g., keratins), contractile proteins (e.g., actin and myosin), immunoproteins (e.g., antibodies), and regulatory proteins (e.g., enzymes) (58). The ability of protein to meet these diverse functions is a result of the various combinations of **amino acids** used to create each protein structure (58, 250). Of the 20 amino acids in the body, there are four nonessential, seven conditionally essential, and nine essential amino acids (table 10.3).

TABLE 10.1 Glycemic Index (GI) for Various Foods Using Glucose (GI = 100) as a Standard

Source	GI	Source	GI
Breakfast cereals		**Snack products**	
Cornflakes	81 ± 6	Chocolate	40 ± 3
Wheat flake biscuits	69 ± 2	Popcorn	65 ± 5
Porridge, rolled oats	55 ± 2	Potato crisps	56 ± 3
Instant oat porridge	79 ± 3	Soft drink	59 ± 3
Rice porridge/congee	78 ± 9	Rice crackers/crisps	87 ± 2
Millet porridge	67 ± 5	**Sugars**	
Muesli	57 ± 2	Fructose	15 ± 4
All-Bran	60 ± 7	Sucrose	65 ± 4
Dairy products and alternatives		Glucose	103 ± 3
Milk (full fat)	39 ± 3	Honey	61 ± 3
Milk (skim)	37 ± 4	Agave	11 ± 1
Ice cream	51 ± 3	**Fruits**	
Yogurt (fruit)	41 ± 2	Apple (raw)	36 ± 2
Soy milk	34 ± 4	Orange (raw)	43 ± 3
Rice milk	86 ± 7	Banana (raw)	51 ± 3
Pasta and noodles		Pineapple (raw)	59 ± 8
Spaghetti (white)	49 ± 2	Mango (raw)	51 ± 5
Spaghetti (whole wheat)	48 ± 5	Watermelon (raw)	76 ± 4
Rice noodles	53 ± 7	Dates (raw)	42 ± 4
Udon noodles	55 ± 7	**Legumes**	
Breads		Chickpeas	28 ± 9
White wheat bread	75 ± 2	Kidney beans	24 ± 4
Whole wheat/whole meal bread	74 ± 2	Lentils	32 ± 5
Specialty grain bread	53 ± 2	Soya beans	16 ± 1
Unleavened wheat bread	70 ± 5	**Vegetables**	
Chapati	52 ± 4	Potato (boiled)	78 ± 4
Wheat roti	62 ± 3	Potato (instant mashed)	87 ± 3
Grains		Potato (French fry)	63 ± 5
Barley	28 ± 2	Carrots (boiled)	39 ± 4
Couscous	65 ± 4	Sweet potato (boiled)	63 ± 6
		Pumpkin (boiled)	64 ± 7
		Plantain	55 ± 6
		Vegetable soup	48 ± 5
		Sweet corn	52 ± 5

Note: High glycemic index (red) ≥70; moderate glycemic index (yellow) = 56-69; low glycemic index (green) ≤55.

TABLE 10.2 Basic Carbohydrate Intake Guidelines for Athletes

Condition	Description of activity	Carbohydrate goals
Injured	Very low–intensity exercise or no activity and minimal energy expenditure	<2 g · kg body mass^{-1} · d^{-1}
Low	Low intensity or skill-based activities with minimal energy expenditure	2-4 g · kg body mass^{-1} · d^{-1}
Moderate	Moderate- to high-intensity exercise lasting about 1 h · d^{-1}	5-7 g · kg body mass^{-1} · d^{-1}
Hard	Moderate- to high-intensity exercise lasting about 1-3 h · d^{-1}	6-8 g · kg body mass^{-1} · d^{-1}
Very hard	Moderate- to high-intensity exercise lasting longer than 4 h · d^{-1}	8-12 g · kg body mass^{-1} · d^{-1}

Note: These basic guidelines should meet the athlete's needs, but individual total energy and specific training needs must be considered.
Adapted from Close, Kasper, and Morton (2021).

TABLE 10.3 Amino Acids

Essential amino acids	Nonessential amino acids	Conditionally essential amino acids
Histidine	Alanine	Arginine
Isoleucine*	Asparagine	Cysteine (cystine)
Leucine*	Aspartic acid	Glutamine
Lysine	Glutamic acid	Glycine
Methionine		Proline
Phenylalanine		Serine
Threonine		Tyrosine
Tryptophan		
Valine*		

*Branched-chain amino acids.

Essential amino acids must be consumed in the diet because the body cannot manufacture them, but **nonessential amino acids** can be synthesized in the body (250). **Conditionally essential amino acids** are not typically considered essential, but in some situations, such as during illness or stress (227), they can become essential and must be obtained through the diet.

There is constant protein turnover throughout the day, allowing damaged proteins to be removed and replaced and new proteins to be formed in response to training (58). Therefore, it is important that adequate amounts of dietary protein are consumed to ensure the availability of the amino acids required to meet these demands.

Protein Quality

The quality of a protein food source is determined by the amino acid content and its digestibility as calculated by the amount of nitrogen absorbed during digestion and the ability to provide the amino acids necessary to support growth, maintenance, and repair (250). High-quality proteins provide all the essential amino acids and are highly digestible, but lower-quality proteins are less digestible and do not provide the essential amino acids. Animal proteins, such as eggs, dairy, red meat, fish, pork, and poultry, contain all the essential amino acids; the only plant-based protein that contains all the essential amino acids is soy protein (250). Plant-based proteins are generally less digestible than animal proteins, but there is some evidence that digestibility can be improved through processing and preparation (186, 250). Although most plant-based foods are deficient in one or more essential amino acids, **vegetarians** and **vegans** can meet their protein needs by consuming a variety of plant-based foods, such as legumes, vegetables, seeds, nuts, rice, and whole grains to ensure all of the essential amino acids are provided (223, 278, 296).

Protein Requirements for Athletes

The amount of protein an athlete requires to support training and adaptation is widely debated within the scientific community, with some researchers suggesting that athletes do not require additional protein in their diets (222) and others saying athletes need to consume significantly more than the 0.8 g · kg body mass^{-1} · day^{-1} typically recommended for nonathletes (58, 126, 212, 213). Despite this ongoing debate, many sport nutritionists and sport scientists recommend that athletes consume between 1.2 and 2.0 g · kg body mass^{-1} · day^{-1} of protein depending on their needs (figure 10.1) (58). A survey of the dietary practices of professional team sport athletes (33, 34, 162) showed these athletes are easily meeting these higher protein requirements. For example, during a 10-day preseason training period, Australian Football League (AFL) players consumed on average 2.2 ± 0.8 g · kg body mass^{-1} · day^{-1} (77). Additionally, during a 7-day in-season training period, players from the English Premier League consumed 2 to 2.5 g · kg body mass^{-1} · day^{-1} (5).

There are some situations in which it may be advisable for athletes to consume protein above this recommended amount (182, 207, 246). For example, during recovery from injury and during immobilization, there is an acceleration of muscle protein breakdown, and the amount of protein required to maintain protein balance increases. Therefore, when an athlete is undergoing rehabilitation from an injury or surgical procedure, protein intake should be increased to between 2 to 3 g · kg body mass^{-1} · day^{-1} (246, 267), with an emphasis on the consumption of about 3 g of **leucine** per protein serving (267). Sometimes referred to as the *anabolic trigger*, leucine is the amino acid primarily responsible for stimulating protein synthesis (197). Consuming food (e.g., chicken, beef, milk, fish) high in leucine is likely to speed up the rehabilitative process (246). Increased protein intake (2-2.5 g · kg body mass^{-1} · d^{-1}) is also recommended during periods of intensified training designed to decrease body fat while maintaining muscle mass (267).

Protein Sources

Several studies have demonstrated that different protein sources elicit different anabolic responses (32, 155, 278). The different rates of digestion and amino acid content of these protein sources dictate the amplitude and duration of the rise of the essential amino acids and leucine, which exert an

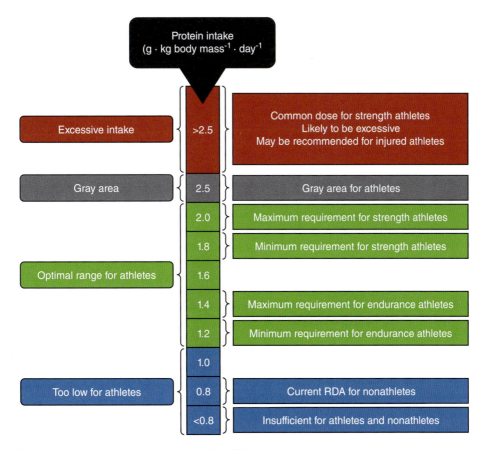

FIGURE 10.1 Proposed protein requirement model for athletes.

Adapted from Close, Kasper, and Morton (2021).

influence on the degree of muscle protein synthesis (MPS) (214). Specifically, whey protein stimulates a greater MPS response postexercise when compared to either casein- or soy-based protein (58, 214). One of the major contributors to these differences is the speed at which whey protein is digested and the concomitant magnitude of the increase in leucine concentration in the blood (214). Similarly, when the postexercise consumption of milk (80% casein and 20% whey) is compared to the consumption of soy-based protein, there is a significantly greater amount of MPS associated with milk consumption (287). The interesting aspect of this study was that although the increase in total amino acids in the blood was slower when milk protein was consumed, there was a significantly greater and prolonged rise in blood leucine concentration compared to soy-based protein consumption (214, 287).

When postexercise consumptions of whey, soy, and casein protein are compared, whey protein results in the largest increase in amino acids (whey > soy > casein) and leucine concentrations (whey > soy > casein) in the blood, as well as MPS (263). The slower appearance of amino acids and reduced leucine concentrations noted for casein consumption are likely a result of a slower rate of digestion (30), which may be of benefit when consumed prior to sleep (272). Specifically, it is now recommended that athletes should consume casein (0.4-0.5 g · kg body mass^{-1}) prior to sleep to provide a sustained delivery of amino acids to the skeletal muscle overnight to facilitate the recovery process and enhance adaptive responses to training (249, 272).

Fat

The term *fat* is often used synonymously with the broader term *lipid*, which includes **triglycerides** and related fatty compounds, such as sterols and phospholipids (250). Of these lipids, triglycerides, fatty acids, phospholipids, and cholesterol are of the greatest significance. Triglycerides, which are formed through the combination of glycerol and three fatty acids, represent the majority of lipids found in the body and in foods (250). Because fatty acids have more carbon and hydrogen molecules relative to oxygen, they provide a greater amount of energy per gram compared to carbohydrate and protein. This is best illustrated by the fact that carbohydrate and protein provide approximately 4 kcals · g^{-1} and fat provides approximately 9 kcals · g^{-1}.

Consumption of fat has historically been linked to cardiovascular disease and obesity (12, 228), so many athletes have sought to eliminate all fat from their diets (58). More recently, researchers have begun to question these beliefs (12, 116). Although the overconsumption of fat is problematic for general health and weight control, the complete elimination of fat is also detrimental to optimal health (58). As highlighted by Close and colleagues (58), the body requires adequate consumption of essential fatty acids (omega-3 and omega-6 fatty acids) and fat-soluble vitamins (A, D, E, and K). Additionally, the complete elimination of high-fat foods can result in micronutrient deficiencies. When carbohydrate stores become depleted, such as during exercise that exceeds 90 minutes, fats become an important fuel source (58).

Fats are generally classified by their chemical structures and are referred to as being saturated or unsaturated (58, 250). **Saturated fats** have their carbon molecules saturated with hydrogen and have no double bonds, and **unsaturated fats** contain some carbon molecules that are joined together with double bonds, making them more chemically reactive (250). **Monounsaturated fatty acids (MUFA)** contain one double bond, and **polyunsaturated fatty acids (PUFA)** contain two or more double bonds (58, 250). A subclass of PUFA is referred to as **essential fatty acids** because the body cannot synthesize these fats; they must be consumed in the diet for optimal health (58). Essential fatty acids are classified as omega-3 and omega-6. Omega-6 fatty acids are abundant in soybean, corn, and safflower oil and foods made with these oils (250). The primary dietary sources of omega-3 fatty acids are fatty fish, such as salmon, herring, halibut, trout, and mackerel, which contain eicosapentaenoic acid (EPA) and docosahexaenoic acid (DHA) (264). Due to the benefits associated with EPA and DHA, athletes are encouraged to regularly consume wild fatty fish (58) or consider omega-3 supplementation (58, 264).

Another classification of fats to consider is partially hydrogenated or trans fats, which are unquestionably harmful and should be removed from the diet (58, 191). These fats are created by adding hydrogen atoms to the fatty acid, which makes them solid at room temperature and better able to withstand repeated heating (58). Due to their unique properties, trans fats are commonly used in the food industry for deep frying, baked goods, packaged snacks, and in shortening (191). Higher intake of trans fatty acids has consistently been associated with an increased risk of coronary heart disease and sudden death (181, 192). Ultimately, trans fats have no health benefit and should be removed from the athlete's diet. Athletes should be encouraged to consume natural fats and make every effort to completely remove processed fats, such as trans fats (e.g., margarine, pastry, confectionary products), from their diets (58).

Hydration

To optimize athletic performance, athletes must be properly hydrated (222). The athlete's state of hydration is based on their daily water balance, which is determined by the net difference between water gain and water loss (235). Gains in water occur via the consumption of liquids or food and the production of metabolic water, and loss of water occurs from respiratory, gastrointestinal, and renal functions, as well as sweat. When water gain and loss are balanced, the athlete has a normal body water content; this is called *euhydration*. Alternatively, when fluids are overconsumed, water gain can exceed water loss resulting in a state of **hyperhydration**. Conversely, if water loss exceeds water gain, a state of **hypohydration** can occur. During exercise, hypohydration is often characterized as *hyperosmotic hypovolemia* because sweat is hypotonic to plasma (235). For simplicity, most sport scientists and coaches use the term *dehydration* to describe body water loss and hypohydration (235). A water loss of more than 2% body mass has the potential to adversely affect performance and increases the risk of potentially life-threatening heat injury; therefore, athletes should strive for euhydration before, during, and after exercise (222).

Electrolytes and Hydration

In addition to water, sweat contains electrolytes such as sodium, chloride, potassium, calcium, and magnesium. For effective hydration, the loss of these electrolytes must also be considered (58). The total amount of sweat loss and the concentration of electrolytes in the sweat dictates the amount of electrolytes lost (235). Sweat typically contains ~35 mEq · L^{-1} (range: 10-70 mEq · L^{-1}) of sodium, ~5 mEq · L^{-1} (range: 3-15 mEq · L^{-1}) of potassium, ~1 mEq · L^{-1} (range: 0.3-2 mEq · L^{-1}) of calcium, ~0.8 mEq · L^{-1} (range: 0.2-1.5 mEq · L^{-1}) of magnesium, and 30 mEq · L^{-1} (range: 5-60 mEq · L^{-1}) of chloride (36). During exercise and competition, sodium loss can range between 2 to 13 g (58) and high losses have been linked to exercise-related muscle cramps (22). Due to the importance of sodium loss, Close and colleagues (58) suggest that when considering hydration strategies, it is important to identify athletes who are salty or heavy sweaters so that personalized hydration strategies can be developed.

Monitoring Hydration Status

Regular estimates of preexercise hydration status are necessary to establish individualized hydration strategies (58). Reasonable estimates of hydration status can be achieved by assessing preexercise urine-specific gravity, osmolality, or color (58, 235). A normal state of hydration is indicated by urine-specific gravities of 1,020 or less (235), osmolality values of less than 700 mOsmol · kg^{-1} (58, 235), or urine being a pale yellow color (11). Note that urine indices of hydration status are sensitive to change in posture, food intake, and body water content (58). Therefore, it is often recommended to use the first urine sample passed after the athlete wakes or samples collected after several hours of stable hydration status to determine whether the athlete is euhydrated (58, 235).

Pretraining and Precompetition Fluid Requirements

The primary goal of pretraining or precompetition hydration strategies is to ensure that the athlete is euhydrated and has normal electrolyte levels prior to the initiation of physical activity. In most instances, if the athlete has consumed sufficient beverages with meals and there is a protracted recovery period (8-12 h) prior to the initiation of physical activity, the athlete will be close to being euhydrated, and less aggressive pretraining or precompetition hydration strategies are required (235). If, however, the athlete has not adequately consumed fluids and electrolytes after suffering a substantial fluid deficit, more aggressive pre-exercise hydration strategies may be warranted. Ultimately, the main goal of preexercise fluid-replacement strategies is to correct any fluid and electrolyte deficits prior to the initiation of exercise (235).

The general pretraining or precompetition fluid-replacement recommendation is to consume 5 to 7 ml · kg body mass^{-1} at least 4 hours prior to exercise (58, 235). Additionally, if the athlete does not produce urine or the urine is dark in color, an additional 3 to 5 ml · kg body mass^{-1} should be consumed about 2 hours before training. The timing of these hydration strategies should allow for fluid absorption and enable urine output to return to normal prior to exercise (58, 235). Additionally, the consumption of sports drinks (instead of water) during this period may also be beneficial because they contain carbohydrates and electrolytes (58).

Fluid Requirements During Training and Competition

The primary goal of fluid consumption during training and competition is to prevent excessive dehydration (>2% body mass loss) and changes to electrolyte balance to avert compromised performance (235). The amount of fluid that needs to be consumed is highly individualized and is affected by the athlete's sweat rate, exercise duration, and the availability of fluid. Therefore, due to the specific metabolic requirements of each sport, it is often difficult to provide prescriptive recommendations for fluid consumption (58). Regardless, the American College of Sports Medicine advises that individualized fluid-replacement strategies that limit body mass loss to less than 2% of pretraining or precompetition levels should be implemented to prevent dehydration (235). Athletes should not attempt to increase mass during this time, because this can lead to **hyponatremia** (a serum sodium concentration of <135 mmol · L^{-1}), which in extreme cases can be fatal (4, 111). To reduce the risk of hyponatremia, the prevailing recommendation is to drink to thirst (111).

To develop fluid-consumption strategies that prevent excessive dehydration, Close and colleagues (58) recommend that athletes weigh themselves nude before and after exercise to determine whether their normal fluid consumption patterns are effective and make changes accordingly. Additionally, habitual fluid consumption during training and competition must be assessed. This can be accomplished by ensuring that each athlete has a labeled drink bottle that can be monitored by support staff (58). Note that cold beverages (10 °C [50 °F]) rather than hot beverages (37-50 °C [99-122 °F]) have been reported to attenuate the rise of body temperature that occurs during exercise (159). Additionally, sports drinks that contain electrolytes and carbohydrates are considered to be superior to water, due to their ability to sustain fluid–electrolyte balance and performance (235). Note, however, that sports drinks should contain no more than 4% to 8% carbohydrate (glucose polymer), because higher concentrations of carbohydrate and greater osmolality can hinder gastric emptying (280). A key step in developing an individualized fluid-replacement strategy is to test various intake strategies to maximize gastric emptying, fluid absorption, and carbohydrate delivery while minimizing the potential for gastrointestinal distress during competition (58).

Posttraining or Postcompetition Rehydration Strategies

The primary goal after training or competition is to fully replace any fluid and electrolyte loss (235). The structure of the strategies employed is largely predicated by the time available. With adequate time, euhydration can be established with the consumption of normal meals and beverages, and targeted hydration strategies may not be warranted (235). If, however, more rapid and complete rehydration is required, the general recommendation is to consume about 1.5 L (51 oz) of fluid for each kilogram of body mass lost during training or competition (58, 235). Additionally, beverages and snacks with sodium can stimulate thirst and fluid retention, which can expedite recovery (178, 235). Fluid and electrolyte consumption should occur over time as opposed to consuming large boluses (150), so as to maximize fluid retention (58).

Energy Intake

It is well-documented that the energy cost of training exerts a major influence on the athlete's overall **energy expenditure (EE)** and that any alterations to the training load that are employed at the macro-, meso-, and microcycle levels of the annual training plan will affect the magnitude of EE (193, 259). Thinking about this logically, it is easy to deduce that **energy intake (EI)** must also be altered to support the training process. For example, Anderson and colleagues (6) report that across a 7-day in-season training period, the daily EE (3,566 ± 585 kcals) of English Premier League soccer players was not statistically different from EI (3,186 ± 367 kcals). Interestingly, on match day, when greater running distances and workloads were encountered, the athletes' EIs were significantly greater (3,789 ± 532 kcals) compared to typical training days (2,956 ± 374 kcals). As an extension of this concept, it would make sense that on nontraining days when overall EE is reduced, the EI should also be reduced to better align with the actual energy needs of the athletes (189).

Based on this line of reasoning, manipulations to EI should be strategically aligned with the various levels of the periodized training plan to account for the effects of training and competition. Proper nutritional strategies will ensure adequate **energy availability (EA)** (259). An adequate EA will offset potential acute and chronic health and performance issues associated with developing relative energy deficiency in sport (RED-S). (See the IOC Consensus Statement written by Mountjoy and colleagues for more information [190].)

It is estimated that proper metabolic function, assuming no alterations to activity level, requires an estimated EA of 40 to 45 kcals · kg fat free mass^{-1} · day^{-1} (table 10.4) (47, 163). Operationally, EA is determined based on the athlete's EI and exercise EE (EEE), which is expressed relative to the body's most metabolically active tissue, fat free mass (FFM) (163):

$$\text{energy availability (kcals · kg FFM}^{-1}) = \frac{\text{energy intake (EI)} - \text{exercise energy expenditure (EEE)}}{\text{fat free mass (FFM) (kg)}}$$

Although the determination of EA is considered important, several challenges make it difficult to accurately quantify, including a lack of standard procedures, the limitations of self-reported EI, and challenges in determining EEE (190).

Currently, there is no standardized protocol (e.g., number of collection days, methods for quantifying EI and EEE or FFM) for assessing EA, and questions exist about the ability to accurately determine EI and EEE during training and competition (48, 57, 190). EI is typically determined with either prospective recording or retrospective analysis of food diaries (paper or electronic). Food diaries are often inaccurate due to underreporting, omission errors, or poorly estimated portion sizes (43). Even though inaccuracies are possible, the use of food diaries is currently a common practice and can give a rough estimate of the athlete's EI.

Another issue related to the quantification of EA is the measurement of EEE. Although EEE can be estimated with global positioning systems (GPS), heart rate monitors, and power meters for sports such as cycling and running, there are limited data on methodologies for its quantification in more complex sports (e.g., resistance training, combat sports) or team sports (e.g., soccer, American football) (48). Recently, some have attempted to use wearable devices to estimate EEE. Based on the available data, these devices appear to underestimate EEE in free-living populations (194) and may not be able to be used across all the training activities an athlete may undertake (48). A classic approach often used to estimate EEE is to examine activity logs to calculate metabolic equivalents of task (3) or to reference existing tables of the energy cost of exercise (28, 35, 48). Although there are issues with these methods, they are commonly used to estimate EEE from the athlete's training activities and can be used when determining EA.

Another potential issue to consider is the ability to gain a reliable and accurate measurement of body composition, which is required when calculating EA (48). The gold standard for measuring body composition is the use of dual X-ray absorptiometry (DXA) (196), which is not always available

TABLE 10.4 Classifications of Energy Availability

Classification	Sex	Energy availability	Comment
High energy availability	Male	>40 kcals · kg FFM^{-1}	Useful for healthy weight gain or weight maintenance
	Female	>45 kcals · kg FFM^{-1}	
Optimal energy availability	Male	≥40 kcals · kg FFM^{-1}	Useful for weight maintenance; provides adequate energy for all physiological functions; useful during injury and going through periods of rehabilitation at low or moderate intensity (~1.5 h · d^{-1})
	Female	≥45 kcals · kg FFM^{-1}	
Subclinical low energy availability	Male	30-40 kcals · kg FFM^{-1}	Can be tolerated for a short time as part of a well-designed weight-loss program
	Female	30-45 kcals · kg FFM^{-1}	
Clinical low energy availability	Male	<30 kcals · kg FFM^{-1}	Associated with health issues and impairments in body system function, adaptation to training, and performance capacity
	Female	<30 kcals · kg FFM^{-1}	

Note: FFM = fat free mass; kcals = nutritional calories.
Adapted from Melin et al. (2019).

to coaches and athletes. If available, DXA can be used as part of the athlete-monitoring process, but it is essential that standardized procedures are rigorously followed to ensure reliable data are collected (196). Although DXA scans are considered the most accurate and are the preferred method, other methods, such as hydrostatic weighing, may give a rough estimate of FFM (218) that can be used to guide nutritional strategies.

Although the estimation of EA can be time-consuming and requires some commitment and compliance from the athlete, it is very useful when designing an integrated periodized training plan that attempts to align the athlete's nutritional strategies with their physical training. To effectively accomplish this goal, the coach must leverage the expertise of sport nutritionists and sport scientists to ensure that the athlete's EA is accurately calculated and that their nutritional interventions are correctly aligned with the periodized training plan.

Nutrient Timing

Nutrient timing is a dietary strategy that involves strategic manipulation of nutrient consumption at specific time points surrounding and during training to enhance acute performance or chronic adaptations (9, 145). Much of the early nutrient-timing research centered on the role of acute carbohydrate consumption on moderate- and high-intensity endurance performance and the rates of muscle glycogen resynthesis (89, 90, 124, 142, 145, 242). Following this work, extensive research has been conducted to examine the acute role of protein ingestion on performance, recovery, and adaptation following both endurance and resistance training (8, 9, 126, 145, 238). As noted by Arent and colleagues (9), a major limitation of the available research is the paucity of longitudinal studies that have directly assessed the effect of nutrient-timing strategies on outcome variables associated with performance, recovery, and adaptation to the training process.

In 2004, based on the available acute nutrient-timing research and the known acute bioenergetic, biochemical, and endocrine responses to exercise, Ivy and Portman (121) proposed a theoretical model for explaining the effect of nutrient timing on chronic adaptations to training. As part of this model, nutrient timing was divided into three critical time points: (1) the energy phase, (2) the anabolic phase, and (3) the growth phase (121). In this model, the energy phase represented the time period during training, and the anabolic phase was proposed to last for about 45 minutes after the completion of training (121). Sometimes referred to as the *anabolic window* or *metabolic window*, this phase was suggested to be a time when the exercised muscle was highly sensitive to nutrient interventions (121). Following the anabolic phase, the growth phase represented the time between the end of the anabolic phase and the initiation of the next training session. In 2014, based on emerging research, Ivy and Ferguson-Stegall (123) revised the original nutrient time model presented in 2004. Specifically, the energy phase was modified to include the 4 hours prior to training and the time allotted for training, and the duration of the anabolic phase or anabolic window was extended to 60 to 90 minutes postexercise. Finally, the phase formerly presented as the growth phase was recategorized as the adaptation phase, but it still extended from the cessation of the anabolic phase to the initiation of the next energy phase.

Although the theoretical constructs that underpin the nutrient-timing model are logical, several researchers have questioned the existence of a postexercise anabolic window (8, 238, 239). In 2013, Schoenfeld and colleagues (239) performed a meta-analytic study to examine the effect of protein timing on strength and hypertrophy. The primary finding of this study was that protein timing did not affect strength and hypertrophic outcomes. Although these findings are interesting, Arent and colleagues (9) suggest that this study should be considered with caution when attempting to ascertain the value of nutrient timing. First, Arent and colleagues (9) noted that only 4 of the 23 studies included in the analysis used resistance-trained subjects. Second, the subject population included a wide range of people, including young men and women, elderly men and women, and older men and women with type 2 diabetes. Third, many of the studies tested only protein consumption in the periexercise period and did not directly examine protein timing. Finally, protein intake across the treatment and control groups was only equated in 2 of the 23 studies analyzed. Arent and colleagues (9) rightfully argue that because of these methodological issues, any conclusions about the effect of nutrient timing are tenuous at best.

Although it is fair to question the existence of an anabolic window based on our current understanding of muscle protein synthesis and breakdown, it is likely that this window of opportunity is much longer than was once thought and should be considered to be a "garage door" (9). Unfortunately, the study by Schoenfeld and colleagues (239) is often used as evidence to discount the benefits of nutrient timing and the existence of the anabolic window, when in fact only protein was examined and other nutritional factors, such as carbohydrate, were not considered. It is likely that the primary takeaway from this study is that there is a need for more research exploring the effect of nutrient timing on aspects of performance other than hypertrophy and strength (9).

Contextually, nutritional interventions designed to optimize performance should be implemented during the periexercise period (i.e., before, during, and after training) (9). Although there is evidence of benefits to consuming specific nutrients at specific times, the greatest benefits may be achieved by consuming nutrients at all time points surrounding training and throughout the day. This may be even more important with athletes who engage in multiple training sessions per day, participate in training and competition that significantly depletes glycogen, and incur significant muscle damage. In these scenarios, athletes should consume carbohydrates and protein during the periexercise period and the remaining time points throughout the day as opportunities to facilitate recovery, adaptation, and, ultimately, performance (9). An example of how a nutrient-timing strategy for a soccer athlete could be structured is presented in figure 10.2. When implementing a nutrient-timing strategy, care should be taken to ensure that each aspect of the program is considered in the context of the athlete's overall caloric need and that pretraining, training, posttraining, and presleep nutritional interventions are not increasing calories above the athlete's needs.

Pretraining Nutritional Strategies

Generally, pretraining nutritional strategies are used within 4 hours of the initiation of a training session, and they are primarily used to ensure that adequate fuel is available to maximize performance (9, 266). Traditionally, the primary pretraining nutritional strategy has been to provide carbohydrate to maximize endogenous glycogen stores (94, 143, 294) and maintain serum glucose during endurance training (63, 143) and resistance training (94, 95, 97, 98). Additionally, the provision of protein and amino acids in this period has been examined to explore their effect on training adaptations when they are consumed in isolation or in combination with carbohydrate (145).

Pretraining Carbohydrate Supplementation

The body's stores of glycogen are limited (63, 64). The body stores carbohydrate as glycogen in the liver (75-100 g or 300-400 kcals) and skeletal muscle (300-500 g or 1,200-2,400 kcals) and provides circulating glucose (15-20 g or 60-80 kcals) (123). The limited carbohydrate stores in the body and their effect on performance form the foundation of the many pretraining carbohydrate-feeding strategies (123). For example, 2 hours of moderate-intensity or 1 hour of high-intensity aerobic exercise can reduce muscle glycogen by up to 70% (89), and 45 minutes of intense resistance training can reduce muscle glycogen by about 40% (94, 95). Therefore, it is likely important to increase pretraining carbohydrate intake to maximize muscle glycogen availability prior to training (9). This recommendation becomes even more important prior to high-intensity or long-duration exercise and when multiple training sessions are performed close to one another.

A classic concern regarding pretraining carbohydrate feeding is the increased potential for rebound hypoglycemia during exercise (9, 137). An increased risk of hypoglycemia occurs in response to the combined effects of insulin, which rises in response to carbohydrate consumption, and muscle contraction–induced translocation of glucose transporter-4 to the sarcolemma, both of which increase glucose uptake into the skeletal muscle. In early research, the consumption of carbohydrate 30 to 45 minutes prior to exercise was shown to cause hypoglycemia and reduce time to exhaustion (80). However, the contemporary body of research appears to show that pre-exercise carbohydrate supplementation does not cause hypoglycemia in all individuals and either does not negatively affect performance (9, 55, 102, 123, 131, 187, 251) or significantly enhances performance (81, 88, 141, 202, 243). Ultimately, pretraining dietary strategies designed to provide 150 to 200 g of carbohydrates 2 to 4 hours before training can significantly increase muscle glycogen stores (64) and may result in improved endurance performance (81, 88, 243).

Though most of the research examining pretraining carbohydrate supplementation has focused on aerobic modalities, it is logical that high-intensity intermittent activities, such as resistance training, would benefit from this type of supplementation (9).

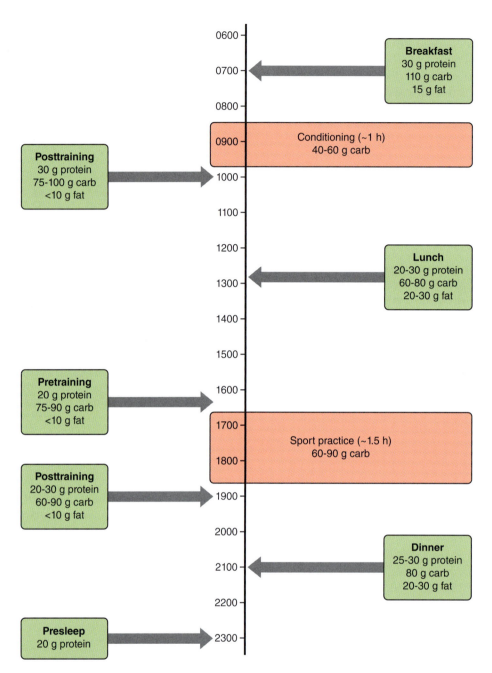

FIGURE 10.2 Example nutrient-timing strategy for a soccer player.
Adapted from Arent, Cintineo, McFadden, et al. (2020).

It is well-documented that there is an approximate 40% reduction in muscle glycogen following high-volume resistance training (95), leading some authors to speculate that carbohydrate availability may not be a limiting factor unless glycogen levels are suboptimal at the start of a training session (9). Although at first glance this contention is logical, one must consider that if the athlete is engaging in multiple training sessions in one day, the provision of carbohydrate prior to resistance training may facilitate glycogen sparing during the training session (94), which would allow subsequent training sessions to be performed with higher training loads or volumes (98).

Another consideration is that pretraining nutrient intake may exert a positive effect on the immune system response after the completion of a bout of endurance or resistance training (9).

For example, Chen and colleagues (54) have reported that consuming meals that contain greater amounts of carbohydrate before training (104 g carbohydrate) results in less immune system disruption in the 2 hours after training compared to consuming meals that contain less carbohydrate (56 g). However, it is important to note that the pretraining provision of carbohydrate more likely positively affects the immune system when higher volumes of resistance training are performed (9). These responses are likely related to training-induced hormonal responses, in particular the cortisol response to high-repetition, high-volume resistance training when compared to moderate- or lower-volume training (151). The ability of carbohydrate supplements to modulate cortisol and immune responses to resistance training may reduce the risk of overtraining (248) and enhance the overall health of the athlete, allowing them to be able to be more available for training and competition (9).

Pretraining Protein and Carbohydrate Supplementation

Researchers have investigated pretraining ingestion of protein and amino acids, either alone or in combination with carbohydrate, to determine whether this enhances resistance training–induced adaptations (144). To investigate this, Tipton and colleagues (269) examined the effect of a carbohydrate plus protein supplement (35 g carbohydrate + 6 g essential amino acids) either before or after a single resistance-training session. The net protein status (breakdown versus synthesis) was found to be greater when carbohydrate and protein were provided before training. Tipton and colleagues (269) speculated that an increased availability of serum amino acids when blood flow was increased likely enhanced protein synthesis. This work provides evidence that providing a carbohydrate and protein beverage before or after resistance training results in an enhanced protein synthesis after the bout of training (144, 268, 269). When the longitudinal effects of pre- and posttraining protein consumption are compared, both feeding strategies were reported to elicit similar strength and hypertrophic adaptations when protein intake was matched between treatment groups (237). Although most of the literature has examined either a pre- or posttraining approach to providing protein or carbohydrate (or both), it has yet to be established whether supplementation during both time frames is more effective (9).

Based on the available literature, the optimal combination of carbohydrate and protein for a pretraining meal depends on several factors, including exercise duration and the athlete's fitness level (144). Generally, it is recommended that a pretraining meal should be consumed 3 to 4 hours prior to training and should provide 1 to 2 g carbohydrate · kg body mass^{-1} and 0.15 to 0.25 g protein · kg body mass^{-1} (144).

During-Training Nutritional Strategies

Nutritional strategies designed to ensure adequate energy for performance during training or competition should be implemented. Probably the most studied intratraining nutritional strategy is the provision of carbohydrate (9), which provides an ergogenic benefit during endurance training (123) and resistance training (95). More recently, the provision of supplements that contain a combination of carbohydrate and protein have been shown to provide ergogenic benefits (9).

Carbohydrate Supplementation During Training

Carbohydrate supplementation during exercise has been reported to offset muscle and liver glycogen use and ensure the maintenance of blood glucose (9). This is particularly important when training intensity is high, lasts longer than 60 minutes, or is comprised of shorter, supramaximal efforts (23, 282). In the absence of carbohydrate supplementation, exercise intensity will diminish (142) in response to a reduction in fuel availability, decreased calcium release from the sarcoplasmic reticulum, and fatigue (205).

It is well-established that endurance performance is improved with the ingestion of carbohydrate during exercise (123). As exercise intensity increases to 70% of $\dot{V}O_2$max or greater, glycogen becomes the primary fuel source (276), and as duration of exercise increases, there is a concomitant reduction in the availability of glycogen. As glycogen becomes less available, metabolism shifts from muscle glycogen toward blood glucose (59, 60). If no carbohydrate is provided, blood glucose levels can decrease to hypoglycemic levels (~3 mmol · L^{-1}) within 2 to 3 hours of cycling. If carbohydrate is consumed, carbohydrate oxidation rates can be maintained for substantially longer (63). Note that carbohydrate supplementation does not seem to spare muscle glycogen from being used for fuel during continuous prolonged exercise performed at intensities of 70% to 75% of $\dot{V}O_2$max; it simply maintains euglycemia and delays the onset of fatigue (63). However, during continuous, low-intensity exercise or variable-intensity exercise, muscle glycogen appears to be spared by carbohydrate supplementation (273, 293, 294).

Carbohydrate supplementation during training has also been reported to benefit resistance training. For example, Wax and colleagues (285) reported that supplementation of 1 g carbohydrate · kg body mass^{-1} immediately before exercise and 0.17 g carbohydrate · kg body mass^{-1} every 6 minutes during exercise resulted in a significantly higher total force output during an isometric resistance-exercise protocol when compared to the consumption of a placebo. Similarly, Haff and colleagues (97) reported that carbohydrate supplementation increased the total amount of work performed during an isokinetic resistance-training session consisting of 16 sets of 10 repetitions performed at 120° · s^{-1}. When considering carbohydrate supplementation and resistance-training performance, note that positive effects are typically seen with high total volumes of work similar to those that would be seen in a general preparation phase that targets hypertrophic or strength–endurance work (95). Additionally, carbohydrate supplementation may be warranted when multiple resistance-training sessions are completed in the same training day (98).

Several investigations demonstrated that the consumption of multiple carbohydrate types (e.g., dextrose, fructose, and maltodextrin) can significantly enhance the rate of exogenous carbohydrate oxidation (85, 130, 132, 133) and performance (66). In fact, the consumption of a carbohydrate supplement that contained a 2:1 ratio of glucose and fructose resulted in an 8% higher power output during a time trial performed after a 120-minute bout of steady-state cycling (66). Based on the available literature, ingesting multiple sources of carbohydrate appears to increase exogenous carbohydrate oxidation, which spares endogenous carbohydrate stores (130). This response likely occurs because the optimization of various intestinal carbohydrate transports results in enhanced rates of carbohydrate absorption beyond what is seen from a single carbohydrate source (123).

Ultimately, based on the available evidence carbohydrate supplementation during training is clearly ergogenic and should be considered part of the athlete's overall training process. Ivy and Ferguson-Stegall (123) recommend that athletes drink a beverage that contains a 3% to 6% carbohydrate solution every 15 to 20 minutes during prolonged exercise (>60 min). Generally, it is recommended that these carbohydrate supplements should supply 30 to 60 g of carbohydrate · hour^{-1} (136). Additionally, Arent and colleagues (9) have recommended that 90 to 144 g of carbohydrate · hour^{-1}, comprised of a 2:1 glucose to fructose mix, should be consumed during endurance exercise that lasts 2 hours or longer. A final consideration is that added calories associated with these intratraining nutritional supplements must be accounted for in the athlete's overall daily caloric intake.

Carbohydrate and Protein Supplementation During Training

The coingestion of carbohydrate and protein has the potential to enhance carbohydrate delivery while minimizing gastrointestinal distress (9). A meta-analytic study by Kloby Nielsen and colleagues (149) found the consumption of carbohydrate and protein produced favorable improvements in time-trial performance and time to exhaustion compared to the consumption of only carbohydrate. This effect remained when nonisocaloric supplements were consumed and when supplements were matched for carbohydrate content (9, 149). However, when the effects of isocaloric supplementation (carbohydrate and protein versus carbohydrate alone) were compared, there were no differences between conditions (9, 149). Although the coingestion of carbohydrate and protein may not result in direct, acute performance improvements, several indirect benefits must be considered. For example, supplementation with a combination of carbohydrate and protein can increase caloric consumption while decreasing carbohydrate intake and potential gastrointestinal distress (9). Additionally, an increased amino acid bioavailability can decrease rates of protein breakdown, be more readily available for gluconeogenesis, and potentially delay central nervous system fatigue (24). During prolonged exercise, skeletal muscle selectively oxidizes branched-chain amino acids (BCAAs) and free tryptophan crosses the blood–brain barrier, increasing serotonin concentrations in the brain and ultimately leading to increased central fatigue and impaired exercise performance (68, 69). The provision of protein during exercise appears to alter the free tryptophan to BCAA ratio, reducing serotonin concentrations in the brain and delaying central fatigue (68).

An additional benefit of consuming carbohydrate and protein during training is that this may protect against muscle damage (123). Saunders and colleagues (232, 233) reported that when supplements that combine carbohydrate and protein are provided during an endurance training session, there are longer times to exhaustion and markers of muscle damage are significantly lower (i.e., creatine kinase). In another study, Saunders and colleagues (234) compared the effects of consuming a carbohydrate (6%) or a combined carbohydrate and protein (6% carbohydrate and 1.8% protein) beverage during and immediately after a 60 km simulated time trial. Plasma creatine kinase and muscle soreness were significantly increased 24 hours after the cessation of the time trial when only carbohydrate was consumed, but there were no increases when the combined carbohydrate and protein beverage was consumed (234). Although the work of Saunders and colleagues (232-234) provides some evidence that consuming carbohydrate and protein during training may serve as a countermeasure for muscle damage and soreness in the 24 hours after training, it is not evident if this effect is simply a response to an increased energy availability. To examine this question, Valentine and colleagues (275) investigated the effect of consuming placebo, carbohydrate (7.75%), carbohydrate plus carbohydrate (9.69%), and carbohydrate plus protein (7.75% carbohydrate and 1.94% protein) beverages every 15 minutes during cycling performed at 75% of $\dot{V}O_2$max to exhaustion. Time to exhaustion did not differ between the two carbohydrate-only drinks, but markers of muscle damage (i.e., creatine kinase and myoglobin) were lower in the carbohydrate plus protein group 24 hours after training. Based on these findings and the existing data, it appears that an intratraining session beverage that includes protein can positively affect markers of muscle damage postexercise (123).

Based on the available evidence, supplements that contain carbohydrate and protein in a 3:1 or 4:1 (carbohydrate:protein) ratio have the potential to increase endurance performance and help the athlete better manage muscle damage (125, 232). Additionally, when these beverages are consumed during resistance training, they have the ability to maintain muscle glycogen stores, offset muscle damage (20), and enhance acute (25, 27) and prolonged (26) training adaptive responses.

Posttraining or Postcompetition Nutritional Strategies

Postexercise nutritional strategies are largely dictated by the type of exercise and the intensity, duration, and frequency of training the athlete undertakes. If the athlete is required to perform multiple training sessions per day, the magnitude of the training stimulus and the resultant glycogen depletion and protein breakdown become increasingly important considerations. Therefore, adequate nutritional provisions must be provided between training sessions so there is necessary fuel to undertake subsequent training and ensure overall recovery and adaptation (9).

Postexercise Carbohydrate Supplementation

The primary goal of posttraining carbohydrate supplementation is replenishing muscle and liver glycogen (58). This goal is particularly important between bouts of carbohydrate-dependent exercise in which performance is the priority during subsequent sessions. The rate of glycogen resynthesis is only about 5% per hour, so it is crucial that carbohydrate intake is optimized ($\sim$1.0-1.5 g $\cdot$ kg body mass^{-1} $\cdot$ h^{-1}) during the 2 hours after training to maximize posttraining glycogen replenishment (9, 46). If carbohydrate consumption is delayed for 2 hours, there is a 50% reduction in muscle glycogen resynthesis over a 4-hour period (124). An additional consideration is that HGI carbohydrates should be consumed in the first few hours posttraining to maximize muscle glycogen replenishment over the 24-hour posttraining period (41). Although in most instances glucose is used during this period, fructose more effectively promotes liver glycogen resynthesis (70). Therefore, it may be warranted to provide the athlete with fructose-rich foods, such as fresh fruit smoothies (58).

An additional benefit of posttraining carbohydrate supplementation is that it attenuates several markers of muscle breakdown and cytokine production, thus improving inflammatory recovery (53, 199, 236). Therefore, during periods of intensified training, such as overreaching, in which immune system suppression can occur (179, 247), the inclusion of carbohydrate supplementation protocols may be an important countermeasure. It is likely that the ingestion of HGI carbohydrates posttraining may aid in the restoration of the immune system, particularly after higher-intensity or strenuous training (9). Based on the contemporary body of scientific evidence, it is generally recommended that to maximize muscle glycogen synthesis, posttraining carbohydrate supplements that deliver 1.2 g · kg body mass^{-1} · hour^{-1} (129) should be consumed hourly for 3 to 4 hours after training (58).

Posttraining Protein Supplementation

The consumption of protein after training plays a critical role in enhancing muscle protein synthesis and optimizing many adaptations that occur in response to training (108). During the posttraining period, there is increased muscle damage and protein breakdown (21, 123) that can be magnified by glycogen depletion (122). Therefore, the provision of protein during the posttraining period can reduce muscle protein breakdown, stimulate muscle protein synthesis, and play an important role in repairing damaged muscle (108). Rapidly digestible, high-quality protein that provides enough essential amino acids, such as whey protein, appears to more effectively stimulate muscle protein synthesis than lower-quality BCAAs or slowly digestible protein (188). Although the specific quantity of protein required to optimize posttraining muscle protein synthesis is unclear, it is likely mediated by the type of exercise session completed (9). Posttraining muscle protein synthesis has been shown to be maximized with the consumption of 20 g of whey protein after resistance training (263, 288) and high-intensity aerobic training (226). However, after resistance training, muscle protein synthesis appears to be greater when 40 g of whey protein are consumed (167). Based on these data, it is generally recommended that 20 to 40 g (0.25-0.40 g · kg body mass^{-1}) of protein that contains about 10 to 12 g of essential amino acids is consumed within 3 to 4 hours of the posttraining period when seeking to maximize muscle protein synthesis and recovery from training (9, 58, 145).

Several authors have postulated that the timing of posttraining protein supplementation may not be as important as the total protein intake when attempting to maximize strength and hypertrophic adaptations (8, 238). Questions about the existence of the anabolic window are based on the fact that muscle protein synthesis is elevated for 24 to 48 hours following high-intensity aerobic training (72) and resistance training (215). However, as pointed out by Arent and colleagues (9), these authors fail to consider that this larger window provides the athlete with an opportunity to capitalize on the benefits of employing multiple time-point feeding strategies. Therefore, it is often recommended that protein (0.25-0.40 g · kg body mass^{-1}) be consumed every 3 to 4 hours after training (9, 58, 145). However, note that rapidly digestible, high-quality proteins, such as whey protein, consumed immediately after the cessation of training can restore protein balance posttraining and can have a beneficial impact on protein synthesis. Protein timing may provide added support for performance and should be considered when attempting to optimize performance.

Posttraining Coingestion of Carbohydrate and Protein

Coingestion of protein and carbohydrate in the posttraining period can enhance muscle glycogen resynthesis (21, 277). There is evidence that the coingestion of protein (0.4 g · kg body mass^{-1} · h^{-1}) and carbohydrate (1.0-1.2 g · kg body mass^{-1} · h^{-1}) during the 2 hours after training results in significantly greater glycogen resynthesis compared to consuming only carbohydrate (21, 277). Additionally, the coingestion of carbohydrate and protein will attenuate muscle protein breakdown and optimize recovery from intensified training. Therefore, based on the available evidence, it is recommended that carbohydrate and protein should be consumed together in the posttraining period. However, much more research is needed to determine the optimal feeding protocols.

Presleep Strategies

Typically, overnight sleep represents the longest post-adsorptive period during which muscle protein breakdown exceeds muscle protein synthesis (272). Both acute and long-term studies show that the consumption of a protein-rich beverage 30 minutes prior to sleep and 2 hours after the last meal of the day is advantageous to muscle protein synthesis, muscle recovery, and overall metabolism (145, 147, 220, 271, 272). Specifically, the consumption of 20 to 40 g of protein 30 minutes prior to sleep has been shown to improve muscle protein synthesis (220), which results in improved long-term adaptive responses to the training process (249). Casein is likely the ideal presleep protein supplement (272), because it is slowly digestible and facilitates a more moderate but prolonged rise in plasma amino acid concentration (211). The sustained postprandial aminoacidemia during overnight sleep likely facilitates muscle protein synthesis throughout the entire night (272), which can facilitate long-term adaptive responses. In support of this contention, Snijders and colleagues (249) clearly demonstrate that the consumption of a casein supplement (13.75 g casein hydrolysate, 13.75 g casein, 15 g carbohydrate, and 0.1 g fat, 178.3 kcals of energy) immediately before bed resulted in enhanced muscle mass and strength gains in response to a 12-week resistance-training program when compared to presleep consumption of a noncaloric placebo beverage. Based on these data, it is evident that a presleep supplement that contains slow (casein) and more rapidly (casein hydrolysate) digestible proteins effectively augments muscle mass and strength gains during long-term resistance training (272). Based on the available evidence it may be warranted for athletes to consume 20-40 g of casein 30 minutes prior sleep to enhance muscle protein synthesis, recovery, and adaptive responses to the training process.

Dietary Supplements

Although a food-first approach is the most prudent nutritional support for training and competition, athletes widely believe that dietary supplements are important (58, 87), and this likely contributes to their widespread use (87, 120). Depending on the sport and level of competition, between 40% and 100% of athletes regularly use dietary supplements (87). Ideally, dietary supplements should be considered only if the athlete's diet is optimized; there is little point in adding supplements to a poor diet (58).

If the athlete's diet is optimal, there may be some benefit from a targeted supplementation plan (58), but this should be done with caution because supplement use can increase the athlete's risk of consuming banned substances or precursors of banned substances (87, 176). There are reports that substances prohibited by the World Anti-Doping Agency are present in 12% to 58% of supplements tested (172). If supplements are incorporated into the athlete's periodized nutrition plan, they must be sourced from reputable companies that have subjected their supplements to third-party batch testing (58, 246). There are several ways to identify whether a supplement has been batch tested, including looking for informed sport (https://www.wetestyoutrust.com) or NSF (https://www.nsfsport.com/index.php) certifications (58, 246) or using mobile applications (e.g., Sport Integrity Australia). The U.S. Anti-Doping Agency has developed a website (https://www.usada.org/athletes/substances/supplement-connect/high-risk-list/) that allows athletes to identify dietary supplements that have an increased risk of causing adverse analytical findings (i.e., doping violations). Batch testing only minimizes the risk of inadvertent doping and is *not* a guarantee that the supplement is drug-free (58). Additionally, the athlete is 100% responsible for what is in their body, and supplement use can increase the risk of inadvertent doping.

The Sport and Exercise Nutrition Register has a decision tree (figure 10.3) to help coaches and athletes decide whether a supplement should be incorporated into the periodized training plan (58). When assessing whether a supplement should be used, determine whether the available evidence supports its use, whether the need can be met through consuming food, and if the supplement has a minimal risk of causing inadvertent doping. Figure 10.4 summarizes some of the most common dietary supplements used by athletes.

Due to the sheer number of dietary supplements available, it is well beyond the scope of this chapter to provide detailed information about all options. Therefore, only brief discussions about creatine monohydrate and β-alanine are provided, because these supplements are extremely popular and there is strong scientific support for their use. For more extensive information on dietary supplements, refer to the A-Z of Nutritional Supplements Series published in the *British Journal of Sports Medicine* (40, 51, 52, 73, 146, 168, 198, 219, 240, 252) and the consensus statement published by the International Olympic Committee (120).

Creatine Monohydrate

Creatine monohydrate (CrM) is one of the most extensively investigated dietary supplements and has repeatedly been shown to improve high-intensity exercise capacity, increase muscle mass and performance, and enhance recovery during intensified training (7, 153, 185, 200, 260, 286). Compelling evidence has shown that creatine supplementation enhances cognitive function (224), provides an anti-inflammatory effect (221), speeds up recovery from traumatic brain injury (TBI) (2), and offers protection against TBI and concussions (164). Due to these wide-ranging benefits, CrM has become one of the most popular nutritional ergogenic aids, with 15% to 40% of athletes and military personnel reporting that they use creatine supplements (153).

A normal diet generally provides 1 to 2 $g \cdot day^{-1}$ of creatine, which allows the skeletal muscle to be about 60% to 80% saturated (153). Through the consumption of oral CrM, individuals with lower

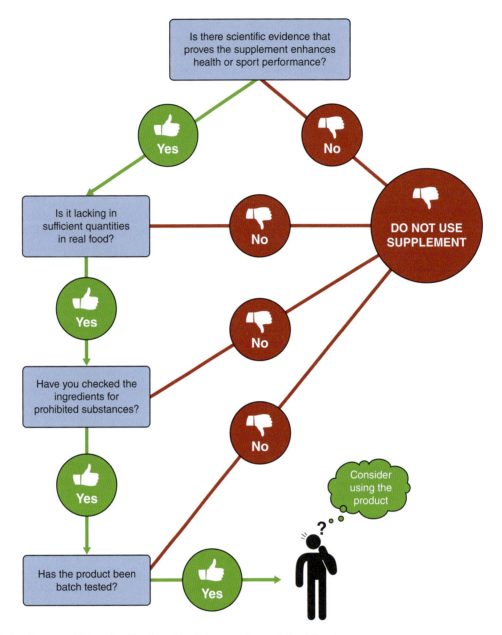

FIGURE 10.3 Sport and Exercise Nutrition Register supplement decision tree.
Adapted from Close, Kasper, and Morton (2021).

skeletal muscle stores of creatine, such as those who eat little meat or fish, are likely to increase the amount of creatine stored in their muscle by 20% to 40%, whereas those with relatively high muscle stores may experience a 10% to 20% increase (37, 152). By increasing the phosphocreatine reservoir, creatine supplementation facilitates a more rapid regeneration of adenosine triphosphate (ATP) during brief, high-intensity exercise bouts, particularly those that are repeated with short recovery periods. It is likely that these benefits will enhance the athlete's ability to undertake and recover from training sessions (37), particularly when training is intensified (260). For example, periods of overreaching may reduce β2-androgen receptor sensitivity (82), which can be offset with a creatine supplementation protocol (260). Additionally, creatine supplementation may upregulate myogenic transcription factors (e.g., myogenin) (109, 208) and satellite cell activity (67, 203), which may also be beneficial for injured athletes.

The most common supplementation strategy is to undertake a loading period during which 0.3 g CrM · kg body mass^{-1} · day^{-1} are consumed in

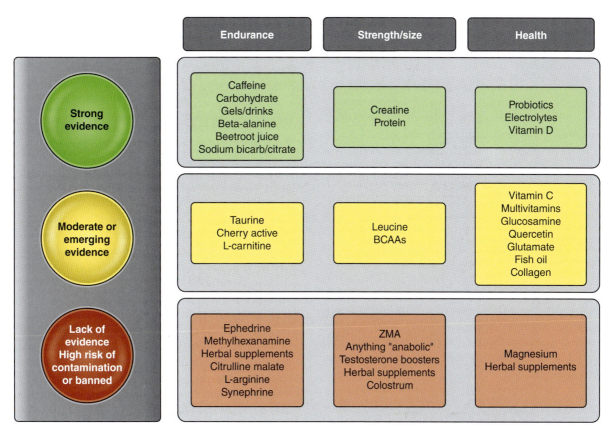

FIGURE 10.4 Summary of some of the most common dietary supplements.

Adapted from G.L. Close, D.L. Hamilton, A. Philp, et al., "New Strategies in Sport Nutrition to Increase Exercise Performance," *Free Radical Biology and Medicine* 98 (2016): 150.

split dosages for 5 to 7 days, followed by a 28-day maintenance period during which 0.03 g CrM · kg body mass^{-1} · day^{-1} are consumed to ensure that creatine stores remain saturated (96, 153). It is generally recommended that CrM supplements are consumed in conjunction with either carbohydrate or carbohydrate and protein to facilitate creatine retention (91, 96, 254). An alternative supplementation approach is to simply consume 3 g CrM · day^{-1}, which can result in an elevation of creatine stores over a 3- to 4-week period (118). This approach provides a more gradual increase in creatine stores but likely has a reduced effect on exercise performance and adaptations to training until creatine stores reach full saturation (153). Once creatine stores are saturated, they can remain elevated for 4 to 6 weeks even when supplementation is ceased (118, 279).

β-Alanine

β-alanine is one of the more popular supplements used by athletes to enhance athletic performance (29, 177). Although this nonproteogenic amino acid does not appear to have any direct ergogenic effects, it is considered the rate-limiting precursor for carnosine synthesis (104). Therefore, the primary role of β-alanine supplementation is to increase carnosine content in skeletal muscle. Supplementation with doses of 4 to 6 g · day^{-1} of β-alanine have been reported to increase carnosine in the skeletal muscle by up to 64% after 4 weeks (104) and 80% after 10 weeks (113). There is, however, a large degree of variability between individual responses to supplementation. For example, Baguet and colleagues (15) report that the consumption of 4.8 g · day^{-1} of β-alanine for 5 to 6 weeks resulted in a 55% increase in muscle carnosine concentrations in high responders and a 15% increase in low responders. The different responses appear to be partially explained by baseline muscle carnosine content and muscle composition (270). Carnosine concentrations tend to be higher in athletes who engage in resistance training and high-intensity exercise (270). Additionally, fast-twitch muscle fibers tend to have higher concentrations of carnosine compared to slow-twitch fibers (270). Finally, men tend to have higher carnosine concentrations compared to women (270). Based on these factors, it is important to consider an individualized approach to supplementation.

Carnosine is an intracellular dipeptide that has buffering, antioxidant, and anti-inflammatory properties (210). It is likely that enhanced buffering explains the meaningful benefits (~0.2%-3.0%) that have been reported for continuous and intermittent maximal exercise performed at durations between 30 seconds and 10 minutes (14, 56, 231). Performance gains are likely correlated with the magnitude of muscle carnosine change associated with supplementation (231). The only noted negative effect of β-alanine supplementation is skin paranesthesia (i.e., tingling), which can be attenuated by spreading the dosage throughout the day or consuming sustained-release tablets (58, 210, 270). Although an emerging body of scientific evidence supports β-alanine supplementation, further work is needed to define specific applications, including targeted sporting events and population-specific recommendations.

Nutritional Considerations for Injury

Injuries are an inescapable aspect of sport participation (267, 283) and can result in short- or long-term removal from full training or competition (246). During the initial stages of the healing process, there is an increased inflammatory response that can last from a few hours to several days, depending on the nature and severity of the injury (267, 283). This inflammatory response initiates numerous processes central to the healing process, so abolishing inflammation during the acute phase may be contraindicated to the healing process (267). However, managing excessive and prolonged inflammation via strategic nutritional strategies may accelerate and enhance the healing process (246). These strategies are likely beneficial for a range of injuries, including minor injuries (e.g., muscular strains, stress fractures, or ankle sprains), injuries that require surgery, and TBI or concussive injury (246).

Nutritional Interventions for Injury Rehabilitation

After an injury, the athlete is in a hypermetabolic state because of the activation of a cascade of inflammatory, immunological, and metabolic responses (246). To meet the hypermetabolic demands and support the healing process, alterations to the macro- and micronutrient compositions of the diet are required. Ideally, nutritional modifications provide enough calories and protein to support the healing process and offset potential lean body mass loss that can be associated with immobilization or reduced training capacity (246, 267). Additionally, dietary strategies can be used to modulate inflammatory and immune response to optimize the recovery and healing process (267). Therefore, when working with an injured athlete, it is important to consider their overall caloric needs and the macro- and micronutrient compositions of their diet.

Caloric Needs

An athlete rehabilitating an injury experiences a stress response that results in an increased energy demand, which will result in an increase in their **basal metabolic rate (BMR)** (246). Ideally, the BMR should be measured via indirect calorimetry, but when this type of measurement is unavailable, it can be estimated using predictive equations (table 10.5) (93, 103).

Once the BMR is established, it should be multiplied by a stress factor to account for the extra caloric demand associated with the rehabilitation process (table 10.6). Specifically, the stress factor accounts for the increased energetic expenditure and protein catabolism associated with the stress response to the injury (246).

TABLE 10.5 Methods of Calculating the Basal Metabolic Rate

Equation name	Equation method	
Harris–Benedict equation	Men	= 66.0 + (13.7 × wt [kg]) + (5.0 × ht [cm]) − (6.8 × age [y])
	Women	= 655.0 + (9.6 × wt [kg]) + (1.8 × ht [cm]) − (4.7 × age [y])
Fat free mass equation		= 370 + (21.6 × FFM [kg])

Note: wt = weight; ht = height; FFM = fat free mass.

TABLE 10.6 Stress Factor for Correction of Basal Metabolic Rate During Injury and Rehabilitation

Injury type	Stress factor
Severe burn	1.5
Major trauma (e.g., ACL surgery)	1.5
Infected wound	1.5
Bone fracture	1.2
Clean wound	1.2
Minor surgery	1.2
Minor injury (e.g., ankle sprain, dislocation)	1.2

Note: High stress (red); moderate stress (yellow).
Adapted from Smith-Ryan, Hirsch, Saylor, et al. (2020).

Additionally, the caloric demand associated with the athlete's physical activity level should be accounted for via the use of an activity-level correction factor (table 10.7). The athlete's total daily caloric requirements while injured can be estimated with the following equation:

total daily energy requirements = BMR × stress factor × activity coefficient

By basing nutritional strategies on the athlete's total daily caloric requirements while injured, the athlete can avoid a negative energy balance that can slow the healing process and exacerbate the potential loss of muscle typically associated with immobilization (246). If the athlete reduces their caloric intake and a negative energy balance occurs, it likely will exacerbate the loss of functional strength, which can prolong the time required to return to play (246). During this time, the athlete may need to follow a diet in which less carbohydrate (i.e., ~40% of total calories) or a 2:1 carbohydrate:protein ratio is consumed to promote positive changes in body composition (157, 158, 246, 274). Smith-Ryan and colleagues (246) suggest that by consuming a greater proportion of protein in combination with complex carbohydrates, the athlete will be able to meet their energetic requirements while minimizing weight and fat mass gain (figure 10.5). In addition, alcohol consumption should be avoided after injury (246, 274) because it can impair protein synthesis, reduce the inflammatory response and impair the healing process, and exacerbate the loss of muscle mass (274).

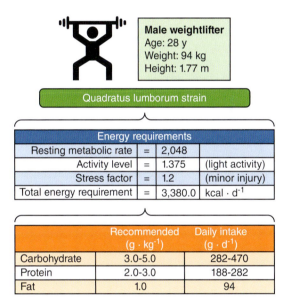

FIGURE 10.5 Example nutritional breakdown for an injured athlete.

Protein Recommendation

After an injury, there is an increased amino acid demand to support wound healing, tissue rebuilding, and glycemic control (289). Inadequate nutritional

TABLE 10.7 Activity-Level Correction of Basal Metabolic Rate

Activity level	Correction factor	Descriptor
Extra active	1.900	Hard exercise two or more sessions per day; training for a long-endurance event
Very active	1.725	Hard exercise every day or exercising two sessions per day
Moderately active	1.550	Moderate exercise or sports 6 to 7 days per week
Lightly active	1.375	Light exercise 1 to 3 days per week
Sedentary	1.200	Little or no exercise; desk job

Adapted from Smith-Ryan, Hirsch, Saylor, et al. (2020).

support leads to an increased catabolism of skeletal muscle to meet the hypermetabolic demand for amino acids (71). The stress response associated with the injury interrupts the homeostatic mechanisms that prevent the loss of lean body mass and increases energy expenditure and protein metabolism (246). This process can increase protein demand by up to 80% and result in an inability to maintain a neutral nitrogen balance. Although it is generally recommended that active individuals consume 1.4 to 2.0 g · kg body mass^{-1} · day^{-1} to maintain a neutral nitrogen balance, it may be warranted to increase this intake to 2.0 to 3.0 g · kg body mass^{-1} · day^{-1} when recovering from an injury (126, 246, 267). An additional consideration is to ensure that 3 g of leucine are consumed per serving, as leucine is considered the anabolic trigger and is primarily responsible for stimulating protein synthesis (197). Animal (e.g., beef, chicken, fish, milk, turkey) and whey proteins, which are high in leucine, should be consumed to accelerate the recovery process (246).

Generally, it is recommended that 20 to 40 g of dietary protein be consumed per sitting (126), with leucine-rich food being consumed at regular intervals throughout the day (246). Consumption should begin within 1 hour of waking and occur every 3 to 4 hours, before and after rehabilitation sessions, and prior to sleep to ensure nitrogen balance is maintained (10, 292).

Complex Carbohydrates

During rehabilitation, carbohydrate-rich foods provide a key source of energy and play an important role in the recovery process (246). Carbohydrate in the diet can facilitate a protein-sparing effect (105), which may help offset any muscle loss due to the hypermetabolic state and increased catabolism associated with injury. It is generally recommended that 3 to 5 g · kg body mass^{-1} (or ~55% of total calories) of carbohydrate should be consumed per day when rehabilitating an injury (265, 266). Complex carbohydrates, such as whole grains, fruits, and vegetables, which are rich in vitamins, minerals, and fiber, should be an important part of the diet during rehabilitation (246). While rehabilitating, the athlete's carbohydrate intake should be no more than 60% of their total caloric intake. Consuming a greater percentage of carbohydrate may lead to hyperglycemia, which can hinder healing and immune function (71, 246). Additionally, processed or refined sugars (i.e., simple carbohydrates) should be avoided, because their consumption can magnify the inflammatory response (195), which could extend the rehabilitative process.

Essential Fatty Acids

A key step in the healing process is the initial inflammatory response that occurs in response to injury (253, 267). Although this acute response is a critical step in the healing process, a prolonged inflammatory response, as seen with severe injury, can be counterproductive to the healing process (50, 161). A key countermeasure to a prolonged inflammatory response is the strategic use of postinjury nutritional strategies, such as the consumption of essential fats (161). During the healing process, fat can provide a critical source of energy and increase cell proliferation, which facilitates the healing process. For example, saturated fatty acids are often used as a fuel source, whereas polyunsaturated and monounsaturated fatty acids are used for cell membrane production (246). Ideally, 0.8 to 2 g · kg body mass^{-1} · day^{-1}, or 20% to 25% of the total daily caloric intake, should come from fat, with 2 g · day^{-1} of omega-3 fatty acids and no more than 10 g · day^{-1} of omega-6 fatty acids recommended (76). Ultimately, high levels of monounsaturated fatty acids and omega-3 fatty acids are important to the recovery process (49, 86, 267). Common sources of omega-3 fatty acids are avocados, olive oil, fish, flax, nuts, and seeds (246). Foods rich in omega-6 fatty acids, such as processed meats, fried and greasy foods, and vegetable oils should be limited due to their proinflammatory responses.

Nutrient Timing for Injury Rehabilitation

Although the athlete's total nutrient intake is an important consideration, the timing of ingestion of these nutrients offers a simple but effective strategy for enhancing adaptation and recovery (8, 9, 65, 246). Nutrient-timing strategies have been reported to stimulate protein synthesis (9), reduce muscle damage (144), enhance recovery (9), and improve body composition (138). Nutrient-timing strategies may be an important consideration when working with injured athletes who are undertaking rehabilitation due to their potential to positively affect lean body mass, strength, and functionality and to shorten the time required to return to play (246). The strategic consumption of nutrients, such as carbohydrate and protein, prior to and after a rehabilitation session is an essential strategy for maximizing the effectiveness of the session (figure 10.6) (145).

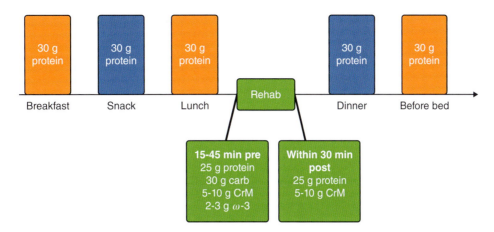

FIGURE 10.6 Example nutrient-timing strategy for injury rehabilitation. CHO: carbohydrate; CrM = creatine monohydrate; ω-3 = omega-3 fatty acids.

Adapted by permission from A.E. Smith-Ryan, K.R. Hirsch, H.E. Saylor, et al., "Nutritional Considerations and Strategies to Facilitate Injury Recovery and Rehabilitation," *Journal of Athletic Training* 55, no. 9 (2020): 918-930.

Nutritional Interventions for Traumatic Brain Injury or Concussion

A cascade of neurological dysregulation can occur in response to TBI and repetitive subconcussive injuries (17). For example, axonal damage, neuroinflammation, and dysregulation of ions (sodium, potassium, calcium) occur in response to a TBI (17). Additionally, the influx of calcium exacerbates damage to the axonal structure and causes mitochondrial dysfunction that contributes to cellular damage (17). It is possible that symptoms associated with TBI can be mitigated by targeted nutritional interventions (246). Based on the available data from several rodent studies, omega-3 fatty acids have the potential to decrease inflammation, cellular death, and axonal damage that occur in response to a TBI (154, 183, 184, 284, 291). In particular, there is compelling evidence that omega-3 fatty acid, curcumin, and CrM supplementation may be useful strategies that can be employed post-TBI.

It is currently believed that consuming 40 mg $\cdot$ kg body mass^{-1} $\cdot$ day^{-1} of omega-3 fatty acids immediately after TBI can be an effective strategy for enhancing the brain's recovery (17). In addition, supplementation with omega-3 fatty acids prior to a TBI or concussive event appears to provide a prophylactic effect by reducing the severity of injury (17, 184). Much more research is required to understand optimal dosing strategies.

An additional strategy for improving recovery after TBI or concussive brain injuries is the use of curcumin supplementation (78, 246). The consumption of 100 mg $\cdot$ kg body mass^{-1} of curcumin that contains 95% curcuminoids has been reported to reduce neuronal apoptosis (184), decrease oxidative stress (78, 290, 297), and improve cognitive function after concussive brain injury or TBI (246, 290). Although the therapeutic effects of curcumin are promising, much more research on the effects of curcumin supplementation is warranted.

An emerging body of evidence supports the use of CrM supplementation as a therapeutic strategy post-TBI or concussion (221, 246). The consumption of CrM post-TBI has the potential to balance the ATP stores and reduce the negative effects on brain energy status associated with the TBI-induced reduction in brain creatine levels (246). When 0.4 g $\cdot$ kg body mass^{-1} $\cdot$ day^{-1} of CrM are consumed post-TBI, there are noted improvements in cognitive function, decreased occurrences of headaches, and reductions in dizziness and fatigue (2, 229, 230). TBI symptoms are likely improved with CrM supplementation via the mitigation of inflammation, mitochondrial dysfunction, nerve damage, and oxidative stress (74). Although these data are promising, it may be necessary to consume more than the typical maintenance dosage of 0.03 g $\cdot$ kg body mass^{-1} $\cdot$ day^{-1} of CrM, as most of the studies used 0.4 g $\cdot$ kg body mass^{-1} $\cdot$ day^{-1}. Even though CrM is a low-risk supplement that may offer significant benefits post-TBI, few studies directly examine CrM supplementation and TBI in humans. CrM should still be considered as part of a post-TBI treatment plan, because it offers significant benefit with little potential risk.

Periodization Strategies

It is well-documented that the adaptive responses that result from a periodized training plan are largely modulated by the programmatic training factors and are amplified or dampened by the athlete's nutritional practices (134, 209, 259). Therefore, to maximize adaptive responses and optimize performance at the appropriate time, targeted nutritional strategies must be integrated into the overall periodized training plan. Ideally, the coach will leverage expert nutritional support and work collaboratively with sport nutritionists to ensure appropriate nutritional strategies. The coach must also understand how periodizing nutrition can positively or negatively affect adaptive responses to training or performance outcomes.

Periodization of Energy Intake

The greatest influence on the athlete's overall EE is the effect of the training loads in their individualized training program. Because the training loads in the macro-, meso-, and microcycles of a periodized training plan vary, it has been postulated that the athlete's EI should also vary between phases, weeks, and training days to better align with training loads (44, 193, 259). Therefore, manipulations of EI must be strategically integrated into the periodized training plan to ensure the athlete is meeting their energy needs. In some situations, the athlete may wish to alter their physique by reducing body fat or body mass or increasing body or muscle mass (259). To meet these needs, EI will be manipulated, but the athlete's diet must be designed to maintain sufficient EI to minimize the chance of developing RED-S (180).

An important step in developing any periodized nutrition plan is performing a complete audit of the athlete's training process (259). Each training session or workout type should be evaluated to estimate its total caloric and substrate use, which can then inform how energy and macronutrients may be manipulated to account for the needs of the athlete's daily training sessions and their overall nutritional goals (265). For example, a training day with a high training load will require a greater EEE, and EI will need to be increased. Conversely, on a recovery day, EEE will be relatively low, and the athlete's EI should be reduced to better align with their needs. It is also important to consider the training demands of each microcycle. For example, the increased training load of a shock microcycle will require an overall increase in the athlete's EEE across the entire microcycle. To ensure that the athlete can tolerate the increased training loads, EI will need to be increased to ensure that the EA aligns with the athlete's needs.

Although it is generally recommended that athletes avoid overmonitoring their EA or EI, they should understand how their general nutritional needs fluctuate from day to day so they can develop habits that can better align their EI with the EEE (259). This alignment may be most important if the athlete is attempting to manipulate body composition to achieve optimal performance (265). Recently referred to as the *periodization of body composition* (112, 256, 259), this practice involves the strategic manipulation of body composition and body mass across different periods and phases of the athlete's annual training plan (256). This concept is best illustrated by Stellingwerff (256), who presented an example of how body composition was periodized during the 9-year career of a female Olympic-level middle-distance runner. In this case study, the athlete's body composition was optimized during competition periods through strategic individualized nutritional strategies because maintaining race body composition year-round was deemed not sustainable for health and performance (256). During the general preparation phase (September to April), the athlete trained at a body mass 2% to 4% above her ideal race weight and body fat percentage, and optimal EA was prioritized in her periodized nutrition plan. Body composition was then optimized during the competition phase (May to August) by employing an energy deficit that was guided by feedback metrics (body mass, performance, and hunger) and applied across an individualized time frame. Ultimately, these strategies resulted in peak performances at the appropriate times while minimizing injury and maximizing training adaptations via the management of EA (45). Additionally, these strategies allowed the athlete to capitalize on the benefits of controlled periods of low energy availability within the framework of endurance training (45).

Periodization of Carbohydrate Intake

Contemporary sport nutrition guidelines have recognized that carbohydrate intake should be considered in the context of carbohydrate availability, in which the daily amount and timing of carbohydrate consumption are aligned with the fuel costs of training or competition schedules (193). It is currently recommended that there should be higher carbohydrate availability on days with higher training loads (i.e., workload, volume, and intensity) or competitions (189, 266), because this will optimize fuel supply for skeletal muscle and central nervous system function (193). In these scenarios, carbohydrate intake should be integrated with other dietary goals to ensure adequate fuel supply from muscle glycogen and exogenous carbohydrate supply and to provide immune system support (193). On days with lower training loads, the amount of carbohydrate consumed can be reduced to better align with the athlete's individual fuel needs. Therefore, the athlete's carbohydrate intake should be varied according to the fuel needs associated with the athlete's individualized energy needs (193). Additionally, based on emerging evidence, carbohydrate availability can also be manipulated to either enhance performance or stimulate specific cell-signaling and gene-expression responses (106).

Training With High Carbohydrate Availability

Training high refers to training under conditions of increased carbohydrate availability, in which muscle and liver glycogen levels are elevated and carbohydrate provisions are provided during training (134). A main benefit of this strategy is that the availability of carbohydrate helps maintain the quality of endurance (117, 295) and high-volume resistance training (98) and reduce symptoms of fatigue and overreaching (1, 100, 101, 244). Additionally, this practice can enhance intestinal function and reduce gastrointestinal problems (135). Although ingesting carbohydrate during prolonged events enhances endurance performance in most events (134), there is a high incidence of gastrointestinal problems in athletes participating in endurance events (135). Because gastric emptying and stomach comfort can be trained, training-high strategies may be useful in reducing incidences of gastrointestinal problems. Specifically, training-high strategies increase the density and activity of sodium-dependent glucose-1 transporters in the intestine, enhancing carbohydrate absorption and oxidation during exercise (135).

The main argument for training high is to maintain the quality of training and optimize long-term training adaptations (134). For example, Simonsen and colleagues (244) reported that across a 4-week training period during which rowers trained twice daily, those who consumed a higher-carbohydrate (10 g · kg body mass^{-1} · d^{-1}) diet increased mean power output during a 2,500 m time trial by 10.7%, whereas those who consumed a lower carbohydrate (5 g · kg body mass^{-1} · d^{-1}) diet improved by only 1.6%. In addition, it is clear that athletes who consume higher-carbohydrate diets experience fewer reductions in performance and fewer symptoms of overreaching during periods of intensified training, despite being able to perform greater amounts of total work during training (1, 100, 101). Based on these data, it is evident that when training quality must be maintained or the athlete is exposed to a period of intensified training or a dense competition schedule, increasing carbohydrate availability is an important nutritional strategy. Therefore, the coach and nutritional support staff must integrate physical training and nutritional interventions so carbohydrate availability matches the training demand to ensure the athlete can maintain a high quality of training.

Training With Low Carbohydrate Availability

Understanding of the important role that muscle glycogen plays in directly and indirectly regulating muscle adaptation has expanded, and several sport nutritionists and scientists now recommend that athletes periodically train under conditions of low glycogen availability (i.e., train low) to enhance training responses (119, 193). Specifically, when an athlete undertakes bouts of exercise with low glycogen availability, there is an upregulation of several key cell-signaling kinases (e.g., AMPK, p38 MAPK), transcriptional factors (e.g., p53, peroxisome proliferator–activated receptor delta), and transcriptional coactivators (e.g., PGC-1α) (18, 119, 216). These cellular-signaling adaptations are likely underpinned by increasing activity of molecules with a glycogen-binding domain, enhancing free fatty acid availability, altering muscle cell osmotic pressure, and increasing catecholamine concentrations (193, 216). Ultimately, these strategies increase mitochondrial enzyme activity or mitochondrial content and increase rates of lipid oxidation, all of which can enhance endurance performance (193).

Based on empirical and practical data, there is a belief that athletes should periodically train with low carbohydrate availability (i.e., train low) to enhance the adaptive response to training (193). Although the long-term implementation of a low-carbohydrate diet can achieve these goals, the periodic reduction of carbohydrate availability around targeted training sessions or time points is likely a more effective strategy for long-term performance enhancement (39). An example of this strategy is performing two training sessions in close succession with minimal carbohydrate intake between sessions, thus creating a scenario in which the second session is performed in a fasted state with only the consumption of water. In this scenario, the athlete would have a low endogenous (i.e., muscle glycogen) and exogenous (i.e., no consumption of carbohydrate during training) carbohydrate availability, which would stimulate specific adaptive responses that have been linked to improved performance (193).

An additional strategy to consider is withholding carbohydrate during the hours after exercise to delay glycogen resynthesis (193). This practice has not been shown to negatively affect the training session and stimulates an upregulation of markers of mitochondrial biogenesis and lipid oxidation during the posttraining recovery phase (19, 156). Mujika and colleagues (193) suggest that this practice offers three major benefits:

1. The athlete can perform their training session with high carbohydrate availability (i.e., train high), increasing the overall quality of the session.
2. The athlete can experience within-day or overnight carbohydrate restriction (i.e., sleep low), which can promote several physiological adaptive responses.
3. The athlete can undertake moderate-intensity training sessions without carbohydrate consumption or in the morning after an overnight fast (i.e., train low) to stimulate specific physiological adaptive responses.

When these basic strategies have been examined with subelite endurance athletes during a single microcycle (170) or a 3-week mesocycle (171), superior training adaptations and performance outcomes were noted when compared to training undertaken with a more balanced distribution of carbohydrate. Mujika and colleagues (193) suggest that these studies provide evidence that individualized carbohydrate consumption strategies (i.e., train high versus train low) can be integrated into the endurance athlete's periodized training plan to enhance the physiological adaptations and performance outcomes targeted by the training plan. Support for periodizing carbohydrate availability with elite endurance athletes has been presented by Stellingwerff (255), who examined the nutritional strategies of three elite marathon runners. Although the integration of strategic manipulations of carbohydrate consumption appears to be a beneficial practice for elite athletes, more research is warranted to further validate this practice.

Integration of Nutrition Strategies Into the Periodized Training Plan

Although the idea of incorporating nutrition into the annual training plan is not a new or novel concept (115, 173, 174), interest in how to optimally integrate nutritional strategies into the athlete's training process has become an increasingly popular topic of scientific inquiry (134, 257, 258, 262). Fundamentally, the periodized training program provides the framework from which nutritional strategies are established (259). Based on this concept, Stellingwerff and colleagues (259) have provided a methodological framework that can be used to guide the integration of nutritional strategies into the athlete's integrated periodized training plan. The framework, shown in figure 10.7, provides a series of questions that can be used to inform nutritional strategies to be implemented at the macrocycle, mesocycle, and microcycle levels of the periodized training plan.

Periodization of Nutrition and the Annual Training Plan

When considering the integration of nutritional strategies into the athlete's periodized training plan, the logical place to begin is at the annual training plan or macrocycle level. Fundamentally, the idea of integrating nutritional practices into the overall periodized training plan centers on aligning nutritional intake with training loads (i.e., volume and intensity) and the goals established for each phase of the annual training plan. For example, during a general preparation phase, the athlete is exposed to higher training volumes that would require them to consume more calories, particularly from carbohydrate food sources (258). Therefore, nutritional strategies that increase carbohydrate intake would be targeted in this phase to ensure that carbohydrate availability aligns with the athlete's energetic needs (figure 10.8).

During this phase of training it also may be warranted to implement creatine-loading protocols, since creatine has been shown to increase work capacity and reduce the risk of overtraining when the athlete is exposed to higher volumes of training

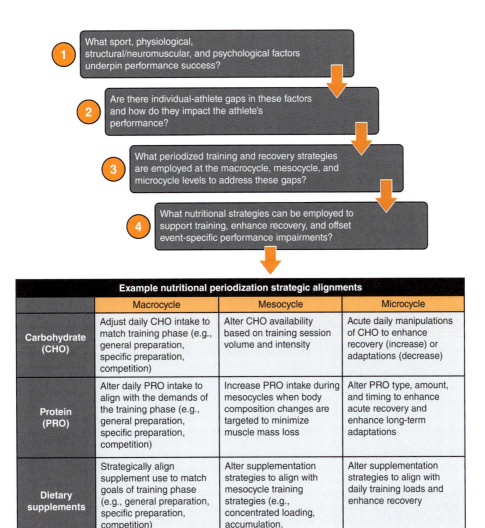

FIGURE 10.7 Theoretical framework for the periodization of nutrition.
Adapted from Stellingwerff, Morton, and Burke (2019).

(260). Alternatively, during a transition phase, the athlete will be exposed to significantly less training load, thus requiring a reduction in overall caloric intake, likely from reduced carbohydrate consumption (258). Reducing caloric intake during transition phases is an important consideration, especially for athletes who compete in weight class–based sports (e.g., weightlifting, boxing, wrestling) or sports that require a specific body weight to optimize performance (e.g., running). During transition phases, athletes often take short rest periods to facilitate mental and physical recovery, and these are often accompanied by significant reductions in training load. Some weight gain is expected, but to ensure that it is not excessive, the athlete's nutritional plan should be formatted to account for these alterations in energetic demand.

Ultimately, at the annual training plan or macrocycle level, several considerations must be aligned with the goals of each training phase (193, 258). The load and density of training in each phase are considered and used to inform nutritional decisions. Therefore, an estimation of the required endogenous and exogenous substrates required during these phases should be used to guide nutritional strategies. EI needs to be aligned with these requirements to ensure that there is adequate EA (258). Additionally, the annual training plan may need to indicate where changes in body composition are targeted and the nutritional strategies being employed. Based on the global goals established in the annual training plan, more specific nutritional strategies can be designed and implemented at the mesocycle level.

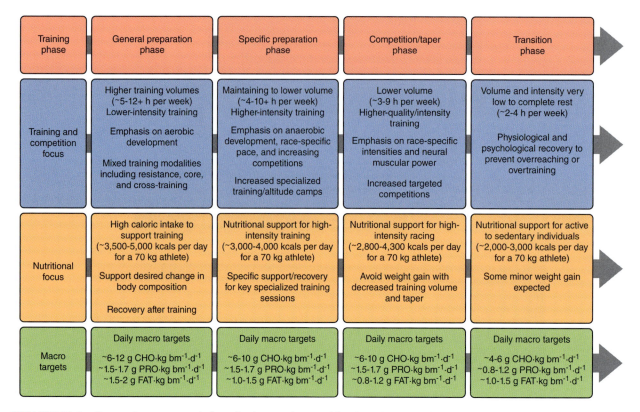

FIGURE 10.8 General recommendations for integrating nutrition into the periodized annual nutritional plan.
Adapted from Stellingwerff, Maughan, and Burke (2011).

Periodization of Nutrition and the Mesocycle

Nutritional strategies employed in the mesocycle must be aligned with the planned training load. For example, if the athlete is exposed to a 2-week overreaching or accentuated loading mesocycle, EI must be increased, primarily by increasing carbohydrate intake, to provide adequate EA and ensure the athlete can tolerate the planned training loads and minimize the risk of injury or overtraining (189). Additionally, due to the increased workload, strategic CrM and omega-3 supplementation strategies may be warranted to enhance the athlete's ability to tolerate the increased training stress. Conversely, as the athlete transitions into a 2-week realization or tapering mesocycle, the overall training load is decreased, which would reduce the EEE. To align with the reduced EEE, the athlete should reduce their EI to ensure that EA aligns with the planned training loads (189).

In addition to matching nutritional interventions with training loads, it is also important to align nutritional strategies with the goals of the mesocycle. For example, during a competitive mesocycle with a particularly dense competition schedule, there should be increased EI, particularly from carbohydrate and protein, to ensure the athlete can tolerate the competitive load. Additionally, targeted nutrient-timing strategies should be implemented to facilitate recovery and ensure that the athlete is properly fueled for each competitive engagement.

Periodization of Nutrition and the Microcycle

When examining each microcycle of a given phase of training, various nutritional strategies can be employed (206). As with the other levels of the periodized training plan, the training load planned for each day is used to guide the nutritional strategies employed across the microcycle. If a strength–power athlete's EEE increases for a given training day, they will need to increase their caloric intake to ensure there is adequate EA to meet the demands of training (189). For example, if the athlete has 70 kg of FFM, expends 300 kcals during a moderate training session, and consumes about 3,450 kcals · day^{-1}, their EA will be 45 kcals · kg FFM^{-1} · day^{-1}. In this instance, the athlete can consume 5 to 7 g carbohydrate · kg body mass^{-1} · day^{-1} to ensure there is enough carbohydrate to meet the training requirements. If, on a subsequent day, the athlete has a particularly hard training session and expends 500 kcals during training, they would need to increase daily caloric intake to about 3,650 kcals to maintain an EA of 45 kcals · kg FFM^{-1} · day^{-1}. Additionally, the athlete would need to increase carbohydrate intake (6-8 g carbohydrate · kg body mass^{-1} · d^{-1}) to meet the demands of intensified training. Conversely, a rest or recovery day with a minimal planned training load would require reducing EI to about 3,150 kcals to maintain an EA of 45 kcals · kg FFM^{-1} · day^{-1}. Although in this scenario it is prudent to reduce the amount of carbohydrate consumed, the athlete must consume at least 3 g · kg body mass^{-1} · day^{-1}, because this is generally recommended as the minimum intake for a strength–power athlete (189, 245).

An alternative approach is manipulating carbohydrate intake to implement train-low or train-high strategies within an individual microcycle (58). Close and colleagues (58) suggest that athletes can strategically employ train-low strategies for predetermined training workloads that can be readily performed with reduced carbohydrate availability. Alternatively, when the highest workloads are encountered for longer durations, adequate carbohydrate availability should be provided in the 24 hours before and during the specific training session (58). Ideally, this would require a day-to-day nutritional periodization strategy implemented in a meal-to-meal manner to maintain metabolic flexibility while allowing the athlete complete high-intensity and prolonged-duration workloads, such as high-intensity interval training above the lactate threshold (58) or multiple training sessions per day. Close and colleagues (58) suggest train-low sessions that are aligned with lower-intensity training sessions performed well below the lactate threshold (e.g., steady-state training). Based on these principles, they presented a theoretical "fuel-for-work" model designed for a soccer player who trains once per day on 4 days and performs resistance training on 3 days and has 2 rest days per week (table 10.8) (58).

As shown in table 10.8, the athlete has five feeding times. Different feeding strategies are employed at key times of the day to integrate train-low and train-high strategies for specific types of training sessions. Note that this is an example of how these strategies could be employed; individualized strategies need to be developed to meet the athlete's sport-specific needs (58). Currently, much more research is warranted to determine how best to periodize nutritional strategies at the microcycle level.

Summary

It is well-established that periodized physical training is a central part of the preparation of athletes and that the physiological and performance adaptations that occur in response to training are modulated by the athlete's nutritional practices. Due to the intimate relationship between nutrition and training adaptation, there is increasing interest in the strategic manipulation of nutrient provision to modulate adaptive and performance responses. Therefore, nutritional periodization is an important part of the athlete's periodized training plan. Nutritional intake should be aligned with training and competition goals and match the energetic requirements of the athlete's training sessions. Through the strategic implementation of specific nutrient-timing strategies throughout the day, it is possible to maximize the interaction between exercise and nutritional intake. Although the athlete should take a food-first approach to nutrition, dietary supplementation should be considered once the athlete's diet is optimized.

TABLE 10.8 Theoretical Fuel-for-Work Model for a Soccer Player

Day	Focus	Breakfast	Lunch	Mid-afternoon snack	Dinner	Evening snack	Comment
Game +1 Sunday	Recovery	High CHO	High CHO	High CHO	High CHO	High CHO	Promote glycogen resynthesis and recovery.
Game +2 Monday	Active recovery	High CHO	High CHO	Low CHO	Medium CHO	Low CHO	Transition to normal eating habits and continue the recovery process.
Game −4 Tuesday	Aerobic	High CHO	Medium CHO	Medium CHO	Low CHO	Low CHO	High total-distance day. Carbohydrate peaking around breakfast, reducing toward evening meal.
Game −3 Wednesday	Anaerobic	High CHO	High CHO	Medium CHO	Low CHO	Low CHO	High-intensity day with high acceleration and deceleration. Carbohydrate peaking around lunch, around field session, and reducing toward evening meal.
Game −2 Thursday	Install	Medium CHO	Medium CHO	Low CHO	Low CHO	Low CHO	Moderate day focusing on competition preparation, mimicking expected opposition play. Moderate carbohydrate peaking around lunch, reducing toward evening meal.
Game −1 Friday	Tactical	High CHO	High CHO	High CHO	High CHO	High CHO	Low day where focus is on preparing for competition by mimicking expected opposition shape. High carbohydrate to facilitate glycogen storage for game.
Game day Saturday	Compete	High CHO	High CHO	High CHO	High CHO	High CHO	High-carbohydrate breakfast and prematch meal to top up glycogen stores prior to game. High-carbohydrate postmatch meals and snacks to ensure optimal postmatch glycogen resynthesis.

Note: CHO = carbohydrate.
Adapted from G.L. Close, A.M. Kasper, and J.P. Morton, "Nutrition for Human Performance," in *Strength and Conditioning for Sports Performance*, edited by I. Jeffreys and J. Moody (New York, NY: Routledge, 2021), 182.

CHAPTER 11

Integration of Monitoring Techniques Into Periodized Training Plans

The process of monitoring training is a rapidly expanding area of study fueled by the never-ending quest for new and better methods of enhancing performance (49, 314). Even with an increased research focus, most of what we know about athlete monitoring is based on personal experience and anecdotal information that is largely unpublished (49, 157). Additionally, although it is well-known that extensive monitoring is integrated into the training processes of elite and professional athletes, much of this information is protected and unpublished (157). Regardless, one can assume that athletes who engage in a better-organized and better-monitored training process will outperform competitors whose training may be less structured or lacks an integrated monitoring program (314). Sands and colleagues (314) suggest that integrating a monitoring process into the athlete's periodized training plan can help shine a light on information that may not be readily apparent without structured data collection, archiving, and measurement. Ultimately, Viru and Viru (372) suggest four major reasons for incorporating monitoring into the athlete's periodized training plan:

1. Documenting the actual training that the athlete completes (e.g., exercises, methods, loads)
2. Providing information about the effects of the training process
3. Determining whether the structure of the training process is adequate for the athlete's specific level of development
4. Determining and assessing the athlete's adaptation characteristics

Similarly, Sands and colleagues (314) suggest three purposes for actively engaging in athlete monitoring:

1. Providing information about the effects of the training process
2. Evaluating the effectiveness of the training plan
3. Assessing the athlete's adaptational characteristics

Any data collected as part of the monitoring process can be retrospectively examined to determine load–performance relationships, enhance the prescription of training loads, help with the avoidance of nonfunctional overreaching, or help determine the athlete's state of preparedness for the demands of competition (157). Another benefit of developing structured monitoring programs is they can enhance communication and relationship building between athletes, support staff, and coaches (157). Halson (157) suggests that when athletes are engaged in a monitoring program, they are empowered and have an increased sense of involvement in and ownership of their training program. Data collected as part of the monitoring program can also foster increased communication between support staff and coaches. Ultimately, all these benefits enhance an athlete's belief in the training process, which may increase their confidence in the support staff and coaches who are guiding their development (157).

Although there are many benefits of a structured monitoring program, the support and coaching staff must remember that the program serves to provide data, which must be analyzed and interpreted to help guide the training process. As such, the monitoring program should never dictate training decisions but should instead be used to inform the coach's decision-making process. Central to the effective implementation of this process, the coach must understand the techniques used in monitoring, how to make the process sustainable, and how to interpret the data garnered from the monitoring program. Additionally, the coach must have a clear rationale for *why* monitoring is being conducted, *what* will be monitored, how *often* monitoring will be conducted, and *how* the data collected will be interpreted and conveyed to the athlete and coaching staff (157). Once these have been determined, the coach can integrate the monitoring program into the overall structure of the periodized annual training plan. Monitoring should be considered an integrated component of periodization used to provide information the coach can use to best optimize the athlete's individualized training and recovery plans (99).

Training Loads

As noted in chapter 4, training load is the quantitative determination of the amount of work completed by the athlete (365). The ability to manipulate the training process to expose the athlete to appropriate training loads so favorable performance outcomes are promoted while reducing the potential for maladaptive responses is a central concept of periodized training (49, 114). A key component of the training process is the integration of a structured methodology for monitoring training loads to provide information about how the athlete is responding to the periodized training plan (figure 11.1) (99).

Ultimately, the model of periodization selected as the foundation for the athlete's training plan will dictate the training loads the athlete is exposed to (147). Conceptually, the application of training loads should be considered a dose–response relationship between the applied training stimulus and the resultant athlete response (5, 23, 114). As such, training load can be considered in the context of being either external or internal (187, 188), depending on if the factor being quantified represents the

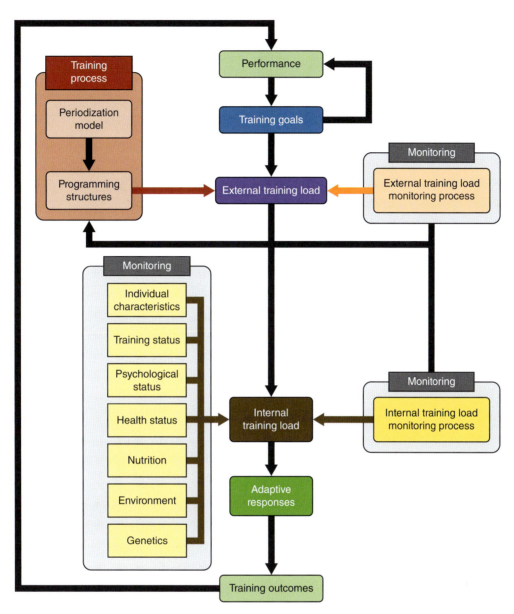

FIGURE 11.1 Theoretical framework of the integration of monitoring into the training process.

applied training stimulus or the athlete's response (184). Ideally, the monitoring process will provide information to the coach about the external and internal load, and this information can be used to make informed decisions about how best to structure the training process.

External Training Load

External load represents the physical work completed by the athlete (114) and has classically served as the foundation for most monitoring programs (157). Due to numerous training activities that an athlete undertakes, external loads are specific to the type of training undertaken (table 11.1) (184). For example, the external load during resistance training is often quantified as the load lifted, the amount of work completed (i.e., volume load = repetitions × weight lifted), or the movement velocity of an exercise (146, 322). In team sports, external load can be determined based on the total distance covered within specific speed bands, metabolic power (i.e., derived from speed–time profiles), speed thresholds, whole body loads (i.e., ground reaction forces), accelerations, decelerations, and rate of acceleration (361). Ultimately, regardless of how it is quantified, the external load dictates the athlete's psychophysiological adaptations (184), and

TABLE 11.1 External Load Variables That Can Be Used to Monitor Training Load and Subsequent Fatigue

Variable	Units and descriptors
Accelerations	Acceleration measures ($m \cdot s^{-1}$)
Distance	Units of distance (m, km, miles)
Frequency	Sessions per day, week, month
Functional neuromuscular tests	Countermovement jumps and drop jump measures
Global positioning system (GPS) measures	Velocity, distance, acceleration, time in zones, location
Movement repetition counts	Activity counts (e.g., steps, jumps, throws)
Player load	Single variable in arbitrary units (time dependent)
Power output	Relative ($W \cdot kg^{-1}$) or absolute power (W)
Repeated efforts	Number of efforts, quality of efforts
Speed	Speed measures ($m \cdot s^{-1}$, $m \cdot min^{-1}$, $km \cdot h^{-1}$)
Time	Units of time (s, min, h, d, wk, y)
Training mode	Resistance training, running, cycling, swimming, and so forth
Volume	Time, volume load, total repetitions/efforts
Work rate	Measure of work rate ($m \cdot min^{-1}$)

it is a major factor affecting the athlete's internal training load.

Internal Training Load

Although the external load has classically been used as part of monitoring programs, it may not accurately represent how the athlete is adapting to the training process (248, 322). As a result, many monitoring programs also assess the athlete's internal load (table 11.2), which represents the athlete's physiological and psychological responses to training (i.e., external load) (121, 147, 184).

Conceptually, measurements of internal load reflect all psychophysiological responses that the athlete's body initiates to cope with the external load (184). In addition to external load, several other modifiable and nonmodifiable factors can affect the athlete's internal load, such as training status, nutritional intake, overall health, psychological status, and genetics (figure 11.1) (363). The athlete's response to a given external load can

TABLE 11.2 Internal Load Variables That Can Be Used to Monitor Training Load and Subsequent Fatigue

Variable	Descriptors
Heart rate	Resting, exercise response, recovery
Heart rate variability (HRV)	Resting
Hormonal response	Baseline, response to exercise
Illness	Incidence, duration
Immunological response	Baseline, response to exercise
Injury	Type, duration
Lactate	Response to exercise
Oxygen consumption	Exercise
Psychological	Stress, anxiety, motivation
Rating of perceived exertion (RPE)	Exercise
Sensations	Hopeful, neutral, hopeless

change as a result of modifications to certain factors, such as training status or nutritional intake. Additionally, changes to the athlete's training environment, such as training in hot conditions, can affect their psychophysiological responses to the training process (184).

External and Internal Load Integration

Even though many technological advancements allow for the more precise quantification of external load, it is generally recommended not to solely monitor athletes using external load (157, 184). For example, Impellizzeri and colleagues (184) suggest that since there are often low and high responders to a given external training load, the incorporation of internal load measurements is required to fully understand the athlete's response to the external load. It is well-documented that the lactate threshold can correspond to different percentages of the maximal oxygen uptake ($\dot{V}O_2$max) (101, 184, 257). It is possible that two athletes exercising at the same percentage of $\dot{V}O_2$max will experience different training-induced adaptations. If $\dot{V}O_2$max is used as the marker of internal load, one might suggest that there is a responder and a nonresponder to the applied external training load. However, it is possible that the percentage of $\dot{V}O_2$max the athletes are training at corresponds to different lactate responses (i.e., internal load) (184, 257).

Impellizzeri and colleagues (184) also suggest that an uncoupling between the internal and external load could potentially be used to determine how the athlete is coping with their training program. For example, an athlete who displays an elevated internal load in response to a standardized external load in similar conditions may be losing fitness or experiencing a fatigue response. Conversely, an athlete who displays a lower internal load in this situation is assumed to be displaying a higher fitness level (184). Measuring internal load by both physiological and psychological measurements may make it possible to isolate the type of fatigue being expressed by the athlete. For example, increases in heart rate and the **rating of perceived exertion (RPE)** are both associated with muscular fatigue (237), whereas mental fatigue results in elevations in RPE (238). Impellizzeri and colleagues (184) suggest that the coach who understands these concepts can better mitigate fatigue by reducing muscle-damaging exercise or employing strategies to enhance sleep hygiene. Ultimately, an effective monitoring program should incorporate measurements of both external and internal load to give the coach a more comprehensive understanding of the training load.

Methods for Monitoring External Training Load

A number of potential markers of external training load can be integrated into the periodized training plan to monitor the training load (table 11.1) (157). For example, external load can be monitored by quantifying power output, speed, acceleration, or other measures that represent what the athlete has actually completed (49). Note that there is limited data on the efficacy of using many of these measures as monitoring tools, and to date there is no single gold-standard workload measurement (121, 157). Ultimately, the choice of which external load metrics to quantify is dictated by the characteristics of the sport being monitored.

Advanced technological solutions are increasingly available, with many offering a wealth of data that may or may not provide information that is valuable to the coach's decision-making process (63, 121, 145, 206, 314). When deciding which monitoring tools to use, coaches need to remember the primary aims of monitoring and select appropriate tools and methods to address those aims. Although it is likely different sports will require unique monitoring solutions, a core set of external load monitoring methods must be understood to adapt them to the athlete's specific situation.

Power Output, Speed, and Acceleration

Numerous technologies can be used to quantify external training loads (157). In cycling, for example, power meters such as the SRM, Garmin Rally, or PowerTap allow for continuous measurement of work rate (i.e., power output) (196, 268). Data can be continuously collected during training and competition and then analyzed to provide information about the athlete's average power, normalized power, speed, and accelerations during the collection period (157). Data collected with a power meter can be used to calculate a **Training Stress Score (TSS)** (7), which takes into account the intensity and duration of each training session or competition to indicate the overall external training load the athlete completed. The TSS can be calculated using the following equation:

$$\text{Training Stress Score} = \frac{\text{duration (s)} \times \text{normalized power (w)} \times \text{intensity factor}}{\text{functional threshold power} \times 3{,}600} \times 100$$

The athlete's TSS is based on a 1-hour time trial performed at their threshold power. Riding for 1 hour at functional threshold power would equate to 100 TSS points and an intensity factor of 1.0 (7). Allen and Coggan (7) suggest that the TSS can be used to quantify the intensity of training and give insight into the duration of recovery (figure 11.2).

Ultimately, the use of a power meter to collect normalized power, intensity factor, and TSS for each training session and competition can give the coach keen insight into the external loads the athlete is exposed to. By tracking these data over time, the coach can leverage this information to guide their decisions about the athlete's periodized training plan. It is also possible that machine learning can be used to model the effects of different TSSs on the progression of training. Ultimately, power meters are very useful tools for quantifying external training loads in cycling.

Time-Motion Analysis

It has become common for team sports to monitor athletes during training and competition with **time-motion analysis** techniques such as global positioning system (GPS) tracking and movement pattern analysis via digital video (i.e., ProZone) (78, 157, 343). For example, Akenhead and Nassis (4) surveyed 41 high-level soccer clubs from Europe, the United States, and Australia and determined that 40 of these clubs used GPS monitoring techniques at every field training session. Due to the small size of modern GPS and accelerometer units, they are easily embedded into monitoring practices because they are noninvasive, easy to wear, and can be seamlessly integrated into all field-based training sessions. In some sports, these devices can be worn during competition (248, 305).

Although the early incarnations of GPS devices were simply used to quantify the distance the athlete traveled during training or competition (248), modern devices measure accelerations, high-intensity distance, impacts, work rate (e.g., m · min^{-1}), and training load derived from other variables (table 11.3) (248, 250, 305). For example, player load, a scoring value that accounts for the intensity and duration of effort, can be quantified based on GPS data. This score is often weighted with an exponentially increasing coefficient (296). Alternatively, the player load can be calculated as the root mean square of the change in acceleration in successive movements (382).

When GPS devices are combined with other microsensor devices, such as accelerometers, magnetometers, and gyroscopes, more accurate measures of the physical demands and activity profiles of sports can be made (248). Variables such as collisions (93), metabolic power (85, 204), and accelerometer load (119) can be determined. In addition, the accumulated mechanical stress on the athlete, such as body load, can be calculated from several metrics by taking the vector magnitude of accelerations, decelerations, changes in direction, and impacts (248). Impacts from running,

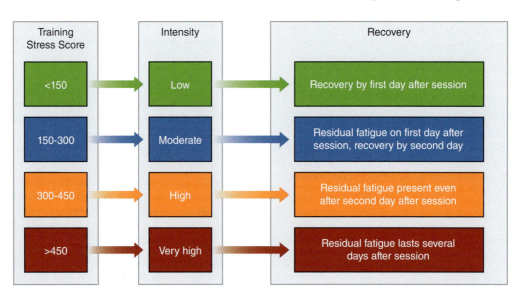

FIGURE 11.2 Training Stress Score and recovery.
Adapted from Allen and Coggan (2010).

TABLE 11.3 GPS Measurements of Training Load

Measure	Description
Total distance covered	Total meters covered
High-speed running distance	≥13.1-15.0 km · h^{-1}
Very high–speed running distance	≥16.9-19.8 km · h^{-1}
Accelerometer-derived load	Player load[a] and body load[b]
Impacts	>2.0-5.0 G

[a]summated zones; [b]vector magnitude calculations
Data from McGuigan (2017).

tackling, jumping, and colliding with other players are generally determined from the summed accelerations from three planes, including front–back, left–right, and up–down (231). This metric can then be categorized by impact zone, ranging from light to heavy (248).

Another metric of interest to coaches and athletes is the amount of high-speed running. For the most part, GPS devices are considered to reliably measure velocity, but as the velocity of movement increases they becomes less reliable (13, 166, 193). Additionally, there are large variations in estimates of change in velocity between GPS units from the same manufacturer (55). Several factors affect the ability of GPS units to quantify acceleration and the velocity of movement. For example, the unit's processing speed can exert a significant influence on the accuracy of measurement, with 10 Hz systems being three times more accurate than 5 Hz systems (362). Additionally, the location, antenna volume, and chipset capacity can affect the instantaneous measurement of velocity (340). Regardless of these issues, practitioners still use GPS devices to monitor time spent in specified velocity zones (340). There is currently no consensus on how to determine specific velocity zones or where to set the threshold for high-speed and very high–speed running. For example, in Australian football, sprint efforts have been defined as activity greater than 4.00 m · s^{-1} (338), and in soccer they are defined as activity greater than 5.50 m · s^{-1} (66). Although speed zones are generally categorized based on the sport being measured, McGuigan (248) suggests that high-speed running is generally defined as activity performed at speeds greater than 14.5 km · h^{-1} (>9 mi · h^{-1} or >4.0 m · s^{-1}) and very high–speed running occurs at speeds greater than 19.1 km · h^{-1} (>11.8 mi · h^{-1} or >5.3 m · s^{-1}). In addition to defining these speed thresholds, it is also common to align various movements with specific speed zones (see table 11.4). In addition to defining speed zones, repeated high-intensity running can be defined as three or more rapid accelerations (e.g., >2.78 m · s^{-1}), high speeds (e.g., >5 m · s^{-1}), or contacts interspersed with less than 21 seconds of recovery between efforts (12, 14, 124, 331).

Although GPS devices can be used with field-based team sports (13), they cannot be used with indoor court-based sports due to an inability to connect with satellites (340). To monitor indoor sports, technologies such as radio frequency–based local positioning systems, including the wireless ad hoc system for positioning, have been developed (107, 168). Generally, local positioning systems tend to have better accuracy compared to GPS as a result of sampling up to 1,000 Hz (332). Although these systems have limited accuracy for peak accelerations and decelerations, they can be used to quantify average changes in velocity or time spent in various acceleration zones. Regardless of the current limitations, local positioning systems are becoming important monitoring tools for indoor court-based sports, such as basketball (113, 377).

TABLE 11.4 General Classification of Speed Zones and Activities

Activity	km · h^{-1}	mi · h^{-1}	m · s^{-1}
Walking	<7.2	<4.5	<2.0
Jogging	7.2-12.9	4.5-8.0	2.0-3.5
Running	13.0-19.8	8.1-12.3	3.6-5.5
Sprinting	>19.8	>12.3	>5.5

Data from McGuigan (2017).

Neuromuscular Function

Measures of **neuromuscular function** are often incorporated into the monitoring programs of athletes (157) in team and individual sports because they are simple to administer and generate minimal fatigue. The two most common neuromuscular function tests are assessments of vertical jump (i.e., countermovement or squat jump) and assessments of isometric force–time curves (157, 278, 335, 354).

Vertical Jump Tests

Vertical jump tests are probably the most popular neuromuscular tests used as part of monitoring programs (343). These types of tests are particularly useful because they reflect stretch-shortening capabilities of the lower body and are considered good tools for evaluating muscular fatigue (212, 343). Common measurements that can be derived from vertical jump tests include jump height, flight time, flight time to contraction time (FT:CT) ratio, peak force, rate of force development (RFD), and impulse (73, 157, 253). The quantification of many of these variables requires the use of a force plate that allows force–time curves to be created and analyzed (253). Although historically force plates have been somewhat expensive and restricted to sport science facilities, these devices are becoming more readily available to coaches (27).

Although the quantification of vertical jump displacement likely yields little information about the athlete's current state of fatigue (81, 217), other metrics derived from the force–time curves collected during vertical jump tests can provide valuable information about the athlete's current state of preparedness. One particularly important variable quantified with a force plate is the FT:CT ratio (81, 82), which appears to be very reflective of the athlete's state of fatigue and may be the most useful countermovement vertical jump variable for assessing neuromuscular fatigue (81). Therefore, coaches may wish to incorporate daily pretraining vertical jump tests that quantify the FT:CT into their monitoring programs.

Several other variables, including the eccentric RFD, average concentric force, and the concentric vertical impulse, have been recommended as part of a comprehensive monitoring program (242). Typically, these measures are made around specific mesocycles (24) and can be used to guide the coach's programming decisions. For example, Mayberry and colleagues (242) suggest that training programs that include specific resistance-training exercises, such as the deadlift, can increase the average concentric force production during the vertical jump. Programs that include deadlifts and squats have been reported to improve the eccentric RFD, average concentric force production, and the concentric vertical impulse during countermovement vertical jumps. Collectively, these data support looking at these metrics around the various mesocycles, phases, and periods of the athlete's annual training plan.

One important aspect of monitoring vertical jump performance is that the data garnered from these simple tests can guide the prescription of training loads (209). For example, Kipp and colleagues (209) reported that artificial neural networks (ANN) can be used to effectively model the effect that changes in resistance training volume load have on jumping performance. Based on this type of advanced training load monitoring, it is possible that the coach may be able to better fine-tune the training process, which may result in a more effective optimization of performance during periods of congested competitions. Ultimately, the use of vertical jump monitoring data and machine learning are expanding areas of research, and much more research is needed to determine the most effective way to use this analysis.

Isometric Tests

Isometric testing allows for the generation of a **force–time curve** that yields a wealth of information about the athlete's neuromuscular function (51, 148). Based on this information, the coach can gauge the athlete's level of adaptation to the training process (50, 335) and determine the athlete's level of preparedness, both of which can inform the coach's decisions about which programming strategies to integrate into the training process. Because isometric testing is time efficient, safe to conduct, and generally not very fatiguing, integrating it into periodized sports-based monitoring programs has become common (140, 335).

The integration of isometric testing into a periodized monitoring program requires the use of a force plate (152), an isokinetic dynamometer (352), a load cell (109, 192), or a custom testing rack (153) to provide the information required for the quantification of the force–time curve characteristics of the specific isometric muscle action being tested (335). The most common quantified force–time curve characteristics include peak force, force at specific predetermined time points, and the RFD (234), which can be quantified with a variety of methods (figure 11.3) (148).

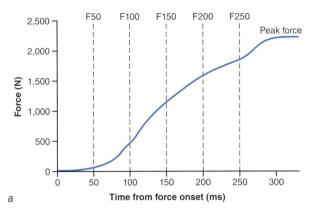
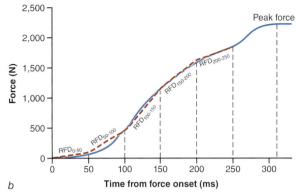

FIGURE 11.3 Example isometric midthigh pull force–time curve measures: *(a)* force measures; *(b)* RFD measures.

The RFD represents the rate at which force is developed and is calculated as follows:

$$\text{rate of force development } (N \cdot s^{-1}) = \frac{\Delta \text{ force (N)}}{\Delta \text{ time (s)}}$$

Typically, the RFD is quantified from the initial inflection point (0 ms) on the force–time curve to predetermined time points (e.g., 0-150 ms or 0-200 ms) (1, 148) or between predetermined time points along the force–time curve (e.g., 100-200 ms) (74, 148). Another popular RFD measure is the peak RFD (pRFD), which represents the steepest part of the force–time curve over a specific epoch. Typically, a 20 ms moving average is considered the most reliable epoch while still providing data sensitive to changes in training status and overall fatigue (152). When the noise-to-signal ratio is determined for the various RFD measurements, this variable can be diagnostic of the athlete's ever-changing state of preparedness (260) and can be reflective of the athlete's response to the training process (151). In addition to the quantification of the RFD, it is now common to quantify the impulse during the same predetermined time points to provide a time history of the contraction, including the influence of the RFD (1). Ultimately, the ability to analyze various components of the isometric force–time curve allows the coach to monitor various aspects of strength and to use these data to guide programming decisions.

In applied sport settings, the most common methods for collecting lower-body isometric force–time curves involve the performance of the **isometric midthigh pull (IMTP)** (figure 11.4*a*) or the **isometric squat (ISQT)** (figure 11.4*b*). Both isometric tests require a custom testing system that allows a stepwise adjustment of the isometric position coupled with a force platform (148, 153). In 1997, Haff and colleagues (153) were one of the first research groups to develop a specialized testing system specifically designed to test the IMTP and ISQT. This system allows a fixed bar made of cold-rolled steel to be adjusted to any position in a stepwise manner with the use of pins and hydraulic jacks (150). In addition, this system uses a single force plate to collect the isometric force–time curve characteristics of preselected positions. Specifically, the IMTP is performed at a position that corresponds to the second pull position of the snatch and clean, which corresponds to a body position in which the trunk is upright (141, 142, 153), the knee angle ranges between 120° and 150° (50), and the hip angle is between 124° and 175° (79). The ISQT is generally performed with an upright trunk position, a knee angle that ranges between 90° and 150° (50, 277), and a hip angle ranging from 110° and 140° (164,

FIGURE 11.4 *(a)* IMTP and *(b)* ISQT.

277). Considering that muscles display different levels of maximal isometric force depending on the length at which they are tested (137), it is critical that the positions used during these two isometric tests are standardized so that they can be replicated between trials and testing sessions. A lack of standardization of these methods can significantly affect the ability of these tests to be used as monitoring tools.

As this test has become more common, the testing system has been modified to incorporate two force platforms, allowing the quantification of force-production asymmetries (figure 11.5) (16, 17). It is generally believed that the ability to determine these force-production asymmetries can be related to sport performance (17) and injury prevention or rehabilitation (198). Regardless of the number of force plates used during the IMTP or ISQT, these simple neuromuscular performance tests are an important and useful part of any monitoring program.

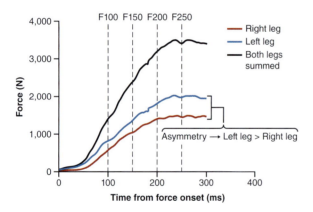

FIGURE 11.5 Example force–time curve asymmetry detection from IMTP test.

Conceptually, isometric tests can be integrated into a monitoring program to assess and provide feedback associated with fatigue management or program efficacy and adaptation (335). For example, Norris and colleagues (278) reported that the IMTP can be used to determine neuromuscular recovery rates after an Australian rules football match. An interesting finding of this work is that the RFD appears to be diagnostic of the rate of recovery for an athlete's neuromuscular performance capacity. Alternatively, Suarez and colleagues (337) report phase-specific changes in the RFD when weightlifters complete a sequential block model of periodization. Note, however, that there are numerous ways to integrate these tests into a monitoring program. Because isometric tests are simple to perform, produce minimal fatigue, and provide a wealth of diagnostic information about the athlete's force-generating capacities, they can be used as part of a monitoring program to assess the athlete's state of preparedness, current training status, and rate of recovery from both training and competition.

Training Volume

The volume of resistance training undertaken is often determined by summing the total number of repetitions completed in an exercise, during a training session, or within a training cycle (i.e., microcycle, mesocycle, macrocycle) (146), but this does not accurately represent the amount of work accomplished because it does not consider the effect of the load lifted on the work completed (146, 174). In fact, the number of repetitions rarely aligns with the amount of work completed during resistance training. For example, McCaulley and colleagues (244) reported that to complete $84.2 \text{ J} \times 10^{-3}$ of work, 37 repetitions need to be completed with 72.8% of 1RM or 33 repetitions need to be completed with 89.3% of 1RM. Based on these data, it is clear that the load lifted affects the amount of work completed, and it can be inferred that the load lifted must be included in the calculation of any measure or volume used to represent the amount of work during resistance training (146, 175, 336). The most common method for accomplishing this is to determine the volume load (146). The volume load concept has also been adapted for sprint training (34, 292).

Volume Load for Resistance Training

The workload associated with resistance training is commonly represented by the **volume load**, which is calculated by multiplying the total number of repetitions (i.e., sets × repetitions) by the load lifted (146). There are two methods for calculating the volume load: the first uses the load lifted, and the second uses a percentage of a defined repetition maximum (RM) (146, 322).

The following equation is used with the load lifted:

volume load (lb or kg) = # of sets × # of repetitions × load lifted (lb or kg)

For example, if an athlete performs the back squat for 3 sets of 10 repetitions with 100 kg, volume load would be calculated as follows:

$$3 \times 10 \times 100 \text{ kg} = 3{,}000 \text{ kg}$$

In the second method for calculating volume load, the number of repetitions is multiplied by the percentage of RM:

$$\text{volume load (A.U.)} = \text{\# of sets} \times \text{\# of repetitions} \times \text{load lifted (\% of RM)}$$

Another way to conceptualize this equation is to consider the percentage as a factor of 100 kg. For example, if the athlete lifted a load that corresponded to 67% of their maximal capacity, the load lifted would be represented as 67 kg. Therefore, if the athlete performed the back squat for 3 sets of 10 repetitions with this load, volume load would be calculated as follows:

$$3 \times 10 \times 67 \text{ kg} = 2{,}010 \text{ kg}$$

When comparing both methods of calculating volume load, note that they yield very different volume load estimates. From a monitoring perspective, using the actual load lifted in the volume load equation gives a much more accurate representation of the workload.

One potential issue with the volume load equations is that they do not typically account for the distance traveled during the exercise (146, 174, 175). As a result, the volume load estimate may result in an under- or overestimation of the amount of work performed, depending on the exercise. One solution suggested by Verkhoshansky and Siff (364) is to correct volume load to account for the displacement during the exercise using a correction coefficient (table 11.5). For example, if an athlete performs the full back squat for 3 sets of 10 repetitions with 130 kg, they complete a volume load of 3,900 kg (table 11.6).

TABLE 11.5 Displacement Correction Coefficients for Weightlifting

Exercise	Correction for total work
Bench press	0.56 × athlete's height (m)
Clean pull	0.50 × athlete's height (m)
Full squat	0.60 × athlete's height (m)
Good morning	0.52 × athlete's height (m)
Half squat	0.37 × athlete's height (m)
Jerk	0.60 × athlete's height (m)
Power clean	0.69 × athlete's height (m)
Snatch pull	0.59 × athlete's height (m)
Split clean	0.77 × athlete's height (m)
Split snatch	0.89 × athlete's height (m)

Adapted by permission from Y. Verkhoshansky and M.C. Siff, *Supertraining* (Rome, Italy: Verkhoshansky, 2009), 330.

If the same number of repetitions is completed for the half squat, the volume load would be identical even though the distance traveled during this exercise is far less than a full squat. If the volume load were corrected for displacement of the barbell during the half squat, much less work would be performed (volume load = 2,540 kg) during the half squat when compared to the full squat (volume load = 4,118 kg). An alternative approach to determining the displacement of movement during a given resistance training exercise is to use a linear position transducer to directly measure each athlete's displacement of movement during training, but this practice is not practical for most training environments. Therefore, it is generally recommended to use the basic volume load metric or correct it with the coefficients (174, 175).

TABLE 11.6 Example Volume Load Calculations

Exercise	Sets	Repetitions	Load (kg)	Correction coefficient	Athlete's height (m)	Volume load (kg)	Corrected volume load (kg)
Squat clean	3	10	100	1.26	1.76	3,000	6,653
Power clean	3	10	100	0.69	1.76	3,000	3,643
Full back squat	3	10	130	0.60	1.76	3,900	4,118
Half back squat	3	10	130	0.37	1.76	3,900	2,540
Full back squat	3	10	130	0.60	1.76	3,900	4,118
Half back squat	3	10	200	0.37	1.76	6,000	3,907

Note: Corrected volume load = volume load × correction coefficient × height (m).

Regardless of how it is determined, volume load is typically represented as the total number of kilograms (or pounds) lifted. An alternative approach to representing the workload encountered during resistance training is to convert the volume load to a **metric ton**, which is equivalent to 1,000 kg (2,205 lb) (35, 146):

$$\text{metric ton} = \frac{\text{volume load (kg)}}{1{,}000 \text{ kg}}$$

or a **short ton**, which is equal to 1,102.3 kg (2,430.1 lb) (35, 146):

$$\text{short ton} = \frac{\text{volume load (kg)}}{1{,}102.3 \text{ kg}}$$

The total volume of the training session would then be represented by the sum of all the volume loads for each exercise in the session (table 11.7).

The volume load of each training session can be used to graphically represent each day's training load and the total workload for each microcycle (figure 11.6). These graphics show the coach how resistance training load varies between training days and microcycles. Ultimately, there are infinite ways volume load can be presented graphically, but the key is to create an easy to understand and interpret visual representation of training load.

Volume Load for Sprint Training

Although volume load is commonly used to determine the workload encountered during resistance training, a similar calculation can be made for sprint training (34, 292). Specifically, when the coach is trying to determine the volume load for speed, speed–endurance, or agility, the intensity of the movement, which is represented as the speed of movement, must be quantified as follows:

TABLE 11.7 Example Volume Load Calculation for a Training Session

Exercise	Sets	Repetitions	Load (kg)	Total repetitions	Volume load (kg)	Metric ton (kg)
Back squat	3	10	150	30	4,500	4.50
Power clean	3	10	90	30	2,700	2.70
Quarter back squat	3	10	220	30	6,600	6.60
Behind neck press	3	10	65	30	1,950	1.95
Total				120	15,750	15.75

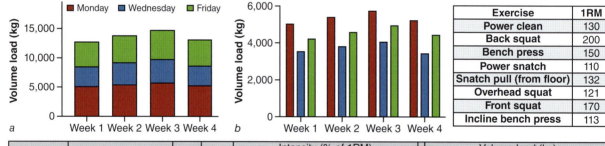

Day	Exercise	Sets	Reps	Intensity (% of 1RM)				Volume load (kg)			
				Week 1	Week 2	Week 3	Week 4	Week 1	Week 2	Week 3	Week 4
Monday	Power clean	5	3	70	75	80	73	1,365	1,463	1,560	1,424
	Back squat	3	5	70	75	80	73	2,100	2,250	2,400	2,190
	Bench press	3	5	70	75	80	73	1,575	1,688	1,800	1,643
	Volume load (kg) =							5,040	5,401	5,760	5,257
Wednesday	Power snatch	5	3	65	70	75	63	1,073	1,155	1,238	1,040
	Overhead squat	3	5	65	70	75	63	1,180	1,271	1,361	1,143
	Snatch pull (from floor)	3	5	65	70	75	63	1,287	1,386	1,485	1,247
	Volume load (kg) =							3,540	3,812	4,084	3,430
Friday	Power clean	5	3	60	65	70	63	1,170	1,268	1,365	1,229
	Front squat	3	5	60	65	70	63	1,530	1,658	1,785	1,607
	Incline bench press	3	5	60	65	70	63	1,530	1,658	1,785	1,607
	Volume load (kg) =							4,230	4,584	4,935	4,443

Note: Volume loads are calculated based on the number of sets and repetitions and the load (kg).
Load is based on the athlete's 1RM for each exercise.

FIGURE 11.6 Presentation of volume load for a mesocycle (*a*) and microcycle (*b*).

$$\text{intensity (m} \cdot \text{s}^{-1}) = \frac{\text{distance (m)}}{\text{time (s)}}$$

For example, if an athlete runs 200 m in 30 seconds, the intensity would be 6.67 m · s⁻¹. Based on this information, the coach could calculate the volume load using the calculated intensity and the distance covered:

$$\text{volume load} = \text{distance (m)} \times \text{intensity (m} \cdot \text{s}^{-1})$$

Because this athlete ran 200 m with an average intensity of 6.67 m · s⁻¹, the volume load for this sprint would be 1,334 m² · s⁻¹. As with the volume load metric used for resistance training, the coach sums all the individual sprint volume loads to calculate the volume load for the training session.

Volume Load to Calculate Monotony and Strain

Once the coach has calculated the volume load for the training session, they can calculate monotony and strain, which can provide valuable information about the athlete's training (table 11.8) (110). The total training load can be calculated for the microcycle (i.e., typically 7 days) by summing the volume loads for each training session during the defined training period (285). Based on these data, **training monotony**, which represents the variation of session training load over the microcycle, can be calculated by dividing the microcycle's mean volume load by its standard deviation (249, 285)

$$\text{monotony (A.U.)} = \frac{\text{mean volume load}}{\text{standard deviation}}$$

If there is little variation in the day-to-day training load, which is represented by a low standard deviation, the monotony of training would be high (248). Conversely, if there is a large degree of variation in training load across the microcycle, the standard deviation will be greater.

The second metric that can be calculated is **training strain**, which represents the product of training loads and the degree of training monotony. This metric is calculated by multiplying the

TABLE 11.8 Volume Load, Monotony, and Strain Calculation for Resistance Training

Day	Session	Volume load (kg)	Daily average (kg)
Monday	a.m.	4,500	4,000
	p.m.	3,500	
Tuesday	a.m.	3,000	3,000
	p.m.		
Wednesday	a.m.	4,200	3,600
	p.m.	3,000	
Thursday	a.m.	2,500	2,500
	p.m.		
Friday	a.m.	4,400	3,700
	p.m.	3,000	
Saturday	a.m.	4,000	4,000
	p.m.		
Sunday	a.m.		
	p.m.		
Total weekly volume load (kg)		32,100.0000	
Daily mean load (kg)		3,466.6667	
Daily standard deviation (kg)		598.8879	
Monotony		5.7885	
Strain		185,811	

Note: The total weekly volume load (kg) is the sum of all the session volume loads. The daily mean (kg) is calculated by taking the average of all the daily averages, and the standard deviation of those daily averages is represented as the daily standard deviation. Monotony is calculated as daily mean load divided by the daily standard deviation. Strain is calculated as total weekly load multiplied by monotony.

microcycle's total volume load by the monotony score (110, 248).

$$\text{strain (A.U.)} = \text{monotony} \times \text{total volume load}$$

If the athlete is exposed to training periods with a high degree of monotony coupled with high degrees of strain, there is an increased risk of illness and injury (110, 285, 297). By monitoring volume load, monotony, and strain over a period of time, the coach will be able to develop individualized external load thresholds that could be indicative of overreaching or overtraining (248). Additionally, by using machine learning or artificial intelligence techniques, the coach may be better able to forecast where to adjust training loads to ensure the athlete continues to progress at the expected rate.

Methods for Monitoring Internal Training Load

Although it is important to quantify external loads, these measures may not provide an accurate picture of how the athlete is responding to the prescribed training or competitive engagements (248). Therefore, it has generally been recommended that monitoring programs should include methods for quantifying both external and internal training loads (184). There are numerous ways to quantify the athlete's internal training load, ranging from measuring the athlete's perceived effort to quantifying physiological responses to the external loads that the athlete completes.

Perceived Exertion

The perception of effort is commonly used to quantify an athlete's training load and can be used as a method for determining exercise intensity (40, 105, 322). Conceptually, the use of the RPE is based on the belief that an athlete can monitor their psychological stress during exercise and retrospectively quantify their perceived effort after training or competition (157). Based on the available literature, the RPE seems to be well-correlated with heart rate during steady-state exercise and high-intensity interval cycling (230), but it is not as well-correlated with heart rate during high-intensity exercise, such as soccer drills (46, 228). Classically, the most common methods for quantifying RPE are the use of the Borg 6-20 scale (37) or the Borg CR-10 scale (where CR stands for category-ratio) (41).

While the CR-10 scale is a popular measure of perceived exertion, the Foster 0-10 scale is more commonly used when quantifying RPE as part of a monitoring program, especially when determining the session RPE (sRPE) (105). The Foster 0-10 scale does not have the same number range or descriptors as the CR-10 scale originally presented by Borg (41). Specifically, the original Borg CR-10 scale included fractions between 0 and 1 (i.e., 0.5) (39), and later versions of Borg's CR-10 scale included fractions between 0 and 3 (i.e., 0.3, 0.5, 1.5, 2.5) and extended the original range above 10 (i.e., 11, 12) (38). Although Foster's 0-10 scale is based on the original CR-10 scale, it has different numerical and psychometric properties (figure 11.7) (105, 112).

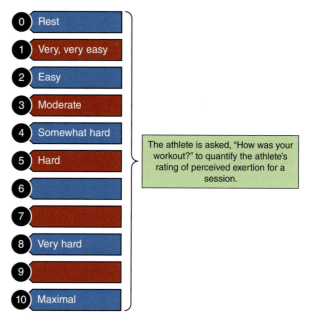

FIGURE 11.7 Foster's 0-10 RPE scale.

Adapted by permission from C. Foster, J.A. Florhaug, J. Franklin, et al., "A New Approach to Monitoring Exercise Training," *The Journal of Strength and Conditioning Research* 15, no. 1 (2001): 111.

Although the CR-10 and the Foster scales are often used with resistance training, researchers have presented data that suggest that these scales do not adequately discriminate intensity during this type of exercise (144, 295, 324). To address these issues, several attempts have been made to modify these scales to better align with the requirements of resistance training performed to failure (figure 11.8) (144, 384).

In this RPE method, the numerical scale is modified and the descriptors are related to the number of repetitions from a maximum effort (i.e., failure) (384). Although this method is interesting, as with other RPE scales, there is a learning curve and a

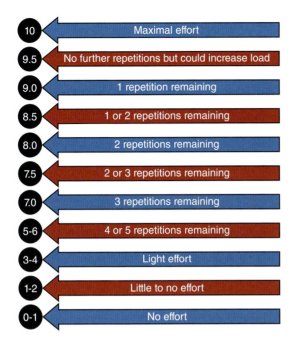

FIGURE 11.8 Resistance training–specific RPE scale.
Adapted from Zourdos, Klemp, Dolan, et al. (2016).

lack of precision in the measurement depending on the athlete's training experience (384) and the number of repetitions away from failure (383). Resistance training to failure has been consistently shown to be a less effective resistance-training loading paradigm (see chapter 13 for more detail) (69, 70), so this method of quantifying training load is questionable at best.

Session Rating of Perceived Exertion

The most common method for quantifying internal training load is the quantification of the sRPE (105). This monitoring method asks the question "How was your workout?", which is then related to a number that corresponds to a descriptor (figure 11.7) (110). Although there are many ways to ask this question, the ultimate goal is to obtain the athlete's global rating of the session (248). Based on the athlete's rating and the duration of the training session, a session load can be calculated using the following equation (111, 112):

$$\text{session load (A.U.)} = \text{session duration (min)} \times \text{session RPE}$$

If, for example, the athlete completes a 70-minute training session and rates the session as being hard (i.e., RPE = 5), the session load would be equivalent to 350 A.U. McGuigan (248) suggests that in team sports, sessions typically range from 300 to 500 A.U. for a low-intensity session and from 700 to 1,000 A.U. for a high-intensity session. However, note that the training load for a given session largely depends on the type of training session completed.

One of the main benefits of quantifying the sRPE is that it can be used with any type of training and allows for every training activity to be quantified on the same scale (249). As such, the coach can quantify the athlete's internal training load for each session, training day, microcycle, and mesocycle (figure 11.9).

To increase the reliability and validity of the sRPE, it must be collected using standardized instructions and anchoring to ensure that the athlete is familiar with the scale (248). Because the sRPE is used to quantify the entire session, it should not be taken immediately following the training session (325) so the last training activity, whether hard or easy, does not exert too large an effect on the rating (110, 325). Classically, it was recommended that the sRPE should be taken 30 minutes after the completion of the session, but several studies have demonstrated that the sRPE can accurately be assessed 10 minutes after the completion of a session and yield a valid and reliable measure of training load (170, 216, 325, 356). Therefore, it is generally accepted that if the sRPE is collected 10 to 15 minutes posttraining, the coach can be assured that a valid measure has been collected (248).

Another use for the sRPE is to guide the prescription of training loads. The sRPE allows the coach to align training with training intensity zones (248). For example, Moreira and colleagues (261) suggest three intensity zones that can be used to prescribe training: low (<4.0 A.U.), moderate (4.0-7.0 A.U.), and high (≥7.0 A.U.). There can be a disconnect between what the coach intends the sRPE to be and how the athlete actually perceives the training session (288). To ensure better alignment between the coach and athlete's sRPE, the coach must regularly examine the athlete's sRPE and improve communication with their athletes. Based on the available evidence, creating open lines of communication has the greatest potential to improve the alignment between the coach's and athlete's sRPEs (288).

As with the volume load, the training load determined based on sRPE can be used to calculate daily and weekly training loads as well as monotony and strain (table 11.9) (110, 249). These metrics provide the coach with valuable information about the athlete's internal load and can be used to track how the athlete is progressing (110). When analyzing these data, the first step is to sum the individual training session loads for each day and then determine

FIGURE 11.9 Example microcycle training load calculated with sRPE.

the daily mean load (i.e., mean of the sessions undertaken). The second step is to determine the standard deviation of the daily mean loads, which can then be used to determine training monotony (i.e., daily mean load divided by standard deviation) (248). The third step is to determine the strain for the microcycle by multiplying the total training load for the microcycle by the monotony score (249). When monotony and strain are both high, the athlete is at a greater risk of illness and injury (80, 110, 297). In fact, Comyns and Hannon (80) suggest that as part of a monitoring program, sRPE is an important tool for minimizing injury risk and maximizing adaptations to the training process.

Heart Rate

A wide range of technologies are available for monitoring athletes. Classically, heart rate (HR) monitors used a chest strap that transmitted wirelessly to a wrist display, but newer devices, such as wristbands or watches, use optical sensors to measure HR directly at the wrist (227). It is commonly accepted that monitors that use a chest strap are more accurate and valid (274, 344).

HR is one of the most common methods for quantifying an athlete's internal training load (157). In fact, Akenhead and Nassis (4) reported that 98% of the professional soccer clubs they surveyed collect HR data from every player at every training session. The basic premise behind HR monitoring during exercise is that there is a linear relationship between HR and the rate of oxygen consumption over a wide range of steady-state exercise (46, 84, 172). Although it is generally accepted that HR can be accurately monitored during exercise, there may be limitations when using this method to monitor exercise intensity in intermittent sports; HR may not accurately reflect the intensity during the brief intense efforts common in these sports (84). Additionally, factors such as the athlete's current state of training, environmental conditions, hydration status, diurnal effects, and medication can all affect the relationship between HR and workload (46). When these factors are appropriately controlled, the accuracy of HR monitoring during exercise can be improved (195, 220).

Heart Rate to RPE Ratio

Another method for garnering information about an athlete's state of fatigue is to examine physiological and perceptual indicators of load during exercise with fixed submaximal loads (157). One way to examine this is to look at the HR:RPE ratio,

TABLE 11.9 Example Training Load, Monotony, and Strain Calculation for a Microcycle for a Professional Mixed Marital Arts Fighter

Day	Type of training	Time of day	Duration (min)	RPE	Session load	Daily average load
Monday	Grappling/BJJ Long-interval HIIT	1100-1300	120	3-5	360-600	420-660
	Strength and conditioning Heavy resistance training	1600-1800	120	4-6	480-720	
Tuesday	Wrestling Technical drilling and long-interval HIIT	1100-1300	120	4-6	480-720	540-780
	Muay Thai/striking Explosive speed and max power, short-interval HIIT	1600-1800	120	5-7	600-840	
Wednesday	MMA sparring Explosive speed and max power, short-interval HIIT	1600-1800	120	8-10	960-1,200	960-1,200
Thursday	Muay Thai/striking Speed/high-tempo striking and short-interval HIIT	1100-1300	120	3-4	360-480	480-660
	Wrestling Anaerobic capacity and lactate tolerance work	1600-1800	120	5-7	600-840	
Friday	Grappling/BJJ Technical drilling and long-interval HIIT	1100-1300	120	2-5	240-600	300-540
	Strength and conditioning Power emphasis Resistance training	1600-1800	120	3-4	360-480	
Saturday	MMA sparring Repeat intervals and lactate tolerance work	1600-1800	120	9-10	1,080-1,200	1,080-1,200
Sunday	Off					
Total weekly volume load						5,520-7,680
Daily mean load						630-840
Daily standard deviation						288.998-314.643
Monotony						2.002-2.907
Strain						11,053-22,323

Note: The total weekly volume load is the sum of all the session loads. The daily mean load is the average of the daily averages, and the standard deviation of those daily averages is represented as the daily standard deviation. Monotony is determined by dividing the daily mean load by the daily standard deviation. The total weekly volume load multiplied by the monotony yields the strain score.

Adapted from D. French, "Combat Sports," in *Science and Application of High-Intensity Interval Training*, edited by P.B. Laursen and M. Buchheit (Champaign, IL: Human Kinetics, 2019), 244.

which has been suggested to be useful in elucidating fatigue (240). Martin and Andersen (240) suggest that the HR:RPE ratio may be an important source of information about the magnitude of training-induced overload, especially when used to examine high-intensity interval training. For example, a lack of change in the HR:RPE ratio over the course of a high-intensity training program may be indicative of the training plan not providing enough overload, which ultimately will result in suboptimal performances. Additionally, if the HR:RPE ratio is reduced as a result of a reduced submaximal HR and an elevated RPE, the internal load may be different when compared to a normal HR:RPE ratio (298). Ultimately, monitoring the HR:RPE ratio is a simple and inexpensive way to garner information about the athlete's internal load and how they are responding to the training regime.

Heart Rate Recovery

It may be useful to implement monitoring activities after the cessation of exercise to gauge the athlete's rate of recovery and training status (221, 283). One popular monitoring method employed during this time is the quantification of **heart rate recovery (HRR)**, which represents the rate at which HR declines after the cessation of exercise. The postexercise HR response is governed by the **autonomic nervous system (ANS)**, specifically parasympathetic activation and sympathetic withdrawal (44, 95, 221). During the postexercise recovery period, there is coordinated interaction between parasympathetic reactivation and sympathetic withdrawal, with parasympathetic reactivation exerting a greater effect on the early reductions in HR (44). Slower HRR may be indicative of fatigue, detraining, or an inability to cope with the training load (44), whereas faster HRR is likely indicative of improvements in fitness and the ability to tolerate training (43, 95). Changes to HRR may also be indicative of overreaching (44), but these findings are not consistent within the literature (247).

Many methods may be used to quantify postexercise HRR, ranging from determining the number of beats completed during a given time period (e.g., 60 s or HRR_{60s}) to signal modeling via linear or monoexponential models (53, 56). Although limited data directly compare time period HRR, Buchheit (53) suggests that monoexponential modeling may provide the best representation of the overall HR response by reflecting the initial fast component of recovery and the delayed recovery phase. In practice, simple HRR variables, such as the HRR_{60s}, have been reported to correlate with changes in endurance performance (95). Although HRR is often suggested as a method for tracking positive changes to high-intensity exercise performance (53), several studies have reported inconsistent relationships between HRR and changes in performance (57, 58).

There are several issues related to the use of HRR that the coach must understand when deciding to use this monitoring tool. First, it is somewhat impractical to use HRR as a daily monitoring tool because it requires a standardized exercise performance test (247). Second, these types of tests tend to have high magnitudes of technical error (221, 351). If the coach decides to use this monitoring tool, it is essential that the chosen procedures are standardized and consistently performed to increase the utility of the test.

Heart Rate Variability

The quantification of resting or postexercise **heart rate variability (HRV)** is one of the most promising methods for monitoring an athlete's adaptation to training (56, 58, 167, 291). In fact, reductions in vagal-related indices of HRV are generally associated with negative adaptive responses to training or nonfunctional overreaching (47, 180, 181). Conversely, increases in vagal-related indices of HRV are thought to be related to elevated fitness (223, 267, 368) and improved performance (10, 58, 126). Although these data seem to indicate that examining HRV is useful for monitoring endurance training adaptations, data on HRV obtained from elite endurance athletes or endurance athletes with extensive training histories are equivocal (54, 182, 235, 284, 294). Additionally, there is a lack of clear association between changes in HRV and performance after strength and HIIT training (321, 347). Alternatively, HRV does seem sensitive to changes in training loads in team sports, such as Australian rules football (57) or team handball (290). Some of the lack of consistency in the findings regarding the utility of HRV measures may be a function of the analysis methods employed.

Fundamentally, HRV is a measure of the normal beat-to-beat intervals, represented as the R-R interval on an **electrocardiogram (ECG)** (44). It is likely that using both weekly and 7-day rolling averages will result in greater validity when compared to single-day measurements (291). Although various HRV measures can be made, the squared difference between the R-R intervals (Ln rMSSD) is generally the preferred method of analysis (53, 157, 291). This analysis method has a higher level of reliability when compared to other indices and is not influenced by breathing frequency, and the data can be collected over short sampling periods (e.g., 60 s) (157). As with all monitoring tools, it is important to longitudinally monitor athletes to understand individual HRV responses to programming strategies such as overreaching, normal training, tapering, and competition.

Although historically the ability to monitor HRV was limited by access to an ECG and specialized analysis software, smartphones and smartwatches can now perform this analysis (100). To effectively measure HRV indices, such as Ln rMSSD, the athlete must lie in a supine position to collect a 10- to 60-second sample of data that is then analyzed with custom software or a spreadsheet (53, 247). It is important to establish a baseline of typical HRV values taken during consistent conditions, such as when the athlete wakes up. Additionally, to increase the effectiveness of this monitoring tool, many assessment points are required to garner a complete understanding of how the athlete responds to various training loads (247). It is generally recommended that HRV is quantified for a minimum of 3 days per week (291). These data points can be analyzed in several ways, including determining a weekly average or using a 7-day rolling average (291). This type of data must be collected consistently over the long term to create a more effective picture of the athlete's individual responses. Finally, when interpreting HRV data, they should be contextualized to the athlete's training history and the structure of the current training phase and collected in combination with psychometric and noninvasive performance markers to effectively monitor the athlete response to the prescribed training (53).

Training Impulse

The quantification of **training impulse (TRIMP)** is a useful method for assessing training load (46, 298) because it represents the total training load imposed on the athlete during the bout of exercise (22, 61). Based on a systems approach that integrates all the components of training into a single factor, this mathematical model of training can be used to describe and estimate the effect of the athlete's training on their performance (45, 46). Conceptually, TRIMP is based on the assumption that physical effort can be quantified based on the athlete's HR response to exercise (266). To calculate TRIMP, the coach must know the athlete's maximal, resting, and average HRs during the session (157, 266, 300). If these are known, TRIMP can be calculated with the following equations:

$$\text{female: TRIMP} = \text{duration} \times \frac{HR_{ex} - HR_{rest}}{HR_{max} - HR_{rest}} \times 0.86e^{1.67x}$$

$$\text{male: TRIMP} = \text{duration} \times \frac{HR_{ex} - HR_{rest}}{HR_{max} - HR_{rest}} \times 0.64e^{1.92x}$$

where

$$e = 2.712$$

$$x = \frac{HR_{ex} - HR_{rest}}{HR_{max} - HR_{rest}}$$

HR_{rest} = average HR during rest

HR_{ex} = average HR during exercise

HR_{max} = maximal HR (45, 46)

Consider a female athlete who completes a 70-minute training session during which her average HR is 145 beats · min^{-1}. If her resting HR is 50 beats · min^{-1} and her maximum HR is 180 beats · min^{-1}, the TRIMP for her session would be calculated as follows:

$$\text{TRIMP} = 70 \times \frac{145 - 50}{180 - 50} \times 0.86e^{1.67x}$$

$$\text{TRIMP} = 70 \times 0.731 \times 0.86 \times 2.712^{(1.67 \times 0.731)}$$

$$\text{TRIMP} = 70 \times 0.731 \times 0.86 \times 3.380 = 148.7$$

An alternative TRIMP approach is the Edwards' method, which is determined by accumulated time in one of five HR zones (zone 1 = 50%-60% of HR_{peak}, zone 2 = 60%-70% of HR_{peak}, zone 3 = 70%-80% of HR_{peak}, zone 4 = 80%-90% of HR_{peak}, zone 5 = 90%-100% of HR_{peak}) multiplied by a weighting factor (45, 103, 300). Based on the time spent in each zone, TRIMP would be calculated as follows:

$$\text{TRIMP} = (\text{duration 1} \times 1) + (\text{duration 2} \times 2) + (\text{duration 3} \times 3) + (\text{duration 4} \times 4) + (\text{duration 5} \times 5)$$

For example, let's say a female athlete completes a 90-minute training session, spending 10 minutes in zone 1, 15 minutes in zone 2, 45 minutes in zone 3, 15 minutes in zone 4, and 5 minutes in zone 5. TRIMP would be calculated as follows:

$$\text{TRIMP} = (10 \times 1) + (15 \times 2) + (45 \times 3) + (15 \times 4) + (5 \times 5) = 260$$

Although this method of determining TRIMP is commonly used, it has some limitations due to the range of HRs within each intensity zone and that fact that small changes in HR can greatly affect the determined training load (45). Borresen and Lambert (45) examined the relationship between this method and sRPE and determined that the Edwards' TRIMP overestimated training loads when athletes spent the majority of their time performing high-intensity or low-intensity activities.

A similar alternative method was developed by Lucia and colleagues (232). The main difference between Lucia's TRIMP and Edwards' TRIMP is that with Lucia's there are only three HR zones based on individually determined lactate thresholds and the onset of blood lactate (157, 233). This concept has resulted in the development of an individualized TRIMP (iTRIMP) for runners (236) and soccer players (6). A key benefit of the iTRIMP is that it reduces the issues that have been previously noted with the use of arbitrary intensity zones and generic weighting factors while better relating to changes in intensity of exercise (6). It is important to note that creating individualized internal load monitoring methods like these takes technical and scientific expertise that may not always be available to coaches and athletes (157).

Lactate

Lactate is sensitive to changes in exercise intensity and duration (28), which might make it a useful measurement as part of a monitoring program (282). For example, as part of a monitoring program in swimming, Olbrecht (282) suggests that monitoring lactate can give insight into the activation and contributions of the aerobic and anaerobic energy systems and give information about the performance of both systems when contextualized with swimming speed.

There are a number of potential limitations for regularly using lactate monitoring (157). Specifically, Halson (157) highlights that inter- and intraindividual differences in lactate accumulation can be affected by several external factors, such as ambient temperature, hydration status, mode of exercise, exercise duration, exercise intensity and rate of exercise intensity change, prior exercise, dietary practices, and muscle glycogen content (191, 339). Additionally, improvements in training status or the occurrence of overtraining have both been associated with reductions in maximal and submaximal lactate concentrations (194, 359), which can lead to erroneous interpretations of lactate measurements when they are used for monitoring practices (339).

One way lactate can be used as a monitoring tool is to create a lactate-to-RPE ratio (329). It has been hypothesized that this ratio may be indicative of an athlete's degree of tiredness or state of overreaching or overtraining (329). Basically, during normal training, the athlete's lactate concentration would be greater than the ratings of perceived exertion, resulting in the ratio of these variables (multiplied by 100) being greater than 100. Conversely, if the athlete is undergoing intensive training, blood lactate concentration can be reduced and the RPE stays the same, resulting in the ratio of these two variables being less than 100. Data supporting this concept were presented by Snyder and colleagues (329), who reported that after 1 week of overtraining there was a 29.1%±3.0% decline in the lactate to RPE ratio, and by 2 weeks of overtraining there was a 48.7%±2.5% decline. Note that similar reductions in this ratio were noted for all workloads greater than 250 W, with significant reductions being associated with maximal workloads (329). In fact, all subjects in the Synder and colleagues (329) study demonstrated a decrease in the lactate-to-RPE ratio at maximal workloads after the completion of an intensive period of interval training (i.e., overreaching). Conversely, after the athletes undertook a 2-week period of recovery training, the ratio elevated and was more reflective of what is seen during periods of normal training. Based on these data, it is evident that the lactate-to-RPE ratio is reflective of changes in the intensity and workload of the training period.

Because this ratio can reflect changes in training intensity and workload and be easily determined by performing fixed loading testing, it might be useful for determining changes in internal load (157, 329). With the increased availability of portable lactate analyzers, this test can be implemented in field-based settings, providing information to the coach within or shortly after a training session (20, 329).

Biochemical, Hormonal, and Immunological Assessments

Much research has examined a range of biochemical, hormonal, and immunological responses to monitor fatigue and minimize the occurrence of excessive fatigue and illness (157). Although the assessment of these factors with blood or saliva analyses can give insight into an athlete's overall health and response to the training process, there are potential limitations associated with these methods. For example, since the causes of fatigue are multifactorial, it is well-accepted that there is no single biochemical, hormonal, or immunological measure that can give definitive insight into the athlete's response to the training process. Additionally, these measures are often expensive, time-consuming, and difficult to undertake in the applied sporting environment (354). Due to these potential limitations, the coach must understand some of the basic measures associated with these assessments and think carefully about whether monitoring biochemical, hormonal, or immunological factors adds value to the monitoring program. A comprehensive review of the literature in this area is well outside the scope of this chapter, but the following sections will highlight some key aspects of these monitoring tools.

Biochemical Assessments

A variety of biochemical measures have been used to evaluate how an athlete is responding to the training process (370). Many are analyzed with blood assays (247). Some of the more common biochemical markers analyzed as part of a monitoring program include creatine kinase, glutamine, and glutamate, as well as several blood parameters (blood count, C-reactive protein, erythrocyte sedimentation rate, urea, creatinine, liver enzymes, ferritin, sodium, and potassium). Although many of these measures are not capable of detecting incidents of overreaching or overtraining, they can provide useful information about the athlete's health status and therefore may be useful in an exclusion diagnosis (255).

Creatine Kinase Athletes exposed to eccentric or unaccustomed exercise show an increase in circulating levels of **creatine kinase (CK)**, an increase that can last for several days to up to a little over a week (357). Although this marker of muscular damage can give insight into the amount of muscular or metabolic strain experienced by the athlete, it is not suitable for determining overreaching or overtraining (255, 358). Athletes exposed to intensified training can show significant increases in CK. For example, Coutts and colleagues (86) reported significant elevations in CK in rugby league players following a 6-week period of overreaching. When training load was reduced during the taper, CK levels returned to baseline, which lends support to the idea that CK levels are reflective of changes in training load. CK levels are also strongly correlated with the number of collisions a player makes in training or competition (251, 252, 355).

Although CK can be used to assess an athlete's level of muscle damage, there is a large amount of individual variability (165), as indicated by high day-to-day variation (coefficient for variation = 27%) (354). Additionally, there is not always a clear relationship between CK levels and performance, so interpretation of these results must be done with caution (247). Although CK is responsive to acute increases in training load (370), its response to long-term training is less clear within the scientific literature, most likely due to the athlete's increased training capacities (52).

Glutamine and Glutamate **Glutamine** and **glutamate** may also be useful markers of internal training load that are responsive to changes in training loads (86). For example, during periods of intensified training, a reduction in plasma glutamine and an elevation of plasma glutamate reduces the glutamine-to-glutamate ratio, which is indicative of suboptimal training adaptations (86, 354). In fact, reductions in this ratio are often found in overreached athletes, where decreases in glutamine are associated with a deteriorated work capacity (138, 326) and an impaired immune system (86, 160, 374), whereas elevations in glutamate are reflective of excessive training stress (183). However, not all studies have reported altered glutamate (86, 160) and glutamine concentrations in athletes who are overreached (86, 160, 374), and other authors have suggested that the glutamine-to-glutamate ratio is a sensitive indicator of nonfunctional overreaching (83, 326). Therefore, measuring glutamine and glutamate may be warranted as part of a comprehensive monitoring program.

Hormonal Assessments

For decades it has been hypothesized that changes in hormones, such as testosterone, cortisol, and the testosterone:cortisol (T:C) ratio, are indicative of the athlete's state of preparedness. Therefore, these hormones are the most commonly monitored ones.

Testosterone **Testosterone** is an **anabolic** hormone that is essential for promoting protein synthesis, red blood cell production, and glycogen replenishment and reducing protein breakdown (224). Even though resting testosterone levels are highly individualized and can vary greatly across a competitive season (224), some researchers have suggested that testosterone may be a useful marker of the athlete's level of preparedness due to its relationship with performance (62, 89, 151, 156). For example, Gaviglio and colleagues (129) have suggested that pregame testosterone levels may be useful for determining the preparedness level of athletes contesting rugby union games. Specifically, pregame testosterone levels are significantly correlated with game ranked outcome (i.e., 1 = bad loss, 2 = unlucky loss, 3 = draw, 4 = average win, 5 = good win, and 6 = good win +) and tend to be significantly ($p < .01$) higher when the team is victorious. These findings are not unexpected, as it is well-documented that resting testosterone levels are linked to psychological aspects of motivation (90) and the expression of maximal power and short-distance speed (91). The relationship of resting testosterone to performance outcome is not only present in team sports but is also documented in individual sports (36, 104, 130, 280, 310). Based on these data, it may be warranted to include assessments of resting testosterone levels as part of a comprehensive monitoring program that seeks to determine the athlete's current state of preparedness. Although the quantification of testosterone is typically performed with blood samples, the ability to quantify testosterone with salivary samples makes the quantification of testosterone less invasive and more practical (136).

Cortisol Cortisol, a glucocorticoid, is released from the adrenal cortex in response to stress (e.g., environmental, psychological, physical) (115, 215, 369). Its production and release are stimulated by **adrenocorticotropic hormone (ACTH)** release from the anterior pituitary (197). Cortisol is often considered a primary stress or catabolic hormone, because it plays an important role in the mobilization of fuel substrates, gluconeogenesis, and immunosuppression (269). Cortisol is also believed to play a role in postexercise tissue remodeling (215). Specifically, muscle protein content is partially regulated by cortisol via the inhibition of muscle protein synthesis (96, 169) and the stimulation of protein degradation (11, 169). Although these catabolic effects affect all skeletal muscle fiber types, they are generally magnified in type II muscle fibers (i.e., fast twitch) (214), which may exert a significant effect on sporting activities that require rapid force production.

The degree to which cortisol is released in response to exercise is modulated by the metabolic demands of the physical exercise. Specifically, duration and intensity play a significant role in regulating the amount of cortisol released (115, 357). For example, aerobic exercise performed above 60% of $\dot{V}O_2$max and anaerobic exercise can produce marked increases in cortisol concentrations (207). In fact, high-volume resistance training can stimulate marked increases in cortisol (213), especially when large mass exercises are performed (254). These elevations can remain elevated for several hours after the completion of an exercise bout (81, 254). For example, team sport athletes, such as Australian football rules players, can display marked increases in cortisol concentrations immediately postmatch (effect size [ES] = 4.05 ± 1.09, 60.8%), 24-hours postmatch (ES = 4.59 ± 1.28, 71.4%), 72-hours postmatch (ES = 1.72 ± 1.34, 22.3%), and 120-hours postmatch (ES = 0.70 ± 10.48, 8.6%) (81). Ultimately, acute cortisol responses are reflective of metabolic stress, whereas chronic responses are more related to tissue homeostasis involving protein metabolism (108).

Cortisol concentrations have also been suggested as being reflective of long-term training stress (214) and have been reported to be elevated when athletes are overtrained (116, 333, 360). Chronic elevations in cortisol may be indicative of a reduced capacity to recover from training, an impaired capacity for protein synthesis, or the occurrence of overreaching or overtraining (72, 224, 342, 366, 367). In fact, Vervoorn and colleagues (366, 367) have reported that cortisol responses to training appear to be mediated by training volume, with greater training volumes corresponding to greater increases in cortisol concentrations. Similarly, Haff and colleagues (151) reported higher cortisol levels in response to higher-volume loads of training during an 11-week training period in elite female weightlifters. Collectively, these studies suggest that cortisol is reflective of training stress and may be a good indicator of an athlete's internal training load.

Due to this relationship, quantifying cortisol levels is an attractive hormonal measure to include in a monitoring program. Although blood measures of cortisol may not be practical, the ability to use salivary samples makes this measure more practical (136, 287).

Testosterone:Cortisol Ratio Because the testosterone:cortisol (T:C) ratio is responsive to changes in training load, it has historically been associated with overreaching and overtraining (2). In fact, the resting T:C ratio has been suggested to be indicative of overall training stress (2, 117) and may represent an approximation of the anabolic to catabolic status of the athlete (2, 334). Generally, when there are increases in training load (i.e., volume load), there are reductions in this ratio (2, 117, 151, 154). Reductions in the T:C ratio are often related to impairments in neuromuscular performance characteristics (155), which are reflective of the athlete's current level of preparedness (151). Therefore, several authors have suggested that monitoring the T:C ratio is an effective way to gauge the athlete's current level of preparedness (2, 36, 151, 243, 367, 371).

A reduction in the T:C ratio of greater than 30% has often been associated with insufficient recovery (2, 21, 357) and been indicative of reductions in the athlete's overall level of preparedness (151,

367). Although it may be debated whether this level of reduction in the T:C ratio is indicative of overtraining, there is ample evidence that decreases in this ratio greater than 30% are related to reductions in performance capacity, especially in activities requiring the expression of high forces or power outputs (151). Therefore, it is generally accepted that monitoring the resting T:C ratio can provide valuable information about the athlete's level of preparedness.

Immunological Assessments

Athletes exposed to excessive training loads can show a suppression of innate and adaptive immunity (135, 255). When athletes are exposed to long-term training periods, a depressed immunity is often noted, especially after periods of intensified training or competition (18, 60, 131-133). Although numerous markers of immune function can be quantified, the most commonly assessed are immunoglobulin A and the cytokines (247).

Immunoglobulin A Found in the mucosal membranes, immunoglobulin A (IgA) represents the first line of defense against viruses and bacteria (65). Several studies have reported that reduced levels of salivary IgA are associated with an increased occurrence of upper respiratory tract infections (URTIs) (94, 134, 258, 276, 302). For example, Neville and colleagues (276) reported a significant reduction in salivary IgA concentrations 3 weeks prior to the occurrence of an URTI. Conversely, 2 weeks after the occurrence of an URTI, salivary IgA levels typically return to baseline.

Interestingly, there appears to be a dose–response relationship between training load and salivary IgA levels (302), with periods of higher training loads being associated with lower IgA levels (76, 77, 106). For example, Coad and colleagues (76) reported that salivary IgA levels are affected by the variation of the in-season Australian Football League match-to-match workloads, with prolonged suppression of salivary IgA lasting greater than 36 hours postmatch depending on the workload encountered. Similarly, Fahlman and Engels (106) reported that the harder the training schedule of American football players, the greater the reductions in salivary IgA and the greater the occurrence of URTIs.

Based on our current understanding about the relationships between training load, salivary IgA levels, and the incidence of illness, it may be warranted to include longitudinal salivary IgA monitoring throughout the competition period of the annual training plan (76). Data garnered from the longitudinal monitoring of salivary IgA levels may also provide insight into workload management decisions, so when significant reductions in salivary IgA are noted, alterations to training loads can be made prior to the occurrence of an illness (239).

Cytokines Several proinflammatory cytokines, including interleukin-6 (IL-6), interleukin-1β (IL-1β), and tumor necrosis factor alpha (TNF-α), have been suggested to be related to systemic inflammation, which has been postulated to be an underlying factor contributing to the occurrence of overtraining (327, 328). Conceptually, when athletes engage in periods of intensive training or competition and there is insufficient time allocated for rest and recovery within their periodized training plan, an acute inflammatory response can occur. In some situations, this response can evolve into chronic inflammation, which can result in systemic inflammatory responses (328). When this occurs, there is an activation of circulating monocytes that stimulate an increase in IL-1β, IL-6, and TNF-α. As these cytokines are increasingly released into the bloodstream, they can access the central nervous system and stimulate specific brain areas, causing depression, loss of appetite, and sleep disturbances, which are commonly associated with overtraining (327, 328). In addition to these responses, cytokines can also stimulate liver cells to reduce the production of certain molecules, such as albumin, and increase the production of other molecules, such as C-reactive protein, to regulate the recovery process. Cytokines also appear to activate the sympathetic nervous system and hypothalamic-pituitary-adrenal axis while concurrently suppressing the activity of the hypothalamic-pituitary-gonadal axis in order to regulate the levels of catecholamines, glucocorticoids, and gonadal hormones within the bloodstream (327, 328). Additionally, immunosuppression can occur in response to the anti-inflammatory factors that accompany the proinflammatory responses that occur in response to systemic inflammation associated with overtraining.

Although monitoring cytokines can be a very informative way to evaluate an athlete's internal load, it is likely that the costs and time-consuming nature of these types of analyses make integrating them into an athlete monitoring program impractical for most athletes (350).

Questionnaires and Diaries

One of the simplest and least expensive methods for monitoring training load is the use of questionnaires and diaries. Both methods rely on the athlete entering subjective information that will need to be corroborated with physiological data (46, 157). Although this method of monitoring has many positives, its main weakness is that it relies on the athlete's subjective responses (172), and these responses may not accurately reflect what the athlete did in training (42). For, example, it is possible that some athletes will attempt to manipulate the data to influence the outcomes of the monitoring program by either over- or underreporting the training load that they have completed, which can affect the coach's interpretation of their training loads.

It is important to consider several factors before implementing questionnaires. For example, the frequency of this type of monitoring and the length of the questionnaire lead to "questionnaire fatigue" (157). Commonly used questionnaires in high-performance sports programs (343) include the Profile of Mood States (POMS) (263), the Brunel Mood Scale (BRUMS) (345, 346), the Recovery–Stress Questionnaire for Athletes (RESTQ-Sport) (202), the Acute Recovery and Stress Scale (ARSS) (210), Daily Analysis of Life Demands for Athletes (DALDA) questionnaire (307), and the Total Quality Recovery (TQR) scale (205).

Profile of Mood States

The POMS is a questionnaire that quantifies an athlete's mood disturbances. It examines six mood states: tension, depression, anger, vigor, fatigue, and confusion (200). To assess these, the athlete completes a 65-item questionnaire in which they rate each item on a 5-point Likert scale from 0 (not at all) to 4 (extremely) (225, 226). Based on the athlete's responses, a global score is calculated by adding the ratings of five negative mood states and subtracting the rating of the one positive mood state (i.e., vigor). Because a negative score is possible, it is generally recommended to add a constant of 100 to the calculated score (263). The POMS is relatively easy to administer, especially when the short version is used, and is highly reliable (29, 226). Additionally, it is often listed as a possible tool for the early identification of overtraining (29).

A seminal study by Morgan and colleagues (263) examined the mood fluctuations of swimmers across a competitive season. Initially, these athletes displayed what is referred to as the *iceberg profile,* which is indicative of a mentally healthy state (263, 264). When these athletes became overtrained, a greater number of mood disturbances were noted, resulting in a profile more reflective of reduced mental health (263). After a period of reduced training load, the swimmers' profiles returned to the iceberg state. Fluctuations in mood state have been reported to be related to changes in training load, with greater mood state disturbances being noted during periods of intensified training and reductions in disturbances occurring when training loads are reduced (200, 263). This dose–response relationship has been verified in several different sports, including swimming (262, 265), speed skating (143), wrestling (263), rowing (201, 301), running (380), cycling (30) and soccer (71).

Brunel Mood Scale

The BRUMS questionnaire is an alternative method for quantifying an athlete's mood state. This questionnaire was developed from the POMS to provide a more rapid assessment of mood states in adolescents and adults (345, 346). This 24-item questionnaire uses the same 5-point Likert scale as the POMS and can be completed in 1 to 2 minutes, which makes it particularly useful in an athlete monitoring program (222). The ability to complete this questionnaire quickly makes it an ideal assessment for quantifying an athlete's current mood state as part of a more comprehensive monitoring program.

Recovery–Stress Questionnaire for Athletes (RESTQ-Sport)

The RESTQ-Sport is one of the few questionnaires that has attempted to address the full complexities associated with stress and recovery (200, 202, 273). It is one of the most widely used questionnaires in athlete monitoring programs (318, 343). This questionnaire is composed of 76 questions subdivided into 19 scales (203) (table 11.10).

Seven of the scales relate to general stress, five relate to general recovery, three relate to stress in sport, and four relate to recovery in sport (248). The athlete rates each item with a Likert scale from 0 (never) to 6 (always). The sums of responses to the 10 stress and 9 recovery scales are determined, and a difference score can also be calculated (248). Note that the relationship between stress and recovery scores is not symmetrical, and they should not be combined (200, 202, 273). It is recommended that the results be presented as a longitudinal graph to represent a recovery–stress profile.

The RESTQ-Sport has been reported to be sensitive to acute and chronic training loads, with one stress (i.e., fatigue) and three recovery (i.e., physical recovery, general well-being, and being in

TABLE 11.10 RESTQ-Sport Scale

Scale	Descriptor	Scale summary
1	General stress	Subjects with high values describe themselves as being frequently mentally stressed, depressed, unbalanced, and listless
2	Emotional stress	Subjects with high values experience frequent irritation, aggression, anxiety, and inhibition
3	Social stress	High values match subjects with frequent arguments, fights, irritation concerning others, general upset, and lack of humor
4	Conflicts and pressure	High values are reached if, in the preceding few days, conflicts were unsettled, unpleasant things had to be done, goals could not be reached, and certain thoughts could not be dismissed
5	Fatigue	Time pressure in job, training, school, and life; being constantly disturbed during important work; overfatigue; and lack of sleep characterize this area of stress
6	Lack of energy	This scale matches ineffective work behavior, such as inability to concentrate and lack of energy and decision making
7	Physical complaints	Physical indisposition and physical complaints related to the whole body are characterized by this scale
8	Success	Success, pleasure at work, and creativity during the past few days are assessed in this area
9	Social recovery	High values are shown by athletes who have frequent pleasurable social contacts and change combined with relaxation and amusement
10	Physical recovery	Physical recovery, physical well-being, and fitness are characterized in this area
11	General well-being	Beside frequent good moods and high well-being, general relaxation and contentment are also in this scale
12	Sleep quality	Enough recovering sleep, an absence of sleeping disorders while falling asleep, and sleeping through the night characterize recovery sleep
13	Disturbed breaks	This scale deals with recovery deficits, interrupted recovery, and situational aspects that get in the way during periods of rest (e.g., teammates, coaches)
14	Burnout or emotional exhaustion	High scores are shown by athletes who feel burned out and want to quit their sport
15	Fitness and injury	High scores signal an acute injury or vulnerability to injuries
16	Fitness and being in shape	Athletes with high scores describe themselves as fit, physically efficient, and vital
17	Burnout and personal accomplishment	High scores are reached by athletes who feel integrated in their team, communicate well with their teammates, and enjoy their sport
18	Self-efficacy	This scale is characterized by how convinced the athlete is that they have trained well and are optimally prepared
19	Self-regulation	The use of mental skills for athletes to prepare, push, motivate, and set goals for themselves are assessed by this scale

Reprinted by permission from M. Kellmann and K.W. Kallus, *Recovery-Stress Questionnaire for Athletes: User Manual* (Champaign, IL: Human Kinetics, 2001), 6-7.

shape) subscales being responsive to fluctuations in training loads (318). Although the subscales can be collapsed into a single score for both stress and recovery, note that the information provided is different than what can be garnered from examining the individual subscales (248, 318). Therefore, it is often recommended that coaches consider monitoring changes in the overall score as well as the subscale scores when using this questionnaire as part of a comprehensive monitoring program.

Although the RESTQ-Sport has been found to be a useful monitoring tool, one of the main complaints is that it is time-consuming (210, 343). As such, it is generally recommended that the original RESTQ-Sport only be used as a weekly monitoring tool (210, 248).

Acute Recovery and Stress Scale

The ARSS questionnaire has 32 adjectives summarized into four stress and four recovery scales that represent physical, emotional, mental, and overall dimensions (210, 211, 272). The four stress and four recovery scales include the following eight categories:

1. Physical performance capabilities
2. Mental performance capabilities
3. Emotional balance
4. Overall recovery
5. Muscular stress
6. Lack of activation
7. Emotional imbalance
8. Overall stress (211)

Each item is rated using a Likert scale from 0 (does not apply at all) to 6 (fully applies) to indicate the extent that it applies to the athlete right now (211). The questionnaire has been found valid and reliable and highly correlated with the scores obtained with the RESTQ-Sport (211, 272). The ARSS can be performed quickly and is easily applied as a daily monitoring tool in high-performance sport settings (211).

Daily Analysis of Life Demands for Athletes

Another method for assessing an athlete's psychological well-being and response to training is the two-part DALDA questionnaire (307). This questionnaire assesses the athlete's daily level of stress. The athlete marks each item as worse than normal, normal, or better than normal. The total number of each response is recorded for each part of the questionnaire.

Part A is used to assess the general stress sources in the athlete's daily life (diet, home life, school or work, friends, training, climate, sleep, recreation, and health) and determine which aspects are particularly stressful. Because performance can deteriorate due to increased general stress, this analysis can provide information about possible causes of poor performances in training and competition (307). Part B is used to determine the athlete's stress-reaction symptoms. The overall number and pattern of negative responses on this part of the questionnaire can be used to determine whether the athlete is being negatively affected by life stressors. If the athlete is unable to cope with life stressors, there will be an increased number of "worse than normal" responses to the items in part B (307).

The DALDA can be used repeatedly throughout the annual training plan and can be easily scored and analyzed to provide a consistent, frequent analysis of the athlete's stress reactions. These data are generally graphed to provide a visual representation of the athlete's ability to cope with training and stress (248, 307). If there are marked increases in the total number of "worse than normal" responses in either part of the questionnaire, the coach can take corrective actions to prevent more serious negative states from occurring (307). Note that this questionnaire is designed for tracking individual athletes over time and not for comparing athletes.

Total Quality Recovery (TQR) Scale

Although many methods can be used to measure the training process, few can be linked directly with the recovery process. The TQR scale emphasizes the athlete's perception of recovery and the importance of countermeasures designed to improve recovery (205). The athlete rates their recovery over the previous 24 hours by answering two questions: "How does it feel?" and "What have you done?" These questions are used to examine daily activities and recovery perceptions, respectively (273). The TQR scale can be used to differentiate between the cause and the consequence of stress, as well as the source and magnitude of the stressors reflected in recovery.

The two scales used are the TQR perceived (TQR_{per}) scale and the TQR action (TQR_{act}) scale (205). The TQR_{per} is adapted from the Borg 6-20 RPE scale (38), and the anchor numbers have been aligned with perceptions of recovery. This scale ranges from no recovery at all (6) to maximal recovery (20). When using the TQR_{act} the athlete collects points based on their nutrition (10 points), sleep and rest (4 points), relaxation and emotional support (3 points), and stretching and cooldown (3 points) over a 24-hour period. A total of 20 points is considered optimal recovery (273). The minimum level of recovery is indicated by a score of 13, and scores below 13 are indicative of incomplete or underrecovery (205).

Ideally, this process would be used to match physical recovery with physical stress and psychological recovery with somatic recovery methods (e.g., social support) (205). Practically speaking, the TQR_{per} and TQR_{act} should be equal to the actual training stress (i.e., RPE rating). This is of particular importance because when training is intensified, the recovery process is believed to be accelerated by the integration of proactive recovery strategies (205). In fact, implementing proactive recovery strategies is generally believed to be more effective than passive rest at restoring the athlete's work capacity (see chapter 9). Even when lower training intensities are undertaken, a minimum level of recovery (TQR_{act} = 13) is required to ensure that the athlete is able to tolerate the prescribed training loads (205).

Another consideration is that the TQR_{per} and TQR_{act} can be compared. If, for example, the athlete has been engaged in a structured recovery plan, an early warning sign that there is an imbalance between training and recovery can be indicated by comparing the TQR_{per} rating to the TQR_{act} score (205). By comparing these two scales, the coach might be able to garner a better understanding of the balance between training and recovery and better modulate training loads and guide the training process.

Sleep

Sleep deprivation can significantly affect performance, motivation, perception of effort, cognition, and numerous biological functions (118, 158). Halson (158) suggests that monitoring sleep quality and quantity can be an important tool in the early detection of significant decrements in performance or health status. For example, the use of sleep diaries and ratings of perceived sleep quality have been used as monitoring tools (67). Although these tools are valuable, biases may exist related to recall, social desirability, and expectations (299) when these tools are integrated into a monitoring program (159). As such, it is often recommended that sleep diaries be used only in conjunction with activity monitoring (159).

The gold standard for providing useful information about the amount and quality of sleep is laboratory-based polysomnography (PSG), but this method is expensive and, for the most part, not practical for applied settings, such as a sport monitoring program (8, 259). The most widely accepted alternative to PSG is actigraphy (97), which requires a small device typically worn on the wrist and uses accelerometer-based technologies to monitor sleep and wake behavior (303). Although actigraphy is more practical than PSG, it may not always be readily available to athletes and coaches.

Recently, technological advances have increased the availability of commercial-grade sleep monitoring devices, such as armbands, rings, and smartphones. These devices have contributed to the increased inclusion of sleep monitoring in many monitoring programs (161, 259). Although some of these devices are reported to be able to provide information about four-stage detection of sleep (i.e., wake, light sleep, slow-wave sleep, and rapid eye movement) based on several metrics including movement detection, HR, HRV, skin conductance, and skin temperature (97, 98, 259), very few have been validated against PSG (97, 98, 323).

Commercial-grade devices can be broadly classified as **wearables** (i.e., worn by athlete) or **nearables** (i.e., placed near the athlete), which have their own distinct advantages and disadvantages (figure 11.10) (159). The main advantages of both types of devices are that they are inexpensive and accessible to most athletes and coaches. When integrated into a monitoring program, they can provide information that can increase the athlete's understanding of their sleep patterns and facilitate conversations between athletes and staff about how to best optimize sleep as a recovery strategy. An additional advantage of wearables is that they can be worn for extended periods. The largest disadvantage of many of these devices is that they lack validation and can cause the athlete to experience increased stress and anxiety about sleep (159). Wearables generally tend to overestimate sleep, and little information is provided to sport scientists by the device's manufacturer about the algorithms used to monitor sleep. Two disadvantages of nearables are that they are not worn by the athlete and may contribute to increased screen time (159), which has often been associated with sleep disturbances (171). Understanding these factors can help the coach determine which method or combination of methods is most appropriate for monitoring the athlete's sleep (159).

Many commercial sleep technologies, as well as sleep diaries and questionnaires, are inexpensive, so these methods are more feasible for an applied sport setting. Due to the growing interest in sleep monitoring technology, it is likely there will be significant advancement in both technology and hardware used to evaluate an athlete's sleep (159). As noted by Professor Shona Halson (159), the increased use of sleep monitoring technologies has a great potential to positively or negatively affect behavior, thus requiring an increased research focus to examine the validity and reliability of these technologies.

Advantages	Method	Disadvantages
Inexpensive Accessible Increase sleep awareness Promote athlete-staff communication Can be worn for extended times May promote further evaluation	Commercial sleep technology: Wearables Fitbit Whoop Oura Ring	Lack of validation Little information on algorithms Likely overestimate sleep May cause stress and anxiety
Inexpensive Accessible Increase sleep awareness Promote athlete-staff communication May promote further evaluation	Commercial sleep technology: Nearables Beddit ResMed S+ Smartphone apps	Lack of validation Device not worn by athlete Apps may increase screen time May cause stress and anxiety
Inexpensive Accessible Provide information on sleep patterns May be more accurate than questionnaires	Sleep diaries Consensus Sleep Diary	Require compliance May be influenced by recall May be influenced by athlete burden
Inexpensive Accessible Provide information on sleep patterns, disorders, daytime sleepiness, and sleep hygiene Can provide behavior information	Sleep questionnaires Athlete Sleep Behavior Athlete Sleep Screening Epworth Sleepiness Scale	May be influenced by recall Lack of standardized data on athletes May be influenced by athlete burden

FIGURE 11.10 Advantages and disadvantages of common sleep monitoring tools.
Adapted from Halson (2019).

Implementing a Monitoring Program

When considering integrating a monitoring program into an athlete's annual training plan, remember that the training process is built on the foundation of superior organization (i.e., periodization) and the systems of training used must be grounded in sound training principles (314). As part of the training process, monitoring adds individual and situation-specific information that can be used to inform the coach's programming decisions (99), potentially predict future performances, and aid in the management of day-to-day training (314). Therefore, the coach must formalize the monitoring program so it contains several methods for evaluating internal and external training loads and performance benchmarking (335). Ideally, data garnered from the monitoring program should be collected longitudinally.

To implement a monitoring program, the coach must understand the various iterations of monitoring programs being used. Although there is no current consensus on the best monitoring practice, the available literature can help the coach make informed decisions about the contents and structure of their monitoring program.

Current Practices

Due to the rapid evolution in the technologies available to monitor internal and external training loads, there has been an increased interest in the investigation and use of monitoring practices in elite sport (4, 75, 317, 343, 353). Despite a growing body of scientific evidence linking effective monitoring practices with the enhancement of numerous aspects of sport performance, many athletes and coaches are still skeptical about the value of implementing monitoring strategies within a periodized annual plan (4, 59). Despite this skepticism, many sport teams implement structured monitoring programs (4, 343) to evaluate the effectiveness of the training process, prevent injuries, maintain performance capacity, and reduce the risk of overtraining (343).

Although it is difficult to quantify the exact monitoring practices within elite sport, several researchers have attempted to determine the best practice methods commonly used as part of a monitoring program (4, 317, 343). For example, Taylor and colleagues (343) surveyed 100 coaches or sport scientists to determine the current state of best practice in high-performance sport. Ninety-one percent of the 55 respondents reported that they had implemented some form of monitoring program. A variety of monitoring methods were reported, with self-report questionnaires (84% respondents) and practical tests of maximal neuromuscular performance (61% of respondents) being the most common. Additionally, GPS systems and accelerometry devices were also cited as important parts of monitoring programs (43%). It is important to point out, however, that this study examined a range of team and individual sports to garner a global understanding of common monitoring techniques in elite sport.

To obtain specific information about the monitoring practices used in professional soccer, Akenhead and Nassis (4) surveyed 41 soccer clubs from Europe, the United States, and Australia. Careful inspection of the data collected in this study revealed that during training, time-motion analysis, HR monitoring, accelerometers, RPE, and other subjective ratings were commonly used to quantify training loads. Additionally, almost all teams surveyed reported using GPS and HR monitors during training. This highlights the unquestionable importance of integrating technology into the monitoring process (353).

At present, there are numerous monitoring tools, including wearable devices that can sense sweat composition, hydration status, glucose or lactate levels, HR, and HRV. The increased use of wearable technologies to monitor individual training responses (63) has contributed to these devices consistently being ranked as one of the most important trends within exercise and sport science (348). As noted by Torres-Ronda and Schelling (353), the implementation of these technologies is often challenging, and it is imperative that research on the usefulness, specificity, validity, and reliability of these devices is used to inform the coach's decisions about if, how, and when to implement them into the overall monitoring program. Burgess (59) suggests that integrating technology into the monitoring process should occur only after there is a full understanding of what the output of the monitoring program represents and time has been taken to fully educate the athletes and coaches about the technology and the meaningfulness of the output.

Individualization of Methods

Monitoring is highly individualized regardless of the sport (157, 311). This is largely because individual athletes respond differently to specific training loads, and the training loads required to stimulate adaptations differ between athletes (157). Through individual monitoring, the coach can determine which athletes are not responding to the training program and potentially diagnose where there is a difference between the external and internal training loads.

Another important consideration that Professor Halson (157) highlights is that an individualized approach allows for the alignment of the internal load intended by the coach with the actual internal load displayed by the athlete. A good example of the potential misalignment of internal load response can be seen in the reported differences noted between the coach's intended session RPE and the athlete's actual session RPE (157, 373). For example, Wallace and colleagues (373) compared the athlete's and coach's perception of internal load during swim training. Interestingly, there was a trend for some athletes to report higher training intensities than the coach during training sessions intentionally designed to be easy. Conversely, some athletes tended to report lower intensities in response to sessions that the coach had intentionally designed to be difficult (373). Based on this example, it is easy to see that monitoring has a high degree of individualization that the coach must consider when developing a monitoring program.

Developing an effective monitoring program is a complex task that requires the coaching staff to design and implement a process based on the primary purpose of the monitoring program (349), the requirements of key stakeholders (e.g., athlete, coach, medical staff), and the available financial resources. Financial resources can often exert a large influence on what types of monitoring activities can be implemented. Regardless, all monitoring programs should be multifaceted and employ several monitoring activities simultaneously.

Most monitoring programs include multiple measures of external load, internal load, wellness, and neuromuscular fatigue (245, 246). The exact methods and number of monitoring activities integrated into the monitoring program will differ depending on the targeted sport. For example, in basketball, external load may be quantified with the use of triaxial accelerometers that determine mechanical load and time spent in predetermined mechanical load zones (9), whereas in weightlifting the external load is determined as the number of lifts completed within certain intensity bands and the volume load completed within the session (3). Although session RPE may be determined for both sports (87), internal load during basketball training may also be examined with several additional measures, including HR monitoring and the calculation of TRIMP or the classification of time spent in individual HR zones (9).

Ideally, multifaceted monitoring programs include evidence-based load-monitoring practices that align with the specific sporting environment (59). Additionally, decisions about what to include or how to implement the monitoring program must be based on several other considerations, such as coaching philosophy, player compliance, and available resources, which can influence the viability of any monitoring program.

Individual Versus Team Sports

Although numerous monitoring strategies can be employed as part of an integrated monitoring program, there are subtle differences in how these strategies can be used in individual and team sport settings. A central consideration when working with team sports, which is different than when working with individual sports, is that the coach is constantly balancing the global needs of the team with the individual performance demands placed on each athlete (149). Therefore, with team sport athletes, the coach needs to develop monitoring strategies that assess how similar training loads individually affect each player and how these responses relate to the whole team (45, 59). This becomes challenging because coaches may have to individually monitor numerous athletes (e.g., 90 players in a National Football League preseason) and compare their data to the team averages, norms, and benchmarks (59). Making this practice even more difficult is that it is common for coaches to employ a suite of load-monitoring strategies designed to quantify multiple external and internal training load metrics (59, 246). Ultimately, due to the volume of data, expert staffing and specific technologies might be required to effectively use the data to make informed decisions that affect the athlete's training process (59, 304).

Interpreting Results

The ability to analyze data collected as part of an athlete monitoring program often depends on the analytical skills of the coach, sport scientist, or data analyst (349). Many tools can be used to derive meaningful information from the collected data, which can then be translated into simple and effective feedback (349). For example, if resources are available, commercial athlete monitoring software can be used to effectively store, analyze, and present data (256). If financial resources are limited or there is a lack of buy-in from other members of the coaching staff, Microsoft Excel or RStudio software may be viable alternatives (349). Regardless of the tools available, several common methods are generally used to analyze monitoring data.

Assessing Meaningful Change

A central factor germane to any monitoring program is the ability to assess clinically or practically relevant changes (157, 311). One method that has gained in popularity is the use of magnitude-based inferences with reference to sport-specific thresholds (25, 26, 157, 199, 298). Although popular in sport science, there has been some debate about the efficacy of this method to determine meaningful change and whether it should be used (275, 308, 309, 376) when analyzing data collected in a monitoring program (199). It may be best to consider this method as a simple descriptive approach (199) and use confidence intervals when attempting to determine meaningful changes (376).

Other metrics that are useful in monitoring practices are determining the smallest worthwhile change (SWC) and the typical error of the estimate, which allow the coach to determine whether a change is meaningful (343) and whether a change requires the coach to take some action (157). Due to differences in the SWC and the varied reliability typically associated with many measurements, Twist and Highton (354) recommend avoiding arbitrary cut-offs, such as 5%, because they may fall within the boundaries of typical variation for a given measure. Therefore, the reliability (coefficient of variation = CV%) of each measurement must be determined to use the SWC more effectively in decision making. The SWC is based on the concepts of Cohen's *d* (349) and is calculated as 0.2 × the between-subject standard deviation (173). If a variable is capable of detecting the SWC using this method, the SWC must be greater than the typical error of the measurement tested (31).

Acute to Chronic Workload Ratio

When examining training load data, there are many ways cumulative load can be calculated, including determining the cumulative load for 7, 14, or 21 days (185, 349). Alternatively, rolling loads are often used in conjunction with the **acute to chronic workload ratio (ACWR)** to provide an indication of the athlete's **acute workload (AWL)** (e.g., 7 days) relative to their **chronic workload (CWL)** (e.g., 28 days), which is represented as a ratio score (177, 270). Although these windows are commonly used as part of many monitoring programs, it may be more appropriate to determine windows more reflective of the sport, training structure, and competition requirements (64). For example, in sports such as basketball that have more frequent competitions (i.e., >1 per week), a shorter acute period, such as 3 days, may be more appropriate (349).

Classically, the ACWR has been associated with injury risk (178, 179, 271) and is often suggested as a useful metric for reducing or preventing injury (123). The use of the ACWR has become so popular it has been the subject of numerous editorials (32, 49, 120, 123, 125, 293) and used as a foundational construct for the development of international guidelines and consensus statements for many organizations, such as the International Olympic Committee (330). Due to its popularity, it is also included in national athlete management systems and commercial monitoring software packages under the assumption that it will reduce the number of injuries within sport (190).

Adaptations to the ACWR have used different methods of calculating the AWL and CWL, including exponentially weighted moving averages (139, 270, 378, 379) and coupled or uncoupled ratios in which the AWL is included or not included in the ACWR calculation (88, 190, 379). However, as pointed out by Impellizzeri and colleagues (185), all these methods have the common characteristic of being a ratio, which can negatively affect the utility of the metric. Specifically, the ACWR should be used with caution because the ratio fails to normalize the numerator by the denominator and there is a significant risk of having unnecessary noise or artifacts in the measurement (229). These risks have largely been ignored within the sport science and training load monitoring literature (32, 49, 120, 123, 125, 139, 293, 349, 379) but must be considered when deciding how to interpret any monitoring data.

The limitations of the ACWR have become a topic of much debate within the scientific literature (185, 189, 190, 375). Impellizzeri and colleagues (185, 189) suggest that the body of evidence does not support the contention that the ACWR is strongly and consistently associated with injury. These authors systematically dismantled the "sweet spot" theory, based on the U-shaped model presented by Hulin and colleagues (178, 179), which was defined as an ACWR between 0.8 and 1.3 and was suggested to be indicative of the lowest injury risk. Based on these data, it has often been recommended to use only small changes in training load between microcycles (330), which fundamentally removes numerous powerful training strategies, such as functional overreaching and tapering for competition. Furthermore, Impellizzeri and colleagues (185) point out that the U-shaped relationship between the ACWR and injury risk that serves as the foundation for the sweet spot theory is not actually present in the work the theory is based on (178, 179). Ultimately, although many coaches, sport scientists, and consumer monitoring programs still use the ACWR as a method for reducing injury risk, this practice is not valid and should be discontinued.

Based on these data, the Australian Institute of Sport has taken the unprecedented step of releasing a bulletin that states that the ACWR should *not* be used as an indicator of injury risk (15). Based on the emerging evidence, Impellizzeri and colleagues (189, 190) suggest that the ACWR be dismissed as a framework and model and that coaches and sport scientists should return to applying core training principles (e.g., overload progression) and using training load, in conjunction with athlete feedback, to monitor whether the athlete is able to complete the planned load progressions.

Quantifying Trends

Although the use of trend analyses and regression analyses to predict future competitive performance is popular, these analyses have largely relied on competition data (314). Sands and colleagues (314) suggest that even though there has been an increased interest in the burgeoning area of sport analytics, there have been limited attempts to use monitoring and training data for predictive purposes. Informal predictions about how an athlete is progressing typically are made by the coach based on a mental model of what training loads the athlete should be able to handle and how they are performing with those loads (314).

Trend analyses may be useful when attempting to determine how an athlete is progressing toward their goals (314) and provide a projection of the level of performance that the athlete may attain at their current rate of gain. For example, a trend analysis could be used to project the performance level that an athlete would need to attain to be successful. This can be illustrated by looking at the trend of the Olympic men's super heavyweight gold medal performances for weightlifting between 1976 to 2021 (figure 11.11).

A linear trend is apparent based on the least-squares regression line presented on the graph. Based on this analysis, it appears that a super heavyweight weightlifter would need to lift at least 484 kg (1,067 lb) at the 2024 Olympics and 492 kg (1,085 lb) in the 2032 Olympics to win the gold medal. This information can help a coach establish important training goals for athletes who are contenders for the Olympic Games; based on this trend, the weightlifter would need to lift at least 484 kg (1,067 lb) to contend for a gold medal.

Trend analyses also can be useful for managing day-to-day training activities (314) or examining changes across several microcycles. Sands and colleagues (314) suggest that to best apply these methods to monitoring, the coach can use a split-middle analysis in which the median slope is determined because it is less sensitive to extreme scores (381). As explained by Wolery and Harris (381) and Sands and colleagues (314), the period of interest is divided in half and the median is determined for each half. After this is completed, a slope is determined connecting the two medians and the split-median line is then extended to reach the beginning and the end of the period of interest. Figure 11.12 shows split-middle trend analysis for the microcycle volume load in an Australian weightlifter's annual training plan.

In this example, an Australian weightlifter was required to compete in four competitions in her annual training plan. The first competition was the Australian Open, which was used to qualify for the state championships (competition 2) and the national championships (competition 3). The fourth competition was the commonwealth cham-

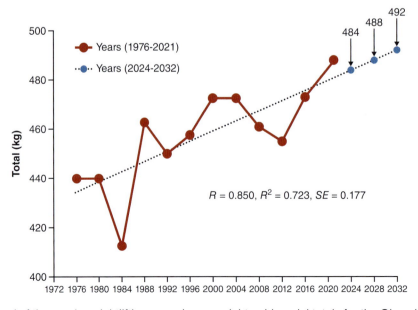

FIGURE 11.11 Trend of the men's weightlifting super heavyweight gold medal totals for the Olympic Games.

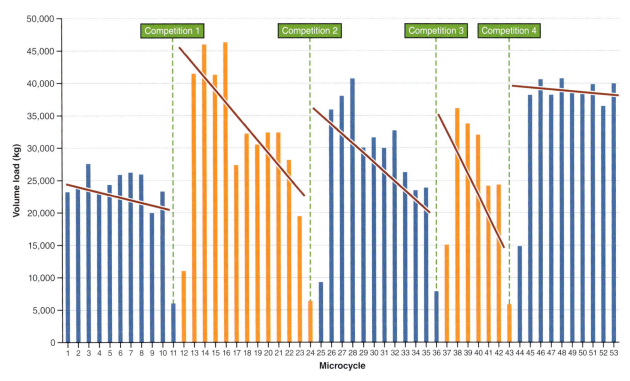

FIGURE 11.12 Split-middle trend analysis for microcycle volume load leading up to an international weightlifting competition.

pionships, her major international competition of the year. When looking at the trend lines, the slope for the time between competition 3 and competition 4 is very steep, which may be indicative of the athlete not being able to accumulate enough training load. This would put her at risk of not being prepared for the final competition of the annual plan. In fact, this athlete performed worse at competition 4 than she did at competition 3. It is easy to see from the split-middle analysis that there was a failure in planning and programming, and she was not adequately prepared for the commonwealth championships.

Trend analyses can be used to examine many factors in a monitoring system besides training load. For example, Sands and colleagues (314) present examples in which this technique was used to look at sleep quality trends, resting heart rate, and body mass relationships. Ultimately, the use of the split-middle technique is an easy-to-perform and informative method for analyzing monitoring data.

Rules-Based Training Management

Training management typically involves identifying unusual data that indicate shifts from normal or that confirm that training can proceed without hesitation or modification (312, 314). One strategy that can be used to evaluate changes in data values as the training program progresses is a **time-series analysis** (314, 316), which involves evaluating trends, detecting outliers, and establishing data behavior based on baselines or specific rules (314). The accurate quantification of the dose of training (i.e., external load) and the athlete's response to the dose (i.e., internal load) provide the data for the time-series analysis. In fact, the quantification of the training process is one of the most important elements of training methodology (279).

It is well-documented that athletes tend to respond to training stress in individualized ways (218, 219, 281, 314). For this reason, Sands and colleagues (314) suggest that group data is of little use because the individual dose responses are lost or obscured by the group. In fact, group means largely obscure the most important outcome of the monitoring program: what happened to each athlete (48, 208, 314).

One strategy used by Sands (313) was to incorporate an artificial intelligence (AI) approach to codify over 200 rules that were extracted from the literature on overtraining, the planning of training, and periodization theory. Based on these rules, data for individual athletes were presented as means and trends and then translated into a list of potential concerns that was used to guide the coach's decisions about the training process. Although this early incarnation of the use of AI was a brute-force method (314), more recent applications appear to offer a method for implementing rules-based monitoring strategies (68). The use of ANN appears ideally suited for analyzing the complex, nonlinear biological responses associated with training (68, 102, 196, 289). Recently, Carrard and colleagues (68) used ANN to separately model and graphically separate adaptation from maladaptation to the training process. As part of this study, they introduced the concept of the Geometric Activity Performance Index (GAPI) to examine adaptive and maladaptive responses. When the GAPI was based on the distance swum (i.e., external load) and the session RPE (i.e., internal load), it was highly related to the performance outcome. Based on these data, Carrard and colleagues (68) suggested that this technique may be useful when attempting to provide information about the training process from which the coach can make subtle modifications to optimize the performance outcome. Ultimately, the use of AI and ANN may be the future of rules-based monitoring strategies, but far more research is needed to develop these systems.

Traffic-Light Systems

When considering rules-based monitoring systems, one strategy that has increased in popularity is the use of traffic-light systems, which use color coding (i.e., green, amber, and red) to indicate the status of the athlete. These systems are used to inform and support decision-making processes (304). Robertson and colleagues (304) suggest that decisions often relate to the type and level of training delivered to the athlete or to the athlete's availability to participate in competition. A traffic-light system can be developed using subjective and objective data derived from the athlete and evidence from historical data. The data incorporated into these systems often include self-reported athlete wellness data (127), musculoskeletal screening scores (157), training loads (92), fitness and fatigue data (122), and physiological testing or benchmarking data (128). The traffic-light system via the alignment of color coding quickly provides information that can be used to adjust the training process to reduce the risk of overtraining, reduce the incidence of injury and illness, and optimize the athlete's overall performance level (304).

Monitoring Techniques and the Periodized Training Plan

When conceptualizing how a monitoring process is integrated into a periodized training plan, it helps to consider monitoring as a decision-support system that provides objective evidence to help the coach make informed decisions (304). Impellizzeri and colleagues (186) suggest that the first step in monitoring and controlling the training process is quantifying the external load, internal load, and training outcome (figure 11.13).

By assessing these three items, the coach can determine whether the external load has stimulated the planned psychophysiological responses (i.e., internal load) and whether these responses have translated into the expected adaptations (i.e., performance outcomes). Failure to meet these targeted responses can be used to guide the coach's decisions about how to fine-tune the training process (186).

Before determining if the prescribed training program is effective or ineffective, the coach must determine whether the athlete has completed the training program as planned (186). Impellizzeri and colleagues (186) suggest this second level of control centers on comparing the training loads completed by the athlete with training load standards planned by the coach (figure 11.14).

If the training load standards are met by the athlete, then training can continue as planned. Conversely, if the athlete fails to meet the standards, then corrective actions can be considered, but only after careful deliberation and attempts to understand why the standards were not met (186). Conceptually, the primary goals of the monitoring program are to determine whether the athlete is doing what is planned by the coach and how the athlete is coping with and tolerating the prescribed training program (186).

To optimize training, the coach can integrate monitoring activities into several different levels of the periodized training plan. Different monitoring strategies can be used at the various levels of the periodized training plan. Specifically, the coach must decide which strategies are used daily and at key time points within the annual training plan.

Training Day

Several monitoring strategies can be integrated into the athlete's daily training program to quantify

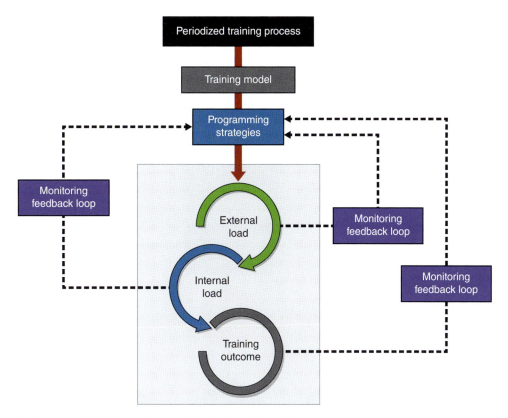

FIGURE 11.13 Framework for integrating monitoring into the training process.
Adapted from Impellizzeri, Menaspà, Coutts, et al. (2020).

internal and external training loads and current state of performance. When employing these strategies, the coach must ensure that the tools used do not unnecessarily burden the athlete and are easy to administer and interpret. An example of a daily monitoring process is presented in figure 11.15.

In this example, several monitoring strategies have been placed throughout the day to help the coach understand how the athlete is responding to the training process and to quantify the internal and external load achieved in each training session. Upon waking, the athlete records their resting HR, sleep duration, sleep quality, and morning body mass (157, 312, 315). These daily metrics allow the coach to examine the athlete's longitudinal response to the training process and potentially provide indicators of when maladaptive responses are occurring (315).

Prior to each training session, the athlete performs countermovement jump testing on a force plate to quantify the FT:CT ratio, peak force, RFD, and impulse (157). During session 1, resistance training, the duration of the session, total repetitions, average training intensity, and overall volume load will be quantified to determine the total external load the athlete completes within the training session. Additionally, the sRPE will be measured and used to quantify a measure of internal training load (sRPE × time[s]). During session 2, which is a HIIT run session, a series of external load metrics can be collected, including duration, pace, and distance covered above the V_{IFT} (peak velocity reached at the end of the 30-15 intermittent fitness test; see chapter 14). Additionally, several internal training load metrics can be collected, including sRPE and average and peak HR. The training loads determined based on sRPE for each training session will be used to determine the daily average training load and then used as part of the microcycle monitoring plan.

Microcycle

Although daily monitoring forms the foundation of the microcycle monitoring plan, additional strategies can be incorporated into this process. For example, McGuigan (245, 246) suggests that wellness and training distress questionnaires can be examined weekly to understand how the athlete is responding to the training process. Additionally, measures of performance, such as the IMTP or ISQT, can be measured weekly or fortnightly to

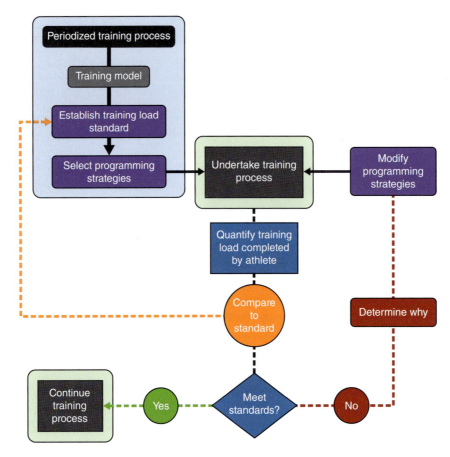

FIGURE 11.14 Monitoring-based decision-making process.
Adapted from Impellizzeri, Menaspà, Coutts, et al. (2020).

provide data that can be used to track the athlete's progress (151). An example of how one might place various monitoring activities into an individual microcycle is presented in figure 11.16.

In this example, each morning the athlete records their resting HR, sleep duration and sleep quality, and body mass. On Monday, the athlete completes an IMTP test from which force–time curve characteristics are analyzed and recorded so that they can be integrated into a longitudinal analysis of the athlete's performance capacities (151). On Wednesday and Saturday, the athlete completes a wellness questionnaire to assess overall wellness, muscle soreness, fatigue, and stress (245, 246).

The most important part of the microcycle monitoring process will be adding all the daily training loads together to determine the total training load accomplished during the microcycle. These data will also be used to calculate monotony and strain scores for the microcycle (see table 11.8, page 279). For most sports this is completed based on the sRPE data, but with strength sports such as weightlifting and powerlifting, the total training load can also be determined by summing the total volume load completed within the microcycle (286). Additionally, monotony and strain can be calculated based on the volume load data (285). In these sports, the training load determined based on sRPE can be used as the internal training load, and the volume load provides an external training load. Regardless of how the training load is calculated for each microcycle, it is important to remember that each individual microcycle training load will be used as part of the mesocycle monitoring process.

Mesocycle

The training loads completed within the mesocycle are a composite of the individual microcycles contained in the mesocycle (see chapter 4). Although direct daily monitoring and microcycle-specific monitoring practices are at the center of the monitoring plan, there are monitoring activities that can be placed strategically at key times during the mesocycle. For example, at the end of each mesocycle, some coaches implement performance

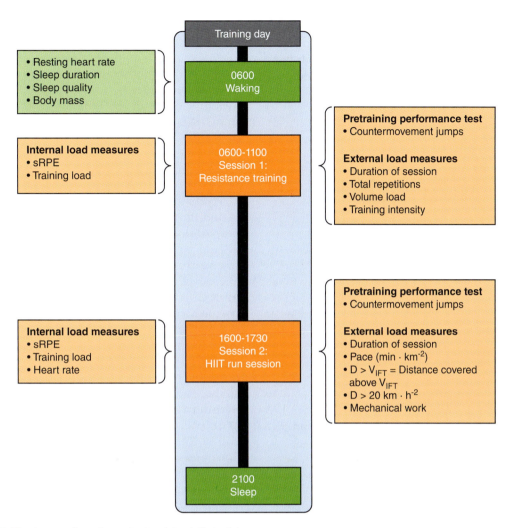

FIGURE 11.15 Integration of monitoring into daily training.

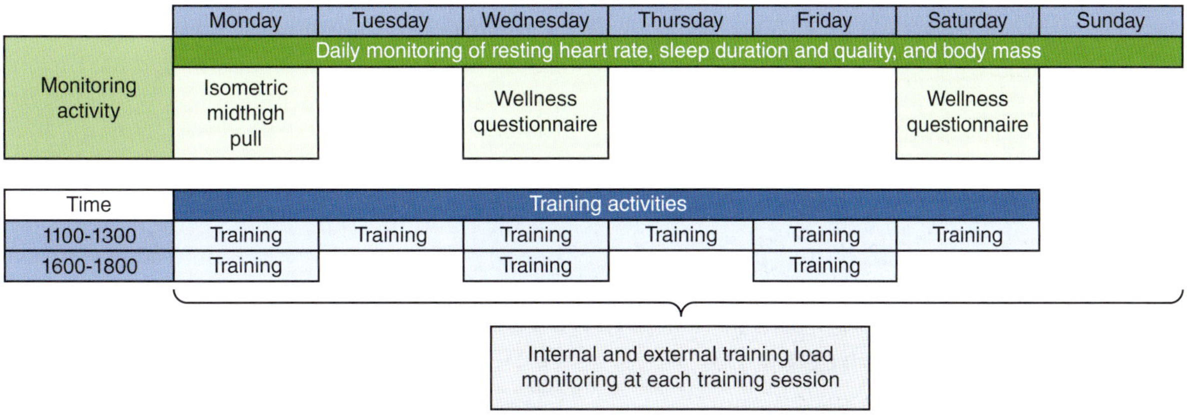

FIGURE 11.16 Integration of monitoring into a microcycle.

tests and assessments of body composition used to gauge how the athlete is responding to the training program (176). This practice is commonly used in resistance training in which the last microcycle of the mesocycle is often used to perform RM testing on key exercises to allow for the recalibration of training loads prescribed for the subsequent mesocycle. Alternatively, testing at this time can be used to examine benchmark tests, such as IMTP, loaded squat jump, 30 m sprint speed, change of direction speed, or body composition, which can be used by the coach to gauge how the athlete is progressing (figure 11.17).

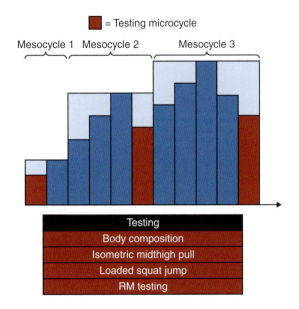

FIGURE 11.17 Integration of monitoring into a mesocycle.

A good example of this monitoring practice was presented by Hornsby and colleagues (176), who examined the maximal strength (IMTP, snatch, and clean and jerk), squat jump (0, 11, and 20 kg [24 and 44 lb]) performance, and body composition of weightlifters at the end of each mesocycle during a 20-week competitive period of the annual training plan. In this study, these data were used to examine how each athlete was progressing into key competitions in the period. When monitoring is integrated into the mesocycle in this manner, it can also be used to inform programming strategies for subsequent mesocycles, allowing the coach to modify programming strategies to ensure that the athlete is progressing according to the goals established by the annual training plan.

Annual Training Plan

As noted in chapter 6, the annual training plan subdivides the year of training into manageable periods (306) so the coach is better able to manage the training process (33). Ideally, these periods also provide a blueprint for when specific medical screening and performance testing can be used during the annual training plan to determine how the athlete is progressing in relationship to preestablished benchmarks. For example, when an athlete initiates a new annual training plan or macrocycle, it would be warranted to perform a medical or physiotherapy screening and an assessment of the athlete's body composition to get an overall account of the athlete's health and injury status. An example of where medical screening, performance testing, and body composition testing can be aligned with various periods and phases of the annual training plan is presented in figure 11.18.

Typically, this type of monitoring can be completed during the first microcycle of the general preparation phase. Although some coaches may decide to perform performance testing (e.g., strength, power, endurance) during the first microcycle after a transition, it may be warranted to wait a few mesocycles before conducting performance testing. Conceptually, at least one mesocycle would allow the athlete to ease into the training process and slowly ramp up training load and intensity prior to testing. Typically, performance testing will be planned for a microcycle at the end or beginning of a specific phase of training (176, 335, 337). For example, in figure 11.18, performance testing is aligned with the end of the general preparation, specific preparation, and main competition phases. Scheduling performance testing at these key times allows the coach to examine how performance changes across the annual training plan. When multiple annual training plans are retrospectively examined, the coach will be able to determine athlete performance progression and, by extension, the effectiveness of the long-term athlete development plan (19). Although numerous performance tests can be used to provide benchmark data, the coach must choose carefully and consider testing items that have a direct association with performance in the sport being monitored. For example, a coach working with basketball players might use the isometric midthigh pull, 20 m sprint, vertical jump, lateral movement, and 20 m multistage shuttle run tests as part of their benchmark testing (163, 319, 320). Alternatively, a coach working with rugby players might implement a 20 m multistage run test, 10 and 40 m sprint tests, a 40 m multiple sprint test, a countermovement jump test, a load squat jump test (60 kg [132 lb]), and an isometric midthigh pull test as part of their benchmark testing (241, 341). The coach may also determine maximal strength with RM testing for the bench press, bench pull, squat, and chin-up (341).

When establishing and integrating benchmark testing into the annual training plan, the coach

Chapter 11 • Integration of Monitoring Techniques Into Periodized Training Plans | **305**

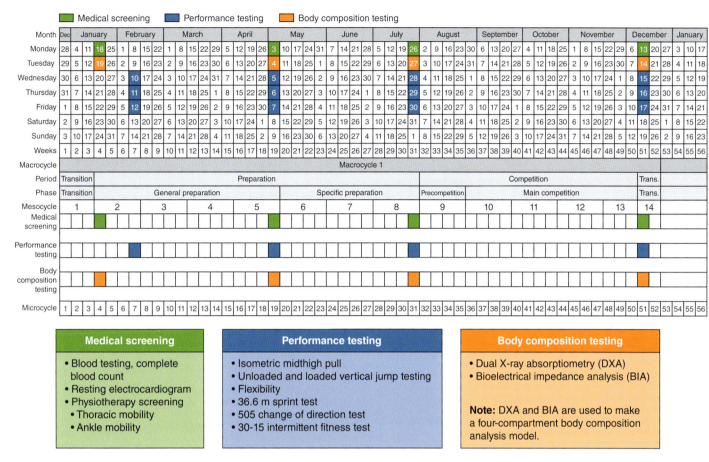

FIGURE 11.18 Integration of monitoring and testing into an American football team's annual training plan.

must establish specific targets for these tests to be evaluated against. For example, Hamilton (162) has presented a series of benchmarks for field hockey based on key strength and conditioning activities (figure 11.19). In this example, a traffic-light system is used to grade the athlete's performance on the key benchmarks. To guide the training process, Hamilton (162) suggests that these benchmark tests be performed at key times throughout the annual training plan, such as preseason, midseason, and 6 weeks prior to the first major international competition. Spacing these tests throughout the annual plan gives the coach sufficient time to make prescriptive changes to the training process and address the specific deficits and needs of each athlete.

Category	Test	Elite	Green	Amber	Red
Acceleration	5 m (s)	0.99	1.04	1.10	1.15
	10 m (s)	1.75	1.80	1.87	1.93
	40 m (s)	5.40	5.65	5.85	6.00
Strength	Isometric midthigh pull peak force (N · N^{-1})	3.75	3.00	2.40	2.00
	Back squat 2RM (kg · kg^{-1})	2.00	1.75	1.50	1.25
	Bench press 2RM (kg · kg^{-1})	1.05	0.90	0.75	0.60
	Wide pull-ups (number)	12.00	9.00	6.00	3.00
Conditioning	Repeated sprint ability (s)	7.20	7.45	7.70	7.90
	30-15 IFT (level)	21.00	20.00	19.50	19.00

FIGURE 11.19 Training benchmarks for field hockey.
Adapted from Hamilton (2019).

Summary

It is essential to integrate monitoring activities into the various levels of the periodized training plan, because this will allow the coach to gauge the athlete's responsiveness to the training process. Central to the ability to effectively use monitoring data is the ability to evaluate the external training loads the athlete is exposed to and determine the internal training loads that occur in response to the training process. Since the coach has many methods to evaluate these training loads, they must consider the cost–benefit ratio of the monitoring plan and each test they choose to incorporate into the plan. Ideally, the coach should create a multifaceted monitoring program composed of several monitoring activities that limit the burden placed on the athlete and maximize the usable information obtained.

The data collected as part of a comprehensive monitoring program provides information to inform the coach's programming decisions. Ideally, the monitoring program illuminates the effectiveness of the training process and the athlete's adaptational characteristics. Additionally, the monitoring program enhances communication among athletes, support staff, and coaches plus gives athletes a sense of involvement and ownership over their programs. Central to the ability of coaches to effectively use data collected through a monitoring program are the methodologies used to analyze the collected data.

Monitoring methods that provide data for assessing meaningful change and determining trends provide the coach valuable information to inform programming decisions. While historically the ACWR was a popular monitoring tool for determining injury risk, based on recent revelations about this method of evaluating monitoring data, it is recommended it no longer be used as part of the monitoring process.

Although there are many ways to analyze the data collected through a monitoring program, the coach must ensure that each aspect of the monitoring program informs their programming decisions. The monitoring program should never dictate the training process but instead guide programming. These decisions should be grounded in sound training theory and be individualized to the athlete. Ultimately, the monitoring process should be considered a key aspect of any periodized training plan.

CHAPTER 12

Periodization Strategies for Optimal Competition Performance

One of the most important goals of any periodized training plan is ensuring that athletes perform at their highest level when it matters most. To accomplish this goal, the coach must carefully craft the annual training plan to ensure that appropriate variations in the training process (e.g., rigorous training, reduced training loads) are implemented in a way that elevates preparedness and performance at the most appropriate times, as dictated by the competitive schedule. Periods of reduced training loads leading into a competition are often referred to as *tapers*. Tapers are used to maximize physiological adaptations while reducing fatigue to stimulate elevations in preparedness and performance, which are often referred to as *peaking* (14, 139).

The process of designing an effective taper is often considered one of the most critical aspects of the periodization process (58) and requires the coach to consider the athlete's response to the tapering process (139) and how this response modulates their level of preparedness. To better prepare athletes for major competitions, the coach must have a comprehensive understanding of the factors that affect the tapering process and must know how to individualize and integrate the taper into the competitive period of the annual training plan. Additionally, the coach must consider when to use tapering strategies and when to use optimization strategies that balance programming strategies to target recovery, loading, and unloading within a competitive microcycle.

Peaking Performance

Ultimately, the goal of a periodized training plan is to direct the training process so the athlete can achieve their best performance at specific competitions throughout the training year. The culmination of the training process is often referred to as *peaking* because the athlete's overall preparedness and performance capacity are elevated to their highest levels prior to and at key competitions (14, 52). Although the training strategies used as part of the peaking process are important, the coach must remember that peaking depends on the training undertaken during the preparation and competition periods, in which the athlete builds their physical and psychological capacities, technical skills, and tactical abilities (14, 52, 67). Therefore, it is in the later stages of the competition period that peak performance is targeted and a structured taper is implemented. As part of this process, the coach will employ specific programming strategies designed to dissipate accumulated fatigue and elevate performance as the athlete moves toward the targeted competition (figure 12.1) (16).

Many factors, including how the coach manipulates the volume, intensity, and frequency of training (52, 58, 94, 150), affect how the athlete responds to the tapering process (14, 161). If the coach correctly manipulates these key training variables and the athlete responds well to these strategies, accumulated fatigue will be dissipated and the athlete will display an increase in physiological and psychological preparedness (58, 102), which ultimately will increase the athlete's overall performance capacity.

Tapering

The process of peaking performance is accomplished with the implementation of a **taper**, where specific programming strategies are prescribed to

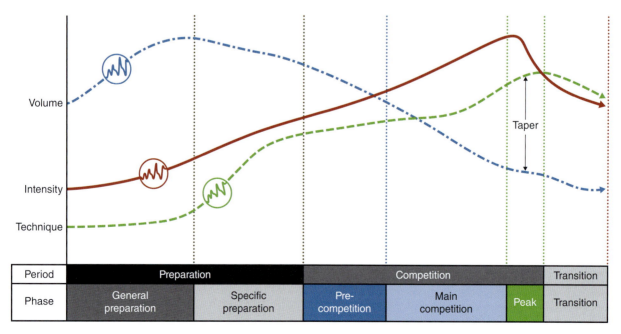

FIGURE 12.1 Example taper phase within a generalized periodization model for strength–power training.
Adapted from Plisk and Stone (2003).

elevate performance in preparation for competition. These strategies are employed by athletes from a variety of individual (43, 60, 63-65, 95, 96, 140, 150, 159) and team sports (34, 75, 81, 89) and are considered a critical aspect of the athlete's overall preparation for competition (58). No matter how well the taper is designed, its ability to elevate preparedness and performance relies on the training periods (i.e., mesocycles and microcycles) that come before its initiation.

There are many ways to describe how an athlete's training plan is modified during the days prior to a major competition (17, 99, 102, 105, 137, 148). Traditionally, the taper has been defined as simply reducing training workload prior to competition to enhance the athlete's performance capacity via the removal of accumulated fatigue (17, 102, 135, 139). More recently, the definition of a taper has been expanded to include factors related to how the taper is designed (100, 102). Specifically, Mujika and Padilla (100) define the taper as "a progressive non-linear reduction of the training load during variable periods of time, in an attempt to reduce the physiological and psychological stress of daily training and optimize sports performance" (page 80). Based on this definition, the coach needs to consider the aim of the taper, the rationale underpinning the taper, and the factors affecting the taper.

Aim of a Taper

The main aim of any taper is to enhance an athlete's ability to compete at a high level. In this regard, the taper is used to leverage the physical capacities, technical and tactical abilities, and psychological capacities developed within the preparation and competition periods of the annual training plan (14, 161). If these capacities and abilities are not established prior to the taper, the ability to optimize performance will be significantly compromised and the athlete will, in most instances, not perform at a high level (94). Conceptually, the coach needs to understand that a taper is simply a period of training during which training loads are reduced to reveal the fitness that has already been developed and to elevate the athlete's level of preparedness, which is masked by accumulated fatigue (102). During the taper there is reduced physiological and psychological fatigue, which increases the athlete's potential for performing at an optimized level.

Rationale of a Taper

The effective implementation of a taper is largely related to the coach's ability to optimize fitness and modulate the time necessary to reduce training fatigue and elevate preparedness (52). The fatigue, fitness, and preparedness relationship presented in chapter 1 (figures 1.17 and 1.18, pages 22-23) can be used to explain the general concepts that underpin a precompetition taper. The training process the athlete undertakes directly affects their level of preparedness via the manipulation of the amount of fitness and the level of fatigue stimulated by the training process (24, 161). Through manipulating the athlete's training program, the coach can modulate and increase the athlete's level of preparedness prior to the planned competitive engagement (52).

The training stress that the athlete is exposed to in the pretaper training period will exert a large effect on the time allocated to the taper, the structure of the taper, and the degree of performance enhancement stimulated by the taper (14, 152, 161). For example, based on the delayed training effects paradigm, if the training period contains higher training loads or is undertaken for extended periods, there will be greater accumulation of fatigue as well as greater increases in the overall levels of fitness (13, 152, 160). In this scenario, a longer or more pronounced taper is necessary to allow the accumulated fatigue to dissipate and to permit the elevated fitness levels developed by the training period to be revealed, resulting in an increase in athlete preparedness and a supercompensation of performance (figure 12.2).

Conversely, lower training loads during the pretaper training period will create less accumulated fatigue, and a shorter taper will be needed to stimulate a performance supercompensation (52) (figure 12.2). Lower training loads in the pretaper training period result in smaller overall fitness adaptations, lower levels of preparedness, and smaller performance gains (i.e., supercompensation) (13, 52, 143). A well-designed taper cannot overcome poor preparation, and a short taper cannot effectively remove the accumulated fatigue stimulated by a training block that contains massive training loads.

Conceptually, the taper is a fatigue-management strategy whereby the coach attempts to use specific programming strategies to modulate training load to reduce accumulated fatigue while maintaining as much of the fitness developed by the pretaper training period as possible to stimulate elevations in performance capacity (i.e., preparedness) (13, 52). Fitness is considered a slow-changing component of athletic preparedness and, depending on the level of fitness achieved, is relatively stable over several minutes, hours, or days (161). Conversely, fatigue can change rapidly and is affected

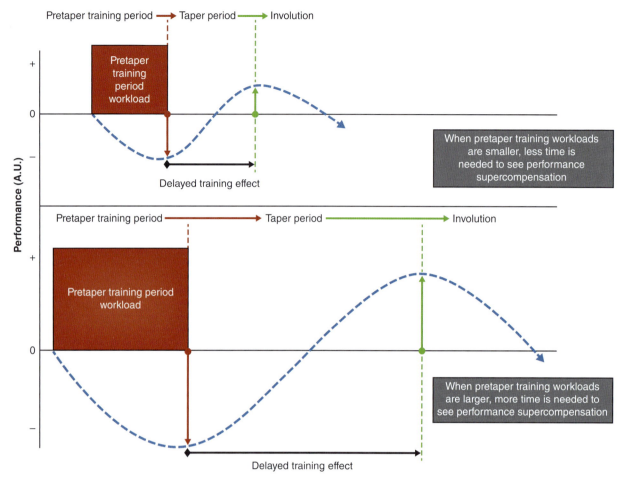

FIGURE 12.2 Delayed training effects and tapers.

Adapted by permission from G.G. Haff, "Peaking for Competition in Individual Sports," in *High-Performance Training for Sports*, edited by D. Joyce and D. Lewindon (Champaign, IL: Human Kinetics, 2022), 333.

by a variety of physiological and psychological stressors (161). Therefore, the coach can manipulate training variables to decrease training loads, which can swiftly reduce accumulated fatigue while maintaining or raising overall fitness and elevating preparedness and performance capacity (52).

Although the basic constructs of employing a taper are straightforward, the actual design and implementation of a taper are much more complex due to the interaction of numerous training- and recovery-based factors that must be considered (13, 52). For example, if the duration of the taper is extended for too long, a state of involution (i.e., detraining) will occur, resulting in a reduction in fitness and preparedness due to the reduced training loads contained within the taper (figures 12.3 and 12.4) (100).

The coach should consider that the athlete's level of preparedness is modulated by a compromise between the extent of the training load reduction and the duration during which this reduction is applied (145). If the training load preceding the taper is relatively low, the coach would implement a shorter taper with smaller reductions in training load to optimize the athlete's level of preparedness for competition. Conversely, if the training load prior to the taper is high, the taper would require a greater reduction in training load, which would be undertaken for a longer time to optimize the athlete's preparedness (15, 74, 145).

Although changes to the athlete's training load are often the most-discussed tapering strategy for modulating fatigue and preparedness, other factors, such as targeted recovery strategies (124, 157), nutritional interventions (124, 157), and sleep hygiene (19), all significantly influence the athlete's ability to modulate fatigue and preparedness during the taper period. Since the effectiveness of a taper is based on numerous factors, the coach should use a holistic approach and not solely focus on training loads.

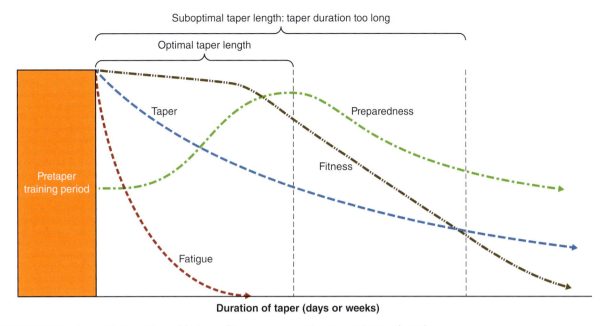

FIGURE 12.3 Interrelationships of fatigue, fitness, preparedness, and taper length.

Adapted by permission from T.O. Bompa and G.G. Haff, *Periodization: Theory and Methodology of Training,* 5th ed., (Champaign, IL: Human Kinetics, 2009), 189.

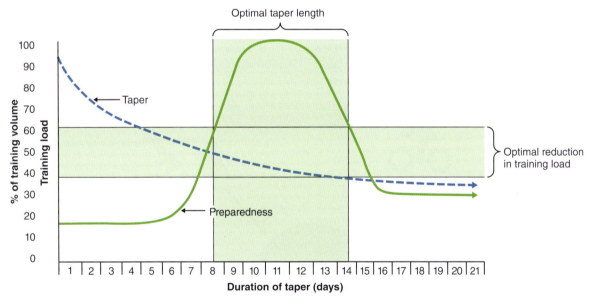

FIGURE 12.4 Relationship between preparedness and the taper length and decrease in training volume.

Adapted from Bompa and Haff (2009).

Effect of a Taper on Performance

In elite sport, small elevations in performance can be the difference between winning and losing (52). For example, in all swimming events at the 2016 Rio Olympics, a 1.3% difference separated the gold medal winner from the fourth-place finisher, and a 1.4% difference separated third from eighth place (52). Similarly, at the 2000 Sydney Olympics, there was a 1.62% difference between the gold medal winner and the fourth-place finisher and a 2.02% difference between third- and eighth-place finishers (104). These data demonstrate that the margins between losing and winning are very small.

In the competition results for weightlifting at the 2016 Rio Olympics, there was a 1.80% difference between the gold medal winner and the fourth-place finisher, with as little as a 0.9% increase in performance resulting in an improvement in placing. Similarly, at the 2012 London Olympics, there was a 2.3% difference between the gold- and bronze-medal performances across all weight classes in weightlifting (52). These data are in line with the within-athlete variability of 2.5% (95% confidence interval = 2.2%-2.9%) in weightlifting performance in the scientific literature (86). Based on these data, a 1.2% increase in the amount of weight lifted can significantly enhance competitive performance.

The effect of a small increase in performance can also be seen in track and field events. These results are very similar to the effect of a 0.4% to 0.5% increase in running performance or a 0.9% to 1.5% increase in field event performance (i.e., throwing and jumping) on an athlete's competitive placing (59).

A taper is one strategy used to enhance performance capacity and increase the chance of competitive success. Generally, a well-crafted taper is expected to enhance competitive performance across a broad spectrum of sports and populations (29). Tapers have been reported to enhance performance in short-duration race events (e.g., 50 m swim, <10 km cycle time trial, 2,000 m row) (8, 30, 31, 106, 141, 148), middle-distance events (e.g., swimming, cycling, and running) (30, 31, 35, 65, 77, 106, 108, 148), and longer-duration events (e.g., duathlon, 40 km cycling time trial, triathlon) (4, 80, 106, 109, 159).

Generally, a preevent taper can stimulate a 0.5% to 8.0% increase in performance in a variety of sporting activities (figure 12.5) (29, 102, 106, 150). In fact, based on the available scientific literature, it is not unreasonable to expect a 2% to 3% improvement in endurance performance in response to a taper (106). Enhancements in performance of this magnitude can exert a significant effect on competitive results; for example, a 3% improvement in a collegiate 8 km runner's performance would translate into a 50-second faster race time (77).

Performance enhancements in responses to a preevent taper can be extended to strength and power performances as well. For example, a 2% to 8% increase in maximal performance would be expected in back squat and bench press performance after a preevent taper (33, 69, 133, 150, 155). Similarly, a preevent taper used in the preparation of track and field athletes has been reported to improve throwing distance by 5% to 6% (5, 158).

It is clear that a properly designed and implemented taper can enhance competitive perfor-

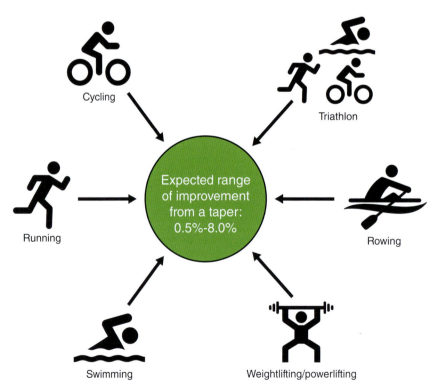

FIGURE 12.5 Expected performance improvement from a taper.

mance (18, 106). The magnitude of this improvement is affected by many factors, including training prior to the taper (52), the type of taper used (102), and how training volume, intensity, and frequency are varied within the taper (18, 52, 102). In general, one would expect a preevent taper to result in a 3% increase in performance, which can differentiate between gold and bronze medal performances at the Olympic Games and in world championships.

Factors Affecting a Taper

Coaches can integrate many programming strategies into the annual training plan to peak the athlete's performance at specifically targeted competitions (18, 52). Regardless of the strategy implemented, the coach should always remember that the primary goal behind any taper is to modulate training loads to dissipate fatigue and elevate preparedness and performance.

To reduce training load and construct a preevent taper, the coach can manipulate training intensity, volume, and frequency (136). Regardless of how these training variables are altered, the overall success of the taper is affected by the training loads undertaken prior to the taper (145), the duration of the taper (88, 137), and the type of taper designed and implemented (17, 73, 102). If the taper is poorly structured, the desired performance gain may not be realized. For example, if the taper is extended for too long, involution (i.e., detraining) will occur, resulting in a reduced level of fitness and preparedness and, ultimately, a decline in performance (100). Conversely, if the training load prior to the taper is very high and the taper is too short and does not adequately reduce training load, the accumulated fatigue from the pretaper period may mask fitness and preparedness, resulting in a reduced performance capacity at the targeted competition (52). Both scenarios can reduce preparedness and compromise performance, so the coach must understand the factors that affect the tapering process to ensure that they choose effective strategies.

Type of Taper

Different strategies can be used to reduce training load during a taper. These strategies are broadly defined within the scientific literature as being either nonprogressive or progressive (figure 12.6) (18, 73, 90, 102).

Nonprogressive Tapers

A **nonprogressive taper**, or **step taper**, leading into a competition uses standard reductions in training load (102). A hallmark of these tapers is a sudden reduction in training load (145) that, if implemented incorrectly, can result in substantial losses in fitness and preparedness over the course of the taper (4). When implemented correctly, however, this strategy can augment the physiological and performance adaptations typically gained from training (53, 56, 64, 65, 82, 102, 113, 133).

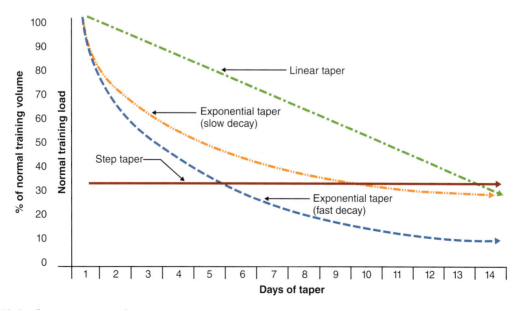

FIGURE 12.6 Common types of tapers.
Adapted from Mujika and Padilla (2003).

Although step tapers can improve performance, this strategy tends to produce smaller performance enhancements than progressive tapers (4, 17, 159). Step tapers have been reported to increase performance by only 1.2% to 1.5%, whereas performance increases of 4.0% to 5.0% have been reported in response to progressive tapers (102). These findings are consistent with the results presented by Banister et al. (4), who also reported greater performance enhancement after a progressive taper compared to a step taper.

Some evidence suggests step tapers may be more effective with some endurance sports (figure 12.7) (4, 18, 90). For example, Bosquet et al. (18) report that progressive tapers are more effective at enhancing swimming and running performance, but a step taper may be a more effective performance enhancement strategy for cycling. These data, however, should be interpreted with caution, because the presented findings may have resulted from small and unequal athlete samples being used in the analysis process (18, 90). Therefore, further scientific inquiry is required to completely understand the value of step tapering strategies leading into cycling competitions.

Progressive Tapers

During a **progressive taper**, there is a systematic linear or exponential reduction in training load leading into a competition (18). With a **linear taper**, there is a systematic linear reduction in training load across a predetermined time period (102). This tapering strategy normally contains higher training loads than those in an exponential taper. An **exponential taper** can be designed with either a slow (i.e., slow decay) or sudden (i.e., fast decay) reduction in training load (52, 90). A **slow exponential taper** tends to have a slower reduction in training load and higher training loads when compared with a fast exponential taper (102). Generally, a **fast exponential taper** tends to result in greater performance gains (3.9%-4.1%) compared to either a slow exponential or linear taper (4, 102, 159).

Other Tapering Strategies

Some coaches use innovative tapering strategies that have not yet been thoroughly investigated in the scientific literature (18, 90). One potential alternative tapering strategy is a **two-phase taper**. The first phase features a reduction in training load, and the second includes a moderate increase in training load during the last days of the taper (figure 12.8) (18, 147). Using mathematical modeling, Thomas et al. (147) used model parameters from competitive swimmers (146) to compare an optimal progressive taper with a two-phase taper. Each taper was designed to last the same duration and use the same basic progressive reduction in training load, but the two-phase taper incorporated a 20% to 30% increase in training load across the final 3 days of the taper. The two-phase taper resulted in a 6 to 25 millisecond improvement in a 60-second event (147). Although these increases were very small, it is possible that further manipulation of the two phases might optimize the training stimulus and lead to greater performance gains.

Another example of an alternative tapering strategy is a **saw taper** (90, 104). In an observational study looking at the final preparation of swimmers before the 2000 Olympic Games, Mujika and colleagues (104) provided a graphical depiction of the 16-week training period for an Australian swimmer, which consisted of 800 km of swimming (i.e., 40-80 km · wk^{-1}) leading into the games. During this athlete's 3-week taper, training load was reduced from about 47 km to 18 km · wk^{-1} (figure 12.9).

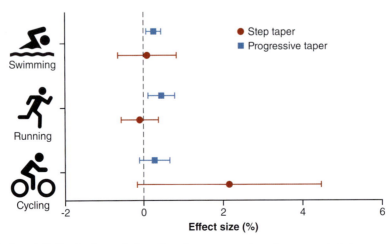

FIGURE 12.7 Effect size statistics for taper-induced endurance sport performance gains.

Data from L. Bosquet, J. Montpetit, D. Arvisais, and I. Mujika, "Effects of Tapering on Performance: A Meta-Analysis," *Medicine & Science in Sports & Exercise* 39 (2007): 1358-1365.

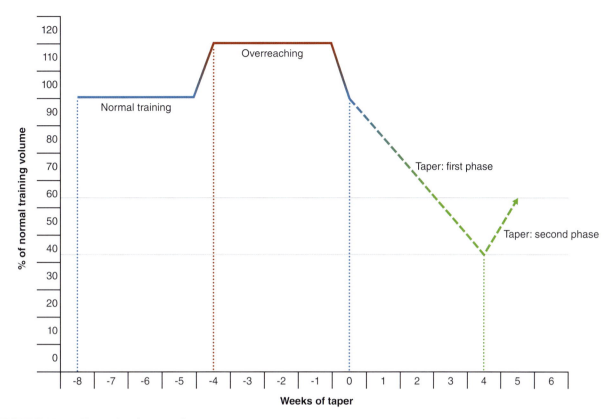

FIGURE 12.8 Example of a two-phase taper.
Adapted from Thomas, Mujika, and Busso (2009).

When examined at the microcycle level, the taper appears to be progressive (104). However, when each day of the 3 weeks of the taper is carefully scrutinized, it is clear there were sharp alterations in training load across this time period. These sharp daily alterations, which oscillated between high and low training loads, are an example of the saw pattern of a saw taper (90). This alternative taper strategy warrants further scientific scrutiny to better understand how it can be employed in the preparation of athletes.

Training Volumes

The manipulation of training volume is one of the more important considerations when planning a preevent taper (52). The two strategies commonly employed to reduce training volume are decreasing the duration of each training session or reducing the frequency of training contained within the taper period (18, 52, 102). Based on the available scientific evidence, reducing the volume of training contained within each training session appears to be a superior programming strategy for reducing the volume of training as this strategy results in greater performance gains compared to reducing training frequency within the taper (18). Additionally, maintaining training frequency also allows the athlete to maintain their confidence in the movements and activities related to their sport.

When considering how much to reduce training volume within the preevent taper, the coach must always consider the training load (i.e., training volume and intensity) that the athlete undertook prior to initiating the taper (52). These training loads exert a significant influence on the required amount of reduction in training volume and the duration of the taper to ensure that preparedness and performance are increased at the appropriate time (52, 145). Ultimately, the interplay between the pretaper training load and the structure of the taper partially explains why there are variable recommendations for volume reductions within the scientific literature (17, 102). For example, tapers that employ 40% to 90% reductions in training volume have been recommended for endurance sports such as swimming (71, 97, 98, 103, 148), cycling (82, 108, 109, 127), and triathlon (4, 110, 159).

Meta-analyses performed on the available scientific research suggest that the optimal performance improvements occur when progressive tapers are

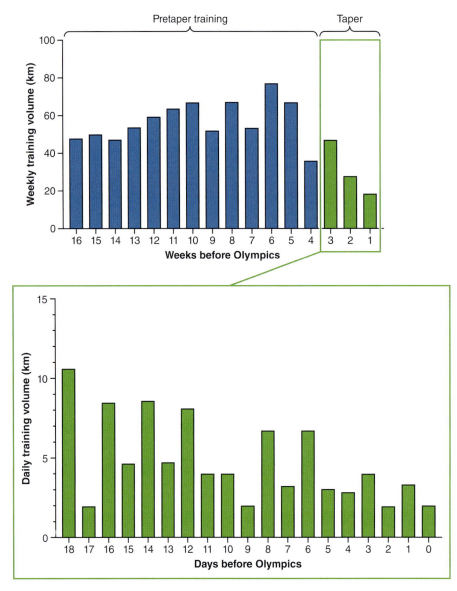

FIGURE 12.9 Example of a saw taper used leading into the Olympic Games.
Adapted from Mujika, Padilla, and Pyne (2002).

designed with 41% to 60% reductions in training volume (16, 18). It is important to reiterate, however, that due to the interrelationship between the pretaper training load and the taper, in some situations greater reductions (i.e., 60%-90% of pretaper training load) in training volume are warranted to dissipate fatigue (102, 145). Additionally, in situations in which greater reductions in volume are employed, it may be warranted to shorten the duration of the taper to offset the potential loss of fitness (74, 94).

Relatively less research is available exploring the optimal reductions in volume necessary for intermittent strength–focused sports (122, 123), such as weightlifting (149), powerlifting (50, 124, 150), strongman (157), and track and field (5, 158). In these types of sports, volume reductions of 30% to 70% of pretaper training loads have been suggested to optimize performance (121, 149, 150). As with endurance athletes, the magnitude of training volume reductions employed within the taper are linked to the pretaper training loads (52).

Training Frequencies

Manipulating training frequency is another strategy that can be used to reduce the amount of training load undertaken during the taper. Some evidence suggests that reducing pretaper training frequency by 50% can increase performance (57, 71). Conversely, there is also evidence that a 2- to 4-week reduction in training frequency only results in a maintenance of performance capacities (61, 62, 64, 82, 85, 102, 105, 112, 127). Although modulating training frequency may be useful in some situations, the maintenance of training frequency appears to be a more effective taper strategy.

When examining the tapering practices of highly trained runners, tapers that contain higher frequencies of training seem to result in greater performance gains compared to tapers with moderate frequencies of training (99). In their meta-analysis, Bosquet and colleagues (18) reported that decreasing the training frequency in the taper does not significantly improve performance. This response is most evident in highly trained athletes who may need greater training frequencies to maintain technical proficiency (102). Note, however, that decreasing training frequency during the taper interacts with other modifiable training factors, including training volume and intensity, which makes it difficult to determine the actual effect of reducing training frequency (91). Based on the current body of scientific knowledge, it is generally recommended that coaches plan tapering periods that maintain training frequency at levels greater than or equal to 80% of pretaper training frequencies (52), especially in technique-dependent sports such as swimming, throwing, and weightlifting (87, 102).

Training Intensity

Another factor that can affect taper effectiveness is the intensity of training (15, 18, 122). When training volume is reduced during a taper, training intensity influences the athlete's ability to maintain the gains established during the pretaper training period (17, 56, 105, 135). When higher training intensities (>90% $\dot{V}O_2$max) are integrated into an endurance athlete's taper, performance tends to supercompensate (135). Conversely, there tends to be a maintenance of or decrease in performance when the taper contains lower training intensities (<70% $\dot{V}O_2$max) (64, 85).

Similarly, there are greater increases in strength when training volume is decreased and higher intensities are incorporated into a strength–power athlete's preevent taper (46, 69, 122, 158). For example, Zaras and colleagues (158) have reported that when track and field throwers (i.e., discus, hammer, shotput) use a high-intensity tapering strategy, there are significantly greater increases in maximal strength, power output, and the rate of force development compared to a lower-intensity tapering strategy.

Although the general recommendation is to increase or maintain intensity during a taper to maximize strength performance outcomes (18, 102, 121, 156), note that when powerlifters substantially reduce training volume and increase high-intensity work, more negative performance outcomes are possible (122). Normal training for these athletes often uses intensities greater than or equal to 85% of maximum; therefore, it may be prudent to simply maintain intensity during the taper (150). Work from Häkkinen et al. (53) and Seppänen (132) supported this contention, showing that performance was improved when strength-trained individuals and powerlifters reduced training volume by 50% to 54% across a 2-week taper while maintaining intensity at about 85% of maximum. Conversely, some evidence in powerlifting supports a slight reduction (~5%) of the training intensity during the taper period to offset fatigue generated during the pretaper training period (124). This is an important consideration and further highlights the symbiotic relationship between the training loads encountered during the pretaper training period and the required volume and intensity modulations employed during the taper period. Much more research is warranted.

Based on the available evidence, it seems prudent to reduce training load by reducing the volume of training while maintaining or slightly increasing intensity during the tapers used by endurance and strength–power athletes. It is, however, important to remember that the tapering process is highly individualized and there may be exceptions to these recommendations.

Taper Duration

Determining the optimal duration of the taper is one of the more difficult decisions the coach needs to make (102). This is largely because the magnitude of fatigue developed by the pretaper training period influences the time necessary to dissipate the accumulated fatigue and elevate the athlete's level of preparedness (145). To remove fatigue and elevate preparedness, the coach will program reductions in training load (i.e., volume and intensity) and choose an effective tapering strategy. The duration of this taper is largely affected by the pretaper training and by how rapidly fatigue needs to be reduced or how much the coach plans to reduce training volume (52). If, for example, the taper features a larger reduction in training load, a short taper lasting less than 15 days is generally recommended (74, 145). Conversely, a longer taper lasting between 15 and 22 days can be employed if more gradual reductions in training load are structured into the taper (52).

The available literature on the duration of a taper shows that physiological, psychological, and performance improvements have been associated with durations of 1 to 4 weeks, with 8 to 14 days recommended as the optimal duration (17, 52, 92). The main benefit of the 8- to 14-day duration is that it provides an effective time for balancing the maintenance of fitness with the need to reduce training load to dissipate cumulative fatigue (17, 74). This duration is short enough to avoid the negative fitness or work capacity effects that can be associated with longer duration tapers, which may occur in response to lower training loads that are performed for prolonged periods of time (52).

While an 8- to 14-day taper is generally considered to be the optimal duration for a preevent taper, it is important to reiterate that the physiological and psychological responses to the reduced training loads encountered within the taper are highly individualized (17, 41, 102, 139). Therefore, it is recommended that the taper duration be personalized to optimize the tapering process for each athlete.

Personalizing the Tapering Process

Within elite sports, the application of tapering strategies is generally based on little or no quantitative data and primarily leverages the personal observations and experiences of the coach and athlete (128, 139). In many instances, coaches base their tapering approaches on the guidelines presented in textbooks (like this one) or the scientific literature on the topic. Once they master the basic tapering constructs, coaches tend to develop their own tapering practices, which are often based on their personal experiences, trial and error, or previously used tapers (128). The coach must constantly examine and reflect on how their athletes respond to the tapering process (e.g., structure, content, implementation) to fine-tune and individualize tapers.

The tapering process does not follow a general prescription or a one-size-fits-all strategy that is applicable to all athletes (128). It is well-documented that elevating an athlete's performance is highly individualized (13, 52), and coaches must approach the taper from a holistic perspective and consider the individual characteristics of their athletes. They should not solely focus on the physiological responses to the taper but also should consider the effect of the taper on the athlete's confidence and the importance of psychological preparation (128). The importance of maintaining the athlete's confidence during the taper cannot be understated, because it is well-documented that confidence is a critical aspect of athletic performance (54). An athlete's confidence can be fragile (48), so strategies that help enhance this psychological factor are important. Psychological preparation should be incorporated into all levels of the periodized training plan, but special attention should be paid to include activities in the taper that maximize the athlete's confidence. Confidence is highly individualized, so the coach must engage in active dialogue with the athlete to ensure their needs are met (128).

Although an experience-based method to designing and implementing a taper is generally effective, an alternative strategy that can more precisely individualize the tapering process is to use mathematical modeling to predict the athlete's physiological and psychological response to alterations in the training process (139, 140, 146). To use mathematical modeling, the coach seeks to establish predictive equations that link tapering strategies to the athlete's regular training load characteristics (139). Support for this approach has been presented by Spilsbury et al. (139), who report that an individualized taper can be modeled to determine the optimal duration, volume, intensity, and frequency of training with endurance runners. In fact, the predictive algorithms were able to explain a large portion of the variance (53%-95%) in tapering strategies in response to a pretaper training load. Spilsbury et al. (139) suggested that these algorithms might be useful tools for coaches when they are considering various tapering strategies.

Mathematical Modeling

A key factor when establishing mathematical models of the tapering process is having data representative of the athlete's internal and external training loads for the training undertaken prior to the initiation of the taper. To predict performance outcomes, the relationship between these training loads can be used to model performance outcomes and predict the potential performances that might occur as the result of the tapering process.

Several models have been used to examine the association between training loads (i.e., internal and external) and performance outcomes (25, 72,

154). Traditionally, a systems-model approach has been used to facilitate our understanding of how the training process might predict an athlete's preparedness and potential for performance (25, 154). This approach was first proposed by Banister and colleagues (3) and was based on the assumption that performance was the balance between two antagonistic responses to training: a positive effect, which is related to adaptation, and a negative effect, which is related to fatigue. To create the model, parameters that are constants, unique to the individual, and characterize the athlete's response to training are incorporated. The model is fitted to each athlete based on their response to a given training program, which allows for the computation of fatigue and adaptation indexes for the specified training period (146). Generally, this approach has provided useful information on the optimal taper duration (95) and how training load should be reduced during the taper to optimize performance (4).

Although the original linear model presented by Banister and colleagues (3) has provided useful information, it is potentially flawed because it assumes that the response to a given training load is independent of the accumulated fatigue stimulated by past training (146). Thomas and colleagues (146) argue that this assumption implies that regardless of the training load encountered prior to a taper, the same duration of reduced training load should be applied. Additionally, based on this model, training should be completely removed for the duration of the taper (42), which conflicts with what we know about detraining (100, 101, 112) and the best way to implement tapering strategies (18, 102).

To address the limitations associated with Banister's linear model, Busso and colleagues (22, 23) used a recursive least-squares algorithm that allowed the parameters incorporated in the model to vary over time. The results of these initial studies clearly demonstrate that a single training session varies according to the difficulty of previous training sessions. To expand on these findings, Busso (21) proposed a nonlinear model that considers the fatigue accumulated during training; this is based on the assumption that the increase in fatigue from a given training session depends on the severity of the fatigue associated with prior training sessions. Busso (21) determined that the magnitude and duration of the fatigue produced by a given training session are increased after repetitive exercise sessions and are reduced when training load is reduced.

In one study, the nonlinear model was able to describe a group of elite swimmers' responses to their training and investigate the effect of the training undertaken prior to the taper on the characteristics (i.e., duration, event, and form of taper) and effectiveness (i.e., performance gain) of the optimal taper (146). To accomplish this goal, Thomas and colleagues (146) used data from two entire swim seasons for four female and four male national and international-class 100 m and 200 m swimmers. The performance modeled exhibited a significant fit with the actual performances registered for these athletes. The results of this study provide further support for the notion that training prior to the taper affects how the taper needs to be designed and implemented. The study also demonstrates that performance is enhanced when the negative effects of training (i.e., fatigue) are reduced and the positive effects of performance (i.e., fitness) are elevated. This model, however, tended to underestimate some of the better performances and overestimate poorer performances. Additionally, the goodness of fit between the model and the actual performances was not as robust with these elite athletes as what was reported by Busso (21) for lower-level athletes in a controlled laboratory training period. One possible explanation for these issues may be related to the complex nature of the training practices of elite athletes, which may affect the accuracy of the quantification of all training variables associated within their training programs (55, 95, 144, 146). Therefore, it is likely that more-advanced modeling techniques that do not rely on deterministic or reductionistic principles are necessary to account for the complex nonlinear relationships that underpin performance (83, 119).

More recently, Kipp and colleagues (72) have used artificial neural networks (ANN) to model the effect of 15 weeks of resistance training on changes in the countermovement vertical jump (CMJ) performance of track and field athletes. To model the association between volume load (i.e., sets × reps × load lifted; see chapter 11) and CMJ performance, a feed-forward ANN was used to create the model. Across 15 weeks of resistance training, the volume load of training completed was monitored and then used as predictor variables in the input layer (see figure 12.10).

Five neurons were used for the hidden layer, and the output consisted of the pre- to postseason changes in CMJ. Twenty-one track and field athletes were randomly divided into training (n = 13), validation (n = 4), and testing (n = 4) sets. The data in the training set was then used to train the weights and biases of the ANN with Levenberg-Marquardt backpropagation (72). To help prevent overfitting and improve generalizability, the validations set was used for "early stopping" of the training process. Finally, the testing set was used

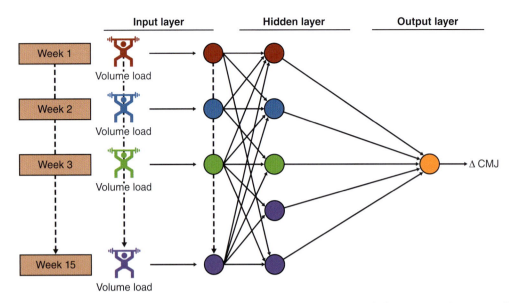

FIGURE 12.10 Artificial neural network architecture used to model the relationship between resistance-training volume load across 15 weeks and changes in countermovement jump.

Adapted by permission from K. Kipp, J. Krzyszkowski, and D. Kant-Hull, "Use of Machine Learning to Model Volume Load Effects on Changes in Jump Performance," *International Journal of Sports Physiology Performance* 15, no. 2 (2020): 286.

to determine how well the ANN would perform when new data (i.e., separate) were applied to the model. The performance of all sets were evaluated with coefficients of determination (r^2), root mean square error (RMSE), and 95% confidence intervals for the RMSE. The connection weights methods were used to calculate the relative importance of the input variable and were then expressed as percentages to show the relative contribution of each predictor on its input-hidden layer weights and the hidden-output layer weights (72, 116). Based on the large coefficients of determination (0.89-0.99) and small RMSE (0.3-0.84) found in this study, the authors concluded that the developed ANN effectively modeled the association of volume load and changes in CMJ performance after 15 weeks of resistance training. One important note about this study is that only resistance-training volume load was tracked and that the fourth, seventh, and fifteenth weeks of training had a large (10%-17%) relative importance in predicting the training-induced changes in CMJ. Interestingly, these weeks all corresponded to unloading or tapering microcycles, which further supports the idea that optimizing CMJ performance requires planned reductions in training volume (i.e., volume load) (72). Although this study provides evidence for the value of using ANN to predict performance outcomes, the fact that the developed model only includes resistance-training volume load as an input variable and does not account for the effect of other training factors or the athlete's response to training (i.e., internal training load) on the CMJ performance is an important consideration. It is likely if more comprehensive monitoring data are integrated into an ANN, more robust modeling of performance can be achieved.

Similarly, Edelmann-Nusser and colleagues (40) used a nonlinear mathematical method of ANN (i.e., multilayer perceptron) to predict 200 m sprint performance from training data. The main differences between this study and that of Kipp and colleagues (72) was that it was based on a single case study from a swimmer competing at the 2000 Sydney Olympic Games and incorporated weekly swim training volume, time spent resistance training, and time spent on other dryland training activities. Interestingly, the developed model was able to predict an Olympic competitive performance of 2:12.59 (min:s), which was very close to the actual competitive performance of 2:12:64 achieved at the Sydney Olympics (40). Based on their data, Edelmann-Nusser and colleagues (40) suggested that once a good model is developed, it could be used to either predict competitive performance or as part of a simulation to determine performance responses of the athlete to subtle changes in the structure of the training process. Ultimately, after a time when training analysis is conducted and the neural networks have been trained, manipulation of the model inputs may allow the coach to simulate how modifications to the training program affect competitive performance. The use of neural networks could enhance programming efficiency by using specific data collected during an integrated monitoring program as part of the input layer used within the ANN modeling techniques.

It seems that the ability to model performance and subtly adjust the athlete's training programs based on changes in various input variables will continue to evolve and become an integral part of the periodization process. For this to occur, integrated monitoring programs (chapter 11) must be developed and incorporated into the athlete's periodized training plan to provide the necessary information about the athlete's internal and external training load needed to effectively use ANN to develop models that can help guide the training process.

Tapering and Team Sport Athletes

Although there is extensive research examining tapering in individual sports, more specifically endurance sports, there is a paucity of experimental and observational research investigating the tapering practices of team sport athletes (93, 125, 151). One of the major differences between athletes who participate in team sports and those who compete in individual sports may be related to how they approach competition. For example, athletes in individual sports have greater flexibility in determining which competitions they target, are able to perform below expectations at some competitions, and can also skip competitions that do not align with the goals of their competitive calendar (89). Conversely, team sport athletes are often required to consistently perform at a high level during each week of a competitive season if they intend to be in contention for a league or world championship (89, 151).

Mujika (89) suggests two ways to conceptualize tapering and peaking for team sport performance. First, preseason training, which is synonymous with a precompetition phase of an annual training plan, could be formatted to ensure each athlete initiates the competitive season in the best possible condition. Second, tapering and peaking strategies could be considered for athletes leading into the Olympic Games, world or national championships, or grand finals (89).

Peaking Performance for a Competitive Season

Most team sport coaches understand that it is not possible to maintain peak physical performance capacity across an entire season (89). It is impossible to undertake a taper that lasts for an entire season or is employed before every competition of the season because of the interplay among training, fatigue, fitness, and preparedness and the overall length of a competitive season in team sports.

One strategy some coaches implement to maximize performance during a competitive season is to place tapering strategies at the end of the preseason to increase performance capacity at the start of the season (33, 93, 115). Support for this practice can be found in work by Coutts and colleagues (33), who employed a period of overreaching (see chapter 9), which was structured similarly to a preseason (i.e., precompetition phase) training period in rugby. This 6-week period used a stepwise increase in training load, which was, on average, 2,136 ± 86 arbitrary units. Following this mesocycle, there were significant reductions (12.3%) in multistage fitness test running performance as well as strength–power and speed performance (−13.8% to −3.7%). Additionally, there were significant alterations to several biochemical markers, such as plasma testosterone: cortisol ratio, creatine kinase, glutamate, and the glutamine:glutamate ratio, that were indicative of overreaching (see chapter 9). After completing this mesocycle of training, a 1-week (i.e., microcycle) taper was employed in which training load was about 38.7% less than the average training load during the overreaching period and was about 56.9% less than the training load in the last microcycle within the period. Following the progressive taper, the authors noted a performance supercompensation for muscular strength, power, and endurance, which they suggested was the result of increased anabolism and a decrease in muscle damage stimulated by the taper (33).

In another study, Bishop and Edge (10) examined the effect of a 6-week overreaching period followed by a 10-day exponential taper on repeated-sprint performance capacity in recreational team sport athletes. Repeated sprint ability (5 × 6 s all-out cycling sprints every 30 s) was tested prior to and after the taper period. The taper resulted in a significant decrease in work decrement (10.2 ± 3.5% vs. 7.9 ± 4.3%, $p <0.05$) and a nonsignificant increase in peak power (+3.2%, $p = 0.18$) and total work (+4.4%, $p = 0.16$). Based on these data, Mujika (89) suggests employing tapering techniques typically used with individual sport athletes in the programming strategies of team sport athletes.

Conceptually, programming an overreaching period during the preseason (i.e., precompetition phase) followed by a taper prior to the start of the season (i.e., main competition phase) aligns with the concepts of the block periodization models (chapter 5) presented by Issurin (68), in which periods of reduced training load are employed after periods of accumulation. Issurin's (68) block model divides training into three stages: accumulation (i.e., overreaching), transmutation (i.e., reduced training load), and realization (i.e., taper). Preseason might be an ideal time to incorporate an accentuated loading block followed by a maintenance block that contains a reduction in training load and induces performance gains. The realization block, which would be representative of a true taper, would then lead into more difficult key competitions such as league championships.

Support for this basic model can be seen in the work of Wahl et al. (153), who examined the use of block periodization models with Spanish soccer players. Athletes were exposed to a 2-week overreaching mesocycle followed by a 4-week transmutation mesocycle in which training loads were substantially reduced, which was designed to simulate a preseason overreaching block followed by a maintenance block of training as used by many coaches (78, 79). Testing was undertaken prior to the start of the overreaching mesocycle and 6 and 25 days after the completion of this block of training. Repeated sprint ability (i.e., mean sprint time and fatigue rate) and Yo-Yo Intermittent Recovery Test Level 2 performance improved significantly from pre-overreaching to 6- and 25-days post-overreaching. Although performance remained elevated at the 25th day after the overreaching testing period, performance tended to decrease in comparison to the 6-day post-overreaching testing period. This is an important consideration when incorporating overreaching and tapering strategies during the preseason, because it appears that after about one mesocycle (i.e., four to six microcycles), it may be warranted to place additional accumulation microcycles into the structure of the in-season training period to maintain capacities throughout the season (2, 120, 142).

Peaking Performance for a Major Tournament

Many team sports have major international tournaments that occur after a long domestic club season (89). Mujika (89) suggests that some nations plan their domestic competition calendars so players can engage in a short transition period followed by a short preparation period before they undertake their national team duties. Conversely, other nations move their domestic schedules so athletes move right from their domestic competitive season into their international competitive schedule. Mujika (89) suggests this is undertaken with the belief that the athletes would be able to maintain competitive shape into the tournament. These two examples of how to structure performance leading into an international tournament have positives and negatives. There is, however, limited research on how best to structure training for these situations.

Many sport teams maintain high-level performance during the main season and then enter a playoff structure in which they must elevate their performance leading to a championship or grand final (19). Depending on the time between the end of the main competitive season and the start of the playoffs, overreaching microcycles followed by microcycles with reduced training loads (i.e., taper) can be programmed. Research by Botonis and colleagues (19) examined this programming strategy with water polo players; a 2-week overreaching mesocycle was followed by a 2-week mesocycle that employed a progressive exponential taper that reduced training loads by about 36%. This tapering strategy resulted in significant improvements in 20 m and 400 m swim performance when compared to postseason values and was aligned with reductions in internal training load (e.g., fatigue perception, muscle soreness, stress levels) after the taper. Based on these data, if time is available between the end of the season and the initiation of the playoffs or tournament, coaches could consider this overload and tapering strategy due to the associated improvements in performance (figure 12.11).

For example, figure 12.12 shows the 2019-2020 National Collegiate Athletic Association (NCAA) American football schedule for the Alabama Crimson Tide. After the last game of the main portion of the competition season (November 30), there were 31 days until the VRBO Citrus Bowl on January 1, 2020.

Based on this schedule, a 1-week transition could be employed after the November 30 game, followed by a 2-week overreaching mesocycle and a 2-week taper, allowing for performance supercompensation at the VRBO Citrus Bowl.

If, however, the team has less time between the end of the season and the playoffs, a different strategy will need to be employed. During the 2019-2020 National Football League (NFL) schedule, the end of in-season play for the Kansas City Chiefs occurred on December 29. The team had 2 weeks until the beginning of the playoffs, which lasted 3 weeks and culminated with the Super Bowl on February 2, 2020 (figure 12.13).

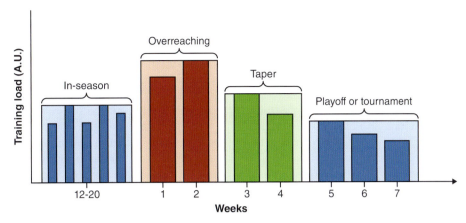

FIGURE 12.11 Playoff or tournament tapering strategy.

FIGURE 12.12 NCAA football season, 2019-2020 Alabama Crimson Tide.

FIGURE 12.13 NFL season, 2019-2020 Kansas City Chiefs.

With this schedule, the team has 13 days between the last in-season game against the Chargers and the first playoff game against the Texans. In this scenario, overreaching could be integrated into the later portions of the end of the microcycle that follows the last game of the season; then, a typical in-season training week could be planned for the microcycle leading into the first playoff game. This strategy could be repeated for the 13 days leading up to the Super Bowl.

There are numerous ways to optimize team sport performance leading into the playoffs or into a major tournament. Although there are some planning strategies in which deliberate overreaching and structured tapering practices can be employed, it is also important to integrate monitoring practices to individualize the training process during this time (see chapter 11). Through smart planning and effective monitoring of both internal and external loads, the coach can enhance programming strategies, which will ultimately increase the athlete's level of preparedness for the key competitive engagements.

Competition Period of the Annual Plan

The primary purpose of a competitive athlete's periodized training plan is to guide the training process toward competition (37). World records and gold medals are not awarded for performances in training. A successful competitive athlete must be able to achieve optimal levels of performance in competition; training results are irrelevant if they do not translate into competitive performance. The coach's role is to help the athlete enhance their competitive performance, and all aspects of the periodized training plan should have a singular focus on the pursuit of this end (37).

In the annual training plan, the structure of the competition period (see chapter 6) largely depends on the number of competitions and their distribution within the plan (117). Central to the success of this period of training is the ability of the coach to craft training interventions that continue to elevate or maintain sport-specific fitness, enhance the psychological traits that underpin performance (e.g., confidence, resilience), and allow the athlete to perfect and consolidate technical and tactical skills in preparation for competition (12). In individual sports, this process is facilitated by aligning key tapering strategies outlined in this chapter with targeted competitions (e.g., championships, Olympic Games) (13). In team sports, this period generally contains a denser competitive schedule, and various programming strategies will be used to optimize performance across the period; tapering strategies will be reserved for the most important competitions. Regardless of the sport, a true peak can only be maintained for a short time (i.e., 8 to 14 days). Therefore, the competition period must be carefully planned to ensure that the athlete's performance is elevated at the most appropriate time and adequate training is provided to maintain physical and psychological attributes that underpin performance.

Classifying Competitions

To understand how to best prepare the athlete for competition, the coach must classify the intended competitions into one of two broad categories: (1) principal or official competitions or (2) training competitions (37).

Principal competitions, or major competitions (13), are the most important competitions in the athlete's annual training plan (13, 37). In individual sports, these competitions provide the key targets for the annual training plan. Due to the overall importance of these competitions and the requirement that the athlete be able to achieve their peak performance at them, a taper is generally used prior to these events. This ensures fatigue is dissipated and the athlete's preparedness is elevated leading into the event (13). In his seminal text, Matveyev (84) suggests that no more than three to five principal competitions that require peak performance should be in an annual training plan. Similarly, Dick (37) suggests that no more than four peak performances that require a comprehensive taper should be included in the annual plan.

In team sports, the competition period generally contains numerous major competitions that require the athlete to perform at a high level more frequently. Because these sports generally have more congested schedules, a true peak performance is reserved for the ultimate competitions (Super Bowl, Grand Final, etc.). Training loads will be varied around each major competition, but the standard taper will be reserved for the most important competition in the annual plan. Since athletes are not able to achieve a true peak performance at every competition, the coach must determine which competitions are the most important in the competitive season so that appropriate tapering strategies can be integrated into the overall training plan.

Exhibition competitions (13), or competitions used for training, play an important role in the athlete's development and competition performance (37). These events test the athlete's current level of development and provide feedback about specific aspects of the training process (13, 37). These competitions should be considered high-intensity training sessions, and the goal should not be focused on victory. Although using competitions as training is an important part of an athlete's development, the coach must always remember that competitions are not a substitute for training (11) and consider the total number of competitions (training and actual) in the annual training plan. The greater the number of competitions in the precompetition and competition periods, the greater the potential for reduced gains in performance and the greater the risks of injury (7, 27, 32, 111).

Planning for Competitions

One of the most important steps in developing the annual training plan is to determine the competitive schedule for the athlete or team (11). The actual dates for major competitions are often set by the sport's governing body and can be used by the coach to set the structure of the competitive period of the annual training plan. In team sports, such as NCAA collegiate football, a preset conference schedule is augmented with nonconference games selected by the university. Regardless of how the schedule is created, the coach needs to determine which competitions require peak performance (i.e., the principal competitions) and plan a structured taper and training competitions that will serve as intense training sessions.

When the coach is establishing the competition period, one of the biggest things to remember is that it is not possible to peak for every competition (89). If the coach attempts to structure the athlete's training plan so the athlete frequently peaks during the season, the athlete will experience a significant reduction in performance capacity due to the reduction in time dedicated to training that enhances the physiological, psychological, tactical, and technical characteristics that underpin performance (11). Therefore, it is generally recommended that the coach target no more than three to five competitions in the annual training plan for which tapering strategies are employed. With the remaining competitions, the coach can optimize performance by employing short unloading periods within the microcycle containing the competition to modulate fatigue.

Ultimately, the structure of the competition period depends on the number of competitions and their distribution over this period (117). If the coach determines the main focus of the annual plan is to target one competition or tournament, a simple competition training period can be used. With this structure, the entirety of the competition period is used to fine-tune the athlete's technical and tactical performance capacities while balancing the development of the physical training components that underpin performance. Prior to the competition, the coach will employ a structured tapering strategy to ensure that the athlete performs at their best at the targeted competitions (117).

If multiple competitions (i.e., two or more consecutive events or tournaments) are targeted, the coach could plan a complex competition training period (117). Olbrect (117) suggests that this type of competition period will contain peak form–inducing or peak form–maintaining periods (i.e., between competition time periods) to allow performance to be maintained across several consecutive competitions. Ultimately, the number of mesocycles in the competition period will be dictated by the athlete's needs and the complexity of the competition period (i.e., simple vs. complex) (117).

An example of a complex competition training period is presented by French (45), who outlines an example annual plan for a taekwondo athlete who is training for the 2012 Olympic Games (figure 12.14) (45). French's annual training plan (45) strategically places groups of competitions at key points followed by periods of training that last several microcycles. This approach, often referred to as the *grouping approach*, has several competitions in a short time followed by a period when the athlete can return to targeted preparation training to continue to develop their physical and performance capacities. Throughout the annual training plan, the coach will leverage different microcycle strategies (see chapter 7) to guide the training process so performance can be optimized or peaked at specific competitions.

Alternatively, competitions can be placed at regular, repeating intervals throughout the competition period (11). This pattern of competition is commonly seen in American football, in which competitions typically occur each weekend. Figure 12.12 shows the competition period for the Alabama Crimson Tide. In this example, the bulk of the competition period occurs between weeks 4 and 17, culminating with the conference championship. During this time, competitive microcycles are employed and training loads are manipulated to optimize performance. The taper is used leading into the conference championship, since there is enough time to engage in an overreaching strategy with another taper prior to the team's bowl game. Similarly, the competition period for the NFL's Kansas City Chiefs (figure 12.13)

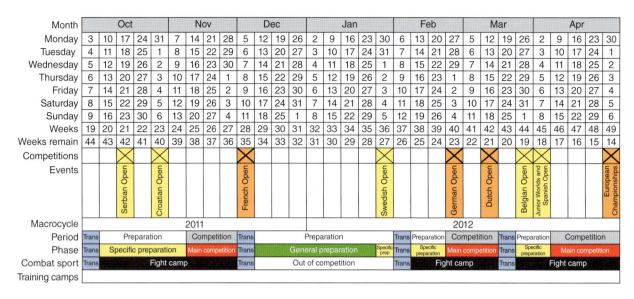

FIGURE 12.14 Example combat sport (taekwondo) macrocycle for Olympic Games preparation.
Adapted from French (2019).

displays the cyclic approach to planning the competition period. Due to the overall length of the competition periods in these two examples, microcycle planning strategies (see chapter 7) are employed to optimize performance during the bulk of the season and then peak for specific competitions.

It is likely that grouped approaches are more aligned with individual sports, and the cyclic approach is better aligned with the competition periods typically undertaken by team sport athletes. The coach can also consider a combination of these two approaches when structuring their annual training plan.

Competition Frequency

Determining how many competitive engagements an athlete undertakes and which competitions employ a taper is a complex planning task. Numerous factors, such as the athlete's individual characteristics (e.g., age, training age) and the sport, affect the coach's decisions about the number and frequency of competitions in the annual training plan (11, 13). An additional consideration is the overall length of the competitive period; the longer the competitive period, the more competitions can be contested (32).

The athlete's chronological and training ages are primary factors that influence the number of competitions the athlete should contest (38). For young athletes who are in the early stages of their long-term athlete development (LTAD) plan, the primary focus should be on developing fundamental movement competencies (44) while deemphasizing competition (51). As the athlete moves through their LTAD plan, the emphasis on competition and the number of competitions in the annual training plan will generally increase (32, 51, 76). Note that if the number of competitions is too high, there is an increased injury risk (126) and a potential negative effect on performance due to reduced time dedicated to training (32, 37).

Although many sports show a pattern in which the number and frequency of competitions increase over time, this may not be the best approach in all sports. For example, in strength and power sports, such as weightlifting and powerlifting (118), there may be an upper limit to the number of competitions athletes should target in an annual training plan. One recommendation for these types of sports is to reduce the number of competitions as the athlete becomes more developed (1, 20). For example, a youth weightlifter (13-15 years old) may engage in 8 to 10 competitions per year with an emphasis on using competition as a training activity (1). As the lifter progresses into the junior ranks (15-20 years old), the number of competitions in their annual training plan will decrease to six to eight per year, and only two or three major competitions per year (i.e., principal competitions) will employ a taper, with the remainder serving as training activities (1). Once the athlete progresses into the senior ranks (>20 years old), the frequency of competition is further reduced to four to six competitions per year with only two competitions serving as principal competitions (1). Ultimately, as the athlete becomes more developed, more focus on training may be warranted to continue to elevate their weightlifting performance. These

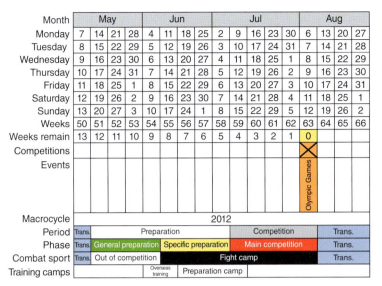

FIGURE 12.14 *(continued)*

recommendations align well with recent research examining the effect of competition frequency on performance progression. Specifically, contesting more than four competitions in a year results in a reduction in progression and competitive success for athletes who compete in strength-focused sports, such as powerlifting (118) or weightlifting.

Ultimately, coaches who work with individual sports, such as weightlifting or track and field, have greater flexibility in the design of the competitive schedule than those who work in team sports (13). In team sports, the frequency of competition is dictated by the schedule of competitions established by the league in which the team competes. For example, NFL teams contest a 17-game regular season between September and December, and if they make postseason play, they can compete in an additional three or four games, for a total of 20 or 21 potential games. The schedule is determined by the NFL via a scheduling algorithm that uses current division alignments and the final division standings from the previous season (114). NFL teams generally compete every week with one bye week each season. In the National Basketball Association, teams typically play 82 regular season games, with two to five games per week across a season that lasts about 5.5 months (47). For the better teams, there can be an additional 2 months of postseason play. Similarly, in the Premier League (soccer), a top team may contest 60 competitions (roughly one game every 3.5-4.5 days) over a period of 270 days, with some players also participating in international competitions (i.e., representing their country) (37). Given these examples, it is easy to see that the coach has little input into the frequency of the team's competitive schedule. Depending on the quality of the team, the coach could establish a player-rotation schedule to reduce playing time for some players, thereby ensuring recovery and optimal play at key times in the season (37).

When the coach is constructing the competitive period of the annual training plan, they must consider the sequence and frequency of competitions (107). Specific attention must be paid to the amount of time between successive competitive engagements, because this time significantly affects the athlete's ability to recover from competition and achieve peak performance at the optimal time (107). To deal with dense competitive schedules, an athlete requires an increased focus on recovery and a reduction in the time dedicated to training. Ultimately, this requirement may impede the athlete's development across the competition period. Additionally, the coach must consider the effect of travel; the more travel required, the greater the potential for the negative effects of jet lag (70) and the chances of travel fatigue (131) (see chapter 9).

When the coach is deciding the frequency of competition and the placement of competitions for an individual sport athlete, they should consider the following general recommendations (9, 11, 13):

- Select the number of competitions based on the athlete's developmental needs so they can achieve and stabilize their top performance.
- Sequence the selected competitions in the annual training plan to progressively increase difficulty, with the most important competition being placed at or toward the end of the annual plan.
- Whenever possible, ensure adequate time between competitions to ensure recovery after the event and adequate time for training activities that further develop the athlete.
- Avoid entering the athlete in too many competitions, which can have a negative effect on the progression of performance and can potentially increase injury risk.
- Consider travel requirements when selecting competitions. Excessive travel during the competition period places additional stress on the athlete and reduces the time that can be dedicated to training. Failing to consider the effect of travel as part of the planning process

can significantly reduce the athlete's ability to compete at their highest level (see chapter 9).

- Target a maximum of four principal competitions in which the athlete employs a full taper. For training competitions, the coach should either consider training through the event or only slightly modulating training loads prior to these events.
- Consider the importance of psychological preparation and the effect of competition on the athlete's confidence. If the athlete requires specific competitive activities to maximize their confidence, this must be considered as part of the planning process.

A coach designing the competitive period for a team sport athlete should consider the following general recommendations (129, 130):

- Determine the time allotted between competitions and how this time relates to the balance between competition and recovery.
- Examine the travel requirements of the schedule provided by the league and determine how to manage travel-related fatigue (see chapter 9).
- Determine where congested competition time periods (e.g., tournaments) exist in the competition period.
- Determine which competitions are the most difficult or will require additional modifications to the training schedule to ensure athletes achieve the appropriate level of recovery prior to the competition.
- Determine where tapering strategies will be employed in the competition period (i.e., pre-competition or main competition phase).

Optimizing Performance for High-Frequency Competition Periods

In many team sports, such as professional soccer or basketball, the competition period of the annual training plan contains numerous competitions (26), and, depending on the sport, these contests may be in a congested schedule (66). It is generally accepted that competition places greater demands on the athlete compared to normal training activities (138) and that **congested competition schedules** in which there is a shorter-than-usual time between competitions can significantly increase the athlete's injury risk (7, 27, 138). For example, simply increasing the number of competitions from one to two within a microcycle can result in a significant increase in injury risk during competition (138). If competitions occur 4 or fewer days apart (6, 28, 36, 39), these risks are further elevated when compared to competitions separated by 6 or more days (138). These periods often require a reduction in training loads so the time between contests can be used to prioritize recovery (138), which reduces the time available for physical training. Ultimately, congested competition periods require the coach to leverage their integrated monitoring program to inform programming decisions and create a better balance between training, competition, and recovery.

The coach must remember that it is impossible to plan for peak performance for every competition. The challenge of ensuring the athlete is prepared for each competition becomes more evident when the competition period is congested. The coach may need to use more fluid strategies, such as **autoregulation** (49, 134) or strategic programming strategies (129, 130), which are based on data collected as part of an integrated monitoring program to better manage the fatigue associated with training, travel, and competition. Because performance and fitness elevate when accumulated fatigue is reduced (146), how training loads are modulated during the competitive period is critical to ensure that the athlete's performance is optimized or peaked at the correct time.

Optimizing Versus Peaking Performance

A coach working in a sport that requires competitive success across a long, possibly congested competition schedule to determine qualification for a playoff and championship must consider how to manage training and competitive stress to ensure success. Attempting to use tapering strategies (i.e., 41-60% reductions in training load for 8 to 14 days) for every competition would result in poor performances over time due to reductions in physical capacities in response to reducing training loads for prolonged periods, so other strategies must be considered.

Conceptually, the coach could implement programming strategies that either optimize or peak performance to their highest possible levels. Peaking, with the use of tapering strategies, employs training strategies designed to minimize fatigue and maximize preparedness and performance capacity for a principal competition. After the completion of a taper, in which full performance peak is achieved, the athlete will need to be exposed to higher training loads for a time. Attempting to employ this strategy within the season can be problematic if the schedule doesn't include any mesocycles without competitions or during which the athlete can be withheld from competition to be exposed to increased training loads.

Alternatively, the coach should employ strategies to optimize performance throughout the season. This process involves programming strategies that reduce accumulated fatigue while elevating preparedness and performance capacity. By leveraging an integrated monitoring system and making informed programming decisions, the coach can optimize competitive in-season performance. To accomplish this task, specific attention must be paid to multiple factors, such as travel, training, and competition fatigue, as well as injuries, all of which affect performance (129, 130).

Although optimization employs similar strategies to peaking, the objective of optimization is to manage fatigue and maintain fitness rather than elevating performance to its highest level. Although some level of fatigue always exists, the coach will employ unloading strategies at strategic times in the competition microcycle. The degree of unloading structured into the athlete's program depends on factors such as the travel required for the competition, the strength of the opposition, and the athlete's ever-changing physiological and psychological responses to competition and training (129, 130). At times, greater or lesser degrees of unloading will be employed. Ultimately, the optimization process is a systematic balancing of training that facilitates recovery and provides loading or unloading during each microcycle of the competition period.

Methods of Manipulating Training

Fundamentally, the optimization process involves manipulating training load across the competitive microcycle to balance the application of training stress, provide the foundation for adaptation, and reduce training load to facilitate recovery. Optimization is generally accomplished by dividing the competitive microcycle into three basic structural components: recovery, loading, and unloading (figure 12.15). As shown in figure 12.15, the two competitions are 7 days apart. The first 2 days after the competition (i.e., game +1 and game +2) target recovery and are designed to reduce the fatigue developed by the first competition and factors associated with that competition (e.g., travel, psychological stress).

There are two basic planning strategies the coach can use to sequence these sessions (figure 12.16). In the first strategy (figure 12.6*a*), the coach plans for the first day after the competition (game +1) to be a day off of training, and the second day (game +2) is a training day featuring low-level training and recovery activities. The second strategy (figure 12.6*b*) plans for the athlete to perform low-level training and recovery activities on the first day after the competition and then have a day off on the second day.

After these recovery days, training load could be elevated for 2 days (i.e., game +3 and game +4) to provide a training stress that maintains the athlete's physical capacities, enhances confidence, and provides technical and tactical training designed to prepare for the coming competition. The overall magnitude of loading will depend on a lot of

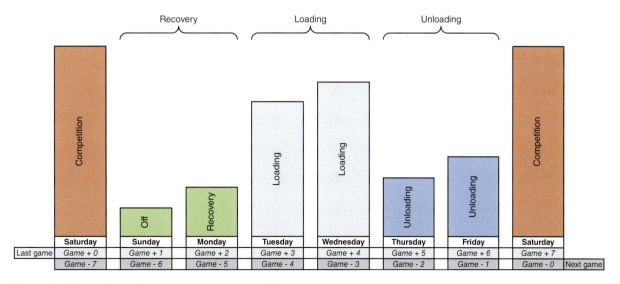

FIGURE 12.15 Optimization strategy for a competition microcycle.

330 | Scientific Foundations and Practical Applications of Periodization

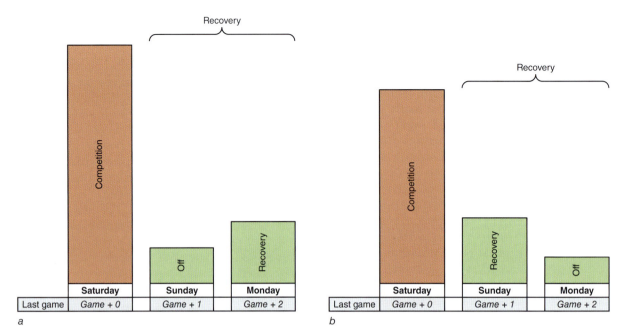

FIGURE 12.16 Two postcompetition recovery training sequences: *(a)* day off followed by recovery training day; *(b)* recovery training day followed by day off.

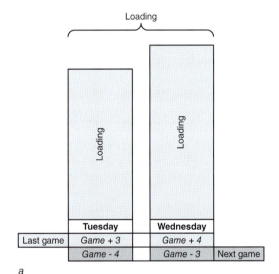

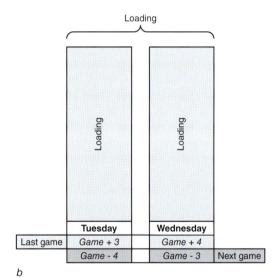

FIGURE 12.17 Loading patterns during a competition microcycle: *(a)* stepwise increase in loading; *(b)* flat loading; *(c)* stepwise decrease in loading.

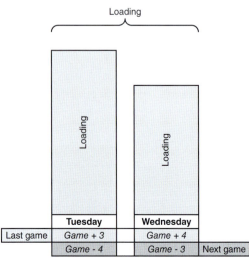

factors, including the athlete's individual rate of recovery, but will generally be structured to deliver moderate to hard training loads (figure 12.17). The focus of training during these loading days is split among physical, technical, and tactical training.

After the loading portion of the microcycle, the coach will reduce training loads (i.e., unload) on the last 2 days before the next competition (i.e., game −2 and game −1), so recovery can occur prior to the subsequent competition (figure 12.18). The most common strategy is to use a stepwise decrease in training load (figure 12.18a) so the lowest load is the day before the competition (game −1). Conversely, training load could be reduced on the first unloading day (game −2) and then elevated on the day prior to the next competition (figure 12.18b). Both strategies have merit and should be considered depending on the athlete's or team's needs.

As noted in chapter 7, various competitive microcycles (figures 7.20, 7.21, and 7.25) can be created to address the number of required competitions in a given period. With more congested competitive schedules, the coach may need to dedicate individual days to recovery, loading, or unloading (figure 12.19). In these microcycles,

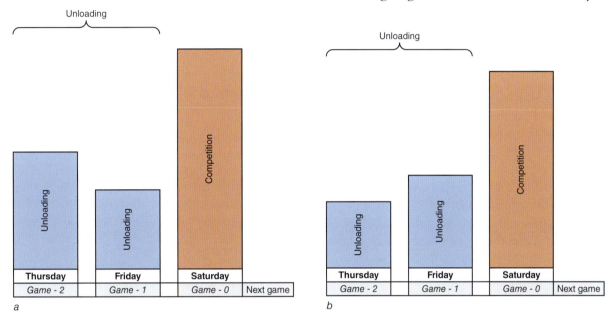

FIGURE 12.18 Precompetition unloading strategies for a competition microcycle: *(a)* unloading with a stepwise decrease in training load; *(b)* unloading with a stepwise increase in training load.

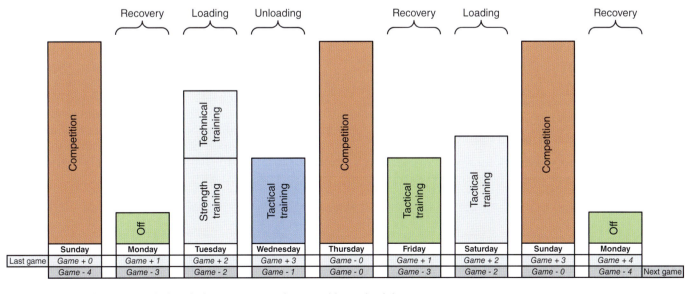

FIGURE 12.19 Loading variation during a congested competition schedule.

Adapted from V. Manzi, S. D'Ottavio, F.M. Impellizzeri, et al., "Profile of Weekly Training Load in Elite Male Professional Basketball Players," *The Journal of Strength & Conditioning Research* 24 (2010): 1399-1406.

postcompetition training days often are classified as recovery sessions but require some loading to ensure maintenance of physical and performance characteristics. Additionally, unloading before a competition will either display a stepwise decrease or increase in training load. Note that these loads are lower in relation to typical loading days. Ultimately, the key to effective microcycles is the ability to manage training loads to minimize fatigue and maximize preparedness as the athlete approaches each competition in each microcycle. Central to this process is the ability to leverage an integrated monitoring system (chapter 11).

Summary

Elevating performance at competitive engagements is a central goal of any periodized training plan. Even though different strategies can be employed to elevate performance depending on the athlete's or team's competitive schedule, there are some basic recommendations about tapering the coach should consider:

- Target two to four principal competitions that will employ structured tapering strategies.
- Use a taper to reduce accumulated fatigue, elevate preparedness, and maintain or elevate fitness to maximize performance capacity.
- Create individualized tapering strategies that last 8 to 14 days to optimize performance. If the taper is preceded by large training loads, the length of the taper may be extended to 4 weeks to reduce accumulated fatigue.
- Decrease training volume by 41% to 60% of the pretaper training volume. If extensive training loads precede the taper, training volume may need to be decreased by 60% to 90%.
- Maintain training frequency at 80% or more of the pretaper training frequency.
- To avoid detraining, ensure the taper includes moderate to high training intensities.
- Use progressive, nonlinear tapering strategies.

The athlete cannot peak for every competition, so the coach must carefully examine the competitive calendar and prioritize specific engagements. At most, the coach should plan for the athlete or team to peak two to four times in the competition period. All other competitions should use optimization strategies in which preplanned unloading is used to reduce accumulated fatigue. For team sports that engage in congested competitive schedules, the taper should be reserved for the playoffs or championship games, with the coach using optimization strategies and strategically manipulating recovery, loading, and unloading to modulate performance capacity prior to each competition.

Ideally, the taper should last 8 to 14 days; this has been shown to produce the optimal performance enhancement. However, if the training load that precedes the taper is very high, it may be warranted to extend the taper to 3 to 4 weeks. Training load should be reduced by 41% to 60% of pretaper training loads, but this can be modified depending on the magnitude of the training loads preceding the taper. If training loads prior to the taper are very high, a greater reduction in training volume (60%-90%) may be warranted. Conversely, if the training loads prior to the taper are very low, a shorter taper may suffice. When reducing training load, the coach should ensure that training frequency is not reduced to less than 80% of pretaper training frequency. Ideally, this reduction in training load should employ a nonlinear tapering strategy. Finally, the coach should ensure that the training intensity is maintained or slightly increased to maintain the physiological and psychological adaptations achieved prior to the initiation of the taper.

The coach must remember that the primary goal of any tapering strategy is to reduce training-induced fatigue and elevate the athlete's level of preparedness. Preparedness should not solely focus on the athlete's physical capacities but should also relate to psychological parameters, such as confidence, which are related to improved performance. The coach should consider integrating psychological training activities into the taper and should have an open dialogue with the athlete to ensure that the athlete's psychological and performance needs are met.

PART IV
TRAINING METHODS

Central to the process of developing periodized plans is the integration of physical training into the process. It is critical for the coach to understand various training methods that can be employed when developing athletes. To help the coach develop a comprehensive understanding of these methods, the final part of this text explores various training methods that can be used as part of a periodized training plan. Chapter 13 examines various aspects of strength and power development and how these training methods can be integrated into a periodized training plan. Chapter 14 presents a detailed discussion about high-intensity interval training methods. Following this discussion, chapter 15 presents training methods for speed and agility development and aligns them with contemporary periodization theory.

CHAPTER 13

Strength, Power, and Hypertrophy Training

Although several factors contribute to an athlete's performance capacity, it is increasingly evident that muscular strength is one of the most important factors underpinning high-level performance. For example, maximal strength is highly correlated with sprinting performance (486); increases in lower-body strength have been clearly shown to translate to improved performance (431), with stronger individuals tending to be faster than their weaker counterparts (29, 83, 227, 309, 317, 546). The ability to jump also seems to be affected by maximal strength (486), with stronger individuals displaying significantly higher vertical jump performances than weaker individuals (28, 227, 283, 428, 442, 546). Furthermore, maximal strength has been reported to affect an athlete's change of direction (COD) ability (486), with stronger athletes demonstrating an enhanced ability to change direction (113, 458, 549) and an increased exit velocity when performing COD activities (457). Based on these data, it is easy to ascertain that maximal strength is important for sporting activities that require the athlete to sprint, jump, and change direction rapidly.

Maximal strength has also been shown to be an important factor modulating endurance performance capacities (32, 470). For example, when maximal strength is added to the training programs of cyclists (31, 33, 38, 338, 398-401), long-distance runners (34, 38, 259, 356), and Nordic skiers (222, 355, 357), athletes show increases in maximal strength that directly translate to improved performance via enhancements in movement economy and efficiency (34).

Higher levels of strength are also related to several sport-specific skills, including tackling ability in rugby (147, 454-456) and throwing speed in cricket (134), baseball (289), handball (98), and water polo (267). Because strength seems to underpin numerous aspects of sporting performance, some have suggested that it is the highest order biomotor ability governing performance (47, 462). Based on the available scientific literature, a hypothetical model can be constructed in which strength is connected to speed, endurance, agility, and power-generation capacities (figure 13.1) (47).

The ability to effectively translate an athlete's strength capacities to sporting performance is directly related to mobility (110, 377). Mobility can be thought of as the **range of motion** through which forces can effectively be applied (377). Due to the importance of mobility to the overall ability to apply maximal strength to sporting performance, Frank Dick (110), the former director of coaching for British Athletics, developed a model of the basic physical characteristics of performance (figure 13.2).

In this model, mobility is central to the development of specific strength, speed, and endurance abilities, which serve as the foundation for sport performance (377). Radcliffe (377) suggests that the basic structure presented by Dick provides a framework from which progressions can be developed so that various attributes are established in alignment with the athlete's individual needs. This concept provides support for incorporating specific physical training activities that build on functional ranges of motion, allowing for maximal strength to be enhanced and translated to improvements in sport performance.

A common question among coaches is, "When is our athlete strong enough?" Fundamentally, an athlete's strength levels exist across a theoretical continuum ranging from a strength deficit (i.e., inadequate strength levels) to what is referred to as a *strength reserve* (56, 122, 486) (figure 13.3). The athlete's strength levels move along this continuum depending on their training history and current training practices. The athlete should seek to increase their strength reserve as much as possible to reduce their overall injury risk while maximizing performance capacity (56, 179, 486). If the athlete's strength levels decline, whether due to injury, poorly designed training programs, or noncompliance to training activities, their performance capacity will be reduced and they will have an increased overall injury risk. Therefore, the coach must seek to implement resistance-training activities that target strength development to ensure the athlete is able to maximize their strength reserve.

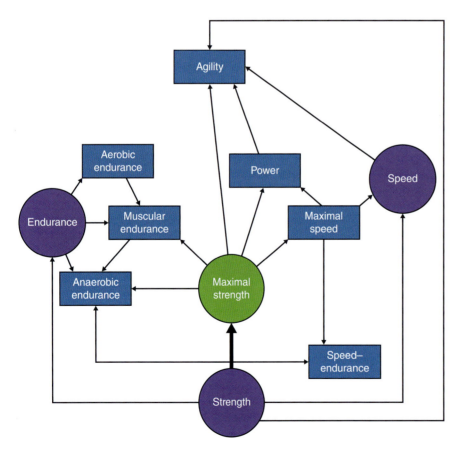

FIGURE 13.1 Interaction of strength, speed, and endurance.
Adapted from Bompa and Haff (2009).

Chapter 13 • Strength, Power, and Hypertrophy Training | **337**

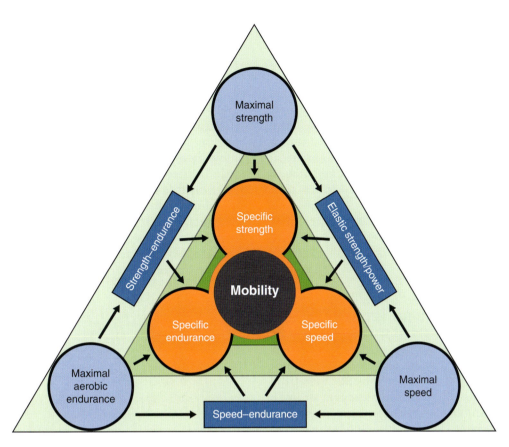

FIGURE 13.2 Hypothetical relationship between basic physical fitness characteristics and their relationship to specific fitness required for sport performance.

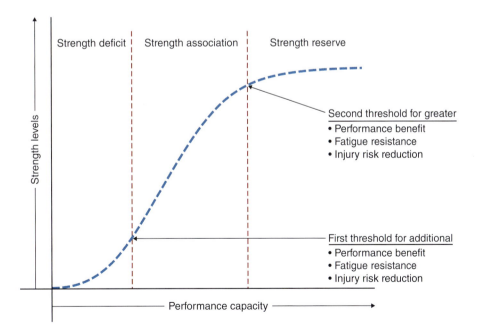

FIGURE 13.3 Theoretical relationship between strength and performance.

Adapted by permission from G.G. Haff, "Isometric and Dynamic Testing," in *Performance Assessments for Strength and Conditioning Coaches*, edited by P. Comfort, P.A. Jones, and J.J. McMahon (Oxon, United Kingdom: Taylor Francis Books, 2019), 167. Reproduced by permission of Taylor and Francis Group, LLC, a division of Informa plc.

Strength and Power Development

Muscular strength is represented as the maximal force or **torque** (i.e., rotational force) that a muscle or group of muscles can generate (47, 115). More specifically, strength is the ability of the neuromuscular system to produce force against an external resistance (472). Greater levels of muscular strength are significantly related to sport performance (486), a more rapid rate of recovery (69, 430), and an overall lower risk of injury (301). A wealth of scientific literature indicates that higher strength levels relate to improved sprint (22, 54, 83, 329), jumping (182, 264, 266, 283, 350), and change of direction performance (264, 266, 346). Additionally, strength has been related to American football (28, 140, 243), soccer (71, 160, 221, 449), volleyball (124, 318), gymnastics (119, 413), rugby league (146, 147), rugby union (120), ice hockey (223), track cycling (468), and aerobic exercise performance (31, 222, 259, 356, 401). As noted by Suchomel and colleagues (485, 486), greater muscular strength underpins many of the attributes associated with overall performance levels and should be an important consideration when creating a periodized training plan. Ultimately, appropriately structured resistance-training interventions integrated into the overall periodized training plan will translate into an enhanced sport performance.

Force and Velocity Relationships

Based on the available scientific evidence, it is easy to see that an athlete's ability to express high levels of force against an external resistance is a very important factor affecting sport performance (187). Given the stated importance of strength, resistance training should be considered an essential part of an athlete's overall training process. The ability of a resistance-training program to translate into sport performance can be partially explained by Newton's second law of motion, in which the sum of the forces acting on an object is equal to the object's mass multiplied by the object's acceleration (486). Based on this relationship, any change in the motion of an object (i.e., acceleration) is directly proportional to the amount of force applied to it. Specifically, the greater the force applied to the object, the greater the acceleration of the object and the greater the velocity of movement (187, 486). Based on this line of reasoning, an increased force-generating capacity, or strength level, is a prerequisite for the expression of high velocities of movement (486).

There is an inverse relationship between force and velocity, whereby the velocity of movement decreases as the external resistance increases (figure 13.4) (187, 265, 533, 552). Reductions in movement velocity continue until a maximum load is lifted (e.g., 1RM, 2RM), resulting in what is referred to as the *minimum* or *terminal velocity threshold*, which represents the point at which muscular failure occurs (241, 533). Fundamentally, it is this relationship that serves as the foundation for velocity-based training (VBT) methods, which will be explored later in this chapter.

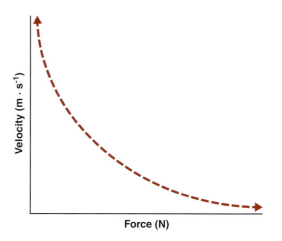

FIGURE 13.4 Force–velocity relationship.

Conceptually, when undertaking a resistance-training program, the programming decisions made can influence various portions of the force–velocity curve (187, 248, 262, 265, 312, 335, 479). It is likely that if heavy resistance training is undertaken, different adaptations will occur when compared to performing resistance training that requires rapid muscle contractions (i.e., ballistic or explosive training methods) (187, 195, 196, 265, 545). For example, if the resistance-training program requires the performance of rapid muscular contractions with low external loads (e.g., ballistic exercises, explosive exercises, plyometrics), it is likely that the low-force portion of the force–velocity curve will be altered (figure 13.5*a*) (187). Conversely, if heavy resistance training is performed, the high-force portion of the force–velocity curve is likely to be altered (figure 13.5*b*) (187). If, however, mixed training methods (i.e., combinations of ballistic and heavy resistance training) are performed as part of a resistance-training program, a more balanced shift of the force–velocity curve can occur (figure 13.5c) (187).

Although these theoretical constructs make sense and to some extent are supported by a sound body of scientific research (187, 248, 262, 265, 312, 335, 479), the athlete's strength levels may actually dictate these responses (80, 81). For example, Cormie and colleagues (81) report that when weaker individuals (back squat 1RM = 1.32 ± 0.14 kg · body mass^{-1}) undertake ballistic resistance training with individualized training loads, the entire force–velocity curve shifted to the right. When stronger individuals (back squat 1RM = 1.97 ± 0.08 kg · body mass^{-1}) completed the same basic training program, only the high-velocity portion of the force–velocity curve shifted to the right. Furthermore, Cormie and colleagues (80) have reported that when weaker individuals (back squat 1RM = 1.28 ± 0.17 kg · body mass^{-1}) undertake heavy resistance training, there is a greater rightward shift in the force–velocity curve then when ballistic training is performed. These two studies clearly show that for weaker individuals, focusing on heavy resistance training is a more effective and efficient methodology for shifting the force–velocity relationship. As the athlete becomes stronger and establishes a higher level of training, the use of more focused ballistic training methods is warranted to shift the high-velocity portion of the force–velocity relationship (80).

An extension of this concept has been presented by Suchomel and colleagues (479), who suggest that various weightlifting derivatives can be used to target specific areas of the force–velocity curve (figure 13.6). Although this construct is interesting and provides a basic framework from which to consider the relationship between various weightlifting derivatives and the force–velocity curve, this is an overly simplistic association that does not consider the effect of the load lifted with each exercise. For example, it is likely that regardless of the exercise performed, the load on the barbell will dictate the velocity of movement. In fact, Haff and Nimphius (187) suggest that warm-up sets performed with

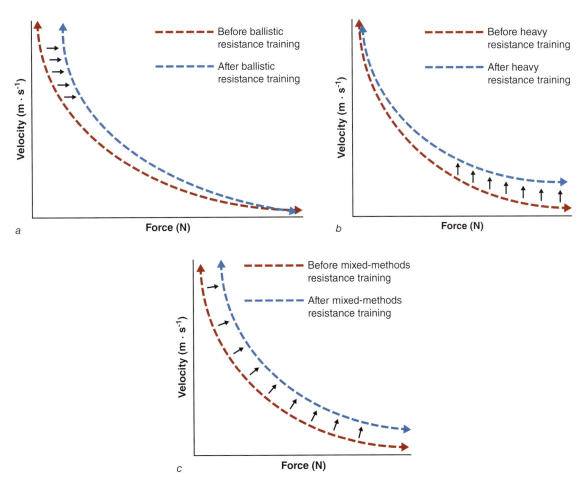

FIGURE 13.5 Theoretical alterations to the force–velocity curve in response to (a) explosive, ballistic, or plyometric exercise; (b) heavy resistance training; (c) mixed-methods resistance training.

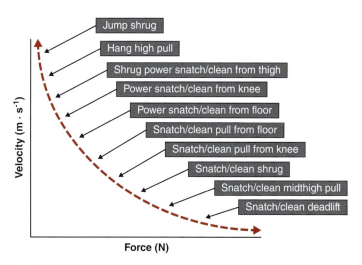

FIGURE 13.6 Aligning weightlifting derivatives with the force–velocity relationship.

Adapted by permission from T.J. Suchomel, P. Comfort, and J.P. Lake, "Enhancing the Force-Velocity Profile of Athletes Using Weightlifting Derivatives," *Strength and Conditioning Journal* 39, no. 1 (2017): 11.

intent provide a very powerful tool for enhancing the high-velocity portion of the force–velocity relationship regardless of the exercise employed.

Rate of Force Development

In many sports, athletes are required to generate high amounts of force against external resistances in relatively short times (187, 265). During sporting movements, the rate of force development (RFD), or explosive muscle strength, represents the rate at which force is generated (3, 187, 486). Typically, the RFD is determined from the slope of the force–time curve (Δ Force/Δ Time) (figure 13.7) (187, 528).

The RFD represents how fast force can be produced and has been consistently shown to be important for sports that involve explosive movements (e.g., sprinting, jumping, throwing, punching, change of direction) (214, 283, 504, 505). These types of activities often require force to be applied in a limited time (50-250 ms) (187), which is generally less than the time required to generate maximal force (>250 ms) (3, 415, 489, 502). Generally, sporting activities that occur in less than 250 milliseconds depend on the RFD, whereas activities that last longer than 250 milliseconds are dominated by maximal strength (i.e., peak force [PF]) (415). Note, however, that maximal strength and the RFD are interrelated (16, 328) and are both related to sport performance.

When examining the effects of various resistance-training activities, it is clear that weaker and untrained individuals will display increases in their maximal force-generating capacity (i.e., PF on the isometric force–time curve) (82, 187) and their RFD (296) in response to training programs that use heavy resistance training (187). In contrast, when stronger athletes undertake heavy-loaded resistance training, it is likely that the main benefit is an enhancement of the athlete's maximal force-generating capacity and strength reserve (187). With these athletes, the optimization of the RFD requires the incorporation of explosive or ballistic exercises (82, 187, 190). Based on these data, the optimization of the force–time curve is affected by different training strategies (figure 13.8).

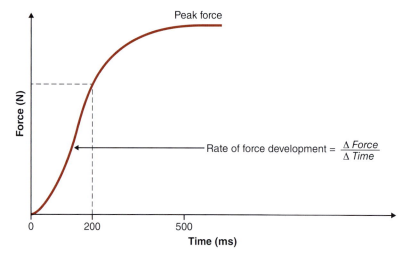

FIGURE 13.7 Isometric force–time curve.

Adapted by permission from G.G. Haff and S. Nimphius, "Training Principles for Power," *Strength and Conditioning Journal* 34 (2012): 5.

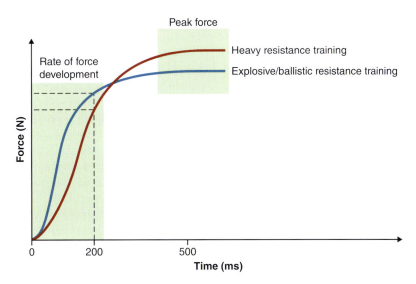

FIGURE 13.8 Effects of various training methods on the isometric force–time curve.

Adapted by permission from G.G. Haff and S. Nimphius, "Training Principles for Power," *Strength and Conditioning Journal* 34 (2012): 5.

Force, Velocity, and Power Relationship

To appreciate how various resistance-training activities enhance the athlete's ability to express high maximal power outputs, the coach must understand how power is mathematically calculated (187). Often referred to as the *rate of doing work* (270), power is generally considered to be the product of force and velocity (187, 265, 344).

$$\text{power} = \frac{\text{work}}{\text{time}} = \frac{\text{force} \times \text{distance}}{\text{time}} = \text{force} \times \text{velocity}$$

Based on the mathematical equations that can be used to calculate power, it is evident that the ability to rapidly apply high levels of force and to express high contraction velocities are central to the ability to express high power outputs (265). When the force–velocity relationship is related to power output (figure 13.9), it is evident that force and velocity are interdependent and that maximal power output is expressed at compromised levels of maximal force and velocity (187, 265, 447).

Haff and Nimphius (187) suggest that there are three key elements that must be considered when attempting to maximize the athlete's power output. First, it is essential that the athlete's muscular strength is maximized due to the well-documented relationship between maximal strength and the RFD. Second, it is important to maximize the RFD, or the speed at which force is applied. Finally, it is important that the athlete develops the ability to express higher forces as the velocity of skeletal

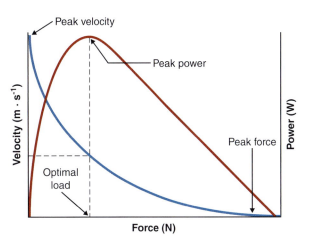

FIGURE 13.9 Force–velocity, force–power, and optimal load relationship.

Reprinted by permission from G.G. Haff and S. Nimphius, "Training Principles for Power," *Strength and Conditioning Journal* 34 (2012): 4.

muscle shortening increases. Careful inspection of these three elements led Haff and Nimphius (187) to conclude that the athlete's maximal strength levels are the main drivers for their ability to express high power outputs. Support for their contention can be found in the scientific literature, where maximal strength is significantly correlated with the RFD (182, 188, 328, 350) and power output (350).

Although maximal strength and the RFD are key contributors to power-generating capacity, the load being overcome will dictate which of these attributes exerts the greatest influence (414, 415). If the load being overcome is decreased, Schmidtbleicher (414, 415) suggests that the contribution of maximal strength to power output will decrease, and the effect of the RFD will increase. Although Schmidtbleicher's (414, 415) theory is logical, remember that maximal strength significantly affects the RFD (182, 188, 328). Therefore, maximal strength, the RFD, and power output are generally considered to be interrelated attributes.

Power-generating capacity or the rate of doing work is generally considered to be the single most important characteristic in sport (190, 265, 312, 414, 473). In fact, several authors have reported that power-generating capacity differentiates between levels of sporting performance (28, 140). When considering the relationships of power output to sporting performance, there are two ways power output is represented: maximal power output and average power output (47). Single-effort maximal performances, such as jumping, sprinting, weightlifting, change of direction, and striking, are typically related to maximal power output (20, 21, 190, 265, 473, 500), whereas average power output is related to the performance of repetitive tasks such as cycling (493), Nordic skiing (355), and running (347).

Factors Affecting Strength

The amount of force an athlete's neuromuscular system can generate depends on seven key concepts (190, 474):

1. The number of motor units recruited
2. The motor unit firing frequency (i.e., rate coding)
3. The amount of motor unit synchronization
4. The degree of neuromuscular inhibition
5. The engagement of the stretch-shortening cycle
6. Muscle fiber type
7. The degree of muscle hypertrophy

Motor Unit Recruitment

The amount of force a muscle can exert is affected by the number of motor units activated (163, 197, 474). The more motor units activated, the greater the amount of force generated by the muscle (190). In their seminal work, Henneman and colleagues (213) determined that the size of the **motor unit** dictates the motor unit's activation threshold. This work established what is known as ***Henneman's size principle***, which suggests that the size of the motor unit dictates its activation. Specifically, Henneman and colleagues (213) determined that smaller motor units, which have a lower activation threshold, are activated earlier than larger motor units, which have a higher activation threshold. Additionally, it is believed that smaller motor units, which are primarily composed of type I muscle fibers, are recruited in response to lower force demands (190). On the other hand, when higher forces are required, higher-threshold motor units, which are primarily comprised of type II muscle fibers, are recruited (102, 190). In addition to the force required, other factors come into play, such as the contraction speed (190), muscle contraction type (117), and the metabolic state of the muscle (247, 332).

Motor Unit Rate Coding

Another strategy for increasing the amount of force generated by a muscle is to increase the firing rate of the motor unit (326), which is referred to as *rate coding* (190). **Rate coding** is often defined as occurring when the frequency of neural impulses sent to an activated motor unit is increased (39). The unique aspect of the rate coding process is that increases in force production occur without additional motor units being recruited (190). In addition to affecting force production, rate coding may also play a significant role in determining the speed of voluntary contractions (519). In support of this contention, several studies have reported that higher motor unit firing rates are associated with higher rates of force development (3, 128, 519, 527). The use of exercises that require high forces and higher power outputs, such as weightlifting or plyometrics, has the potential to change the rate coding of motor units because these exercises increase the frequency of the stimulation of higher-threshold motor units (102, 190).

Motor Unit Synchronization

The asynchronous firing of motor units occurs in response to low-intensity muscle actions with brief dynamic twitches (474). When this occurs, one motor unit deactivates while another is being activated, resulting in a relatively smooth tension production that allows for a relatively smooth movement to occur (474). Historically, it has been thought that as force output is increased, there can be a **synchronization** of motor unit activation that occurs due to the simultaneous activation of numerous motor units (148, 271). The relationship between force production and motor unit synchronization is partially supported by the fact that strength-trained athletes display higher incidences of motor unit synchronization (436). More recently, it has been suggested that motor unit synchronization may not directly enhance maximal force output or strength (434, 547). Based on these data, it appears that motor unit synchronization may exert its greatest influence on the RFD during rapid muscle contractions (434). Additionally, the greatest influence of motor unit synchronization may be exerted on the performance of activities that require the coactivation of multiple muscles at the same time (434).

Neuromuscular Inhibition

Neuromuscular inhibition can be conceptualized as being conscious or somatic reflexive (474). Stone and colleagues (474) suggest that conscious inhibition involves the perception that a given weight may result in injury or is impossible to lift. Somatic-reflexive inhibition would be related to neural feedback from various muscle and joint receptors that result in a reduction in force production (148, 208). A good example of a receptor that operates to prevent the generation of harmful muscular forces during maximal or near maximal efforts is the **Golgi tendon organ** (148). If, through training, the activation patterns of these protective mechanisms are altered, a disinhibition response can occur and force-generating capacity may increase (5, 260, 531). For example, Aagaard and colleagues (4) report that undertaking heavy resistance training can significantly reduce neuromuscular inhibitory responses, which partially explains some of the increases in force-generating capacity as a result of training.

Stretch-Shortening Cycle

A stretch-shortening cycle (SSC) consists of a plyometric muscle action in which an eccentric muscle action (i.e., lengthening of the muscle) precedes a concentric muscle action (i.e., shortening of the muscle) (272, 474). One of the main effects of an SSC is an enhancement of the force generated during the concentric muscle action (145), which results in enhancements in performance during the concentric phase of the cycle (84, 173, 272). Even though there is debate about the exact mechanisms that underpin the performance increases associated with the SSC (173), it is likely that these responses occur because of the storage of elastic energy during the eccentric muscle action (67, 272, 506), activation of the stretch reflex (271, 506), and optimization of muscle activation and activation patterns (4, 42). Enhancements to both the eccentric and concentric portions of the SSC appear to be augmented by increases in maximal strength (4, 84, 392), suggesting that resistance training is essential when attempting to maximize the effect of the SSC.

Muscle Fiber Type

The athlete's muscle fiber type can also exert an influence on their maximal strength and ability to perform rapid muscular contractions (i.e., RFD) (474). In fact, based on the available research, it can be concluded that having a greater percentage and a large cross-sectional area of type II (fast-twitch) muscle fibers may be advantageous for maximizing dynamic force production (141, 142, 374, 375, 496). Support for this contention can be garnered from the numerous cross-sectional studies that reported strength and power athletes' high percentages of type II muscle fibers (53%-60%) (141, 142, 198, 201, 374, 438, 496). For example, Serrano and colleagues (438) reported that weightlifters display very high concentrations of pure **myosin heavy chain (MHC)** IIa concentrations (67.3% ± 13%), and world-class female weightlifters display the highest concentrations of these fiber types (71% ± 17%). Although it is well-accepted that strength and power athletes display greater amounts of type II muscle fibers, there is some debate as to how these fiber type concentrations relate to strength- and power-based performances (141, 438). For example, Fry and colleagues (141) reported that there are significant correlations between MHC IIa concentrations and maximal weight lifted in the snatch ($r = .94$) and the competition total ($r = .80$), whereas Serrano and colleagues (438) reported no correlations between fiber type and strength performance. Serrano and colleagues (438) suggest that the total type II fiber area may be a better determinant of maximal strength than the percentage of type II fibers. It is likely that the percentage of type II fibers affects the RFD more than the maximal force production (51, 299, 396). Because the RFD is a contributor to vertical jump performance (315), one might expect the percentages of type II muscle fibers to relate to jumping performance. In support of this contention, Fry and colleagues (141) reported significant correlations between the percentage of type IIa fibers and static vertical jump (SVJ) height ($r = .79$), SVJ power ($r = .75$), and countermovement vertical jump power output ($r = .83$).

Alternatively, endurance athletes tend to have higher percentages of type I (slow-twitch) muscle fibers (37, 496), which generally correspond to higher maximal oxygen consumption rates (37) and lower capacities for maximal force production (47). In fact, the percentage of type II muscle fibers is inversely correlated with the number of repetitions that can be completed in a back squat test performed to muscular failure with 80% 1RM (202).

Ultimately, based on the available evidence, athletes with higher concentrations of type II muscle fiber concentrations appear to have an advantage in strength- and power-based sports, but having higher type I fiber concentrations is advantageous for endurance-based performances (47).

Muscle Hypertrophy

It is generally accepted that resistance training can induce alterations to a muscle's cross-sectional area (CSA) (i.e., **hypertrophy**) that can be translated into increases in the maximal force-generating capacity of skeletal muscle (2, 128, 228, 485, 490). It is likely that these increases in force-generating capacity are partially related to an increase in the number of contractile elements associated with an increased muscle CSA (11, 128, 540). In fact, Trezise and colleagues (511) suggest that muscle CSA and architecture (i.e., fascicle angulation) exert a significant effect on maximal force production. Approximately 50% to 60% of the force production following a short-term resistance-training program can be accounted for by increases in muscle CSA and alterations to muscle architecture (342). Additionally, it is likely these alterations in force production are modulated by changes in the CSA of type II muscle fibers and the type II:I CSA ratio (321, 322, 511). Overall, based on the available data, there are strong relationships between CSA and greater force production (194, 511).

The effect of muscle hypertrophy on maximal strength has been questioned by several researchers (57, 58, 293, 294). For example, Buckner and colleagues (57, 58) suggest that changes in muscle size and strength are "separate and unrelated adaptations" (58, page 1012). These authors argue that the effect of changes in muscle CSA on force-generating capacity is related to the fact that, in some instances, muscle strength can be increased or decreased without increases or decreases in muscle CSA (13, 72). Although these observations are not new (382, 383), it is important to note that in 1955, Rasch (382) indicated that direct correlations between changes in CSA and force-generating capacity are difficult because "increase in hypertrophy may be due to increases in the number of capillaries and quantity of fluids in exercised muscles, and these do not contribute directly to increases in strength" (page 528). More recent evidence affirms the observations of Rasch (382) and indicates that muscle size can be significantly affected by muscle swelling, the number of capillaries, muscle glycogen content, and other noncontractile elements (417). These issues are most evident when examining the effect of changes in muscle CSA and its influence on force production with relatively untrained individuals (88).

Although there is still debate about the effect of muscle hypertrophy on maximal strength, the consensus in the scientific literature is that changes in CSA can result in alterations in force-production capacity (2, 24, 128, 228, 485, 490). From a practical perspective, the relationship between muscle size and strength can be seen in body weight–class sports, such as weightlifting and powerlifting, in which bigger individuals lift significantly greater loads.

Physiological Adaptations to Resistance Training

Generally, the adaptive response to resistance training can be categorized as being neurological or morphological (128). Neurological adaptations to resistance training include alterations to motor unit recruitment patterns (190), motor unit synchronization (261, 326, 434-437), motor unit firing rate (100, 102), and reflex activation (128). Morphological adaptations include changes to whole-muscle fiber size (73, 128), hypertrophy (128, 348, 416), fiber type transitions (509, 543), and alterations to muscle architecture (2, 128, 510, 511). During the early phases of a resistance-training program, it is generally believed that the primary adaptations are neurological, whereas longer-term training adaptations are associated with morphological changes (figure 13.10) (407).

Classically, neurological adaptations have been reported to dominate during the first 6 to 20 weeks from the initiation of a resistance-training regime (68, 408, 537). Conversely, some researchers have suggested that muscle hypertrophy occurs much sooner than originally thought, with increases being noted in as little as 3 weeks from the initiation of training (440). More recently, it has been suggested that these earlier hypertrophic responses are primarily a result of muscle damage and cel-

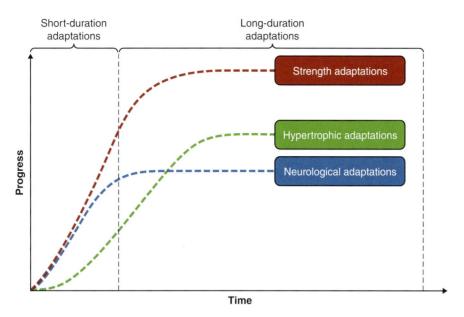

FIGURE 13.10 Time frame for neurological and morphological adaptations to resistance training.
Adapted from Sale (1988).

lular swelling, whereas longer-term adaptations are responses to actual hypertrophic adaptations (89, 90).

One factor that can affect the course of neuromuscular adaptations is the type of exercises employed and the structure of the training program (68, 408, 537). For example, complex resistance-training exercises that engage more than one joint and a large muscle mass (e.g., weightlifting derivatives, squats, snatches, cleans) may require more time for neural adaptations to occur and thus a longer time before hypertrophic adaptations become predominant (68). Support for this contention can be found in the work of Chilibeck and colleagues (68), who reported that neurological adaptations in the upper arm occurred very rapidly, and hypertrophy was noted by the 10th week of training with biceps curls. Conversely, hypertrophy of the legs was not noted until after 20 weeks of leg press training. Collectively, these data provide evidence that the complexity of the exercises contained in a resistance-training program can mitigate the time frame of neurological and morphological adaptations. However, although more complex multijoint exercises take longer to exhibit these changes (68), they appear to be more beneficial for long-term hypertrophic and maximal strength gains (155, 361). In fact, evidence suggests that if a resistance-training program is comprised of multijoint exercises, there is little, if any, benefit from adding single-joint exercises (155).

Neurological Adaptations

Primary adaptive responses to a resistance-training program are affected by motor learning and changes in coordination (405). These adaptations are very specific to the movement patterns targeted by the resistance-training program and the muscle activation sequence that occurs during the trained exercises (128, 410, 544). Collectively, these data highlight that the expression of strength is a skill (59).

Resistance training–induced neurological adaptations can include alterations to motor unit recruitment patterns (190, 519), rate coding (3, 102, 190, 519), and synchronization (434), which affects force-generating capacity or the RFD (190). For example, explosive or heavy resistance training can lower the motor unit recruitment threshold (190, 519), allowing for higher-threshold motor units (i.e., type II) to be recruited sooner or in concert with lower-threshold motor units (i.e., type I) (103, 327, 494), which increases force-generating capacity. Additionally, these types of training can also increase the occurrence of motor unit rate coding (3, 102, 519) and can increase rapid force-production capacity (117, 519). Heavy resistance training also seems to increase motor unit synchronization (434, 435), which can significantly increase the RFD. Finally, heavy resistance training can downregulate the Ib afferent feedback from the Golgi tendon organs in the muscle tendon complex to the spinal motor neuron pool, resulting in a reduction in neuromuscular inhibition, which can facilitate increases in force production (4, 148).

Morphological Adaptations

The primary morphological adaptation associated with resistance training is an increase in myofibrillar size and number, which results in an increase in the CSA of the individual muscle fibers and whole muscle (128). Commonly known as hypertrophy, this morphological adaptation can occur after a few months of resistance training (99, 128, 139, 199, 215, 460) and is often fiber-type specific (139). It is well-documented that there is preferential hypertrophy of the type II muscle fibers in response to a resistance-training program (63, 460, 495, 503, 509). Data presented by Häkkinen and colleagues (199) provide evidence supporting the belief that type II fibers have a greater plasticity, which is indicated by a more rapid rate of hypertrophy in response to resistance training and a more rapid rate of atrophy in response to detraining. Therefore, it is not surprising that short-duration studies (6-10 weeks) have reported significant hypertrophy of the type II fibers (2, 41, 111, 232, 503), whereas longer-duration studies have reported significant increases in type I and type II fiber areas (199, 297). Generally, the proportion of type II fibers is significantly correlated with resistance training–induced hypertrophy (200) and increases in strength (111). With increased hypertrophy there is an increase in the CSA of the skeletal muscle fibers, which can result in an increase in contractile material (128) and changes to the angle of pennation (2, 128, 510, 511). Collectively, these morphological adaptations can significantly enhance resistance training–induced strength adaptations (2, 128).

Another factor that contributes to the morphological adaptations is the training interventions used (139). For example, it appears that eccentric muscle actions are critical for the optimization of muscle hypertrophy (210, 424). Therefore, resistance-training exercises that contain eccentric muscle actions result in a greater stimulus for hypertrophic and strength gains (518). Furthermore, explosive strength training appears to significantly increase type II fiber size and significantly alter the ratio of type II to type I muscle fiber CSA, which enhances maximal strength- and power-generating capacity (139, 191, 474). In support of this contention, Fry (139) reports that the type II to type I ratio is greater in weightlifters than powerlifters and bodybuilders. Based on these data, it is easy to see that the exercises used in a resistance-training program directly affect the morphological adaptations of skeletal muscle.

An additional morphological adaptation to resistance training that must be considered is an alteration to muscle fiber type (128, 507, 543). A reduction in type IIx fiber content with a concomitant increase in type IIa fiber content is the most common resistance training–induced muscle fiber adaptation (63, 128, 200, 460, 543). Bompa and Haff (47) have suggested that these findings may be related to the analytical techniques used when analyzing muscle fiber type. Based on newer analytical methods, it appears that skeletal muscle has an even greater plasticity, and greater fiber-type alterations may be expected in response to training or detraining (300, 508, 543).

The classic fiber-typing methods rely on the histochemical straining properties of the myosin adenosine triphosphatase enzyme found in the globular region of the myosin head (139). Based on this process, the three major fiber types are identified as I, IIa, and IIx. These fiber types can be placed on a continuum from the slowest (type I) to the fastest (type IIx), resulting in the common terminology of slow and fast skeletal muscle (139). More recently, researchers have begun to examine MHC content to identify both major and hybrid fiber types (300, 508, 543). It appears that in addition to the major categories of MHC (i.e., type I, type IIa, type IIx), there is a pool of hybrid fibers (i.e., type I/IIa, type I/IIa/IIx, type IIa/IIx) that can be altered in response to training or detraining (149, 508, 543). As the hybrid pool is altered, there is a concomitant modification of the type IIx, IIa, and type I fibers, which partially explains the different fiber-type classifications typically associated with strength athletes (table 13.1).

Characteristics of Strength

An appropriately structured resistance-training program can be used to develop a variety of strength characteristics. By understanding the various characteristics that can be developed with appropriate training methods, the coach can improve the degree of transfer of strength development into sport-specific performance gains (47, 427, 498). Some characteristics of strength that the coach should consider are strength–endurance, maximal strength, relative strength, speed–strength, power, and supramaximal strength.

TABLE 13.1 Fiber-Type Distribution of Various Strength-Trained Athletes

Population	Fiber-type distribution (%)			
	I	IIa	IIx	Hybrids
Resistance-trained men (10, 446, 540, 543)	34	58	<1	8
Resistance-trained women (543)	35	53	<1	12
National-caliber bodybuilders (268)	35	39	0	26
Novice bodybuilders (87)	27	47	9	17
World-class female weightlifters (438)	17	71	0	12
National-class female weightlifters (438)	25	67	0	7
National-class male weightlifters (438)	25	63	9	3
National-class male weightlifters (141)	35	64	1	NA
Weightlifters (438)	23	67	3	8
Male powerlifters (298)	51	45	4	NA
Female powerlifters (298)	46	54	0	NA

Note: All percentages based on myosin heavy chain data. NA = not available.

Strength–Endurance

The ability to repetitively produce muscular force over extended periods of time is referred to as *strength–endurance* (47). In resistance training the number of repetitions performed with a given load is generally considered to be a test of strength–endurance (183).

Maximal Strength

The highest amount of force the neuromuscular system can generate during a maximal voluntary contraction is referred to as **maximal strength** (47). Maximal strength is often measured as the heaviest load that the athlete can lift for one repetition (1RM). Based on the available scientific literature, greater maximal strength levels significantly underpin many physical and performance attributes, such as enhanced force–time curve characteristics (e.g., RFD, maximal force) and general skills performance (e.g., jumping, sprinting, change of direction) (486). Additionally, greater maximal strength also serves as a protective mechanism that reduces overall injury risk (301).

Relative Strength

The most basic way to represent **relative strength** is to create a ratio between an athlete's maximal strength and their body mass or lean body mass (469). Although this ratio-scaling method is commonly used, it fails to account for body dimensionality (244, 469). Additionally, this ratio-scaling method is based on the assumption that there is a linear relationship between strength and body size. It is clear from the existing literature that strength does not increase linearly with increases in body mass (18, 129, 263, 343, 469). In fact, simple ratio-scaling methods tend to bias results toward smaller individuals (18, 555). Conceptually, strength is proportional to body height (H^2) or to body mass to the two-thirds power ($bm^{0.67}$) (244), as represented with the following equations:

$$\text{allometric scaling} = \frac{\text{load}}{\text{body mass}^{0.67}}$$

$$\text{height scaling} = \frac{\text{load}}{\text{height}^2}$$

The use of the allometric scaling methods are generally recognized as the preferred method for representing an athlete's relative strength and both allometric scaling and height scaling are commonly used in the scientific literature (35, 244, 469).

Speed–Strength

The ability to develop force rapidly during high-velocity movements is often referred to as *speed–strength* (47, 498). This type of strength is based on a foundation of maximal strength and is maximized with activities that enhance the maximal RFD (479). Speed–strength is often considered to be related to the expression of power.

Power

Power is the product of force and velocity and is often used to represent the intensity of an activity (77). The ability to express high amounts of power is predicated by having high levels of maximal strength and an ability to express a high RFD (486). High power outputs are often considered to be one of the most important characteristics related to sport performance (21, 333, 462, 486).

Supramaximal Strength

Supramaximal strength, or eccentric maximal strength, represents the maximal force that can be produced during an **eccentric muscle action** (207, 498). Specifically, these forces are in excess of those achieved during maximal isometric (536) and concentric (206) muscle actions. Due to the unique nature of this type of strength, Harden and colleagues (206) recommend that it be tested with specific methodologies because estimating it from tests of maximal concentric or isometric strength do not allow for accurate assessment.

Methods of Resistance Training

The various methods of resistance training affect maximal strength, the RFD, power output, and the ability to repetitively produce force. When considering the classification of strength, a hierarchy ranging from ballistic to supramaximal resistance-training methods can be conceptualized (table 13.2) (498).

Ballistic Methods

Training methods that require acceleration throughout the entire concentric movement are often referred to as *ballistic exercises* (82, 485). The most employed ballistic exercises include plyometrics, jump squats, bench throws, and medicine ball throws (478, 480, 485, 498). Ballistic exercises have been shown to produce greater forces, velocities of movement, power outputs, and muscle activation when compared to the same exercise performed quickly (286, 345). These types of exercises may lead to a lowering of the motor unit recruitment threshold (103, 519) and a more rapid activation of the entire motor neuron pool (116). Ultimately, due to these alterations to motor unit recruitment, ballistic exercises exert a significant influence on the RFD, which can directly translate to an enhanced power output (485). When compared to traditional resistance-training exercises, such as the back squat, bench press, and deadlift, ballistic exercises have a greater ability to enhance the RFD, especially in stronger individuals (80-82).

Although ballistic exercise can be incorporated throughout the annual training plan, the goal of the training phase will affect which ballistic exercise is used (485). For example, during a general preparation phase that targets hypertrophy, loaded jump squats would be avoided due to the phase's focus on increasing work capacity and muscle CSA (485). It would be far better to incorporate this exercise into a strength–speed or speed–strength phase of training because the goals of the exercise and the phase would better align. Although it is often recommended that all athletes can benefit from ballistic exercises (485), the athlete must establish an appropriate strength base prior to incorporating these exercises (80, 81).

Speed–Strength Methods

The primary goals of speed–strength (i.e., explosiveness) training methods are to enhance the RFD and increase power development (479, 548). Verkhoshansky and Siff (522) suggest that when targeting speed–strength, the development of speed against resistance is vital and overall strength development is less important. The development of speed–strength is accomplished with loaded sport movements (498), lifting movements with loads 40% to 60% of 1RM (339), or depth jumps (548). Exercises such as loaded bench throws and jumps performed with relatively low loads (≤50% of 1RM) are commonly used to develop speed–strength. Kettlebells (485) and medicine balls can also be used to target speed–strength development (548).

Some authors suggest that performing weightlifting movements and their derivatives with relatively light loads is useful for the development of speed–strength (254, 479). For example, Suchomel and colleagues (479) suggest the jump shrug (482) and the hang high pull (481) are useful training exercises for enhancing speed–strength. Ideally, if maximizing speed–strength is the primary focus of the training phase, strength or power training should be performed twice per week (209).

Strength–Speed Methods

Although both speed–strength and strength–speed resistance-training methods develop the RFD and increase power development (479), strength–speed methods also target the continued development of

TABLE 13.2 Classification of Resistance-Training Methods

Method	Reps per set	Number of sets	Set structure	Cluster sets	Intensity	Exercise types
Ballistic	1-6	3-6	Traditional sets	Standard	0%-50% 1RM	Plyometrics, throws, loaded jumps
Speed–strength	2-4	3-6	Traditional sets	Ascending, standard, undulating, wave loaded	70%-80% 1RM for weightlifting exercises 70%-110% 1RM for weightlifting pulling derivatives 40%-60% 1RM for nonweightlifting exercises 0%-50% 1RM for ballistic exercises	Weightlifting movements, depth jumps, resistance training, ballistic exercises
Strength–speed	2-4	3-6	Traditional sets	Ascending, standard, undulating, wave loaded	70%-90% 1RM for weightlifting exercises 90%-110% 1RM for weightlifting pulling derivatives 75%-90% 1RM for nonweightlifting exercises 30%-70% 1RM for ballistic exercises	Weightlifting movements, resistance training, ballistic exercises
Maximal strength	1-6	3-6	Traditional sets	Ascending, standard, undulating, wave loaded	80%-100% 1RM	Resistance-training methods, weightlifting derivatives, machines, isometrics
Supramaximal strength	1-6	3-6	Traditional sets	Ascending, standard, undulating, wave loaded	105%-140% 1RM for eccentrics 105%-120% (eccentric)/50%-100% (concentric) 1RM for accentuated eccentric loading	Eccentrics, accentuated eccentric loading
Hypertrophy	8-12	3-6	Traditional sets	Ascending, descending, standard	65%-80% 1RM	Resistance-training methods, weightlifting derivatives, machines
Strength–endurance	>12	3-6	Traditional sets	Ascending, standard, undulating, wave loaded	<65% 1RM	Resistance-training methods, weightlifting derivatives, machines

maximal strength (479). DeWeese and colleagues (104) suggest that the primary goal of strength–speed resistance-training methods is moving relatively heavy loads quickly to enhance the RFD and continue to develop strength. Weightlifting (e.g., snatch, clean, jerk) and the weightlifting derivatives (e.g., clean and snatch pull, push jerk) are ideally suited for the development of strength–speed (104). Based on figure 13.6, various weightlifting derivatives can be selected to target specific aspects of the force–velocity curve. For example, the high-force end of the curve can be targeted with the use of the snatch/clean deadlift, midthigh pull (107, 480), pull from the knee (109), and pull from the floor (108, 480). Alternatively, the jump shrug (482), the hang high pull (477), power snatch/clean from the knee (76, 483), and power snatch/clean from the thigh (74, 75) can be used to target the higher-velocity end of the force–velocity curve.

Maximal Strength Methods

Numerous resistance-training strategies can target the development of maximal strength. Generally, optimal strength gains occur in response to training within what is referred to as the *strength zone* (422). This zone requires the performance of one to six repetitions per set, with loads of 80% to 100% of 1RM (365, 443, 479, 492, 498). It is generally believed that training within this zone enhances neuromuscular adaptations that facilitate force production (246, 422). In fact, Jenkins and colleagues (246) reported greater increases in percentage of voluntary activation and electromyographic amplitude after 6 weeks of training with loads that correspond to 80% of 1RM compared to training with 30% of 1RM.

Generally, we see a dose–response relationship between load lifted and the amount of strength gained (422). For example, significantly greater strength gains occur when training in the strength zone compared to training within the hypertrophy zone (i.e., 8-12 repetitions per set) (63, 302, 419, 426). Although it is clear that training with heavier loads is essential for maximizing muscular strength, consistently training to muscular failure is not necessary (92, 127, 171, 501) and may be detrimental to long-term strength gains (65, 66). For example, Carroll and colleagues (66) reported that consistently training to failure (i.e., RM loads) results in an increased training strain, monotony, and overall injury risk, whereas training based on percentages of RM, with heavy and light days, results in superior maximal strength gains and improvements in RFD and vertical jump performance. Additionally, training with percentages of RM results in greater increases in type II muscle fiber CSA, type I muscle fiber CSA, and anatomical CSA when compared to training to failure (65).

It is likely that frequently training to failure creates a fatigue-management problem that impedes the athlete's ability to recover (331) and adapt to the training stimulus, which can negatively affect the ability to increase maximal strength. Morán-Navarro and colleagues (331) reported that the time necessary to recover from training to failure is significantly longer than not training to failure. The effect of training to failure and the associated slower rate of recovery may be magnified when resistance training is integrated into the preparation of athletes who use multiple and more frequent training activities (359, 360).

Based on the overwhelming evidence presented in the scientific literature, frequently training to failure in an attempt to maximize strength gains is unnecessary (66, 92, 127) and should be used sparingly (92). Ideally, when the main goal of a resistance-training program is maximal strength, training not performed to failure is recommended (92, 127, 171, 501).

An additional consideration when constructing resistance-training programs that target maximal strength is the duration of the inter-set rest interval. It is well-documented that inter-set rest intervals of at least 2 to 3 minutes are required to maximize strength gains (12, 62, 172). It is likely that longer rest intervals are most important when using multijoint resistance-training exercises. It is generally recommended that multijoint resistance-training exercises make up the majority of a resistance-training program due to their more efficient stimulation of maximal strength (361), so it is important to ensure adequate inter-set rest to maintain training intensity.

Supramaximal Strength Methods

Generally, an individual can lower a heavier load than they can lift. Therefore, when employing traditional strength-training methods where the load is limited by concentric maximal strength, the load prescribed will not provide an overload for the eccentric portion of the lift (204). To address this issue, supramaximal resistance-training methods can be integrated into a resistance-training program. With this training method, loads that are in excess of concentric maximums are applied during targeted eccentric training (439) or with accentuated eccentric loading strategies (discussed in more detail later in the chapter) (529, 530, 532).

Generally, the use of supramaximal training methods (i.e., eccentric training) may stimulate fiber-type shifts toward faster MHC isoforms (135, 136), which are commonly associated with increases in force and power production (1, 135). Furthermore, the unique loading parameters associated with supramaximal training can also increase fascicle lengths (130, 131, 157), which may lead to faster maximal shortening velocities and translate into increased potential for power development (292,

341). Therefore, supramaximal training methods may be useful for maximizing the adaptive responses to the resistance-training program.

Supramaximal training methods use eccentric loads that range between 105% and 140% of concentric 1RM depending on the targeted outcome. It is important to note that this type of training is very intense and can create significant muscle damage if not programmed correctly (205, 387, 532). Although Thibaudeau (498) suggests that these methods should be used only during shock microcycles and for no more than two microcycles (i.e., short mesocycle), research shows that these methods can be very effective when employed for a 4-week mesocycle (205) or two successive 5-week mesocycles (532).

Hypertrophy Methods

When training to increase muscular size, it is generally believed that performing 8 to 12 repetitions per set (i.e., the zone of hypertrophy) with loads of 65% to 80% of 1RM provides the most efficient stimulus (184, 422). Although it is often said that training to failure is necessary to stimulate muscle growth, there is an emerging body of evidence that suggests that training to failure is not necessary for maximizing muscle hypertrophy (65, 285, 411, 526). In fact, when training loads of 65% to 80% of 1RM are used, there is convincing evidence that not training to failure is a more effective method for stimulating muscle hypertrophy (285). Conversely, if lower loads (i.e., 30%-50% of 1RM) are used, training to failure appears to be a prerequisite for stimulating muscle hypertrophy (287, 334, 420). However, hypertrophy training performed to failure creates greater fatigue (331, 412), delayed rates of recovery (420), and greater levels of discomfort (412). Based on the available research, if resistance training is performed within the hypertrophy zone, training to failure is not necessary and training not performed to failure is a better training approach.

Although the load employed in resistance-training programs that target muscle hypertrophy is important, it is likely that the volume load (sets × reps × load) of training is a more important factor for enhancing muscle hypertrophy (55, 137, 287, 295). For example, several studies reported that training with more sets per muscle group, which results in an overall increase in volume load, resulted in greater increases in muscle hypertrophy (55, 284, 418). Ultimately, muscle hypertrophy follows a dose–response relationship, with greater gains being achieved with higher volume loads of training (418, 423).

Classically, shorter inter-set rest intervals coupled with higher volumes (i.e., 8-12 repetitions) of resistance training have been recommended to target acute hormonal responses when hypertrophy is the goal of a resistance-training program (280). Although the acute hormonal response is often cited as a rationale for using short rest intervals, research suggests that acute hormonal fluctuations play a minor role in stimulating hypertrophy, and mechanical loading factors (538, 539), such as volume load, likely exert a greater influence. Support for this contention can be found in research that reported that longer inter-set rest intervals allow for greater volume loads of training, which translate into greater hypertrophic gains (425). Ultimately, it appears that employing rest intervals of 2 to 3 minutes during resistance training targeting hypertrophy results in the greatest adaptive responses.

Finally, the type of exercise used also seems to influence the hypertrophy stimulated by the training program. Generally, it is recommended that resistance-training programs should contain combinations of multijoint and single-joint exercises (385). Although some evidence shows that these combinations can result in increased muscle hypertrophy (27, 53), research has questioned the efficacy of this practice (26). Specifically, the addition of single-joint exercises to a resistance-training program that contains multijoint exercises has been reported to offer no additional muscular adaptations in untrained individuals (26, 156) or trained individuals (26, 95). Although there continues to be debate about the need to incorporate single-joint exercises into a resistance-training program (53), research indicates that these exercises do not seem to affect hypertrophy (349). Remember, however, that strength is maximized when multijoint exercises are placed before single-joint exercises.

Strength–Endurance Methods

Strength–endurance can be defined as the ability to resist muscular fatigue when performing resistance training with submaximal loads (391). It is often targeted with resistance-training programs that employ more than 12 repetitions and loads that are less than 65% of 1RM (184, 443). This type of resistance training has been proposed to enhance buffering and oxidative capacity, increase mitochondrial density, enhance metabolic enzymatic activity, and increase capillary density (443). Classically, the inter-set rest interval is recommended to be 30 seconds or less for strength–endurance (184). Short inter-set rest intervals stimulate greater oxygen consumption (i.e., 30 s > 60 s > 120 s > 180 s), which may partially explain the common physiological adaptations associated with this type of training (386). Depending on the structure of the training session and the exercises used, the inter-set rest intervals can be short (<1 min) or long (1-2 min). If multijoint exercises are used, longer inter-set rest intervals will be needed to maintain performance. Specifically, if short rest intervals (i.e., 30-60 s) are used, the load lifted may have to be reduced by 5% to 15% across each set performed to maintain training volume (386).

Basic Training Factor Manipulation

Effective strength and conditioning programs require the systematic manipulation of multiple training factors to align with the key strategies established by the periodized training plan. Generally, these programming decisions result in alterations to the athlete's external training load. Although the intensity and number of repetitions are common variables that can be manipulated within the training plan, it is also important to consider other variables, such as the **inter-set**, **intra-set**, and **inter-repetition rest intervals** that can be varied to stimulate different physiological adaptations and performance gains (figure 13.11).

Repetitions

Although the number of repetitions and the intensity of training are often discussed in isolation, the number of repetitions that can be completed is a function of the load. Fundamentally, the higher the training load, the lower the repetitions that can be performed (47, 219, 220, 445, 484, 497). Table 13.3 shows the general relationship between the number of repetitions completed and training load.

If a **repetition maximum (RM)** test is performed, the coach can use the reconversion factors in table 13.3 to estimate maximal loads that can be lifted for other repetition schemes. For example, if the athlete completes five repetitions with a load of 120 kg (265 lb) in the bench press, their estimated 1RM would be 140 kg (i.e., 120 × 1.163) (309 lb). These estimations are generally more accurate when less than five repetitions are completed during an RM test (291, 484). Additionally, because the number of repetitions performed with a given percentage of 1RM is affected by training status, muscle mass engaged, type of exercise, and sex, it can be challenging to make definitive connections between the percentage of 1RM and the number of repetitions completed (17, 47, 220, 258, 393, 445). For example, Julio and colleagues (258) reported that recreationally trained men can perform a wide range of maximal repetitions in the bench press when performed at 70% (11-20 reps), 80% (5-15 reps), and 90% (2-7 reps) of 1RM. Additionally, Shimano and colleagues (445) reported that training status and exercise type affect the number of

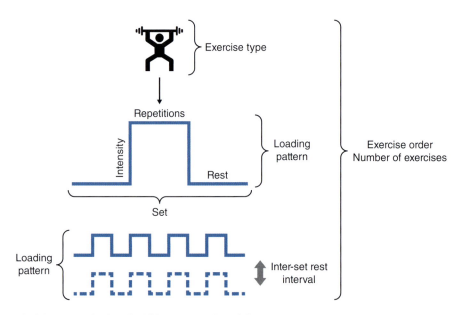

FIGURE 13.11 Variables manipulated within a strength-training program.

TABLE 13.3 Load to Repetition Relationship

Percentage of 1RM	Number of repetitions	Reconvert factor
100	1	1.000
95	2	1.053
92	3	1.087
90	4	1.111
86	5	1.163
83	6	1.205
81	7	1.235
79	8	1.266
77	9	1.299
75	10	1.333
71	11	1.408
69	12	1.449
68	13	1.471
66	14	1.493
65	15	1.538

Note: The reconvert factor is multiplied by the load lifted for the given repetitions to predict the one-repetition maximum (1RM). For example, if the athlete's 3RM is 120 kg (265 lb), we would multiply this by 1.087 to determine the 1RM would be estimated to be 130 kg (287 lb).

repetitions an individual can perform at a given percentage of 1RM. For example, when lifting a load that was equivalent to 60% of 1RM, untrained men performed 35.9 ± 13.4 repetitions of the back squat, 21.6 ± 3.7 repetitions of the bench press, and 17.2 ± 3.7 repetitions of the arm curl. Trained men who used the same load performed 29.9 ± 7.4 repetitions of the back squat, 21.7 ± 3.8 repetitions of the bench press, and 19.0 ± 2.0 repetitions of the arm curl. Suchomel and colleagues (484) suggest that based on these data, using percentages of 1RM may result in inconsistent training stimuli and divergent performance adaptations.

Although there are limitations to the load to repetition relationship, the coach might consider the modified versions of the relationships presented in table 13.4. For example, Thibaudeau (497) suggests that one possible solution is to align the association table with the athlete's fiber type. If an athlete is classified as type I fiber dominant (i.e., endurance athlete), they can likely do more repetitions with higher percentages of their 1RM. If the athlete is classified as type II fiber dominant (i.e., strength–power athlete), they will most likely be able to perform lower repetitions with higher percentages of their maximum. Although this method of aligning repetitions and percentages of 1RM is not perfect and needs to be validated with

TABLE 13.4 Alternative Load to Repetition Relationships

Number of repetitions	Type II fiber dominant		Balanced fiber ratio		Type I fiber dominant	
	% of 1RM	Reconvert factor	% of 1RM	Reconvert factor	% of 1RM	Reconvert factor
1	100	1.000	100	1.000	100	1.000
2	92	1.087	95	1.053	98	1.020
3	87	1.149	92	1.087	96	1.042
4	82	1.220	90	1.111	94	1.064
5	79	1.266	86	1.163	92	1.087
6	76	1.316	83	1.205	90	1.111
7	73	1.370	81	1.235	88	1.136
8	70	1.429	79	1.266	86	1.163
9	67	1.493	77	1.299	84	1.190
10	64	1.563	75	1.333	82	1.220
11	61	1.639	71	1.408	80	1.250
12	58	1.724	69	1.449	78	1.282
13	55	1.818	68	1.471	76	1.316
14	52	1.923	67	1.493	74	1.351
15	50	2.000	65	1.538	72	1.389

Adapted from Thibaudeau (2006).

controlled scientific studies, it does allow the coach to better align the load to repetition relationship with different classifications of athletes.

The manipulation of repetition schemes in a resistance-training program can result in specific physiological adaptations (63). Generally, low-repetition schemes (1-6 reps) are better for developing maximal strength and power, and higher-repetition schemes (>10 reps) are associated with enhanced muscular endurance (63, 125, 313, 492). High-intensity endurance (short duration) appears to be enhanced with repetition ranges between 10 and 15 (63, 125), and low-intensity endurance (long duration) is improved when more than 25 repetitions are performed (63). The most efficient stimulation of hypertrophy seems to occur when 8 to 12 repetitions are performed (422, 443). However, hypertrophy can be stimulated with a variety of repetition schemes, depending on the total number of sets completed and if sets are performed to failure or not (334, 422).

Based on the relationships presented between repetitions and adaptive responses, a repetition maximum (RM) continuum can be created (figure 13.12). The continuum concept illustrates where the training emphasis is aligned with a specific RM load. Training benefits are blended for any given load, and this continuum simply presents the most efficient repetition range for stimulating a targeted adaptive response. Additionally, although the continuum is presented in many texts (45, 48, 125, 443), note that training adaptations are not solely dictated by the repetition scheme. In fact, adaptive responses are affected by numerous factors, including the number of sets and the load lifted.

Sets

A **set** is a series of repetitions grouped together and performed continuously without any inter-repetition rest (181). It is well-documented that training programs that use single sets are not as effective for stimulating muscular hypertrophy or maximizing strength gains as those that use multiple sets (365, 366, 381, 388, 389). When looking at the number of sets that can be performed for a given exercise within a training program, there is a dose–response relationship; single-set protocols offer a minimal stimulus for strength gains, whereas a minimum of three sets may be required to maximize strength gains (366, 389). For example, Rhea and colleagues (389) suggest that a minimum of four sets is required to maximize strength gains in both trained and untrained individuals. Similarly, Peterson and colleagues (366) suggest that four sets are needed to maximize strength gains for untrained and trained individuals, and highly trained athletes may need as many as eight sets. Additionally, Krieger (284) reported that multiple sets produce 40% greater hypertrophy compared to single sets, with the greatest effects being associated with four to six sets. Ultimately, it appears that hypertrophy training follows a dose–response relationship, with greater gains being associated with greater numbers of sets (418).

When considering how many sets to incorporate into the athlete's periodized training plan, the coach must consider several factors. First, the number of sets that optimizes maximal strength or hypertrophic responses is affected by the athlete's training status. Second, the number of sets in the training plan will be dictated by the training period and phase in which the program appears (47). For example, during the general preparation phase when a greater number of repetitions are performed, fewer sets may be incorporated into the training plan. Conversely, when the athlete is in the specific preparation phase when fewer repetitions are performed, more sets may be planned to maximize the training stimulus. Third, training adaptations are dictated not only by the number of repetitions and sets performed but also the load, the structure of each set, and the exercises programmed (47).

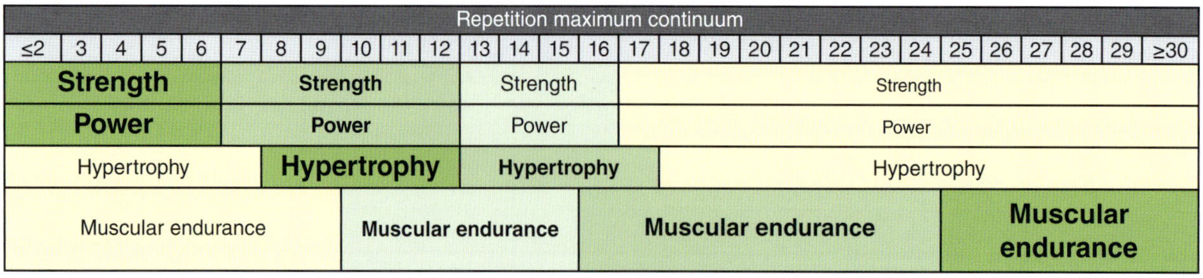

Note: The bolder the text, the greater the efficiency for the targeted characteristic.

FIGURE 13.12 Continuum of strength-training methods.

Volume

Often coaches represent training volume as the total number of repetitions completed (14, 125, 176) or the total number of sets performed (47, 423). These methods are not ideal because they can misrepresent the amount of work completed (176). For example, the completion of three sets of five repetitions would yield the same number of repetitions as five sets of three repetitions. Although both protocols result in 15 repetitions, the two protocols would create vastly different amounts of total work or physiological stress (176). A far better approach is to calculate the volume load (176, 464, 467) by multiplying the weight lifted by the number of sets and repetitions completed (see chapter 11 for more detail). Ultimately, volume load is a reasonable indicator of the amount of work accomplished during resistance training (310) because it accounts for the load lifted (184). For example, if an athlete's 1RM in the back squat is 130 kg (287 lb) and they perform three sets of five repetitions with 112 kg (247 lb), they would complete 1,680 kg (3,704 lb) of work. If this same athlete performed five sets of three repetitions with 120 kg (265 lb), they would complete 1,800 kg (3,968 lb) of work. Based on these calculations, even though the athlete performed 15 repetitions with each training scheme, it is easy to see that the volume load is substantially higher when five sets of three repetitions were performed.

When calculating the volume load, coaches employ different strategies, such as only using repetitions with loads greater than 80% of 1RM (14, 368) for all of the repetitions completed (176, 368). Regardless of strategy, the volume load of training for a given exercise or within a training session, training day, microcycle, mesocycle, or annual plan can be calculated to represent the volume and total amount of work completed (47).

Intensity

Generally, the amount of weight or resistance used represents the **training intensity** or load. The intensity of a training session, training day, microcycle, or mesocycle can be calculated by dividing the volume load by the total number of repetitions completed (184).

Several strategies are commonly used when prescribing training intensity for strength and conditioning (168, 484, 557):

- Percentage-based methods
- RM training
- RM zones
- Velocity-based training (VBT) methods
- Rating of perceived exertion
- Repetitions in reserve

Percentage-Based Methods

In typical resistance-training programs, the load assigned can be expressed as a percentage of a 1RM load (figure 13.13). Classically, a 1RM is established by performing a test to determine the heaviest load that can be lifted one time with proper technique (443). Because of the relationship between the load that can be lifted and the number of repetitions, it is possible to predict the 1RM from other RM tests (e.g., 2RM, 3RM, 5RM) (tables 13.3 and 13.4) (47, 219, 220, 445, 484, 497). However, the ability to predict the 1RM is less valid when higher RMs are used (291). After the 1RM is determined with these methods, the training load can be aligned with a targeted training load designator (figure 13.13). For example, if an athlete has a 200 kg (441 lb) 1RM for the back squat, a load of 180 to 188 kg (397-414 lb) would be a heavy load, and a light load would be 140 to 148 kg (309-326 lb).

Descriptor	Abbreviation	% of repetition maximum
Supramaximal	SMX	>100
Maximum	MX	100
Very heavy	VH	95-99
Heavy	H	90-94
Moderately heavy	MH	85-89
Moderate	M	80-84
Moderately light	ML	75-79
Light	L	70-74
Very light	VL	≤69

FIGURE 13.13 Relative intensity for strength training.

Although the use of the % 1RM to prescribe training load is well-established, there are shortcomings associated with this method (484). Several authors suggest that the 1RM varies dramatically from day to day, and this variation can result in a significant mismatch between the load prescribed and the athlete's actual capacities (23, 112, 162, 253, 304, 305). Interestingly, when examined at the microcycle level, the 1RM is very stable and varies 5% to 10% depending on the structure of the microcycle (25, 233). For example, Banyard and colleagues (25) demonstrated that when the 1RM back squat is tested on three nonconsecutive days (e.g., Monday, Wednesday, and Friday), the variation in maximal strength is less than 5%. Similarly,

Hughes and colleagues (233) report that when the back squat 1RM is tested on three consecutive days at 24 hours after the first 1RM test, maximal strength is decreased by about 10%, and by 48 hours, strength is decreased by about 5% from the first day. Collectively, these data lend support for the common practice of prescribing 5% to 10% variations in the % 1RM across a microcycle (106, 184, 464, 479) to account for the effect of fatigue on the athlete's maximal strength levels (figure 13.14). Additionally, by prescribing a percentage range for each training load, the coach can assess the athlete while they are training and then autoregulate the training load within a predetermined intensity band based on the athlete's current state.

An alternative approach is to prescribe the training load based on a percentage of the maximum performance capacity for a given set–repetition scheme (106, 464) (figure 13.15). For example, if the athlete's training program requires them to perform three sets of five repetitions with a moderately heavy load, the athlete would use a load that corresponds to 85% to 89% of their estimated 6RM training load, which corresponds to 71% to 74% of their 1RM. A main benefit of this method of prescribing training load is that it accounts for multiple sets being performed at a targeted training load and allows for the integration of a degree of autoregulation because the athlete is prescribed an intensity band in which to complete their training.

Strength can change across the mesocycle, so periodic RM testing may be warranted to recalibrate the prescribed training loads. Although it may be impossible to perform frequent 1RM testing, the coach can fold RM loadings (e.g., 3RM, 5RM) into the program to test maximal capacities. From these data, the coach can estimate the athlete's 1RM via the use of the reconvert factors presented in tables 13.3 and 13.4. This method of prescribing intensity can generally maximize performance gains while minimizing maladaptive responses (65, 66, 358-360).

Repetition Maximum Training

Repetition maximum (RM) training requires the athlete to select the heaviest load that can be lifted for a given number of repetitions (e.g., 1RM, 3RM, 5RM) (184, 274, 542). For example, if a 3RM load is prescribed, the athlete will use a resistance that

#	Microcycle Average intensity	Monday	Tuesday	Wednesday	Thursday	Friday	Saturday	Sunday
1	ML (75%-79%)	MH (85%-89%)	L (70%-74%)	Recovery day	ML (75%-79%)	Recovery day	L (70%-74%)	Recovery day
2	M (80%-84%)	H (90%-94%)	ML (75%-79%)	Recovery day	M (80%-84%)	Recovery day	ML (75%-79%)	Recovery day
3	MH (85%-89%)	VH (95%-99%)	M (80%-84%)	Recovery day	H (90%-94%)	Recovery day	M (80%-84%)	Recovery day
4	L (70%-74%)	L (70%-74%)	L (70%-74%)	Recovery day	ML (75%-79%)	Recovery day	L (70%-74%)	Recovery day

FIGURE 13.14 Example of training load variation across a microcycle based on percentage of repetition maximum. VH = very heavy; H = heavy; MH = moderately heavy; M = moderate; ML = moderately light; L = light; VL = very light.

Relative intensities															
Repetition maximum	1	2	3	4	5	6	7	8	9	10	11	12	13	14	15
Percentage	100%	95%	92%	90%	86%	83%	81%	79%	77%	75%	71%	69%	68%	67%	65%
Reconvert factor	1.000	1.053	1.087	1.111	1.163	1.205	1.235	1.266	1.299	1.333	1.408	1.449	1.471	1.493	1.538

Descriptor	Percentage	Absolute intensities (% of 1RM)														
Maximum	100%	100%	95%	92%	90%	86%	83%	81%	79%	77%	75%	71%	69%	68%	67%	65%
Very heavy	99% / 95%	99% / 95%	94% / 90%	91% / 87%	89% / 86%	85% / 82%	82% / 79%	80% / 77%	78% / 75%	76% / 73%	74% / 71%	70% / 67%	68% / 66%	67% / 65%	66% / 64%	64% / 62%
Heavy	94% / 90%	94% / 90%	89% / 86%	86% / 83%	85% / 81%	81% / 77%	78% / 75%	76% / 73%	74% / 71%	72% / 69%	71% / 68%	67% / 64%	65% / 62%	64% / 61%	63% / 60%	61% / 59%
Moderately heavy	89% / 85%	89% / 85%	85% / 81%	82% / 78%	80% / 77%	77% / 73%	74% / 71%	72% / 69%	70% / 67%	69% / 65%	67% / 64%	63% / 60%	61% / 59%	61% / 58%	60% / 57%	58% / 55%
Moderate	84% / 80%	84% / 80%	80% / 76%	77% / 74%	76% / 72%	72% / 69%	70% / 66%	68% / 65%	66% / 63%	65% / 62%	63% / 60%	60% / 57%	58% / 55%	57% / 54%	56% / 54%	55% / 52%
Moderately light	79% / 75%	79% / 75%	75% / 71%	73% / 69%	71% / 68%	68% / 65%	66% / 62%	64% / 61%	62% / 59%	61% / 58%	59% / 56%	56% / 53%	55% / 52%	54% / 51%	53% / 50%	51% / 49%
Light	74% / 70%	74% / 70%	70% / 67%	68% / 64%	67% / 63%	64% / 60%	61% / 58%	60% / 57%	58% / 55%	57% / 54%	55% / 53%	53% / 50%	51% / 48%	50% / 48%	50% / 47%	48% / 46%
Very light	69% / 65%	69% / 65%	66% / 62%	63% / 60%	62% / 59%	59% / 56%	57% / 54%	56% / 53%	55% / 51%	53% / 50%	52% / 49%	49% / 46%	48% / 45%	47% / 44%	46% / 44%	45% / 42%

FIGURE 13.15 Training load and intensity zone relationship.

allows them to perform only three repetitions; if they attempt a fourth repetition, they will not be able to complete it. If the athlete can perform more than three repetitions, the load on subsequent sets is increased until only three repetitions can be performed. Conversely, if the athlete cannot perform three repetitions, the load would be reduced on subsequent sets.

Proponents of this method of prescribing training load suggest that it removes some of the limitations associated with the use of the percentage of 1RM method (% 1RM) because the load for each exercise is adjusted to the athlete's current physiological state (66, 484). Fundamentally, this method of prescribing intensity is a form of training to failure, which results in every exercise within the training session being performed at maximal intensity (figure 13.15). Because training to failure is maximal training, it is possible that this loading method will produce a fatigue-management problem, which could negatively affect adaptive responses and result in physiological consequences, such as nonfunctional overreaching and overtraining (242, 366).

A growing body of scientific knowledge clearly demonstrates that training to failure is a suboptimal methodology for resistance training when targeting strength (66, 92, 171, 308, 366, 501, 526) or hypertrophic adaptations (65, 285, 308, 411). Additionally, when this methodology is used as part of a concurrent training program, there is a muted development compared to training based on the % 1RM (240). Ultimately, these maladaptive responses are a result of fatigue-management issues associated with chronic maximal training. Additionally, this method of loading results in significantly higher training loads, monotony of training, and training strain, which increase injury risk compared to % 1RM training (66, 359). Ultimately, based on the available scientific evidence, it appears that using loads based on a % 1RM is a more efficient and beneficial method for prescribing training loads.

Repetition Maximum Zones

Another method that has been proposed to address some of the issues associated with the % 1RM loading method is to use **repetition maximum (RM) zones** (66, 274, 484). Like the RM method of prescribing load, this method allows the athlete to select a training load at which they complete repetitions within a predetermined range (e.g., 1-3RM, 4-6RM, 8-12RM) (274). For example, if a 4RM to 6RM is prescribed and the athlete can perform more than six repetitions or fewer than four repetitions, the load will be modified so the athlete can perform the prescribed repetitions. Even though improvements in maximal strength have been associated with training with RM zones (63, 225, 390), this method of prescribing training load has some of the same shortcomings as RM training. Specifically, the relative intensity will always be indicative of a maximal intensity because the athlete is required to train to failure (358). This is problematic because it creates a fatigue-management problem that can negatively affect the development of maximal strength, power, and the RFD, which are best optimized with a mixed-methods approach that employs variations in training loads (187, 484). Kraemer and Fleck (278) suggest that RM zone-based training can be used to incorporate training load variations similar to % 1RM-based training methods. Specifically, they classify training loads as very light (16-20RM), light (13-15RM), moderate (8-10RM), heavy (3-5RM), and very heavy (1-3RM) based on the amount of muscle tissue activated when performing the training activity. At first glance this seems logical, but due to the higher amount of total work performed and the implementation of training to failure during the very light day, there will be significantly more fatigue compared to a moderate, heavy, or very heavy session (36). Ultimately, because this loading method requires the athlete to train to failure, all the loading zones proposed by Kraemer and Fleck (278) are essentially maximal loads, which obviates the ability to introduce variation in training load into the training program. Ample research shows that resistance training with RM zones is less effective compared to % 1RM-based training programs (66, 358-360). Like RM training, the use of RM zones to program training load results in a significantly greater total training load, monotony of training, and training strain, which significantly increase injury risk compared to programs that use % 1RM training loads (359).

Although RM zones do address some of the issues associated with using %RM, the chronic use of this loading method will result in a maladaptive response to training (501), such as nonfunctional overreaching or overtraining. Therefore, the use of % 1RM loading methods or methods that allow for submaximal loading will result in more positive training outcomes.

Velocity-Based Training Methods

Although many coaches consider **velocity-based training (VBT) methods** the new, revolutionary method of prescribing resistance-training intensity, using velocity to guide resistance-training intensity is not a new or novel concept (23, 325, 394). In fact, there are reports of German (394) and American weightlifters (325) using linear transducers to quantify movement velocity in the 1970s. In fact, in 1976, Zhekov recommended various mechanical systems that could quantify movement velocity during weightlifting movements (216). Additionally, in the 1990s, Hiskia (216) presented a revolutionary portable weightlifting analysis system called the V-scope that could quantify movement velocity during resistance-training exercise. However, these early methods of quantifying movement velocity were limited by cumbersome equipment or excessive costs. Numerous technological advances have improved the availability of affordable velocity measurement devices, such as linear position transducers, accelerometers, and inertial movement sensors, making it incrementally easier for modern coaches to measure velocity. The ability to integrate technology into the weight room is appealing and has resulted in an increase in research examining this technology's ability to guide training.

Although at first glance VBT methods may seem ideal for prescribing training loads, the application of this method may not be as effective as many suggest (484). To truly understand why so many people are jumping on the VBT bandwagon, it is important to understand the theoretical framework underpinning this method of prescribing training intensity. It is well-documented that as the external load lifted increases, there is a concomitant reduction in the velocity of movement (241, 245, 533). This decline in movement velocity continues until 1RM is achieved, which corresponds to what is referred to as the *minimal* or *terminal velocity threshold* (241, 533). Generally, there is a near-linear relationship between the load lifted and the velocity of movement. Due to this relationship, it has been suggested that resistance-training intensity should be prescribed based on a load-velocity (LV) profile (23, 363, 533) or a 1RM that is predicted from the LV profile (23, 253, 533).

One of the biggest arguments used by proponents of VBT to support the use of the LV profile to predict the 1RM is that the 1RM varies dramatically from session to session. This variation results in a mismatch between maximal capacity for each day and the athlete's current 1RM (23, 253). Therefore, several authors suggest that using velocity to predict the 1RM for the training session off the warm-up sets (253) or by associating training zones with the LV profile will better align with the athlete's current strength levels to provide a more effective way to prescribe training loads (23, 253, 533). Although at first glance this contention seems reasonable, these constructs are not fully supported by the available scientific literature. The premise that the 1RM changes dramatically and the velocity of movement is more accurate has been questioned by Banyard and colleagues (25). Using a novel study design, they assessed (25) the back squat 1RM on 3 nonconsecutive days while simultaneously measuring velocity. With this design, they determined that the 1RM across a microcycle was extremely stable (intraclass correlation [ICC] = 0.99, standard error of the measurement [SEM] = 2.9 kg, coefficient of variation [CV] = 2.1%), but the velocity at 1RM was completely unstable (ICC = 0.42, SEM = 0.05 m · s^{-1}, CV = 22.5%) and varied dramatically from day to day. Additionally, when the warm-up sets were used to estimate the actual 1RM on each testing day, they consistently overestimated the athlete's actual maximal strength that day (loads up to 60% = +30 kg, +21%; 80% = +22 kg, +16%; 90% = +19 kg, +14%). These findings clearly demonstrate that there may be a mismatch between the athlete's maximal strength and the velocity of movement during the back squat. Due to this mismatch, it is likely that if velocity metrics are used to estimate the athlete's maximal strength on a given training day, incorrect and possibly excessive loads will be prescribed.

The second method that has been recommended is to create individualized LV profiles for each athlete and each exercise to be trained with VBT methods (23, 533). The creation of the LV profile requires the athlete to perform a series of progressively loaded attempts while simultaneously measuring velocity, which can then be used to create LV profiles for the tested exercises (figure 13.16).

The LV profile is created with the use of a regression analysis that fits the velocity (data points) of movement with different loads (kg or %RM) during the lift (23). Although greater accuracy is achieved with more testing loads (e.g., 10 loads), this may not be feasible when testing numerous athletes. Therefore, using a light load (about 40% of 1RM) and a heavy load (about 80% of 1RM) has been suggested as a viable option for generating the LV profile (150, 151). At this point, the coach can create an intensity-alignment table that provides velocity zones the athlete will use to guide the load lifted (figure 13.17). Regardless of which method is used to create the LV profile, the coach would need to create an individualized LV profile for every athlete and exercise they intend to use VBT methods with in their training program.

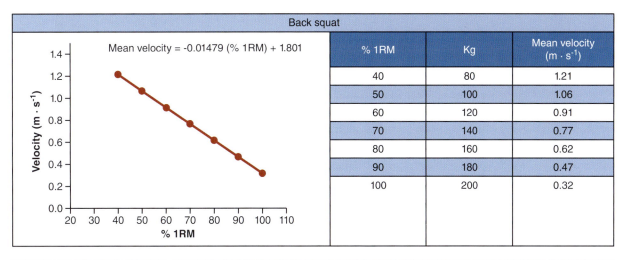
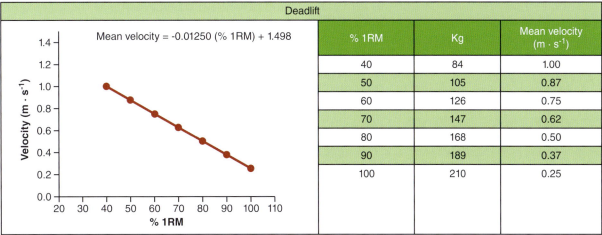
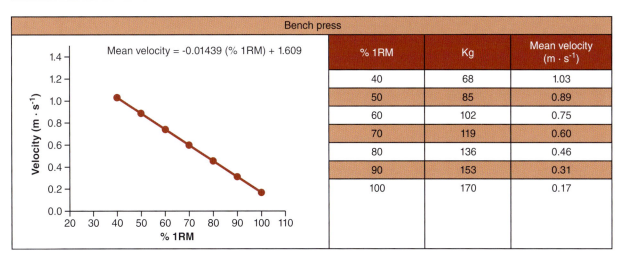

FIGURE 13.16 Example LV profiles for the back squat, deadlift, and bench press.

An alternative approach to using velocity to guide resistance training is to set velocity thresholds (484). It is well-documented that when resistance training uses sets of repetitions performed continuously, there is a concomitant reduction in movement velocity across the set (188, 515, 516). One strategy is to set a velocity-loss threshold to either the volume or relative intensity of the set (533-535). With this method of prescribing intensity, the athlete is given a set percentage velocity decline (e.g., 10%, 20%, 30%) of the first repetition of the set (533). Using smaller velocity thresholds

Descriptor	Abbreviation	Back squat (m · s⁻¹)	Deadlift (m · s⁻¹)	Bench press (m · s⁻¹)
Maximum	MX	≤ 0.32	≤ 0.25	≤ 0.17
Very heavy	VH	0.40 – 0.34	0.31 – 0.26	0.24 – 0.18
Heavy	H	0.47 – 0.41	0.37 – 0.32	0.31 – 0.26
Moderately heavy	MH	0.54 – 0.48	0.44 – 0.39	0.39 – 0.33
Moderate	M	0.62 – 0.56	0.50 – 0.45	0.46 – 0.40
Moderately light	ML	0.69 – 0.63	0.56 – 0.51	0.53 – 0.47
Light	L	0.77 – 0.71	0.62 – 0.57	0.60 – 0.54
Very light	VL	≥ 0.78	≥ 0.64	≥ 0.63

FIGURE 13.17 Example intensity alignment for mean velocity zones for the back squat, bench press, and deadlift. Alignments are based on the load-velocity profiles shown in figure 13.16.

(e.g., 10% of the first repetition of the set) will better maintain velocity across a set (535), whereas larger thresholds (e.g., 30% of the first repetition of the set) will result in greater accumulated fatigue (362, 533). If the athlete exceeds the prescribed threshold, the load is reduced for the subsequent set. Conversely if the athlete does not achieve the targeted threshold, the load can be increased. Alternatively, the set can be terminated when the threshold is crossed (533). Suchomel and colleagues (484) suggest this method allows for a form of flexible programming that may allow the athlete to better manage fatigue as the load or volume changes in response to the current state.

Although the addition of velocity-monitoring technology and the implementation of these programming strategies may be appealing, there are several disadvantages if this method is not applied correctly. If the athlete solely focuses on attainment of the highest possible velocity without maintaining appropriate technique during the lift, inefficient motor patterns will likely manifest, which may reduce the effectiveness of the training exercise (484). Therefore, it is essential that the athlete has solidified their technique before using VBT methods (303). This concept has largely been ignored in the VBT literature because most of the research in this space has been performed with the Smith machine, which has a fixed movement pattern, rather than with free weights, where technique is more important (484).

Although VBT methods are clearly better than training to failure (RM or RM zones), there is limited research that has directly compared this methodology to percentage-based training methods (112, 354). There is, however, emerging evidence that this method of prescribing training is no better than the classic percentage-based methodologies (353). Ultimately, more research directly comparing VBT and percentage-based training methods is required to fully elucidate the value of VBT methods.

One promising application of VBT training may be to modulate training loads during the competitive period of the annual training plan in which the athlete will display ever-changing fatigue states because of the competition, travel, and training schedules. VBT methods such as velocity-loss thresholds or velocity bands may allow the athlete to better autoregulate their training. Support for this contention can be found in the work of Orange and colleagues (354), who have suggested that using VBT methods during the competition period may optimize the training stimulus.

Rating of Perceived Exertion

Traditionally, the rating of perceived exertion (RPE) has been used to gauge the exertion and intensity of aerobic exercise (212). First developed by Gunnar Borg (49), the original RPE scale rated exertion between 6 and 20, which roughly represented heart rate (i.e., 60-200 bpm). Due to its relationship to heart rate, this scale has limited utility when applied to the prescription of resistance-training intensities (212). Alternatively, the Borg CR-10 scale (50) and the OMNI scale (123, 340, 395) have been used to provide an indicator of effort during resistance training. To gauge training intensity, Helms and colleagues (212) suggest that the RPE can be obtained from the athlete after each exercise or group of exercises in the resistance-training session. Alternatively, the RPE can be obtained within 10 to 30 minutes of the completion of a resistance-training session to provide session RPE (sRPE) (see chapter 11 for more detail) (314). Although sRPE is more commonly used as a monitoring tool (94), the RPE has been suggested to be a useful method for prescribing resistance-training intensity on a set-by-set basis (175, 212). Ultimately, the main limitation of RPE to prescribe training intensity is that, in most instances, athletes give RPE scores below maximum even when training is performed to volitional failure (175, 376, 445, 520). Due to this limitation, alternative methods of prescribing training intensity should be used when designing resistance-training interventions.

Repetitions in Reserve

An alternative method for prescribing resistance-training intensity is **repetitions in reserve (RIR)** (211, 212, 557). Fundamentally, the RIR scale is a modification of the classic Borg CR-10 scale in which an RPE value is aligned with an estimated number of repetitions the athlete can complete prior to volitional failure (figure 11.8, page 281) (212, 512). Hackett and colleagues (175) reported that although athletes could not accurately gauge the RPE during resistance training, they did exhibit a higher degree of accuracy in estimating the number of repetitions remaining in a set prior to volitional failure, and their accuracy increased as they were closer to volitional failure. Based on this work, Zourdos and colleagues (557) modified the Borg CR-10 scale so it corresponded to a RIR score. Interestingly, the RIR method of quantifying intensity is more accurate when the athlete has a higher resistance-training age (557) and the training session uses training loads that are closer to volitional failure (556). Due to these limitations, the use of RIR methods to prescribe training loads should be avoided with athletes who have limited resistance-training experience (484). Additionally, the ability to estimate the RIR is diminished during higher-repetition sets (e.g., >12 reps) and sets performed with lower relative intensities (e.g., >4 RIR) (556). Suchomel and colleagues (484) point out that this can be problematic because the inability to accurately gauge lower-intensity training and the need to be near muscular failure may make it difficult to employ light and heavy training days. Therefore, the use of RIR as a programming strategy is limited and may need to be coupled with other strategies such as % 1RM or VBT methods.

Rest Intervals

When designing a resistance-training program, the coach must understand the basic terminology used to describe the rest intervals that can be employed. The prefixes *inter-* (between) and *intra-* (within) refer to the location of the rest interval related to the sets of the training program (513). Inter-set, intra-set, and inter-repetition rest intervals can be incorporated into a resistance-training program (figure 13.18).

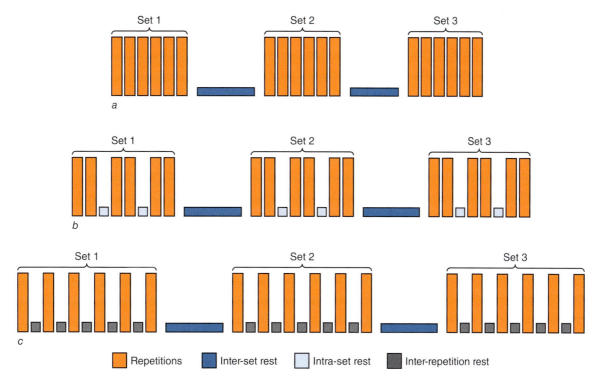

FIGURE 13.18 Example *(a)* inter-set, *(b)* intra-set, and *(c)* inter-repetition rest intervals.

Inter-Set Rest Intervals

The rest interval between a series of sets is referred to as the *inter-set rest interval* (513). The time allotted for the inter-set rest interval can play a distinct role in modulating the substrate replenishment between sets. For example, after 30 seconds of rest, about 70% of adenosine triphosphate (ATP) can be restored, and complete restoration can occur by 3 to 5 minutes (232). After 2 minutes of rest, phosphocreatine (PCr) can be about 84% restored and completely restored after 8 minutes of recovery (208, 234, 235). Ultimately, inter-set rest intervals of 1 minute or less may result in inadequate recovery (541), which can result in a 12% to 44% reduction in force- and power-generating capacity (9, 367, 476). Conversely, if the inter-set rest interval is extended to 2 to 5 minutes, force- and power-generating capacity can be almost completely restored depending on the workload (9, 40, 406, 476). Based on these data, longer inter-set rest intervals (2-5 min) are preferred when training to maximize strength and power.

Based on the available research, shorter rest intervals (≤1 min) do not allow enough recovery to sustain training intensities across multiple sets of resistance training, which could negatively affect both strength and power development (97, 541). Therefore, it is generally recommended that when training to enhance muscular strength and power development, rest intervals between 2 and 5 minutes should be used (184, 443). Conversely, rest intervals between 30 seconds and 1.5 minutes are often recommended for training programs that target hypertrophy (97, 274, 282, 541). It is important to consider that shorter rest intervals (i.e., <2 min) result in a reduced ability to maintain force production; this effect may be magnified when coupled with higher volumes. Recently, Schoenfeld and colleagues (425) examined the effect of short (i.e., 1 min) and long (i.e., 3 min) rest intervals on muscle hypertrophy after 8 weeks of resistance training. As expected, the longer inter-set rest interval group displayed significantly greater strength gains. Unexpectedly, this group displayed significantly greater hypertrophy than the short rest interval group and equal muscular endurance. Careful examination of these data reveals that the longer inter-set rest interval allowed the subjects to lift heavier weights more frequently, resulting in a greater overall volume load, which may have exerted a greater stimulus for muscular adaptation. When considering hypertrophy, it is possible that the volume load the athlete completes is more important than the inter-set rest interval (137). Based on this line of reasoning, Schoenfeld and colleagues (425) suggest that resistance-training programs that target hypertrophy should use a minimum inter-set rest interval of 2 minutes.

It is plausible that shorter inter-set rest intervals are advantageous for the development of muscular endurance. When shorter rest intervals are used with higher-volume resistance-training programs, several physiological adaptations occur, such as increase in capillary density, mitochondrial density, and buffering capacity (47, 541). Ultimately, these adaptations may translate into enhanced endurance performance. Although the current recommendation is to use short inter-set rest intervals when targeting muscular endurance (443, 541), an emerging body of evidence suggests longer inter-set rest intervals coupled with higher-volume training can result in similar gains in muscular endurance while stimulating greater strength gains (425).

Inter-Repetition Rest Intervals

The inter-repetition rest interval is the rest interval between each repetition in a predefined set (513). Traditionally, sets are performed continuously with no inter-repetition rest (figure 13.18a). However, with cluster sets (see Advanced Resistance-Training Methods section), 15- and 45-second rest intervals between each repetition can significantly alter the training stimulus as well as the quality of each repetition (figure 13.18c) (181, 186, 255). Theoretically, these rest intervals provide an opportunity for partial recovery, allowing for an enhanced recovery via the maintenance of PCr stores and an increased metabolite clearance (101, 159, 352). Short inter-repetition rest intervals may increase the availability of ATP and PCr, which could translate into a maintenance of movement velocity across the set and potentially the entire training session (513). Ultimately, the modulation of the inter-repetition rest allows for the training stress to be altered to ensure the goals of the set are met.

Intra-Set Rest Intervals

The intra-set rest interval is the rest between groups of repetitions within a defined set structure (figure 13.18b) (513). Like the inter-repetition rest interval, this rest interval is used to create cluster sets. For example, three sets of six repetitions separated by a 2-minute inter-set rest could be subdivided into clusters of three pairs of two repetitions each, separated by a 15- to 45-second intra-set rest interval (181, 186). The duration of the intra-set rest interval is dictated by the number of repetitions within the cluster and the targeted physiological and performance outcomes. For example, if a set of 12 repetitions is subdivided into clusters of four repetitions, a longer (i.e., 30-45 s) intra-set rest interval may be applied to ensure performance is maintained. If, however, the goal of the set is to enhance muscular endurance, then shorter intra-set rest intervals (i.e., 15-25 s) may be applied.

Exercise Selection

When designing a resistance-training program, the coach selects the exercises that make up the program. To make informed exercise selections, the coach must understand the various types of resistance exercises (443).

Most resistance-training exercises can be classified as either core or assistance exercises. Exercises that recruit large amounts of muscle mass and involve two or more primary joints (i.e., **multijoint exercises**) while activating synergistic muscles are classified as **core exercises** because of their importance to strength and power development (184, 443). When these exercises (e.g., power clean, squat, front squat) load the axial skeleton (i.e., place load on the spine), they can also be classified as **structural exercises** (184). A good example of a structural exercise is the back squat because the barbell loads the axial skeleton and the musculature of the torso must maintain a near-erect position throughout the duration of the exercise (184). If the structural exercise is performed rapidly, such as a power clean or jump shrug, it can also be classified as a **power exercise** or **explosive exercise**. Overall, core exercises are the cornerstones of a resistance-training program because they provide a multidimensional training stimulus that engages a large amount of muscle mass and more readily transfer to enhanced performance (521).

Alternatively, exercises that recruit smaller amounts of muscle mass and use one primary joint (i.e., **single-joint exercises**) are classified as **assistance exercises** (184). Because these exercises isolate a specific muscle or muscle group, they are commonly used as part of injury-prevention and rehabilitation protocols (184, 443). These exercises often address muscles that are predisposed to injury due to the unique demands of the sport or require reconditioning after an injury (443). Even though these exercises have a place in a resistance-training program, they should not be the primary component of the training program because they are generally considered less important than the core exercises in maximizing sport performance (443).

Exercise Order

The overall effectiveness of a resistance-training program can be influenced by the order of exercises in the training session (19, 385, 441, 450, 459). For example, when multijoint exercises (e.g., bench press, squat, leg press, shoulder press) are placed later in a training session, performance will decline compared to when they are performed earlier in the session (450-452). Therefore, due to the fundamental importance of large-mass, multijoint exercises to strength development, it is generally recommended that these exercises are placed early in the session when the athlete has less fatigue (184, 384, 443). After these exercises are completed, the athlete can progress to smaller-mass, single-joint exercises (384).

Another way to think about exercise order is to consider the type of exercise (i.e., power, core, or assistance) being programmed. Generally, exercises that target power development (e.g., power cleans, jump squats) should be performed prior to core exercises (i.e., large-mass, multijoint exercises). Assistance exercises (i.e., small-mass, single-joint exercises) should be performed at the end of the training session (184). Although this basic exercise order is effective for most athletes, in some situations it may be warranted for advanced athletes who are attempting to maximize strength and power development to perform explosive (312, 432) or heavy-loaded, multijoint exercises (312) prior to the performance of a plyometric or sprint activity (187, 404). This exercise ordering strategy creates a strength–power potentiation complex (471), which will be further discussed in the Advanced Resistance-Training Methods section of this chapter.

Another approach to exercise order is alternating between upper- and lower-body or agonist–antagonist exercises (450-452). Although this ordering method may be useful for circuit-based resistance-training programs, it is considered inappropriate for training programs that target the maximization of strength and power development (465).

Training Frequency

The number of times a muscle group is trained or the number of training sessions completed per week can be used to define training frequency (14, 91, 126, 421). Based on the scientific literature, greater strength gains occur in response to training programs that contain more frequent training (158, 166, 167, 236, 316, 366, 371). In the seminal paper by Gillam (158), data were presented that showed a progressive increase in strength as training frequency increased from one to five sessions per week. Specifically, strength gains were the greatest with three (increase of 32%) and five (increase of 41%) sessions per week when compared to one (increase of 19%) and two (increase of 24%) sessions per week. More recently, Grgic and colleagues (169) concluded there is a progressive increase in strength as training frequency increases, with training frequencies of four or more times per week exerting the greatest effect on strength gains. These effects were most noted when multijoint exercises were part of the training program (figure 13.19).

However, it is interesting to note that when the frequency of training is compared with volume-equalized training programs, there is relatively no difference between strength gains achieved (86, 133, 169, 380, 444). A similar finding has also been noted when looking at the effect of training frequency on hypertrophy (170). Based on these data, it appears that the main benefit of increasing training frequency is the ability to increase the overall volume of training exposing the athlete to a greater overall training stimulus (169, 170).

When considering training frequency recommendations, it is generally accepted that strength gains are optimized when full-body resistance training is performed for 2 or 3 resistance-training days per week with novice individuals or athletes (15, 64, 389). As these individuals develop, the frequency of training must be increased to meet the athlete's training needs. Intermediate athletes should increase their training frequency to 3 or 4 resistance-training days per week (15, 316, 389). Although this frequency of training will meet the needs of most athletes, it is possible more advanced athletes will require additional training days per week to provide enough training stimulus for continued adaptation and performance gains.

Although there is great variability in the amount of training that can be employed with more advanced athletes, it is likely that 4 to 6 training days per week may be warranted to maximize strength gains (15, 224). Support for this contention can be found in the scientific literature, which shows that athletes who use higher-frequency resistance training display greater strength gains (224). For example, university-level American football players who complete 4 or 5 resistance-training days per week display significantly greater strength gains compared to those who perform fewer training sessions per week (224). Additionally, it is not uncommon for elite weightlifters to train 5 or 6 days per week (6-8, 14, 475, 491).

Another strategy for increasing training volume is increasing the number of sessions in each training day. In fact, Greek (114), Soviet (152), Chinese (61), and American (251, 252, 466) weightlifters all employ two training sessions per day as part of their training programs. Bulgarian weightlifters, on the other hand, may use as many as six 45-minute training sessions per day (6-8, 249). Ultimately, Aján and Baroga (14) suggest that multiple training sessions per day is necessary to maximize weight-lifting performance.

Although it is likely the main benefit of more frequent training is the ability to increase the overall volume of training, it is plausible that breaking longer training sessions into smaller, more frequent, shorter bouts of training may allow for very effective micro-dosing of the strength stimuli (86, 269). It is hypothesized that shorter, more frequent training sessions followed by recovery and nutritional interventions will result in an increased quality of training. Support for this hypothesis can be found in the work of Häkkinen and Kallinen (192), who report that when a targeted training load is split into two shorter sessions, strength athletes display significantly greater muscle hypertrophy, neuromuscular adaptations, and force-production capacity compared to one training session per day. Based on the available data, if the athlete's primary goal is to increase hypertrophy, strength, or power-generation capacity, more frequent training may be warranted (47).

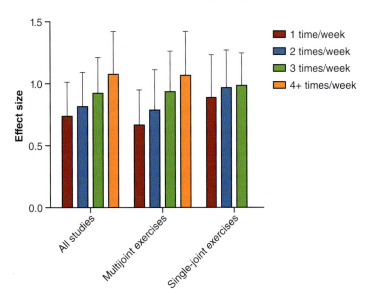

FIGURE 13.19 Mean effect sizes and 95% confidence intervals for strength gains and training frequency.

Data from J. Grgic, B.J. Schoenfeld, T.B. Davies, et al., "Effect of Resistance Training Frequency on Gains in Muscular Strength: A Systematic Review and Meta-Analysis," *Sports Medicine* 48 (2018): 1207-1220.

Although a case can be made for increasing training frequency, the actual training frequency an athlete can tolerate is highly individualized. Many factors, such as the athlete's chronological age, training age or status, type of strength needed, the period or phase of the training plan, and the overall targeted goals of the training process can all influence a coach's decision about the optimal training frequency. An additional consideration is that most athletes use resistance training to enhance the performance of other sporting activities (47). These athletes may be able to perform only two or three resistance-training sessions per week because they are performing other training activities, such as metabolic conditioning, sprint training, and technical and tactical training. Finally, the frequency of training may vary throughout the annual training plan. For example, during the general preparation phase, the frequency of resistance training is likely higher compared to the main competition phase, which might show a slight reduction in training frequency during the taper leading into the most important competition targeted in the annual plan.

Loading Patterns

When designing a resistance-training program, the loading pattern employed is an important consideration because it directly affects the physiological adaptations associated with training. The most used and effective loading pattern is a flat loaded target set structure (figure 13.20).

With these set structures, the athlete first completes several warm-up sets with progressively increasing loads, then performs target sets at the same flat load, and finally performs a set with a reduced intensity (i.e., down set). Generally, when targeting the development of maximal strength, the prescribed training load for the target sets will range between 80% and 100% of 1RM (161, 193). In the flat loaded target sets presented in figure 13.20, the load for the target sets is 80% of 1RM; then it is reduced by 20% for the down set. This reduction in training load stimulates a postactivation performance enhancement (PAPE) effect that results in an increase in movement velocity and power output (471) and an increase in growth hormone release (164). Based on the available literature, it appears that performance is maximized with training loads between 70% and 85% of 1RM for most athletes (161, 554). For example, 35% of the yearly training volume of Russian weightlifters was reported to be between 70% and 80% of 1RM, 26% was between 80% and 90% of 1RM, and only 7% was between 90% and 100% of 1RM (554). If too much of the athlete's training volume is in the 90% to 100% range, performance may stagnate and signs of overtraining may occur (138). Therefore, it is essential the coach design systematic variations in training load at the session, microcycle, and mesocycle levels of the training process.

Another popular loading pattern is the **pyramid set structure**, which is sometimes referred to as the *ascending pyramid* (43, 44, 46, 47). This loading pattern features a progressive increase

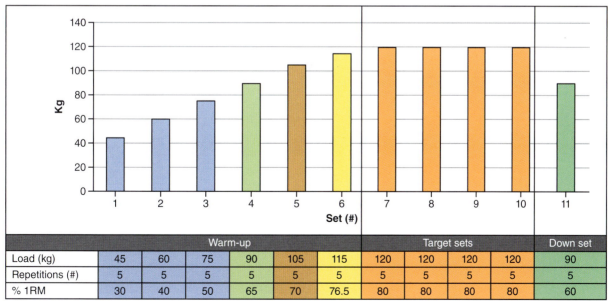

	Warm-up						Target sets				Down set
Set (#)	1	2	3	4	5	6	7	8	9	10	11
Load (kg)	45	60	75	90	105	115	120	120	120	120	90
Repetitions (#)	5	5	5	5	5	5	5	5	5	5	5
% 1RM	30	40	50	65	70	76.5	80	80	80	80	60

Note: Loading based on a maximum front squat of 150 kg. Intensities based on figure 13.15.

FIGURE 13.20 Flat loaded target sets for the front squat.

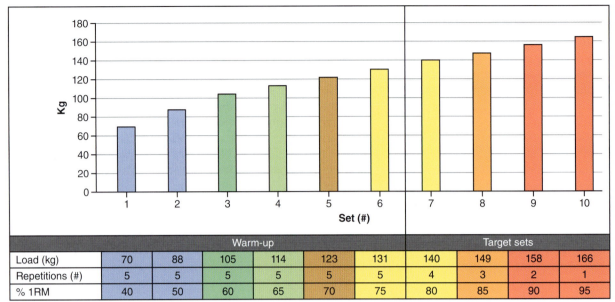

FIGURE 13.21 Ascending pyramid using the power clean.

in the training load as the repetitions decrease (figure 13.21).

To maximize strength gains, the athlete should avoid going to failure on any sets in the pyramid. Load should increase only 10% to 15% from the first set to the last set of the pyramid (i.e., steps contained within the target sets) (44, 46, 47). Increases of greater than 15% in loads across the steps should be avoided because accumulated fatigue may impair strength development (46).

In a modified version called the **double pyramid** (44, 46, 47) or simply a *pyramid* (553), the load is increased up to a maximal attempt while the repetitions are decreased. After the heaviest load is lifted, the load is progressively decreased while the repetitions increase (figure 13.22) (47, 553).

Although the double pyramid, or pyramid, loading structure is useful in some contexts, Zatsiorsky and colleagues (553) recently suggested that this loading model has been virtually abandoned by

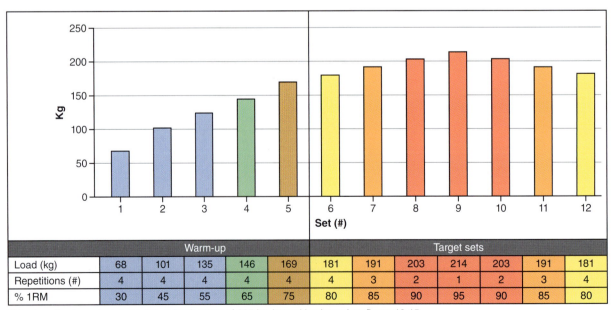

FIGURE 13.22 Double pyramid using the back squat.

Olympic-caliber athletes due to the premature levels of fatigue that occur on the ascending portion of the pyramid. To account for this issue, Bompa and Buzzichelli (45) suggested a better approach would be to keep the number of repetitions constant while performing only five or six target sets (figure 13.23). Additionally, they suggested the maximal load should not exceed 90% of 1RM (45). It is likely that this loading pattern accounts for the issues noted by Zatsiorsky and colleagues (553) and has the potential to stimulate a PAPE response during the descending portion of the pyramid (471).

Another modification of the pyramid loading pattern is called the **skewed pyramid** (44, 46, 47). Bompa (43) suggests this is an improved variant of the double pyramid because the load is progressively increased across a series of sets and then a down set is performed for four to six repetitions with the intent to move as fast as possible (figure 13.24). As with flat loaded target sets, the incorporation of a down set would be expected to result in a PAPE effect (471).

Another advanced loading structure commonly used in weightlifting is **wave loading** (492), which

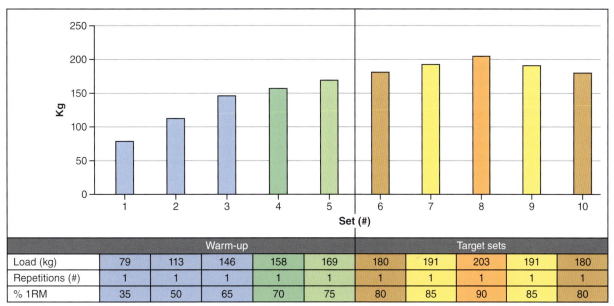

Note: Loading based on a maximum back squat of 225 kg. Intensities based on figure 13.15.

FIGURE 13.23 Modified double pyramid using the back squat.

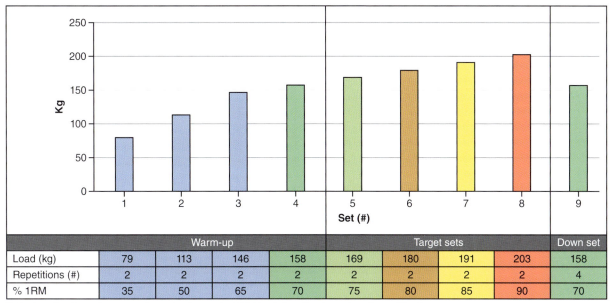

Note: Loading based on a maximum back squat of 225 kg. Intensities based on figure 13.15.

FIGURE 13.24 Skewed pyramid using the back squat.

is sometimes referred to as **segment work** (250). The load is increased in an undulating or wave-like manner (figure 13.25). It is likely that this method of loading creates a PAPE effect with the lighter loads performed after the completion of the heavy loads. Although it would be logical to expect a PAPE effect with wave loading, this has yet to be validated in the scientific literature. This loading structure is ideally suited for weightlifting exercises (e.g., snatches, power snatches, cleans, power cleans) because it allows coaches to spot technical errors during the lifts of heavier loads that can be corrected with lighter loads (250).

An alternative to wave loading is what Jones (250) refers to as **double stimulation**, in which the athlete alternates between high-repetition sets and sets that have a single repetition performed with 10% to 15% more load (figure 13.26). This method is generally recommended for strength exercises (e.g., back squats, pulls, presses) (250).

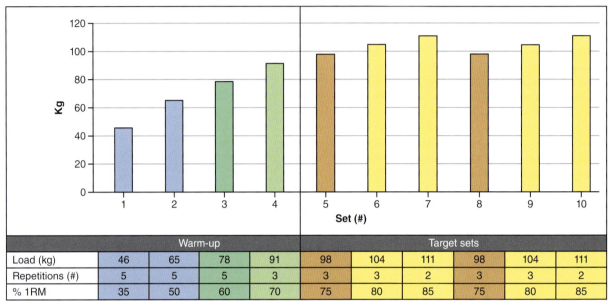

Note: Loading based on a maximum snatch of 130 kg. Intensities based on figure 13.15.

FIGURE 13.25 Wave loading using the snatch.

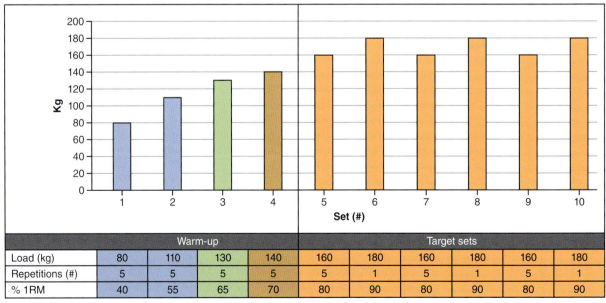

Note: Loading based on a maximum back squat of 200 kg. Intensities based on figure 13.15.

FIGURE 13.26 Double stimulation using the back squat.

Advanced Resistance-Training Methods

Advanced athletes may need more complex resistance-training methods to continue to stimulate physiological adaptations that lead to performance gains. Numerous advanced training methods can be employed; some of the most common include cluster sets, accentuated eccentric methods, and strength–power potentiation complexes.

Cluster Sets

One technique for altering the training stimulus delivered by a resistance-training program is to modify the set structure (181, 186, 513). Traditionally, sets are performed continuously with only inter-set rest (186, 189) (figure 13.27a). Alternatively, the set can be modified to provide inter-repetition rest (figure 13.27b) or intra-set rest (figure 13.27c). Rest intervals last 15 to 40 seconds. The practice of including periodic rest intervals within the set while maintaining the inter-set rest is commonly referred to as a *cluster set* in the scientific (93, 181, 186, 189, 288, 513) and applied literature (323, 370, 379, 397, 448, 499). Although research investigating cluster sets has become popular and this advanced training technique is a popular practice in modern strength and conditioning, it is not a new concept. The roots of the cluster set can be traced back to the late 1950s, when Perry Rader discussed the implementation of a 10-second rest between repetitions in an article in *IronMan Magazine* (379). Even though the cluster set has a rich history, the term has been mistakenly used as an umbrella term for any modification to the traditional set (256, 306, 307, 319, 351, 513, 517).

Historically, the cluster set was first referred to as the *rest-pause method*; a short rest interval (8-10 s), referred to as a *pause*, was placed between the repetitions in a period of defined work (i.e., set) (379). Over time, the rest-pause terminology morphed into the current cluster set taxonomy when inter-repetition (189, 397, 448) and intra-set rest intervals were introduced (181). In 1987, Roll and Omer (397) described the cluster set as a predetermined set of two to six repetitions with 20 to 30 seconds of inter-repetition rest to ensure maximal intensity was achieved on each repetition. In 1999, Siff and Verkhoshansky (448) suggested that a cluster set can be created by performing one or more repetitions with 10 to 20 seconds of inter-repetition or intra-set rest provided within the set structure. Furthermore, they proposed two subcategories of the cluster set: the extensive cluster set and the intensive cluster set.

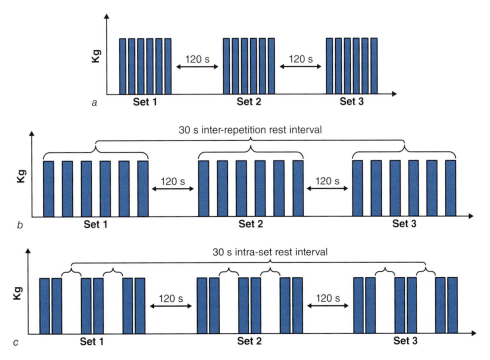

FIGURE 13.27 Basic set structures used in resistance training: *(a)* traditional set; *(b)* basic cluster set with inter-repetition rest intervals; *(c)* basic cluster set with intra-set rest intervals.

They recommended that the extensive cluster set should contain four to six repetitions performed with a 4RM to 6RM load separated by 10 seconds of inter-repetition or intra-set rest. The intensive cluster set was recommended to be performed for four to six repetitions with loads at 75% to 90% of 1RM and 20 seconds of inter-repetition or intra-set rest.

A further evolution of the cluster set was proposed in 2008, when Haff and colleagues (181, 186) suggested that the loading pattern of each repetition or group of repetitions could be modified to alter the training stimulus. Based on this recommendation, there are five possible variations to the cluster set (table 13.5): basic (figure 13.27), undulating, wave, ascending, and descending (figure 13.28).

- *Basic cluster set:* The load is maintained across the set and only the inter-repetition or intra-set rest interval is modified (figure 13.27*b* and 13.27*c*) (181, 186). This set structure generally results in a maintenance of movement velocity across each repetition in the set.

- *Undulating cluster set:* The load is applied in a pyramid fashion (figure 13.28*a*) (181, 186). This method of loading is thought to stimulate a PAPE response, which results in an increased velocity of movement during the descending portion of the pyramid (189).

- *Wave loaded cluster set:* The load alternates intensity between repetitions (figure 13.28*b*) or between groups of repetitions. During the repetitions performed with lighter loads, it has been hypothesized that a PAPE response will occur and the velocity of movement will increase.

- *Ascending cluster set:* The load lifted across the set is increased, with the highest load lifted on the last repetition of the set (figure 13.28*c*) (181). It is hypothesized that during the set following the inter-set rest, the velocity of movement will be enhanced because of a PAPE response that is stimulated by the higher load repetitions at the end of the previous set.

- *Descending cluster set:* The first repetition of the set is a maximal or near maximal attempt, and the load is progressively reduced on the subsequent repetitions (figure 13.28*d*).

Although many of these cluster set loading paradigms are used in strength and conditioning settings, much more research is warranted to fully understand the benefits of these structures and how best to implement them as part of a resistance-training program.

An additional consideration when employing cluster sets is the number of repetitions in the set. Through selecting different cluster set configurations, the coach can modulate the velocity loss across the set, which can alter the training outcome. For example, cluster sets of four repetitions will result in a greater velocity decline than sets of two repetitions (515). Using individual repetitions or pairs of repetitions to create the cluster set means

TABLE 13.5 Example Loading Patterns for Cluster Sets

Type of cluster	Sets	×	Repetitions	Intensity (% 1RM)	Inter-repetition rest (s)	Intra-set rest (s)	Clusters in the set (%/repetition)					Inter-set rest (s)
Basic	1-5	×	5/1	80%	30		80/1	80/1	80/1	80/1	80/1	120
	1-5	×	6/2	80%		30	80/2	80/2	80/2			120
Undulating	1-5	×	5/1	80%	30		75/1	82/1	88/1	80/1	75/1	120
	1-5	×	6/2	80%		30	77/2	86/2	77/2			120
Wave	1-5	×	5/1	80%	30		77/1	85/1	77/1	85/1	77/1	120
	1-5	×	8/2	80%		30	77/2	86/2	77/2	86/2		120
Ascending	1-5	×	5/1	80%	30		70/1	75/1	80/1	85/1	90/1	120
	1-5	×	6/2	80%		30	75/2	80/2	85/2			120
Descending	1-5	×	5/1	80%	30		90/1	85/1	80/1	75/1	70/1	120
	1-5	×	6/2	80%		30	85/2	80/2	75/2			120

Note: 5/1 = 5 total repetitions/1 cluster repetition; 6/2 = 6 total repetitions/2 cluster repetitions; 8/2 = 8 total repetitions/2 cluster repetitions.

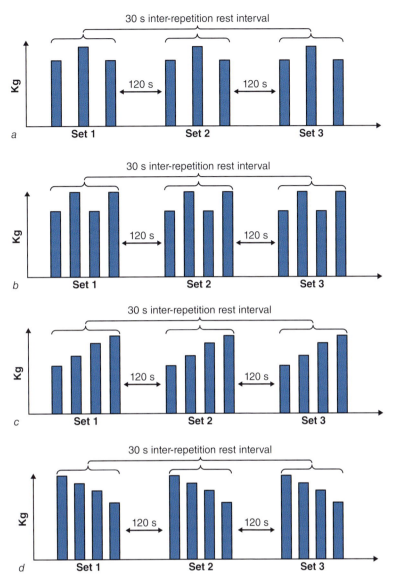

FIGURE 13.28 Examples of *(a)* undulating, *(b)* wave, *(c)* ascending, and *(d)* descending cluster sets.

less velocity loss across the set, which may translate into a maximization of muscular power development (186). Conversely, if the targeted training outcome is the maximization of muscle hypertrophy, cluster sets that contain more repetitions and higher training loads allow for a greater velocity decline across each group of repetitions (362) and a higher time under tension and total work (514), which may provide a more effective hypertrophic stimulus. Interestingly, if the load is aligned with the RM for the number of repetitions in the cluster set, a similar velocity loss can occur when comparing high-volume traditional and cluster sets (514). For example, similar velocity declines are noted when the following are performed: sets of 12 repetitions at 60% of 1RM, clusters of four repetitions at 75% of 1RM with 30 seconds intra-set rest, and clusters of two repetitions at 80% of 1RM with 30 seconds intra-set rest (514). Interestingly, the heavier-loaded cluster sets performed with fewer repetitions resulted in a higher concentric time under tension (514), which may result in an enhanced hypertrophic stimulus (416). This highlights an important aspect of cluster sets first noted by Rader (379) in 1958 that is often not considered by modern sport scientists and coaches: Using cluster sets allows for heavier loads to be lifted.

When implementing cluster sets, the inter-repetition or intra-set rest interval can be aligned with specific training targets. For example, if strength–power endurance or hypertrophy is the training goal, a shorter rest interval of 5 to 15 seconds might be selected (185). Conversely, if maximal strength is the target of the training program, inter-repetition and intra-set rest intervals of 15 to 30 seconds can be used. Remember that the shorter the rest interval, the greater the focus on endurance (185). If the cluster set has groups of multiple repetitions, a longer intra-set rest interval should be used. Ideally, cluster sets are best suited for exercises such as the snatch or clean or weightlifting derivatives and ballistic exercises such as the jump squat and bench throw.

Although a lot of research looks at the acute effects of cluster sets (288, 513) and some research explores the chronic effects of cluster sets (93, 257), limited research exists explaining how to use these set structures in a periodized training plan (397). In the classic coaching literature, cluster sets generally are recommended for the specific preparation and precompetition (i.e., preseason) phases (397). For example, Roll and Omer (397) suggest that cluster sets should be used in the precompetition phase when strength and power are the focus of the annual training plan for a collegiate American football team. Similarly, Miller (324) suggests that competitive weightlifters should use cluster sets during the specific preparation and precompetition phases of their annual training plans.

Historically, cluster sets appear best suited for the specific preparation and precompetition phases, but recently it has been proposed that cluster sets can be implemented in other phases of the annual training plan (figure 13.29) (181, 186). For example, Haff and Harden (185) suggest that traditional sets, basic cluster sets, and ascending cluster sets can be employed in any phase of the annual training plan. Additionally, they suggest that undulating cluster sets are best suited for the specific preparation, precompetition, and main competition phases, whereas wave loaded cluster sets may be best suited for the precompetition and main competition phases. Finally, descending cluster sets are best suited for the general and specific preparation phases.

Accentuated Eccentric Methods

Accentuated eccentric loading (AEL) refers to the application of loads that are more than the concentric load during the performance of the eccentric portion of coupled eccentric (i.e., lengthening) and concentric (i.e., shortening) muscle actions (487, 530). For example, weight releasers may be used during a back squat to provide additional load during the eccentric portion of the lift. During the transition between the eccentric and concentric phases of the lift, the weight releaser allows for the seamless removal of a portion of

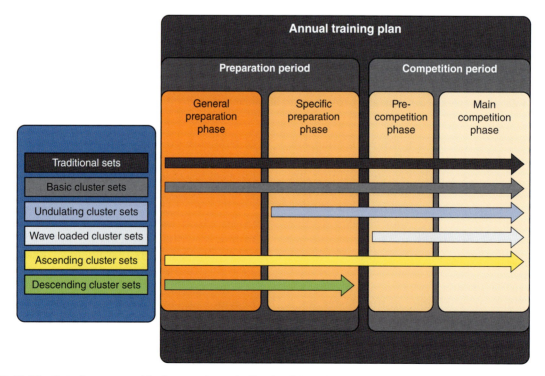

FIGURE 13.29 Set alignments with phases of a periodized training plan.

the load with minimal alteration to the athlete's technique (487, 499, 530). Alternatively, an AEL can be created with a customized leg press device (Sportesse, Somerset, United Kingdom) in which pneumatically applied loads (up to 420 kg [926 lb]) can augment the load during the eccentric portion of the lift. Upon reaching a predetermined end position (i.e., end of the eccentric portion of the lift), the pneumatic load is automatically removed, reducing the load during the concentric portion of the lift (207). Fundamentally, each method of applying an AEL augments the load during the eccentric phase of the lift and removes that augmentation prior to the initiation of the concentric phase of the lift to better align the training load with the athlete's eccentric and concentric maximal strength levels.

Muscles can produce more force during eccentric versus isometric (i.e., constant length) or concentric muscle actions (118, 206, 231). In fact, several researchers suggest that individuals can be up to 50% stronger during maximal eccentric exercise compared to maximal concentric exercise (118, 206, 226, 231). However, emerging evidence seems to indicate clear variability in the amount of additional force an individual can produce during eccentric muscle actions compared to concentric and isometric muscle actions (206). This variability may be partially attributed to the athlete's relative strength levels (218) and their familiarity with the eccentric task (204).

During multijoint AEL exercises, supramaximal loads of up to 150% of the athlete's concentric 1RM can be applied (207), although not all trained athletes are able to tolerate loads approaching 150% of their concentric 1RM (206, 207, 218, 387). For example, Refsnes (387) suggests that stronger individuals may benefit more from using lighter relative eccentric loads (e.g., 105%-110% of concentric 1RM), whereas weaker individuals may benefit from using heavier eccentric loads (e.g., 120%-130% of concentric 1RM). Although this programming recommendation provides the coach with a sound starting point, much more research is required to develop a full understanding of the optimal eccentric loading strategies for the application of AEL training methods.

An additional consideration when programming AEL methods is the ratio between eccentric and concentric loads. For example, Suchomel and colleagues (488) suggest as a basic rule that the difference between the eccentric and concentric loads should be greater than 30% of 1RM. In support of this contention, Merrigan and colleagues (320) recommend a ratio of 120% eccentric load to 65% concentric load of concentric 1RM, which would create a difference of 55% between the eccentric and concentric phases of the lift. Furthermore, Refsnes (387) suggests that the concentric load applied during AEL methods should not exceed 50% of 1RM. Although these recommendations provide some basic direction, much more research on the optimal loading ratio for AEL exercises is warranted.

Several strategies can be used to program AEL exercises, each of which directly affects the strategy used to program each set. For example, a traditional set can be employed if the AEL is applied to only the first repetition of the set (figure 13.30a) (204, 320, 488). For example, an eccentric load of 120% and a concentric load of 65% of concentric 1RM can be used on repetition 1 of a set of four repetitions (figure 13.30a). After the eccentric phase of the lift is completed for repetition 1, the weight releaser removes 55% of the load, and the remaining three reps are performed with 65% of 1RM for both the eccentric and concentric phases of the lift. If, however, the AEL is to be applied to every repetition, a cluster set would be required to allow the athlete or coach to reattach the weight releaser to the barbell (figure 13.30b).

Overall, AEL training methods are ideally suited for enhancing maximal strength and power gains (488) and, depending on the loading parameters applied, can be used in all phases of a periodized training plan. In the general preparation phase, AEL methods may be applied to increase the time under tension and potentially stimulate greater gains in hypertrophy (387). During the specific preparation phase, AEL may be employed to increase maximal strength levels, whereas in the precompetition and main competition phases, AEL may be used to maximize strength–speed and speed–strength (204). Note that because of the increased eccentric load, the coach must carefully consider the overall volume of AEL incorporated into the plan.

Strength–Power Potentiation Complexes

A growing body of evidence shows that strength–power potentiation complexes (SPPCs) or complex pairs (217, 430) can result in an enhanced performance (290, 471). Generally, an SPPC involves the performance of a high-force (174, 432, 433) or high-power (378, 432, 433) resistance-training exercise followed by the performance of a high-power or high-velocity movement, such as a plyometric activity (471). For example, heavy squats may be

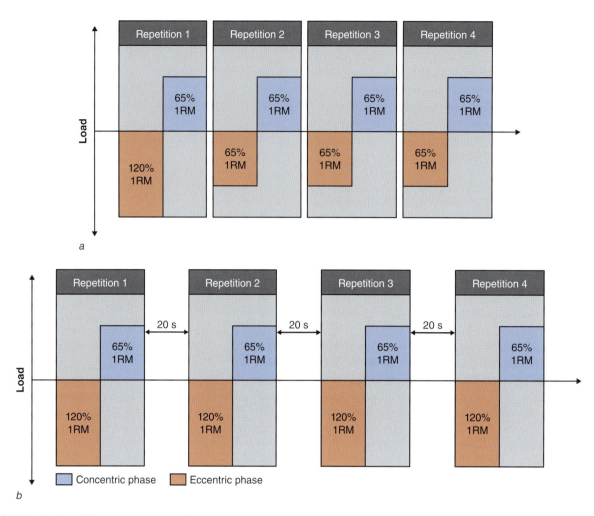

FIGURE 13.30 AEL strategies: *(a)* AEL applied on first repetition; *(b)* AEL applied on all repetitions using cluster sets.

used to produce a PAPE response (85, 373) during the performance of vertical jumps (165, 311, 330, 428), horizontal plyometrics (404), or sprints (311). Ultimately, it is thought that the acute performance increase associated with the incorporation of SPPCs into the athlete's training program will translate to greater performance gains over time.

Stone and colleagues (471) suggest that the fitness–fatigue model (see chapter 1) offers a theoretical framework for understanding SPPCs. They postulate that the ability to express a PAPE is affected by the degree of potentiation, which is a function of the net balance between the fitness and fatigue stimulated by the conditioning activity (430). Performance will decrease if fatigue dominates, remain unaltered if it is equal to the fitness gain, or increase if fatigue is minimized while fitness is elevated (430, 471). Applying this theory to an SPPC, the conditioning activity acutely increases the athlete's fitness and fatigue. On termination of the conditioning activity, the preparedness decreases due to the masking of the acute fitness gain by fatigue. As fatigue is dissipated, there is a concomitant increase in the level of preparedness, which, in this construct, is considered a form of potentiation (471). Note that the potentiation effect will not last indefinitely but will be a function of the workload encountered during the conditioning activity and the duration of rest prior to the performance of the high-velocity or high-power movement.

Conditioning activities that use higher intensities (≥85% of 1RM) or plyometric activities generally result in greater PAPEs. For example, conditioning activities that employ high-intensity shallow back squats (i.e., above parallel) result in greater performance effects than moderate-intensity (30%-84%) back squats performed to a depth above or below parallel (430). The degree of PAPE is generally affected by three critical factors, which are strength levels (70, 428, 430, 471), the level of fatigue stimulated (409), and the athlete's past training experience (203).

In a meta-analysis, Seitz and Haff (430) provide convincing evidence that stronger individuals (i.e., back squat ≥1.75 of body weight for men and >1.5 of body weight for women; bench press ≥1.35 of body weight for men) with more resistance-training experience produce significantly greater PAPE responses. After the completion of a conditioning exercise, stronger individuals maximize the potentiation response earlier (5-7 min) than weaker individuals who need longer recovery before optimal performance occurs (≥8 min) (figure 13.31).

Additionally, stronger individuals display greater potentiation effects from conditioning activities that employ single sets with near maximal loads, whereas weaker individuals display greater effects from multiple-set conditioning activities that employ submaximal loads (430).

Overall, due to the effect of maximal strength on the expression of PAPEs, the use of SPPCs may be reserved for stronger, more-developed athletes. As part of a periodized training plan, there are numerous ways SPPCs can be integrated into a resistance-training session. For example, three repetitions of the quarter back squat performed at 85% of 1RM could be followed by 5 minutes of rest and then three repetitions of box jumps to a 75 cm (30 in.) box. Alternatively, three repetitions of the power clean could be performed at 80% of 1RM followed by 3 to 5 minutes of recovery and a series of five hurdle hops. In both examples, multiple sets could be performed depending on the athlete's level of ability (429).

SPPCs appear to be ideally suited for developing strength–speed or speed–strength. Depending on the exercises chosen and the loading patterns used, the coach can target specific outcomes and then align these outcomes with the goals established for each phase of the annual training plan.

Periodization Methods for Strength, Power, and Hypertrophy Development

When considering the periodization of strength training, it is often difficult to understand the scientific literature due to the continued confusion that many researchers have regarding periodization and programming. In fact, most of the research that purports to investigate the periodization of resistance training examines various programming strategies and does not actually investigate periodization methodologies (461). Only three models of periodization can be applied to resistance training: parallel, sequential, and emphasis (see chapter 5 and figure 5.4, page 111) (178, 180, 339).

Parallel Model

In resistance training, the most common parallel model is a **daily undulating periodization (DUP)** model. Even though many authors falsely call this a periodization model (276, 390), it is in fact a programming strategy that aligns with the concepts of a parallel periodization model. First presented by Professor Kraemer in the 1990s at the Pennsylvania State University (273, 553), this strategy programs training sessions with different distinct training targets across a microcycle. The most common RM zones used in DUP protocols are between two and four repetitions for power-based exercises (40%-70% of 1RM), 4-6RM when targeting strength development, 8-12RM when targeting hypertrophy, and 12-15RM when targeting strength–endurance (209). These basic zones are all trained within a microcycle as follows (553):

Monday: Four sets of 12RM to 15RM (strength–endurance zone)

Tuesday: Four sets of 4RM to 6RM (strength zone)

Wednesday: Rest

Thursday: Four sets of 8RM to 12RM (hypertrophy zone)

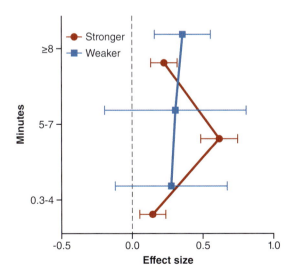

FIGURE 13.31 Effect sizes for the time frame of potentiation after a conditioning activity.

Adapted by permission from L.B. Seitz and G.G. Haff, "Factors Modulating Post-Activation Potentiation of Jump, Sprint, Throw and Upper-Body Ballistic Performances: A Systematic Review with Meta-Analysis," *Sports Medicine* 46 (2016): 231-240, Springer Nature.

Friday: Five sets of three for power exercises at 40% to 70% of 1RM (power zone)

Saturday: Rest

Sunday: Rest

The primary goal of this programming strategy is to simultaneously target hypertrophic and neurological factors associated with strength in each microcycle (553). Because this model relies on RM zones, it requires the athlete to train to failure at every training session except the one that targets power development. Each microcycle is presented with the same basic rotation within the mesocycle or multiple mesocycles, so there is less overall training variation compared to sequential or emphasis models (209). The lack of novel training stimulus could be problematic, because this can impede overall development (461) and lead to maladaptive training responses.

In a series of papers, Painter and colleagues (359, 360) offered some very interesting data that question the efficacy of the DUP programming model presented by Kraemer and Fleck (275). Specifically, the DUP model was shown to provide less training variation as indicated by the high monotony score when compared to a sequential model of training. Additionally, the track athletes who completed the DUP program completed 60% more volume load (i.e., work) and had a significantly higher strain score. As noted by McGuigan and Foster (314), the risk of injury or illness increases when training monotony and strain are high. In fact, Painter and colleagues (359) reported that 100% of the athletes who completed the DUP program experienced an injury or illness not related to resistance training, whereas only 40% of the athletes who undertook a block periodization model experienced an injury or illness during the time frame of testing. Based on these data, the DUP programming strategy appears to result in poor fatigue management and an increased risk of overtraining and injury risk for athletes (359).

Although some research supports the use of the DUP programming strategy (154, 279, 281, 372), many of the studies that demonstrated improvements in performance used relatively untrained individuals (78, 79, 96, 279, 372). Because parallel models of training can be effective with untrained or novice athletes, it is not surprising that these populations can have positive outcomes in response to a DUP programming strategy. Due to some of the fatigue-management issues related to the DUP programming strategy, it is likely that intermediate and advanced athletes will not maximize strength gains or performance with parallel models of periodization that employ the DUP model.

Sequential Model

The literature on the periodization of resistance training commonly uses the term *linear periodization* when discussing sequential models (209, 453), but this is incorrect (369) because the load dynamics are undulatory rather than linear (52, 238). Therefore, terms such as *linear* or *reverse linear periodization* should be removed from the taxonomy related to the periodization of resistance training. Alternatively, these models should be referred to as *sequential periodization models* because there is a sequential development of physical and performance capacities. Fundamentally, sequential models allow for the athlete's training to be saturated with a unidirectional, focused stimulus while minimizing the athlete's risk of approaching a maximal level of training tolerance (see figure 5.9, page 114) and deemphasizing other fitness characteristics (524, 525). By sequencing the training into discrete blocks of time, the residual training effects associated with each block can be summated to maximize preparedness and performance at specific times.

The basic premise of sequential models is that training targets are placed into a logical, sequential pattern that facilitates the development of specific physiological and performance outcomes. For example, Zamparo and colleagues (550) suggest a basic sequential pattern for developing power or speed in which training is sequenced into three major targets: hypertrophy, maximal strength, and power or speed development (see figure 5.10, page 114). Support for this basic sequence is provided by Schmidtbleicher (415), who suggests strength and power gains are facilitated after periods of training dedicated to developing muscle mass. In fact, the seminal study by Stone and colleagues (463) presents a sequential resistance-training model in which periods of time are dedicated to hypertrophic, strength, strength and power, and power maximization. Ultimately, a lot of evidence shows that sequential models work well with resistance training (65, 66, 229, 461).

Central to the effectiveness of sequential models is the use of a concentrated or accentuated loading block of training that targets very few related characteristics, such as strength and RFD (461, 523, 524). As noted by Issurin (239), these types of blocks result in residual training effects that can persist for several weeks and can potentiate the next block of training. Stone and colleagues (461) suggest that residual effects should be considered in the context of reversibility, because the acquired fitness attributes decline toward baseline after the cessation of a concentrated loading block. For example, after the cessation of strength training, maximal strength tends to decrease by 2% or less after 2 weeks (153, 230) and by about 12% after 12 weeks (195) of detraining. Stone and colleagues (461) also report that the ability to express high power outputs declines more rapidly than strength–endurance, and strength tends to be maintained for days to weeks (rate of decline: power > strength–endurance > maximal strength). These rates of decline can be influenced by training state and training that continues after the target attribute is removed (336, 337). The ability to slow a residual decline allows for the results of sequenced training blocks to persist across and potentially facilitate subsequent training blocks (461) through what is often called *phase potentiation*. As a result of these basic concepts, the progression of training in a sequential model of resistance training must be logically structured. The basic principles of sequential training models described in the literature serve as the foundation for block training, summated microcycles, and conjugated sequential models.

Block Training Models

In resistance training, the most noted sequential model of periodization is block periodization (461, 485). In a block model, a series of concentrated loads are sequenced over time to produce superior results (105, 485). For example, three mesocycle blocks can be sequenced such that block 1 targets strength–endurance, block 2 targets maximal strength, and block 3 targets strength–power (177). Due to the sequence of these blocks, the residuals from each block summate to stimulate a performance supercompensation after the completion of the sequence (figure 13.32).

A lot of scientific evidence supports using sequential models of periodization when constructing resistance-training interventions (30, 359, 360, 461). For example, Painter and colleagues (359, 360) used a three-block sequence with the following progression: strength–endurance, strength, and power (figure 13.33). In this sequence there are variations in intensity, volume, and training focus depending

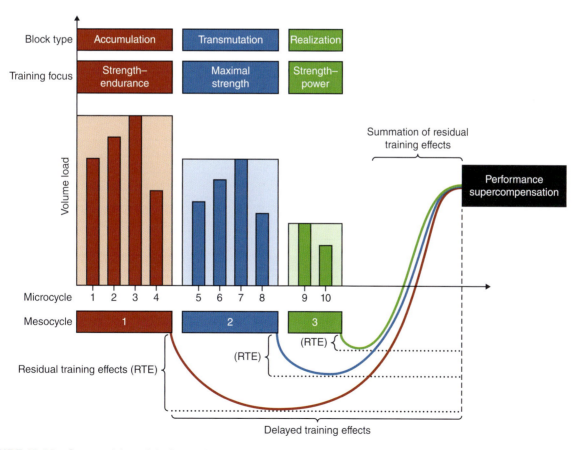

FIGURE 13.32 Sequential model of periodization applied to resistance training.

on the targeted goal for each mesocycle (359, 360). Ultimately, the sequential structure results in superior performance gains, efficiency of training, and fatigue management, and lower injury risk when compared to parallel models, such as DUP.

Summated Microcycle Model

An alternative sequential model could be referred to as a *weekly undulating* (60) or *summated microcycle* (369). Summated microcycles typically are based on a 4-week mesocycle that progresses from

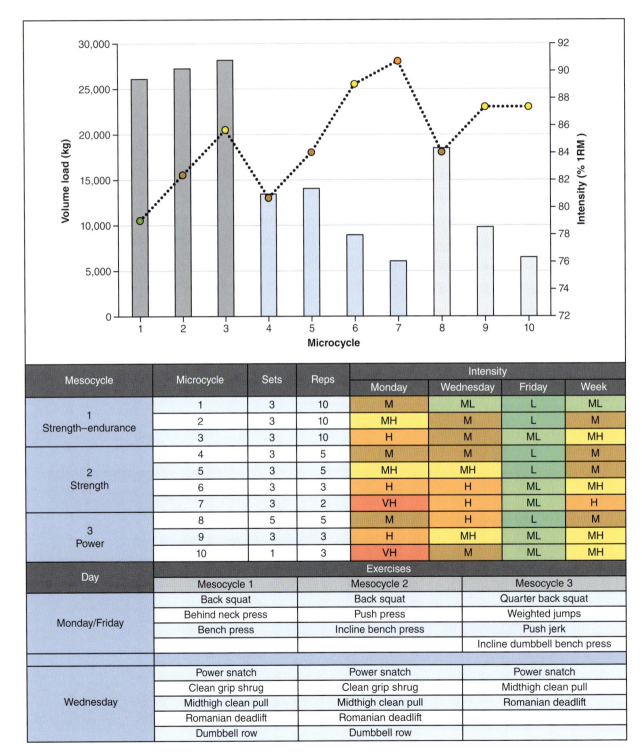

FIGURE 13.33 Sequential periodization model for resistance training.

extensive to intensive workloads and ends with a microcycle focused on recovery. The method distribution is altered so the microcycle, rather than the mesocycle, is allocated to strength–endurance, maximal strength, and speed–strength (369). Generally, there is an increase in volume and intensity across the first three microcycles, followed by an unloading microcycle. The third week of the mesocycle contains the greatest workloads and results in the greatest amount of fatigue. This strategy has been suggested to offer two benefits (143, 144, 369, 403):

1. It provides a form of intramesocycle variation that increases the probability of training effects converging while minimizing the risk of nonfunctional overreaching or overtraining.
2. It provides a form of intramesocycle contrast that may facilitate long-term adaptive responses.

In the limited research that has explored the use of summated microcycles, it appears that this method stimulates superior performance gains (60) compared to parallel models, such as DUP. For example, Buford and colleagues (60) reported greater improvements in bench press and leg press strength compared to a DUP model but similar results to that of a traditional block model. Because relatively untrained subjects were used in this study, it is possible summated microcycles may be more beneficial for athletes with a higher training age. In fact, Plisk and Stone (369) suggest that this model should not be used with novices and is better suited for intermediate athletes.

Conjugated Sequential Model

An advanced block model that can be used in the resistance-training programs of advanced athletes is referred to as a *conjugate sequence* (369). Plisk and Stone (369) suggest that this model should be considered an intermesocycle variation strategy that incorporates periods of accumulation followed by periods of restitution. Classically, this model places 4-week mesocycle blocks into a specific sequence. For example, if targeting the development of speed–strength, the first 4-week block in the sequence focuses on high-volume, low-intensity strength training and the maintenance of other attributes (369). This block is designed to saturate the system with strength–endurance training (i.e., concentrated load) that results in temporary reductions in preparedness. In the subsequent block, the focus shifts toward speed–strength development, allowing for preparedness to rebound due to the effect of the delayed training effects and the reductions in training load. After the completion of the first two blocks, the sequence is repeated with progressively increasing workloads and intensities (figure 13.34) (369).

An alternative conjugated sequential model was presented by Poliquin (370) in which the duration of each block was reduced to only 2 weeks. This

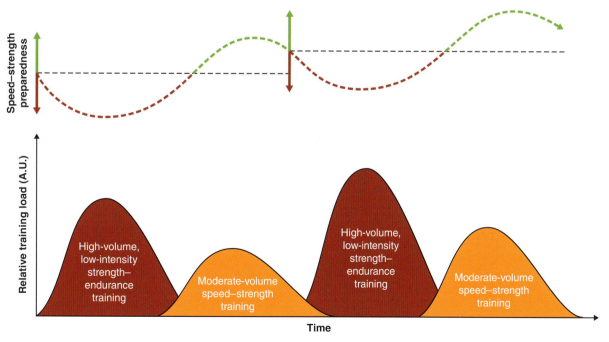

FIGURE 13.34 Basic conjugated sequence model applied to resistance training targeting speed–strength development.
Adapted from Verkhoshansky and Siff (2009).

model could be considered a variant of the conjugated sequential model because it requires the athlete to alternate between mesocycle blocks of accumulation and intensification (table 13.6).

In this model, each mesocycle lasts 2 weeks (i.e., two microcycles). The focus of each mesocycle alternates between higher-volume and higher-intensity training as the athlete moves through a 12-week training period. It has been hypothesized that this approach provides an undulatory stimulus that may optimize adaptive responses (364). However, this has yet to be confirmed in the scientific literature.

Emphasis Model

An alternative approach to planning strength training that may be ideal for team sport athletes (402), individual sport athletes with dense competitive cycles (132, 339), or those in tactical environments (e.g., military, police) is the emphasis, or pendulum, training model. This model allows for a blending of the key constructs of both parallel and sequential models of training. Specifically, several key training factors can be trained simultaneously (parallel approach) with varying degrees of emphasis over time (sequential approach) to align with the targeted outcomes (178, 180, 551). The contemporary literature presents several applications of the emphasis model, including the advanced daily undulating model and the multitargeted block model.

Advanced Daily Undulating Model

The advanced daily undulating (ADUP) model can be classified as an emphasis model of periodization. Although the traditional DUP model uses an equal distribution of strength-training targets over the course of two mesocycles, the ADUP model requires the coach to establish a focused emphasis for the mesocycle. For example, if the focus of a series of three mesocycles is the development of maximal strength, more sessions during the mesocycle will be dedicated to strength development and the frequency of other targets will be reduced (277, 553). Although this programming strategy can be classified as an emphasis model, it contains the same basic programming flaws associated with traditional DUP models. Specifically, every training session is maximal intensity because it requires training to be performed with RM loads, which can negatively affect monotony, strain, and injury risk. Conceptually, it may be possible to modify this model to remove RM loads and replace them with percentages of RMs, but this has yet to be examined in the scientific literature. Until extensive research exploring the efficacy of the ADUP model is completed, it should not be used to prescribe resistance training for athletes.

Multitargeted Block Model

The block-emphasis model, or **multitargeted block periodization training model** (237), appears to be necessary for sports that require the development of several abilities to achieve competitive success. In this model, each block of training is vertically integrated so complementary training factors are trained with varying degrees of emphasis (parallel approach) and sequenced over time (sequential approach) to facilitate phase potentiation (178). For example, if targeting the development of maximal strength and the RFD, a basic three-block model could be constructed (178) (figure 13.35).

In the first block, the factors to be targeted are strength–endurance and power–endurance while maximal strength is maintained. Strength–speed and speed–strength will not be targeted during this

TABLE 13.6 Example Conjugate Sequence Approach to Strength Development

Focus	Hypertrophy		Maximal strength		Hypertrophy		Maximal strength		Hypertrophy		Maximal strength	
Mesocycle	1		2		3		4		5		6	
Total reps	60-72		40-60		64-80		30-50		40-48		24-36	
Microcycle	1	2	3	4	5	6	7	8	9	10	11	12
Sets	3	3	5	5	4	4	5	5	4	4	6	6
Reps per set	10-12	10-12	4-6	4-6	8-10	8-10	3-5	3-5	5-7	5-7	2-3	2-3
Total reps	30-36	30-36	20-30	20-30	32-40	32-40	15-25	15-25	20-28	20-28	12-18	12-18
Intensity	69%-75%	69%-75%	83%-90%	83%-90%	75%-79%	75%-79%	85%-90%	85%-90%	81%-86%	81%-86%	90%-95%	90%-95%

Adapted from C. Poliquin, "Five Steps to Increasing the Effectiveness of Your Strength Training Program," *NSCA Journal* 10 (1998): 34-39.

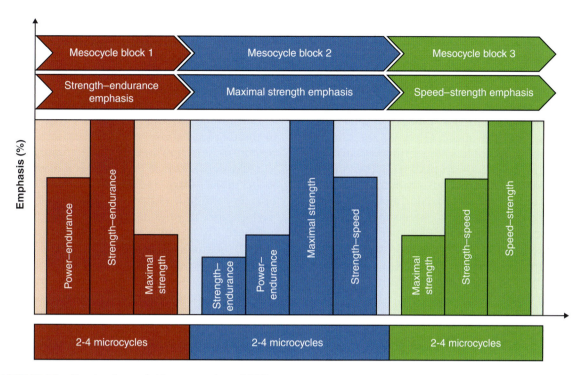

FIGURE 13.35 Emphasis model for strength and RFD.

block. As the athlete moves into the second block of training, the main emphasis shifts toward the development of maximal strength and strength–speed while strength–endurance and power–endurance are maintained with the use of down sets. In the last block of training, the emphasis is on speed–strength and strength–speed while maximal strength is maintained.

Another example of the application of this model was presented by Munroe and Haff (339) (figure 13.36).

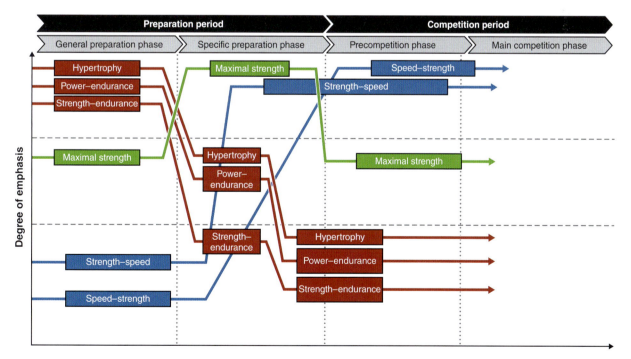

FIGURE 13.36 Emphasis model for resistance training for track cyclists (sprinters).

Adapted by permission from L. Munroe and G.G. Haff, "Sprint Cycling," in *Routledge Handbook of Strength and Conditioning: Sport-Specific Programming for High Performance,* edited by A. Turner (New York, NY: Routledge, 2018), 518.

In this example, early in the general preparation phase, the athlete will focus on increasing muscle CSA (i.e., muscle mass) that may have been lost during the previous competition period (121). As the athlete shifts into the specific preparation phase, the primary emphasis will be to increase maximal strength with a secondary emphasis on developing strength–speed (339). As the competition period approaches, the primary emphasis will shift toward speed–strength with a secondary emphasis on strength–speed. Although maximal strength is important, the goal during this period is simply to maintain the gains established during the specific preparation period. Ultimately, this example provides an idea of how the resistance-training emphasis may shift across a macrocycle. The basic principles presented in figure 13.36 can be adapted for team sport athletes.

Summary

The integration of resistance training into a periodized training plan is essential because resistance training develops the most important physical attributes that underpin sport performance. Not only is strength the foundation for the expression of high power outputs, but it also is essential for maintaining repetitive muscular contractions (i.e., muscular endurance) and reducing overall injury risk. The physiological adaptations of the neuromuscular system are specific to the structure of the resistance-training program. An essential component of any resistance-training program is the provision of novel training stimuli to stimulate the body's adaptive processes. When implementing a resistance-training program, remember that variations in training load are essential to maximize adaptive responses. It is, however, unwise to frequently train to muscular failure as this has been demonstrated to be unnecessary and increases the overall risk of injury without enhancing maximal strength or performance beyond not training to failure.

There are infinite ways to vary the training stimuli introduced during a resistance-training program, several of which have been presented in this chapter. The important thing to remember is that the resistance-training program should not be constructed in isolation but instead should be integrated into the athlete's overall periodized training plan. Otherwise, it is likely to provide little benefit to the athlete. Several models can be employed to construct a periodized training plan including parallel, sequential, and emphasis models. Novice athletes can benefit from a parallel periodization model, whereas intermediate to advanced athletes should implement sequential models. With team sports, tactical environments, or sports with very dense competition calendars, it may be warranted to use an emphasis approach.

CHAPTER 14

High-Intensity Interval Training

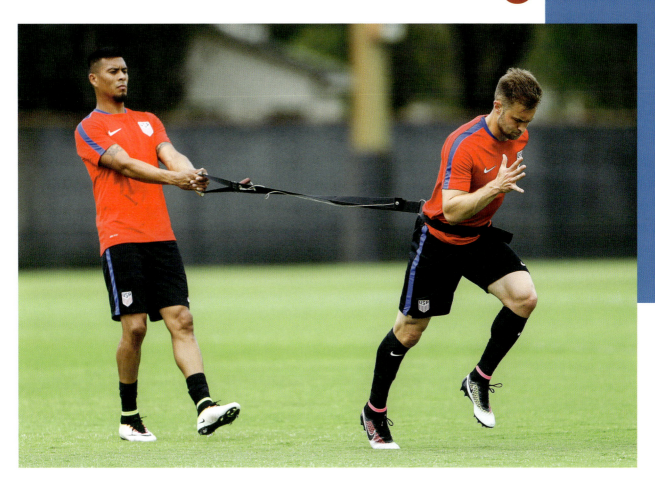

Although high-intensity interval training (HIIT) has received a lot of recent attention in the scientific (13, 14, 33, 34, 115) and coaching literature (5, 26), and whole books (117) have been written to explain it, athletes have used HIIT for more than a century (13). In 1912, Hannes Kolehmainen (from Finland) used interval training as part of his preparations for the Olympic 10,000 m race (13). In the 1920s and 1930s, coach Lauri Pihkala (also from Finland) expanded these early HIIT methods with Paavo Nurmi, who used HIIT methods as part of his training and became one of the best middle- and long-distance runners of all time (13, 116). After the second world war, interval training became widely used by European runners, the most famous of these being Emil Zátopek from Czechoslovakia. In the 1950s, with his coach Josef Hron, Zátopek began to use bouts of short interval training performed at a pace near his critical velocity (13, 117). In fact, Zátopek appears to have manipulated many of the variables commonly examined in modern HIIT methodologies, including altering exercise and recovery intensities to alter the metabolic demands of his training sessions (117). Although many more athletes have contributed to our early understanding of HIIT (see Billat [13] for a detailed history), it appears that these early innovators provided the first evidence of the effectiveness of HIIT and provided the foundation for the modern application of HIIT with athletes.

In the United Kingdom in the 1970s, Tom Reilly, who is widely considered to be the father of soccer science, suggested that HIIT may be an important aspect of the preparation of team sport athletes (117). In 1994, Bangsbo, in his seminal text *Fitness Training in Soccer: A Scientific Approach* (6) and in a scientific paper on the physiology of soccer (7), provided the foundation for the modern application of HIIT in team sports. Starting in 2001, the interest in HIIT increased incrementally starting with the work of Professor Billat, who examined the effects of aerobic (13) and anaerobic (14) interval training for runners. These works were expanded on by Laursen and Jenkins (118) in 2002, when they reviewed the physiological basis for interval training with endurance athletes. By 2013, our understanding of the importance of HIIT had expanded incrementally, resulting in Buchheit and Laursen's (33, 34) seminal review papers on the topic. In 2019, Laursen and Buchheit (117) expanded these review papers into their comprehensive text *Science and Application of High-Intensity Interval Training: Solutions to the Programming Puzzle*, which readers are encouraged to explore if they want to maximize their understanding of HIIT. Based on these resources, the goal of this chapter is to highlight key aspects of HIIT to help the coach understand how to integrate HIIT into an athlete's periodized training plan. To accomplish this goal, we will first explore the basic concepts that underpin HIIT.

Types of High-Intensity Interval Training

HIIT can include repeated long duration (≥60 s) to short duration (<60 s) bouts of high-intensity exercise or all-out sprints performed for short (≤10 s, repeated sprint training [RST]) or long (>20-45 s, sprint interval training [SIT]) durations interspersed with periods of recovery (34, 35). Additionally, HIIT training also can incorporate game-based HIIT **(GBHIIT)**, activities typically performed for 2 to 4 minutes at game intensity (35). Each of these methods provides a variety of training activities for the coach to manipulate and guide the physiological and performance outcomes targeted in a periodized training plan. To effectively use these methods, the coach must understand the nuances of each HIIT training strategy.

Long Interval High-Intensity Interval Training

Long interval training bouts generally last 2 to 5 minutes and are performed at 80% to 85% of the peak speed reached at the end of the 30-15 intermittent fitness test (V_{IFT}) or 95% to 100% of the peak incremental test speed ($V_{IncTest}$) (35). These bouts are typically interspersed with recovery periods of 1 to 4 minutes. Passive rest is used if short rest intervals are employed, and active recovery performed at 45% of V_{IFT} or 60% of $V_{IncTest}$ is used with longer recovery periods (35).

Short Interval High-Intensity Interval Training

Short interval (SIT) training bouts use repeated efforts that last 10 to 60 seconds and are performed at intensities 90% to 105% of V_{IFT} or 100% to 120% of $V_{IncTest}$ (34, 35). Generally, the recovery interval between bouts is 10 to 60 seconds. Passive rest is used if short recovery periods are employed, and active recovery performed at 45% of V_{IFT} or 60% of $V_{IncTest}$ is used with longer rest periods (35).

Repeated Sprint Training

Repeated sprint training (RST) is a very high–intensity form of interval training that is used to develop high-end capacities or the anaerobic speed reserve or anaerobic power reserve (35). This format requires all-out efforts performed for 3 to 10 seconds interspersed with 15- to 60-second rest intervals. Passive rest is used for short recovery periods, and active recovery performed at 45% of V_{IFT} or 60% of $V_{IncTest}$ is used with longer recovery periods (35).

Sprint Interval Training

Sprint interval training (SIT) requires the athlete to perform a longer all-out sprint that lasts 20 to 45 seconds (35, 86). Due to the taxing nature of this format of HIIT, passive recovery of 1 to 4 minutes is planned between exercise bouts (35).

Game-Based High-Intensity Interval Training

Game-based HIIT (GBHIIT) incorporates sport-specific, game-based activities that last 2 to 5 minutes. These activities are performed at game-level intensity, which is often difficult to quantify (35). These activities typically use passive recovery periods of 90 seconds to 4 minutes. A unique aspect of this format is that decision making and interactions with opponents and teammates are incorporated into the work period (48, 57). A key aspect of GBHIIT is the inclusion of different task constraints used to concurrently target development of the athlete's tactical and technical abilities, physiological and physical adaptations, and psychological factors associated with high levels of performance (48, 57, 58, 143).

Prescribing High-Intensity Interval Training for Athletes

Several approaches can be used to prescribe the intensity of training used in a HIIT session (33, 37). A central component of this process is to ensure that the prescribed intensities are individualized and allow each athlete to reach the intensity of training required to stimulate the targeted physiological adaptations. Although the most accurate method to calibrate HIIT is using laboratory-based testing methods, several field-based maximal critical-speed and power analysis methods may be more practical and effective for achieving the targeted performance (37).

Track and Field Approach

The traditional approach to programming HIIT for endurance runners is determined from running speeds based on set times for predetermined distances without physiological data, such as the $\dot{V}O_2$max or the lactate threshold (13, 33). Buchheit and Laursen (33, 37) suggest that one of the main benefits of this method is that the athlete's entire locomotor profile can be used to construct individualized HIIT sessions. For example, with short intervals that last 10 to 60 seconds, the reference running time can be based off a percentage of a maximal 100 to 400 m sprint, and longer intervals (e.g., 2-4 min or 6-8 min) can be based off the speed maintained over 800 to 1,500 m or 2,000 to 3,000 m (33, 37). Although this method has traditionally been successful, it is impossible to manipulate the acute physiological load and precisely target specific adaptive responses to the prescribed HIIT session (figure 14.1).

This method of programming tends to be reserved for highly experienced coaches who work with well-trained athletes for whom running times for several distances are known (33, 37). Buchheit and Laursen (33, 37) suggest that this method is

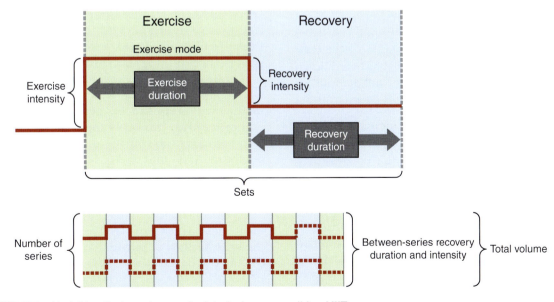

FIGURE 14.1 Variables that can be manipulated when prescribing HIIT.

Adapted from Buchheit and Laursen (2019).

difficult to translate to non-track-and-field athletes and that it is not appropriate, practical, or effective to use it with all athletes.

Rating of Perceived Exertion Approach

Due to its simplicity and versatility, using the rating of perceived exertion (RPE) is an appealing approach for programming the intensity of a HIIT session (69). With this method there is no requirement to monitor heart rate (HR); the coach simply prescribes the duration or distance of work and the relief interval (166). The use of RPE allows the athlete to self-regulate the intensity of exercise based on how they feel.

When using RPE, the intensity of an exercise bout is typically based on the maximal intensity of exercise perceived as sustainable (hard to very hard) and is typically categorized with the Borg CR-10 scale (≥6) or the 6-20 scale (≥15). It is believed that the RPE represents "the conscious sensation of how hard, heavy and strenuous exercise is" (128) in relation to the combined effects of the physiological (61), biomechanical, and psychological (129) stress or fatigue the athlete is exposed to during exercise. Ultimately, the RPE responses to exercise are gender independent (83) and comparable between free versus constant-paced exercise (82).

One of the main benefits of using RPE to guide HIIT intensity is that no testing and no knowledge of the athlete's fitness level is required to implement the session (165, 166). Another benefit of the RPE method is that it is a universal exercise regulator irrespective of the mode of exercise or the conditions under which the exercise is completed (33, 37). Although much more research is needed to examine the efficacy of RPE-guided HIIT with athletes, guiding training with RPE has been shown to result in similar physiological adaptations as those achieved with 6 weeks of HR-based training in young women (54).

The primary limitation of the RPE method is that it does not allow the coach to precisely manipulate the training stimulus to stimulate specific physiological responses to the prescribed HIIT session (33, 37). Ultimately, this can limit the ability to target specific adaptive responses and is potentially problematic in team sports (33). Ultimately, although using the RPE is a common method for prescribing HIIT, Buchheit and Laursen (37) suggest when used without other markers of performance, such as speed or power, and markers of physiological responses, such as HR or lactate, it can create a level of uncertainty in the athlete's overall training program.

Maximal Aerobic Speed and Power

A useful reference intensity when programming HIIT is the speed (or power) associated with $\dot{V}O_2max$: v/p$\dot{V}O_2max$, which is referred to as the **maximal aerobic speed** (v$\dot{V}O_2max$) or **maximal aerobic power** (p$\dot{V}O_2max$) (13-15, 100, 118). Conceptually, the v/p$\dot{V}O_2max$ is an integrated measure of both the $\dot{V}O_2max$ and the energetic cost of running or cycling that directly represents the athlete's locomotor ability (15, 33). Since the v/p$\dot{V}O_2max$ is the lowest speed or power necessary to elicit $\dot{V}O_2max$, it is logical to use it as a reference for prescribing training (15, 33, 37, 118, 136).

Several direct methods may be used to determine or estimate the v/p$\dot{V}O_2max$.

- The running speed for a given $\dot{V}O_2max$ can be calculated based on the linear relationship between $\dot{V}O_2$ and running speed established at submaximal speed (63) or from the individual metabolic cost of running, either with (67) or without (114) resting $\dot{V}O_2$.

- Direct measurement (i.e., pulmonary gas exchange) during an incremental ramp-like test to exhaustion performed on a treadmill, ergometer (i.e., cycling, rowing), or track can be used to estimate the v/p$\dot{V}O_2max$. When performed on a track, the University of Montreal Track Test (UM-TT) (121) is typically used with team sport athletes (26, 71), although the VAM-Eval, which employs smoother speed increments and shorter intercone distances, can also be used (46, 130). Generally, the VAM-Eval has been used with young populations and nondistance running specialists because it is easier to administer when compared the UM-TT (33, 37, 46, 130). When working with cycling, progressive incremental tests can be performed on a cycle ergometer with protocols that employ fast ramp step increases (i.e., 30 W · min^{-1}) can be used to determine p$\dot{V}O_2max$ (120). Similar protocols can be undertaken with rowing (59) or ski ergometers (181) to determine the p$\dot{V}O_2max$.

To establish a true v/p$\dot{V}O_2max$ during an incremental test, a measure of $\dot{V}O_2$ is needed to establish the lowest speed or power that elicits $\dot{V}O_2max$ (33, 37). At the end of these tests, the final speed or power achieved (V/P$_{IncTest}$) is only an approximation of the v/p$\dot{V}O_2max$ (33). Although these two speeds or powers are almost perfectly correlated ($r > .90$)

(121), the V/P$_{IncTest}$ can be 5% to 10% greater than the v/pV̇O$_2$max (33). Additionally, athletes who have greater anaerobic reserves tend to display a greater v/pV̇O$_2$max–V/P$_{IncTest}$ difference (33, 37).

Indirect methods that can be used to predict the v/pV̇O$_2$max are generally considered to be more practical for field settings (33). Several methods including those specific to running, cycling, and rowing can be used.

- *Running:* Since the average time to exhaustion at vV̇O$_2$max ranges between 4 and 8 minutes (15, 101), a 5-minute run to exhaustion can be used to determine vV̇O$_2$max (12). The vV̇O$_2$max calculated based on this test has been reported to be almost perfectly correlated with the V$_{IncTest}$ established with the UM-TT (r = .94) and ramp treadmill tests (r = .97) (11). However, pacing strategies can affect the results of the 5-minute test, so it may be most appropriate for trained runners who can run at vV̇O$_2$max for about 5 minutes (37). A comparable approach typically applied in field sports, such as Australian rules football, involves a 2 km (1.2 mi) time trial that typically lasts 6 to 7 minutes and may be easier to administer (60).

- *Cycling:* The power output that can be sustained over 4 minutes, or the **maximal mean power output (MMP)**, is closely related to the pV̇O$_2$max (119, 120, 152). As such, performing 4-minute, all-out cycling power tests in the laboratory or in the field using a power meter provides a means for monitoring performance. The use of power meters is common in cycling (3) and, when coupled with related software packages, can be used to determine the pV̇O$_2$max or v/pV̇O$_2$max (referred to as the 4-minute MMP) (37).

- *Rowing:* Similar to running and cycling, a time trial on a rowing ergometer can be used to determine the pV̇O$_2$max (142). Typically, a 2 km (1.2 mi) time trial (~6-8 min) is performed on a Concept II rowing ergometer. This test is very specific to the demands of rowing as most rowing events are determined over this competition distance (53, 147).

Regardless of how the V/P$_{IncTest}$ and the v/pV̇O$_2$max are determined, these measures are method (100) and protocol (134) dependent. For example, a measured vV̇O$_2$max (16) or V/P$_{IncTest}$ (15, 91) tends to be higher than an estimated vV̇O$_2$max (63, 67). Additionally, protocols that contain longer-duration stages tend to result in lower v/pV̇O$_2$max values (134), and stages with larger speed or power increments will result in a shorter test and higher speed or power values (37). Regardless, similar performance gains occur when training is prescribed based on a V$_{IncTest}$ or a vV̇O$_2$max (127). Based on these findings, the V$_{IncTest}$ is considered to be a viable field measure that can guide HIIT prescription. Traditional field-based tests, such as the UM-TT (121) or VAM-Eval (46, 130), can also be used to establish the V$_{IncTest}$ without sophisticated equipment, such as a metabolic cart (37).

Heart Rate–Based Prescription

Over the last 30 years, monitoring the athlete's HR has become one of the most widely used methods for measuring and controlling the intensity of training in field settings (1). Although using HR zones works well for prolonged and submaximal exercise bouts, its effectiveness for setting or adjusting intensity during HIIT may be limited (37). For example, measuring HR in isolation cannot yield information about work performed above the speed or power associated with V̇O$_2$max, which is an important aspect of HIIT exercise prescription (13, 14, 33, 37, 118). Additionally, HR does not always reach maximal values (>90%-95% of HR$_{max}$) when performing very short (<30 s) (135) and medium (1-2 min) (165) intervals, even though it is expected to reach these levels during exercise at or below the speed or power associated with V̇O$_2$max (33). This occurs due to the HR response at the onset of exercise being slower than the V̇O$_2$ response (55). Additionally, the HR inertia during recovery periods can be problematic because it can result in an overestimation of the actual work or physiological load that occurs during this time (165). Furthermore, similar HR responses can be found in response to different types of HIIT (run-based HIIT [165] or small-sided games [SSGs] [131]) even though these sessions have different lactate responses. Therefore, due to the temporal dissociation between V̇O$_2$, blood lactate, HR, and workload during HIIT, the ability to use only HR to determine the intensity of a HIIT session is limited (33).

When HR-based HIIT prescriptions (90%-95% of HR$_{max}$) are compared to prescriptions based on the speed reached at the end of the V$_{IFT}$, it has been reported that greater performance improvements occur when V$_{IFT}$ is used to prescribe training intensity (153). Therefore, Buchheit and Laursen (37) suggest that HR should be used only to monitor the athlete's response to the training session and over time. When employed in team sports, the HR responses to a standardized HIIT session that uses individualized targeted running distances can serve as discrete monitoring points throughout the season, fundamentally serving as a fitness test without a formal testing session (37). For example, Buchheit and colleagues (47) employed HR monitoring during 4-minute HIIT sessions with a 15-second work to 15-second rest interval to determine if HR response was maintained during an Australian rules football team's 2-week Christmas break.

Team Sport Approach

Due to the requirements of team sports, there is a lot of interest in game- (40, 48, 52, 77, 97, 105, 138, 182) and skills-based (79, 80) conditioning activities. Although there is a limited understanding of the $\dot{V}O_2$ responses to SSGs or GBHIIT (42, 51, 52), it appears that a significant amount of time can be spent at $\dot{V}O_2$max during these activities (42). For example, Buchheit and colleagues (42) have reported that national-level handball players spend 70% of an SSG (i.e., 5:30 min of an 8-min session) at $\dot{V}O_2$max. Although it is well-documented that SSGs are useful conditioning strategies (4, 40, 48, 64, 96, 105, 182), the coach should consider using less-specific (i.e., run-based) but more controlled HIIT activities during certain phases of the athlete's annual training plan (i.e., general preparation phase). Although the physiological load can be manipulated by changing the technical rules (48, 182), number of players (154, 182), and the pitch size (122, 154) during the implementation of SSGs, the overall training loads of SSGs cannot be precisely standardized (37). In fact, the within-athlete responses to SSG-based training are highly variable (95, 96), and there is greater between-player variability in the cardiovascular response when compared to run-based HIIT (97). Additionally, the average $\dot{V}O_2$ achieved during SSGs has been reported to be inversely related to the athlete's $\dot{V}O_2$max (42), which may be indicative of a possible ceiling effect for the development of $\dot{V}O_2$max in fitter players (37).

Another consideration with SSGs is that the frequent changes in direction or movement patterns coupled with the alternating work and rest periods may produce variations in muscular venous pump action, which may limit the maintenance of a high stroke volume during exercise, leading to compromised long-term adaptation (103). When considering changes in stroke volume, it is possible to roughly estimate these changes with the use of the $\dot{V}O_2$:HR ratio (37, 180). When the $\dot{V}O_2$:HR ratio is examined, it is likely lower during SSGs when compared to run-based interval training (42, 51, 52). Buchheit and Laursen (37) suggest that because of this issue, it is possible the assessment of cardiopulmonary responses during SSGs or competitions with the use of HR may be misleading (131). Additionally, the $\dot{V}O_2$:speed (42) and the HR:speed (131) relationships tend to be higher during SSGs when compared to generic running, most likely a result of the engagement of a greater amount of muscle mass (37).

Although GBHIIT and SSG-based conditioning activities are often considered to be more sport specific (4), this may not always be the case because athletes have more space to run and tend to reach speeds of up to 85% to 90% of maximal sprinting speed during competitions (37, 50, 68, 132), which creates different metabolic demands compared to these types of training activities. Another important consideration highlighted by Buchheit and Laursen (37) is that due to the frequent accelerations, decelerations, and changes in direction, SSGs likely result in a higher neuromuscular load compared to more traditional, run-based HIIT activities. The potential for higher neuromuscular loads must be considered when implementing GBHIIT and SSGs as part of the athlete's overall training plan.

When examining the HR responses to various forms of soccer training activities (e.g., tactical training, SSGs, HIIT circuits, run-based HIIT), it should be noted that SSGs can expose the athlete to high workloads (i.e., near 90% of HR_{max}) that are only slightly less than what can be achieved with circuit or HIIT activities (97).

Based on these data, it is evident that SSG and GBHIIT are important training activities the coach can add to their training toolbox. If the coach understands their strengths and limitations, they can be effectively integrated into the athlete's physical development plan.

Anaerobic Speed Reserve and Anaerobic Power Reserve

The anaerobic speed reserve (ASR) and **anaerobic power reserve (APR)** represent the difference between v/p$\dot{V}O_2$max and the **maximal sprinting speed (MSS)** and **anaerobic peak power (MMP_{5s})** (33, 37). Although many coaches fail to consider the ASR or APR when designing their HIIT programs, some track and field coaches have indirectly used these concepts to set intensity (33, 37). Scientific support for the use of the ASR was first noted in 2001 by Blondel and colleagues (19), who reported that the time to exhaustion at intensities above v$\dot{V}O_2$max was more related to the ASR and the

MSS than the athlete's $v\dot{V}O_2max$. Additionally, the proportion of the ASR used is related to performance during all-out efforts that last a few seconds to several minutes (49, 178, 179). Although these studies have focused on continuous exercise, more recent research has examined the relationship between the ASR and MSS during high-intensity intermittent running (30, 44) and repeated sprint performance (27, 45, 133, 174). In a field setting, a group of athletes could be required to complete a HIIT session at the same $v\dot{V}O_2max$ (72), but each athlete may perform this session at a different percentage of their ASR (figure 14.2), which will result in each athlete being exposed to different physiological demands (25).

Due to the potential effect of the ASR or APR on the intensity of a HIIT session, Buchheit and Laursen (37) recommend that the ASR or APR, MSS or maximal peak power, and $v/p\dot{V}O_2max$ should be quantified to individualize the training session.

Recently, Sandford and colleagues (162) recommended a three-step approach to applying the ASR or APR construct from a macro and micro training plan perspective (figure 14.3). The first step of this

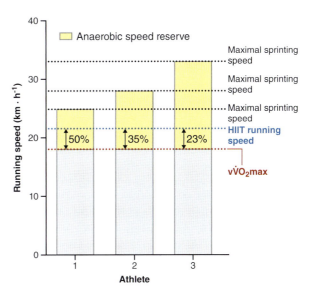

FIGURE 14.2 An illustration of the anaerobic speed reserve (ASR) of three athletes with similar $v\dot{V}O_2max$ but different maximal sprinting speeds during a HIIT session. Athlete 3 has the greatest ASR, and thus works at a lower percentage of this ASR and has a lower exercise load than athletes 1 and 2. Athlete 2 has a lower exercise load than athlete 1.

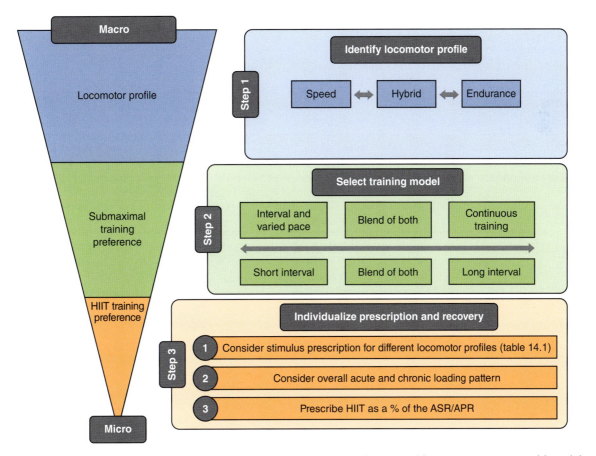

FIGURE 14.3 A practical guide to using the anerobic speed reserve or the anaerobic power reserve to guide training.

Adapted by permission from G.N. Sandford, P.B. Laursen, and M. Buchheit, "Anaerobic Speed/Power Reserve and Sport Performance: Scientific Basis, Current Applications and Future Directions," *Sports Medicine* 51, no. 10 (2021): 2017-2028, Springer Nature.

process is to determine the athlete's individual dominance for speed versus endurance aptitude to establish a locomotor profile (table 14.1). Based on the existing research, the locomotor profile for a group of elite athletes is somewhat diverse regardless of whether the athletes participate in individual (123, 161, 163) or team sports (30, 109, 130). As a result, Sandford and colleagues (162) recommend calibrating the training approach to each athlete's locomotor profile.

The second step is to align the athlete's profile with an appropriate training model (162). For example, an athlete who has an endurance profile may be best suited for continuous, higher-volume training that can include long HIIT sessions. Additionally, this type of athlete may have a greater tolerance for overload training (e.g., training days with multiple sessions) and periodic increases in intensity (9, 164, 172). Conversely, if an athlete with a speed profile was given this type of program, they would likely experience maladaptive responses or overreaching (9).

Finally, the coach must make numerous day-to-day decisions about the intensity, duration, frequency, and training load integrated into the athlete's program. Because athletes' adaptive responses are variable (112, 123, 124, 176), Sandford and colleagues (162) suggest that coaches consider a framework that aligns aerobic development methods with the various locomotor profiles (figure 14.4).

30-15 Intermittent Fitness Test

The **30-15 intermittent fitness test (30-15 IFT)** (http://30-15ift.com) was developed to facilitate the prescription of intermittent exercise and **change of direction–based HIIT** (21, 24, 25, 33). Specifically, the test was designed to account for the proportion of the ASR used, the individual's metabolic iner-

TABLE 14.1 Estimated Fiber Type Continuum and Locomotor Profile

Profile type	Estimated fiber type dominance	Anaerobic speed reserve or anaerobic power reserve	Locomotor profile
Speed	Fast twitch	Large	Low MAS or MAP
			Moderate MSS or MPP
Hybrid	Intermediate	Moderate	Moderate MAS or MAP
			Moderate MSS or MPP
Endurance	Slow twitch	Small	High MAS or MAP
			Low MSS or MPP

Note: MAS = maximal aerobic speed; MAP = maximal aerobic power; MSS = maximal sprinting speed; MPP = maximal peak power.

Adapted by permission from G.N. Sandford, P.B. Laursen, and M. Buchheit, "Anaerobic Speed/Power Reserve and Sport Performance: Scientific Basis, Current Applications and Future Directions," *Sports Medicine* 51, no. 10 (2021): 2017-2028, Springer Nature.

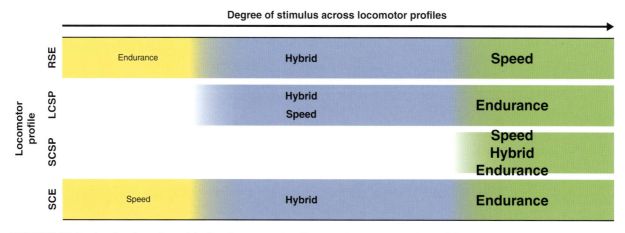

FIGURE 14.4 Application of aerobic development stimuli across locomotor profiles. SCE = slow continuous effort; SCSP = short critical speed or power; LCSP = long critical speed or power; RSE = repeated sprint effort. Note: Application of these methods is driven by context depending on profile subgroup. The bolder the text, the greater the degree of stimulus.

Adapted from Sandford, Laursen, and Buchheit (2021).

tia (e.g., $\dot{V}O_2$ kinetics) at the onset of each short interval, the recovery capacity between each interval, and the athlete's change of direction (COD) abilities (24, 25). Therefore, the 30-15 IFT elicits a maximal HR and $\dot{V}O_2$ while providing measures of the athlete's ASR; repeated effort ability; and acceleration, deceleration, and COD capacities (23, 24, 28). This test consists of 30-second shuttle runs interspersed with 15 seconds of recovery, and it is typically initiated at a velocity of 8 km · h^{-1} with increases of 0.5 km · h^{-1} for each subsequent stage (21, 24). The speed achieved at the final stage of the test is referred to as the V_{IFT}, which can be used to estimate the athlete's $\dot{V}O_2$max (25):

$$\dot{V}O_2 max_{30-15IFT} = 28.3 - 2.15G - 0.741A$$
$$- 0.741A - 0.0357W + 0.0586A \times V_{IFT} + 1.03V_{IFT}$$

where G stands for gender (female = 2; male = 1), A stands for age, and W stands for weight (25).

Buchheit (25) suggests that the 30-15 IFT is highly specific to the training sessions commonly used in intermittent sports. In fact, only the V_{IFT} determined from the 30-15 IFT can be used to accurately prescribe HIIT (33). For example, in contrast to the V_{IFT}, the velocity achieved at the end of the Yo-Yo Intermittent Recovery Test Level 1 (vYo-YoIR1) cannot be used for training prescription because its relationship with the $V_{IncTest}$ and $v\dot{V}O_2$max has been shown to be speed dependent (73). Additionally, when running at vYo-YoIR1, fitter athletes tend to run below their $v\dot{V}O_2$max, whereas unfit athletes use a greater portion of their ASR (33). Finally, the V_{IFT} has been reported to be a reliable (coefficient of variation = 1.6%, 95% confidence interval = 1.4-1.8) (22) and accurate method for determining V_{IFT} (33). However, the V_{IFT} tends to be 15% to 25% (2-5 km · h^{-1}) faster than the $v\dot{V}O_2$max or $V_{IncTest}$ (21, 25, 37, 42) and thus needs to be adjusted when used for programming HIIT (37). Typically, HIIT is performed around $v\dot{V}O_2$max, somewhere between 100% to 120% of this velocity (13, 14), with the V_{IFT} representing the upper limit for these exercises (i.e., 100% except for very short intervals or maximal RST) (37). Ultimately, the 30-15 IFT allows for precise, individualized prescription of the intensity and duration of HIIT within an intensity range of 85% to 105% of the V_{IFT} (40-42, 66, 140).

Once the athlete's V_{IFT} is determined, the results can be used to individualize the HIIT session (88). For example, if an athlete who has a V_{IFT} = 18 km · h^{-1} is performing a 15 second–15 second HIIT running session (i.e., run = 15 s; passive rest = 15 s) performed at 95% of V_{IFT}, the target running distance would be 71 m (233 ft) (88). This distance would be calculated as follows:

$$V_{IFT} (m \cdot s^{-1}) = \frac{V_{IFT}(km \cdot h^{-1})}{3.6} = \frac{18}{3.6} = 5$$

$$\text{distance (m)} = V_{IFT}(m \cdot s^{-1}) \times \%V_{IFT}$$
$$\times \text{time (s)} = 5 \times 0.95 \times 15 = 71$$

Fundamentally, this process could be completed for a group of athletes to develop individualized training sessions. For example, if a group of athletes were prescribed a straight-line HIIT running session with a 15-second work to 15-second rest interval, each athlete would be required to complete an individualized running distance based on their V_{IFT} (figure 14.5) (26).

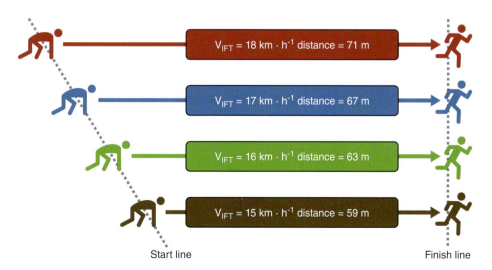

FIGURE 14.5 Example running area for straight line HIIT training (15s–15s at 95% of V_{IFT}).
Adapted from Buchheit (2013).

If these runs must be completed with COD, as is the case for many sports, the coach must consider the time necessary to complete each COD when calculating the targeted running distance to ensure that the cardiovascular load is similar to that of straight-line running (26). In fact, if the same distance is covered with COD during the same time, there is a substantial increase in the relative intensity (65), which is related to the number of CODs and their effect on running speed (31). Although there is a lack of scientific evidence on the exact correction factor that is needed for HIIT sessions that contain COD (26, 37), Buchheit (26) suggests that the correction factor can range between 3% and 30%. The athlete's height and training volume may also need to be accounted for when individualizing these corrections; smaller athletes who are more trained generally present a better COD ability (31), thereby requiring the use of a smaller correction factor. Ultimately, Buchheit and Laursen (37) suggest that the adjusted difference will generally be no greater that 1 to 2 m (3-7 ft) and that the shuttle distance can be modified as needed.

All-Out Sprinting

Repeated all-out sprinting efforts, or RST, are comprised of all-out sprinting over a given distance or for a predetermined duration (84, 85, 104). Generally, these sessions are classified as RST if short (3-10 s) sprints are performed or SIT if longer (30-45 s) sprints are performed (37). Because the intensity of these bouts of exercise are all-out, or maximal, there is no need to pretest the athlete to calibrate the training intensity (37).

Variables Used to Program High-Intensity Interval Training

When prescribing HIIT sessions, coaches can manipulate several variables of the training process to alter the training stimulus and target specific physiological adaptations (figure 14.1) (21, 35, 38, 171). Globally, these factors are related to the structure of the exercise period or work undertaken and the organization of the recovery periods in and between each series of HIIT exercise (33).

Exercise Intensity

The most influential programming factor associated with a HIIT session is the intensity of work performed (21, 35). Conceptually, imagine a spectrum of intensities; the critical speed or lactate steady state (i.e., an intensity that can be maintained for 30-60 min) is on the lower-intensity end of the spectrum, and maximal sprinting speed, or instantaneous power, represents the higher-intensity end of the spectrum (35).

When considering the determinants of maximal power output or speed, the athlete's individual motor unit phenotype or the predominance of slow-twitch (type I) and fast-twitch (type II) muscle fiber types affects these performances (35, 151, 162). Based on histochemical straining for myosin adenosine triphosphatase content, the three major fiber-type classifications are type I, type IIa, and type IIx. Each fiber classification displays distinctly different contractile characteristics (173). Type I fibers are generally efficient, fatigue resistant, and rely on aerobic energy supply but have a limited potential for rapid force development (89, 173). Type II fibers are the exact opposite; they are inefficient, fatigable, produce force rapidly, and are related to high power outputs (89). Alternatively, scientists have examined myosin heavy chain content and determined that there are a vast area of hybrid fibers that contribute to training adaptations (145, 146) and that can be related to the performance of the various HIIT methods (35, 162). Additionally, the athlete's total amount of muscle mass or volume of motor units in the functional muscle group or per cross-sectional area is related to their ability to perform all-out maximal speed or power (99, 141).

Exercise Duration

The duration of exercise during a HIIT session is directly influenced by the intensity of the exercise (35) and is a key factor influencing the athlete's physiological response to the session (33). Buchheit and Laursen (35) suggest that the maximum duration an exercise task can be undertaken at a constant speed or power output is an inverse and curvilinear function of the intensity of exercise and is specific to the muscle fiber type or the volume of engaged muscle fibers. Fundamentally, the higher the intensity of the exercise, the shorter the duration it can be maintained. Basically, the power or speed time continuum represents the interplay or trade-off between the intensity and duration of an exercise bout an individual can complete.

If maximal-intensity exercise is performed for varying durations, a classic power law distribution profile can be created from a plot of power or speed achieved versus duration (35). Based on these relationships, two key concepts can be examined: the critical power or critical velocity model and the anaerobic work capacity.

Critical Power or Critical Velocity Model

The **critical power (CP)** or **critical velocity (CV)** model describes the capacity of the athlete to sustain a given work rate as a function of time (35, 108) and represents the physiological landmark that is the boundary between heavy- and severe-intensity exercise domains (figure 14.6) (56).

Figure 14.6 shows the hyperbolic relationship between power (or speed) and the time for which it can be sustained (98, 137, 139, 149). Based on this figure, sustainable power (or speed) falls as a function of exercise duration, and the point at which the power (or velocity) curve intensity and duration distribution begins to level out, known mathematically as the *asymptote*, represents the CP (or CV) (35, 108, 148). Roughly, the CP or CV is the intensity of exercise that can be sustained for 20 to 30 minutes (107). Although it has been suggested that the CP or CV corresponds to the maximum lactate steady state (MLSS) (i.e., the highest speed or power output that does not result in a rise in blood lactate >1.0 mmol · L^{-1}) (10, 35), there is evidence that the CP is significantly higher than the power output at the MLSS (150). Therefore, the CP or CV should be considered a marker of a different intensity domain when compared to the MLSS.

Anaerobic Work Capacity

The **anaerobic work capacity (W')** represents the amount of work that can be completed above the CP or CV threshold (108) and the finite amount of energy that is available above the CP or CV (35). In figure 14.6, the W' is represented by different-sized boxes (i.e., boxes 1-4) that account for different intensity and duration combinations. As noted in the figure, some boxes are tall and skinny (i.e., box 1), whereas others are long and skinny (i.e., box 4). The size or volume of each box represents a theoretical W' and a finite source of energy (35). Theoretically, these boxes represent the stored phosphagen (i.e., adenosine triphosphate, phosphocreatine) and fast glycolytic energy (i.e., glycogen) availability (see chapter 2). This reflects the finite amount of energy available to perform HIIT before needing to recover (35). Although there are numerous ways to use this energy (i.e., boxes 1-4), the take-home message is that there is a limited amount available. Buchheit and Laursen (35) equated the W' to a battery with limited amounts of stored energy. When HIIT is performed above the CP or CV, the amount of available energy in the W' battery will be reduced. When adequate recovery is provided during the HIIT session, the battery's energy can be restored (35). Conversely, if inadequate recovery is provided during the HIIT session, the W' battery becomes depleted.

Exercise Modality

When considering the modality of exercise used with HIIT, the main factor dictating what type of exercise is performed is the demands of the sport. For example, running is the preferred modality of HIIT for run-based sports, cycling is the preferred modality for cyclists, and rowing is preferred for rowers (35). However, in some situations, modifications to the modality of exercise can be used to alter the locomotor, neuromuscular, and musculoskeletal strain associated with the HIIT session. Conceptually, the coach can modify the type of exercise performed (e.g., running, swimming, rowing, skiing) or the conditions associated with the mode employed to alter the training stress and stimulus (35). For example, a run-based HIIT session can be performed on grass or sand, uphill

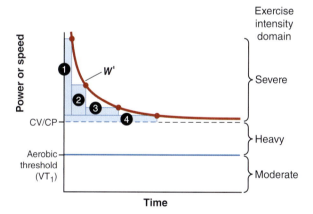

FIGURE 14.6 Critical power or velocity and anaerobic work capacity (W'). The concept of W' is described further with the boxes labeled 1 through 4, which allows for different usage of W' across varying combinations of intensities and duration. In this example, all W' boxes display the same total finite volume. VT$_1$: ventilatory threshold (anaerobic threshold).

Adapted by permission from A.M. Jones, A. Vanhatalo, M. Burnley, et al., "Critical Power: Implications for Determination of V̇O$_2$max and Exercise Tolerance," *Medicine & Science in Sports & Exercise* 42, no. 10 (2010): 1876-1890.

or downhill, with additional load (i.e., weighted vest), or as a shuttle or in a straight line.

Through manipulating the exercise mode, the coach can increase or decrease the locomotor, neuromuscular or musculoskeletal, and/or metabolic strain depending on the athlete's situation (35). For example, a reserve rugby player could perform a run-based HIIT session with a greater number of CODs than they would typically perform to increase the neuromuscular load associated with the session to account for the lack of playing time. Conversely, a starting basketball player may maintain their cardiovascular fitness with the use of a treadmill based HIIT session, while minimizing neuromuscular load developed during games (35).

A modification that can be made with team or racket sport athletes is to use more specific modes to replace run-only methods (35). For example, the soccer player may incorporate passing and shooting into their short-interval HIIT session (102, 103). Hoff and colleagues (103) developed a soccer-specific dribbling track that can be used to incorporate several soccer-specific skills into an athlete's HIIT session (figure 14.7). The dribble track requires the athlete to navigate a predetermined course while dribbling a soccer ball around the cones and over 30 cm (12 in.) hurdles, to run backward at a predetermined zone, and to maintain an HR of 90% to 95% of maximum (i.e., 84.5% of $\dot{V}O_2$max) for 4 minutes (102, 103). Ideally, four 4-minute bouts separated by 4 minutes of low-intensity active recovery are used with the dribble track, providing a significant stimulus for improving soccer-specific fitness. One of the main benefits of structuring HIIT in this manner is that athletes generally demonstrate greater motivation for sport-specific activities such as these. However, since this is a closed-skill activity and there is no interaction with opponents and no decision making, it is considered different from SSGs or GBHIIT (35).

Although there are many ways that the coach can manipulate the mode of exercise used in the HIIT session, they must consider the neuromuscular and metabolic effects of these modifications and ensure that whatever modification they make meets the individual needs of their athletes.

Recovery Period

There is a lot of debate about how to structure the recovery periods in a HIIT session. Some coaches believe that an active recovery is required to facilitate the removal of blood lactate that has accumulated in the muscle during the high-intensity work (35, 110, 175). Although the main support for this belief comes from research that has examined the effect of active recovery on blood lactate concentrations (2, 8), there is limited research suggesting that changes in blood lactate concentrations are reflective of muscle lactate concentrations (111, 175). More recently, the concept that lactate is related to fatigue has been questioned (76, 90), and it has been reported that neither blood (87, 177) nor muscle (111) lactate has any direct relationship with performance capacities. As such, there is little evidence to support the notion that active recovery is essential.

Alternatively, Buchheit and Laursen (35) suggest that a better way to think of the recovery period is to contextualize it to energy availability and the time needed to replenish these resources. In this context, the availability of muscle phosphocreatine (PCr) stores used to replenish adenosine triphosphate can be related to the W'. Specifically, when PCr stores are high, W' is also high, and W' is low when PCr stores are also low (35). Additionally, the availability of muscle glycogen can be considered in the context of maintaining the W', especially when considering longer HIIT sessions (78). Based on these metabolic constraints, one could suggest that the recovery period is simply used to recharge the athlete's W', which may provide additional adaptive stimuli (35).

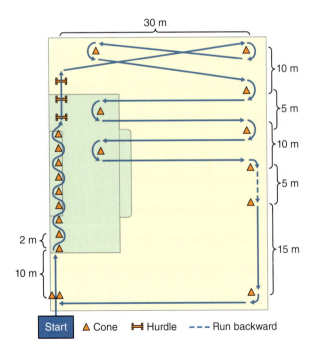

FIGURE 14.7 High-intensity interval training: soccer-specific dribble track.

Adapted by permission from J. Hoff, U. Wisløff, L.C. Engen, et al., "Soccer Specific Aerobic Endurance Training," *British Journal of Sports Medicine* 36 (2002): 219, with permission from BMJ Publishing Group Ltd.

When the recovery period is considered in the context of the interplay between the intensity and duration, it is obvious that the longer the duration and the lower the intensity of the recovery period, the greater the recovery of the W' (35). Conversely, if the recovery period is shortened or the intensity is increased (i.e., toward critical power), there is an increase in the overall workload and metabolic rate associated with the HIIT session (35). For example, Dupont and colleagues (74) examined the effect of passive versus active (40% of $\dot{V}O_2max$) recovery on how long subjects could repeat a series of 15 second–15 second (i.e., exercise–recovery) high-intensity exercise bouts. Recovery was twice as long using passive recovery (962 ± 314 s) compared to active recovery (427 ± 118 s). More recently, Perrier-Melo and colleagues (144) reported meta-analytic data that provide further evidence that passive recovery results in greater performance recuperation compared to active recovery. Therefore, it is logical to suggest that the use passive recovery allows for a better maintenance of the athlete's W' (35).

However, active recovery evidently provides an additional training stressor when examined in the context of how it affects the metabolic cost of the HIIT session (35). Dupont and colleagues (74) reported that the average metabolic power associated with a passive recovery period resulted in a marginally lower aerobic power when compared to the active recovery period (48.9 ± 4.9 versus 52.6 ± 4.6 mL · kg^{-1} · min^{-1}). When oxyhemoglobin saturation was examined with near-infrared spectroscopy, there was an overall slower rate of decline associated with the use of a passive recovery period compared to an active recovery period. Additionally, it was noted that the passive recovery may also provide a higher reoxygenation of myoglobin and a higher PCr resynthesis rate, which may partially explain an enhanced performance capacity and a better W' recovery rate (35, 74).

The effects of the employment of passive and active recovery strategies have also been examined during RST (29). Buchheit and colleagues (29) examined the effect of active and passive recovery on all-out running performance and the physiological responses to a series of six maximal 4-second sprints interspersed with 21 seconds of active (2 m · s^{-1}) or passive (standing) recovery on a nonmotorized treadmill. Overall, the mean running speed was significantly lower (active = 3.79 ± 0.28 m · s^{-1} versus passive = 4.09 ± 0.28 m · s^{-1}, $p < 0.001$) and the percentage of speed decrement was significantly lower (active = 7.2% ± 3.7% versus passive 3.2% ± 1.3%) when passive recovery was compared to active recovery. Additionally, when active recovery was performed there was a greater metabolic demand, as indicated by a higher oxygen uptake, increased blood lactate levels, and higher deoxyhemoglobin levels (29). Ultimately, these data provide further support for the notion that passive recovery is better able to maintain the athlete's W', allowing for greater performances levels during subsequent bouts of sprint interval training.

Clearly the duration and intensity of the recovery bout are important considerations modulating the physiological stress and performance capacity associated with a HIIT session. If performance during the HIIT session is the key targeted outcome, then longer passive recovery should be used. Conversely, if the workload accomplished in the session is important, then short, higher-intensity active recovery activities can be implemented to ensure that higher workloads are accomplished (29). Based on the available research, Buchheit and colleagues (29) indicate that 2 minutes of passive or easy walking offers the best recovery for the vast majority of long-interval HIIT sessions.

Series Duration

Conceptually, the series duration which is impacted by the number of HIIT intervals (i.e., work-to-rest intervals) performed in the series can affect the metabolic responses needed to meet the energetic demands of the prescribed training session. For example, the longer the duration of the series of interval, the greater the amount of work performed (i.e., more intervals or repetitions) and the more taxed the PCr and glycolytic systems become, resulting in a greater reliance on aerobic metabolism (170) unless the recovery period is prolonged and passive (35). Furthermore, if the recovery period between intervals or series is reduced and active recovery is performed, this response can be further magnified.

The structure of the series of intervals prescribed in the HIIT session provides an additional way to guide the adaptive responses targeted by the training session. For example, if the series duration is reduced, the metabolic rate will be enhanced, resulting in an increased quality of training, which may be important when a training session is targeting technical and tactical elements related to performance (35). Conversely, the series duration can be lengthened to target the development of endurance or fatigue resistance, which may be particularly important for sports that rely on endurance performance capacities (35).

Buchheit and Laursen (35) suggest one programming strategy that can be used with team sport athletes is to implement several shorter series of intervals, so the athlete can complete a greater amount of high-quality work compared to one longer series. For example, two series of 4-minute bouts that are separated by a longer recovery period may be a better option than a single 8-minute period of HIIT when targeting the completion of higher-quality or higher-intensity work (35). However, if aerobic adaptations are targeted, the duration of the series of intervals should not be less than 3 minutes to allow the athlete to achieve a $\dot{V}O_2$ plateau. Generally, high-quality series tend to last around 4 minutes, whereas endurance-focused series can last up to 14 minutes (35).

Number of Interval Series

The total duration of the session and total workload contained within the session will also increase if the number of series contained within the HIIT session increases (35). A primary result of this increase is an increased aerobic demand, which stimulates greater aerobic adaptations unless the rest interval between series is prolonged and passive. Conversely, if the number of series contained within the session is reduced, the total volume and workload of the session will also be reduced, which stimulates an elevated quality of training and potentially a higher intensity of training within the session.

Recovery Intensity and Duration Between Series

During the recovery period between series, if the intensity of the recovery activity is reduced or if the duration of the recovery period is lengthened, the speed of W' recovery will be increased (35). Conversely, if the recovery duration is shortened and the intensity of the recovery activity is increased, there will be an increased metabolic rate during recovery, resulting in a reduced rate of W' recovery (35). Based on these relationships, the coach can increase the quality of work performed in subsequent training series by using passive and longer between-series recoveries that allow for a more complete W' recovery. If a greater metabolic demand or greater aerobic load is needed, the between-series recovery period can be active or shortened to reduce the recovery rate of the W'.

Total Volume or Work Performed

The total volume or work performed in a HIIT session is based on the structure of the number of series performed and the recovery duration and intensity between each series (35). The total work or volume can be quantified using a combination of methods, including acute cardiovascular load (HR), neuromuscular and musculoskeletal load (e.g., indirectly from power meters, accelerometers, or GPS), and overall training load (e.g., session rating of perceived exertion) (36). The coach must understand the total volume or work performed by the athlete to ensure that appropriate training progression occurs and that overtraining is avoided (35).

Program Considerations for High-Intensity Interval Training

When designing HIIT sessions and integrating them into the athlete's periodized training plan, the coach must consider several factors that affect the desired acute physiological responses to each HIIT session (33) and dictate which types of HIIT activities will be integrated into the athlete's periodized training plan (figure 14.8).

First, the coach must consider the athlete's sport to ensure that the HIIT methods used are specific to the physical demands associated with that sport (figure 14.9). For example, an American football player requires a greater proportion of anaerobic-based HIIT sessions compared to an Australian rules football player who requires more aerobic-based HIIT sessions (17, 60). Additionally, these factors must be considered in the context of the targeted long-term training adaptations required for success in the targeted sport.

Second, the coach must create an individualized athlete profile that presents the athlete's strengths and weaknesses. Based on the athlete's profile, it is likely that different types of HIIT sessions will be required for each athlete (116).

Third, the coach must consider what long-term adaptive responses to target and how these sessions align with the periods and phases of the periodized training plan (116). For example, during the general preparation phase, more generic HIIT sessions may be used to develop a fitness foundation, whereas during the precompetition and competition phases, more sport-specific anaerobic HIIT sessions may be employed (33).

Ultimately, choosing appropriate HIIT sessions and integrating these sessions into a periodized training plan is not an easy task and is largely based on the basic principles of good program

Chapter 14 • High-Intensity Interval Training | **397**

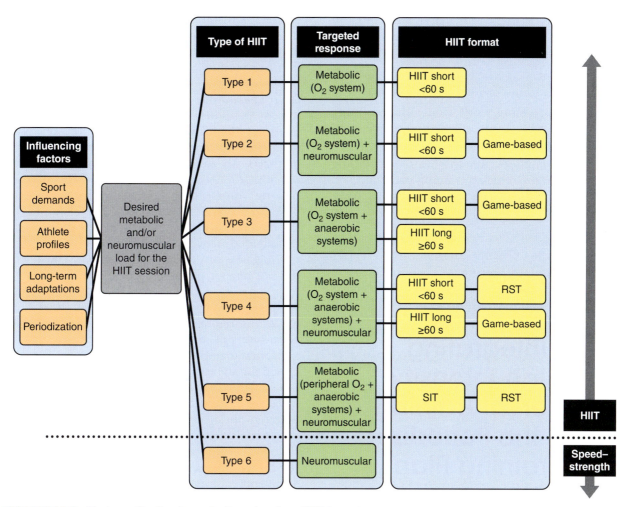

FIGURE 14.8 Factors affecting the selection of various HIIT formats.
Adapted from Buchheit and Laursen (2013); Laursen and Buchheit (2019).

FIGURE 14.9 Physical demands of various sports relative to speed, strength, and endurance.
Reprinted by permission from P.B. Laursen and M. Buchheit, "Genesis and Evolution of High-Intensity Interval Training," in *Science and Application of High-Intensity Interval Training,* edited by P.B. Laursen and M. Buchheit (Champaign, IL: Human Kinetics, 2019), 13.

design (34). To help guide the HIIT programming process, Laursen and Buchheit (116) recommend that the coach consider:

- the desired acute metabolic and neuromuscular responses to the planned HIIT session,
- how the training loads from other training sessions affect or are affected by the planned HIIT session,
- the time required to recover from each training session in the athlete's training plan, and
- the effect of the HIIT session on the quality of and athlete's ability to complete subsequent training sessions.

The coach who carefully considers these factors can better align the outcomes of the HIIT session with the overall periods and phases in the athlete's individualized annual training plan.

Integrating High-Intensity Interval Training Into the Periodized Training Plan

Overall, there is relatively little scientific data on how to optimally integrate HIIT into a periodized annual training plan; only a few studies examine programming strategies that have been integrated into individual (70, 159) or multiple sequenced mesocycles (156, 158, 160). Although these data provide some evidence of how HIIT can be used within a periodized training program, much more research exploring this area is warranted. As a result of the limited available research, most of the recommendations about integrating HIIT into a periodized training plan are based on a fundamental understanding of periodization theory, practical experience, and information garnered from the concurrent training literature (18, 81).

When considering the best strategies for integrating HIIT into a periodized training plan, it is helpful to remember that training typically progresses from general to specific targets as the athlete moves through the annual training plan or macrocycle (20). Based on this progression, the coach may implement HIIT strategies that incorporate straight-line running during the general preparation phase and then include some SSGs or GBHIIT activities during the specific preparation phase. During the competitive phase, the coach may decide to primarily employ HIIT methods that use various SSG and GBHIIT strategies and only occasionally implement straight-line running HIIT. These strategies will be modulated based on the competition schedule and density (32), as well as the mechanical work experienced in response to tactical, technical, and other physical training methods. An additional consideration centers on the athlete's needs by accounting for the athlete's playing volume and loading history across the past days or microcycles (32). For example, on the days following a competition, the starters will complete a recovery session (game +1) and light training sessions (game +2, game +3). Those who did not play or played minimally will complete a training session of multiple HIIT formats (game +1) that target both mechanical work (type 4 via SSGs) and high-speed running (type 2 or 4, with short intervals) to ensure they are exposed to the appropriate amount of loading so fitness is maintained throughout the competition period (32, 113).

Ultimately, the integration of HIIT into the athlete's periodized training plan is dictated by the targeted physiological outcomes, the structure of the technical and tactical training sessions, the placement of other physical training factors, and the competitive schedule (32). As noted in chapter 4, understanding the various training load factors associated with different training activities will help the coach better select appropriate periodization models and structure the individual microcycles in the annual training plan.

Periodization Models and High-Intensity Interval Training

When considering the various methods of implementing HIIT, the most common periodization models that have been employed are the sequential and emphasis models.

Sequential Models of Periodization

In the literature exploring the periodization of HIIT, the sequential model (i.e., block model) of periodization is commonly presented as a useful methodology for guiding the training process of endurance athletes (156, 158, 168). Although short-term studies generally report enhanced physiological and performance gains when block periodization models are used with HIIT, relatively few studies have directly examined the long-term effect of macro-, meso- and microcycle training interventions on world-class endurance athletes (157, 167, 168). Rønnestad and Hansen (157) presented an interesting case study for an elite cyclist to describe the long-term effect of a systematic sequential model of periodization. These researchers examined the physiological and performance responses to a 58-week training intervention that incorporated HIIT, low-intensity training, moderate-intensity training, and strength training with an elite cyclist. Interestingly, the employment of a sequential model of periodization resulted in large improvements in the performance-related factors tested (157). When the effects of this training period were compared to the cyclist's best performance in the 10 preceding years, he was able to elevate his $\dot{V}O_2$max by 13.7%, peak aerobic power (W_{max}) by 12.6%, and power output at 3 mmol · L^{-1} blood lactate concentration (Power$_{3la-}$) by 19.5% across the 58-week training period. What makes these data particularly interesting is that this athlete already had a high physiological performance capacity and age (37 years), further highlighting the magnitude of these performance gains (125). In fact, this athlete ended this training period with a $\dot{V}O_2$max of 87 mL · kg^{-1} · min^{-1}, W_{max} of 73.5 W · kg^{-1}, and a Power$_{3la-}$ of 4.9 W · kg^{-1}, which would move them from an elite to a world-class cyclist classification (106, 157).

In another study, Solli and colleagues (168) examined the effect of sequential and parallel periodization models on the performance of a world-class cross-country skier. Interestingly, the sequential model exposed the athlete to overall lower training volumes and greater amounts of HIIT. Although the parallel model exposed the athlete to a progressive increase in HIIT toward the competition period, the sequential model provided larger amounts of HIIT from the first preparation period followed by a gradual reduction as the athlete moved toward the competition period. Seven dedicated HIIT blocks of training fundamentally served as accumulation or overreaching blocks of training. These blocks lasted 7 to 11 days and each contained 8 to 13 HIIT sessions and was strategically placed in the annual training plan. After each HIIT block of training, essential reductions in training load were incorporated. The take-home message from this study is that sequential models of periodization can be used to effectively integrate HIIT into the annual training plans of elite endurance athletes.

Emphasis Models of Periodization

Most of the available scientific literature examining the use of different models of periodization when programming HIIT used endurance sports, such as cycling or running (92-94, 169). Although often referred to as *block periodization* (93), these studies have actually examined a form of emphasis modeling (i.e., multitargeted block model). For example, Hebisz and colleagues (93) compared two mesocycles (8 microcycles or 56 days) of training, one that used an emphasis model and one that used a parallel model (i.e., polarized training). The parallel model contained the same percentage contributions of SIT, low-intensity interval training (LIIT), HIIT, and passive rest across each 2-week mesocycle block. In the emphasis model, the training focus varied between two types of blocks: (1) low-intensity emphasis = 52.9% LIIT, 11.8% SIT, 5.9% HIIT, and 29.4% recovery, and (2) high-intensity emphasis = 0.0% LIIT, 27.3% SIT, 45.5% HIIT, and 27.3% recovery (figure 14.10).

Although the emphasis and parallel models resulted in similar maximal aerobic power and power achieved at ventilatory threshold, the parallel model was more effective at elevating the $\dot{V}O_2$max in this population of cyclists. However,

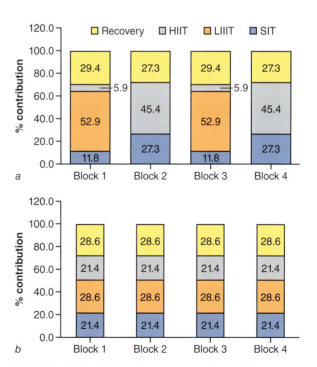

FIGURE 14.10 *(a)* Emphasis versus *(b)* parallel periodization model: high-intensity interval training.

Data from Hebisz, Hebisz, and Drelak (2021).

there are many ways an emphasis model can be constructed, and it is possible that the various training factors included in this study were not optimally integrated or sequenced, resulting in a mismanagement of training stress.

Based on the current scientific literature, the use of sequential models of periodization seems to be superior to the emphasis models that have been tested. However, due to the overall paucity of studies that directly examine the long-term effect of incorporating HIIT as part of emphasis periodization models, much more research is required to determine the optimal sequence and integration of the various HIIT methods as part of the emphasis model.

Integrating High-Intensity Interval Training Into the Microcycle

When considering the use of HIIT as part of the athlete's training process, the athlete must be exposed to the full **high-speed running (HSR)** velocity spectrum (39, 126) to reduce overall injury risk (75). Although many coaches are afraid to have their athletes engage in maximal sprinting during training due to a misguided fear that this practice increases the risk of acute muscle strains, the reality is that injury risk can ultimately be reduced as a result of exposing athletes to HSR in training (75). In fact, even though resistance training, especially that which increases the eccentric strength of the hamstrings (155), can protect against acute muscle strains, the neuromuscular demands of sprint activities are unique and cannot be replicated with resistance-training methodologies (39, 155). Therefore, how HSR is integrated and managed within a periodized training program is of particular importance to many athletes, especially team sport athletes. Although it is clear that HSR is an important countermeasure to acute muscle strains (75), it is of equal importance to consider how HSR and the mechanical work associated with accelerations, decelerations, and COD are programmed (39). Although conceptually the integration of HSR into that athlete's periodized training plan appears to be a simple process, the actual programming of this type of training in the context of the competing demands associated with the preparation of team sport athletes is actually a complex undertaking.

As the coach begins the programming process, they must always consider the period and phase of the annual training plan in which the microcycle is placed. This allows the coach to better align their programming decisions with the goals and directions set forth within the annual training plan. When deciding on the type and format of HIIT to employ, the coach should consider the neuromuscular demands associated with the technical and tactical training sessions contained in the individual microcycle (39). For example, if the technical and tactical training session on a given day incorporates a large amount of HSR, it would be warranted to use HIIT methods with a lower overall neuromuscular load (i.e., type 1 HIIT, figure 14.8) or fewer game-based activities that contain a high amount of mechanical work (i.e., acceleration, deceleration, or COD) (39). Alternatively, if the goal of the session is to provide an overload stimulus to prepare that athlete for a match-based worst-case scenario (62), then a type 2 HIIT session that targets HSR could be implemented (43). If, however, the technical or tactical session contains a large amount of mechanical work, choosing a HIIT session format that contains HSR would be warranted due to the mechanical differences between the types of training.

When considering the programming strategies used between competitive engagements, the coach must understand the overall construct of the training plan and consider the overall locomotor load associated with the competition (39). If the athlete plays more overall minutes in the preceding competition and there is a short duration between competitions within the microcycle, there will be less need for HSR and training with a high level of mechanical work (39). Conversely, athletes who do not engage in a lot of competitive minutes or do not participate in the competition will require HIIT that spans the gamut of possible options as well as HSR activities. This is particularly important when there are more than 5 days between competitions (32, 39).

Summary

Although the use of HIIT has a long and rich history, emerging evidence has begun to elucidate the overall importance of this type of training for the development of individual and team sport athletes. Central to the effectiveness of this method of conditioning is the ability to individualize the training stimulus the athlete is exposed to. Specifically, if the athlete's V_{IFT} and MSS are determined, the coach can more precisely individualize the training stimulus and target specific metabolic and neuromuscular responses. By understanding the response to each of the six available HIIT types (figure 14.8), the coach can better align the training process with the athlete's requirements. Once a HIIT type is selected, the coach can miniplate several key variables (figure 14.1) to fine-tune the athlete's physiological responses to the training. Ultimately, when designing HIIT sessions, the coach must remember to consider the acute metabolic and neuromuscular responses to the session, how the training loads from various training factors interact, the time frame of recovery associated with each training session, and the ways the HIIT session may affect subsequent sessions. Based on these considerations, the coach can more effectively design each micro- and mesocycle of training and ensure that any interference effects associated with concurrent training are mitigated. Although there is limited research directly exploring how HIIT sessions should be structured to align with the strategies established in the three major periodization models (i.e., parallel, sequential, and emphasis), emerging evidence shows that HIIT session are most effectively programmed in the context of sequential models of periodization.

CHAPTER 15

Speed and Agility Development

The ability to outrun an opponent is considered by many coaches and athletes to be a hallmark of superior sport performance. In fact, the ability to engage in high-speed movements, such as sprinting, is fundamental for success in many team sports, including American football (89), rugby league (91, 93), rugby union (78, 305), and soccer (105). Sprinting speed has been reported to be a major factor discriminating between levels of play (78, 89, 92, 93), with elite athletes being able to accelerate faster over 10, 20, and 40 m compared to age-matched subelite athletes (245). Additionally, sprint speed discriminates between starters and nonstarters, with starters being faster (91). When speed is considered in the context of team sports, the ability to express high speeds or accelerate over relatively short distances (<40 m) seems to be a major contributor to success (94, 125).

Many coaches use the word *speed* as an umbrella term to describe athletes who display the skills and abilities to achieve high movement velocities or rapidly change direction, velocity, or mode of movement (71). This term is also used to describe agile athletes who can rapidly change direction, velocity, or movement mode in response to a stimulus or tactical situation (208). Ultimately, although speed is important to sport success, the athlete's ability to change direction rapidly can mute an opponent's speed advantage or provide a tactical advantage during competition (71). Therefore, when coaches talk about speed, they often are referring to a composite of the athlete's ability to express high movement velocities, change direction rapidly, and display high levels of agility.

Due to the importance of both speed and agility, it is essential that structured training practices are developed to maximize them (136). To accomplish this goal, the coach must understand the factors that affect speed and agility performance and translate this knowledge into a periodized training plan that specifically develops these important characteristics. This chapter will help the coach understand the major factors that contribute to speed, **change of direction ability**, and agility. Additionally, information is provided about how these training targets can be integrated into a periodized training plan.

Speed

In the context of sport, speed is defined as the rate at which an athlete can cover a specific distance (136, 201). Although the terms *speed* and *velocity* are often used interchangeably, these terms must be considered separately (71). Specifically, speed is a scalar quantity that describes only how fast an object covers a given distance, whereas **velocity** is a vector quantity that describes how fast an object is traveling and the direction it is traveling. Based on this understanding, velocity should be considered as speed that is expressed in a direction (71).

Generally, speed is an integral factor associated with successful performances in a wide variety of sports (136, 161, 199, 321, 322). To highlight how important speed is to successful sport performance, the axiom "speed kills" is often stated within coaching circles (136). Although once considered to be solely a genetic trait that is not greatly affected by training (124), it is now widely accepted that well-structured and scientifically sound periodized training programs can significantly improve an athlete's ability to perform high-speed movements (136, 139, 200, 215).

In a sporting context, speed can either be categorized as linear or multidirectional (71). **Linear speed**, more commonly referred to as *sprinting*, significantly affects success in several track and field events, as well as during open field running in team sports (71, 136). Although linear speed is important for team sport athletes, the ability to express **multidirectional speed** is a more critical determinant of success. In team sport scenarios, the athlete's ability to respond to the everchanging environment with fast, efficient changes of direction should be referred to as *game speed* (136). Fundamentally, **game speed** is the application of speed in a sport-specific context in a manner that maximizes sport performance (136). On the other hand, linear speed requires the ability to accelerate and attain a maximal velocity and maintain it for as long as possible (69, 199).

The rate of change in velocity that allows for maximal velocity to be achieved in a minimal amount of time is referred to as **acceleration** (161, 294). An athlete's ability to accelerate determines performance over short distances (e.g., 5-30 m) (203, 306) and is highly correlated with the maximal velocity achieved by the athlete during a sprinting activity (235, 258). For example, Slawinski and colleagues (258) reported that males need to accelerate to a maximal velocity of about 11.53 m · s^{-1} (41.5 km · h^{-1}) and females need to accelerate to a maximal velocity of about 10.39 m · s^{-1} (37.4 km · h^{-1}) to achieve a world-class 100 m performance. Interestingly, elite male and female sprinters achieve the same average mean acceleration (males = 1.83 ± 0.24 m · s^{-2}; females = 1.82 ± 0.22 m · s^{-2}) but males can accelerate for a longer duration (males = 6.44 ± 0.86 s; females = 5.70 ± 0.69 s). Additionally, it is evident that the ability to accelerate can be used to differentiate between athletes of various competitive levels (5, 69, 199). For example, when examining the 100 m race, elite sprinters accelerate for longer durations and may not achieve maximal sprinting speed until 70 to 80 m (5), whereas untrained sprinters tend to reach maximal sprinting speeds within 10 to 36 m (69). The ability to accelerate at a faster rate also appears to be related to maximal lower-body strength, with faster sprinters being significantly stronger than their slower counterparts (15, 63, 188, 247). In fact, maximal strength has been significantly correlated to the ability to accelerate (40, 168, 280), with stronger individuals displaying higher rates of acceleration. Although maximal strength is generally considered to be an important factor affecting sprint performance (25, 41, 196, 197, 246, 315), an even more important factor is likely the ability to produce force rapidly, which is often referred to as the *rate of force development (RFD)* (71).

When considered in the context of team sports, such as soccer or American football, acceleration abilities underpin successful competitive performance (121, 161, 203). NCAA Division 1 college football players engage in frequent accelerations with sprint distances that range from 7.7 to 315.8 m, depending on the position they play (301). Soccer players also engage in numerous accelerations during training and match play (97), with an average sprint distance of about 17 m (1.5-105 m) (19). Often, sprints are initiated when the athlete is moving at a slower speed (i.e., cruising) (315) and accelerates in an attempt to break away from the competition or initiate a tackle (203, 232). Therefore, the ability to rapidly accelerate in the first few steps appears to be an integral part of effective match play (203). Based on this information, it is clear that maximizing the athlete's ability to rapidly accelerate is a critical aspect of the training process (315).

During a sprint, there is typically a period of acceleration followed by the attainment of a maximal running velocity (71, 201). In some instances, an athlete may have great acceleratory capacities and lack the ability to achieve and maintain high sprint velocities (315), which supports the contention that acceleration and maximal-speed running are specific sprinting qualities (68). As noted by Bompa and Haff (35), the differences in the kinematics of acceleration and maximal velocity sprinting support this contention and provide evidence for the belief that running mechanics (203, 315) and specific strength qualities underpin the capacity to express maximal running speeds (124, 187). It is therefore likely that different training methods will likely affect the ability to accelerate and express high-speed movements (22, 199).

After achieving a maximal velocity during a sprint, the athlete will attempt to maintain that speed for as long as possible (69, 71, 199, 201). Fatigue will begin to develop, resulting in an impaired ability to maintain force output and effective running mechanics, which ultimately results in a reduced ability to maintain maximal running speed (226). There are many factors that contribute to fatigue. Generally, fatigue that occurs in response to running at maximal speeds is related to both peripheral and central fatigue mechanisms (234, 235). As the duration of the sprint is extended, there is a gradual decline in anaerobic adenosine triphosphate (ATP) production and an increased accumulation of adenosine diphosphate, which occurs in response to a reduced availability of phosphocreatine (PCr) and a reduced glycolytic flux (185). If the sprint activity lasts longer than 30 seconds, an increased accumulation of hydrogen may adversely affect the contractile machinery or stimulate reductions in glycolytic flux (98, 267), which can reduce the athlete's ability to exert force (268) and maintain efficient running mechanics. To increase the athlete's buffering and fatigue-management capacities, several training strategies, including short- and long-interval sprinting programs (see chapter 14), have been effectively implemented to allow the athlete to maintain sprinting performance for longer durations (67, 152, 227).

Conceptually, speed is an expression of a series of skills and abilities that converge to allow the athlete to achieve high movement velocities (226). Although it is often suggested that these abilities and skills are unrelated, they are in fact interrelated and can be developed with targeted training activities that can enhance the athlete's ability to express high-speed movements (207, 226, 234, 235, 290). The application of appropriate sprint training methods, including sprint- and run-specific drills, strength training and plyometrics, resisted or assisted sprint training, and interval-based sprinting activities, can exert a positive effect on sprint performance (e.g., acceleration, achievement of maximal velocities, maintenance of high velocities) (152, 207, 227). To enhance competitive performance, these sprint training activities must be integrated into the athlete's overall periodized training plan to ensure that appropriate performance progressions are established (35).

Technical Model of Sprinting

Sprinting is a ballistic activity comprised of a series of coupled flight and support phases, known as *strides*, that are used to launch the body forward with a maximal acceleration or velocity over brief distances (35, 71, 226). Generally, the flight phase, which is sometimes referred to as the *nonsupport phase* (35), contains the recovery and ground preparations of the swing leg, whereas the support phase requires the athlete to perform an eccentric breaking action prior to performing a concentric propulsive action (35, 71, 226). As the speed of movement increases, the time spent in the flight phase will increase and the time spent in the support phase will decrease (4, 35). As time spent in the support phase decreases, it becomes increasingly important that high levels of force be expressed rapidly (i.e., increase RFD) to maintain or continue to increase running speed (35).

Ultimately, the speed at which an athlete can run or sprint depends on the interaction between stride rate and stride length (figure 15.1) (71, 74, 151, 226, 315). As an athlete accelerates and approaches maximal velocity, their stride rate will increase to a greater extent than their stride length (226). Stride length is individualized because of its relationship to body height and limb length (195), so it is not as trainable as stride rate (226) when attempting to enhance sprinting speed. However, during a sprint, elite sprinters tend to achieve greater stride rates and lengths in short periods of time (226), suggesting that both can be optimized by appropriate training methodologies (35).

The underlying factor for maximizing stride length and frequency is the ability to rapidly produce force (i.e., RFD) (71). In fact, the most important factor affecting sprinting speed is the amount force that can be rapidly applied during the support phase (44, 176, 303, 304). When force production is considered in the context of stride length, the application of force is required to displace a mass. Stride length represents a displacement of mass (71). Elite sprinters who tend to be stronger (52) can achieve stride lengths of about 2.70 m at maximal velocity, whereas novice sprinters who tend to be weaker display stride lengths of about 2.56 m at maximum velocity (figure 15.2) (176).

In addition to displaying increased stride lengths, elite sprinters also demonstrate faster stride rates (4.63 steps · s^{-1}) compared to novice

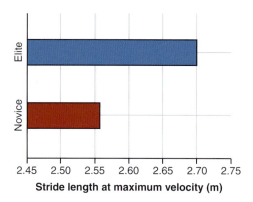

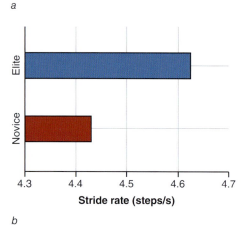

FIGURE 15.2 *(a)* Stride length and *(b)* stride rate of elite and novice sprinters.

Reprinted by permission from B.H. DeWeese and S. Nimphius, "Program Design and Technique for Speed and Agility Training," in *Essentials of Strength Training and Conditioning*, edited by G.G. Haff and N.T. Triplett (Champaign, IL: Human Kinetics, 2016), 528.

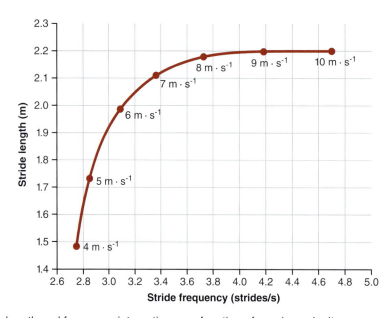

FIGURE 15.1 Stride length and frequency interaction as a function of running velocity.

Reprinted by permission from B.H. DeWeese and S. Nimphius, "Program Design and Technique for Speed and Agility Training," in *Essentials of Strength Training and Conditioning*, edited by G.G. Haff and N.T. Triplett (Champaign, IL: Human Kinetics, 2016), 528.

sprinters (4.43 steps · s⁻¹) (176). DeWeese and Nimphius (71) suggest that elite sprinters need less **ground contact time** to exert the forces needed to displace their body mass. Faster sprinters spend more time in the flight phase as a result of their higher stride rates (4, 35). However, the time they spend repositioning their swing leg is similar to slower sprinters (71, 176, 304). Ultimately, elite sprinters are better able to propel themselves because of properly directed vertical forces (71) that are achieved via the optimization of knee height at maximal knee flexion of the recovering leg (176). Mann and Murphy (176) suggest that a higher knee height provides a greater time for force production and subsequent ground clearance. By employing this technique, the elite sprinter can produce most of their force during the initial parts of the support phase (71).

Additionally, the continuous application of high forces during short support phases allows faster sprinters to achieve higher velocities by performing longer strides at a faster rate (71). Although it is easy to deduce that force production is the major limiting factor dictating how fast a sprinter can run, technical efficiency and a properly structured periodized training plan also affect the development of sprinting speed.

Linear sprinting speed is comprised of three phases: start (figure 15.3), acceleration (figure 15.4), and maximal velocity (figure 15.5).

Start

The optimal starting position for initiating a sprint is a medium heel-to-toe stance, regardless of whether the position uses a two-point (standing), three-point (crouching), or four-point (crouching) stance (226). When initiating the sprint from a static start position, the sprinter must aggressively extend both legs to produce the requisite forces (~905 N) during the start clearance (~0.28 s) to overcome the static start position (71). As the front leg extends, the athlete swings their back leg to the front side of the body in preparation for initiation of the support phase. In concert with this movement, the arm opposite the leg swinging forward will move forward and upward with the elbow flexed at a 90° angle and the hand moving toward the forehead (226). As the front leg moves into the support phase, the opposite arm swings backward with the elbow extended as the contralateral (front) leg completes a triple extension of the hip, knee, and ankle (34, 226). When this movement series is correctly performed, the athlete's body will move forward at an angle of 45° from horizontal as they exit the starting position (34, 226) (see figure 15.4).

It is well-documented that faster sprinters generate larger horizontal block impulses than slower sprinters (27). These higher impulses are partially explained by faster sprinters being able to apply

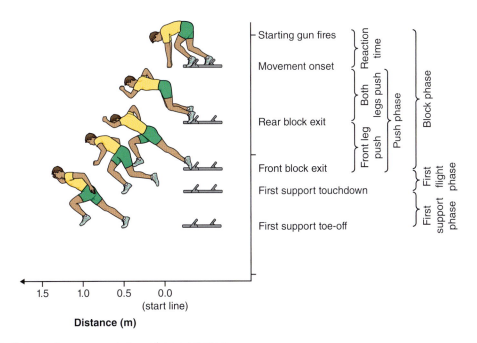

FIGURE 15.3 Schematic representation of a sprint start.

Adapted by permission from N.E. Bezodis, S. Willwacher, and A.I.T. Salo, "The Biomechanics of the Track and Field Sprint Start: A Narrative Review," *Sports Medicine* 49 (2019): 1347. Distributed under the terms of the Creative Commons Attribution 4.0 International License (http://creativecommons.org/licenses/by/4.0/).

FIGURE 15.4 Sprint technique during the acceleration phase.

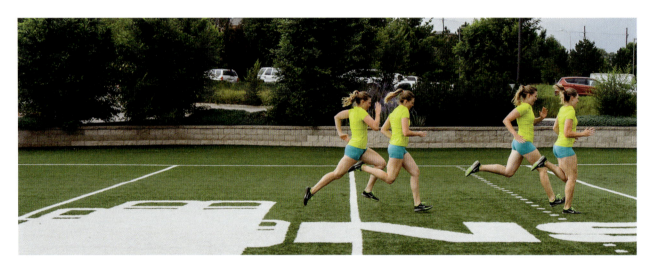

FIGURE 15.5 Sprint technique at maximum velocity: from left to right, late flight to early support; early support; mid-support; late support to toe-off.

greater peak and average forces (26, 309) and display higher RFD during the start (257). Ultimately, due to the intimate relationship between maximal strength, the RFD, and impulse, it is evident that integrating properly designed strength-training interventions into the athlete's periodized training plan can be very beneficial when attempting to maximize the efficiency of the sprint start (27, 68, 236).

Acceleration

As the athlete transitions from the static start position into the initial acceleration phase of the sprint, body angle will progressively climb from about 45° to a more upright position as the athlete approaches maximal velocity (figure 15.5) (226, 315). The forward lean that occurs during the acceleration period allows the athlete to assume what is sometimes referred to as the *power line* position, in which the leg is fully extended and in line with the body's longitudinal axis at the completion of the drive phase (226). From this position, the knee is driven forward so it is in front of the hip. This allows the athlete to achieve a position in which the thigh is perpendicular to the trunk and the lower leg is parallel to the trunk (226). Once in this position (i.e., ground preparation position), the leg moves into the support phase, in which it extends down and backward while striking the ground with smaller hip and knee angles then those seen when running at maximal velocity (226, 315). During the support phase, the athlete will transition between two subphases—eccentric braking and concentric propulsive (226)—that are coupled to engage a stretch-shortening cycling action and maximize force production. To continue to accelerate, greater ground reaction forces must be developed (142).

Overall, the arm action should originate from the shoulder and be performed with the arm flexed at about 90° to facilitate leg drive and offset the axial **momentum** generated by the contralateral leg and hip that occurs during the acceleration phase (226). As the front side leg enters the support phase, the opposite arm moves close to the body as the hand swings upward and forward from hip to shoulder height (153, 226, 250).

During the initial acceleration phase, which typically occurs within the first 15 to 20 m, both stride rate and frequency increase (174), with increases in stride frequency exerting the greatest effect on running velocity (174, 203). As the athlete transitions into the later stages of acceleration, increases in stride length will exert a greater influence on running velocity (174).

Maximal Velocity

Fundamentally, sprinting at maximal velocities requires the athlete to move their lower limbs at maximal speeds through an alternating series of support and flight phases (71, 244). As the athlete moves into the support phase, they transition from an eccentric braking action into a concentric propulsive action (71). This sequence of muscle actions engages the stretch-shortening cycle (SSC) (4, 226), resulting in a powerful and impulsive triple extension of the hip, knee, and ankle that maximizes the ground reaction forces generated (226). Ideally, during the support phase, ground contact is made on the front side of the athlete's body (178, 226). After the triple extension is completed, the athlete will initiate a triple flexion of the ankle, knee, and hip on the back side of the body, resulting in the athlete's heel being close to the buttocks (34, 226). This recovery movement allows the knee to be rapidly moved toward the front side of the body in preparation for a rapid foot descent, during which the foot accelerates down and backward on ground strike (226).

As the sprinter achieves maximal sprinting speed, the trunk will be in a more upright position (226, 315) and the stride rate and length will be major contributors to the velocity of movement (5, 199, 304). During the initial support phase, the rapid application of vertical ground reaction forces during each foot strike results in the maximization of the time spent in the nonsupport phase to provide sufficient time for the swing leg to be repositioned in preparation for the next support phase (304). The ability to rapidly apply higher vertical ground reaction forces during the support phase of a sprint underpins the athlete's ability to reach and maintain faster running speeds (199, 298, 304). In fact, Weyand and colleagues (304) suggest that athletes who display faster top speeds can more rapidly apply higher vertical ground reaction forces per unit of body mass during the support phase of the sprint than their slower counterparts. Additionally, because these forces must be applied in a relatively short time (i.e., 85-160 ms) during each foot strike, the athlete's ability to exert a maximal RFD is critical (177, 184, 257, 303). Collectively, these data support the contention that strength, specifically relative maximal strength, is an important contributor to maximal speed development. Additionally, these data support the belief that targeted strength-training activities are essential components of a periodized training plan that focuses on speed development.

Physiological Factors Affecting Speed

The coach must understand the various physiological factors that underpin the athlete's ability to perform high-speed movements, such as those seen when performing sprinting activities. The ability to perform high-speed movements can be affected by several different energetic, genetic, morphological, and neurophysiological factors (35, 71, 235).

Energetic Factors Affecting Speed

The ability to sprint requires the athlete to sustain a very high power output over a relatively short time. To accomplish this goal, a rapid release of energy is required to maintain a high crossbridge cycling rate within the skeletal muscle and ensure a rapid and repetitive production of muscular force (35, 185). Although all three energetic systems (phosphagen, glycolytic, and oxidative) contribute to this energetic supply (185), the phosphagen (ATP-PC) and glycolytic systems (fast and slow glycolysis) predominate during most sprinting activities (56). The oxidative contribution to energy supply generally depends on the structure of the sprint training session; the duration, length, and number of sprints performed and the rest interval employed dictate the magnitude of contribution from the oxidative system (234). For example, if longer-duration sprints

(≥30 s) are repeated several times and relatively short rest intervals are employed, the contribution of the oxidative system to energetic supply will progressively increase (185). Therefore, it is easy to deduce that the structure of the training program can significantly affect the enzymatic adaptations, substrate storage, and ability to tolerate the accumulation of fatigue-inducing metabolites (234).

Enzymatic Activity Sprinting can significantly reduce muscular stores of ATP and PCr (3, 127). These reductions are greater in the type IIa and type IIx fiber types (3). Interestingly, faster sprinters tend to display a significantly faster rate of PCr breakdown (127). This increased use of PCr is likely mediated by an increased rate of creatine kinase (CK) activity, which can be enhanced with chronic sprint training (203, 216, 283). Additionally, to more rapidly resynthesize ATP and meet the energetic demands of sprinting, it is likely that chronic sprint training stimulates increased myokinase enzyme activity (3, 67, 233, 234).

In addition to the alterations associated with the phosphagen system, several key enzymes associated with the glycolytic system are also affected by various forms of sprint training (234). For example, both short (<10 s) and long (>10 s) sprints are associated with increased **phosphorylase** activity, which is responsible for stimulating the breakdown of muscle glycogen (46, 173, 216, 234). Additionally, short, long, and combined sprint training activities are associated with an increased **phosphofructokinase (PFK)** activity (46, 133, 173, 233, 234). PFK, the enzyme responsible for regulating the rate of glycolytic flux, also regulates the rate at which energy is supplied from the glycolytic systems and has been related to performance in high-intensity activities, such as sprinting (279). Finally, both short- and long-duration sprinting has been shown to stimulate increases in **lactate dehydrogenase** activity, which enhances the ability to convert pyruvate to lactate (see chapter 2) (173, 216, 228, 234). However, the more concentrated the sprint training program, the greater the changes in the glycolytic enzymes (216).

When multiple long sprints (≥30 s) are performed, there is a significant decrease in the glycolytic flux, which results in a reduction in maximal power output and speed (33). This reduction in the rate of the glycolytic system likely occurs in response to elevated hydrogen concentrations reducing the activity of PFK, resulting in a reduced production of lactate and increased contribution of the oxidative energy system (18, 33, 126, 259). The duration of the sprint (18, 259) and the rest interval between sprints (17, 173) exert the greatest influence on the contribution of the oxidative system to energetic supply during sprinting. For example, oxidative contribution to energetic supply increases when multiple longer sprints are performed with shorter rest intervals between each sprint. This leads to increased succinate dehydrogenase and citrate synthase activity, which facilitates the ability of this pathway to meet the energetic demands (3, 46, 133).

Ultimately, the enzymatic adaptations that occur in response to chronic sprint training result in improved rates of ATP supply from the phosphagen and glycolytic systems. Additionally, when performed in interval formats (i.e., multiple sprints with varying rest interval durations), the superior training stimulus offers a better transfer of training effect to team sports (see chapter 14).

Energy Substrate Storage The availability and rapid use of PCr and glycogen are significantly related to the athlete's ability to perform high-intensity exercise (see chapter 2) (3, 77, 234). As a result of the energetic demands of sprinting, the PCr stores of elite sprint athletes can be reduced by about 62% during a 60 m sprint and about 71% during a 100 m sprint (127). Because of the rapid reductions in PCr, sprint performance is also associated with a more rapid rate of glycogenolysis (3). When examining the metabolic contributions of PCr and glycogen during a 100 m sprint, it appears that both energetic stores are used during the early phases of the sprint. As the athlete transitions into the maximum speed phase, the contribution of PCr is reduced, and by the end of the sprint (i.e., deceleration phase), glycogen becomes the primary energetic substrate (127).

Because both PCr and glycogen are important to sprint performance, it is logical to hypothesize that sprint training can result in positive chronic adaptations to substrate storage, allowing for improved substrate availability during sprinting (3). In support of this contention, Parra and colleagues (216) reported that chronic sprint training focused on short sprints can result in elevated PCr and glycogen levels, whereas training with longer-duration sprints tends to only elevate glycogen levels. Based on these findings, it appears that chronic sprint training can result in alterations in the amount of energy substrates stored within skeletal muscle, and it is likely that these alterations underpin the performance gains associated with structured sprint training (216).

Fatigue-Inducing Metabolites When glycolytic flux is high, the glycolytic system produces ATP at a higher rate, resulting in the accumulation of lactic acid (160, 302) that is rapidly converted to lactate (83, 118). When lactic acid is dissociated into lactate, there is an increase in hydrogen ion concentration, which can inhibit PFK activity (120). In response to an increased hydrogen ion concentration, there is a decrease in calcium transport rate (157, 238) and a reduction in the crossbridge cycling rate in the skeletal muscle (198). If these hydrogen ions are not buffered and continue to accumulate, the ability to sprint—and more importantly, repetitively sprint—will be impaired (152).

High-intensity interval training (HIIT) exposes an athlete to increased hydrogen ion concentrations that facilitate an increased buffering capacity (190, 302). Elevations in buffering capacity allow for the maintenance of a higher glycolytic flux, which facilitates energy supply and the maintenance of sprinting performance capacity. Ultimately, the athlete must be exposed to training activities that increase buffering capacity to prepare them to better tolerate metabolic fatigue-inducing factors, such as lactic acid or hydrogen (35). For more information on HIIT activities, refer to chapter 14.

Genetic Factors Affecting Speed

Some athletes appear naturally talented, and there seems to be a genetic component associated with sport performance (224, 307). In fact, there is a significant genetic influence on anaerobic capacity, explosive power (47), maximal strength, and the ability to respond to strength training (281), all of which are related to the ability to move at high speeds.

Due to the important role of alpha-actinin-3 (ACTN3) in fast-twitch skeletal muscle, several researchers have suggested that there may be subtle differences in performance between individuals with different ACTN3 R577x genotypes (24, 169, 172, 223). MacArthur and North (172) suggested that individuals who express ACTN3 with an RR or RX genotype may have an advantage in sprint or power performance compared to those who are ACTN3 deficient. In fact, Yang and colleagues (313) reported that both male and female sprint athletes have a significantly higher frequency of the ACTN3 577R allele (either RR or RX), whereas endurance athletes tend to have a higher frequency of the ACTN3 577xx allele. Interestingly, there is a trend toward a predominance of the ACTN3 577R allele in Olympic sprint athletes. MacArthur and North (172) suggest that because female athletes have lower testosterone levels, the ACTN3 genotype may be a more important discriminator of athletic performance in females. Based on these findings, some researchers have referred to ACT3 577R as the speed gene (24, 172, 223).

Because of emerging data linking specific genetic markers with aspects of sport performance, we have seen an increase in the number of direct-to-consumer (DTC) genetic tests that claim to be able to identify athletic talents (296, 300). Although these tests may be appealing to some, a growing consensus in the scientific community posits that genetic testing should not be a part of a sport talent identification process (296, 300). In fact, Webborn and colleagues (300) strongly discourage the use of DTC genetic testing and explicitly state that this type of testing should not be used as a method of talent identification.

Skeletal Muscle Factors Affecting Speed

Human skeletal muscle fiber type is typically determined based on its myosin heavy chain (MHC) isoform composition (37, 221). Generally, there are three MHC isoforms (I, IIa, IIx) that form three pure MHC fiber types (I, IIa, and IIx) and combine to form three hybrid fiber types (I/IIa, IIa/IIx, I/IIa/IIx) (222, 308). These MHC fiber types can be placed on a continuum of slow- to fast-twitch fiber types (figure 15.6). Force- and power-generating capacities also can be placed on this continuum, with type I MHC isoforms exhibiting the lowest force- and power-generating capacity and type IIx MHC isoforms exhibiting the highest force- and power-generating capacity (38, 39).

It is well-documented that MHC isoform type plays an influential role in determining contractile speed and power output in skeletal muscle (37, 221, 287). Based on these relationships, it is logical to conclude that an athlete's fiber type may influence their ability to sprint. In support of this contention, it is well-documented that sprint athletes tend to have a higher percentage of type IIa muscle fibers (11, 60, 101, 148, 220, 287) compared to endurance athletes (61, 119) and healthy nonathletes (10, 202, 308). Additionally, Trappe and colleagues (287) reported that the muscle fiber type of a sprinter who was a former world record holder in the 60 m (7.30 s) and 110 m hurdles (12.91 s) displayed a total fast-twitch population of 71% with an abundance of type IIx (24%) muscle fibers (figure 15.7). When this athlete's single muscle fiber contractile speed and power were analyzed, researchers found they followed a hierarchal pattern (IIx > IIa/x > IIa > I)

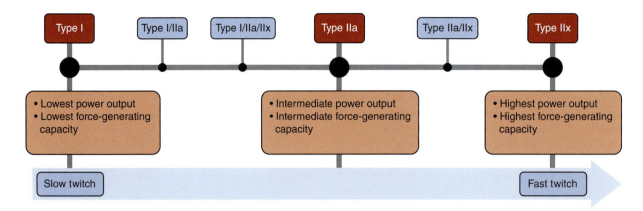

FIGURE 15.6 Myosin heavy chain continuum.

across the continuum with, MHC IIx fibers being 50% faster and 78% more powerful than the MHC IIa fibers (287). Based on these data, it is likely that training-induced changes to muscle fiber composition may partially explain improvements in sprinting performance.

Training-induced alterations to the muscle fiber partially depend on individual differences and the athlete's genetic predisposition to training (81, 157, 159, 234). For example, prolonged endurance training stimulates an MHC fiber type shift from a type II toward a type I profile via reductions in the hybrid fibers (e.g., decreased II/a and decreased I/IIa/IIx), which is disadvantageous for sprint performance (286). Conversely, type II fiber content tends to increase in response to structured sprint training (60, 81, 133, 134), which in some instances occurs in response to a bidirectional shift, with an increase in type IIa fibers resulting from a decrease in both type I and type IIx fibers (9, 11, 234). If, however, endurance training is included in the athlete's training plan, these favorable adaptations to the skeletal muscle fiber type compositions can be muted (234). Additionally, if inadequate rest is provided between repetitions or sets of sprint efforts (122, 158, 234) or the athlete exclusively trains with long-duration sprints (46, 155, 234, 255), a fiber-type transition similar to that seen with endurance training can occur.

Because the way an athlete trains influences skeletal muscle fiber type and the transition of the hybrid fiber types, the coach must be careful when constructing the athlete's periodized training plan to ensure that it aligns with the targeted training outcomes. The first programming consideration revolves around whether to include traditional endurance training (e.g., long slow distance activities). When working with athletes who must express high levels of sprinting speed, traditional endurance training should generally be avoided. Second, shorter rest intervals or longer sprint intervals should be reserved for the general preparation phase of the athlete's annual training plan if they are deemed necessary for the athlete's development. As the athlete moves from the general preparation phase into the specific preparation phase, shorter sprints with longer rest intervals can be used to develop higher-speed movements (35).

Neural Factors Affecting Speed

A high level of neuromuscular activation is required during the performance of high-velocity movements, such as maximal sprinting (140, 211, 234, 235). Specifically, the temporal sequencing of

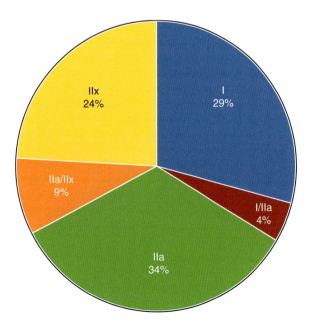

FIGURE 15.7 Vastus lateralis myosin heavy chain distribution for a world champion sprinter.

Adapted from Trappe, Luden, Minchev, et al. (2015).

muscle activation, the use of the SSC, the stretch reflex, and the development of neural fatigue can all affect sprinting ability (234, 235).

Muscle Activation During complex movement tasks, such as sprinting, a multitude of muscles must be activated at specific times in specific sequences and with appropriate intensities to optimize movement speed (235). Through the training process, the athlete can refine neural activation patterns and enhance the development of an efficient motor program to underpin high-speed movements (194, 235). These improvements in movement speed may be achieved via the optimization of the timing of the agonist and antagonist muscle activation patterns, resulting in a decreased co-contraction at an appropriate time during contraction (235). Additionally, as muscle contraction speed is altered, the ratio of the contribution from the coagonist muscles is altered (48, 235). Ultimately, it is likely these responses are facilitated by task-specific training, which can allow for greater overall activation during a given activity.

Additionally, the ability to fully or selectively recruit type II muscle fibers appears to be important when attempting to optimize sprint performance (235). Supporting this contention is evidence from one cross-sectional study in which sprint athletes displayed a greater ability to selectively recruit type II motor units compared to endurance athletes or untrained individuals (240). Although these data are far from conclusive, they may be interpreted as evidence that sprint training might enhance the athlete's ability to recruit motor units that are able to rapidly contract and relax (235). Additionally, this response can be enhanced when sprint athletes integrate other explosive or ballistic training activities, such as weightlifting and plyometrics, into their training programs, because these activities have been shown to alter motor unit recruitment patterns so type II fibers are recruited sooner (114).

Stretch-Shortening Cycle It is well-documented that the SSC contributes to the propulsive forces during running (71, 73, 235). Fundamentally, the SSC is an eccentric–concentric coupling phenomenon during which the muscle–tendon complexes are rapidly and forcefully lengthened (stretch loaded) and then immediately shortened in a reactive or elastic manner (71, 146). Simplistically, the SSC is best demonstrated in activities that require a rapid transition from an eccentric action to a concentric action, such as running, jumping, and hopping (146).

The SSC actions generally exploit the intrinsic muscle–tendon behavior and the force length reflex feedback to the nervous system (7, 45, 74). Although SSC actions acutely use elastic energy to increase mechanical efficiency and impulse, they tend to chronically enhance muscle stiffness and neuromuscular activation, which leads to long-term performance gain (71, 146, 147, 241, 242).

When training to enhance SSC performance, activities should

- involve multijoint movements that transmit forces through the kinetic chain,
- exploit the elastic-reflexive mechanism, and
- emphasize work quality and technique via sessions that are structured around brief periods of work or clusters separated by frequent rest intervals (71).

To accomplish these requirements, combinations of progressive heavy resistance and plyometric training methods are typically used. Potential advanced resistance-training strategies that can be used to enhance the SSC include complex methods (182) in which SSC and heavy resistance-training activities are alternated within the same training session (59, 156). Although this training modality is increasing in popularity among advanced athletes, it is likely not appropriate for novices or youth athletes (71), and these athletes should focus on maximizing maximal strength with the use of heavy resistance-training.

Stretch Reflex When considered in the context of sprinting, the **stretch reflex** plays a role in force production and controlling muscle stiffness. Because ground contact during sprinting can be less than 100 milliseconds, the rapid time frame of the reflex contribution to force production makes it very applicable to sprinting (235).

When sprinting, the preactivation of the numerous leg muscles associated with generating propulsive forces likely results in increases in muscle spindle sensitivity, allowing for a potentiation of the stretch reflex contribution force production (100, 104, 151). Training-induced adaptations to the muscle spindle sensitivity may occur in response to sprint training (146) and strength and power training (144), which can improve muscle stiffness on ground contact (235). Additionally, increases in tendomuscular stiffness may affect the storage and use of elastic energy as part of the SSC and ultimately be related to maximal running velocity and speed maintenance (50, 164). Specifically, increases in tendomuscular stiffness result in a decreased contact time during the support phase of sprinting via increases in both the RFD and the peak forces generated (235).

Neural Fatigue Neural fatigue is a potential performance limiter during and after maximal sprint exercise (228, 235). Fatigue during the later stages of a 100 m sprint causes a decreased stride rate, which corresponds to a reduction in sprinting speed (5, 235, 284). These reductions in stride rate appear to occur in response to altered motor unit recruitment patterns and changes in the motor unit firing rate, which are representative of acute neural fatigue. Specifically, after the acceleration phase of a 100 m sprint, there is a 4.9% to 8.7% reduction in muscle activation that likely occurs in response to fatigue at the neuromuscular junction, a reduced motor unit firing rate, and a decreased recruitment of higher threshold motor units (type IIx) (197, 235). It is likely that the progressive reduction in motor unit recruitment is a result of a less-than-optimal output from the motor cortex (235).

An additional potential cause of acute neural fatigue is related to a reduction in reflex sensitivity (235) that can influence propulsive force output during running (73). One factor that may reduce the sensitivity of these reflexes is the accumulation of lactate. Lactate is known to act on group III and IV muscle afferents, and when lactate accumulates, it may potentially limit the SSC contribution to the propulsive phase of sprinting (193, 256). Ultimately, even relatively small changes in reflex sensitivity may negatively affect the quality of the sprint performance (235).

In contrast to acute neural fatigue, lasting neural fatigue can continue long after the cessation of exercise (235). Although the origin of long-lasting neural fatigue is likely multifaceted, it has been hypothesized that it occurs via afferent feedback loops either as a result of the influence of muscle damage or peripheral fatigue feedback (235). Longer-lasting fatigue can affect reflex output as well as proprioception, which ultimately can affect sprinting technique. As a result, many coaches consider neural fatigue and its time frame for recovery when planning the timing and frequency of training sessions that target maximal speed development (85, 86, 218). To address this, it is commonly recommended to provide 48 to 72 hours between maximal sprint activities (124). Ultimately, the coach must consider the time allotted between high-intensity training activities in order to better manage fatigue when structuring the athlete's training program.

Spring–Mass Model and Speed

Strength and speed training have been linked to an increased preactivation of the musculature engaged during sprinting (143, 147). With the onset of pre-tension, the sensitivity of the muscle spindles can be increased. Reductions in the time required for feedback from the muscle spindles ultimately results in greater muscle stiffness and tendon compliance (71, 144, 151, 235). These factors support the SSC, which underpins the **spring–mass model (SMM)** (71, 123, 272). This mathematical model represents sprinting as a type of locomotion in which the lower limb acts as the spring and the body's center of mass serves as the mass (29, 65, 79, 82, 123).

During a complete running cycle, one spring compresses and then propels the sprinter's body forward, and the other spring moves forward in preparation for ground contact (71). At ground contact (i.e., foot strike), compression of the spring is initiated, and a sudden brief deceleration assists in propelling the swing leg forward in preparation for ground contact. As the center of mass moves in front of the foot, the sprinter moves into the mid-stance phase, where the center of mass is lowered and the spring is compressed to its lowest point (71). During the push-off segment of the stance phase, there is a return of energy via the extension of the coiled spring, resulting in a forward projection of the sprinter (71).

Although the SMM provides a framework for understanding the basic actions associated with upright running, its ability to describe the stance phase of elite sprinters may be limited (71). Specifically, elite sprinters produce more of their vertical forces during the first half of ground contact, which is different from the pattern typically presented by the SMM, in which vertical force is more symmetrically applied (52, 71). Regardless, the SMM should be considered a basic framework to be used to describe the interaction of the SSC, muscle stiffness, and sprinting. The increase in muscle stiffness due to the increase in stride frequency is one of the most important factors associated with the leg spring (82).

Performance Factors Affecting Speed

To perform the techniques associated with high-speed movements, an athlete is required to express high amounts of force, often in a very short time (71). **Force** is a vector quantity that has both a magnitude (i.e., size) and a direction and is the product of mass and acceleration. Force is traditionally described as a push or pull exerted on an object that results in the movement of that object. This movement changes the object's velocity, which is represented as an acceleration (71). As long as force is applied to the object, acceleration will continue to cause a change in velocity. Fundamentally, muscular strength should be considered the ability to exert force on an external object or source of resistance (254, 269, 276). The athlete's ability to apply force is largely related to their maximal strength levels (247). When considered in the context of sprinting, it is evident that high levels of muscular strength are required for the athlete to exert the requisite forces against gravity to accelerate and achieve high-speed movements (276).

Force must also be considered in the context of the time available to produce it; there is limited time available during most athletic activities. Two variables that describe force relative to the time available to produce it are the RFD and impulse (71). The RFD is the rate at which force is produced and can be considered as the ability to develop force in a minimal amount of time (2, 7). **Impulse** is the product of the force generated and the time required for its production or the integral of force with respect to time. Based on the impulse–momentum relationship, the magnitude of the change of momentum of an object is dictated by the impulse applied (71). Ultimately, the ability to apply high impulses during rapid stance phases is a key factor dictating maximal running speeds.

When considering the expression of speed, the coach must consider the importance of the athlete's maximal strength levels, their ability to express a high RFD, and their ability to apply high impulses. The available literature shows strong relationships between maximal strength levels and the ability to express higher sprint velocities (15, 248), which may be explained by an ability to produce a higher peak ground reaction force, impulse, and RFD during each foot strike while running (247).

Strength

Faster sprint performances generally are related to a greater force application, shorter ground contact times, and greater stride lengths (304). In fact, faster sprinters can apply greater ground reaction forces during the first half of their support phase (52), and the amount of force generated is highly related to the athlete's overall maximal lower-body strength levels (247). Numerous studies have reported significant correlations between maximal lower-body strength and sprint performance (i.e., sprint times or higher speeds) (15, 55, 165, 186, 248, 276, 312). In fact, Suchomel and colleagues (276) suggested that 85% of the studies they examined for their review reported moderate or greater relationships between maximal lower-body strength levels and sprinting performances. These findings were further supported by a meta-analytic study by Seitz and colleagues (247) in which increasing lower-body strength was reported to positively transfer to sprinting performance. Although the majority of the literature indicates that stronger individuals are able to produce faster sprinting performances than their weaker counterparts (21, 63, 128, 186, 191, 312), several studies have reported no relationship between strength and sprint performance (16, 63). One potential explanation for these conflicting findings is that these divergent studies (16, 63) examined absolute strength and did not consider how relative maximal strength related to sprint performance.

Rate of Force Development

The RFD, also referred to as *explosive strength*, is the rate that force is generated during sporting movements (2, 187), and it exerts a significant functional importance in fast and forceful muscle contractions (2). The importance of the RFD is highlighted by the fact that performing rapid movements (e.g., jumping, sprinting) limits the amount of time (~50-250 ms) force can be produced, and longer periods of time (>300 ms) are required to apply maximal forces (1, 2, 277, 282). A limited time for force application is clearly present during sprint performance, in which the average ground contact time ranges from 85 to 110 milliseconds (mean = 96 ± 7 ms) (184). Therefore, one of the most important factors underpinning sprint performance is the ability to express forces rapidly during the brief ground contact times associated with sprinting (299, 303). To further highlight the importance of the RFD to sprint performance, Suchomel and colleagues (276) reported that the RFD has large correlations with sprint performance.

Intuitively, maximal strength and the RFD are interrelated, with stronger individuals generally being able to develop greater forces in shorter periods of time (112, 113, 299). In fact, maximal strength explains 80% of the variance in the RFD (150-250 ms) (12), and increasing strength with the use of structured resistance-training methods positively affects the ability to express high RFD (figure 15.8) (2, 13, 112, 117, 291).

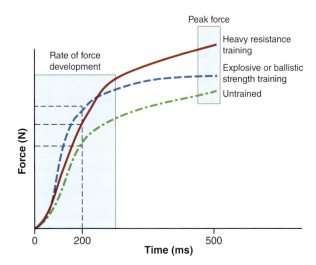

FIGURE 15.8 Isometric force–time curve depicting the RFD and maximal force-generating capacity.

Reprinted by permission from G.G. Haff and S. Nimphius, "Training Principles for Power," *Strength & Conditioning Journal* 34 (2012): 6. Original adapted from R.U. Newton and W.J. Kraemer, "Developing Explosive Muscular Power: Implications for a Mixed Methods Training Strategy," *Strength & Conditioning Journal* 16 (1994): 24.

Heavy resistance training can increase maximal strength (58, 112, 206) and increase the RFD in weaker and untrained individuals (167). For stronger, more experienced athletes, the optimization of the RFD may require the incorporation of explosive or ballistic exercises, such as weightlifting derivatives, plyometrics, and jump squats (58, 112, 114). Although explosive and ballistic exercises can significantly affect the RFD, these training activities cannot increase or maintain maximal strength levels to the same extent as heavy resistance training (112). Because maximal strength serves as the foundation for the RFD, it is important that a mixed-methods training approach that targets maximal strength and the RFD is incorporated into the athlete's periodized annual training plan. In support of this contention, Stone and colleagues (271) suggest that if the training program is appropriately structured, maximal strength and the RFD can be enhanced simultaneously.

Impulse

The ability of an object to move is predicated by the forces applied to produce a change in velocity. When contextualized to sprinting, the application of force is never instantaneous because it is applied throughout the support phase (71). The time spent in this phase is referred to as the *ground contact time*. The product of the amount of force applied to the ground and the duration of ground contact is represented as impulse and is graphically presented as the area under the force–time curve (figure 15.9). Ultimately, changes in impulse alter the athlete's momentum, which directly affects the athlete's ability to accelerate or decelerate (71, 214).

When looking at the acceleration and maximal velocity phases of a sprint, one can see how the vertical and horizontal forces differ. Figure 15.9 illustrates the braking phase, during which there is negative horizontal force, and the propulsive phase, during which there is a positive horizontal

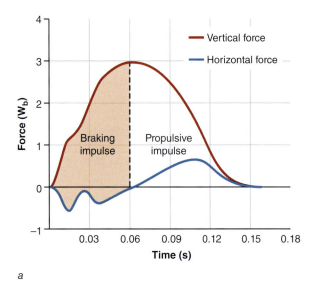
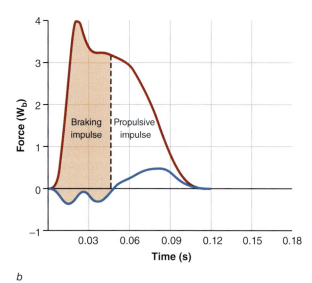

FIGURE 15.9 Sprint ground reaction force and impulse during *(a)* acceleration and *(b)* maximal velocity phases.

Reprinted by permission from B.H. DeWeese and S. Nimphius, "Program Design and Technique for Speed and Agility Training," in *Essentials of Strength Training and Conditioning*, edited by G.G. Haff and N.T. Triplett (Champaign, IL: Human Kinetics, 2016), 524.

force. The two areas under the vertical force–time curve separated by the black line represent the braking and propulsive impulses (71). Interestingly, during the maximal velocity phase (figure 15.9), force production is asymmetrical and the RFD is very high, which facilitates shorter ground contact times compared to the acceleration phase of a sprint (71). Ultimately, if the time frame for force application is the same, the only way for the athlete to increase the amount of impulse is to generate greater force. Therefore, when designing training programs to enhance sprinting ability, it is essential that training enhances maximal strength, impulse, and the RFD (71).

Training for Speed

The development of coordination and speed, strength, technique, specific endurance, and mobility underpins the athlete's stride length and frequency while sprinting (figure 15.10) (310). This is a key consideration when training for speed.

The overall effectiveness of a training program that targets speed development is a result of a well-organized periodized program that organically develops and matures the skills required to optimize sprint performance (71). A well-designed training program targets the development of specific components in a phasic manner to fully maximize the athlete's sprint performance capacity (71).

Sprint Training

Central to the ability to develop sprinting speed is an enhanced ability to rapidly generate high levels of force in a short time (178, 195, 303). This ability is best developed through long-term training plans that focus on developing maximal strength, RFD, and impulse (2, 270). Although squatting exercises typically are used to maximize lower-body strength, weightlifting movements and plyometric training activities, which engage the SSC, are used to enhance the RFD and impulse (114). Similarly, the SSC is engaged during upright running (i.e., high velocity phase of a sprint), which has led some to suggest that high-speed running is a plyometric activity (71). An additional consideration is that exposure to movements that engage the SSC can increase muscle stiffness, which is considered beneficial for maximizing sprinting performance (82, 272).

Although a variety of training stimuli are important for the optimization of an athlete's performance capacity, maximal velocity sprinting is likely the most effective training activity for enhancing running speed (71). Maximal velocity running requires a high degree of central nervous system (CNS) activity to maximally activate the skeletal muscle. Central to this process is increasing the frequency of the signal from the CNS to the motor unit, commonly referred to as *rate coding* (149, 235). Rate coding is particularly important because when signal frequency reaches a threshold, the skeletal muscle may not completely relax between stimulations (149), resulting in a more forceful contraction and a higher RFD in subsequent contractions (205). It is possible that chronically exposing the athlete to high-speed running will improve the ability of the CNS to rapidly activate the skeletal muscle, ultimately leading to enhanced force-production characteristics that facilitate the expression of speed.

To enhance sprint performance, there has been an increased interest in the use of resisted and assisted sprint training techniques because they may enhance force production or target specific neuromuscular adaptations (64, 129, 219, 236). The coach needs to be familiar with potential benefits and disadvantages of these techniques prior to deciding whether to implement them into an athlete's periodized training plan (tables 15.1 and 15.2).

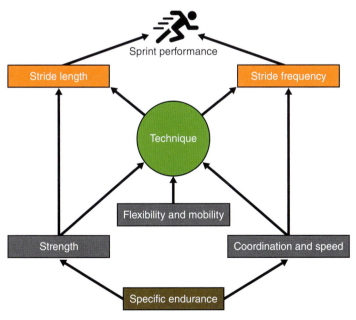

FIGURE 15.10 Interaction of major contributors to sprint performance.

Adapted by permission from G. Winckler, "An Examination of Speed Endurance," *New Studies in Athletics* 61 (1991): 28.

TABLE 15.1 Potential Benefits and Disadvantages of Assisted Sprint Training

Type of assistance	Potential benefits	Potential disadvantages
Downhill running	↑ running speed	↓ muscle activation
	↑ acceleration	↓ propulsive force production
	↑ stride rate	↑ occurrence of chop step
	↑ stride length	↑ exposure to high eccentric loads
		Altered foot placement that may affect the stretch-shortening cycle
Elastic cord–assisted running	↑ acceleration	Altered running mechanics with towing forces greater than 3.8%
	↓ ground contact time	↓ muscle activation
	↑ stride rate	↓ propulsive force production
		↑ occurrence of chop step
		↑ braking forces
Assisted towing	↑ running speed	Altered running mechanics with towing forces greater than 3.8%
	↑ acceleration	↓ muscle activation
	↑ stride rate	↓ propulsive force production
	Improved sprint kinematics	↑ occurrence of chop step
		↑ braking forces

Note: ↑ = increased; ↓ = decreased.

TABLE 15.2 Potential Benefits and Disadvantages of Resisted Sprint Training

Type of assistance	Potential benefits	Potential disadvantages
Sled pushing, sled towing, parachute running, weighted vest sprinting, incline running	↑ acceleration (light loads)	↑ ground contact times with heavier loads
	↑ maximum speed (heavy loads)	↓ stride lengths
	Overloads acceleration phase	If slopes are too great, improper sprint biomechanics and sprinting technique can be reinforced.
	Accentuates the biomechanics of the acceleration phase	Sled pushing may alter natural sprinting gait cycle due to arm action removal.
	↑ propulsive forces	
	↑ rate of force development	
	↑ acceleration	

Note: ↑ = increased; ↓ = decreased.

Assisted Sprint Training During assisted sprint training, sometimes referred to as *overspeed training* (71, 154), the athlete can achieve supramaximal running velocities (236) that are believed to enhance sprinting performance. The most common assisted sprint training methods use towing devices (i.e., assisted towing, elastic cord assisted running, motorized pulling) or feature downhill running (71, 236, 293). Some of the potential benefits of assisted sprint training include increased stride rate and stride frequency and improved accelerations (71, 154, 236, 293). In addition, Leyva and colleagues (154) suggest that assisted sprint activities provide a novel training stimulus that can translate into performance gains depending on how they are implemented (table 15.3).

Assisted sprint training also has several disadvantages, including reductions in muscle activation and propulsive force production and increases in braking forces and alterations to running mechanics (71).

TABLE 15.3 Example Programming for Assisted and Resisted Sprint Training

Assisted sprint training							
Method	Frequency (# per wk)	Duration (wk)	Intensity	Set	Reps	Distance (m)	Inter-set rest (min)
Downhill running	3	8	3.4°-5.8°	1-3	4-6	20	2-10
Elastic cord running	6	3	4%-30% body weight	1-3	5-9	30	2-6
Assisted towed running	3	4	40-50 N	1-3	8-10	20	2-3
Resisted sprint training							
Method	Frequency (# per wk)	Duration (wk)	Intensity	Set	Reps	Distance (m)	Inter-set rest (min)
Sled towing	2-3	4-8	10%-12.6% or 30% body weight	1-4	3-5	20-40	2-6
Parachute running	2-3	4	Medium (1.2 × 1.2 m) or large (1.4 × 1.4 m)	1-4	4	20-30	4-6
Weighted vest sprinting	2-3	4-7	8%-20% body weight	1-4	3-5	20-50	3-4

Adapted from Leyva et al. (2017).

Prior to implementing assisted sprint training, the coach must determine whether the potential benefits outweigh the disadvantages. There is a paucity of research exploring assisted sprint training, and much more research is warranted to better understand how to use these novel training methods.

Resisted Sprint Training Resisted sprint training is used as a strength-specific training activity to enhance the acceleration phase of the sprint (6). There are several ways to incorporate resistance into sprint training, including **resisted sled training (RST)**, parachute pulling, wearing weights (170, 171), and incline sprint training (71, 154). The most common form is RST, which involves towing a sled device while sprinting (6, 219). This method increases horizontal trunk lean, which allows for a greater amount of horizontal force to be produced. This might be beneficial for the acceleration phase but is likely detrimental for the maximal velocity phase of a sprint (219). Due to the increased load, it is possible that RST will increase muscular strength or peak force (62, 204, 212) or the RFD (62, 183). Due to the strong relationship between maximal strength, the RFD, and sprinting performance, it is likely that RST is an effective method for enhancing sprint performance.

Based on the meta-analysis conducted by Alcaraz and colleagues (6), RST is an effective method for enhancing the early acceleration phase (≤10 m), but it exerts only a small effect on the maximum velocity phase of the sprint. There is no consensus on the optimal load for the application of RST, but to best model the demands of sprinting (i.e., movement patterns, load, and movement velocity), RST should be performed with only a slight overload (≤20% of body mass) (6). The athlete's maximal lower-body strength may mitigate the optimal load for RST, with stronger athletes requiring higher loads to optimize performance (14, 162).

Although RST does offer some training benefits, there are some potential disadvantages (71). If a load greater than 20% of body mass is used, ground contact time can increase in weaker athletes, altering the athlete's sprint mechanics (6), such as shortening the athlete's stride length (71). Ultimately, it is up to the coach to determine the cost–benefit relationship of this method of training prior to integrating it into the athlete's training program.

To address some of the disadvantages associated with RST, there has been increased interest in the use of wearable resistance (170, 171). This method allows the athlete to perform movement-specific resisted training, which hypothetically would increase the transfer of training effect due to alignment with the principles of specificity (171). The modern incarnation of this resisted sprint training method uses compression garments that permit weighted resistance to be attached (using Velcro) to different parts of the body. Wearable resistance has been reported to increase sprint times for distances greater than 10 m when compared to unloaded sprinting when loads of 2% or more of body mass are used with arm loading or 5% or more of body mass are used with leg and trunk loading (171). Based on the available literature, it may be warranted to integrate wearable resistance into various phases of a sprint training program. However, additional research is needed to better understand the longitudinal effect of this practice and the best ways to optimize these novel resisted sprint training strategies.

Strength Training

When considering the effect of strength training on sprinting performance, it is important to look at the principle of dynamic correspondence (51, 274). Based on this principle, biomechanical specificity is not simply focused on the external movement characteristics but on the function of the inherent biomechanics of the training and sport tasks (51). The coach must consider the following dynamic correspondence criteria (103):

- *Categories of transfer of training effects.* Three categories explain how a transfer of training might be achieved. A primary transfer occurs because of a high degree of specificity in which the training task is directly correlated to improvements in the target sport performance (103). A secondary transfer occurs when the gains achieved from training have a less-direct transfer to the targeted sport performance. In this case, the adaptations stimulated by training result in improvements in factors that underpin the performance of more specific activities and likely are more important for long-term athlete development. For example, hypertrophic gains may not directly result in increases in sprinting speed but will directly affect the development of strength, which facilitates the maximization of power output and leads to improvements in sprint performance. Finally, a tertiary transfer occurs when there is no obvious mechanism for the transfer of training effects to performance (103). A good example of this type of transfer is the reduction of injury risk that occurs because of improvements in maximal strength.

- *Acceptance of generality.* Strength-training activities are general, and the primary aim of this process is not to replicate the movement but to provide a significant overload and therefore stimulate adaptation in other components that underpin performance. Goodwin and Cleather (103) suggest the critical factor when deciding on which exercises to employ is to understand which components of the athlete's functional abilities are weak or of very high importance. Additionally, it is important to consider that overload can take the form of any of the force-production characteristics (e.g., peak force, RFD, joint moment). When applied to a periodized training plan, it may be important to model the correspondence in exercise selection through different periods of the annual training plan, in some instances providing a significant overload to a specific characteristic while allowing another characteristic to decrease due to less emphasis (103).

- *Combination with variation.* If the coach is overfocused on specificity, they can design programs that focus only on exercises with the highest correspondence to the targeted performance (103). Training programs designed in this way are generally suboptimal and lack the capacity to improve general strength-related qualities or structural capacities. Through the application of this dynamic correspondence criteria, the coach can ensure that even though there is programmed variation, specific key movement themes can be retained within the targeted training exercises (103).

- *Direction of forces relative to the athlete.* There is general confusion about how to differentiate between force vectors as oriented to the global (i.e., relative to the earth's surface) or local (i.e., relative to the athlete's body) frames (103). This confusion is most evident in the force–vector theory, which contends that horizontal exercises are more specific to horizontal sport skills (84), such as sprinting (166). Advocates for this theory argue that during acceleration there are greater horizontal forces relative to the global frame, and during high-speed running there are greater vertical ground reaction forces (84). Due to this belief, exercises that target horizontal force production, such as the hip thrust or glute thrust, have been recommended when training to maximizing sprint performance (57, 166). To understand why exercises such as the hip thrust, or glute thrust, do not adhere to the principles of dynamic correspondence, the coach must consider the orientation of the force vectors in relation to the local frame. For example, when the ground reaction forces during acceleration are contextualized to the athlete's body, they are largely oriented vertically (figure 15.11). When the forces applied during the hip thrust are examined in relation to the athlete's body, it is clear they are anteriorly directed (i.e., horizontally to the athlete's body) (53), which is a different force application when compared to acceleration (figure 15.12). Therefore, it is evident that the hip thrust violates the principle of dynamic correspondence because its force application relative to the local frame does not correspond to the activity of sprinting. Based on this line of reasoning, it is easy to deduce that this strength-training exercise offers little to no benefit for the development of sprinting performance capacity.

Based on these four key concepts, the coach should further consider the criteria for practically applying the principles of dynamic correspond-

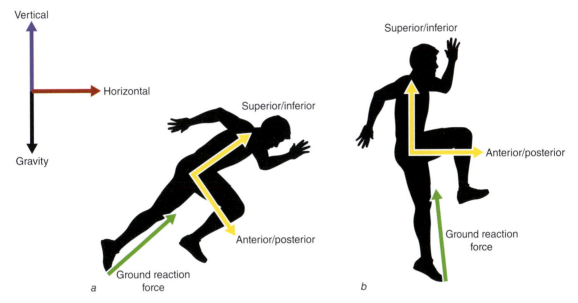

FIGURE 15.11 Relationship between global (relative to the earth) and local (relative to the athlete's body) frame: *(a)* The athlete is accelerating and is experiencing ground reaction forces (light green arrow) that display substantial horizontal and vertical components relative to the global frame. *(b)* If the local and global frames are aligned (the athlete is rotated), the ground reaction forces are largely vertical when oriented to the local frame.

Adapted from Fitzpatrick et al. (2019); Cleather (2021).

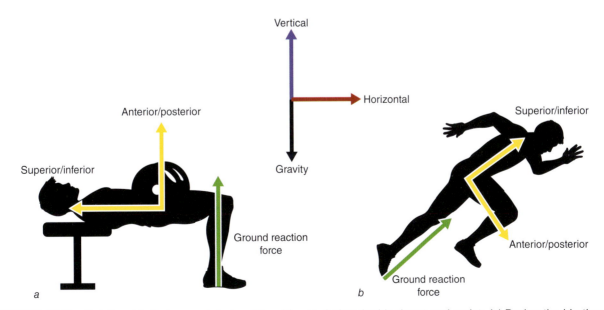

FIGURE 15.12 Relationship between global and local frame during the hip thrust and sprint: *(a)* During the hip thrust, forces are vertical to the global frame but are anterior or posterior to the local frame (the athlete's body). *(b)* During acceleration, forces are horizontal relative to the global frame but are superior or inferior to the local frame.

Adapted from Cleather (2021).

ence presented in table 15.4 when designing strength-training programs to enhance sprinting performance.

It is well-documented that strength and, more importantly, the RFD are critical factors that underpin high sprinting speed (21, 63, 128, 186, 191, 247, 312). For example, there are large to very large relationships between maximal lower-body strength, as measured using the back squat, and sprint performance (15, 54, 186, 247, 248, 312). Furthermore, Seitz and colleagues (247) reported that increases in lower-body strength can translate into a mean sprint improvement of about 3.11% due to improvements in performance during the accel-

TABLE 15.4 Principle of Dynamic Correspondence: Six Practical Criteria for Strength Training

Criteria		General recommendations
1	Amplitude and direction	*Exercise types:* Closed-chain exercises that target the development of ground reaction forces should be the primary target.
		General preparation phase: There should be a greater focus on multijoint, full range of motion exercises, such as squats, presses, and pulls, to build and develop the musculature most relevant to sprinting (or sport of interest).
		Specific preparation and competition phases: Training emphasis should shift toward exercises with similar ranges of motion to those seen in the sporting activity, such as partial squats and weightlifting derivatives.
2	Accentuated regions of force production	A larger emphasis on developing general strength should be a priority when working with weaker athletes. This should be prioritized prior to incorporating ballistic training methods.
		Incorporating bands and chains with traditional resistance-training exercises should be avoided when the primary goal is maximizing the transfer of training effects.
		Specific preparation and competition phases: Traditional resistance training should be supplemented with ballistic exercises, such as jump squats, bench throws, and other plyometric exercises.
3	Dynamics of effort	Training should be sequenced so there is a greater emphasis on high-velocity movements closer to competition.
		The concentric phase of all lifts should be performed with maximal intent.
		All phases: Weightlifting movements, cluster sets, and contrast or complex training should be used throughout the annual plan to maximize both force- and velocity-specific adaptations.
		All phases: A mixed-methods training approach should be used in which all aspects of the force–velocity relationship are targeted. Specifically, high-load, low-velocity and low-load, high-velocity movements should be performed.
4	Rate and time of maximum force production	The improvement of sport-specific rate of force development should be a primary focus of the training process.
		Strength and plyometric exercises should be incorporated to improve the rate of force development.
		Exercises that require short ground contact times should be implemented when targeting sprint performance.
5	Regime of muscular work	Most of the training plan should be made up of exercises that consist of eccentric and concentric muscle actions.
		Training exercises that accentuate the eccentric load can be employed when targeting size and architectural changes to the muscle.
		Training should progress from a general to specific focus as the athlete approaches the competitive periods and phases.
6	Segmental interrelation	Exercise selection needs to be considered based on the interrelationship of the global (i.e., body), segmental (i.e., joint), and muscular actions during athletic movements.
		The function of specific muscle groups within the kinetic chain and the control strategy for the entire kinetic chain must be considered in relation to the multijoint movement patterns associated with the sport.

eration phase. It is likely that these improvements stem from an increased ability to produce higher peak ground reaction forces, impulses, and RFD during each stance phase, which translates into greater sprinting speeds.

Additionally, emerging evidence shows that weightlifting movements, such as the power clean, are significantly correlated with sprint performance (15, 128). The integration of weightlifting derivatives into the athlete's training program also have been reported to result in large improvements in performance during the acceleration phase (275). For example, Suchomel and colleagues (275) reported that the integration of various weightlifting, weightlifting-derivative, and traditional strength-training exercises can result in significant improvements in 10, 20, and 30 m sprint performance. The ability of weightlifting exercises and their derivatives to translate to sprint performance is logical if one considers the principles of dynamic correspondence; specifically, these exercises engage a triple extension in a dynamic manner similar to the engagement seen during sprinting.

Ideally, a key aspect of integrating strength training into the athlete's periodized training plan when targeting speed development is the ability to maximize strength and enhance speed–strength qualities (116). The exercises selected should provide the most benefit for enhancing motor unit rate coding and later type II muscle fiber architecture (90, 115). Based on an emerging body of evidence, strength-training programs targeting the development of sprint speed should have a foundation of squatting, weightlifting, and weightlifting derivatives.

Plyometric Training

Plyometric exercises are characterized by three specific phases: (1) preactivation (i.e., eccentric), (2) amortization (i.e., isometric), and (3) shortening (i.e., concentric) (66, 292). Plyometric training activities can strengthen the elastic properties of the connective tissue, improve the mechanical characteristics of the muscle–tendon complex, optimize crossbridge mechanics, and enhance motor unit activation (179, 230, 292). These adaptations increase joint stiffness, improve muscle strength, increase contraction speed, improve dynamic stability, and enhance neuromuscular control (179, 230, 239). Ultimately, adaptations to plyometric training have the potential to translate into improvements in sprinting speed (231, 318).

A recent meta-analysis by van de Hoef and colleagues (292) reported that plyometric training significantly increased 20 m and 40 m sprint speed. Similarly, in another meta-analysis, Oxfeldt and colleagues (213) reported that plyometric training significantly improved sprint performance. Specifically, 4 to 8 weeks of plyometric training resulted in a −2.3% to −13.7% reduction in sprint time. Similarly, Davies and colleagues (66) suggest that plyometric training may be most applicable when attempting to improve the initial portions of the sprint (10-40 m). Based on the available research, plyometric training should be considered an important part of a periodized training program designed to develop sprinting speed. It is likely the combination of strength and plyometric training provides the greatest enhancement of sprinting performance (247, 292).

Mobility Training

DeWeese and Nimphius (71) suggest that tissue manipulation is an increasingly popular practice when targeting the development of speed. Activities such as stretching, chiropractic care, massage, and myofascial release are often applied to optimize mobility during dynamic movements. Mobility should be defined as the ability of the athlete's limb to move through a desired range of motion. To ensure that the athlete can properly perform the various movement patterns required to engage in sprinting activities, they must have the required mobility.

As noted earlier in this chapter, to sprint efficiently, the athlete must apply ground reaction forces as rapidly as possible in a short time (247). Because this characteristic underpins the athlete's ability to produce optimal stride lengths and forward propulsion, DeWeese and Nimphius (71) suggest that the athlete's mobility may limit them during the flight phase of the sprint. The athlete may possess the ability to express forces correctly, but due to limitations in their mobility, these forces may be misdirected. When this occurs, an erroneous ground contact results in a dampened sprint speed and an increased overall injury risk.

Training for Speed and Speed–Endurance

Two major subgroups of training are often highlighted when developing sprint performance (88): technical and energy system components. Technical components include effective sprinting mechanics and effective starting and acceleration techniques (88). Energy system components associated with sprinting are related to how the phosphagen, glycolytic, and oxidative systems interact to produce the energy required for sprinting. Specific energetic responses can be targeted by implementing specific training activities, such as speed, speed endurance, and tempo endurance training (88). For example, an athlete can develop short speed–endurance by targeting the ATP-PC system through short sprints (50-80 m) at 90% to 95% of maximum speed with longer rest intervals between reps (1-2 min) and sets (5-7 min). Training activities that target various aspects of speed and speed–endurance can be found in table 15.5.

Agility

It is well-documented that success in multidirectional sports is influenced by the ability to change speeds or rapidly change direction in response to an external cue (30, 76, 141, 208, 251, 320). When examining these types of movements, the coach must consider the difference between change of direction (COD) ability, **agility**, and **maneuverability** (figure 15.13) (208).

COD is the physical ability to perform a planned or unplanned change of direction (209). Agility is a COD performed in response to an external stimulus (252) or to information (208) that is rapidly processed. Maneuverability is a COD ability that requires the athlete to maintain velocity or to change their mode of travel (e.g., transition to crossover, shuffle, or backpedal) (71, 208). Since these three abilities are interrelated, superior COD ability is demonstrated when COD speed, agility, and maneuverability overlap as presented in figure 15.13 (208). Because of this interdependence, agility should be considered a complex set of interrelated skills that allows the athlete to

TABLE 15.5 Methods for Targeting Specific Energetic Systems Associated With Speed and Speed–Endurance

Type of training	Targeted energy system		Objectives	Distance (m)	% of best	Recovery time	
	Global	Specific				Repetitions	Sets
Speed	Anaerobic	ATP-PC	Speed	20-80	90-95	3-5 min	6-8 min
		Glycolytic	Anaerobic power	20-80	95-100	3-5 min	6-8 min
Speed–endurance	Anaerobic	ATP-PC	Short speed endurance	50-80	90-95	1-2 min	5-7 min
			Anaerobic power	50-80	95-100	2-3 min	7-10 min
		Glycolytic	Short speed endurance	<80	90-95	1 min	3-4 min
			Anaerobic power	<80	95-100	1 min	4 min
		ATP-PC and glycolytic	Speed endurance	80-150	90-95	5-6 min	
			Anaerobic power	80-150	95-100	6-10 min	
Tempo	Intensive	Mixed	Glycolytic and oxidative	Anaerobic capacity	>80	80-90	30 s-5 min	2-3 min
	Extensive	Aerobic	Oxidative metabolism	Aerobic capacity	>200	<70	<45 s	<2 min
			Aerobic power	>100	70-79	30-90 s	2-3 min
Special endurance	Anaerobic	ATP-PC and glycolytic	Long speed endurance	150-300	90-95	10-12 min	
		Glycolytic	Anaerobic power	150-300	95-100	12-15 min	
			Lactate tolerance	300-600	95-100	Complete recovery	

Adapted by permission from W.H. Freeman, *Peak When It Counts: Periodization for American Track & Field,* 4th ed., (Mountain View, CA: Tafnews Press, 2001), 110.

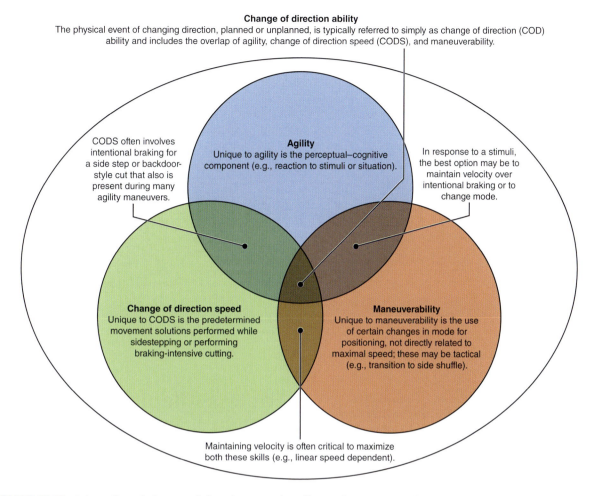

FIGURE 15.13 Interaction of change of direction speed, agility, and maneuverability.

Reprinted by permission from S. Nimphius, "Agility Training," in *High-Performance Training for Sports,* edited by D. Joyce and D. Lewindon (Champaign, IL: Human Kinetics, 2022).

process information and rapidly change direction in training and competitive environments. When considering agility, the coach must remember that various perceptual–cognitive abilities and the multiple physical qualities that underpin COD speed or maneuverability work in concert to maximize agility (figure 15.14) (208, 252, 321).

Perceptual-Cognitive Speed

A key aspect of the agility model presented in figure 15.14 is the effect of perceptual–cognitive speed on an athlete's agility (208). The importance of perceptual–cognitive speed is most noted during competition; the athlete must be able to visually scan the field, recognize patterns based on their tactical knowledge, and then rapidly change direction based on the information gathered (35, 192, 208, 217). In fact, Menezes and colleagues (192) suggest that the ability to rapidly diagnose a tactical situation and then maneuver into position is a key characteristic of some of the world's best team sport athletes. In some instances, a highly developed perceptual–cognitive speed can offset some physical deficits. This is most noted in older, more experienced players who may not be as physically gifted as their younger counterparts but are able to assess a tactical environment more rapidly prior to changing direction.

Due to their overall importance, these perceptual and cognitive skills must be developed when attempting to maximize an athlete's agility (208). Nimphius (208) suggests that these skills should be considered long-term athlete development goals that are primarily addressed in the coaching of sport skill, because this maximizes the ecological validity and translation into enhanced perceptual–

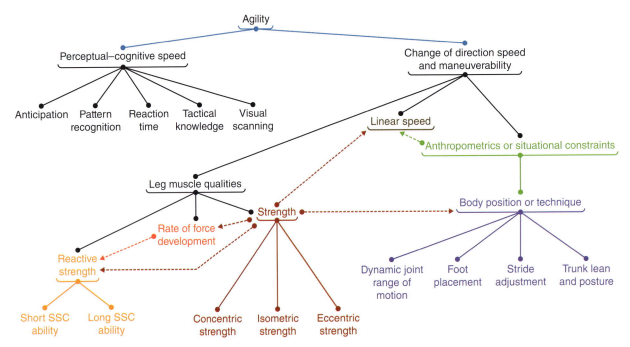

FIGURE 15.14 Model of components affecting agility.

cognitive performance in the competitive environment. Further support for this contention can be garnered from the reported differences in the information response during offensive and defensive agility movements (262). Because the brain processes offensive and defensive responses differently, training activities must engage the athlete in relevant tactical decisions to train the perceptual–cognitive and neuromuscular aspects of agility in ways that directly translate into optimized performance in the competitive environment (208).

An athlete's perceptual and cognitive training can be enhanced in many ways (217). At the center of this training is the athlete's understanding of the tactics of their sport and the details of both offensive and defensive strategies. This is largely based on experience but can be developed or enhanced with activities such as film study (217). In addition, the athlete should be exposed to open-skill agility activities that train decision making and COD performance simultaneously (35). These activities include **reactive agility drills**, in which the athlete must respond to visual or auditory stimuli as part of the agility training session. Open-skill agility also can be implemented as part of a small-sided game (SSG) that requires high-speed decisions and sport-specific movements. Paul and colleagues (217) suggest that SSGs are a superior method for developing agility performance due to the speed of decision making required in the small, confined areas typically used to create SSGs.

Factors Affecting Change of Direction Speed and Maneuverability

When considering COD speed and maneuverability, the coach must understand the effects of linear speed, leg muscle qualities, and the technique employed (figure 15.14) (71, 252, 321).

Linear Speed

Many coaches think linear speed is a primary determinant of an athlete's COD speed (252) or maneuverability. Although maximal sprinting speed is related, it explains only a small amount of the variability seen in COD performances (208, 209, 252, 321, 322). Therefore, linear speed and COD speed should be considered distinct locomotor skills (295, 317) that require specific targeted training activities (252, 322).

In the transfer of training effects from linear speed training to agility performance, the more complex the agility task, the less linear speed will transfer to the task (322). In most instances, focusing only on linear speed development will result in virtually no improvement in multidirectional COD task performance (252, 322). An additional consideration that can enhance the transfer of training effect is the inclusion of the ball or other implement (e.g., hockey stick, lacrosse stick) into the training process. The inclusion of these objects can significantly alter the athlete's ability to perform multidirectional COD tasks (252, 322) and straight-line running tasks (317). Therefore, to maximize COD speed and maneuverability, the athlete must engage in training activities that include straight-line sprinting and a variety of COD tasks (319, 322) with and without implements (e.g., balls, hockey sticks) (317).

Leg Muscle Qualities

Strength, RFD, and **reactive strength** all exert an influence on the athlete's COD speed and maneuverability (71, 168, 252, 321). For example, maximal lower body strength has been reported to be highly correlated ($r = -.70$, $p < .01$) to COD performance, with the back squat explaining 51% of the variance in performance (e.g., 505 agility test) and the combination of the back squat and deadlift explaining 56% of the variance in performance (278). Additionally, Townsend and colleagues (285) reported that isometric peak force explains 43% of the variance on the pro agility test and 27% of the variance on the Lane Agility test. When the body of literature is critically evaluated, depending on the strength and agility tests used, strength measures can explain between 10% to 79% of the variance in an athlete's COD performance (276). Clearly, based on these data, strength is an important attribute that must be developed if one wishes to maximize COD abilities.

Although maximal strength plays a major role in COD performance, due to the relatively short time required to apply force during COD activities, the ability to express high RFD likely exerts a greater influence on the athlete's ability to perform these activities (276). When examining COD performance, the plant phase can range between 23 and 77 milliseconds depending on the entry velocity and severity of the COD angle required (181, 262, 263). Therefore, the ability to express high forces in periods that last between 0 and 150 milliseconds is of greater importance. In support of this contention, Wang and colleagues (299) reported significant correlations between RFD at 0 to 30 milliseconds ($r = -.518$, $p = .048$), 0 to 50 milliseconds ($r = -.528$, $p = .044$), 0 to 90 milliseconds ($r = -.528$, $p = .043$), 0 to 100 milliseconds ($r = -.518$, $p = .048$), and the peak RFD ($r = -.523$, $p = .045$) and COD performance. Due to these significant relationships, athletes should employ training activities, such as weightlifting, weightlifting derivatives, and plyometrics (114), to maximize their abilities to express high RFD.

In addition to maximal strength and the RFD, the ability to express high levels of reactive strength is important when attempting to maximize COD ability (95, 135, 321). Reactive strength represents the athlete's ability to effectively employ the SSC, which is the ability of the musculotendinous unit to produce a rapid and forceful concentric muscle action immediately following a rapid eccentric muscle action (135). This series of actions often occurs in response to impact forces that induce a stretch response (145, 289). The magnitude of the impact forces and the athlete's ability to tolerate them will dictate the nature of the SSC (i.e., short/fast ≤250 ms or long/slow >250 ms) (135, 243). Ultimately, reactive strength represents the athlete's ability to produce force rapidly, which is commonly associated with COD (189), sprint (237), and jump (32, 297) performance.

The **reactive strength index (RSI)** is a metric used to quantify the athlete's ability to use the SSC (314) and is typically measured using a drop jump (180) or repeated jump (163) test. Key goals of the task, regardless of the test, are to minimize ground contact time and maximize the displacement of the jump (be it vertical or horizontal) (135, 314), which are similar to the cutting steps associated with COD performances (76). During a COD task, the ability to engage the SSC in response to an eccentric load results in greater forces being generated during the concentric phase of the COD task (144), resulting in a more rapid acceleration when changing direction. Support for the importance of reactive strength can be found in a recent meta-analysis by Jarvis and colleagues (135) in which the RSI was determined to be significantly associated with COD speed ($r = -.565$, $p < .0001$).

Based on the available data, it is evident that to maximize COD speed and maneuverability, the athlete must maximize their maximal strength, RFD, and reactive strength. These physical capacities can be addressed with sound strength and conditioning methods, including targeted strength development with multijoint exercises, such as squatting and weightlifting derivatives, as well as plyometric training activities (96, 130).

Technique

In most sports, athletes constantly vary their body postures in response to situational or tactical scenarios or to change the pace or direction of play (208). To illustrate the various movements that contribute to COD ability, Nimphius and Kadlec (210) provided a framework that relates the mode of travel, transitional movements, and cut-style COD (figure 15.15). This framework clearly illustrates that agility cannot be trained through a single technique because numerous factors contribute to overall COD ability (71).

Modes of travel	Transitional movements	Cut-style COD
Typically form part of many CODS tests (linear) or maneuverability tests (curvilinear or different mode other than linear)	Often link various modes of travel, change velocities, or change orientation of body	The "typified" COD with higher deceleration prior to or within COD intended to evade or react. Very effective but often discussed due to injury risk.

• Forward linear running*
  • Normal
  • With trunk rotations
• Curvilinear running
  • Single curve with various bends
  • Multiple curves (e.g., Illinois Agility)
• Backward running (backpedaling)
• Lateral shuffling
  • Without crossover
  • With crossover
	• Linear running with change in speeds
	  • Jog-sprint-jog
	  • Walk-sprint-jog
	  • Any additional variations
	• Acceleration from various start positions
	  • Front-on
	  • Side-on
	    • Crossover step**
	    • Drop step**
	  • Backward
	  • Ground based
	• Transition to and from linear running
	  • Lateral movements
	  • Backpedaling
		• Side step
		  • Various angles less than 90°
		  • With various entry velocities
		  • With varying penultimate braking
		• Crossover step
		  • Typically with less than 45°
		  • Variations as above
		• Backdoor or cut-back
		  • Angles greater than 90° (cut-back)
		  • Backdoor typified by 180°
		  • Variations as above

→ Increasing complexity of movement due to combining modes of travel or increasing joint loading in early stance of cutting

*Maximal sprinting (part of linear running development) will have the highest joint loading, but it is rare to transition while at maximal speed or change direction at maximal speed; therefore, the increasing progression arrow is in context of typical speeds prior to COD and from a skill acquisition perspective and is not intended to be strict in progression but dependent on athlete limitations and context.

**It is not recommended to coach the feet or these movements. Use of constraints (e.g., back or face against wall taking away ability to drop step and crossover option respectively) will allow the athlete to develop a movement solution for the situation. This approach will increase athlete autonomy and likelihood of transfer into actual situations in the absence of coaching or verbal instruction.

FIGURE 15.15 Physical movements related to COD ability.

Reprinted by permission from S. Nimphius and D. Kadlec, "Framework for Different Physical Movements that Relate to Overarching Change of Direction Ability," *Figure Share* (2020), https://doi.org/10.6084/m6089.figshare.11589486.v11589481. Distributed under the terms of the Creative Commons Attribution 4.0 International License (http://creativecommons.org/licenses/by/4.0/).

Although COD ability is a complex interaction of a variety of movements, the athlete's body position during braking and reacceleration, leg action, and arm action all affect the ability to express high levels of agility (71). As the athlete decelerates, they will decrease their stride rate and increase their body lean to allow their base of support to move farther from their center of gravity (226). As they enter the stance phase, they will reorient their trunk and hips toward the direction of intended travel to facilitate reacceleration on completing the COD (49). A key aspect of this series of events is to ensure alignment of the ankle, knee, and hip through to the trunk and shoulders (71). Additionally, as the athlete enters or exits the COD, the body's center of mass is lowered. If performing a side-shuffling COD, this lowered center of gravity is essential (253). Ultimately, these series of movements allow the athlete to maintain dynamic stability (226) while facilitating a rapid COD (252).

An additional consideration is the actions of the arms (71), which are a fundamental component of multidirectional movement (225, 226). The actions of the arms should not cause a decrease in speed or movement efficiency but should contribute to leg drive (71, 225, 226). An inefficient arm drive, whether because of poor arm mechanics or a mistimed movement pattern, can decrease speed, resulting in an overall reduction in the COD speed (71).

Central to effective COD mechanics is the ability to effectively dissipate and tolerate the eccentric braking loads through an effective knee range of motion (76, 260, 262). Different braking strategies and techniques will be used depending on different angled directional changes (figure 15.16) (76). Ultimately, the sharper the angle required during the COD, the greater the eccentric braking load (76) and the greater the importance of eccentric strength levels (265). The ability to tolerate the eccentric loads associated with a COD is related to overall strength levels (128) and the technique used to perform the COD task (225, 226).

Physiological Considerations of Change of Direction and Agility

In addition to the physiological factors associated with speed development, DeWeese and Nimphius (71) highlight several additional factors associated with COD and agility performance. First, they note that the ground contact times during the acceleration (0.17-2.0 s) (8) and maximal velocity (0.09-0.11 s) phases during sprinting (303, 304) are shorter than

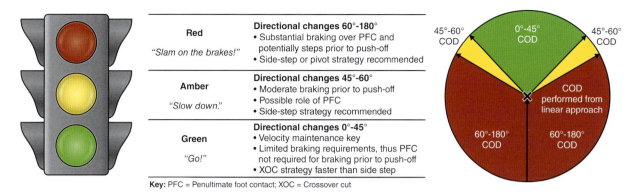

FIGURE 15.16 Traffic light system indicating braking strategy and COD technique strategies.

Reprinted by permission from T. Dos'Santos, C. Thomas, P. Comfort, and P.A. Jones, "The Effect of Angle and Velocity on Change of Direction Biomechanics: An Angle-Velocity Trade-Off," *Sports Medicine* 48 (2018): 2243. Distributed under the terms of the Creative Commons Attribution 4.0 International License (http://creativecommons.org/licenses/by/4.0/).

those reported during the plant phase in COD (0.44-0.72 s) (20, 181) or agility (0.23-0.25 s) (71) performances. Therefore, they suggest that most COD and agility performances engage longer-duration SSC activities (71). Second, they highlight that effective braking is a critical aspect of agility performance (262, 264) and that training strategies that include high-velocity and high-force eccentric muscle actions are necessary when targeting the enhancement of COD and agility performances (71). Finally, they highlight the collective effects of visual search scanning, anticipation, decision making, reaction time (251), and tactical situations (i.e., offensive versus defensive tactics) on the perceptual–cognitive demands associated with agility and the effect on the brain strategy required (71, 261, 266).

Programming Considerations

The development of a speed- or agility-based training program requires the coach to plan at several distinct levels, including the annual training plan, macrocycle, mesocycle, and microcycle (35). Central to this planning process is considering the requirements of the athlete's sport (99) and the time allotted for speed and agility development. As part of the programming process, the coach must consider each variable of training both individually and in the context of the collective training process (71). Additionally, the coach must consider the athlete's needs, the athlete's responsiveness to training, and the feedback from an integrated monitoring program when manipulating the key programming variables associated with speed and agility training (71).

Basic Principles of Speed and Agility Development

When designing training programs that target speed and agility, the coach must consider several basic principles to maximize effectiveness (72).

Quality of Training

Speed and agility training activities are physiologically stressful to the athlete (72) and must be meticulously and systematically programmed (226). Programming strategies must emphasize the quality of training while managing the associated fatigue. Typically, training is structured with brief work bouts and frequent rest periods to maximize the quality of learning and training effects (226).

The coach must ensure that the athlete consistently uses appropriate techniques in all training activities; the quality of training is of the utmost importance. An additional consideration is that speed and agility training should not be performed under fatigue or with excessively short rest intervals (226). If possible, it is beneficial to distribute daily training activities into training units separated by long recovery breaks or subdivided into bouts of work that are implemented as small clusters separated by frequent rest pauses (226). Additionally, the coach must ensure that the athlete is focused on developing disciplined habits that facilitate high-quality training.

Technical Precision

When implementing speed and agility training activities, the coach must ensure technical precision in all training drills and activities (72). The coach must continuously reinforce the axiom "how you do small things is how you do all things," because using sloppy or poor technique during warm-ups, sprint training, plyometrics, or strength training can negatively affect the development of speed and agility.

Conceptually, if the athlete performs a drill with inefficient or poor technique, they will be practicing and potentially stabilizing this inappropriate movement pattern. If this occurs regularly, the ability to maximize or optimize the expression of high-speed movement or agility can become compromised (35). To ensure this does not occur, the coach must provide the athlete with adequate rest to avoid excessive fatigue and also must provide the athlete with appropriate technical cues (23).

Specificity of Speed and Agility Training

As with all training activities, the principles of specificity apply to the development of both speed and agility. The demands of the sport should drive not only the bioenergetic characteristics of the training activities but also the decisions about the types of drills and strength training that will be implemented (71). For example, in American football, the ability to rapidly accelerate and change direction are key aspects of elite performance (175). Therefore, the speed and agility program should focus on maximizing acceleration, deceleration, and the ability to rapidly change direction in response to an external stimulus. Additionally, due to the importance of maximal strength and the RFD to both acceleration and COD performance, the strength-training program should focus on developing these characteristics.

Although rugby also requires an ability to rapidly accelerate and change direction, the characteristics of the sport require different agility-based training activities (249). It may also be warranted to include speed and agility training activities that require the rugby player to carry and pass the ball to increase the degree of sport specificity in the training activities (245). Although including the ball in both speed and agility training activities is important, the coach must remember that this would only be implemented after specific skills and performance capacities are mastered in a controlled environment (71). The coach should consider speed and agility as being developed across a continuum or framework that progresses from basic to advanced skill sets.

Multifactorial Development

The athlete's ability to perform high-speed and agile movements is affected by numerous factors, including maximal strength, RFD, and impulse (72, 208, 252, 321), as well as the programming and periodization strategies employed (71). Therefore, the importance of integrating strength training into the athlete's overall sprint and agility training plan cannot be underestimated and must be considered foundational to speed and agility development.

The coach must also consider the bioenergetic demands of the various sprint and agility training methods integrated into the training plan and how these activities relate to the competitive activity (35). Understanding the physiological and bioenergetic demands of the sport and aligning the training activities with these demands becomes increasingly important when developing speed endurance (see chapter 14) (227).

Instruction, Cueing, and Feedback

An essential aspect of the coaching process is the ability to communicate information to the athlete so performance can be enhanced (23). During practice or competition, this is generally accomplished through verbal instruction, cues, and feedback. Verbal communication should focus the athlete's attention on some key aspect of performance (23). The coach's language has a direct effect on how the athlete focuses during movement, so the coach must know what to say and when to say it so the athlete receives the appropriate information at the right time (311).

When using verbal instruction, the coach can use medium to long task-focused phrases (three or more words) delivered prior to the performance of a motor skill (23). For example, the coach may provide an externally focused instruction, such as "focus on explosively pushing the ground away," during the acceleration phase of a sprint. The use of externally focused instruction has been reported to be more effective at enhancing sprinting speed (23) and agility performance.

The coach may also use cues, which are short task-focused phrases (one to two words) delivered prior to or during the performance of a motor skill (23). For example, the coach might use action verbs, such as *explode*, *push*, or *drive*, to focus the athlete's attention (23, 311). Cues are powerful tools because they are usually the last thing the coach instructs the athlete to focus on prior to movement (311). Winkelman (311) suggests that coaches give only one cue at a time so as not to overload the athlete's working memory. Additionally, the coach should deliver an external cue, because this focuses that athlete's intention in relation to the environment they are trying to navigate (311). Finally, the coach must align their cues to the athlete's needs.

In addition to instruction and cues, the coach must give the athlete subjective and objective feedback throughout the training process (23, 35, 72). For example, subjective feedback can include perceptions of maximum speed, and objective feedback can be given as recorded times or video analysis of performance (72). Regular video feedback has been linked to positive changes in COD (70, 75) and sprint (80) technique. However, video feedback should be used sparingly and with a specific purpose. Using video feedback excessively may compromise the athlete's long-term development (36).

Motivation and Discipline

Motivation is a central component underpinning the development of speed and agility (72). Due to the high intensities and the potential fatigue associated with this type of training, especially when targeting speed endurance (225, 226), the athlete needs a high degree of motivation to endure the effort required to increase performance (288). Ultimately, motivation is fostered by a sense of purpose (273, 288) that fuels the athlete's desire to undertake the prescribed training (42). Although motivation is important to the training process, it is not without limits. Without discipline and the habits that come from a disciplined approach to the training process, the athlete will not be able to maximize speed and agility performance capacity, regardless of how motivated they are (42).

Programming Variables

When constructing a speed, speed–endurance, or agility-based training program, the coach must consider several key factors, including the frequency of training, density of training, duration and distance of the prescribed training, intensity of training, volume of training, exercise order, and rest intervals used during each training session. Through the appropriate manipulation of these factors, the coach can better direct the athlete's training process and ensure training is appropriately integrated and sequenced within the periodized training plan.

Frequency

The number of training sessions during a defined time (e.g., a day, microcycle, or mesocycle) is the frequency of training (71, 226). Speed training is typically performed two or three times per week depending on the focus of the training block that contains the speed training and the focus of the athlete's training program.

As few as two 15-minute agility training sessions per week can result in significant improvements in agility performance within 3 weeks of training (249). As noted by Jeffreys (138), these activities can easily be integrated into the athlete's warm-up prior to technical and tactical training sessions (see chapter 8). Alternatively, DeWeese and Nimphius (71) recommend one to three agility sessions per week depending on the focus of the training block.

Density

The training completed within a given period of time is the density of training (71, 72). When considering speed, speed–endurance, or agility training, the density of a training session is represented as the ratio of work to recovery contained in a set or series of repeated sprints or agility drills (71, 72, 226).

Duration and Distance

The two most common considerations when prescribing speed, speed–endurance, or agility training are the duration of the activity and the distance covered during the activity (226). For example, the coach can require the athlete to sprint 150 m (distance) in 22 seconds (duration), yielding a distance and duration from which the intensity and volume load of training can be calculated.

The primary bioenergetic pathway used during the activity is largely determined by the duration and distance covered during the activity (see chapter 2) (35). For example, the phosphagen system will supply most of the energy during short-duration or short-distance sprinting events used to develop acceleration or speed. Conversely, longer-distance and longer-duration activities will rely more on the oxidative system to meet energetic demands. Additionally, the rest period between bouts of sprint, speed–endurance, or agility training activities can influence which energetic system is the primary supplier of energy for the training activity.

The duration and distance covered can also be related to the targeted performance outcome. For example, shorter-duration and -distance sprinting activities, such as 10 to 40 m sprints, are often used to develop the athlete's ability to accelerate, whereas longer-distance sprinting activities, such as 50 to 60 m sprints, are often used to target maximal speed development (34). These activities can be incorporated into their own training sessions or into the sport-specific warm-up prior to technical and tactical training sessions (137).

Intensity

The intensity of speed, speed–endurance, or agility-based training activities is often quantified based on the maximal velocity or speed of movement (35):

$$\text{intensity (m} \cdot \text{s}^{-1}) = \frac{\text{distance (m)}}{\text{time (s)}}$$

Based on this equation, if an athlete sprints 200 m in 30 seconds, the intensity of this bout would be 6.7 m · s⁻¹. To alter the intensity of the bout, the coach can increase the distance of the run or decrease the time allotted to complete the activity. For example, if the time allotted to complete a 200 m sprint is decreased to 25 seconds, the intensity will increase to 8.0 m · s⁻¹. Alternatively, if the distance covered is reduced to 150 m and the time is held constant at 30 seconds, the intensity of the bout would decrease to 5.0 m · s⁻¹. This calculation can be used to either monitor or plan the intensity of training for the speed or agility session.

When designing a speed training session, the coach will prescribe training intensity zones based on the athlete's maximal sprinting speed (MSS) for a given distance (table 15.6).

To create the intensity zones, the coach takes the maximal intensity for the distance being trained and multiplies it by the targeted percentage:

$$\text{percentage maximum velocity (m} \cdot \text{s}^{-1}) =$$
$$\text{max intensity (m} \cdot \text{s}^{-1}) \times \text{percent}$$

If, for example, the athlete's MSS for a 150 m is 7.58 m · s⁻¹, their 90% intensity would be 6.82 m · s⁻¹:

$$90\% \text{ intensity (m} \cdot \text{s}^{-1}) =$$
$$7.58 \text{ (m} \cdot \text{s}^{-1}) \times 0.90 = 6.82 \text{ (m} \cdot \text{s}^{-1})$$

If the training session is prescribed to be in zone 5 (6.82-7.58 m · s⁻¹), the limits for the time allocated for each sprint would be calculated with the following equation:

$$\text{time (s)} = \frac{\text{distance (m)}}{\text{percentage maximum velocity (m} \cdot \text{s}^{-1})}$$

$$90\% \text{ training time (s)} = \frac{150 \text{ (m)}}{6.82 \text{ (m} \cdot \text{s}^{-1})} = 22.0 \text{ (s)}$$

Based on this equation, the session would require the athlete to complete each 150 m sprint in 19.8 to 22.0 seconds.

Ultimately, the coach can use these calculations to determine the average intensity of the speed training session (figure 15.17). If an agility training session is planned, the coach will need to adjust the calculation to account for the time it would take to complete each COD. This may be accomplished by adding 1 to 2 m to the total distance to account for the CODs in the drill (43).

Volume

The volume of a training session is represented by the number of repetitions completed at a prescribed intensity or for a specific task (106, 226). Although this method of quantifying volume gives a rough estimate of total work completed, a more accurate method of quantifying volume is to calculate volume load, which is the product of the intensity and distance completed per repetition (226). This metric estimates the total work completed or training stress associated with the speed and agility training session (106, 226).

Volume load is calculated based on running speed (i.e., intensity) and the distance covered (226) using the following equation:

$$\text{volume load (m}^2 \cdot \text{s}^{-1}) =$$
$$\text{velocity (m} \cdot \text{s}^{-1}) \times \text{distance (m)}$$

If, for example, an athlete completes a 150 m sprint in 6.82 m · s⁻¹, the volume load would be 1,022.73 m² · s⁻¹. If the distance of the sprint remains 150 m and the speed of the sprint is increased to 7.58 m · s⁻¹,

TABLE 15.6 Sprint Training Intensity Zones

Zone	Descriptor	Percentage	Velocity (m · s⁻¹)	Time (s)
6	Supramaximal	>100	>7.7	<13.0
5	Maximal	90-100	6.9-7.7	14.4-13.0
4	Heavy	80-89	6.2-6.8	16.3-14.6
3	Moderate	70-79	5.4-6.1	18.6-16.5
2	Low	60-69	4.6-5.3	21.7-18.8
1	Very low	<60	<4.6	>21.7

Note: Times are based on a best 100 m sprint time of 13 seconds.

Workout 1				Workout 2				Workout 3			
Best 250 m = 35.0 s Velocity = 7.14 m · s⁻¹				Best 200 m = 26.9 s Velocity = 7.43 m · s⁻¹				Best 150 m = 19.8 s Velocity = 7.58 m · s⁻¹			
Session intensity: Zone 3				Session intensity: Zone 4				Session intensity: Zone 5			
Distance (m)	Time (s)	Intensity (m · s⁻¹)	Volume load (A.U.)	Distance (m)	Time (s)	Intensity (m · s⁻¹)	Volume load (A.U.)	Distance (m)	Time (s)	Intensity (m · s⁻¹)	Volume load (A.U.)
250	44.3	5.64	1,410.84	200	30.2	6.62	1,324.50	150	19.8	7.58	1,136.36
250	45.0	5.56	1,388.89	200	31.5	6.35	1,269.84	150	20.1	7.46	1,119.40
250	46.3	5.40	1,349.89	200	32.0	6.25	1,250.00	150	20.5	7.32	1,097.56
				200	32.5	6.15	1,230.77	150	21.1	7.11	1,066.35
								150	21.9	6.85	1,027.40
Training intensity =	5.53			Training intensity =	6.34			Training intensity =	7.26		
Session volume load =	4,149.62			Session volume load =	5,075.11			Session volume load =	5,447.07		

FIGURE 15.17 Volume load and average intensity for sprint training sessions.

the volume load would increase to 1,136.36 m² · s⁻¹, representing an increase in workload.

Much like the volume load calculation in resistance training, this metric can be a valuable tool that allows the coach to estimate or monitor the total workload of a training session, referred to as the *training session volume load*. An example of how this calculation can be used to determine the workload associated with various training sessions is presented in figure 15.17. Ultimately, through programming variations in volume load, the coach can better manage the athlete's levels of fatigue while maximizing fitness and preparedness at predetermined times (35).

Exercise Order

When designing a speed, speed–endurance, and agility-based training program, a key factor to consider is the order of the exercises in each training session (226). Because speed and agility training activities have high metabolic, neuromuscular, and coordinative demands, their placement in a training session and training day must be carefully considered. Central to determining the order of training is the management of fatigue, because speed and agility training should be undertaken when the athlete has a minimal level of fatigue (150, 226). Therefore, sprint and agility training activities generally are done after the completion of a dynamic warm-up but prior to other training activities, such as sport-specific technical and tactical training (150, 226).

Ideally, athletes should engage in speed and agility training sessions when fully recovered after a day of rest or after a light technical training session that focuses on sprint and agility mechanics (150). For example, Bompa and Buzzichelli (34) suggest that speed training should be done in the morning after a rest day (e.g., 9:00 a.m.) with speed–endurance or strength training performed later in the day (e.g., 4:00 p.m.). When deciding on the order of training, the coach must consider the time needed for recovery after speed and agility training and the interaction of speed and agility training with other training activities.

For a speed and agility session, it is recommended to separate brief work periods with frequent rest intervals of 2 to 3 minutes or to use work-to-rest ratios of 1:12 or 1:20 (226). For a speed–endurance session, it is best to use the various HIIT methods explained in chapter 14.

Rest Intervals

The physiological stress and performance outcomes associated with speed, speed–endurance, or agility training can be influenced by manipulating the inter-repetition or inter-set rest intervals. When attempting to maximize speed development, longer rest intervals often are programmed to ensure the athlete is recovered and able to provide a maximal effort during each sprint (88). For example, to ensure an almost complete replenishment of stored phosphagens and a maximization of power output, longer rest intervals (work-to-rest ratio of 1:12-1:20) should be used when targeting maximal speed. When focusing on the development of high-intensity interval endurance, shorter rest intervals (work-to-rest ratio of 1:3-1:5) can be used (see chapter 14). Finally, when targeting the oxidative system, the shortest rest intervals (work-to-rest ratio of 1:0-1:3) are typically used (56, 126, 227).

A central factor in setting appropriate rest intervals for a training session is determining the targeted outcome and ensuring that the training activities align with the demands of the sport. For example, the work-to-rest intervals most commonly seen in American football are around 1:6 (227), whereas in soccer they are 1:7 to 1:8 (161) and in rugby they are 1:1 to 1.9 to 1 to 1.9:1 (78). By analyzing the work-to-rest ratios experienced by the athlete in competition, the coach can better align training activities with competitive demands and thus better prepare the athlete for the physical demands of competition.

Training Session Intensity

The overall intensity of a training session can be determined based on the total volume load and distance covered during the training session. This metric represents the average intensity of all the activities in the session and is calculated with the following equation:

$$\text{training intensity (m} \cdot \text{s}^{-1}) = \frac{\text{training session volume load (m}^2 \cdot \text{s}^{-1})}{\text{total distance covered (m)}}$$

Based on the example training sessions presented in figure 15.17, a volume load of 4,149.62 m² · s⁻¹ and a total distance of 750 m were completed in workout 1, resulting in a training intensity of 5.53 m · s⁻¹.

$$\text{training intensity (m} \cdot \text{s}^{-1}) = \frac{4,149.62 \ (\text{m}^2 \cdot \text{s}^{-1})}{750 \ (\text{m})} = 5.53 \ (\text{m} \cdot \text{s}^{-1})$$

Periodization Models: Speed and Agility Training

A periodized training program can be constructed in multiple ways to develop both speed and agility. The overall success of the periodized training program is predicated on how the training factors in the plan align with the specific goals established by the periods and phases of the macrocycle or annual training plan. The most common periodization models used for the development of speed and agility are sequential and emphasis periodization models (71, 85, 102).

Sequential Models of Periodization

The sequential model of periodization is based on the principle of delayed training effects; the training effects from one period can influence the responses to subsequent training periods (108, 109, 131, 132, 323). Fundamental to this concept is breaking training into focused mesocycle blocks that are then sequenced to drive adaptive responses and performance gains toward a predetermined training outcome.

Applying Sequential Models of Periodization to Speed Development

The development of speed generally occurs through the maturation of acceleration abilities prior to exposing the athlete to maximal velocity efforts (71). A basic sequential development pattern requires the athlete to develop their acceleration abilities followed by maximal speed development (71, 229). This model represents what is often referred to as the *short-to-long method* for developing speed (71, 85). DeWeese and Nimphius (71) suggest that when this model is implemented, the athlete begins the training year focused on improving propulsive forces via training activities that expose them to short sprints that are designed to improve the mechanics associated with the acceleration phase of the sprint. Later in the training year, the focus of the athlete's training transitions to longer sprint work to enhance maximal speed through the development of upright running mechanics (figure 15.18) (71). Central to this model is the belief that the greatest improvements in sprinting speed occur because of an optimization of the rate and timing of force application via the development of the athlete's ability to accelerate (71).

FIGURE 15.18 Sequential model for speed development.

Applying Sequential Models of Periodization to Agility Development

The development of agility requires periodized training strategies. Random programming or solely focusing on sport-specific methods, such as SSGs, are less effective strategies for developing and maximizing agility performance (31, 71). Generally, it is recommended to develop agility sequentially. Start by enhancing the physical capacities that underpin COD and agility performance and then leverage these capacities to develop COD mechanics and abilities with preplanned COD drills (figure 15.19) (208).

Once the athlete develops COD mechanics and abilities, focus shifts toward the development of agility with the application of specific agility drills (208, 316). After it is developed, agility is applied in sport-specific contexts through activities such as sport-specific drills like SSGs (316).

Although sequential periodization models are popular for developing speed and agility in amateur and professional sports around the world, these models may not be the best strategies for optimizing performance (85). As noted in chapter 5, a primary issue associated with using sequential models to target speed development is the reduction in fitness and strength that would be expected before the athlete is exposed to significant speed work, ultimately reducing the time the athlete is exposed to these high-speed training activities (85). Therefore, it is common for elite sprint coaches to not use pure sequential models of periodization and preferentially use various forms of emphasis modeling (124).

Emphasis Models of Periodization

The emphasis model of periodization may be ideally suited for the development of sprint and agility performance because it addresses some of the major issues associated with sequential models (71, 85). In this model, multiple training targets are simultaneously scheduled within the program, but the amount of time or volume allocated to each training target is manipulated to vertically integrate and horizontally sequence the training process.

Applying Emphasis Models of Periodization to Speed Development

The most noted example of the application of the emphasis model of periodization for speed development is Charlie Francis' vertical integration model (85). Francis used a short-to-long training model in which multiple training objects are targeted within a training period (85, 87). Key to this model is the use of polarized sprint training methods in which sprint training is performed at either 95% or greater maximal velocity (speed work) or less than 75% maximal velocity (tempo work) (85, 87, 124). This is done to avoid midrange intensities (~75%-95% of maximum), which Francis considered not beneficial for performance or recovery (85, 87). Additionally, plyometrics, strength training, core conditioning, and electromyostimulation are integrated into the periodized training plan (85, 87). A key aspect of this model is that all six training objects are simultaneously trained, and only the volumes of training allotted to each factor are manipulated within the microcycle or mesocycle (85, 87). This planning strategy allows the coach to ensure that the athlete is exposed to enough high-velocity running and allows the athlete to better maintain maximal strength and explosiveness.

Although the vertical integration model is a great example of an emphasis periodization model (85, 87), there are alternative ways to implement this model to better align with the athlete's needs (108, 110). For example, in a three mesocycle sequence, training activities focused on maximal strength, speed, power, and speed–endurance (i.e., plyometrics) are programmed with varying degrees of

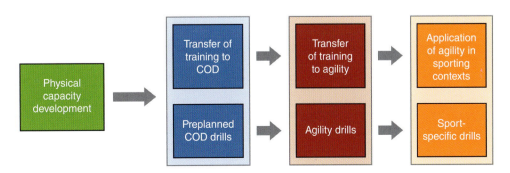

FIGURE 15.19 Sequential progression for agility development.

emphasis (figure 15.20). For example, in block 1, the primary focus of training is the development of maximal strength because it provides the foundation for speed development (71). During this block, the secondary and tertiary emphases focus on the maintenance of muscular power and speed development, whereas a minimum amount of training (quaternary focus) targets speed–endurance training. As the athlete moves to the next block of training, the focus shifts toward the development of muscular power and speed while strength and speed endurance receive maintenance loading. In the final block, the maximization of speed is the primary emphasis, and the development of speed–endurance is a secondary emphasis. At this time, both muscular power and maximal strength are targeted with maintenance loading strategies.

Ultimately, the emphasis model allows the athlete to target multiple training factors simultaneously with varying degrees of focus that shift to align with the demands of the periodized training plan (107, 109, 324). The strength of this model is that it is ideally suited for developing speed for sports with long competitive seasons because the blocks of training can be manipulated every 2 to 3 weeks to align with the competitive season.

Applying Emphasis Models of Periodization to Agility Development

Similar to speed development, the use of an emphasis model can be highly beneficial for the development of agility. Because maximal strength (i.e., eccentric and concentric), the RFD, and the ability to engage the SSC are critical aspects that underpin the development of COD abilities and agility, they should be integrated into any emphasis model of periodization that focuses on the development of agility. However, if only the interplay of COD ability, maneuverability, and agility is considered, these factors can be contextualized as part of a periodized training plan that uses an emphasis model. For example, if a 12-week training program was designed to improve high-velocity COD performance, maneuverability, and agility, a basic emphasis model of periodization could be employed to allocate training time to these targeted abilities (figure 15.21).

	Block 1	Block 2	Block 3
Primary focus	Maximal strength	Muscular power	Speed
Secondary focus	Muscular power	Speed	Speed–endurance
Tertiary focus	Speed	Maximal strength	Muscular power
Quaternary focus	Speed–endurance	Speed–endurance	Maximal strength
Duration (wk)	2-6	2-4	1-2

FIGURE 15.20 Emphasis model applied to sprint training.

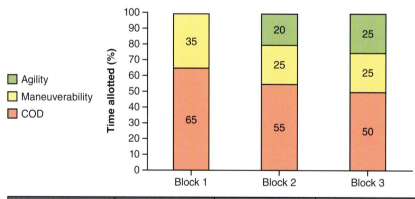

	Block 1	Block 2	Block 3
Primary focus	COD	COD	COD
Secondary focus	Maneuverability	Maneuverability	Agility
Tertiary focus		Agility	Maneuverability
Period	Preparation		Competition
Season	Off-season		Preseason
Duration (wk)	4	4	4
Sessions (per wk)	2-3	2-3	1-2

FIGURE 15.21 Emphasis model applied to agility training.
Data from DeWeese and Nimphius (2016).

Figure 15.21 shows three, 4-week blocks of training in which the amount of time allotted to COD ability, maneuverability, and agility is integrated and sequenced (71). For example, in block 1, 65% of the allotted training time is focused on developing COD ability, and the remaining time is used to develop maneuverability. In block 2, the amounts of time dedicated to COD ability (55%) and maneuverability (25%) are reduced to open time for agility training (20%). In the third block, the amount of time dedicated to COD ability (50%) is further reduced, time allocated to agility training (25%) is increased, and time spent focused on maneuverability remains constant (25%). Based on this basic sequence and integration plan, the coach can design specific training activities to target the development of these abilities to address the athlete's needs (71).

Periodization of Training: Integration of Training Factors

A central factor underpinning the successful development of speed and agility is the construction of a periodized training plan that integrates and sequences the key training factors associated with the targeted performance outcomes. Crucial to this process is the development of an annual training plan that provides the scaffolding and timelines required by the targeted sport. The macrocycles, mesocycles, and microcycles are designed based on the annual training plan.

As mentioned, the basic structure is dictated by the demands of the sport. For example, an elite sprinter will typically use a bi-cycle annual training plan (88), but a team sport athlete may not, depending on the sport and the league in which they compete (35). Various training targets can be emphasized or deemphasized in specific periods and phases of the sprinter's annual training plan. Figure 15.22 presents training targets for each phase of the sprinter's annual training plan. Based on this figure, the coach can select specific training activities (tables 15.5 and 15.7) to address the targeted emphasis. For example, in the specific preparation phase, anaerobic endurance can be targeted with short speed–endurance training activities. Ultimately, this is only an example of how various training factors could be integrated into the training plan for a sprint athlete.

The dynamics of the annual training plan are very different when working with team sports because the competition period is generally longer and dictated by the league or conference. Although there are many ways to construct an annual training plan in these situations, an emphasis model may be ideally suited for the optimization of performance during dense competitive periods. A basic example of how to integrate four training foci (strength, plyometric, speed, and agility training) into an annual training plan for a team sport is outlined in figure 15.23 (229).

For the speed development, a sequential progression is presented in which acceleration is developed in the general preparation phase, speed is maximized in the early part of the specific preparation phase, and speed–endurance is elevated in the late specific preparation phase and the precompetition phase. In the main competition phase, training is focused on maintaining speed

Period	Preparation		Competition
Phase	General preparation	Specific preparation	Main competition
Primary emphasis	General endurance	Anaerobic endurance	Speed
	Strength–endurance	Short speed–endurance	Short speed–endurance
	Running technique	General strength	Long speed–endurance
Secondary emphasis	Aerobic capacity	Specific strength	Special endurance
	Aerobic power	Speed	Tactics
	Flexibility	Running technique	Running technique
Tertiary emphasis	Speed	General endurance	General strength
	Anaerobic capacity	Aerobic power	Specific strength
		Anaerobic capacity	Flexibility
		Flexibility	Aerobic power

FIGURE 15.22 Integrated annual training plan for a sprinter.

Adapted from Freeman (2001); Bompa and Haff (2009).

TABLE 15.7 General Sprint Training Recommendations

Training method	Distance (m)	Intensity (%)	Recovery (min)	Total session volume (m)	Initiation	Time to next HIS (h)	Footwear and surface
Acceleration	10-50	>98	2-7	100-300	Block/three-point/crouched	48	Spikes on track
Maximal velocity	10-30a	>98	4-15	50-150a	20-40 m flying start	48-72	Spikes on track
Sprint-specific endurance	80-150	>95	8-30	300-900	Standing start	48-72	Spikes on track
Speed–endurance	60-80	90-95	2-4 (8-15)	600-2,000	Standing start	48-72	Spikes on track
Resisted sprints	10-30	80-95b	3-6	50-200	Three-point/crouched	48	Optional
Assisted sprints	10-30a	≤105	5-15	≤100a	20-40 m flying start	48	Spikes on track
Tempo	100-300	60-70	1-3	1,000-2,000	Standing start	24	Trainers on grass

Note: Intensity = a percentage of maximal velocity; recovery = time between repetitions (sets); HIS = high-intensity session.
aFlying distance is excluded.
bPerceived effort is maximal, so the velocity decline is caused by resistance loading.

Reprinted by permission from T. Haugen, S. Seiler, Ø. Sandbakk, et al., "The Training and Development of Elite Sprint Performance: An Integration of Scientific and Best Practice Literature," *Sports Medicine* Open 5, no. 44 (2019): 7. Distributed under the terms of the Creative Commons Attribution 4.0 International License (http://creativecommons.org/licenses/by/4.0/).

Period	Preparation		Competition	
Phase	General preparation	Specific preparation	Precompetition	Main competition
Strength training	Hypertrophy/strength–endurance	Maximal strength	Strength/power	Strength and power maintenance
Plyometric training	Basic jump and toss progressions	Bound and hop progressions	Combination and shock method progressions	Plyometric maintenance routines
Speed training	Acceleration	Speed	Speed–endurance	Speed maintenance routines
Agility training	Posture, balance, stability, and mobility progressions	Speed and power cut-specific progressions	Reactionary agility progressions	Sport-specific agility drills

FIGURE 15.23 Annual training plan integrating speed, agility, and strength training for a team sport.
Adapted by permission from J.C. Radcliffe, *Functional Training for Athletes at All Levels* (Berkeley, CA: Ulysses Press, 2007), 32.

throughout the competitive season. A sequential development pattern is also used for the development of agility. In the general preparation phase, agility development starts with posture, balance, stability, and mobility progressions that develop the physical literacy that underpins the ability to change direction and maximize agility. The early part of the specific preparation phase uses specific COD development strategies. As the athlete transitions into the later stages of the specific preparation and precompetition phases, reactive agility progressions become the primary focus. Note that strength and plyometric training are also integrated into the annual training plan (229).

In another example, Plisk (226) presents the preparation period for an emphasis model of periodization for a hypothetical university or professional American football program (figure 15.24). In this example, four training targets (i.e., strength, speed and agility, speed–endurance, and special endurance) are implemented with varying training frequencies and densities to rotate which training targets are emphasized within each mesocycle. For example, in the first 3-week mesocycle, 12 training sessions (4 per week) are dedicated to strength training (i.e., primary focus) and 6 training sessions (2 per week) are allotted to both speed and agility and speed–endurance training (i.e., secondary emphasis). Speed and agility and speed–endurance training are completed within the same session, with the focus varying between sessions, or in separate sessions depending on time constraints (35, 111, 226). In this block, speed–endurance is developed based on the principles of tactical metabolic training (227) with the use of HIIT strategies performed with short intervals (work = 10-60 s; rest = 100-60 s; intensity = 90%-105% V_{IFT}) (28).

For the second mesocycle, the emphasis of training shifts. The density and frequency of strength training is reduced to three sessions per microcycle (12 sessions over 4 microcycles), and the density and frequency of both speed and agility and speed–endurance training are increased (12 sessions, 3 per microcycle). In this mesocycle, the focus of the speed and agility training is to execute sound movement mechanics at submaximal speed, whereas speed–endurance training uses repeated sprint training methods (work = 3-10 s; rest = 15-60 s; intensity = all out).

In the third mesocycle, the emphasis on strength training increases (12 sessions, 4 per microcycle), and the density of both speed and agility and speed–endurance training (6 sessions per microcycle) decreases. In the fourth mesocycle, the density and frequency of strength training are reduced (12 sessions over 4 microcycles) and the objectives are the same as the third mesocycle. The special endurance training in this mesocycle uses HIIT training methods in which the work-to-rest intervals are aligned with those typically seen during an American football game (111, 226, 227). Density and frequency of both speed and agility training are increased and special endurance training is integrated into the mesocycle (12 sessions, 3 per microcycle).

Once the coach outlines the mesocycle structures, they can begin to construct the individual microcycles. A critical aspect of the organization of speed, agility, and speed–endurance training within the microcycle is managing fatigue (226). The coach must understand the effect of fatigue on the athlete's ability to perform speed- and

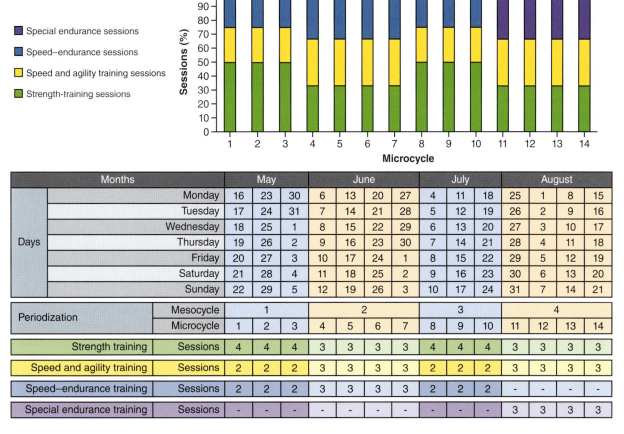

FIGURE 15.24 Emphasis periodization model applied to university or professional American football.
Adapted from Bompa and Haff (2009).

Month	Dates	Mesocycle	Weeks	Emphasis	Monday	Tuesday	Wednesday	Thursday	Friday	Saturday	Sunday
May	5/16 to 6/5	1	1-3	Strength training	Lower body	Upper body		Lower body	Upper body		
				Speed and agility training		▓			▓		
				Speed–endurance training			▓				
				Special endurance training							
June	6/6 to 7/3	2	4-7	Strength training	Mixed		Mixed		Mixed		
				Speed and agility training		▓		▓			
				Speed–endurance training			▓				
				Special endurance training							
July	7/4 to 7/24	3	8-10	Strength training	Lower body	Upper body		Lower body	Upper body		
				Speed and agility training		▓			▓		
				Speed–endurance training			▓		▓		
				Special endurance training							
August	7/25 to 8/21	4	11-14	Strength training	Mixed		Mixed		Mixed		
				Speed and agility training		▓		▓			
				Speed–endurance training							
				Special endurance training	▓				▓		

FIGURE 15.25 Mesocycle and microcycle breakdown for an emphasis periodization model applied to college or professional American football.

agility-based drills with appropriate technique (35). To ensure the athlete doesn't use poor technique, these activities should be performed under a minimum amount of fatigue, typically after a well-structured warm-up based on the raise, activate, mobilize, and potentiate protocols discussed in chapter 8. If time is available, multiple training sessions should be scheduled within the training day to minimize the effect of fatigue on training and maximize the quality of the speed and agility training sessions. For example, based on the American football example presented in figure 15.24, the coach can create a microcycle model (figure 15.25).

In this model, the frequency and density of training are altered to focus on different training targets within each mesocycle. When multiple training factors are targeted on the same training day, fatigue management becomes increasingly important. If possible, training targets should be split into distinct training sessions that are spaced throughout the training day.

Summary

In many sports, speed, agility, and speed–endurance are important components of competitive success. To optimally develop these abilities, the coach must understand the fundamental physiological and performance factors that underpin each ability. The coach must remember that maximal strength development serves as a foundation for the optimization of both speed and agility performance. An athlete who possesses inadequate strength levels will not be able to express high enough RFD and impulses to produce high-speed linear or multilinear speed. Although maximal strength development is essential for the long-term development of the athlete, specialized training activities, such as plyometrics and reactive strength training, are also necessary components of the training process. If these training activities are structured correctly and appropriately integrated into the athlete's training plan, they can provide a foundation for the development of speed, COD, maneuverability, and agility. In addition, high-speed running and sport-specific agility activities are also critical components of the athlete's training program.

The optimization of speed, COD, maneuverability, and agility is enhanced when these qualities are appropriately integrated and sequenced into a periodized training plan. Generally, sequential or emphasis periodization models are recommended for targeting development of these abilities. In most instances, emphasis models provide the best approach for integrating and sequencing training so detraining effects do not negatively affect the development of high-speed movement and agility.

APPENDIX

Training Session and Training Plan Templates

Training Session Template 442

Mesocycle Training Plan Template 443

Annual Training Plan Templates 444

Training Session Template

Athlete:	

Training session:		Session start time (HR:MIN)	
		Session stop time (HR:MIN)	
Date (month/day/year):			

| Location: | | Equipment needed | |

Objective:	

Element	Duration	Activities	Notes
Introduction			

Warm-up		Activity	Dosage	Notes

Main body		Activity	Dosage	Notes

Cool-down		Activity	Dosage	Notes

Session notes	

From G. Gregory Haff, *Scientific Foundations and Practical Applications of Periodization* (Champaign, IL: Human Kinetics, 2025).

Mesocycle Training Plan Template

Mesocycle template

Mesocycle #: _____ Dates: _____ to _____

Objectives/goals

Areas of focus	Foci and goals

Periodization

Training period		Notes:
Training phase		
Mesocycle type		
Number of microcycles		

	Microcycle number						Notes
	1	2	3	4	5	6	
Date of week start							
Peaking index (1-10)							
Total training time (hr:min)							
Average sRPE							
Total training load (A.U.)							
Testing dates/week							
Recovery weeks							

Technical and tactical training

	1	2	3	4	5	6	Notes
Technical primary focus							
Weekly sessions							
Total training time (hr:min)							
Tactical primary focus							
Weekly sessions							
Total training time (hr:min)							

Resistance training

	1	2	3	4	5	6	Notes
Primary focus							
Weekly sessions							
Total training time (hr:min)							
Daily sessions							
Average session time (hr:min)							

Plyometric training

	1	2	3	4	5	6	Notes
Primary focus							
Weekly sessions							
Total training time (hr:min)							
Average session time (hr:min)							
Total lower-body touches (#)							
Total upper-body touches (#)							

Agility and COD training

	1	2	3	4	5	6	Notes
Primary focus							
Weekly sessions							
Total training time (hr:min)							
Average session time (hr:min)							

Sprint training

	1	2	3	4	5	6	Notes
Primary focus							
Weekly sessions							
Total training time (hr:min)							
Average session time (hr:min)							

Metabolic conditioning

	1	2	3	4	5	6	Notes
Primary focus							
Weekly sessions							
Total training time (hr:min)							
Average session time (hr:min)							

From G. Gregory Haff, *Scientific Foundations and Practical Applications of Periodization* (Champaign, IL: Human Kinetics, 2025).

Annual Training Plan Templates

Example 1

			Performance goals							
Objectives										
Macrocycle										
Period										
Phase										
Month										
	Monday									
	Tuesday									
	Wednesday									
	Thursday									
	Friday									
	Saturday									
	Sunday									
	Week		1	2	3	4	5	6	7	8
Peaking index										
Competition calendar	Opponent	Competition 1								
		Home								
		Away								
		Date								
		Location								
		Travel method								
		Competition 2								
		Home								
		Away								
		Date								
		Location								
		Travel method								
		Competition 3								
		Home								
		Away								
		Date								
		Location								
		Travel method								
Training camp										
Holiday/vacation										
Performance testing										
Medical screening										
Mesocycle										
		Mesocycle type								
Microcycle			1	2	3	4	5	6	7	8
		Microcycle type								
Periodization	Technical and tactical training	Tactical training								
		Technical training								
	Physical training	Resistance training								
		Metabolic conditioning								
		Speed training								
		Agility and COD training								
		Plyometric training								
	Nutrition, psychology, and recovery	Nutrition focus								
		Psychological training								
		Recovery method focus								

Training factors	Peaking index	%								
Volume	1	100								
Intensity	2	90								
Peaking	3	80								
Physical prep	4	70								
Technical prep	5	60								
Tactical prep	6	50								
Psych prep	7	40								
	8	30								
	9	20								
	10	10								

From G. Gregory Haff, *Scientific Foundations and Practical Applications of Periodization* (Champaign, IL: Human Kinetics, 2025).

Annual Training Plan Templates
Example 2

			Performance goals							
Competition calendar	Objectives									
	Macrocycle									
	Period									
	Phase									
	Month									
		Monday								
		Tuesday								
		Wednesday								
		Thursday								
		Friday								
		Saturday								
		Sunday								
		Week	1	2	3	4	5	6	7	8
	Peaking index									
	Opponent	Competition 1								
		Home								
		Away								
		Date								
		Location								
		Travel method								
	Training camp									
	Holiday/vacation									
	Performance testing									
	Medical screening									
	Mesocycle									
		Mesocycle type								
	Microcycle		1	2	3	4	5	6	7	8
		Microcycle type								
Periodization	Technical and tactical training	Tactical training								
		Technical training								
	Physical training	Resistance training								
		Metabolic conditioning								
		Speed training								
		Agility and COD training								
		Plyometric training								
	Nutrition, psychology, and recovery	Nutrition focus								
		Psychological training								
		Recovery method focus								

Training factors	Peaking index	%
Volume	1	100
Intensity	2	90
Peaking	3	80
Physical prep	4	70
Technical prep	5	60
Tactical prep	6	50
Psych prep	7	40
	8	30
	9	20
	10	10

From G. Gregory Haff, *Scientific Foundations and Practical Applications of Periodization* (Champaign, IL: Human Kinetics, 2025).

Annual Training Plan Templates

Example 3

			Performance goals							
	Objectives									
	Macrocycle									
	Period										
	Phase										
	Month										
		Monday									
		Tuesday									
		Wednesday									
		Thursday									
		Friday									
		Saturday									
		Sunday									
		Week	1	2	3	4	5	6	7	8
	Peaking index									
Competition calendar	Opponent	Competition 1								
		Home									
		Away									
		Date									
		Location									
		Travel method									
		Competition 2									
		Home									
		Away									
		Date									
		Location									
		Travel method									
		Competition 3									
		Home									
		Away									
		Date									
		Location									
		Travel method									
	Training camp										
	Holiday/vacation										
	Performance testing										
	Medical screening										
	Mesocycle										
		Mesocycle type									
	Microcycle		1	2	3	4	5	6	7	8
		Microcycle type									
Organization of training factors	Tactical training										
		Focus									
		Number of sessions									
		Total time (min:s)									
		Average sRPE									
		Training load (A.U.)									
	Technical training										
		Focus									
		Number of sessions									
		Total time (min:s)									
		Average sRPE									
		Training load (A.U.)									

Organization of training factors (cont.)

Resistance training	Focus									
	Number of sessions									
	Total time (min:s)									
	Main exercises									
	Sets									
	Reps									
	Intensity									
	Assistance exercises									
	Sets									
	Reps									
	Intensity									
	Average sRPE									
	Training load (A.U.)									
High-intensity interval training	Focus									
	Total time (min:s)									
	Number of sessions									
	Long interval (#)									
	Type 1									
	Type 2									
	Type 3									
	Type 4									
	Type 5									
	Type 6									
	Short interval (#)									
	Type 1									
	Type 2									
	Type 3									
	Type 4									
	Type 5									
	Type 6									
	Repeated sprint training (#)									
	Type 1									
	Type 2									
	Type 3									
	Type 4									
	Type 5									
	Type 6									
	Sprint interval training (#)									
	Type 1									
	Type 2									
	Type 3									
	Type 4									
	Type 5									
	Type 6									
	Small-sided games (#)									
	Type 1									
	Type 2									
	Type 3									
	Type 4									
	Type 5									
	Type 6									
	Average sRPE									
	Training load (A.U.)									
Plyometric training	Focus									
	Number of sessions									
	Total time (min:s)									
	Total touches									
	Lower body									
	Upper body									
	Average sRPE									
	Training load (A.U.)									
Agility and COD	Focus									
	Total time (min:s)									
	Number of sessions									
	Agility									
	COD									
	Average sRPE									
	Training load (A.U.)									
	Average sRPE									
	Total training load (A.U.)									
	Monotony (A.U.)									
	Strain (A.U.)									

Training factors		Peaking index	%							
Training load	——	1	100							
Monotony	– – –	2	90							
Strain	····	3	80							
Peaking index	▬▬	4	70							
		5	60							
		6	50							
		7	40							
		8	30							
		9	20							
		10	10							

From G. Gregory Haff, *Scientific Foundations and Practical Applications of Periodization* (Champaign, IL: Human Kinetics, 2025).

Annual Training Plan Templates

Example 4

		Performance goals							
Competition calendar	Objectives								
	Macrocycle								
	Period								
	Phase								
	Month								
	Monday								
	Tuesday								
	Wednesday								
	Thursday								
	Friday								
	Saturday								
	Sunday								
	Week	1	2	3	4	5	6	7	8
	Peaking index								
	Opponent — Competition 1 — Home								
	Away								
	Date								
	Location								
	Travel method								
	Competition 2 — Home								
	Away								
	Date								
	Location								
	Travel method								
	Competition 3 — Home								
	Away								
	Date								
	Location								
	Travel method								
	Training camp								
	Holiday/vacation								
	Performance testing								
	Medical screening								
	Mesocycle								
	Mesocycle type								
	Microcycle	1	2	3	4	5	6	7	8
	Microcycle type								
Organization of training factors	Tactical training								
	Focus								
	Number of sessions								
	Total time (min:s)								
	Average sRPE								
	Training load (A.U.)								
	Technical training								
	Focus								
	Number of sessions								
	Total time (min:s)								
	Average sRPE								
	Training load (A.U.)								

Appendix

Organization of training factors (cont.)

Resistance training
Focus	
Number of sessions	
Total time (min:s)	
Main exercises	
Sets	
Reps	
Intensity	
Assistance exercises	
Sets	
Reps	
Intensity	
Average sRPE	
Training load (A.U.)	

High-intensity interval training
Focus	
Total time (min:s)	
Number of sessions	
Long interval (#)	
Short interval (#)	
Repeated sprint training (#)	
Sprint interval training (#)	
Small-sided games (#)	
Average sRPE	
Training load (A.U.)	

Plyometric training
Focus	
Number of sessions	
Total time (min:s)	
Total touches	
Lower body	
Upper body	
Average sRPE	
Training load (A.U.)	

Agility and COD
Focus	
Total time (min:s)	
Number of sessions	
Agility	
COD	
Average sRPE	
Training load (A.U.)	

Summary
Average sRPE	
Total training load (A.U.)	
Monotony (A.U.)	
Strain (A.U.)	

Training factors

Training factors	Peaking index	%
Training load —	1	100
Monotony - - -	2	90
Strain ⋯⋯	3	80
Peaking index ▬	4	70
	5	60
	6	50
	7	40
	8	30
	9	20
	10	10

From G. Gregory Haff, *Scientific Foundations and Practical Applications of Periodization* (Champaign, IL: Human Kinetics, 2025).

Annual Training Plan Templates

Example 5

			Performance goals							
Competition calendar	**Objectives**									
	Macrocycle									
	Period									
	Phase									
	Month									
		Monday								
		Tuesday								
		Wednesday								
		Thursday								
		Friday								
		Saturday								
		Sunday								
		Week	1	2	3	4	5	6	7	8
	Peaking index									
	Opponent	Competition 1								
		Home								
		Away								
		Date								
		Location								
		Travel method								
	Training camp									
	Holiday/vacation									
	Performance testing									
	Medical screening									
	Mesocycle									
		Mesocycle type								
	Microcycle		1	2	3	4	5	6	7	8
		Microcycle type								
Organization of training factors	**Tactical training**									
		Focus								
		Number of sessions								
		Total time (min:s)								
		Average sRPE								
		Training load (A.U.)								
	Technical training									
		Focus								
		Number of sessions								
		Total time (min:s)								
		Average sRPE								
		Training load (A.U.)								
	Resistance training	Focus								
		Number of sessions								
		Total time (min:s)								
		Main exercises								
		Sets								
		Reps								
		Intensity								
		Assistance exercises								
		Sets								
		Reps								
		Intensity								
		Average sRPE								
		Training load (A.U.)								

Organization of training factors (cont.)	**High-intensity interval training**	Focus								
		Total time (min:s)								
		Number of sessions								
		Long interval (#)								
		Type 1								
		Type 2								
		Type 3								
		Type 4								
		Type 5								
		Type 6								
		Short interval (#)								
		Type 1								
		Type 2								
		Type 3								
		Type 4								
		Type 5								
		Type 6								
		Repeated sprint training (#)								
		Type 1								
		Type 2								
		Type 3								
		Type 4								
		Type 5								
		Type 6								
		Sprint interval training (#)								
		Type 1								
		Type 2								
		Type 3								
		Type 4								
		Type 5								
		Type 6								
		Small-sided games (#)								
		Type 1								
		Type 2								
		Type 3								
		Type 4								
		Type 5								
		Type 6								
		Average sRPE								
		Training load (A.U.)								
	Plyometric training	Focus								
		Number of sessions								
		Total time (min:s)								
		Total touches								
		Lower body								
		Upper body								
		Average sRPE								
		Training load (A.U.)								
	Agility and COD	Focus								
		Total time (min:s)								
		Number of sessions								
		Agility								
		COD								
		Average sRPE								
		Training load (A.U.)								
		Average sRPE								
		Total training load (A.U.)								
		Monotony (A.U.)								
		Strain (A.U.)								

Training factors	Peaking index	%							
Training load ——	1	100							
Monotony – – –	2	90							
Strain ▪▪▪▪	3	80							
Peaking index ▬	4	70							
	5	60							
	6	50							
	7	40							
	8	30							
	9	20							
	10	10							

From G. Gregory Haff, *Scientific Foundations and Practical Applications of Periodization* (Champaign, IL: Human Kinetics, 2025).

Annual Training Plan Templates
Example 6

			Performance goals							
Competition calendar	**Objectives**									
	Macrocycle									
	Period									
	Phase									
	Month									
		Monday								
		Tuesday								
		Wednesday								
		Thursday								
		Friday								
		Saturday								
		Sunday								
		Week	1	2	3	4	5	6	7	8
	Peaking index									
	Opponent	Competition 1								
		Home								
		Away								
		Date								
		Location								
		Travel method								
	Training camp									
	Holiday/vacation									
	Performance testing									
	Medical screening									
	Mesocycle									
		Mesocycle type								
	Microcycle		1	2	3	4	5	6	7	8
		Microcycle type								
Organization of training factors	Tactical training									
	Focus									
	Number of sessions									
	Total time (min:s)									
	Average sRPE									
	Training load (A.U.)									
	Technical training									
	Focus									
	Number of sessions									
	Total time (min:s)									
	Average sRPE									
	Training load (A.U.)									

Organization of training factors (cont.)

Resistance training
Focus	
Number of sessions	
Total time (min:s)	
Main exercises	
Sets	
Reps	
Intensity	
Assistance exercises	
Sets	
Reps	
Intensity	
Average sRPE	
Training load (A.U.)	

High-intensity interval training
Focus	
Number of sessions	
Long interval (#)	
Short interval (#)	
Repeated sprint training (#)	
Sprint interval training (#)	
Small-sided games (#)	
Total time (min:s)	
Average sRPE	
Training load (A.U.)	

Plyometric training
Focus	
Number of sessions	
Total time (min:s)	
Total touches	
Lower body	
Upper body	
Average sRPE	
Training load (A.U.)	

Agility and COD
Focus	
Number of sessions	
Agility	
COD	
Total time (min:s)	
Average sRPE	
Training load (A.U.)	

Average sRPE	
Total training load (A.U.)	
Monotony (A.U.)	
Strain (A.U.)	

Training factors	Peaking index	%
Training load —	1	100
Monotony – – –	2	90
Strain ······	3	80
Peaking index ▬	4	70
	5	60
	6	50
	7	40
	8	30
	9	20
	10	10

From G. Gregory Haff, *Scientific Foundations and Practical Applications of Periodization* (Champaign, IL: Human Kinetics, 2025).

GLOSSARY

30-15 intermittent fitness test (30-15 IFT)—An intermittent test used to determine the speed from which training intensities are prescribed.

absolute density—The ratio of the effective work the athlete performs to the absolute volume or duration of the training session.

absolute volume—The total volume or duration of work that is performed in a session.

acceleration—The rate of change in velocity.

accentuated eccentric loading (AEL)—A training method in which higher loads are used during the eccentric portion of a resistance-training exercise; often accomplished with the use of weight releasers.

accentuated loading—A short period in which training loads are increased dramatically; also called *concentrated loading*.

accumulation block—A mesocycle of training that contains substantial training loads that are typically used to develop general physical capacities, such as aerobic endurance, muscle strength, or general movement technique; also referred to as a *concentrated loading, overreaching,* or *developmental block*.

accumulation mesocycle—A block of training that contains substantial training loads that are typically used to develop general physical capacities, such as aerobic endurance, muscle strength, or general movement technique; also referred to as a *concentrated loading, overreaching,* or *developmental block*.

acidosis—An accumulation of hydrogen ions that results in an increase in muscle acidity.

active warm-up—Using dynamic activities such as jogging, calisthenics, cycling, or rowing to increase muscle and core temperature prior to exercising or competing.

acute to chronic workload ratio (ACWR)—A ratio of the acute workload, typically 7 days, to the chronic workload, typically 28 days, which is commonly used as part of monitoring programs.

acute training effects—The physiological and performance responses to a single exercise or series of exercises.

acute workload (AWL)—The recent or short-term training load typically measured over a week or shorter duration. It represents the immediate training stress placed on the athlete's body due to training or competition.

acyclic skills—A series of integrated functions that are performed in one action.

adaptation—The process by which an organism adjusts to its environment.

adaptive potential—The athlete's ability to respond to a training load. This is typically affected by the athlete's genetics and pretraining level of phenotype, which is the athlete's fitness level at the start of the training intervention; can be affected by other factors such as chronological age, training history, and injury and health status.

adenosine diphosphate (ADP)—A high-energy phosphate compound that plays a critical role in energy metabolism; can be used to create adenosine triphosphate (ATP).

adenosine monophosphate (AMP)—A nucleotide involved in energy metabolism and signal transduction that serves as a precursor for the synthesis of other important molecules in the body. Formed when inorganic phosphate is removed from adenosine diphosphate and attached to another adenosine diphosphate by the myokinase reaction.

adenosine triphosphatase (ATPase)—The enzyme that breaks adenosine triphosphate into adenosine diphosphate, inorganic phosphate, and hydrogen.

adenosine triphosphate (ATP)—A high-energy phosphate compound that functions as the primary energy currency in cells; releases energy when its phosphate bonds are broken.

adrenocorticotropic hormone (ACTH)—An important component of the hypothalamic-pituitary-adrenal axis. It is often produced in response to increased stress, and it stimulates the production and release of cortisol.

aerobic—In the presence of oxygen.

aftereffects—The residual effects associated with a training exercise or session.

agility—The ability to rapidly change direction and accelerate in response to information or an external stimulus.

amino acids—Molecules that, when combined, form proteins; they are classified as essential, nonessential, or conditionally essential.

anabolic—Refers to a process that promotes building, growth, or synthesis of complex molecules from simpler molecules.

anabolism—A metabolic process that involves the synthesis of complex molecules from smaller molecules.

anaerobic—Without oxygen.

anaerobic peak power (MMP_{5s})—The highest power output that can be achieved in an all-out 5-second test.

anaerobic power reserve (APR)—The difference between the power at $\dot{V}O_2max$ and the maximal anaerobic power.

anaerobic speed reserve (ASR)—The difference between the athlete's velocity at $\dot{V}O_2max$ and their maximal sprinting speed.

anaerobic work capacity (W')—The theoretical limited energy supply above critical power.

annual training plan—An entire year of training that is subdivided into periods and phases; is the key aspect of the macromanagement of the training process.

ascending pyramid—An increase in training load and a decrease in the number of repetitions across a series of sets.

assistance exercises—Generally single-joint exercises that play a minor role in resistance-training programs.

autonomic nervous system (ANS)—A control system that regulates bodily function, such as heart rate, digestion, respiratory rate, pupillary response, urination, and sexual arousal.

autoregulation—A process by which an athlete's training is adjusted in accordance with their performance or perception of their ability to perform.

basal metabolic rate (BMR)—The lowest rate of body metabolism (energy use) that can sustain life.

beta-oxidation—The breakdown of free fatty acids into acetyl-CoA.

bi-cycle annual training plan—An annual plan that contains two competitive seasons and targets two competitive peaks.

bioenergetics—Term given to the study of metabolic processes that produce or use energy.

bioenergetic specificity—The relationship of the energetic profile of a training activity to the profile of the targeted performance; also known as *metabolic specificity*.

biomotor ability—A physical capacity such as strength, speed, or endurance. An athlete's biomotor abilities may be genetically determined, but they are widely influenced by training practices.

block-emphasis model—A subcategory of the emphasis model in which multiple training factors are simultaneously developed; these factors are vertically integrated and horizontally sequenced.

block periodization—A training model in which mesocycle structures are designated as accumulation, transmutation, or realization. This model is typically classified as a sequential model of training, but if structured with multiple training targets, it could be designed as an emphasis model.

block training—A sequential approach to structuring training in which a series of training mesocycles are linked.

catabolism—Breaking larger molecules into smaller molecules.

central fatigue—The inability of the central nervous system to activate or maintain the activation of skeletal muscle.

change of direction ability—The ability to change direction, whether planned or unplanned.

change of direction–based HIIT—A form of HIIT that incorporates changes of direction.

chronic workload (CWL)—The chronic workload represents the long-term or historical training load, typically quantified across a mesocycle lasting 28 days. It represents the average or accumulated stress experienced by the athlete over time.

chronological age—The age of the athlete.

cold water immersion (CWI)—Submerging all or part of the body in water that is between 10 and 20 °C (50-68 °F).

competition microcycle—Consists of the period prior to and including the competition; often structured around the demands of the competitive period.

competition period—Outlines the competitive season in an annual plan. It is typically divided into the precompetition and main competition phases. The main goal of the competition period is competitive success.

competitive exercises—Exercises that contain movements used in competition.

complex pair—Involves performing a heavy resistance exercise prior to performing an explosive movement with similar biomechanical characteristics.

complex training model—A parallel training model where general development, specialized preparatory, specialized developmental, and competitive exercises are trained simultaneously.

complex variational training model—A parallel model of training in which multiple factors are trained simultaneously, but the means for targeting these factors changes every 2 to 6 weeks.

concentrated loading—A period in which training loads are increased dramatically; also called *accentuated loading* or *overreaching*.

concentrated unidirectional training model—A model of training developed by Professor Yuri Verkhoshansky that uses concentrated workloads followed by periods of recovery.

conditionally essential amino acids—Amino acids that are not typically essential but can become essential under certain conditions; must be consumed in the diet.

congested competition schedules—Schedules that have frequent competitions with short periods of time between them.

conjugated sequential loading model—A training model in which training is sequenced to take advantage of training residuals developed with periods of concentrated loading; also referred to as the *coupled successive system*.

contrast therapy—Alternations of thermotherapy and cryotherapy techniques.

contrast water therapy (CWT)—A water immersion strategy in which the individual alternates between cold water immersion and hot water immersion, typically ending with cold water immersion.

core exercises—The primary, multijoint exercises used in a resistance-training program.

cortisol—A corticosteroid hormone released from the adrenal cortex that stimulates the catabolism of proteins, spares glucose use, stimulates gluconeogenesis, and increases free fatty acid mobilization.

coupled successive system—A training model that is sequenced to take advantage of training residuals developed with periods of concentrated loading; also referred to as the *conjugated sequential loading model*.

creatine kinase (CK)—An enzyme in the phosphagen system that is found in skeletal muscles and other tissues. It removes a phosphate from phosphocreatine and forms inorganic phosphate, which is then added to adenosine diphosphate to form adenosine triphosphate and creatine. It becomes elevated in the blood when muscle is damaged.

critical power (CP)—Represents the capacity to sustain a particular work rate as a function of time and represents the physiological landmark that is the boundary between heavy- and severe-intensity exercise domains.

critical velocity (CV)—The capacity to sustain a particular work rate as a function of time and represents the physiological landmark that is the boundary between heavy- and severe-intensity exercise domains.

cryostimulation (CRY)—A cryotherapy technique in which the athlete is exposed to very cold air or gas (−110 to −160 °C [−166 to −256 °F]) for brief periods (2-5 min).

cumulative training effects—The physiological and motor or technical responses to a series of training sessions or to a specific training program.

cyclic skills—Sporting activities or skills that contain repetitive movement patterns.

cytokine theory of overtraining—Suggests that microtrauma and inadequate recovery lead to systematic inflammation and that overtraining is largely regulated by cytokine responses to this trauma.

Daily Analysis of Life Demands for Athletes (DALDA)—A psychological questionnaire used to assess an athlete's life stress.

daily undulating periodization (DUP)—A programming model in which all resistance-training targets (e.g., strength–endurance, hypertrophy, strength, power) are trained within a training week; it is used in parallel models of periodization.

dehydration—A water loss greater than 2% of body mass that can negatively affect performance and be life threatening in some instances.

delayed onset muscle soreness (DOMS)—Muscle soreness and pain that can occur for 24 to 72 hours after the completion of exercise.

delayed recovery—The long-term recovery and supercompensation effects associated with training; also called *delayed training effects*.

delayed training effects—The long-term responses to a training session or period of training.

density—The frequency with which an athlete performs a series of training sessions per unit of time.

density of training—The number of training sessions in a given period; also referred to as *frequency of training*.

detraining—The partial or complete loss of training-induced adaptations in response to a cessation of training or a reduction in training load.

detraining load—Training load that does not stimulate or maintain current physiological adaptations or performance levels.

detraining syndrome—A type of detraining that occurs after the cessation of training and results in maladaptive responses such as insomnia, anxiety, depression, and altered cardiovascular function; also referred to as Entlastungssyndrom, *exercise dependency syndrome,* or *exercise abstinence syndrome.*

double pyramid—Occurs when a series of sets are performed with increasing loads and decreasing repetitions. After the heaviest set is completed, the load is progressively decreased while the repetitions are increased across subsequent sets.

double-shock microcycle—Two successive shock microcycles.

double stimulation—A modification of wave loading in which the athlete alternates between sets of high repetitions and single repetitions that are performed with 10% to 15% more load.

dynamic strength–endurance—The application of considerable force in an uninterrupted manner or the repetitive application of force with different short rest intervals.

dynamic stretching—Preparing for activity with the use of movement patterns that are related to the activity of interest.

dynamic warm-up—The use of movement patterns that are related to the sporting activity to prepare the athlete for performance; typically uses mobility drills or dynamic stretching.

eccentric muscle action—A lengthening action.

electrocardiogram (ECG)—Test that records electrical signals from the heart and is used to monitor or evaluate the function of the heart.

emphasis training model—Model used to simultaneously train multiple factors with varying degrees of focus.

endergonic reaction—A type of chemical reaction that requires the input of energy in order to proceed.

endurance—The ability to withstand stress over a prolonged period.

energy—The ability or capacity to perform work.

energy availability (EA)—Calculated by subtracting the amount of energy expended during exercise from the energy intake and then dividing by fat free mass.

energy expenditure (EE)—The number of calories that are expended.

energy intake (EI)—The number of calories that are consumed.

essential amino acids—Amino acids that cannot be synthesized by the body and must be consumed in the diet.

essential fatty acids—A subclass of polyunsaturated fats that cannot be synthesized by the body and must be consumed within the diet.

euhydration—State of normal body water content in which water gain and loss are balanced.

excess postexercise oxygen consumption (EPOC)—Elevated oxygen consumption that occurs after the cessation of exercise; also known as *oxygen debt*.

exergonic reaction—A type of chemical reaction that releases energy as a result of the reaction.

exploitation—Making use of some resource to increase the benefits realized.

explosive exercises—Exercises that focus on rapidly contracting muscles to generate maximum force in a short amount of time. Common examples include plyometrics, jump squats, weightlifting movements, and weightlifting derivatives.

exponential taper—A systematic decrease in training load with a slow or fast decay.

external load—The physical work encountered by the athlete.

fast exponential taper—An exponential taper in which a more rapid reduction in training load is employed.

fast glycolysis—One of the two glycolytic pathways; it results in the production of lactate from the breakdown of glucose or glycogen. It has a faster rate of energy supply than slow glycolysis.

fat—An organic compound with limited water solubility that exists in the body as triglycerides, free fatty acids, phospholipids, and steroids.

fatigue—A sense of tiredness, reduced energy, or lack of motivation that is often accompanied by a reduction in muscular performance capacity.

fitness—A slow-changing component of an athlete's preparedness.

fitness–fatigue model—Explains the relationship between fitness, fatigue, and preparedness.

foam roller—A self-massage device that relies on body weight to apply pressure to the soft tissues using a rolling motion.

force—A vector quantity that has both a magnitude and a direction and is the product of mass and acceleration.

force–time curve—Represents the time of force production during a given period; typically created from isometric muscle actions or vertical jump performances.

frequency—How often training is undertaken (i.e., number of sessions) within a given time.

frequency of training—The number of training sessions in a given period; also referred to as *density of training*.

fructose—A monosaccharide found in many plants; also called *fruit sugar*.

functional overreaching (FOR)—Occurs when performance is enhanced after a period of intentionally increased training, such as concentrated loading.

functional threshold power—Ninety-five percent of the average power output achieved during a 20-minute cycling time trial.

FUNdamental training—General training activities designed to increase movement literacy.

galactose—A monosaccharide that when bound to glucose forms lactose; also called *milk sugar*.

game-based HIIT (GBHIIT)—Form of HIIT that incorporates sport-specific, game-based activities that last between 2 and 5 minutes interspersed with recovery periods that last between 1.5 and 4 minutes.

game speed—The expression of speed in a sport-specific context that maximizes sport performance; often synonymous with *multidirectional speed*.

general adaptive syndrome—An explanation of how the body responds to stress first proposed by Hans Selye.

general physical training (GPT)—Training that focuses on establishing the physiological base that underpins sport performance; it is generally established with higher volumes and moderate intensities.

general preparation phase—Contains the highest training volumes and workloads; typically occurs in the early portion of the preparatory period and is designed to increase work capacity and set the foundation for the competitive period.

general preparatory exercises—Exercises that do not repeat any movements from the competitive exercises. They are a means of all-around physical development.

general training age—The number of years a youth athlete has been participating in general or FUNdamental training activities.

general warm-up—Consists of slow aerobic activity that is used to increase heart rate, blood flow, muscle temperature, and respiration rate while reducing the viscosity of the joint fluids.

global strength–endurance—The ability to repetitively produce force using many muscle groups.

gluconeogenesis—The synthesis of glucose from amino acids, lactate, glycerol, and other carbon-chain molecules.

glucose—A monosaccharide and the most common form of carbohydrate transported by the body.

glucose transporter-4 (GLUT4)—A contraction-sensitive glucose transport protein that aids in the uptake of glucose into the skeletal muscle.

glutamate—A free amino acid in the brain that is at the crossroads of multiple metabolic pathways.

glutamine—The most abundant free amino acid in the body; it plays an important role in immune function and metabolism.

glycemic index—A numerical ranking system that ranks how quickly and to what extent a carbohydrate-containing food raises blood glucose after consumption compared to pure glucose or white bread.

glycogen—A form of carbohydrate that is stored in the skeletal muscle and liver.

glycogenolysis—The breakdown of glycogen.

glycolysis—Metabolic pathway in the sarcoplasm that uses glucose and glycogen to resynthesize adenosine triphosphate.

glycolytic flux—Rate of progression for the glycolytic system.

Golgi tendon organ—A sensory receptor within tendons that monitors tension.

ground contact time—The amount of time spent in contact with the ground, typically during the stance phase of sprinting.

heart rate recovery (HRR)—The rate at which heart rate declines after the cessation of exercise.

heart rate variability (HRV)—A measure of beat-to-beat intervals, represented as the R-R interval on an electrocardiogram.

hemoglobin—The iron-containing compound in blood that binds oxygen.

Henneman's size principle—Hypothesizes that the size of the motor unit and its force-generating capacity dictates its activation.

heteropolysaccharide—A polysaccharide formed from two or more different monosaccharides that are bound together.

high-intensity exercise endurance (HIEE) training—Training that involves repetitively engaging in high-intensity movements or sustaining activities 2 minutes or less.

high-intensity interval training (HIIT)—Repeated bouts of high-intensity work performed above critical speed, power, or lactate threshold and interspersed with periods of low-intensity exercise or complete rest.

high-intensity overtraining—Overtraining caused by excessive use of high intensities of training; it is commonly associated with resistance training or strength sports such as weightlifting and powerlifting.

high-speed running (HSR)—Running performed at maximal speeds.

high-volume overtraining—Overtraining caused by excessive use of high volumes of training; it is commonly seen in endurance and team sports.

homopolysaccharide—A polysaccharide formed from two monosaccharides that are bound together.

horizontal sequencing—Planning training so the residual training effects of one training period affect a subsequent training period.

hot water immersion (HWI)—A form of hydrotherapy in which all or part of the body is submerged in water warmer than 36 °C (97 °F).

hydrostatic pressure—Stimulates the displacement of fluids from the extremities toward the central cavity of the body.

hyperhydration—Fluid gain exceeds fluid loss.

hypertrophy—An increase in muscle size.

hypohydration—Fluid loss exceeds fluid gain.

hyponatremia—Abnormally low concentration of sodium in the blood.

immediate training effects—The physiological and performance responses that occur immediately after an individual training session.

impulse—The product of the amount of force applied to the duration of that application.

individualization—Developing training interventions to address the specific attributes or needs of an individual.

inorganic phosphate (P_i)—A stimulator of cellular metabolism. When adenosine triphosphate (ATP) is broken down, it splits into P_i and adenosine diphosphate (ADP), allowing energy to be released. It can be combined with ADP to form ATP.

intensity—A qualitative element of training that can be represented as speed, power, velocity, heart rate, or percentage of maximal strength. In resistance training, intensity is often represented based on a repetition maximum test.

interexercise recovery—Bioenergetic activity that occurs during a training bout to ensure that energy is available to meet the demands of the physical activity being performed.

internal load—The athlete's response to the external load.

inter-repetition rest interval—The rest between repetitions contained within a set.

inter-set rest interval—The rest interval between sets.

intra-set rest interval—The rest interval between clusters or groups of repetitions contained within a set.

introductory microcycle—Used to introduce new skills or training activities and establish or reestablish general athletic abilities.

involution—The rate of decay, often used to describe a reduction in preparedness or performance capacity.

isometric midthigh pull (IMTP)—An isometric test that models the second pull position associated with the clean; it is performed in a specialized rack in conjunction with a force plate.

isometric squat (ISQT)—An isometric test performed in a partial squat corresponding to a knee angle between 90° and 150° and a hip angle between 110° and 140°; it is performed in a specialized rack in conjunction with a force plate.

isometric strength–endurance—The application of isometric tension of varying magnitudes and durations or the maintenance of static posture.

jet lag—The desynchronization between the body's circadian rhythms and the external 24-hour light–dark cycle; typically occurs when crossing multiple time zones.

kinematic profile—A description of the displacement, velocity, power, or rate of force development during a movement; is commonly discussed when referring to mechanical specificity.

kinetic profile—A description of the forces generated during a movement; is commonly discussed when referring to mechanical specificity.

Krebs cycle—A metabolic pathway within the mitochondria in which energy is transferred from carbohydrates, fats, or amino acids to nicotinamide adenine dinucleotide (NAD^+) for subsequent production of adenosine triphosphate (ATP) in the electron transport chain.

lactate—A salt formed from lactic acid. It is a fuel that can be used to create glucose and can be metabolized by skeletal muscle and the heart. It is not believed to be related to fatigue.

lactate dehydrogenase—An enzyme contained in the glycolytic energy system that converts pyruvate to lactate.

lactate threshold (LT)—The point at which lactate concentration abruptly increases in response to increase in exercise intensity; typically represented as a 1 mmol · L^{-1} increase in comparison to baseline during a graded exercise test.

lactic acid—The end product of fast glycolysis. It is often associated with fatigue because it can inhibit calcium binding to troponin, interfere with crossbridge attachment, and stimulate nociceptors (i.e., pain receptors).

lactormone—The autocrine-, paracrine-, and endocrine-like actions of lactate.

leucine—An essential amino acid that is often referred to as the *anabolic trigger* because of its role in stimulating protein synthesis.

linear speed—The velocity of movement in a straight line.

linear taper—A systematic linear reduction of training load.

lipid—Organic molecules that are not soluble in water; they store energy and are sometimes referred to as *fat*.

local strength–endurance—The ability to repetitively produce muscular force or maintain force production of a single muscle group.

long-lasting delayed training effects (LDTE)—Training aftereffects of a concentrated loading period.

long-term athlete development (LTAD)—A multiyear process that is used to guide athlete development, improve health and fitness, and enhance physical performance; typically aligns stages of development with the development of key physiological attributes.

long-term residual training effects—Training adaptations that are maintained for years or are potentially permanent.

low-intensity exercise endurance (LIEE) training—Training that involves long-duration aerobic activity performed below the lactate threshold.

machine learning—A subdiscipline of artificial intelligence (AI) used to develop algorithms and modules that enable computers to learn and make predictions or decisions without explicit programming.

macrocycle—A long-term planning structure that contains preparation, competition, and transition periods; typically aligns with the seasons being contested in the annual training plan.

main competition phase—Contains all the competitions the athlete is targeting. The goal of this phase is to maximize preparedness at key times to optimize competitive performance.

maneuverability—A change of direction ability that requires the athlete to maintain velocity (often curvilinear in pattern) or requires a change in the mode of travel (e.g., transition to crossover, shuffle, or backpedal).

maximal aerobic power—The power output associated with the $\dot{V}O_2$max.

maximal aerobic speed—The speed associated with the $\dot{V}O_2$max.

maximal lactate steady state (MLSS)—The highest exercise intensity (speed or power output) at which blood lactate does not increase more than 1.0 mmol · L^{-1} during constant load exercise, representing an equilibrium between lactate production and removal.

maximal mean power output (MMP)—The power output that can be sustained over 4 minutes; it is closely related to the power at $\dot{V}O_2$max (p$\dot{V}O_2$max).

maximal oxygen uptake ($\dot{V}O_2$max)—The greatest rate of oxygen uptake by the body measured during dynamic exercise; also referred to as *maximal aerobic power*.

maximal sprinting speed (MSS)—The maximal speed that can be achieved during a given sprint, typically represented as km · h^{-1}.

maximal strength—The highest amount of force the neuromuscular system can generate during a maximal voluntary contraction.

maximal voluntary contraction (MVC)—The maximal amount of force an athlete can produce in a specific isometric exercise.

mechanical specificity—The relationship of the kinematic and kinetic profile of the training activities with the targeted performance outcome.

mediator—An intermediate step that explains the association between the observed variable and the outcome.

medium-term residual training effects—Training factors that are maintained for several months.

mesocycle—A training cycle of 2 to 6 weeks, with the most common duration being 4 weeks. Also referred to as a block.

metabolic acidosis—A substantial increase in acid production or loss of bicarbonate, which results in an imbalance in the body's acid–base balance.

metabolic specificity—The relationship of the energetic profile of a training activity to the profile of the targeted performance; also known as *bioenergetic specificity*.

metabolism—The sum of all the catabolic and anabolic reactions within the body.

metric ton—A unit equal to 1,000 kg (2,205 lb).

microcycle—A training cycle of 2 to 14 days, with the most common duration being 7 days.

mitochondria—The subcellular organelle responsible for producing adenosine triphosphatase in the presence of oxygen; often called the *powerhouse* of the cell. It contains the enzymes for the Krebs cycle and the electron transport chain.

mobility—The range of motion through which force can effectively be applied. Mobility frames flexibility as a dynamic quality in which the athlete must demonstrate control, coordination, and force through a specified range of motion.

model microcycle—Used to reproduce the distribution of work and rest within a competitive microcycle; it prepares the athlete for the stressors associated with competitive microcycles.

moderator—A factor that modifies a given variable's effect on an outcome.

momentum—The relationship between the mass of an object and the velocity of movement.

mono-cycle annual training plan—Contains only one competitive season and targets one major competitive peak.

monosaccharide—The simplest carbohydrate molecule; often referred to as *simple sugar*.

monotonous program overtraining—A reduction or stagnation in performance gain that occurs in response to a lack of training variation.

monounsaturated fatty acids (MUFA)—Unsaturated fats that contain one double bond.

motor unit—The motor nerve and all the muscle fibers it innervates.

multidirectional speed—The athlete's ability to change speed and direction in response to ever-changing game scenarios; also referred to as *game speed*.

multijoint exercises—Exercises that recruit a large amount of muscle and involve two or more primary joints.

multitargeted block periodization training models—A block training model that targets several training factors within a training block. Typically, two or three physical training factors are trained with varying emphasis within the block while technical and tactical training are maintained.

multiyear training plan—A long-term planning structure that is created by linking several annual training plans to guide specific development outcomes. The most common multiyear plan is the quadrennial training plan.

myoglobin—A molecule similar to hemoglobin that is found in skeletal muscle and carries oxygen from the cell membrane to the mitochondria.

myosin heavy chain (MHC)—Consists primarily of the head of the crossbridge and is typically associated with muscle fiber type.

nearables—A consumer tracking device, such as Beddit or Early Sense, placed near the athlete, typically over or under their mattress to monitor sleeping.

neuromuscular function—Refers to the interaction and coordination between the nervous system and the muscular system. Involves the complex interplay between nerve impulses and muscle contractions, allowing for movement, strength, control, and coordination.

nonessential amino acids—Amino acids that can be synthesized by the body and do not need to be consumed in the diet.

nonfunctional overreaching (NFOR)—Occurs when recovery takes longer than 2 weeks and performance is not enhanced or supercompensated after a period of intentionally increased training, such as concentrated loading.

nonprogressive taper—Taper strategy that uses a standard reduction in training load to elevate performance prior to competition; also known as a *step taper*.

nutrient timing—A dietary strategy that involves the strategic manipulation of nutrient consumption at specific time points surrounding and during training in an attempt to amplify adaptive responses and enhance performance.

nutritional periodization—The planned, structured, and strategic manipulation of nutritional interventions to enhance the adaptive response to the training process to optimize long-term performance.

oligosaccharides—Monosaccharides that are bound together.

onset of blood lactate accumulation (OBLA)—The intensity of exercise at which the blood lactate reaches 4 mmol · L^{-1} during an incremental exercise test.

optimization—Making the best use of a situation or resource.

ordinary microcycle—Contains submaximal intensities and lower training loads that can be sequenced to informally increase the training loads across several microcycles.

overload—The amount of training load that provides a greater stress or load on the body than what the body is normally exposed to.

overreaching—A short period of planned overtraining that occurs within 2 weeks of a period of intensified training, such as concentrated loading.

overtraining—An accumulation of training and nontraining stressors that results in a long-term performance reduction.

overtraining syndrome (OTS)—Numerous symptoms and conditions that collectively contribute to impaired performance.

oxidative system—The most complex of the three energy systems; often referred to as the *aerobic energy system*. It occurs in the mitochondria and requires oxygen to make energy.

oxygen debt—The elevated postexercise oxygen consumption; it is related to the replenishment of phosphocreatine (PCr) and the resynthesis of glucose from lactate and to elevated body temperature, heart rate, and breathing postexercise.

oxygen deficit—The difference between the oxygen uptake during the first few minutes of exercise and an equal time period during steady-state exercise; the anaerobic contribution to the total energy cost of exercise.

parallel-emphasis model—A subdivision of the emphasis model in which several training factors are simultaneously trained at varying intensities.

parallel training model—A multilateral training model that allows for several biomotor abilities to be trained concurrently; it works well for novice athletes.

parasympathetic overtraining—Represents advanced stages of overtraining in which parasympathetic activity dominates at rest and during exercise and there is sympathetic inhibition.

passive warm-up—Using external methods, such as saunas, hot showers, hot baths, heating pads, or diathermy, to increase muscle and core temperature without depleting energy substrates.

peaking—A period in which preparedness and performance are elevated in response to a taper.

peaking index—A numerical designator that aligns with the athlete's level of preparedness; also referred to as the *preparedness index*. It is used in the annual training plan to define the expected level of preparedness.

perceived fatigability—Fatigability attributed to psychological factors that modulate performance.

performance fatigability—A decline in an objective measure of performance over a specific period that depends on the capacity of the nervous system to provide adequate activation of the muscles involved in performing a task.

periods—A subcategory of the macrocycle that is used to define the major overbridging goal of the unit of time. Three periods are often defined as preparation, competitive, and transition periods.

periodization—A cyclical training approach in which the logical integration and sequencing of modifiable training parameters (i.e., volume, intensity, training density, training frequency, exercise selection, and mode) are planned to optimize the athlete's performance outcomes at appropriate times.

peripheral fatigue—Occurs when the regulatory or support systems are unable to maintain muscle contractility or the bioenergetic energy supply and waste removal necessary to preserve physical activity.

phases—Used to define the goals within a period; often aligned with the major training goals.

phase potentiation—The stimulation of increased adaptation to a training plan based on the delayed training effects from a previous training block.

phosphagen system—Anaerobic energy system that provides energy for short-term and high-intensity activities; also known as the *ATP-PC system*.

phosphocreatine (PCr)—A phosphorylated creatine molecule and component of the phosphagen system that serves as a rapid supply of high-energy phosphates in skeletal muscle and the brain to buffer adenosine triphosphate (ATP) and provide energy for muscle actions by maintaining ATP stores.

phosphofructokinase (PFK)—The rate-limiting enzyme in the glycolytic system.

phosphorylase—The enzyme responsible for stimulating muscle glycogen breakdown.

planning—The development or implementation of a training load model that is aligned with the training process established by periodization.

polysaccharide—A complex carbohydrate composed of more than 10 monosaccharides; can be classified as homopolysaccharide or heteropolysaccharide depending on structure.

polyunsaturated fatty acids (PUFA)—Unsaturated fats that contain two or more double bonds; sometimes referred to as *essential fatty acids*.

postactivation performance enhancement (PAPE)—A phenomenon that occurs after the performance of a high-force or high-power-output conditioning activity; often represented as an increased movement velocity, power output, or maximal force.

postactivation potentiation (PAP)—An enhanced muscle contractile response after an intense voluntary contraction.

postexercise recovery—The period after the cessation of exercise that is needed to return to homeostasis.

power—The rate of doing work (power = work/time); also represented as the product of force and velocity divided by time (power = [force × velocity]/time).

power exercises—Exercises that require a rapid force production, such as the power clean or power snatch.

precompetition phase—Phase of training that links the specific preparation phase and the main competition phase. It often contains exhibitions or friendlies as training tools. Competitive success is not the primary goal of this phase.

precompetitive microcycle—Used to elevate the athlete's performance in preparation for competition. This type of microcycle is often used to transition the athlete into a competitive microcycle.

preparation period—Contains the highest workloads in the annual training plan. It is broken into the general and specific preparation phases and is designed to increase the athlete's work capacity.

preparedness—An athlete's potential to perform. When elevated, the athlete will have an increased performance potential; if suppressed, the athlete will have a decreased performance capacity.

preparedness index—A numerical designator that aligns with the athlete's level of preparedness; also referred to as the *peaking index*. This index is used in the annual training plan to define the expected level of preparedness.

priming exercises—Used prior to a competitive engagement in an attempt to stimulate an elevation in the athlete's level of preparedness and competition performance. These exercises are typically employed within a priming session.

priming session—A training session that is 4 to 12 hours prior to a competition and is used to elevate the athlete's preparedness for and performance in the competition.

principle of dynamic correspondence—An exercise or training program's ability to directly affect an athlete's performance; also referred to as a *transfer effect*.

Profile of Mood States (POMS)—A psychological rating scale used to assess distinct, transient mood states.

programming—The prescription of precise manipulations of specific training factors to stimulate a specific physiological and performance response.

progressive overload—The gradual increase of training stress (e.g., workload, volume, intensity, frequency) above a normal magnitude.

progressive taper—A systematic reduction in training load prior to a competition.

pyramid set structure—An increase in training load as the number of repetitions contained within each set decreases; also known as an *ascending pyramid*.

pyruvate—The end product of slow glycolysis. It can be converted to lactate by lactate dehydrogenase or transported into the mitochondria, where it is oxidized.

raise, activate and mobilize, and potentiate (RAMP)—An alternative approach to warming up in which the athlete goes through a progressive warm-up that is designed to better prepare them for training or competition and is used as an important developmental training activity.

range of motion—The extent of movement of a joint measured in degrees of a circle.

rate coding—The motor unit firing rate.

rate of force development (RFD)—The rate at which force is produced during a muscular contraction, typically quantified from a force–time curve during an isometric muscle action or vertical jump.

rating of perceived exertion (RPE)—A measure quantified based on the Borg CR-10 scale or the Borg 6-20 scale.

reactive agility drills—Drills that require the athlete to change direction in response to visual or auditory stimuli.

reactive strength—The ability of the musculotendinous unit to produce a rapid and forceful concentric muscle action immediately following a rapid eccentric muscle action.

reactive strength index (RSI)—A metric to quantify the athlete's ability to use the stretch-shortening cycle; typically measured with a drop jump or repeated jump test.

realization block—A training block designed to stimulate recovery; classically referred to as a *taper*.

realization mesocycle—Designed to stimulate recovery; classically referred to as a *taper*.

recovery microcycle—Contains a reduced training load that is marked by reductions in volume and intensity used to provide the athlete with rest; also called a *restorative microcycle*. This microcycle can be used as a transition microcycle that links mesocycles.

Recovery–Stress Questionnaire for Athletes (RESTQ-Sport)—A psychological rating scale used to assess recovery.

relative density—The percentage of work volume performed compared to the total volume of the training session.

relative strength—The ratio between maximal strength and body weight or lean body mass.

relative volume—The total amount of time (i.e., the duration) of the training session.

remote coach—A coach who works with an athlete remotely through streaming or video review; also called a *video coach*.

repeated sprint training (RST)—Short sprints that generally consist of 3- to 10-second efforts at all-out maximal intensity interspersed with short recovery periods that are passive or at lower intensities.

repetition maximum (RM)—The heaviest weight that can be lifted for a predetermined number of repetitions (e.g., a 3RM is the heaviest load that can be lifted three times).

repetition maximum (RM) training—Performing all training sets at RM load; a training to failure method.

repetition maximum (RM) zones—Lifting the heaviest load possible for a given number of repetitions that are represented as a zone (e.g., the hypertrophy zone is 8-12 reps, so the athlete would lift the heaviest load they can for 8-12 reps); a training to failure method.

repetitions—The number of completed work intervals in a set.

repetitions in reserve (RIR)—The number of repetitions the athlete has left prior to achieving a repetition maximum.

residual training effects—The time frame in which the training effect dissipates.

resisted sled training (RST)—Towing or pulling a sled while sprinting.

retaining load—Training load that maintains the athlete's current level of preparedness but does not provide enough overload to stimulate positive adaptations.

reversibility—The reversal of the effects of training after the cessation or reduction of a training stimulus.

rolling devices—Used to roll and compress targeted muscle; examples include foam rollers or massage sticks.

running economy—The efficiency of movement while running, often determined by quantifying the oxygen or energy cost of movement.

sarcoplasmic reticulum—A network of tubules and sacs within the skeletal muscle that plays an important role in muscle contraction and relaxation by releasing and storing calcium.

saturated fats—Fats that have their carbon molecule saturated with hydrogen and have no double bonds.

saw taper—A taper that uses daily dramatic alterations in training loads.

segment work—Involves alternating higher- and lower-load sets; also called *wave loading*.

sequential training model—A model of training used to arrange an individual or limited number of training factors into a logical pattern to guide the athlete's training toward a targeted outcome.

session rating of perceived exertion (sRPE) scale—A subjective scale used in monitoring in which 0 is rest and 10 is maximal exertion. Session RPE is multiplied by the duration of the session to indicate of training load in arbitrary units.

set—A grouping of repetitions or units of work.

shock microcycle—Contains a sudden dramatic increase in training load, which is designed to saturate the athlete with a training stimulus to bring them out of a state of stagnation; also called *concentrated loading* or *overreaching microcycle*.

short-term residual training effects—Training factors that are retained for a few days to a number of weeks.

short ton—A unit equal to 1,102.3 kg (2,430.1 lb).

single-joint exercises—Exercises that involve smaller amounts of muscle mass and use one primary joint, such as a biceps curl.

skewed pyramid—Increasing the load across a series of sets and then performing a down set for four to six repetitions.

slow exponential taper—An exponential taper in which a slower reduction in training load is employed with higher training loads.

slow glycolysis—One of the two glycolytic pathways; breaks down glucose or glycogen resulting in the formation of pyruvate, which is then shuttled into the mitochondria where it is used in the Krebs cycle.

small-sided game (SSG)—A method of high-intensity training that integrates technical, tactical, and physical training factors into one activity.

specialized developmental exercises—Exercises that repeat parts of the competitive movement pattern; they serve as the entry point into sports form.

specialized preparatory exercises—Exercises that use similar muscle groups but do not repeat parts of the competitive movements.

specificity—The extent to which something is related to a specific attribute or condition.

specific preparation phase—Occurs in the later portions of the preparation period and is designed to elevate preparedness and prepare the athlete for the competitive period through the use of sport-specific training means.

specific training age—The number of years a youth athlete has been participating in sport-specific training interventions.

specific warm-up—Using sport-specific movement patterns that mirror the skills that will be performed in the training session.

speed—The ability to cover a distance in the fastest time possible.

speed–endurance—The ability to prolong the duration of motion at near maximal speed or the ability to repetitively produce maximal or near maximal speeds.

speed–strength—Involves aspects of speed and strength, with speed exerting a greater influence than strength on the performance variable. It is related to the expression of power and represents the ability to develop force rapidly and at high velocities.

sporting form—An athlete's readiness to perform in their given sport.

sports form—Refers to how an athlete maximizes adaptations in response to training that manifest in various stages, ultimately leading toward the maximization of sport performance. Sometimes considered analogous to preparedness and peaking.

sport-specific physical training (SSPT)—Training that specifically targets aspects of sport performance; it closely models sporting performance.

spring–mass model (SMM)—Model that represents sprinting as a form of locomotion in which the lower limb acts as the spring and the body's center of mass serves as the mass.

sprint interval training (SIT)—All-out maximal sprinting efforts that last between 20 and 45 seconds and are interspersed with recovery periods that last between 1 and 4 minutes.

static stretching—A slow, constant stretch with the end position held for 15 to 30 seconds.

step taper—A nonprogressive taper that uses a sudden reduction in training load.

stimulating load—Training load that provides overload and results in positive adaptations that elevate preparedness.

strength—The maximal force or torque a muscle or group of muscles can generate.

strength–endurance—The ability to repetitively produce muscular force or maintain force production for a time; also called *muscular endurance*.

strength–power potentiation complex (SPPC)—Created when a high-force or high-power activity is used to stimulate a postactivation performance enhancement (PAPE) response in a subsequent high-power or high-velocity movement.

strength–speed—Involves aspects of strength and speed, with strength exerting a greater influence than speed on the performance variable; related to the expression of power.

stretch reflex—The contraction of a muscle in response to a stretch; also referred to as the *myotatic reflex*.

stretch-shortening cycle (SSC)—An eccentric–concentric coupling phenomenon in which the muscle–tendon complexes are rapidly and forcibly lengthened (stretch loaded) and immediately shortened in a reactive or elastic manner; an active stretch or eccentric muscle action that precedes a shortening or concentric muscle action of the same muscle.

structural exercises—Exercises that place load on the axial skeleton, such as a squat; they are often multijoint exercises that involve a large amount of muscle mass.

summated microcycles—A series of microcycles with an extensive to intensive workload progression and a brief restoration period.

supramaximal strength—The maximal force that can be generated during an eccentric muscle action.

sympathetic overtraining—Representative of prolonged stress and related to increases in sympathetic nervous system activity at rest.

synchronization—The simultaneous activation of numerous motor units; it is related to the rate of force development.

tactical metabolic training—Training interventions that mirror the work intervals and work-to-rest ratios encountered in competition.

taper—A period in which training load is reduced prior to a competition; typically lasts between 8 and 14 days.

tedium—A state of training monotony that can induce training boredom and hinder development.

testosterone—The predominant male sex hormone; it is produced in the testes in men and in the adrenal cortex and the ovaries in women. It is used as an index of anabolism.

testosterone:cortisol (T:C) ratio—An indicator of the anabolic–catabolic balance; related to preparedness.

time-motion analysis—A monitoring technique that uses technology such as global positioning systems or video analysis to track movement patterns.

time-series analysis—An analysis of a sequence of measures taken over time to evaluate trends, detect outliers, and establish data behavior.

torque—The rotational force a muscle or group of muscles can generate.

training—Structured interventions that are designed to develop a specific performance characteristic.

training block—A 2- to 6-week training period (the most common duration is 4 weeks); also called a *mesocycle*.

training day—One or more training sessions used to deliver specific training units.

training effect—The cumulative physiological, psychological, and performance responses to a training exercise, session, or program; can be classified as acute, immediate, delayed, cumulative, or residual.

training impulse (TRIMP)—A representation of the training load that is imposed on the athlete during a bout of exercise; based on the athlete's heart rate response to the bout of exercise.

training intensity—The intensity of the training session; often calculated by taking the volume load and dividing it by the number of repetitions completed.

training load—The overall workload experienced in training.

training monotony—The variation of the training load over a microcycle. It is calculated by dividing the microcycle's average load by its standard deviation.

training session—The smallest unit of planning contained within a periodized training plan; also called a *workout*. It generally contains less than 40 minutes of rest between bouts of activity.

training strain—The product of the training load and the degree of monotony.

Training Stress Score (TSS)—A metric that considers intensity and duration of each training session to determine an external training load; based on a 1-hour time-trial performance at threshold power and an intensity factor.

training unit—A specific task or activity that is performed as part of a training session.

transition period—A period of reduced training loads that serves as a bridge between macrocycles, annual training plans, and multiyear training plans. It is used to reduce both psychological and physical fatigue and prepare athletes for subsequent training periods.

transmutation block—A training block that uses workloads to develop sport-specific abilities; also referred to as *normal training*. These blocks of training come after accentuated loading.

transmutation mesocycle—Contains workloads that develop sport-specific abilities; also called *normal training*. These blocks come after accumulation mesocycles.

travel fatigue—Occurs in response to frequent travel across multiple time zones.

tri-cycle annual training plan—Contains three competitive seasons and targets three competitive peaks.

triglycerides—The body's most concentrated energy source and the most-stored fat in the body.

two-phase taper—A taper period in which the first phase uses a progressive reduction in training and the last 3 days of the taper employ an increase in training load of 50% to 80% of normal training.

undertraining—Insufficient training that results in a stagnation or reduction in performance.

unsaturated fats—Fats that contain some carbon molecules that are joined together with double bonds, making them more reactive.

variation—A change in a stimulus applied to the training process.

variational training model—A parallel training model in which multiple training factors are trained simultaneously and the means of targeting these training factors change every 2 to 6 weeks.

vegan—A person who abstains from the use or consumption of animal products.

vegetarian—A person who does not consume meat.

velocity—A vector quantity that describes how fast an object is traveling and the direction it is traveling.

velocity-based training (VBT) methods—Based on the linear relationship between force and velocity. Proponents of these methods suggest that they are a better way to prescribe resistance-training intensity or focus.

vertical integration—A process through which compatible training factors are grouped within training periods; allows complementary training factors to be trained while minimizing interference effects.

vertical integration model—An emphasis model developed by Charlie Francis in which multiple factors are simultaneously trained but with differing emphasis.

volume—A quantitative element of the training process that can be represented as time, duration, distance, or number of repetitions performed; the total quantity of the activity performed.

volume load—A representation of the work completed during resistance training or sprinting. When used with resistance training, it is calculated by multiplying the total number of repetitions (sets × repetitions) by the load lifted; when used with sprinting, it is calculated by multiplying distance by intensity.

wave loading—Involves manipulating the load on a set-to-set basis; on every other set, the load increases, and on the alternate set, it decreases.

wearables—Electronic devices, such as smartwatches, which are worn by the athlete to monitor physiological and performance metrics.

zone of optimization—Nonstatic zone in which training adaptation is optimized.

Chapter 1

1. Agostinete, RR, Rossi, FE, Magalhaes, AJ, Rocha, AP, Parmezzani, SS, Gerosa-Neto, J, Cholewa, JM, and Lira, FS. Immunometabolic responses after short and moderate rest intervals to strength exercise with and without similar total volume. *Front Physiol* 7:444, 2016.
2. Ahtiainen, JP, Pakarinen, A, Kraemer, WJ, and Hakkinen, K. Acute hormonal and neuromuscular responses and recovery to forced vs maximum repetitions multiple resistance exercises. *Int J Sports Med* 24:410-418, 2003.
3. Areta, JL, and Hopkins, WG. Skeletal muscle glycogen content at rest and during endurance exercise in humans: A meta-analysis. *Sports Med* 48:2091-2102, 2018.
4. Baar, K, Nader, G, and Bodine, S. Resistance exercise, muscle loading/unloading and the control of muscle mass. *Essays Biochem* 42:61-74, 2006.
5. Banister, EW, Carter, JB, and Zarkadas, PC. Training theory and taper: Validation in triathlon athletes. *Eur J Appl Physiol Occup Physiol* 79:182-191, 1999.
6. Behm, DG, Reardon, G, Fitzgerald, J, and Drinkwater, E. The effect of 5, 10, and 20 repetition maximums on the recovery of voluntary and evoked contractile properties. *J Strength Cond Res* 16:209-218, 2002.
7. Bompa, TO, and Haff, GG. Basis for training. In *Periodization: Theory and Methodology of Training*. 5th ed. Champaign, IL: Human Kinetics, 3-30, 2009.
8. Bondarchuk, AP. A brief overview of the transfer of training. In *Transfer of Training in Sports*. Michigan, USA: Ultimate Athlete Concepts, 1-57, 2007.
9. Buckner, SL, Mouser, JG, Dankel, SJ, Jessee, MB, Mattocks, KT, and Loenneke, JP. The general adaptation syndrome: Potential misapplications to resistance exercise. *J Sci Med Sport* 20:1015-1017, 2017.
10. Burgomaster, KA, Heigenhauser, GJ, and Gibala, MJ. Effect of short-term sprint interval training on human skeletal muscle carbohydrate metabolism during exercise and time-trial performance. *J Appl Physiol* 100:2041-2047, 2006.
11. Burke, L. Nutrition for recovery after competition and training. In *Clinical Sports Nutrition*. 2nd ed. Burke, L, Deakin, V, eds. Roseville, Australia: McGraw-Hill Australia, 759, 2000.
12. Burke, LM, van Loon, LJC, and Hawley, JA. Postexercise muscle glycogen resynthesis in humans. *J Appl Physiol (1985)* 122:1055-1067, 2017.
13. Burleson, MA, Jr., O'Bryant, HS, Stone, MH, Collins, MA, and Triplett-McBride, T. Effect of weight training exercise and treadmill exercise on post-exercise oxygen consumption. *Med Sci Sports Exerc* 30:518-522, 1998.
14. Burt, DG, Lamb, K, Nicholas, C, and Twist, C. Effects of exercise-induced muscle damage on resting metabolic rate, sub-maximal running and post-exercise oxygen consumption. *Eur J Sport Sci* 14:337-344, 2014.
15. Carriker, CR. Components of fatigue: Mind and body. *J Strength Cond Res* 31:3170-3176, 2017.
16. Carroll, TJ, Taylor, JL, and Gandevia, SC. Recovery of central and peripheral neuromuscular fatigue after exercise. *J Appl Physiol (1985)* 122:1068-1076, 2017.
17. Cavalcante, PAM, Gregnani, MF, Henrique, JS, Ornellas, FH, and Araujo, RC. Aerobic but not resistance exercise can induce inflammatory pathways via toll-like 2 and 4: A systematic review. *Sports Med Open* 3:42, 2017.
18. Chen, TC, Nosaka, K, Lin, MJ, Chen, HL, and Wu, CJ. Changes in running economy at different intensities following downhill running. *J Sports Sci* 27:1137-1144, 2009.
19. Chesley, A, MacDougall, JD, Tarnopolsky, MA, Atkinson, SA, and Smith, K. Changes in human muscle protein synthesis after resistance exercise. *J Appl Physiol* 73:1383-1388, 1992.
20. Chiu, LZ, and Barnes, JL. The fitness-fatigue model revisited: Implications for planning short- and long-term training. *Strength Cond J* 25:42-51, 2003.
21. Chiu, LZ, and Schilling, BK. A primer on weightlifting: From sport to sports training. *Strength Cond J* 27:42-48, 2005.
22. Coffey, VG, and Hawley, JA. The molecular bases of training adaptation. *Sports Med* 37:737-763, 2007.
23. Coffey, VG, and Hawley, JA. Concurrent exercise training: Do opposites distract? *J Physiol* 595:2883-2896, 2017.
24. Conchola, EC, Thiele, RM, Palmer, TB, Smith, DB, and Thompson, BJ. Acute postexercise time course responses of hypertrophic vs. power-endurance squat exercise protocols on maximal and rapid torque of the knee extensors. *J Strength Cond Res* 29:1285-1294, 2015.
25. Connolly, F, and White, P. *Game Changer*. Victory Belt, 2017.
26. Costill, DL, Gollnick, PD, Jansson, ED, Saltin, B, and Stein, EM. Glycogen depletion pattern in human muscle fibres during distance running. *Acta Physiol Scand* 89:374-383, 1973.
27. Costill, DL, Pascoe, DD, Fink, WJ, Roberts, RA, Barr, SI, and Pearson, D. Impaired muscle glycogen resynthesis after eccentric exercise. *J Appl Physiol* 69:46-50, 1990.
28. Coyle, EF. Substrate utilization during exercise in active people. *Am J Clin Nutr* 61:968S-979S, 1995.
29. Coyle, EF. Physical activity as a metabolic stressor. *Am J Clin Nutr* 72:512S-520S, 2000.

30. Cross, MJ, Williams, S, Trewartha, G, Kemp, SP, and Stokes, KA. The influence of in-season training loads on injury risk in professional Rugby Union. *Int J Sports Physiol Perform* 11:350-355, 2016.
31. Cunanan, AJ, DeWeese, BH, Wagle, JP, Carroll, KM, Sausaman, R, Hornsby, WG, 3rd, Haff, GG, Triplett, NT, Pierce, KC, and Stone, MH. Authors' reply to Buckner et al.: Comment on: "The General Adaptation Syndrome: A Foundation for the Concept of Periodization". *Sports Med* 48:1755-1757, 2018.
32. Cunanan, AJ, DeWeese, BH, Wagle, JP, Carroll, KM, Sausaman, R, Hornsby, WG, 3rd, Haff, GG, Triplett, NT, Pierce, KC, and Stone, MH. The general adaptation syndrome: A foundation for the concept of periodization. *Sports Med* 48:787-797, 2018.
33. Dankel, SJ, Mattocks, KT, Jessee, MB, Buckner, SL, Mouser, JG, Counts, BR, Laurentino, GC, and Loenneke, JP. Frequency: The overlooked resistance training variable for inducing muscle hypertrophy? *Sports Med* 47:799-805, 2017.
34. Davies, RW, Carson, BP, and Jakeman, PM. The effect of whey protein supplementation on the temporal recovery of muscle function following resistance training: A systematic review and meta-analysis. *Nutrients* 10, 2018.
35. Davis, JM. Central and peripheral factors in fatigue. *J Sports Sci* 13:S49-53, 1995.
36. Dennis, R, Farhart, P, Goumas, C, and Orchard, J. Bowling workload and the risk of injury in elite cricket fast bowlers. *J Sci Med Sport* 6:359-367, 2003.
37. DeWeese, BH, Hornsby, G, Stone, M, and Stone, MH. The training process: Planning for strength–power training in track and field. Part 1: Theoretical aspects. *J Sport Health Sci* 4:308-317, 2015.
38. Dick, FW. Planning the programme. In *Sports Training Principles*. 3rd ed. London: A&C Black, 253-304, 1997.
39. Dick, FW. *Sports Training Principles*. 4th ed. London: A&C Black, 2002.
40. Dotan, R, Mitchell, C, Cohen, R, Gabriel, D, Klentrou, P, and Falk, B. Child-adult differences in the kinetics of torque development. *J Sports Sci* 31:945-953, 2013.
41. Dotan, R, Mitchell, C, Cohen, R, Klentrou, P, Gabriel, D, and Falk, B. Child-adult differences in muscle activation—a review. *Pediatr Exerc Sci* 24:2-21, 2012.
42. Drew, MK, and Finch, CF. The relationship between training load and injury, illness and soreness: A systematic and literature review. *Sports Med* 46:861-883, 2016.
43. El-Hewie, MF. *Essentials of Weightlifting & Strength Training*. 1st ed. Lodi, NJ: Shaymaa Publishing Corporation, 2003.
44. Falk, B, Usselman, C, Dotan, R, Brunton, L, Klentrou, P, Shaw, J, and Gabriel, D. Child-adult differences in muscle strength and activation pattern during isometric elbow flexion and extension. *Appl Physiol Nutr Metab* 34:609-615, 2009.
45. Febbraio, MA, and Dancey, J. Skeletal muscle energy metabolism during prolonged, fatiguing exercise. *J Appl Physiol* 87:2341-2347, 1999.
46. Ferguson, BS, Rogatzki, MJ, Goodwin, ML, Kane, DA, Rightmire, Z, and Gladden, LB. Lactate metabolism: Historical context, prior misinterpretations, and current understanding. *Eur J Appl Physiol* 118:691-728, 2018.
47. Ferreira, DV, Gentil, P, Ferreira-Junior, JB, Soares, SRS, Brown, LE, and Bottaro, M. Dissociated time course between peak torque and total work recovery following bench press training in resistance trained men. *Physiol Behav* 179:143-147, 2017.
48. Fitts, RH. The cross-bridge cycle and skeletal muscle fatigue. *J Appl Physiol* 104:551-558, 2008.
49. Fitz-Clarke, JR, Morton, RH, and Banister, EW. Optimizing athletic performance by influence curves. *J Appl Physiol* 71:1151-1158, 1991.
50. Ford, P, De Ste Croix, M, Lloyd, R, Meyers, R, Moosavi, M, Oliver, J, Till, K, and Williams, C. The long-term athlete development model: Physiological evidence and application. *J Sports Sci* 29:389-402, 2011.
51. Foster, C. Monitoring training in athletes with reference to overtraining syndrome. *Med Sci Sports Exerc* 30:1164-1168, 1998.
52. Foster, C, de Koning, JJ, Rundell, KW, and Snyder, AC. Physiology of speed skating. In *Exercise and Sport Science*. Garrett, WE, Kirkendall, DT, eds. Philadelphia, PA: Lippincott Williams and Wilkins, 885-893, 2000.
53. Fry, AC. The role of training intensity in resistance exercise overtraining and overreaching. In *Overtraining in Sport*. Kreider, RB, Fry, AC, O'Toole, ML, eds. Champaign, IL: Human Kinetics, 107-127, 1998.
54. Fry, AC, Kraemer, WJ, van Borselen, F, Lynch, JM, Marsit, JL, Roy, EP, Triplett, NT, and Knuttgen, HG. Performance decrements with high-intensity resistance exercise overtraining. *Med Sci Sports Exerc* 26:1165-1173, 1994.
55. Fry, AC, Schilling, BK, Weiss, LW, and Chiu, LZ. Beta2-adrenergic receptor downregulation and performance decrements during high-intensity resistance exercise overtraining. *J Appl Physiol* 101:1664-1672, 2006.
56. Gabbett, TJ. The training-injury prevention paradox: Should athletes be training smarter and harder? *Br J Sports Med* 50:273-280, 2016.
57. Gabbett, TJ, Hulin, BT, Blanch, P, and Whiteley, R. High training workloads alone do not cause sports injuries: How you get there is the real issue. *Br J Sports Med* 50:444-445, 2016.
58. Gabbett, TJ, Kennelly, S, Sheehan, J, Hawkins, R, Milsom, J, King, E, Whiteley, R, and Ekstrand, J. If overuse injury is a "training load error", should undertraining be viewed the same way? *Br J Sports Med* 50:1017-1018, 2016.
59. Galliven, EA, Singh, A, Michelson, D, Bina, S, Gold, PW, and Deuster, PA. Hormonal and metabolic responses to exercise across time of day and menstrual cycle phase. *J Appl Physiol* 83:1822-1831, 1997.
60. Gallo, TF, Cormack, SJ, Gabbett, TJ, and Lorenzen, CH. Self-reported wellness profiles of professional Australian football players during the competition phase of the season. *J Strength Cond Res* 31:495-502, 2017.
61. Gamble, P. Specificity and transfer of training effects. In *Strength and Conditioning for Team Sports: Sport-Specific Physical Preparation for High Performance*. London: Routledge, 1-9, 2013.

62. Garcia-Lopez, D, de Paz, JA, Jimenez-Jimenez, R, Bresciani, G, De Souza-Teixeira, F, Herrero, JA, Alvear-Ordenes, I, and Gonzalez-Gallego, J. Early explosive force reduction associated with exercise-induced muscle damage. *J Physiol Biochem* 62:163-169, 2006.

63. Garhammer, J. Periodization of strength training for athletes. *Track Tech* 73:2398-2399, 1979.

64. Garrandes, F, Colson, SS, Pensini, M, and Legros, P. Time course of mechanical and neuromuscular characteristics of cyclists and triathletes during a fatiguing exercise. *Int J Sports Med* 28:148-156, 2007.

65. Garrandes, F, Colson, SS, Pensini, M, Seynnes, O, and Legros, P. Neuromuscular fatigue profile in endurance-trained and power-trained athletes. *Med Sci Sports Exerc* 39:149-158, 2007.

66. Georgiades, E, Klissouras, V, Baulch, J, Wang, G, and Pitsiladis, Y. Why nature prevails over nurture in the making of the elite athlete. *BMC Genomics* 18:835, 2017.

67. Gillam, GM. Effects of frequency of weight training on muscle strength enhancement. *J Sports Med* 21:432-436, 1981.

68. Gonzalez-Badillo, JJ, Rodriguez-Rosell, D, Sanchez-Medina, L, Ribas, J, Lopez-Lopez, C, Mora-Custodio, R, Yanez-Garcia, JM, and Pareja-Blanco, F. Short-term recovery following resistance exercise leading or not to failure. *Int J Sports Med* 37:295-304, 2016.

69. Gorostiaga, EM, Navarro-Amezqueta, I, Calbet, JA, Hellsten, Y, Cusso, R, Guerrero, M, Granados, C, Gonzalez-Izal, M, Ibanez, J, and Izquierdo, M. Energy metabolism during repeated sets of leg press exercise leading to failure or not. *PLoS One* 7:e40621, 2012.

70. Gorostiaga, EM, Navarro-Amezqueta, I, Calbet, JA, Sanchez-Medina, L, Cusso, R, Guerrero, M, Granados, C, Gonzalez-Izal, M, Ibanez, J, and Izquierdo, M. Blood ammonia and lactate as markers of muscle metabolites during leg press exercise. *J Strength Cond Res* 28:2775-2785, 2014.

71. Gorostiaga, EM, Navarro-Amezqueta, I, Cusso, R, Hellsten, Y, Calbet, JA, Guerrero, M, Granados, C, Gonzalez-Izal, M, Ibanez, J, and Izquierdo, M. Anaerobic energy expenditure and mechanical efficiency during exhaustive leg press exercise. *PLoS One* 5:e13486, 2010.

72. Goto, K, Higashiyama, M, Ishii, N, and Takamatsu, K. Prior endurance exercise attenuates growth hormone response to subsequent resistance exercise. *Eur J Appl Physiol* 94:333-338, 2005.

73. Grgic, J, Schoenfeld, BJ, Davies, TB, Lazinica, B, Krieger, JW, and Pedisic, Z. Effect of resistance training frequency on gains in muscular strength: A systematic review and meta-analysis. *Sports Med* 48:1207-1220, 2018.

74. Guezennec, Y, Leger, L, Lhoste, F, Aymonod, M, and Pesquies, PC. Hormone and metabolite response to weight-lifting training sessions. *Int J Sports Med* 7:100-105, 1986.

75. Haff, GG. The essentials of periodisation. In *Strength and Conditioning for Sports Performance*. Jeffreys, I, Moody, J, eds. Abingdon, Oxon: Routledge, 404-448, 2016.

76. Haff, GG. Periodization and power integration. In *Developing Power*. McGuigan, M, ed. Champaign, IL: Human Kinetics, 33-62, 2017.

77. Haff, GG, Burgener, M, Faigenbaum, AD, Kilgore, JL, Lavalle, ME, Nitka, M, Rippetoe, M, and Proulx, C. Roundtable discussion: Youth resistance training. *Strength and Cond J* 25:49-64, 2003.

78. Haff, GG, and Burgess, SJ. Resistance training for endurance sports. In *Developing Endurance*. Reuter, BH, ed. Champaign, IL: Human Kinetics, 135-180, 2012.

79. Haff, GG, and Haff, EE. Resistance training program design. In *Essentials Of Periodization*. 2nd ed. Malek, MH, Coburn, JW, eds. Champaign, IL: Human Kinetics, 359-401, 2012.

80. Haff, GG, and Haff, EE. Training integration and periodization. In *Strength and Conditioning Program Design*. Hoffman, J, ed. Champaign, IL: Human Kinetics, 209-254, 2012.

81. Haff, GG, Koch, AJ, Potteiger, JA, Kuphal, KE, Magee, LM, Green, SB, and Jakicic, JJ. Carbohydrate supplementation attenuates muscle glycogen loss during acute bouts of resistance exercise. *Int J Sport Nutr Exerc Metab* 10:326-339, 2000.

82. Haff, GG, Kraemer, WJ, O'Bryant, HS, Pendlay, G, Plisk, S, and Stone, MH. Roundtable discussion: Periodization of training—part 2. *NSCA J* 26:56-70, 2004.

83. Haff, GG, Stone, MH, Warren, BJ, Keith, R, Johnson, RL, Nieman, DC, Williams, F, and Kirksey, KB. The effect of carbohydrate supplementation on multiple sessions and bouts of resistance exercise. *J Strength Cond Res* 13:111-117, 1999.

84. Häkkinen, K, and Kallinen, M. Distribution of strength training volume into one or two daily sessions and neuromuscular adaptations in female athletes. *Electromyogr Clin Neurophysiol* 34:117-124, 1994.

85. Hall, MM, Rajasekaran, S, Thomsen, TW, and Peterson, AR. Lactate: Friend or foe. *PM&R* 8:S8-S15, 2016.

86. Harre, D. *Principles of Sports Training*. Berlin, Germany: Democratic Republic: Sportverlag, 1982.

87. Harre, D, Harre, D, and Barsch, J. The formation of the standard of athletic performance. In *Principles of Sports Training: Introduction to the Theory and Methods of Training*. Michigan, USA: Ultimate Athlete Concepts, 70-112, 2012.

88. Harre, D, Harre, D, and Barsch, J. *Principles of Sports Training: Introduction to the Theory and Methods of Training*. Michigan, USA: Ultimate Athlete Concepts, 2012.

89. Harris, RC, Edwards, RH, Hultman, E, Nordesjo, LO, Nylind, B, and Sahlin, K. The time course of phosphorylcreatine resynthesis during recovery of the quadriceps muscle in man. *Pflugers Arch* 367:137-142, 1976.

90. Hartman, MJ, Clark, B, Bembens, DA, Kilgore, JL, and Bemben, MG. Comparisons between twice-daily and once-daily training sessions in male weight lifters. *Int J Sports Physiol Perform* 2:159-169, 2007.

91. Hayes, LD, Grace, FM, Baker, JS, and Sculthorpe, N. Exercise-induced responses in salivary testosterone, cortisol, and their ratios in men: A meta-analysis. *Sports Med* 45:713-726, 2015.

92. Herda, TJ, and Cramer, JT. Bioenergetics of exercise and training. In *Essentials of Strength Training and Conditioning*. 4th ed. Haff, GG, Triplett, N, eds. Champaign, IL: Human Kinetics, 43-63, 2016.

93. Hirvonen, J, Rehunen, S, Rusko, H, and Harkonen, M. Breakdown of high-energy phosphate compounds and lactate accumulation during short supramaximal exercise. *Eur J Appl Physiol* 56:253-259, 1987.

94. Hodges, NJ, Hayes, S, Horn, RR, and Williams, AM. Changes in coordination, control and outcome as a result of extended practice on a novel motor skill. *Ergonomics* 48:1672-1685, 2005.

95. Hulin, BT, Gabbett, TJ, Caputi, P, Lawson, DW, and Sampson, JA. Low chronic workload and the acute:chronic workload ratio are more predictive of injury than between-match recovery time: A two-season prospective cohort study in elite rugby league players. *Br J Sports Med* 50, 2016.

96. Hultman, E, Greenhaff, PL, Ren, JM, and Soderlund, K. Energy metabolism and fatigue during intense muscle contraction. *Biochem Soc Trans* 19:347-353, 1991.

97. Hultman, E, and Sjoholm, H. Biochemical causes of fatigue. In *Human Muscle Power.* Jones, NL, ed. Champaign, IL: Human Kinetics, 343-363, 1986.

98. Hyldahl, RD, and Hubal, MJ. Lengthening our perspective: Morphological, cellular, and molecular responses to eccentric exercise. *Muscle Nerve* 49:155-170, 2014.

99. Ide, BN, Leme, TC, Lopes, CR, Moreira, A, Dechechi, CJ, Sarraipa, MF, Da Mota, GR, Brenzikofer, R, and Macedo, DV. Time course of strength and power recovery after resistance training with different movement velocities. *J Strength Cond Res* 25:2025-2033, 2011.

100. Ijichi, T, Hasegawa, Y, Morishima, T, Kurihara, T, Hamaoka, T, and Goto, K. Effect of sprint training: Training once daily versus twice every second day. *Eur J Sport Sci* 15:143-150, 2015.

101. Issurin, V. *Building the Modern Athlete: Scientific Advancement & Training Innovation.* Michigan, USA: Ultimate Athlete Concepts, 2015.

102. Izquierdo, M, Ibanez, J, Gonzalez-Badillo, JJ, Hakkinen, K, Ratamess, NA, Kraemer, WJ, French, DN, Eslava, J, Altadill, A, Asiain, X, and Gorostiaga, EM. Differential effects of strength training leading to failure versus not to failure on hormonal responses, strength, and muscle power gains. *J Appl Physiol* 100:1647-1656, 2006.

103. Jamurtas, AZ, Koutedakis, Y, Paschalis, V, Tofas, T, Yfanti, C, Tsiokanos, A, Koukoulis, G, Kouretas, D, and Loupos, D. The effects of a single bout of exercise on resting energy expenditure and respiratory exchange ratio. *Eur J Appl Physiol* 92:393-398, 2004.

104. Johnson, U, and Ivarsson, A. Psychosocial factors and sport injuries: Prediction, prevention and future research directions. *Curr Opin Psychol* 16:89-92, 2017.

105. Karlsson, J, Nordesjo, LO, Jorfeldt, L, and Saltin, B. Muscle lactate, ATP, and CP levels during exercise after physical training in man. *J Appl Physiol* 33:199-203, 1972.

106. Karlsson, J, and Ollander, B. Muscle metabolites with exhaustive static exercise of different duration. *Acta Physiol Scand* 86:309-314, 1972.

107. Khong, TK, Selvanayagam, VS, Sidhu, SK, and Yusof, A. Role of carbohydrate in central fatigue: A systematic review. *Scand J Med Sci Sports* 27:376-384, 2017.

108. Kiely, J. Periodization paradigms in the 21st century: Evidence-led or tradition-driven? *Int J Sports Physiol Perform* 7:242-250, 2012.

109. Kiely, J. Periodization theory: Confronting an inconvenient truth. *Sports Med* 48:753-764, 2018.

110. Kjaer, M, Kiens, B, Hargreaves, M, and Richter, EA. Influence of active muscle mass on glucose homeostasis during exercise in humans. *J Appl Physiol* 71:552-557, 1991.

111. Kraemer, WJ, Ratamess, NA, and Nindl, BC. Recovery responses of testosterone, growth hormone, and IGF-1 after resistance exercise. *J Appl Physiol (1985)* 122:549-558, 2017.

112. Kramer, JB, Stone, MH, O'Bryant, HS, Conley, MS, Johnson, RL, Nieman, DC, Honeycutt, DR, and Hoke, TP. Effects of single vs. multiple sets of weight training: Impact of volume, intensity, and variation. *J Strength Cond Res* 11:143-147, 1997.

113. Kubo, K, Teshima, T, Ikebukuro, T, Hirose, N, and Tsunoda, N. Tendon properties and muscle architecture for knee extensors and plantar flexors in boys and men. *Clin Biomech (Bristol, Avon)* 29:506-511, 2014.

114. Kurz, T. *Science of Sports Training.* 2nd ed. Island Pond, VT: Stadion Publishing, 2001.

115. Lacome, M, Carling, C, Hager, JP, Dine, G, and Piscione, J. Workload, fatigue, and muscle damage in an under-20 Rugby Union team over an intensified international tournament. *Int J Sports Physiol Perform* 13:1059-1066, 2018.

116. LaForgia, J, Withers, RT, and Gore, CJ. Effects of exercise intensity and duration on the excess post-exercise oxygen consumption. *J Sports Sci* 24:1247-1264, 2006.

117. Lebon, V, Dufour, S, Petersen, KF, Ren, J, Jucker, BM, Slezak, LA, Cline, GW, Rothman, DL, and Shulman, GI. Effect of triiodothyronine on mitochondrial energy coupling in human skeletal muscle. *J Clin Invest* 108:733-737, 2001.

118. Leeder, JD, van Someren, KA, Gaze, D, Jewell, A, Deshmukh, NI, Shah, I, Barker, J, and Howatson, G. Recovery and adaptation from repeated intermittent-sprint exercise. *Int J Sports Physiol Perform* 9:489-496, 2014.

119. Lexell, J, Sjostrom, M, Nordlund, AS, and Taylor, CC. Growth and development of human muscle: A quantitative morphological study of whole vastus lateralis from childhood to adult age. *Muscle Nerve* 15:404-409, 1992.

120. Lloyd, RS, Cronin, JB, Faigenbaum, AD, Haff, GG, Howard, R, Kraemer, WJ, Micheli, LJ, Myer, GD, and Oliver, JL. National Strength and Conditioning Association position statement on long-term athletic development. *J Strength Cond Res* 30:1491-1509, 2016.

121. Lloyd, RS, Oliver, JL, Faigenbaum, AD, Howard, R, De Ste Croix, MB, Williams, CA, Best, TM, Alvar, BA, Micheli, LJ, Thomas, DP, Hatfield, DL, Cronin, JB, and Myer, GD. Long-term athletic development—part 1: A pathway for all youth. *J Strength Cond Res* 29:1439-1450, 2015.

122. Lloyd, RS, Oliver, JL, Faigenbaum, AD, Howard, R, De Ste Croix, MBA, Williams, CA, Best, TM, Alvar, BA, Micheli, LJ, Thomas, DP, Hatfield, DL, Cronin, JB, and Myer, GD. Long-term athletic development—part 2: Barriers to success and potential solutions. *J Strength Cond Res* 29:1451-1464, 2015.

123. Lloyd, RS, Oliver, JL, Meyers, RW, Moody, JA, and Stone, MH. Long-term athletic development and its application to youth weightlifting. *Strength & Conditioning Journal* 34:55-66, 2012.

124. MacDougall, D, and Sale, D. *The Physiology of Training for High Performance*. Oxford, United Kingdom: Oxford University Press, 2014.

125. MacDougall, D, and Sale, D. Training for strength, power, and speed. In *The Physiology of Training for High Performance*. Oxford, United Kingdom: Oxford University Press, 246-307, 2014.

126. MacDougall, JD, Gibala, MJ, Tarnopolsky, MA, MacDonald, JR, Interisano, SA, and Yarasheski, KE. The time course for elevated muscle protein synthesis following heavy resistance exercise. *Can J Appl Physiol* 20:480-486, 1995.

127. MacDougall, JD, Ray, S, McCartney, N, Sale, D, Lee, P, and Gardner, S. Substrate utilization during weight lifting (abstract). *Med Sci Sports Exerc* 20:S66, 1988.

128. MacDougall, JD, Ray, S, Sale, DG, McCartney, N, Lee, P, and Garner, S. Muscle substrate utilization and lactate production during weightlifting. *Can J Appl Physiol* 24:209-215, 1999.

129. MacIntosh, BR, and Shahi, MR. A peripheral governor regulates muscle contraction. *Applied physiology, nutrition, and metabolism [Physiologie appliquee, nutrition et metabolisme]* 36:1-11, 2011.

130. MacIntyre, DL, Sorichter, S, Mair, J, Berg, A, and McKenzie, DC. Markers of inflammation and myofibrillar proteins following eccentric exercise in humans. *Eur J Appl Physiol* 84:180-186, 2001.

131. Mackey, AL, and Kjaer, M. The breaking and making of healthy adult human skeletal muscle in vivo. *Skelet Muscle* 7:24, 2017.

132. Malisoux, L, Frisch, A, Urhausen, A, Seil, R, and Theisen, D. Monitoring of sport participation and injury risk in young athletes. *J Sci Med Sport* 16:504-508.

133. Mangine, GT, Hoffman, JR, Gonzalez, AM, Townsend, JR, Wells, AJ, Jajtner, AR, Beyer, KS, Boone, CH, Miramonti, AA, Wang, R, LaMonica, MB, Fukuda, DH, Ratamess, NA, and Stout, JR. The effect of training volume and intensity on improvements in muscular strength and size in resistance-trained men. *Physiol Rep* 3, 2015.

134. Mann, JB, Bryant, KR, Johnstone, B, Ivey, PA, and Sayers, SP. Effect of physical and academic stress on illness and injury in Division 1 college football players. *J Strength Cond Res* 30:20-25, 2016.

135. Mcardle, WD, Katch, FI, and Katch, VL. Dynamics of pulmonary ventilation. In *Exercise Physiology: Energy, Nutrition, and Human Performance*. 7th ed. Baltimore, MD: Lippincott, Williams & Wilkins, 286-302, 2010.

136. McCann, DJ, Mole, PA, and Caton, JR. Phosphocreatine kinetics in humans during exercise and recovery. *Med Sci Sports Exerc* 27:378-389, 1995.

137. McGarvey, W, Jones, R, and Petersen, S. Excess post-exercise oxygen consumption following continuous and interval cycling exercise. *International Journal of Sport Nutrition & Exercise Metabolism* 15:28-37, 2005.

138. McGuigan, M. Athlete monitoring guidelines for individual sports. In *Monitoring Training and Performance in Athletes*. Champaign, IL: Human Kinetics, 171-188, 2017.

139. McGuigan, M. Athlete monitoring guidelines for team sports. In *Monitoring Training and Performance in Athletes*. Champaign, IL: Human Kinetics, 189-201, 2017.

140. McMillan, JL, Stone, MH, Sartin, J, Keith, R, Marple, D, Brown, C, and Lewis, RD. 20-hour physiological responses to a single weight-training session. *J Strength Cond Res* 7:9-21, 1993.

141. Medvedyev, AS. *A system of multi-year training in weightlifting*. Moscow Russia: Fizkultura i Sport, 1986.

142. Melby, C, Scholl, C, Edwards, G, and Bullough, R. Effect of acute resistance exercise on postexercise energy expenditure and resting metabolic rate. *J Appl Physiol* 75:1847-1853, 1993.

143. Michaut, A, Pousson, M, Millet, G, Belleville, J, and Van Hoecke, J. Maximal voluntary eccentric, isometric and concentric torque recovery following a concentric isokinetic exercise. *Int J Sports Med* 24:51-56, 2003.

144. Milanez, VF, Ramos, SP, Okuno, NM, Boullosa, DA, and Nakamura, FY. Evidence of a non-linear dose-response relationship between training load and stress markers in elite female futsal players. *J Sports Sci Med* 13:22-29, 2014.

145. Millet, GP, Candau, RB, Barbier, B, Busso, T, Rouillon, JD, and Chatard, JC. Modelling the transfers of training effects on performance in elite triathletes. *Int J Sports Med* 23:55-63, 2002.

146. Millet, GY, Tomazin, K, Verges, S, Vincent, C, Bonnefoy, R, Boisson, RC, Gergele, L, Feasson, L, and Martin, V. Neuromuscular consequences of an extreme mountain ultra-marathon. *PLoS One* 6:e17059, 2011.

147. Molina, R, and Denadai, BS. Dissociated time course recovery between rate of force development and peak torque after eccentric exercise. *Clin Physiol Funct Imaging* 32:179-184, 2012.

148. Morán-Navarro, R, Perez, CE, Mora-Rodriguez, R, de la Cruz-Sanchez, E, Gonzalez-Badillo, JJ, Sanchez-Medina, L, and Pallares, JG. Time course of recovery following resistance training leading or not to failure. *Eur J Appl Physiol* 117:2387-2399, 2017.

149. Mul, JD, Stanford, KI, Hirshman, MF, and Goodyear, LJ. Exercise and regulation of carbohydrate metabolism. *Prog Mol Biol Transl Sci* 135:17-37, 2015.

150. Muller, E, Benko, U, Raschner, C, and Schwameder, H. Specific fitness training and testing in competitive sports. *Med Sci Sports Exerc* 32:216-220, 2000.

151. Nicol, C, Avela, J, and Komi, PV. The stretch-shortening cycle: A model to study naturally occurring neuromuscular fatigue. *Sports Med* 36:977-999, 2006.

152. Nieman, DC, and Pedersen, BK. Exercise and immune function: Recent developments. *Sports Med* 27:73-80, 1999.

153. Noakes, TD, Peltonen, JE, and Rusko, HK. Evidence that a central governor regulates exercise performance during acute hypoxia and hyperoxia. *J Exp Biol* 204:3225-3234, 2001.

154. O'Toole, ML. Overreaching and overtraining in endurance athletes. In *Overtraining in Sport*. Kreider, RB, Fry, AC, O'Toole, ML, eds. Champaign, IL: Human Kinetics, 3-18, 1998.

155. Olbrect, J. *The Science of Winning: Planning, Periodizing, and Optimizing Swim Training*. Luton, England: Swimshop, 2000.

156. Oliver, JL, and Smith, PM. Neural control of leg stiffness during hopping in boys and men. *J Electromyogr Kinesiol* 20:973-979, 2010.
157. Ortenblad, N, Nielsen, J, Saltin, B, and Holmberg, HC. Role of glycogen availability in sarcoplasmic reticulum Ca2+ kinetics in human skeletal muscle. *J Physiol* 589:711-725, 2011.
158. Owens, DJ, Twist, C, Cobley, JN, Howatson, G, and Close, GL. Exercise-induced muscle damage: What is it, what causes it and what are the nutritional solutions? *Eur J Sport Sci*:1-15, 2018.
159. Pareja-Blanco, F, Rodriguez-Rosell, D, Sanchez-Medina, L, Ribas-Serna, J, Lopez-Lopez, C, Mora-Custodio, R, Yanez-Garcia, JM, and Gonzalez-Badillo, JJ. Acute and delayed response to resistance exercise leading or not leading to muscle failure. *Clin Physiol Funct Imaging* 37:630-639, 2017.
160. Parolin, ML, Chesley, A, Matsos, MP, Spriet, LL, Jones, NL, and Heigenhauser, GJ. Regulation of skeletal muscle glycogen phosphorylase and PDH during maximal intermittent exercise. *Am J Physiol* 277:E890-900, 1999.
161. Peake, JM, Neubauer, O, Della Gatta, PA, and Nosaka, K. Muscle damage and inflammation during recovery from exercise. *J Appl Physiol (1985)* 122:559-570, 2017.
162. Peterson, MD, Rhea, MR, and Alvar, BA. Applications of the dose-response for muscular strength development: A review of meta-analytic efficacy and reliability for designing training prescription. *J Strength Cond Res* 19:950-958, 2005.
163. Pickering, C, and Kiely, J. ACTN3: More than just a gene for speed. *Front Physiol* 8, 2017.
164. Plisk, SS. Effective needs analysis and functional training principles. In *Strength and Conditioning for Sports Performance*. Jeffreys, I, Moody, J, eds. New York, New York: Routledge, 181-200, 2016.
165. Plisk, SS, and Gambetta, V. Tactical metabolic training: Part 1. *Strength Cond J* 19:44-53, 1997.
166. Plisk, SS, and Stone, MH. Periodization strategies. *Strength Cond J* 25:19-37, 2003.
167. Rumpf, MC, Lockie, RG, Cronin, JB, and Jalilvand, F. Effect of different sprint training methods on sprint performance over various distances: A brief review. *J Strength Cond Res* 30:1767-1785, 2016.
168. Sahlin, K, Tonkonogi, M, and Soderlund, K. Energy supply and muscle fatigue in humans. *Acta Physiol Scand* 162:261-266, 1998.
169. Sands, WA. Monitoring elite female gymnasts. *Natl Strength Cond Assoc J* 13:66-71, 1991.
170. Schiphof-Godart, L, Roelands, B, and Hettinga, FJ. Drive in sports: How mental fatigue affects endurance performance. *Front Psychol* 9, 2018.
171. Schwellnus, M, Soligard, T, Alonso, J-M, Bahr, R, Clarsen, B, Dijkstra, HP, Gabbett, TJ, Gleeson, M, Hägglund, M, Hutchinson, MR, Janse Van Rensburg, C, Meeusen, R, Orchard, JW, Pluim, BM, Raftery, M, Budgett, R, and Engebretsen, L. How much is too much? (Part 2) International Olympic Committee consensus statement on load in sport and risk of illness. *Br J Sports Med* 50:1043-1052, 2016.
172. Selye, H. Stress and the general adaptation syndrome. *Br Med J* 1:1383, 1950.
173. Selye, H. Confusion and controversy in the stress field. *J Human Stress* 1:37-44, 1975.
174. Selye, H. Forty years of stress research: Principal remaining problems and misconceptions. *Can Med Assoc J* 115:53-56, 1976.
175. Selye, H. A code for coping with stress. *AORN J* 25:35-42, 1977.
176. Selye, H. Stress and holistic medicine. *Fam Community Health* 3:85-88, 1980.
177. Selye, H. The Stress Concept: Past, Present, and Future. In *Stress Research: Issues for the Eighties*. Cooper, CL, ed. New York: Wiley, 1-20, 1983.
178. Sheppard, JM, and Triplett, NT. Program design for resistance training. In *Essentials of Strength Training and Conditioning*. Haff, GG, Triplett, NT, eds. Champaign, IL: Human Kinetics, 439-470, 2016.
179. Siff, MC. Functional training revisited. *Strength Cond J* 24:42-46, 2002.
180. Silva, JR, Rumpf, MC, Hertzog, M, Castagna, C, Farooq, A, Girard, O, and Hader, KJSM. Acute and residual soccer match-related fatigue: A systematic review and meta-analysis. *Sports Med* 48:539-583, 2018.
181. Smiles, WJ, Hawley, JA, and Camera, DM. Effects of skeletal muscle energy availability on protein turnover responses to exercise. *J Exp Biol* 219:214-225, 2016.
182. Smith, LL. Cytokine hypothesis of overtraining: A physiological adaptation to excessive stress? *Med Sci Sports Exerc* 32:317-331, 2000.
183. Soligard, T, Schwellnus, M, Alonso, J-M, Bahr, R, Clarsen, B, Dijkstra, HP, Gabbett, T, Gleeson, M, Hägglund, M, Hutchinson, MR, Janse van Rensburg, C, Khan, KM, Meeusen, R, Orchard, JW, Pluim, BM, Raftery, M, Budgett, R, and Engebretsen, L. How much is too much? (Part 1) International Olympic Committee consensus statement on load in sport and risk of injury. *Br J Sports Med* 50:1030-1041, 2016.
184. 1Sousa, AC, Marinho, DA, Gil, MH, Izquierdo, M, Rodriguez-Rosell, D, Neiva, HP, and Marques, MC. Concurrent training followed by detraining: Does the resistance training intensity matter? *J Strength Cond Res* 32:632-642, 2018.
185. Speakman, JR, and Selman, C. Physical activity and resting metabolic rate. *Proc Nutr Soc* 62:621-634, 2003.
186. Stepto, NK, Martin, DT, Fallon, KE, and Hawley, JA. Metabolic demands of intense aerobic interval training in competitive cyclists. *Med Sci Sports Exerc* 33:303-310, 2001.
187. Stone, MH, Collins, D, Plisk, S, Haff, G, and Stone, ME. Training principles: Evaluation of modes and methods of resistance training. *Strength Cond J* 22:65, 2000.
188. Stone, MH, Keith, R, Kearney, JT, Wilson, GD, and Fleck, S, J,. Overtraining: A review of the signs and symptoms of overtraining. *J Strength Cond Res* 5:35-50, 1991.
189. Stone, MH, and O'Bryant, HO. *Weight Training: A Scientific Approach*. Edina, MN: Burgess, 1987.
190. Stone, MH, O'Bryant, HS, and Garhammer, J. A theoretical model of strength training. *NSCA J* 3:36-39, 1982.
191. Stone, MH, Plisk, S, and Collins, D. Training principles: Evaluation of modes and methods of resistance-training—a coaching perspective. *Sport Biomech* 1:79-104, 2002.

192. Stone, MH, Stone, ME, and Sands, WA. Bioenergetic and metabolic factors. In *Principles and Practice of Resistance Training*. Champaign, IL: Human Kinetics, 61-86, 2007.

193. Stone, MH, Stone, ME, and Sands, WA. The concept of periodization. In *Principles and Practice of Resistance Training*. Champaign, IL: Human Kinetics, 259-286, 2007.

194. Stone, MH, Stone, ME, and Sands, WA. Introduction, definitions, objectives, tasks, and principles of training. In *Principles and Practice of Resistance Training*. Champaign, IL: Human Kinetics, 1-12, 2007.

195. Stone, MH, Stone, ME, and Sands, WA. Physical and physiological adaptations to resistance training. In *Principles and Practice of Resistance Training*. Champaign, IL: Human Kinetics, 201-228, 2007.

196. Stone, MH, Stone, ME, and Sands, WA. *Principles and Practice of Resistance Training*. Champaign, IL: Human Kinetics, 2007.

197. Stults-Kolehmainen, MA, Bartholomew, JB, and Sinha, R. Chronic psychological stress impairs recovery of muscular function and somatic sensations over a 96-hour period. *J Strength Cond Res* 28:2007-2017, 2014.

198. Sundberg, CW, Hunter, SK, Trappe, SW, Smith, CS, and Fitts, RH. Effects of elevated H+ and Pi on the contractile mechanics of skeletal muscle fibres from young and old men: implications for muscle fatigue in humans. *J Physiol* 596:3992-4015, 2018.

199. Tang, JE, Perco, JG, Moore, DR, Wilkinson, SB, and Phillips, SM. Resistance training alters the response of fed state mixed muscle protein synthesis in young men. *Am J Physiol Regul Integr Comp Physiol* 294:R172-178, 2008.

200. Ten Haaf, T, van Staveren, S, Oudenhoven, E, Piacentini, MF, Meeusen, R, Roelands, B, Koenderman, L, Daanen, HAM, Foster, C, and de Koning, JJ. Prediction of functional overreaching from subjective fatigue and readiness to train after only 3 days of cycling. *Int J Sports Physiol Perform* 12:S287-S294, 2017.

201. Tesch, P, Sjodin, B, Thorstensson, A, and Karlsson, J. Muscle fatigue and its relation to lactate accumulation and LDH activity in man. *Acta Physiol Scand* 103:413-420, 1978.

202. Tesch, PA, Ploutz-Snyder, LL, Yström, L, Castro, M, and Dudley, G. Skeletal muscle glycogen loss evoked by resistance exercise. *J Strength Cond Res* 12:67-73, 1998.

203. Thibaudeau, C. *The Black Book of Training Secrets*. Quebec, Canada: F.Lepine Publishing, 2006.

204. Thomas, K, Brownstein, CG, Dent, J, Parker, P, Goodall, S, and Howatson, G. Neuromuscular fatigue and recovery after heavy resistance, jump, and sprint training. *Med Sci Sports Exerc* 50:2526-2535, 2018.

205. Tucker, R, and Collins, M. What makes champions? A review of the relative contribution of genes and training to sporting success. *Br J Sports Med* 46:555-561, 2012.

206. Tucker, WJ, Angadi, SS, and Gaesser, GA. Excess postexercise oxygen consumption after high-intensity and sprint interval exercise, and continuous steady-state exercise. *J Strength Cond Res* 30:3090-3097, 2016.

207. Turner, A, and Comfort, P. Periodisation. In *Advanced Strength and Conditioning: An Evidence-Based Approach*. Turner, A, Comfort, P, eds. London: Routledge Taylor Francis, 116-136, 2018.

208. Twomey, R, Aboodarda, SJ, Kruger, R, Culos-Reed, SN, Temesi, J, and Millet, GY. Neuromuscular fatigue during exercise: Methodological considerations, etiology and potential role in chronic fatigue. *Neurophysiol Clin* 47:95-110, 2017.

209. Van Praagh, E, and Dore, E. Short-term muscle power during growth and maturation. *Sports Med* 32:701-728, 2002.

210. Verkhoshansky, Y, and Siff, MC. Adaptations and training effect. In *Supertraining: Expanded Version*. 6th ed. Rome, Italy: Verkhoshansky, 82-94, 2009.

211. Verkhoshansky, Y, and Siff, MC. *Supertraining*. 6th (expanded) ed. Rome, Italy: Verkhoshansky, 2009.

212. Verkhoshansky, Y, and Verkhoshansky, N. *Special Strength Training Manual for Coaches*. Rome, Italy: Verkhoshansky, 2011.

213. Viru, A. *Adaptations in Sports Training*. Boca Raton, FL: CRC Press, 1995.

214. Wakeling, JM. Motor units are recruited in a task-dependent fashion during locomotion. *J Exp Biol* 207:3883-3890, 2004.

215. Waugh, CM, Korff, T, Fath, F, and Blazevich, AJ. Rapid force production in children and adults: Mechanical and neural contributions. *Med Sci Sports Exerc* 45, 2013.

216. Weigert, K. *Neue Auffassung der Zellwucherung Auf Äussere Reize*. 1873.

217. Westerblad, H, Allen, DG, and Lannergren, J. Muscle fatigue: Lactic acid or inorganic phosphate the major cause? *News Physiol Sci* 17:17-21, 2002.

218. Wiese-Bjornstal, DM. Psychology and socioculture affect injury risk, response, and recovery in high-intensity athletes: A consensus statement. *Scand J Med Sci Sports* 20:103-111, 2010.

219. Windt, J, and Gabbett, TJ. How do training and competition workloads relate to injury? The workload-injury aetiology model. *Br J Sports Med* 51:428-435, 2017.

220. Yamada, AK, Verlengia, R, and Bueno Junior, CR. Mechanotransduction pathways in skeletal muscle hypertrophy. *J Recept Signal Transduct Res* 32:42-44, 2012.

221. Zainuddin, Z, Sacco, P, Newton, M, and Nosaka, K. Light concentric exercise has a temporarily analgesic effect on delayed-onset muscle soreness, but no effect on recovery from eccentric exercise. *Appl Physiol Nutr Metab* 31:126-134, 2006.

222. Zatsiorsky, VM, Kraemer, WJ, and Fry, AC. Basic concepts of training theory. In *Science and Practice of Strength Training*. 3rd ed. Champaign, IL: Human Kinetics, 3-16, 2021.

223. Zatsiorsky, VM, Kraemer, WJ, and Fry, AC. *Science and Practice of Strength Training*. 3rd ed. Champaign, IL: Human Kinetics, 2021.

Chapter 2

1. Abernethy, PJ, Jurimae, J, Logan, PA, Taylor, AW, and Thayer, RE. Acute and chronic response of skeletal muscle to resistance exercise. *Sports Med* 17:22-38, 1994.

2. Abernethy, PJ, Thayer, R, and Taylor, AW. Acute and chronic responses of skeletal muscle to endurance and sprint exercise. A review. *Sports Med* 10:365-389, 1990.

3. Ahlborg, G, and Felig, P. Influence of glucose ingestion on fuel-hormone response during prolonged exercise. *J Appl Physiol* 41:683-688, 1976.
4. Ahlborg, G, and Felig, P. Lactate and glucose exchange across the forearm, legs, and splanchnic bed during and after prolonged leg exercise. *J Clin Invest* 69:45-54, 1982.
5. Bahr, R, Gronnerod, O, and Sejersted, OM. Effect of supramaximal exercise on excess postexercise O2 consumption. *Med Sci Sports Exerc* 24:66-71, 1992.
6. Baker, JS, McCormick, MC, and Robergs, RA. Interaction among skeletal muscle metabolic energy systems during intense exercise. *J Nutr Metab* 2010:905612, 2010.
7. Balsom, PD, Soderlund, K, Sjodin, B, and Ekblom, B. Skeletal muscle metabolism during short duration high-intensity exercise: Influence of creatine supplementation. *Acta Physiol Scand* 154:303-310, 1995.
8. Barclay, CJ. Energy demand and supply in human skeletal muscle. *J Muscle Res Cell Motil* 38:143-155, 2017.
9. Barnard, RJ, Edgerton, VR, Furukawa, T, and Peter, JB. Histochemical, biochemical, and contractile properties of red, white, and intermediate fibers. *American Journal of Physiology* 220:410-414, 1971.
10. Bassett, DR, Jr., and Howley, ET. Limiting factors for maximum oxygen uptake and determinants of endurance performance. *Med Sci Sports Exerc* 32:70-84, 2000.
11. Bemben, MG, and Lamont, HS. Creatine supplementation and exercise performance: Recent findings. *Sports Med* 35:107-125, 2005.
12. Beneke, R, Hutler, M, and Leithauser, RM. Maximal lactate-steady-state independent of performance. *Med Sci Sports Exerc* 32:1135-1139, 2000.
13. Bentley, DJ, McNaughton, LR, Thompson, D, Vleck, VE, and Batterham, AM. Peak power output, the lactate threshold, and time trial performance in cyclists. *Med Sci Sports Exerc* 33:2077-2081, 2001.
14. Bentley, DJ, Newell, J, and Bishop, D. Incremental exercise test design and analysis: Implications for performance diagnostics in endurance athletes. *Sports Med* 37:575-586, 2007.
15. Berg, WE. Individual differences in respiratory gas exchange during recovery from moderate exercise. *Am J Physiol* 149:597-610, 1947.
16. Bickham, DC. Extracellular K+ accumulation: A physiological framework for fatigue during intense exercise. *J Physiol* 554:593, 2004.
17. Billat, LV. Use of blood lactate measurements for prediction of exercise performance and for control of training: Recommendations for long-distance running. *Sports Med* 22:157-175, 1996.
18. Billat, VL. VO2 slow component and performance in endurance sports. *Br J Sports Med* 34:83-85, 2000.
19. Billat, VL, Demarle, A, Slawinski, J, Paiva, M, and Koralsztein, JP. Physical and training characteristics of top-class marathon runners. *Med Sci Sports Exerc* 33:2089-2097, 2001.
20. Billat, VL, Sirvent, P, Py, G, Koralsztein, JP, and Mercier, J. The concept of maximal lactate steady state: A bridge between biochemistry, physiology and sport science. *Sports Med* 33:407-426, 2003.
21. Bishop, D, Edge, J, Thomas, C, and Mercier, J. Effects of high-intensity training on muscle lactate transporters and postexercise recovery of muscle lactate and hydrogen ions in women. *Am J Physiol Regul Integr Comp Physiol* 295:R1991-1998, 2008.
22. Bogdanis, GC, Nevill, ME, Boobis, LH, and Lakomy, HK. Contribution of phosphocreatine and aerobic metabolism to energy supply during repeated sprint exercise. *J Appl Physiol* 80:876-884, 1996.
23. Bogdanis, GC, Nevill, ME, Boobis, LH, Lakomy, HK, and Nevill, AM. Recovery of power output and muscle metabolites following 30 s of maximal sprint cycling in man. *J Physiol* 482:467-480, 1995.
24. Bompa, TO, and Haff, GG. Basis for training. In *Periodization: Theory and Methodology of Training*. 5th ed. Champaign, IL: Human Kinetics, 3-30, 2009.
25. Bompa, TO, and Haff, GG. Endurance Training. In *Periodization: Theory and Methodology of Training*. 5th ed. Champaign, IL: Human Kinetics, 287-314, 2009.
26. Bonen, A. The expression of lactate transporters (MCT1 and MCT4) in heart and muscle. *Eur J Appl Physiol* 86:6-11, 2001.
27. Boobis, I, Williams, C, and Wooten, SN. Influence of sprint training on muscle metabolism during maximal exercise in man. *J Appl Physiol* 342:36P-37P, 1983.
28. Borsheim, E, and Bahr, R. Effect of exercise intensity, duration and mode on post-exercise oxygen consumption. *Sports Med* 33:1037-1060, 2003.
29. Brooks, GA. Amino acid and protein metabolism during exercise and recovery. *Med Sci Sports Exerc* 19:S150-156, 1987.
30. Brooks, GA. Cell-cell and intracellular lactate shuttles. *J Physiol* 587:5591-5600, 2009.
31. Brooks, GA, Brauner, KE, and Cassens, RG. Glycogen synthesis and metabolism of lactic acid after exercise. *Am J Physiol* 224:1162-1166, 1973.
32. Brooks, GA, Fahey, TD, and Baldwin, KM. The maintenance of ATP homeostasis in energetics and human movement. In *Exercise Physiology: Human Bioenergetics and Its Applications*. 4th ed. ed. Boston: McGraw-Hill, 31-42, 2005.
33. Buchheit, M, and Laursen, PB. High-intensity interval training, solutions to the programming puzzle: Part I: Cardiopulmonary emphasis. *Sports Med* 43:313-338, 2013.
34. Buchheit, M, and Laursen, PB. High-intensity interval training, solutions to the programming puzzle: Part II: Anaerobic energy, neuromuscular load and practical applications. *Sports Med* 43:927-954, 2013.
35. Burke, LM, Kiens, B, and Ivy, JL. Carbohydrates and fat for training and recovery. *J Sports Sci* 22:15-30, 2004.
36. Burke, LM, van Loon, LJC, and Hawley, JA. Postexercise muscle glycogen resynthesis in humans. *J Appl Physiol (1985)* 122:1055-1067, 2017.
37. Busa, WB, and Nuccitelli, R. Metabolic regulation via intracellular pH. *Am J Physiol* 246:R409-438, 1984.
38. Carling, D. AMP-activated protein kinase: Balancing the scales. *Biochimie* 87:87-91, 2005.
39. Carter, H, Jones, AM, and Doust, JH. Effect of 6 weeks of endurance training on the lactate minimum speed. *J Sports Sci* 17:957-967, 1999.

40. Cerretelli, P, Ambrosoli, G, and Fumagalli, M. Anaerobic recovery in man. *Eur J Appl Physiol Occup Physiol* 34:141-148, 1975.
41. Chasiotis, D, Sahlin, K, and Hultman, E. Regulation of glycogenolysis in human muscle at rest and during exercise. *J Appl Physiol Respir Environ Exerc Physiol* 53:708-715, 1982.
42. Coggan, AR, and Coyle, EF. Reversal of fatigue during prolonged exercise by carbohydrate infusion or ingestion. *J Appl Physiol* 63:2388-2395, 1987.
43. Conley, M. Bioenergetics of Exercise Training. In *Essentials of Strength Training and Conditioning*. 2nd ed. Baechle, TR, Earle, RW, eds. Champaign, IL: Human Kinetics, 73-90, 2000.
44. Conley, MS, Stone, MH, O'Bryant, HS, Johnson, RL, Honeycutt, DR, and Hoke, TP. Peak power versus power at maximal oxygen uptake. Presented at National Strength and Conditioning Association Annual Convention, Las Vegas,NE, 1993.
45. Constantin-Teodosiu, D, Greenhaff, PL, McIntyre, DB, Round, JM, and Jones, DA. Anaerobic energy production in human skeletal muscle in intense contraction: A comparison of 31P magnetic resonance spectroscopy and biochemical techniques. *Exp Physiol* 82:593-601, 1997.
46. Coyle, EF. Integration of the physiological factors determining endurance performance ability. *Exerc Sport Sci Rev* 23:25-63, 1995.
47. Coyle, EF, Hagberg, JM, Hurley, BF, Martin, WH, Ehsani, AA, and Holloszy, JO. Carbohydrate feeding during prolonged strenuous exercise can delay fatigue. *J Appl Physiol* 55:230-235, 1983.
48. Davis, JA, Frank, MH, Whipp, BJ, and Wasserman, K. Anaerobic threshold alterations caused by endurance training in middle-aged men. *J Appl Physiol Respir Environ Exerc Physiol* 46:1039-1046, 1979.
49. Denadai, BS, Ortiz, MJ, Greco, CC, and de Mello, MT. Interval training at 95% and 100% of the velocity at VO2 max: Effects on aerobic physiological indexes and running performance. *Appl Physiol Nutr Metab* 31:737-743, 2006.
50. Di Prampero, PE, Capelli, C, Pagliaro, P, Antonutto, G, Girardis, M, Zamparo, P, and Soule, RG. Energetics of best performances in middle-distance running. *J Appl Physiol* 74:2318-2324, 1993.
51. Dolny, DG, and Lemon, PW. Effect of ambient temperature on protein breakdown during prolonged exercise. *J Appl Physiol (1985)* 64:550-555, 1988.
52. Dudley, GA. Metabolic consequences of resistive-type exercise. *Med Sci Sports Exerc* 20:S158-161, 1988.
53. Dudley, GA, and Murray, TF. Exercise physiology corner: energy for sport. *Strength Cond J* 4:14-15, 1982.
54. Dudley, GA, and Terjung, RL. Influence of aerobic metabolism on IMP accumulation in fast-twitch muscle. *Am J Physiol* 248:C37-42, 1985.
55. Dufaux, B, Assmann, G, and Hollmann, W. Plasma lipoproteins and physical activity: A review. *Int J Sports Med* 3:123-136, 1982.
56. Dumke, CL, Brock, DW, Helms, BH, and Haff, GG. Heart rate at lactate threshold and cycling time trials. *J Strength Cond Res* 20:601-607, 2006.
57. Esfarjani, F, and Laursen, PB. Manipulating high-intensity interval training: Effects on VO2max, the lactate threshold and 3000 m running performance in moderately trained males. *J Sci Med Sport* 10:27-35, 2007.
58. Essen, B. Glycogen depletion of different fibre types in human skeletal muscle during intermittent and continuous exercise. *Acta Physiol Scand* 103:446-455, 1978.
59. Fabiato, A, and Fabiato, F. Effects of pH on the myofilaments and the sarcoplasmic reticulum of skinned cells from cardiac and skeletal muscles. *J Physiol Lond* 276:233-255, 1978.
60. Farrell, PA, Wilmore, JH, Coyle, EF, Billing, JE, and Costill, DL. Plasma lactate accumulation and distance running performance. *Med Sci Sports* 11:338-344, 1979.
61. Farrell, PA, Wilmore, JH, Coyle, EF, Billing, JE, and Costill, DL. Plasma lactate accumulation and distance running performance. 1979. *Med Sci Sports Exerc* 25:1091-1097, 1993.
62. Ferguson, BS, Rogatzki, MJ, Goodwin, ML, Kane, DA, Rightmire, Z, and Gladden, LB. Lactate metabolism: Historical context, prior misinterpretations, and current understanding. *Eur J Appl Physiol* 118:691-728, 2018.
63. Fiorenza, M, Hostrup, M, Gunnarsson, TP, Shirai, Y, Schena, F, Iaia, FM, and Bangsbo, J. Neuromuscularfatigue and metabolism during high-intensity intermittent exercise. *Med Sci Sports Exerc* 51:1642-1652, 2019.
64. Freund, H, and Gendry, P. Lactate kinetics after short strenuous exercise in man. *Eur J Appl Physiol* 39:123-135, 1978.
65. Fuchs, F, Reddy, Y, and Briggs, FN. The interaction of cations with the calcium-binding site of troponin. *Biochim Biophys Acta* 221:407-409, 1970.
66. Gaesser, GA, and Brooks, GA. Metabolic bases of excess post-exercise oxygen consumption: A review. *Med Sci Sports Exerc* 16:29-43, 1984.
67. Gaitanos, GC, Williams, C, Boobis, LH, and Brooks, S. Human muscle metabolism during intermittent maximal exercise. *J Appl Physiol* 75:712-719, 1993.
68. Gamble, P. Implications and applications of training specificity for coaches and athletes. *Strength Cond J* 28:54-58, 2006.
69. Gastin, PB. Energy system interaction and relative contribution during maximal exercise. *Sports Med* 31:725-741, 2001.
70. Gollnick, PD, Armstrong, RB, Saltin, B, Saubert, CW, 4th, Sembrowich, WL, and Shepherd, RE. Effect of training on enzyme activity and fiber composition of human skeletal muscle. *J Appl Physiol* 34:107-111, 1973.
71. Gollnick, PD, Armstrong, RB, Saubert, CW, Piehl, K, and Saltin, B. Enzyme activity and fiber composition in skeletal muscle of untrained and trained men. *J Appl Physiol* 33:312-319, 1972.
72. Gollnick, PD, and Bayle, WM. Biochemical training adaptations and maximal power. In *Human Muscle Power*. Jones, NL, McCartney, N, McComas, AJ, eds. Champaign, IL: Human Kinetics, 255-267, 1986.
73. Gollnick, PD, and Bayly, WM. Biochemical training adaptations and maximal power. In *Human Muscle Power*. Jones, NL, ed. Champaign IL: Human Kinetics, 334-340, 1986.

74. Gollnick, PD, Bayly, WM, and Hodgson, DR. Exercise intensity, training, diet, and lactate concentration in muscle and blood. *Med Sci Sports Exerc* 18:334-340, 1986.

75. Gollnick, PD, and Saltin, B. Significance of skeletal muscle oxidative enzyme enhancement with endurance training. *Clin Physiol* 2:1-12, 1982.

76. Gonzalez, JT, Fuchs, CJ, Betts, JA, and van Loon, LJ. Liver glycogen metabolism during and after prolonged endurance-type exercise. *Am J Physiol Endocrinol Metab* 311:E543-E553, 2016.

77. Goodman, MN, and Ruderman, NB. Influence of muscle use on amino acid metabolism. *Exerc Sport Sci Rev* 10:1-26, 1982.

78. Graham, TE, Rush, JWE, and MacLean, DA. Skeletal muscle oxidative enzyme enhancement with endurance training. In *Exercise Metabolism*. Hargreaves, M, Spriet, LL, eds. Champaign, IL: Human Kinetics, 41-72, 2006.

79. Green, HJ, Duhamel, TA, Holloway, GP, Moule, J, Ouyang, J, Ranney, D, and Tupling, AR. Muscle metabolic responses during 16 hours of intermittent heavy exercise. *Can J Physiol Pharmacol* 85:634-645, 2007.

80. Haff, GG, Koch, AJ, Potteiger, JA, Kuphal, KE, Magee, LM, Green, SB, and Jakicic, JJ. Carbohydrate supplementation attenuates muscle glycogen loss during acute bouts of resistance exercise. *Int J Sport Nutr Exerc Metab* 10:326-339, 2000.

81. Häkkinen, K, Alen, M, Kraemer, WJ, Gorostiaga, E, Izquierdo, M, Rusko, H, Mikkola, J, Hakkinen, A, Valkeinen, H, Kaarakainen, E, Romu, S, Erola, V, Ahtiainen, J, and Paavolainen, L. Neuromuscular adaptations during concurrent strength and endurance training versus strength training. *Eur J Appl Physiol* 89:42-52, 2003.

82. Hall, MM, Rajasekaran, S, Thomsen, TW, and Peterson, AR. Lactate: Friend or foe. *PM&R* 8:S8-S15, 2016.

83. Halson, SL, Bridge, MW, Meeusen, R, Busschaert, B, Gleeson, M, Jones, DA, and Jeukendrup, AE. Time course of performance changes and fatigue markers during intensified training in trained cyclists. *J Appl Physiol* 93:947-956, 2002.

84. Harris, RC, Edwards, RH, Hultman, E, Nordesjo, LO, Nylind, B, and Sahlin, K. The time course of phosphorylcreatine resynthesis during recovery of the quadriceps muscle in man. *Pflugers Arch* 367:137-142, 1976.

85. Hearris, MA, Hammond, KM, Fell, JM, and Morton, JP. Regulation of muscle glycogen metabolism during exercise: Implications for endurance performance and training adaptations. *Nutrients* 10, 2018.

86. Heck, H, Mader, A, Hess, G, Mucke, S, Muller, R, and Hollmann, W. Justification of the 4-mmol/L lactate threshold. *Int J Sports Med* 6:117-130, 1985.

87. Henritze, J, Weltman, A, Schurrer, RL, and Barlow, K. Effects of training at and above the lactate threshold on the lactate threshold and maximal oxygen uptake. *Eur J Appl Physiol Occup Physiol* 54:84-88, 1985.

88. Henry, FM. Aerobic oxygen consumption and alactic debt in muscular work. *J Appl Physiol* 3:427-438, 1951.

89. Herda, TJ, and Cramer, JT. Bioenergetics of exercise and training. In *Essentials of Strength Training and Conditioning*. 4th ed. Haff, GG, Triplett, N, eds. Champaign, IL: Human Kinetics, 43-63, 2016.

90. Hermansen, L. Effect of metabolic changes on force generation in skeletal muscle during maximal exercise. *Ciba Found Symp* 82:75-88, 1981.

91. Hermansen, L, and Stensvold, I. Production and removal of lactate during exercise in man. *Acta Physiol Scand* 86:191-201, 1972.

92. Hermansen, L, and Vaage, O. Lactate disappearance and glycogen synthesis in human muscle after maximal exercise. *Am J Physiol* 233:E422-429, 1977.

93. Hickson, RC, Rosenkoetter, MA, and Brown, MM. Strength training effects on aerobic power and short-term endurance. *Med Sci Sports Exerc* 12:336-339, 1980.

94. Hill, A, and Lupton, M. L H. Muscular exercise, lactic acid, and the supply and utilization of oxygen. *QJ Med* 16:135-171, 1923.

95. Hirvonen, J, Rehunen, S, Rusko, H, and Harkonen, M. Breakdown of high-energy phosphate compounds and lactate accumulation during short supramaximal exercise. *Eur J Appl Physiol* 56:253-259, 1987.

96. Hultman, E, Bergstrom, J, and Anderson, NM. Breakdown and resynthesis of phosphorylcreatine and adenosine triphosphate in connection with muscular work in man. *Scand J Clin Lab Invest* 19:56-66, 1967.

97. Hultman, E, and Sjoholm, H. Biochemical causes of fatigue. In *Human Muscle Power*. Jones, NL, ed. Champaign, IL: Human Kinetics, 343-363, 1986.

98. Impellizzeri, F, Sassi, A, Rodriguez-Alonso, M, Mognoni, P, and Marcora, S. Exercise intensity during off-road cycling competitions. *Med Sci Sports Exerc* 34:1808-1813, 2002.

99. Ivy, JL, Katz, AL, Cutler, CL, Sherman, WM, and Coyle, EF. Muscle glycogen synthesis after exercise: Effect of time of carbohydrate ingestion. *J Appl Physiol* 64:1480-1485, 1988.

100. Jacobs, I. Blood lactate: Implications for training and sports performance. *Sports Med* 3:10-25, 1986.

101. Jacobs, I, Tesch, PA, Bar Or, O, Karlsson, J, and Dotan, R. Lactate in human skeletal muscle after 10 and 30 s of supramaximal exercise. *J Appl Physiol* 55:365-367, 1983.

102. Jones, AM. A five year physiological case study of an Olympic runner. *Br J Sports Med* 32:39-43, 1998.

103. Jones, AM, and Carter, H. The effect of endurance training on parameters of aerobic fitness. *Sports Med* 29:373-386, 2000.

104. Joyner, MJ, and Coyle, EF. Endurance exercise performance: The physiology of champions. *J Physiol* 586:35-44, 2008.

105. Juel, C. Intracellular pH recovery and lactate efflux in mouse soleus muscles stimulated in vitro: The involvement of sodium/proton exchange and a lactate carrier. *Acta Physiol Scand* 132:363-371, 1988.

106. Karlsson, J, Nordesjo, LO, Jorfeldt, L, and Saltin, B. Muscle lactate, ATP, and CP levels during exercise after physical training in man. *J Appl Physiol* 33:199-203, 1972.

107. Karlsson, J, and Ollander, B. Muscle metabolites with exhaustive static exercise of different duration. *Acta Physiol Scand* 86:309-314, 1972.

108. Keith, SP, Jacobs, I, and McLellan, TM. Adaptations to training at the individual anaerobic threshold. *Eur J Appl Physiol Occup Physiol* 65:316-323, 1992.

109. Khong, TK, Selvanayagam, VS, Sidhu, SK, and Yusof, A. Role of carbohydrate in central fatigue: A systematic review. *Scand J Med Sci Sports* 27:376-384, 2017.

110. Kindermann, W, Simon, G, and Keul, J. The significance of the aerobic-anaerobic transition for the determination of work load intensities during endurance training. *Eur J Appl Physiol Occup Physiol* 42:25-34, 1979.

111. Knuttgen, HG, and Komi, PV. Basic definitions for exercise. In *Strength and Power in Sport*. Komi, PV, ed. Oxford: Blackwell Scientific, 3-8, 2003.

112. Kraemer, WJ, Noble, BJ, Clark, MJ, and Culver, BW. Physiologic responses to heavy-resistance exercise with very short rest periods. *Int J Sports Med* 8:247-252, 1987.

113. Kunz, P, Engel, FA, Holmberg, HC, and Sperlich, B. A meta-comparison of the effects of high-intensity interval training to those of small-sided games and other training protocols on parameters related to the physiology and performance of youth soccer players. *Sports Med Open* 5:7, 2019.

114. LaForgia, J, Withers, RT, and Gore, CJ. Effects of exercise intensity and duration on the excess post-exercise oxygen consumption. *J Sports Sci* 24:1247-1264, 2006.

115. Lambert, CP, Flynn, MG, Boone, JB, Michaud, TJ, and Rodriguez-Zayas, J. Effects of carbohydrate feeding on multiple-bout resistance exercise. *J Appl Sport Sci Res* 5:192-197, 1991.

116. Lanza, IR, Wigmore, DM, Befroy, DE, and Kent-Braun, JA. In vivo ATP production during free-flow and ischaemic muscle contractions in humans. *J Physiol* 577:353-367, 2006.

117. Laursen, PB, and Buchheit, M. Genesis and evolution of high-intensity interval training. In *Science and Application of High-Intensity Interval Training*. Laursen, PB, Buchheit, M, eds. Champaign, IL: Human Kinetics, 3-16, 2019.

118. Laursen, PB, and Buchheit, M. Manipulating HIIT variables. In *Science and Application of High-Intensity Interval Training*. Laursen, PB, Buchheit, M, eds. Champaign, IL: Human Kinetics, 51-72, 2019.

119. Laursen, PB, and Buchheit, M. Physiological targets of HIIT. In *Science and Application of High-Intensity Interval Training*. Laursen, PB, Buchheit, M, eds. Champaign, IL: Human Kinetics, 3-50, 2019.

120. Laursen, PB, and Buchheit, M. Using HIIT weapons. In *Science and Application of High-Intensity Interval Training*. Laursen, PB, Buchheit, M, eds. Champaign, IL: Human Kinetics, 73-118, 2019.

121. Laursen, PB, and Jenkins, DG. The scientific basis for high-intensity interval training: optimising training programmes and maximising performance in highly trained endurance athletes. *Sports Med* 32:53-73, 2002.

122. Laursen, PB, Shing, CM, Peake, JM, Coombes, JS, and Jenkins, DG. Interval training program optimization in highly trained endurance cyclists. *Med Sci Sports Exerc* 34:1801-1807, 2002.

123. Lehmann, M, and Keul, J. Free plasma catecholamines, heart rates, lactate levels, and oxygen uptake in competition weight lifters, cyclists, and untrained control subjects. *Int J Sports Med* 7:18-21, 1986.

124. Lemon, PW, and Mullin, JP. Effect of initial muscle glycogen levels on protein catabolism during exercise. *J Appl Physiol* 48:624-629, 1980.

125. Londeree, BR. Effect of training on lactate/ventilatory thresholds: A meta-analysis. *Med Sci Sports Exerc* 29:837-843, 1997.

126. MacDougall, D, and Sale, D. Biochemical basis for performance. In *The Physiology of Training for High Performance*. Oxford, United Kingdom: Oxford University Press, 16-37, 2014.

127. MacDougall, D, and Sale, D. Introduction to training for high performance. In *The Physiology of Training for High Performance*. Oxford, United Kingdom: Oxford University Press, 3-15, 2014.

128. MacDougall, D, and Sale, D. Neuromuscular bases for performance. In *The Physiology of Training for High Performance*. Oxford, United Kingdom: Oxford University Press, 147-216, 2014.

129. MacDougall, JD, Ward, GR, Sale, DG, and Sutton, JR. Biochemical adaptation of human skeletal muscle to heavy resistance training and immobilization. *J Appl Physiol* 43:700-703, 1977.

130. Maughan, R, and Gleeson, M. *The Biochemical Basis of Sports Performance*. 2nd ed. New York, NY: Oxford University Press, 2010.

131. Maughan, R, and Gleeson, M. The endurance athlete. In *The Biochemical Basis of Sports Performance*. 2nd ed. New York, NY: Oxford University Press, 127-173, 2010.

132. Maughan, R, and Gleeson, M. Middle distance events. In *The Biochemical Basis of Sports Performance*. 2nd ed. New York, NY: Oxford University Press, 99-126, 2010.

133. Maughan, R, and Gleeson, M. The sprinter. In *The Biochemical Basis of Sports Performance*. 2nd ed. New York, NY: Oxford University Press, 74-98, 2010.

134. Maughan, R, and Gleeson, M. The weightlifter. In *The Biochemical Basis of Sports Performance*. 2nd ed. New York, NY: Oxford University Press, 14-72, 2010.

135. Mcardle, WD, Katch, FI, and Katch, VL. Energy transfer during exercise. In *Exercise Physiology: Nutrition, Energy, and Human Performance*. 7th ed. Baltimore, MD: Lippincot, Williams, Wilkins, 162-177, 2010.

136. Mcardle, WD, Katch, FI, and Katch, VL. Energy transfer in the body. In *Exercise Physiology: Nutrition, Energy, and Human Performance*. 7th ed. Baltimore, MD: Lippincot, Williams, Wilkins, 134-161, 2010.

137. McCann, DJ, Mole, PA, and Caton, JR. Phosphocreatine kinetics in humans during exercise and recovery. *Med Sci Sports Exerc* 27:378-389, 1995.

138. McCardle, WD, Katch, FI, and Katch, VL. Dynamics of pulmonary ventilation. In *Exercise Physiology: Energy, Nutrition, and Human Performance*. 7th ed. Philadelphia: Lea & Febiger, 286-302, 2010.

139. McCardle, WD, Katch, FI, and Katch, VL. Dynamics of pulmonary ventilation. In *Exercise physiology: energy, nutrition, and human performance*. 8th ed. Philadelphia: Lippincott Williams and Wilkins, 286-301, 2015.

140. McCardle, WD, Katch, FI, and Katch, VL. Fuel for exercise: Bioenergetics and muscle metabolism. In *Exercise Physiology: Energy, Nutrition, and Human Performance*. 8th ed. Philadelphia: Lippincott Williams and Wilkins, 51-72, 2015.

141. McCartney, N, Spriet, LL, Heigenhauser, GJ, Kowalchuk, JM, Sutton, JR, and Jones, NL. Muscle power and metabolism in maximal intermittent exercise. *J Appl Physiol* 60:1164-1169, 1986.

142. McMillan, JL, Stone, MH, Sartin, J, Keith, R, Marple, D, Brown, C, and Lewis, RD. 20-hour physiological responses to a single weight-training session. *J Strength Cond Res* 7:9-21, 1993.

143. Medbo, JI, and Burgers, S. Effect of training on the anaerobic capacity. *Med Sci Sports Exerc* 22:501-507, 1990.

144. Meyer, RA, and Foley, JM. Cellular processes integrating the metabolic response to exercise. In *Handbook of Physiology*. Roswell, LB, Shepard, JT, eds. Bethesda, MD: Oxford University Press / Am. Physiol. Soc, 841-869, 1996.

145. Morton, JP, and Close, GL. The bioenergetics of sports performance. In *Strength and Conditioning for Sports Performance*. Jeffreys, I, Moody, J, eds. Abingdon, Oxon: Routledge, 67-91, 2016.

146. Mul, JD, Stanford, KI, Hirshman, MF, and Goodyear, LJ. Exercise and regulation of carbohydrate metabolism. *Prog Mol Biol Transl Sci* 135:17-37, 2015.

147. Murray, B, and Rosenbloom, C. Fundamentals of glycogen metabolism for coaches and athletes. *Nutr Rev* 76:243-259, 2018.

148. Nader, GA. Concurrent strength and endurance training: from molecules to man. *Med Sci Sports Exerc* 38:1965-1970, 2006.

149. Nakamaru, Y, and Schwartz, A. The influence of hydrogen ion concentration on calcium binding and release by skeletal muscle sarcoplasmic reticulum. *J Gen Physiol* 59:22-32, 1972.

150. Nielsen, JJ, Mohr, M, Klarskov, C, Kristensen, M, Krustrup, P, Juel, C, and Bangsbo, J. Effects of high-intensity intermittent training on potassium kinetics and performance in human skeletal muscle. *J Physiol* 554:857-870, 2004.

151. O'Reilly, KP, Warhol, MJ, Fielding, RA, Frontera, WR, Meredith, CN, and Evans, WJ. Eccentric exercise-induced muscle damage impairs muscle glycogen repletion. *J Appl Physiol* 63:252-256, 1987.

152. Opie, LH, and Newsholme, EA. The activities of fructose 1,6-diphosphatase, phosphofructokinase and phosphoenolpyruvate carboxykinase in white muscle and red muscle. *Biochem J* 103:391-399, 1967.

153. Padilla, S, Mujika, I, Angulo, F, and Goiriena, JJ. Scientific approach to the 1-h cycling world record: A case study. *J Appl Physiol* 89:1522-1527, 2000.

154. Palmer, GS, Borghouts, LB, Noakes, TD, and Hawley, JA. Metabolic and performance responses to constant-load vs. variable-intensity exercise in trained cyclists. *J Appl Physiol (1985)* 87:1186-1196, 1999.

155. Parkhouse, WS, McKenzie, DC, Hochochka, PW, Mommsen, TP, Ovalle, WK, Shinn, SL, and Rhodes, EC. The relationship between carnosine levels, buffering capacity, fiber type, and anaerobic capacity in elite athletes. In *Biochemistry of Exercise*. Knuttgen, HG, Vogel, JA, Poortmans, J, eds. Champaign, IL: Human Kinetics, 590-594, 1983.

156. Parkin, JA, Carey, MF, Martin, IK, Stojanovska, L, and Febbraio, MA. Muscle glycogen storage following prolonged exercise: Effect of timing of ingestion of high glycemic index food. *Med Sci Sports Exerc* 29:220-224, 1997.

157. Pierce, K, Rozenek, R, and Stone, MH. Effects of high volume weight training on lactate, heart rate, and perceived exertion. *J Strength Cond Res* 7:211-215, 1993.

158. Pilegaard, H, Terzis, G, Halestrap, A, and Juel, C. Distribution of the lactate/H+ transporter isoforms MCT1 and MCT4 in human skeletal muscle. *Am J Physiol* 276:E843-848, 1999.

159. Plisk, SS. Anaerobic metabolic conditioning: A brief review of theory, strategy and practical application. *J Strength Cond Res* 5:22-34, 1991.

160. Plisk, SS, and Gambetta, V. Tactical metabolic training: Part 1. *Strength Cond J* 19:44-53, 1997.

161. Powers, SK, and Howley, ET. Bioenergetics. In *Exercise Physiology: Theory and Application to Fitness and Performance*. 5th ed. Sydney, Australia: McGraw Hill, 39-63, 2014.

162. Powers, SK, and Howley, ET. Exercise metabolism. In *Exercise Physiology: Theory and Application to Fitness and Performance*. 5th ed. Sydney, Australia: McGraw Hill, 64-83, 2014.

163. Reed, JP, Schilling, BK, and Murlasits, Z. Acute neuromuscular and metabolic responses to concurrent endurance and resistance exercise. *J Strength Cond Res* 27:793-801, 2013.

164. Richter, EA, Kiens, B, Saltin, B, Christensen, NJ, and Savard, G. Skeletal muscle glucose uptake during dynamic exercise in humans: Role of muscle mass. *Am J Physiol* 254:E555-561, 1988.

165. Robergs, RA, Ghiasvand, F, and Parker, D. Biochemistry of exercise-induced metabolic acidosis. *Am J Physiol Regul Integr Comp Physiol* 287:R502-R516, 2004.

166. Robergs, RA, Pearson, DR, Costill, DL, Fink, WJ, Pascoe, DD, Benedict, MA, Lambert, CP, and Zachweija, JJ. Muscle glycogenolysis during differing intensities of weight-resistance exercise. *J Appl Physiol* 70:1700-1706, 1991.

167. Roberts, AD, Billeter, R, and Howald, H. Anaerobic muscle enzyme changes after interval training. *Int J Sports Med* 3:18-21, 1982.

168. Rozenek, R, Rosenau, L, Rosenau, P, and Stone, MH. The effect of intensity on heart rate and blood lactate response to resistance exercise. *J Strength Cond Res* 7:51-54, 1993.

169. Sahlin, K. Muscle energetics during explosive activities and potential effects of nutrition and training. *Sports Med* 44:167-173, 2014.

170. Sahlin, K, Tonkonogi, M, and Soderlund, K. Energy supply and muscle fatigue in humans. *Acta Physiol Scand* 162:261-266, 1998.

171. Saltin, B, and Gollnick, PD. Skeletal muscle adaptability: Significance for metabolism and performance. *Compr Physiol*:555-631, 2010.

172. Saltin, B, and Karlsson, J. Muscle glycogen utilization during work of different intensities. In *Muscle Metabolism During Exercise*. Pernow, P, Saltin, B, eds. New York: Plenum Press, 289-300, 1971.

173. Seiler, S, and Sylta, O. How does interval-training prescription affect physiological and perceptual responses? *Int J Sports Physiol Perform* 12:S280-S286, 2017.

174. Sherman, WM, and Wimer, GS. Insufficient dietary carbohydrate during training: Does it impair athletic performance? *Int J Sport Nutr* 1:28-44, 1991.

175. Shimizu, K, and Matsuoka, Y. Regulation of glycolytic flux and overflow metabolism depending on the source of energy generation for energy demand. *Biotechnol Adv* 37:284-305, 2019.

176. Sjödin, B, and Jacobs, I. Onset of blood lactate accumulation and marathon running performance. *Int J Sports Med* 2:23-26, 1981.

177. Sjödin, B, Jacobs, I, and Svedenhag, J. Changes in onset of blood lactate accumulation (OBLA) and muscle enzymes after training at OBLA. *Eur J Appl Physiol Occup Physiol* 49:45-57, 1982.

178. Sjodin, B, Thorstensson, A, Frith, K, and Karlsson, J. Effect of physical training on LDH activity and LDH isozyme pattern in human skeletal muscle. *Acta Physiol Scand* 97:150-157, 1976.

179. Sjogaard, G. Changes in skeletal muscles capillarity and enzyme activity with training and detraining. In *Physiological Chemistry of Training and Detraining*. Marconnet, P, Poortmans, J, Hermansen, L, eds. New York: Karger, 202-214, 1984.

180. Smith, SA, Montain, SJ, Matott, RP, Zientara, GP, Jolesz, FA, and Fielding, RA. Creatine supplementation and age influence muscle metabolism during exercise. *J Appl Physiol* 85:1349-1356, 1998.

181. Sporer, BC, and Wenger, HA. Effects of aerobic exercise on strength performance following various periods of recovery. *J Strength Cond Res* 17:638-644, 2003.

182. Stainsby, WN, and Barclay, JK. Exercise metabolism: O2 deficit, steady level O2 uptake and O2 uptake for recovery. *Med Sci Sports* 2:177-181, 1970.

183. Stone, MH, Stone, ME, and Sands, WA. Bioenergetic and metabolic factors. In *Principles and Practice of Resistance Training*. Champaign, IL: Human Kinetics, 61-86, 2007.

184. Svedahl, K, and MacIntosh, BR. Anaerobic threshold: The concept and methods of measurement. *Can J Appl Physiol* 28:299-323, 2003.

185. Taylor, DJ, Styles, P, Matthews, PM, Arnold, DA, Gadian, DG, Bore, P, and Radda, GK. Energetics of human muscle: Exercise-induced ATP depletion. *Magn Reson Med* 3:44-54, 1986.

186. Tesch, P. Muscle fatigue in man: With special reference to lactate accumulation during short term intense exercise. *Acta Physiol Scand Suppl* 480:1-40, 1980.

187. Tesch, PA, Ploutz-Snyder, LL, Yström, L, Castro, M, and Dudley, G. Skeletal muscle glycogen loss evoked by resistance exercise. *J Strength Cond Res* 12:67-73, 1998.

188. Tomlin, DL, and Wenger, HA. The relationship between aerobic fitness and recovery from high intensity intermittent exercise. *Sports Med* 31:1-11, 2001.

189. Tucker, WJ, Angadi, SS, and Gaesser, GA. Excess postexercise oxygen consumption after high-intensity and sprint interval exercise, and continuous steady-state exercise. *J Strength Cond Res* 30:3090-3097, 2016.

190. van Hall, G. Lactate kinetics in human tissues at rest and during exercise. *Acta Physiol (Oxf)* 199:499-508, 2010.

191. van Loon, LJ, Greenhaff, PL, Constantin-Teodosiu, D, Saris, WH, and Wagenmakers, AJ. The effects of increasing exercise intensity on muscle fuel utilisation in humans. *J Physiol* 536:295-304, 2001.

192. Vanhelder, WP, Radomski, MW, Goode, RC, and Casey, K. Hormonal and metabolic response to three types of exercise of equal duration and external work output. *Eur J Appl Physiol* 54:337-342, 1985.

193. Venckunas, T, Krusnauskas, R, Snieckus, A, Eimantas, N, Baranauskiene, N, Skurvydas, A, Brazaitis, M, and Kamandulis, S. Acute effects of very low-volume high-intensity interval training on muscular fatigue and serum testosterone level vary according to age and training status. *Eur J Appl Physiol* 119:1725-1733, 2019.

194. Warren, BJ, Stone, MH, Kearney, JT, Fleck, SJ, Johnson, RL, Wilson, GD, and Kraemer, WJ. Performance measures, blood lactate and plasma ammonia as indicators of overwork in elite junior weightlifters. *Int J Sports Med* 13:372-376, 1992.

195. Wells, JG, Balke, B, and Van Fossan, DD. Lactic acid accumulation during work: A suggested standardization of work classification. *J Appl Physiol* 10:51-55, 1957.

196. Weltman, A, Seip, RL, Snead, D, Weltman, JY, Haskvitz, EM, Evans, WS, Veldhuis, JD, and Rogol, AD. Exercise training at and above the lactate threshold in previously untrained women. *Int J Sports Med* 13:257-263, 1992.

197. Weston, AR, Myburgh, KH, Lindsay, FH, Dennis, SC, Noakes, TD, and Hawley, JA. Skeletal muscle buffering capacity and endurance performance after high-intensity interval training by well-trained cyclists. *Eur J Appl Physiol Occup Physiol* 75:7-13, 1997.

198. Whipp, BJ, Seard, C, and Wasserman, K. Oxygen deficit-oxygen debt relationships and efficiency of anaerobic work. *J Appl Physiol* 28:452-456, 1970.

199. Wilson, JM, Marin, PJ, Rhea, MR, Wilson, SM, Loenneke, JP, and Anderson, JC. Concurrent training: A meta-analysis examining interference of aerobic and resistance exercises. *J Strength Cond Res* 26:2293-2307, 2012.

200. Wojtaszewski, JF, Nielsen, P, Kiens, B, and Richter, EA. Regulation of glycogen synthase kinase-3 in human skeletal muscle: Effects of food intake and bicycle exercise. *Diabetes* 50:265-269, 2001.

201. Wyatt, FB. Comparison of lactate and ventilatory threshold to maximal oxygen consumption: A meta-analysis. *J Strength Cond Res* 13:67-71, 1999.

202. Yoshida, T, Chida, M, Ichioka, M, and Suda, Y. Blood lactate parameters related to aerobic capacity and endurance performance. *Eur J Appl Physiol Occup Physiol* 56:7-11, 1987.

203. Zehnder, M, Muelli, M, Buchli, R, Kuehne, G, and Boutellier, U. Further glycogen decrease during early recovery after eccentric exercise despite a high carbohydrate intake. *Eur J Nutr* 43:148-159, 2004.

Chapter 3

1. Arnett, MG, DeLuccia, D, and Gilmartin, K. Male and female differences and the specificity of fatigue on skill acquisition and transfer performance. *Res Q Exerc Sport* 71:201-205, 2000.

2. Baker, D, and Nance, S. The relation between running speed and measures of strength and power in professional rugby league players. *J Strength Cond Res* 13:230-235, 1999.

3. Baker, DG. Comparison of strength levels between players from within the same club who were selected vs. not selected to play in the grand final of the national rugby league competition. *J Strength Cond Res* 31:1461-1467, 2017.

4. Balague, G. Periodization of psychological skills training. *J Sci Med Sport* 3:230-237, 2000.

5. Balsalobre-Fernandez, C, Santos-Concejero, J, and Grivas, GV. Effects of strength training on running economy in highly trained runners: a systematic review with meta-analysis of controlled trials. *J Strength Cond Res* 30:2361-2368, 2016.

6. Barnes, KR, Hopkins, WG, McGuigan, MR, Northuis, ME, and Kilding, AE. Effects of resistance training on running economy and cross-country performance. *Med Sci Sports Exerc*, 2013.

7. Barnes, KR, and Kilding, AE. Strategies to improve running economy. *Sports Med* 45:37-56, 2015.

8. Blagrove, RC, Howatson, G, and Hayes, PR. Effects of strength training on the physiological determinants of middle- and long-distance running performance: A systematic review. *Sports Med* 48:1117-1149, 2018.

9. Bompa, TO, and Buzzichelli, CA. Strength, power, and muscular endurance in sports. In *Periodization Training for Sports*. 3rd ed. Champaign, IL: Human Kinetics, 3-18, 2015.

10. Bompa, TO, and Buzzichelli, CA. Basis of training. In *Periodization: Theory and Methodology of Training*. 6th ed. Champaign, IL: Human Kinetics, 3-27, 2019.

11. Bompa, TO, and Buzzichelli, CA. Preparation for Training. In *Periodization: Theory and Methodology of Training*. 6th ed. Champaign, IL: Human Kinetics, 51-70, 2019.

12. Bompa, TO, and Carrera, MC. *Periodization Training for Sports: Science-Based strength and Conditioning Plans for 20 Sports*. 2nd ed. Champaign, IL: Human Kinetics, 2005.

13. Bompa, TO, and Haff, GG. Basis for training. In *Periodization: Theory and Methodology of Training*. 5th ed. Champaign, IL: Human Kinetics, 3-30, 2009.

14. Bompa, TO, and Haff, GG. Preparation for training. In *Periodization: Theory and Methodology of Training*. 5th ed. Champaign, IL: Human Kinetics, 57-78, 2009.

15. Bompa, TO, and Haff, GG. Strength development. In *Periodization: Theory and Methodology of Training*. 5th ed. Champaign, IL: Human Kinetics, 261-286, 2009.

16. Bondarchuk, AP. A brief overview of the transfer of training. In *Transfer of Training in Sports*. Michigan, USA: Ultimate Athlete Concepts, 1-57, 2007.

17. Bondarchuk, AP. *Transfer of Training in Sports: Volume I*. Michigan, USA: Ultimate Athlete Concepts, 2007.

18. Bondarchuk, AP. Cycles of sports form development and training transfer. In *Transfer of Training in Sport: Volume II*. Michigan, USA: Ultimate Athlete Concepts, 12-51, 2010.

19. Bondarchuk, AP. *Transfer of Training In Sport: Volume II*. Michigan, USA: Ultimate Athlete Concepts, 2010.

20. Bret, C, Rahmani, A, Dufour, AB, Messonnier, L, and Lacour, JR. Leg strength and stiffness as ability factors in 100 m sprint running. *J Sports Med Phys Fitness* 42:274-281, 2002.

21. Buchheit, M, Lacome, M, Cholley, Y, and Simpson, BM. Neuromuscular responses to conditioned soccer sessions assessed via GPS-embedded accelerometers: Insights into tactical periodization. *Int J Sports Physiol Perform* 13:577-583, 2018.

22. Buchheit, M, and Laursen, PB. High-intensity interval training, solutions to the programming puzzle: Part I: Cardiopulmonary emphasis. *Sports Med* 43:313-338, 2013.

23. Buchheit, M, and Laursen, PB. High-intensity interval training, solutions to the programming puzzle: Part II: Anaerobic energy, neuromuscular load and practical applications. *Sports Med* 43:927-954, 2013.

24. Chambers, R, Gabbett, TJ, Cole, MH, and Beard, A. The use of wearable microsensors to quantify sport-specific movements. *Sports Med*:1-17, 2015.

25. Chaouachi, A, Brughelli, M, Chamari, K, Levin, GT, Ben Abdelkrim, N, Laurencelle, L, and Castagna, C. Lower limb maximal dynamic strength and agility determinants in elite basketball players. *J Strength Cond Res* 23:1570-1577, 2009.

26. Clemente, FM, Couceiro, MS, Martins, FM, Mendes, R, and Figueiredo, AJ. Measuring tactical behaviour using technological metrics: Case study of a football game. *Int J Sports Sci Coach* 8:723-739, 2013.

27. Collins, D, and MacNamara, Á. The rocky road to the top. *Sports Med* 42:907-914, 2012.

28. Conley, DL, and Krahenbuhl, GS. Running economy and distance running performance of highly trained athletes. *Med Sci Sports Exerc* 12:357-360, 1980.

29. Coughlan, EK, Williams, AM, McRobert, AP, and Ford, PR. How experts practice: A novel test of deliberate practice theory. *J Exp Psychol Learn Mem Cogn* 40:449, 2014.

30. Coutts, AJ. Evolution of football match analysis research. *J Sports Sci* 32:1829-1830, 2014.

31. Di Russo, F, Bultrini, A, Brunelli, S, Delussu, AS, Polidori, L, Taddei, F, Traballesi, M, and Spinelli, D. Benefits of sports participation for executive function in disabled athletes. *J Neurotrauma* 27:2309-2319, 2010.

32. Dick, FW. Perceptual-motor learning. In *Sports Training Principles*. 4th ed. London: A and C Black, 183-203, 2002.

33. Duckworth, A, and Gross, JJ. Self-control and grit: Related but separable determinants of success. *Curr Dir Psychol Sci* 23:319-325, 2014.

34. Duckworth, AL, Peterson, C, Matthews, MD, and Kelly, DR. Grit: Perseverance and passion for long-term goals. *J Pers Soc Psychol* 92:1087-1101, 2007.

35. Dunlavy, JK, Sands, WA, McNeal, JR, Stone, MH, Smith, SA, Jemni, M, and Haff, GG. Strength performance assessment in a simulated men's gymnastics still rings cross. *J Sports Sci Medicine* 6:93-97, 2007.

36. Ericsson, KA, Krampe, RT, and Tesch-Römer, C. The role of deliberate practice in the acquisition of expert performance. *Psychol Rev* 100:363-406, 1993.

37. Eskreis-Winkler, L, Shulman, EP, Beal, SA, and Duckworth, AL. The grit effect: Predicting retention in the military, the workplace, school and marriage. *Front Psychol* 5:36, 2014.

38. Farlinger, CM, and Fowles, JR. The effect of sequence of skating-specific training on skating performance. *Int J Sports Physiol Perform* 3:185-198, 2008.

39. Farrow, D, and Robertson, S. Development of a skill acquisition periodisation framework for high-performance sport. *Sports Med* 47:1043-1054, 2017.
40. Florescu, C, Dumitrescu, V, and Predescu, A. *Metodologia desvoltari calitatilor fizice (The methodology of developing physical qualities)*. Bucharest: National Sports Council, 1969.
41. Ford, PR, Coughlan, EK, Hodges, NJ, and Williams, AM. Deliberate practice in sport. In *Routledge Handbook of Sport Expertise*. London; New York: Routledge, 373-388, 2015.
42. Ford, PR, Hodges, NJ, Williams, AM, Kaufmann, S, and Simonton, D. Creating champions: The development of expertise in sport. In *The Complexity of Greatness*. Kaufmann, S, ed. New York: Oxford University Press, 391-413, 2013.
43. Foster, C, and Lucia, A. Running economy. *Sports Med* 37:316-319, 2007.
44. Fox, JL, Scanlan, AT, and Stanton, R. A review of player monitoring approaches in basketball: Current trends and future directions. *J Strength Cond Res* 31:2021-2029, 2017.
45. Gabbett, TJ. The training-injury prevention paradox: Should athletes be training smarter and harder? *Br J Sports Med* 50:273-280, 2016.
46. Gabbett, TJ, Hulin, BT, Blanch, P, and Whiteley, R. High training workloads alone do not cause sports injuries: How you get there is the real issue. *Br J Sports Med* 50:444-445, 2016.
47. Gabbett, TJ, and Whiteley, R. Two training-load paradoxes: Can we work harder and smarter, can physical preparation and medical be teammates? *Int J Sports Physiol Perform* 12:S250-S254, 2017.
48. Gamble, P. Metabolic conditioning. In *Strength and Conditioning for Team Sports: Sport-Specific Physical Preparation for High Performance*. London: Routledge, 53-72, 2013.
49. Garcia-Pinillos, F, Soto-Hermoso, VM, and Latorre-Roman, PA. How does high-intensity intermittent training affect recreational endurance runners? Acute and chronic adaptations: A systematic review. *J Sport Health Sci* 6:54-67, 2017.
50. Gray, AJ, Shorter, K, Cummins, C, Murphy, A, and Waldron, M. Modelling movement energetics using global positioning system devices in contact team sports: Limitations and solutions. *Sports Med* 48:1357-1368, 2018.
51. Guadagnoli, MA, and Lee, TD. Challenge point: A framework for conceptualizing the effects of various practice conditions in motor learning. *J Mot Behav* 36:212-224, 2004.
52. Gulbin, JP, Oldenziel, KE, Weissensteiner, JR, and Gagné, F. A look through the rear view mirror: Developmental experiences and insights of high performance athletes. *Talent Development and Excellence* 2:149-164, 2010.
53. Hadi, G, Akkus, H, and Harbili, E. Three-dimensional kinematic analysis of the snatch technique for lifting different barbell weights. *J Strength Cond Res* 26:1568-1576, 2012.
54. Haff, GG. Periodization strategies for youth development. In *Strength and Conditioning for Young Athletes: Science and Application*. Lloyd, RS, Oliver, JL, eds. London: Routledge, Taylor & Francis Group, 149-168, 2014.
55. Haff, GG. The essentials of periodisation. In *Strength and Conditioning for Sports Performance*. Jeffreys, I, Moody, J, eds. Abingdon, Oxon: Routledge, 404-448, 2016.
56. Hardy, L, Barlow, M, Evans, L, Rees, T, Woodman, T, and Warr, C. Great British medalists: Psychosocial biographies of super-elite and elite athletes from Olympic sports. *Prog Brain Res* 232:1-119, 2017.
57. Hausler, J, Halaki, M, and Orr, R. Application of global positioning system and microsensor technology in competitive rugby league match-play: A systematic review and meta-analysis. *Sports Med* 46:559-588, 2016.
58. Hodges, NJ, Ford, PR, Hendry, DT, and Williams, AM. Getting gritty about practice and success: Motivational characteristics of great performers. *Prog Brain Res* 232:167-173, 2017.
59. Hoff, J, Helgerud, J, and Wisløff, U. Maximal strength training improves work economy in trained female cross-country skiers. *Med Sci Sports Exerc* 31:870-877, 1999.
60. Howard, RM, Conway, R, and Harrison, AJ. Muscle activity in sprinting: A review. *Sports Biomech* 17:1-17, 2018.
61. Hübner, K, and Schärer. Relationship between swallow, support scale and iron cross on rings and their specific preconditioning strengthening exercises. *Science of Gymnastics Journal* 7:59-68, 2015.
62. Hulin, BT, Gabbett, TJ, Caputi, P, Lawson, DW, and Sampson, JA. Low chronic workload and the acute:chronic workload ratio are more predictive of injury than between-match recovery time: A two-season prospective cohort study in elite rugby league players. *Br J Sports Med* 50, 2016.
63. Junge, A. The influence of psychological factors on sports injuries: Review of the literature. *Am J Sports Med* 28:S10-15, 2000.
64. Kelly, VG, and Coutts, AJ. Planning and monitoring training loads during the competition phase in team sports. *Strength Cond J* 29:32-37, 2007.
65. Laursen, PB, and Buchheit, M, eds. *Science and Application of High-Intensity Interval Training*. Champaign, IL: Human Kinetics, 2019.
66. Lee, S, DeRosia, KD, and Lamie, LM. Evaluating the contribution of lower extremity kinetics to whole body power output during the power snatch. *Sports Biomech* 17:554-556, 2018.
67. Lee, TD, Swinnen, SP, and Serrien, DJ. Cognitive effort and motor learning. *Quest* 46:328-344, 1994.
68. Leirdal, S, Roeleveld, K, and Ettema, G. Coordination specificity in strength and power training. *Int J Sports Med* 29:225-231, 2008.
69. Lloyd, RS, Cronin, JB, Faigenbaum, AD, Haff, GG, Howard, R, Kraemer, WJ, Micheli, LJ, Myer, GD, and Oliver, JL. National Strength and Conditioning Association position statement on long-term athletic development. *J Strength Cond Res* 30:1491-1509, 2016.
70. Macnamara, BN, Moreau, D, and Hambrick, DZ. The relationship between deliberate practice and performance in sports: A meta-analysis. *Perspect Psychol Sci* 11:333-350, 2016.
71. Malone, JJ, Lovell, R, Varley, MC, and Coutts, AJ. Unpacking the black box: Applications and considerations for

using GPS devices in sport. *Int J Sports Physiol Perform* 12:S218-S226, 2017.

72. Malone, S, Hughes, B, Doran, DA, Collins, K, and Gabbett, TJ. Can the workload-injury relationship be moderated by improved strength, speed and repeated-sprint qualities? *J Sci Med Sport* 22:29-34, 2019.

73. Marcora, SM, Staiano, W, and Manning, V. Mental fatigue impairs physical performance in humans. *J Appl Physiol* 106:857-864, 2009.

74. McCann, DJ, and Higginson, BK. Training to maximize economy of motion in running gait. *Curr Sports Med Rep* 7:158-162, 2008.

75. Moore, IS. Is there an economical running technique? A review of modifiable biomechanical factors affecting running economy. *Sports Med* 46:793-807, 2016.

76. Mujika, I, Halson, S, Burke, L, Balagué, G, and Farrow, D. An integrated, multifactorial approach to periodization for optimal performance in individual and team sports. *Int J Sports Physiol Perform* 13:538-561, 2018.

77. Nádori, L, and Granek, I. *Theoretical and Methodological Basis of Training Planning With Special Considerations Within a Microcycle.* Lincoln, NE: NSCA, 1989.

78. Olthof, SBH, Frencken, WGP, and Lemmink, K. A match-derived relative pitch area facilitates the tactical representativeness of small-sided games for the official soccer match. *J Strength Cond Res* 33:523-530, 2019.

79. Ortega-Toro, E, Garcia-Angulo, A, Gimenez-Egido, JM, Garcia-Angulo, FJ, and Palao, JM. Design, validation, and reliability of an observation instrument for technical and tactical actions of the offense phase in soccer. *Front Psychol* 10:22, 2019.

80. Østerås, H, Helgerud, J, and Hoff, J. Maximal strength-training effects on force-velocity and force-power relationships explain increases in aerobic performance in humans. *Eur J Appl Physiol* 88:255-263, 2002.

81. Paavolainen, L, Häkkinen, K, Hamalainen, I, Nummela, A, and Rusko, H. Explosive-strength training improves 5-km running time by improving running economy and muscle power. *J Appl Physiol* 86:1527-1533, 1999.

82. Paavolainen, L, Häkkinen, K, and Rusko, H. Effects of explosive type strength training on physical performance characteristics in cross-country skiers. *Eur J Appl Physiol Occup Physiol* 62:251-255, 1991.

83. Paquette, MR, Peel, SA, Smith, RE, Temme, M, and Dwyer, JN. The impact of different cross-training modalities on performance and injury-related variables in high school cross country runners. *J Strength Cond Res* 32:1745-1753, 2018.

84. Plisk, SS, and Gambetta, V. Tactical metabolic training: Part 1. *Strength Cond J* 19:44-53, 1997.

85. Plisk, SS, and Stone, MH. Periodization strategies. *Strength Cond J* 25:19-37, 2003.

86. Rein, R, and Memmert, D. Big data and tactical analysis in elite soccer: Future challenges and opportunities for sports science. *Springerplus* 5:1410, 2016.

87. Robertson, S, and Joyce, D. Evaluating strategic periodisation in team sport. *J Sports Sci* 36:279-285, 2018.

88. Robertson, SJ, and Joyce, DG. Informing in-season tactical periodisation in team sport: Development of a match difficulty index for Super Rugby. *J Sports Sci* 33:99-107, 2015.

89. Rønnestad, BR, Hansen, EA, and Raastad, T. In-season strength maintenance training increases well-trained cyclists' performance. *Eur J Appl Physiol* 110:1269-1282, 2010.

90. Rønnestad, BR, Hansen, J, Hollan, I, and Ellefsen, S. Strength training improves performance and pedaling characteristics in elite cyclists. *Scand J Med Sci Sports* 25:e89-e98, 2015.

91. Rønnestad, BR, and Mujika, I. Optimizing strength training for running and cycling endurance performance: A review. *Scand J Med Sci Sports* 24:603-612, 2014.

92. Royal, KA, Farrow, D, Mujika, I, Halson, SL, Pyne, D, and Abernethy, B. The effects of fatigue on decision making and shooting skill performance in water polo players. *J Sports Sci* 24:807-815, 2006.

93. Rozin, E. The influence of anthropometric parameters on successful learning in gymnastics. *Yessis Review of Soviet Physical Education Sports* 9:16-21, 1974.

94. Sampson, JA, Murray, A, Williams, S, Halseth, T, Hanisch, J, Golden, G, and Fullagar, HHK. Injury risk-workload associations in NCAA American college football. *J Sci Med Sport* 21:1215-1220, 2018.

95. Sarmento, H, Clemente, FM, Araujo, D, Davids, K, McRobert, A, and Figueiredo, A. What performance analysts need to know about research trends in association football (2012-2016): A systematic review. *Sports Med* 48:799-836, 2018.

96. Saunders, PU, Pyne, DB, Telford, RD, and Hawley, JA. Factors affecting running economy in trained distance runners. *Sports Med* 34:465-485, 2004.

97. Schmolinsky, G. Basic elements of track and field training. In *Track and Field: The East German Textbook of Athletics.* Toronto, Canada: Sports Book Publisher, 17-119, 2004.

98. Seitz, LB, Reyes, A, Tran, TT, de Villarreal, ES, and Haff, GG. Increases in lower-body strength transfer positively to sprint performance: A systematic review with meta-analysis. *Sports Med* 44:1693-1702, 2014.

99. Smith, DJ. A framework for understanding the training process leading to elite performance. *Sports Med* 33:1103-1126, 2003.

100. Smith, MR, Zeuwts, L, Lenoir, M, Hens, N, De Jong, LM, and Coutts, AJ. Mental fatigue impairs soccer-specific decision-making skill. *J Sports Sci* 34:1297-1304, 2016.

101. Speranza, MJ, Gabbett, TJ, Johnston, RD, and Sheppard, JM. Muscular strength and power correlates of tackling ability in semiprofessional rugby league players. *J Strength Cond Res* 29:2071-2078, 2015.

102. Speranza, MJA, Gabbett, TJ, Greene, DA, Johnston, RD, and Sheppard, JM. Changes in Rugby League Tackling Ability During a Competitive Season: The Relationship With Strength and Power Qualities. *J Strength Cond Res* 31:3311-3318, 2017.

103. Spurrs, RW, Murphy, AJ, and Watsford, ML. The effect of plyometric training on distance running performance. *Eur J Appl Physiol* 89:1-7, 2003.

104. Stone, MH, Sands, WA, Pierce, KC, Newton, RU, Haff, GG, and Carlock, J. Maximum strength and strength training: A relationship to endurance? *Strength and Cond J* 28:44-53, 2006.

105. Stone, MH, Wilson, D, Rozenek, R, and Newton, H. Anaerobic capacity: Physiological basis. *Strength Cond J* 5:40-40, 1983.
106. Suchomel, TJ, Comfort, P, and Lake, JP. Enhancing the force–velocity profile of athletes using weightlifting derivatives. *Strength Cond J* 39:10-20, 2017.
107. Suchomel, TJ, Nimphius, S, and Stone, MH. The importance of muscular strength in athletic performance. *Sports Med* 46:1419-1449, 2016.
108. Tam, N, Tucker, R, Santos-Concejero, J, Prins, D, and Lamberts, RP. Running economy: Neuromuscular and joint stiffness contributions in trained runners. *Int J Sports Physiol Perform*:1-22, 2018.
109. Taylor, J. A tactical metabolic training model for collegiate basketball. *Strength Cond J* 26:22-29, 2004.
110. Tropin, Y. Analysis of technical tactical training of highly skilled fighters of Greco-Roman wrestling. *Physical Education of Students* 2:59-63, 2013.
111. Verkhoshansky, Y, and Siff, MC. Factors influencing strength production. In *Supertraining*. 6th (expanded) ed. Rome Italy: Verkhoshansky, 125-200, 2009.
112. Verkhoshansky, Y, and Siff, MC. Strength training methods. In *Supertraining*. 6th (expanded) ed. Rome, Italy: Verkhoshansky, 393-420, 2009.
113. Verkhoshansky, Y, and Siff, MC. *Supertraining*. 6th (expanded) ed. Rome, Italy: Verkhoshansky, 2009.
114. Wang, CH, Chang, CC, Liang, YM, Shih, CM, Chiu, WS, Tseng, P, Hung, DL, Tzeng, OJ, Muggleton, NG, and Juan, CH. Open vs. closed skill sports and the modulation of inhibitory control. *PLoS One* 8:e55773, 2013.
115. Windt, J, Zumbo, BD, Sporer, B, MacDonald, K, and Gabbett, TJ. Why do workload spikes cause injuries, and which athletes are at higher risk? Mediators and moderators in workload-injury investigations. *Br J Sports Med* 51:993-994, 2017.

Chapter 4

1. Abadjiev, I. Basic training principles for Bulgarian elite. *Can Weightlifting Fed Official Newsletter* 5:13-18, 1976.
2. Abadjiev, I. Basic training principles for Bulgarian elite. *Inter Olympic Lifter* 3:12-13, 1976.
3. Abadjiev, I. Basic training principles for Bulgarian elite. *New Brunswick Weightlifting Association Newsletter* 4:19-24, 1977.
4. Abadjiev, I. Preparation of the Bulgarian weightlifters for the Olympic Games 1984. *Australian Weightlifter* Oct:25-29, 1981.
5. Adlercreutz, H, Harkonen, M, Kuoppasalmi, K, Naveri, H, Huhtaniemi, I, Tikkanen, H, Remes, K, Dessypris, A, and Karvonen, J. Effect of training on plasma anabolic and catabolic steroid hormones and their response during physical exercise. *Int J Sports Med* 7 Suppl 1:27-28, 1986.
6. Akubat, I, Barrett, S, and Abt, G. Integrating the internal and external training loads in soccer. *Int J Sports Physiol Perform* 9:457-462, 2014.
7. Alén, M, Pakarinen, A, Häkkinen, K, and Komi, PV. Responses of serum androgenic-anabolic and catabolic hormones to prolonged strength training. *Int J Sports Med* 9:229-233, 1988.
8. Allen, H. Using a power meter. In *Cycling Science*. Cheung, SS, Zabala, M, eds. Champaign, IL: Human Kinetics, 362-370, 2017.
9. American College of Sports Medicine. American College of Sports Medicine position stand: Progression models in resistance training for healthy adults. *Med Sci Sports Exerc* 41:687-708, 2009.
10. Androulakis-Korakakis, P, Fisher, JP, Kolokotronis, P, Gentil, P, and Steele, J. Reduced volume "daily max" training compared to higher volume periodized training in powerlifters preparing for competition: A pilot study. *Sports (Basel)* 6, 2018.
11. Aubry, A, Hausswirth, C, Louis, J, Coutts, AJ, and Y, LEM. Functional overreaching: The key to peak performance during the taper? *Med Sci Sports Exerc* 46:1769-1777, 2014.
12. Axe, MJ, Windley, TC, and Snyder-Mackler, L. Data-based interval throwing programs for collegiate softball players. *J Athl Train* 37:194-203, 2002.
13. Bakshi, NK, Inclan, PM, Kirsch, JM, Bedi, A, Agresta, C, and Freehill, MT. Current workload recommendations in baseball pitchers: A systematic review. *Am J Sports Med*:363546519831010, 2019.
14. Bartlett, JD, O'Connor, F, Pitchford, N, Torres-Ronda, L, and Robertson, SJ. Relationships between internal and external training load in team-sport athletes: Evidence for an individualized approach. *Int J Sports Physiol Perform* 12:230-234, 2017.
15. Baumert, P, Lake, MJ, Stewart, CE, Drust, B, and Erskine, RM. Genetic variation and exercise-induced muscle damage: Implications for athletic performance, injury and ageing. *Eur J Appl Physiol* 116:1595-1625, 2016.
16. Ben Abdelkrim, N, Castagna, C, Jabri, I, Battikh, T, El Fazaa, S, and El Ati, J. Activity profile and physiological requirements of junior elite basketball players in relation to aerobic-anaerobic fitness. *J Strength Cond Res* 24:2330-2342, 2010.
17. Berger, J, Harre, D, and Ritter, I. Principles of athletic training. In *Principles of Sports Training: Introduction to the Theory and Methods of Training*. Harre, D, ed. Michigan: Ultimate Athlete Concepts, 113-150, 2012.
18. Billat, V, Lepretre, PM, Heugas, AM, Laurence, MH, Salim, D, and Koralsztein, JP. Training and bioenergetic characteristics in elite male and female Kenyan runners. *Med Sci Sports Exerc* 35:297-304; discussion 305-296, 2003.
19. Billat, VL, Demarle, A, Slawinski, J, Paiva, M, and Koralsztein, JP. Physical and training characteristics of top-class marathon runners. *Med Sci Sports Exerc* 33:2089-2097, 2001.
20. Bompa, TO, and Buzzichelli, CA. Basis of training. In *Periodization: Theory and Methodology of Training*. 6th ed. Champaign, IL: Human Kinetics, 3-27, 2019.
21. Bompa, TO, and Buzzichelli, CA. Principles of training. In *Periodization: Theory and Methodology of Training*. 6th ed. Champaign, IL: Human Kinetics, 29-49, 2019.
22. Bompa, TO, and Haff, GG. Basis for training. In *Periodization: Theory and Methodology of Training*. 5th ed. Champaign, IL: Human Kinetics, 3-30, 2009.
23. Bompa, TO, and Haff, GG. Principles of Training. In *Periodization: Theory and Methodology of Training*. 5th ed. Champaign, IL: Human Kinetics Publishers, 31-56, 2009.

24. Bompa, TO, and Haff, GG. Variables of training. In *Periodization: Theory and Methodology of Training*. 5th ed. Champaign, IL: Human Kinetics, 79-96, 2009.

25. Bondarchuk, A. Problem status and its further training ways. In *Periodization of Training In Sports*. Kiev, Ukraine: New Training Concepts, 13-42, 2011.

26. Borsheim, E, and Bahr, R. Effect of exercise intensity, duration and mode on post-exercise oxygen consumption. *Sports Med* 33:1037-1060, 2003.

27. Bourdon, PC, Cardinale, M, Murray, A, Gastin, P, Kellmann, M, Varley, MC, Gabbett, TJ, Coutts, AJ, Burgess, DJ, Gregson, W, and Cable, NT. Monitoring athlete training loads: Consensus statement. *Int J Sports Physiol Perform* 12:S2161-S2170, 2017.

28. Brady, F. A theoretical and empirical review of the contextual interference effect and the learning of motor skills. *Quest* 50:266-293, 1998.

29. Brooks, GA, Fahey, TD, and Baldwin, KM. The maintenance of ATP homeostasis in energetics and human movement. In *Exercise Physiology: Human Bioenergetics and Its Applications*. 4th ed. Boston: McGraw-Hill, 31-42, 2005.

30. Bruin, G, Kuipers, H, Keizer, HA, and Vander Vusse, GJ. Adaptation and overtraining in horses subjected to increasing training loads. *J Appl Physiol* 76:1908-1913, 1994.

31. Buchheit, M, and Laursen, PB. High-intensity interval training, solutions to the programming puzzle: Part I: Cardiopulmonary emphasis. *Sports Med* 43:313-338, 2013.

32. Buckner, SL, Jessee, MB, Mouser, JG, Dankel, SJ, Mattocks, KT, Bell, ZW, Abe, T, and Loenneke, JP. The basics of training for muscle size and strength: A brief review on the theory. *Med Sci Sports Exerc* 52:645-653, 2020.

33. Calleja-Gonzalez, J, Mielgo-Ayuso, J, Ostojic, SM, Jones, MT, Marques-Jimenez, D, Caparros, T, and Terrados, N. Evidence-based post-exercise recovery strategies in rugby: A narrative review. *Phys Sportsmed* 47:137-147, 2019.

34. Clemente, FM, Mendes, B, Nikolaidis, PT, Calvete, F, Carrico, S, and Owen, AL. Internal training load and its longitudinal relationship with seasonal player wellness in elite professional soccer. *Physiol Behav* 179:262-267, 2017.

35. Coffey, VG, and Hawley, JA. Concurrent exercise training: Do opposites distract? *J Physiol* 595:2883-2896, 2017.

36. Coffey, VG, Zhong, Z, Shield, A, Canny, BJ, Chibalin, AV, Zierath, JR, and Hawley, JA. Early signaling responses to divergent exercise stimuli in skeletal muscle from well-trained humans. *Faseb J* 20:190-192, 2006.

37. Conceicao, F, Fernandes, J, Lewis, M, Gonzalez-Badillo, JJ, and Jimenez-Reyes, P. Movement velocity as a measure of exercise intensity in three lower limb exercises. *J Sports Sci* 34:1099-1106, 2016.

38. Conley, M. Bioenergetics of exercise training. In *Essentials of Strength Training and Conditioning*. 2nd ed. Baechle, TR, Earle, RW, eds. Champaign, IL: Human Kinetics, 73-90, 2000.

39. Conley, MS, Stone, MH, O'Bryant, HS, Johnson, RL, Honeycutt, DR, and Hoke, TP. Peak power versus power at maximal oxygen uptake. Presented at National Strength and Conditioning Association Annual Convention, Las Vegas, NE, 1993.

40. Coutts, AJ, Wallace, LK, and Slattery, KM. Monitoring changes in performance, physiology, biochemistry, and psychology during overreaching and recovery in triathletes. *Int J Sports Med* 28:125-134, 2007.

41. Cummins, C, Orr, R, O'Connor, H, and West, C. Global positioning systems (GPS) and microtechnology sensors in team sports: A systematic review. *Sports Med* 43:1025-1042, 2013.

42. Dankel, SJ, Mattocks, KT, Jessee, MB, Buckner, SL, Mouser, JG, Counts, BR, Laurentino, GC, and Loenneke, JP. Frequency: The overlooked resistance training variable for inducing muscle hypertrophy? *Sports Med* 47:799-805, 2017.

43. Davies, RW, Carson, BP, and Jakeman, PM. The effect of whey protein supplementation on the temporal recovery of muscle function following resistance training: A systematic review and meta-analysis. *Nutrients* 10, 2018.

44. Del Vecchio, L, Stanton, R, Reaburn, P, Macgregor, C, Meerkin, J, Villegas, J, and Korhonen, MT. Effects of combined strength and sprint training on lean mass, strength, power, and sprint performance in masters road cyclists. *J Strength Cond Res* 33:66-79, 2019.

45. Deuster, PA, Contreras-Sesvold, CL, O'Connor, FG, Campbell, WW, Kenney, K, Capacchione, JF, Landau, ME, Muldoon, SM, Rushing, EJ, and Heled, Y. Genetic polymorphisms associated with exertional rhabdomyolysis. *Eur J Appl Physiol* 113:1997-2004, 2013.

46. DeWeese, BH, Gray, HS, Sams, ML, Scruggs, SK, and Serrano, AJ. Revising the definition of periodization: Merging historical principles with modern concerns. *Olympic Coach Magazine* 24:5-19, 2015.

47. DeWeese, BH, Hornsby, G, Stone, M, and Stone, MH. The training process: Planning for strength–power training in track and field. Part 1: Theoretical aspects. *Journal of Sport and Health Science* 4:308-317, 2015.

48. Dick, FW. Fitness. In *Sports Training Principles*. 4th ed. London: A and C Black, 218-228, 2002.

49. Duchateau, J, Semmler, JG, and Enoka, RM. Training adaptations in the behavior of human motor units. *J Appl Physiol* 101:1766-1775, 2006.

50. Faria, EW, Parker, DL, and Faria, IE. The science of cycling: Physiology and training—part 1. *Sports Med* 35:285-312, 2005.

51. Ferguson, BS, Rogatzki, MJ, Goodwin, ML, Kane, DA, Rightmire, Z, and Gladden, LB. Lactate metabolism: Historical context, prior misinterpretations, and current understanding. *Eur J Appl Physiol* 118:691-728, 2018.

52. Fernandez-Fernandez, J, Sanz-Rivas, D, Sarabia, JM, and Moya, M. Preseason training: The effects of a 17-day high-intensity shock microcycle in elite tennis players. *J Sports Sci Med* 14:783-791, 2015.

53. Fiskerstrand, A, and Seiler, KS. Training and performance characteristics among Norwegian international rowers 1970-2001. *Scand J Med Sci Sports* 14:303-310, 2004.

54. Foster, C. Monitoring training in athletes with reference to overtraining syndrome. *Med Sci Sports Exerc* 30:1164-1168, 1998.

55. Fox, JL, Stanton, R, Sargent, C, Wintour, SA, and Scanlan, AT. The association between training load and perfor-

55. ...mance in team sports: A systematic review. *Sports Med* 48:2743-2774, 2018.

56. Fry, AC. The role of training intensity in resistance exercise overtraining and overreaching. In *Overtraining in Sport*. Kreider, RB, Fry, AC, O'Toole, ML, eds. Champaign, IL: Human Kinetics, 107-127, 1998.

57. Fry, AC, and Kraemer, WJ. Resistance exercise overtraining and overreaching: Neuroendocrine responses. *Sports Med* 23:106-129, 1997.

58. Fry, AC, Kraemer, WJ, Stone, MH, Koziris, LP, Thrush, JT, and Fleck, SJ. Relationships between serum testosterone, cortisol, and weightlifting performance. *J Strength Cond Res* 14:338-343, 2000.

59. Fry, AC, Kraemer, WJ, Stone, MH, Warren, BJ, Fleck, SJ, Kearney, JT, and Gordon, SE. Endocrine responses to overreaching before and after 1 year of weightlifting. *Can J Appl Physiol* 19:400-410, 1994.

60. Fry, AC, Webber, JM, Weiss, LW, Fry, MD, and Li, Y. Impaired performance with excessive high-intensity free-weight training. *J Strength Cond Res* 14:54-61, 2000.

61. Fry, RW, Morton, AR, and Keast, D. Periodisation and the prevention of overtraining. *Can J Sport Sci* 17:241-248, 1992.

62. Fry, RW, Morton, AR, and Keast, D. Periodisation of training stress—a review. *Can J Sport Sci* 17:234-240, 1992.

63. Gabbett, TJ. Science of Rugby League football: A review. *J Sports Sci* 23:961-976, 2005.

64. Gabbett, TJ. Relationship between accelerometer load, collisions, and repeated high-intensity effort activity in Rugby League players. *J Strength Cond Res* 29:3424-3431, 2015.

65. Gabbett, TJ. The training-injury prevention paradox: Should athletes be training smarter and harder? *Br J Sports Med* 50:273-280, 2016.

66. Gabbett, TJ. Workload monitoring and athlete management. In *Advanced Strength and Conditioning: An Evidence-Based Approach*. Turner, A, Comfort, P, eds. Abingdon, Oxon: Routledge, 137-150, 2018.

67. Gabbett, TJ. Debunking the myths about training load, injury and performance: Empirical evidence, hot topics and recommendations for practitioners. *Br J Sports Med* 54:58-66, 2020.

68. Gao, J. A study on pre-game training characteristics of Chinese elite swimmers. *J Beijing Sport Univ* 31:832-834, 2008.

69. Garvican, LA, Ebert, TR, Quod, MJ, Gardner, SA, Gregory, J, Osbourne, MA, and Martin, DT. High-performance cyclists. In *Physiology Tests for Athletes*. 2nd ed. Tanner, RK, Gore, CJ, eds. Champaign, IL: Human Kinetics, 299-322, 2013.

70. Gillam, GM. Effects of frequency of weight training on muscle strength enhancement. *J Sports Med* 21:432-436, 1981.

71. Gorostiaga, EM, Granados, C, Ibanez, J, Gonzalez-Badillo, JJ, and Izquierdo, M. Effects of an entire season on physical fitness changes in elite male handball players. *Med Sci Sports Exerc* 38:357-366, 2006.

72. Gorostiaga, EM, Navarro-Amezqueta, I, Calbet, JA, Hellsten, Y, Cusso, R, Guerrero, M, Granados, C, Gonzalez-Izal, M, Ibanez, J, and Izquierdo, M. Energy metabolism during repeated sets of leg press exercise leading to failure or not. *PLoS One* 7:e40621, 2012.

73. Gorostiaga, EM, Navarro-Amezqueta, I, Calbet, JA, Sanchez-Medina, L, Cusso, R, Guerrero, M, Granados, C, Gonzalez-Izal, M, Ibanez, J, and Izquierdo, M. Blood ammonia and lactate as markers of muscle metabolites during leg press exercise. *J Strength Cond Res* 28:2775-2785, 2014.

74. Grgic, J, Schoenfeld, BJ, Davies, TB, Lazinica, B, Krieger, JW, and Pedisic, Z. Effect of resistance training frequency on gains in muscular strength: A systematic review and meta-analysis. *Sports Med* 48:1207-1220, 2018.

75. Guellich, A, Seiler, S, and Emrich, E. Training methods and intensity distribution of young world-class rowers. *Int J Sports Physiol Perform* 4:448-460, 2009.

76. Gullich, A, and Emrich, E. Considering long-term sustainability in the development of world class success. *Eur J Sport Sci* 14 Suppl 1:S383-397, 2014.

77. Haff, GG. Quantifying workloads in resistance training: A brief review. *Prof Strength and Cond* 10:31-40, 2010.

78. Haff, GG. The essentials of periodisation. In *Strength and Conditioning for Sports Performance*. Jeffreys, I, Moody, J, eds. Abingdon, Oxon: Routledge, 404-448, 2016.

79. Haff, GG. Periodization and power integration. In *Developing Power*. McGuigan, M, ed. Champaign, IL: Human Kinetics, 33-62, 2017.

80. Haff, GG. Periodization for tactical populations. In *NSCA's Essentials of Tactical Strength and Conditioning*. Alvar, BA, Sell, K, Deuster, PA, eds. Champaign, IL: Human Kinetics, 181-204, 2017.

81. Haff, GG. Periodization and programming of individual sports. In *NSCA's Essentials of Sport Science*. French, D, Torres Ronda, L, eds. Champaign, IL: Human Kinetics, 27-42, 2022.

82. Haff, GG, and Dumke, C. Submaximal exercise testing. In *Laboratory Manual for Exercise Physiology, 2E*. Champaign, IL: Human Kinetics, 159-180, 2018.

83. Haff, GG, and Haff, EE. Resistance training program design. In *Essentials of Periodization*. 2nd ed. Malek, MH, Coburn, JW, eds. Champaign, IL: Human Kinetics, 359-401, 2012.

84. Haff, GG, and Haff, EE. Training integration and periodization. In *Strength and Conditioning Program Design*. Hoffman, J, ed. Champaign, IL: Human Kinetics, 209-254, 2012.

85. Haff, GG, Jackson, JR, Kawamori, N, Carlock, JM, Hartman, MJ, Kilgore, JL, Morris, RT, Ramsey, MW, Sands, WA, and Stone, MH. Force-time curve characteristics and hormonal alterations during an eleven-week training period in elite women weightlifters. *J Strength Cond Res* 22:433-446, 2008.

86. Haff, GG, Kraemer, WJ, O'Bryant, HS, Pendlay, G, Plisk, S, and Stone, MH. Roundtable discussion: Periodization of training—part 1. *NSCA J* 26:50-69, 2004.

87. Haff, GG, Kraemer, WJ, O'Bryant, HS, Pendlay, G, Plisk, S, and Stone, MH. Roundtable discussion: Periodization of training—part 2. *NSCA J* 26:56-70, 2004.

88. Haff, GG, Whitley, A, and Potteiger, JA. A brief review: Explosive exercises and sports performance. *Strength Cond J* 23:13-20, 2001.

89. Häkkinen, K. Neuromuscular and hormonal adaptations during strength and power training. A review. *J Sports Med Phys Fitness* 29:9-26, 1989.

90. Häkkinen, K. Neuromuscular adaptations during strength training, aging, detraining, and immobilization. *Crit Rev Physic Rehab Med* 6:161-198, 1994.

91. Häkkinen, K, Alen, M, and Komi, PV. Changes in isometric force- and relaxation-time, electromyographic and muscle fibre characteristics of human skeletal muscle during strength training and detraining. *Acta Physiol Scand* 125:573-585, 1985.

92. Häkkinen, K, and Kallinen, M. Distribution of strength training volume into one or two daily sessions and neuromuscular adaptations in female athletes. *Electromyogr Clin Neurophysiol* 34:117-124., 1994.

93. Häkkinen, K, Kallinen, M, Komi, PV, and Kauhanen, H. Neuromuscular adaptations during short-term "normal" and reduced training periods in strength athletes. *Electromyogr Clin Neurophysiol* 31:35-42, 1991.

94. Häkkinen, K, Keskinen, KL, Alen, M, Komi, PV, and Kauhanen, H. Serum hormone concentrations during prolonged training in elite endurance-trained and strength-trained athletes. *Eur J Appl Physiol* 59:233-238, 1989.

95. Häkkinen, K, and Komi, PV. Effect of explosive type strength training on electromyographic and force production characteristics of leg extensor muscles during concentric and various stretch-shortening cycle exercises. *Scand J Sports Sci* 7:65-76, 1985.

96. Häkkinen, K, Pakarinen, A, Alen, M, Kauhanen, H, and Komi, PV. Neuromuscular and hormonal adaptations in athletes to strength training in two years. *J Appl Physiol* 65:2406-2412, 1988.

97. Halson, SL, Bridge, MW, Meeusen, R, Busschaert, B, Gleeson, M, Jones, DA, and Jeukendrup, AE. Time course of performance changes and fatigue markers during intensified training in trained cyclists. *J Appl Physiol* 93:947-956, 2002.

98. Harries, SK, Lubans, DR, and Callister, R. Systematic review and meta-analysis of linear and undulating periodized resistance training programs on muscular strength. *J Strength Cond Res* 29:1113-1125, 2015.

99. Harris, GR, Stone, MH, O'Bryant, HS, Proulx, CM, and Johnson, RL. Short-term performance effects of high power, high force, or combined weight-training methods. *J Strength Cond Res* 14:14-20, 2000.

100. Haugen, T, Seiler, S, Sandbakk, O, and Tønnessen, E. The training and development of elite sprint performance: An integration of scientific and best practice literature. *Sports Med Open* 5:44, 2019.

101. Hawley, JA. Sending the signal: Muscle glycogen availability as a regulator of training adaptation. In *Hormones, Metabolism and the Benefits of Exercise*. Spiegelman, B, ed. Cham: Springer International, 43-55, 2017.

102. Hearris, MA, Hammond, KM, Fell, JM, and Morton, JP. Regulation of muscle glycogen metabolism during exercise: Implications for endurance performance and training adaptations. *Nutrients* 10, 2018.

103. Hellebrandt, F, and Houtz, S. Mechanisms of muscle training in man: Experimental demonstration of the overload principle. *Phys Ther Rev* 36:371-383, 1956.

104. Henderson, B, Cook, J, Kidgell, DJ, and Gastin, PB. Game and training load differences in elite junior Australian football. *J Sports Sci Med* 14:494-500, 2015.

105. Herda, TJ, and Cramer, JT. Bioenergetics of exercise and training. In *Essentials of Strength Training and Conditioning*. 4th ed. Haff, GG, Triplett, N, eds. Champaign, IL: Human Kinetics, 43-63, 2016.

106. Hodges, NJ, Hayes, S, Horn, RR, and Williams, AM. Changes in coordination, control and outcome as a result of extended practice on a novel motor skill. *Ergonomics* 48:1672-1685, 2005.

107. Hoffman, JR, Wendell, M, Cooper, J, and Kang, J. Comparison between linear and nonlinear in-season training programs in freshman football players. *J Strength Cond Res* 17:561-565, 2003.

108. Hornsby, WG, Gentles, JA, MacDonald, CJ, Mizuguchi, S, Ramsey, MW, and Stone, MH. Maximum strength, rate of force development, jump height, and peak power alterations in weightlifters across five months of training. *Sports* 5:78, 2017.

109. Hornsby, WG, Gentles, JA, and Stone, MH. Application to Training. In *Performance Assessment in Strength and Conditioning*. Comfort, P, Jones, PA, McMahon, JJ, eds., 332-353, 2019.

110. Impellizzeri, FM, Rampinini, E, and Marcora, SM. Physiological assessment of aerobic training in soccer. *J Sports Sci* 23:583-592, 2005.

111. Ingham, SA, Fudge, BW, and Pringle, JS. Training distribution, physiological profile, and performance for a male international 1500-m runner. *Int J Sports Physiol Perform* 7:193-195, 2012.

112. Ishida, Y, Yamagishi, T, Mujika, I, Nakamura, M, Suzuki, E, and Yamashita, D. Training cessation and subsequent retraining of a world-class female Olympic sailor after Tokyo 2020: A case study. *Physiol Rep* 11:e15593, 2023.

113. Issurin, V. Block periodization versus traditional training theory: A review. *J Sports Med Phys Fitness* 48:65-75, 2008.

114. Issurin, V. Training effects. In *Principles and Basics of Advanced Athletic Training*. Yessis, M, ed. Michigan, USA: Ultimate Athlete Concepts, 45-79, 2008.

115. Issurin, V. Training effects. In *Building the Modern Athlete: Scientific Advancement & Training Innovation*. Thome, M, ed. Michigan, USA: Ultimate Athlete Concepts, 31-73, 2015.

116. Issurin, VB. New horizons for the methodology and physiology of training periodization. *Sports Med* 40:189-206, 2010.

117. Jaspers, A, Brink, MS, Probst, SG, Frencken, WG, and Helsen, WF. Relationships between training load indicators and training outcomes in professional soccer. *Sports Med* 47:533-544, 2017.

118. Klika, RJ, Alderdice, MS, Kvale, JJ, and Kearney, JT. Efficacy of cycling training based on a power field test. *J Strength Cond Res* 21:265-269, 2007.

119. Knuttgen, HG, and Komi, PV. Basic definitions for exercise. In *Strength and Power in Sport*. Komi, PV, ed. Oxford: Blackwell Scientific, 3-8, 1992.

120. Knuttgen, HG, and Komi, PV. Basic definitions for exercise. In *Strength and Power in Sport*. Komi, PV, ed. Oxford: Blackwell Scientific, 3-8, 2003.

121. Kraemer, WJ, and Ratamess, NA. Hormonal responses and adaptations to resistance exercise and training. *Sports Med* 35:339-361, 2005.

122. Lambert, EV, St Clair Gibson, A, and Noakes, TD. Complex systems model of fatigue: Integrative homoeostatic control of peripheral physiological systems during exercise in humans. *Br J Sports Med* 39:52-62, 2005.

123. Laursen, PB, Shing, CM, Peake, JM, Coombes, JS, and Jenkins, DG. Interval training program optimization in highly trained endurance cyclists. *Med Sci Sports Exerc* 34:1801-1807, 2002.

124. Lazu, AL, Love, SD, Butterfield, TA, English, R, and Uhl, TL. The relationship between pitching volume and arm soreness in collegiate baseball pitchers. *Int J Sports Phys Ther* 14:97-106, 2019.

125. Leutshenko, AV, and Berestovskaya, AL. The main elements in the planning of training for elite discus throwers. In *The Throws: Contemporary Theory, Technique, and Training*. 5th ed. Jarver, J, ed. Mountain View, CA: Tafnews Press, 106-108, 2000.

126. Mackinnon, L, and Hooper, S. Overtraining and recovery in elite athletes. Belconnen ACT, Australia: The University of Queensland, 1991.

127. Matveyev, LP. Introductory characteristics of sports training. In *Fundamentals of Sports Training*. Moscow: Fizkultua i Sport, 29-59, 1977.

128. Maughan, R, and Gleeson, M. The endurance athlete. In *The Biochemical Basis of Sports Performance*. 2nd ed. New York: Oxford University Press, 127-173, 2010.

129. Maughan, R, and Gleeson, M. The sprinter. In *The Biochemical Basis of Sports Performance*. 2nd ed. New York: Oxford University Press, 74-98, 2010.

130. McGuigan, M. Measures of fitness and fatigue. In *Monitoring Training and Performance in Athletes*. Champaign, IL: Human Kinetics, 103-134, 2017.

131. McGuigan, MR, and Foster, C. A new approach to monitoring resistance training. *Strength Cond J* 26:42-47, 2004.

132. McMaster, DT, Gill, N, Cronin, J, and McGuigan, M. The development, retention and decay rates of strength and power in elite Rugby Union, Rugby League and American football: A systematic review. *Sports Med* 43:367-384, 2013.

133. McMillan, JL, Stone, MH, Sartin, J, Keith, R, Marple, D, Brown, C, and Lewis, RD. 20-hour physiological responses to a single weight-training session. *J Strength Cond Res* 7:9-21, 1993.

134. Melchiorri, G, Ronconi, M, Triossi, T, Viero, V, De Sanctis, D, Tancredi, V, Salvati, A, Padua, E, and Alvero Cruz, JR. Detraining in young soccer players. *J Sports Med Phys Fitness* 54:27-33, 2014.

135. Meyer, T, Wegmann, M, Poppendieck, W, and Fullagar, HH. Regenerative interventions in professional football. *Sport-Orthopädie-Sport-Traumatologie-Sports Orthopaedics and Traumatology* 30:112-118, 2014.

136. Minetti, AE. On the mechanical power of joint extensions as affected by the change in muscle force (or cross-sectional area), ceteris paribus. *Eur J Appl Physiol* 86:363-369, 2002.

137. Moore, DR. Nutrition to support recovery from endurance exercise: Optimal carbohydrate and protein replacement. *Curr Sports Med Rep* 14:294-300, 2015.

138. Mujika, and Padilla, S. Muscular characteristics of detraining in humans. *Med Sci Sports Exerc* 33:1297-1303., 2001.

139. Mujika, I. Olympic preparation of a world-class female triathlete. *Int J Sports Physiol Perform* 9:727-731, 2014.

140. Mujika, I, Halson, S, Burke, L, Balagué, G, and Farrow, D. An integrated, multifactorial approach to periodization for optimal performance in individual and team sports. *Int J Sports Physiol Perform* 13:538-561, 2018.

141. Myakinchenko, EB, Kriuchkov, AS, Adodin, NV, and Feofilaktov, V. The annual periodization of training volumes of international-level cross-country skiers and biathletes. *Int J Sports Physiol Perform* 15:1181-1188, 2020.

142. Nádori, L. Theoretical and methodological basis of training planning. In *Theoretical and Methodological Basis of Training Planning With Special Considerations Within a Microcycle*. Nádori, L, Granek, I, eds. Lincoln, NE: National Strength and Conditioning Association, 1-25, 1989.

143. Neal, CM, Hunter, AM, and Galloway, SD. A 6-month analysis of training-intensity distribution and physiological adaptation in Ironman triathletes. *J Sports Sci* 29:1515-1523, 2011.

144. Nedelec, M, McCall, A, Carling, C, Legall, F, Berthoin, S, and Dupont, G. Recovery in soccer: Part II—recovery strategies. *Sports Med* 43:9-22, 2013.

145. O'Toole, ML. Overreaching and overtraining in endurance athletes. In *Overtraining in Sport*. Kreider, RB, Fry, AC, O'Toole, ML, eds. Champaign, IL: Human Kinetics, 3-18, 1998.

146. Ochi, E, Maruo, M, Tsuchiya, Y, Ishii, N, Miura, K, and Sasaki, K. Higher training frequency is important for gaining muscular strength under volume-matched training. *Front Physiol* 9:744, 2018.

147. Olbrect, J. Definitions and principles of training. In *The Science of Winning: Planning, Periodizing, and Optimizing Swim Training*. Luton, England: Swimshop, 1-13, 2000.

148. Olbrect, J. *The Science of Winning: Planning, Periodizing, and Optimizing Swim Training*. Luton, England: Swimshop, 2000.

149. Painter, K, Haff, G, Triplett, N, Stuart, C, Hornsby, G, Ramsey, M, Bazyler, C, and Stone, M. Resting hormone alterations and injuries: Block vs. DUP weight-training among D-1 track and field athletes. *Sports* 6:3, 2018.

150. Pareja-Blanco, F, Villalba-Fernandez, A, Cornejo-Daza, PJ, Sanchez-Valdepenas, J, and Gonzalez-Badillo, JJ. Time course of recovery following resistance exercise with different loading magnitudes and velocity loss in the set. *Sports (Basel)* 7, 2019.

151. Passfield, L, Hopker, JG, Jobson, S, Friel, D, and Zabala, M. Knowledge is power: Issues of measuring training and performance in cycling. *J Sports Sci* 35:1426-1434, 2017.

152. Pickering, C, and Kiely, J. ACTN3: More than just a gene for speed. *Front Physiol* 8, 2017.

153. Pickering, C, and Kiely, J. Hamstring injury prevention: A role for genetic information? *Med Hypotheses* 119:58-62, 2018.

154. Pickering, C, Kiely, J, Suraci, B, and Collins, D. The magnitude of Yo-Yo test improvements following an aerobic training intervention are associated with total genotype score. *PloS One* 13:e0207597, 2018.

155. Plisk, SS, and Stone, MH. Periodization strategies. *Strength and Cond J* 25:19-37, 2003.

156. Rago, V, Brito, J, Figueiredo, P, Costa, J, Barreira, D, Krustrup, P, and Rebelo, A. Methods to collect and interpret external training load using microtechnology incorporating GPS in professional football: A systematic review. *Res Sports Med* 28:437-458, 2020.

157. Ranchordas, MK, Dawson, JT, and Russell, M. Practical nutritional recovery strategies for elite soccer players when limited time separates repeated matches. *J Int Soc Sports Nutr* 14:35, 2017.

158. Rawson, ES, Miles, MP, and Larson-Meyer, DE. Dietary supplements for health, adaptation, and recovery in athletes. *Int J Sport Nutr Exerc Metab* 28:188-199, 2018.

159. Reuter, BH, and Dawes, JJ. Program design and technique for aerobic endurance training. In *Essentials of Strength Training and Conditioning*. 4th ed. Haff, GG, Triplett, N, eds. Champaign, IL: Human Kinetics, 559-582, 2016.

160. Richard, NA, and Koehle, MS. Optimizing recovery to support multi-evening cycling competition performance. *Eur J Sport Sci* 19:811-823, 2019.

161. Rønnestad, BR, and Hansen, J. A scientific approach to improve physiological capacity of an elite cyclist. *Int J Sports Physiol Perform* 13:390-393, 2018.

162. Rowbottom, DG. Periodization of training. In *Exercise and Sport Science*. Garrett, WE, Kirkendall, DT, eds. Philadelphia, PA: Lippicott Williams and Wilkins, 499-512, 2000.

163. Sands, WA, Kavanaugh, AA, Murray, SR, McNeal, JR, and Jemni, M. Modern techniques and technologies applied to training and performance monitoring. *Int J Sports Physiol Perform* 12:S263-S272, 2017.

164. Schneider, C, Hanakam, F, Wiewelhove, T, Doweling, A, Kellmann, M, Meyer, T, Pfeiffer, M, and Ferrauti, A. Heart rate monitoring in team sports: A conceptual framework for contextualizing heart rate measures for training and recovery prescription. *Front Physiol* 9:639, 2018.

165. Schoenfeld, BJ, Ogborn, D, and Krieger, JW. Effects of resistance training frequency on measures of muscle hypertrophy: A systematic review and meta-analysis. *Sports Med* 46:1689-1697, 2016.

166. Schumacher, YO, and Mueller, P. The 4000-m team pursuit cycling world record: theoretical and practical aspects. *Med Sci Sports Exerc* 34:1029-1036, 2002.

167. Seitz, LB, Reyes, A, Tran, TT, de Villarreal, ES, and Haff, GG. Increases in lower-body strength transfer positively to sprint performance: A systematic review with meta-analysis. *Sports Med* 44:1693-1702, 2014.

168. Siewierski, M. Volume and structure of training loads of top swimmers in direct starting preparation phase for main competition. *Polish Journal of Sport & Tourism* 17, 2010.

169. Skorski, S, and Abbiss, CR. The manipulation of pace within endurance sport. *Front Physiol* 8:102, 2017.

170. Smith, CM, Housh, TJ, Hill, EC, Schmidt, RJ, and Johnson, GO. Time course of changes in neuromuscular responses at 30% versus 70% 1 repetition maximum during dynamic constant external resistance leg extensions to failure. *Int J Exerc Sci* 10:365-378, 2017.

171. Smith, DJ. A framework for understanding the training process leading to elite performance. *Sports Med* 33:1103-1126, 2003.

172. Sollie, O, Jeppesen, PB, Tangen, DS, Jerneren, F, Nellemann, B, Valsdottir, D, Madsen, K, Turner, C, Refsum, H, Skalhegg, BS, Ivy, JL, and Jensen, J. Protein intake in the early recovery period after exhaustive exercise improves performance the following day. *J Appl Physiol (1985)* 125:1731-1742, 2018.

173. Spencer, M, Bishop, D, Dawson, B, and Goodman, C. Physiological and metabolic responses of repeated-sprint activities: Specific to field-based team sports. *Sports Med* 35:1025-1044, 2005.

174. Stanula, AJ, Gabrys, TT, Roczniok, RK, Szmatlan-Gabrys, UB, Ozimek, MJ, and Mostowik, AJ. Quantification of the demands during an ice-hockey game based on intensity zones determined from the incremental test outcomes. *J Strength Cond Res* 30:176-183, 2016.

175. Stølen, T, Chamari, K, Castagna, C, and Wisløff, U. Physiology of soccer: An update. *Sports Med* 35:501-536, 2005.

176. Stone, MH, and Fry, AC. Increased training volume in strength/power athletes. In *Overtraining in Sport*. Kreider, RB, Fry, AC, O'Toole, ML, eds. Champaign, IL: Human Kinetics, 87-106, 1998.

177. Stone, MH, Keith, R, Kearney, JT, Wilson, GD, and Fleck, S, J,. Overtraining: A review of the signs and symptoms of overtraining. *Journal of Applied Sport Science Research* 5:35-50, 1991.

178. Stone, MH, O'Bryant, H, and Garhammer, J. A hypothetical model for strength training. *J Sports Med* 21:342-351, 1981.

179. Stone, MH, and O'Bryant, HS. Letter to the editor. *J Strength Cond Res* 9:125-127, 1995.

180. Stone, MH, Potteiger, JA, Pierce, KC, Proulx, CM, O'Bryant, HS, Johnson, RL, and Stone, ME. Comparison of the effects of three different weight-training programs on the one repetition maximum squat. *J Strength Cond Res* 14:332-337, 2000.

181. Stone, MH, Stone, ME, and Sands, WA. Bioenergetic and metabolic factors. In *Principles and Practice of Resistance Training*. Champaign, IL: Human Kinetics, 61-86, 2007.

182. Stone, MH, Stone, ME, and Sands, WA. The concept of periodization. In *Principles and Practice of Resistance Training*. Champaign, IL: Human Kinetics Publishers, 259-286, 2007.

183. Stone, MH, Stone, ME, and Sands, WA. Developing resistance training programs. In *Principles and Practice of Resistance Training*. Champaign, IL: Human Kinetics, 287-294, 2007.

184. Stone, MH, Stone, ME, and Sands, WA. Introduction, definitions, objectives, tasks, and principles of training. In *Principles and Practice of Resistance Training*. Champaign, IL: Human Kinetics, 1-12, 2007.

185. Stone, MH, and Wathen, D. Letter to the editor. *Strength Cond J* 23:7-9, 2001.

186. Stults-Kolehmainen, MA, Bartholomew, JB, and Sinha, R. Chronic psychological stress impairs recovery of muscular function and somatic sensations over a 96-hour period. *J Strength Cond Res* 28:2007-2017, 2014.

187. Stults-Kolehmainen, MA, and Sinha, R. The effects of stress on physical activity and exercise. *Sports Med* 44:81-121, 2014.

188. Suchomel, TJ, Nimphius, S, Bellon, CR, and Stone, MH. The importance of muscular strength: Training considerations. *Sports Med* 48:765-785, 2018.

189. Sweeting, AJ, Cormack, SJ, Morgan, S, and Aughey, RJ. When is a sprint a sprint? A review of the analysis of team-sport athlete activity profile. *Front Physiol* 8:432, 2017.

190. Tanaka, H, Monahan, KD, and Seals, DR. Age-predicted maximal heart rate revisited. *J Am Coll Cardiol* 37:153-156, 2001.

191. Taylor, JB, Wright, AA, Dischiavi, SL, Townsend, MA, and Marmon, AR. Activity demands during multi-directional team sports: A systematic review. *Sports Med* 47:2533-2551, 2017.

192. Ten Haaf, T, van Staveren, S, Oudenhoven, E, Piacentini, MF, Meeusen, R, Roelands, B, Koenderman, L, Daanen, HAM, Foster, C, and de Koning, JJ. Prediction of functional overreaching from subjective fatigue and readiness to train after only 3 days of cycling. *Int J Sports Physiol Perform* 12:S287-S294, 2017.

193. Tjelta, LI. A longitudinal case study of the training of the 2012 European 1500 m track champion. *Int J Appl Sports Sci* 25:11-18, 2013.

194. Tjelta, LI, Tønnessen, E, and Enoksen, E. A case study of the training of nine times New York Marathon winner Grete Waitz. *Int J Sports Sci Coach* 9:139-158, 2014.

195. Toji, H, and Kaneko, M. Effect of multiple-load training on the force-velocity relationship. *J Strength Cond Res* 18:792-795, 2004.

196. Toji, H, Suei, K, and Kaneko, M. Effects of combined training loads on relations among force, velocity, and power development. *Can J Appl Physiol* 22:328-336, 1997.

197. Tønnessen, E, Svendsen, IS, Ronnestad, BR, Hisdal, J, Haugen, TA, and Seiler, S. The annual training periodization of 8 world champions in orienteering. *Int J Sports Physiol Perform* 10:29-38, 2015.

198. Tønnessen, E, Sylta, O, Haugen, TA, Hem, E, Svendsen, IS, and Seiler, S. The road to gold: Training and peaking characteristics in the year prior to a gold medal endurance performance. *PLoS One* 9:e101796, 2014.

199. Tufano, JJ, Conlon, JA, Nimphius, S, Brown, LE, Banyard, HG, Williamson, BD, Bishop, LG, Hopper, AJ, and Haff, GG. Cluster sets: Permitting greater mechanical stress without decreasing relative velocity. *Int J Sports Physiol Perform* 12:463-469, 2017.

200. Tufano, JJ, Conlon, JA, Nimphius, S, Oliver, JM, Kreutzer, A, and Haff, GG. Different cluster sets result in similar metabolic, endocrine, and perceptual responses in trained men. *J Strength Cond Res* 33:346-354, 2019.

201. Turner, A, and Comfort, P. Periodisation. In *Advanced Strength and Conditioning: An Evidence-Based Approach*. Turner, A, Comfort, P, eds. London: Routledge Taylor Francis, 116-136, 2018.

202. Urhausen, A, Gabriel, H, and Kindermann, W. Blood hormones as markers of training stress and overtraining. *Sports Med* 20:251-276, 1995.

203. Varley, MC, Jaspers, A, Helsen, WF, and Malone, JJ. Methodological considerations when quantifying high-intensity efforts in team sport using global positioning system technology. *Int J Sports Physiol Perform* 12:1059-1068, 2017.

204. Verkhoshansky, Y, and Siff, MC. Factors influencing strength production. In *Supertraining*. 6th (expanded) ed. Rome, Italy: Verkhoshansky, 125-200, 2009.

205. Verkhoshansky, Y, and Siff, MC. Organisation of training. In *Supertraining*. 6th (expanded) ed. Rome, Italy: Verkhoshansky, 313-393, 2009.

206. Verkhoshansky, Y, and Siff, MC. Preparedness and training load. In *Supertraining*. 6th (expanded) ed. Rome, Italy: Verkhoshansky, 313-367, 2009.

207. Verkhoshansky, Y, and Siff, MC. Programming and organisation of training. In *Supertraining*. 6th (expanded) ed. Rome, Italy: Verkhoshansky, 313-392, 2009.

208. Verkhoshansky, Y, and Siff, MC. Strength and the muscular system. In *Supertraining*. 6th ed. Rome, Italy: Verkhoshansky, 1-82, 2009.

209. Winter, EM, and Fowler, N. Exercise defined and quantified according to the Systeme International d'Unites. *J Sports Sci* 27:447-460, 2009.

210. Zamparo, P, Minetti, AE, and di Prampero, PE. Interplay among the changes of muscle strength, cross-sectional area and maximal explosive power: Theory and facts. *Eur J Appl Physiol* 88:193-202, 2002.

211. Zapico, AG, Calderon, FJ, Benito, PJ, Gonzalez, CB, Parisi, A, Pigozzi, F, and Di Salvo, V. Evolution of physiological and haematological parameters with training load in elite male road cyclists: A longitudinal study. *J Sports Med Phys Fitness* 47:191-196, 2007.

212. Zatsiorsky, VM, Kraemer, WJ, and Fry, AC. Basic concepts of training theory. In *Science and Practice of Strength Training*. 3rd ed. Champaign, IL: Human Kinetics Publishers, 3-16, 2021.

213. Zatsiorsky, VM, Kraemer, WJ, and Fry, AC. Timing in strength training. In *Science and Practice of Strength Training*. 3rd ed. Champaign, IL: Human Kinetics Publishers, 79-98, 2021.

214. Zourdos, MC, Dolan, C, Quiles, JM, Klemp, A, Jo, E, Loenneke, JP, Blanco, R, and Whitehurst, M. Efficacy of daily one-repetition maximum training in well-trained powerlifters and weightlifters: A case series. *Nutr Hosp* 33:437-443, 2016.

Chapter 5

1. Afonso, J, Nikolaidis, PT, Sousa, P, and Mesquita, I. Is empirical research on periodization trustworthy? A comprehensive review of conceptual and methodological issues. *J Sports Sci Med* 16:27-34, 2017.

2. Afonso, J, Rocha, T, Nikolaidis, PT, Clemente, FM, Rosemann, T, and Knechtle, B. A systematic review of meta-analyses comparing periodized and non-periodized exercise programs: Why we should go back to original research. *Front Physiol* 10:1023, 2019.

3. Arruda, AF, Carling, C, Zanetti, V, Aoki, MS, Coutts, AJ, and Moreira, A. Effects of a very congested match schedule on body-load impacts, accelerations, and running measures in youth soccer players. *Int J Sports Physiol Perform* 10:248-252, 2015.

4. Bartolomei, S, Hoffman, JR, Merni, F, and Stout, JR. A comparison of traditional and block periodized strength training programs in trained athletes. *J Strength Cond Res* 28:990-997, 2014.

5. Bartolomei, S, Hoffman, JR, Stout, JR, Zini, M, Stefanelli, C, and Merni, F. Comparison of block versus weekly undulating periodization models on endocrine and strength changes in male athletes. *Kineziologija* 48:71-78, 2016.

6. Bartolomei, S, Stout, JR, Fukuda, DH, Hoffman, JR, and Merni, F. Block vs. weekly undulating periodized resistance training programs in women. *J Strength Cond Res* 29:2679-2687, 2015.

7. Berger, J, Harre, D, and Ritter, I. Principles of athletic training. In *Principles of Sports Training: Introduction to the Theory and Methods of Training.* Harre, D, ed. Michigan: Ultimate Athlete Concepts, 113-150, 2012.

8. Bompa, TO. Antrenamentul in perooda, pregatitoare. *Caiet Pentre Sporturi Nautice* 3:22-24, 1956.

9. Bompa, TO. Criteria pregatirii a unui plan departra ani. *Cultura Fizica si Sport* 2:11-19, 1968.

10. Bompa, TO. *Periodization of Strength.* Toronto, ON: Veritas Publishing, 1993.

11. Bompa, TO. *Theory and Methodology of Training: The Key to Athletic Performance.* Dubuque, IA: Kendall/Hunt Publishing Company, 1994.

12. Bompa, TO. *Periodization: Theory and Methodology of Training.* 4th ed. Champaign, IL: Human Kinetics, 1999.

13. Bompa, TO. *Total Training for Coaching Team Sports: A Self-Help Guide.* Toronto, ON: Sports Books, 2006.

14. Bompa, TO, Blumenstein, B, Orbach, I, and Hoffman, J. Present state of the art. In *Integrated Periodization in Sports Training & Athletic Development.* Bompa, TO, Blumenstein, B, Hoffman, J, Howell, S, Orbach, I, eds. Ann Arbor, MI: Meyer & Meyer Sport, 12-22, 2019.

15. Bompa, TO, and Buzzichelli, CA. Periodization as planning and programming of sport training. In *Periodization Training for Sports.* 3rd ed. Champaign, IL: Human Kinetics, 87-98, 2015.

16. Bompa, TO, and Buzzichelli, CA. Periodization of biomotor abilities. In *Periodization: Theory and Methodology of Training.* 6th ed. Champaign, IL: Human Kinetics, 91-114, 2019.

17. Bompa, TO, and Haff, GG. Annual training plan. In *Periodization: Theory and Methodology of Training.* 5th ed. Champaign, IL: Human Kinetics, 125-185, 2009.

18. Bompa, TO, and Haff, GG. Principles of training. In *Periodization: Theory and Methodology of Training.* 5th ed. Champaign, IL: Human Kinetics, 31-56, 2009.

19. Bondarchuk, A. Periodization of sports training. *Legkaya Atletika* 12:8-9, 1986.

20. Bondarchuk, A. Problem status and its further training ways. In *Periodization of Training In Sports.* Kiev, Ukraine: New Training Concepts, 13-42, 2011.

21. Bondarchuk, AP. Track and field training. *Legkaya Atletika* 12:8-9, 1986.

22. Bondarchuk, AP. Constructing a training system. *Track Tech* 102:254-269, 1988.

23. Bondarchuk, AP. The role and sequence of using different training-load intensities. *Fit Sports Rev Inter* 29:202-204, 1994.

24. Bondarchuk, AP. *Transfer of Training in Sports: Volume I.* Michigan, USA: Ultimate Athlete Concepts, 2007.

25. Bondarchuk, AP. Cycles of sports form development and training transfer. In *Transfer of Training in Sport: Volume II.* Michigan, USA: Ultimate Athlete Concepts, 12-51, 2010.

26. Bondarchuk, AP. *Transfer of Training in Sport: Volume II.* Michigan, USA: Ultimate Athlete Concepts, 2010.

27. Bosquet, L, Montpetit, J, Arvisais, D, and Mujika, I. Effects of tapering on performance: A meta-analysis. *Med Sci Sports Exerc* 39:1358-1365, 2007.

28. Breil, FA, Weber, SN, Koller, S, Hoppeler, H, and Vogt, M. Block training periodization in alpine skiing: Effects of 11-day HIT on VO(2max) and performance. *Eur J Appl Physiol* 109:1077-1086, 2010.

29. Buckner, SL, Jessee, MB, Mouser, JG, Dankel, SJ, Mattocks, KT, Bell, ZW, Abe, T, and Loenneke, JP. The basics of training for muscle size and strength: A brief review on the theory. *Med Sci Sports Exerc* 52:645-653, 2020.

30. Cissik, J, Hedrick, A, and Barnes, M. Challenges applying the research on periodization. *Strength Cond J* 30:45-51, 2008.

31. Coffey, VG, and Hawley, JA. Concurrent exercise training: Do opposites distract? *J Physiol* 595:2883-2896, 2017.

32. Colquhoun, RJ, Gai, CM, Walters, J, Brannon, AR, Kilpatrick, MW, D'Agostino, DP, and Campbell, WI. Comparison of powerlifting performance in trained men using traditional and flexible daily undulating periodization. *J Strength Cond Res* 31:283-291, 2017.

33. Connolly, F, and White, P. The evolution of preparation. In *Game Changer.* Canada: Victory Belt Publishing, 247-264, 2017.

34. Counsilman, JE, and Counsilman, BE. *The New Science of Swimming.* Englewood Cliffs, NJ: Prentice Hall, 1994.

35. Cunanan, AJ, DeWeese, BH, Wagle, JP, Carroll, KM, Sausaman, R, Hornsby, WG, 3rd, Haff, GG, Triplett, NT, Pierce, KC, and Stone, MH. The general adaptation syndrome: A foundation for the concept of periodization. *Sports Med* 48:787-797, 2018.

36. DeWeese, BH, Gray, HS, Sams, ML, Scruggs, SK, and Serrano, AJ. Revising the definition of periodization: Merging historical principles with modern concerns. *Olympic Coach Magazine* 24:5-19, 2015.

37. DeWeese, BH, Hornsby, G, Stone, M, and Stone, MH. The training process: Planning for strength–power training in track and field. Part 1: Theoretical aspects. *J Sport Health Sci* 4:308-317, 2015.

38. Drees, L. *Olympia: Gods, Artists, and Athletes.* New York: Praeger, 1968.

39. Ekstrand, J, Walden, M, and Hagglund, M. A congested football calendar and the wellbeing of players: Correlation between match exposure of European footballers before the World Cup 2002 and their injuries and performances during that World Cup. *Br J Sports Med* 38:493-497, 2004.

40. Evans, M. Strength and conditioning for cycling. In *Strength and Conditioning for Sports Performance.* Jeffreys, I, Moody, J, eds. Abingdon, Oxon: Routledge, 642-646, 2016.

41. Fleck, SJ. Periodized strength training: A critical review. *J Strength Cond Res* 13:82-89, 1999.
42. Fleck, SJ, and Kraemer, WJ. Periodized training. In *The Ultimate Training System: Periodization Breakthrough*. New York: Advanced Research Press, 17-22, 1996.
43. Fleck, SJ, and Kraemer, WJ. Advanced training strategies. In *Designing Resistance Training Programs*. 3rd ed. Champaign, IL: Human Kinetics, 209-240, 2004.
44. Francis, C. *Structure of Training for Speed*. CharlieFrancis.com, 2008.
45. Freeman, WH. The big picture—planning from setting long-term goals to the annual plan. In *Peak When It Counts: Periodization for American Track & Field*. 4th ed. Mountain View, CA: Tafnews Press, 43-50, 2001.
46. Fry, RW, Morton, AR, and Keast, D. Periodisation of training stress—a review. *Can J Sport Sci* 17:234-240, 1992.
47. Gamble, P. Planning and scheduling: Periodisation of training. In *Strength and Conditioning for Team Sports: Sport-Specific Physical Preparation for High Performance*. London: Routledge, 204-220, 2013.
48. Garcia-Pallares, J, Garcia-Fernandez, M, Sanchez-Medina, L, and Izquierdo, M. Performance changes in world-class kayakers following two different training periodization models. *Eur J Appl Physiol* 110:99-107, 2010.
49. Gardiner, EN. *Athletics in the Ancient World*. Mineola, NY: Dover, 2002.
50. Gavanda, S, Geisler, S, Quittmann, OJ, and Schiffer, T. The effect of block versus daily undulating periodization on strength and performance in adolescent football players. *Int J Sports Physiol Perform* 14:814-821, 2019.
51. Grgic, J, Mikulic, P, Podnar, H, and Pedisic, Z. Effects of linear and daily undulating periodized resistance training programs on measures of muscle hypertrophy: A systematic review and meta-analysis. *PeerJ* 5:e3695, 2017.
52. Haff, GG. Periodization of training. In *Conditioning for Strength and Human Performance*. 2nd ed. Brown, LE, Chandler, J, eds. Philadelphia, PA: Wolters Kluwer, Lippincott, Williams & Wilkins, 326-345, 2012.
53. Haff, GG. Peaking for competition in individual sports. In *High-Performance Training for Sports*. Joyce, D, Lewindon, D, eds., 524-540, 2014.
54. Haff, GG. Periodization strategies for youth development. In *Strength and Conditioning for Young Athletes: Science and Application*. Lloyd, RS, Oliver, JL, eds. London: Routledge, Taylor & Francis Group, 149-168, 2014.
55. Haff, GG. The essentials of periodisation. In *Strength and Conditioning for Sports Performance*. Jeffreys, I, Moody, J, eds. Abingdon, Oxon: Routledge, 404-448, 2016.
56. Haff, GG. Periodization and power integration. In *Developing Power*. McGuigan, M, ed. Champaign, IL: Human Kinetics, 33-62, 2017.
57. Haff, GG. Periodization strategies for youth development. In *Strength and Conditioning for Young Athletes: Science and Application*. 2nd ed. Lloyd, R, Oliver, JL, eds. London: Routledge, 281-299, 2019.
58. Haff, GG. Peaking for competition in individual sports. In *High-Performance Training for Sports*. 2nd ed. Joyce, D, Lewindon, D, eds. Champaign, IL: Human Kinetics, 524-541, 2022.
59. Haff, GG. Periodization and programming of individual sports. In *NSCA's Essentials of Sport Science*. French, D, Torres Ronda, L, eds. Champaign, IL: Human Kinetics, 27-42, 2022.
60. Haff, GG, and Haff, EE. Training integration and periodization. In *Strength and Conditioning Program Design*. Hoffman, J, ed. Champaign, IL: Human Kinetics, 209-254, 2012.
61. Haff, GG, and Kendall, K. Strength and conditioning. In *Coaching for Sports Performance*. Baghurst, T, ed. New York: Routledge, 310-350, 2019.
62. Haff, GG, Kraemer, WJ, O'Bryant, HS, Pendlay, G, Plisk, S, and Stone, MH. Roundtable discussion: Periodization of training—part 1. *NSCA J* 26:50-69, 2004.
63. Harre, D. Principles of athletic training. In *Principles of Sports Training: Introduction to the Theory and Methods of Training*. Harre, D, ed. Berlin, Germany: Sportverlag, 73-94, 1982.
64. Harre, D. *Principles of Sports Training*. Berlin, Germany: Sportverlag, 1982.
65. Harre, D. *Trainingslehre*. Berlin, Germany: Sportverlag, 1982.
66. Harris, GR, Stone, MH, O'Bryant, HS, Proulx, CM, and Johnson, RL. Short-term performance effects of high power, high force, or combined weight-training methods. *J Strength Cond Res* 14:14-20, 2000.
67. Issurin, V, ed. *Advanced Athlete Training*. Michigan, USA: Ultimate Athlete Concepts, 2008.
68. Issurin, V. Block periodization in applications to different sports. In *Building the Modern Athlete: Scientific Advancements & Training Innovations*. Michigan, USA: Ultimate Athlete Concepts, 191-212, 2008.
69. Issurin, V. Block periodization training models as an alternative to traditional approach. In *Advanced Athlete Training*. Michigan, USA: Ultimate Athlete Concepts, 164-190, 2008.
70. Issurin, V. Block periodization versus traditional training theory: A review. *J Sports Med Phys Fitness* 48:65-75, 2008.
71. Issurin, V. Block periodization vs. traditional theory. In *Block Periodization: Breakthrough in Sports Training*. Yessis, M, ed. Michigan, USA: Ultimate Athlete Concepts, 1-36, 2008.
72. Issurin, V. The workout: General concepts and structure guidelines. In *Block Periodization: Breakthrough in Sports Training*. Yessis, M, ed. Michigan, USA: Ultimate Athlete Concepts, 37-77, 2008.
73. Issurin, V. Periodization training from ancient precursors to structured block models. *Kinesiology* 46:3-9, 2014.
74. Issurin, V. *Building the Modern Athlete: Scientific Advancement & Training Innovation*. Michigan, USA: Ultimate Athlete Concepts, 2015.
75. Issurin, V, and Kaverin, V. Planning and design of annual preparation cycle in canoe-kayak paddling. In *Grebnoj Sport [Rowing, Canoeing, Kayaking]*. Moscow: Fizkultura i Sport, 25-29, 1985.
76. Issurin, VB. New horizons for the methodology and physiology of training periodization. *Sports Med* 40:189-206, 2010.
77. Issurin, VB. Benefits and limitations of block periodized training approaches to athletes' preparation: A review. *Sports Med* 46:329-338, 2016.

78. Issurin, VB. Biological background of block periodized endurance training: A review. *Sports Med* 49:31-39, 2019.
79. James, LP, Haff, GG, Kelly, VG, and Beckman, EM. Towards a determination of the physiological characteristics distinguishing successful mixed martial arts athletes: A systematic review of combat sport literature. *Sports Med* 46:1525-1551, 2016.
80. Jeffreys, I. Quadrennial planning for the high school athlete. *Strength Cond J* 30:74-83, 2008.
81. Jovanović, M. Planning. In *Strength Training Manual: The Agile Periodization Approach: Volume 2*. Belgrade, Serbia: Complementary Training, 9-63, 2019.
82. Kaverin, V, and Issurin, V. Performance analysis and preparation: Concept of the USSR canoe-kayak national team in the XXIV Seoul Olympic Games. *Sport-Science Gerald* 17:45-47, 1989.
83. Kiely, J. New horizons for the methodology and physiology of training periodization: Block periodization: New horizon or a false dawn? *Sports Med* 40:803-805, 2010.
84. Kiely, J. Periodization paradigms in the 21st century: Evidence-led or tradition-driven? *Int J Sports Physiol Perform* 7:242-250, 2012.
85. Kiely, J. Periodization theory: Confronting an inconvenient truth. *Sports Med* 48:753-764, 2018.
86. Kotov, B. Olympic sport. *Guidelines for Track and Field*, 1916.
87. Kraemer, WJ, and Fleck, SJ. Periodization of resistance training. In *Optimizing Strength Training*. Champaign, IL: Human Kinetics, 1-26, 2007.
88. Kraemer, WJ, and Ratamess, NA. Fundamentals of resistance training: Progression and exercise prescription. *Med Sci Sports Exerc* 36:674-688, 2004.
89. Kraemer, WJ, Torine, JC, Dudley, J, and Martin, GJ. Nonlinear periodization: Insights for use in collegiate and professional American football resistance training programs. *Strength Cond J* 37:17-36, 2015.
90. Lloyd, RS, Oliver, JL, Faigenbaum, AD, Howard, R, De Ste Croix, MB, Williams, CA, Best, TM, Alvar, BA, Micheli, LJ, Thomas, DP, Hatfield, DL, Cronin, JB, and Myer, GD. Long-term athletic development—part 1: A pathway for all youth. *J Strength Cond Res* 29:1439-1450, 2015.
91. Lloyd, RS, Oliver, JL, Faigenbaum, AD, Howard, R, De Ste Croix, MBA, Williams, CA, Best, TM, Alvar, BA, Micheli, LJ, Thomas, DP, Hatfield, DL, Cronin, JB, and Myer, GD. Long-term athletic development—part 2: Barriers to success and potential solutions. *J Strength Cond Res* 29:1451-1464, 2015.
92. Loturco, I, Nakamura, FY, Kobal, R, Gil, S, Pivetti, B, Pereira, LA, and Roschel, H. Traditional periodization versus optimum training load applied to soccer players: Effects on neuromuscular abilities. *Int J Sports Med* 37:1057-1059, 2016.
93. Mallo, J. Effect of block periodization on performance in competition in a soccer team during four consecutive seasons: A case study. *Int J Perform Anal Sport* 11:476-485, 2011.
94. Mallo, J. Effect of block periodization on physical fitness during a competitive soccer season. *Int J Perform Anal Sport* 12:64-67, 2012.
95. Manchado, C, Cortell-Tormo, JM, and Tortosa-Martinez, J. Effects of two different training periodization models on physical and physiological aspects of elite female team handball players. *J Strength Cond Res* 32:280-287, 2018.
96. Marques, L, Franchini, E, Drago, G, Aoki, MS, and Moreira, A. Physiological and performance changes in national and international judo athletes during block periodization training. *Biol Sport* 34:371-378, 2017.
97. Mattocks, KT, Dankel, SJ, Buckner, SL, Jessee, MB, Counts, BR, Mouser, JG, Laurentino, GC, and Loenneke, JP. Periodization: What is it good for? *Journal of Trainology* 5:6-12, 2016.
98. Matveyev, L. *Periodization of Sports Training*. Moscow: Fizkultura i Sport, 1965.
99. McNamara, JM, and Stearne, DJ. Flexible nonlinear periodization in a beginner college weight training class. *J Strength Cond Res* 24:2012-2017, 2010.
100. McNamara, JM, and Stearne, DJ. Effect of concurrent training, flexible nonlinear periodization, and maximal-effort cycling on strength and power. *J Strength Cond Res* 27:1463-1470, 2013.
101. Meeusen, R, Duclos, M, Foster, C, Fry, A, Gleeson, M, Nieman, D, Raglin, J, Rietjens, G, Steinacker, J, Urhausen, A, European College of Sport Science, and American College of Sports Medicine. Prevention, diagnosis, and treatment of the overtraining syndrome: Joint consensus statement of the European College of Sport Science and the American College of Sports Medicine. *Med Sci Sports Exerc* 45:186-205, 2013.
102. Miarka, B, Vecchio, FB, Camey, S, and Amtmann, JA. Comparisons: Technical-tactical and time-motion analysis of mixed martial arts by outcomes. *J Strength Cond Res* 30:1975-1984, 2016.
103. Mujika, I, Goya, A, Padilla, S, Grijalba, A, Gorostiaga, E, and Ibanez, J. Physiological responses to a 6-d taper in middle-distance runners: Influence of training intensity and volume. *Med Sci Sports Exerc* 32:511-517, 2000.
104. Mujika, I, Halson, S, Burke, L, Balagué, G, and Farrow, D. An integrated, multifactorial approach to periodization for optimal performance in individual and team sports. *Int J Sports Physiol Perform* 13:538-561, 2018.
105. Mujika, I, and Padilla, S. Scientific bases for precompetition tapering strategies. *Med Sci Sports Exerc* 35:1182-1187, 2003.
106. Munroe, L, and Haff, GG. Sprint cycling. In *Routledge Handbook of Strength and Conditioning*. Turner, A, ed. New York: Routledge, 506-525, 2018.
107. Nádori, L. *Training and Competition*. Budapest, Hungary: Sport, 1962.
108. Nádori, L. *Theory of Training and Exercise*. Budapest, Hungary: Sport, 1968.
109. Nádori, L. Theoretrical and methodological basis of training planning. In *Theoretical and Methodological Basis of Training Planning With Special Considerations Within a Microcycle*. Nádori, L, Granek, I, eds. Lincoln, NE: National Strength and Conditioning Association, 1-25, 1989.
110. Nádori, L, and Granek, I. *Theoretical and Methodological Basis of Training Planning With Special Considerations*

111. Norris, SR, and Smith, DJ. Planning, periodization, and sequencing training and competition: The rationale for a competently planned, optimally executed training and competition program, supported by a multidisciplinary team. In *Enhancing Recovery: Preventing Underperformance in Athletes*. Kellmann, M, ed. Champaign, IL: Human Kinetics, 121-141, 2002.

112. Olbrect, J. Basics of training planning. In *The Science of Winning: Planning, Periodizing, and Optimizing Swim Training*. Luton, England: Swimshop, 171-192, 2000.

113. Olbrect, J. Definitions and principles of training. In *The Science of Winning: Planning, Periodizing, and Optimizing Swim Training*. Luton, England: Swimshop, 1-13, 2000.

114. Ozolin, N. *Sovremennaia Systema Sportivnoi Trenirovky [Athlete's Training System for Competition]*. Moscow: Fizkultura i Sport, 1971.

115. Painter, K, Haff, G, Ramsey, M, McBride, J, Triplett, T, Sands, W, Lamont, H, Stone, M, and Stone, M. Strength gains: Block versus daily undulating periodization weight training among track and field athletes. *Int J Sports Physiol Perform* 7:161-169, 2012.

116. Painter, K, Haff, G, Triplett, N, Stuart, C, Hornsby, G, Ramsey, M, Bazyler, C, and Stone, M. Resting hormone alterations and injuries: Block vs. DUP weight-training among D-1 track and field athletes. *Sports* 6:3, 2018.

117. Painter, KB, Haff, GG, Ramsey, MW, McBride, J, Triplett, T, Sands, WA, Lamont, HS, Stone, ME, and Stone, MH. Strength Gains: Block Vs Dup Weight-Training Among Track and Field Athletes. *Int J Sports Physiol Perform* 7:161-169, 2012.

118. Pihkala, L. Allgemeine Richtlinien fur das athletische Training. In *Athletik Handbuch der Lebenswichtigen Leibesubungen*. Krummel, GK, ed. Munchen: Lehmann, 185-190, 1930.

119. Platonov, V. The basis of modern training process periodization in high-performance athletes for year preparation. *Res Yearb* 12:176-180, 2006.

120. Platonov, VN. *Teoria General del Entrenamiento Deportivo Olimpico*. Badalona, Spain: Paidotribo Editorial, 2002.

121. Pliauga, V, Lukonaitiene, I, Kamandulis, S, Skurvydas, A, Sakalauskas, R, Scanlan, AT, Stanislovaitiene, J, and Conte, D. The effect of block and traditional periodization training models on jump and sprint performance in collegiate basketball players. *Biol Sport* 35:373-382, 2018.

122. Plisk, SS, and Stone, MH. Periodization strategies. *Strength and Cond J* 25:19-37, 2003.

123. Prestes, J, De Lima, C, Frollini, AB, Donatto, FF, and Conte, M. Comparison of linear and reverse linear periodization effects on maximal strength and body composition. *J Strength Cond Res* 23:266-274, 2009.

124. Pyne, D, and Touretski, G. An analysis of the training of Olympic sprint champion Alexandre Popov. *Australian Swim Coach* 10:5-14, 1993.

125. Robertson, S, and Joyce, D. Evaluating strategic periodisation in team sport. *J Sports Sci* 36:279-285, 2018.

126. Robertson, SJ, and Joyce, DG. Informing in-season tactical periodisation in team sport: Development of a match difficulty index for Super Rugby. *J Sports Sci* 33:99-107, 2015.

127. Robinson, RS. *Sources for the History of Greek Athletics*. Cincinnati: Ares Pub, 1955.

128. Rønnestad, BR, Ellefsen, S, Nygaard, H, Zacharoff, EE, Vikmoen, O, Hansen, J, and Hallén, J. Effects of 12 weeks of block periodization on performance and performance indices in well-trained cyclists. *Scand J Med Sci Sports* 24:327-335, 2014.

129. Rønnestad, BR, Hansen, J, and Ellefsen, S. Block periodization of high-intensity aerobic intervals provides superior training effects in trained cyclists. *Scand J Med Sci Sports* 24:34-42, 2014.

130. Rønnestad, BR, Hansen, J, Thyli, V, Bakken, TA, and Sandbakk, Ø. 5-week block periodization increases aerobic power in elite cross-country skiers. *Scand J Med Sci Sports* 26:140-146, 2016.

131. Rønnestad, BR, Ofsteng, SJ, and Ellefsen, S. Block periodization of strength and endurance training is superior to traditional periodization in ice hockey players. *Scand J Med Sci Sports* 29:180-188, 2019.

132. Satori, J, and Tschiene, P. The further development of training theory: New elements and tendencies. *Sci Period Res Technol Sport* 8, 1988.

133. Schwellnus, M, Soligard, T, Alonso, J-M, Bahr, R, Clarsen, B, Dijkstra, HP, Gabbett, TJ, Gleeson, M, Hägglund, M, Hutchinson, MR, Janse Van Rensburg, C, Meeusen, R, Orchard, JW, Pluim, BM, Raftery, M, Budgett, R, and Engebretsen, L. How much is too much? (Part 2) International Olympic Committee consensus statement on load in sport and risk of illness. *Br J Sports Med* 50:1043-1052, 2016.

134. Smith, DJ. A framework for understanding the training process leading to elite performance. *Sports Med* 33:1103-1126, 2003.

135. Soligard, T, Schwellnus, M, Alonso, J-M, Bahr, R, Clarsen, B, Dijkstra, HP, Gabbett, T, Gleeson, M, Hägglund, M, Hutchinson, MR, Janse van Rensburg, C, Khan, KM, Meeusen, R, Orchard, JW, Pluim, BM, Raftery, M, Budgett, R, and Engebretsen, L. How much is too much? (Part 1) International Olympic Committee consensus statement on load in sport and risk of injury. *Br J Sports Med* 50:1030-1041, 2016.

136. Solli, GS, Tønnessen, E, and Sandbakk, Ø. Block vs. traditional periodization of HIT: Two different paths to success for the world's best cross-country skier. *Front Physiol* 10:375, 2019.

137. Stone, MH, and Fry, AC. Increased training volume in strength/power athletes. In *Overtraining in Sport*. Kreider, RB, Fry, AC, O'Toole, ML, eds. Champaign, IL: Human Kinetics, 87-106, 1998.

138. Stone, MH, Keith, R, Kearney, JT, Wilson, GD, and Fleck, S, J,. Overtraining: A review of the signs and symptoms of overtraining. *J Strength Cond Res* 5:35-50, 1991.

139. Stone, MH, O'Bryant, H, and Garhammer, J. A hypothetical model for strength training. *J Sports Med* 21:342-351, 1981.

140. Stone, MH, O'Bryant, HS, and Garhammer, J. A theoretical model of strength training. *NSCA J* 3:36-39, 1982.

141. Stone, MH, Potteiger, JA, Pierce, KC, Proulx, CM, O'Bryant, HS, Johnson, RL, and Stone, ME. Comparison of the

141. effects of three different weight-training programs on the one repetition maximum squat. *J Strength Cond Res* 14:332-337, 2000.
142. Suarez, DG, Mizuguchi, S, Hornsby, WG, Cunanan, AJ, Marsh, DJ, and Stone, MH. Phase-specific changes in rate of force development and muscle morphology throughout a block periodized training cycle in weightlifters. *Sports* 7:129, 2019.
143. Touretski, G. Preparation of sprint events: 1998 ASCTA Convention. Canberra, ACT: Australian Institute of Sport, 1998.
144. Tschiene, P. A necessary direction in training: The integration of biological adaptation in the training program. *Coach Sport Sci J* 1:2-14, 1995.
145. Turner, A, and Comfort, P. Periodisation. In *Advanced Strength and Conditioning: An Evidence-Based Approach*. Turner, A, Comfort, P, eds. London: Routledge Taylor Francis, 116-136, 2018.
146. Verkhoshansky, U. Preliminary methodological remarks. In *The Block Training System in Endurance Running*. Rome, Italy: Verkhoshansky, 16-18, 2007.
147. Verkhoshansky, Y, and Siff, MC. Application of special strength training means. In *Supertraining*. 6th (expanded) ed. Rome, Italy: Verkhoshansky, 287-294, 2009.
148. Verkhoshansky, Y, and Siff, MC. The methods of special strength training. In *Supertraining*. 6th ed. Rome, Italy: Verkhoshansky, 257-312, 2009.
149. Verkhoshansky, Y, and Siff, MC. Organisation of training. In *Supertraining*. 6th (expanded) ed. Rome, Italy: Verkhoshansky, 313-393, 2009.
150. Verkhoshansky, Y, and Siff, MC. Programming and organisation of training. In *Supertraining*. 6th (expanded) ed. Rome, Italy: Verkhoshansky, 313-392, 2009.
151. Verkhoshansky, Y, and Verkhoshansky, N. Combined method of special strength training. In *Special Strength Training Manual for Coaches*. Rome, Italy: Verkhoshansky, 105-116, 2011.
152. Verkhoshansky, Y, and Verkhoshansky, N. The contribution of Yuri Verkhoshansky to the development of sport science. In *Special Strength Trainng Manual for Coaches*. Rome, Italy: Verkhoshansky, 263-284, 2011.
153. Verkhoshansky, Y, and Verkhoshansky, N. Organization of special strength training in the training process and the block training system. In *Special Strength Training Manual for Coaches*. Rome, Italy: Verkhoshansky, 117-144, 2011.
154. Verkhoshansky, YU. Perspectives in the development of speed-strength preparation in the development of jumpers. *Track and Field* 9:11-12, 1966.
155. Verkhoshansky, YU. *Osnovi Spetsialnoi Silovoi Podgotovki i Sporte [Fundamentals of Special Strength Training in Sport]*. Moscow: Fizkultura i Sport, 1977.
156. Verkhoshansky, YU. How to set up a training program. *Sov Sports Rev* 16:123-136, 1981.
157. Verkhoshansky, YU. *Programming and Organization of Training*. Moscow: Fizkultura i Sport, 1985.
158. Verkhoshansky, YU. *Fundamentals of Special Strength Training in Sport*. Livonia, MI: Sportivy Press, 1986.
159. Verkhoshansky, YU. The end of "periodization" in the training of high performance sport. *National Fitness Council of South Australia* 37:14-18, 1999.
160. Verkhoshansky, YU. *Special Strength Training: A Practical Manual for Coaches*. Michigan, USA: Ultimate Athlete Concepts, 2006.
161. Verkhoshansky, YU. Theory and methodology of sport preparation: Block training system for top-level athletes. *Teoria i Practica Physicheskoj Culturi* 4:2-14, 2007.
162. Verkhoshansky, YU, and Verkhoshansky, N. *Special Strength Training Manual for Coaches*. Rome, Italy: Verkhosansky, 2011.
163. Verkhoshansky, YV. Forms of constructing training with respect to organization. In *Programming and Organization of Training*. Livonia, MI: Sportivny Press, 127-177, 1988.
164. Verkhoshansky, YV. The principle connection between the athlete's state and training load. In *Programming and Organization of Training*. Livonia, MI: Sportivny Press, 82-124, 1988.
165. Viru, A. Planning macrocycles. *Mod Athlete Coach* 26:7-10, 1988.
166. Viru, A. *Adaptations in Sports Training*. Boca Raton, FL: CRC Press, 1995.
167. Viru, A. Physiological aspects of selected problems of training methodology (training strategy). In *Adaptations in Sports Training*. Boca Raton, FL: CRC Press, 281-300, 1995.
168. Werchoshanski, J. Specific training principles for power. *Mod Athlete Coach* 17:11-13, 1979.
169. Zamparo, P, Minetti, AE, and di Prampero, PE. Interplay among the changes of muscle strength, cross-sectional area and maximal explosive power: Theory and facts. *Eur J Appl Physiol* 88:193-202, 2002.
170. Zatsiorsky, VM, Kraemer, WJ, and Fry, AC. Basic concepts of training theory. In *Science and Practice of Strength Training*. 3rd ed. Champaign, IL: Human Kinetics, 3-14, 2021.
171. Zatsiorsky, VM, Kraemer, WJ, and Fry, AC. *Science and Practice of Strength Training*. 3rd ed. Champaign, IL: Human Kinetics, 2021.
172. Zatsiorsky, VM, Kraemer, WJ, Fry, AC. Timing in strength training. In *Science and Practice of Strength Training*. 3rd ed. Champaign, IL: Human Kinetics, 79-98, 2021.

Chapter 6

1. Andersen, LL, Andersen, JL, Magnusson, SP, Suetta, C, Madsen, JL, Christensen, LR, and Aagaard, P. Changes in the human muscle force-velocity relationship in response to resistance training and subsequent detraining. *J Appl Physiol* 99:87-94, 2005.
2. Anshel, MH, and Novak, J. Effects of different intensities of fatigue on performing a sport skill requiring explosive muscular effort: A test of the specificity of practice principle. *Percept Mot Skills* 69:1379-1389, 1989.
3. Baekeland, F. Exercise deprivation: Sleep and psychological reactions. *Arch Gen Psychiatry* 22:365-369, 1970.
4. Baker, D. Applying the in-season periodization of strength and power training to football. *Strength Cond J* 20:18-27, 1998.

5. Balyi, I. Quadrennial and double quadrennial planning of athletic training. Victoria, BC: Canadian Coaches Association, 1990.
6. Balyi, I. Sport system building and long-term athlete development in British Columbia. British Columbia, Canada: SportMed BC, 2001.
7. Balyi, I, and Hamilton, A. Long-term athlete development: Trainability in childhood and adolescence. *Olympic Coach* 16:4-9, 1993.
8. Balyi, I, and Hamilton, A. Long-term athlete development: Trainability in childhood and adolescence: Windows of opportunity, optimal trainability. Victoria, BC: National Coaching Institute British Columbia & Advanced Training and Performance, 2004.
9. Berger, J, Harre, D, and Ritter, I. Principles of athletic training. In *Principles of Sports Training: Introduction to the Theory and Methods of Training*. Harre, D, ed. Michigan: Ultimate Athlete Concepts, 113-150, 2012.
10. Bernards, J, Blaisdell, R, Light, TJ, and Stone, MH. Prescribing an annual plan for the competitive surf athlete: Optimal methods and barriers to implementation. *Strength Cond J* 39:36-45, 2017.
11. Bompa, TO, and Buzzichelli, CA. Periodization of the annual plan. In *Periodization: Theory and Methodology of Training*. Champaign, IL: Human Kinetics, 165-206, 2019.
12. Bompa, TO, and Haff, GG. Annual training plan. In *Periodization: Theory and Methodology of Training*. Champaign, IL: Human Kinetics, 125-185, 2009.
13. Buchheit, M, Morgan, W, Wallace, J, Bode, M, and Poulos, N. Physiological, psychometric, and performance effects of the Christmas break in Australian football. *Int J Sports Physiol Perform* 10:120-123, 2015.
14. Coyle, EF, Martin, WH, 3rd, Sinacore, DR, Joyner, MJ, Hagberg, JM, and Holloszy, JO. Time course of loss of adaptations after stopping prolonged intense endurance training. *J Appl Physiol* 57:1857-1864, 1984.
15. Dick, FW. Periodising the year. In *Sports Training Principles*. London: A and C Black, 305-311, 2007.
16. Ehsani, AA, Hagberg, JM, and Hickson, RC. Rapid changes in left ventricular dimensions and mass in response to physical conditioning and deconditioning. *American Journal of Cardiology* 42:52-56, 1978.
17. Ford, P, De Ste Croix, M, Lloyd, R, Meyers, R, Moosavi, M, Oliver, J, Till, K, and Williams, C. The long-term athlete development model: Physiological evidence and application. *J Sports Sci* 29:389-402, 2011.
18. Foster, C, Florhaug, JA, Franklin, J, Gottschall, L, Hrovatin, LA, Parker, S, Doleshal, P, and Dodge, C. A new approach to monitoring exercise training. *J Strength Cond Res* 15:109-115, 2001.
19. Freeman, WH. The big picture—planning from setting long-term goals to the annual plan. In *Peak When It Counts: Periodization for American Track & Field*. Mountain View, CA: Tafnews Press, 43-50, 2001.
20. Freeman, WH. The language of periodization. In *Peak When It Counts: Periodization for American Track & Field*. Mountain View, CA: Tafnews Press, 17-22, 2001.
21. Freeman, WH. Planning the details—from the annual plan to the daily workout. In *Peak When It Counts: Periodization for American Track & Field*. Mountain View, CA: Tafnews Press, 51-61, 2001.
22. French, D. Combat sports. In *Science and Application of High-Intensity Interval Training*. Laursen, PB, Buchheit, M, eds. Champaign, IL: Human Kinetics, 227-246, 2019.
23. Gabbett, TJ. The training-injury prevention paradox: Should athletes be training smarter and harder? *Br J Sports Med* 50:273-280, 2016.
24. Gabbett, TJ. Workload monitoring and athlete management. In *Advanced Strength and Conditioning: An Evidence-Based Approach*. Turner, A, Comfort, P, eds. Abingdon, Oxon: Routledge, 137-150, 2018.
25. Gabbett, TJ. Debunking the myths about training load, injury and performance: Empirical evidence, hot topics and recommendations for practitioners. *Br J Sports Med* 54:58-66, 2020.
26. Gay, RA. A comparison of four strength maintenance programs for football players. Thesis. Texas Tech University, 1969.
27. Haff, GG. The essentials of periodisation. In *Strength and Conditioning for Sports Performance*. Jeffreys, I, Moody, J, eds. Abingdon, Oxon: Routledge, 404-448, 2016.
28. Haff, GG. Periodization. In *Essentials of Strength Training and Conditioning*. Haff, GG, Triplett, NT, eds. Champaign, IL United States: Human Kinetics, 583-604, 2016.
29. Haff, GG. Periodization strategies for youth development. In *Strength and Conditioning for the Young Athlete: Science and Application*. Lloyd, R, Oliver, JL, eds. London, England: Routledge, 281-299, 2019.
30. Haff, GG. The essentials of periodisation. In *Strength and Conditioning for Sports Performance*. Jeffreys, I, Moody, J, eds. Abingdon, Oxon: Routledge, 394-444, 2021.
31. Haff, GG. Peaking for competition in individual sports. In *High-Performance Training for Sports*. Joyce, D, Lewindon, D, eds. Champaign, IL: Human Kinetics, 524-541, 2022.
32. Haff, GG. Periodization and programming of individual sports. In *NSCA's Essentials of Sport Science*. French, D, Torres Ronda, L, eds. Champaign, IL: Human Kinetics, 27-42, 2022.
33. Haff, GG, and Burgess, SJ. Resistance training for endurance sports. In *Developing Endurance*. Reuter, BH, ed. Champaign, IL: Human Kinetics, 135-180, 2012.
34. Haff, GG, and Haff, EE. Training integration and periodization. In *Strength and Conditioning Program Design*. Hoffman, J, ed. Champaign, IL: Human Kinetics, 209-254, 2012.
35. Häkkinen, K, Alen, M, and Komi, PV. Changes in isometric force- and relaxation-time, electromyographic and muscle fibre characteristics of human skeletal muscle during strength training and detraining. *Acta Physiol Scand* 125:573-585, 1985.
36. Häkkinen, K, and Komi, PV. Electromyographic changes during strength training and detraining. *Med Sci Sports Exerc* 15:455-460, 1983.
37. Häkkinen, K, Komi, PV, and Tesch, PA. Effect of combined concentric and eccentric strength training and detraining on force-time, muscle fiber and metabolic characteristics of leg extensor muscles. *Scand J Sports Sci* 3:50-58, 1981.

38. Harre, D, Hoger, H, Thieb, G, Heinz, W, Bringmann, W, Muller, S, and Winter, R. Training: Objectives, tasks and principles. In *Principles of Sports Training: Introduction to the Theory and Methods of Training*. Harre, D, ed. Michigan: Ultimate Athlete Concepts, 70-112, 2012.

39. Hochrein, M, and Schleicher, I. Circulatory maladjustment syndrome. *Medizinische Monatsschrift* 12:234-240, 1958.

40. Hortobagyi, T, Houmard, JA, Stevenson, JR, Fraser, DD, Johns, RA, and Israel, RG. The effects of detraining on power athletes. *Med Sci Sports Exerc* 25:929-935, 1993.

41. Houmard, JA, Hortobagyi, T, Johns, RA, Bruno, NJ, Nute, CC, Shinebarger, MH, and Welborn, JW. Effect of short-term training cessation on performance measures in distance runners. *Int J Sports Med* 13:572-576, 1992.

42. Israel, S. Das akute entlastungssyndrom des leistungssportlers. *Sportarzt u Sportmed* 18:185-190, 1967.

43. Issurin, V. Designing the training programs. In *Principles and Basics of Advanced Athlete Training*. Michigan: Ultimate Athlete Concepts, 121-187, 2008.

44. Issurin, V. Long-Term Periodization. In *Building the Modern Athlete: Scientific Advancement & Training Innovation*. Thome, M, ed. Michigan, USA: Ultimate Athlete Concepts, 120-344, 2015.

45. Izquierdo, M, Ibanez, J, Gonzalez-Badillo, JJ, Ratamess, NA, Kraemer, WJ, Häkkinen, K, Bonnabau, H, Granados, C, French, DN, and Gorostiaga, EM. Detraining and tapering effects on hormonal responses and strength performance. *J Strength Cond Res* 21:768-775, 2007.

46. Jeffreys, I. Quadrennial planning for the high school athlete. *Strength and Cond J* 30:74-83, 2008.

47. Jensen, M. Pedagogy of coaching. In *Coaching for Sports Performance*. Baghurst, T, ed. New York, NY: Routledge, 38-74, 2020.

48. Jones, L. Training programs: Major events dictate yearly plan. *Weightlifting USA* VIII:12-13, 1990.

49. Joo, CH. The effects of short term detraining and retraining on physical fitness in elite soccer players. *PloS One* 13:e0196212-e0196212, 2018.

50. Kiely, J. Periodization theory: Confronting an inconvenient truth. *Sports Med* 48:753-764, 2018.

51. Kim, H-D, and Cruz, AB. The influence of coaches' leadership styles on athletes' satisfaction and team cohesion: A meta-analytic approach. *Int J Sports Sci Coach* 11:900-909, 2016.

52. Kraemer, WJ, Koziris, LP, Ratamess, NA, Hakkinen, K, NT, TR-M, Fry, AC, Gordon, SE, Volek, JS, French, DN, Rubin, MR, Gomez, AL, Sharman, MJ, Michael Lynch, J, Izquierdo, M, Newton, RU, and Fleck, SJ. Detraining produces minimal changes in physical performance and hormonal variables in recreationally strength-trained men. *J Strength Cond Res* 16:373-382, 2002.

53. Kuipers, H, and Keizer, HA. Overtraining in elite athletes: Review and directions for the future. *Sports Med* 6:79-92, 1988.

54. Kurz, T. Cycles in sports training. In *Science of Sports Training*. Island Pond, VT: Stadion Publishing, 51-98, 2001.

55. Lidor, R, Tenenbaum, G, Ziv, G, and Issurin, V. Achieving expertise in sport: Deliberate practice, adaptation, and periodization of training. *Kinesiol Rev* 5:129-141, 2016.

56. Malone, JJ, Michele, RD, Morgans, R, Burgess, D, Morton, JP, and Drust, B. Seasonal training-load quantification in elite English Premier League soccer players. *Int J Sports Physiol Perform* 10:489, 2015.

57. Matveyev, LP. Annual and semi-annual training cycles. In *Fundamentals of Sports Training*. Moscow: Fizkultua i Sport, 259-287, 1977.

58. McGuigan, M. Quantifying training stress. In *Monitoring Training and Performance in Athletes*. Champaign, IL: Human Kinetics, 69-101, 2017.

59. Mujika, and Padilla, S. Muscular characteristics of detraining in humans. *Med Sci Sports Exerc* 33:1297-1303., 2001.

60. Mujika, I, Halson, S, Burke, L, Balagué, G, and Farrow, D. An integrated, multifactorial approach to periodization for optimal performance in individual and team sports. *Int J Sports Physiol Perform* 13:538-561, 2018.

61. Mujika, I, and Padilla, S. Detraining: loss of training-induced physiological and performance adaptations. Part I: short term insufficient training stimulus. *Sports Med* 30:79-87., 2000.

62. Mujika, I, and Padilla, S. Detraining: Loss of training-induced physiological and performance adaptations. Part II: Long term insufficient training stimulus. *Sports Med* 30:145-154, 2000.

63. Norris, SR, and Smith, DJ. Planning, periodization, and sequencing training and competition: The rationale for a competently planned, optimally executed training and competition program, supported by a multidisciplinary team. In *Enhancing Recovery: Preventing Underperformance in Athletes*. Kellmann, M, ed. Champaign, IL: Human Kinetics, 121-141, 2002.

64. Olbrect, J. Basics of training planning. In *The Science of Winning: Planning, Periodizing, and Optimizing Swim Training*. Luton, England: Swimshop, 171-192, 2000.

65. Purdom, TM, Levers, KS, McPherson, CS, Giles, J, and Brown, L. A longitudinal prospective study: The effect of annual seasonal transition and coaching influence on aerobic capacity and body composition in Division I female soccer players. *Sports (Basel)* 8, 2020.

66. Radcliffe, JC. The programs. In *Functional Training for Athletes at All Levels*. Berkeley, CA: Ulysses Press, 27-58, 2007.

67. Reilly, T, Drust, B, and Clarke, N. Muscle fatigue during football match-play. *Sports Med* 38:357-367, 2008.

68. Robertson, S, and Joyce, D. Evaluating strategic periodisation in team sport. *J Sports Sci* 36:279-285, 2018.

69. Robertson, SJ, and Joyce, DG. Informing in-season tactical periodisation in team sport: Development of a match difficulty index for Super Rugby. *J Sports Sci* 33:99-107, 2015.

70. Rodríguez-Fernández, A, Sánchez-Sánchez, J, Ramirez-Campillo, R, Rodríguez-Marroyo, JA, Villa Vicente, JG, and Nakamura, FY. Effects of short-term in-season break detraining on repeated-sprint ability and intermittent endurance according to initial performance of soccer player. *PloS One* 13:e0201111-e0201111, 2018.

71. Rowbottom, DG. Periodization of training. In *Exercise and Sport Science*. Garrett, WE, Kirkendall, DT, eds. Philadelphia, PA: Lippicott Williams and Wilkins, 499-512, 2000.

72. Sanna, G, and O'Connor, KM. Fatigue-related changes in stance leg mechanics during sidestep cutting maneuvers. *Clin Biomech (Bristol, Avon)*, 2008.

73. Schmolinsky, G. Walking and running. In *Track and Field: The East German Textbook of Athletics*. Toronto, Canada: Sports Book Publisher, 120-221, 2004.
74. Shaffick, B. A theoretical training plan and facility for Ontario-based Olympic weightlifters. *American Journal of Recreation and Sports* 2:1-28, 2023.
75. Silva, JR, Brito, J, Akenhead, R, and Nassis, GP. The transition period in soccer: A window of opportunity. *Sports Med* 46:305-313, 2016.
76. Silva, JR, Nassis, GP, and Rebelo, A. Strength training in soccer with a specific focus on highly trained players. *Sports Med Open* 1:17-17, 2015.
77. Sousa, AC, Neiva, HP, Izquierdo, M, Cadore, EL, Alves, AR, and Marinho, DA. Concurrent training and detraining: Brief review on the effect of exercise intensities. *Int J Sports Med* 40:747-755, 2019.
78. Staron, RS, Leonardi, MJ, Karapondo, DL, Malicky, ES, Falkel, JE, Hagerman, FC, and Hikida, RS. Strength and skeletal muscle adaptations in heavy-resistance-trained women after detraining and retraining. *J Appl Physiol* 70:631-640, 1991.
79. Stone, MH, and O'Bryant, HO. Training theory and its application to resistance training. In *Weight Training: A Scientific Approach*. Edina, MN: Burgess, 121-126, 1987.
80. Thompson, JK, and Blanton, P. Energy conservation and exercise dependence: A sympathetic arousal hypothesis. *Med Sci Sports Exerc* 19:91-99, 1987.
81. Tønnessen, E, Svendsen, IS, Olsen, IC, Guttormsen, A, and Haugen, T. Performance development in adolescent track and field athletes according to age, sex and sport discipline. *PLoS One* 10:e0129014, 2015.
82. Urhausen, A, and Kindermann, W. Echocardiographic findings in strength- and endurance-trained athletes. *Sports Med* 13:270-284, 1992.
83. Verkhoshansky, Y, and Siff, MC. Organisation of training. In *Supertraining: Expanded Edition*. Rome, Italy: Verkhoshansky, 313-393, 2009.
84. Viru, A. Physiological aspects of selected problems of training methodology (training strategy). In *Adaptations in Sports Training*. Boca Raton, FL: CRC Press, 281-300, 1995.
85. Waldén, M, Hägglund, M, and Ekstrand, J. Time-trends and circumstances surrounding ankle injuries in men's professional football: An 11-year follow-up of the UEFA Champions League injury study. *Br J Sports Med* 47:748-753, 2013.
86. Zatsiorsky, VM, Kraemer, WJ, and Fry, AC. Basic concepts of training theory. In *Science and Practice of Strength Training,* 3rd ed. Champaign, IL: Human Kinetics, 3-16, 2021.
87. Zatsiorsky, VM, Kraemer, WJ, and Fry, AC. Timing in strength training. In *Science and Practice of Strength Training,* 3rd ed. Champaign, IL: Human Kinetics, 79-98, 2021.

Chapter 7

1. Berger, J, Harre, D, and Ritter, I. Principles of athletic training. In *Principles of Sports Training: Introduction to the Theory and Methods of Training*. Harre, D, ed. Michigan, USA: Ultimate Athlete Concepts, 113-150, 2012.
2. Bishop, DJ, Bartlett, J, Fyfe, J, and Lee, M. Methodological considerations for concurrent training. In *Concurrent Aerobic and Strength Training*. Schumann, M, Ronnestad, B, eds. Cham, Switzerland: Springer, 183-196, 2019.
3. Bompa, TO, and Haff, GG. Training cycles. In *Periodization: Theory and Methodology of Training*. 5th ed. Champaign, IL: Human Kinetics, 203-234, 2009.
4. Bondarchuk, AP. Constructing a training system. *Track Tech* 102:254-269, 1988.
5. Bruin, G, Kuipers, H, Keizer, HA, and Vander Vusse, GJ. Adaptation and overtraining in horses subjected to increasing training loads. *J Appl Physiol* 76:1908-1913, 1994.
6. Busso, T, Benoit, H, Bonnefoy, R, Feasson, L, and Lacour, JR. Effects of training frequency on the dynamics of performance response to a single training bout. *J Appl Physiol* 92:572-580, 2002.
7. Counsilman, JE, and Counsilman, BE. Advanced theories in the planning of training. In *The New Science of Swimming*. Englewood Cliffs, NJ: Prentice Hall, 229-255, 1994.
8. Coutts, A, Hocking, J, and Bilsborough, JC. Australian football. In *Science and Application of High-Intensity Interval Training*. Laursen, PB, Buchheit, M, eds. Champaign, IL: Human Kinetics, 393-410, 2019.
9. DeWeese, BH, Hornsby, G, Stone, M, and Stone, MH. The training process: Planning for strength–power training in track and field. Part 1: Theoretical aspects. *J Sport Health Sci* 4:308-317, 2015.
10. Dick, FW. Units, microcycles, mesocycles, and macrocycles. In *Sports Training Principles*. 5th ed. London: A and C Black, 319-328, 2007.
11. Dolci, F, Kilding, AE, Chivers, P, Piggott, B, and Hart, NH. High-intensity interval training shock microcycle for enhancing sport performance: a brief review. *J Strength Cond Res* 34:1188-1196, 2020.
12. Eston, R. Use of ratings of perceived exertion in sports. *Int J Sports Physiol Perform* 7:175-182, 2012.
13. Foster, C. Monitoring training in athletes with reference to overtraining syndrome. *Med Sci Sports Exerc* 30:1164-1168, 1998.
14. Foster, C, Daines, E, Hector, L, Snyder, AC, and Welsh, R. Athletic performance in relation to training load. *Wis Med J* 95:370-374, 1996.
15. Foster, C, Florhaug, JA, Franklin, J, Gottschall, L, Hrovatin, LA, Parker, S, Doleshal, P, and Dodge, C. A new approach to monitoring exercise training. *J Strength Cond Res* 15:109-115, 2001.
16. Freeman, WH. Periodized training for jumpers. In *Peak When It Counts: Periodization for American Track & Field*, 4th ed. Mountain View, CA: Tafnews Press, 120-130, 2001.
17. French, D. Combat sports. In *Science and Application of High-Intensity Interval Training*. Laursen, PB, Buchheit, M, eds. Champaign, IL: Human Kinetics, 227-246, 2019.
18. Fry, RW, Morton, AR, and Keast, D. Periodisation and the prevention of overtraining. *Can J Sport Sci* 17:241-248, 1992.
19. Fry, RW, Morton, AR, and Keast, D. Periodisation of training stress—a review. *Can J Sport Sci* 17:234-240, 1992.
20. Fyfe, J, Buchheit, M, and Laursen, PB. Incorporating HIIT into a concurrent training program. In *Science and*

Application of High-Intensity Interval Training. Laursen, PB, Buchheit, M, eds. Champaign, IL: Human Kinetics, 119-136, 2019.

21. Haff, GG. Periodization of training. In *Conditioning for Strength and Human Performance*. 2nd ed. Brown, LE, Chandler, J, eds. Philadelphia, PA: Wolters Kluwer, Lippincott, Williams & Wilkins, 326-345, 2012.
22. Haff, GG. The essentials of periodisation. In *Strength and Conditioning for Sports Performance*. Jeffreys, I, Moody, J, eds. Abingdon, Oxon: Routledge, 404-448, 2016.
23. Haff, GG. Periodization for tactical populations. In *NSCA's Essentials of Tactical Strength and Conditioning*. Alvar, BA, Sell, K, Deuster, PA, eds. Champaign, IL: Human Kinetics, 181-204, 2017.
24. Haff, GG. Periodization and programming of individual sports. In *NSCA's Essentials of Sport Science*. French, D, Torres Ronda, L, eds. Champaign, IL: Human Kinetics, 27-42, 2022.
25. Haff, GG, and Haff, EE. Training integration and periodization. In *Strength and Conditioning Program Design*. Hoffman, J, ed. Champaign, IL: Human Kinetics, 209-254, 2012.
26. Hamilton, D. Field Hockey. In *Science and Application of High-Intensity Interval Training*. Laursen, PB, Buchheit, M, eds. Champaign, IL: Human Kinetics, 455-476, 2019.
27. Issurin, V. Block periodization versus traditional training theory: A review. *J Sports Med Phys Fitness* 48:65-75, 2008.
28. Issurin, V. Designing the training programs. In *Principles and Basics of Advanced Athlete Training*. Michigan, USA: Ultimate Athlete Concepts, 121-187, 2008.
29. Issurin, V. Microcycles, mesocycles, and training stages. In *Block Periodization: Breakthrough in Sports Training*. Michigan, USA: Ultimate Athlete Concepts, 78-127, 2008.
30. Issurin, V, and Kaverin, V. Planning and design of annual preparation cycle in canoe-kayak paddling. In *Grebnoj Sport [Rowing, Canoeing, Kayaking]*. Moscow: Fizkultura i Sport, 25-29, 1985.
31. Issurin, VB. New horizons for the methodology and physiology of training periodization. *Sports Med* 40:189-206, 2010.
32. Issurin, VB. Benefits and limitations of block periodized training approaches to athletes' preparation: A review. *Sports Med* 46:329-338, 2016.
33. Kurz, T. Cycles in sports training. In *Science of Sports Training*. 2nd ed. Island Pond, VT: Stadion Publishing, 51-98, 2001.
34. Mann, JB, Bryant, KR, Johnstone, B, Ivey, PA, and Sayers, SP. Effect of physical and academic stress on illness and injury in Division 1 college football players. *J Strength Cond Res* 30:20-25, 2016.
35. Matveyev, LP. Fundamentals of the structure of training and its initial links. In *Fundamentals of Sports Training*. Moscow: Fizkultua i Sport, 245-259, 1977.
36. McGuigan, M. Quantifying training stress. In *Monitoring Training and Performance in Athletes*. Champaign, IL: Human Kinetics, 69-101, 2017.
37. McGuigan, MR, and Foster, C. A new approach to monitoring resistance training. *Strength Cond J* 26:42-47, 2004.
38. Mujika, I, Halson, S, Burke, L, Balagué, G, and Farrow, D. An integrated, multifactorial approach to periodization for optimal performance in individual and team sports. *Int J Sports Physiol Perform* 13:538-561, 2018.
39. Nádori, L. Theoretrical and methodological basis of training planning. In *Theoretical and Methodological Basis of Training Planning With Special Considerations Within a Microcycle*. Nádori, L, Granek, I, eds. Lincoln, NE: National Strength and Conditioning Association, 1-25, 1989.
40. Plisk, SS, and Stone, MH. Periodization strategies. *Strength and Cond J* 25:19-37, 2003.
41. Poulos, N. Rugby Sevens. In *Science and Application of High-Intensity Interval Training*. Laursen, PB, Buchheit, M, eds. Champaign, IL: Human Kinetics, 525-546, 2019.
42. Pyne, D, and Touretski, G. An analysis of the training of Olympic sprint champion Alexandre Popov. *Australian Swim Coach* 10:5-14, 1993.
43. Robineau, J, Babault, N, Piscione, J, Lacome, M, and Bigard, AX. Specific training effects of concurrent aerobic and strength exercises depend on recovery duration. *J Strength Cond Res* 30:672-683, 2016.
44. Rowbottom, DG. Periodization of training. In *Exercise and Sport Science*. Garrett, WE, Kirkendall, DT, eds. Philadelphia, PA: Lippicott Williams and Wilkins, 499-512, 2000.
45. Sale, DG, Jacobs, I, MacDougall, JD, and Garner, S. Comparison of two regimens of concurrent strength and endurance training. *Med Sci Sports Exerc* 22:348-356, 1990.
46. Stone, MH, Stone, ME, and Sands, WA. Introduction, definitions, objectives, tasks, and principles of training. In *Principles and Practice of Resistance Training*. Champaign, IL: Human Kinetics, 1-12, 2007.
47. Tønnessen, E, Svendsen, IS, Ronnestad, BR, Hisdal, J, Haugen, TA, and Seiler, S. The annual training periodization of 8 world champions in orienteering. *Int J Sports Physiol Perform* 10:29-38, 2015.
48. Tønnessen, E, Sylta, O, Haugen, TA, Hem, E, Svendsen, IS, and Seiler, S. The road to gold: Training and peaking characteristics in the year prior to a gold medal endurance performance. *PLoS One* 9:e101796, 2014.
49. Touretski, G. Preparation of sprint events: 1998 ASCTA Convention. Canberra, ACT: Australian Institute of Sport, 1998.
50. Verkhoshansky, Y, and Siff, MC. Organisation of training. In *Supertraining*. 6th (expanded) ed. Rome, Italy: Verkhoshansky, 313-393, 2009.
51. Verkhoshansky, Y, and Siff, MC. Programming and organisation of training. In *Supertraining*. 6th (expanded) ed. Rome, Italy: Verkhoshansky, 313-392, 2009.
52. Williams, S, Trewartha, G, Cross, MJ, Kemp, SPT, and Stokes, KA. Monitoring what matters: A systematic process for selecting training-load measures. *Int J Sports Physiol Perform* 12:S2-101-S102-106, 2017.
53. Zatsiorsky, VM, Kraemer, WJ, and Fry, AC. Timing in strength training. In *Science and Practice of Strength Training*. 3rd ed. Champaign, IL: Human Kinetics, 79-98, 2021.

Chapter 8

1. Abadjiev, I. Basic training principles for Bulgarian elite. *Can Weightlifting Fed Official Newsletter* 5:13-18, 1976.

2. Allen, DG, Lee, JA, and Westerblad, H. Intracellular calcium and tension during fatigue in isolated single muscle fibres from Xenopus laevis. *J Physiol* 415:433-458, 1989.
3. Andrews, TR, Mackey, T, Inkrott, TA, Murray, SR, Clark, IE, and Pettitt, RW. Effect of hang cleans or squats paired with countermovement vertical jumps on vertical displacement. *J Strength Cond Res* 25:2448-2452, 2011.
4. Anshel, MH, and Novak, J. Effects of different intensities of fatigue on performing a sport skill requiring explosive muscular effort: A test of the specificity of practice principle. *Percept Mot Skills* 69:1379-1389, 1989.
5. Barcroft, H, and Edholm, OG. The effect of temperature on blood flow and deep temperature in the human forearm. *J Physiol* 102:5-20, 1943.
6. Barcroft, J, and King, WO. The effect of temperature on the dissociation curve of blood. *J Physiol* 39:374-384, 1909.
7. Beato, M, Bigby, AEJ, De Keijzer, KL, Nakamura, FY, Coratella, G, and McErlain-Naylor, SA. Post-activation potentiation effect of eccentric overload and traditional weightlifting exercise on jumping and sprinting performance in male athletes. *PLoS One* 14:e0222466, 2019.
8. Bennett, B. The video coach—reflections on the use of ICT in high-performance sport. *Int Sport Coach J* 7:220-228, 2020.
9. Bennett, BC. My video coach—a phenomenographic interpretation of athlete perceptions of coaching through a live video feed. *Qual Res Sport Exerc Health*:1-18, 2020.
10. Bentley, DJ, Smith, PA, Davie, AJ, and Zhou, S. Muscle activation of the knee extensors following high intensity endurance exercise in cyclists. *Eur J Appl Physiol* 81:297-302, 2000.
11. Bentley, DJ, Zhou, S, and Davie, AJ. The effect of endurance exercise on muscle force generating capacity of the lower limbs. *J Sci Med Sport* 1:179-188, 1998.
12. Bishop, D. Warm up I: Potential mechanisms and the effects of passive warm up on exercise performance. *Sports Med* 33:439-454, 2003.
13. Bishop, D. Warm up II: Performance changes following active warm up and how to structure the warm up. *Sports Med* 33:483-498, 2003.
14. Bishop, DJ, Bartlett, J, Fyfe, J, and Lee, M. Methodological considerations for concurrent training. In *Concurrent Aerobic and Strength Training*. Schumann, M, Ronnestad, B, eds. Cham, Switzerland: Springer, 183-196, 2019.
15. Bishop, PA, Jones, E, and Woods, AK. Recovery from training: A brief review. *J Strength Cond Res* 22:1015-1024, 2008.
16. Bixler, B, and Jones, RL. High-school football injuries: Effects of a post-halftime warm-up and stretching routine. *Fam Pract Res J* 12:131-139, 1992.
17. Blazevich, AJ, and Babault, N. Post-activation potentiation versus post-activation performance enhancement in humans: Historical perspective, underlying mechanisms, and current issues. *Front Physiol* 10, 2019.
18. Bobbert, MF, Hollander, AP, and Huijing, PA. Factors in delayed onset muscular soreness of man. *Med Sci Sports Exerc* 18:75-81, 1986.
19. Bogdanis, GC, Nevill, ME, Lakomy, HK, Graham, CM, and Louis, G. Effects of active recovery on power output during repeated maximal sprint cycling. *Eur J Appl Physiol Occup Physiol* 74:461-469, 1996.
20. Bompa, TO, and Buzzichelli, CA. Planning the training sessions. In *Periodization: Theory and Methodology of Training*. 6th ed. Champaign, IL: Human Kinetics, 115-136, 2019.
21. Bompa, TO, and Haff, GG. Workout planning. In *Periodization: Theory and Methodology of Training*. 5th ed. Champaign, IL: Human Kinetics, 235-256, 2009.
22. Bondarchuk, A. Organization and implementation of training sessions, microcycles and mesocycles. In *Soviet Sport Methods: A Detailed Look Inside the World's Greatest System*. Thome, M, Mann, BJ, eds. Michigan, USA: Ultimate Athlete Concepts, 128-168, 2016.
23. Boratto, L, Carta, S, Mulas, F, and Pilloni, P. An e-coaching ecosystem: Design and effectiveness analysis of the engagement of remote coaching on athletes. *Pers Ubiquitous Comput* 21:689-704, 2017.
24. Branscheidt, M, Kassavetis, P, Anaya, M, Rogers, D, Huang, HD, Lindquist, MA, and Celnik, P. Fatigue induces long-lasting detrimental changes in motor-skill learning. *Elife* 8, 2019.
25. Busso, T, Benoit, H, Bonnefoy, R, Feasson, L, and Lacour, JR. Effects of training frequency on the dynamics of performance response to a single training bout. *J Appl Physiol* 92:572-580, 2002.
26. Chaabene, H, Behm, DG, Negra, Y, and Granacher, U. Acute effects of static stretching on muscle strength and power: An attempt to clarify previous caveats. *Front Physiol* 10:1468, 2019.
27. Charron, J, Garcia, JEV, Roy, P, Ferland, P-M, and Comtois, AS. Physiological responses to repeated running sprint ability tests: A systematic review. *Int J Exerc Sci* 13:1190, 2020.
28. Cheung, K, Hume, P, and Maxwell, L. Delayed onset muscle soreness: Treatment strategies and performance factors. *Sports Med* 33:145-164, 2003.
29. Chiu, LZ, Fry, AC, Weiss, LW, Schilling, BK, Brown, LE, and Smith, SL. Postactivation potentiation response in athletic and recreationally trained individuals. *J Strength Cond Res* 17:671-677, 2003.
30. Coggan, AR, and Coyle, EF. Carbohydrate ingestion during prolonged exercise: Effects on metabolism and performance. *Exerc Sport Sci Rev* 19:1-40, 1991.
31. Coito, N, Davids, K, Folgado, H, Bento, T, and Travassos, B. Capturing and quantifying tactical behaviors in small-sided and conditioned games in soccer: A systematic review. *Res Q Exerc Sport* 93:189-203, 2022.
32. Costa, PB, Medeiros, HBO, and Fukuda, DH. Warm-up, stretching, and cool-down strategies for combat sports. *Strength Cond J* 33:71-79, 2011.
33. Craig, BW, Lucas, J, Pohlman, R, and Schilling, H. The effect of running, weightlifting and a combination of both on growth hormone release. *J Appl Sport Sci Res* 5:198-203, 1991.
34. D'Amico, AP, and Gillis, J. Influence of foam rolling on recovery from exercise-induced muscle damage. *J Strength Cond Res* 33:2443-2452, 2019.
35. Dankel, SJ, Mattocks, KT, Jessee, MB, Buckner, SL, Mouser, JG, Counts, BR, Laurentino, GC, and Loenneke, JP. Frequency: The overlooked resistance training variable for

35. inducing muscle hypertrophy? *Sports Med* 47:799-805, 2017.
36. Davis, JM. Central and peripheral factors in fatigue. *J Sports Sci* 13 Spec No:S49-53, 1995.
37. Davis, JM, Alderson, NL, and Welsh, RS. Serotonin and central nervous system fatigue: Nutritional considerations. *Am J Clin Nutr* 72:573S-578S, 2000.
38. Di Blasio, A, Tranquilli, A, Di Santo, S, Marchetti, G, Bergamin, M, Bullo, V, Cugusi, L, Tavoletta, S, Gallazzi, A, Bucci, I, and Napolitano, G. Does the cool-down content affect cortisol and testosterone production after a whole-body workout? A pilot study. *Sport Sciences for Health* 14:579-586, 2018.
39. Dupuy, O, Douzi, W, Theurot, D, Bosquet, L, and Dugué, B. An evidence-based approach for choosing post-exercise recovery techniques to reduce markers of muscle damage, soreness, fatigue, and inflammation: a systematic review with meta-analysis. *Front Physiol* 9, 2018.
40. Edwards, RHT. Human muscle function and fatigue. In *Human Muscle Fatigue: Physiological Mechanisms*. Porter, R, Whelan, J, eds. London: Pitman, 1-18, 1981.
41. Eston, R. Use of ratings of perceived exertion in sports. *Int J Sports Physiol Perform* 7:175-182, 2012.
42. Faulkner, SH, Ferguson, RA, Gerrett, N, Hupperets, M, Hodder, SG, and Havenith, G. Reducing muscle temperature drop after warm-up improves sprint cycling performance. *Med Sci Sports Exerc* 45:359-365, 2013.
43. Fletcher, IM, and Jones, B. The effect of different warm-up stretch protocols on 20 meter sprint performance in trained rugby union players. *J Strength Cond Res* 18:885-888, 2004.
44. Freeman, WH. Planning the details—from the annual plan to the daily workout. In *Peak When It Counts: Periodization for American Track & Field*. 4th ed. Mountain View, CA: Tafnews Press, 51-61, 2001.
45. Fry, AC, Stone, MH, Thrush, JT, and Fleck, SJ. Precompetition training sessions enhance competitive performance of high anxiety junior weightlifters. *J Strength Cond Res* 9:37-42, 1995.
46. Funk, DC, Swank, AM, Mikla, BM, Fagan, TA, and Farr, BK. Impact of prior exercise on hamstring flexibility: A comparison of proprioceptive neuromuscular facilitation and static stretching. *J Strength Cond Res* 17:489-492, 2003.
47. Fyfe, J, Buchheit, M, and Laursen, PB. Incorporating HIIT into a concurrent training program. In *Science and Application of High-Intensity Interval Training*. Laursen, PB, Buchheit, M, eds. Champaign, IL: Human Kinetics, 119-136, 2019.
48. Gandevia, SC. Spinal and supraspinal factors in human muscle fatigue. *Physiol Rev* 81:1725-1789, 2001.
49. Garhammer, J, and Takano, B. Training for weightlifting. In *Strength and Power in Sport*. 2nd ed. Komi, PV, ed. Oxford, UK: Blackwell Scientific, 502-515, 2003.
50. Grange, RW, Cory, CR, Vandenboom, R, and Houston, ME. Myosin phosphorylation augments force-displacement and force-velocity relationships of mouse fast muscle. *Am J Physiol* 269:C713-724, 1995.
51. Güllich, A, and Schmidtbleicher, D. MVC-induced short-term potentiation of explosive force. *New Studies in Athletics* 11:67-81, 1996.
52. Haff, GG. The essentials of periodisation. In *Strength and Conditioning for Sports Performance*. Jeffreys, I, Moody, J, eds. Abingdon, Oxon: Routledge, 404-448, 2016.
53. Haff, GG. The essentials of periodisation. In *Strength and Conditioning for Sports Performance*. 2nd ed. Jeffreys, I, Moody, J, eds. Abingdon, Oxon: Routledge, 394-444, 2021.
54. Haff, GG, and Haff, EE. Training integration and periodization. In *Strength and Conditioning Program Design*. Hoffman, J, ed. Champaign, IL: Human Kinetics, 209-254, 2012.
55. Haff, GG, Hobbs, RT, Haff, EE, Sands, WA, Pierce, KC, and Stone, MH. Cluster training: A novel method for introducing training program variation. *Strength Cond J* 30:67-76, 2008.
56. Haff, GG, Lehmkuhl, MJ, McCoy, LB, and Stone, MH. Carbohydrate supplementation and resistance training. *J Strength Cond Res* 17:187-196, 2003.
57. Häkkinen, K, and Kallinen, M. Distribution of strength training volume into one or two daily sessions and neuromuscular adaptations in female athletes. *Electromyogr Clin Neurophysiol* 34:117-124, 1994.
58. Halouani, J, Chtourou, H, Gabbett, T, Chaouachi, A, and Chamari, K. Small-sided games in team sports training: A brief review. *J Strength Cond Res* 28:3594-3618, 2014.
59. Harrison, PW, James, LP, McGuigan, MR, Jenkins, DG, and Kelly, VG. Resistance priming to enhance neuromuscular performance in sport: Evidence, potential mechanisms and directions for future research. *Sports Med* 49:1499-1514, 2019.
60. Harrison, PW, James, LP, McGuigan, MR, Jenkins, DG, and Kelly, VG. Prevalence and application of priming exercise in high performance sport. *J Sci Med Sport* 23:297-303, 2020.
61. Hearris, MA, Hammond, KM, Fell, JM, and Morton, JP. Regulation of muscle glycogen metabolism during exercise: Implications for endurance performance and training adaptations. *Nutrients* 10, 2018.
62. Hodgson, M, Docherty, D, and Robbins, D. Post-activation potentiation: Underlying physiology and implications for motor performance. *Sports Med* 35:585-595, 2005.
63. Holcomb, WR. Stretching and warm-up. In *Essentials of Strength and Conditioning*. 2nd ed. Baechle, TR, Earle, RW, eds. Champaign, IL: Human Kinetics, 321-342, 2000.
64. Hornery, DJ, Farrow, D, Mujika, I, and Young, W. Fatigue in tennis: Mechanisms of fatigue and effect on performance. *Sports Med* 37:199-212, 2007.
65. Issurin, V. Block periodization versus traditional training theory: A review. *J Sports Med Phys Fitness* 48:65-75, 2008.
66. Issurin, V. The workout: General concepts and structure guidelines. In *Block Periodization: Breakthrough in Sports Training*. Yessis, M, ed. Michigan, USA: Ultimate Athlete Concepts, 37-77, 2008.
67. Issurin, V. The workout: General concepts and structure guidelines. In *Building the Modern Athlete: Scientific Advancement & Training Innovation*. Thome, M, ed. Michigan, USA: Ultimate Athlete Concepts, 235-269, 2015.
68. Ivy, J, and Portman, R. Nutrient timing. In *The Future of Sports Nutrition: Nutrient Timing*. North Bergan, NJ: Basic Health Publications, 7-14, 2004.
69. Jeffreys, I. Warm-up revisited: The ramp method of optimizing warm-ups. *Prof Strength Cond* 6:12-18, 2007.

70. Jeffreys, I. Providing effective feedback and instruction: Internal versus external focus. *Prof Strength Cond* 20:30-32, 2010.

71. Jeffreys, I. Warm-up and flexibility training. In *Essentials of Strength Training and Conditioning*. 4th ed. Haff, GG, Triplett, N, eds. Champaign, IL: Human Kinetics, 317-350, 2016.

72. Jeffreys, I. RAMP warm-ups: More than simply short-term preparation. *Prof Strength Cond* 44:17-23, 2017.

73. Jeffreys, I. The activation and mobilization phase. In *The Warm-Up: Maximise Performance and Improve Long-Term Athlete Development*. Champaign, IL: Human Kinetics, 53-142, 2019.

74. Jeffreys, I. Agility and quickness program design. In *Developing Agility and Quickness*. Dawes, J, ed. Champaign, IL: Human Kinetics, 153-162, 2019.

75. Jeffreys, I. The potentiation phase. In *The Warm-Up: Maximise Performance and Improve Long-Term Athlete Development*. Champaign, IL: Human Kinetics, 143-168, 2019.

76. Jeffreys, I. The raise phase. In *The Warm-Up: Maximise Performance and Improve Long-Term Athlete Development*. Champaign, IL: Human Kinetics, 27-52, 2019.

77. Jeffreys, I. *The Warm-Up: Maximise Performance and Improve Long-Term Athlete Development*. Champaign, IL: Human Kinetics, 2019.

78. Jeffreys, I. Why we warm up. In *The Warm-Up: Maximise Performance and Improve Long-Term Athlete Development*. Champaign, IL: Human Kinetics, 1-8, 2019.

79. Jemni, M, Sands, WA, Friemel, F, and Delamarche, P. Effect of active and passive recovery on blood lactate and performance during simulated competition in high level gymnasts. *Can J Appl Physiol* 28:240-256, 2003.

80. Jensen, M. Pedagogy of coaching. In *Coaching for Sports Performance*. Baghurst, T, ed. New York: Routledge, 38-74, 2020.

81. Jo, E, Judelson, DA, Brown, LE, Coburn, JW, and Dabbs, NC. Influence of recovery duration after a potentiating stimulus on muscular power in recreationally trained individuals. *J Strength Cond Res* 24:343-347, 2010.

82. Jones, TW, and Howatson, G. Immediate effects of endurance exercise on subsequent strength performance. In *Concurrent Aerobic and Strength Training: Scientific Basics and Practical Applications*. Schumann, M, Ronnestad, BR, eds. Cham, Switzerland: Springer, 139-154, 2019.

83. Kay, AD, and Blazevich, AJ. Effect of acute static stretch on maximal muscle performance: A systematic review. *Med Sci Sports Exerc* 44:154-164, 2012.

84. Kellmann, M, Bertollo, M, Bosquet, L, Brink, M, Coutts, AJ, Duffield, R, Erlacher, D, Halson, SL, Hecksteden, A, Heidari, J, Kallus, KW, Meeusen, R, Mujika, I, Robazza, C, Skorski, S, Venter, R, and Beckmann, J. Recovery and performance in sport: Consensus statement. *Int J Sports Physiol Perform* 13:240-245, 2018.

85. Kilduff, LP, Finn, CV, Baker, JS, Cook, CJ, and West, DJ. Preconditioning strategies to enhance physical performance on the day of competition. *Int J Sports Physiol Perform* 8:677-681, 2013.

86. Kurz, T. Cycles in sports training. In *Science of Sports Training*. 2nd ed. Island Pond, VT: Stadion Publishing, 51-98, 2001.

87. LaForgia, J, Withers, RT, and Gore, CJ. Effects of exercise intensity and duration on the excess post-exercise oxygen consumption. *J Sports Sci* 24:1247-1264, 2006.

88. Macdonald, GZ, Button, DC, Drinkwater, EJ, and Behm, DG. Foam rolling as a recovery tool after an intense bout of physical activity. *Med Sci Sports Exerc* 46:131-142, 2014.

89. MacDonald, GZ, Penney, MD, Mullaley, ME, Cuconato, AL, Drake, CD, Behm, DG, and Button, DC. An acute bout of self-myofascial release increases range of motion without a subsequent decrease in muscle activation or force. *J Strength Cond Res* 27:812-821, 2013.

90. MacIntosh, BR, and Rassier, DE. What is fatigue? *Can J Appl Physiol* 27:42-55., 2002.

91. Malareki, I. Investigation of physiological justification of so-called "warming up". *Acta Physiol Pol* 5:543-546, 1954.

92. Mancinelli, CA, Davis, DS, Aboulhosn, L, Brady, M, Eisenhofer, J, and Foutty, S. The effects of massage on delayed onset muscle soreness and physical performance in female college athletes. *Phys Ther Sport* 7:5-13, 2006.

93. Mason, B, McKune, A, Pumpa, K, and Ball, N. The use of acute exercise interventions as game day priming strategies to improve physical performance and athlete readiness in team-sport athletes: A systematic review. *Sports Med* 50:1943-1962, 2020.

94. McBride, JM, Nimphius, S, and Erickson, TM. The acute effects of heavy-load squats and loaded countermovement jumps on sprint performance. *J Strength Cond Res* 19:893-897, 2005.

95. McGuigan, M. Measures of fitness and fatigue. In *Monitoring Training and Performance in Athletes*. Champaign, IL: Human Kinetics, 103-134, 2017.

96. McGuigan, M. Quantifying training stress. In *Monitoring Training and Performance in Athletes*. Champaign, IL: Human Kinetics, 69-101, 2017.

97. McMillan, JL, Stone, MH, Sartin, J, Keith, R, Marple, D, Brown, C, and Lewis, RD. 20-hour physiological responses to a single weight-training session. *J Strength Cond Res* 7:9-21, 1993.

98. McMorris, T, Barwood, M, and Corbett, J. Central fatigue theory and endurance exercise: Toward an interoceptive model. *Neurosci Biobehav Rev* 93:93-107, 2018.

99. Merlau, S. Recovery time optimization to facilitate motor learning during sprint intervals. *Strength Cond J* 27:68, 2005.

100. Mika, A, Mika, P, Fernhall, B, and Unnithan, VB. Comparison of recovery strategies on muscle performance after fatiguing exercise. *Am J Phys Med Rehabil* 86:474-481, 2007.

101. Millet, GY, and Lepers, R. Alterations of neuromuscular function after prolonged running, cycling and skiing exercises. *Sports Med* 34:105-116, 2004.

102. Mohr, AR, Long, BC, and Goad, CL. Effect of foam rolling and static stretching on passive hip-flexion range of motion. *J Sport Rehabil* 23:296-299, 2014.

103. Monedero, J, and Donne, B. Effect of recovery interventions on lactate removal and subsequent performance. *Int J Sports Med* 21:593-597, 2000.

104. Moriarty, TA, Mermier, C, Kravitz, L, Gibson, A, Beltz, N, and Zuhl, M. Acute aerobic exercise based cognitive and

motor priming: Practical applications and mechanisms. *Front Psychol* 10, 2019.
105. Mujika, I, Halson, S, Burke, L, Balagué, G, and Farrow, D. An integrated, multifactorial approach to periodization for optimal performance in individual and team sports. *Int J Sports Physiol Perform* 13:538-561, 2018.
106. Murlasits, Z, Kneffel, Z, and Thalib, L. The physiological effects of concurrent strength and endurance training sequence: A systematic review and meta-analysis. *J Sports Sci* 36:1212-1219, 2018.
107. Noakes, TD. Physiological models to understand exercise fatigue and the adaptations that predict or enhance athletic performance. *Scand J Med Sci Sports* 10:123-145, 2000.
108. Orlick, T, and Partington, J. The sport psychology consultant: Analysis of critical components as viewed by Canadian Olympic athletes. *The Sport Psychologist* 1:4-17, 1987.
109. Ortenblad, N, Nielsen, J, Saltin, B, and Holmberg, HC. Role of glycogen availability in sarcoplasmic reticulum Ca2+ kinetics in human skeletal muscle. *J Physiol* 589:711-725, 2011.
110. Paris, HL, Sinai, EC, Shei, RJ, Keller, AM, and Mickleborough, TD. The influence of carbohydrate ingestion on peripheral and central fatigue during exercise in hypoxia: A narrative review. *Eur J Sport Sci*:1-13, 2020.
111. Pelka, M, Kölling, S, Ferrauti, A, Meyer, T, Pfeiffer, M, and Kellmann, M. Acute effects of psychological relaxation techniques between two physical tasks. *J Sports Sci* 35:216-223, 2017.
112. Pooley, S, Spendiff, O, Allen, M, and Moir, HJ. Static stretching does not enhance recovery in elite youth soccer players. *BMJ Open Sport Exerc Med* 3:e000202, 2017.
113. Popp, JK, Bellar, DM, Hoover, DL, Craig, BW, Leitzelar, BN, Wanless, EA, and Judge, LW. Pre- and post-activity stretching practices of collegiate athletic trainers in the United States. *J Strength Cond Res* 31:2347-2354, 2017.
114. Poulos, N. Rugby Sevens. In *Science and Application of High-Intensity Interval Training*. Laursen, PB, Buchheit, M, eds. Champaign, IL: Human Kinetics, 525-546, 2019.
115. Prieske, O, Behrens, M, Chaabene, H, Granacher, U, and Maffiuletti, NA. Time to differentiate postactivation "potentiation" from "performance enhancement" in the strength and conditioning community. *Sports Med* 50:1559-1565, 2020.
116. Radcliffe, JC, and Radcliffe, JL. Effects of different warm-up protocols on peak power output during a single response jump task. *Med Sci Sports Exerc* 28:S189, 1996.
117. Reilly, T, and Ekblom, B. The use of recovery methods post-exercise. *J Sports Sci* 23:619-627, 2005.
118. Richard, NA, and Koehle, MS. Optimizing recovery to support multi-evening cycling competition performance. *Eur J Sport Sci* 19:811-823, 2019.
119. Robergs, RA, Pearson, DR, Costill, DL, Fink, WJ, Pascoe, DD, Benedict, MA, Lambert, CP, and Zachweija, JJ. Muscle glycogenolysis during differing intensities of weight-resistance exercise. *J Appl Physiol* 70:1700-1706, 1991.
120. Rodacki, AL, Fowler, NE, and Bennett, SJ. Vertical jump coordination: Fatigue effects. *Med Sci Sports Exerc* 34:105-116, 2002.
121. Ruben, RM, Molinari, MA, Bibbee, CA, Childress, MA, Harman, MS, Reed, KP, and Haff, GG. The acute effects of an ascending squat protocol on performance during horizontal plyometric jumps. *J Strength Cond Res* 24:358-369, 2010.
122. Sale, DG. Postactivation potentiation: Role in human performance. *Exerc Sport Sci Rev* 30:138-143, 2002.
123. Schiphof-Godart, L, Roelands, B, and Hettinga, FJ. Drive in sports: How mental fatigue affects endurance performance. *Front Psychol* 9, 2018.
124. Schroeder, AN, and Best, TM. Is self myofascial release an effective preexercise and recovery strategy? A literature review. *Curr Sports Med Rep* 14:200-208, 2015.
125. Scott, DJ, Ditroilo, M, and Marshall, PA. Complex Training: The Effect of Exercise Selection and Training Status on Postactivation Potentiation in Rugby League Players. *J Strength Cond Res* 31:2694-2703, 2017.
126. Seitz, L, Saez de Villarreal, E, and Haff, GG. The temporal profile of postactivation potentiation is related to strength level. *J Strength Cond Res* 28:706-715, 2014.
127. Seitz, LB, and Haff, GG. Application of methods of inducing postactivation potentiation during the preparation of rugby players. *Strength Cond J* 37:40-49, 2015.
128. Seitz, LB, and Haff, GG. Factors modulating post-activation potentiation of jump, sprint, throw and upper-body ballistic performances: A systematic review with meta-analysis. *Sports Med* 46:231-240, 2016.
129. Seitz, LB, Trajano, GS, and Haff, GG. The back squat and the power clean elicit different degrees of potentiation. *Int J Sports Physiol Perform* 9:643-649, 2014.
130. Seitz, LB, Trajano, GS, Haff, GG, Dumke, CC, Tufano, JJ, and Blazevich, AJ. Relationships between maximal strength, muscle size, and myosin heavy chain isoform composition and postactivation potentiation. *Appl Physiol Nutr Metab* 41:491-497, 2016.
131. Shrier, I. Does stretching improve performance? A systematic and critical review of the literature. *Clin J Sport Med* 14:267-273, 2004.
132. Silva, LM, Neiva, HP, Marques, MC, Izquierdo, M, and Marinho, DA. Effects of warm-up, post-warm-up, and re-warm-up strategies on explosive efforts in team sports: A systematic review. *Sports Med* 48:2285-2299, 2018.
133. Sporer, BC, and Wenger, HA. Effects of aerobic exercise on strength performance following various periods of recovery. *J Strength Cond Res* 17:638-644, 2003.
134. Stone, MH, Sands, WA, Pierce, KC, Ramsey, MW, and Haff, GG. Power and power potentiation among strength power athletes: Preliminary study. *Int J Sports Physiol Perf* 3:55-67, 2008.
135. Tan, B. Manipulating resistance training program variables to optimize maximum strength in men: A review. *J Strength Cond Res* 13:289-304, 1999.
136. Taylor, JL, and Gandevia, SC. A comparison of central aspects of fatigue in submaximal and maximal voluntary contractions. *J Appl Physiol* 104:542-550, 2008.
137. Tessitore, A, Meeusen, R, Pagano, R, Benvenuti, C, Tiberi, M, and Capranica, L. Effectiveness of active versus passive recovery strategies after futsal games. *J Strength Cond Res* 22:1402-1412, 2008.

138. Van Hooren, B, and Peake, JM. Do we need a cool-down after exercise? A narrative review of the psychophysiological effects and the effects on performance, injuries and the long-term adaptive response. *Sports Med* 48:1575-1595, 2018.
139. Vetter, RE. Effects of six warm-up protocols on sprint and jump performance. *J Strength Cond Res* 21:819-823, 2007.
140. Viru, A. Physiological aspects of selected problems of training methodology (training strategy). In *Adaptations in Sports Training*. Boca Raton, FL: CRC Press, 241-280, 1995.
141. Winchester, JB, Nelson, AG, Landin, D, Young, MA, and Schexnayder, IC. Static stretching impairs sprint performance in collegiate track and field athletes. *J Strength Cond Res* 22:13-19, 2008.
142. Woods, K, Bishop, P, and Jones, E. Warm-up and stretching in the prevention of muscular injury. *Sports Med* 37:1089-1099, 2007.
143. Yetter, M, and Moir, GL. The acute effects of heavy back and front squats on speed during forty-meter sprint trials. *J Strength Cond Res* 22:159-165, 2008.
144. Young, WB, and Behm, DG. Should static stretching be used during a warm-up for strength and power activities? *Strength Cond J* 24:33-37, 2002.
145. Young, WB, and Behm, DG. Effects of running, static stretching and practice jumps on explosive force production and jumping performance. *J Sports Med Phys Fitness* 43:21-27, 2003.
146. Zatsiorsky, VM, Kraemer, WJ, and Fry, AC. Timing in strength training. In *Science and Practice of Strength Training*. 3rd ed. Champaign, IL: Human Kinetics, 79-98, 2021.

Chapter 9

1. Abbiss, CR, and Laursen, PB. Models to explain fatigue during prolonged endurance cycling. *Sports Med* 35:865-898, 2005.
2. Adamczyk, JG, Krasowska, I, Boguszewski, D, and Reaburn, P. The use of thermal imaging to assess the effectiveness of ice massage and cold-water immersion as methods for supporting post-exercise recovery. *J Therm Biol* 60:20-25, 2016.
3. Adlercreutz, H, Harkonen, M, Kuoppasalmi, K, Naveri, H, Huhtaniemi, I, Tikkanen, H, Remes, K, Dessypris, A, and Karvonen, J. Effect of training on plasma anabolic and catabolic steroid hormones and their response during physical exercise. *Int J Sports Med* 7:27-28, 1986.
4. Agu, O, Baker, D, and Seifalian, AM. Effect of graduated compression stockings on limb oxygenation and venous function during exercise in patients with venous insufficiency. *Vascular* 12:69-76, 2004.
5. Ahokas, EK, Ihalainen, JK, Kyrolainen, H, and Mero, AA. Effects of water immersion methods on postexercise recovery of physical and mental performance. *J Strength Cond Res* 33:1488-1495, 2019.
6. Allen, DG, Lannergren, J, and Westerblad, H. Muscle cell function during prolonged activity: Cellular mechanisms of fatigue. *Exp Physiol* 80:497-527, 1995.
7. Amann, M, and Dempsey, JA. Locomotor muscle fatigue modifies central motor drive in healthy humans and imposes a limitation to exercise performance. *J Physiol* 586:161-173, 2008.
8. Angus, S. Massage therapy for sprinters and runners. *Clin Podiatr Med Surg* 18:329-336, 2001.
9. Argus, CK, Broatch, JR, Petersen, AC, Polman, R, Bishop, DJ, and Halson, S. Cold-water immersion and contrast water therapy: No improvement of short-term recovery after resistance training. *Int J Sports Physiol Perform* 12:886-892, 2017.
10. Argus, CK, Driller, MW, Ebert, TR, Martin, DT, and Halson, SL. The effects of 4 different recovery strategies on repeat sprint-cycling performance. *Int J Sports Physiol Perform* 8:542-548, 2013.
11. Azevedo, RA, Silva-Cavalcante, MD, Lima-Silva, AE, and Bertuzzi, R. Fatigue development and perceived response during self-paced endurance exercise: State-of-the-art review. *Eur J Appl Physiol* 121:687-696, 2021.
12. Banfi, G, Lombardi, G, Colombini, A, and Melegati, G. Whole-body cryotherapy in athletes. *Sports Med* 40:509-517, 2010.
13. Banfi, G, Melegati, G, Barassi, A, Dogliotti, G, d'Eril, GM, Dugué, B, and Corsi, MM. Effects of whole-body cryotherapy on serum mediators of inflammation and serum muscle enzymes in athletes. *J Therm Biol* 34:55-59, 2009.
14. Barnett, A. Using recovery modalities between training sessions in elite athletes: Does it help? *Sports Med* 36:781-796, 2006.
15. Beckham, G, Suchomel, T, and Mizuguchi, S. Force plate use in performance monitoring and sport science testing. *New Studies in Athletics* 29:25-37, 2014.
16. Bell, L, Ruddock, A, Maden-Wilkinson, T, and Rogerson, D. Overreaching and overtraining in strength sports and resistance training: A scoping review. *J Sports Sci* 38:1897-1912, 2020.
17. Best, TM, Hunter, R, Wilcox, A, and Haq, F. Effectiveness of sports massage for recovery of skeletal muscle from strenuous exercise. *Clin J Sport Med* 18:446-460, 2008.
18. Bieuzen, F, Bleakley, CM, and Costello, JT. Contrast water therapy and exercise induced muscle damage: A systematic review and meta-analysis. *PLoS One* 8:e62356, 2013.
19. Birk, TJ, McGrady, A, MacArthur, RD, and Khuder, S. The effects of massage therapy alone and in combination with other complementary therapies on immune system measures and quality of life in human immunodeficiency virus. *J Altern Complement Med* 6:405-414, 2000.
20. Birrer, D, and Morgan, G. Psychological skills training as a way to enhance an athlete's performance in high-intensity sports. *Scand J Med Sci Sports* 20:78-87, 2010.
21. Bishop, PA, Jones, E, and Woods, AK. Recovery from training: A brief review. *J Strength Cond Res* 22:1015-1024, 2008.
22. Bleakley, CM, Bieuzen, F, Davison, GW, and Costello, JT. Whole-body cryotherapy: Empirical evidence and theoretical perspectives. *Open Access J Sports Med* 5:25-36, 2014.
23. Bochmann, RP, Seibel, W, Haase, E, Hietschold, V, Rodel, H, and Deussen, A. External compression increases forearm perfusion. *J Appl Physiol (1985)* 99:2337-2344, 2005.
24. Bompa, TO, and Haff, GG. Rest and recovery. In *Periodization: Theory and Methodology of Training*. 5th ed. Champaign, IL: Human Kinetics, 97-122, 2009.

25. Bonde-Petersen, F, Schultz-Pedersen, L, and Dragsted, N. Peripheral and central blood flow in man during cold, thermoneutral, and hot water immersion. *Aviat Space Environ Med* 63:346-350, 1992.
26. Bonen, A, Ness, GW, Belcastro, AN, and Kirby, RL. Mild exercise impedes glycogen repletion in muscle. *J Appl Physiol* 58:1622-1629, 1985.
27. Borges, N, Reaburn, P, Driller, M, and Argus, C. Age-related changes in performance and recovery kinetics in masters athletes: A narrative review. *J Aging Phys Act* 24:149-157, 2016.
28. Born, DP, Sperlich, B, and Holmberg, HC. Bringing light into the dark: Effects of compression clothing on performance and recovery. *Int J Sports Physiol Perform* 8:4-18, 2013.
29. Borsheim, E, and Bahr, R. Effect of exercise intensity, duration and mode on post-exercise oxygen consumption. *Sports Med* 33:1037-1060, 2003.
30. Brennan, MJ, and Miller, LT. Overview of treatment options and review of the current role and use of compression garments, intermittent pumps, and exercise in the management of lymphedema. *Cancer* 83:2821-2827, 1998.
31. Broatch, JR, Petersen, A, and Bishop, DJ. Cold-water immersion following sprint interval training does not alter endurance signaling pathways or training adaptations in human skeletal muscle. *Am J Physiol Regul Integr Comp Physiol* 313:R372-R384, 2017.
32. Broatch, JR, Petersen, A, and Bishop, DJ. The influence of post-exercise cold-water immersion on adaptive responses to exercise: A review of the literature. *Sports Med* 48:1369-1387, 2018.
33. Brown, F, Gissane, C, Howatson, G, van Someren, K, Pedlar, C, and Hill, J. Compression garments and recovery from exercise: A meta-analysis. *Sports Med* 47:2245-2267, 2017.
34. Buchheit, M, Horobeanu, C, Mendez-Villanueva, A, Simpson, BM, and Bourdon, PC. Effects of age and spa treatment on match running performance over two consecutive games in highly trained young soccer players. *J Sports Sci* 29:591-598, 2011.
35. Budgett, R, Newsholme, E, Lehmann, M, Sharp, C, Jones, D, Peto, T, Collins, D, Nerurkar, R, and White, P. Redefining the overtraining syndrome as the unexplained underperformance syndrome. *Br J Sports Med* 34:67-68, 2000.
36. Burke, LM, Hawley, JA, Jeukendrup, A, Morton, JP, Stellingwerff, T, and Maughan, RJ. Toward a common understanding of diet-exercise strategies to manipulate fuel availability for training and competition preparation in endurance sport. *Int J Sport Nutr Exerc Metab* 28:451-463, 2018.
37. Byrne, B. Deep vein thrombosis prophylaxis: The effectiveness and implications of using below-knee or thigh-length graduated compression stockings. *Heart Lung* 30:277-284, 2001.
38. Byrne, C, Twist, C, and Eston, R. Neuromuscular function after exercise-induced muscle damage: Theoretical and applied implications. *Sports Med* 34:49-69, 2004.
39. Cadegiani, FA, and Kater, CE. Hormonal aspects of overtraining syndrome: A systematic review. *BMC Sports Sci Med Rehabil* 9:14, 2017.
40. Cadegiani, FA, Silva, PHL, Abrao, TCP, and Kater, CE. Novel markers of recovery from overtraining syndrome: The EROS-LONGITUDINAL study. *Int J Sports Physiol Perform* 16:1175-1184, 2021.
41. Cafarelli, E, and Flint, F. The role of massage in preparation for and recovery from exercise: An overview. *Sports Med* 14:1-9, 1992.
42. Caia, J, Kelly, VG, and Halson, SL. The role of sleep in maximising performance in elite athletes. In *Sport, Recovery, and Performance: Interdisciplinary Insights.* Kellmann, M, Beckmann, J, eds. Abingdon: Routledge, Taylor Francis Group, 151-167, 2018.
43. Calleja-Gonzalez, J, Mielgo-Ayuso, J, Ostojic, SM, Jones, MT, Marques-Jimenez, D, Caparros, T, and Terrados, N. Evidence-based post-exercise recovery strategies in rugby: A narrative review. *Phys Sportsmed* 47:137-147, 2019.
44. Carriker, CR. Components of fatigue: Mind and body. *J Strength Cond Res* 31:3170-3176, 2017.
45. Carroll, TJ, Taylor, JL, and Gandevia, SC. Recovery of central and peripheral neuromuscular fatigue after exercise. *J Appl Physiol (1985)* 122:1068-1076, 2017.
46. Cheatham, SW, Kolber, MJ, Cain, M, and Lee, M. The effects of self-myofascial release using a foam roll or roller massager on joint range of motion, muscle recovery, and performance: A systematic review. *Int J Sports Phys Ther* 10:827-838, 2015.
47. Chicharro, JL, Lopez-Mojares, LM, Lucia, A, Perez, M, Alvarez, J, Labanda, P, Calvo, F, and Vaquero, AF. Overtraining parameters in special military units. *Aviat Space Environ Med* 69:562-568, 1998.
48. Chleboun, GS, Howell, JN, Baker, HL, Ballard, TN, Graham, JL, Hallman, HL, Perkins, LE, Schauss, JH, and Conatser, RR. Intermittent pneumatic compression effect on eccentric exercise-induced swelling, stiffness, and strength loss. *Arch Phys Med Rehabil* 76:744-749, 1995.
49. Choi, D, Cole, KJ, Goodpaster, BH, Fink, WJ, and Costill, DL. Effect of passive and active recovery on the resynthesis of muscle glycogen. *Med Sci Sports Exerc* 26:992-996, 1994.
50. Choy, M, and Salbu, RL. Jet lag: Current and potential therapies. *P T* 36:221-231, 2011.
51. Claudino, JG, Cronin, J, Mezencio, B, McMaster, DT, McGuigan, M, Tricoli, V, Amadio, AC, and Serrao, JC. The countermovement jump to monitor neuromuscular status: A meta-analysis. *J Sci Med Sport* 20:397-402, 2017.
52. Cochrane, DJ. Alternating hot and cold water immersion for athlete recovery: A review. *Physical Therapy in Sport* 5:26-32, 2004.
53. Cormack, SJ, Newton, RU, and McGuigan, MR. Neuromuscular and endocrine responses of elite players to an Australian rules football match. *Int J Sports Physiol Perform* 3:359-374, 2008.
54. Costill, DL, Flynn, MG, Kirwan, JP, Houmard, JA, Mitchell, JB, Thomas, R, and Park, SH. Effects of repeated days of intensified training on muscle glycogen and swimming performance. *Med Sci Sports Exerc* 20:249-254, 1988.
55. Costill, DL, Pascoe, DD, Fink, WJ, Robergs, RA, Barr, SI, and Pearson, D. Impaired muscle glycogen resynthesis after eccentric exercise. *J Appl Physiol* 69:46-50, 1990.

56. Costill, DL, Sherman, WM, Fink, WJ, Maresh, C, Witten, M, and Miller, JM. The role of dietary carbohydrates in muscle glycogen resynthesis after strenuous running. *Am J Clin Nutr* 34:1831-1836, 1981.

57. Cote, DJ, Prentice, WE, Jr., Hooker, DN, and Shields, EW. Comparison of three treatment procedures for minimizing ankle sprain swelling. *Phys Ther* 68:1072-1076, 1988.

58. Coyle, EF. Timing and method of increased carbohydrate intake to cope with heavy training, competition and recovery. *J Sports Sci* 9 Spec No:29-51, 1991.

59. Crowe, MJ, O'Connor, D, and Rudd, D. Cold water recovery reduces anaerobic performance. *Int J Sports Med* 28:994-998, 2007.

60. Crowther, F, Sealey, R, Crowe, M, Edwards, A, and Halson, S. Influence of recovery strategies upon performance and perceptions following fatiguing exercise: A randomized controlled trial. *BMC Sports Sci Med Rehabil* 9:25, 2017.

61. Cunanan, AJ, DeWeese, BH, Wagle, JP, Carroll, KM, Sausaman, R, Hornsby, WG, 3rd, Haff, GG, Triplett, NT, Pierce, KC, and Stone, MH. The general adaptation syndrome: A foundation for the concept of periodization. *Sports Med* 48:787-797, 2018.

62. Dantzer, R, Bluthe, RM, Gheusi, G, Cremona, S, Laye, S, Parnet, P, and Kelley, KW. Molecular basis of sickness behavior. *Ann N Y Acad Sci* 856:132-138, 1998.

63. Davies, V, Thompson, KG, and Cooper, SM. The effects of compression garments on recovery. *J Strength Cond Res* 23:1786-1794, 2009.

64. Davis, HL, Alabed, S, and Chico, TJA. Effect of sports massage on performance and recovery: A systematic review and meta-analysis. *BMJ Open Sport Exerc Med* 6:e000614, 2020.

65. Decorte, N, Lafaix, PA, Millet, GY, Wuyam, B, and Verges, S. Central and peripheral fatigue kinetics during exhaustive constant-load cycling. *Scand J Med Sci Sports* 22:381-391, 2012.

66. Dedrick, ME, and Clarkson, PM. The effects of eccentric exercise on motor performance in young and older women. *Eur J Appl Physiol Occup Physiol* 60:183-186, 1990.

67. DeWeese, BH, Gray, HS, Sams, ML, Scruggs, SK, and Serrano, AJ. Revising the definition of periodization: Merging historical principles with modern concerns. *Olympic Coach Magazine* 24:5-19, 2015.

68. Didehdar, D, and Sobhani, S. The effect of cold-water immersion on physical performance. *J Bodyw Mov Ther* 23:258-261, 2019.

69. Dunn, AJ, and Swiergiel, AH. The role of cytokines in infection-related behavior. *Ann N Y Acad Sci* 840:577-585, 1998.

70. Elenkov, IJ, and Chrousos, GP. Stress hormones, Th1/Th2 patterns, pro/anti-inflammatory cytokines and susceptibility to disease. *Trends Endocrinol Metab* 10:359-368, 1999.

71. Enoka, RM. Morphological features and activation patterns of motor units. *J Clin Neurophysiol* 12:538-559, 1995.

72. Enoka, RM, and Duchateau, J. Translating fatigue to human performance. *Med Sci Sports Exerc* 48:2228-2238, 2016.

73. Enoka, RM, and Fuglevand, AJ. Motor unit physiology: Some unresolved issues. *Muscle Nerve* 24:4-17, 2001.

74. Enoka, RM, and Stuart, DG. Neurobiology of muscle fatigue. *J Appl Physiol* 72:1631-1648, 1992.

75. Eston, R, and Peters, D. Effects of cold water immersion on the symptoms of exercise-induced muscle damage. *J Sports Sci* 17:231-238, 1999.

76. Exelmans, L, and Van den Bulck, J. Bedtime mobile phone use and sleep in adults. *Soc Sci Med* 148:93-101, 2016.

77. Fallon, KE. Blood tests in tired elite athletes: Expectations of athletes, coaches and sport science/sports medicine staff. *Br J Sports Med* 41:41-44, 2007.

78. Fiscus, KA, Kaminski, TW, and Powers, ME. Changes in lower-leg blood flow during warm-, cold-, and contrast-water therapy. *Arch Phys Med Rehabil* 86:1404-1410, 2005.

79. Fitts, RH. Cellular mechanisms of muscle fatigue. *Physiol Rev* 74:49-94, 1994.

80. Fitts, RH. The muscular system: Fatigue process. In *ACSM's Advanced Exercise Physiology*. Tipton, CM, ed. Philadelphia, PA: Lippincott, Williams & Wilkins, 178-196, 2006.

81. Fitts, RH. The cross-bridge cycle and skeletal muscle fatigue. *Journal of applied physiology* 104:551-558, 2008.

82. Frohlich, M, Faude, O, Klein, M, Pieter, A, Emrich, E, and Meyer, T. Strength training adaptations after cold-water immersion. *J Strength Cond Res* 28:2628-2633, 2014.

83. Fry, AC. The role of training intensity in resistance exercise overtraining and overreaching. In *Overtraining in Sport*. Kreider, RB, Fry, AC, O'Toole, ML, eds. Champaign, IL: Human Kinetics, 107-127, 1998.

84. Fry, AC, and Kraemer, WJ. Resistance exercise overtraining and overreaching: Neuroendocrine responses. *Sports Med* 23:106-129, 1997.

85. Fry, AC, Kraemer, WJ, van Borselen, F, Lynch, JM, Marsit, JL, Roy, EP, Triplett, NT, and Knuttgen, HG. Performance decrements with high-intensity resistance exercise overtraining. *Med Sci Sports Exerc* 26:1165-1173, 1994.

86. Fry, AC, Webber, JM, Weiss, LW, Fry, MD, and Li, Y. Impaired performance with excessive high-intensity free-weight training. *J Strength Cond Res* 14:54-61, 2000.

87. Fullagar, HH, Duffield, R, Skorski, S, Coutts, AJ, Julian, R, and Meyer, T. Sleep and recovery in team sport: Current sleep-related issues facing professional team-sport athletes. *Int J Sports Physiol Perform* 10:950-957, 2015.

88. Fyfe, JJ, Broatch, JR, Trewin, AJ, Hanson, ED, Argus, CK, Garnham, AP, Halson, SL, Polman, RC, Bishop, DJ, and Petersen, AC. Cold water immersion attenuates anabolic signaling and skeletal muscle fiber hypertrophy, but not strength gain, following whole-body resistance training. *J Appl Physiol (1985)* 127:1403-1418, 2019.

89. Gabbett, TJ. Performance changes following a field conditioning program in junior and senior Rugby League players. *J Strength Cond Res* 20:215-221, 2006.

90. Gabbett, TJ. The training-injury prevention paradox: Should athletes be training smarter and harder? *Br J Sports Med* 50:273-280, 2016.

91. Gabbett, TJ. Workload monitoring and athlete management. In *Advanced Strength and Conditioning: An Evidence-Based Approach*. Turner, A, Comfort, P, eds. Abingdon, Oxon: Routledge, 137-150, 2018.

92. Gabbett, TJ. Debunking the myths about training load, injury and performance: Empirical evidence, hot topics

and recommendations for practitioners. *Br J Sports Med* 54:58-66, 2020.

93. Gabriel, H, Urhausen, A, and Kindermann, W. Mobilization of circulating leucocyte and lymphocyte subpopulations during and after short, anaerobic exercise. *Eur J Appl Physiol* 65:164-170, 1992.

94. Gaesser, GA, and Brooks, GA. Metabolic bases of excess post-exercise oxygen consumption: A review. *Med Sci Sports Exerc* 16:29-43, 1984.

95. Gandevia, SC. Spinal and supraspinal factors in human muscle fatigue. *Physiol Rev* 81:1725-1789, 2001.

96. Gill, ND, Beaven, CM, and Cook, C. Effectiveness of post-match recovery strategies in rugby players. *Br J Sports Med* 40:260-263, 2006.

97. Grandou, C, Wallace, L, Impellizzeri, FM, Allen, NG, and Coutts, AJ. Overtraining in resistance exercise: An exploratory systematic review and methodological appraisal of the literature. *Sports Med* 50:815-828, 2020.

98. Granter, R. Treatments used for musculoskeletal conditions: More choices and more evidence. In *Bruckner and Kan's Clinical Sports Medicine*. Brukner, P, ed. New South Whales, Australia: McGraw Hill Australia, 164-209, 2012.

99. Green, HJ. Mechanisms of muscle fatigue in intense exercise. *J Sports Sci* 15:247-256, 1997.

100. Gulick, DT, Kimura, IF, Sitler, M, Paolone, A, and Kelly, JD. Various treatment techniques on signs and symptoms of delayed onset muscle soreness. *J Athl Train* 31:145-152, 1996.

101. Gupta, L, Morgan, K, and Gilchrist, S. Does elite sport degrade sleep quality? A systematic review. *Sports Med* 47:1317-1333, 2017.

102. Haff, GG, Jackson, JR, Kawamori, N, Carlock, JM, Hartman, MJ, Kilgore, JL, Morris, RT, Ramsey, MW, Sands, WA, and Stone, MH. Force-time curve characteristics and hormonal alterations during an eleven-week training period in elite women weightlifters. *J Strength Cond Res* 22:433-446, 2008.

103. Haff, GG, Stone, MH, O'Bryant, HS, Harman, E, Dinan, CN, Johnson, R, and Han, KH. Force-time dependent characteristics of dynamic and isometric muscle actions. *J Strength Cond Res* 11:269-272, 1997.

104. Hahn, AG. Training, recovery and overtraining: The role of the autonomic nervous system. *Sports Coach*:29-30, 1994.

105. Halson, SL. Does the time frame between exercise influence the effectiveness of hydrotherapy for recovery? *Int J Sports Physiol Perform* 6:147-159, 2011.

106. Halson, SL. Monitoring training load to understand fatigue in athletes. *Sports Med* 44 Suppl 2:S139-147, 2014.

107. Halson, SL. Sleep monitoring in athletes: Motivation, methods, miscalculations and why it matters. *Sports Med* 49:1487-1497, 2019.

108. Halson, SL, Bartram, J, West, N, Stephens, J, Argus, CK, Driller, MW, Sargent, C, Lastella, M, Hopkins, WG, and Martin, DT. Does hydrotherapy help or hinder adaptation to training in competitive cyclists? *Med Sci Sports Exerc* 46:1631-1639, 2014.

109. Halson, SL, Bridge, MW, Meeusen, R, Busschaert, B, Gleeson, M, Jones, DA, and Jeukendrup, AE. Time course of performance changes and fatigue markers during intensified training in trained cyclists. *J Appl Physiol* 93:947-956, 2002.

110. Halson, SL, Burke, LM, and Pearce, J. Nutrition for travel: From jetlag to catering. *Int J Sport Nutr Exerc Metab* 29:228-235, 2019.

111. Halson, SL, and Jeukendrup, AE. Does overtraining exist? An analysis of overreaching and overtraining research. *Sports Med* 34:967-981, 2004.

112. Haun, CT, Roberts, MD, Romero, MA, Osburn, SC, Mobley, CB, Anderson, RG, Goodlett, MD, Pascoe, DD, and Martin, JS. Does external pneumatic compression treatment between bouts of overreaching resistance training sessions exert differential effects on molecular signaling and performance-related variables compared to passive recovery? An exploratory study. *PLoS One* 12:e0180429, 2017.

113. Hausswirth, C, Louis, J, Bieuzen, F, Pournot, H, Fournier, J, Filliard, JR, and Brisswalter, J. Effects of whole-body cryotherapy vs. far-infrared vs. passive modalities on recovery from exercise-induced muscle damage in highly-trained runners. *PLoS One* 6:e27749, 2011.

114. Hausswirth, C, Schaal, K, Le Meur, Y, Bieuzen, F, Filliard, JR, Volondat, M, and Louis, J. Parasympathetic activity and blood catecholamine responses following a single partial-body cryostimulation and a whole-body cryostimulation. *PLoS One* 8:e72658, 2013.

115. Heishman, AD, Daub, BD, Miller, RM, Freitas, EDS, and Bemben, MG. Monitoring external training loads and neuromuscular performance for Division I basketball players over the preseason. *J Sports Sci Med* 19:204-212, 2020.

116. Hemmings, B. Psychological and immunological effects of massage after sport. *Br J Ther Rehabil* 7:516-519, 2000.

117. Hemmings, B, Smith, M, Graydon, J, and Dyson, R. Effects of massage on physiological restoration, perceived recovery, and repeated sports performance. *Br J Sports Med* 34:109-114, 2000.

118. Hettchen, M, Glockler, K, von Stengel, S, Piechele, A, Lotzerich, H, Kohl, M, and Kemmler, W. Effects of compression tights on recovery parameters after exercise induced muscle damage: A randomized controlled crossover study. *Evid Based Complement Alternat Med* 2019:5698460, 2019.

119. Higgins, D, and Kaminski, TW. Contrast therapy does not cause fluctuations in human gastrocnemius intramuscular temperature. *J Athl Train* 33:336-340, 1998.

120. Higgins, TR, Heazlewood, IT, and Climstein, M. A random control trial of contrast baths and ice baths for recovery during competition in U/20 Rugby Union. *J Strength Cond Res* 25:1046-1051, 2011.

121. Hill, J, Howatson, G, van Someren, K, Leeder, J, and Pedlar, C. Compression garments and recovery from exercise-induced muscle damage: A meta-analysis. *Br J Sports Med* 48:1340-1346, 2014.

122. Horgan, BG, Halson, SL, Drinkwater, EJ, West, NP, Tee, N, Alcock, RD, Chapman, DW, and Haff, GG. No effect of repeated post-resistance exercise cold or hot water immersion on in-season body composition and performance responses in academy rugby players: A randomised controlled cross-over design. *Eur J Appl Physiol* 123:351-359, 2023.

123. Horgan, BG, West, NP, Tee, N, Drinkwater, EJ, Halson, SL, Vider, J, Fonda, CJ, Haff, GG, and Chapman, DW. Acute inflammatory, anthropometric, and perceptual (muscle soreness) effects of postresistance exercise water immersion in junior international and subelite male volleyball athletes. *J Strength Cond Res* 36:3473-3484, 2022.

124. Hornsby, WG, Gentles, JA, MacDonald, CJ, Mizuguchi, S, Ramsey, MW, and Stone, MH. Maximum strength, rate of force development, jump height, and peak power alterations in weightlifters across five months of training. *Sports* 5:78, 2017.

125. Hornsby, WG, Haff, GG, Suarez, DG, Ramsey, MW, Triplett, NT, Hardee, JP, Stone, ME, and Stone, MH. Alterations in adiponectin, leptin, resistin, testosterone, and cortisol across eleven weeks of training among Division One collegiate throwers: A preliminary study. *J Funct Morphol Kinesiol* 5:44, 2020.

126. Howatson, G, Gaze, D, and van Someren, KA. The efficacy of ice massage in the treatment of exercise-induced muscle damage. *Scand J Med Sci Sports* 15:416-422, 2005.

127. Hung, TC, Liao, YH, Tsai, YS, Ferguson-Stegall, L, Kuo, CH, and Chen, CY. Hot water bathing impairs training adaptation in elite teen archers. *Chin J Physiol* 61:118-123, 2018.

128. Issurin, V. Block periodization versus traditional training theory: A review. *J Sports Med Phys Fitness* 48:65-75, 2008.

129. Ivy, J, and Portman, R. NTS growth phase. In *Nutrient Timing*. North Bergen, NJ: Basic Health Publications, 67-82, 2004.

130. Janse van Rensburg, DCC, Jansen van Rensburg, A, Fowler, P, Fullagar, H, Stevens, D, Halson, S, Bender, A, Vincent, G, Claassen-Smithers, A, Dunican, I, Roach, GD, Sargent, C, Lastella, M, and Cronje, T. How to manage travel fatigue and jet lag in athletes? A systematic review of interventions. *Br J Sports Med* 54:960-968, 2020.

131. Jaworska, J, Rodziewicz-Flis, E, Kortas, J, Kozłowska, M, Micielska, K, Babińska, A, Laskowski, R, Lombardi, G, and Ziemann, E. Short-term resistance training supported by whole-body cryostimulation induced a decrease in myostatin concentration and an increase in isokinetic muscle strength. *Int J Environ Res Public Health* 17:5496, 2020.

132. Jo, E, Judelson, DA, Brown, LE, Coburn, JW, and Dabbs, NC. Influence of recovery duration after a potentiating stimulus on muscular power in recreationally trained individuals. *J Strength Cond Res* 24:343-347, 2010.

133. Jones, JJ, Kirschen, GW, Kancharla, S, and Hale, LJSH. Association between late-night tweeting and next-day game performance among professional basketball players. *Sleep Health* 5:68-71, 2019.

134. Jones, NA, and Field, T. Massage and music therapies attenuate frontal EEG asymmetry in depressed adolescents. *Adolescence* 34:529-534, 1999.

135. Juliff, LE, Halson, SL, Bonetti, DL, Versey, NG, Driller, MW, and Peiffer, JJ. Influence of contrast shower and water immersion on recovery in elite netballers. *J Strength Cond Res* 28:2353-2358, 2014.

136. Jurimae, J, Maestu, J, Jurimae, T, Mangus, B, and von Duvillard, SP. Peripheral signals of energy homeostasis as possible markers of training stress in athletes: A review. *Metabolism* 60:335-350, 2011.

137. Kay, D, and Marino, FE. Fluid ingestion and exercise hyperthermia: Implications for performance, thermoregulation, metabolism and the development of fatigue. *J Sports Sci* 18:71-82, 2000.

138. Kay, D, Marino, FE, Cannon, J, St Clair Gibson, A, Lambert, MI, and Noakes, TD. Evidence for neuromuscular fatigue during high-intensity cycling in warm, humid conditions. *Eur J Appl Physiol* 84:115-121, 2001.

139. Kayser, B. Exercise starts and ends in the brain. *Eur J Appl Physiol* 90:411-419, 2003.

140. Kellmann, M. Psychological assessment of under recovery. In *Enhancing Recovery: Preventing Underperformance in Athletes*. Kellmann, M, ed. Champaign, IL: Human Kinetics, 37-55, 2002.

141. Kellmann, M. Underrecovery and overtraining: Different concepts—similar impact? In *Enhancing Recovery: Preventing Underperformance in Athletes*. Kellmann, M, ed. Champaign, IL: Human Kinetics, 3-24, 2002.

142. Kellmann, M, Bertollo, M, Bosquet, L, Brink, M, Coutts, A, Duffield, R, Erlacher, D, Halson, S, Hecksteden, A, Heidari, J, Meeusen, R, Mujika, I, Robazza, C, Skorski, S, Venter, R, and Beckmann, J. Recovery and performance in sport: Consensus statement. *Int J Sports Physiol Perform* 13:240-245, 2018.

143. Kenttä, G, and Hassmén, P. Overtraining and recovery: A conceptual model. *Sports Med* 26:1-16, 1998.

144. Kenttä, G, Hassmén, P, and Raglin, JS. Training practices and overtraining syndrome in Swedish age-group athletes. *Int J Sports Med* 22:460-465, 2001.

145. Kerksick, CM, Arent, S, Schoenfeld, BJ, Stout, JR, Campbell, B, Wilborn, CD, Taylor, L, Kalman, D, Smith-Ryan, AE, Kreider, RB, Willoughby, D, Arciero, PJ, VanDusseldorp, TA, Ormsbee, MJ, Wildman, R, Greenwood, M, Ziegenfuss, TN, Aragon, AA, and Antonio, J. International Society of Sports Nutrition position stand: Nutrient timing. *J Int Soc Sports Nutr* 14:33, 2017.

146. Keyser, RE. Peripheral fatigue: High-energy phosphates and hydrogen ions. *PM R* 2:347-358, 2010.

147. Khosla, SS, and DuBois, AB. Fluid shifts during initial phase of immersion diuresis in man. *J Appl Physiol* 46:703-708, 1979.

148. King, M, and Duffield, R. The effects of recovery interventions on consecutive days of intermittent sprint exercise. *J Strength Cond Res* 23:1795-1802, 2009.

149. Kluger, BM, Krupp, LB, and Enoka, RM. Fatigue and fatigability in neurologic illnesses: Proposal for a unified taxonomy. *Neurology* 80:409-416, 2013.

150. Ko, DS, Lerner, R, Klose, G, and Cosimi, AB. Effective treatment of lymphedema of the extremities. *Arch Surg* 133:452-458, 1998.

151. Kölling, S, Duffield, R, Erlacher, D, Venter, R, and Halson, SL. Sleep-related issues for recovery and performance in athletes. *Int J Sports Physiol Perform* 14:144-148, 2019.

152. Kraemer, WJ, Bush, JA, Wickham, RB, Denegar, CR, Gomez, AL, Gotshalk, LA, Duncan, ND, Volek, JS, Newton, RU, and Putukian, M. Continuous compression as an effective therapeutic intervention in treating eccentric-exercise-induced muscle soreness. *J Sport Rehabil* 10:11-23, 2001.

153. Kraemer, WJ, Bush, JA, Wickham, RB, Denegar, CR, Gomez, AL, Gotshalk, LA, Duncan, ND, Volek, JS, Putukian, M, and Sebastianelli, WJ. Influence of compression therapy on symptoms following soft tissue injury from maximal eccentric exercise. *J Orthop Sports Phys Ther* 31:282-290, 2001.

154. Kraemer, WJ, Flanagan, SD, Comstock, BA, Fragala, MS, Earp, JE, Dunn-Lewis, C, Ho, JY, Thomas, GA, Solomon-Hill, G, Penwell, ZR, Powell, MD, Wolf, MR, Volek, JS, Denegar, CR, and Maresh, CM. Effects of a whole body compression garment on markers of recovery after a heavy resistance workout in men and women. *J Strength Cond Res* 24:804-814, 2010.

155. Kreider, RB, Kalman, DS, Antonio, J, Ziegenfuss, TN, Wildman, R, Collins, R, Candow, DG, Kleiner, SM, Almada, AL, and Lopez, HL. International Society of Sports Nutrition position stand: Safety and efficacy of creatine supplementation in exercise, sport, and medicine. *J Int Soc Sports Nutr* 14:18, 2017.

156. Kruger, M, de Marees, M, Dittmar, KH, Sperlich, B, and Mester, J. Whole-body cryotherapy's enhancement of acute recovery of running performance in well-trained athletes. *Int J Sports Physiol Perform* 10:605-612, 2015.

157. Kuipers, H, and Keizer, HA. Overtraining in elite athletes: Review and directions for the future. *Sports Med* 6:79-92, 1988.

158. Kuligowski, LA, Lephart, SM, Giannantonio, FP, and Blanc, RO. Effect of whirlpool therapy on the signs and symptoms of delayed-onset muscle soreness. *J Athl Train* 33:222-228, 1998.

159. Kurz, T. Natural means of recovery. In *Science of Sports Training*. 2nd ed. Island Pond, VT: Stadion Publishing, 121-134, 2001.

160. LaForgia, J, Withers, RT, and Gore, CJ. Effects of exercise intensity and duration on the excess post-exercise oxygen consumption. *J Sports Sci* 24:1247-1264, 2006.

161. Lanier, AB. Use of nonsteroidal anti-inflammatory drugs following exercise-induced muscle injury. *Sports Med* 33:177-186, 2003.

162. Lastella, M, Roach, GD, Halson, SL, and Sargent, C. Sleep/wake behaviours of elite athletes from individual and team sports. *Eur J Sport Sci*:1-7, 2014.

163. Laukkanen, JA, Laukkanen, T, and Kunutsor, SK. Cardiovascular and other health benefits of sauna bathing: A review of the evidence. *Mayo Clin Proc* 93:1111-1121, 2018.

164. Leeder, J, Gissane, C, van Someren, K, Gregson, W, and Howatson, G. Cold water immersion and recovery from strenuous exercise: A meta-analysis. *Br J Sports Med* 46:233-240, 2012.

165. Lehmann, M, Baumgartl, P, Wiesenack, C, Seidel, A, Baumann, H, Fischer, S, Spori, U, Gendrisch, G, Kaminski, R, and Keul, J. Training-overtraining: Influence of a defined increase in training volume vs training intensity on performance, catecholamines and some metabolic parameters in experienced middle- and long-distance runners. *Eur J Appl Physiol Occup Physiol* 64:169-177., 1992.

166. Lehmann, M, Gastmann, U, Petersen, KG, Bachl, N, Seidel, A, Khalaf, AN, Fischer, S, and Keul, J. Training-overtraining: performance, and hormone levels, after a defined increase in training volume versus intensity in experienced middle- and long-distance runners. *Br J Sports Med* 26:233-242., 1992.

167. Leivadi, S, Hernandez-Reif, M, Field, T, O'Rourke, M, D'Arienzo, S, Lewis, D, del Pino, N, Schanberg, S, and Kuhn, C. Massage therapy and relaxation effects on university dance students. *J Dance Med Sci* 3:108-112, 1999.

168. Lepers, R, Maffiuletti, NA, Rochette, L, Brugniaux, J, and Millet, GY. Neuromuscular fatigue during a long-duration cycling exercise. *J Appl Physiol (1985)* 92:1487-1493, 2002.

169. Maier, SF, and Watkins, LR. Cytokines for psychologists: Implications of bidirectional immune-to-brain communication for understanding behavior, mood, and cognition. *Psychol Rev* 105:83-107, 1998.

170. Malone, S, Hughes, B, Doran, DA, Collins, K, and Gabbett, TJ. Can the workload-injury relationship be moderated by improved strength, speed and repeated-sprint qualities? *J Sci Med Sport* 22:29-34, 2019.

171. Malta, ES, Dutra, YM, Broatch, JR, Bishop, DJ, and Zagatto, AM. The effects of regular cold-water immersion use on training-induced changes in strength and endurance performance: A systematic review with meta-analysis. *Sports Med* 51:161-174, 2021.

172. Mancinelli, CA, Davis, DS, Aboulhosn, L, Brady, M, Eisenhofer, J, and Foutty, S. The effects of massage on delayed onset muscle soreness and physical performance in female college athletes. *Phys Ther Sport* 7:5-13, 2006.

173. Marchetti, B, Gallo, F, Farinella, Z, Tirolo, C, Testa, N, Romeo, C, and Morale, MC. Luteinizing hormone-releasing hormone is a primary signaling molecule in the neuroimmune network. *Ann N Y Acad Sci* 840:205-248, 1998.

174. Marques-Jimenez, D, Calleja-Gonzalez, J, Arratibel, I, Delextrat, A, and Terrados, N. Are compression garments effective for the recovery of exercise-induced muscle damage? A systematic review with meta-analysis. *Physiol Behav* 153:133-148, 2016.

175. Martin, JS, Kephart, WC, Haun, CT, McCloskey, AE, Shake, JJ, Mobley, CB, Goodlett, MD, Kavazis, A, Pascoe, DD, Zhang, L, and Roberts, MD. Impact of external pneumatic compression target inflation pressure on transcriptome-wide RNA expression in skeletal muscle. *Physiol Rep* 4, 2016.

176. Martin, NA, Zoeller, RF, Robertson, RJ, and Lephart, SM. The comparative effects of sports massage, active recovery, and rest in promoting blood lactate clearance after supramaximal leg exercise. *J Athl Train* 33:30-35, 1998.

177. Martinez-Guardado, I, Rojas-Valverde, D, Gutierrez-Vargas, R, Ugalde Ramirez, A, Gutierrez-Vargas, JC, and Sanchez-Urena, B. Intermittent pneumatic compression and cold water immersion effects on physiological and perceptual recovery during multi-sports international championship. *J Funct Morphol Kinesiol* 5, 2020.

178. Matos, NF, Winsley, RJ, and Williams, CA. Prevalence of nonfunctional overreaching/overtraining in young English athletes. *Med Sci Sports Exerc* 43:1287-1294, 2011.

179. Mcardle, WD, Katch, FI, and Katch, VL. Energy Transfer During Exercise. In *Exercise Physiology: Nutrition, Energy, and Human Performance*. 7th ed. Baltimore, MD: Lippincot, Williams, Wilkins, 161-176, 2015.

180. McGorm, H, Roberts, LA, Coombes, JS, and Peake, JM. Turning up the heat: An evaluation of the evidence for heating to promote exercise recovery, muscle rehabilitation and adaptation. *Sports Med* 48:1311-1328, 2018.

181. McMorris, T, Barwood, M, and Corbett, J. Central fatigue theory and endurance exercise: Toward an interoceptive model. *Neurosci Biobehav Rev* 93:93-107, 2018.

182. Meeusen, R, and De Pauw, K. Overtraining syndrome. In *Recovery for Performance in Sport*. Hausswirth, C, Mujika, I, eds. Champaign, IL: Human Kinetics, 9-20, 2013.

183. Meeusen, R, and De Pauw, K. Overtraining—what do we know? In *Sport, Recovery, and Performance: Interdisciplinary Insights*. Kellmann, M, Beckmann, J, eds. Abingdon, Oxon: Routledge, 51-62, 2018.

184. Meeusen, R, Duclos, M, Foster, C, Fry, A, Gleeson, M, Nieman, D, Raglin, J, Rietjens, G, Steinacker, J, Urhausen, A, European College of Sport Science, and American College of Sports Medicine. Prevention, diagnosis, and treatment of the overtraining syndrome: Joint consensus statement of the European College of Sport Science and the American College of Sports Medicine. *Med Sci Sports Exerc* 45:186-205, 2013.

185. Meeusen, R, Duclos, M, Gleeson, M, Rietjens, G, Steinacker, JM, and Urhausen, A. Prevention, diagnosis and treatment of overtraining syndrome. *Eur J Sport Science* 6:1-14, 2006.

186. Meeusen, R, Piacentini, MF, Busschaert, B, Buyse, L, De Schutter, G, and Stray-Gundersen, J. Hormonal responses in athletes: The use of a two bout exercise protocol to detect subtle differences in (over)training status. *Eur J Appl Physiol* 91:140-146, 2004.

187. Mero, A, Tornberg, J, Mäntykoski, M, and Puurtinen, R. Effects of far-infrared sauna bathing on recovery from strength and endurance training sessions in men. *Springerplus* 4:321, 2015.

188. Mika, A, Mika, P, Fernhall, B, and Unnithan, VB. Comparison of recovery strategies on muscle performance after fatiguing exercise. *Am J Phys Med Rehabil* 86:474-481, 2007.

189. Millet, GY, and Lepers, R. Alterations of neuromuscular function after prolonged running, cycling and skiing exercises. *Sports Med* 34:105-116, 2004.

190. Monedero, J, and Donne, B. Effect of recovery interventions on lactate removal and subsequent performance. *Int J Sports Med* 21:593-597, 2000.

191. Moore, CA, and Fry, AC. Nonfunctional overreaching during off-season training for skill position players in collegiate American football. *J Strength Cond Res* 21:793-800, 2007.

192. Morel, PA, and Oriss, TB. Crossregulation between Th1 and Th2 cells. *Crit Rev Immunol* 18:275-303, 1998.

193. Morgan, W, O'Connor, P, Sparling, P, and Pate, R. Psychological characterization of the elite female distance runner. *Int J Sports Med* 8:S124-S131, 1987.

194. Morgan, WP, Brown, DR, Raglin, JS, O'Connor, PJ, and Ellickson, KA. Psychological monitoring of overtraining and staleness. *Br J Sports Med* 21:107-114, 1987.

195. Morgan, WP, O'Connor, PJ, Ellickson, KA, and Bradley, PW. Personality structure, mood states, and performance in elite male distance runners. *Int J Sport Psychol* 19:247-263, 1988.

196. Morton, RH. Contrast water immersion hastens plasma lactate decrease after intense anaerobic exercise. *J Sci Med Sport* 10:467-470, 2007.

197. Mujika, I, Halson, S, Burke, L, Balagué, G, and Farrow, D. An integrated, multifactorial approach to periodization for optimal performance in individual and team sports. *Int J Sports Physiol Perform* 13:538-561, 2018.

198. Myrer, JW, Draper, DO, and Durrant, E. Contrast therapy and intramuscular temperature in the human leg. *J Athl Train* 29:318-322, 1994.

199. Nedelec, M, McCall, A, Carling, C, Legall, F, Berthoin, S, and Dupont, G. Recovery in soccer: Part I—post-match fatigue and time course of recovery. *Sports Med* 42:997-1015, 2012.

200. Nederhof, E, Lemmink, KA, Visscher, C, Meeusen, R, and Mulder, T. Psychomotor speed: Possibly a new marker for overtraining syndrome. *Sports Med* 36:817-828, 2006.

201. Nemet, D, Meckel, Y, Bar-Sela, S, Zaldivar, F, Cooper, DM, and Eliakim, A. Effect of local cold-pack application on systemic anabolic and inflammatory response to sprint-interval training: A prospective comparative trial. *Eur J Appl Physiol* 107:411-417, 2009.

202. Nilsson, S. Overtraining. In *An Update on Sports Medicine: Proceedings From the Second Scandinavian Conference on Sports Medicine, Soria Maria, Oslo Norway, March 9-15*. Maehlum, S, Nilsson, S, Renstrom, P, eds. Oslo, Norway: Danish and Norwegian Sports Medicine Association, Swedish Society of Sports Medicine, 97-104, 1986.

203. Noakes, TD. Physiological models to understand exercise fatigue and the adaptations that predict or enhance athletic performance. *Scand J Med Sci Sports* 10:123-145, 2000.

204. Oliver, JL, and Harrison, CB. Aerobic and anaerobic training for young athletes. In *Strength and Conditioning for Young Athletes: Science and Application*. 2nd ed. Lloyd, R, Oliver, JL, eds. New York: Routledge, 248-264, 2020.

205. Ortenblad, N, Nielsen, J, Saltin, B, and Holmberg, HC. Role of glycogen availability in sarcoplasmic reticulum Ca2+ kinetics in human skeletal muscle. *J Physiol* 589:711-725, 2011.

206. Partridge, EM, Cooke, J, McKune, A, and Pyne, DB. Whole-body cryotherapy: Potential to enhance athlete preparation for competition? *Front Physiol* 10, 2019.

207. Peacock, CA, Krein, DD, Silver, TA, Sanders, GJ, and KA, VONC. An acute bout of self-myofascial release in the form of foam rolling improves performance testing. *Int J Exerc Sci* 7:202-211, 2014.

208. Pearcey, GE, Bradbury-Squires, DJ, Kawamoto, JE, Drinkwater, EJ, Behm, DG, and Button, DC. Foam rolling for delayed-onset muscle soreness and recovery of dynamic performance measures. *J Athl Train* 50:5-13, 2015.

209. Pinniger, GJ, Steele, JR, and Groeller, H. Does fatigue induced by repeated dynamic efforts affect hamstring muscle function? *Med Sci Sports Exerc* 32:647-653, 2000.

210. Piras, A, Campa, F, Toselli, S, Di Michele, R, and Raffi, M. Physiological responses to partial-body cryotherapy performed during a concurrent strength and endurance session. *Appl Physiol Nutr Metab* 44:59-65, 2019.

211. Pires, FO, Lima-Silva, AE, Bertuzzi, R, Casarini, DH, Kiss, MA, Lambert, MI, and Noakes, TD. The influence of peripheral afferent signals on the rating of perceived exertion and time to exhaustion during exercise at different intensities. *Psychophysiology* 48:1284-1290, 2011.

212. Plisk, SS, and Stone, MH. Periodization strategies. *Strength and Cond J* 25:19-37, 2003.

213. Poppendieck, W, Faude, O, Wegmann, M, and Meyer, T. Cooling and performance recovery of trained athletes: A meta-analytical review. *Int J Sports Physiol Perform* 8:227-242, 2013.

214. Poppendieck, W, Wegmann, M, Ferrauti, A, Kellmann, M, Pfeiffer, M, and Meyer, T. Massage and performance recovery: A meta-analytical review. *Sports Med* 46:183-204, 2016.

215. Poppendieck, W, Wegmann, M, Hecksteden, A, Darup, A, Schimpchen, J, Skorski, S, Ferrauti, A, Kellmann, M, Pfeiffer, M, and Meyer, T. Does cold-water immersion after strength training attenuate training adaptation? *Int J Sports Physiol Perform* 16:304-310, 2020.

216. Pournot, H, Bieuzen, F, Duffield, R, Lepretre, PM, Cozzolino, C, and Hausswirth, C. Short term effects of various water immersions on recovery from exhaustive intermittent exercise. *Eur J Appl Physiol* 111:1287-1295, 2011.

217. Powers, SK, and Howley, ET. Exercise metabolism. In *Exercise Physiology: Theory and Application to Fitness and Performance.* 5th ed. Sydney, Australia: McGraw Hill, 64-83, 2014.

218. Qu, C, Wu, Z, Xu, M, Qin, F, Dong, Y, Wang, Z, and Zhao, J. Cryotherapy models and timing-sequence recovery of exercise-induced muscle damage in middle- and long-distance runners. *J Athl Train* 55:329-335, 2020.

219. Raglin, J, and Wilson, G. Overtraining and staleness in athletes. In *Emotions in Sports.* Hanin, YL, ed. Champaign, IL: Human Kinetics, 191-207, 200.

220. Ragupathi, D, Ibrahim, N, Tan, KA, and Andrew, BN. Relations of bedtime mobile phone use to cognitive functioning, academic performance, and sleep quality in undergraduate students. *Int J Environ Res Public Health* 17, 2020.

221. Ratel, S, Duche, P, and Bedu, M. Effect of recovery duration on the time course of maximal power during high intensity intermittent exercise in children and adults. *Sci & Sports* 16:40-42, 2001.

222. Reilly, T, and Brooks, GA. Exercise and the circadian variation in body temperature measures. *Int J Sports Med* 7:358-362, 1986.

223. Reilly, T, Cable, NT, and Dowzer, CN. The efficacy of deep-water running. In *Contemporary Ergonomics.* McCabe, PT, ed. London: Taylor & Francis, 162-166, 2002.

224. Reilly, T, Drust, B, and Clarke, N. Muscle fatigue during football match-play. *Sports Med* 38:357-367, 2008.

225. Reilly, T, and Ekblom, B. The use of recovery methods post-exercise. *J Sports Sci* 23:619-627, 2005.

226. Reilly, T, and Rigby, M. Effect of an active warm-down following competitive soccer. In *Science and Football IV.* Spinks, W, Reilly, T, Murphy, A, eds. London: Routledge, 226-229, 2002.

227. Reilly, T, Waterhouse, J, and Edwards, B. Jet lag and air travel: Implications for performance. *Clin Sports Med* 24:367-380, 2005.

228. Rexilius, SJ, Mundt, C, Erickson Megel, M, and Agrawal, S. Therapeutic effects of massage therapy and handling touch on caregivers of patients undergoing autologous hematopoietic stem cell transplant. *Oncol Nurs Forum* 29:E35-E44, 2002.

229. Rey, E, Padrón-Cabo, A, Barcala-Furelos, R, Casamichana, D, and Romo-Pérez, V. Practical active and passive recovery strategies for soccer players. *Strength Cond J* 40:45-57, 2018.

230. Rey, E, Padrón-Cabo, A, Costa, PB, and Barcala-Furelos, R. Effects of foam rolling as a recovery tool in professional soccer players. *J Strength Cond Res* 33:2194-2201, 2019.

231. Ribeiro, J, Sarmento, H, Silva, AF, and Clemente, FM. Practical postexercise recovery strategies in male adult professional soccer players: A systematic review. *Strength Cond J* 43:7-22, 2021.

232. Rice, SM, Purcell, R, De Silva, S, Mawren, D, McGorry, PD, and Parker, AG. The mental health of elite athletes: A narrative systematic review. *Sports Med* 46:1333-1353, 2016.

233. Richard, NA, and Koehle, MS. Optimizing recovery to support multi-evening cycling competition performance. *Eur J Sport Sci* 19:811-823, 2019.

234. Rietjens, GJ, Kuipers, H, Adam, JJ, Saris, WH, van Breda, E, van Hamont, D, and Keizer, HA. Physiological, biochemical and psychological markers of strenuous training-induced fatigue. *Int J Sports Med* 26:16-26, 2005.

235. Rissanen, JA, Häkkinen, A, Laukkanen, J, Kraemer, WJ, and Häkkinen, K. Acute neuromuscular and hormonal responses to different exercise loadings followed by a sauna. *J Strength Cond Res* 34:313-322, 2020.

236. Roberts, LA, Raastad, T, Markworth, JF, Figueiredo, VC, Egner, IM, Shield, A, Cameron-Smith, D, Coombes, JS, and Peake, JM. Post-exercise cold water immersion attenuates acute anabolic signaling and long-term adaptations in muscle to strength training. *J Physiol* 593:4285-4301, 2015.

237. Robertson, CV, and Marino, FE. A role for the prefrontal cortex in exercise tolerance and termination. *J Appl Physiol (1985)* 120:464-466, 2016.

238. Rogalski, B, Dawson, B, Heasman, J, and Gabbett, TJ. Training and game loads and injury risk in elite Australian footballers. *J Sci Med Sport* 16:499-503, 2013.

239. Romagnani, S. Development of Th 1- or Th 2-dominated immune responses: What about the polarizing signals? *Int J Clin Lab Res* 26:83-98, 1996.

240. Romyn, G, Robey, E, Dimmock, JA, Halson, SL, and Peeling, P. Sleep, anxiety and electronic device use by athletes in the training and competition environments. *Eur J Sport Sci* 16:301-308, 2016.

241. Rose, C, Edwards, KM, Siegler, J, Graham, K, and Caillaud, C. Whole-body cryotherapy as a recovery technique after exercise: A review of the literature. *Int J Sports Med* 38:1049-1060, 2017.

242. Roth, SM, Martel, GF, Ivey, FM, Lemmer, JT, Metter, EJ, Hurley, BF, and Rogers, MA. High-volume, heavy-resistance strength training and muscle damage in young and older women. *J Appl Physiol* 88:1112-1118, 2000.

243. Rutkove, SB. Effects of temperature on neuromuscular electrophysiology. *Muscle Nerve* 24:867-882, 2001.

244. Samuels, C. Sleep, recovery, and performance: The new frontier in high-performance athletics. *Phys Med Rehabil Clin N Am* 20:149-159, ix, 2009.

245. Samuels, CH. Jet lag and travel fatigue: A comprehensive management plan for sport medicine physicians and high-performance support teams. *Clin J Sport Med* 22:268-273, 2012.

246. Sanchez-Medina, L, and Gonzalez-Badillo, JJ. Velocity loss as an indicator of neuromuscular fatigue during resistance training. *Med Sci Sports Exerc* 43:1725-1734, 2011.

247. Sands, WA, McNeal, JR, Murray, SR, and Stone, MH. Dynamic compression enhances pressure-to-pain threshold in elite athlete recovery: exploratory study. *J Strength Cond Res* 29:1263-1272, 2015.

248. Sands, WA, Murray, MB, Murray, SR, McNeal, JR, Mizuguchi, S, Sato, K, and Stone, MH. Peristaltic pulse dynamic compression of the lower extremity enhances flexibility. *J Strength Cond Res* 28:1058-1064, 2014.

249. Sargent, C, Lastella, M, Halson, SL, and Roach, GD. The impact of training schedules on the sleep and fatigue of elite athletes. *Chronobiol Int* 31:1160-1168, 2014.

250. Schafer, LU, Hayes, M, and Dekerle, J. The magnitude of neuromuscular fatigue is not intensity dependent when cycling above critical power but relates to aerobic and anaerobic capacities. *Exp Physiol* 104:209-219, 2019.

251. Schimpchen, J, Wagner, M, Ferrauti, A, Kellmann, M, Pfeiffer, M, and Meyer, T. Can cold water immersion enhance recovery in elite Olympic weightlifters? An individualized perspective. *J Strength Cond Res* 31:1569-1576, 2017.

252. Schniepp, J, Campbell, TS, Powell, KL, and Pincivero, DM. The effects of cold-water immersion on power output and heart rate in elite cyclists. *J Strength Cond Res* 16:561-566, 2002.

253. Schobitz, B, Reul, JM, and Holsboer, F. The role of the hypothalamic-pituitary-adrenocortical system during inflammatory conditions. *Crit Rev Neurobiol* 8:263-291, 1994.

254. Scoon, GS, Hopkins, WG, Mayhew, S, and Cotter, JD. Effect of post-exercise sauna bathing on the endurance performance of competitive male runners. *J Sci Med Sport* 10:259-262, 2007.

255. Seitz, L, Saez de Villarreal, E, and Haff, GG. The temporal profile of postactivation potentiation is related to strength level. *J Strength Cond Res* 28:706-715, 2014.

256. Selsby, JT, Rother, S, Tsuda, S, Pracash, O, Quindry, J, and Dodd, SL. Intermittent hyperthermia enhances skeletal muscle regrowth and attenuates oxidative damage following reloading. *J Appl Physiol (1985)* 102:1702-1707, 2007.

257. Shimokochi, Y, Kuwano, S, Yamaguchi, T, Abutani, H, and Shima, N. Effects of wearing a compression garment during night sleep on recovery from high-intensity eccentric-concentric quadriceps muscle fatigue. *J Strength Cond Res* 31:2816-2824, 2017.

258. Shiraishi, M, Schou, M, Gybel, M, Christensen, NJ, and Norsk, P. Comparison of acute cardiovascular responses to water immersion and head-down tilt in humans. *J Appl Physiol* 92:264-268, 2002.

259. Siff, MC, and Verkhoshansky, YU. Designing sport specific strength programmes. In *Supertraining*. 4th ed. Denver, CO: Supertraining International, 411-452, 1999.

260. Skorski, S, Mujika, I, Bosquet, L, Meeusen, R, Coutts, AJ, and Meyer, T. The temporal relationship between exercise, recovery processes, and changes in performance. *Int J Sports Physiol Perform* 14:1015-1021, 2019.

261. Skorski, S, Schimpchen, J, Pfeiffer, M, Ferrauti, A, Kellmann, M, and Meyer, T. Effects of postexercise sauna bathing on recovery of swim performance. *Int J Sports Physiol Perform* 15:1-7, 2019.

262. Smith, LL. Cytokine hypothesis of overtraining: A physiological adaptation to excessive stress? *Med Sci Sports Exerc* 32:317-331, 2000.

263. Smith, LL. Tissue trauma: The underlying cause of overtraining syndrome? *J Strength Cond Res* 18:185-193, 2004.

264. Smith, RS, Efron, B, Mah, CD, and Malhotra, A. The impact of circadian misalignment on athletic performance in professional football players. *Sleep* 36:1999-2001, 2013.

265. Smith, RS, Guilleminault, C, and Efron, B. Circadian rhythms and enhanced athletic performance in the National Football League. *Sleep* 20:362-365, 1997.

266. Snyder, AC. Overtraining and glycogen depletion hypothesis. *Med Sci Sports Exerc* 30:1146-1150, 1998.

267. Spencer, M, Bishop, D, Dawson, B, Goodman, C, and Duffield, R. Metabolism and performance in repeated cycle sprints: Active versus passive recovery. *Med Sci Sports Exerc* 38:1492-1499, 2006.

268. St Clair Gibson, A, Lambert, EV, Rauch, LH, Tucker, R, Baden, DA, Foster, C, and Noakes, TD. The role of information processing between the brain and peripheral physiological systems in pacing and perception of effort. *Sports Med* 36:705-722, 2006.

269. St Clair Gibson, A, Lambert, ML, and Noakes, TD. Neural control of force output during maximal and submaximal exercise. *Sports Med* 31:637-650, 2001.

270. Stanley, J, Buchheit, M, and Peake, JM. The effect of post-exercise hydrotherapy on subsequent exercise performance and heart rate variability. *Eur J Appl Physiol* 112:951-961, 2012.

271. Stanley, J, Halliday, A, D'Auria, S, Buchheit, M, and Leicht, AS. Effect of sauna-based heat acclimation on plasma volume and heart rate variability. *Eur J Appl Physiol* 115:785-794, 2015.

272. Stephens, JM, Halson, S, Miller, J, Slater, GJ, and Askew, CD. Cold water immersion for athletic recovery: One size does not fit all. *Int J Sports Physiol Perform* 12:2-9, 2017.

273. Stone, MH, and Fry, AC. Increased training volume in strength/power athletes. In *Overtraining in Sport*. Kreider, RB, Fry, AC, O'Toole, ML, eds. Champaign, IL: Human Kinetics, 87-106, 1998.

274. Stone, MH, Keith, R, Kearney, JT, Wilson, GD, and Fleck, S, J,. Overtraining: A review of the signs and symptoms of overtraining. *J Strength Cond Res* 5:35-50, 1991.

275. Stone, MH, O'Bryant, HS, Hornsby, G, Cunanan, A, Mizuguchi, S, Suarez, DG, South, M, Marsh, D, Haff, GG, and Ramsey, MW. Using the isometric mid-thigh pull in the monitoring of weightlifters: 25+ years of experience. *Professional Strength and Conditioning* 54:19-26, 2019.

276. Stone, MH, Stone, ME, and Sands, WA. Physical and physiological adaptations to resistance training. In *Principles*

277. Suarez, DG, Mizuguchi, S, Hornsby, WG, Cunanan, AJ, Marsh, DJ, and Stone, MH. Phase-specific changes in rate of force development and muscle morphology throughout a block periodized training cycle in weightlifters. *Sports* 7:129, 2019.

278. Swenson, C, Sward, L, and Karlsson, J. Cryotherapy in sports medicine. *Scand J Med Sci Sports* 6:193-200, 1996.

279. Szczepanska-Gieracha, J, Borsuk, P, Pawik, M, and Rymaszewska, J. Mental state and quality of life after 10 session whole-body cryotherapy. *Psychol Health Med* 19:40-46, 2014.

280. Takeuchi, K, Hatade, T, Wakamiya, S, Fujita, N, Arakawa, T, and Miki, A. Heat stress promotes skeletal muscle regeneration after crush injury in rats. *Acta Histochem* 116:327-334, 2014.

281. Tanaka, M, and Watanabe, Y. Supraspinal regulation of physical fatigue. *Neurosci Biobehav Rev* 36:727-734, 2012.

282. Taoutaou, Z, Granier, P, Mercier, B, Mercier, J, Ahmaidi, S, and Prefaut, C. Lactate kinetics during passive and partially active recovery in endurance and sprint athletes. *Eur J Appl Physiol Occup Physiol* 73:465-470, 1996.

283. Taylor, DJ, Kemp, GJ, Thompson, CH, and Radda, GK. Ageing: Effects on oxidative function of skeletal muscle in vivo. *Mol Cell Biochem* 174:321-324, 1997.

284. Taylor, JL, Amann, M, Duchateau, J, Meeusen, R, and Rice, CL. Neural contributions to muscle fatigue: From the brain to the muscle and back again. *Med Sci Sports Exerc* 48:2294-2306, 2016.

285. Taylor, JL, and Gandevia, SC. A comparison of central aspects of fatigue in submaximal and maximal voluntary contractions. *J Appl Physiol* 104:542-550, 2008.

286. Thomas, K, Brownstein, CG, Dent, J, Parker, P, Goodall, S, and Howatson, G. Neuromuscular fatigue and recovery after heavy resistance, jump, and sprint training. *Med Sci Sports Exerc* 50:2526-2535, 2018.

287. Thomas, K, Elmeua, M, Howatson, G, and Goodall, S. Intensity-dependent contribution of neuromuscular fatigue after constant-load cycling. *Med Sci Sports Exerc* 48:1751-1760, 2016.

288. Tipton, MJ, Collier, N, Massey, H, Corbett, J, and Harper, M. Cold water immersion: Kill or cure? *Exp Physiol* 102:1335-1355, 2017.

289. Tucker, WJ, Angadi, SS, and Gaesser, GA. Excess postexercise oxygen consumption after high-intensity and sprint interval exercise, and continuous steady-state exercise. *J Strength Cond Res* 30:3090-3097, 2016.

290. Urhausen, A, Gabriel, H, and Kindermann, W. Blood hormones as markers of training stress and overtraining. *Sports Med* 20:251-276, 1995.

291. Urhausen, A, Gabriel, HH, Weiler, B, and Kindermann, W. Ergometric and psychological findings during overtraining: A long-term follow-up study in endurance athletes. *Int J Sports Med* 19:114-120, 1998.

292. Uusitalo, AL. Overtraining: Making a difficult diagnosis and implementing targeted treatment. *Phys Sportsmed* 29:35-50, 2001.

293. Vaile, J, Halson, S, Gill, N, and Dawson, B. Effect of hydrotherapy on recovery from fatigue. *Int J Sports Med* 29:539-544, 2008.

294. Vaile, J, Halson, S, Gill, N, and Dawson, B. Effect of hydrotherapy on the signs and symptoms of delayed onset muscle soreness. *Eur J Appl Physiol* 102:447-455, 2008.

295. Vaile, JM, Gill, ND, and Blazevich, AJ. The effect of contrast water therapy on symptoms of delayed onset muscle soreness. *J Strength Cond Res* 21:697-702, 2007.

296. Verkhoshansky, Y, and Siff, MC. Designing sport specific strength programmes. In *Supertraining*. 6th ed. Rome: Verkhoshansky, 421-480, 2009.

297. Verkhoshansky, Y, and Siff, MC. Programming and organisation of training. In *Supertraining*. 6th (expanded) ed. Rome, Italy: Verkhoshansky, 313-392, 2009.

298. Vernon, A, Joyce, C, and Banyard, HG. Readiness to train: Return to baseline strength and velocity following strength or power training. *Int J Sports Sci Coach* 15:204-211, 2020.

299. Versey, N, Halson, S, and Dawson, B. Effect of contrast water therapy duration on recovery of cycling performance: A dose-response study. *Eur J Appl Physiol* 111:37-46, 2011.

300. Versey, NG, Halson, SL, and Dawson, BT. Effect of contrast water therapy duration on recovery of running performance. *Int J Sports Physiol Perform* 7:130-140, 2012.

301. Versey, NG, Halson, SL, and Dawson, BT. Water immersion recovery for athletes: Effect on exercise performance and practical recommendations. *Sports Med* 43:1101-1130, 2013.

302. Vervoorn, C, Quist, AM, Vermulst, LJ, Erich, WB, de Vries, WR, and Thijssen, JH. The behaviour of the plasma free testosterone/cortisol ratio during a season of elite rowing training. *Int J Sports Med* 12:257-263, 1991.

303. Viitasalo, JT, Niemela, K, Kaappola, R, Korjus, T, Levola, M, Mononen, HV, Rusko, HK, and Takala, TE. Warm underwater water-jet massage improves recovery from intense physical exercise. *Eur J Appl Physiol Occup Physiol* 71:431-438, 1995.

304. Viru, A, and Viru, M. Preconditioning of the performance in power events by endogenous testosterone: In memory of Professor Carmelo Bosco. *J Strength Cond Res* 19:6-8, 2005.

305. Vitale, KC, Owens, R, Hopkins, SR, and Malhotra, A. Sleep hygiene for optimizing recovery in athletes: Review and recommendations. *Int J Sports Med* 40:535-543, 2019.

306. Vrijkotte, S, Roelands, B, Pattyn, N, and Meeusen, R. The overtraining syndrome in soldiers: Insights from the sports domain. *Mil Med* 184:e192-e200, 2019.

307. Wahl, P, Guldner, M, and Mester, J. Effects and sustainability of a 13-day high-intensity shock microcycle in soccer. *J Sports Sci Med* 13:259-265, 2014.

308. Washington, LL, Gibson, SJ, and Helme, RD. Age-related differences in the endogenous analgesic response to repeated cold water immersion in human volunteers. *Pain* 89:89-96, 2000.

309. Waterhouse, J, Atkinson, G, Edwards, B, and Reilly, T. The role of a short post-lunch nap in improving cogni-

tive, motor, and sprint performance in participants with partial sleep deprivation. *J Sports Sci* 25:1557-1566, 2007.
310. Waterhouse, J, Reilly, T, and Edwards, B. The stress of travel. *J Sports Sci* 22:946-965, 2004.
311. Watts, PB, Daggett, M, Gallagher, P, and Wilkins, B. Metabolic response during sport rock climbing and the effects of active versus passive recovery. *Int J Sports Med* 21:185-190, 2000.
312. Weavil, JC, and Amann, M. Corticospinal excitability during fatiguing whole body exercise. *Prog Brain Res* 240:219-246, 2018.
313. Weavil, JC, and Amann, M. Neuromuscular fatigue during whole body exercise. *Curr Opin Physiol* 10:128-136, 2019.
314. Webb, NP, Harris, NK, Cronin, JB, and Walker, C. The relative efficacy of three recovery modalities after professional Rugby League matches. *J Strength Cond Res* 27:2449-2455, 2013.
315. Weerapong, P, Hume, PA, and Kolt, GS. The mechanisms of massage and effects on performance, muscle recovery and injury prevention. *Sports Med* 35:235-256, 2005.
316. Weinber, R, Jackson, A, and Kolodny, K. The relationship of massage and exercise to mood enhancement. *Sport Psychol* 2:202-211, 1988.
317. Weir, JP, Beck, TW, Cramer, JT, and Housh, TJ. Is fatigue all in your head? A critical review of the central governor model. *Br J Sports Med* 40:573-586, 2006.
318. Weston, CF, O'Hare, JP, Evans, JM, and Corrall, RJ. Haemodynamic changes in man during immersion in water at different temperatures. *Clin Sci (Lond)* 73:613-616, 1987.
319. Whitney, JD, and Wickline, MM. Treating chronic and acute wounds with warming: Review of the science and practice implications. *J Wound Ostomy Continence Nurs* 30:199-209, 2003.
320. Wiewelhove, T, Döweling, A, Schneider, C, Hottenrott, L, Meyer, T, Kellmann, M, Pfeiffer, M, and Ferrauti, A. A meta-analysis of the effects of foam rolling on performance and recovery. *Front Physiol* 10:376, 2019.
321. Wilcock, IM, Cronin, JB, and Hing, WA. Physiological response to water immersion: A method for sport recovery? *Sports Med* 36:747-765, 2006.
322. Wilcock, IM, Cronin, JB, and Hing, WA. Water immersion: Does it enhance recovery from exercise? *Int J Sports Physiol Perf* 1:195-206, 2006.
323. Williams, ER, McKendry, J, Morgan, PT, and Breen, L. Enhanced cycling time-trial performance during multiday exercise with higher-pressure compression garment wear. *Int J Sports Physiol Perform* 16:287, 2020.
324. Yamane, M, Teruya, H, Nakano, M, Ogai, R, Ohnishi, N, and Kosaka, M. Post-exercise leg and forearm flexor muscle cooling in humans attenuates endurance and resistance training effects on muscle performance and on circulatory adaptation. *Eur J Appl Physiol* 96:572-580, 2006.
325. Yessis, M. Making the most of Soviet restorative measures. In *Secrets of Russian Sports Fitness and Training*. Michigan, USA: Ultimate Athlete Concepts, 247-261, 2008.
326. Yona, M. Effects of cold stimulation of human skin on motor unit activity. *Jpn J Physiol* 47:341-348, 1997.
327. Zalessky, M. Pedagogical, physiological, and psychological means of restoration. *Legkaya Atletika* 7:20-22, 1979.
328. Zandvoort, CS, de Zwart, JR, van Keeken, BL, Viroux, PJF, and Tiemessen, IJH. A customised cold-water immersion protocol favours one-size-fits-all protocols in improving acute performance recovery. *Eur J Sport Sci* 18:54-61, 2018.
329. Zarzissi, S, Bouzid, MA, Zghal, F, Rebai, H, and Hureau, TJ. Aging reduces the maximal level of peripheral fatigue tolerable and impairs exercise capacity. *Am J Physiol Regul Integr Comp Physiol* 319:R617-R625, 2020.
330. Zatsiorsky, VM, Kraemer, WJ, and Fry, AC. Basic concepts of training theory. In *Science and Practice of Strength Training*. 3rd ed. Champaign, IL: Human Kinetics, 3-14, 2021.
331. Zatsiorsky, VM, Kraemer, WJ, and Fry, AC. Overreaching, overtraining, and recovery. In *Science and Practice of Strength Training*. 3rd ed. Champaign, IL: Human Kinetics, 177-194, 2021.
332. Zeitlin, D, Keller, SE, Shiflett, SC, Schleifer, SJ, and Bartlett, JA. Immunological effects of massage therapy during academic stress. *Psychosom Med* 62:83-84, 2000.
333. Zelikovski, A, Kaye, CL, Fink, G, Spitzer, SA, and Shapiro, Y. The effects of the modified intermittent sequential pneumatic device (MISPD) on exercise performance following an exhaustive exercise bout. *Br J Sports Med* 27:255-259, 1993.
334. Zhang, H, Huizenga, C, Arens, E, and Yu, T. Considering individual physiological differences in a human thermal model. *J Therm Biol* 26:401-408, 2001.

Chapter 10

1. Achten, J, Halson, SL, Moseley, L, Rayson, MP, Casey, A, and Jeukendrup, AE. Higher dietary carbohydrate content during intensified running training results in better maintenance of performance and mood state. *J Appl Physiol* 96:1331-1340, 2004.
2. Ainsley Dean, PJ, Arikan, G, Opitz, B, and Sterr, A. Potential for use of creatine supplementation following mild traumatic brain injury. *Concussion* 2:CNC34, 2017.
3. Ainsworth, BE, Haskell, WL, Whitt, MC, Irwin, ML, Swartz, AM, Strath, SJ, O'Brien, WL, Bassett, DR, Jr., Schmitz, KH, Emplaincourt, PO, Jacobs, DR, Jr., and Leon, AS. Compendium of physical activities: An update of activity codes and MET intensities. *Med Sci Sports Exerc* 32:S498-504, 2000.
4. Almond, CS, Shin, AY, Fortescue, EB, Mannix, RC, Wypij, D, Binstadt, BA, Duncan, CN, Olson, DP, Salerno, AE, Newburger, JW, and Greenes, DS. Hyponatremia among runners in the Boston Marathon. *N Engl J Med* 352:1550-1556, 2005.
5. Anderson, L, Naughton, RJ, Close, GL, Di Michele, R, Morgans, R, Drust, B, and Morton, JP. Daily distribution of macronutrient intakes of professional soccer players from the English Premier League. *Int J Sport Nutr Exerc Metab* 27:491-498, 2017.
6. Anderson, L, Orme, P, Naughton, RJ, Close, GL, Milsom, J, Rydings, D, O'Boyle, A, Di Michele, R, Louis, J, Hambly, C, Speakman, JR, Morgans, R, Drust, B, and Morton, JP.

Energy intake and expenditure of professional soccer players of the English Premier League: Evidence of carbohydrate periodization. *Int J Sport Nutr Exerc Metab* 27:128-138, 2017.

7. Antonio, J, Candow, DG, Forbes, SC, Gualano, B, Jagim, AR, Kreider, RB, Rawson, ES, Smith-Ryan, AE, VanDusseldorp, TA, Willoughby, DS, and Ziegenfuss, TN. Common questions and misconceptions about creatine supplementation: What does the scientific evidence really show? *J Int Soc Sports Nutr* 18:13, 2021.

8. Aragon, AA, and Schoenfeld, BJ. Nutrient timing revisited: Is there a post-exercise anabolic window? *J Int Soc Sports Nutr* 10:5, 2013.

9. Arent, SM, Cintineo, HP, McFadden, BA, Chandler, AJ, and Arent, MA. Nutrient timing: A garage door of opportunity? *Nutrients* 12:1948, 2020.

10. Areta, JL, Burke, LM, Ross, ML, Camera, DM, West, DW, Broad, EM, Jeacocke, NA, Moore, DR, Stellingwerff, T, Phillips, SM, Hawley, JA, and Coffey, VG. Timing and distribution of protein ingestion during prolonged recovery from resistance exercise alters myofibrillar protein synthesis. *J Physiol* 591:2319-2331, 2013.

11. Armstrong, LE. Assessing hydration status: The elusive gold standard. *J Am Coll Nutr* 26:575S-584S, 2007.

12. Astrup, A, Magkos, F, Bier, DM, Brenna, JT, de Oliveira Otto, MC, Hill, JO, King, JC, Mente, A, Ordovas, JM, Volek, JS, Yusuf, S, and Krauss, RM. Saturated fats and health: A reassessment and proposal for food-based recommendations: JACC state-of-the-art review. *J Am Coll Cardiol* 76:844-857, 2020.

13. Atkinson, FS, Brand-Miller, JC, Foster-Powell, K, Buyken, AE, and Goletzke, J. International tables of glycemic index and glycemic load values 2021: A systematic review. *Am J Clin Nutr* 114:1625-1632, 2021.

14. Baguet, A, Bourgois, J, Vanhee, L, Achten, E, and Derave, W. Important role of muscle carnosine in rowing performance. *J Appl Physiol* 109:1096-1101, 2010.

15. Baguet, A, Reyngoudt, H, Pottier, A, Everaert, I, Callens, S, Achten, E, and Derave, W. Carnosine loading and washout in human skeletal muscles. *J Appl Physiol* 106:837-842, 2009.

16. Barber, TM, Kabisch, S, Pfeiffer, AFH, and Weickert, MO. The health benefits of dietary fibre. *Nutrients* 12:3209, 2020.

17. Barrett, EC, McBurney, MI, and Ciappio, ED. Omega-3 fatty acid supplementation as a potential therapeutic aid for the recovery from mild traumatic brain injury/concussion. *Adv Nutr* 5:268-277, 2014.

18. Bartlett, JD, Hawley, JA, and Morton, JP. Carbohydrate availability and exercise training adaptation: Too much of a good thing? *Eur J Sport Sci* 15:3-12, 2015.

19. Bartlett, JD, Louhelainen, J, Iqbal, Z, Cochran, AJ, Gibala, MJ, Gregson, W, Close, GL, Drust, B, and Morton, JP. Reduced carbohydrate availability enhances exercise-induced p53 signaling in human skeletal muscle: Implications for mitochondrial biogenesis. *Am J Physiol Regul Integr Comp Physiol* 304:R450-458, 2013.

20. Baty, JJ, Hwang, H, Ding, Z, Bernard, JR, Wang, B, Kwon, B, and Ivy, JL. The effect of a carbohydrate and protein supplement on resistance exercise performance, hormonal response, and muscle damage. *J Strength Cond Res* 21:321-329, 2007.

21. Beelen, M, Burke, LM, Gibala, MJ, and van Loon, LJ. Nutritional strategies to promote postexercise recovery. *Int J Sport Nutr Exerc Metab* 20:515-532, 2010.

22. Bergeron, MF. Heat cramps: Fluid and electrolyte challenges during tennis in the heat. *J Sci Med Sport* 6:19-27, 2003.

23. Bergstrom, J, Hermansen, L, Hultman, E, and Saltin, B. Diet, muscle glycogen and physical performance. *Acta Physiol Scand* 71:140-150, 1967.

24. Betts, JA, and Stevenson, E. Should protein be included in CHO-based sports supplements? *Med Sci Sports Exerc* 43:1244-1250, 2011.

25. Bird, SP, Tarpenning, KM, and Marino, FE. Effects of liquid carbohydrate/essential amino acid ingestion on acute hormonal response during a single bout of resistance exercise in untrained men. *Nutrition* 22:367-375, 2006.

26. Bird, SP, Tarpenning, KM, and Marino, FE. Independent and combined effects of liquid carbohydrate/essential amino acid ingestion on hormonal and muscular adaptations following resistance training in untrained men. *Eur J Appl Physiol* 97:225-238, 2006.

27. Bird, SP, Tarpenning, KM, and Marino, FE. Liquid carbohydrate/essential amino acid ingestion during a short-term bout of resistance exercise suppresses myofibrillar protein degradation. *Metabolism* 55:570-577, 2006.

28. Black, K, Slater, J, Brown, RC, and Cooke, R. Low energy availability, plasma lipids, and hormonal profiles of recreational athletes. *J Strength Cond Res* 32:2816-2824, 2018.

29. Blancquaert, L, Everaert, I, and Derave, W. Beta-alanine supplementation, muscle carnosine and exercise performance. *Curr Opin Clin Nutr Metab Care* 18:63-70, 2015.

30. Boirie, Y, Dangin, M, Gachon, P, Vasson, MP, Maubois, JL, and Beaufrere, B. Slow and fast dietary proteins differently modulate postprandial protein accretion. *Proc Natl Acad Sci U S A* 94:14930-14935, 1997.

31. Bonilla, DA, Perez-Idarraga, A, Odriozola-Martinez, A, and Kreider, RB. The 4R's framework of nutritional strategies for post-exercise recovery: A review with emphasis on new generation of carbohydrates. *Int J Environ Res Public Health* 18:103, 2021.

32. Bos, C, Metges, CC, Gaudichon, C, Petzke, KJ, Pueyo, ME, Morens, C, Everwand, J, Benamouzig, R, and Tome, D. Postprandial kinetics of dietary amino acids are the main determinant of their metabolism after soy or milk protein ingestion in humans. *J Nutr* 133:1308-1315, 2003.

33. Bradley, WJ, Cavanagh, B, Douglas, W, Donovan, TF, Twist, C, Morton, JP, and Close, GL. Energy intake and expenditure assessed "in-season" in an elite European Rugby Union squad. *Eur J Sport Sci* 15:469-479, 2015.

34. Bradley, WJ, Cavanagh, BP, Douglas, W, Donovan, TF, Morton, JP, and Close, GL. Quantification of training load, energy intake, and physiological adaptations during a rugby preseason: A case study from an elite European Rugby Union squad. *J Strength Cond Res* 29:534-544, 2015.

35. Braun, H, von Andrian-Werburg, J, Schanzer, W, and Thevis, M. Nutrition status of young elite female German football players. *Pediatr Exerc Sci* 30:157-167, 2018.

36. Brouns, F. Heat—sweat—dehydration—rehydration: A praxis oriented approach. *J Sports Sci* 9 Spec No:143-152, 1991.
37. Buford, TW, Kreider, RB, Stout, JR, Greenwood, M, Campbell, B, Spano, M, Ziegenfuss, T, Lopez, H, Landis, J, and Antonio, J. International Society of Sports Nutrition position stand: Creatine supplementation and exercise. *J Int Soc Sports Nutr* 4:6, 2007.
38. Burke, LM. Nutrition strategies for the marathon: Fuel for training and racing. *Sports Med* 37:344-347, 2007.
39. Burke, LM. Re-examining high-fat diets for sports performance: Did we call the "nail in the coffin" too soon? *Sports Med* 45 33-49, 2015.
40. Burke, LM, Castell, LM, and Stear, SJ. BJSM reviews: A-Z of supplements: Dietary supplements, sports nutrition foods and ergogenic aids for health and performance: Part 1. *Br J Sports Med* 43:728-729, 2009.
41. Burke, LM, Collier, GR, and Hargreaves, M. Muscle glycogen storage after prolonged exercise: Effect of the glycemic index of carbohydrate feedings. *J Appl Physiol* 75:1019-1023, 1993.
42. Burke, LM, Collier, GR, and Hargreaves, M. Glycemic index—a new tool in sport nutrition? *Int J Sport Nutr* 8:401-415, 1998.
43. Burke, LM, Cox, GR, Culmmings, NK, and Desbrow, B. Guidelines for daily carbohydrate intake: Do athletes achieve them? *Sports Med* 31:267-299, 2001.
44. Burke, LM, and Hawley, JA. Swifter, higher, stronger: What's on the menu? *Science* 362:781-787, 2018.
45. Burke, LM, Jeukendrup, AE, Jones, AM, and Mooses, M. Contemporary nutrition strategies to optimize performance in distance runners and race walkers. *Int J Sport Nutr Exerc Metab* 29:117-129, 2019.
46. Burke, LM, Kiens, B, and Ivy, JL. Carbohydrates and fat for training and recovery. *J Sports Sci* 22:15-30, 2004.
47. Burke, LM, Loucks, AB, and Broad, N. Energy and carbohydrate for training and recovery. *J Sports Sci* 24:675-685, 2006.
48. Burke, LM, Lundy, B, Fahrenholtz, IL, and Melin, AK. Pitfalls of conducting and interpreting estimates of energy availability in free-living athletes. *Int J Sport Nutr Exerc Metab* 28:350-363, 2018.
49. Calder, PC. n-3 fatty acids, inflammation and immunity: New mechanisms to explain old actions. *Proc Nutr Soc* 72:326-336, 2013.
50. Calder, PC, Albers, R, Antoine, JM, Blum, S, Bourdet-Sicard, R, Ferns, GA, Folkerts, G, Friedmann, PS, Frost, GS, Guarner, F, Lovik, M, Macfarlane, S, Meyer, PD, M'Rabet, L, Serafini, M, van Eden, W, van Loo, J, Vas Dias, W, Vidry, S, Winklhofer-Roob, BM, and Zhao, J. Inflammatory disease processes and interactions with nutrition. *Br J Nutr* 101:S1-45, 2009.
51. Castell, LM, Burke, LM, Stear, SJ, and Maughan, RJ. BJSM reviews: A-Z of nutritional supplements: Dietary supplements, sports nutrition foods and ergogenic aids for health and performance: Part 8. *Br J Sports Med* 44:468-470, 2010.
52. Castell, LM, Burke, LM, Stear, SJ, McNaughton, LR, and Harris, RC. BJSM reviews: A-Z of nutritional supplements: Dietary supplements, sports nutrition foods and ergogenic aids for health and performance: Part 5. *Br J Sports Med* 44:77-78, 2010.
53. Chan, MA, Koch, AJ, Benedict, SH, and Potteiger, JA. Influence of carbohydrate ingestion on cytokine responses following acute resistance exercise. *Int J Sport Nutr Exerc Metab* 13:454-465, 2003.
54. Chen, YJ, Wong, SH, Wong, CK, Lam, CW, Huang, YJ, and Siu, PM. The effect of a pre-exercise carbohydrate meal on immune responses to an endurance performance run. *Br J Nutr* 100:1260-1268, 2008.
55. Chryssanthopoulos, C, and Williams, C. Pre-exercise carbohydrate meal and endurance running capacity when carbohydrates are ingested during exercise. *Int J Sports Med* 18:543-548, 1997.
56. Chung, W, Shaw, G, Anderson, ME, Pyne, DB, Saunders, PU, Bishop, DJ, and Burke, LM. Effect of 10 week beta-alanine supplementation on competition and training performance in elite swimmers. *Nutrients* 4:1441-1453, 2012.
57. Cialdella-Kam, L, Guebels, CP, Maddalozzo, GF, and Manore, MM. Dietary intervention restored menses in female athletes with exercise-associated menstrual dysfunction with limited impact on bone and muscle health. *Nutrients* 6:3018-3039, 2014.
58. Close, GL, Kasper, AM, and Morton, JP. Nutrition for human performance. In *Strength and Conditioning for Sports Performance*. 2nd ed. Jeffreys, I, Moody, J, eds. New York: Routledge, 153-184, 2021.
59. Coggan, AR, and Coyle, EF. Reversal of fatigue during prolonged exercise by carbohydrate infusion or ingestion. *J Appl Physiol* 63:2388-2395, 1987.
60. Coggan, AR, and Coyle, EF. Effect of carbohydrate feedings during high-intensity exercise. *J Appl Physiol* 65:1703-1709, 1988.
61. Costill, DL. Carbohydrate for athletic training and performance. *Bol Asoc Med P R* 83:350-353, 1991.
62. Coyle, EF. Timing and method of increased carbohydrate intake to cope with heavy training, competition and recovery. *J Sports Sci* 9 Spec No:29-51, 1991.
63. Coyle, EF, Coggan, AR, Hemmert, MK, and Ivy, JL. Muscle glycogen utilization during prolonged strenuous exercise when fed carbohydrate. *J Appl Physiol* 61:165-172, 1986.
64. Coyle, EF, Coggan, AR, Hemmert, MK, Lowe, RC, and Walters, TJ. Substrate usage during prolonged exercise following a preexercise meal. *J Appl Physiol* 59:429-433, 1985.
65. Cribb, PJ, and Hayes, A. Effects of supplement timing and resistance exercise on skeletal muscle hypertrophy. *Med Sci Sports Exerc* 38:1918-1925, 2006.
66. Currell, K, and Jeukendrup, AE. Superior endurance performance with ingestion of multiple transportable carbohydrates. *Med Sci Sports Exerc* 40:275-281, 2008.
67. Dangott, B, Schultz, E, and Mozdziak, PE. Dietary creatine monohydrate supplementation increases satellite cell mitotic activity during compensatory hypertrophy. *Int J Sports Med* 21:13-16, 2000.
68. Davis, JM, Alderson, NL, and Welsh, RS. Serotonin and central nervous system fatigue: Nutritional considerations. *Am J Clin Nutr* 72:573S-578S, 2000.

69. Davis, JM, and Bailey, SP. Possible mechanisms of central nervous system fatigue during exercise. *Med Sci Sports Exerc* 29:45-57, 1997.
70. Decombaz, J, Jentjens, R, Ith, M, Scheurer, E, Buehler, T, Jeukendrup, A, and Boesch, C. Fructose and galactose enhance postexercise human liver glycogen synthesis. *Med Sci Sports Exerc* 43:1964-1971, 2011.
71. Demling, RH. Nutrition, anabolism, and the wound healing process: An overview. *Eplasty* 9:e9, 2009.
72. Di Donato, DM, West, DW, Churchward-Venne, TA, Breen, L, Baker, SK, and Phillips, SM. Influence of aerobic exercise intensity on myofibrillar and mitochondrial protein synthesis in young men during early and late postexercise recovery. *Am J Physiol Endocrinol Metab* 306:E1025-E1032, 2014.
73. DiMarco, NM, West, NP, Burke, LM, Stear, SJ, and Castell, LM. A-Z of nutritional supplements: Dietary supplements, sports nutrition foods and ergogenic aids for health and performance: Part 30. *Br J Sports Med* 46:299-300, 2012.
74. Dolan, E, Gualano, B, and Rawson, ES. Beyond muscle: The effects of creatine supplementation on brain creatine, cognitive processing, and traumatic brain injury. *Eur J Sport Sci* 19:1-14, 2019.
75. Donaldson, CM, Perry, TL, and Rose, MC. Glycemic index and endurance performance. *Int J Sport Nutr Exerc Metab* 20:154-165, 2010.
76. European Food Safety Authority. Scientific opinion on the tolerable upper intake level of eicosapentaenoic acid (EPA), docosahexaenoic acid (DHA) and docosapentaenoic acid (DPA). *EFSA Journal* 10:2815, 2012.
77. Falkenberg, E, Aisbett, B, Lastella, M, Roberts, S, and Condo, D. Nutrient intake, meal timing and sleep in elite male Australian football players. *J Sci Med Sport* 24:7-12, 2021.
78. Farkhondeh, T, Samarghandian, S, Roshanravan, B, and Peivasteh-Roudsari, L. Impact of curcumin on traumatic brain injury and involved molecular signaling pathways. *Recent Pat Food Nutr Agric* 11:137-144, 2020.
79. Ferrugem, LC, Martini, GL, and De Souza, CG. Influence of the glycemic index of pre-exercise meals in sports performance: A systematic review. *International Journal of Medical Reviews* 5:151-158, 2018.
80. Foster, C, Costill, DL, and Fink, WJ. Effects of preexercise feedings on endurance performance. *Med Sci Sports* 11:1-5, 1979.
81. Francescato, MP, and Puntel, I. Does a pre-exercise carbohydrate feeding improve a 20-km cross-country ski performance? *J Sports Med Phys Fitness* 46:248-256, 2006.
82. Fry, AC, Schilling, BK, Weiss, LW, and Chiu, LZ. Beta2-adrenergic receptor downregulation and performance decrements during high-intensity resistance exercise overtraining. *J Appl Physiol* 101:1664-1672, 2006.
83. Fry, RW, Morton, AR, and Keast, D. Periodisation and the prevention of overtraining. *Can J Sport Sci* 17:241-248, 1992.
84. Fry, RW, Morton, AR, and Keast, D. Periodisation of training stress—a review. *Can J Sport Sci* 17:234-240, 1992.
85. Fuchs, CJ, Gonzalez, JT, and van Loon, LJC. Fructose co-ingestion to increase carbohydrate availability in athletes. *J Physiol* 597:3549-3560, 2019.
86. Galland, L. Diet and inflammation. *Nutr Clin Pract* 25:634-640, 2010.
87. Garthe, I, and Maughan, RJ. Athletes and supplements: Prevalence and perspectives. *Int J Sport Nutr Exerc Metab* 28:126-138, 2018.
88. Gleeson, M, Maughan, RJ, and Greenhaff, PL. Comparison of the effects of pre-exercise feeding of glucose, glycerol and placebo on endurance and fuel homeostasis in man. *Eur J Appl Physiol Occup Physiol* 55:645-653, 1986.
89. Gollnick, PD, Armstrong, RB, Saubert, CW, Sembrowich, WL, Shepherd, RE, and Saltin, B. Glycogen depletion patterns in human skeletal muscle fibers during prolonged work. *Pflugers Arch* 344:1-12, 1973.
90. Gollnick, PD, Karlsson, J, Piehl, K, and Saltin, B. Selective glycogen depletion in skeletal muscle fibres of man following sustained contractions. *J Physiol Lond* 241:59-67, 1974.
91. Green, AL, Hultman, E, Macdonald, IA, Sewell, DA, and Greenhaff, PL. Carbohydrate ingestion augments skeletal muscle creatine accumulation during creatine supplementation in humans. *Am J Physiol* 271:E821-826, 1996.
92. Haff, GG. Carbohydrates. In *Essentials of Sports Nutrition and Supplements*. Antonio, J, Kalman, D, Stout, JR, Greenwood, M, Willoughby, DS, Haff, GG, eds. Totowa, NJ: Humana Press, 281-311, 2008.
93. Haff, GG, and Dumke, C. Resting metabolic rate determinations. In *Laboratory Manual for Exercise Physiology*. 2nd ed. Champaign, IL: Human Kinetics, 135-148, 2018.
94. Haff, GG, Koch, AJ, Potteiger, JA, Kuphal, KE, Magee, LM, Green, SB, and Jakicic, JJ. Carbohydrate supplementation attenuates muscle glycogen loss during acute bouts of resistance exercise. *Int J Sport Nutr Exerc Metab* 10:326-339, 2000.
95. Haff, GG, Lehmkuhl, MJ, McCoy, LB, and Stone, MH. Carbohydrate supplementation and resistance training. *J Strength Cond Res* 17:187-196, 2003.
96. Haff, GG, and Potteiger, JA. Creatine supplementation for the strength/power athlete. *Strength and Cond* 19:72-74, 1997.
97. Haff, GG, Schroeder, CA, Koch, AJ, Kuphal, KE, Comeau, MJ, and Potteiger, JA. The effects of supplemental carbohydrate ingestion on intermittent isokinetic leg exercise. *J Sports Med Phys Fitness* 41:216-222., 2001.
98. Haff, GG, Stone, MH, Warren, BJ, Keith, R, Johnson, RL, Nieman, DC, Williams, F, and Kirksey, KB. The effect of carbohydrate supplementation on multiple sessions and bouts of resistance exercise. *J Strength Cond Res* 13:111-117, 1999.
99. Hallfrisch, J, Facn, and Behall, KM. Mechanisms of the effects of grains on insulin and glucose responses. *J Am Coll Nutr* 19:320S-325S, 2000.
100. Halson, SL, Bridge, MW, Meeusen, R, Busschaert, B, Gleeson, M, Jones, DA, and Jeukendrup, AE. Time course of performance changes and fatigue markers during intensified training in trained cyclists. *J Appl Physiol* 93:947-956, 2002.
101. Halson, SL, Lancaster, GI, Achten, J, Gleeson, M, and Jeukendrup, AE. Effects of carbohydrate supplementation on performance and carbohydrate oxidation after intensified cycling training. *J Appl Physiol (1985)* 97:1245-1253, 2004.

102. Hargreaves, M, Costill, DL, Fink, WJ, King, DS, and Fielding, RA. Effect of pre-exercise carbohydrate feedings on endurance cycling performance. *Med Sci Sports Exerc* 19:33-36, 1987.

103. Harris, JA, and Benedict, FG. A biometric study of human basal metabolism. *Proc Natl Acad Sci U S A* 4:370-373, 1918.

104. Harris, RC, Tallon, MJ, Dunnett, M, Boobis, L, Coakley, J, Kim, HJ, Fallowfield, JL, Hill, CA, Sale, C, and Wise, JA. The absorption of orally supplied beta-alanine and its effect on muscle carnosine synthesis in human vastus lateralis. *Amino Acids* 30:279-289, 2006.

105. Hart, DW, Wolf, SE, Zhang, XJ, Chinkes, DL, Buffalo, MC, Matin, SI, DebRoy, MA, Wolfe, RR, and Herndon, DN. Efficacy of a high-carbohydrate diet in catabolic illness. *Crit Care Med* 29:1318-1324, 2001.

106. Hawley, JA. Sending the signal: Muscle glycogen availability as a regulator of training adaptation. In *Hormones, Metabolism and the Benefits of Exercise*. Spiegelman, B, ed. Cham, Switzerland: Springer International, 43-55, 2017.

107. Hawley, JA, and Leckey, JJ. Carbohydrate dependence during prolonged, intense endurance exercise. *Sports Med* 45:S5-12, 2015.

108. Hawley, JA, Tipton, KD, and Millard-Stafford, ML. Promoting training adaptations through nutritional interventions. *J Sports Sci* 24:709-721, 2006.

109. Hespel, P, Op't Eijnde, B, Van Leemputte, M, Urso, B, Greenhaff, PL, Labarque, V, Dymarkowski, S, Van Hecke, P, and Richter, EA. Oral creatine supplementation facilitates the rehabilitation of disuse atrophy and alters the expression of muscle myogenic factors in humans. *J Physiol* 536:625-633, 2001.

110. Heung-Sang Wong, S, Sun, FH, Chen, YJ, Li, C, Zhang, YJ, and Ya-Jun Huang, W. Effect of pre-exercise carbohydrate diets with high vs low glycemic index on exercise performance: A meta-analysis. *Nutr Rev* 75:327-338, 2017.

111. Hew-Butler, T, Almond, C, Ayus, JC, Dugas, J, Meeuwisse, W, Noakes, T, Reid, S, Siegel, A, Speedy, D, Stuempfle, K, Verbalis, J, and Weschler, L. Consensus statement of the 1st International Exercise-Associated Hyponatremia Consensus Development Conference, Cape Town, South Africa 2005. *Clin J Sport Med* 15:208-213, 2005.

112. Heydenreich, J, Kayser, B, Schutz, Y, and Melzer, K. Total energy expenditure, energy intake, and body composition in endurance athletes across the training season: A systematic review. *Sports Med Open* 3:8, 2017.

113. Hill, CA, Harris, RC, Kim, HJ, Harris, BD, Sale, C, Boobis, LH, Kim, CK, and Wise, JA. Influence of beta-alanine supplementation on skeletal muscle carnosine concentrations and high intensity cycling capacity. *Amino Acids* 32:225-233, 2007.

114. Hofeins, J. An overview of macronutrients. In *Essentials of Sports Nutrition and Supplements*. Antonio, J, Kalman, D, Stout, JR, Greenwood, M, Willoughby, DS, Haff, GG, eds. Totowa, NJ: Humana Press, 237-250, 2008.

115. Hoffman, J, and Howell, S. Fundamentals of sports nutrition. In *Integrated Periodization in Sports Training and Athletic Development*. Bompa, TO, Blumenstein, B, Hoffman, J, Howell, S, Orbach, I, eds. Aachen, Germany: Meyer and Meyr Sport, 23-61, 2019.

116. Hu, FB. Are refined carbohydrates worse than saturated fat? *Am J Clin Nutr* 91:1541-1542, 2010.

117. Hulston, CJ, Venables, MC, Mann, CH, Martin, C, Philp, A, Baar, K, and Jeukendrup, AE. Training with low muscle glycogen enhances fat metabolism in well-trained cyclists. *Med Sci Sports Exerc* 42:2046-2055, 2010.

118. Hultman, E, Soderlund, K, Timmons, JA, Cederblad, G, and Greenhaff, PL. Muscle creatine loading in men. *J Appl Physiol* 81:232-237, 1996.

119. Impey, SG, Hearris, MA, Hammond, KM, Bartlett, JD, Louis, J, Close, GL, and Morton, JP. Fuel for the work required: A theoretical framework for carbohydrate periodization and the glycogen threshold hypothesis. *Sports Med* 48:1031-1048, 2018.

120. International Olympic Committee Expert Group on Dietary Supplements in Athletes. International Olympic Committee expert group statement on dietary supplements in athletes. *Int J Sport Nutr Exerc Metab* 28:102-103, 2018.

121. Ivy, J, and Portman, R. Nutrient timing. In *The Future of Sports Nutrition: Nutrient Timing*. North Bergan, NJ: Basic Health Publications, 7-14, 2004.

122. Ivy, JL. Regulation of muscle glycogen repletion, muscle protein synthesis and repair following exercise. *J Sports Sci Med* 3:131-138, 2004.

123. Ivy, JL, and Ferguson-Stegall, LM. Nutrient timing: The means to improved exercise performance, recovery, and training adaptation. *Am J Lifestyle Med* 8:246-259, 2014.

124. Ivy, JL, Katz, AL, Cutler, CL, Sherman, WM, and Coyle, EF. Muscle glycogen synthesis after exercise: Effect of time of carbohydrate ingestion. *J Appl Physiol* 64:1480-1485, 1988.

125. Ivy, JL, Res, PT, Sprague, RC, and Widzer, MO. Effect of a carbohydrate-protein supplement on endurance performance during exercise of varying intensity. *Int J Sport Nutr Exerc Metab* 13:382-395, 2003.

126. Jäger, R, Kerksick, CM, Campbell, BI, Cribb, PJ, Wells, SD, Skwiat, TM, Purpura, M, Ziegenfuss, TN, Ferrando, AA, Arent, SM, Smith-Ryan, AE, Stout, JR, Arciero, PJ, Ormsbee, MJ, Taylor, LW, Wilborn, CD, Kalman, DS, Kreider, RB, Willoughby, DS, Hoffman, JR, Krzykowski, JL, and Antonio, J. International Society of Sports Nutrition position stand: Protein and exercise. *J Int Soc Sports Nutr* 14:20, 2017.

127. Jandrain, BJ, Pallikarakis, N, Normand, S, Pirnay, F, Lacroix, M, Mosora, F, Pachiaudi, C, Gautier, JF, Scheen, AJ, Riou, JP, and et al. Fructose utilization during exercise in men: Rapid conversion of ingested fructose to circulating glucose. *J Appl Physiol* 74:2146-2154, 1993.

128. Jenkins, DJ, Wolever, TM, Taylor, RH, Barker, H, Fielden, H, Baldwin, JM, Bowling, AC, Newman, HC, Jenkins, AL, and Goff, DV. Glycemic index of foods: A physiological basis for carbohydrate exchange. *Am J Clin Nutr* 34:362-366, 1981.

129. Jentjens, R, and Jeukendrup, A. Determinants of post-exercise glycogen synthesis during short-term recovery. *Sports Med* 33:117-144, 2003.

130. Jentjens, RL, Achten, J, and Jeukendrup, AE. High oxidation rates from combined carbohydrates ingested during exercise. *Med Sci Sports Exerc* 36:1551-1558, 2004.

131. Jentjens, RL, Cale, C, Gutch, C, and Jeukendrup, AE. Effects of pre-exercise ingestion of differing amounts of carbohydrate on subsequent metabolism and cycling performance. *Eur J Appl Physiol* 88:444-452, 2003.

132. Jeukendrup, AE. Carbohydrate intake during exercise and performance. *Nutrition* 20:669-677, 2004.

133. Jeukendrup, AE. Carbohydrate and exercise performance: The role of multiple transportable carbohydrates. *Curr Opin Clin Nutr Metab Care* 13:452-457, 2010.

134. Jeukendrup, AE. Periodized nutrition for athletes. *Sports Med* 47:51-63, 2017.

135. Jeukendrup, AE. Training the gut for athletes. *Sports Med* 47:101-110, 2017.

136. Jeukendrup, AE, Jentjens, RL, and Moseley, L. Nutritional considerations in triathlon. *Sports Med* 35:163-181, 2005.

137. Jeukendrup, AE, and Killer, SC. The myths surrounding pre-exercise carbohydrate feeding. *Ann Nutr Metab* 57:18-25, 2010.

138. Josse, AR, Tang, JE, Tarnopolsky, MA, and Phillips, SM. Body composition and strength changes in women with milk and resistance exercise. *Med Sci Sports Exerc* 42:1122-1130, 2010.

139. Kabir, M, Rizkalla, SW, Champ, M, Luo, J, Boillot, J, Bruzzo, F, and Slama, G. Dietary amylose-amylopectin starch content affects glucose and lipid metabolism in adipocytes of normal and diabetic rats. *J Nutr* 128:35-43, 1998.

140. Kanungo, S, Wells, K, Tribett, T, and El-Gharbawy, A. Glycogen metabolism and glycogen storage disorders. *Ann Transl Med* 6:474, 2018.

141. Karamanolis, IA, Laparidis, KS, Volaklis, KA, Douda, HT, and Tokmakidis, SP. The effects of pre-exercise glycemic index food on running capacity. *Int J Sports Med* 32:666-671, 2011.

142. Karlsson, J, and Saltin, B. Diet, muscle glycogen, and endurance performance. *J Appl Physiol* 31:203-206, 1971.

143. Kavouras, SA, Troup, JP, and Berning, JR. The influence of low versus high carbohydrate diet on a 45-min strenuous cycling exercise. *Int J Sport Nutr Exerc Metab* 14:62-72, 2004.

144. Kerksick, C, Harvey, T, Stout, J, Campbell, B, Wilborn, C, Kreider, R, Kalman, D, Ziegenfuss, T, Lopez, H, Landis, J, Ivy, JL, and Antonio, J. International Society of Sports Nutrition position stand: Nutrient timing. *J Int Soc Sports Nutr* 5:17, 2008.

145. Kerksick, CM, Arent, S, Schoenfeld, BJ, Stout, JR, Campbell, B, Wilborn, CD, Taylor, L, Kalman, D, Smith-Ryan, AE, Kreider, RB, Willoughby, D, Arciero, PJ, VanDusseldorp, TA, Ormsbee, MJ, Wildman, R, Greenwood, M, Ziegenfuss, TN, Aragon, AA, and Antonio, J. International Society of Sports Nutrition position stand: Nutrient timing. *J Int Soc Sports Nutr* 14:33, 2017.

146. King, DS, Baskerville, R, Hellsten, Y, Senchina, DS, Burke, LM, Stear, SJ, and Castell, LM. A-Z of nutritional supplements: Dietary supplements, sports nutrition foods and ergogenic aids for health and performance: Part 34. *Br J Sports Med* 46:689-690, 2012.

147. Kinsey, AW, and Ormsbee, MJ. The health impact of nighttime eating: Old and new perspectives. *Nutrients* 7:2648-2662, 2015.

148. Kleyn, J, and Hough, J. The microbiology of brewing. *Annu Rev Microbiol* 25:583-608, 1971.

149. Kloby Nielsen, LL, Tandrup Lambert, MN, and Jeppesen, PB. The effect of ingesting carbohydrate and proteins on athletic performance: A systematic review and meta-analysis of randomized controlled trials. *Nutrients* 12:1483, 2020.

150. Kovacs, EM, Schmahl, RM, Senden, JM, and Brouns, F. Effect of high and low rates of fluid intake on post-exercise rehydration. *Int J Sport Nutr Exerc Metab* 12:14-23, 2002.

151. Kraemer, WJ, and Ratamess, NA. Hormonal responses and adaptations to resistance exercise and training. *Sports Med* 35:339-361, 2005.

152. Kreider, RB. Sports application of creatine. In *Essentials of Sports Nutrition and Supplements*. Antonio, J, Kalman, D, Stout, JR, Greenwood, M, Willoughby, DS, Haff, GG, eds. Totowa, NJ: Humana Press, 417-440, 2008.

153. Kreider, RB, Kalman, DS, Antonio, J, Ziegenfuss, TN, Wildman, R, Collins, R, Candow, DG, Kleiner, SM, Almada, AL, and Lopez, HL. International Society of Sports Nutrition position stand: Safety and efficacy of creatine supplementation in exercise, sport, and medicine. *J Int Soc Sports Nutr* 14:18, 2017.

154. Kumar, PR, Essa, MM, Al-Adawi, S, Dradekh, G, Memon, MA, Akbar, M, and Manivasagam, T. Omega-3 fatty acids could alleviate the risks of traumatic brain injury: A mini review. *J Tradit Complement Med* 4:89-92, 2014.

155. Lacroix, M, Bos, C, Leonil, J, Airinei, G, Luengo, C, Dare, S, Benamouzig, R, Fouillet, H, Fauquant, J, Tome, D, and Gaudichon, C. Compared with casein or total milk protein, digestion of milk soluble proteins is too rapid to sustain the anabolic postprandial amino acid requirement. *Am J Clin Nutr* 84:1070-1079, 2006.

156. Lane, SC, Camera, DM, Lassiter, DG, Areta, JL, Bird, SR, Yeo, WK, Jeacocke, NA, Krook, A, Zierath, JR, Burke, LM, and Hawley, JA. Effects of sleeping with reduced carbohydrate availability on acute training responses. *J Appl Physiol (1985)* 119:643-655, 2015.

157. Layman, DK. Dietary guidelines should reflect new understandings about adult protein needs. *Nutr Metab (Lond)* 6:12, 2009.

158. Layman, DK, Boileau, RA, Erickson, DJ, Painter, JE, Shiue, H, Sather, C, and Christou, DD. A reduced ratio of dietary carbohydrate to protein improves body composition and blood lipid profiles during weight loss in adult women. *J Nutr* 133:411-417, 2003.

159. Lee, JK, and Shirreffs, SM. The influence of drink temperature on thermoregulatory responses during prolonged exercise in a moderate environment. *J Sports Sci* 25:975-985, 2007.

160. Lehninger, AL, Nelson, DL, and Cox, MM. Carbohydrates. In *Principles of Biochemistry*. 2nd ed. New York: Worth, 298-323, 1993.

161. Lin, E, Kotani, JG, and Lowry, SF. Nutritional modulation of immunity and the inflammatory response. *Nutrition* 14:545-550, 1998.

162. Lohman, R, Carr, A, and Condo, D. Nutritional intake in Australian football players: Sports nutrition knowledge

163. Loucks, AB, Kiens, B, and Wright, HH. Energy availability in athletes. *J Sports Sci* 29:S7-S15, 2011.

164. Lucke-Wold, BP, Logsdon, AF, Nguyen, L, Eltanahay, A, Turner, RC, Bonasso, P, Knotts, C, Moeck, A, Maroon, JC, Bailes, JE, and Rosen, CL. Supplements, nutrition, and alternative therapies for the treatment of traumatic brain injury. *Nutr Neurosci* 21:79-91, 2018.

165. Ludwig, DS. Dietary glycemic index and the regulation of body weight. *Lipids* 38:117-121, 2003.

166. Ludwig, DS, Majzoub, JA, Al-Zahrani, A, Dallal, GE, Blanco, I, and Roberts, SB. High glycemic index foods, overeating, and obesity. *Pediatrics* 103:E26, 1999.

167. Macnaughton, LS, Wardle, SL, Witard, OC, McGlory, C, Hamilton, DL, Jeromson, S, Lawrence, CE, Wallis, GA, and Tipton, KD. The response of muscle protein synthesis following whole-body resistance exercise is greater following 40 g than 20 g of ingested whey protein. *Physiol Rep* 4:e1289, 2016.

168. Manore, M, Meeusen, R, Roelands, B, Moran, S, Popple, AD, Naylor, MJ, Burke, LM, Stear, SJ, and Castell, LM. BJSM reviews: A-Z of nutritional supplements: Dietary supplements, sports nutrition foods and ergogenic aids for health and performance: Part 16. *Br J Sports Med* 45:73-74, 2011.

169. Marangoni, F, Pellegrino, L, Verduci, E, Ghiselli, A, Bernabei, R, Calvani, R, Cetin, I, Giampietro, M, Perticone, F, Piretta, L, Giacco, R, La Vecchia, C, Brandi, ML, Ballardini, D, Banderali, G, Bellentani, S, Canzone, G, Cricelli, C, Faggiano, P, Ferrara, N, Flachi, E, Gonnelli, S, Macca, C, Magni, P, Marelli, G, Marrocco, W, Miniello, VL, Origo, C, Pietrantonio, F, Silvestri, P, Stella, R, Strazzullo, P, Troiano, E, and Poli, A. Cow's milk consumption and health: A health professional's guide. *J Am Coll Nutr* 38:197-208, 2019.

170. Marquet, L-A, Hausswirth, C, Molle, O, Hawley, J, Burke, L, Tiollier, E, and Brisswalter, J. Periodization of carbohydrate intake: Short-term effect on performance. *Nutrients* 8:755, 2016.

171. Marquet, LA, Brisswalter, J, Louis, J, Tiollier, E, Burke, LM, Hawley, JA, and Hausswirth, C. Enhanced endurance performance by periodization of carbohydrate intake: "Sleep low" strategy. *Med Sci Sports Exerc* 48:663-672, 2016.

172. Martinez-Sanz, JM, Sospedra, I, Ortiz, CM, Baladia, E, Gil-Izquierdo, A, and Ortiz-Moncada, R. Intended or unintended doping? A review of the presence of doping substances in dietary supplements used in sports. *Nutrients* 9:1093, 2017.

173. Matveyev, LP. Fundamentals of the structure of training and its initial links. In *Fundamentals of Sports Training*. Moscow: Fizkultua i Sport, 245-259, 1977.

174. Matveyev, LP. Introductory characteristics of sports training. In *Fundamentals of Sports Training*. Moscow: Fizkultua i Sport, 29-59, 1977.

175. Maughan, R, and Gleeson, M. Middle distance events. In *The Biochemical Basis of Sports Performance*. 2nd ed. New York: Oxford University Press, 99-126, 2010.

176. Maughan, RJ, Burke, LM, Dvorak, J, Larson-Meyer, DE, Peeling, P, Phillips, SM, Rawson, ES, Walsh, NP, Garthe, I, Geyer, H, Meeusen, R, van Loon, LJC, Shirreffs, SM, Spriet, LL, Stuart, M, Vernec, A, Currell, K, Ali, VM, Budgett, RG, Ljungqvist, A, Mountjoy, M, Pitsiladis, YP, Soligard, T, Erdener, U, and Engebretsen, L. IOC consensus statement: Dietary supplements and the high-performance athlete. *Br J Sports Med* 52:439-455, 2018.

177. Maughan, RJ, Greenhaff, PL, and Hespel, P. Dietary supplements for athletes: Emerging trends and recurring themes. *J Sports Sci* 29:S57-S66, 2011.

178. Maughan, RJ, and Shirreffs, SM. Development of individual hydration strategies for athletes. *Int J Sport Nutr Exerc Metab* 18:457-472, 2008.

179. Meeusen, R, Duclos, M, Foster, C, Fry, A, Gleeson, M, Nieman, D, Raglin, J, Rietjens, G, Steinacker, J, Urhausen, A, European College of Sport Science, and American College of Sports Medicine. Prevention, diagnosis, and treatment of the overtraining syndrome: Joint consensus statement of the European College of Sport Science and the American College of Sports Medicine. *Med Sci Sports Exerc* 45:186-205, 2013.

180. Melin, AK, Heikura, IA, Tenforde, A, and Mountjoy, M. Energy availability in athletics: Health, performance, and physique. *Int J Sport Nutr Exerc Metab* 29:152-164, 2019.

181. Mente, A, de Koning, L, Shannon, HS, and Anand, SS. A systematic review of the evidence supporting a causal link between dietary factors and coronary heart disease. *Arch Intern Med* 169:659-669, 2009.

182. Mettler, S, Mitchell, N, and Tipton, KD. Increased protein intake reduces lean body mass loss during weight loss in athletes. *Med Sci Sports Exerc* 42:326-337, 2010.

183. Mills, JD, Bailes, JE, Sedney, CL, Hutchins, H, and Sears, B. Omega-3 fatty acid supplementation and reduction of traumatic axonal injury in a rodent head injury model. *J Neurosurg* 114:77-84, 2011.

184. Mills, JD, Hadley, K, and Bailes, JE. Dietary supplementation with the omega-3 fatty acid docosahexaenoic acid in traumatic brain injury. *Neurosurgery* 68:474-481, 2011.

185. Mills, S, Candow, DG, Forbes, SC, Neary, JP, Ormsbee, MJ, and Antonio, J. Effects of creatine supplementation during resistance training sessions in physically active young adults. *Nutrients* 12:1880, 2020.

186. Millward, DJ, Layman, DK, Tome, D, and Schaafsma, G. Protein quality assessment: Impact of expanding understanding of protein and amino acid needs for optimal health. *Am J Clin Nutr* 87:1576S-1581S, 2008.

187. Mitchell, JB, Braun, WA, Pizza, FX, and Forrest, M. Pre-exercise carbohydrate and fluid ingestion: Influence of glycemic response on 10-km treadmill running performance in the heat. *J Sports Med Phys Fitness* 40:41-50, 2000.

188. Moore, DR. Maximizing post-exercise anabolism: The case for relative protein intakes. *Front Nutr* 6:147, 2019.

189. Mota, JA, Nuckols, G, and Smith-Ryan, AE. Nutritional periodization: Applications for the strength athlete. *Strength Cond J* 41:69-78, 2019.

190. Mountjoy, M, Sundgot-Borgen, J, Burke, L, Ackerman, KE, Blauwet, C, Constantini, N, Lebrun, C, Lundy, B, Melin, A, Meyer, N, Sherman, R, Tenforde, AS, Torstveit, MK, and Budgett, R. International Olympic Committee (IOC)

consensus statement on relative energy deficiency in sport (RED-S): 2018 update. *Int J Sport Nutr Exerc Metab* 28:316-331, 2018.

191. Mozaffarian, D. Dietary and policy priorities for cardiovascular disease, diabetes, and obesity: A comprehensive review. *Circulation* 133:187-225, 2016.

192. Mozaffarian, D, Katan, MB, Ascherio, A, Stampfer, MJ, and Willett, WC. Trans fatty acids and cardiovascular disease. *N Engl J Med* 354:1601-1613, 2006.

193. Mujika, I, Halson, S, Burke, L, Balagué, G, and Farrow, D. An integrated, multifactorial approach to periodization for optimal performance in individual and team sports. *Int J Sports Physiol Perform* 13:538-561, 2018.

194. Murakami, H, Kawakami, R, Nakae, S, Nakata, Y, Ishikawa-Takata, K, Tanaka, S, and Miyachi, M. Accuracy of wearable devices for estimating total energy expenditure: Comparison with metabolic chamber and doubly labeled water method. *JAMA Intern Med* 176:702-703, 2016.

195. Myles, IA. Fast food fever: Reviewing the impacts of the Western diet on immunity. *Nutr J* 13:61, 2014.

196. Nana, A, Slater, GJ, Stewart, AD, and Burke, LM. Methodology review: Using dual-energy X-ray absorptiometry (DXA) for the assessment of body composition in athletes and active people. *Int J Sport Nutr Exerc Metab* 25:198-215, 2015.

197. Nicastro, H, Artioli, GG, Costa Ados, S, Solis, MY, da Luz, CR, Blachier, F, and Lancha, AH, Jr. An overview of the therapeutic effects of leucine supplementation on skeletal muscle under atrophic conditions. *Amino Acids* 40:287-300, 2011.

198. Nieman, DC, Laupheimer, MW, Ranchordas, MK, Burke, LM, Stear, SJ, and Castell, LM. A-Z of nutritional supplements: Dietary supplements, sports nutrition foods and ergogenic aids for health and performance: Part 33. *Br J Sports Med* 46:618-620, 2012.

199. Nieman, DC, and Mitmesser, SH. Potential impact of nutrition on immune system recovery from heavy exertion: A metabolomics perspective. *Nutrients* 9:513, 2017.

200. Nunes, JP, Ribeiro, AS, Schoenfeld, BJ, Tomeleri, CM, Avelar, A, Trindade, MC, Nabuco, HC, Cavalcante, EF, Junior, PS, Fernandes, RR, Carvalho, FO, and Cyrino, ES. Creatine supplementation elicits greater muscle hypertrophy in upper than lower limbs and trunk in resistance-trained men. *Nutr Health* 23:223-229, 2017.

201. O'Reilly, J, Wong, SH, and Chen, Y. Glycaemic index, glycaemic load and exercise performance. *Sports Med* 40:27-39, 2010.

202. Okano, G, Takeda, H, Morita, I, Katoh, M, Mu, Z, and Miyake, S. Effect of pre-exercise fructose ingestion on endurance performance in fed men. *Med Sci Sports Exerc* 20:105-109, 1988.

203. Olsen, S, Aagaard, P, Kadi, F, Tufekovic, G, Verney, J, Olesen, JL, Suetta, C, and Kjaer, M. Creatine supplementation augments the increase in satellite cell and myonuclei number in human skeletal muscle induced by strength training. *J Physiol* 573:525-534, 2006.

204. Ormsbee, MJ, Bach, CW, and Baur, DA. Pre-exercise nutrition: The role of macronutrients, modified starches and supplements on metabolism and endurance performance. *Nutrients* 6:1782-1808, 2014.

205. Ortenblad, N, Nielsen, J, Saltin, B, and Holmberg, HC. Role of glycogen availability in sarcoplasmic reticulum Ca2+ kinetics in human skeletal muscle. *J Physiol* 589:711-725, 2011.

206. Pallotta, H. Practical strategies for carbohydrate periodization in football: An integrated approach with reference to training periodization. *Journal of Australian Strength and Conditioning* 27:51-63, 2019.

207. Papadopoulou, SK. Rehabilitation nutrition for injury recovery of athletes: The role of macronutrient intake. *Nutrients* 12:2449, 2020.

208. Parise, G, Mihic, S, MacLennan, D, Yarasheski, KE, and Tarnopolsky, MA. Effects of acute creatine monohydrate supplementation on leucine kinetics and mixed-muscle protein synthesis. *J Appl Physiol* 91:1041-1047, 2001.

209. Parr, EB, Heilbronn, LK, and Hawley, JA. A time to eat and a time to exercise. *Exerc Sport Sci Rev* 48:4-10, 2020.

210. Peeling, P, Castell, LM, Derave, W, de Hon, O, and Burke, LM. Sports foods and dietary supplements for optimal function and performance enhancement in track-and-field athletes. *Int J Sport Nutr Exerc Metab* 29:198-209, 2019.

211. Pennings, B, Boirie, Y, Senden, JM, Gijsen, AP, Kuipers, H, and van Loon, LJ. Whey protein stimulates postprandial muscle protein accretion more effectively than do casein and casein hydrolysate in older men. *Am J Clin Nutr* 93:997-1005, 2011.

212. Phillips, SM. Protein requirements and supplementation in strength sports. *Nutrition* 20:689-695, 2004.

213. Phillips, SM. Dietary protein for athletes: From requirements to metabolic advantage. *Appl Physiol Nutr Metab* 31:647-654, 2006.

214. Phillips, SM. The science of muscle hypertrophy: making dietary protein count. *Proc Nutr Soc* 70:100-103, 2011.

215. Phillips, SM, Tipton, KD, Aarsland, A, Wolf, SE, and Wolfe, RR. Mixed muscle protein synthesis and breakdown after resistance exercise in humans. *Am J Physiol* 273:E99-E107, 1997.

216. Philp, A, Hargreaves, M, and Baar, K. More than a store: Regulatory roles for glycogen in skeletal muscle adaptation to exercise. *Am J Physiol Endocrinol Metab* 302:E1343-E1351, 2012.

217. Plisk, SS, and Stone, MH. Periodization strategies. *Strength and Cond J* 25:19-37, 2003.

218. Pollock, ML, Graves, JE, and Garzarella, L. The measurement of body composition. In *Physiological Assessment of Human Fitness*. Maud, PJ, Foster, C, eds. Champaign, IL: Human Kinetics, 169-204, 1995.

219. Ranchordas, MK, Burd, N, Senchina, DS, Burke, LM, Stear, SJ, and Castell, LM. A-Z of nutritional supplements: Dietary supplements, sports nutrition foods and ergogenic aids for health and performance: Part 29. *Br J Sports Med* 46:155-156, 2012.

220. Reis, CEG, Loureiro, LMR, Roschel, H, and da Costa, THM. Effects of pre-sleep protein consumption on muscle-related outcomes: A systematic review. *J Sci Med Sport* 24:177-182, 2021.

221. Riesberg, LA, Weed, SA, McDonald, TL, Eckerson, JM, and Drescher, KM. Beyond muscles: The untapped potential of creatine. *Int Immunopharmacol* 37:31-42, 2016.

222. Rodriguez, NR, Di Marco, NM, and Langley, S. American College of Sports Medicine position stand: Nutrition and athletic performance. *Med Sci Sports Exerc* 41:709-731, 2009.
223. Rogerson, D. Vegan diets: Practical advice for athletes and exercisers. *J Int Soc Sports Nutr* 14:36, 2017.
224. Roschel, H, Gualano, B, S, MO, and E, SR. Creatine supplementation and brain health. *Nutrients* 13:586, 2021.
225. Routledge, HE, Leckey, JJ, Lee, MJ, Garnham, A, Graham, S, Burgess, D, Burke, LM, Erskine, RM, Close, GL, and Morton, JP. Muscle glycogen utilisation during an Australian rules football game. *Int J Sports Physiol Perform* 14:122-124, 2019.
226. Rowlands, DS, Nelson, AR, Phillips, SM, Faulkner, JA, Clarke, J, Burd, NA, Moore, D, and Stellingwerff, T. Protein-leucine fed dose effects on muscle protein synthesis after endurance exercise. *Med Sci Sports Exerc* 47:547-555, 2015.
227. Rozga, M, Cheng, FW, Moloney, L, and Handu, D. Effects of micronutrients or conditional amino acids on COVID-19-related outcomes: An evidence analysis center scoping review. *J Acad Nutr Diet* 121:1354-1363, 2021.
228. Sacks, FM, Lichtenstein, AH, Wu, JHY, Appel, LJ, Creager, MA, Kris-Etherton, PM, Miller, M, Rimm, EB, Rudel, LL, Robinson, JG, Stone, NJ, Van Horn, LV, and American Heart Association. Dietary fats and cardiovascular disease: A presidential advisory from the American Heart Association. *Circulation* 136:e1-e23, 2017.
229. Sakellaris, G, Kotsiou, M, Tamiolaki, M, Kalostos, G, Tsapaki, E, Spanaki, M, Spilioti, M, Charissis, G, and Evangeliou, A. Prevention of complications related to traumatic brain injury in children and adolescents with creatine administration: An open label randomized pilot study. *J Trauma Acute Care Surg* 61:322-329, 2006.
230. Sakellaris, G, Nasis, G, Kotsiou, M, Tamiolaki, M, Charissis, G, and Evangeliou, A. Prevention of traumatic headache, dizziness and fatigue with creatine administration: A pilot study. *Acta Paediatr* 97:31-34, 2008.
231. Saunders, B, Elliott-Sale, K, Artioli, GG, Swinton, PA, Dolan, E, Roschel, H, Sale, C, and Gualano, B. Beta-alanine supplementation to improve exercise capacity and performance: A systematic review and meta-analysis. *Br J Sports Med* 51:658-669, 2017.
232. Saunders, MJ, Kane, MD, and Todd, MK. Effects of a carbohydrate-protein beverage on cycling endurance and muscle damage. *Med Sci Sports Exerc* 36:1233-1238, 2004.
233. Saunders, MJ, Luden, ND, and Herrick, JE. Consumption of an oral carbohydrate-protein gel improves cycling endurance and prevents postexercise muscle damage. *J Strength Cond Res* 21:678-684, 2007.
234. Saunders, MJ, Moore, RW, Kies, AK, Luden, ND, and Pratt, CA. Carbohydrate and protein hydrolysate coingestions improvement of late-exercise time-trial performance. *Int J Sport Nutr Exerc Metab* 19:136-149, 2009.
235. Sawka, MN, Burke, LM, Eichner, ER, Maughan, RJ, Montain, SJ, and Stachenfeld, NS. American College of Sports Medicine position stand: Exercise and fluid replacement. *Med Sci Sports Exerc* 39:377-390, 2007.
236. Scharhag, J, Meyer, T, Auracher, M, Gabriel, HH, and Kindermann, W. Effects of graded carbohydrate supplementation on the immune response in cycling. *Med Sci Sports Exerc* 38:286-292, 2006.
237. Schoenfeld, BJ, Aragon, A, Wilborn, C, Urbina, SL, Hayward, SE, and Krieger, J. Pre- versus post-exercise protein intake has similar effects on muscular adaptations. *PeerJ* 5:e2825, 2017.
238. Schoenfeld, BJ, and Aragon, AA. Is there a postworkout anabolic window of opportunity for nutrient consumption? Clearing up controversies. *J Orthop Sports Phys Ther* 48:911-914, 2018.
239. Schoenfeld, BJ, Aragon, AA, and Krieger, JW. The effect of protein timing on muscle strength and hypertrophy: A meta-analysis. *J Int Soc Sports Nutr* 10:53, 2013.
240. Senchina, DS, Bermon, S, Stear, SJ, Burke, LM, and Castell, LM. BJSM reviews: A-Z of nutritional supplements: Dietary supplements, sports nutrition foods and ergogenic aids for health and performance: Part 17. *Br J Sports Med* 45:150-151, 2011.
241. Shaw, AD, and Davies, GJ. Lactose intolerance: problems in diagnosis and treatment. *J Clin Gastroenterol* 28:208-216, 1999.
242. Sherman, WM, Costill, DL, Fink, WJ, and Miller, JM. Effect of exercise-diet manipulation on muscle glycogen and its subsequent utilization during performance. *Int J Sports Med* 2:114-118, 1981.
243. Sherman, WM, Peden, MC, and Wright, DA. Carbohydrate feedings 1 h before exercise improves cycling performance. *Am J Clin Nutr* 54:866-870, 1991.
244. Simonsen, JC, Sherman, WM, Lamb, DR, Dernbach, AR, Doyle, JA, and Strauss, R. Dietary carbohydrate, muscle glycogen, and power output during rowing training. *J Appl Physiol* 70:1500-1505, 1991.
245. Slater, G, and Phillips, SM. Nutrition guidelines for strength sports: Sprinting, weightlifting, throwing events, and bodybuilding. *J Sports Sci* 29:S67-S77, 2011.
246. Smith-Ryan, AE, Hirsch, KR, Saylor, HE, Gould, LM, and Blue, MNM. Nutritional considerations and strategies to facilitate injury recovery and rehabilitation. *J Athl Train* 55:918-930, 2020.
247. Smith, LL. Cytokine hypothesis of overtraining: A physiological adaptation to excessive stress? *Med Sci Sports Exerc* 32:317-331, 2000.
248. Smith, LL. Tissue trauma: The underlying cause of overtraining syndrome? *J Strength Cond Res* 18:185-193, 2004.
249. Snijders, T, Res, PT, Smeets, JS, van Vliet, S, van Kranenburg, J, Maase, K, Kies, AK, Verdijk, LB, and van Loon, LJ. Protein ingestion before sleep increases muscle mass and strength gains during prolonged resistance-type exercise training in healthy young men. *J Nutr* 145:1178-1184, 2015.
250. Spano, M. Basic nutrition factors in health. In *Essentials of Strength Training and Conditioning*. 4th ed. Haff, GG, Triplett, N, eds. Champaign, IL: Human Kinetics, 175-200, 2016.
251. Sparks, MJ, Selig, SS, and Febbraio, MA. Pre-exercise carbohydrate ingestion: Effect of the glycemic index on endurance exercise performance. *Med Sci Sports Exerc* 30:844-849, 1998.
252. Stear, SJ, Castell, LM, Burke, LM, and Spriet, LL. BJSM reviews: A-Z of nutritional supplements: Dietary supplements,

sports nutrition foods and ergogenic aids for health and performance: Part 6. *Br J Sports Med* 44:297-298, 2010.

253. Stechmiller, JK. Understanding the role of nutrition and wound healing. *Nutr Clin Pract* 25:61-68, 2010.

254. Steenge, GR, Simpson, EJ, and Greenhaff, PL. Protein- and carbohydrate-induced augmentation of whole body creatine retention in humans. *J Appl Physiol* 89:1165-1171, 2000.

255. Stellingwerf, T. Case study: Nutrition and training periodization in three elite marathon runners. *Int J Sport Nutr Exerc Metab* 22:392-400, 2012.

256. Stellingwerff, T. Case study: Body composition periodization in an Olympic-level female middle-distance runner over a 9-year career. *Int J Sport Nutr Exerc Metab* 28:428-433, 2018.

257. Stellingwerff, T, Boit, MK, Res, PT, and International Association of Athletics Federations. Nutritional strategies to optimize training and racing in middle-distance athletes. *J Sports Sci* 25:S17-S28, 2007.

258. Stellingwerff, T, Maughan, RJ, and Burke, LM. Nutrition for power sports: Middle-distance running, track cycling, rowing, canoeing/kayaking, and swimming. *J Sports Sci* 29:S79-S89, 2011.

259. Stellingwerff, T, Morton, JP, and Burke, LM. A framework for periodized nutrition for athletics. *Int J Sport Nutr Exerc Metab* 29:141-151, 2019.

260. Sterczala, A, Fry, A, Chiu, L, Schilling, B, Weiss, L, and Nicoll, J. Beta2-adrenergic receptor maladaptations to high power resistance exercise overreaching. *Hum Physiol* 43:446-454, 2017.

261. Swagerty, DL, Jr., Walling, AD, and Klein, RM. Lactose intolerance. *Am Fam Physician* 65:1845-1850, 2002.

262. Sygo, J, Kendig Glass, A, Killer, SC, and Stellingwerff, T. Fueling for the field: Nutrition for jumps, throws, and combined events. *Int J Sport Nutr Exerc Metab* 29:95-105, 2019.

263. Tang, JE, Moore, DR, Kujbida, GW, Tarnopolsky, MA, and Phillips, SM. Ingestion of whey hydrolysate, casein, or soy protein isolate: Effects on mixed muscle protein synthesis at rest and following resistance exercise in young men. *J Appl Physiol* 107:987-992, 2009.

264. Thielecke, F, and Blannin, A. Omega-3 fatty acids for sport performance: Are they equally beneficial for athletes and amateurs? A narrative review. *Nutrients* 12:3712, 2020.

265. Thomas, DT, Erdman, KA, and Burke, LM. American College of Sports Medicine joint position statement: Nutrition and athletic performance. *Med Sci Sports Exerc* 48:543-568, 2016.

266. Thomas, DT, Erdman, KA, and Burke, LM. Position of the Academy of Nutrition and Dietetics, Dietitians of Canada, and the American College of Sports Medicine: Nutrition and athletic performance. *J Acad Nutr Diet* 116:501-528, 2016.

267. Tipton, KD. Nutritional support for exercise-induced injuries. *Sports Med* 45:93-104, 2015.

268. Tipton, KD, Elliott, TA, Ferrando, AA, Aarsland, AA, and Wolfe, RR. Stimulation of muscle anabolism by resistance exercise and ingestion of leucine plus protein. *Appl Physiol Nutr Metab* 34:151-161, 2009.

269. Tipton, KD, Rasmussen, BB, Miller, SL, Wolf, SE, Owens-Stovall, SK, Petrini, BE, and Wolfe, RR. Timing of amino acid-carbohydrate ingestion alters anabolic response of muscle to resistance exercise. *Am J Physiol Endocrinol Metab* 281:E197-E206, 2001.

270. Trexler, ET, Smith-Ryan, AE, Stout, JR, Hoffman, JR, Wilborn, CD, Sale, C, Kreider, RB, Jager, R, Earnest, CP, Bannock, L, Campbell, B, Kalman, D, Ziegenfuss, TN, and Antonio, J. International Society of Sports Nutrition position stand: Beta-alanine. *J Int Soc Sports Nutr* 12:30, 2015.

271. Trommelen, J, Holwerda, AM, Kouw, IW, Langer, H, Halson, SL, Rollo, I, Verdijk, LB, and van Loon, LJ. Resistance exercise augments postprandial overnight muscle protein synthesis rates. *Med Sci Sports Exerc* 48:2517-2525, 2016.

272. Trommelen, J, and van Loon, LJ. Pre-sleep protein ingestion to improve the skeletal muscle adaptive response to exercise training. *Nutrients* 8:763, 2016.

273. Tsintzas, OK, Williams, C, Boobis, L, and Greenhaff, P. Carbohydrate ingestion and glycogen utilization in different muscle fibre types in man. *J Physiol Lond* 489:243-250, 1995.

274. Turnagol, HH, Kosar, SN, Guzel, Y, Aktitiz, S, and Atakan, MM. Nutritional considerations for injury prevention and recovery in combat sports. *Nutrients* 14:53, 2021.

275. Valentine, RJ, Saunders, MJ, Todd, MK, and St Laurent, TG. Influence of carbohydrate-protein beverage on cycling endurance and indices of muscle disruption. *Int J Sport Nutr Exerc Metab* 18:363-378, 2008.

276. van Loon, LJ, Greenhaff, PL, Constantin-Teodosiu, D, Saris, WH, and Wagenmakers, AJ. The effects of increasing exercise intensity on muscle fuel utilisation in humans. *J Physiol* 536:295-304, 2001.

277. van Loon, LJ, Saris, WH, Kruijshoop, M, and Wagenmakers, AJ. Maximizing postexercise muscle glycogen synthesis: Carbohydrate supplementation and the application of amino acid or protein hydrolysate mixtures. *Am J Clin Nutr* 72:106-111, 2000.

278. van Vliet, S, Burd, NA, and van Loon, LJ. The skeletal muscle anabolic response to plant- versus animal-based protein consumption. *J Nutr* 145:1981-1991, 2015.

279. Vandenberghe, K, Goris, M, Van Hecke, P, Van Leemputte, M, Vangerven, L, and Hespel, P. Long-term creatine intake is beneficial to muscle performance during resistance training. *J Appl Physiol* 83:2055-2063, 1997.

280. Vist, GE, and Maughan, RJ. The effect of osmolality and carbohydrate content on the rate of gastric emptying of liquids in man. *J Physiol (Lond)* 486:523-531, 1995.

281. Volek, J. Enhancing exercise performance: Nutritional implications. In *Exercise and Sport Science*. Garrett, WE, Kirkendall, DT, eds. Philadelphia, PA: Lippincott Williams and Wilkins, 980, 2000.

282. Vollestad, NK, Tabata, I, and Medbo, JI. Glycogen breakdown in different human muscle fibre types during exhaustive exercise of short duration. *Acta Physiol Scand* 144:135-141, 1992.

283. Wall, BT, Morton, JP, and van Loon, LJ. Strategies to maintain skeletal muscle mass in the injured athlete: Nutritional considerations and exercise mimetics. *Eur J Sport Sci* 15:53-62, 2015.

284. Wang, T, Van, KC, Gavitt, BJ, Grayson, JK, Lu, YC, Lyeth, BG, and Pichakron, KO. Effect of fish oil supplementation in a rat model of multiple mild traumatic brain injuries. *Restor Neurol Neurosci* 31:647-659, 2013.

285. Wax, B, Brown, SP, Webb, HE, and Kavazis, AN. Effects of carbohydrate supplementation on force output and time to exhaustion during static leg contractions superimposed with electromyostimulation. *J Strength Cond Res* 26:1717-1723, 2012.

286. Wax, B, Kerksick, CM, Jagim, AR, Mayo, JJ, Lyons, BC, and Kreider, RB. Creatine for exercise and sports performance, with recovery considerations for healthy populations. *Nutrients* 13:1915, 2021.

287. Wilkinson, SB, Tarnopolsky, MA, Macdonald, MJ, Macdonald, JR, Armstrong, D, and Phillips, SM. Consumption of fluid skim milk promotes greater muscle protein accretion after resistance exercise than does consumption of an isonitrogenous and isoenergetic soy-protein beverage. *Am J Clin Nutr* 85:1031-1040, 2007.

288. Witard, OC, Jackman, SR, Breen, L, Smith, K, Selby, A, and Tipton, KD. Myofibrillar muscle protein synthesis rates subsequent to a meal in response to increasing doses of whey protein at rest and after resistance exercise. *Am J Clin Nutr* 99:86-95, 2014.

289. Wolfe, RR, Goodenough, RD, Burke, JF, and Wolfe, MH. Response of protein and urea kinetics in burn patients to different levels of protein intake. *Ann Surg* 197:163-171, 1983.

290. Wu, A, Ying, Z, and Gomez-Pinilla, F. Dietary curcumin counteracts the outcome of traumatic brain injury on oxidative stress, synaptic plasticity, and cognition. *Exp Neurol* 197:309-317, 2006.

291. Wu, A, Ying, Z, and Gomez-Pinilla, F. Dietary strategy to repair plasma membrane after brain trauma: Implications for plasticity and cognition. *Neurorehabil Neural Repair* 28:75-84, 2014.

292. Yang, Y, Breen, L, Burd, NA, Hector, AJ, Churchward-Venne, TA, Josse, AR, Tarnopolsky, MA, and Phillips, SM. Resistance exercise enhances myofibrillar protein synthesis with graded intakes of whey protein in older men. *Br J Nutr*:1-9, 2012.

293. Yaspelkis, BB, and Ivy, JL. Effect of carbohydrate supplements and water on exercise metabolism in the heat. *J Appl Physiol* 71:680-687, 1991.

294. Yaspelkis, BB, Patterson, JG, Anderla, PA, Ding, Z, and Ivy, JL. Carbohydrate supplementation spares muscle glycogen during variable-intensity exercise. *J Appl Physiol* 75:1477-1485, 1993.

295. Yeo, WK, Paton, CD, Garnham, AP, Burke, LM, Carey, AL, and Hawley, JA. Skeletal muscle adaptation and performance responses to once a day versus twice every second day endurance training regimens. *J Appl Physiol* 105:1462-1470, 2008.

296. Young, VR, and Pellett, PL. Plant proteins in relation to human protein and amino acid nutrition. *Am J Clin Nutr* 59:1203S-1212S, 1994.

297. Zhu, HT, Bian, C, Yuan, JC, Chu, WH, Xiang, X, Chen, F, Wang, CS, Feng, H, and Lin, JK. Curcumin attenuates acute inflammatory injury by inhibiting the TLR4/MyD88/NF-kappaB signaling pathway in experimental traumatic brain injury. *J Neuroinflammation* 11:59, 2014.

Chapter 11

1. Aagaard, P, Simonsen, EB, Andersen, JL, Magnusson, P, and Dyhre-Poulsen, P. Increased rate of force development and neural drive of human skeletal muscle following resistance training. *J Appl Physiol* 93:1318-1326, 2002.

2. Adlercreutz, H, Harkonen, M, Kuoppasalmi, K, Naveri, H, Huhtaniemi, I, Tikkanen, H, Remes, K, Dessypris, A, and Karvonen, J. Effect of training on plasma anabolic and catabolic steroid hormones and their response during physical exercise. *Int J Sports Med* 7:27-28, 1986.

3. Aján, T, and Baroga, L. The structure of the training process. In *Weightlifting: Fitness for All Sports*. Budapest: International Weightlifting Federation, 183-395, 1988.

4. Akenhead, R, and Nassis, GP. Training load and player monitoring in high-level football: Current practice and perceptions. *Int J Sports Physiol Perform* 11:587-593, 2016.

5. Akubat, I, Barrett, S, and Abt, G. Integrating the internal and external training loads in soccer. *Int J Sports Physiol Perform* 9:457-462, 2014.

6. Akubat, I, Patel, E, Barrett, S, and Abt, G. Methods of monitoring the training and match load and their relationship to changes in fitness in professional youth soccer players. *J Sports Sci* 30:1473-1480, 2012.

7. Allen, H, and Coggan, AR. Beyond average power. In *Training and Racing with a Power Meter*. Boulder, CO: Velo Press, 117-142, 2010.

8. Ancoli-Israel, S, Cole, R, Alessi, C, Chambers, M, Moorcroft, W, and Pollak, CP. The role of actigraphy in the study of sleep and circadian rhythms. *Sleep* 26:342-392, 2003.

9. Aoki, MS, Ronda, LT, Marcelino, PR, Drago, G, Carling, C, Bradley, PS, and Moreira, A. Monitoring training loads in professional basketball players engaged in a periodized training program. *J Strength Cond Res* 31:348-358, 2017.

10. Atlaoui, D, Pichot, V, Lacoste, L, Barale, F, Lacour, JR, and Chatard, JC. Heart rate variability, training variation and performance in elite swimmers. *Int J Sports Med* 28:394-400, 2007.

11. Auclair, D, Garrel, DR, Chaouki Zerouala, A, and Ferland, LH. Activation of the ubiquitin pathway in rat skeletal muscle by catabolic doses of glucocorticoids. *Am J Physiol* 272:C1007-C1016, 1997.

12. Aughey, RJ. Australian football player work rate: Evidence of fatigue and pacing? *Int J Sports Physiol Perform* 5:394-405, 2010.

13. Aughey, RJ. Applications of GPS technologies to field sports. *Int J Sports Physiol Perform* 6:295-310, 2011.

14. Austin, D, Gabbett, T, and Jenkins, D. Repeated high-intensity exercise in professional Rugby Union. *J Sports Sci* 29:1105-1112, 2011.

15. Australian Institute of Sport. Athlete management system: Recent developments in athlete workload and health monitoring. 2022. http://subscribe.ausport.gov.au/t/r-2CAD3E99D6C6144D2540EF23F30FEDED. Accessed October 9, 2022/.

16. Bailey, CA, Sato, K, Alexander, R, Chiang, C, and Stone, MH. Isometric force production symmetry and jumping performance in college athletes. *J Trainology* 2:1-5, 2013.
17. Bailey, CA, Sato, K, Burnett, A, and Stone, MH. Force production asymmetry in male and female athletes of differing strength. *Int J Sports Physiol Perform* 10:504-508, 2015.
18. Baj, Z, Kantorski, J, Majewska, E, Zeman, K, Pokoca, L, Fornalczyk, E, Tchorzewski, H, Sulowska, Z, and Lewicki, R. Immunological status of competitive cyclists before and after the training season. *Int J Sports Med* 15:319-324, 1994.
19. Baker, DG. 10-year changes in upper body strength and power in elite professional Rugby League players: The effect of training age, stage, and content. *J Strength Cond Res* 27:285-292, 2013.
20. Baldari, C, Bonavolonta, V, Emerenziani, GP, Gallotta, MC, Silva, AJ, and Guidetti, L. Accuracy, reliability, linearity of Accutrend and Lactate Pro versus EBIO plus analyzer. *Eur J Appl Physiol* 107:105-111, 2009.
21. Banfi, G, Marinelli, M, Roi, GS, and Agape, V. Usefulness of free testosterone/cortisol ratio during a season of elite speed skating athletes. *Int J Sports Med* 14:373-379, 1993.
22. Banister, EW, Calvert, TW, Savage, MV, and Back, A. A system model of training for athletic performance. *Aus J Sports Med* 7:170-176, 1975.
23. Bartlett, JD, O'Connor, F, Pitchford, N, Torres-Ronda, L, and Robertson, SJ. Relationships between internal and external training load in team-sport athletes: Evidence for an individualized approach. *Int J Sports Physiol Perform* 12:230-234, 2017.
24. Batra, A, Wetmore, AB, Hornsby, WG, Lipinska, P, Staniak, Z, Surala, O, and Stone, MH. Strength, endocrine, and body composition alterations across four blocks of training in an elite 400 m sprinter. *J Funct Morphol Kinesiol* 6:25, 2021.
25. Batterham, AM, and Hopkins, WG. Making meaningful inferences about magnitudes. *Int J Sports Physiol Perform* 1:50-57, 2006.
26. Batterham, AM, and Hopkins, WG. The problems with "The Problem with 'Magnitude-Based Inference'". *Med Sci Sports Exerc* 51:599, 2019.
27. Beckham, G, Suchomel, T, and Mizuguchi, S. Force plate use in performance monitoring and sport science testing. *New Studies in Athletics* 29:25-37, 2014.
28. Beneke, R, Leithauser, RM, and Ochentel, O. Blood lactate diagnostics in exercise testing and training. *Int J Sports Physiol Perform* 6:8-24, 2011.
29. Berger, BG, and Motl, RW. Exercise and mood: A selective review and synthesis of research employing the profile of mood states. *J Appl Sport Psychol* 12:69-92, 2000.
30. Berger, BG, Motl, RW, Butki, BD, Martin, DT, Wilkinson, JG, and Owen, DR. Mood and cycling performance in response to three weeks of high-intensity, short-duration overtraining, and a two-week taper. *Sport Psychol* 13:444-457, 1999.
31. Bernards, J, Sato, K, Haff, G, and Bazyler, C. Current research and statistical practices in sport science and a need for change. *Sports* 5:87, 2017.
32. Blanch, P, and Gabbett, TJ. Has the athlete trained enough to return to play safely? The acute:chronic workload ratio permits clinicians to quantify a player's risk of subsequent injury. *Br J Sports Med* 50:471-475, 2016.
33. Bompa, TO, and Haff, GG. Annual training plan. In *Periodization: Theory and Methodology of Training*. 5th ed. Champaign, IL: Human Kinetics, 125-185, 2009.
34. Bompa, TO, and Haff, GG. Speed and agility. In *Periodization: Theory and Methodology of Training*. 5th ed. Champaign, IL: Human Kinetics, 315-342, 2009.
35. Bompa, TO, and Haff, GG. Strength and power development. In *Periodization: Theory and Methodology of Training*. 5th ed. Champaign, IL: Human Kinetics, 259-286, 2009.
36. Booth, A, Shelley, G, Mazur, A, Tharp, G, and Kittok, R. Testosterone, and winning and losing in human competition. *Horm Behav* 23:556-571, 1989.
37. Borg, G. Perceived exertion as an indicator of somatic stress. *Scand J Rehabil Med* 2:92-98, 1970.
38. Borg, G. Administration of the Borg Scales. In *Borg's Perceived Exertion and Pain Scales*. Champaign, IL: Human Kinetics, 44-53, 1998.
39. Borg, G. The Borg CR10 Scale. In *Borg's Perceived Exertion and Pain Scales*. Champaign, IL: Human Kinetics, 39-43, 1998.
40. Borg, GA. Perceived exertion. *Exerc Sport Sci Rev* 2:131-153, 1974.
41. Borg, GA. Psychophysical bases of perceived exertion. *Med Sci Sports Exerc* 14:377-381, 1982.
42. Borresen, J, and Lambert, M. Validity of self-reported training duration. *Int J Sports Sci Coach* 1:353-359, 2006.
43. Borresen, J, and Lambert, MI. Changes in heart rate recovery in response to acute changes in training load. *Eur J Appl Physiol* 101:503-511, 2007.
44. Borresen, J, and Lambert, MI. Autonomic control of heart rate during and after exercise: Measurements and implications for monitoring training status. *Sports Med* 38:633-646, 2008.
45. Borresen, J, and Lambert, MI. Quantifying training load: A comparison of subjective and objective methods. *Int J Sports Physiol Perform* 3:16-30, 2008.
46. Borresen, J, and Lambert, MI. The quantification of training load, the training response and the effect on performance. *Sports Med* 39:779-795, 2009.
47. Bosquet, L, Merkari, S, Arvisais, D, and Aubert, AE. Is heart rate a convenient tool to monitor over-reaching? A systematic review of the literature. *Br J Sports Med* 42:709-714, 2008.
48. Bouffard, M. The perils of averaging data in adapted physical activity research. *Adapt Phys Activ Q* 10:371-391, 1993.
49. Bourdon, PC, Cardinale, M, Murray, A, Gastin, P, Kellmann, M, Varley, MC, Gabbett, TJ, Coutts, AJ, Burgess, DJ, Gregson, W, and Cable, NT. Monitoring athlete training loads: Consensus statement. *Int J Sports Physiol Perform* 12:S2161-S2170, 2017.
50. Brady, CJ, Harrison, AJ, and Comyns, TM. A review of the reliability of biomechanical variables produced during

the isometric mid-thigh pull and isometric squat and the reporting of normative data. *Sports Biomech*:1-25, 2018.

51. Brady, CJ, Harrison, AJ, Flanagan, EP, Haff, GG, and Comyns, TM. A comparison of the isometric mid-thigh pull and isometric squat: Intraday reliability, usefulness and the magnitude of difference between tests. *Int J Sports Physiol Perform* 13:844-852, 2018.

52. Brancaccio, P, Maffulli, N, and Limongelli, FM. Creatine kinase monitoring in sport medicine. *Br Med Bull* 81-82:209-230, 2007.

53. Buchheit, M. Monitoring training status with HR measures: Do all roads lead to Rome? *Front Physiol* 5:73, 2014.

54. Buchheit, M, Al Haddad, H, Mendez-Villanueva, A, Quod, MJ, and Bourdon, PC. Effect of maturation on hemodynamic and autonomic control recovery following maximal running exercise in highly trained young soccer players. *Front Physiol* 2:69, 2011.

55. Buchheit, M, Al Haddad, H, Simpson, BM, Palazzi, D, Bourdon, PC, Di Salvo, V, and Mendez-Villanueva, A. Monitoring accelerations with GPS in football: Time to slow down? *Int J Sports Physiol Perform* 9:442-445, 2014.

56. Buchheit, M, Papelier, Y, Laursen, PB, and Ahmaidi, S. Noninvasive assessment of cardiac parasympathetic function: Postexercise heart rate recovery or heart rate variability? *Am J Physiol Heart Circ Physiol* 293:H8-H10, 2007.

57. Buchheit, M, Racinais, S, Bilsborough, JC, Bourdon, PC, Voss, SC, Hocking, J, Cordy, J, Mendez-Villanueva, A, and Coutts, AJ. Monitoring fitness, fatigue and running performance during a pre-season training camp in elite football players. *J Sci Med Sport*, 2013.

58. Buchheit, M, Simpson, MB, Al Haddad, H, Bourdon, PC, and Mendez-Villanueva, A. Monitoring changes in physical performance with heart rate measures in young soccer players. *Eur J Appl Physiol* 112:711-723, 2012.

59. Burgess, DJ. The research doesn't always apply: Practical solutions to evidence-based training-load monitoring in elite team sports. *Int J Sports Physiol Perform* 12:S2136-S2141, 2017.

60. Bury, T, Marechal, R, Mahieu, P, and Pirnay, F. Immunological status of competitive football players during the training season. *Int J Sports Med* 19:364-368, 1998.

61. Calvert, TW, Banister, EW, and Savage, MV. A systems model of the effects of training on physical performance. *IEEE Trans Syst Man Cybern* 2:94-102, 1976.

62. Cardinale, M, and Stone, MH. Is testosterone influencing explosive performance? *J Strength Cond Res* 20:103-107, 2006.

63. Cardinale, M, and Varley, MC. Wearable training-monitoring technology: Applications, challenges, and opportunities. *Int J Sports Physiol Perform* 12:S255-S262, 2017.

64. Carey, DL, Blanch, P, Ong, KL, Crossley, KM, Crow, J, and Morris, ME. Training loads and injury risk in Australian football-differing acute:chronic workload ratios influence match injury risk. *Br J Sports Med* 51:1215-1220, 2017.

65. Carins, J, and Booth, C. Salivary immunoglobulin-A as a marker of stress during strenuous physical training. *Aviat Space Environ Med* 73:1203-1207, 2002.

66. Carling, C, Le Gall, F, and Dupont, G. Analysis of repeated high-intensity running performance in professional soccer. *J Sports Sci* 30:325-336, 2012.

67. Carney, CE, Buysse, DJ, Ancoli-Israel, S, Edinger, JD, Krystal, AD, Lichstein, KL, and Morin, CM. The consensus sleep diary: Standardizing prospective sleep self-monitoring. *Sleep* 35:287-302, 2012.

68. Carrard, J, Kloucek, P, and Gojanovic, B. Modelling training adaptation in swimming using artificial neural network geometric optimisation. *Sports (Basel)* 8:8, 2020.

69. Carroll, KM, Bazyler, CD, Bernards, JR, Taber, CB, Stuart, CA, DeWeese, BH, Sato, K, and Stone, MH. Skeletal muscle fiber adaptations following resistance training using repetition maximums or relative intensity. *Sports* 7:169, 2019.

70. Carroll, KM, Bernards, JR, Bazyler, CD, Taber, CB, Stuart, CA, DeWeese, BH, Sato, K, and Stone, MH. Divergent performance outcomes following resistance training using repetition maximums or relative intensity. *Int J Sports Physiol Perform* 14:46-54, 2019.

71. Casanova, N, Palmeira, DEOA, Pereira, A, Crisostomo, L, Travassos, B, and Costa, AM. Cortisol, testosterone and mood state variation during an official female football competition. *J Sports Med Phys Fitness* 56:775-781, 2016.

72. Cevada, T, Vasques, PE, Moraes, H, and Deslandes, A. Salivary cortisol levels in athletes and nonathletes: A systematic review. *Horm Metab Res* 46:905-910, 2014.

73. Chavda, S, Bromley, T, Jarvis, P, Williams, S, Bishop, C, Turner, AN, Lake, JP, and Mundy, PD. Force-time characteristics of the countermovement jump: Analyzing the curve in Excel. *Strength Cond J* 40:67-77, 2018.

74. Chavda, S, Turner, AN, Comfort, P, Haff, GG, Williams, S, Bishop, C, and Lake, JP. A practical guide to analyzing the force-time curve of isometric tasks in Excel. *Strength Cond J* 42:26-37, 2020.

75. Clubb, J, and McGuigan, M. Developing cost-effective, evidence-based load monitoring systems in strength and conditioning practice. *Strength Cond J* 40:75-81, 2018.

76. Coad, S, Gray, B, and McLellan, C. Seasonal analysis of mucosal immunological function and physical demands in professional Australian rules footballers. *Int J Sports Physiol Perform* 11:574-580, 2016.

77. Coad, S, Gray, B, Wehbe, G, and McLellan, C. Physical demands and salivary immunoglobulin A responses of elite Australian rules football athletes to match play. *Int J Sports Physiol Perform* 10:613-617, 2015.

78. Colomer, CME, Pyne, DB, Mooney, M, McKune, A, and Serpell, BG. Performance analysis in Rugby Union: A critical systematic review. *Sports Med Open* 6:4, 2020.

79. Comfort, P, Dos'Santos, T, Beckham, GK, Stone, MH, Guppy, SN, and Haff, GG. Standardization and methodological considerations for the isometric mid-thigh pull. *Strength Cond J* 41:57-79, 2019.

80. Comyns, T, and Hannon, A. Strength and conditioning coaches' application of the session rating of perceived exertion method of monitoring within professional Rugby Union. *J Hum Kinet* 61:155-166, 2018.

81. Cormack, SJ, Newton, RU, and McGuigan, MR. Neuromuscular and endocrine responses of elite players to

82. Cormack, SJ, Newton, RU, McGuigan, MR, and Cormie, P. Neuromuscular and endocrine responses of elite players during an Australian rules football match. *Int J Sports Physiol Perform* 3:359-374, 2008.

82. Cormack, SJ, Newton, RU, McGuigan, MR, and Cormie, P. Neuromuscular and endocrine responses of elite players during an Australian rules football season. *Int J Sports Physiol Perform* 3:439-453, 2008.

83. Coutts, A, Reaburn, P, Piva, TJ, and Murphy, A. Changes in selected biochemical, muscular strength, power, and endurance measures during deliberate overreaching and tapering in Rugby League players. *Int J Sports Med* 28:116-124, 2007.

84. Coutts, AJ, and Cormack, S. Monitoring training response. In *High-Performance Training for Sports*. Joyce, D, Lewindon, D, eds. Champaign, IL: Human Kinetics, 71-84, 2014.

85. Coutts, AJ, Kempton, T, Sullivan, C, Bilsborough, J, Cordy, J, and Rampinini, E. Metabolic power and energetic costs of professional Australian football match-play. *J Sci Med Sport* 18:219-224, 2015.

86. Coutts, AJ, Reaburn, P, Piva, TJ, and Rowsell, GJ. Monitoring for overreaching in Rugby League players. *Eur J Appl Physiol* 99:313-324, 2007.

87. Coyne, JOC, Coutts, AJ, Newton, RU, and Haff, GG. The influence of mental fatigue on sessional ratings of perceived exertion in elite open and closed skill sports athletes. *J Strength Cond Res* 35:963-969, 2021.

88. Coyne, JOC, Nimphius, S, Newton, RU, and Haff, GG. Does mathematical coupling matter to the acute to chronic workload ratio? A case study from elite sport. *Int J Sports Physiol Perform* 14:1447-1454, 2019.

89. Crewther, BT, and Cook, C. Relationships between salivary testosterone and cortisol concentrations and training performance in Olympic weightlifters. *J Sports Med Phys Fitness* 50:371-375, 2010.

90. Crewther, BT, Kilduff, LP, and Cook, CJ. Trained and untrained males show reliable salivary testosterone responses to a physical stimulus, but not a psychological stimulus. *J Endocrinol Invest* 37:1065-1072, 2014.

91. Crewther, BT, Lowe, T, Weatherby, RP, Gill, N, and Keogh, J. Neuromuscular performance of elite Rugby Union players and relationships with salivary hormones. *J Strength Cond Res* 23:2046-2053, 2009.

92. Cross, MJ, Williams, S, Trewartha, G, Kemp, SP, and Stokes, KA. The influence of in-season training loads on injury risk in professional Rugby Union. *Int J Sports Physiol Perform* 11:350-355, 2016.

93. Cummins, C, and Orr, R. Analysis of physical collisions in elite national Rugby League match play. *Int J Sports Physiol Perform* 10:732-739, 2015.

94. Cunniffe, B, Griffiths, H, Proctor, W, Davies, B, Baker, JS, and Jones, KP. Mucosal immunity and illness incidence in elite Rugby Union players across a season. *Med Sci Sports Exerc* 43:388-397, 2011.

95. Daanen, HA, Lamberts, RP, Kallen, VL, Jin, A, and Van Meeteren, NL. A systematic review on heart-rate recovery to monitor changes in training status in athletes. *Int J Sports Physiol Perform* 7:251-260, 2012.

96. Dardevet, D, Sornet, C, Savary, I, Debras, E, Patureau-Mirand, P, and Grizard, J. Glucocorticoid effects on insulin- and IGF-I-regulated muscle protein metabolism during aging. *J Endocrinol* 156:83-89, 1998.

97. de Zambotti, M, Cellini, N, Goldstone, A, Colrain, IM, and Baker, FC. Wearable sleep technology in clinical and research settings. *Med Sci Sports Exerc* 51:1538-1557, 2019.

98. de Zambotti, M, Rosas, L, Colrain, IM, and Baker, FC. The sleep of the ring: Comparison of the OURA sleep tracker against polysomnography. *Behav Sleep Med* 17:124-136, 2019.

99. DeWeese, BH, Gray, HS, Sams, ML, Scruggs, SK, and Serrano, AJ. Revising the definition of periodization: Merging historical principles with modern concerns. *Olympic Coach Magazine* 24:5-19, 2015.

100. Dobbs, WC, Fedewa, MV, MacDonald, HV, Holmes, CJ, Cicone, ZS, Plews, DJ, and Esco, MR. The accuracy of acquiring heart rate variability from portable devices: A systematic review and meta-analysis. *Sports Med* 49:417-435, 2019.

101. Dumke, CL, Brock, DW, Helms, BH, and Haff, GG. Heart rate at lactate threshold and cycling time trials. *J Strength Cond Res* 20:601-607, 2006.

102. Edelmann-Nusser, J, Hohmann, A, and Henneberg, B. Modeling and prediction of competitive performance in swimming upon neural networks. *Eur J Sport Sci* 2:1-10, 2002.

103. Edwards, S. High performance training and racing. In *The Heart Rate Monitor Book*. Edwards, S, ed. Sacramento, CA: Feet Fleet Press, 113-123, 1993.

104. Elias, M. Serum cortisol, testosterone, and testosterone-binding globulin responses to competitive fighting in human males. *Aggress Behav* 7:215-224, 1981.

105. Eston, R. Use of ratings of perceived exertion in sports. *Int J Sports Physiol Perform* 7:175-182, 2012.

106. Fahlman, MM, and Engels, HJ. Mucosal IgA and URTI in American college football players: A year longitudinal study. *Med Sci Sports Exerc* 37:374-380, 2005.

107. Figueira, B, Goncalves, B, Folgado, H, Masiulis, N, Calleja-Gonzalez, J, and Sampaio, J. Accuracy of a basketball indoor tracking system based on standard Bluetooth low energy channels (NBN23). *Sensors (Basel)* 18:1940, 2018.

108. Florini, JR. Hormonal control of muscle growth. *Muscle & Nerve* 10:577-598, 1987.

109. Folland, JP, Buckthorpe, MW, and Hannah, R. Human capacity for explosive force production: Neural and contractile determinants. *Scand J Med Sci Sports* 24:894-906, 2014.

110. Foster, C. Monitoring training in athletes with reference to overtraining syndrome. *Med Sci Sports Exerc* 30:1164-1168, 1998.

111. Foster, C, Daines, E, Hector, L, Snyder, AC, and Welsh, R. Athletic performance in relation to training load. *Wis Med J* 95:370-374, 1996.

112. Foster, C, Florhaug, JA, Franklin, J, Gottschall, L, Hrovatin, LA, Parker, S, Doleshal, P, and Dodge, C. A new approach to monitoring exercise training. *J Strength Cond Res* 15:109-115, 2001.

113. Fox, JL, Green, J, and Scanlan, AT. Not all about the effort? A comparison of playing intensities during winning and

losing game quarters in basketball. *Int J Sports Physiol Perform* 16:1-4, 2021.

114. Fox, JL, Stanton, R, Sargent, C, Wintour, SA, and Scanlan, AT. The association between training load and performance in team sports: A systematic review. *Sports Med* 48:2743-2774, 2018.

115. Fragala, MS, Kraemer, WJ, Denegar, CR, Maresh, CM, Mastro, AM, and Volek, JS. Neuroendocrine-immune interactions and responses to exercise. *Sports Med* 41:621-639, 2011.

116. Fry, AC, and Kraemer, WJ. Resistance exercise overtraining and overreaching: Neuroendocrine responses. *Sports Med* 23:106-129, 1997.

117. Fry, AC, Kraemer, WJ, Stone, MH, Koziris, LP, Thrush, JT, and Fleck, SJ. Relationships between serum testosterone, cortisol, and weightlifting performance. *J Strength Cond Res* 14:338-343, 2000.

118. Fullagar, HH, Skorski, S, Duffield, R, Hammes, D, Coutts, AJ, and Meyer, T. Sleep and athletic performance: The effects of sleep loss on exercise performance, and physiological and cognitive responses to exercise. *Sports Med* 45:161-186, 2015.

119. Gabbett, TJ. Relationship between accelerometer load, collisions, and repeated high-intensity effort activity in Rugby League players. *J Strength Cond Res* 29:3424-3431, 2015.

120. Gabbett, TJ. The training-injury prevention paradox: Should athletes be training smarter and harder? *Br J Sports Med* 50:273-280, 2016.

121. Gabbett, TJ. Workload monitoring and athlete management. In *Advanced Strength and Conditioning: An Evidence-Based Approach*. Turner, A, Comfort, P, eds. Abingdon, Oxon: Routledge, 137-150, 2018.

122. Gabbett, TJ, and Domrow, N. Relationships between training load, injury, and fitness in sub-elite collision sport athletes. *J Sports Sci* 25:1507-1519, 2007.

123. Gabbett, TJ, Hulin, BT, Blanch, P, and Whiteley, R. High training workloads alone do not cause sports injuries: How you get there is the real issue. *Br J Sports Med* 50:444-445, 2016.

124. Gabbett, TJ, Jenkins, DG, and Abernethy, B. Physical demands of professional Rugby League training and competition using microtechnology. *J Sci Med Sport* 15:80-86, 2012.

125. Gabbett, TJ, and Whiteley, R. Two training-load paradoxes: Can we work harder and smarter, can physical preparation and medical be teammates? *Int J Sports Physiol Perform* 12:S250-S254, 2017.

126. Garet, M, Tournaire, N, Roche, F, Laurent, R, Lacour, JR, Barthelemy, JC, and Pichot, V. Individual interdependence between nocturnal ANS activity and performance in swimmers. *Med Sci Sports Exerc* 36:2112-2118, 2004.

127. Gastin, P, B., Meyer, D, and Robinson, D. Perceptions of wellness to monitor adaptive responses to training and competition in elite Australian football. *J Strength Cond Res* 27:2518-2526, 2013.

128. Gastin, PB, Meyer, D, Huntsman, E, and Cook, J. Increase in injury risk with low body mass and aerobic-running fitness in elite Australian football. *Int J Sports Physiol Perform* 10:458-463, 2015.

129. Gaviglio, CM, Crewther, BT, Kilduff, LP, Stokes, KA, and Cook, CJ. Relationship between pregame concentrations of free testosterone and outcome in Rugby Union. *Int J Sports Physiol Perform* 9:324-331, 2014.

130. Gladue, BA, Boechler, M, and McCaul, KD. Hormonal response to competition in human males. *Aggress Behav* 15:409-422, 1989.

131. Gleeson, M. Mucosal immune responses and risk of respiratory illness in elite athletes. *Exerc Immunol Rev* 6:5-42, 2000.

132. Gleeson, M. Immune function and exercise. *Eur J Sport Sci* 4:52-66, 2004.

133. Gleeson, M, Bishop, N, Oliveira, M, McCauley, T, Tauler, P, and Muhamad, AS. Respiratory infection risk in athletes: Association with antigen-stimulated IL-10 production and salivary IgA secretion. *Scand J Med Sci Sports* 22:410-417, 2012.

134. Gleeson, M, and Bishop, NC. URI in athletes: Are mucosal immunity and cytokine responses key risk factors? *Exerc Sport Sci Rev* 41:148-153, 2013.

135. Gleeson, M, and Walsh, NP. The BASES expert statement on exercise, immunity, and infection. *J Sports Sci* 30:321-324, 2012.

136. Gonzalez-Bono, E, Salvador, A, Serrano, MA, and Ricarte, J. Testosterone, cortisol, and mood in a sports team competition. *Horm Behav* 35:55-62, 1999.

137. Gordon, AM, Huxley, AF, and Julian, FJ. The variation in isometric tension with sarcomere length in vertebrate muscle fibres. *J Physiol* 184:170-192, 1966.

138. Greenham, G, Buckley, JD, Garrett, J, Eston, R, and Norton, K. Biomarkers of physiological responses to periods of intensified, non-resistance-based exercise training in well-trained male athletes: A systematic review and meta-analysis. *Sports Med* 48:2517-2548, 2018.

139. Griffin, A, Kenny, IC, Comyns, TM, and Lyons, M. The association between the acute:chronic workload ratio and injury and its application in team sports: A systematic review. *Sports Med* 50:561-580, 2020.

140. Guppy, SN, Brady, CJ, Comfort, P, and Haff, GG. The isometric mid-thigh pull: Review and methodology—part I. *Prof Strength and Cond* 51:13-19, 2018.

141. Guppy, SN, Brady, CJ, Kotani, Y, Stone, MH, Medic, N, and Haff, GG. The effect of altering body posture and barbell position on the between-session reliability of force-time curve characteristics in the isometric mid-thigh pull. *Sports* 6:162-177, 2018.

142. Guppy, SN, Brady, CJ, Kotani, Y, Stone, MH, Medic, N, and Haff, GG. Effect of altering body posture and barbell position on the within-session reliability and magnitude of force-time curve characteristics in the isometric midthigh pull. *J Strength Cond Res* 33:3252-3262, 2019.

143. Gutmann, MC, Pollock, ML, Foster, C, and Schmidt, D. Training stress in Olympic speed skaters: A psychological perspective. *Phys Sportsmed* 12:45-57, 1984.

144. Hackett, DA, Johnson, NA, Halaki, M, and Chow, CM. A novel scale to assess resistance-exercise effort. *J Sports Sci* 30:1405-1413, 2012.

145. Hader, K, Rumpf, MC, Hertzog, M, Kilduff, LP, Girard, O, and Silva, JR. Monitoring the athlete match response:

Can external load variables predict post-match acute and residual fatigue in soccer? A systematic review with meta-analysis. *Sports Med Open* 5:48, 2019.

146. Haff, GG. Quantifying workloads in resistance training: A brief review. *Prof Strength and Cond* 10:31-40, 2010.

147. Haff, GG. Periodization for tactical populations. In *NSCA's Essentials of Tactical Strength and Conditioning*. Alvar, BA, Sell, K, Deuster, PA, eds. Champaign, IL: Human Kinetics, 181-204, 2017.

148. Haff, GG. Strength-isometric and dynamic testing. In *Performance Assessment in Strength and Conditioning*. Comfort, P, Jones, PA, McMahon, JJ, eds. New York: Routledge, Taylor Francis Group, 166-192, 2019.

149. Haff, GG. Periodization and programming of individual sports. In *NSCA's Essentials of Sport Science*. French, D, Torres Ronda, L, eds. Champaign, IL: Human Kinetics, 27-42, 2022.

150. Haff, GG, Carlock, JM, Hartman, MJ, Kilgore, JL, Kawamori, N, Jackson, JR, Morris, RT, Sands, WA, and Stone, MH. Force-time curve characteristics of dynamic and isometric muscle actions of elite women Olympic weightlifters. *J Strength Cond Res* 19:741-748, 2005.

151. Haff, GG, Jackson, JR, Kawamori, N, Carlock, JM, Hartman, MJ, Kilgore, JL, Morris, RT, Ramsey, MW, Sands, WA, and Stone, MH. Force-time curve characteristics and hormonal alterations during an eleven-week training period in elite women weightlifters. *J Strength Cond Res* 22:433-446, 2008.

152. Haff, GG, Ruben, RP, Lider, J, Twine, C, and Cormie, P. A comparison of methods for determining the rate of force development during isometric midthigh clean pulls. *J Strength Cond Res* 29:386-395, 2015.

153. Haff, GG, Stone, MH, O'Bryant, HS, Harman, E, Dinan, CN, Johnson, R, and Han, KH. Force-time dependent characteristics of dynamic and isometric muscle actions. *J Strength Cond Res* 11:269-272, 1997.

154. Häkkinen, K, Pakarinen, A, Alen, M, Kauhanen, H, and Komi, PV. Relationships between training volume, physical performance capacity, and serum hormone concentrations during prolonged training in elite weight lifters. *Int J Sports Med* 8 Suppl 1:61-65, 1987.

155. Häkkinen, K, Pakarinen, A, Alen, M, and Komi, PV. Serum hormones during prolonged training of neuromuscular performance. *Eur J Appl Physiol* 53:287-293, 1985.

156. Häkkinen, K, Pakarinen, A, and Kallinen, M. Neuromuscular adaptations and serum hormones in women during short-term intensive strength training. *Eur J Appl Physiol Occup Physiol* 64:106-111, 1992.

157. Halson, SL. Monitoring training load to understand fatigue in athletes. *Sports Med* 44:S139-147, 2014.

158. Halson, SL. Sleep in elite athletes and nutritional interventions to enhance sleep. *Sports Med* 44 Suppl 1:S13-23, 2014.

159. Halson, SL. Sleep monitoring in athletes: Motivation, methods, miscalculations and why it matters. *Sports Med* 49:1487-1497, 2019.

160. Halson, SL, Lancaster, GI, Jeukendrup, AE, and Gleeson, M. Immunological responses to overreaching in cyclists. *Med Sci Sports Exerc* 35:854-861, 2003.

161. Halson, SL, Peake, JM, and Sullivan, JP. Wearable technology for athletes: Information overload and pseudoscience? *Int J Sports Physiol Perform* 11:705-706, 2016.

162. Hamilton, D. Field Hockey. In *Science and Application of High-Intensity Interval Training*. Laursen, PB, Buchheit, M, eds. Champaign, IL: Human Kinetics, 455-476, 2019.

163. Harley, RA, Doust, J, and Mills, SH. Basketball. In *Sport and Exercise Physiology Guidelines: The British Association of Sport and Exercise Sciences Guide*. Winter, EM, Jones, AM, Davison, RCR, Bromley, PD, Mercer, TH, eds. London: Routledge, Taylor and Francis Group, 232-240, 2007.

164. Hart, NH, Nimphius, S, Spiteri, T, and Newton, RU. Leg strength and lean mass symmetry influences kicking performance in Australian football. *J Sports Sci Med* 13:157-165, 2014.

165. Hartmann, U, and Mester, J. Training and overtraining markers in selected sport events. *Med Sci Sports Exerc* 32:209-215, 2000.

166. Hausler, J, Halaki, M, and Orr, R. Application of global positioning system and microsensor technology in competitive Rugby League match-play: A systematic review and meta-analysis. *Sports Med* 46:559-588, 2016.

167. Hautala, AJ, Kiviniemi, AM, and Tulppo, MP. Individual responses to aerobic exercise: The role of the autonomic nervous system. *Neurosci Biobehav Rev* 33:107-115, 2009.

168. Hedley, M, Mackintosh, C, Shuttleworth, R, Humphrey, D, Sathyan, T, and Ho, P. Wireless tracking system for sports training indoors and outdoors. *Procedia Engineering* 2:2999-3004, 2010.

169. Hickson, RC, Czerwinski, SM, Falduto, MT, and Young, AP. Glucocorticoid antagonism by exercise and androgenic-anabolic steroids. *Med Sci Sports Exerc* 22:331-340, 1990.

170. Hiscock, DJ, Dawson, B, Donnelly, CJ, and Peeling, P. Muscle activation, blood lactate, and perceived exertion responses to changing resistance training programming variables. *Eur J Sport Sci* 16:536-544, 2016.

171. Hisler, GC, Hasler, BP, Franzen, PL, Clark, DB, and Twenge, JM. Screen media use and sleep disturbance symptom severity in children. *Sleep Health* 6:731-742, 2020.

172. Hopkins, WG. Quantification of training in competitive sports. Methods and applications. *Sports Med* 12:161-183, 1991.

173. Hopkins, WG, Marshall, SW, Batterham, AM, and Hanin, J. Progressive statistics for studies in sports medicine and exercise science. *Med Sci Sports Exerc* 41:3-13, 2009.

174. Hornsby, W, Gentles, J, Comfort, P, Suchomel, T, Mizuguchi, S, and Stone, M. Resistance training volume load with and without exercise displacement. *Sports* 6:137, 2018.

175. Hornsby, WG. Application to training. In *Performance Assessment in Strength and Conditioning*. Comfort, P, Jones, PA, McMahon, JJ, eds. New York: Routledge, 332-353, 2019.

176. Hornsby, WG, Gentles, JA, MacDonald, CJ, Mizuguchi, S, Ramsey, MW, and Stone, MH. Maximum strength, rate of force development, jump height, and peak power alterations in weightlifters across five months of training. *Sports* 5:78, 2017.

177. Hulin, BT, and Gabbett, TJ. Indeed association does not equal prediction: The never-ending search for the perfect acute:chronic workload ratio. *Br J Sports Med* 53:144-145, 2019.

178. Hulin, BT, Gabbett, TJ, Blanch, P, Chapman, P, Bailey, D, and Orchard, JW. Spikes in acute workload are associated with increased injury risk in elite cricket fast bowlers. *Br J Sports Med* 48:708-712, 2014.

179. Hulin, BT, Gabbett, TJ, Lawson, DW, Caputi, P, and Sampson, JA. The acute:chronic workload ratio predicts injury: High chronic workload may decrease injury risk in elite rugby league players. *Br J Sports Med* 50:231-236, 2016.

180. Hynynen, E, Uusitalo, A, Konttinen, N, and Rusko, H. Heart rate variability during night sleep and after awakening in overtrained athletes. *Med Sci Sports Exerc* 38:313-317, 2006.

181. Hynynen, E, Uusitalo, A, Konttinen, N, and Rusko, H. Cardiac autonomic responses to standing up and cognitive task in overtrained athletes. *Int J Sports Med* 29:552-558, 2008.

182. Iellamo, F, Legramante, JM, Pigozzi, F, Spataro, A, Norbiato, G, Lucini, D, and Pagani, M. Conversion from vagal to sympathetic predominance with strenuous training in high-performance world class athletes. *Circulation* 105:2719-2724, 2002.

183. Ikonen, JN, Joro, R, Uusitalo, AL, Kyrolainen, H, Kovanen, V, Atalay, M, and Tanskanen-Tervo, MM. Effects of military training on plasma amino acid concentrations and their associations with overreaching. *Exp Biol Med (Maywood)* 245:1029-1038, 2020.

184. Impellizzeri, FM, Marcora, SM, and Coutts, AJ. Internal and external training load: 15 years on. *Int J Sports Physiol Perform* 14:270-273, 2019.

185. Impellizzeri, FM, McCall, A, Ward, P, Bornn, L, and Coutts, AJ. Training load and its role in injury prevention, part 2: Conceptual and methodologic pitfalls. *J Athl Train* 55:893-901, 2020.

186. Impellizzeri, FM, Menaspa, P, Coutts, AJ, Kalkhoven, J, and Menaspa, MJ. Training load and its role in injury prevention, part I: Back to the future. *J Athl Train* 55:885-892, 2020.

187. Impellizzeri, FM, Rampinini, E, Coutts, AJ, Sassi, A, and Marcora, SM. Use of RPE-based training load in soccer. *Med Sci Sports Exerc* 36:1042-1047, 2004.

188. Impellizzeri, FM, Rampinini, E, and Marcora, SM. Physiological assessment of aerobic training in soccer. *J Sports Sci* 23:583-592, 2005.

189. Impellizzeri, FM, Tenan, MS, Kempton, T, Novak, A, and Coutts, AJ. Acute:chronic workload ratio: Conceptual issues and fundamental pitfalls. *Int J Sports Physiol Perform* 15:907–913, 2020.

190. Impellizzeri, FM, Woodcock, S, Coutts, AJ, Fanchini, M, McCall, A, and Vigotsky, AD. What role do chronic workloads play in the acute to chronic workload ratio? Time to dismiss ACWR and its underlying theory. *Sports Med* 51:581-592, 2021.

191. Jacobs, I. Blood lactate: Implications for training and sports performance. *Sports Med* 3:10-25, 1986.

192. James, LP, Roberts, LA, Haff, GG, Kelly, VG, and Beckman, EM. Validity and reliability of a portable isometric mid-thigh clean pull. *J Strength Cond Res* 31:1378-1386, 2017.

193. Jennings, D, Cormack, S, Coutts, AJ, Boyd, L, and Aughey, RJ. The validity and reliability of GPS units for measuring distance in team sport specific running patterns. *Int J Sports Physiol Perform* 5:328-341, 2010.

194. Jeukendrup, AE, and Hesselink, MK. Overtraining—what do lactate curves tell us? *Br J Sports Med* 28:239-240, 1994.

195. Jeukendrup, AE, and Van Diemen, A. Heart rate monitoring during training and competition in cyclists. *J Sport Sci* 16:S91-S99, 1998.

196. Jobson, SA, Passfield, L, Atkinson, G, Barton, G, and Scarf, P. The analysis and utilization of cycling training data. *Sports Med* 39:833-844, 2009.

197. Jones, MT, and Gillham, B. Factors involved in the regulation of adrenocorticotropic hormone/beta-lipotropic hormone. *Physiol Rev* 68:743-818, 1988.

198. Jordan, MJ, Aagaard, P, and Herzog, W. Lower limb asymmetry in mechanical muscle function: A comparison between ski racers with and without ACL reconstruction. *Scand J Med Sci Sports* 25:e301-e309, 2014.

199. Jovanovic, M, Torres Ronda, L, and French, DM. Statistical modeling. In *NSCA's Essentials of Sport Science*. French, DM, Torres Ronda, L, eds. Champaign, IL: Human Kinetics, 257-287, 2022.

200. Kellmann, M. Psychological assessment of under recovery. In *Enhancing Recovery: Preventing Underperformance in Athletes*. Kellmann, M, ed. Champaign, IL: Human Kinetics, 37-55, 2002.

201. Kellmann, M, and Gunther, KD. Changes in stress and recovery in elite rowers during preparation for the Olympic Games. *Med Sci Sports Exerc* 32:676-683, 2000.

202. Kellmann, M, and Kallus, KW. Construction of the Recovery-Stress Questionnaire for Athletes. In *Recovery-Stress Questionnaire for Athletes*. Champaign, IL: Human Kinetics, 29-34, 2001.

203. Kellmann, M, and Kallus, KW. Description of the Recovery-Stress Questionnaire for Athletes. In *Recovery-Stress Questionnaire for Athletes: User Manual*. Champaign, IL: Human Kinetics, 5-10, 2001.

204. Kempton, T, Sirotic, AC, Rampinini, E, and Coutts, AJ. Metabolic power demands of Rugby League match play. *Int J Sports Physiol Perform* 10:23-28, 2015.

205. Kenttä, G, and Hassmén, P. Overtraining and recovery: A conceptual model. *Sports Med* 26:1-16, 1998.

206. Kiely, M, Warrington, G, McGoldrick, A, and Cullen, S. Physiological and performance monitoring in competitive sporting environments: A review for elite individual sports. *Strength Cond J* 41:62-74, 2019.

207. Kindermann, W, Schnabel, A, Schmitt, WM, Biro, G, Cassens, J, and Weber, F. Catecholamines, growth hormone, cortisol, insulin, and sex hormones in anaerobic and aerobic exercise. *Eur J Appl Physiol* 49:389-399, 1982.

208. Kinugasa, T, Cerin, E, and Hooper, S. Single-subject research designs and data analyses for assessing elite athletes' conditioning. *Sports Med* 34:1035-1050, 2004.

209. Kipp, K, Krzyszkowski, J, and Kant-Hull, D. Use of machine learning to model volume load effects on

changes in jump performance. *Int J Sports Physiol Perform* 15:285-287, 2020.

210. Kölling, S, Hitzschke, B, Holst, T, Ferrauti, A, Meyer, T, Pfeiffer, M, and Kellmann, M. Validity of the acute recovery and stress scale: Training monitoring of the German junior national field hockey team. *Int J Sports Sci Coach* 10:529-542, 2015.

211. Kölling, S, Schaffran, P, Bibbey, A, Drew, M, Raysmith, B, Nassi, A, and Kellmann, M. Validation of the Acute Recovery and Stress Scale (ARSS) and the Short Recovery and Stress Scale (SRSS) in three English-speaking regions. *J Sports Sci* 38:130-139, 2020.

212. Komi, PV. Stretch-shortening cycle: A powerful model to study normal and fatigued muscle. *J Biomech* 33:1197-1206, 2000.

213. Kraemer, WJ. Endocrine response and adaptation to strength training. In *Strength and Power in Sport*. Komi, PV, ed. Oxford: Blackwell Scientific, 291-304, 1992.

214. Kraemer, WJ, and Ratamess, N. Endocrine Responses and Adaptations to Strength and Power Training. In *Strength and Power in Sport*. Komi, PV, ed. Oxford: Blackwell Scientific, 361-286, 2003.

215. Kraemer, WJ, and Ratamess, NA. Hormonal responses and adaptations to resistance exercise and training. *Sports Med* 35:339-361, 2005.

216. Kraft, JA, Green, JM, and Gast, TM. Work distribution influences session ratings of perceived exertion response during resistance exercise matched for total volume. *J Strength Cond Res* 28:2042-2046, 2014.

217. Krustrup, P, Zebis, M, Jensen, JM, and Mohr, M. Game-induced fatigue patterns in elite female soccer. *J Strength Cond Res* 24:437-441, 2010.

218. Lacey, JI, Bateman, DE, and Vanlehn, R. Autonomic response specificity: An experimental study. *Psychosom Med* 15:8-21, 1953.

219. Lacey, JI, and Lacey, BC. Verification and extension of the principle of autonomic response-stereotypy. *Am J Psychol* 71:50-73, 1958.

220. Lambert, MI, Mbambo, ZH, and St Clair Gibson, A. Heart rate during training and competition for long-distance running. *J Sports Sci* 16:S85-S90, 1998.

221. Lamberts, RP, Lemmink, KA, Durandt, JJ, and Lambert, MI. Variation in heart rate during submaximal exercise: Implications for monitoring training. *J Strength Cond Res* 18:641-645, 2004.

222. Lan, MF, Lane, AM, Roy, J, and Hanin, NA. Validity of the Brunel Mood Scale for use with Malaysian athletes. *J Sports Sci Med* 11:131-135, 2012.

223. Lee, CM, Wood, RH, and Welsch, MA. Influence of short-term endurance exercise training on heart rate variability. *Med Sci Sports Exerc* 35:961-969, 2003.

224. Lee, EC, Fragala, MS, Kavouras, SA, Queen, RM, Pryor, JL, and Casa, DJ. Biomarkers in sports and exercise: Tracking health, performance, and recovery in athletes. *J Strength Cond Res* 31:2920-2937, 2017.

225. Leunes, A. Updated bibliography on the profile of mood states in sport and exercise psychology research. *J Appl Sport Psychol* 12:110-113, 2000.

226. Leunes, A, and Burger, J. Profile of mood states research in sport and exercise psychology: Past, present, and future. *J Appl Sport Psychol* 12:5-15, 2000.

227. Li, RT, Kling, SR, Salata, MJ, Cupp, SA, Sheehan, J, and Voos, JE. Wearable performance devices in sports medicine. *Sports Health* 8:74-78, 2016.

228. Little, T, and Williams, AG. Measures of exercise intensity during soccer training drills with professional soccer players. *J Strength Cond Res* 21:367-371, 2007.

229. Lolli, L, Batterham, AM, Hawkins, R, Kelly, DM, Strudwick, AJ, Thorpe, RT, Gregson, W, and Atkinson, G. The acute-to-chronic workload ratio: An inaccurate scaling index for an unnecessary normalisation process? *Br J Sports Med* 53:1510-1512, 2019.

230. Losnegard, T, Skarli, S, Hansen, J, Roterud, S, Svendsen, IS, Rønnestad, BR, and Paulsen, G. Is rating of perceived exertion a valuable tool for monitoring exercise intensity during steady-state conditions in elite endurance athletes? *Int J Sports Physiol Perform* 16:1589-1595, 2021.

231. Lovell, TW, Sirotic, AC, Impellizzeri, FM, and Coutts, AJ. Factors affecting perception of effort (session rating of perceived exertion) during Rugby League training. *Int J Sports Physiol Perform* 8:62-69, 2013.

232. Lucia, A, Hoyos, J, Perez, M, and Chicharro, JL. Heart rate and performance parameters in elite cyclists: A longitudinal study. *Med Sci Sports Exerc* 32:1777-1782., 2000.

233. Lucia, A, Hoyos, J, Santalla, A, Earnest, C, and Chicharro, JL. Tour de France versus Vuelta a Espana: Which is harder? *Med Sci Sports Exerc* 35:872-878., 2003.

234. Maffiuletti, NA, Aagaard, P, Blazevich, AJ, Folland, J, Tillin, N, and Duchateau, J. Rate of force development: Physiological and methodological considerations. *Eur J Appl Physiol* 116:1091-1116, 2016.

235. Manzi, V, Castagna, C, Padua, E, Lombardo, M, D'Ottavio, S, Massaro, M, Volterrani, M, and Iellamo, F. Dose-response relationship of autonomic nervous system responses to individualized training impulse in marathon runners. *Am J Physiol Heart Circ Physiol* 296:H1733-H1740, 2009.

236. Manzi, V, Iellamo, F, Impellizzeri, F, D'Ottavio, S, and Castagna, C. Relation between individualized training impulses and performance in distance runners. *Med Sci Sports Exerc* 41:2090-2096, 2009.

237. Marcora, SM, Bosio, A, and de Morree, HM. Locomotor muscle fatigue increases cardiorespiratory responses and reduces performance during intense cycling exercise independently from metabolic stress. *Am J Physiol Regul Integr Comp Physiol* 294:R874-R883, 2008.

238. Marcora, SM, Staiano, W, and Manning, V. Mental fatigue impairs physical performance in humans. *J Appl Physiol* 106:857-864, 2009.

239. Mariscal, G, Vera, P, Platero, JL, Bodi, F, de la Rubia Orti, JE, and Barrios, C. Changes in different salivary biomarkers related to physiologic stress in elite handball players: The case of females. *Sci Rep* 9:19554, 2019.

240. Martin, DT, and Andersen, MB. Heart rate-perceived exertion relationship during training and taper. *J Sports Med Phys Fitness* 40:201-208, 2000.

241. Martin, EA, and Beckham, GK. Isometric mid-thigh pull performance in rugby players: A systematic literature review. *J Funct Morphol Kinesiol* 5:91, 2020.

242. Mayberry, JK, Patterson, B, and Wagner, P. Improving vertical jump profiles through prescribed movement plans. *J Strength Cond Res* 32:1619-1626, 2018.

243. Mazur, A, and Booth, A. Testosterone and dominance in men. *Behav Brain Sci* 21:353-363, 1998.

244. McCaulley, GO, McBride, JM, Cormie, P, Hudson, MB, Nuzzo, JL, Quindry, JC, and Travis Triplett, N. Acute hormonal and neuromuscular responses to hypertrophy, strength and power type resistance exercise. *Eur J Appl Physiol* 105:695-704, 2009.

245. McGuigan, M. Athlete monitoring guidelines for individual sports. In *Monitoring Training and Performance in Athletes*. Champaign, IL: Human Kinetics, 171-188, 2017.

246. McGuigan, M. Athlete monitoring guidelines for team sports. In *Monitoring Training and Performance in Athletes*. Champaign, IL: Human Kinetics, 189-201, 2017.

247. McGuigan, M. Measures of fitness and fatigue. In *Monitoring Training and Performance in Athletes*. Champaign, IL: Human Kinetics, 103-134, 2017.

248. McGuigan, M. Quantifying training stress. In *Monitoring Training and Performance in Athletes*. Champaign, IL: Human Kinetics, 69-101, 2017.

249. McGuigan, MR, and Foster, C. A new approach to monitoring resistance training. *Strength Cond J* 26:42-47, 2004.

250. McLaren, SJ, Macpherson, TW, Coutts, AJ, Hurst, C, Spears, IR, and Weston, M. The relationships between internal and external measures of training load and intensity in team sports: A meta-analysis. *Sports Med* 48:641-658, 2018.

251. McLellan, CP, Lovell, DI, and Gass, GC. Biochemical and endocrine responses to impact and collision during elite Rugby League match play. *J Strength Cond Res* 25:1553-1562, 2011.

252. McLellan, CP, Lovell, DI, and Gass, GC. Markers of post-match fatigue in professional Rugby League players. *J Strength Cond Res* 25:1030-1039, 2011.

253. McMahon, JJ, Lake, JP, and Suchomel, TJ. Vertical jump testing. In *Performance Assessment in Strength and Conditioning*. Comfort, P, Jones, PA, McMahon, JJ, eds. New York: Routledge, 96-116, 2019.

254. McMillan, JL, Stone, MH, Sartin, J, Keith, R, Marple, D, Brown, C, and Lewis, RD. 20-hour physiological responses to a single weight-training session. *J Strength Cond Res* 7:9-21, 1993.

255. Meeusen, R, Duclos, M, Foster, C, Fry, A, Gleeson, M, Nieman, D, Raglin, J, Rietjens, G, Steinacker, J, Urhausen, A, European College of Sport Science, and American College of Sports Medicine. Prevention, diagnosis, and treatment of the overtraining syndrome: Joint consensus statement of the European College of Sport Science and the American College of Sports Medicine. *Med Sci Sports Exerc* 45:186-205, 2013.

256. Menaspa, MJ, Menaspa, P, Clark, SA, and Fanchini, M. Validity of the online athlete management system to assess training load. *Int J Sports Physiol Perform* 13:750-754, 2018.

257. Meyer, T, Gabriel, HH, and Kindermann, W. Is determination of exercise intensities as percentages of VO2max or HRmax adequate? *Med Sci Sports Exerc* 31:1342-1345, 1999.

258. Milanez, VF, Ramos, SP, Okuno, NM, Boullosa, DA, and Nakamura, FY. Evidence of a non-linear dose-response relationship between training load and stress markers in elite female futsal players. *J Sports Sci Med* 13:22-29, 2014.

259. Miller, DJ, Lastella, M, Scanlan, AT, Bellenger, C, Halson, SL, Roach, GD, and Sargent, C. A validation study of the WHOOP strap against polysomnography to assess sleep. *J Sports Sci* 38:2631-2636, 2020.

260. Moeskops, S, Oliver, JL, Read, PJ, Cronin, JB, Myer, GD, Haff, GG, and Lloyd, RS. Within- and between-session reliability of the isometric midthigh pull in young female athletes. *J Strength Cond Res* 32:1892-1901, 2018.

261. Moreira, A, Bilsborough, JC, Sullivan, CJ, Ciancosi, M, Aoki, MS, and Coutts, AJ. Training periodization of professional Australian football players during an entire Australian Football League season. *Int J Sports Physiol Perform* 10:566-571, 2015.

262. Morgan, W, O'Connor, P, Sparling, P, and Pate, R. Psychological characterization of the elite female distance runner. *Int J Sports Med* 8:S124-S131, 1987.

263. Morgan, WP, Brown, DR, Raglin, JS, O'Connor, PJ, and Ellickson, KA. Psychological monitoring of overtraining and staleness. *Br J Sports Med* 21:107-114, 1987.

264. Morgan, WP, and Costill, DL. Selected psychological characteristics and health behaviors of aging marathon runners: A longitudinal study. *Int J Sports Med* 17:305-312, 1996.

265. Morgan, WP, Costill, DL, Flynn, MG, Raglin, JS, and O'Connor, PJ. Mood disturbance following increased training in swimmers. *Med Sci Sports Exerc* 20:408-414, 1988.

266. Morton, RH, Fitz-Clarke, JR, and Banister, EW. Modeling human performance in running. *J Appl Physiol* 69:1171-1177, 1990.

267. Mourot, L, Bouhaddi, M, Tordi, N, Rouillon, JD, and Regnard, J. Short- and long-term effects of a single bout of exercise on heart rate variability: Comparison between constant and interval training exercises. *Eur J Appl Physiol* 92:508-517, 2004.

268. Mujika, I. Quantification of training and competition loads in endurance sports: Methods and applications. *Int J Sports Physiol Perform* 12:S29-S217, 2017.

269. Munck, A, Guyre, PM, and Holbrook, NJ. Physiological functions of glucocorticoids in stress and their relation to pharmacological actions. *Endocr Rev* 5:25-44, 1984.

270. Murray, NB, Gabbett, TJ, Townshend, AD, and Blanch, P. Calculating acute:chronic workload ratios using exponentially weighted moving averages provides a more sensitive indicator of injury likelihood than rolling averages. *Br J Sports Med* 51:749-754, 2017.

271. Murray, NB, Gabbett, TJ, Townshend, AD, Hulin, BT, and McLellan, CP. Individual and combined effects of acute and chronic running loads on injury risk in elite Australian footballers. *Scand J Med Sci Sports* 27:990-998, 2017.

272. Nässi, A, Ferrauti, A, Meyer, T, Pfeiffer, M, and Kellmann, M. Development of two short measures for recovery and stress in sport. *Eur J Sport Sci* 17:894-903, 2017.

273. Nässi, A, Ferrauti, A, Meyer, T, Pfeiffer, M, and Kellmann, M. Psychological tools used for monitoring training responses of athletes. *Perform Enhanc Health* 5:125-133, 2017.

274. Navalta, JW, Montes, J, Bodell, NG, Salatto, RW, Manning, JW, and DeBeliso, M. Concurrent heart rate validity of wearable technology devices during trail running. *PLoS One* 15:e0238569, 2020.

275. Nevill, AM, Williams, AM, Boreham, C, Wallace, ES, Davison, GW, Abt, G, Lane, AM, and Winter, EEB. Can we trust "magnitude-based inference"? *J Sports Sci* 36:2769-2770, 2018.

276. Neville, V, Gleeson, M, and Folland, JP. Salivary IgA as a risk factor for upper respiratory infections in elite professional athletes. *Med Sci Sports Exerc* 40:1228-1236, 2008.

277. Newton, RU, Hakkinen, K, Hakkinen, A, McCormick, M, Volek, J, and Kraemer, WJ. Mixed-methods resistance training increases power and strength of young and older men. *Med Sci Sports Exerc* 34:1367-1375, 2002.

278. Norris, D, Joyce, D, Siegler, J, Clock, J, and Lovell, R. Recovery of force-time characteristics following Australian rules football matches: Examining the utility of the isometric mid-thigh pull. *Int J Sports Physiol Perform* 14:765-770, 2019.

279. Norris, SR, and Smith, DJ. Planning, periodization, and sequencing training and competition: The rationale for a competently planned, optimally executed training and competition program, supported by a multidisciplinary team. In *Enhancing Recovery: Preventing Underperformance in Athletes.* Kellmann, M, ed. Champaign, IL: Human Kinetics, 121-141, 2002.

280. Obmiński, Z. Pre- and post-start hormone levels in blood as an indicator of psycho-physiological load with junior judo competitors. *Polish Journal of Sport & Tourism* 16:158-165, 2009.

281. Obrist, PA. Heart rate and somatic-motor coupling during classical aversive conditioning in humans. *J Exp Psychol* 77:180-193, 1968.

282. Olbrecht, J. Determining training intensity and content. In *The Science of Winning: Planning, Periodizing, and Optimizing Swim Training.* Luton, England: Swimshop, 95-166, 2000.

283. Otter, RT, Brink, MS, van der Does, HT, and Lemmink, KA. Monitoring perceived stress and recovery in relation to cycling performance in female athletes. *Int J Sports Med* 37:12-18, 2016.

284. Pagani, M, and Lucini, D. Can autonomic monitoring predict results in distance runners? *Am J Physiol Heart Circ Physiol* 296:H1721-H1722, 2009.

285. Painter, K, Haff, G, Triplett, N, Stuart, C, Hornsby, G, Ramsey, M, Bazyler, C, and Stone, M. Resting hormone alterations and injuries: Block vs. DUP weight-training among D-1 track and field athletes. *Sports* 6:3, 2018.

286. Painter, KB, Haff, GG, Ramsey, MW, McBride, J, Triplett, T, Sands, WA, Lamont, HS, Stone, ME, and Stone, MH. Strength gains: Block vs DUP weight-training among track and field athletes. *Int J Sports Physiol Perform* 7:161-169, 2012.

287. Papacosta, E, Nassis, GP, and Gleeson, M. Salivary hormones and anxiety in winners and losers of an international judo competition. *J Sports Sci* 34:1281-1287, 2016.

288. Paul, D, Read, P, Farooq, A, and Jones, L. Factors influencing the association between coach and athlete rating of exertion: A systematic review and meta-analysis. *Sports Med Open* 7:1, 2021.

289. Pfeiffer, M, and Hohmann, A. Applications of neural networks in training science. *Hum Mov Sci* 31:344-359, 2012.

290. Plews, DJ, Laursen, PB, Kilding, AE, and Buchheit, M. Heart rate variability in elite triathletes, is variation in variability the key to effective training? A case comparison. *Eur J Appl Physiol* 112:3729-3741, 2012.

291. Plews, DJ, Laursen, PB, Stanley, J, Kilding, AE, and Buchheit, M. Training adaptation and heart rate variability in elite endurance athletes: Opening the door to effective monitoring. *Sports Med* 43:779-781, 2014.

292. Plisk, SS. Speed, agility, and speed-endurance development. In *Essentials of Strength Training and Conditioning.* 3rd ed. Baechle, TR, Earle, RW, eds. Champaign, IL: Human Kinetics, 2008.

293. Pluim, BM, and Drew, MK. It's not the destination, it's the "road to load" that matters: A tennis injury prevention perspective. *Br J Sports Med* 50:641-642, 2016.

294. Portier, H, Louisy, F, Laude, D, Berthelot, M, and Guezennec, CY. Intense endurance training on heart rate and blood pressure variability in runners. *Med Sci Sports Exerc* 33:1120-1125, 2001.

295. Pritchett, RC, Green, JM, Wickwire, PJ, and Kovacs, M. Acute and session RPE responses during resistance training: Bouts to failure at 60% and 90% of 1RM. *S Afr J Sports Med* 21:23-26, 2009.

296. Prudholme, DC, Coburn, JW, Lynn, SK, and Lockie, RG. Relationships between sprint, acceleration, and deceleration metrics with training load in Division I collegiate women's soccer players. *J Hum Kinet* 85:53-62, 2022.

297. Putlur, P, Foster, C, Miskowski, JA, Kane, MK, Burton, SE, Scheett, TP, and McGuigan, MR. Alteration of immune function in women collegiate soccer players and college students. *J Sports Sci Med* 3:234-243, 2004.

298. Pyne, DB, and Martin, DT. Fatigue—insights from individual and team sports. In *Regulation of Fatigue in Exercise.* New York: Nova Science, 177-185, 2011.

299. Quante, M, Kaplan, ER, Rueschman, M, Cailler, M, Buxton, OM, and Redline, S. Practical considerations in using accelerometers to assess physical activity, sedentary behavior, and sleep. *Sleep Health* 1:275-284, 2015.

300. Rabbani, A, Kargarfard, M, Castagna, C, Clemente, FM, and Twist, C. Associations between selected training-stress measures and fitness changes in male soccer players. *Int J Sports Physiol Perform* 14:1050-1057, 2019.

301. Raglin, JS, Morgan, WP, and Luchsinger, AE. Mood and self-motivation in successful and unsuccessful female rowers. *Med Sci Sports Exerc* 22:849-853, 1990.

302. Rico-Gonzalez, M, Clemente, FM, Oliveira, R, Bustamante-Hernandez, N, and Pino-Ortega, J. Part I: Relationship among training load management, salivary immuno-

globulin A, and upper respiratory tract infection in team sport: A systematic review. *Healthcare (Basel)* 9:366, 2021.

303. Roach, GD, Schmidt, WF, Aughey, RJ, Bourdon, PC, Soria, R, Claros, JC, Garvican-Lewis, LA, Buchheit, M, Simpson, BM, Hammond, K, Kley, M, Wachsmuth, N, Gore, CJ, and Sargent, C. The sleep of elite athletes at sea level and high altitude: A comparison of sea-level natives and high-altitude natives (ISA3600). *Br J Sports Med* 47:i114-i120, 2013.

304. Robertson, S, Bartlett, JD, and Gastin, PB. Red, amber, or green? Athlete monitoring in team sport: The need for decision-support systems. *Int J Sports Physiol Perform* 12:S273-S279, 2017.

305. Robineau, J, Marrier, B, Le Meur, Y, Piscione, J, Peeters, A, and Lacome, M. "Road to Rio": A case study of workload periodization strategy in rugby-7s during an Olympic season. *Front Sports Act Living* 1:72, 2020.

306. Rowbottom, DG. Periodization of training. In *Exercise and Sport Science*. Garrett, WE, Kirkendall, DT, eds. Philadelphia, PA: Lippicott Williams and Wilkins, 499-512, 2000.

307. Rushall, BS. A tool for measuring stress tolerance in elite athletes. *J Appl Sport Psychol* 2:51-66, 1990.

308. Sainani, KL. The problem with "magnitude-based inference". *Med Sci Sports Exerc* 50:2166-2176, 2018.

309. Sainani, KL. Response. *Med Sci Sports Exerc* 51:600, 2019.

310. Salvador, A, Simon, V, Suay, F, and Llorens, L. Testosterone and cortisol responses to competitive fighting in human males: A pilot study. *Aggress Behav* 13:9-13, 1987.

311. Sands, W, Cardinale, M, McNeal, J, Murray, S, Sole, C, Reed, J, Apostolopoulos, N, and Stone, M. Recommendations for measurement and management of an elite athlete. *Sports* 7:105, 2019.

312. Sands, W, and Stone, M. Are you progressing and how would you know? *Olympic Coach* 17:4-10, 2005.

313. Sands, WA. Monitoring elite female gymnasts. *Natl Strength Cond Assoc J* 13:66-71, 1991.

314. Sands, WA, Kavanaugh, AA, Murray, SR, McNeal, JR, and Jemni, M. Modern techniques and technologies applied to training and performance monitoring. *Int J Sports Physiol Perform* 12:S263-S272, 2017.

315. Sands, WA, and McNeal, JR. Predicting athlete preparation and performance. *J Sport Behav* 23:289-310, 2000.

316. Sands, WA, McNeal, JR, and Stone, MH. Plaudits and pitfalls in studying elite athletes. *Percept Mot Skills* 100:22-24, 2005.

317. Saw, AE, Main, LC, and Gastin, PB. Role of a self-report measure in athlete preparation. *J Strength Cond Res* 29:685-691, 2015.

318. Saw, AE, Main, LC, and Gastin, PB. Monitoring the athlete training response: Subjective self-reported measures trump commonly used objective measures: A systematic review. *Br J Sports Med* 50:281-291, 2016.

319. Scanlan, AT, Wen, N, Guy, JH, Elsworthy, N, Lastella, M, Pyne, DB, Conte, D, and Dalbo, VJ. The isometric midthigh pull in basketball: An effective predictor of sprint and jump performance in male, adolescent players. *Int J Sports Physiol Perform* 15:409–415, 2020.

320. Scanlan, AT, Wen, N, Pyne, DB, Stojanovic, E, Milanovic, Z, Conte, D, Vaquera, A, and Dalbo, VJ. Power-related determinants of modified agility T-test performance in male adolescent basketball players. *J Strength Cond Res* 35:2248-2254, 2021.

321. Schneider, C, Wiewelhove, T, Raeder, C, Flatt, AA, Hoos, O, Hottenrott, L, Schumbera, O, Kellmann, M, Meyer, T, Pfeiffer, M, and Ferrauti, A. Heart rate variability monitoring during strength and high-intensity interval training overload microcycles. *Front Physiol* 10, 2019.

322. Scott, BR, Duthie, GM, Thornton, HR, and Dascombe, BJ. Training monitoring for resistance exercise: Theory and applications. *Sports Med* 46:687-698, 2016.

323. Shambroom, JR, Fabregas, SE, and Johnstone, J. Validation of an automated wireless system to monitor sleep in healthy adults. *J Sleep Res* 21:221-230, 2012.

324. Shimano, T, Kraemer, WJ, Spiering, BA, Volek, JS, Hatfield, DL, Silvestre, R, Vingren, JL, Fragala, MS, Maresh, CM, Fleck, SJ, Newton, RU, Spreuwenberg, LP, and Hakkinen, K. Relationship between the number of repetitions and selected percentages of one repetition maximum in free weight exercises in trained and untrained men. *J Strength Cond Res* 20:819-823, 2006.

325. Singh, F, Foster, C, Tod, D, and McGuigan, MR. Monitoring different types of resistance training using session rating of perceived exertion. *Int J Sports Physiol Perform* 2:34-45, 2007.

326. Smith, DJ, and Norris, SR. Changes in glutamine and glutamate concentrations for tracking training tolerance. *Med Sci Sports Exerc* 32:684-689, 2000.

327. Smith, LL. Cytokine hypothesis of overtraining: A physiological adaptation to excessive stress? *Med Sci Sports Exerc* 32:317-331, 2000.

328. Smith, LL. Tissue trauma: The underlying cause of overtraining syndrome? *J Strength Cond Res* 18:185-193, 2004.

329. Snyder, AC, Jeukendrup, AE, Hesselink, MK, Kuipers, H, and Foster, C. A physiological/psychological indicator of over-reaching during intensive training. *Int J Sports Med* 14:29-32, 1993.

330. Soligard, T, Schwellnus, M, Alonso, J-M, Bahr, R, Clarsen, B, Dijkstra, HP, Gabbett, T, Gleeson, M, Hägglund, M, Hutchinson, MR, Janse van Rensburg, C, Khan, KM, Meeusen, R, Orchard, JW, Pluim, BM, Raftery, M, Budgett, R, and Engebretsen, L. How much is too much? (Part 1) International Olympic Committee consensus statement on load in sport and risk of injury. *Br J Sports Med* 50:1030-1041, 2016.

331. Spencer, M, Lawrence, S, Rechichi, C, Bishop, D, Dawson, B, and Goodman, C. Time-motion analysis of elite field hockey, with special reference to repeated-sprint activity. *J Sports Sci* 22:843-850, 2004.

332. Stevens, TG, de Ruiter, CJ, van Niel, C, van de Rhee, R, Beek, PJ, and Savelsbergh, GJ. Measuring acceleration and deceleration in soccer-specific movements using a local position measurement (LPM) system. *Int J Sports Physiol Perform* 9:446-456, 2014.

333. Stone, MH, and Fry, AC. Increased training volume in strength/power athletes. In *Overtraining in Sport*. Kreider, RB, Fry, AC, O'Toole, ML, eds. Champaign, IL: Human Kinetics, 87-106, 1998.

334. Stone, MH, Keith, R, Kearney, JT, Wilson, GD, and Fleck, SJ. Overtraining: A review of the signs and symptoms of overtraining. *J Strength Cond Res* 5:35-50, 1991.

335. Stone, MH, O'Bryant, HS, Hornsby, G, Cunanan, A, Mizuguchi, S, Suarez, DG, South, M, Marsh, D, Haff, GG, and Ramsey, MW. Using the isometric mid-thigh pull in the monitoring of weightlifters: 25+ years of experience. *Professional Strength and Conditioning* 54:19-26, 2019.

336. Stone, MH, Stone, ME, and Sands, WA. Modes of resistance training. In *Principles and Practice of Resistance Training*. Champaign, IL: Human Kinetics, 241-258, 2007.

337. Suarez, DG, Mizuguchi, S, Hornsby, WG, Cunanan, AJ, Marsh, DJ, and Stone, MH. Phase-specific changes in rate of force development and muscle morphology throughout a block periodized training cycle in weightlifters. *Sports* 7:129, 2019.

338. Sullivan, C, Bilsborough, JC, Cianciosi, M, Hocking, J, Cordy, J, and Coutts, AJ. Match score affects activity profile and skill performance in professional Australian football players. *J Sci Med Sport* 17:326-331, 2014.

339. Swart, J, and Jennings, C. Use of blood lactate concentration as a marker of training status. *S Afr J Sports Med* 16:1-5, 2004.

340. Sweeting, AJ, Cormack, SJ, Morgan, S, and Aughey, RJ. When is a sprint a sprint? A review of the analysis of team-sport athlete activity profile. *Front Physiol* 8:432, 2017.

341. Tang, RJ, and Wiltshire, HD. Rugby Union. In *Sport and Exercise Physiology Testing Guidelines: The British Association of Sport and Exercise Science Guide*. Winter, EM, Jones, AM, Davison, RCR, Bromley, PD, Mercer, TH, eds. London: Routledge, Taylor & Francis, 262-271, 2007.

342. Tanskanen, MM, Kyröläinen, H, Uusitalo, AL, Huovinen, J, Nissilä, J, Kinnunen, H, Atalay, M, and Häkkinen, K. Serum sex hormone-binding globulin and cortisol concentrations are associated with overreaching during strenuous military training. *J Strength Cond Res* 25:787-797, 2011.

343. Taylor, K, Chapman, D, Cronin, J, Newton, MJ, and Gill, N. Fatigue monitoring in high performance sport: A survey of current trends. *J Aust Strength Cond* 20:12-23, 2012.

344. Terbizan, DJ, Dolezal, BA, and Albano, C. Validity of seven commercially available heart rate monitors. *Measurement in Physical Education and Exercise Science* 6:243-247, 2002.

345. Terry, PC, Lane, AM, and Fogarty, GJ. Construct validity of the Profile of Mood States–Adolescents for use with adults. *Psychol Sport Exerc* 4:125-139, 2003.

346. Terry, PC, Lane, AM, Lane, HJ, and Keohane, L. Development and validation of a mood measure for adolescents. *J Sports Sci* 17:861-872, 1999.

347. Thamm, A, Freitag, N, Figueiredo, P, Doma, K, Rottensteiner, C, Bloch, W, and Schumann, M. Can heart rate variability determine recovery following distinct strength loadings? A randomized cross-over trial. *Int J Environ Res Public Health* 16:4353, 2019.

348. Thompson, WR. Worldwide survey of fitness trends for 2020. *ACSMs Health Fit J* 23:10-18, 2019.

349. Thornton, HR, Delaney, JA, Duthie, GM, and Dascombe, BJ. Developing athlete monitoring systems in team sports: Data analysis and visualization. *Int J Sports Physiol Perform* 14:698-705, 2019.

350. Thorpe, RT, Atkinson, G, Drust, B, and Gregson, W. Monitoring fatigue status in elite team-sport athletes: Implications for practice. *Int J Sports Physiol Perform* 12:S227-S234, 2017.

351. Thorpe, RT, Strudwick, AJ, Buchheit, M, Atkinson, G, Drust, B, and Gregson, W. Monitoring fatigue during the in-season competitive phase in elite soccer players. *Int J Sports Physiol Perform* 10:958-964, 2015.

352. Tillin, NA, Pain, MT, and Folland, JP. Contraction type influences the human ability to use the available torque capacity of skeletal muscle during explosive efforts. *Proc Biol Sci* 279:2106-2115, 2012.

353. Torres-Ronda, L, and Schelling, X. Critical process for the implementation of technology in sport organizations. *Strength Cond J* 39:54-59, 2017.

354. Twist, C, and Highton, J. Monitoring fatigue and recovery in Rugby League players. *Int J Sports Physiol Perform* 8:467-474, 2013.

355. Twist, C, Waldron, M, Highton, J, Burt, D, and Daniels, M. Neuromuscular, biochemical and perceptual post-match fatigue in professional Rugby League forwards and backs. *J Sports Sci* 30:359-367, 2012.

356. Uchida, MC, Teixeira, LF, Godoi, VJ, Marchetti, PH, Conte, M, Coutts, AJ, and Bacurau, RF. Does the timing of measurement alter session-RPE in boxers? *J Sports Sci Med* 13:59-65, 2014.

357. Urhausen, A, Gabriel, H, and Kindermann, W. Blood hormones as markers of training stress and overtraining. *Sports Med* 20:251-276, 1995.

358. Urhausen, A, Gabriel, HH, and Kindermann, W. Impaired pituitary hormonal response to exhaustive exercise in overtrained endurance athletes. *Med Sci Sports Exerc* 30:407-414, 1998.

359. Urhausen, A, Gabriel, HH, Weiler, B, and Kindermann, W. Ergometric and psychological findings during overtraining: A long-term follow-up study in endurance athletes. *Int J Sports Med* 19:114-120, 1998.

360. Uusitalo, AL. Overtraining: Making a difficult diagnosis and implementing targeted treatment. *Phys Sportsmed* 29:35-50, 2001.

361. Vanrenterghem, J, Nedergaard, NJ, Robinson, MA, and Drust, B. Training load monitoring in team sports: A novel framework separating physiological and biomechanical load-adaptation pathways. *Sports Med* 47:2135-2142, 2017.

362. Varley, MC, Fairweather, IH, and Aughey, RJ. Validity and reliability of GPS for measuring instantaneous velocity during acceleration, deceleration, and constant motion. *J Sports Sci* 30:121-127, 2012.

363. Vellers, HL, Kleeberger, SR, and Lightfoot, JT. Inter-individual variation in adaptations to endurance and resistance exercise training: Genetic approaches towards understanding a complex phenotype. *Mamm Genome* 29:48-62, 2018.

364. Verkhoshansky, Y, and Siff, MC. Organisation of training. In *Supertraining*. 6th (expanded) ed. Rome, Italy: Verkhoshansky, 313-393, 2009.

365. Verkhoshansky, Y, and Siff, MC. Preparedness and training load. In *Supertraining*. 6th (expanded) ed. Rome, Italy: Verkhoshansky, 313-367, 2009.
366. Vervoorn, C, Quist, AM, Vermulst, LJ, Erich, WB, de Vries, WR, and Thijssen, JH. The behaviour of the plasma free testosterone/cortisol ratio during a season of elite rowing training. *Int J Sports Med* 12:257-263, 1991.
367. Vervoorn, C, Vermulst, LJ, Boelens-Quist, AM, Koppeschaar, HP, Erich, WB, Thijssen, JH, and de Vries, WR. Seasonal changes in performance and free testosterone: Cortisol ratio of elite female rowers. *Eur J Appl Physiol Occup Physiol* 64:14-21, 1992.
368. Vesterinen, V, Häkkinen, K, Hynynen, E, Mikkola, J, Hokka, L, and Nummela, A. Heart rate variability in prediction of individual adaptation to endurance training in recreational endurance runners. *Scand J Med Sci Sports* 23:171-180, 2013.
369. Viru, A, and Viru, M. Hormones as tools for training monitoring. In *Biochemical Monitoring of Sport Training*. Champaign, IL: Human Kinetics, 73-112, 2001.
370. Viru, A, and Viru, M. Metabolites and substrates. In *Biochemical Monitoring of Sport Training*. Champaign, IL: Human Kinetics, 29-60, 2001.
371. Viru, A, and Viru, M. Preconditioning of the performance in power events by endogenous testosterone: In memory of Professor Carmelo Bosco. *J Strength Cond Res* 19:6-8, 2005.
372. Viru, M, and Viru, A. Monitoring of training. *Modern Athlete and Coach* 40:3-6, 2002.
373. Wallace, LK, Slattery, KM, and Coutts, AJ. The ecological validity and application of the session-RPE method for quantifying training loads in swimming. *J Strength Cond Res* 23:33-38, 2009.
374. Walsh, NP, Blannin, AK, Robson, PJ, and Gleeson, M. Glutamine, exercise and immune function: Links and possible mechanisms. *Sports Med* 26:177-191, 1998.
375. Wang, C, Vargas, JT, Stokes, T, Steele, R, and Shrier, I. Analyzing activity and injury: Lessons learned from the acute:chronic workload ratio. *Sports Med* 50:1243-1254, 2020.
376. Welsh, AH, and Knight, EJ. "Magnitude-based inference": A statistical review. *Med Sci Sports Exerc* 47:874-884, 2015.
377. Williams, MNC, Dalbo, VJ, Fox, JL, O'Grady, CJ, and Scanlan, AT. Comparing weekly training and game demands according to playing position in a semiprofessional basketball team. *Int J Sports Physiol Perform* 16:772-778, 2021.
378. Williams, S, West, S, Cross, MJ, and Stokes, KA. Better way to determine the acute:chronic workload ratio? *Br J Sports Med* 51:209-210, 2017.
379. Windt, J, and Gabbett, T. Injury risk model. In *NSCA's Essentials of Sport Science*. French, D, Torres Ronda, L, eds. Champaign, IL: Human Kinetics, 287-300, 2022.
380. Wittig, AF, Houmard, JA, and Costill, DL. Psychological effects during reduced training in distance runners. *Int J Sports Med* 10:97-100, 1989.
381. Wolery, M, and Harris, SR. Interpreting results of single-subject research designs. *Phys Ther* 62:445-452, 1982.
382. Young, CM, Gastin, PB, Sanders, N, Mackey, L, and Dwyer, DB. Player load in elite netball: Match, training, and positional comparisons. *Int J Sports Physiol Perform* 11:1074-1079, 2016.
383. Zourdos, MC, Goldsmith, JA, Helms, ER, Trepeck, C, Halle, JL, Mendez, KM, Cooke, DM, Haischer, MH, Sousa, CA, Klemp, A, and Byrnes, RK. Proximity to failure and total repetitions performed in a set influences accuracy of intraset repetitions in reserve-based rating of perceived exertion. *J Strength Cond Res* 35:S158-S165, 2021.
384. Zourdos, MC, Klemp, A, Dolan, C, Quiles, JM, Schau, KA, Jo, E, Helms, E, Esgro, B, Duncan, S, Garcia Merino, S, and Blanco, R. Novel resistance training-specific rating of perceived exertion scale measuring repetitions in reserve. *J Strength Cond Res* 30:267-275, 2016.

Chapter 12

1. Aján, T, and Baroga, L. The structure of the training process. In *Weightlifting: Fitness for All Sports*. Budapest: International Weightlifting Federation, 183-395, 1988.
2. Baker, D. Applying the in-season periodization of strength and power training to football. *Strength Cond J* 20:18-27, 1998.
3. Banister, EW, Calvert, TW, Savage, MV, and Back, A. A system model of training for athletic performance. *Aus J Sports Med* 7:170-176, 1975.
4. Banister, EW, Carter, JB, and Zarkadas, PC. Training theory and taper: Validation in triathlon athletes. *Eur J Appl Physiol Occup Physiol* 79:182-191, 1999.
5. Bazyler, CD, Mizuguchi, S, Harrison, AP, Sato, K, Kavanaugh, AA, DeWeese, BH, and Stone, MH. Changes in muscle architecture, explosive ability, and track and field throwing performance throughout a competitive season and following a taper. *J Strength Cond Res* 31:2785-2793, 2017.
6. Bengtsson, H, Ekstrand, J, and Hagglund, M. Muscle injury rates in professional football increase with fixture congestion: An 11-year follow-up of the UEFA Champions League injury study. *Br J Sports Med* 47:743-747, 2013.
7. Bengtsson, H, Ekstrand, J, Walden, M, and Hagglund, M. Muscle injury rate in professional football is higher in matches played within 5 days since the previous match: A 14-year prospective study with more than 130 000 match observations. *Br J Sports Med* 52:1116-1122, 2018.
8. Berger, BG, Motl, RW, Butki, BD, Martin, DT, Wilkinson, JG, and Owen, DR. Mood and cycling performance in response to three weeks of high-intensity, short-duration overtraining, and a two-week taper. *Sport Psychol* 13:444-457, 1999.
9. Berger, J, Harre, D, and Ritter, I. Principles of athletic training. In *Principles of Sports Training: Introduction to the Theory and Methods of Training*. Harre, D, ed. Michigan, USA: Ultimate Athlete Concepts, 113-150, 2012.
10. Bishop, D, and Edge, J. The effects of a 10-day taper on repeated-sprint performance in females. *J Sci Med Sport* 8:200-209, 2005.
11. Bompa, TO, and Buzzichelli, CA. Peaking for competition. In *Periodization: Theory and Methodology of Training*. 6th ed. Champaign, IL: Human Kinetics, 207-225, 2019.

12. Bompa, TO, and Haff, GG. Annual training plan. In *Periodization: Theory and Methodology of Training*. 5th ed. Champaign, IL: Human Kinetics, 125-185, 2009.
13. Bompa, TO, and Haff, GG. Peaking for competition. In *Periodization: Theory and Methodology of Training*. 5th ed. Champaign, IL: Human Kinetics, 187-202, 2009.
14. Bompa, TO, and Haff, GG. *Periodization: Theory and Methodology of Training*. 5th ed. Champaign, IL: Human Kinetics, 2009.
15. Bompa, TO, Hoffman, J, Blumenstein, B, and Orbach, I. Tapering and peaking for competitions. In *Integrated Periodization in Sports Training & Athletic Development*. Bompa, TO, Blumenstein, B, Hoffman, J, Howell, S, Orbach, I, eds. Ann Arbor, MI: Meyer & Meyer Sport, 174-197, 2019.
16. Bosquet, L, Berryman, N, and Mujika, I. Managing the training load of overreached athletes: Insights from detraining and tapering literature. In *Sport, Recovery, and Performance: Interdisciplinary Insights*. Kellmann, M, Beckmann, J, eds. New York: Routledge, 87-107, 2018.
17. Bosquet, L, Leger, L, and Legros, P. Methods to determine aerobic endurance. *Sports Med* 32:675-700, 2002.
18. Bosquet, L, Montpetit, J, Arvisais, D, and Mujika, I. Effects of tapering on performance: A meta-analysis. *Med Sci Sports Exerc* 39:1358-1365, 2007.
19. Botonis, PG, Toubekis, AG, and Platanou, TI. Training loads, wellness and performance before and during tapering for a water-polo tournament. *J Hum Kinet* 66:131-141, 2019.
20. Buitrago, M, and Ma, J. The training plan and training diary. In *Chinese Weightlifting: Technical Mastery and Training*. China: Ma Strength, 221-240, 2018.
21. Busso, T. Variable dose-response relationship between exercise training and performance. *Med Sci Sports Exerc* 35:1188-1195, 2003.
22. Busso, T, Benoit, H, Bonnefoy, R, Feasson, L, and Lacour, JR. Effects of training frequency on the dynamics of performance response to a single training bout. *J Appl Physiol* 92:572-580, 2002.
23. Busso, T, Denis, C, Bonnefoy, R, Geyssant, A, and Lacour, JR. Modeling of adaptations to physical training by using a recursive least squares algorithm. *J Appl Physiol* 82:1685-1693, 1997.
24. Busso, T, Hakkinen, K, Pakarinen, A, Carasso, C, Lacour, JR, Komi, PV, and Kauhanen, H. A systems model of training responses and its relationship to hormonal responses in elite weight-lifters. *Eur J Appl Physiol* 61:48-54, 1990.
25. Busso, T, and Thomas, L. Using mathematical modeling in training planning. *Int J Sports Physiol Perform* 1:400-405, 2006.
26. Carling, C, McCall, A, Le Gall, F, and Dupont, G. The impact of in-season national team soccer play on injury and player availability in a professional club. *J Sports Sci* 33:1751-1757, 2015.
27. Carling, C, McCall, A, Le Gall, F, and Dupont, G. What is the extent of exposure to periods of match congestion in professional soccer players? *J Sports Sci* 33:2116-2124, 2015.
28. Carling, C, McCall, A, Le Gall, F, and Dupont, G. The impact of short periods of match congestion on injury risk and patterns in an elite football club. *Br J Sports Med* 50:764-768, 2016.
29. Chtourou, H, Chaouachi, A, Driss, T, Dogui, M, Behm, DG, Chamari, K, and Souissi, N. The effect of training at the same time of day and tapering period on the diurnal variation of short exercise performances. *J Strength Cond Res* 26:697-708, 2012.
30. Costill, DL, King, DS, Thomas, R, and Hargreaves, M. Effects of reduced training on muscular power in swimmers. *Phys Sportsmed* 13:94-101, 1985.
31. Costill, DL, Thomas, R, Robergs, RA, Pascoe, D, Lambert, C, Barr, S, and Fink, WJ. Adaptations to swimming training: Influence of training volume. *Med Sci Sports Exerc* 23:371-377, 1991.
32. Counsilman, JE, and Counsilman, BE. International sports training theory. In *The New Science of Swimming*. Englewood Cliffs, NJ: Prentice Hall, 187-228, 1994.
33. Coutts, A, Reaburn, P, Piva, TJ, and Murphy, A. Changes in selected biochemical, muscular strength, power, and endurance measures during deliberate overreaching and tapering in Rugby League players. *Int J Sports Med* 28:116-124, 2007.
34. Coutts, AJ, Reaburn, P, Piva, TJ, and Rowsell, GJ. Monitoring for overreaching in Rugby League players. *Eur J Appl Physiol* 99:313-324, 2007.
35. D'acquisto, L, Bone, M, Takahashi, S, Langhans, G, Barzdukas, A, and Troup, J. Changes in aerobic power and swimming economy as a result of reduced training volume. In *Biomechanics and Medicine in Swimming, VI*. London: E & FN Spon, 201-205, 1992.
36. Dellal, A, Lago-Penas, C, Rey, E, Chamari, K, and Orhant, E. The effects of a congested fixture period on physical performance, technical activity and injury rate during matches in a professional soccer team. *Br J Sports Med* 49:390-394, 2015.
37. Dick, FW. Competition period. In *Sports Training Principles*. 4th ed. London: A and C Black, 351-359, 2002.
38. Drabik, J. Training loads and children. In *Children and Sports Training*. Island Pond, VT: Stadion Publishing, 41-54, 1995.
39. Dupont, G, Nedelec, M, McCall, A, McCormack, D, Berthoin, S, and Wisloff, U. Effect of 2 soccer matches in a week on physical performance and injury rate. *Am J Sports Med* 38:1752-1758, 2010.
40. Edelmann-Nusser, J, Hohmann, A, and Henneberg, B. Modeling and prediction of competitive performance in swimming upon neural networks. *Eur J Sport Sci* 2:1-10, 2002.
41. Ferland, PM, and Comtois, AS. Classic powerlifting performance: A systematic review. *J Strength Cond Res* 33:S194-S201, 2019.
42. Fitz-Clarke, JR, Morton, RH, and Banister, EW. Optimizing athletic performance by influence curves. *J Appl Physiol* 71:1151-1158, 1991.
43. Flynn, MG, Pizza, FX, Boone, JB, Jr., Andres, FF, Michaud, TA, and Rodriguez-Zayas, JR. Indices of training stress during competitive running and swimming seasons. *Int J Sports Med* 15:21-26, 1994.
44. Ford, P, De Ste Croix, M, Lloyd, R, Meyers, R, Moosavi, M, Oliver, J, Till, K, and Williams, C. The long-term athlete

development model: Physiological evidence and application. *J Sports Sci* 29:389-402, 2011.

45. French, D. Combat sports. In *Science and Application of High-Intensity Interval Training*. Laursen, PB, Buchheit, M, eds. Champaign, IL: Human Kinetics, 227-246, 2019.

46. Gibala, MJ, MacDougall, JD, and Sale, DG. The effects of tapering on strength performance in trained athletes. *Int J Sports Med* 15:492-497, 1994.

47. Gonzalez, AM, Hoffman, JR, Rogowski, JP, Burgos, W, Manalo, E, Weise, K, Fragala, MS, and Stout, JR. Performance changes in NBA basketball players vary in starters vs. nonstarters over a competitive season. *J Strength Cond Res* 27:611-615, 2013.

48. Gould, D, Guinan, D, Greenleaf, C, Medbery, R, and Peterson, K. Factors affecting Olympic performance: Perceptions of athletes and coaches from more and less successful teams. *Sport Psychol* 13:371-394, 1999.

49. Greig, L, Stephens Hemingway, BH, Aspe, RR, Cooper, K, Comfort, P, and Swinton, PA. Autoregulation in resistance training: Addressing the inconsistencies. *Sports Med* 50:1873-1887, 2020.

50. Grgic, J, and Mikulic, P. Tapering practices of Croatian open-class powerlifting champions. *J Strength Cond Res* 31:2371-2378, 2017.

51. Haff, GG. Periodization strategies for youth development. In *Strength and Conditioning for Young Athletes: Science and Application*. 2nd ed. Lloyd, R, Oliver, JL, eds. London: Routledge, 281-299, 2019.

52. Haff, GG. Peaking for competition in individual sports. In *High-Performance Training for Sports*. 2nd ed. Joyce, D, Lewindon, D, eds. Champaign, IL: Human Kinetics, 524-541, 2022.

53. Häkkinen, K, Kallinen, M, Komi, PV, and Kauhanen, H. Neuromuscular adaptations during short-term "normal" and reduced training periods in strength athletes. *Electromyogr Clin Neurophysiol* 31:35-42, 1991.

54. Hays, K, Thomas, O, Maynard, I, and Bawden, M. The role of confidence in world-class sport performance. *J Sports Sci* 27:1185-1199, 2009.

55. Hellard, P, Avalos, M, Lacoste, L, Barale, F, Chatard, JC, and Millet, GP. Assessing the limitations of the Banister model in monitoring training. *J Sports Sci* 24:509-520, 2006.

56. Hickson, RC, Foster, C, Pollock, ML, Galassi, TM, and Rich, S. Reduced training intensities and loss of aerobic power, endurance, and cardiac growth. *J Appl Physiol* 58:492-499, 1985.

57. Hickson, RC, and Rosenkoetter, MA. Reduced training frequencies and maintenance of increased aerobic power. *Med Sci Sports Exerc* 13:13-16, 1981.

58. Hooper, SL, Mackinnon, LT, and Ginn, EM. Effects of three tapering techniques on the performance, forces and psychometric measures of competitive swimmers. *Eur J Appl Physiol Occup Physiol* 78:258-263, 1998.

59. Hopkins, WG. Competitive performance of elite track and field athletes: Variability and smallest worthwhile enhancements. *Sportscience* 9:17-20, 2005.

60. Houmard, JA. Tapering for the competitive cyclist. *Performance Conditioning for Cyclists* 2:1-8, 1996.

61. Houmard, JA, Costill, DL, Mitchell, JB, Park, SH, Fink, WJ, and Burns, JM. Testosterone, cortisol, and creatine kinase levels in male distance runners during reduced training. *Int J Sports Med* 11:41-45, 1990.

62. Houmard, JA, Costill, DL, Mitchell, JB, Park, SH, Hickner, RC, and Roemmich, JN. Reduced training maintains performance in distance runners. *Int J Sports Med* 11:46-52, 1990.

63. Houmard, JA, and Johns, RA. Effects of taper on swim performance: Practical implications. *Sports Med* 17:224-232, 1994.

64. Houmard, JA, Kirwan, JP, Flynn, MG, and Mitchell, JB. Effects of reduced training on submaximal and maximal running responses. *Int J Sports Med* 10:30-33, 1989.

65. Houmard, JA, Scott, BK, Justice, CL, and Chenier, TC. The effects of taper on performance in distance runners. *Med Sci Sports Exerc* 26:624-631, 1994.

66. Howle, K, Waterson, A, and Duffield, R. Injury incidence and workloads during congested schedules in football. *Int J Sports Med* 41:75-81, 2020.

67. Issurin, V. Microcycles, mesocycles, and training stages. In *Block Periodization: Breakthrough in Sports Training*. Michigan, USA: Ultimate Athlete Concepts, 78-127, 2008.

68. Issurin, V. Block periodization in applications to different sports. In *Building the Modern Athlete: Scientific Advancement & Training Innovation*. Thome, M, ed. Michigan, USA: Ultimate Athlete Concepts, 191-212, 2015.

69. Izquierdo, M, Ibanez, J, Gonzalez-Badillo, JJ, Ratamess, NA, Kraemer, WJ, Häkkinen, K, Bonnabau, H, Granados, C, French, DN, and Gorostiaga, EM. Detraining and tapering effects on hormonal responses and strength performance. *J Strength Cond Res* 21:768-775, 2007.

70. Janse van Rensburg, DCC, Jansen van Rensburg, A, Fowler, P, Fullagar, H, Stevens, D, Halson, S, Bender, A, Vincent, G, Claassen-Smithers, A, Dunican, I, Roach, GD, Sargent, C, Lastella, M, and Cronje, T. How to manage travel fatigue and jet lag in athletes? A systematic review of interventions. *Br J Sports Med* 54:960-968, 2020.

71. Johns, RA, Houmard, JA, Kobe, RW, Hortobagyi, T, Bruno, NJ, Wells, JM, and Shinebarger, MH. Effects of taper on swim power, stroke distance, and performance. *Med Sci Sports Exerc* 24:1141-1146, 1992.

72. Kipp, K, Krzyszkowski, J, and Kant-Hull, D. Use of machine learning to model volume load effects on changes in jump performance. *Int J Sports Physiol Perform* 15:285-287, 2020.

73. Krespi, M, Sporis, G, and Trajkovic, N. Effects of two different tapering protocols on fitness and physical match performance in elite junior soccer players. *J Strength Cond Res* 34:1731-1740, 2020.

74. Kubukeli, ZN, Noakes, TD, and Dennis, SC. Training techniques to improve endurance exercise performances. *Sports Med* 32:489-509, 2002.

75. Le Meur, Y, Hausswirth, C, and Mujika, I. Tapering for competition: A review. *Science & Sports* 27:77-87, 2012.

76. Lloyd, RS, Oliver, JL, Faigenbaum, AD, Howard, R, De Ste Croix, MB, Williams, CA, Best, TM, Alvar, BA, Micheli, LJ, Thomas, DP, Hatfield, DL, Cronin, JB, and Myer, GD.

Long-term athletic development—part 1: A pathway for all youth. *J Strength Cond Res* 29:1439-1450, 2015.

77. Luden, N, Hayes, E, Galpin, A, Minchev, K, Jemiolo, B, Raue, U, Trappe, TA, Harber, MP, Bowers, T, and Trappe, S. Myocellular basis for tapering in competitive distance runners. *J Appl Physiol* 108:1501-1509, 2010.

78. Mallo, J. Effect of block periodization on performance in competition in a soccer team during four consecutive seasons: A case study. *Int J Perform Anal Sport* 11:476-485, 2011.

79. Mallo, J. Effect of block periodization on physical fitness during a competitive soccer season. *Int J Perform Anal Sport* 12:64-67, 2012.

80. Margaritis, I, Palazzetti, S, Rousseau, AS, Richard, MJ, and Favier, A. Antioxidant supplementation and tapering exercise improve exercise-induced antioxidant response. *J Am Coll Nutr* 22:147-156, 2003.

81. Marrier, B, Robineau, J, Piscione, J, Lacome, M, Peeters, A, Hausswirth, C, Morin, JB, and Le Meur, Y. Supercompensation kinetics of physical qualities during a taper in team-sport athletes. *Int J Sports Physiol Perform* 12:1163-1169, 2017.

82. Martin, DT, Scifres, JC, Zimmerman, SD, and Wilkinson, JG. Effects of interval training and a taper on cycling performance and isokinetic leg strength. *Int J Sports Med* 15:485-491, 1994.

83. Maszczyk, A, Roczniok, R, Waskiewicz, Z, Czuba, M, Mikolajec, K, Zajac, A, and Stanula, A. Application of regression and neural models to predict competitive swimming performance. *Percept Mot Skills* 114:610-626, 2012.

84. Matveyev, LP. Annual and semi-annual training cycles. In *Fundamentals of Sports Training*. Moscow: Fizkultua i Sport, 259-287, 1977.

85. McConell, GK, Costill, DL, Widrick, JJ, Hickey, MS, Tanaka, H, and Gastin, PB. Reduced training volume and intensity maintain aerobic capacity but not performance in distance runners. *Int J Sports Med* 14:33-37, 1993.

86. McGuigan, MR, and Kane, MK. Reliability of performance of elite Olympic weightlifters. *J Strength Cond Res* 18:650-653, 2004.

87. McNeely, E, and David Sandler, M. Tapering for endurance athletes. *Strength Cond J* 29:18, 2007.

88. Meline, T, Mathieu, L, Borrani, F, Candau, R, and Sanchez, AM. Systems model and individual simulations of training strategies in elite short-track speed skaters. *J Sports Sci* 37:347-355, 2019.

89. Mujika, I. Thoughts and considerations for team-sport peaking. *Olympic Coach* 18:9-11, 2007.

90. Mujika, I. Basics of tapering. In *Tapering and Peaking for Optimal Performance*. Champaign, IL: Human Kinetics, 1-14, 2009.

91. Mujika, I. Reduction of the training load. In *Tapering and Peaking for Optimal Performance*. Champaign, IL: Human Kinetics, 71-87, 2009.

92. Mujika, I. *Tapering and Peaking for Optimal Performance*. Champaign, IL: Human Kinetics Publishers, 2009.

93. Mujika, I. Unique aspects of team sport tapering. In *Tapering and Peaking for Optimal Performance*. Champaign, IL: Human Kinetics, 113-119, 2009.

94. Mujika, I. Intense training: The key to optimal performance before and during the taper. *Scand J Med Sci Sports* 20:24-31, 2010.

95. Mujika, I, Busso, T, Lacoste, L, Barale, F, Geyssant, A, and Chatard, JC. Modeled responses to training and taper in competitive swimmers. *Med Sci Sports Exerc* 28:251-258, 1996.

96. Mujika, I, Chatard, J-C, Busso, T, Geyssant, A, Barale, F, and Lacoste, L. Use of swim-training profiles and performances data to enhance training effectiveness. *J Swim Res* 11:23-29, 1996.

97. Mujika, I, Chatard, JC, and Geyssant, A. Effects of training and taper on blood leucocyte populations in competitive swimmers: relationships with cortisol and performance. *Int J Sports Med* 17:213-217, 1996.

98. Mujika, I, Chatard, JC, Padilla, S, Guezennec, CY, and Geyssant, A. Hormonal responses to training and its tapering off in competitive swimmers: relationships with performance. *Eur J Appl Physiol Occup Physiol* 74:361-366, 1996.

99. Mujika, I, Goya, A, Ruiz, E, Grijalba, A, Santisteban, J, and Padilla, S. Physiological and performance responses to a 6-day taper in middle-distance runners: Influence of training frequency. *Int J Sports Med* 23:367-373, 2002.

100. Mujika, I, and Padilla, S. Detraining: loss of training-induced physiological and performance adaptations. Part I: Short term insufficient training stimulus. *Sports Med* 30:79-87, 2000.

101. Mujika, I, and Padilla, S. Detraining: Loss of training-induced physiological and performance adaptations. Part II: Long term insufficient training stimulus. *Sports Med* 30:145-154, 2000.

102. Mujika, I, and Padilla, S. Scientific bases for precompetition tapering strategies. *Med Sci Sports Exerc* 35:1182-1187, 2003.

103. Mujika, I, Padilla, S, Geyssant, A, and Chatard, JC. Hematological responses to training and taper in competitive swimmers: Relationships with performance. *Arch Physiol Biochem* 105:379-385, 1998.

104. Mujika, I, Padilla, S, and Pyne, D. Swimming performance changes during the final 3 weeks of training leading to the Sydney 2000 Olympic Games. *Int J Sports Med* 23:582-587, 2002.

105. Mujika, I, Padilla, S, Pyne, D, and Busso, T. Physiological changes associated with the pre-event taper in athletes. *Sports Med* 34:891-927, 2004.

106. Murach, KA, and Bagley, JR. Less is more: The physiological basis for tapering in endurance, strength, and power athletes. *Sports* 3:209-218, 2015.

107. Nádori, L. Theoretrical and methodological basis of training planning. In *Theoretical and Methodological Basis of Training Planning With Special Considerations Within a Microcycle*. Nádori, L, Granek, I, eds. Lincoln, NE: National Strength and Conditioning Association, 1-25, 1989.

108. Neary, JP, Bhambhani, YN, and McKenzie, DC. Effects of different stepwise reduction taper protocols on cycling performance. *Can J Appl Physiol* 28:576-587, 2003.

109. Neary, JP, Martin, TP, and Quinney, HA. Effects of taper on endurance cycling capacity and single muscle fiber properties. *Med Sci Sports Exerc* 35:1875-1881, 2003.

110. Neary, JP, Martin, TP, Reid, DC, Burnham, R, and Quinney, HA. The effects of a reduced exercise duration taper programme on performance and muscle enzymes of endurance cyclists. *Eur J Appl Physiol Occup Physiol* 65:30-36, 1992.

111. Nedelec, M, McCall, A, Carling, C, Legall, F, Berthoin, S, and Dupont, G. Recovery in soccer: Part I—post-match fatigue and time course of recovery. *Sports Med* 42:997-1015, 2012.

112. Neufer, PD. The effect of detraining and reduced training on the physiological adaptations to aerobic exercise training. *Sports Med* 8:302-320, 1989.

113. Neufer, PD, Costill, DL, Fielding, RA, Flynn, MG, and Kirwan, JP. Effect of reduced training on muscular strength and endurance in competitive swimmers. *Med Sci Sports Exerc* 19:486-490, 1987.

114. NFL. Creating the NFL schedule. 2020. https://operations.nfl.com/the-game/creating-the-nfl-schedule. Accessed December 31, 2020.

115. Nunes, JA, Moreira, A, Crewther, BT, Nosaka, K, Viveiros, L, and Aoki, MS. Monitoring training load, recovery-stress state, immune-endocrine responses, and physical performance in elite female basketball players during a periodized training program. *J Strength Cond Res* 28:2973-2980, 2014.

116. Nuzzo, JL, Anning, JH, and Scharfenberg, JM. The reliability of three devices used for measuring vertical jump height. *J Strength Cond Res* 25:2580-2590, 2011.

117. Olbrect, J. Basics of training periodization. In *The Science of Winning: Planning, Periodizing, and Optimizing Swim Training*. Luton, England: Swimshop, 193-202, 2000.

118. Pearson, J, Spathis, JG, van den Hoek, DJ, Owen, PJ, Weakley, J, and Latella, C. Effect of competition frequency on strength performance of powerlifting athletes. *J Strength Cond Res* 34:1213-1219, 2020.

119. Pfeiffer, M, and Hohmann, A. Applications of neural networks in training science. *Hum Mov Sci* 31:344-359, 2012.

120. Plisk, SS, and Stone, MH. Periodization strategies. *Strength and Cond J* 25:19-37, 2003.

121. Pritchard, H, Keogh, J, Barnes, M, and McGuigan, M. Effects and mechanisms of tapering in maximizing muscular strength. *Strength Cond J* 37:72-83, 2015.

122. Pritchard, HJ, Barnes, MJ, Stewart, RJ, Keogh, JW, and McGuigan, MR. Higher- versus lower-intensity strength-training taper: Effects on neuromuscular performance. *Int J Sports Physiol Perform* 14:458-463, 2019.

123. Pritchard, HJ, Barnes, MJ, Stewart, RJC, Keogh, JWL, and McGuigan, MR. Short-term training cessation as a method of tapering to improve maximal strength. *J Strength Cond Res* 32:458-465, 2018.

124. Pritchard, HJ, Tod, DA, Barnes, MJ, Keogh, JW, and McGuigan, MR. Tapering practices of New Zealand's elite raw powerlifters. *J Strength Cond Res* 30:1796-1804, 2016.

125. Pyne, DB, Mujika, I, and Reilly, T. Peaking for optimal performance: Research limitations and future directions. *J Sports Sci* 27:195-202, 2009.

126. Quarrie, KL, Raftery, M, Blackie, J, Cook, CJ, Fuller, CW, Gabbett, TJ, Gray, AJ, Gill, N, Hennessy, L, Kemp, S, Lambert, M, Nichol, R, Mellalieu, SD, Piscione, J, Stadelmann, J, and Tucker, R. Managing player load in professional Rugby Union: A review of current knowledge and practices. *Br J Sports Med* 51:421-427, 2017.

127. Rietjens, GJ, Keizer, HA, Kuipers, H, and Saris, WH. A reduction in training volume and intensity for 21 days does not impair performance in cyclists. *Br J Sports Med* 35:431-434, 2001.

128. Ritchie, D, Allen, JB, and Kirkland, A. Where science meets practice: Olympic coaches' crafting of the tapering process. *J Sports Sci* 36:1145-1154, 2018.

129. Robertson, S, and Joyce, D. Evaluating strategic periodisation in team sport. *J Sports Sci* 36:279-285, 2018.

130. Robertson, SJ, and Joyce, DG. Informing in-season tactical periodisation in team sport: Development of a match difficulty index for Super Rugby. *J Sports Sci* 33:99-107, 2015.

131. Samuels, CH. Jet lag and travel fatigue: A comprehensive management plan for sport medicine physicians and high-performance support teams. *Clin J Sport Med* 22:268-273, 2012.

132. Seppänen, S. Effects of two different tapering models on maximal strength gains in recreationally strength trained men. Thesis. Jyväskylä, Finland: University of Jyväskylä, 2018.

133. Seppänen, S, and Häkkinen, K. Step vs. two-phase gradual volume reduction tapering protocols in strength training: Effects on neuromuscular performance and serum hormone concentrations. *J Strength Cond Res* 36:2771-2779, 2022.

134. Shattock, K, and Tee, JC. Autoregulation in resistance training: A comparison of subjective versus objective methods. *J Strength Cond Res* 36:641-648, 2022.

135. Shepley, B, MacDougall, JD, Cipriano, N, Sutton, JR, Tarnopolsky, MA, and Coates, G. Physiological effects of tapering in highly trained athletes. *J Appl Physiol* 72:706-711, 1992.

136. Skovgaard, C, Almquist, NW, Kvorning, T, Christensen, PM, and Bangsbo, J. Effect of tapering after a period of high-volume sprint interval training on running performance and muscular adaptations in moderately trained runners. *J Appl Physiol* 124:259-267, 2018.

137. Smith, DJ. A framework for understanding the training process leading to elite performance. *Sports Med* 33:1103-1126, 2003.

138. Soligard, T, Schwellnus, M, Alonso, J-M, Bahr, R, Clarsen, B, Dijkstra, HP, Gabbett, T, Gleeson, M, Hägglund, M, Hutchinson, MR, Janse van Rensburg, C, Khan, KM, Meeusen, R, Orchard, JW, Pluim, BM, Raftery, M, Budgett, R, and Engebretsen, L. How much is too much? (Part 1) International Olympic Committee consensus statement on load in sport and risk of injury. *Br J Sports Med* 50:1030-1041, 2016.

139. Spilsbury, KL, Fudge, BW, Ingham, SA, Faulkner, SH, and Nimmo, MA. Tapering strategies in elite British endurance runners. *Eur J Sport Sci* 15:367-373, 2015.

140. Spilsbury, KL, Nimmo, MA, Fudge, BW, Pringle, JSM, Orme, MW, and Faulkner, SH. Effects of an increase in intensity during tapering on 1500-m running performance. *Appl Physiol Nutr Metab* 44:783-790, 2019.

141. Steinacker, JM, Lormes, W, Kellmann, M, Liu, Y, Reissnecker, S, Opitz-Gress, A, Baller, B, Gunther, K, Petersen,

KG, Kallus, KW, Lehmann, M, and Altenburg, D. Training of junior rowers before world championships: Effects on performance, mood state and selected hormonal and metabolic responses. *J Sports Med Phys Fitness* 40:327-335, 2000.

142. Stone, MH, Stone, ME, and Sands, WA. Developing resistance training programs. In *Principles and Practice of Resistance Training*. Champaign, IL: Human Kinetics, 287-294, 2007.

143. Stone, MH, Stone, ME, and Sands, WA. *Principles and Practice of Resistance Training*. Champaign, IL: Human Kinetics, 2007.

144. Taha, T, and Thomas, SG. Systems modelling of the relationship between training and performance. *Sports Med* 33:1061-1073, 2003.

145. Thomas, L, and Busso, T. A theoretical study of taper characteristics to optimize performance. *Med Sci Sports Exerc* 37:1615-1621, 2005.

146. Thomas, L, Mujika, I, and Busso, T. A model study of optimal training reduction during pre-event taper in elite swimmers. *J Sports Sci* 26:643-652, 2008.

147. Thomas, L, Mujika, I, and Busso, T. Computer simulations assessing the potential performance benefit of a final increase in training during pre-event taper. *J Strength Cond Res* 23:1729-1736, 2009.

148. Trappe, S, Costill, D, and Thomas, R. Effect of swim taper on whole muscle and single muscle fiber contractile properties. *Med Sci Sports Exerc* 32:48-56, 2000.

149. Travis, SK, Mizuguchi, S, Stone, MH, Sands, WA, and Bazyler, CD. Preparing for a national weightlifting championship: A case series. *J Strength Cond Res* 34:1842-1850, 2020.

150. Travis, SK, Mujika, I, Gentles, JA, Stone, MH, and Bazyler, CD. Tapering and peaking maximal strength for powerlifting performance: A review. *Sports* 8:125, 2020.

151. Vachon, A, Berryman, N, Mujika, I, Paquet, JB, Arvisais, D, and Bosquet, L. Effects of tapering on neuromuscular and metabolic fitness in team sports: A systematic review and meta-analysis. *Eur J Sport Sci* 21:300-311, 2021.

152. Viru, A. *Adaptations in Sports Training*. Boca Raton, FL: CRC Press, 1995.

153. Wahl, P, Guldner, M, and Mester, J. Effects and sustainability of a 13-day high-intensity shock microcycle in soccer. *J Sports Sci Med* 13:259-265, 2014.

154. Wallace, LK, Slattery, KM, and Coutts, AJ. A comparison of methods for quantifying training load: Relationships between modelled and actual training responses. *Eur J Appl Physiol* 114:11-20, 2014.

155. Williams, TD, Esco, MR, Fedewa, MV, and Bishop, PA. Bench press load-velocity profiles and strength after overload and taper microcycles in male powerlifters. *J Strength Cond Res* 34:3338-3345, 2020.

156. Wilson, JM, and Wilson, GJ. A practical approach to the taper. *Strength Cond J* 30:10-17, 2008.

157. Winwood, PW, Dudson, MK, Wilson, D, McLaren-Harrison, JKH, Redjkins, V, Pritchard, HJ, and Keogh, JWL. Tapering practices of strongman athletes. *J Strength Cond Res* 32:1181-1196, 2018.

158. Zaras, ND, Angeliki-Nikoletta, ES, Krase, AA, Methenitis, SK, Karampatsos, GP, Georgiadis, GV, Spengos, KM, and Terzis, GD. Effects of tapering with light vs. heavy loads on track and field throwing performance. *J Strength Cond Res* 28:3484-3495, 2014.

159. Zarkadas, PC, Carter, JB, and Banister, EW. Modelling the effect of taper on performance, maximal oxygen uptake, and the anaerobic threshold in endurance triathletes. *Adv Exp Med Biol* 393:179-186, 1995.

160. Zatsiorsky, VM, Kraemer, WJ, and Fry, AC. *Science and Practice of Strength Training*. 3rd ed. Champaign, IL: Human Kinetics, 2021.

161. Zatsiorsky, VM, Kraemer, WJ, and Fry, AC. Basic concepts of training theory. In *Science and Practice of Strength Training*. 3rd ed. Champaign, IL: Human Kinetics, 3-16, 2021.

Chapter 13

1. Aagaard, P, and Andersen, JL. Correlation between contractile strength and myosin heavy chain isoform composition in human skeletal muscle. *Med Sci Sports Exerc* 30:1217-1222, 1998.

2. Aagaard, P, Andersen, JL, Dyhre-Poulsen, P, Leffers, AM, Wagner, A, Magnusson, SP, Halkjaer-Kristensen, J, and Simonsen, EB. A mechanism for increased contractile strength of human pennate muscle in response to strength training: Changes in muscle architecture. *J Physiol* 534:613-623, 2001.

3. Aagaard, P, Simonsen, EB, Andersen, JL, Magnusson, P, and Dyhre-Poulsen, P. Increased rate of force development and neural drive of human skeletal muscle following resistance training. *J Appl Physiol* 93:1318-1326, 2002.

4. Aagaard, P, Simonsen, EB, Andersen, JL, Magnusson, SP, Halkjaer-Kristensen, J, and Dyhre-Poulsen, P. Neural inhibition during maximal eccentric and concentric quadriceps contraction: Effects of resistance training. *J Appl Physiol* 89:2249-2257, 2000.

5. Aagaard, P, and Thorstensson, A. Neuromuscular aspects of exercise—adaptive responses evoked by strength training. In *Textbook of Sports Medicine: Basic Science and Clinical Aspects of Sports Injury and Physical Activity*. Kjaer, M, Magnusson, M, eds. Chester, England: Whiley Publishers, 70-106, 2003.

6. Abadjiev, I. Basic training principles for Bulgarian elite. *Can Weightlifting Fed Official Newsletter* 5:13-18, 1976.

7. Abadjiev, I. Basic training principles for Bulgarian elite. *New Brunswick Weightlifting Association Newsletter* 4:19-24, 1977.

8. Abadjiev, I. Preparation of the Bulgarian weightlifters for the Olympic Games 1984. *Australian Weightlifter* Oct:25-29, 1981.

9. Abdessemed, D, Duche, P, Hautier, C, Poumarat, G, and Bedu, M. Effect of recovery duration on muscular power and blood lactate during the bench press exercise. *Int J Sports Med* 20:368-373, 1999.

10. Adams, GR, Hather, BM, Baldwin, KM, and Dudley, GA. Skeletal muscle myosin heavy chain composition and resistance training. *J Appl Physiol* 74:911-915, 1993.

11. Ahtiainen, JP, Pakarinen, A, Alen, M, Kraemer, WJ, and Hakkinen, K. Muscle hypertrophy, hormonal adaptations and strength development during strength training in strength-trained and untrained men. *Eur J Appl Physiol* 89:555-563, 2003.

12. Ahtiainen, JP, Pakarinen, A, Alen, M, Kraemer, WJ, and Hakkinen, K. Short vs. long rest period between the sets in hypertrophic resistance training: Influence on muscle strength, size, and hormonal adaptations in trained men. *J Strength Cond Res* 19:572-582, 2005.
13. Ahtiainen, JP, Walker, S, Peltonen, H, Holviala, J, Sillanpaa, E, Karavirta, L, Sallinen, J, Mikkola, J, Valkeinen, H, Mero, A, Hulmi, JJ, and Hakkinen, K. Heterogeneity in resistance training-induced muscle strength and mass responses in men and women of different ages. *Age (Dordr)* 38:10, 2016.
14. Aján, T, and Baroga, L. The structure of the training process. In *Weightlifting: Fitness for All Sports*. Budapest: International Weightlifting Federation, 183-395, 1988.
15. American College of Sports Medicine. American College of Sports Medicine position stand: Progression models in resistance training for healthy adults. *Med Sci Sports Exerc* 41:687-708, 2009.
16. Andersen, LL, and Aagaard, P. Influence of maximal muscle strength and intrinsic muscle contractile properties on contractile rate of force development. *Eur J Appl Physiol* 96:46-52, 2006.
17. Arazi, H, and Asadi, A. The relationship between the selected percentages of one repetition maximum and the number of repetitions in trained and untrained males. *Electron Physician* 9:25-33, 2011.
18. Atkins, SJ. Normalizing expressions of strength in elite Rugby League players. *J Strength Cond Res* 18:53-58, 2004.
19. Augustsson, J, Thomee, R, Hornstedt, P, Lindblom, J, Karlsson, J, and Grimby, G. Effect of pre-exhaustion exercise on lower-extremity muscle activation during a leg press exercise. *J Strength Cond Res* 17:411-416, 2003.
20. Baker, D. Comparison of upper-body strength and power between professional and college-aged rugby league players. *J Strength Cond Res* 15:30-35, 2001.
21. Baker, D. A series of studies on the training of high-intensity muscle power in Rugby League football players. *J Strength Cond Res* 15:198-209, 2001.
22. Baker, D, and Nance, S. The relation between running speed and measures of strength and power in professional Rugby League players. *J Strength Cond Res* 13:230-235, 1999.
23. Balsalobre-Fernández, C, and Torres-Ronda, L. The implementation of velocity-based training paradigm for team sports: Framework, technologies, practical recommendations and challenges. *Sports* 9:47, 2021.
24. Balshaw, TG, Massey, GJ, Maden-Wilkinson, TM, Lanza, MB, and Folland, JP. Effect of long-term maximum strength training on explosive strength, neural, and contractile properties. *Scand J Med Sci Sports* 32:685-697, 2022.
25. Banyard, HG, Nosaka, K, and Haff, GG. Reliability and validity of the load-velocity relationship to predict the 1RM back squat. *J Strength Cond Res* 31:1897-1904, 2017.
26. Barbalho, M, Coswig, VS, Raiol, R, Steele, J, Fisher, J, Paoli, A, and Gentil, P. Effects of adding single joint exercises to a resistance training programme in trained women. *Sports (Basel)* 6:160, 2018.
27. Barbalho, M, Coswig, VS, Raiol, R, Steele, J, Fisher, JP, Paoli, A, Bianco, A, and Gentil, P. Does the addition of single joint exercises to a resistance training program improve changes in performance and anthropometric measures in untrained men? *Eur J Transl Myol* 28:7827, 2018.
28. Barker, M, Wyatt, TJ, Johnson, RL, Stone, MH, O'Bryant, HS, Poe, C, and Kent, M. Performance factors, physiological assessment, physical characteristic, and football playing ability. *J Strength Cond Res* 7:224-233, 1993.
29. Barr, MJ, Sheppard, JM, Agar-Newman, DJ, and Newton, RU. Transfer effect of strength and power training to the sprinting kinematics of international rugby players. *J Strength Cond Res* 28:2585-2596, 2014.
30. Bartolomei, S, Hoffman, JR, Merni, F, and Stout, JR. A comparison of traditional and block periodized strength training programs in trained athletes. *J Strength Cond Res* 28:990-997, 2014.
31. Bastiaans, JJ, van Diemen, AB, Veneberg, T, and Jeukendrup, AE. The effects of replacing a portion of endurance training by explosive strength training on performance in trained cyclists. *Eur J Appl Physiol* 86:79-84., 2001.
32. Bazyler, CD, Abbott, HA, Bellon, CR, Taber, CB, and Stone, MH. Strength training for endurance athletes: Theory to practice. *Strength Cond J* 37:1-12, 2015.
33. Beattie, K, Carson, BP, Lyons, M, and Kenny, IC. The effect of maximal- and explosive-strength training on performance indicators in cyclists. *Int J Sports Physiol Perform* 12:470-480, 2017.
34. Beattie, K, Kenny, IC, Lyons, M, and Carson, BP. The effect of strength training on performance in endurance athletes. *Sports Med* 44:845-865, 2014.
35. Beckham, G, Mizuguchi, S, Carter, C, Sato, K, Ramsey, M, Lamont, H, Hornsby, G, Haff, G, and Stone, M. Relationships of isometric mid-thigh pull variables to weightlifting performance. *J Sports Med Phys Fitness* 53:573-581, 2013.
36. Behm, DG, Reardon, G, Fitzgerald, J, and Drinkwater, E. The effect of 5, 10, and 20 repetition maximums on the recovery of voluntary and evoked contractile properties. *J Strength Cond Res* 16:209-218, 2002.
37. Bergh, U, Thorstensson, A, Sjodin, B, Hulten, B, Piehl, K, and Karlsson, J. Maximal oxygen uptake and muscle fiber types in trained and untrained humans. *Med Sci Sports* 10:151-154, 1978.
38. Berryman, N, Mujika, I, Arvisais, D, Roubeix, M, Binet, C, and Bosquet, L. Strength training for middle- and long-distance performance: A meta-analysis. *Int J Sports Physiol Perform* 13:57, 2018.
39. Bigland, B, and Lippold, OC. Motor unit activity in the voluntary contraction of human muscle. *J Physiol* 125:322-335, 1954.
40. Bilcheck, HM, Kraemer, WJ, Maresh, CM, and M.A., Z. The effect of isokinetic fatigue on recovery of maximal isokinetic concentric and eccentric strength in women. *J Strength Cond Res* 7:43-50, 1993.
41. Blocquiaux, S, Gorski, T, Van Roie, E, Ramaekers, M, Van Thienen, R, Nielens, H, Delecluse, C, De Bock, K, and Thomis, M. The effect of resistance training, detraining and retraining on muscle strength and power, myofibre size, satellite cells and myonuclei in older men. *Exp Gerontol* 133:110860, 2020.

42. Bobbert, MF, and van Soest, AJ. Why do people jump the way they do? *Exerc Sport Sci Rev* 29:95-102, 2001.
43. Bompa, TO. Training methods for maximal strength. In *Periodization of Strength*. Toronto, ON: Veritas, 146-171, 1993.
44. Bompa, TO, and Buzzichelli, CA. Manipulating the training variables. In *Periodization: Training for Sports*. Champaign, IL: Human Kinetics, 125-156, 2015.
45. Bompa, TO, and Buzzichelli, CA. Strength and power development. In *Periodization: Theory and Methodology of Training*. 6th ed. Champaign, IL: Human Kinetics, 229-264, 2019.
46. Bompa, TO, and Carrera, MC. Manipulation of training variables. In *Periodization Training for Sports: Science-Based Strength and Conditioning Plans for 20 Sports*. 2nd ed. Champaign, IL: Human Kinetics, 63-84, 2005.
47. Bompa, TO, and Haff, GG. Strength and power development. In *Periodization: Theory and Methodology of Training*. 5th ed. Champaign, IL: Human Kinetics, 259-286, 2009.
48. Bompa, TO, and Haff, GG. Strength development. In *Periodization: Theory and Methodology of Training*. 5th ed. Champaign, IL: Human Kinetics, 261-286, 2009.
49. Borg, G. Perceived exertion as an indicator of somatic stress. *Scand J Rehabil Med* 2:92-98, 1970.
50. Borg, GA. Psychophysical bases of perceived exertion. *Med Sci Sports Exerc* 14:377-381, 1982.
51. Bottinelli, R, Pellegrino, MA, Canepari, M, Rossi, R, and Reggiani, C. Specific contributions of various muscle fibre types to human muscle performance: An in vitro study. *J Electromyogr Kinesiol* 9:87-95, 1999.
52. Bradley-Popovich, GE, and Haff, GG. Nonlinear versus linear periodization models. *Strength Cond J* 23:42-44, 2001.
53. Brandão, L, de Salles Painelli, V, Lasevicius, T, Silva-Batista, C, Brendon, H, Schoenfeld, BJ, Aihara, AY, Cardoso, FN, de Almeida Peres, B, and Teixeira, EL. Varying the order of combinations of single- and multi-joint exercises differentially affects resistance training adaptations. *J Strength Cond Res* 34:1254-1263, 2020.
54. Bret, C, Rahmani, A, Dufour, AB, Messonnier, L, and Lacour, JR. Leg strength and stiffness as ability factors in 100 m sprint running. *J Sports Med Phys Fitness* 42:274-281, 2002.
55. Brigatto, FA, Lima, LEM, Germano, MD, Aoki, MS, Braz, TV, and Lopes, CR. High resistance-training volume enhances muscle thickness in resistance-trained men. *J Strength Cond Res* 36:22-30, 2022.
56. Buchner, DM, Beresford, SA, Larson, EB, LaCroix, AZ, and Wagner, EH. Effects of physical activity on health status in older adults: II. Intervention studies. *Annu Rev Public Health* 13:469-488, 1992.
57. Buckner, SL, Dankel, SJ, Mattocks, KT, Jessee, MB, Grant Mouser, J, and Loenneke, JP. Muscle size and strength: Another study not designed to answer the question. *Eur J Appl Physiol* 117:1273-1274, 2017.
58. Buckner, SL, Dankel, SJ, Mattocks, KT, Jessee, MB, Mouser, JG, Counts, BR, and Loenneke, JP. The problem of muscle hypertrophy: Revisited. *Muscle Nerve* 54:1012-1014, 2016.
59. Buckner, SL, Jessee, MB, Mattocks, KT, Mouser, JG, Counts, BR, Dankel, SJ, and Loenneke, JP. Determining strength: A case for multiple methods of measurement. *Sports Med* 47:193-195, 2017.
60. Buford, TW, Rossi, SJ, Smith, DB, and Warren, AJ. A comparison of periodization models during nine weeks with equated volume and intensity for strength. *J Strength Cond Res* 21:1245-1250, 2007.
61. Buitrago, M, and Ma, J. The training plan and training diary. In *Chinese Weightlifting: Technical Mastery and Training*. China: Ma Strength, 221-240, 2018.
62. Buresh, R, Berg, K, and French, J. The effect of resistive exercise rest interval on hormonal response, strength, and hypertrophy with training. *J Strength Cond Res* 23:62-71, 2009.
63. Campos, GE, Luecke, TJ, Wendeln, HK, Toma, K, Hagerman, FC, Murray, TF, Ragg, KE, Ratamess, NA, Kraemer, WJ, and Staron, RS. Muscular adaptations in response to three different resistance-training regimens: Specificity of repetition maximum training zones. *Eur J Appl Physiol* 88:50-60., 2002.
64. Candow, DG, and Burke, DG. Effect of short-term equal-volume resistance training with different workout frequency on muscle mass and strength in untrained men and women. *J Strength Cond Res* 21:204-207, 2007.
65. Carroll, KM, Bazyler, CD, Bernards, JR, Taber, CB, Stuart, CA, DeWeese, BH, Sato, K, and Stone, MH. Skeletal muscle fiber adaptations following resistance training using repetition maximums or relative intensity. *Sports* 7:169, 2019.
66. Carroll, KM, Bernards, JR, Bazyler, CD, Taber, CB, Stuart, CA, DeWeese, BH, Sato, K, and Stone, MH. Divergent performance outcomes following resistance training using repetition maximums or relative intensity. *Int J Sports Physiol Perform* 14:46-54, 2019.
67. Cavagna, GA, Saibene, FP, and Margaria, R. Effect of negative work on the amount of positive work performed by an isolated muscle. *J Appl Physiol* 20:157-158, 1965.
68. Chilibeck, PD, Calder, AW, Sale, DG, and Webber, CE. A comparison of strength and muscle mass increases during resistance training in young women. *Eur J Appl Physiol* 77:170-175, 1998.
69. Chiu, LZ, and Barnes, JL. The fitness-fatigue model revisited: Implications for planning short- and long-term training. *Strength Cond J* 25:42-51, 2003.
70. Chiu, LZ, Fry, AC, Weiss, LW, Schilling, BK, Brown, LE, and Smith, SL. Postactivation potentiation response in athletic and recreationally trained individuals. *J Strength Cond Res* 17:671-677, 2003.
71. Christou, M, Smilios, I, Sotiropoulos, K, Volaklis, K, Pilianidis, T, and Tokmakidis, SP. Effects of resistance training on the physical capacities of adolescent soccer players. *J Strength Cond Res* 20:783-791, 2006.
72. Churchward-Venne, TA, Tieland, M, Verdijk, LB, Leenders, M, Dirks, ML, de Groot, LCPGM, and van Loon, LJC. There are no nonresponders to resistance-type exercise training in older men and women. *J Am Med Dir Assoc* 16:400-411, 2015.
73. Coffey, VG, and Hawley, JA. The molecular bases of training adaptation. *Sports Med* 37:737-763, 2007.
74. Comfort, P, Allen, M, and Graham-Smith, P. Kinetic comparisons during variations of the power clean. *J Strength Cond Res* 25:3269-3273, 2011.

75. Comfort, P, Fletcher, C, and McMahon, JJ. Determination of optimal loading during the power clean, in collegiate athletes. *J Strength Cond Res* 26:2970-2974, 2012.

76. Comfort, P, McMahon, JJ, and Fletcher, C. No kinetic differences during variations of the power clean in inexperienced female collegiate athletes. *J Strength Cond Res* 27:363-368, 2013.

77. Conley, MS, Stone, MH, O'Bryant, HS, Johnson, RL, Honeycutt, DR, and Hoke, TP. Peak power versus power at maximal oxygen uptake. Presented at National Strength and Conditioning Association Annual Convention, Las Vegas,NE, 1993.

78. Conlon, JA, Newton, RU, Tufano, JJ, Banyard, HG, Hopper, AJ, Ridge, AJ, and Haff, GG. Periodization strategies in older adults: Impact on physical function and health. *Med Sci Sports Exerc* 48:2426-2436, 2016.

79. Conlon, JA, Newton, RU, Tufano, JJ, Penailillo, LE, Banyard, HG, Hopper, AJ, Ridge, AJ, and Haff, GG. The efficacy of periodised resistance training on neuromuscular adaptation in older adults. *Eur J Appl Physiol* 117:1181-1194, 2017.

80. Cormie, P, McGuigan, MR, and Newton, RU. Adaptations in athletic performance following ballistic power vs strength training. *Med Sci Sports Exerc* 42:1582-1598, 2010.

81. Cormie, P, McGuigan, MR, and Newton, RU. Influence of strength on magnitude and mechanisms of adaptation to power training. *Med Sci Sports Exerc* 42:1566-1581, 2010.

82. Cormie, P, McGuigan, MR, and Newton, RU. Developing maximal neuromuscular power: Part 2—training considerations for improving maximal power production. *Sports Med* 41:125-146, 2011.

83. Cronin, JB, and Hansen, KT. Strength and power predictors of sports speed. *J Strength Cond Res* 19:349-357, 2005.

84. Cronin, JB, McNair, PJ, and Marshall, RN. The role of maximal strength and load on initial power production. *Med Sci Sports Exerc* 32:1763-1769, 2000.

85. Cuenca-Fernandez, F, Smith, IC, Jordan, MJ, MacIntosh, BR, Lopez-Contreras, G, Arellano, R, and Herzog, W. Nonlocalized postactivation performance enhancement (PAPE) effects in trained athletes: A pilot study. *Appl Physiol Nutr Metab* 42:1122-1125, 2017.

86. Cuthbert, M, Haff, GG, Arent, SM, Ripley, N, McMahon, JJ, Evans, M, and Comfort, P. Effects of variations in resistance training frequency on strength development in well-trained populations and implications for in-season athlete training: A systematic review and meta-analysis. *Sports Med* 51:1697-1982, 2021.

87. D'Antona, G, Lanfranconi, F, Pellegrino, MA, Brocca, L, Adami, R, Rossi, R, Moro, G, Miotti, D, Canepari, M, and Bottinelli, R. Skeletal muscle hypertrophy and structure and function of skeletal muscle fibres in male body builders. *J Physiol* 570:611-627, 2006.

88. Damas, F, Libardi, CA, and Ugrinowitsch, C. The development of skeletal muscle hypertrophy through resistance training: The role of muscle damage and muscle protein synthesis. *Eur J Appl Physiol* 118:485-500, 2018.

89. Damas, F, Phillips, S, Vechin, FC, and Ugrinowitsch, C. A review of resistance training-induced changes in skeletal muscle protein synthesis and their contribution to hypertrophy. *Sports Med* 45:801-807, 2015.

90. Damas, F, Phillips, SM, Libardi, CA, Vechin, FC, Lixandrao, ME, Jannig, PR, Costa, LA, Bacurau, AV, Snijders, T, Parise, G, Tricoli, V, Roschel, H, and Ugrinowitsch, C. Resistance training-induced changes in integrated myofibrillar protein synthesis are related to hypertrophy only after attenuation of muscle damage. *J Physiol* 594:5209-5222, 2016.

91. Dankel, SJ, Mattocks, KT, Jessee, MB, Buckner, SL, Mouser, JG, Counts, BR, Laurentino, GC, and Loenneke, JP. Frequency: The overlooked resistance training variable for inducing muscle hypertrophy? *Sports Med* 47:799-805, 2017.

92. Davies, T, Orr, R, Halaki, M, and Hackett, D. Effect of Training leading to repetition failure on muscular strength: A systematic review and meta-analysis. *Sports Med* 46:487-502, 2016.

93. Davies, TB, Tran, DL, Hogan, CM, Haff, GG, and Latella, C. Chronic effects of altering resistance training set configurations using cluster sets: A systematic review and meta-analysis. *Sports Med* 51:707-736, 2021.

94. Day, ML, McGuigan, MR, Brice, G, and Foster, C. Monitoring exercise intensity during resistance training using the session RPE scale. *J Strength Cond Res* 18:353-358, 2004.

95. de Franca, HS, Branco, PA, Guedes Junior, DP, Gentil, P, Steele, J, and Teixeira, CV. The effects of adding single-joint exercises to a multi-joint exercise resistance training program on upper body muscle strength and size in trained men. *Appl Physiol Nutr Metab* 40:822-826, 2015.

96. de Lima, C, Boullosa, DA, Frollini, AB, Donatto, FF, Leite, RD, Gonelli, PR, Montebello, MI, Prestes, J, and Cesar, MC. Linear and daily undulating resistance training periodizations have differential beneficial effects in young sedentary women. *Int J Sports Med* 33:723-727, 2012.

97. de Salles, BF, Simão, R, Miranda, F, da Silva Novaes, J, Lemos, A, and Willardson, JM. Rest interval between sets in strength training. *Sports Med* 39:765-777 2009.

98. Debanne, T, and Laffaye, G. Predicting the throwing velocity of the ball in handball with anthropometric variables and isotonic tests. *J Sports Sci* 29:705-713, 2011.

99. Defreitas, JM, Beck, TW, Stock, MS, Dillon, MA, and Kasishke, PR, 2nd. An examination of the time course of training-induced skeletal muscle hypertrophy. *Eur J Appl Physiol* 111:2785-2790, 2011.

100. Del Vecchio, A, Casolo, A, Negro, F, Scorcelletti, M, Bazzucchi, I, Enoka, R, Felici, F, and Farina, D. The increase in muscle force after 4 weeks of strength training is mediated by adaptations in motor unit recruitment and rate coding. *J Physiol* 597:1873-1887, 2019.

101. Denton, J, and Cronin, JB. Kinematic, kinetic, and blood lactate profiles of continuous and intraset rest loading schemes. *J Strength Cond Res* 20:528-534, 2006.

102. Deschenes, M. Short review: Rate coding and motor unit recruitment patterns. *J Appl Sports Sci Res* 3:33-39, 1989.

103. Desmedt, JE, and Godaux, E. Ballistic contractions in man: Characteristic recruitment pattern of single motor units of the tibialis anterior muscle. *J Physiol (Lond)* 264:673-693, 1977.

104. DeWeese, BH, Bellon, C, Magrum, E, Taber, CB, and Suchomel, TJ. Strengthening the springs: Improving sprint performance via strength training. *Techniques for Track & Field and Cross Country* 9:8-23, 2016.

105. DeWeese, BH, Hornsby, G, Stone, M, and Stone, MH. The training process: Planning for strength–power training in track and field. Part 1: Theoretical aspects. *J Sport Health Sci* 4:308-317, 2015.
106. DeWeese, BH, Hornsby, G, Stone, M, and Stone, MH. The training process: Planning for strength–power training in track and field. Part 2: Practical and applied aspects. *J Sport Health Sci* 4:318-324, 2015.
107. DeWeese, BH, Serrano, AJ, Scruggs, SK, and Burton, JD. The midthigh pull: Proper application and progressions of a weightlifting movement derivative. *Strength Cond J* 35:54-58, 2013.
108. DeWeese, BH, Serrano, AJ, Scruggs, SK, and Sams, ML. The clean pull and snatch pull: Proper technique for weightlifting movement derivatives. *Strength Cond J* 34:82-86, 2012.
109. DeWeese, BH, Suchomel, TJ, Serrano, AJ, Burton, JD, Scruggs, SK, and Taber, CB. Pull from the knee: Proper technique and application. *Strength Cond J* 38:79-85, 2016.
110. Dick, FW. Fitness. In *Sports Training Principles*. 4th ed. London: A and C Black, 218-228, 2002.
111. Dons, B, Bollerup, K, Bonde-Petersen, F, and Hancke, S. The effect of weight-lifting exercise related to muscle fiber composition and muscle cross-sectional area in humans. *Eur J Appl Physiol* 40:95-106, 1979.
112. Dorrell, HF, Smith, MF, and Gee, TI. Comparison of velocity-based and traditional percentage-based loading methods on maximal strength and power adaptations. *J Strength Cond Res* 34:46-53, 2020.
113. Dos'Santos, T, Thomas, C, Comfort, P, McMahon, JJ, and Jones, PA. Relationships between isometric force-time characteristics and dynamic performance. *Sports (Basel)* 5:68, 2017.
114. Dreschler, A. Putting it all together: Developing the training plan. In *The Weightlifting Encyclopedia: A Guide to World Class Performance*. Flushing, NY: A IS A Communications, 245-320, 1998.
115. Duchateau, J, and Baudry, S. Training adaptation of the neuromuscular system. *Neuromuscular Aspects of Sport Performance*:216-253, 2011.
116. Duchateau, J, and Hainaut, K. Mechanisms of muscle and motor unit adaptation to explosive power training. In *Strength and Power in Sport*. 2nd ed. Komi, PV, ed. Oxford: Blackwell Science, 315-330, 2003.
117. Duchateau, J, Semmler, JG, and Enoka, RM. Training adaptations in the behavior of human motor units. *J Appl Physiol* 101:1766-1775, 2006.
118. Dufour, SP, Lampert, E, Doutreleau, S, Lonsdorfer-Wolf, E, Billat, VL, Piquard, F, and Richard, R. Eccentric cycle exercise: Training application of specific circulatory adjustments. *Med Sci Sports Exerc* 36:1900-1906, 2004.
119. Dunlavy, JK, Sands, WA, McNeal, JR, Stone, MH, Smith, SA, Jemni, M, and Haff, GG. Strength performance assessment in a simulated men's gymnastics still rings cross. *J Sports Sci Medicine* 6:93-97, 2007.
120. Dymond, C, Flanagan, EP, and Turner, AP. The relationship between maximal strength and plyometric ability in rugby players. Presented at ISBS-Conference Proceedings Archive, 2011.
121. Evans, M. Strength and conditioning for cycling. In *Strength and Conditioning for Sports Performance*. Jeffreys, I, Moody, J, eds. Abingdon, Oxon: Routledge, 642-646, 2016.
122. Faigenbaum, AD, MacDonald, JP, and Haff, GG. Are young athletes strong enough for sport? DREAM on. *Curr Sports Med Rep* 18:6-8, 2019.
123. Faulkner, J, and Eston, RG. Perceived exertion research in the 21st century: Developments, reflections and questions for the future. *J Exerc Sci Fit* 6:1-14, 2008.
124. Ferris, DP, Signorile, JF, and Caruso, JF. The relationship between physical and physiological variables and volleyball spiking velocity. *J Strength Cond Res* 9:32-36, 1995.
125. Fleck, S, and Kraemer, WJ. Developing the individualised resistance training workout. In *Designing Resistance Training Programs*. 3rd ed. Champaign, IL: Human Kinetics, 151-186, 2004.
126. Fleck, S, and Kraemer, WJ. Types of strength training. In *Designing Resistance Training Programs*. 3rd ed. Champaign, IL: Human Kinetics, 13-52, 2004.
127. Folland, JP, Irish, CS, Roberts, JC, Tarr, JE, and Jones, DA. Fatigue is not a necessary stimulus for strength gains during resistance training. *Br J Sports Med* 36:370-373, 2002.
128. Folland, JP, and Williams, AG. The adaptations to strength training: Morphological and neurological contributions to increased strength. *Sports Med* 37:145-168, 2007.
129. Ford, LE, Detterline, AJ, Ho, KK, and Cao, W. Gender- and height-related limits of muscle strength in world weightlifting champions. *J Appl Physiol* 89:1061-1064, 2000.
130. Franchi, MV, Atherton, PJ, Reeves, ND, Fluck, M, Williams, J, Mitchell, WK, Selby, A, Beltran Valls, RM, and Narici, MV. Architectural, functional and molecular responses to concentric and eccentric loading in human skeletal muscle. *Acta Physiol (Oxf)* 210:642-654, 2014.
131. Franchi, MV, Wilkinson, DJ, Quinlan, JI, Mitchell, WK, Lund, JN, Williams, JP, Reeves, ND, Smith, K, Atherton, PJ, and Narici, MV. Early structural remodeling and deuterium oxide-derived protein metabolic responses to eccentric and concentric loading in human skeletal muscle. *Physiol Rep* 3, 2015.
132. Francis, C. *Structure of Training for Speed*. CharlieFrancis.com, 2008.
133. Franco, CMC, Carneiro, MAS, de Sousa, JFR, Gomes, GK, and Orsatti, FL. Influence of high- and low-frequency resistance training on lean body mass and muscle strength gains in untrained men. *J Strength Cond Res*, 2019.
134. Freeston, JL, Carter, T, Whitaker, G, Nicholls, O, and Rooney, KB. Strength and power correlates of throwing velocity on subelite male cricket players. *J Strength Cond Res* 30:1646-1651, 2016.
135. Friedmann-Bette, B, Bauer, T, Kinscherf, R, Vorwald, S, Klute, K, Bischoff, D, Muller, H, Weber, MA, Metz, J, Kauczor, HU, Bartsch, P, and Billeter, R. Effects of strength training with eccentric overload on muscle adaptation in male athletes. *Eur J Appl Physiol* 108:821-836, 2010.
136. Friedmann, B, Kinscherf, R, Vorwald, S, Muller, H, Kucera, K, Borisch, S, Richter, G, Bartsch, P, and Billeter, R. Muscular adaptations to computer-guided strength training with eccentric overload. *Acta Physiol Scand* 182:77-88, 2004.

137. Frobose, I, Verdonck, A, Duesberg, F, and Mucha, C. Effects of various load intensities in the framework of postoperative stationary endurance training on performance deficit of the quadriceps muscle of the thigh. *Z Orthop Ihre Grenzgeb* 131:164-167, 1993.

138. Fry, AC. The role of training intensity in resistance exercise overtraining and overreaching. In *Overtraining in Sport*. Kreider, RB, Fry, AC, O'Toole, ML, eds. Champaign, IL: Human Kinetics, 107-127, 1998.

139. Fry, AC. The role of resistance exercise intensity on muscle fibre adaptations. *Sports Med* 34:663-679, 2004.

140. Fry, AC, and Kraemer, WJ. Physical performance characteristics of American collegiate football players. *J Appl Sport Sci Res* 5:126-138, 1991.

141. Fry, AC, Schilling, BK, Staron, RS, Hagerman, FC, Hikida, RS, and Thrush, JT. Muscle fiber characteristics and performance correlates of male Olympic-style weightlifters. *J Strength Cond Res* 17:746-754, 2003.

142. Fry, AC, Webber, JM, Weiss, LW, Harber, MP, Vaczi, M, and Pattison, NA. Muscle fiber characteristics of competitive power lifters. *J Strength Cond Res* 17:402-410, 2003.

143. Fry, RW, Morton, AR, and Keast, D. Periodisation and the prevention of overtraining. *Can J Sport Sci* 17:241-248, 1992.

144. Fry, RW, Morton, AR, and Keast, D. Periodisation of training stress—a review. *Can J Sport Sci* 17:234-240, 1992.

145. Fukutani, A, Isaka, T, and Herzog, W. Evidence for muscle cell-based mechanisms of enhanced performance in stretch-shortening cycle in skeletal muscle. *Front Physiol* 11:609553, 2020.

146. Gabbett, TJ. Science of Rugby League football: A review. *J Sports Sci* 23:961-976, 2005.

147. Gabbett, TJ. Influence of fatigue on tackling ability in Rugby League players: Role of muscular strength, endurance, and aerobic qualities. *PLoS One* 11:e0163161, 2016.

148. Gabriel, DA, Kamen, G, and Frost, G. Neural adaptations to resistive exercise: Mechanisms and recommendations for training practices. *Sports Med* 36:133-149, 2006.

149. Gallagher, P, Trappe, S, Harber, M, Creer, A, Mazzetti, S, Trappe, T, Alkner, B, and Tesch, P. Effects of 84-days of bedrest and resistance training on single muscle fibre myosin heavy chain distribution in human vastus lateralis and soleus muscles. *Acta Physiol Scand* 185:61-69, 2005.

150. Garcia-Ramos, A, Haff, GG, Pestana-Melero, FL, Perez-Castilla, A, Rojas, FJ, Balsalobre-Fernandez, C, and Jaric, S. Feasibility of the 2-Point Method for Determining the 1-Repetition Maximum in the Bench Press Exercise. *Int J Sports Physiol Perform* 13:474-481, 2018.

151. Garcia-Ramos, A, and Jaric, S. Two-point method: A quick and fatigue-free procedure for assessment of muscle mechanical capacities and the one-repetition maximum. *Strength Cond J* 40:54-65, 2018.

152. Garhammer, J, and Takano, B. Training for weightlifting. In *Strength and Power in Sport*. 2nd ed. Komi, PV, ed. Oxford, UK: Blackwell Scientific, 502-515, 2003.

153. Gavanda, S, Geisler, S, Quittmann, OJ, Bauhaus, H, and Schiffer, T. Three weeks of detraining does not decrease muscle thickness, strength or sport performance in adolescent athletes. *Int J Exerc Sci* 13:633-644, 2020.

154. Gavanda, S, Geisler, S, Quittmann, OJ, and Schiffer, T. The effect of block versus daily undulating periodization on strength and performance in adolescent football players. *Int J Sports Physiol Perform* 14:814-821, 2019.

155. Gentil, P, Fisher, J, and Steele, J. A review of the acute effects and long-term adaptations of single- and multi-joint exercises during resistance training. *Sports Med* 47:843-855, 2017.

156. Gentil, P, Soares, SR, Pereira, MC, da Cunha, RR, Martorelli, SS, Martorelli, AS, and Bottaro, M. Effect of adding single-joint exercises to a multi-joint exercise resistance-training program on strength and hypertrophy in untrained subjects. *Appl Physiol Nutr Metab* 38:341-344, 2013.

157. Geremia, JM, Baroni, BM, Bini, RR, Lanferdini, FJ, de Lima, AR, Herzog, W, and Vaz, MA. Triceps surae muscle architecture adaptations to eccentric training. *Front Physiol* 10:1456, 2019.

158. Gillam, GM. Effects of frequency of weight training on muscle strength enhancement. *J Sports Med* 21:432-436, 1981.

159. Girman, JC, Jones, MT, Matthews, TD, and Wood, RJ. Acute effects of a cluster-set protocol on hormonal, metabolic and performance measures in resistance-trained males. *Eur J Sport Sci* 14:151-159, 2014.

160. Gissis, I, Papadopoulos, C, Kalapotharakos, VI, Sotiropoulos, A, Komsis, G, and Manolopoulos, E. Strength and speed characteristics of elite, subelite, and recreational young Gonzalez-Badillo, JJ, Izquierdo, M, and Gorostiaga, EM. Moderate volume of high relative training intensity produces greater strength gains compared with low and high volumes in competitive weightlifters. *J Strength Cond Res* 20:73-81, 2006.

161. Gonzalez-Badillo, JJ, Izquierdo, M, and Gorostiaga, EM. Moderate volume of high relative training intensity produces greater strength gains compared with low and high volumes in competitive weightlifters. *J Strength Cond Res* 20:73-81, 2006.

162. Gonzalez-Badillo, JJ, and Sanchez-Medina, L. Movement velocity as a measure of loading intensity in resistance training. *Int J Sports Med* 31:347-352, 2010.

163. Gordon, T, Thomas, CK, Munson, JB, and Stein, RB. The resilience of the size principle in the organization of motor unit properties in normal and reinnervated adult skeletal muscles. *Can J Physiol Pharmacol* 82:645-661, 2004.

164. Goto, K, Sato, K, and Takamatsu, K. A single set of low intensity resistance exercise immediately following high intensity resistance exercise stimulates growth hormone secretion in men. *J Sports Med Phys Fitness* 43:243-249, 2003.

165. Gourgoulis, V, Aggeloussis, N, Kasimatis, P, Mavromatis, G, and Garas, A. Effect of a submaximal half-squats warm-up program on vertical jumping ability. *J Strength Cond Res* 17:342-344, 2003.

166. Graves, JE, Pollock, ML, Foster, D, Leggett, SH, Carpenter, DM, Vuoso, R, and Jones, A. Effect of training frequency and specificity on isometric lumbar extension strength. *Spine* 15:504-509, 1990.

167. Graves, JE, Pollock, ML, Leggett, SH, Braith, RW, Carpenter, DM, and Bishop, LE. Effect of reduced training frequency on muscular strength. *Int J Sports Med* 9:316-319, 1988.

168. Greig, L, Stephens Hemingway, BH, Aspe, RR, Cooper, K, Comfort, P, and Swinton, PA. Autoregulation in resistance training: Addressing the inconsistencies. *Sports Med* 50:1873-1887, 2020.

169. Grgic, J, Schoenfeld, BJ, Davies, TB, Lazinica, B, Krieger, JW, and Pedisic, Z. Effect of resistance training frequency on gains in muscular strength: A systematic review and meta-analysis. *Sports Med* 48:1207-1220, 2018.

170. Grgic, J, Schoenfeld, BJ, and Latella, C. Resistance training frequency and skeletal muscle hypertrophy: A review of available evidence. *J Sci Med Sport* 22:361-370, 2019.

171. Grgic, J, Schoenfeld, BJ, Orazem, J, and Sabol, F. Effects of resistance training performed to repetition failure or non-failure on muscular strength and hypertrophy: A systematic review and meta-analysis. *J Sport Health Sci* 11:202-211, 2022.

172. Grgic, J, Schoenfeld, BJ, Skrepnik, M, Davies, TB, and Mikulic, P. Effects of rest interval duration in resistance training on measures of muscular strength: A systematic review. *Sports Med* 48:137-151, 2018.

173. Groeber, M, Reinhart, L, Kornfeind, P, and Baca, A. The contraction modalities in a stretch-shortening cycle in animals and single joint movements in humans: A systematic review. *J Sports Sci Med* 18:604-614, 2019.

174. Güllich, A, and Schmidtbleicher, D. MVC-induced short-term potentiation of explosive force. *New Studies in Athletics* 11:67-81, 1996.

175. Hackett, DA, Johnson, NA, Halaki, M, and Chow, CM. A novel scale to assess resistance-exercise effort. *J Sports Sci* 30:1405-1413, 2012.

176. Haff, GG. Quantifying workloads in resistance training: A brief review. *Prof Strength and Cond* 10:31-40, 2010.

177. Haff, GG. Periodization of training. In *Conditioning for Strength and Human Performance*. 2nd ed. Brown, LE, Chandler, J, eds. Philadelphia, PA: Wolters Kluwer, Lippincott, Williams & Wilkins, 326-345, 2012.

178. Haff, GG. Periodization and power integration. In *Developing Power*. McGuigan, M, ed. Champaign, IL: Human Kinetics, 33-62, 2017.

179. Haff, GG. Isometric and dynamic testing. In *Performance Assessments for Strength and Conditioning Coaches*. Comfort, P, Jones, PA, McMahon, JJ, eds. Oxon, UK: Taylor Francis, 168-194, 2019.

180. Haff, GG. Periodization and programming of individual sports. In *NSCA's Essentials of Sport Science*. French, D, Torres Ronda, L, eds. Champaign, IL: Human Kinetics, 27-42, 2022.

181. Haff, GG, Burgess, S, and Stone, MH. Cluster training: Theoretical and practical applications for the strength and conditioning professional. *Prof Strength and Cond* 12:12-17, 2008.

182. Haff, GG, Carlock, JM, Hartman, MJ, Kilgore, JL, Kawamori, N, Jackson, JR, Morris, RT, Sands, WA, and Stone, MH. Force-time curve characteristics of dynamic and isometric muscle actions of elite women Olympic weightlifters. *J Strength Cond Res* 19:741-748, 2005.

183. Haff, GG, and Dumke, C. Musculoskeletal fitness measurements. In *Laboratory Manual for Exercise Physiology*. 2nd ed. Human Kinetics, 253-286, 2018.

184. Haff, GG, and Haff, EE. Resistance training program design. In *Essentials of Periodization*. 2nd ed. Malek, MH, Coburn, JW, eds. Champaign, IL: Human Kinetics, 359-401, 2012.

185. Haff, GG, and Harden, M. Cluster sets: Scientific background and practical applications. In *Advanced Strength and Conditioning: An Evidence-Based Approach*. 2nd ed. Turner, A, Comfort, P, eds. London: Routledge Taylor Francis, 213-232, 2022.

186. Haff, GG, Hobbs, RT, Haff, EE, Sands, WA, Pierce, KC, and Stone, MH. Cluster training: A novel method for introducing training program variation. *Strength Cond J* 30:67-76, 2008.

187. Haff, GG, and Nimphius, S. Training principles for power. *Strength Cond J* 34:2-12, 2012.

188. Haff, GG, Stone, MH, O'Bryant, HS, Harman, E, Dinan, CN, Johnson, R, and Han, KH. Force-time dependent characteristics of dynamic and isometric muscle actions. *J Strength Cond Res* 11:269-272, 1997.

189. Haff, GG, Whitley, A, McCoy, LB, O'Bryant, HS, Kilgore, JL, Haff, EE, Pierce, K, and Stone, MH. Effects of different set configurations on barbell velocity and displacement during a clean pull. *J Strength Cond Res* 17:95-103, 2003.

190. Haff, GG, Whitley, A, and Potteiger, JA. A brief review: Explosive exercises and sports performance. *Strength Cond J* 23:13-20, 2001.

191. Häkkinen, K. Neuromuscular adaptations during strength training, aging, detraining, and immobilization. *Crit Rev Physic Rehab Med* 6:161-198, 1994.

192. Häkkinen, K, and Kallinen, M. Distribution of strength training volume into one or two daily sessions and neuromuscular adaptations in female athletes. *Electromyogr Clin Neurophysiol* 34:117-124, 1994.

193. Häkkinen, K, Kauhanen, H, and Kuoppa, T. Neural, muscular and hormonal adaptations, changes in muscle strength and weightlifting results with respect to variations in training during one year follow-up period in Finnish elite weightlifters. *World Weightlifting (IWF)* 87:2-10, 1987.

194. Häkkinen, K, and Keskinen, KL. Muscle cross-sectional area and voluntary force production characteristics in elite strength- and endurance-trained athletes and sprinters. *Eur J Appl Physiol* 59:215-220, 1989.

195. Häkkinen, K, and Komi, PV. Changes in electrical and mechanical behavior of leg extensor muscles during heavy resistance strength training. *Scand J Sports Sci* 7:55-64, 1985.

196. Häkkinen, K, and Komi, PV. Effect of explosive type strength training on electromyographic and force production characteristics of leg extensor muscles during concentric and various stretch-shortening cycle exercises. *Scand J Sports Sci* 7:65-76, 1985.

197. Häkkinen, K, and Komi, PV. Training-induced changes in neuromuscular performance under voluntary and reflex conditions. *Eur J Appl Physiol Occup Physiol* 55:147-155, 1986.

198. Häkkinen, K, Komi, PV, Alen, M, and Kauhanen, H. EMG, muscle fibre and force production characteristics during a 1 year training period in elite weight-lifters. *Eur J Appl Physiol* 56:419-427, 1987.

199. Häkkinen, K, Komi, PV, and Tesch, PA. Effect of combined concentric and eccentric strength training and detraining on force-time, muscle fiber and metabolic characteristics of leg extensor muscles. *Scand J Sports Sci* 3:50-58, 1981.

200. Häkkinen, K, Newton, RU, Gordon, SE, McCormick, M, Volek, JS, Nindl, BC, Gotshalk, LA, Campbell, WW, Evans, WJ, Häkkinen, A, Humphries, BJ, and Kraemer, WJ. Changes in muscle morphology, electromyographic activity, and force production characteristics during progressive strength training in young and older men. *J Gerontol A Biol Sci Med Sci* 53:B415-423., 1998.

201. Häkkinen, K, Pakarinen, A, Alen, M, Kauhanen, H, and Komi, PV. Neuromuscular and hormonal adaptations in athletes to strength training in two years. *J Appl Physiol* 65:2406-2412, 1988.

202. Hall, ECR, Lysenko, EA, Semenova, EA, Borisov, OV, Andryushchenko, ON, Andryushchenko, LB, Vepkhvadze, TF, Lednev, EM, Zmijewski, P, Popov, DV, Generozov, EV, and Ahmetov, II. Prediction of muscle fiber composition using multiple repetition testing. *Biol Sport* 38:277-283, 2021.

203. Hamada, T, Sale, DG, MacDougall, JD, and Tarnopolsky, MA. Postactivation potentiation, fiber type, and twitch contraction time in human knee extensor muscles. *J Appl Physiol* 88:2131-2137, 2000.

204. Harden, M, Comfort, P, and Haff, GG. Eccentric training: Scientific background and practical applications. In *Advanced Strength and Conditioning: An Evidence-Based Approach*. 2nd ed. Turner, A, Comfort, P, eds. London: Routledge Taylor Francis, 190-212, 2022.

205. Harden, M, Wolf, A, Evans, M, Hicks, KM, Thomas, K, and Howatson, G. Four weeks of augmented eccentric loading using a novel leg press device improved leg strength in well-trained athletes and professional sprint track cyclists. *PLoS One* 15:e0236663, 2020.

206. Harden, M, Wolf, A, Haff, GG, Hicks, KM, and Howatson, G. Repeatability and specificity of eccentric force output and the implications for eccentric training load prescription. *J Strength Cond Res* 33:676-683, 2019.

207. Harden, M, Wolf, A, Russell, M, Hicks, KM, French, D, and Howatson, G. An evaluation of supramaximally loaded eccentric leg press exercise. *J Strength Cond Res* 32:2708-2714, 2018.

208. Harris, RC, Edwards, RH, Hultman, E, Nordesjo, LO, Nylind, B, and Sahlin, K. The time course of phosphorylcreatine resynthesis during recovery of the quadriceps muscle in man. *Pflugers Arch* 367:137-142, 1976.

209. Hartmann, H, Wirth, K, Keiner, M, Mickel, C, Sander, A, and Szilvas, E. Short-term periodization models: Effects on strength and speed-strength performance. *Sports Med* 45:1373-1386, 2015.

210. Hather, BM, Tesch, PA, Buchanan, P, and Dudley, GA. Influence of eccentric actions on skeletal muscle adaptations to resistance training. *Acta Physiol Scand* 143:177-185, 1991.

211. Helms, ER, Brown, SR, Cross, MR, Storey, A, Cronin, J, and Zourdos, MC. Self-rated accuracy of rating of perceived exertion-based load prescription in powerlifters. *J Strength Cond Res* 31:2938-2943, 2017.

212. Helms, ER, Cronin, J, Storey, A, and Zourdos, MC. Application of the repetitions in reserve-based rating of perceived exertion scale for resistance training. *Strength Cond J* 38:42-49, 2016.

213. Henneman, E, Somjen, G, and Carpenter, DO. Excitability and inhibitability of motoneurons of different sizes. *J Neurophysiol* 28:599-620, 1965.

214. Hernandez-Davo, JL, Sabido, R, Moya-Ramon, M, and Blazevich, AJ. Load knowledge reduces rapid force production and muscle activation during maximal-effort concentric lifts. *Eur J Appl Physiol* 115:2571-2581, 2015.

215. Higbie, EJ, Cureton, KJ, Warren, GL, 3rd, and Prior, BM. Effects of concentric and eccentric training on muscle strength, cross-sectional area, and neural activation. *J Appl Physiol* 81:2173-2181, 1996.

216. Hiskia, G. Advanced electronic technology for real-time biomechanical analysis of weightlifting. Presented at Proceedings of the Weightlifting Symposium, Greece, 1993.

217. Hodgson, M, Docherty, D, and Robbins, D. Post-activation potentiation: Underlying physiology and implications for motor performance. *Sports Med* 35:585-595, 2005.

218. Hody, S, Croisier, JL, Bury, T, Rogister, B, and Leprince, P. Eccentric muscle contractions: Risks and benefits. *Front Physiol* 10:536, 2019.

219. Hoeger, WWK, Barette, SL, Hale, DF, and Hopkins, DR. Relationship between repetitions and selected percentages of one repetition maximum. *J Appl Sport Sci Res* 1:11-13, 1987.

220. Hoeger, WWK, Hopkins, DR, Barette, SL, and Hale, DF. Relationship between repetitions and selected percentages of one repetition maximum: A comparison between untrained and trained males and females. *J Appl Sports Sci Res* 4:47-54, 1990.

221. Hoff, J, and Helgerud, J. Endurance and strength training for soccer players: Physiological considerations. *Sports Med* 34:165-180, 2004.

222. Hoff, J, Helgerud, J, and Wisløff, U. Maximal strength training improves work economy in trained female cross-country skiers. *Med Sci Sports Exerc* 31:870-877, 1999.

223. Hoff, J, Kemi, OJ, and Helgerud, J. Strength and endurance differences between elite and junior elite ice hockey players: The importance of allometric scaling. *Int J Sports Med* 26:537-541, 2005.

224. Hoffman, JR, Maresh, CM, Armstrong, LE, and Kraemer, WJ. Effects of off-season and in-season resistance training programs on a collegiate male basketball team. *J Human Muscle Perf* 1:48-55, 1991.

225. Hoffman, JR, Ratamess, NA, Klatt, M, Faigenbaum, AD, Ross, RE, Tranchina, NM, McCurley, RC, Kang, J, and Kraemer, WJ. Comparison between different off-season resistance training programs in Division III American college football players. *J Strength Cond Res* 23:11-19, 2009.

226. Hollander, DP, Kraemer, RR, Kilpatrick, MW, Ramadan, AG, Reeves, GV, Francois, M, Herbert, EP, and Tryniecki, JL. Maximal eccentric and concentric strength discrepancies between young men and women for dynamic resistance exercise. *J Strength Cond Res* 21:34-40, 2007.

227. Hori, N, Newton, RU, Andrews, WA, Kawamori, N, McGuigan, MR, and Nosaka, K. Does performance of hang power clean differentiate performance of jumping,

228. Hornsby, WG, Gentles, JA, Haff, GG, Stone, MH, Buckner, SL, Dankel, SJ, Bell, ZW, Abe, T, and Loenneke, JP. What is the impact of muscle hypertrophy on strength and sport performance? *Strength Cond J* 40:99-111, 2018.

227. [sprinting, and changing of direction? *J Strength Cond Res* 22:412-418, 2008.]

229. Hornsby, WG, Gentles, JA, MacDonald, CJ, Mizuguchi, S, Ramsey, MW, and Stone, MH. Maximum strength, rate of force development, jump height, and peak power alterations in weightlifters across five months of training. *Sports* 5:78, 2017.

230. Hortobagyi, T, Houmard, JA, Stevenson, JR, Fraser, DD, Johns, RA, and Israel, RG. The effects of detraining on power athletes. *Med Sci Sports Exerc* 25:929-935, 1993.

231. Hortobagyi, T, and Katch, FI. Eccentric and concentric torque-velocity relationships during arm flexion and extension: Influence of strength level. *Eur J Appl Physiol Occup Physiol* 60:395-401, 1990.

232. Houston, ME, Froese, EA, Valeriote, SP, Green, HJ, and Ranney, DA. Muscle performance, morphology and metabolic capacity during strength training and detraining: A one leg model. *Eur J Appl Physiol* 51:25-35, 1983.

233. Hughes, LJ, Banyard, HG, Dempsey, AR, and Scott, BR. Using a load-velocity relationship to predict one repetition maximum in free-weight exercise: A comparison of the different methods. *J Strength Cond Res* 33:2409-2419, 2019.

234. Hultman, E, Bergstrom, J, and Anderson, NM. Breakdown and resynthesis of phosphorylcreatine and adenosine triphosphate in connection with muscular work in man. *Scand J Clin Lab Invest* 19:56-66, 1967.

235. Hultman, E, and Sjoholm, H. Biochemical causes of fatigue. In *Human Muscle Power.* Jones, NL, ed. Champaign, IL: Human Kinetics, 343-363, 1986.

236. Hunter, GR. Changes in body composition, body build and performance associated with different weight training frequencies in males and females. *NSCA J* 7:26-28, 1985.

237. Issurin, V. Block periodization training models as an alternative to traditional approach. In *Advanced Athlete Training.* Michigan, USA: Ultimate Athlete Concepts, 164-190, 2008.

238. Issurin, VB. New horizons for the methodology and physiology of training periodization. *Sports Med* 40:189-206, 2010.

239. Issurin, VB. Benefits and limitations of block periodized training approaches to athletes' preparation: A review. *Sports Med* 46:329-338, 2016.

240. Izquierdo-Gabarren, M, Gonzalez de Txabarri Exposito, R, Garcia-Pallares, J, Sanchez-Medina, L, Saez de Villarreal E, S, and Izquierdo, M. Concurrent endurance and strength training not to failure optimizes performance gains. *Med Sci Sports Exerc* 42:1191-1199, 2010.

241. Izquierdo, M, Gonzalez-Badillo, JJ, Hakkinen, K, Ibanez, J, Kraemer, WJ, Altadill, A, Eslava, J, and Gorostiaga, EM. Effect of loading on unintentional lifting velocity declines during single sets of repetitions to failure during upper and lower extremity muscle actions. *Int J Sports Med* 27:718-724, 2006.

242. Izquierdo, M, Ibanez, J, Gonzalez-Badillo, JJ, Hakkinen, K, Ratamess, NA, Kraemer, WJ, French, DN, Eslava, J, Altadill, A, Asiain, X, and Gorostiaga, EM. Differential effects of strength training leading to failure versus not to failure on hormonal responses, strength, and muscle power gains. *J Appl Physiol* 100:1647-1656, 2006.

243. Jacobson, BH, Conchola, EC, Smith, DB, Akehi, K, and Glass, RG. Relationship between selected strength and power assessments to peak and average velocity of the drive block in offensive line play. *J Strength Cond Res* 30:2202-2205, 2016.

244. Jaric, S. Muscle strength testing: Use of normalisation for body size. *Sports Med* 32:615-631, 2002.

245. Jaric, S. Force-velocity relationship of muscles performing multi-joint maximum performance tasks. *Int J Sports Med* 36:699-704, 2015.

246. Jenkins, NDM, Miramonti, AA, Hill, EC, Smith, CM, Cochrane-Snyman, KC, Housh, TJ, and Cramer, JT. Greater neural adaptations following high- vs. low-load resistance training. *Front Physiol* 8:331, 2017.

247. Jensen, BR, Pilegaard, M, and Sjogaard, G. Motor unit recruitment and rate coding in response to fatiguing shoulder abductions and subsequent recovery. *Eur J Appl Physiol* 83:190-199, 2000.

248. Jones, K, Bishop, P, Hunter, G, and Fleisig, G. The effects of varying resistance-training loads on intermediate- and high-velocity-specific adaptations. *J Strength Cond Res* 15:349-356., 2001.

249. Jones, L. Training programs: Do Bulgarian methods lead the way for the USA? *Weightlifting USA* 9:10-11, 1991.

250. Jones, L. Coaching platform: Advanced training programs. *Weightlifting USA* 4:8-11, 1992.

251. Jones, L. Coaching platform: Advanced training programs. *Weightlifting USA* November:8, 1992.

252. Jones, L. Coaching platform: Advanced training programs. *Weightlifting USA* July:10-11, 1992.

253. Jovanić, M, and Flanagan, EP. Researched applications of velocity based strength training. 22:58-69, 2014.

254. Judge, LW. Developing speed strength: In-season training program for the collegiate thrower. *Strength Cond J* 29:42, 2007.

255. Jukic, I, Ramos, AG, Helms, ER, McGuigan, MR, and Tufano, JJ. Acute effects of cluster and rest redistribution set structures on mechanical, metabolic, and perceptual fatigue during and after resistance training: A systematic review and meta-analysis. *Sports Med* 50:2209-2236, 2020.

256. Jukic, I, and Tufano, JJ. Shorter but more frequent rest periods: No effect on velocity and power compared to traditional sets not performed to failure. *J Hum Kinet* 66:257-268, 2019.

257. Jukic, I, Van Hooren, B, Ramos, AG, Helms, ER, McGuigan, MR, and Tufano, JJ. The effects of set structure manipulation on chronic adaptations to resistance training: A systematic review and meta-analysis. *Sports Med* 51:1061-1086, 2021.

258. Julio, U, Panissa, V, and Franchini, E. Prediction of one repetition maximum from the maximum number of repetitions with submaximal loads in recreationally strength-trained men. *Science & Sports* 27:e69-e76, 2012.

259. Jung, AP. The impact of resistance training on distance running performance. *Sports Med* 33:539-552, 2003.

260. Kamen, G. The acquisition of maximal isometric plantar flexor strength: A force time curve analysis. *J Motor Behav* 15:63-73, 1983.

261. Kamen, G, and Roy, A. Motor unit synchronization in young and elderly adults. *Eur J Appl Physiol* 81:403-410, 2000.

262. Kaneko, M, Fuchimoto, T, Toji, H, and Suei, K. Training effect of different loads on the force-velocity relationship and mechanical power output in human muscle. *Scand J Sports Sci* 5:50-55, 1983.

263. Kauhanen, H, Komi, PV, and Hakkinen, K. Standardization and validation of the body weight adjustment regression equations in Olympic weightlifting. *J Strength Cond Res* 16:58-74, 2002.

264. Kawamori, N, Crum, AJ, Blumert, P, Kulik, J, Childers, J, Wood, J, Stone, MH, and Haff, GG. Influence of different relative intensities on power output during the hang power clean: Identification of the optimal load. *J Strength Cond Res* 19:698-708, 2005.

265. Kawamori, N, and Haff, GG. The optimal training load for the development of muscular power. *J Strength Cond Res* 18:675-684, 2004.

266. Kawamori, N, Rossi, SJ, Justice, BD, Haff, EE, Pistilli, EE, O'Bryant, HS, Stone, MH, and Haff, GG. Peak force and rate of force development during isometric and dynamic mid-thigh clean pulls performed at various intensities. *J Strength Cond Res* 20:483-491, 2006.

267. Keiner, M, Rahse, H, Wirth, K, Hartmann, H, Fries, K, and Haff, GG. Influence of maximal strength on in-water and dry-land performance in young water polo players. *J Strength Cond Res* 34:1999-2005, 2020.

268. Kesidis, N, Metaxas, TI, Vrabas, IS, Stefanidis, P, Vamvakoudis, E, Christoulas, K, Mandroukas, A, Balasas, D, and Mandroukas, K. Myosin heavy chain isoform distribution in single fibres of bodybuilders. *Eur J Appl Physiol* 103:579-583, 2008.

269. Kilen, A, Hjelvang, LB, Dall, N, Kruse, NL, and Nordsborg, NB. Adaptations to short, frequent sessions of endurance and strength training are similar to longer, less frequent exercise sessions when the total volume is the same. *J Strength Cond Res* 29:S46-S51, 2015.

270. Knudson, DV. Correcting the use of the term "power" in the strength and conditioning literature. *J Strength Cond Res* 23:1902-1908, 2009.

271. Komi, PV. Training of muscle strength and power: Interaction of neuromotoric, hypertrophic, and mechanical factors. *Int J Sports Med* 7:10-15, 1986.

272. Komi, PV. Stretch-shortening cycle: A powerful model to study normal and fatigued muscle. *J Biomech* 33:1197-1206, 2000.

273. Kraemer, WJ. A series of studies—the physiological basis for strength training in American football: Fact over philosophy. *J Strength Cond Res* 11:131-142, 1997.

274. Kraemer, WJ, and Fleck, SJ. Acute programming variables. In *Optimizing Strength Training: Designing Nonlinear Periodization Workouts*. Champaign, IL: Human Kinetics, 41-64, 2007.

275. Kraemer, WJ, and Fleck, SJ. *Optimizing Strength Training: Designing Nonlinear Periodization Workouts*. Champaign, IL: Human Kinetics, 2007.

276. Kraemer, WJ, and Fleck, SJ. Periodization of resistance training. In *Optimizing Strength Training*. Champaign, IL: Human Kinetics, 1-26, 2007.

277. Kraemer, WJ, and Fleck, SJ. Practical considerations. In *Optimizing Strength Training: Designing Nonlinear Periodization Workouts*. Champaign, IL: Human Kinetics, 65-86, 2007.

278. Kraemer, WJ, and Fleck, SJ. Workout design. In *Optimizing Strength Training: Designing Nonlinear Periodization Workouts*. Champaign, IL: Human Kinetics, 87-100, 2007.

279. Kraemer, WJ, Hakkinen, K, Triplett-Mcbride, NT, Fry, AC, Koziris, LP, Ratamess, NA, Bauer, JE, Volek, JS, McConnell, T, Newton, RU, Gordon, SE, Cummings, D, Hauth, J, Pullo, F, Lynch, JM, Fleck, SJ, Mazzetti, SA, and Knuttgen, HG. Physiological changes with periodized resistance training in women tennis players. *Med Sci Sports Exerc* 35:157-168, 2003.

280. Kraemer, WJ, Marchitelli, L, Gordon, SE, Harman, E, Dziados, JE, Mello, R, Frykman, P, McCurry, D, and Fleck, SJ. Hormonal and growth factor responses to heavy resistance exercise protocols. *J Appl Physiol* 69:1442-1450, 1990.

281. Kraemer, WJ, Ratamess, N, Fry, AC, Triplett-McBride, T, Koziris, LP, Bauer, JA, Lynch, JM, and Fleck, SJ. Influence of resistance training volume and periodization on physiological and performance adaptations in collegiate women tennis players. *Am J Sports Med* 28:626-633, 2000.

282. Kraemer, WJ, and Ratamess, NA. Fundamentals of resistance training: Progression and exercise prescription. *Med Sci Sports Exerc* 36:674-688, 2004.

283. Kraska, JM, Ramsey, MW, Haff, GG, Fethke, N, Sands, WA, Stone, ME, and Stone, MH. Relationship between strength characteristics and unweighted and weighted vertical jump height. *Int J Sports Physiol Perform* 4:461-473, 2009.

284. Krieger, JW. Single vs. multiple sets of resistance exercise for muscle hypertrophy: A meta-analysis. *J Strength Cond Res* 24:1150-1159, 2010.

285. Lacerda, LT, Marra-Lopes, RO, Diniz, RCR, Lima, FV, Rodrigues, SA, Martins-Costa, HC, Bemben, MG, and Chagas, MH. Is performing repetitions to failure less important than volume for muscle hypertrophy and strength? *J Strength Cond Res* 34:1237-1248, 2020.

286. Lake, J, Lauder, M, Smith, N, and Shorter, K. A comparison of ballistic and nonballistic lower-body resistance exercise and the methods used to identify their positive lifting phases. *J Appl Biomech* 28:431-437, 2012.

287. Lasevicius, T, Schoenfeld, BJ, Silva-Batista, C, Barros, TdS, Aihara, AY, Brendon, H, Longo, AR, Tricoli, V, Peres, BdA, and Teixeira, EL. Muscle failure promotes greater muscle hypertrophy in low-load but not in high-load resistance training. *J Strength Cond Res* 36:346-351, 2022.

288. Latella, C, Teo, WP, Drinkwater, EJ, Kendall, K, and Haff, GG. The acute neuromuscular responses to cluster set resistance training: A systematic review and meta-analysis. *Sports Med* 49:1861-1877, 2019.

289. Lehman, G, Drinkwater, EJ, and Behm, DG. Correlation of throwing velocity to the results of lower-body field tests in male college baseball players. *J Strength Cond Res* 27:902-908, 2013.

290. Lepkowski, M, Leiting, KA, and Koch, AJ. Practical considerations and applications of postactivation performance

enhancement in group training: Delayed performance enhancing triplexes. *Strength Cond J* 43:62-67, 2021.

291. LeSuer, DA, McCormick, JH, Mayhew, JL, Wasserstein, RL, and Arnold, MD. The accuracy of prediction equations for estimating 1-RM performance in the bench press, squat, and deadlift. *J Strength Cond Res* 11:211-213, 1997.

292. Lieber, RL, and Friden, J. Functional and clinical significance of skeletal muscle architecture. *Muscle Nerve* 23:1647-1666, 2000.

293. Loenneke, JP, Buckner, SL, Dankel, SJ, and Abe, T. Exercise-induced changes in muscle size do not contribute to exercise-induced changes in muscle strength. *Sports Med* 49:987-991, 2019.

294. Loenneke, JP, Dankel, SJ, Bell, ZW, Buckner, SL, Mattocks, KT, Jessee, MB, and Abe, T. Is muscle growth a mechanism for increasing strength? *Med Hypotheses* 125:51-56, 2019.

295. Longo, AR, Silva-Batista, C, Pedroso, K, de Salles Painelli, V, Lasevicius, T, Schoenfeld, BJ, Aihara, AY, de Almeida Peres, B, Tricoli, V, and Teixeira, EL. Volume load rather than resting interval influences muscle hypertrophy during high-intensity resistance training. *J Strength Cond Res* 36:1554-1559, 2022.

296. Lovell, DI, Cuneo, R, and Gass, GC. The effect of strength training and short-term detraining on maximum force and the rate of force development of older men. *Eur J Appl Physiol* 109:429-435, 2010.

297. MacDougall, JD, Elder, GC, Sale, DG, Moroz, JR, and Sutton, JR. Effects of strength training and immobilization on human muscle fibres. *Eur J Appl Physiol* 43:25-34, 1980.

298. Machek, SB, Hwang, PS, Cardaci, TD, Wilburn, DT, Bagley, JR, Blake, DT, Galpin, AJ, and Willoughby, DS. Myosin heavy chain composition, creatine analogues, and the relationship of muscle creatine content and fast-twitch proportion to Wilks coefficient in powerlifters. *J Strength Cond Res* 34:3022-3030, 2020.

299. Maffiuletti, NA, Aagaard, P, Blazevich, AJ, Folland, J, Tillin, N, and Duchateau, J. Rate of force development: Physiological and methodological considerations. *Eur J Appl Physiol* 116:1091-1116, 2016.

300. Malisoux, L, Francaux, M, and Theisen, D. What do single-fiber studies tell us about exercise training? *Med Sci Sports Exerc* 39:1051-1060, 2007.

301. Malone, S, Hughes, B, Doran, DA, Collins, K, and Gabbett, TJ. Can the workload-injury relationship be moderated by improved strength, speed and repeated-sprint qualities? *J Sci Med Sport* 22:29-34, 2019.

302. Mangine, GT, Hoffman, JR, Gonzalez, AM, Townsend, JR, Wells, AJ, Jajtner, AR, Beyer, KS, Boone, CH, Miramonti, AA, Wang, R, LaMonica, MB, Fukuda, DH, Ratamess, NA, and Stout, JR. The effect of training volume and intensity on improvements in muscular strength and size in resistance-trained men. *Physiol Rep* 3, 2015.

303. Mann, JB. *Developing Explosive Athletes: Use of Velocity Based Training in Athletes*. Michigan, USA: Ultimate Athlete Concepts, 2021.

304. Mann, JB, Ivey, PA, and Sayers, SP. Velocity-based training in football. *Strength Cond J* 37:52-57, 2015.

305. Mann, JB, Thyfault, JP, Ivey, PA, and Sayers, SP. The effect of autoregulatory progressive resistance exercise vs. linear periodization on strength improvement in college athletes. *J Strength Cond Res* 24:1718-1723, 2010.

306. Marshall, P. Acute muscle activation and fatigue following the rest-pause resistance exercise method. *J Sci Med Sport* 14:e88-e89, 2011.

307. Marshall, PW, Robbins, DA, Wrightson, AW, and Siegler, JC. Acute neuromuscular and fatigue responses to the rest-pause method. *J Sci Med Sport* 15:153-158, 2012.

308. Martorelli, S, Cadore, EL, Izquierdo, M, Celes, R, Martorelli, A, Cleto, VA, Alvarenga, JG, and Bottaro, M. Strength training with repetitions to failure does not provide additional strength and muscle hypertrophy gains in young women. *Eur J Transl Myol* 27, 2017.

309. McBride, JM, Blow, D, Kirby, TJ, Haines, TL, Dayne, AM, and Triplett, NT. Relationship between maximal squat strength and five, ten, and forty yard sprint times. *J Strength Cond Res* 23:1633-1636, 2009.

310. McBride, JM, McCaulley, GO, Cormie, P, Nuzzo, JL, Cavill, MJ, and Triplett, NT. Comparison of methods to quantify volume during resistance exercise. *J Strength Cond Res* 23:106-110, 2009.

311. McBride, JM, Nimphius, S, and Erickson, TM. The acute effects of heavy-load squats and loaded countermovement jumps on sprint performance. *J Strength Cond Res* 19:893-897, 2005.

312. McBride, JM, Triplett-McBride, T, Davie, A, and Newton, RU. The effect of heavy- vs. light-load jump squats on the development of strength, power, and speed. *J Strength Cond Res* 16:75-82, 2002.

313. McDonagh, MJ, and Davies, CT. Adaptive response of mammalian skeletal muscle to exercise with high loads. *Eur J Appl Physiol Occup Physiol* 52:139-155., 1984.

314. McGuigan, MR, and Foster, C. A new approach to monitoring resistance training. *Strength Cond J* 26:42-47, 2004.

315. McLellan, CP, Lovell, DI, and Gass, GC. The role of rate of force development on vertical jump performance. *J Strength Cond Res* 25:379-385, 2011.

316. McLester, JR, Bishop, P, and Guilliams, ME. Comparison of 1 day and 3 day per week of equal volume resistance training in experienced subjects. *J Strength Cond Res* 14:273-281, 2000.

317. Meckel, Y, Atterbom, H, Grodjinovsky, A, Ben-Sira, D, and Rotstein, A. Physiological characteristics of female 100 metre sprinters of different performance levels. *J Sports Med Phys Fitness* 35:169-175, 1995.

318. Melrose, DR, Spaniol, FJ, Bohling, ME, and Bonnette, RA. Physiological and performance characteristics of adolescent club volleyball players. *J Strength Cond Res* 21:481-486, 2007.

319. Merrigan, JJ, Jones, MT, Padecky, J, Malecek, J, Omcirk, D, Scott, BR, and Tufano, JJ. Impact of rest-redistribution on fatigue during maximal eccentric knee extensions. *J Hum Kinet* 74:205-214, 2020.

320. Merrigan, JJ, Tufano, JJ, Flalzone, M, and Jones, MT. Effectiveness of accentuated eccentric loading: Contingent on concentric load. *Int J Sports Physiol Perform* 16:66-72, 2020.

321. Methenitis, S, Karandreas, N, Spengos, K, Zaras, N, Stasinaki, AN, and Terzis, G. Muscle fiber conduction velocity,

muscle fiber composition, and power performance. *Med Sci Sports Exerc* 48:1761-1771, 2016.

322. Methenitis, S, Spengos, K, Zaras, N, Stasinaki, AN, Papadimas, G, Karampatsos, G, Arnaoutis, G, and Terzis, G. Fiber type composition and rate of force development in endurance and resistance trained individuals. *J Strength Cond Res* 33:2388-2397, 2019.

323. Miller, C. Cluster training. In *The Sport of Olympic-Style Weightlifting*. Santa Fe, NM: Sunstone Press, 89-92, 2011.

324. Miller, C. *The Sport of Olympic-Style Weightlifting*. Santa Fe, NM: Sunstone Press, 2011.

325. Miller, C. Timing the speed of the bar. In *Olympic Lifting: A Training Manual*. Santa Fe, NM: Sonstone Press, 108-110, 2018.

326. Milner-Brown, HS, Stein, RB, and Lee, RG. Synchronization of human motor units: Possible roles of exercise and supraspinal reflexes. *Electroencephalogr Clin Neurophysiol* 38:245-254, 1975.

327. Minigawa, TH, Matoba, H, Kawai, Y, and Niu, H. Physiological properties of motor units. In *Biomechanics VI-A*. Assmussen, E, Jorgensen, K, eds. Baltimore, MD: University Park Press, 201-206, 1978.

328. Mirkov, DM, Nedeljkovic, A, Milanovic, S, and Jaric, S. Muscle strength testing: Evaluation of tests of explosive force production. *Eur J Appl Physiol* 91:147-154, 2004.

329. Möck, S, Hartmann, R, Wirth, K, Rosenkranz, G, and Mickel, C. Relationship between maximal dynamic force in the deep back squat and sprinting performance in consecutive segments up to 30 m. *J Strength Cond Res* 35:1039-1043, 2021.

330. Moir, GL, Mergy, D, Witmer, C, and Davis, SE. The acute effects of manipulating volume and load of back squats on countermovement vertical jump performance. *J Strength Cond Res* 25:1486-1491, 2011.

331. Morán-Navarro, R, Perez, CE, Mora-Rodriguez, R, de la Cruz-Sanchez, E, Gonzalez-Badillo, JJ, Sanchez-Medina, L, and Pallares, JG. Time course of recovery following resistance training leading or not to failure. *Eur J Appl Physiol* 117:2387-2399, 2017.

332. Moritani, T. Neuromuscular adaptations during the acquisition of muscle strength, power and motor tasks. *J Biomech* 26:95-107, 1993.

333. Morrissey, MC, Harman, EA, and Johnson, MJ. Resistance training modes: Specificity and effectiveness. *Med Sci Sports Exerc* 27:648-660, 1995.

334. Morton, RW, Colenso-Semple, L, and Phillips, SM. Training for strength and hypertrophy: An evidence-based approach. *Curr Opin Physiol* 10:90-95, 2019.

335. Moss, BM, Refsnes, PE, Abildgaard, A, Nicolaysen, K, and Jensen, J. Effects of maximal effort strength training with different loads on dynamic strength, cross-sectional area, load-power and load-velocity relationships. *Eur J Appl Physiol* 75:193-199, 1997.

336. Mujika, I, and Padilla, S. Detraining: Loss of training-induced physiological and performance adaptations. Part I: Short term insufficient training stimulus. *Sports Med* 30:79-87, 2000.

337. Mujika, I, and Padilla, S. Detraining: Loss of training-induced physiological and performance adaptations. Part II: Long term insufficient training stimulus. *Sports Med* 30:145-154, 2000.

338. Mujika, I, Rønnestad, BR, and Martin, DT. Effects of increased muscle strength and muscle mass on endurance-cycling performance. *Int J Sports Physiol Perform* 11:283-289, 2016.

339. Munroe, L, and Haff, GG. Sprint cycling. In *Routledge Handbook of Strength and Conditioning*. Turner, A, ed. New York: Routledge, 506-525, 2018.

340. Naclerio, F, Rodriguez-Romo, G, Barriopedro-Moro, MI, Jimenez, A, Alvar, BA, and Triplett, NT. Control of resistance training intensity by the OMNI perceived exertion scale. *J Strength Cond Res* 25:1879-1888, 2011.

341. Narici, M. Human skeletal muscle architecture studied in vivo by non-invasive imaging techniques: Functional significance and applications. *J Electromyogr Kinesiol* 9:97-103, 1999.

342. Narici, MV, Hoppeler, H, Kayser, B, Landoni, L, Claassen, H, Gavardi, C, Conti, M, and Cerretelli, P. Human quadriceps cross-sectional area, torque and neural activation during 6 months strength training. *Acta Physiol Scand* 157:175-186, 1996.

343. Nevill, AM, and Holder, RL. Scaling, normalizing, and per ratio standards: An allometric modeling approach. *J Appl Physiol* 79:1027-1031, 1995.

344. Newton, RU, and Kraemer, WJ. Developing explosive muscular power: Implications for a mixed methods training strategy. *Strength Cond J* 16:20-31, 1994.

345. Newton, RU, Kraemer, WJ, Häkkinen, K, Humphries, BJ, and Murphy, AJ. Kinematics, kinetics, and muscle activation during explosive upper body movements. *J Appl Biomech* 12:31-41, 1996.

346. Nimphius, S, McGuigan, MR, and Newton, RU. Relationship between strength, power, speed, and change of direction performance of female softball players. *J Strength Cond Res* 24:885-895, 2010.

347. Noakes, TD. Implications of exercise testing for prediction of athletic performance: A contemporary perspective. *Med Sci Sports Exerc* 20:319-330, 1988.

348. Norrbrand, L, Fluckey, JD, Pozzo, M, and Tesch, PA. Resistance training using eccentric overload induces early adaptations in skeletal muscle size. *Eur J Appl Physiol* 102:271-281, 2008.

349. Nunes, JP, Grgic, J, Cunha, PM, Ribeiro, AS, Schoenfeld, BJ, de Salles, BF, and Cyrino, ES. What influence does resistance exercise order have on muscular strength gains and muscle hypertrophy? A systematic review and meta-analysis. *Eur J Sport Sci* 21:149-157, 2021.

350. Nuzzo, JL, McBride, JM, Cormie, P, and McCaulley, GO. Relationship between countermovement jump performance and multijoint isometric and dynamic tests of strength. *J Strength Cond Res* 22:699-707, 2008.

351. Oliver, JM, Jagim, AR, Sanchez, AC, Mardock, MA, Kelly, KA, Meredith, HJ, Smith, GL, Greenwood, M, Parker, JL, Riechman, SE, Fluckey, JD, Crouse, SF, and Kreider, RB. Greater gains in strength and power with intraset rest intervals in hypertrophic training. *J Strength Cond Res* 27:3116-3131, 2013.

352. Oliver, JM, Kreutzer, A, Jenke, S, Phillips, MD, Mitchell, JB, and Jones, MT. Acute response to cluster sets in trained and untrained men. *Eur J Appl Physiol* 115:2383-2393, 2015.

353. Orange, ST, Hritz, A, Pearson, L, Jeffries, O, Jones, TW, and Steele, J. Comparison of the effects of velocity-based vs. traditional resistance training methods on adaptations in strength, power, and sprint speed: A systematic review, meta-analysis, and quality of evidence appraisal. *J Sports Sci* 40:1220-1234, 2022.

354. Orange, ST, Metcalfe, JW, Robinson, A, Applegarth, MJ, and Liefeith, A. Effects of in-season velocity- versus percentage-based training in academy Rugby League players. *Int J Sports Physiol Perform* 15:554-561, 2020.

355. Østerås, H, Helgerud, J, and Hoff, J. Maximal strength-training effects on force-velocity and force-power relationships explain increases in aerobic performance in humans. *Eur J Appl Physiol* 88:255-263, 2002.

356. Paavolainen, L, HÄkkinen, K, Hamalainen, I, Nummela, A, and Rusko, H. Explosive-strength training improves 5-km running time by improving running economy and muscle power. *J Appl Physiol* 86:1527-1533, 1999.

357. Paavolainen, L, Häkkinen, K, and Rusko, H. Effects of explosive type strength training on physical performance characteristics in cross-country skiers. *Eur J Appl Physiol Occup Physiol* 62:251-255, 1991.

358. Painter, K, Haff, G, Ramsey, M, McBride, J, Triplett, T, Sands, W, Lamont, H, Stone, M, and Stone, M. Strength gains: Block versus daily undulating periodization weight training among track and field athletes. *Int J Sports Physiol Perform* 7:161-169, 2012.

359. Painter, K, Haff, G, Triplett, N, Stuart, C, Hornsby, G, Ramsey, M, Bazyler, C, and Stone, M. Resting hormone alterations and injuries: Block vs. DUP weight-training among D-1 track and field athletes. *Sports* 6:3, 2018.

360. Painter, KB, Haff, GG, Ramsey, MW, McBride, J, Triplett, T, Sands, WA, Lamont, HS, Stone, ME, and Stone, MH. Strength gains: Block versus daily undulating periodization weight training among track and field athletes. *Int J Sports Physiol Perform* 7:161-169, 2012.

361. Paoli, A, Gentil, P, Moro, T, Marcolin, G, and Bianco, A. Resistance training with single vs. multi-joint exercises at equal total load volume: Effects on body composition, cardiorespiratory fitness, and muscle strength. *Front Physiol* 8:1105, 2017.

362. Pareja-Blanco, F, Rodriguez-Rosell, D, Sanchez-Medina, L, Sanchis-Moysi, J, Dorado, C, Mora-Custodio, R, Yanez-Garcia, JM, Morales-Alamo, D, Perez-Suarez, I, Calbet, JAL, and Gonzalez-Badillo, JJ. Effects of velocity loss during resistance training on athletic performance, strength gains and muscle adaptations. *Scand J Med Sci Sports* 27:724-735, 2017.

363. Pareja-Blanco, F, Walker, S, and Hakkinen, K. Validity of using velocity to estimate intensity in resistance exercises in men and women. *Int J Sports Med* 41:1047-1055, 2020.

364. Pedemonte, J. Updated acquisitions about training periodization: Part one. *Strength Cond J* 4:56-60, 1982.

365. Peterson, MD, Rhea, MR, and Alvar, BA. Maximizing strength development in athletes: A meta-analysis to determine the dose-response relationship. *J Strength Cond Res* 18:377-382, 2004.

366. Peterson, MD, Rhea, MR, and Alvar, BA. Applications of the dose-response for muscular strength development: A review of meta-analytic efficacy and reliability for designing training prescription. *J Strength Cond Res* 19:950-958, 2005.

367. Pincivero, DM, Gear, WS, Moyna, NM, and Robertson, RJ. The effects of rest interval on quadriceps torque and perceived exertion in healthy males. *J Sports Med Phys Fitness* 39:294-299, 1999.

368. Pistilli, EE, Kaminsky, DE, Totten, L, and Miller, D. An 8-week periodized mesocycle leading to a national level weightlifting competition. *Strength Cond J* 26:62-68, 2004.

369. Plisk, SS, and Stone, MH. Periodization strategies. *Strength Cond J* 25:19-37, 2003.

370. Poliquin, C. Poliquin's top 10 set/rep programs for maximal strength. In *Modern Trends in Strength Training: Volume 1—Reps and Sets*. 2nd ed. East Greenwich, RI: CharlesPoliquin.net, 33-51, 2001.

371. Pollock, ML, Graves, JE, Bamman, MM, Leggett, SH, Carpenter, DM, Carr, C, Cirulli, J, Matkozich, J, and Fulton, M. Frequency and volume of resistance training: Effect on cervical extension strength. *Arch Phys Med Rehabil* 74:1080-1086, 1993.

372. Prestes, J, Frollini, AB, de Lima, C, Donatto, FF, Foschini, D, de Cassia Marqueti, R, Figueira, A, Jr., and Fleck, SJ. Comparison between linear and daily undulating periodized resistance training to increase strength. *J Strength Cond Res* 23:2437-2442, 2009.

373. Prieske, O, Behrens, M, Chaabene, H, Granacher, U, and Maffiuletti, NA. Time to differentiate postactivation "potentiation" from "performance enhancement" in the strength and conditioning community. *Sports Med* 50:1559-1565, 2020.

374. Prince, FP, Hikida, RS, and Hagerman, FC. Human muscle fiber types in power lifters, distance runners and untrained subjects. *Pflugers Arch* 363:19-26, 1976.

375. Prince, FP, Hikida, RS, Hagerman, FC, Staron, RS, and Allen, WH. A morphometric analysis of human muscle fibers with relation to fiber types and adaptations to exercise. *J Neurol Sci* 49:165-179., 1981.

376. Pritchett, RC, Green, JM, Wickwire, PJ, and Kovacs, M. Acute and session RPE responses during resistance training: Bouts to failure at 60% and 90% of 1RM. *S Afr J Sports Med* 21:23-26, 2009.

377. Radcliffe, JC. Overview. In *Functional Training for Athletes at All Levels*. Berkeley, CA: Ulysses Press, 1-26, 2007.

378. Radcliffe, JC, and Radcliffe, JL. Effects of different warm-up protocols on peak power output during a single response jump task. *Med Sci Sports Exerc* 28:S189, 1996.

379. Rader, P. Workouts for the working man. *IronMan Magazine* 18:22-23, 1958.

380. Ralston, GW, Kilgore, L, Wyatt, FB, Buchan, D, and Baker, JS. Weekly training frequency effects on strength gain: A meta-analysis. *Sports Med Open* 4:36, 2018.

381. Ralston, GW, Kilgore, L, Wyatt, FB, Dutheil, F, Jaekel, P, Buchan, DS, and Baker, JS. Re-examination of 1- vs. 3-sets of resistance exercise for pre-spaceflight muscle conditioning: A systematic review and meta-analysis. *Front Physiol* 10:864, 2019.

382. Rasch, PJ. The problem of muscle hypertrophy: A review. *J Am Osteopath Assoc* 54:525-528, 1955.

383. Rasch, PJ, and Morehouse, LE. Effect of static and dynamic exercises on muscular strength and hypertrophy. *J Appl Physiol* 11:29-34, 1957.

384. Ratamess, N. Developing resistance training programs. In *NSCA's Essentials of Tactical Strength and Conditioning*. Alvar, BA, Sell, K, Deuster, PA, eds. Champaign, IL: Human Kinetics, 157-180.

385. Ratamess, NA, Alvar, BA, Evotoch, TK, Housh, TJ, Kibler, WB, Kraemer, WJ, and Triplett, NT. American College of Sports Medicine position stand: Progression models in resistance training for healthy adults. *Med Sci Sports Exerc* 41:687-708, 2009.

386. Ratamess, NA, Falvo, MJ, Mangine, GT, Hoffman, JR, Faigenbaum, AD, and Kang, J. The effect of rest interval length on metabolic responses to the bench press exercise. *Eur J Appl Physiol* 100:1-17, 2007.

387. Refsnes, PE. Testing and training for top Norwegian athletes. In *Science in Elite Sport*. Müller, E, Ludescher, F, Zallinger, G, eds. New York: Routledge, 96-114, 1999.

388. Rhea, MR, Alvar, BA, and Burkett, LN. Single versus multiple sets for strength: A meta-analysis to address the controversy. *Res Q Exerc Sport* 73:485-488, 2002.

389. Rhea, MR, Alvar, BA, Burkett, LN, and Ball, SD. A meta-analysis to determine the dose response for strength development. *Med Sci Sports Exerc* 35:456-464, 2003.

390. Rhea, MR, Ball, SD, Phillips, WT, and Burkett, LN. A comparison of linear and daily undulating periodized programs with equated volume and intensity for strength. *J Strength Cond Res* 16:250-255, 2002.

391. Ribeiro, AS, Dos Santos, ED, Nunes, JP, and Schoenfeld, BJ. Acute effects of different training loads on affective responses in resistance-trained men. *Int J Sports Med* 40:850-855, 2019.

392. Rice, PE, and Nimphius, S. When task constraints delimit movement strategy: Implications for isolated joint training in dancers. *Front Sports Act Living* 2:1-8, 2020.

393. Richens, B, and Cleather, DJ. The relationship between the number of repetitions performed at given intensities is different in endurance and strength trained athletes. *Biol Sport* 31:157-161, 2014.

394. Richter, G. Ein trainergerat zur objektivierung der sportartspezifischen schnellkraftfahigkeit und zur trainingssteuerung im gewichtheben. *Theor Prax Leistungssports* 11:241-263, 1973.

395. Robertson, RJ, Goss, FL, Rutkowski, J, Lenz, B, Dixon, C, Timmer, J, Frazee, K, Dube, J, and Andreacci, J. Concurrent validation of the OMNI perceived exertion scale for resistance exercise. *Med Sci Sports Exerc* 35:333-341, 2003.

396. Rodríguez-Rosell, D, Pareja-Blanco, F, Aagaard, P, and González-Badillo, JJ. Physiological and methodological aspects of rate of force development assessment in human skeletal muscle. 38:743-762, 2018.

397. Roll, F, and Omer, J. Football: Tulane football winter program. *Strength Cond J* 9:34-38, 1987.

398. Rønnestad, BR, Hansen, EA, and Raastad, T. Effect of heavy strength training on thigh muscle cross-sectional area, performance determinants, and performance in well-trained cyclists. *Eur J Appl Physiol* 108:965-975, 2010.

399. Rønnestad, BR, Hansen, EA, and Raastad, T. In-season strength maintenance training increases well-trained cyclists' performance. *Eur J Appl Physiol* 110:1269-1282, 2010.

400. Rønnestad, BR, Hansen, J, Hollan, I, Spencer, M, and Ellefsen, S. In-season strength training cessation impairs performance variables in elite cyclists. *Int J Sports Physiol Perform* 11:727-735, 2016.

401. Rønnestad, BR, and Mujika, I. Optimizing strength training for running and cycling endurance performance: A review. *Scand J Med Sci Sports* 24:603-612, 2014.

402. Rønnestad, BR, Ofsteng, SJ, and Ellefsen, S. Block periodization of strength and endurance training is superior to traditional periodization in ice hockey players. *Scand J Med Sci Sports* 29:180-188, 2019.

403. Rowbottom, DG. Periodization of training. In *Exercise and Sport Science*. Garrett, WE, Kirkendall, DT, eds. Philadelphia, PA: Lippicott Williams and Wilkins, 499-512, 2000.

404. Ruben, RM, Molinari, MA, Bibbee, CA, Childress, MA, Harman, MS, Reed, KP, and Haff, GG. The acute effects of an ascending squat protocol on performance during horizontal plyometric jumps. *J Strength Cond Res* 24:358-369, 2010.

405. Rutherford, OM, and Jones, DA. The role of learning and coordination in strength training. *Eur J Appl Physiol Occup Physiol* 55:100-105, 1986.

406. Sahlin, K, and Ren, JM. Relationship of contraction capacity to metabolic changes during recovery from a fatiguing contraction. *J Appl Physiol* 67:648-654, 1989.

407. Sale, DG. Influence of exercise and training on motor unit activation. *Exerc Sport Sci Rev* 15:S95-S151, 1987.

408. Sale, DG. Neural adaptation to resistance training. *Med Sci Sports Exerc* 20:S135-S145, 1988.

409. Sale, DG. Postactivation potentiation: Role in human performance. *Exerc Sport Sci Rev* 30:138-143, 2002.

410. Sale, DG, MacDougall, JD, Upton, AR, and McComas, AJ. Effect of strength training upon motoneuron excitability in man. *Med Sci Sports Exerc* 15:57-62, 1983.

411. Sampson, JA, and Groeller, H. Is repetition failure critical for the development of muscle hypertrophy and strength? *Scand J Med Sci Sports* 26:1427-1439, 2016.

412. Santos, W, Vieira, CA, Bottaro, M, Nunes, VA, Ramirez-Campillo, R, Steele, J, Fisher, JP, and Gentil, P. Resistance training performed to failure or not to failure results in similar total volume, but with different fatigue and discomfort levels. *J Strength Cond Res* 35:1372-1379, 2021.

413. Schärer, C, Huber, S, Bucher, P, Capelli, C, and Hübner, K. Maximum strength benchmarks for difficult static elements on rings in male elite gymnastics. *Sports* 9:78, 2021.

414. Schmidtbleicher, D. Strength training (Part 2): Structural analysis of motor strength qualities and its application to training. *Science Periodical on Research and Technology* 5:1-10, 1985.

415. Schmidtbleicher, D. Training for power events. In *Strength and Power in Sport*. Komi, PV, ed. Oxford: Blackwell, 381-385, 1992.

416. Schoenfeld, BJ. The mechanisms of muscle hypertrophy and their application to resistance training. *J Strength Cond Res* 24:2857-2872, 2010.

417. Schoenfeld, BJ. Mechanisms of hypertrophy. In *Science and Development of Muscle Hypertrophy*. Champaign, IL: Human Kinetics, 29-50, 2016.

418. Schoenfeld, BJ, Contreras, B, Krieger, J, Grgic, J, Delcastillo, K, Belliard, R, and Alto, A. Resistance training volume enhances muscle hypertrophy but not strength in trained men. *Med Sci Sports Exerc* 51:94-103, 2019.

419. Schoenfeld, BJ, Contreras, B, Vigotsky, AD, and Peterson, M. Differential effects of heavy versus moderate loads on measures of strength and hypertrophy in resistance-trained men. *J Sports Sci Med* 15:715-722, 2016.

420. Schoenfeld, BJ, and Grgic, J. Does training to failure maximize muscle hypertrophy? *Strength Cond J* 41:108-113, 2019.

421. Schoenfeld, BJ, Grgic, J, and Krieger, J. How many times per week should a muscle be trained to maximize muscle hypertrophy? A systematic review and meta-analysis of studies examining the effects of resistance training frequency. *J Sports Sci* 37:1286-1295, 2019.

422. Schoenfeld, BJ, Grgic, J, Van Every, DW, and Plotkin, DL. Loading recommendations for muscle strength, hypertrophy, and local endurance: A re-examination of the repetition continuum. *Sports* 9:32, 2021.

423. Schoenfeld, BJ, Ogborn, D, and Krieger, JW. Dose-response relationship between weekly resistance training volume and increases in muscle mass: A systematic review and meta-analysis. *Journal of Sports Sciences* 35:1073-1082, 2017.

424. Schoenfeld, BJ, Ogborn, DI, Vigotsky, AD, Franchi, MV, and Krieger, JW. Hypertrophic effects of concentric vs. eccentric muscle actions: A systematic review and meta-analysis. *J Strength Cond Res* 31:2599-2608, 2017.

425. Schoenfeld, BJ, Pope, ZK, Benik, FM, Hester, GM, Sellers, J, Nooner, JL, Schnaiter, JA, Bond-Williams, KE, Carter, AS, Ross, CL, Just, BL, Henselmans, M, and Krieger, JW. Longer interset rest periods enhance muscle strength and hypertrophy in resistance-trained men. *J Strength Cond Res* 30:1805-1812, 2016.

426. Schoenfeld, BJ, Ratamess, NA, Peterson, MD, Contreras, B, Sonmez, GT, and Alvar, BA. Effects of different volume-equated resistance training loading strategies on muscular adaptations in well-trained men. *J Strength Cond Res* 28:2909-2918, 2014.

427. Schröder, W, Harre, D, and Bauersfeld, M. Characteristics of strength abilities. In *Principles of Sports Training: Introduction to the Theory and Methodology of Training.* Harre, D, ed. Michigan, USA: Ultimate Athlete Concepts, 151-155, 2012.

428. Seitz, L, Saez de Villarreal, E, and Haff, GG. The temporal profile of postactivation potentiation is related to strength level. *J Strength Cond Res* 28:706-715, 2014.

429. Seitz, LB, and Haff, GG. Application of methods of inducing postactivation potentiation during the preparation of rugby players. *Strength Cond J* 37:40-49, 2015.

430. Seitz, LB, and Haff, GG. Factors modulating post-activation potentiation of jump, sprint, throw and upper-body ballistic performances: A systematic review with meta-analysis. *Sports Med* 46:231-240, 2016.

431. Seitz, LB, Reyes, A, Tran, TT, de Villarreal, ES, and Haff, GG. Increases in lower-body strength transfer positively to sprint performance: A systematic review with meta-analysis. *Sports Med* 44:1693-1702, 2014.

432. Seitz, LB, Trajano, GS, and Haff, GG. The back squat and the power clean elicit different degrees of potentiation. *Int J Sports Physiol Perform* 9:643-649, 2014.

433. Seitz, LB, Trajano, GS, Haff, GG, Dumke, CC, Tufano, JJ, and Blazevich, AJ. Relationships between maximal strength, muscle size, and myosin heavy chain isoform composition and postactivation potentiation. *Appl Physiol Nutr Metab* 41:491-497, 2016.

434. Semmler, JG. Motor unit synchronization and neuromuscular performance. *Exerc Sport Sci Rev* 30:8-14, 2002.

435. Semmler, JG, Kornatz, KW, Dinenno, DV, Zhou, S, and Enoka, RM. Motor unit synchronisation is enhanced during slow lengthening contractions of a hand muscle. *J Physiol* 545:681-695, 2002.

436. Semmler, JG, and Nordstrom, MA. Motor unit discharge and force tremor in skill- and strength-trained individuals. *Exp Brain Res* 119:27-38, 1998.

437. Semmler, JG, Sale, MV, Meyer, FG, and Nordstrom, MA. Motor-unit coherence and its relation with synchrony are influenced by training. *J Neurophysiol* 92:3320-3331, 2004.

438. Serrano, N, Colenso-Semple, LM, Lazauskus, KK, Siu, JW, Bagley, JR, Lockie, RG, Costa, PB, and Galpin, AJ. Extraordinary fast-twitch fiber abundance in elite weightlifters. *PLoS One* 14:e0207975, 2019.

439. Sevilmiş, E, and Atalağ, O. Effects of post activation potentiation on eccentric loading: Is it possible to do more repetitions after supra-maximal loading? *Journal of Human Sport and Exercise* 14:1-7, 2019.

440. Seynnes, OR, de Boer, M, and Narici, MV. Early skeletal muscle hypertrophy and architectural changes in response to high-intensity resistance training. *J Appl Physiol* 102:368-373, 2007.

441. Sforzo, GA, and Touey, PR. Manipulating exercise order affects muscular performance during a resistance exercise training session. *J Strength Cond Res* 10:20-24, 1996.

442. Sheppard, JM, Cronin, JB, Gabbett, TJ, McGuigan, MR, Etxebarria, N, and Newton, RU. Relative importance of strength, power, and anthropometric measures to jump performance of elite volleyball players. *J Strength Cond Res* 22:758-765, 2008.

443. Sheppard, JM, and Triplett, NT. Program design for resistance training. In *Essentials of Strength Training and Conditioning.* 4th ed. Haff, GG, Triplett, NT, eds. Champaign, IL: Human Kinetics, 439-470, 2016.

444. Shiau, K, Tsao, TH, and Yang, CB. Effects of single versus multiple bouts of resistance training on maximal strength and anaerobic performance. *J Hum Kinet* 62:231-240, 2018.

445. Shimano, T, Kraemer, WJ, Spiering, BA, Volek, JS, Hatfield, DL, Silvestre, R, Vingren, JL, Fragala, MS, Maresh, CM, Fleck, SJ, Newton, RU, Spreuwenberg, LP, and Hakkinen, K. Relationship between the number of repetitions and selected percentages of one repetition maximum in free weight exercises in trained and untrained men. *J Strength Cond Res* 20:819-823, 2006.

446. Shoepe, TC, Stelzer, JE, Garner, DP, and Widrick, JJ. Functional adaptability of muscle fibers to long-term resistance exercise. *Med Sci Sports Exerc* 35:944-951, 2003.

447. Siegel, JA, Gilders, RM, Staron, RS, and Hagerman, FC. Human muscle power output during upper- and lower-body exercises. *J Strength Cond Res* 16:173-178, 2002.

448. Siff, MC, and Verkhoshansky, YU. Strength training methods. In *Supertraining*. 4th ed. Denver, CO: Supertraining International, 390-410, 1999.

449. Silvestre, R, Kraemer, WJ, West, C, Judelson, DA, Spiering, BA, Vingren, JL, Hatfield, DL, Anderson, JM, and Maresh, CM. Body composition and physical performance during a National Collegiate Athletic Association Division I men's soccer season. *J Strength Cond Res* 20:962-970, 2006.

450. Simão, R, de Salles, BF, Figueiredo, T, Dias, I, and Willardson, JM. Exercise order in resistance training. *Sports Med* 42:251-265, 2012.

451. Simão, R, Farinatti Pde, T, Polito, MD, Maior, AS, and Fleck, SJ. Influence of exercise order on the number of repetitions performed and perceived exertion during resistance exercises. *J Strength Cond Res* 19:152-156, 2005.

452. Simão, R, Farinatti Pde, T, Polito, MD, Viveiros, L, and Fleck, SJ. Influence of exercise order on the number of repetitions performed and perceived exertion during resistance exercise in women. *J Strength Cond Res* 21:23-28, 2007.

453. Souza, EO, Ugrinowitsch, C, Tricoli, V, Roschel, H, Lowery, RP, Aihara, AY, Leao, AR, and Wilson, JM. Early adaptations to six weeks of non-periodized and periodized strength training regimens in recreational males. *J Sports Sci Med* 13:604-609, 2014.

454. Speranza, MJ, Gabbett, TJ, Johnston, RD, and Sheppard, JM. Muscular strength and power correlates of tackling ability in semiprofessional Rugby League players. *J Strength Cond Res* 29:2071-2078, 2015.

455. Speranza, MJ, Gabbett, TJ, Johnston, RD, and Sheppard, JM. Effect of strength and power training on tackling ability in semiprofessional Rugby League players. *J Strength Cond Res* 30:336-343, 2016.

456. Speranza, MJA, Gabbett, TJ, Greene, DA, Johnston, RD, and Sheppard, JM. Changes in Rugby League tackling ability during a competitive season: The relationship with strength and power qualities. *J Strength Cond Res* 31:3311-3318, 2017.

457. Spiteri, T, Cochrane, JL, Hart, NH, Haff, GG, and Nimphius, S. Effect of strength on plant foot kinetics and kinematics during a change of direction task. *Eur J Sport Sci* 13:646-652, 2013.

458. Spiteri, T, Newton, RU, Binetti, M, Hart, NH, Sheppard, JM, and Nimphius, S. Mechanical determinants of faster change of direction and agility performance in female basketball athletes. *J Strength Cond Res* 29:2205-2214, 2015.

459. Spreuwenberg, LP, Kraemer, WJ, Spiering, BA, Volek, JS, Hatfield, DL, Silvestre, R, Vingren, JL, Fragala, MS, Häkkinen, K, Newton, RU, Maresh, CM, and Fleck, SJ. Influence of exercise order in a resistance-training exercise session. *J Strength Cond Res* 20:141-144, 2006.

460. Staron, RS, Malicky, ES, Leonardi, MJ, Falkel, JE, Hagerman, FC, and Dudley, GA. Muscle hypertrophy and fast fiber type conversions in heavy resistance-trained women. *Eur J Appl Physiol* 60:71-79, 1990.

461. Stone, MH, Hornsby, WG, Haff, GG, Fry, AC, Suarez, DG, Liu, J, Gonzalez-Rave, JM, and Pierce, KC. Periodization and block periodization in sports: Emphasis on strength-power training—a provocative and challenging narrative. *J Strength Cond Res* 35:2351-2371, 2021.

462. Stone, MH, Moir, G, Glaister, M, and Sanders, R. How much strength is necessary? *Physical Therapy in Sport* 3:88-96, 2002.

463. Stone, MH, O'Bryant, H, and Garhammer, J. A hypothetical model for strength training. *J Sports Med* 21:342-351, 1981.

464. Stone, MH, and O'Bryant, HO. Practical considerations for weight training. In *Weight Training: A Scientific Approach*. Edina, MN: Burgess, 137-165, 1987.

465. Stone, MH, O'Bryant, HS, and Garhammer, J. A theoretical model of strength training. *NSCA J* 3:36-39, 1982.

466. Stone, MH, Pierce, K, Sands, WA, and Stone, M. Weightlifting: Program design. *Strength Cond J* 28:10-17, 2006.

467. Stone, MH, Plisk, S, and Collins, D. Training principles: Evaluation of modes and methods of resistance-training—a coaching perspective. *Sport Biomech* 1:79-104, 2002.

468. Stone, MH, Sands, WA, Carlock, J, Callan, S, Dickie, D, Daigle, K, Cotton, J, Smith, SL, and Hartman, M. The importance of isometric maximum strength and peak rate-of-force development in sprint cycling. *J Strength Cond Res* 18:878-884, 2004.

469. Stone, MH, Sands, WA, Pierce, KC, Carlock, J, Cardinale, M, and Newton, RU. Relationship of maximum strength to weightlifting performance. *Med Sci Sports Exerc* 37:1037-1043, 2005.

470. Stone, MH, Sands, WA, Pierce, KC, Newton, RU, Haff, GG, and Carlock, J. Maximum strength and strength training: A relationship to endurance? *Strength and Cond J* 28:44-53, 2006.

471. Stone, MH, Sands, WA, Pierce, KC, Ramsey, MW, and Haff, GG. Power and power potentiation among strength power athletes: Preliminary study. *Int J Sports Physiol Perf* 3:55-67, 2008.

472. Stone, MH, Stone, ME, and Sands, WA. Biomechanics of resistance training. In *Principles and Practice of Resistance Training*. Champaign, IL: Human Kinetics, 45-62, 2007.

473. Stone, MH, Stone, ME, and Sands, WA. Modes of resistance training. In *Principles and Practice of Resistance Training*. Champaign, IL: Human Kinetics, 241-258, 2007.

474. Stone, MH, Stone, ME, and Sands, WA. Physical and physiological adaptations to resistance training. In *Principles and Practice of Resistance Training*. Champaign, IL: Human Kinetics, 201-228, 2007.

475. Storey, A, and Smith, HK. Unique aspects of competitive weightlifting: Performance, training and physiology. *Sports Med* 42:769-790, 2012.

476. Stull, GA, and Clarke, DH. Patterns of recovery following isometric and isotonic strength decrement. *Med Sci Sports* 3:135-139., 1971.

477. Suchomel, TJ, Beckham, GK, and Wright, GA. Effect of various loads on the force-time characteristics of the hang high pull. *J Strength Cond Res* 29:1295-1301, 2015.

478. Suchomel, TJ, and Comfort, P. Developing muscular strength and power. In *Advanced Strength and Conditioning: An Evidence Based Approach*. Turner, A, Comfort, P, eds. New York: Routledge, 13-38, 2018.

479. Suchomel, TJ, Comfort, P, and Lake, JP. Enhancing the force–velocity profile of athletes using weightlifting derivatives. *Strength Cond J* 39:10-20, 2017.

480. Suchomel, TJ, Comfort, P, and Stone, MH. Weightlifting pulling derivatives: Rationale for implementation and application. *Sports Med* 45:823-839, 2015.
481. Suchomel, TJ, DeWeese, BH, Beckham, GK, Serrano, AJ, and French, SM. The hang high pull: A progressive exercise into weightlifting derivatives. *Strength Cond J* 36:79-83, 2014.
482. Suchomel, TJ, DeWeese, BH, Beckham, GK, Serrano, AJ, and Sole, CJ. The jump shrug: A progressive exercise into weightlifting derivatives. *Strength Cond J* 36:43-47, 2014.
483. Suchomel, TJ, DeWeese, BH, and Serrano, AJ. The power clean and power snatch from the knee. *Strength Cond J* 38:98-105, 2016.
484. Suchomel, TJ, Nimphius, S, Bellon, CR, Hornsby, WG, and Stone, MH. Training for muscular strength: Methods for monitoring and adjusting training intensity. *Sports Med* 51:2051-2066, 2021.
485. Suchomel, TJ, Nimphius, S, Bellon, CR, and Stone, MH. The importance of muscular strength: Training considerations. *Sports Med* 48:765-785, 2018.
486. Suchomel, TJ, Nimphius, S, and Stone, MH. The importance of muscular strength in athletic performance. *Sports Med* 46:1419-1449, 2016.
487. Suchomel, TJ, Wagle, JP, Douglas, J, Taber, CB, Harden, M, Haff, GG, and Stone, MH. Implementing eccentric resistance training—part 1: A brief review of existing methods. *J Funct Morphol Kinesiol* 4:38, 2019.
488. Suchomel, TJ, Wagle, JP, Douglas, J, Taber, CB, Harden, M, Haff, GG, and Stone, MH. Implementing eccentric resistance training—part 2: Practical recommendations. *J Funct Morphol Kinesiol* 4:55, 2019.
489. Sukop, J, and Nelson, R. Effect of isometric training on the force-time characteristics of muscle contraction. In *Biomechanics IV*. Nelson, RC, Morehouse, CA, eds. Baltimore, MD: University Park Press, 440-447, 1974.
490. Taber, CB, Vigotsky, A, Nuckols, G, and Haun, CT. Exercise-induced myofibrillar hypertrophy is a contributory cause of gains in muscle strength. *Sports Med* 49, 2019.
491. Takano, B. The Bulgarian single-week training cycle. *Natl Strength Cond Assoc J* 13:26-27, 1991.
492. Tan, B. Manipulating resistance training program variables to optimize maximum strength in men: A review. *J Strength Cond Res* 13:289-304, 1999.
493. Tanaka, H, and Swensen, T. Impact of resistance training on endurance performance: A new form of cross-training? *Sports Med* 25:191-200, 1998.
494. ter Haar Romeny, BM, Denier van der Gon, JJ, and Gielen, CC. Changes in recruitment order of motor units in the human biceps muscle. *Exp Neurol* 78:360-368, 1982.
495. Tesch, PA. Skeletal muscle adaptations consequent to long-term heavy resistance exercise. *Med Sci Sports Exerc* 20:S132-S134, 1988.
496. Tesch, PA, and Karlsson, J. Muscle fiber types and size in trained and untrained muscles of elite athletes. *J Appl Physiol* 59:1716-1720, 1985.
497. Thibaudeau, C. Planning intensity. In *The Black Book of Training Secrets*. Quebec, Canada: F.Lepine Publishing, 87-108, 2006.
498. Thibaudeau, C. Training methods. In *The Black Book of Training Secrets*. Quebec, Canada: F.Lepine Publishing, 43-58, 2006.
499. Thibaudeau, C. Training tools: Weight releasers. In *Theory and Application of Modern Strength and Power Methods*. F.Lepine Publishing, 72-77, 2006.
500. Thomas, M, Fiatarone, MA, and Fielding, RA. Leg power in young women: Relationship to body composition, strength, and function. *Med Sci Sports Exerc* 28:1321-1326, 1996.
501. Thompson, SW, Rogerson, D, Ruddock, A, and Barnes, A. The effectiveness of two methods of prescribing load on maximal strength development: A systematic review. *Sports Med* 50:919-938, 2020.
502. Thorstensson, A, Grimby, G, and Karlsson, J. Force-velocity relations and fiber composition in human knee extensor muscles. *J Appl Physiol* 40:12-16, 1976.
503. Thorstensson, A, Hulten, B, von Dobeln, W, and Karlsson, J. Effect of strength training on enzyme activities and fibre characteristics in human skeletal muscle. *Acta Physiol Scand* 96:392-398, 1976.
504. Tillin, NA, Jimenez-Reyes, P, Pain, MT, and Folland, JP. Neuromuscular performance of explosive power athletes versus untrained individuals. *Med Sci Sports Exerc* 42:781-790, 2010.
505. Tillin, NA, Pain, MTG, and Folland, J. Explosive force production during isometric squats correlates with athletic performance in Rugby Union players. *J Sports Sci* 31:66-76, 2013.
506. Tomalka, A, Weidner, S, Hahn, D, Seiberl, W, and Siebert, T. Power amplification increases with contraction velocity during stretch-shortening cycles of skinned muscle fibers. *Front Physiol* 12:644981, 2021.
507. Trappe, S, Godard, M, Gallagher, P, Carroll, C, Rowden, G, and Porter, D. Resistance training improves single muscle fiber contractile function in older women. *Am J Physiol Cell Physiol* 281:C398-406, 2001.
508. Trappe, S, Harber, M, Creer, A, Gallagher, P, Slivka, D, Minchev, K, and Whitsett, D. Single muscle fiber adaptations with marathon training. *J Appl Physiol* 101:721-727, 2006.
509. Travis, SK, Ishida, A, Taber, CB, Fry, AC, and Stone, MH. Emphasizing task-specific hypertrophy to enhance sequential strength and power performance. *J Funct Morphol Kinesiol* 5:76, 2020.
510. Trezise, J, and Blazevich, AJ. Anatomical and neuromuscular determinants of strength change in previously untrained men following heavy strength training. *Front Physiol* 10:1001, 2019.
511. Trezise, J, Collier, N, and Blazevich, AJ. Anatomical and neuromuscular variables strongly predict maximum knee extension torque in healthy men. *Eur J Appl Physiol* 116:1159-1177, 2016.
512. Tuchscherer, M. RPEs. In *The Reactive Training Manual: Developing Your Own Custom Training Program for Powerlifting*. Michael Tuschscher, 14-17, 1990.
513. Tufano, JJ, Brown, LE, and Haff, GG. Theoretical and practical aspects of different cluster set structures: A systematic review. *J Strength Cond Res* 31:848-867, 2017.

514. Tufano, JJ, Conlon, JA, Nimphius, S, Brown, LE, Banyard, HG, Williamson, BD, Bishop, LG, Hopper, AJ, and Haff, GG. Cluster sets: Permitting greater mechanical stress without decreasing relative velocity. *Int J Sports Physiol Perform* 12:463-469, 2017.

515. Tufano, JJ, Conlon, JA, Nimphius, S, Brown, LE, Seitz, LB, Williamson, BD, and Haff, GG. Maintenance of velocity and power with cluster sets during high-volume back squats. *Int J Sports Physiol Perform* 11:885-892, 2016.

516. Tufano, JJ, Conlon, JA, Nimphius, S, Oliver, JM, Kreutzer, A, and Haff, GG. Different cluster sets result in similar metabolic, endocrine, and perceptual responses in trained men. *J Strength Cond Res* 33:346-354, 2019.

517. Tufano, JJ, Omcirk, D, Malecek, J, Pisz, A, Halaj, M, and Scott, BR. Traditional sets vs rest-redistribution: A laboratory-controlled study of a specific cluster set configuration at fast and slow velocities. *Appl Physiol Nutr Metab* 45:421-430, 2020.

518. Ünlü, G, Cevikol, C, and Melekoglu, T. Comparison of the effects of eccentric, concentric, and eccentric-concentric isotonic resistance training at two velocities on strength and muscle hypertrophy. *J Strength Cond Res* 34:337-344, 2020.

519. Van Cutsem, M, Duchateau, J, and Hainaut, K. Changes in single motor unit behaviour contribute to the increase in contraction speed after dynamic training in humans. *J Physiol* 513:295-305, 1998.

520. Vasquez, LM, McBride, JM, Paul, JA, Alley, JR, Carson, LT, and Goodman, CL. Effect of resistance exercise performed to volitional failure on ratings of perceived exertion. *Percept Mot Skills* 117:881-891, 2013.

521. Verkhoshansky, Y, and Siff, MC. Designing sport specific strength programmes. In *Supertraining*. 6th ed. Rome, Italy: Verkhoshansky, 421-480, 2009.

522. Verkhoshansky, Y, and Siff, MC. Factors influencing strength production. In *Supertraining*. 6th (expanded) ed. Rome, Italy: Verkhoshansky, 125-200, 2009.

523. Verkhoshansky, Y, and Siff, MC. *Supertraining*. 6th (expanded) ed. Rome, Italy: Verkhoshansky, 2009.

524. Verkhoshansky, YU. How to set up a training program. *Sov Sports Rev* 16:123-136, 1981.

525. Verkhoshansky, YU. *Programming and organization of training*. Moscow: Fizkultura i Sport, 1985.

526. Vieira, AF, Umpierre, D, Teodoro, JL, Lisboa, SC, Baroni, BM, Izquierdo, M, and Cadore, EL. Effects of resistance training performed to failure or not to failure on muscle strength, hypertrophy, and power output: A systematic review with meta-analysis. *J Strength Cond Res* 35:1165-1175, 2021.

527. Viitasalo, JT, and Komi, PV. Interrelationships between electromyographic, mechanical, muscle structure and reflex time measurements in man. *Acta Physiol Scand* 111:97-103, 1981.

528. Viitasalo, JT, and Komi, PV. Rate of force development, muscle structure and fatigue. In *Biomechanics VII-A: Proceedings of the 7th International Congress of Biomechanics*. Morecki, A, Kazimirz, F, Kedzior, K, Wit, A, eds. Baltimore, MD: University Park Press, 136-141, 1981.

529. Wagle, JP, Cunanan, AJ, Carroll, KM, Sams, ML, Wetmore, A, Bingham, GE, Taber, CB, DeWeese, BH, Sato, K, Stuart, CA, and Stone, MH. Accentuated eccentric loading and cluster set configurations in the back squat: A kinetic and kinematic analysis. *J Strength Cond Res* 35:420-427, 2021.

530. Wagle, JP, Taber, CB, Cunanan, AJ, Bingham, GE, Carroll, KM, DeWeese, BH, Sato, K, and Stone, MH. Accentuated eccentric loading for training and performance: A review. *Sports Med* 47:2473-2495, 2017.

531. Walker, S. Evidence of resistance training-induced neural adaptation in older adults. *Exp Gerontol* 151:111408, 2021.

532. Walker, S, Blazevich, AJ, Haff, GG, Tufano, JJ, Newton, RU, and Häkkinen, K. Greater strength gains after training with accentuated eccentric than traditional isoinertial loading loads in already strength-trained men. *Front Physiol* 7:149-161, 2016.

533. Weakley, J, Mann, B, Banyard, H, McLaren, S, Scott, T, and Garcia-Ramos, A. Velocity-based training: From theory to application. *Strength Cond J* 43:31-49, 2021.

534. Weakley, J, McLaren, S, Ramirez-Lopez, C, Garcia-Ramos, A, Dalton-Barron, N, Banyard, H, Mann, B, Weaving, D, and Jones, B. Application of velocity loss thresholds during free-weight resistance training: Responses and reproducibility of perceptual, metabolic, and neuromuscular outcomes. *J Sports Sci* 38:477-485, 2020.

535. Weakley, J, Ramirez-Lopez, C, McLaren, S, Dalton-Barron, N, Weaving, D, Jones, B, Till, K, and Banyard, H. The effects of 10%, 20%, and 30% velocity loss thresholds on kinetic, kinematic, and repetition characteristics during the barbell back squat. *Int J Sports Physiol Perform* 15:180-188, 2020.

536. Webber, S, and Kriellaars, D. Neuromuscular factors contributing to in vivo eccentric moment generation. *J Appl Physiol (1985)* 83:40-45, 1997.

537. Wernbom, M, Augustsson, J, and Thomee, R. The influence of frequency, intensity, volume and mode of strength training on whole muscle cross-sectional area in humans. *Sports Med* 37:225-264, 2007.

538. West, DW, Kujbida, GW, Moore, DR, Atherton, P, Burd, NA, Padzik, JP, De Lisio, M, Tang, JE, Parise, G, Rennie, MJ, Baker, SK, and Phillips, SM. Resistance exercise-induced increases in putative anabolic hormones do not enhance muscle protein synthesis or intracellular signalling in young men. *J Physiol* 587:5239-5247, 2009.

539. West, DW, and Phillips, SM. Anabolic processes in human skeletal muscle: Restoring the identities of growth hormone and testosterone. *Phys Sportsmed* 38:97-104, 2010.

540. Widrick, JJ, Stelzer, JE, Shoepe, TC, and Garner, DP. Functional properties of human muscle fibers after short-term resistance exercise training. *Am J Physiol Regul Integr Comp Physiol* 283:R408-R416, 2002.

541. Willardson, JM. A brief review: Factors affecting the length of the rest interval between resistance exercise sets. *J Strength Cond Res* 20:978-984, 2006.

542. Willardson, JM, Norton, L, and Wilson, G. Training to failure and beyond in mainstream resistance exercise programs. *Strength Cond J* 32:21-29, 2010.

543. Williamson, DL, Gallagher, PM, Carroll, CC, Raue, U, and Trappe, SW. Reduction in hybrid single muscle fiber proportions with resistance training in humans. *J Appl Physiol* 91:1955-1961, 2001.

544. Wilson, GJ, Murphy, AJ, and Walshe, A. The specificity of strength training: The effect of posture. *Eur J Appl Physiol Occup Physiol* 73:346-352, 1996.

545. Wilson, GJ, Newton, RU, Murphy, AJ, and Humphries, BJ. The optimal training load for the development of dynamic athletic performance. *Med Sci Sports Exerc* 25:1279-1286, 1993.

546. Wisløff, U, Castagna, C, Helgerud, J, Jones, R, and Hoff, J. Strong correlation of maximal squat strength with sprint performance and vertical jump height in elite soccer players. *Br J Sports Med* 38:285-288, 2004.

547. Yao, W, Fuglevand, RJ, and Enoka, RM. Motor-unit synchronization increases EMG amplitude and decreases force steadiness of simulated contractions. *J Neurophysiol* 83:441-452, 2000.

548. Yessis, M. Speed-strength training: A Soviet breakthrough. In *Secrets of Russian Sports Fitness and Training*. Michigan, USA: Ultimate Athlete Concepts, 144-166, 2008.

549. Young, WB, Miller, IR, and Talpey, SW. Physical qualities predict change-of-direction speed but not defensive agility in Australian rules football. *J Strength Cond Res* 29:206-212, 2015.

550. Zamparo, P, Minetti, AE, and di Prampero, PE. Interplay among the changes of muscle strength, cross-sectional area and maximal explosive power: Theory and facts. *Eur J Appl Physiol* 88:193-202, 2002.

551. Zatsiorsky, VM, Kraemer, WJ, and Fry, AC. Timing in strength training. In *Science and Practice of Strength Training*. 3rd ed. Champaign, IL: Human Kinetics, 79-98, 2021.

552. Zatsiorsky, VM, Kraemer, WJ, and Fry, AC. Task-specific strength. In *Science and Practice of Strength Training*. 3rd ed. Champaign, IL: Human Kinetics, 15-40, 2021.

553. Zatsiorsky, VM, Kraemer, WJ, and Fry, AC. Timing in strength training. In *Science and Practice of Strength Training*. 3rd ed. Champaign, IL: Human Kinetics, 79-98, 2021.

554. Zatsiorsky, VM, Kraemer, WJ, and Fry, AC. Training intensity. In *Science and Practice of Strength Training*. 3rd ed. Champaign, IL: Human Kinetics, 61-78, 2021.

555. Zoeller, RF, Ryan, ED, Gordish-Dressman, H, Price, TB, Seip, RL, Angelopoulos, TJ, Moyna, NM, Gordon, PM, Thompson, PD, and Hoffman, EP. Allometric scaling of biceps strength before and after resistance training in men. *Med Sci Sports Exerc* 39:1013-1019, 2007.

556. Zourdos, MC, Goldsmith, JA, Helms, ER, Trepeck, C, Halle, JL, Mendez, KM, Cooke, DM, Haischer, MH, Sousa, CA, Klemp, A, and Byrnes, RK. Proximity to failure and total repetitions performed in a set influences accuracy of intraset repetitions in reserve-based rating of perceived exertion. *J Strength Cond Res* 35:S158-S165, 2021.

557. Zourdos, MC, Klemp, A, Dolan, C, Quiles, JM, Schau, KA, Jo, E, Helms, E, Esgro, B, Duncan, S, Garcia Merino, S, and Blanco, R. Novel resistance training-specific rating of perceived exertion scale measuring repetitions in reserve. *J Strength Cond Res* 30:267-275, 2016.

Chapter 14

1. Achten, J, and Jeukendrup, AE. Heart rate monitoring: applications and limitations. *Sports Med* 33:517-538, 2003.

2. Ahmaidi, S, Granier, P, Taoutaou, Z, Mercier, J, Dubouchaud, H, and Prefaut, C. Effects of active recovery on plasma lactate and anaerobic power following repeated intensive exercise. *Med Sci Sports Exerc* 28:450-456, 1996.

3. Allen, H, and Coggan, AR. Interpreting data. In *Training and Racing With a Power Meter*. Boulder, CO: Velo Press, 93-116, 2010.

4. Arslan, E, Orer, GE, and Clemente, FM. Running-based high-intensity interval training vs. small-sided game training programs: Effects on the physical performance, psychophysiological responses and technical skills in young soccer players. *Biol Sport* 37:165-173, 2020.

5. Baker, D. Recent trends in high-intensity aerobic training for field sports. *Professional Strength and Conditioning* 22:3-8, 2011.

6. Bangsbo, J. *Fitness Training in Soccer: A Scientific Approach*. Spring City, PA: Reedswain Publishing, 1994.

7. Bangsbo, J. The physiology of soccer—with special reference to intense intermittent exercise. *Acta Physiol Scand Suppl* 619:1-155, 1994.

8. Belcastro, AN, and Bonen, A. Lactic acid removal rates during controlled and uncontrolled recovery exercise. *J Appl Physiol* 39:932-936, 1975.

9. Bellinger, P, Desbrow, B, Derave, W, Lievens, E, Irwin, C, Sabapathy, S, Kennedy, B, Craven, J, Pennell, E, Rice, H, and Minahan, C. Muscle fiber typology is associated with the incidence of overreaching in response to overload training. *J Appl Physiol (1985)* 129:823-836, 2020.

10. Beneke, R. Anaerobic threshold, individual anaerobic threshold, and maximal lactate steady state in rowing. *Med Sci Sports Exerc* 27:863-867, 1995.

11. Berthon, P, and Fellmann, N. General review of maximal aerobic velocity measurement at laboratory: Proposition of a new simplified protocol for maximal aerobic velocity assessment. *J Sports Med Phys Fitness* 42:257-266, 2002.

12. Berthon, P, Fellmann, N, Bedu, M, Beaune, B, Dabonneville, M, Coudert, J, and Chamoux, A. A 5-min running field test as a measurement of maximal aerobic velocity. *Eur J Appl Physiol Occup Physiol* 75:233-238, 1997.

13. Billat, LV. Interval training for performance: A scientific and empirical practice. Special recommendations for middle- and long-distance running. Part I: Aerobic interval training. *Sports Med* 31:13-31, 2001.

14. Billat, LV. Interval training for performance: A scientific and empirical practice. Special recommendations for middle- and long-distance running. Part II: Anaerobic interval training. *Sports Med* 31:75-90, 2001.

15. Billat, LV, and Koralsztein, JP. Significance of the velocity at VO2max and time to exhaustion at this velocity. *Sports Med* 22:90-108, 1996.

16. Billat, V, Renoux, JC, Pinoteau, J, Petit, B, and Koralsztein, JP. Reproducibility of running time to exhaustion at VO2max in subelite runners. *Med Sci Sports Exerc* 26:254-257, 1994.

17. Bilsborough, JC, and Cabrera, M. Football. In *Science and Application of High-Intensity Interval Training*. Laursen, PB, Buchheit, M, eds. Champaign, IL: Human Kinetics, 379-392, 2019.

18. Bishop, BJ, Bartlett, J, Fyfe, J, and Lee, M. Methodological considerations for concurrent training. In *Concurrent*

Aerobic and Strength Training: Scientific Basics and Practical Applications. Schumann, M, Ronnestad, BR, eds. Cham, Switzerland: Springer, 183-197, 2019.

19. Blondel, N, Berthoin, S, Billat, V, and Lensel, G. Relationship between run times to exhaustion at 90, 100, 120, and 140% of vVO2max and velocity expressed relatively to critical velocity and maximal velocity. *Int J Sports Med* 22:27-33, 2001.

20. Bompa, TO, and Haff, GG. Annual training plan. In *Periodization: Theory and Methodology of Training.* 5th ed. Champaign, IL: Human Kinetics, 125-185, 2009.

21. Buchheit, M. The 30-15 intermittent fitness test: A new intermittent running field test for intermittent sport players—part 1. *Approches du Handball* 87:27-34, 2005.

22. Buchheit, M. The 30-15 intermittent fitness test: Reliability and implication for interval training of intermittent sport players. Presented at 10th European Congress of Sport Science, Belgrade, Serbia, Jul 13-16, 2005.

23. Buchheit, M. 30-15 intermittent fitness test et répétition de sprints. *Science & Sports* 23:26-28, 2008.

24. Buchheit, M. The 30-15 intermittent fitness test: Accuracy for individualizing interval training of young intermittent sport players. *J Strength Cond Res* 22:365-374, 2008.

25. Buchheit, M. Le 30-15 intermittent fitness test: 10 year review. *Myorobie Journal* 1:1-9, 2010.

26. Buchheit, M. Individualizing high-intensity interval training in intermittent sport athletes with the 30-15 intermittent fitness test. Colorado Springs: NSCA, 2013.

27. Buchheit, M, Abbiss, CR, Peiffer, JJ, and Laursen, PB. Performance and physiological responses during a sprint interval training session: Relationships with muscle oxygenation and pulmonary oxygen uptake kinetics. *Eur J Appl Physiol* 112:767-779, 2012.

28. Buchheit, M, Al Haddad, H, Millet, GP, Lepretre, PM, Newton, M, and Ahmaidi, S. Cardiorespiratory and cardiac autonomic responses to 30-15 intermittent fitness test in team sport players. *J Strength Cond Res* 23:93-100, 2009.

29. Buchheit, M, Cormie, P, Abbiss, CR, Ahmaidi, S, Nosaka, KK, and Laursen, PB. Muscle deoxygenation during repeated sprint running: Effect of active vs. passive recovery. *Int J Sports Med* 30:418-425, 2009.

30. Buchheit, M, Hader, K, and Mendez-Villanueva, A. Tolerance to high-intensity intermittent running exercise: Do oxygen uptake kinetics really matter? *Front Physiol* 3:406, 2012.

31. Buchheit, M, Haydar, B, Hader, K, Ufland, P, and Ahmaidi, S. Assessing running economy during field running with changes of direction: Application to 20 m shuttle runs. *Int J Sports Physiol Perform* 6:380-395, 2011.

32. Buchheit, M, Lacome, M, and Simpson, B. Soccer. In *Science and Application of High-Intensity Interval Training.* Laursen, PB, Buchheit, M, eds. Champaign, IL: Human Kinetics, 547-564, 2019.

33. Buchheit, M, and Laursen, PB. High-intensity interval training, solutions to the programming puzzle: Part I: Cardiopulmonary emphasis. *Sports Med* 43:313-338, 2013.

34. Buchheit, M, and Laursen, PB. High-intensity interval training, solutions to the programming puzzle: Part II: Anaerobic energy, neuromuscular load and practical applications. *Sports Med* 43:927-954, 2013.

35. Buchheit, M, and Laursen, PB. Manipulating HIIT variables. In *Science and Application of High-Intensity Interval Training.* Buchheit, M, Laursen, PB, eds. Champaign, IL: Human Kinetics, 51-72, 2019.

36. Buchheit, M, and Laursen, PB. Quantifying training load. In *Science and Application of High-Intensity Interval Training.* Buchheit, M, Laursen, PB, eds. Champaign, IL: Human Kinetics, 161-178, 2019.

37. Buchheit, M, and Laursen, PB. Traditional methods of HIIT programming. In *Science and Application of High-Intensity Interval Training.* Laursen, PB, Buchheit, M, eds. Champaign, IL: Human Kinetics, 17-33, 2019.

38. Buchheit, M, and Laursen, PB. Aerobic power training. In *High Performance Training for Sports.* 2nd ed. Joyce, D, Lewindon, D, eds. Champaign, IL: Human Kinetics, 208-221, 2022.

39. Buchheit, M, and Laursen, PB. Periodization and programming for team sports. In *NSCA's Essentials of Sport Science.* French, D, Torres Ronda, L, eds. Champaign, IL: Human Kinetics, 43-56, 2022.

40. Buchheit, M, Laursen, PB, Kuhnle, J, Ruch, D, Renaud, C, and Ahmaidi, S. Game-based training in young elite handball players. *Int J Sports Med* 30:251-258, 2009.

41. Buchheit, M, Laursen, PB, Millet, GP, Pactat, F, and Ahmaidi, S. Predicting intermittent running performance: Critical velocity versus endurance index. *Int J Sports Med* 29:307-315, 2008.

42. Buchheit, M, Lepretre, PM, Behaegel, AL, Millet, GP, Cuvelier, G, and Ahmaidi, S. Cardiorespiratory responses during running and sport-specific exercises in handball players. *J Sci Med Sport* 12:399-405, 2009.

43. Buchheit, M, and Mayer, N. Restoring players' specific fitness and performance capacity in relation to match physical and technical demands. In *Muscle Injury Guide: Prevention of and Return to Play from Muscle Injuries.* Pruna, R, Anderson, TE, Clarsen, B, McCall, A, eds. Spain: Barca Innovation Hub, 29-37, 2019.

44. Buchheit, M, and Mendez-Villanueva, A. Supramaximal intermittent running performance in relation to age and locomotor profile in highly-trained young soccer players. *J Sports Sci* 31:1402-1411, 2013.

45. Buchheit, M, and Mendez-Villanueva, A. Changes in repeated-sprint performance in relation to change in locomotor profile in highly-trained young soccer players. *J Sports Sci* 32:1309-1317, 2014.

46. Buchheit, M, Mendez-Villanueva, A, Simpson, BM, and Bourdon, PC. Match running performance and fitness in youth soccer. *Int J Sports Med* 31:818-825, 2010.

47. Buchheit, M, Morgan, W, Wallace, J, Bode, M, and Poulos, N. Physiological, psychometric, and performance effects of the Christmas break in Australian football. *Int J Sports Physiol Perform* 10:120-123, 2015.

48. Bujalance-Moreno, P, Latorre-Roman, PA, and Garcia-Pinillos, F. A systematic review on small-sided games in football players: Acute and chronic adaptations. *J Sports Sci* 37:921-949, 2019.

49. Bundle, MW, Hoyt, RW, and Weyand, PG. High-speed running performance: A new approach to assessment and prediction. *J Appl Physiol (1985)* 95:1955-1962, 2003.

50. Casamichana, D, Castellano, J, and Castagna, C. Comparing the physical demands of friendly matches and small-sided games in semiprofessional soccer players. *J Strength Cond Res* 26:837-843, 2012.
51. Castagna, C, Belardinelli, R, Impellizzeri, FM, Abt, GA, Coutts, AJ, and D'Ottavio, S. Cardiovascular responses during recreational 5-a-side indoor-soccer. *J Sci Med Sport* 10:89-95, 2007.
52. Castagna, C, Impellizzeri, FM, Chaouachi, A, Ben Abdelkrim, N, and Manzi, V. Physiological responses to ball-drills in regional level male basketball players. *J Sports Sci* 29:1329-1336, 2011.
53. Cataldo, A, Cerasola, D, Russo, G, Zangla, D, and Traina, M. Mean power during 20 sec all-out test to predict 2000 m rowing ergometer performance in national level young rowers. *J Sports Med Phys Fitness* 55:872-877, 2015.
54. Celine, CG, Monnier-Benoit, P, Groslambert, A, Tordi, N, Perrey, S, and Rouillon, JD. The perceived exertion to regulate a training program in young women. *J Strength Cond Res* 25:220-224, 2011.
55. Cerretelli, P, and Di Prampero, PE. Kinetics of respiratory gas exchange and cardiac output at the onset of exercise. *Scand J Respir Dis Suppl* 77:35a-35g, 1971.
56. Chorley, A, and Lamb, KL. The application of critical power, the work capacity above critical power (W'), and its reconstitution: A narrative review of current evidence and implications for cycling training prescription. *Sports (Basel)* 8:123, 2020.
57. Clemente, FM, Ramirez-Campillo, R, Afonso, J, Sarmento, H, Rosemann, T, and Knechtle, B. A meta-analytical comparison of the effects of small-sided games vs. running-based high-intensity interval training on soccer players' repeated-sprint ability. *Int J Environ Res Public Health* 18:2781, 2021.
58. Clemente, FM, and Sarmento, H. The effects of small-sided soccer games on technical actions and skills: A systematic review. *Hum Mov* 21:100-119, 2020.
59. Cosgrove, MJ, Wilson, J, Watt, D, and Grant, SF. The relationship between selected physiological variables of rowers and rowing performance as determined by a 2000 m ergometer test. *J Sports Sci* 17:845-852, 1999.
60. Coutts, A, Hocking, J, and Bilsborough, JC. Australian football. In *Science and Application of High-Intensity Interval Training*. Laursen, PB, Buchheit, M, eds. Champaign, IL: Human Kinetics, 393-410, 2019.
61. Coutts, AJ, Rampinini, E, Marcora, SM, Castagna, C, and Impellizzeri, FM. Heart rate and blood lactate correlates of perceived exertion during small-sided soccer games. *J Sci Med Sport* 12:79-84, 2009.
62. Cunningham, DJ, Shearer, DA, Carter, N, Drawer, S, Pollard, B, Bennett, M, Eager, R, Cook, CJ, Farrell, J, Russell, M, and Kilduff, LP. Assessing worst case scenarios in movement demands derived from global positioning systems during international Rugby Union matches: Rolling averages versus fixed length epochs. *PLoS One* 13:e0195197, 2018.
63. Daniels, J, Scardina, N, Hayes, J, and Foley, P. Elite and subelite female middle-and long-distance runners. In *Sport and Elite Performers*. Landers, DM, ed. Champaign, IL: Human Kinetics, 57-72, 1984.
64. Dellal, A, Hill-Haas, S, Lago-Penas, C, and Chamari, K. Small-sided games in soccer: Amateur vs. professional players' physiological responses, physical, and technical activities. *J Strength Cond Res* 25:2371-2381, 2011.
65. Dellal, A, Keller, D, Carling, C, Chaouachi, A, Wong del, P, and Chamari, K. Physiologic effects of directional changes in intermittent exercise in soccer players. *J Strength Cond Res* 24:3219-3226, 2010.
66. Dellal, A, Varliette, C, Owen, A, Chirico, EN, and Pialoux, V. Small-sided games versus interval training in amateur soccer players: effects on the aerobic capacity and the ability to perform intermittent exercises with changes of direction. *J Strength Cond Res* 26:2712-2720, 2012.
67. Di Prampero, P, Atchou, G, Brückner, J-C, and Moia, C. The energetics of endurance running. *Eur J Appl Physiol Occup Physiol* 55:259-266, 1986.
68. Di Salvo, V, Baron, R, Gonzalez-Haro, C, Gormasz, C, Pigozzi, F, and Bachl, N. Sprinting analysis of elite soccer players during European Champions League and UEFA Cup matches. *J Sports Sci* 28:1489-1494, 2010.
69. Dishman, RK, Patton, RW, Smith, J, Weinberg, R, and Jackson, A. Using perceived exertion to prescribe and monitor exercise training heart rate. *Int J Sports Med* 8:208-213, 1987.
70. Dolci, F, Kilding, AE, Chivers, P, Piggott, B, and Hart, NH. High-intensity interval training shock microcycle for enhancing sport performance: A brief review. *J Strength Cond Res* 34:1188-1196, 2020.
71. Dupont, G, Akakpo, K, and Berthoin, S. The effect of in-season, high-intensity interval training in soccer players. *J Strength Cond Res* 18:584-589, 2004.
72. Dupont, G, Blondel, N, Lensel, G, and Berthoin, S. Critical velocity and time spent at a high level of VO2 for short intermittent runs at supramaximal velocities. *Can J Appl Physiol* 27:103-115., 2002.
73. Dupont, G, Defontaine, M, Bosquet, L, Blondel, N, Moalla, W, and Berthoin, S. Yo-Yo Intermittent Recovery Test versus the Universite de Montreal Track Test: Relation with a high-intensity intermittent exercise. *J Sci Med Sport* 13:146-150, 2010.
74. Dupont, G, Moalla, W, Guinhouya, C, Ahmaidi, S, and Berthoin, S. Passive versus active recovery during high-intensity intermittent exercises. *Med Sci Sports Exerc* 36:302-308, 2004.
75. Edouard, P, Mendiguchia, J, Guex, K, Lahti, J, Samozino, P, and Morin, J-B. Sprinting: A potential vaccine for hamstring injury? *Sport Perform Sci Reports* 1:1-2, 2019.
76. Ferguson, BS, Rogatzki, MJ, Goodwin, ML, Kane, DA, Rightmire, Z, and Gladden, LB. Lactate metabolism: Historical context, prior misinterpretations, and current understanding. *Eur J Appl Physiol* 118:691-728, 2018.
77. Fernandez-Fernandez, J, Sanz-Rivas, D, Sanchez-Munoz, C, de la Aleja Tellez, JG, Buchheit, M, and Mendez-Villanueva, A. Physiological responses to on-court vs running interval training in competitive tennis players. *J Sports Sci Med* 10:540-545, 2011.
78. Fiorenza, M, Hostrup, M, Gunnarsson, TP, Shirai, Y, Schena, F, Iaia, FM, and Bangsbo, J. Neuromuscular fatigue and metabolism during high-intensity intermittent exercise. *Med Sci Sports Exerc* 51:1642-1652, 2019.

79. Gabbett, TJ. Skill-based conditioning games as an alternative to traditional conditioning for Rugby League players. *J Strength Cond Res* 20:309-315, 2006.

80. Gabbett, TJ. Do skill-based conditioning games offer a specific training stimulus for junior elite volleyball players? *J Strength Cond Res* 22:509-517, 2008.

81. Gamble, P. Periodization of training for team sports athletes. *Strength Cond J* 28:56, 2006.

82. Garcin, M, Danel, M, and Billat, V. Perceptual responses in free vs. constant pace exercise. *Int J Sports Med* 29:453-459, 2008.

83. Garcin, M, Fleury, A, Mille-Hamard, L, and Billat, V. Sex-related differences in ratings of perceived exertion and estimated time limit. *Int J Sports Med* 26:675-681, 2005.

84. Gibala, MJ, and Jones, AM. Physiological and performance adaptations to high-intensity interval training. *Nestle Nutr Inst Workshop Ser* 76:51-60, 2013.

85. Gibala, MJ, and McGee, SL. Metabolic adaptations to short-term high-intensity interval training: A little pain for a lot of gain? *Exerc Sport Sci Rev* 36:58-63, 2008.

86. Gist, NH, Fedewa, MV, Dishman, RK, and Cureton, KJ. Sprint interval training effects on aerobic capacity: A systematic review and meta-analysis. *Sports Med* 44:269-279, 2014.

87. Gorostiaga, EM, Asiain, X, Izquierdo, M, Postigo, A, Aguado, R, Alonso, JM, and Ibanez, J. Vertical jump performance and blood ammonia and lactate levels during typical training sessions in elite 400-m runners. *J Strength Cond Res* 24:1138-1149, 2010.

88. Haff, GG, and Dumke, C. High-intensity fitness testing. In *Laboratory Manual for Exercise Physiology*. 2nd ed. Champaign, IL: Human Kinetics, 195-218, 2018.

89. Haff, GG, Whitley, A, and Potteiger, JA. A brief review: Explosive exercises and sports performance. *Strength Cond J* 23:13-20, 2001.

90. Hall, MM, Rajasekaran, S, Thomsen, TW, and Peterson, AR. Lactate: Friend or foe. *PM&R* 8:S8-S15, 2016.

91. Harling, SA, Tong, RJ, and Mickleborough, TD. The oxygen uptake response running to exhaustion at peak treadmill speed. *Med Sci Sports Exerc* 35:663-668, 2003.

92. Hebisz, P, and Hebisz, R. The effect of polarized training (SIT, HIIT, and ET) on muscle thickness and anaerobic power in trained cyclists. *Int J Environ Res Public Health* 18:6547, 2021.

93. Hebisz, P, Hebisz, R, and Drelak, M. Comparison of aerobic capacity changes as a result of a polarized or block training program among trained mountain bike cyclists. *Int J Environ Res Public Health* 18:8865, 2021.

94. Hebisz, P, Hebisz, R, Zaton, M, Ochmann, B, and Mielnik, N. Concomitant application of sprint and high-intensity interval training on maximal oxygen uptake and work output in well-trained cyclists. *Eur J Appl Physiol* 116:1495-1502, 2016.

95. Hill-Haas, S, Coutts, A, Rowsell, G, and Dawson, B. Variability of acute physiological responses and performance profiles of youth soccer players in small-sided games. *J Sci Med Sport* 11:487-490, 2008.

96. Hill-Haas, S, Rowsell, G, Coutts, A, and Dawson, B. The reproducibility of physiological responses and performance profiles of youth soccer players in small-sided games. *Int J Sports Physiol Perform* 3:393-396, 2008.

97. Hill-Haas, SV, Dawson, B, Impellizzeri, FM, and Coutts, AJ. Physiology of small-sided games training in football: A systematic review. *Sports Med* 41:199-220, 2011.

98. Hill, AV. The physiological basis of athletic records. *Sci Mon* 21:409-428, 1925.

99. Hill, AV. The dimensions of animals and their muscular dynamics. *Sci Prog* 38:209-230, 1950.

100. Hill, DW, and Rowell, AL. Running velocity at VO2max. *Med Sci Sports Exerc* 28:114-119, 1996.

101. Hill, DW, and Rowell, AL. Significance of time to exhaustion during exercise at the velocity associated with VO2max. *Eur J Appl Physiol Occup Physiol* 72:383-386, 1996.

102. Hoff, J, and Helgerud, J. Endurance and strength training for soccer players: Physiological considerations. *Sports Med* 34:165-180, 2004.

103. Hoff, J, Wisløff, U, Engen, LC, Kemi, OJ, and Helgerud, J. Soccer specific aerobic endurance training. *Br J Sports Med* 36:218-221, 2002.

104. Iaia, FM, and Bangsbo, J. Speed endurance training is a powerful stimulus for physiological adaptations and performance improvements of athletes. *Scand J Med Sci Sports* 20:11-23, 2010.

105. Impellizzeri, FM, Marcora, SM, Castagna, C, Reilly, T, Sassi, A, Iaia, FM, and Rampinini, E. Physiological and performance effects of generic versus specific aerobic training in soccer players. *Int J Sports Med* 27:483-492, 2006.

106. Jeukendrup, AE, Craig, NP, and Hawley, JA. The bioenergetics of world class cycling. *J Sci Med Sport* 3:414-433, 2000.

107. Jones, AM, Burnley, M, Black, MI, Poole, DC, and Vanhatalo, A. The maximal metabolic steady state: Redefining the "gold standard". *Physiol Rep* 7:e14098, 2019.

108. Jones, AM, and Vanhatalo, A. The "critical power" concept: Applications to sports performance with a focus on intermittent high-intensity exercise. *Sports Med* 47:65-78, 2017.

109. Julio, UF, Panissa, VLG, Paludo, AC, Alves, ED, Campos, FAD, and Franchini, E. Use of the anaerobic speed reserve to normalize the prescription of high-intensity interval exercise intensity. *Eur J Sport Sci* 20:166-173, 2020.

110. Kemi, OJ, Fowler, E, McGlynn, K, Primrose, D, Smirthwaite, R, and Wilson, J. Intensity-dependence of exercise and active recovery in high-intensity interval training. *J Sports Med Phys Fitness* 59:1937-1943, 2019.

111. Krustrup, P, Mohr, M, Steensberg, A, Bencke, J, Kjaer, M, and Bangsbo, J. Muscle and blood metabolites during a soccer game: Implications for sprint performance. *Med Sci Sports Exerc* 38:1165-1174, 2006.

112. Krustrup, P, Söderlund, K, Mohr, M, González-Alonso, J, and Bangsbo, J. Recruitment of fibre types and quadriceps muscle portions during repeated, intense knee-extensor exercise in humans. *Pflugers Arch* 449:56-65, 2004.

113. Lacome, M, Simpson, BM, Cholley, Y, Lambert, P, and Buchheit, M. Small-sided games in elite soccer: Does one size fit all? *Int J Sports Physiol Perform* 13:568-576, 2018.

114. Lacour, J, Padilla-Magunacelaya, S, Barthelemy, J, and Dormois, D. The energetics of middle-distance running. *Eur J Appl Physiol Occup Physiol* 60:38-43, 1990.

115. Laursen, PB. Training for intense exercise performance: High-intensity or high-volume training? *Scand J Med Sci Sports* 20:1-10, 2010.
116. Laursen, PB, and Buchheit, M. Genesis and evolution of high-intensity interval training. In *Science and Application of High-Intensity Interval Training*. Laursen, PB, Buchheit, M, eds. Champaign, IL: Human Kinetics, 3-16, 2019.
117. Laursen, PB, and Buchheit, M, eds. *Science and Application of High-Intensity Interval Training*. Champaign, IL: Human Kinetics, 2019.
118. Laursen, PB, and Jenkins, DG. The scientific basis for high-intensity interval training: Optimising training programmes and maximising performance in highly trained endurance athletes. *Sports Med* 32:53-73, 2002.
119. Laursen, PB, Shing, CM, and Jenkins, DG. Reproducibility of the cycling time to exhaustion at VO2peak in highly trained cyclists. *Can J Appl Physiol* 28:605-615, 2003.
120. Laursen, PB, Shing, CM, Peake, JM, Coombes, JS, and Jenkins, DG. Interval training program optimization in highly trained endurance cyclists. *Med Sci Sports Exerc* 34:1801-1807, 2002.
121. Leger, L, and Boucher, R. An indirect continuous running multistage field test: The Universite de Montreal track test. *Can J Appl Sport Sci* 5:77-84, 1980.
122. Lemes, JC, Luchesi, M, Diniz, LBF, Bredt, S, Chagas, MH, and Praca, GM. Influence of pitch size and age category on the physical and physiological responses of young football players during small-sided games using GPS devices. *Res Sports Med* 28:206-216, 2020.
123. Lievens, E, Bellinger, P, Van Vossel, K, Vancompernolle, J, Bex, T, Minahan, C, and Derave, W. Muscle typology of world-class cyclists across various disciplines and events. *Med Sci Sports Exerc* 53:816-824, 2021.
124. Lievens, E, Klass, M, Bex, T, and Derave, W. Muscle fiber typology substantially influences time to recover from high-intensity exercise. *J Appl Physiol (1985)* 128:648-659, 2020.
125. Lundby, C, and Robach, P. Performance enhancement: What are the physiological limits? *Physiology (Bethesda)* 30:282-292, 2015.
126. Malone, S, Roe, M, Doran, DA, Gabbett, TJ, and Collins, K. High chronic training loads and exposure to bouts of maximal velocity running reduce injury risk in elite Gaelic football. *J Sci Med Sport* 20:250-254, 2017.
127. Manoel, FA, da Silva, DF, Lima, JRP, and Machado, FA. Peak velocity and its time limit are as good as the velocity associated with VO2max for training prescription in runners. *Sports Med Int Open* 1:E8-E15, 2017.
128. Marcora, SM. Role of feedback from group III and IV muscle afferents in perception of effort, muscle pain, and discomfort. *J Appl Physiol (1985)* 110:1499, 2011.
129. Marcora, SM, Staiano, W, and Manning, V. Mental fatigue impairs physical performance in humans. *J Appl Physiol* 106:857-864, 2009.
130. Mendez-Villanueva, A, Buchheit, M, Kuitunen, S, Poon, TK, Simpson, B, and Peltola, E. Is the relationship between sprinting and maximal aerobic speeds in young soccer players affected by maturation? *Pediatr Exerc Sci* 22:497-510, 2010.
131. Mendez-Villanueva, A, Buchheit, M, Simpson, B, and Bourdon, PC. Match play intensity distribution in youth soccer. *Int J Sports Med* 34:101-110, 2013.
132. Mendez-Villanueva, A, Buchheit, M, Simpson, B, Peltola, E, and Bourdon, P. Does on-field sprinting performance in young soccer players depend on how fast they can run or how fast they do run? *J Strength Cond Res* 25:2634-2638, 2011.
133. Mendez-Villanueva, A, Hamer, P, and Bishop, D. Fatigue in repeated-sprint exercise is related to muscle power factors and reduced neuromuscular activity. *Eur J Appl Physiol* 103:411-419, 2008.
134. Midgley, A, McNaughton, L, and Carroll, S. Time at VO2max during intermittent treadmill running: Test protocol dependent or methodological artefact? *Int J Sports Med* 28:934-939, 2007.
135. Midgley, AW, McNaughton, LR, and Carroll, S. Reproducibility of time at or near VO2max during intermittent treadmill running. *Int J Sports Med* 28:40-47, 2007.
136. Midgley, AW, McNaughton, LR, and Wilkinson, M. Is there an optimal training intensity for enhancing the maximal oxygen uptake of distance runners? Empirical research findings, current opinions, physiological rationale and practical recommendations. *Sports Med* 36:117-132, 2006.
137. Monod, H, and Scherrer, J. The work capacity of a synergic muscular group. *Ergonomics* 8:329-338, 1965.
138. Moran, J, Blagrove, RC, Drury, B, Fernandes, JFT, Paxton, K, Chaabene, H, and Ramirez-Campillo, R. Effects of small-sided games vs. conventional endurance training on endurance performance in male youth soccer players: A meta-analytical comparison. *Sports Med* 49:731-742, 2019.
139. Moritani, T, Nagata, A, Devries, HA, and Muro, M. Critical power as a measure of physical work capacity and anaerobic threshold. *Ergonomics* 24:339-350, 1981.
140. Mosey, T. High intensity interval training in youth soccer players—using fitness testing results practically. *Journal of Australian Strength and Conditioning* 17:49-51, 2009.
141. Nedeljkovic, A, Mirkov, DM, Bozic, P, and Jaric, S. Tests of muscle power output: The role of body size. *Int J Sports Med* 30:100-106, 2009.
142. Ní Chéilleachair, NJ, Harrison, AJ, and Warrington, GD. HIIT enhances endurance performance and aerobic characteristics more than high-volume training in trained rowers. *J Sports Sci* 35:1052-1058, 2017.
143. Ometto, L, Vasconcellos, FV, Cunha, FA, Teoldo, I, Souza, CRB, Dutra, MB, O'Sullivan, M, and Davids, K. How manipulating task constraints in small-sided and conditioned games shapes emergence of individual and collective tactical behaviours in football: A systematic review. *Int J Sports Sci Coach* 13:1200-1214, 2018.
144. Perrier-Melo, RJ, D'Amorim, I, Meireles Santos, T, Caldas Costa, E, Rodrigues Barbosa, R, and M, DACC. Effect of active versus passive recovery on performance-related outcome during high-intensity interval exercise. *J Sports Med Phys Fitness* 61:562-570, 2021.
145. Pette, D, and Staron, RS. Mammalian skeletal muscle fiber type transitions. *Int Rev Cytol* 170:143-223., 1997.
146. Pette, D, and Staron, RS. Myosin isoforms, muscle fiber types, and transitions. *Microsc Res Tech* 50:500-509., 2000.

147. Plews, D. Rowing. In *Science and Application of High-Intensity Interval Training*. Laursen, PB, Buchheit, M, eds. Champaign, IL: Human Kinetics, 311-324, 2019.

148. Poole, DC, Burnley, M, Vanhatalo, A, Rossiter, HB, and Jones, AM. Critical power: An important fatigue threshold in exercise physiology. *Med Sci Sports Exerc* 48:2320-2334, 2016.

149. Poole, DC, Ward, SA, Gardner, GMW, and Whipp, BJ. Metabolic and respiratory profile of the upper limit for prolonged exercise in man. *Ergonomics* 31:1265-1279, 1988.

150. Pringle, JS, and Jones, AM. Maximal lactate steady state, critical power and EMG during cycling. *Eur J Appl Physiol* 88:214-226, 2002.

151. Qaisar, R, Bhaskaran, S, and Van Remmen, H. Muscle fiber type diversification during exercise and regeneration. *Free Radic Biol Med* 98:56-67, 2016.

152. Quod, MJ, Martin, DT, Martin, JC, and Laursen, PB. The power profile predicts road cycling MMP. *Int J Sports Med* 31:397-401, 2010.

153. Rabbani, A, and Buchheit, M. Heart rate-based versus speed-based high-intensity interval training in young soccer players. In *International Research in Science and Soccer II*. Favero, T, Drust, B, Dawson, B, eds. New York: Routledge, 133-144, 2015.

154. Rampinini, E, Impellizzeri, FM, Castagna, C, Abt, G, Chamari, K, Sassi, A, and Marcora, SM. Factors influencing physiological responses to small-sided soccer games. *J Sports Sci* 25:659-666, 2007.

155. Raya-Gonzalez, J, Castillo, D, and Clemente, FM. Injury prevention of hamstring injuries through exercise interventions. *J Sports Med Phys Fitness* 61:1242-1251, 2021.

156. Rønnestad, BR, Ellefsen, S, Nygaard, H, Zacharoff, EE, Vikmoen, O, Hansen, J, and Hallén, J. Effects of 12 weeks of block periodization on performance and performance indices in well-trained cyclists. *Scand J Med Sci Sports* 24:327-335, 2014.

157. Rønnestad, BR, and Hansen, J. A scientific approach to improve physiological capacity of an elite cyclist. *Int J Sports Physiol Perform* 13:390-393, 2018.

158. Rønnestad, BR, Hansen, J, and Ellefsen, S. Block periodization of high-intensity aerobic intervals provides superior training effects in trained cyclists. *Scand J Med Sci Sports* 24:34-42, 2014.

159. Rønnestad, BR, Hansen, J, Thyli, V, Bakken, TA, and Sandbakk, O. 5-week block periodization increases aerobic power in elite cross-country skiers. *Scand J Med Sci Sports* 26:140-146, 2016.

160. Rønnestad, BR, Ofsteng, SJ, and Ellefsen, S. Block periodization of strength and endurance training is superior to traditional periodization in ice hockey players. *Scand J Med Sci Sports* 29:180-188, 2019.

161. Sandford, GN, Allen, SV, Kilding, AE, Ross, A, and Laursen, PB. Anaerobic speed reserve: A key component of elite male 800-m running. *Int J Sports Physiol Perform* 14:501-508, 2019.

162. Sandford, GN, Laursen, PB, and Buchheit, M. Anaerobic speed/power reserve and sport performance: Scientific basis, current applications and future directions. *Sports Med* 51:2017-2028, 2021.

163. Sandford, GN, and Stellingwerff, T. "Question your categories": The misunderstood complexity of middle-distance running profiles with implications for research methods and application. *Front Sports Act Living* 1:28, 2019.

164. Seiler, S. What is best practice for training intensity and duration distribution in endurance athletes? *Int J Sports Physiol Perform* 5:276-291, 2010.

165. Seiler, S, and Hetlelid, KJ. The impact of rest duration on work intensity and RPE during interval training. *Med Sci Sports Exerc* 37:1601-1607, 2005.

166. Seiler, S, and Sjursen, JE. Effect of work duration on physiological and rating scale of perceived exertion responses during self-paced interval training. *Scand J Med Sci Sports* 14:318-325, 2004.

167. Solli, GS, Tønnessen, E, and Sandbakk, Ø. The training characteristics of the world's most successful female cross-country skier. *Front Physiol* 8:1069, 2017.

168. Solli, GS, Tønnessen, E, and Sandbakk, Ø. Block vs. traditional periodization of HIT: Two different paths to success for the world's best cross-country skier. *Front Physiol* 10:375, 2019.

169. Stöggl, T, and Sperlich, B. Polarized training has greater impact on key endurance variables than threshold, high intensity, or high volume training. *Frontiers in Physiology* 5, 2014.

170. Tabata, I. Tabata training: one of the most energetically effective high-intensity intermittent training methods. *J Thibault, G. A graphical model for interval training. New Studies in Athletics* 18:49-56, 2003.

171. Thibault, G. A graphical model for interval training. *New Studies in Athletics* 18:49-56, 2003.

172. Tjelta, LI. The training of international level distance runners. *Int J Sports Sci Coach* 11:122-134, 2016.

173. Triplett, NT. Structure and function of body systems. In *Essentials of Strength Training and Conditioning*. 4th ed. Haff, GG, Triplett, NT, eds. Champaign, IL: Human Kinetics, 1-18, 2016.

174. Ufland, P, Ahmaidi, S, and Buchheit, M. Repeated-sprint performance, locomotor profile and muscle oxygen uptake recovery: Effect of training background. *Int J Sports Med* 34:924-930, 2013.

175. Van Hooren, B, and Peake, JM. Do we need a cool-down after exercise? A narrative review of the psychophysiological effects and the effects on performance, injuries and the long-term adaptive response. *Sports Med* 48:1575-1595, 2018.

176. Vollaard, NB, Constantin-Teodosiu, D, Fredriksson, K, Rooyackers, O, Jansson, E, Greenhaff, PL, Timmons, JA, and Sundberg, CJ. Systematic analysis of adaptations in aerobic capacity and submaximal energy metabolism provides a unique insight into determinants of human aerobic performance. *J Appl Physiol (1985)* 106:1479-1486, 2009.

177. Weltman, A, Stamford, BA, and Fulco, C. Recovery from maximal effort exercise: Lactate disappearance and subsequent performance. *J Appl Physiol Respir Environ Exerc Physiol* 47:677-682, 1979.

178. Weyand, PG, and Bundle, MW. Energetics of high-speed running: Integrating classical theory and contemporary

observations. *Am J Physiol Regul Integr Comp Physiol* 288:R956-965, 2005.

179. Weyand, PG, Lin, JE, and Bundle, MW. Sprint performance-duration relationships are set by the fractional duration of external force application. *Am J Physiol Regul Integr Comp Physiol* 290:R758-765, 2006.

180. Whipp, BJ, Higgenbotham, MB, and Cobb, FC. Estimating exercise stroke volume from asymptotic oxygen pulse in humans. *J Appl Physiol (1985)* 81:2674-2679, 1996.

181. Wisløff, U, and Helgerud, J. Methods for evaluating peak oxygen uptake and anaerobic threshold in upper body of cross-country skiers. *Med Sci Sports Exerc* 30:963-970, 1998.

182. Zanin, M, Ranaweera, J, Darrall-Jones, J, Weaving, D, Till, K, and Roe, G. A systematic review of small sided games within rugby: Acute and chronic effects of constraints manipulation. *J Sports Sci* 39:1633-1660, 2021.

Chapter 15

1. Aagaard, P. Training-induced changes in neural function. *Exerc Sport Sci Rev* 31:61-67, 2003.

2. Aagaard, P, Simonsen, EB, Andersen, JL, Magnusson, P, and Dyhre-Poulsen, P. Increased rate of force development and neural drive of human skeletal muscle following resistance training. *J Appl Physiol* 93:1318-1326, 2002.

3. Abernethy, PJ, Thayer, R, and Taylor, AW. Acute and chronic responses of skeletal muscle to endurance and sprint exercise: A review. *Sports Med* 10:365-389, 1990.

4. Adrian, MJ, and Cooper, JM. Biomechanics of running. In *Biomechanics of Human Movement*. New York: WCB McGraw-Hill, 295-314, 1995.

5. Ae, M, Ito, A, and Suzuki, M. The men's 100 metres. *New Studies in Athletics* 7:47-52, 1992.

6. Alcaraz, PE, Carlos-Vivas, J, Oponjuru, BO, and Martínez-Rodríguez, A. The effectiveness of resisted sled training (RST) for sprint performance: A systematic review and meta-analysis. *Sports Med* 48:2143-2165, 2018.

7. Alexander, RM. Mechanics of skeleton and tendons. In *Handbook of Physiology: The Nervous System: Motor Control*. Brookhardt, JM, Mountcastle, VB, Brooks, VB, Greiger, SR, eds. Bethesda, MD: American Physiological Society, 17-42, 1981.

8. Alexander, RM. Walking, running, and hopping. In *Principles of Animal Locomotion*. Princeton, NJ: Princeton Union Press, 103-145, 2002.

9. Allemeier, CA, Fry, AC, Johnson, P, Hikida, RS, Hagerman, FC, and Staron, RS. Effects of sprint cycle training on human skeletal muscle. *J Appl Physiol* 77:2385-2390, 1994.

10. Andersen, JL, Klitgaard, H, Bangsbo, J, and Saltin, B. Myosin heavy chain isoforms in single fibres from m. vastus lateralis of soccer players: Effects of strength-training. *Acta Physiol Scand* 150:21-26, 1994.

11. Andersen, JL, Klitgaard, H, and Saltin, B. Myosin heavy chain isoforms in single fibres from m. vastus lateralis of sprinters: Influence of training. *Acta Physiol Scand* 151:135-142, 1994.

12. Andersen, LL, and Aagaard, P. Influence of maximal muscle strength and intrinsic muscle contractile properties on contractile rate of force development. *Eur J Appl Physiol* 96:46-52, 2006.

13. Andersen, LL, Andersen, JL, Zebis, MK, and Aagaard, P. Early and late rate of force development: Differential adaptive responses to resistance training? *Scand J Med Sci Sports* 20:e162-e169, 2010.

14. Andre, MJ, Fry, AC, and Lane, MT. Appropriate loads for peak-power during resisted sprinting on a non-motorized treadmill. *J Hum Kinet* 38:161-167, 2013.

15. Baker, D, and Nance, S. The relation between running speed and measures of strength and power in professional Rugby League players. *J Strength Cond Res* 13:230-235, 1999.

16. Baker, DG, and Newton, RU. Comparison of lower body strength, power, acceleration, speed, agility, and sprint momentum to describe and compare playing rank among professional Rugby League players. *J Strength Cond Res* 22:153-158, 2008.

17. Balsom, PD, Seger, JY, Sjodin, B, and Ekblom, B. Maximal-intensity intermittent exercise: Effect of recovery duration. *Int J Sports Med* 13:528-533, 1992.

18. Balsom, PD, Seger, JY, Sjodin, B, and Ekblom, B. Physiological responses to maximal intensity intermittent exercise. *Eur J Appl Physiol* 65:144-149, 1992.

19. Bangsbo, J. The physiology of soccer—with special reference to intense intermittent exercise. *Acta Physiol Scand Suppl* 619:1-155, 1994.

20. Barnes, JL, Schilling, BK, Falvo, MJ, Weiss, LW, Creasy, AK, and Fry, AC. Relationship of jumping and agility performance in female volleyball athletes. *J Strength Cond Res* 21:1192-1196, 2007.

21. Barr, MJ, Sheppard, JM, Agar-Newman, DJ, and Newton, RU. Transfer effect of strength and power training to the sprinting kinematics of international rugby players. *J Strength Cond Res* 28:2585-2596, 2014.

22. Beato, M, Drust, B, and Iacono, AD. Implementing high-speed running and sprinting training in professional soccer. *Int J Sports Med* 42:295-299, 2021.

23. Benz, A, Winkelman, N, Porter, J, and Nimphius, S. Coaching instructions and cues for enhancing sprint performance. *Strength Cond J* 38:1-11, 2016.

24. Berman, Y, and North, KN. A gene for speed: The emerging role of alpha-actinin-3 in muscle metabolism. *Physiology (Bethesda)* 25:250-259, 2010.

25. Berthoin, S, Dupont, G, Mary, P, and Gerbeaux, M. Predicting sprint kinematic parameters from anaerobic field tests in physical education students. *J Strength Cond Res* 15:75-80, 2001.

26. Bezodis, NE, Walton, SP, and Nagahara, R. Understanding the track and field sprint start through a functional analysis of the external force features which contribute to higher levels of block phase performance. *J Sports Sci* 37:560-567, 2019.

27. Bezodis, NE, Willwacher, S, and Salo, AIT. The biomechanics of the track and field sprint start: A narrative review. *Sports Med* 49:1345-1364, 2019.

28. Bilsborough, JC, and Cabrera, M. Football. In *Science and Application of High-Intensity Interval Training*. Laursen, PB, Buchheit, M, eds. Champaign, IL: Human Kinetics, 379-392, 2019.

29. Blickhan, R. The spring-mass model for running and hopping. *J Biomech* 22:1217-1227, 1989.
30. Bloomfield, J, Polman, R, and O'Donoghue, P. Physical demands of different positions in FA Premier League soccer. *J Sports Sci Med* 6:63-70, 2007.
31. Bloomfield, J, Polman, R, O'Donoghue, P, and McNaughton, L. Effective speed and agility conditioning methodology for random intermittent dynamic type sports. *J Strength Cond Res* 21:1093-1100, 2007.
32. Bobbert, M, and Casius, LJR. Is the effect of a countermovement on jump height due to active state development? *Med Sci Sports Exerc* 37:440-446, 2005.
33. Bogdanis, GC, Nevill, ME, Boobis, LH, and Lakomy, HK. Contribution of phosphocreatine and aerobic metabolism to energy supply during repeated sprint exercise. *J Appl Physiol* 80:876-884, 1996.
34. Bompa, TO, and Buzzichelli, CA. Speed and agility training. In *Periodization: Theory and Methodology of Training*. 6th ed. Champaign, IL: Human Kinetics, 301-324, 2019.
35. Bompa, TO, and Haff, GG. Speed and agility. In *Periodization: Theory and Methodology of Training*. 5th ed. Champaign, IL: Human Kinetics, 315-342, 2009.
36. Born, P, and GER, TV. Video analysis and video feedback in tennis: Using mobile devices to benefit digital teaching and learning. *Coaching & Sport Science Review* 75:29-30, 2018.
37. Bottinelli, R. Functional heterogeneity of mammalian single muscle fibres: Do myosin isoforms tell the whole story? *Pflugers Arch* 443:6-17, 2001.
38. Bottinelli, R, Canepari, M, Pellegrino, MA, and Reggiani, C. Force-velocity properties of human skeletal muscle fibres: Myosin heavy chain isoform and temperature dependence. *J Physiol* 495:573-586, 1996.
39. Bottinelli, R, Pellegrino, MA, Canepari, M, Rossi, R, and Reggiani, C. Specific contributions of various muscle fibre types to human muscle performance: An in vitro study. *J Electromyogr Kinesiol* 9:87-95, 1999.
40. Brady, CJ, Harrison, AJ, Flanagan, EP, Haff, GG, and Comyns, TM. The relationship between isometric strength and sprint acceleration in sprinters. *Int J Sports Physiol Perform* 15:38-45, 2020.
41. Bret, C, Rahmani, A, Dufour, AB, Messonnier, L, and Lacour, JR. Leg strength and stiffness as ability factors in 100 m sprint running. *J Sports Med Phys Fitness* 42:274-281, 2002.
42. Bubbs, M. Leadership and great coaching. In *Peak: The New Science of Athletic Performance That Is Revolutionizing Sports*. London: Chelsea Green Publishing, 297-318, 2019.
43. Buchheit, M, and Laursen, PB. Traditional methods of HIIT programming. In *Science and Application of High-Intensity Interval Training*. Laursen, PB, Buchheit, M, eds. Champaign, IL: Human Kinetics, 17-33, 2019.
44. Bundle, MW, Hoyt, RW, and Weyand, PG. High-speed running performance: A new approach to assessment and prediction. *J Appl Physiol (1985)* 95:1955-1962, 2003.
45. Burke, R. Motor units: Anatomy, physiology, and functional organization. *Compr Physiol*:345-422, 2011.
46. Cadefau, J, Casademont, J, Grau, JM, Fernandez, J, Balaguer, A, Vernet, M, Cusso, R, and Urbano-Marquez, A. Biochemical and histochemical adaptation to sprint training in young athletes. *Acta Physiol Scand* 140:341-351, 1990.
47. Calvo, M, Rodas, G, Vallejo, M, Estruch, A, Arcas, A, Javierre, C, Viscor, G, and Ventura, JL. Heritability of explosive power and anaerobic capacity in humans. *Eur J Appl Physiol* 86:218-225., 2002.
48. Carpentier, A, Duchateau, J, and Hainaut, K. Velocity dependent muscle strategy during plantarflexion in humans. *J Electromyogr Kinesiol* 6:225-233, 1996.
49. Castillo-Rodriguez, A, Fernandez-Garcia, JC, Chinchilla-Minguet, JL, and Carnero, EA. Relationship between muscular strength and sprints with changes of direction. *J Strength Cond Res* 26:725-732, 2012.
50. Chelly, SM, and Denis, C. Leg power and hopping stiffness: Relationship with sprint running performance. *Med Sci Sports Exerc* 33:326-333, 2001.
51. Chiu, LZ, and Schilling, BK. A primer on weightlifting: From sport to sports training. *Strength and Cond J* 27:42-48, 2005.
52. Clark, KP, and Weyand, PG. Are running speeds maximized with simple-spring stance mechanics? *J Appl Physiol (1985)* 117:604-615, 2014.
53. Cleather, DJ. Force-vector theory. In *Force: The Biomechanics of Training*. Prague, Czech Republic: KMA Press, 69-74, 2021.
54. Comfort, P, Bullock, N, and Pearson, SJ. A comparison of maximal squat strength and 5-, 10-, and 20-meter sprint times, in athletes and recreationally trained men. *J Strength Cond Res* 26:937-940, 2012.
55. Comfort, P, Stewart, A, Bloom, L, and Clarkson, B. Relationships between strength, sprint, and jump performance in well-trained youth soccer players. *J Strength Cond Res* 28:173-177, 2014.
56. Conley, M. Bioenergetics of exercise training. In *Essentials of Strength Training and Conditioning*. 2nd ed. Baechle, TR, Earle, RW, eds. Champaign, IL: Human Kinetics, 73-90, 2000.
57. Contreras, B, Vigotsky, AD, Schoenfeld, BJ, Beardsley, C, McMaster, DT, Reyneke, JH, and Cronin, JB. Effects of a six-week hip thrust vs. front squat resistance training program on performance in adolescent males: a randomized controlled trial. *J Strength Cond Res* 31:999-1008, 2017.
58. Cormie, P, McGuigan, MR, and Newton, RU. Developing maximal neuromuscular power: Part 2—training considerations for improving maximal power production. *Sports Med* 41:125-146, 2011.
59. Cormier, P, Freitas, TT, Rubio-Arias, JA, and Alcaraz, PE. Complex and contrast training: Does strength and power training sequence affect performance-based adaptations in team sports? A systematic review and meta-analysis. *J Strength Cond Res* 34:1461-1479, 2020.
60. Costill, DL, Daniels, J, Evans, W, Fink, W, Krahenbuhl, G, and Saltin, B. Skeletal muscle enzymes and fiber composition in male and female track athletes. *J Appl Physiol* 40:149-154, 1976.

61. Costill, DL, Fink, WJ, and Pollock, ML. Muscle fiber composition and enzyme activities of elite distance runners. *Med Sci Sports* 8:96-100, 1976.
62. Cottle, CA, Carlson, LA, and Lawrence, MA. Effects of sled towing on sprint starts. *J Strength Cond Res* 28:1241-1245, 2014.
63. Cronin, JB, and Hansen, KT. Strength and power predictors of sports speed. *J Strength Cond Res* 19:349-357, 2005.
64. Cross, MR, Samozino, P, Brown, SR, and Morin, JB. A comparison between the force-velocity relationships of unloaded and sled-resisted sprinting: Single vs. multiple trial methods. *Eur J Appl Physiol* 118:563-571, 2018.
65. Dalleau, G, Belli, A, Bourdin, M, and Lacour, JR. The spring-mass model and the energy cost of treadmill running. *Eur J Appl Physiol Occup Physiol* 77:257-263, 1998.
66. Davies, G, Riemann, BL, and Manske, R. Current concepts of plyometric exercise. *Int J Sports Phys Ther* 10:760-786, 2015.
67. Dawson, B, Fitzsimons, M, Green, S, Goodman, C, Carey, M, and Cole, K. Changes in performance, muscle metabolites, enzymes and fibre types after short sprint training. *Eur J Appl Physiol* 78:163-169, 1998.
68. Delecluse, C. Influence of strength training on sprint running performance: Current findings and implications for training. *Sports Med* 24:147-156, 1997.
69. Delecluse, CH, Van Coppenolle, H, Willems, E, Diels, R, Goris, M, Van Leemputte, M, and Vuylsteke, M. Analysis of 100 m sprint performance as a multi-dimensional skill. *Journal of Human Movement Studies* 28:87-101, 1995.
70. Dempsey, AR, Lloyd, DG, Elliott, BC, Steele, JR, and Munro, BJ. Changing sidestep cutting technique reduces knee valgus loading. *Am J Sports Med* 37:2194-2200, 2009.
71. DeWeese, BH, and Nimphius, S. Program design and technique for speed and agility training. In *Essentials of Strength Training and Conditioning*. 4th ed. Haff, GG, Triplett, NT, eds. Champaign, IL: Human Kinetics, 521-548, 2016.
72. Dick, FW. Theory and practice of speed development. In *Sports Training Principles*. 5th ed. London: A and C Black, 255-270, 2007.
73. Dietz, V, Schmidtbleicher, D, and Noth, J. Neuronal mechanisms of human locomotion. *J Neurophysiol* 42:1212-1222, 1979.
74. Dillman, CJ. Kinematic analyses of running. *Exerc Sport Sci Rev* 3:193-218, 1975.
75. Dos'Santos, T, McBurnie, A, Thomas, C, Comfort, P, and Jones, PA. Biomechanical comparison of cutting techniques: A review and practical applications. *Strength Cond J* 41:40-54, 2019.
76. Dos'Santos, T, Thomas, C, Comfort, P, and Jones, PA. The effect of angle and velocity on change of direction biomechanics: An angle-velocity trade-off. *Sports Med* 48:2235-2253, 2018.
77. Duffield, R, Dawson, B, and Goodman, C. Energy system contribution to 100-m and 200-m track running events. *J Sci Med Sport* 7:302-313, 2004.
78. Duthie, G, Pyne, D, and Hooper, S. Applied physiology and game analysis of Rugby Union. *Sports Med* 33:973-991, 2003.
79. Dutto, DJ, and Smith, GA. Changes in spring-mass characteristics during treadmill running to exhaustion. *Med Sci Sports Exerc* 34:1324-1331, 2002.
80. Dyal, A. Using expert modeling and video feedback to improve starting block execution with track and field sprinters. Thesis. Tampa, FL: University of South Florida, 2016.
81. Esbjornsson, M, Hellsten-Westing, Y, Balsom, PD, Sjodin, B, and Jansson, E. Muscle fibre type changes with sprint training: Effect of training pattern. *Acta Physiol Scand* 149:245-246, 1993.
82. Farley, CT, and Gonzalez, O. Leg stiffness and stride frequency in human running. *J Biomech* 29:181-186, 1996.
83. Ferguson, BS, Rogatzki, MJ, Goodwin, ML, Kane, DA, Rightmire, Z, and Gladden, LB. Lactate metabolism: Historical context, prior misinterpretations, and current understanding. *Eur J Appl Physiol* 118:691-728, 2018.
84. Fitzpatrick, DA, Cimadoro, G, and Cleather, DJ. The magical horizontal force muscle? A preliminary study examining the "force-vector" theory. *Sports (Basel)* 7, 2019.
85. Francis, C. *Structure of Training for Speed*. CharlieFrancis.com, 2008.
86. Francis, C, and Coplon, J. *Speed Trap: Inside the Biggest Scandal in Olympic History*. New York: St. Martin's Press, 1991.
87. Francis, C, and Patterson, P. Planning and periodization. In *The Charlie Francis Training System*. Ottawa, Ontario: TBLI Publications, 75-93, 1992.
88. Freeman, WH. Periodized training for sprinters and hurdles. In *Peak When It Counts: Periodization for American Track & Field*. 4th ed. Mountain View, CA: Tafnews Press, 106-119, 2001.
89. Fry, AC, and Kraemer, WJ. Physical performance characteristics of American collegiate football players. *J Appl Sport Sci Res* 5:126-138, 1991.
90. Fry, AC, Schilling, BK, Staron, RS, Hagerman, FC, Hikida, RS, and Thrush, JT. Muscle fiber characteristics and performance correlates of male Olympic-style weightlifters. *J Strength Cond Res* 17:746-754, 2003.
91. Gabbett, T, Kelly, J, Ralph, S, and Driscoll, D. Physiological and anthropometric characteristics of junior elite and sub-elite Rugby League players, with special reference to starters and non-starters. *J Sci Med Sport* 12:215-222, 2009.
92. Gabbett, TJ. Physiological and anthropometric characteristics of amateur Rugby League players. *Br J Sports Med* 34:303, 2000.
93. Gabbett, TJ. Physiological characteristics of junior and senior Rugby league players. *Br J Sports Med* 36:334-339, 2002.
94. Gabbett, TJ. Sprinting patterns of national Rugby League competition. *J Strength Cond Res* 26:121-130, 2012.
95. Gabbett, TJ, Kelly, JN, and Sheppard, JM. Speed, change of direction speed, and reactive agility of Rugby League players. *J Strength Cond Res* 22:174-181, 2008.
96. García-Valverde, A, Manresa-Rocamora, A, Hernández-Davó, JL, and Sabido, R. Effect of weightlifting training on jumping ability, sprinting performance and squat strength: A systematic review and meta-analysis. *Int J Sports Sci Coach* 17:917-939, 2022.

97. Gimenez, JV, Jimenez-Linares, L, Leicht, AS, and Gomez, MA. Predictive modelling of the physical demands during training and competition in professional soccer players. *J Sci Med Sport* 23:603-608, 2020.

98. Girard, O, Mendez-Villanueva, A, and Bishop, D. Repeated-sprint ability—part I: Factors contributing to fatigue. *Sports Med* 41:673-694, 2011.

99. Gleason, BH, Kramer, JB, and Stone, MH. Agility training for American football. *Strength Cond J* 37:65-71, 2015.

100. Gollhofer, A, Schopp, A, Rapp, W, and Stroinik, V. Changes in reflex excitability following isometric contraction in humans. *Eur J Appl Physiol Occup Physiol* 77:89-97, 1998.

101. Gollnick, PD, Armstrong, RB, Saubert, CW, Piehl, K, and Saltin, B. Enzyme activity and fiber composition in skeletal muscle of untrained and trained men. *J Appl Physiol* 33:312-319, 1972.

102. Goodwin, J, Tawiah-Dodoo, J, Waghorn, R, and Wild, J. Sprint running. In *Routledge Handbook of Strength and Conditioning*. Turner, A, ed. New York: Routledge, 473-505, 2018.

103. Goodwin, JE, and Cleather, DJ. The biomechanical basis of training. In *Strength and Conditioning for Sports Performance*. 2nd ed. Jeffreys, I, Moody, J, eds. New York: Routledge, 61-86, 2021.

104. Gottlieb, GL, Agarwal, GC, and Jaeger, RJ. Response to sudden torques about ankle in man. IV: A functional role of alpha-gamma linkage. *J Neurophysiol* 46:179-190, 1981.

105. Gravina, L, Gil, SM, Ruiz, F, Zubero, J, Gil, J, and Irazusta, J. Anthropometric and physiological differences between first team and reserve soccer players aged 10-14 years at the beginning and end of the season. *J Strength Cond Res* 22:1308-1314, 2008.

106. Haff, GG. Quantifying workloads in resistance training: A brief review. *Prof Strength and Cond* 10:31-40, 2010.

107. Haff, GG. Periodization and power integration. In *Developing Power*. McGuigan, M, ed. Champaign, IL: Human Kinetics, 33-62, 2017.

108. Haff, GG. The essentials of periodisation. In *Strength and Conditioning for Sports Performance*. 2nd ed. Jeffreys, I, Moody, J, eds. Abingdon, Oxon: Routledge, 394-444, 2021.

109. Haff, GG. Periodization and programming of individual sports. In *NSCA's Essentials of Sport Science*. French, D, Torres Ronda, L, eds. Champaign, IL: Human Kinetics, 27-42, 2022.

110. Haff, GG, and Haff, EE. Training integration and periodization. In *Strength and Conditioning Program Design*. Hoffman, J, ed. Champaign, IL: Human Kinetics, 209-254, 2012.

111. Haff, GG, Kraemer, WJ, O'Bryant, HS, Pendlay, G, Plisk, S, and Stone, MH. Roundtable discussion: Periodization of training—part 2. *NSCA J* 26:56-70, 2004.

112. Haff, GG, and Nimphius, S. Training principles for power. *Strength Cond J* 34:2-12, 2012.

113. Haff, GG, Stone, MH, O'Bryant, HS, Harman, E, Dinan, CN, Johnson, R, and Han, KH. Force-time dependent characteristics of dynamic and isometric muscle actions. *J Strength Cond Res* 11:269-272, 1997.

114. Haff, GG, Whitley, A, and Potteiger, JA. A brief review: Explosive exercises and sports performance. *Strength Cond J* 23:13-20, 2001.

115. Häkkinen, K. Neuromuscular adaptations during strength training, aging, detraining, and immobilization. *Crit Rev Physic Rehab Med* 6:161-198, 1994.

116. Häkkinen, K, and Komi, PV. Changes in electrical and mechanical behavior of leg extensor muscles during heavy resistance strength training. *Scand J Sports Sci* 7:55-64, 1985.

117. Häkkinen, K, Komi, PV, and Alen, M. Effect of explosive type strength training on isometric force- and relaxation-time, electromyographic and muscle fibre characteristics of leg extensor muscles. *Acta Physiol Scand* 125:587-600, 1985.

118. Hall, MM, Rajasekaran, S, Thomsen, TW, and Peterson, AR. Lactate: Friend or foe. *PM&R* 8:S8-S15, 2016.

119. Harber, M, and Trappe, S. Single muscle fiber contractile properties of young competitive distance runners. *J Appl Physiol* 105:629-636, 2008.

120. Hargreaves, M, McKenna, MJ, Jenkins, DG, Warmington, SA, Li, JL, Snow, RJ, and Febbraio, MA. Muscle metabolites and performance during high-intensity, intermittent exercise. *J Appl Physiol* 84:1687-1691, 1998.

121. Harper, DJ, Carling, C, and Kiely, J. High-intensity acceleration and deceleration demands in elite team sports competitive match play: A systematic review and meta-analysis of observational studies. *Sports Med* 49:1923-1947, 2019.

122. Harridge, SD, Bottinelli, R, Canepari, M, Pellegrino, M, Reggiani, C, Esbjornsson, M, Balsom, PD, and Saltin, B. Sprint training, in vitro and in vivo muscle function, and myosin heavy chain expression. *J Appl Physiol* 84:442-449, 1998.

123. Haugen, T, McGhie, D, and Ettema, G. Sprint running: From fundamental mechanics to practice—a review. *Eur J Appl Physiol* 119:1273-1287, 2019.

124. Haugen, T, Seiler, S, Sandbakk, O, and Tønnessen, E. The training and development of elite sprint performance: An integration of scientific and best practice literature. *Sports Med Open* 5:44, 2019.

125. Haugen, T, Tønnessen, E, Hisdal, J, and Seiler, S. The role and development of sprinting speed in soccer. *Int J Sports Physiol Perform* 9:432-441, 2014.

126. Herda, TJ, and Cramer, JT. Bioenergetics of exercise and training. In *Essentials of Strength Training and Conditioning*. 4th ed. Haff, GG, Triplett, N, eds. Champaign, IL: Human Kinetics, 43-63, 2016.

127. Hirvonen, J, Rehunen, S, Rusko, H, and Harkonen, M. Breakdown of high-energy phosphate compounds and lactate accumulation during short supramaximal exercise. *Eur J Appl Physiol* 56:253-259, 1987.

128. Hori, N, Newton, RU, Andrews, WA, Kawamori, N, McGuigan, MR, and Nosaka, K. Does performance of hang power clean differentiate performance of jumping, sprinting, and changing of direction? *J Strength Cond Res* 22:412-418, 2008.

129. Hrysomallis, C. The effectiveness of resisted movement training on sprinting and jumping performance. *J Strength Cond Res* 26:299-306, 2012.

130. İnce, İ. Effects of split style Olympic weightlifting training on leg stiffness vertical jump change of direction and

131. Issurin, V. Block periodization versus traditional training theory: A review. *J Sports Med Phys Fitness* 48:65-75, 2008.
132. Issurin, VB. New horizons for the methodology and physiology of training periodization. *Sports Med* 40:189-206, 2010.
133. Jacobs, I, Esbjornsson, M, Sylven, C, Holm, I, and Jansson, E. Sprint training effects on muscle myoglobin, enzymes, fiber types, and blood lactate. *Med Sci Sports Exerc* 19:368-374, 1987.
134. Jansson, E, Esbjornsson, M, Holm, I, and Jacobs, I. Increase in the proportion of fast-twitch muscle fibres by sprint training in males. *Acta Physiol Scand* 140:359-363, 1990.
135. Jarvis, P, Turner, A, Read, P, and Bishop, C. Reactive strength index and its associations with measures of physical and sports performance: A systematic review with meta-analysis. *Sports Med* 52:301-330, 2022.
136. Jeffreys, I. The nature of speed. In *Developing Speed*. Jeffreys, I, ed. Champaign, IL: Human Kinetics, 1-18, 2013.
137. Jeffreys, I. RAMP warm-ups: More than simply short-term preparation. *Prof Strength Cond* 44:17-23, 2017.
138. Jeffreys, I. The raise phase. In *The Warm-Up: Maximise Performance and Improve Long-Term Athlete Development*. Champaign, IL: Human Kinetics, 27-52, 2019.
139. Jeffreys, I, Huggins, S, and Davies, N. Delivering a gamespeed-focused speed and agility development program in an English Premier League soccer academy. *Strength Cond J* 40:23-32, 2018.
140. Jonhagen, S, Ericson, MO, Nemeth, G, and Eriksson, E. Amplitude and timing of electromyographic activity during sprinting. *Scand J Med Sci Sports* 6:15-21, 1996.
141. Karcher, C, and Buchheit, M. On-court demands of elite handball, with special reference to playing positions. *Sports Med* 44:797-814, 2014.
142. Keller, TS, Weisberger, AM, Ray, JL, Hasan, SS, Shiavi, RG, and Spengler, DM. Relationship between vertical ground reaction force and speed during walking, slow jogging, and running. *Clin Biomech (Bristol, Avon)* 11:253-259, 1996.
143. Komi, P. Neuromuscular performance: Factors influencing force and speed production. *Scand J Sports Sci* 1:2-15, 1979.
144. Komi, PV. Training of muscle strength and power: Interaction of neuromotoric, hypertrophic, and mechanical factors. *Int J Sports Med* 7:10-15, 1986.
145. Komi, PV. Stretch-shortening cycle: A powerful model to study normal and fatigued muscle. *J Biomech* 33:1197-1206, 2000.
146. Komi, PV. Stretch-shortening cycle. In *Strength and Power in Sport*. 2nd ed. Komi, PV, ed. Oxford, UK: Blackwell Science, 184-202, 2003.
147. Komi, PV, and Nicol, C. Stretch–shortening cycle of muscle function. In *Neuromuscular Aspects of Sport Performance*. Komi, PV, ed. Chichester, West Sussex: Wiley-Blackwell, 15-31, 2011.
148. Korhonen, MT, Cristea, A, Alen, M, Hakkinen, K, Sipila, S, Mero, A, Viitasalo, JT, Larsson, L, and Suominen, H. Aging, muscle fiber type, and contractile function in sprint-trained athletes. *J Appl Physiol* 101:906-917, 2006.
149. Kraemer, WJ, and Looney, DP. Underlying mechanisms and physiology of muscular power. *Strength Cond J* 34:13-19, 2012.
150. Kurz, T. Speed. In *Science of Sports Training*. 2nd ed. Island Pond, VT: Stadion Publishing, 179-194, 2001.
151. Kyröläinen, H, Komi, PV, and Belli, A. Changes in muscle activity patterns and kinetics with increasing speed. *J Strength Cond Res* 13:400-406, 1999.
152. Laursen, PB, and Jenkins, DG. The scientific basis for high-intensity interval training: Optimising training programmes and maximising performance in highly trained endurance athletes. *Sports Med* 32:53-73, 2002.
153. Lentz, D, and Hardyk, A. Speed training. In *Training for Speed, Agility, and Quickness*. 2nd ed. Brown, LE, Ferrigno, VA, eds. Champaign, IL: Human Kinetics, 17-70, 2005.
154. Leyva, WD, Wong, MA, and Brown, LE. Resisted and assisted training for sprint speed: A brief review. *Journal of Physical Fitness, Medicine & Treatment in Sports* 1:555554, 2017.
155. Liljedahl, ME, Holm, I, Sylven, C, and Jansson, E. Different responses of skeletal muscle following sprint training in men and women. *Eur J Appl Physiol* 74:375-383, 1996.
156. Lim, JJH, and Barley, CI. Complex training for power development: Practical applications for program design. *Strength Cond J* 38:33-43, 2016.
157. Linnamo, V, Häkkinen, K, and Komi, PV. Neuromuscular fatigue and recovery in maximal compared to explosive strength loading. *Eur J Appl Physiol Occup Physiol* 77:176-181, 1998.
158. Linossier, MT, Denis, C, Dormois, D, Geyssant, A, and Lacour, JR. Ergometric and metabolic adaptation to a 5-s sprint training programme. *Eur J Appl Physiol* 67:408-414, 1993.
159. Linossier, MT, Dormois, D, Geyssant, A, and Denis, C. Performance and fibre characteristics of human skeletal muscle during short sprint training and detraining on a cycle ergometer. *Eur J Appl Physiol* 75:491-498, 1997.
160. Linossier, MT, Dormois, D, Perier, C, Frey, J, Geyssant, A, and Denis, C. Enzyme adaptations of human skeletal muscle during bicycle short-sprint training and detraining. *Acta Physiol Scand* 161:439-445, 1997.
161. Little, T, and Williams, AG. Specificity of acceleration, maximum speed, and agility in professional soccer players. *J Strength Cond Res* 19:76-78, 2005.
162. Lizana, JA, Bachero-Mena, B, Calvo-Lluch, A, Sanchez-Moreno, M, Pereira, LA, Loturco, I, and Pareja-Blanco, F. Do faster, stronger, and more powerful athletes perform better in resisted sprints? *J Strength Cond Res* 36:1826-1832, 2022.
163. Lloyd, RS, Oliver, JL, Hughes, MG, and Williams, CA. Reliability and validity of field-based measures of leg stiffness and reactive strength index in youths. *J Sports Sci* 27:1565-1573, 2009.
164. Locatelli, E. The importance of anaerobic glycolysis and stiffness in the sprints (60, 100, 200 metres). *N Stud Athletics* 11:121-125, 1996.

165. Lockie, RG, Murphy, AJ, Knight, TJ, and de Jonge, XAKJ. Factors that differentiate acceleration ability in field sport athletes. *J Strength Cond Res* 25:2704-2714, 2011.

166. Loturco, I, Contreras, B, Kobal, R, Fernandes, V, Moura, N, Siqueira, F, Winckler, C, Suchomel, T, and Pereira, LA. Vertically and horizontally directed muscle power exercises: Relationships with top-level sprint performance. *PLoS One* 13:e0201475, 2018.

167. Lovell, DI, Cuneo, R, and Gass, GC. The effect of strength training and short-term detraining on maximum force and the rate of force development of older men. *Eur J Appl Physiol* 109:429-435, 2010.

168. Lum, D, Haff, GG, and Barbosa, TM. The relationship between isometric force-time characteristics and dynamic performance: A systematic review. *Sports* 8:63, 2020.

169. Ma, F, Yang, Y, Li, X, Zhou, F, Gao, C, Li, M, and Gao, L. The association of sport performance with ACE and ACTN3 genetic polymorphisms: A systematic review and meta-analysis. *PLoS One* 8:e54685, 2013.

170. Macadam, P, Cronin, JB, and Simperingham, KD. The effects of Wearable resistance training on metabolic, kinematic and kinetic variables during walking, running, sprint running and jumping: A systematic review. *Sports Med* 47:887-906, 2017.

171. Macadam, P, Cronin, JB, Uthoff, AM, and Feser, EH. Effects of different wearable resistance placements on sprint-running performance: A review and practical applications. *Strength Cond J* 41:79-96, 2019.

172. MacArthur, DG, and North, KN. A gene for speed? The evolution and function of alpha-actinin-3. *Bioessays* 26:786-795, 2004.

173. MacDougall, JD, Hicks, AL, MacDonald, JR, McKelvie, RS, Green, HJ, and Smith, KM. Muscle performance and enzymatic adaptations to sprint interval training. *J Appl Physiol* 84:2138-2142, 1998.

174. Mackala, K. Optimisation of performance through kinematic analysis of the different phases of the 100 metres. *New Studies in Athletics* 22:7, 2007.

175. Mann, JB, Ivey, PA, Mayhew, JL, Schumacher, RM, and Brechue, WF. Relationship between agility tests and short sprints: Reliability and smallest worthwhile difference in National Collegiate Athletic Association Division I football players. *J Strength Cond Res* 30:893-900, 2016.

176. Mann, R, and Murphy, A. *The Mechanics of Sprinting and Hurdling*. Lexington, KY: CreateSpace, 2018.

177. Mann, RV, and Murphy, A. Critical general performance descriptors for the short sprint at maximal velocity. In *The Mechanics of Sprinting and Hurdling*. Scotts Valley, CA: CreateSpace Independent Publishing Platform, 144-152, 2018.

178. Mann, RV, and Murphy, A. Understanding the sprint performance. In *The Mechanics of Sprinting and Hurdling*. Scotts Valley, CA: CreateSpace Independent Publishing Platform, 60-97, 2018.

179. Markovic, G, and Mikulic, P. Neuro-musculoskeletal and performance adaptations to lower-extremity plyometric training. *Sports Med* 40:859-895, 2010.

180. Markwick, WJ, Bird, SP, Tufano, JJ, Seitz, LB, and Haff, GG. The intraday reliability of the reactive strength index (RSI) calculated from a drop jump in professional men's basketball. *Int J Sports Physiol Perform* 10:482-488, 2015.

181. Marshall, BM, Franklyn-Miller, AD, King, EA, Moran, KA, Strike, SC, and Falvey, ÉC. Biomechanical factors associated with time to complete a change of direction cutting maneuver. *J Strength Cond Res* 28:2845-2851, 2014.

182. Marshall, J, Bishop, C, Turner, A, and Haff, GG. Optimal training sequences to develop lower body force, velocity, power, and jump height: A systematic review with meta-analysis. *Sports Med* 51:1245-1271, 2021.

183. Martinez-Valencia, MA, Romero-Arenas, S, Elvira, JL, Gonzalez-Rave, JM, Navarro-Valdivielso, F, and Alcaraz, PE. Effects of sled towing on peak force, the rate of force development and sprint performance during the acceleration phase. *J Hum Kinet* 46:139-148, 2015.

184. Mattes, K, Wolff, S, and Alizadeh, S. Kinematic stride characteristics of maximal sprint running of elite sprinters: Verification of the "swing-pull technique". *J Hum Kinet* 77:15-24, 2021.

185. Maughan, R, and Gleeson, M. The sprinter. In *The Biochemical Basis of Sports Performance*. 2nd ed. New York: Oxford University Press, 74-98, 2010.

186. McBride, JM, Blow, D, Kirby, TJ, Haines, TL, Dayne, AM, and Triplett, NT. Relationship between maximal squat strength and five, ten, and forty yard sprint times. *J Strength Cond Res* 23:1633-1636, 2009.

187. McBride, JM, Triplett-McBride, T, Davie, A, and Newton, RU. A comparison of strength and power characteristics between power lifters, Olympic lifters, and sprinters. *J Strength Cond Res* 13:58-66, 1999.

188. McBride, JM, Triplett-McBride, T, Davie, A, and Newton, RU. The effect of heavy- vs. light-load jump squats on the development of strength, power, and speed. *J Strength Cond Res* 16:75-82, 2002.

189. McCormick, BT, Hannon, JC, Hicks-Little, CA, Newton, M, Shultz, B, Detling, N, and Young, WB. The relationship between change of direction speed in the frontal plane, power, reactive strength, and strength. *Int J Exerc Sci* 7:260-270, 2014.

190. McKenna, MJ, Harmer, AR, Fraser, SF, and Li, JL. Effects of training on potassium, calcium and hydrogen ion regulation in skeletal muscle and blood during exercise. *Acta Physiol Scand* 156:335-346, 1996.

191. Meckel, Y, Atterbom, H, Grodjinovsky, A, Ben-Sira, D, and Rotstein, A. Physiological characteristics of female 100 metre sprinters of different performance levels. *J Sports Med Phys Fitness* 35:169-175, 1995.

192. Menezes, GB, Oliveira, RS, Ferreira, ABM, Assis, TVL, Batista, ES, Oliver, JL, Lloyd, RS, and Mortatti, AL. Does motor coordination influence perceptual-cognitive and physical factors of agility in young soccer players in a sport-specific agility task? *Sports Biomech*:1-14, 2021.

193. Mense, S. Nervous outflow from skeletal muscle following chemical noxious stimulation. *J Physiol* 267:75-88, 1977.

194. Mero, A, and Komi, PV. Effects of supramaximal velocity on biomechanical variables in sprinting. *Int J Sport Biomech* 1:240-252, 1985.

195. Mero, A, Komi, PV, and Gregor, RJ. Biomechanics of sprint running: A review. *Sports Med* 13:376-392, 1992.

196. Mero, A, Luhtanen, P, Viitasalo, JT, and Komi, PV. Relationships between maximal running velocity, muscle fiber characteristics, force production and force relaxation of sprinters. *Scand J Sports Sci* 3:16-22, 1981.
197. Mero, A, and Peltola, E. Neural activation fatigued and non-fatigued conditions of short and long sprint running. *Biol Sport* 6:43-58, 1989.
198. Metzger, JM, and Moss, RL. pH modulation of the kinetics of a Ca2(+)-sensitive cross-bridge state transition in mammalian single skeletal muscle fibres. *J Physiol* 428:751-764, 1990.
199. Moir, G, Sanders, R, Button, C, and Glaister, M. The effect of periodized resistance training on accelerative sprint performance. *Sports Biomech* 6:285-300, 2007.
200. Moran, J, Ramirez-Campillo, R, Liew, B, Chaabene, H, Behm, DG, Garcia-Hermoso, A, Izquierdo, M, and Granacher, U. Effects of bilateral and unilateral resistance training on horizontally orientated movement performance: A systematic review and meta-analysis. *Sports Med* 51:225-242, 2021.
201. Morin, JB. Speed training. In *High-Performance Training for Sports*. Joyce, D, Lweindon, D, eds. Champaign, IL: Human Kinetics, 149-162, 2022.
202. Murach, K, Raue, U, Wilkerson, B, Minchev, K, Jemiolo, B, Bagley, J, Luden, N, and Trappe, S. Single muscle fiber gene expression with run taper. *PLoS One* 9:e108547, 2014.
203. Murphy, AJ, Lockie, RG, and Coutts, AJ. Kinematic determinants of early acceleration in field sport athletes. *J Sports Sci and Med* 2:144-150, 2003.
204. Murray, A, Aitchison, TC, Ross, G, Sutherland, K, Watt, I, McLean, D, and Grant, S. The effect of towing a range of relative resistances on sprint performance. *J Sports Sci* 23:927-935, 2005.
205. Naczk, M, Naczk, A, Brezenczek-Owczarzak, W, Arlet, J, and Adach, Z. Relationship between maximal rate of force development and maximal voluntary contraction. *Studies in Physical Culture and Tourism* 17, 2010.
206. Newton, RU, and Kraemer, WJ. Developing explosive muscular power: Implications for a mixed methods training strategy. *Strength Cond J* 16:20-31, 1994.
207. Nicholson, B, Dinsdale, A, Jones, B, and Till, K. The training of short distance sprint performance in football code athletes: A systematic review and meta-analysis. *Sports Med* 51:1179-1207, 2021.
208. Nimphius, S. Agility training. In *High-Performance Training for Sports*. Joyce, D, Lweindon, D, eds. Champaign, IL: Human Kinetics, 181-196, 2022.
209. Nimphius, S, Callaghan, SJ, Bezodis, NE, and Lockie, RG. Change of direction and agility tests: Challenging our current measures of performance. *Strength Cond J* 40:26-38, 2018.
210. Nimphius, S, and Kadllec, D. Framework for different physical movements that relate to overarching change of direction ability. 2020. https://doi.org/10.6084/m9.figshare.11589486.v1.
211. Nummela, A, Rusko, H, and Mero, A. EMG activities and ground reaction forces during fatigued and nonfatigued sprinting. *Med Sci Sports Exerc* 26:605-609, 1994.
212. Okkonen, O, and Häkkinen, K. Biomechanical comparison between sprint start, sled pulling, and selected squat-type exercises. *J Strength Cond Res* 27:2662-2673, 2013.
213. Oxfeldt, M, Overgaard, K, Hvid, LG, and Dalgas, U. Effects of plyometric training on jumping, sprint performance, and lower body muscle strength in healthy adults: A systematic review and meta-analyses. *Scand J Med Sci Sports* 29:1453-1465, 2019.
214. Pandy, MG, Lai, AKM, Schache, AG, and Lin, YC. How muscles maximize performance in accelerated sprinting. *Scand J Med Sci Sports* 31:1882-1896, 2021.
215. Pardos-Mainer, E, Lozano, D, Torrontegui-Duarte, M, Carton-Llorente, A, and Roso-Moliner, A. Effects of strength vs. plyometric training programs on vertical jumping, linear sprint and change of direction speed performance in female soccer players: A systematic review and meta-analysis. *Int J Environ Res Public Health* 18:401, 2021.
216. Parra, J, Cadefau, JA, Rodas, G, Amigo, N, and Cusso, R. The distribution of rest periods affects performance and adaptations of energy metabolism induced by high-intensity training in human muscle. *Acta Physiologica Scandinavica* 169:157-165, 2000.
217. Paul, DJ, Gabbett, TJ, and Nassis, GP. Agility in team sports: Testing, training and factors affecting performance. *Sports Med* 46:421-442, 2016.
218. Penfold, L, and Jenkins, D. Training for speed. *Training for Speed and Endurance*:24-41, 1996.
219. Petrakos, G, Morin, J-B, and Egan, B. Resisted sled sprint training to improve sprint performance: A systematic review. *Sports Med* 46:381-400, 2016.
220. Pette, D. Training effects on the contractile apparatus. *Acta Physiol Scand* 162:367-376, 1998.
221. Pette, D, Peuker, H, and Staron, RS. The impact of biochemical methods for single muscle fibre analysis. *Acta Physiol Scand* 166:261-277, 1999.
222. Pette, D, and Staron, RS. Myosin isoforms, muscle fiber types, and transitions. *Microsc Res Tech* 50:500-509., 2000.
223. Pickering, C, and Kiely, J. ACTN3: More than just a gene for speed. *Front Physiol* 8, 2017.
224. Pickering, C, Kiely, J, Grgic, J, Lucia, A, and Del Coso, J. Can genetic testing identify talent for sport? *Genes (Basel)* 10:972, 2019.
225. Plisk, SS. The angle on agility. *Training and Conditioning* 10:37-43, 2000.
226. Plisk, SS. Speed, agility, and speed-endurance development. In *Essentials of Strength Training and Conditioning*. 3rd ed. Baechle, TR, Earle, RW, eds. Champaign, IL: Human Kinetics, 2008.
227. Plisk, SS, and Gambetta, V. Tactical metabolic training: Part 1. *Strength Cond J* 19:44-53, 1997.
228. Racinais, S, Bishop, D, Denis, R, Lattier, G, Mendez-Villaneuva, A, and Perrey, S. Muscle deoxygenation and neural drive to the muscle during repeated sprint cycling. *Med Sci Sports Exerc* 39:268-274, 2007.
229. Radcliffe, JC. The programs. In *Functional Training for Athletes at All Levels*. Berkeley, CA: Ulysses Press, 27-58, 2007.
230. Ramirez-Campillo, R, Burgos, CH, Henriquez-Olguin, C, Andrade, DC, Martinez, C, Alvarez, C, Castro-Sepulveda,

M, Marques, MC, and Izquierdo, M. Effect of unilateral, bilateral, and combined plyometric training on explosive and endurance performance of young soccer players. *J Strength Cond Res* 29:1317-1328, 2015.

231. Ramirez-Campillo, R, Gentil, P, Negra, Y, Grgic, J, and Girard, O. Effects of plyometric jump training on repeated sprint ability in athletes: A systematic review and meta-analysis. *Sports Med* 51:2165-2179, 2021.

232. Rienzi, E, Drust, B, Reilly, T, Carter, JE, and Martin, A. Investigation of anthropometric and work-rate profiles of elite South American international soccer players. *J Sports Med Phys Fitness* 40:162-169, 2000.

233. Roberts, AD, Billeter, R, and Howald, H. Anaerobic muscle enzyme changes after interval training. *Int J Sports Med* 3:18-21, 1982.

234. Ross, A, and Leveritt, M. Long-term metabolic and skeletal muscle adaptations to short-sprint training: Implications for sprint training and tapering. *Sports Med* 31:1063-1082, 2001.

235. Ross, A, Leveritt, M, and Riek, S. Neural influences on sprint running: Training adaptations and acute responses. *Sports Med* 31:409-425, 2001.

236. Rumpf, MC, Lockie, RG, Cronin, JB, and Jalilvand, F. Effect of different sprint training methods on sprint performance over various distances: A brief review. *J Strength Cond Res* 30:1767-1785, 2016.

237. Saez de Villarreal, E, Requena, B, and Cronin, JB. The effects of plyometric training on sprint performance: A meta-analysis. *J Strength Cond Res* 26:575-584, 2012.

238. Sahlin, K. Muscle fatigue and lactic acid accumulation. *Acta Physiol Scand Suppl* 556:83-91, 1986.

239. Sale, DG. Neural adaptation to resistance training. *Med Sci Sports Exerc* 20:S135-S145, 1988.

240. Saplinskas, JS, Chobotas, MA, and Yashchaninas, II. The time of completed motor acts and impulse activity of single motor units according to the training level and sport specialization of tested persons. *Electromyogr Clin Neurophysiol* 20:529-539, 1980.

241. Schmidtbleicher, D. Strength training (part 1): Structural analysis of motor strength qualities and its application to training. *Sci Per Res Tech Sport: Phys Training/Strength* 4:1-12, 1985.

242. Schmidtbleicher, D. Strength training (part 2): Structural analysis of motor strength qualities and its application to training. *Sci Per Res Tech Sport: Phys Training/Strength* 5:1-10, 1985.

243. Schmidtbleicher, D. Training for power events. In *The Encyclopedia of Sports Medicine Vol 3: Strength and Power Sports*. Komi, PV, ed. Oxford: Blackwell, 169-179, 1992.

244. Schmolinsky, G. Walking and running. In *Track and Field: The East German Textbook of Athletics*. Toronto, Canada: Sports Book, 120-221, 2004.

245. Seitz, LB, Barr, M, and Haff, GG. Effects of sprint training with or without ball carry in elite rugby players. *Int J Sports Physiol Perform* 10:761-766, 2015.

246. Seitz, LB, and Haff, GG. Factors modulating post-activation potentiation of jump, sprint, throw and upper-body ballistic performances: A systematic review with meta-analysis. *Sports Med* 46:231-240, 2016.

247. Seitz, LB, Reyes, A, Tran, TT, de Villarreal, ES, and Haff, GG. Increases in lower-body strength transfer positively to sprint performance: A systematic review with meta-analysis. *Sports Med* 44:1693-1702, 2014.

248. Seitz, LB, Trajano, GS, and Haff, GG. The back squat and the power clean elicit different degrees of potentiation. *Int J Sports Physiol Perform* 9:643-649, 2014.

249. Serpell, BG, Young, WB, and Ford, M. Are the perceptual and decision-making components of agility trainable? A preliminary investigation. *J Strength Cond Res* 25:1240-1248, 2011.

250. Sheppard, J. The nature of speed. In *Developing Speed*. Jeffreys, I, ed. Champaign, IL: Human Kinetics, 19-30, 2013.

251. Sheppard, JM, Dawes, JJ, Jeffreys, I, Spiteri, T, and Nimphius, S. Broadening the view of agility: A scientific review of the literature. *Journal of Australian Strength and Conditioning* 22, 2014.

252. Sheppard, JM, and Young, WB. Agility literature review: Classifications, training and testing. *J Sports Sci* 24:919-932, 2006.

253. Shimokochi, Y, Ide, D, Kokubu, M, and Nakaoji, T. Relationships among performance of lateral cutting maneuver from lateral sliding and hip extension and abduction motions, ground reaction force, and body center of mass height. *J Strength Cond Res* 27:1851-1860, 2013.

254. Siff, MC. Biomechanical foundations of strength and power. In *Biomechanics in Sport*. Zatsiorsky, VM, ed. London: Blackwell Scientific, 103-139, 2001.

255. Simoneau, JA, Lortie, G, Boulay, MR, Marcotte, M, Thibault, MC, and Bouchard, C. Human skeletal muscle fiber type alteration with high-intensity intermittent training. *Eur J Appl Physiol Occup Physiol* 54:250-253, 1985.

256. Sinoway, LI, Hill, JM, Pickar, JG, and Kaufman, MP. Effects of contraction and lactic acid on the discharge of group III muscle afferents in cats. *J Neurophysiol* 69:1053-1059, 1993.

257. Slawinski, J, Bonnefoy, A, Levêque, J-M, Ontanon, G, Riquet, A, Dumas, R, and Chèze, L. Kinematic and kinetic comparisons of elite and well-trained sprinters during sprint start. *J Strength Cond Res* 24:896-905, 2010.

258. Slawinski, J, Termoz, N, Rabita, G, Guilhem, G, Dorel, S, Morin, JB, and Samozino, P. How 100-m event analyses improve our understanding of world-class men's and women's sprint performance. *Scand J Med Sci Sports* 27:45-54, 2017.

259. Spencer, M, Bishop, D, Dawson, B, and Goodman, C. Physiological and metabolic responses of repeated-sprint activities: Specific to field-based team sports. *Sports Med* 35:1025-1044, 2005.

260. Spiteri, T, Cochrane, JL, Hart, NH, Haff, GG, and Nimphius, S. Effect of strength on plant foot kinetics and kinematics during a change of direction task. *Eur J Sport Sci* 13:646-652, 2013.

261. Spiteri, T, Cochrane, JL, and Nimphius, S. The evaluation of a new lower-body reaction time test. *J Strength Cond Res* 27:174-180, 2013.

262. Spiteri, T, Hart, NH, and Nimphius, S. Offensive and defensive agility: A sex comparison of lower body

kinematics and ground reaction force. *J Appl Biomech* 30:514-520, 2014.

263. Spiteri, T, Newton, RU, Binetti, M, Hart, NH, Sheppard, JM, and Nimphius, S. Mechanical determinants of faster change of direction and agility performance in female basketball athletes. *J Strength Cond Res* 29:2205-2214, 2015.

264. Spiteri, T, and Nimphius, S. Relationship between timing variables and plant foot kinetics during change of direction movements. *Journal of Australian Strength and Conditioning* 21:73-77, 2013.

265. Spiteri, T, Nimphius, S, Hart, NH, Specos, C, Sheppard, JM, and Newton, RU. Contribution of strength characteristics to change of direction and agility performance in female basketball athletes. *J Strength Cond Res* 28:2415-2423, 2014.

266. Spiteri, T, Nimphius, S, and Wilkie, J. Comparison of running times during reactive offensive and defensive agility protocols. *Journal of Australian Strength and Conditioning* 20:73-78, 2012.

267. Spriet, LL, Lindinger, MI, McKelvie, RS, Heigenhauser, GJ, and Jones, NL. Muscle glycogenolysis and H+ concentration during maximal intermittent cycling. *J Appl Physiol* 66:8-13, 1989.

268. Stackhouse, SK, Reisman, DS, and Binder-Macleod, SA. Challenging the role of pH in skeletal muscle fatigue. *Phys Ther* 81:1897-1903, 2001.

269. Stone, MH. Literature review: Explosive exercises and training. *Natl Strength Cond Assoc J* 15:17-19, 1993.

270. Stone, MH, Sanborn, K, O'Bryant, HS, Hartman, M, Stone, ME, Proulx, C, Ward, B, and Hruby, J. Maximum strength-power-performance relationships in collegiate throwers. *J Strength Cond Res* 17:739-745, 2003.

271. Stone, MH, Stone, ME, and Sands, WA. Testing, measurement, and evaluation. In *Principles and Practice of Resistance Training*. Champaign, IL: Human Kinetics, 157-180, 2007.

272. Struzik, A, Karamanidis, K, Lorimer, A, Keogh, JWL, and Gajewski, J. Application of leg, vertical, and joint stiffness in running performance: A literature overview. *Appl Bionics Biomech* 2021:9914278, 2021.

273. Stulberg, S, and Magness, S. *Peak Performance*. New York: Rodale Books, 2017.

274. Suarez, DG, Wagle, JP, Cunanan, AJ, Sausaman, RW, and Stone, MH. Dynamic correspondence of resistance training to sport: A brief review. *Strength Cond J* 41:80-89, 2019.

275. Suchomel, TJ, McKeever, SM, and Comfort, P. Training with weightlifting derivatives: The effects of force and velocity overload stimuli. *J Strength Cond Res* 34:1808-1818, 2020.

276. Suchomel, TJ, Nimphius, S, and Stone, MH. The importance of muscular strength in athletic performance. *Sports Med* 46:1419-1449, 2016.

277. Sukop, J, and Nelson, R. Effect of isometric training on the force-time characteristics of muscle contraction. In *Biomechanics IV*. Nelson, RC, Morehouse, CA, eds. Baltimore, MD: University Park Press, 440-447, 1974.

278. Swinton, PA, Lloyd, R, Keogh, JW, Agouris, I, and Stewart, AD. Regression models of sprint, vertical jump and change of direction performance. *J Strength Cond Res* 28:1839-1848, 2014.

279. Tesch, PA, Wright, JE, Vogel, JA, Daniels, WL, Sharp, DS, and Sjödin, B. The influence of muscle metabolic characteristics on physical performance. *Eur J Appl Physiol Occup Physiol* 54:237-243, 1985.

280. Thomas, C, Comfort, P, Chiang, C, and Jones, PA. Relationship between isometric mid-thigh pull variables and sprint and change of direction performance in collegiate athletes. *J Trainology* 4:6-10, 2015.

281. Thomis, MA, Beunen, GP, Maes, HH, Blimkie, CJ, Van Leemputte, M, Claessens, AL, Marchal, G, Willems, E, and Vlietinck, RF. Strength training: Importance of genetic factors. *Med Sci Sports Exerc* 30:724-731, 1998.

282. Thorstensson, A, Karlsson, J, Viitasalo, JH, Luhtanen, P, and Komi, PV. Effect of strength training on EMG of human skeletal muscle. *Acta Physiol Scand* 98:232-236, 1976.

283. Thorstensson, A, Sjodin, B, and Karlsson, J. Enzyme activities and muscle strength after "sprint training" in man. *Acta Physiol Scand* 94:313-318, 1975.

284. Tomazin, K, Morin, JB, Strojnik, V, Podpecan, A, and Millet, GY. Fatigue after short (100-m), medium (200-m) and long (400-m) treadmill sprints. *Eur J Appl Physiol* 112:1027-1036, 2012.

285. Townsend, JR, Bender, D, Vantrease, W, Hudy, J, Huet, K, Williamson, C, Bechke, E, Serafini, P, and Mangine, GT. Isometric mid-thigh pull performance is associated with athletic performance and sprinting kinetics In Division I men and women's basketball players. *J Strength Cond Res* 33:2665-2673, 2019.

286. Trappe, S, Harber, M, Creer, A, Gallagher, P, Slivka, D, Minchev, K, and Whitsett, D. Single muscle fiber adaptations with marathon training. *J Appl Physiol* 101:721-727, 2006.

287. Trappe, S, Luden, N, Minchev, K, Raue, U, Jemiolo, B, and Trappe, TA. Skeletal muscle signature of a champion sprint runner. *J Appl Physiol (1985)* 118:1460-1466, 2015.

288. Turner, AN, Bishop, C, Cree, J, Carr, P, McCann, A, Bartholomew, B, and Halsted, L. Building a high-performance model for sport: A human development-centered approach. *Strength Cond J* 41:100-107, 2019.

289. Turner, AN, and Jeffreys, I. The stretch-shortening cycle: Proposed mechanisms and methods for enhancement. *Strength Cond J* 32:87-99, 2010.

290. Uthoff, A, Oliver, J, Cronin, J, Harrison, C, and Winwood, P. Sprint-specific training in youth: Backward running vs. forward running training on speed and power measures in adolescent male athletes. *J Strength Cond Res* 34:1113-1122, 2020.

291. Van Cutsem, M, Duchateau, J, and Hainaut, K. Changes in single motor unit behaviour contribute to the increase in contraction speed after dynamic training in humans. *J Physiol* 513:295-305, 1998.

292. van de Hoef, PA, Brauers, JJ, van Smeden, M, Backx, FJG, and Brink, MS. The effects of lower-extremity plyometric training on soccer-specific outcomes in adult male soccer players: A systematic review and meta-analysis. *Int J Sports Physiol Perform* 15:3-17, 2019.

293. van den Tillaar, R. Comparison of development of step-kinematics of assisted 60 m sprints with different pulling

294. Varley, MC, and Aughey, RJ. Acceleration profiles in elite Australian soccer. *Int J Sports Med* 34:34-39, 2013.

295. Vescovi, JD, and McGuigan, MR. Relationships between sprinting, agility, and jump ability in female athletes. *J Sports Sci* 26:97-107, 2008.

296. Vlahovich, N, Fricker, PA, Brown, MA, and Hughes, D. Ethics of genetic testing and research in sport: A position statement from the Australian Institute of Sport. *Br J Sports Med* 51:5-11, 2017.

297. Voigt, M, Bojsen-Moller, F, Simonsen, EB, and Dyhre-Poulsen, P. The influence of tendon Youngs modulus, dimensions and instantaneous moment arms on the efficiency of human movement. *J Biomech* 28:281-291, 1995.

298. von Lieres und Wilkau, HC, Irwin, G, Bezodis, NE, Simpson, S, and Bezodis, IN. Phase analysis in maximal sprinting: An investigation of step-to-step technical changes between the initial acceleration, transition and maximal velocity phases. *Sports Biomech* 19:141-156, 2020.

299. Wang, R, Hoffman, JR, Tanigawa, S, Miramonti, AA, La Monica, MB, Beyer, KS, Church, DD, Fukuda, DH, and Stout, JR. Isometric mid-thigh pull correlates with strength, sprint, and agility performance in collegiate Rugby Union players. *J Strength Cond Res* 30:3051-3056, 2016.

300. Webborn, N, Williams, A, McNamee, M, Bouchard, C, Pitsiladis, Y, Ahmetov, I, Ashley, E, Byrne, N, Camporesi, S, Collins, M, Dijkstra, P, Eynon, N, Fuku, N, Garton, FC, Hoppe, N, Holm, S, Kaye, J, Klissouras, V, Lucia, A, Maase, K, Moran, C, North, KN, Pigozzi, F, and Wang, G. Direct-to-consumer genetic testing for predicting sports performance and talent identification: Consensus statement. *Br J Sports Med* 49:1486-1491, 2015.

301. Wellman, AD, Coad, SC, Goulet, GC, and McLellan, CP. Quantification of competitive game demands of NCAA Division I college football players using global positioning systems. *J Strength Cond Res* 30:11-19, 2016.

302. Weston, AR, Myburgh, KH, Lindsay, FH, Dennis, SC, Noakes, TD, and Hawley, JA. Skeletal muscle buffering capacity and endurance performance after high-intensity interval training by well-trained cyclists. *Eur J Appl Physiol Occup Physiol* 75:7-13, 1997.

303. Weyand, PG, Sandell, RF, Prime, DN, and Bundle, MW. The biological limits to running speed are imposed from the ground up. *J Appl Physiol (1985)* 108:950-961, 2010.

304. Weyand, PG, Sternlight, DB, Bellizzi, MJ, and Wright, S. Faster top running speeds are achieved with greater ground forces not more rapid leg movements. *J Appl Physiol* 89:1991-1999, 2000.

305. Wheeler, KW, Askew, CD, and Sayers, MG. Effective attacking strategies in Rugby Union. *Eur J Sport Sci* 10:237-242, 2010.

306. Wild, JJ, Bezodis, IN, North, JS, and Bezodis, NE. Characterising initial sprint acceleration strategies using a whole-body kinematics approach. *J Sports Sci* 40:203-214, 2022.

307. Williams, AM, and Reilly, T. Talent identification and development in soccer. *J Sports Sci* 18:657-667, 2000.

308. Williamson, DL, Gallagher, PM, Carroll, CC, Raue, U, and Trappe, SW. Reduction in hybrid single muscle fiber proportions with resistance training in humans. *J Appl Physiol* 91:1955-1961, 2001.

309. Willwacher, S, Herrmann, V, Heinrich, K, Funken, J, Strutzenberger, G, Goldmann, JP, Braunstein, B, Brazil, A, Irwin, G, Potthast, W, and Bruggemann, GP. Sprint Start Kinetics of Amputee and Non-Amputee Sprinters. *PLoS One* 11:e0166219, 2016.

310. Winckler, G. An examination of speed endurance. *New Studies in Athletics* 61:27-33, 1991.

311. Winkelman, N. Cueing for training and performance. In *High-Performance Training for Sports*. Joyce, D, Lweindon, D, eds. Champaign, IL: Human Kinetics, 223-232, 2022.

312. Wisløff, U, Castagna, C, Helgerud, J, Jones, R, and Hoff, J. Strong correlation of maximal squat strength with sprint performance and vertical jump height in elite soccer players. *Br J Sports Med* 38:285-288, 2004.

313. Yang, N, MacArthur, DG, Gulbin, JP, Hahn, AG, Beggs, AH, Easteal, S, and North, K. ACTN3 genotype is associated with human elite athletic performance. *Am J Hum Genet* 73:627-631, 2003.

314. Young, W. Laboratory strength assessment of athletes. *N Stud Athletics* 10:89-96, 1995.

315. Young, W, Benton, D, Duthie, G, and Pryor, J. Resistance training for short sprints and maximum-speed sprints. *Strength Cond J* 23:7-13, 2001.

316. Young, W, and Farrow, D. The importance of a sport-specific stimulus for training agility. *Strength Cond J* 35:39-43, 2013.

317. Young, W, Hawken, M, and McDonald, L. Relationship between speed, agility and strength qualities in Australian rules football. *Strength Cond Coach* 4:3-6, 1996.

318. Young, W, McLean, B, and Ardagna, J. Relationship between strength qualities and sprinting performance. *J Sports Med Phys Fitness* 35:13-19, 1995.

319. Young, WB. Transfer of strength and power training to sports performance. *Int J Sports Physiol Perf* 1:74-83, 2006.

320. Young, WB, Dawson, B, and Henry, GJ. Agility and change-of-direction speed are independent skills: Implications for training for agility in invasion sports. *Int J Sports Sci Coach* 10:159-169, 2015.

321. Young, WB, James, R, and Montgomery, I. Is muscle power related to running speed with changes of direction? *J Sports Med Phys Fitness* 42:282-288, 2002.

322. Young, WB, McDowell, MH, and Scarlett, BJ. Specificity of sprint and agility training methods. *J Strength Cond Res* 15:315-319, 2001.

323. Zamparo, P, Minetti, AE, and di Prampero, PE. Interplay among the changes of muscle strength, cross-sectional area and maximal explosive power: Theory and facts. *Eur J Appl Physiol* 88:193-202, 2002.

324. Zatsiorsky, VM, Kraemer, WJ, and Fry, AC. Timing in strength training. In *Science and Practice of Strength Training*. 3rd ed. Champaign, IL: Human Kinetics, 79-98, 2021.

INDEX

Note: The italicized f and t following page numbers refer to figures and tables, respectively.

A

absolute density 82
acceleration 273, 404, 416
acceleration phase 408f, 408-409
accelerometers 272
accentuated eccentric loading (AEL) 372-373, 374f
accentuated loading 114
accumulated fatigue 15, 94, 217, 309-310
accumulated mechanical stress 272
accumulation mesocycle block 115-116, 153, 155t
acetyl coenzyme A 36-37
active recovery 32, 189, 222, 395
active rest 136, 138
active warm-up 182-183
activity logs 245
Acute Recovery and Stress Scale (ARSS) 292
acute to chronic workload ratio (ACWR) 297-298
acute training effects 77
acute workload (AWL) 297
acyclic combined skills 52
acyclic skills 52
adaptation(s)
   definition of 7
   factors that affect 22f, 202f
   fatigue and 230
   individualized nature of 9
   intensity of training and 87
   in long-term athlete development 420
   morphological 344, 345f, 346
   neurological 344-346, 345f
   neuromuscular 345, 350
   overload. *See* overload
   performance capacity and 7
   physical training for 56, 58
   physiological stress and 5
   psychological stress and 5
   resistance training 344-346, 345f
   reversibility of 13
   scientific principles and 4
   specificity 12-13
   stimulation of 56, 58, 77, 109
   training loads for 6, 90-91, 113
   training stimuli for 3, 7f, 8f
   variation 10-12
   volume of training and 87
adaptive potential 77
adenosine diphosphate (ADP) 26-27, 27f, 203
adenosine monophosphate (AMP) 27, 27f
adenosine triphosphatase (ATPase) 26
adenosine triphosphate (ATP)
   aerobic energy systems as source of 46, 46f
   anaerobic energy systems as source of 45f, 45-46, 46f
   chemical structure of 27f
   description of 17, 26
   energy systems and 28-29, 38, 38t
   fatigue caused by depletion of 39
   intensity of training and 83
   for maximal efforts lasting 15 to 60 seconds 41t, 43
   muscular stores of 83
   phosphocreatine and 28
   repletion of 39, 217
   skeletal muscle storage of 26-27
   sprinting effects on 405, 410
   sprint training use of 45-46
   substrates for 35
adrenocorticotropic hormone (ACTH) 288
advanced athletes 120, 132, 164, 218, 364
advanced daily undulating (ADUP) model 380
aerobic endurance 48-49, 123t
aerobic energy systems 28, 46, 46f, 47f, 48f
aerobic training 31, 49, 86t, 247
aftereffects 22, 23f
age 14, 81, 129, 191, 218, 326
agility
   change of direction ability 424-425
   components of 426f
   development of 429-431
   importance of 404
   in long-term athlete development 425
   open-skill 426
   overview of 424-425
   perceptual–cognitive speed effects on 425-426
   physiological considerations of 428-429
   reactive drills 426
   training sessions that develop 188
agility training
   cueing in 430-431
   density of 431
   discipline in 431
   duration of 431
   emphasis training model application to 436f, 436-437
   exercise order in 433
   fatigue in 433
   feedback in 431
   frequency of 431
   instruction in 430-431
   intensity of 432, 434
   motivation in 431
   multifactorial development in 430
   periodization models applied to 434-437
   periodized training plan for 437
   programming of 429-434
   rest intervals in 433-434
   sequential training model application to 435, 435f
   sessions 431
   technical precision in 429-430
   volume of 432-433
alarm phase, of general adaptive syndrome 20, 20f
all-out sprinting 392
alpha-actinin-3 77, 411
aminoacidemia 252
amino acids 37-38, 238, 240t, 241, 249
ammonia 38
amylopectin 237
amylose 237
anabolic trigger 241
anabolic window 246-247
anabolism 26, 26f, 215
anaerobic capacity 42
anaerobic endurance 123t
anaerobic energy systems 28, 35, 45f, 45-46, 46f, 47f, 48f
anaerobic peak power 388
anaerobic power reserve (APR) 388-390, 389f
anaerobic speed reserve (ASR) 85, 388-390, 389f
anaerobic sports 49
anaerobic training 31, 39, 44
anaerobic work capacity (W') 393
animal polysaccharides 237

annual training plans. *See also* training plans
  accumulation mesocycle in 158*f*
  benchmark testing integrated into 304-305, 305*f*
  bi-cycle 140*f*, 142*f*, 142-144, 143*f*
  classification of 138-139
  competition period of 133-135, 143-145, 324-328
  construction of 148-150, 149*t*
  definition of 130
  general preparation phase of 131, 132*f*, 133*f*, 138
  goals of 149
  macrocycles in 130-135, 132*f*, 133*f*, 142-144, 149
  main competition phase of 134-135
  Matveyev's classic model of 139*f*
  mesocycle design from 152
  microcycle in 400
  monitoring program integration into 304-305, 305*f*
  mono-cycle 139-142, 140*f*, 141*f*
  multiyear training plan and 149
  peaking strategies 313
  precompetition phase of 134
  preparation period of 131-133, 132*f*, 143, 145
  realization mesocycle in 158*f*
  specific preparation phase of 131-133, 132*f*, 133*f*
  sport-specific structure of 437
  sprint training 437, 437*f*
  for team sports 110, 139, 437, 438*f*
  transition period of. *See* transition period
  transmutation mesocycle in 158*f*
  tri-cycle 140*f*, 144*f*, 144-145
anthropometric characteristics 14
artificial intelligence 299
artificial neural networks (ANNs) 274, 300, 319-321, 320*f*
ascending cluster set 370, 370*t*, 371*f*
ascending pyramid pattern 365-366, 366*f*
assessment training sessions 180
assistance exercise 363
assisted sprint training 418*t*, 418-419, 419*t*
asymptote 393
athlete(s). *See also* advanced athletes; elite athletes; novice athletes
  carbohydrate requirements for 238, 240*t*
  current health status of 90
  current training status of 191
  current work capacity of 14
  fitness level of 14, 191
  genetic endowment of 4, 4*f*
  individual anaerobic threshold of 86
  maximal heart rate of 85-86
  monitoring of 267-268
  performance capacity of 4*f*, 4-5
  protein requirements for 240-241, 241*f*
  psychological state of 14
  rate of development of 148
  training age of 14, 81, 191
  training history of 14
  training load determination for 6-7
  training volume affected by 80
athlete development
  long-term. *See* long-term athlete development (LATD)
  training day based on level of 182
  volume of training and 80
Australian Institute of Sport 297
autonomic nervous system (ANS) 284
autoregulation 328

B

ballistic resistance training 338, 339*f*, 348, 349*t*, 416
banned substances 253
benchmark testing 304-305, 305*f*
bench press 359*f*
beta-oxidation 31, 37
bi-cycle annual training plans 140*f*, 142*f*, 142-144, 143*f*
big data technological stack 64, 65*f*
biochemical assessments 286-287
bioenergetic limiters
  for explosive events lasting less than 2 seconds 41
  for maximal efforts lasting 12 to 15 seconds 41*t*, 41-42
  phosphagens as 40
bioenergetics
  adenosine diphosphate in 26-27, 27*f*
  adenosine triphosphate in 26, 38
  definition of 26
  in sprint events 431
  systems 28*f*
bioenergetic specificity 12, 46-49, 48*t*
biomotor abilities 52-55, 53*f*, 54*f*
biomotor ability 11, 11*f*
block complex model 116, 117*f*
block complex variational model 116, 117*f*
block-emphasis model 121-124
block periodization 110, 115-118, 116*f*, 117*f*, 118*f*, 152, 217, 322, 377, 399
block training 115-118, 116*f*, 117*f*, 118*f*, 377-378, 437. *See also* training blocks
blood lactate 30-35, 34*f*, 43, 394
blood sugar. *See* glucose
body composition 245-246, 304
Bondarchuk, Anatoliy 57-58, 58*f*, 112*f*, 115-116, 117*f*, 152-153, 154*f*
Borg CR-10 scale 280, 360-361
branched-chain amino acids (BCAAs) 38, 250
breathing exercises 189
Brunel Mood Scale (BRUMES) 290
build-up mesocycles 156-157

C

calcium 17, 190
carbohydrates
  athlete requirements for 238, 240*t*
  in beverages 250
  complex 237
  during-training supplementation of 249-251
  glycemic index of 238
  monosaccharides 236
  muscle damage prevention using 251
  oligosaccharides 237
  oxidation of 36, 250
  polysaccharides 237
  postexercise consumption of 40, 217, 251-252
  posttraining supplementation of 251-252
  pretraining supplementation of 247-249
  protein and 250-252
  resistance training use of 247-248, 250
casein protein 242, 252
catabolic phase 17
catabolism 26, 26*f*, 215
cell-mediated immunity 216
central fatigue 17, 191, 203-204
central governor model, of fatigue 15
change of direction ability (COD)
  arms in 428
  description of 404, 424-425
  emphasis training model for 436-437
  factors that affect 426-428
  high-intensity interval training based on 390-392, 400
  leg muscle qualities that affect 427
  linear speed in 426-427
  maneuverability. *See* maneuverability
  maximal strength in 335, 427
  physical movements related to 428, 428*f*
  physiological considerations of 428-429
  reactive strength in 427
  sequential periodization model for developing 435
  speed in 426-427
  technique 427-428, 428*f*
children, training programs for 13-14
chronic workload (CWL) 297
chronological age 129, 326
chronotype 219
chunking 52
circadian rhythms 218
clinical low energy availability 245*t*
closed-skill sport 51-52
cluster sets 369*f*, 369-372, 370*f*, 371*f*, 372*f*
coach 324, 327, 430
cognitive effort 62

cold packs 225
cold-water immersion (CWI) 224-228, 230-231
combined training sessions 180
competition
    classification of 324-325
    coach's role in 324
    congested schedules 328, 331*f*
    exhibition 324-325
    fluid requirements 243-244
    frequency of 326-328
    in individual sports 324, 326
    multiple 325
    peaking performance for 321-322
    planning for 325-326
    priming session on day of 195
    principal 324
    in regular, repeating intervals 325-326
    rehydration after 244
    sleep patterns affected by 222
    sodium loss during 243
    in team sports 324-325
    training days between 65
    training load for 324
    training purposes of 324-325
competition microcycle 163, 174, 231, 232*f*, 329*f*, 330*f*, 331
competition period
    in annual training plan 133-135, 143-145, 324-328
    goals during 231
    length of 326
    mesocycles for 152, 155, 157
    microcycles for 161, 162*f*, 170
    recovery methods in 231, 232*f*
    training load for 133, 328
    two-peak microcycle in 167, 171*f*
competitive performance 63, 195, 312-313
complementary training factors 122, 123*f*
complex carbohydrates 237
complex pair 188
complex training models 111-112, 112*f*
complex variational training model 111-114, 112*f*
compression garments 229, 231
concentrated loading 96-100, 97*f*, 110, 114, 115*f*, 207
concentrated unidirectional training model 115
conditionally essential amino acids 240
congested competition schedules 328, 331*f*
conjugated sequential loading models 118-119, 119*f*, 120*f*, 379-380
conjugate sequence 379, 380*t*
conscientiousness 69-70
contractile proteins 238
contrast water therapy (CWT) 226, 228
cool-down 189*f*, 189-190, 222
core exercises 363
cortisol 15, 97-98, 288

coupled successive system 118
courage 69
CR-10 scale 280, 360-361
creatine kinase 224, 287
creatine supplementation 42
critical power (CP) 393
critical velocity (CV) 393
crossbridge cycling 29
cross-sectional area of muscle 344, 350
cryostimulation (CRY) 224-225
cryotherapy 224-225
cueing 430-431
cumulative training effects 77
current health status 90
current work capacity 14
cyclic skills 52
cycling
    biomotor ability for 53
    heart rate monitoring in 86
    maximal aerobic speed and power for 387
    power-based training zones in 86, 87*t*
    power meters used in 271
cytochromes 36
cytokines 289
cytokine theory of overtraining 216

D

Daily Analysis of Life Demands for Athletes (DALDA) 215, 292
daily undulating periodization (DUP) 375
decision making, monitoring-based 302*f*
dehydration 243-244
delayed onset muscle soreness (DOMS) 17-18, 190
delayed recovery 217
delayed training effects 77-78, 78*f*, 162, 207, 309, 310*f*
deliberate environment 70
deliberate practice 61
descending cluster set 370, 370*t*, 371*f*
detraining
    description of 6, 9, 13, 18
    long-term 136, 137*t*
    passive rest as cause of 135
    short-term 136, 137*t*
    transition period and 135-139, 137*f*
detraining load 91
detraining syndrome 135-136
developmental mesocycle 115-116
diaries 289-293
dietary supplements 253-255, 254*f*
direct-to-consumer genetic tests 411
discipline 431
docosahexaenoic acid (DHA) 242
double pyramid loading pattern 366*f*, 366-367
double-shock microcycle 162-163
double stimulation loading pattern 368, 368*f*
double sugars 237

dual X-ray absorptiometry (DXA) 245-246
during-training period 249-251
dynamic correspondence principle 12, 420-422, 422*t*
dynamic external pneumatic compression 229
dynamic strength–endurance 55
dynamic stretching 184
dynamic warm-up 184, 184*f*

E

eccentric braking loads 428
eicosapentaenoic acid (EPA) 242
electrocardiogram (ECG) 284
electrolytes 243-244
elite athletes 6, 9, 113, 127, 168*f*, 318, 403, 406-407
emphasis training model
    agility development application of 436*f*, 436-437
    block-emphasis 121-124
    description of 120-121
    high-intensity interval training and 399-400
    mesocycles in 439-440, 440*f*
    parallel-emphasis 121
    resistance training uses of 381*f*
    sample 121
    speed development application of 435-436, 436*f*
    sports for 125
    sprint training application of 435-436, 436*f*
    strength training uses of 380-382
    for team sports 438-439, 439*f*
    vertical integration model 121-122, 435
endergonic reaction 26, 26*f*
endurance
    as biomotor ability 52-55, 53*f*, 54*f*
    high-intensity exercise 59-60
    locomotor profile 390, 390*f*, 390*t*
    low-intensity exercise 59
    speed and 336*f*
    strength and 336*f*. *See also* strength–endurance
    training sessions that develop 188
endurance athletes
    high-volume overtraining risks in 209
    muscle fibers in 343-344
    sauna benefits for 226
    sequential periodization model for 398
    short-term detraining effects on 136
endurance capacity
    maximal strength benefits for 336
    training methods to develop 59
endurance sports
    energy systems used in 41*t*, 43
    training factors integrated into mesocycle for 161*f*
    volume of training in 133

endurance training
  aerobic 48-49
  carbohydrate supplementation benefits for 249
  resting energy metabolism after 18
  running economy affected by 60
energetic profile of sport 12
energy 25-26
energy availability (EA) 245t, 245-246
energy expenditure (EE) 244
energy intake (EI) 244-246
energy systems
  adenosine triphosphate production 28-29, 38, 38t
  aerobic 28
  anaerobic 28
  for endurance events lasting up to 40 minutes 41t, 43
  for explosive events lasting less than 2 seconds 41, 41t
  glycolysis. See glycolysis
  interrelationship of 45-46
  for long-distance events lasting several hours 41t, 43-44
  for maximal efforts lasting 15 to 60 seconds 41t, 42-43
  for maximal efforts lasting 12 to 15 seconds 41t, 41-42
  for maximal efforts lasting up to 6 minutes 41t, 43
  oxidative system. See oxidative system
  phosphagen (ATP-PC) system 28-29, 38
  rapid 28
  in sprinting 409, 423-424
Entlastungssyndrom 135
essential amino acids 240-241
essential fatty acids 242
euhydration 243-244
excellence 70
excessive training load 8, 8f
excess postexercise oxygen consumption (EPOC) 18, 44-45, 83, 217
excitation–contraction coupling 29, 203
exercise(s)
  adenosine triphosphate use during 27
  aerobic contributions to 44-45
  anaerobic contributions to 44-45
  assistance 363
  carbohydrate consumption after 40, 217
  carbohydrate supplementation during 249-251
  core 363
  eccentric muscle actions in 17
  explosive 363
  foam rolling after 223-224
  force-generating capacity after 18
  general preparatory 112, 113t
  glucose uptake during 17
  in high-intensity interval training 392-394

multijoint 363, 373
muscle damage secondary to 18
order of 363, 433
oxygen consumption after 18, 44
power 363
preparedness affected by 23
rebound hyperglycemia during 247
recovery after 17-18
resistance training 363
resting energy metabolism after 18
single-joint 363
sodium loss during 243
specialized developmental 58f, 59, 113t
specialized preparatory 58f, 59, 113t
structural 363
exercise abstinence syndrome 135
exercise dependency syndrome 135
exercise energy expenditure (EEE) 244
exercise-induced fatigue 15, 17, 222
exercising, training versus 4
exergonic reaction 26, 26f
exhibition competitions 324-325
expectation maximization algorithm 64
exploitation 4-6
explosive exercises 363
explosive strength 340, 415
exponential taper 314
external pneumatic compression 229
external training load
  description of 76, 76f, 269-270
  internal load and, integration of 271
  monitoring of 271-280
  neuromuscular function 274-276, 275f
  power meters for measuring 271-272
  power output 271-272
  in resistance training 269
  time-motion analysis 272-273
  variables in 270t

F

fast exponential taper 314
fast glycolysis 28-35, 43, 83
fast-twitch muscle fibers 28, 343
fat(s)
  classification of 242
  definition of 242
  monounsaturated 242
  oxidation of 37
  partially hydrogenated 242
  polyunsaturated 242
  saturated 242
  trans 242-243
  unsaturated 242
fat free mass (FFM) 245-246
fatigue
  accumulated 94, 217, 309-310
  adaptations and 230
  adenosine triphosphate depletion as cause of 39
  aftereffects of 23
  in agility training 433

central 17, 191, 203-204, 405
cognitive effort as cause of 62
contributing factors 405
definition of 203
exercise-induced 15, 17, 222
exercise task and 204
in fitness–fatigue model 22-23
general preparation phase as cause of 131
lactic acid effects on 17, 29
manifestations of 190
mediators of 204
mental 191, 220
in metabolic acidosis 29-30
metabolites induced by 410-411
negative effects of 22
neural 414
neuromuscular 213
neurotransmitter alterations caused by 191
overreaching and 205, 206f
overtraining and 205, 206f
performance capacity affected by 131
peripheral 15, 29-30, 190-191, 203-204, 405, 414
physical training levels and 56
preparedness and 145, 317, 374
recovery and 204-205, 205f
rest interval manipulation for 19
shock microcycle as cause of 162
in speed training 433
in sport-specific training 88
strategies for dealing with 191
stress and 204-205, 205f
taper for management of 309, 311f
training load and 19, 22
travel 218, 219f
volume of training as cause of 87-89
fat-soluble vitamins 242
fatty acids 43, 242
fiber 237
Finnish sauna 225
fitness aftereffects 22-23
fitness–fatigue model 22-23, 23f, 374
5-point peaking index 146, 146t
flat loaded target set 365, 365f
flat loading 93-94, 94f, 100
flavin adenine dinucleotide (FADH2) 36
flight time to contraction time ratio (FT:CT) 213, 274
fluid consumption 244
fluid requirements 243-244
foam roller/rolling 223-224, 231
food 239t, 240
force 414-415. See also rate of force development
force-generating capacity 18, 338, 340, 344-345
force–power relationship 341-342
force–time curve
  isometric 212, 212f, 274, 275f, 340f, 341f, 416f

force–time curve *(continued)*
  vertical jump performance 213
force–vector theory 420
force–velocity relationships
  description of 338-341
  graph of 338*f*
  power output and 341
  weightlifting and 339, 340*f*
forecasting 107
Foster 0-10 scale 280, 280*f*
Francis, Charlie 121-122, 435
free fatty acids 37
fructose 236, 239*t*
functional overreaching (FOR) 207, 207*f*
functional threshold power 86
FUNdamental training 129

G

gait cycle 52
galactose 236
Galen 106
game-based high-intensity interval training 384-385, 388, 394
game speed 404
game theory 107
general adaptive syndrome 20*f*, 20-22, 21*f*, 205, 206*f*
general physical training (GPT) 56-60, 57*f*, 58*f*, 131-132
general preparation phase 131, 133*f*, 138
general preparatory exercises 112, 113*t*
general training age 129
general warm-up 184, 184*f*
genetic ceiling 4
genetic endowment 4, 4*f*
Geometric Activity Performance Index (GAPI) 300
global strength–endurance 55
gluconeogenesis 32, 37, 236
glucose 17, 36, 236, 239*t*
glucose transporter-4 (GLUT4) 17, 247
glutamate 287
glutamine 287
glycemic index (GI) 237-238, 239*t*
glycogen
  body storage of 237, 247
  branching of 237
  depletion of 39-40, 40*f*, 43
  description of 15, 17
  during-training levels of 249
  galactose storage as 236
  intramyofibrillar 203
  muscle concentrations of 39-40, 43, 247-248
  performance benefits of 238
  postexercise recovery of 18, 40, 217
  pretraining 247
  repletion of 39-40, 251
  resynthesis of 251
  skeletal muscle storage of 39
  in sprint performance 410
  synthesis of 237

glycogenolysis 39, 237, 410
glycogen synthase 40
glycolysis
  definition of 29
  fast. *See* fast glycolysis
  glucose in 36
  slow 28-29, 35
glycolytic flux 29, 41-42, 405, 410-411
glycolytic system 29, 30*f*, 410
Golgi tendon organ 343
GPS 63, 80, 85, 245, 272-273, 273*t*
graded exercise tests 85
grit 69-70, 70*f*
ground contact time 407, 416
ground reaction forces 420, 421*f*, 423
grouping approach 325
group training sessions 178*f*, 178-179
guanine triphosphate (GTP) 36
"Gymnasticus" 106
gyroscopes 272

H

Halson, Shona 293, 295
handouts 182
heart rate
  high-intensity interval training programming using 387-388
  maximal 85-86
  monitoring of 282-285
  rating of perceived exertion and 280, 282-284
  workload and 85
heart rate monitoring 85
heart rate recovery (HRR) 284
heart rate variability (HRV) 284-285
heavy resistance training 338-339, 339*f*, 343, 345, 416
hemoglobin 183, 217
Henneman's size principle 342
heteropolysaccharide 237
high-demand microcycles 167, 170*f*
high energy availability 245*t*
high-frequency competition periods 328-332
high glycemic index 238
high-intensity exercise
  adenosine triphosphate use during 27-28
  anaerobic energy systems for 45
  carbohydrates for 35
  fast glycolysis in 43
  glycogen as energy source for 39
  heart rate:rating of perceived exertion scale ratio 283
  lactate accumulation after 31
  phosphocreatine repletion after 39
high-intensity exercise endurance (HIEE) 59-60
high-intensity interval training (HIIT)
  anaerobic peak power 388
  anaerobic power reserve 388-390, 389*f*

  anaerobic speed reserve 388-390, 389*f*
  anaerobic work capacity 393
  benefits of 49
  calibration methods for 385
  change of direction-based 390-392, 400
  critical power 393
  critical velocity 393
  definition of 49, 60
  emphasis models and 399-400
  exercise duration in 392-393
  exercise intensity in 392
  exercise modality in 393-394
  factors that affect 397*f*
  game-based 384-385, 388, 394
  heart rate-based prescription of 387-388
  high-intensity exercise endurance development using 60
  history of 383-384
  hydrogen ion concentrations affected by 411
  lactate accumulation after 31, 34-35
  long interval 384
  maximal aerobic power for 386-387
  maximal aerobic speed for 386-387
  maximal sprinting speed 388-389, 389*f*
  microcycle integration of 400
  ordering of training for 194
  periodization models and 398-400
  periodized training plan integration of 398-400
  program considerations for 396-398, 397*f*
  rating of perceived exertion approach 386
  recovery period in 394-396
  run-based 393-394
  series of intervals in 395-396
  sessions 396
  short interval 384
  small-sided game 35
  sport-specific design of 396-398, 397*f*
  team sport approach 388, 394
  30-15 intermittent fitness test 390-392
  total volume in 396
  track-and-field approach 385-386
  variables in 385*f*
  variables used for programming of 392-396
  work performed in 396
high-intensity overtraining 210*f*, 210-211, 215
high-intensity training 19*f*
high-speed running 273, 400
high-volume overtraining 209-210
hip thrust 421*f*
homopolysaccharide 237
horizontal sequencing 79
hormonal assessments 286-289
hot–cold contrast therapy 226

hot-water immersions (HWI) 225-226, 228
Hron, Josef 383-384
humoral immunity 216
hydration 243-244
hydrogen 41t, 42
hydrostatic pressure 226-227
hydrotherapy 226-228
hyperglycemia, rebound 247
hyperhydration 243
hypertrophy
   description of 114, 246, 344
   maximal strength effects of 344
   as morphological adaptation 346
   resistance training for 344, 349t, 351
   sets for 354
   timing of 344
   training loads for 351
   training to failure for 351
hypohydration 243
hyponatremia 244

I

ice bags 225
iceberg profile 290
ice massage 225
immediate training effects 77
immune system 248-249
immunoglobulin A 289
immunological assessments 289
immunology 216
immunoproteins 238
impulse 415-417
individual anaerobic threshold (IAS) 86
individualization, of training programs 13-14
individual sports
   coaches in 327
   competitions in 324, 326
   microcycles for 172f
   monitoring program for 296
   sleep patterns in 221
   team sports versus 321
   training sessions for 178f, 179
inertial measurement units (IMUs) 63
injury
   acute to chronic workload ratio and 297
   protein intake during 241
   psychological stress and 14
   training load and 6, 8-9, 56
inorganic phosphate (P_i) 26, 27f, 29, 203
interexercise recovery 217
interleukin-1β 289
interleukin-6 289
intermediate athletes 120
intermuscular task specificity 12-13
internal training load
   description of 76f, 76-77, 85
   external load and, integration of 271
   factors that affect 270
   measurements of 270-271
   monitoring of. *See* internal training load monitoring
   variables in 270t
internal training load monitoring
   biochemical assessments for 286-287
   diaries used in 289-293
   heart rate for 282-285
   heart rate recovery 284
   heart rate variability 284-285
   hormonal assessments for 286-289
   immunological assessments for 289
   lactate for 286
   perceived exertion 280f, 280-281, 281f
   questionnaires used in 289-293
   session rating of perceived exertion scale for 281-282, 282f
   training impulse for 285-286
inter-repetition rest intervals 352, 361f, 362, 369, 371
inter-set rest intervals 350-352, 361f, 362
intramuscular task specificity 12-13
intramyofibrillar glycogen 203
intra-set rest intervals 352, 361f, 362-363, 369, 371
in-travel 219, 220f
introductory microcycle 162
involution 9, 9f, 13, 18, 310
iron cross 55-56
isometric force–time curve 212, 212f, 274, 275f, 340f, 341f, 416f
isometric midthigh pull (IMTP) 212, 275, 275f, 301-302, 304
isometric squat (ISQT) 275, 275f, 301
isometric strength–endurance 55
isometric tests 274-276, 275f, 276f
Issurin, Vladimir 116

J

jet lag 218-219, 219f

K

kinematic profile 12
kinetic profile 12
Kolehmainen, Hannes 383
Kotov, Boris 106
Krebs cycle 28, 35-36, 37f

L

lactate
   accumulation of 29-33, 33f, 43, 83
   blood levels of 30-35, 43, 394
   description of 15
   in fast glycolysis 29-35
   gluconeogenesis of 32
   high-intensity interval training effects on 31, 34-35
   internal training load monitoring uses of 286
   maximal lactate steady state 35
   monitoring uses of 286
   monocarboxylate transporter protein and 31-32, 32f
   muscle levels of 30-31
   onset of blood lactate accumulation 33-35, 34f, 43
   oxidation of 44-45
   postexercise removal of 32
   stretch-shortening cycle affected by 414
   usage of 31, 32f
lactate dehydrogenase 410
lactate dehydrogenase heart 31
lactate dehydrogenase reaction 29
lactate threshold (LT) 32-35, 34f, 43, 271
lactic acid 15, 17, 29, 411
lactormone 30-31
lactose 237
lactose intolerance 237
lateral prefrontal cortex 204
learning technique 61-62
leucine 241
levulose 236
linear loading 93
linear periodization 375
linear speed 404, 407f, 407-409, 408f, 426-427
linear taper 314
lipid 242
liver glycogen resynthesis 251
load. *See* training load(s); volume load
loading patterns
   ascending pyramid 365-366, 366f
   for cluster sets 370t
   double pyramid 366f, 366-367
   double stimulation 368, 368f
   flat loaded target set 365, 365f
   modified double pyramid 367, 367f
   pyramid 366f, 366-367
   pyramid set structure 365-366, 366f
   for resistance training 365f, 365-368, 366f, 367f, 368f
   skewed pyramid 367, 367f
   wave 367-368, 368f
load velocity (LV) profile 358, 359f
local positioning systems 273
local strength–endurance 55
locomotor profile 390, 390f, 390t
long-distance events 41t, 43-44
long-duration training session 181, 190
long interval high-intensity interval training 384
long-lasting delayed training effects (LDTE) 115
long-term athlete development (LTAD)
   adaptations in 420
   agility in 425
   models 127, 129, 148
   multilateral training for 124
   multiyear training plans for 129f, 129-130
   periodization modeling and 129f
   in young athletes 326
long-term detraining 136, 137t
long-term goals 70

long-term recovery 217
long-term residual training effects 78
long-term training 148, 288
lower body
   isometric force–time curves 275
   priming exercises for 196f
   strength of 422
low-intensity exercise 40, 44, 44f
low-intensity exercise endurance (LIEE) 59-60
low-intensity interval training (LIIT) 399

M

machine learning algorithms 64
macrocycles
   in annual training plans 130-135, 132f, 133f, 149
   in bi-cycle annual training plan 142f, 142-144, 143f
   description of 110
   example of 326f-327f
   preparation period of 131-133, 132f
   in tri-cycle annual training plan 144f, 145
macronutrients
   carbohydrates. See carbohydrates
   definition of 236
   fat. See fat(s)
   protein. See protein
magnetometers 272
main competition phase 134-135
maltose 237
malt sugar 237
maneuverability 424, 426-427
massage 223-225
massage stick 223-224
mathematical modeling, of taper 318-321
Matveyev, Leonid P. 106
maximal aerobic power (p$\dot{V}O_2$max) 386-387
maximal aerobic speed (v$\dot{V}O_2$max) 386-387
maximal exercise 31
maximal heart rate 85-86
maximal lactate steady state (MLSS) 35
maximal oxygen uptake ($\dot{V}O_2$max)
   description of 32-33
   exercise performance affected by 43-44
   glycogenolysis and 39
   intensity of exercise and 38
   maximal velocity and 84
maximal sprinting speed (MSS) 388-389, 389f, 432
maximal strength. See also muscular strength
   acceleration and 404
   in change of direction ability 427
   change of direction ability affected by 335
   definition of 347
   endurance performance capabilities affected by 336
   muscle hypertrophy effects on 344
   overtraining and 214
   performance capacity affected by 335
   rate of force development affected by 341-342, 415-416
   rate of force development and 415
   resistance-training methods for 349t, 350
maximal velocity 84, 405, 408f, 409, 416, 435
maximal voluntary contraction (MVC) 17
mechanical specificity 12-13
mediator 56
medium-duration training structure 110
medium-term residual training effects 78
mental fatigue 191, 220
mesocycles
   accumulation block 116-117, 153, 155t, 158f
   annual training plan for designing of 152
   build-up 156-157
   competition period 152, 155, 157
   construction of 160-161
   definition of 152
   description of 10, 109-110
   developmental 115-116
   duration of 152-153
   in emphasis training model 439-440, 440f
   example of 159, 160f, 161f
   loading patterns 156-159
   monitoring program integration into 302-304
   periodization model alignment with 152, 153f
   preparation period 152, 156f
   realization block 116-118, 153, 155t, 158f
   restorative 115-116
   retention 115-116
   sequencing of 153, 155-156, 156f, 158f
   step loaded 156-157, 157f
   strength during 356
   strength training focus of 439
   taxonomy of 152-153, 154t, 155f
   training factors 159-160
   training load in 159-160
   transmutation block 116-117, 153, 155t, 158f
   types of 152-155, 153f, 154t
   volume load for 278f
   workloads for 153
metabolic acidosis 29-30
metabolic equivalents 245
metabolic specificity 12, 26, 46
metabolic window 246
metabolism 26, 26f
metric ton 278
microcycles
   competition. See competition microcycle
   in competition period 161, 162f, 170
   construction of 173-174
   definition of 161
   description of 10, 18, 90, 94
   design of 171
   double-shock 162-163
   duration of 161
   high-demand 167
   high-demand training with 170f, 171f
   high-intensity interval training integration into 400
   for individual sports 172f
   integration of 169-173, 174f
   introductory 162
   loading patterns for 165-169
   model 163
   monitoring program integration into 301-302, 303f
   monotony calculation for 283t
   one-peak 167, 169f
   ordinary 162
   precompetitive 163
   in preparation period 161, 162f
   preseason 168f
   recovery 163
   restorative 163
   sequencing of 163-164
   session rating of perceived exertion scale for determining 282f
   sessions in 164, 165f, 166f, 167f
   shock 162-163, 218
   as short-duration training structure 110
   step loaded mesocycles broken into 157f
   strain calculation for 283t
   structure of 161, 164-165, 165f, 166f, 167f, 168f
   summated 95, 378-379
   for team sports 172f, 173f, 174
   three-peak 169, 171f
   training load in 165, 283t
   two-peak 167, 170f, 171f
   types of 161-163
   volume load for 278f
   work-to-rest ratios for 157
microsensor technology 63
milk sugar 236
minimal velocity threshold 338, 358
mitochondria 35
mixed training sessions 179
mobility 185, 336
mobility training 423
model microcycle 163
moderate-duration training session 181, 190
moderate glycemic index 238
moderator 56

modified double pyramid loading pattern 367, 367*f*
momentum 409
monitoring
   athlete 267-268
   decision making based on 302*f*
   external training load 271-280
   GPS 272-273, 273*f*
   individualization of 295-296
   internal training load. *See* internal training load monitoring
   local positioning systems for 273
   overview of 267-268
   reasons for 268
   sleep quality 293, 294*t*
monitoring program
   acute to chronic workload ratio 297-298
   annual training plan integration of 304-305, 305*f*
   assessing changes from 296-297
   current practices in 295
   goals of 300
   implementation of 294-296
   individualization of methods 295-296
   for individual sports 296
   isometric testing in 274-275
   mesocycle integration of 302-304
   microcycle integration of 301-302, 303*f*
   results of 296-300
   rules-based training management 299-300
   structured 268
   for team sports 296
   traffic-light systems 300, 305, 429*f*
   training day integration of 300-301, 303*f*
   trend analyses 298*f*, 298-299, 299*f*
monocarboxylate transporter (MCT) proteins, 31-32, 32*f*
mono-cycle annual training plans 139-142, 140*f*, 141*f*
monosaccharides 236
monotonous program overtraining 10
monotonous training load 8, 8*f*, 10, 89, 211
monotony 279*t*, 279-280, 302
monounsaturated fatty acids (MUFA) 242
mood disturbances 214-215
morphological adaptations 344, 345*f*, 346
motor units 342-343
multidirectional speed 404
multijoint exercises 363, 373
multilateral training 111, 124
multiplanar movements 186
multiple-session training days 194-195
multitarget block model 380-382
multitask training sessions 188
multiyear training plans 128*f*, 128-130, 147-149, 148*t*, 151

muscle
   cross-sectional area of 344, 350
   glycogen concentrations 39-40, 43, 247-248
   hypertrophy of. *See* hypertrophy
   lactate levels in 30-31
   oxygen delivery to 183
   skeletal. *See* skeletal muscle
muscle fibers
   exercise intensity based on 392
   fast-twitch 28, 343, 392
   lactate production in 31
   locomotor profile based on 390*t*
   morphological adaptation to resistance training by 346
   repetitions and 353
   slow-twitch 28, 392
   strength and 343-344
   in strength-trained athletes 347*t*
   training-induced alterations to 412
   types of 343-344, 392, 412
   type II 344, 346
muscle protein synthesis (MPS) 18, 242, 246, 252
muscle pumping action 226
muscle soreness, delayed onset 17-18, 190
muscular endurance 53
muscular strength 218, 338, 340. *See also* maximal strength; strength
myoglobin 183, 217
myokinase reaction 29
myosin heavy chain (MHC) 343, 411-412, 412*f*

N

naps 222
nearables 293
neural fatigue 414
neuromuscular adaptations 345, 350
neuromuscular fatigue 213
neuromuscular function tests 274-276, 275*f*, 276*f*
neuromuscular inhibition 343
neurotransmitters 191
Newton's second law of motion 338
nicotinamide adenine dinucleotide (NADH) 29, 36
nonessential amino acids 240
nonfunctional overreaching (NFOR) 207-208, 211
nonprogressive taper 313-314
nonsupport phase 405
novice athletes 6, 9, 90, 113, 132, 164, 218
nutrient timing
   anabolic phase of 246
   definition of 246
   energy phase of 246
   example of 248*f*
   growth phase of 246

nutrition
   during-training 249-251
   in nonfunctional overreaching 208
   pretraining 247-249
nutritional periodization
   carbohydrates. *See* carbohydrates
   definition of 235, 236
   energy intake 244-246
   fat. *See* fat(s)
   fluid requirements 243-244
   hydration 243-244
   macronutrients 236-243
   pretraining 247-249
   protein. *See* protein
   strategies of 236

O

older athletes 218
oligosaccharides 237
Olympic Games 43, 70, 106, 115-116, 128, 134, 218, 222, 298, 311-312, 314, 316*f*
omega-3 fatty acids 242
omega-6 fatty acids 242
one-factor theory of supercompensation 15. *See also* supercompensation
one-peak microcycle 167, 169*f*
1RM 352-353, 355, 357, 365. *See also* maximal strength
onset of blood lactate accumulation (OBLA) 33-35, 43
"On the Preservation of Health" 106
open-skill agility 426
open-skill sport 51-52
optimal energy availability 245*t*
optimization, zone of 6, 6*f*
optimization of training 4, 6-7, 10-12, 329
ordinary microcycle 162
orienteering 159
overload
   definition of 7, 201
   performance capacity affected by 92
   progressive 9, 91, 93*f*, 94
   technical training application of 62
   training loads for 7-8, 8*f*
   variation and 10
overreaching. *See also* supercompensation
   causes of 205, 207
   continuum of 205, 206*f*
   definition of 207
   description of 9-10, 56, 205-207
   fatigue and 205, 206*f*
   functional 207, 207*f*
   general adaptive syndrome and 206*f*
   nonfunctional 207-208, 211
   planned 96
   psychological symptoms of 220
   in team sports athletes 321
overspeed training 418

overtraining
    characteristics of 208
    continuum of 205, 206f
    cytokine theory of 216
    definition of 6
    fatigue and 205, 206f
    general adaptive syndrome and 206f
    high-intensity 210f, 210-211, 215
    high-volume 209-210
    injury risks 56, 114
    maximal strength decreases as indicator of 214
    monitoring of 211-216
    monotonous program 10
    mood disturbances associated with 214-215
    nonfunctional overreaching versus 208
    parasympathetic 208-209, 209t
    performance testing to prevent 211-214
    psychological symptoms of 214-215, 220
    rate of force development as indicator of 212, 212f, 214
    in resistance training 210f
    signs of 214, 214f
    speed of movement as indicator of 212-213
    strength testing as indicator of 214
    sympathetic 208-209, 209t
    training load and 20, 114, 170
    training stimulus and 8, 8f, 18
    velocity of movement as indicator of 212-213
    zone of 6f
overtraining syndrome (OTS)
    continuum of 206f
    definition of 207
    hormones related to 215-216
    immunologic findings in 216
    mood disturbances associated with 214-215
    nonfunctional overreaching versus 208
    performance changes associated with 211
    psychological symptoms of 214-215
    testosterone to cortisol ratio in 215
oxidative phosphorylation 36
oxidative system
    carbohydrate oxidation 36
    definition of 35
    fat oxidation 37
    protein oxidation 37-38
    substrates used in 35
oxygen consumption
    excess postexercise 18, 44-45, 83, 217
    in low-intensity exercise 44, 44f
    measurement of 44
    muscle fibers and 344
    postexercise 18, 44-45, 83

oxygen debt 44
oxygen deficit 44
oxygen delivery 183

P
parallel-emphasis model 121
parallel training models
    complex training models 111-112, 112f
    definition of 111
    high-intensity interval training and 399
    for resistance training 375-376
    sports for 125
    variational training models 111-114, 112f
parasympathetic overtraining 208-209, 209t
partially hydrogenated fats 242
passive recovery 189, 221-223, 395
passive rest 135-136
passive warm-up 182
peak 135
peak force 274
peaking index 145-147, 146f
peaking performance
    for competitive season 321-322
    description of 308
    in high-frequency competition periods 328-329
    tapering for 328
    for tournaments 322-324, 323t
peak rate of force development (pRFD) 275
perceived exertion 280f, 280-281, 281f
perceived fatigability 203
perceptual–cognitive speed 425-426
perfectionism 70
performance. See also competitive performance
    biomotor abilities in 52-55
    cold-water immersion effects on 227
    frequency of training effects on 18
    glycemic index effects on 238
    high-intensity training effects on 19f
    intensity of training and 86
    peaking 308
    physical characteristics of 336, 337f
    sleep effects on 221, 221f
    stagnation in 8
    strength and 337f
    taper effects on 311-313, 312f
    training activity and, transferability between 12
    training loads and 318-319
    training processes to improve 109
performance capacity
    adaptation and 7
    in competition period 133
    concentrated load effects on 115
    description of 4f, 4-5
    fatigue effects on 131

    maximal strength effects on 335
    overload effects on 92
    supercompensation of 96
    taper effects on 312
    testosterone:cortisol ratio and 98
    training load effect on 8f, 8-9, 9f
    training stimuli for 417
performance fatigability 203
performance tests
    overtraining monitoring and prevention through 211-214
    rate of force development 212, 212f, 214
    after resistance training 303
    speed of movement 212-213
    strength testing 214
    velocity of movement 212-213
    vertical jump performance 213-214
periodization
    block. See block periodization
    daily undulating 375
    definition of 107
    description of 10, 105-106
    game theory and 107
    general adaptive syndrome and 20f
    goals of 109
    hierarchical structures of 109-111, 110f
    high-volume overtraining managed with 210
    history of 106
    individualization of 90, 91f
    of learning technique 61-62
    linear 375
    misuse of 107
    nutritional. See nutritional periodization
    planning and 107-109, 108f
    programming and 107-109, 108f
    reverse linear 375
    as scaffolding framework 107
    skill acquisition in 61-62
    of training load 76, 88-89
    training models used in. See periodization models
    variation and 10, 107
periodization models
    agility training application of 434-437
    categories of 111f
    conjugated sequential loading models 118-119, 119f, 120f
    development of 108
    emphasis training model. See emphasis training model
    high-intensity interval training and 398-400
    mesocycles aligned with 152, 153f
    parallel. See parallel training models
    selection of 124-126
    sequential. See sequential training models
    speed training application of 434-437

sport-specific selection of 125
training load based on 76
periodized training plans
  agility training application of 437
  construction of 110
  designing of 109
  goals of 307
  high-intensity interval training integration in 398-400
  individualization of 90
  long-term development goals of 109
  microcycles in 110-111
  monitoring techniques and 300-305
  peaking performance as goal of 308
  psychological training integrated into 71, 71f, 72f
  purpose of 324
  recovery methods integrated into 230, 231f
  sets in 354
  speed training application of 437
  sprint training application of 437
  step loading in 96
  strength training in 423
  training loads in 89, 91-92
  variation in 107
peripheral fatigue 15, 29-30, 190-191, 203-204, 405, 414
peripheral governor model, of fatigue 15
perseverance 70
phase potentiation 99, 99f, 377
phenotype 77
Philostratus 106
phosphagens 39, 42
phosphagen (ATP-PC) system 28-29, 38, 83, 410
phosphocreatine (PCr)
  active recovery effects on 222
  depletion of 39
  description of 15, 17, 28
  inter-set rest intervals for 362
  muscular stores of 83
  repletion of 39, 217, 394
  skeletal muscle levels of 17, 41-42
  sprinting effects on 405, 410
  in sprint performance 410
phosphofructokinase (PFK) 42, 410
phosphorylase 410
physical training
  description of 55-56
  general 56-60, 57f, 58f, 131-132
  inadequacies in 56
  in microcycle 174
  multilateral approach to 58
  physiological adaptations stimulated by 56, 58, 77
  sequential approach to 57f
  sport-specific 56-60, 57f, 58f, 131-132
  technical abilities affected by 55-56
  technique affected by 60
physical training sessions 180

physiological stress
  energy demand affected by 87
  training adaptations and 5
Pihkala, Lauri 106, 383
planned overreaching 96
planning, periodization and 107-109, 108f
plant polysaccharides 237
plateau 208
player load 272
plyometric training 60, 339f, 374, 423
polysaccharides 237
polysomnography (PSG) 293
polyunsaturated fatty acids (PUFA) 242
postactivation performance enhancement (PAPE) 183, 365, 367, 374-375
postactivation potentiation (PAP) 183
postexercise period
  carbohydrate supplementation in 251-252
  protein supplementation in 252
  recovery in 217
posttraining period 251-252
posttravel 220, 220f
power
  calculation of 341
  definition of 348
  development of 338
  force–power relationship 341-342
power-based training zones 86, 87t
power–endurance 380
power exercises 363
power-generating capacity 341-342
power index rankings 66, 67t, 68t
power line position 408
power meters 271-272
power output 271-272, 341
power training 99, 99f, 100f, 123t
precompetition phase 134
precompetitive microcycle 163
preparation period
  description of 131-133, 132f, 143, 145
  for emphasis model 438, 439f
  goals in 231
  mesocycles for 152, 156f
  microcycles for 161, 162f
  recovery in 231
preparedness
  athlete's performance potential 145
  in competition period 133
  dynamics of 88f
  fatigue and 145, 317, 374
  in fitness–fatigue model 22, 24f
  fluctuations in 88, 88f
  overload as source of 201
  supercompensation as source of 15, 201
  taper and 311f
  testosterone:cortisol ratio and 98
  training focus effects on 24f
  in training plan 88f
preparedness index 145-147, 146f

preseason 321
pretraining period
  amino acid supplementation in 249
  carbohydrate supplementation in 247-249
  nutritional strategies for 247-249
  protein supplementation in 249
pretravel 219, 220f
primary transfer, of training effects 420
priming exercises 195, 196f
priming sessions 195
principal competitions 324
principle of dynamic correspondence 12
Profile of Mood States (POMS) 215, 290
programming process
  fatigue considerations 191
  hierarchical levels in 110f
  mesocycles in. See mesocycles
  microcycles in. See microcycles
  periodization and 107-109, 108f
  stages of 151-152
progression, in technical training 62
progressive overload 9, 91, 93f, 94
progressive taper 314, 314f
proinflammatory cytokines 216, 289
protein
  amino acids in. See amino acids
  athlete requirements for 240-241, 241f
  carbohydrates and 250-252
  casein 242
  contractile 238
  during-training supplementation of 250-251
  functions of 238
  immunoproteins 238
  oxidation of 37-38
  posttraining supplementation of 252
  presleep ingestion of 252-253
  pretraining supplementation of 249
  quality of 240
  regulatory 238
  sources of 241-242
  soy 242
  structural 238
  supplementation of 249-252
  timing of 246
  whey 242, 252
psychological skills 71
psychological state 14
psychological stress. See also stress
  general adaptive syndrome affected by 21f
  injury risks 14
  intensity of training affected by 83
  recovery affected by 21, 220-221
  training adaptations and 5
psychological training
  conscientiousness 69-70
  courage 69
  excellence 70
  integration of 70-71, 71f
  long-term goals 70

psychological training *(continued)*
    periodization plan integration of 71, 71*f*, 72*f*
    resilience 70
    self-confidence and 71
    volitional skills targeted by 220
pyramid loading pattern 366*f*, 366-367
pyramid set structure 365-366, 366*f*
pyruvate 35-36

Q

qualitative variation 11*f*, 11-12
quantitative variation 10-11
questionnaires 289-293

R

raise, activate and mobilize, and potentiate (RAMP) protocol 185*f*, 185-186, 187*t*
range of motion 336
rate coding 342, 417
rate of doing work 341
rate of force development (RFD)
    calculation of 275
    definition of 212, 340, 405, 415
    description of 340, 376
    heavy resistance training effects on 345, 416
    maximal strength effects on 341-342, 415-416
    mesocycle targets and 212*f*
    peak 275
    sprinting and 415-416, 422
    in start phase of sprint 408
    stress–recovery imbalance and 214
    vertical jump test for determination of 274
rating of perceived exertion (RPE)
    applications of 360
    definition of 271
    heart rate and 280
    high-intensity interval training programming using 386
    history of 360
    lactate and 286
    session. *See* session rating of perceived exertion (sRPE) scale
reactive agility drills 426
reactive strength 427
reactive strength index (RSI) 427
realization mesocycle block 116-118, 153
rebound hyperglycemia 247
recovery
    active 32, 189, 222, 395
    Acute Recovery and Stress Scale 292
    aerobic training for 49
    age effects on 218
    in competition period 231, 232*f*
    in concentrated loading 96, 97*f*
    delayed 217
    description of 17-18, 216

factors that affect 22*f*, 202*f*, 218-220
fatigue and 204-205, 205*f*
in high-intensity interval training 394-396
interexercise 217
intersession strategies for 195
intervention strategies for 230-231
lactate removal effects on 32
length of 194
long-term 217
massage for 223-225
methods for enhancing 222-230
modalities for 221-230
muscular strength effects on 218
of older athletes 218
passive 189, 221-223, 395
postcompetition 330*f*
postexercise 217
in preparation period 231
psychological aspects of 220-221
sleep patterns 221, 221*f*
stress and 204-205, 205*f*, 215
structured 230
training load and 92
training sessions for 180
training status effects on 218
Training Stress Score and 272*f*
travel effects on 218-220
variations in 20*f*
volume of training based on 81
recovery methods
    cold-water immersion 224-228, 230-231
    combined use of 230
    in competition period 231, 232*f*
    compression garments 229, 231
    contrast water therapy 226, 228
    cryotherapy 224-225
    external pneumatic compression 229
    foam roller/rolling 223-224, 231
    hot-water immersion 225-226, 228
    hydrotherapy 226-228
    ice massage 225
    periodization of 230-233
    periodized training plan integration of 230, 231*f*
    self-massage 223-224
    thermotherapy 225-226
recovery microcycle 163
Recovery–Stress Questionnaire for Athletes (RESTQ-Sport) 215, 290-291, 291*t*
recovery time 15, 21, 81-82
regulatory proteins 238
rehydration 244
Reilly, Tom 384
relative density 82
relative strength 347
relative volume 82
relaxation exercises 189
remote coach 179
repeated sprint training (RST) 384, 395

repetition(s)
    in cluster sets 370-371
    description of 80
    rest intervals between 352, 361*f*, 362
    training load and 352, 353*t*
repetition maximum (RM)
    description of 276-277, 352-353
    training for 356-357
    zones 357, 375
repetitions in reserve (RIR) 361
residual training effects 78*f*, 78-79
resilience 70
resistance phase, of general adaptive syndrome 20, 20*f*, 22
resistance training
    accentuated eccentric loading 372-373, 374*f*
    acute hormonal response to 350
    adaptations to 344-346, 345*f*
    ballistic 338, 339*f*, 348, 349*t*, 416
    block periodization in 377-378
    carbohydrate supplementation for 247-248, 250
    cluster sets for 369*f*, 369-372, 370*f*, 371*f*, 372*f*
    compression garments after 229
    conjugated sequence model applied to 119*f*
    eccentric muscle actions in 346
    emphasis model for 381*f*
    energy systems for 39
    exercise order and selection for 363
    external load during 269
    force–velocity relationships in 338
    frequency of 363-365
    glycogen concentrations affected by 39-40, 40*f*
    heavy 338-339, 339*f*, 343, 345, 416
    high-intensity overtraining associated with 210*f*, 210-211
    for hypertrophy 349*t*, 351
    immediate training effects after 77
    intensity of 84, 85*t*
    inter-set rest intervals in 350-352
    loading patterns for 365*f*, 365-368, 366*f*, 367*f*, 368*f*
    for maximal strength 349*t*, 350
    monotony for 279*t*
    morphological adaptations to 344, 345*f*, 346
    muscle hypertrophy from 344
    muscle protein synthesis after 252
    myofibrillar size affected by 346
    neurological adaptations to 344-346, 345*f*
    neuromuscular fatigue during 213
    overtraining in 210*f*
    performance benefits of 338
    performance testing at end of 303
    periodization of 376
    phosphagens in 40
    physiological adaptations to 344-346

Index | 583

rating of perceived exertion scale for 281*f*
repetitions in 354
responses to 19
resting energy metabolism after 18
sequential model for 376-380, 377*f*, 378*f*
short-term 344
single-joint exercises in 350
for speed–strength 348, 349*t*
strain for 279*t*
strength affected by 346
for strength–endurance 349*t*, 351-352
for strength–speed 348-350, 349*t*
stress continuum in 210*f*
for supramaximal strength 349*t*, 350-351
volume load for 276-278, 277*t*, 279*t*, 320*f*
resisted sled training (RST) 419
resisted sprint training 418*t*, 419*t*, 419-420
rest
  active 136, 138
  in-travel 219
  passive 135-136
resting energy metabolism 18
rest intervals
  in agility training 433-434
  description of 19
  inter-repetition 352, 361*f*, 362, 369, 371
  inter-set 350-352, 361*f*, 362
  intra-set 352, 361*f*, 362-363, 371
  in speed training 433-434
  in sprint training 433-434
restorative mesocycle 115-116
restorative microcycle 163
rest-pause method 369
retaining load 91
retention mesocycle 115-116
reverse linear periodization 375
reversibility 13, 62
rolling devices 223
rowing 387
R-R interval 284
rules-based training management 299-300
running 387, 400, 417
running economy 60
running gait 52
running velocity 406*f*

S

sarcoplasmic reticulum 16, 17, 190
saturated fats 242
sauna bathing 225-226
saw taper 314-315, 316*f*
scientific disciplines 4-5, 5*f*
seasons 138, 138*f*
secondary transfer, of training effects 420

segment work 368
self-confidence 71
self-massage 223-224
sequential training models
  accentuated loading 114
  agility development application of 435, 435*f*
  block training 115-118, 116*f*, 117*f*, 118*f*
  concentrated loading 114, 115*f*
  definition of 114
  endurance performance use of 114*f*
  functional overreaching and 207
  high-intensity interval training and 398-400
  power development use of 114*f*
  resistance training 376-380, 377*f*, 378*f*
  speed development application of 434, 434*f*, 437-438
  sports that use 114-115
serotonin 191
session rating of perceived exertion (sRPE) scale
  definition of 167
  internal training loads and 281-282, 282*f*, 295, 301
  monitoring uses of 360
  peaking index from 146
  training impulse and 285
  training loads based on 281-282, 282*f*
  training sessions and 181, 181*f*
set(s)
  cluster 369*f*, 369-372, 370*f*, 371*f*, 372*f*
  definition of 354
  flat loaded target set 365, 365*f*
  pyramid set structure 365-366, 366*f*
  rest intervals between 350-352, 361*f*, 362
shock microcycle 162-163, 218
short-duration training session 181
short-duration training structures 110
short interval high-intensity interval training 384
short-term detraining 136, 137*t*
short-term residual training effects 78
short-term resistance training 344
shot putters 11-12
single-joint exercises 350, 363
single-session training days 194
skeletal muscle
  adenosine triphosphate storage in 26-27
  external pneumatic compression effects on 229
  functional adaptations 125*f*
  glycogen storage in 39
  lactate accumulation in 43
  phosphocreatine levels in 17, 41-42
  power output in 411
  speed affected by 411-412
skewed pyramid loading pattern 367, 367*f*

skills
  psychological 71
  sporting. *See* sporting skills
sleep
  monitoring of 293, 294*t*
  patterns of 221, 221*f*
  protein ingestion before 252-253
sleep debt 222
sleep deprivation 293
sleep diaries 293
sleep hygiene 222
slow exponential taper 314
slow glycolysis 28, 29, 35
slow-twitch muscle fibers 28
small-sided game (SSG) 35, 388, 394, 426
smartphones 222
Smith, Lucille 216
sodium 243
soy protein 242
specialized developmental exercises 58*f*, 59, 113*t*
specialized preparatory exercises 58*f*, 59, 113*t*
specific adaptation to imposed demands (SAID) principle 12, 25-26
specificity
  in agility training 430
  bioenergetic 12
  definition of 12-13, 25, 46
  mechanical 12-13
  metabolic 12, 26
  in speed training 430
  in technical training 62
  of training effect paradox 13
specific training age 129
specific warm-up 184
speed. *See also* sprinting speed
  as biomotor ability 52-55, 53*f*, 54*f*
  definition of 403-404
  development of 429-431
  endurance and 336*f*
  energetic factors affecting 409-410, 424*t*
  game 404
  genetic factors that affect 411
  linear 404, 407*f*, 407-409, 408*f*, 426-427
  locomotor profile 390, 390*f*, 390*t*
  multidirectional 404
  neural factors that affect 412-414
  perceptual–cognitive 425-426
  performance factors that affect 414-417
  physiological factors affecting 409-414
  skeletal muscle factors that affect 411-412
  spring–mass model and 414
  sprint training for. *See* sprint training
  strength and 336*f*
  strength training for 420-423, 421*f*, 422*t*
  training sessions that develop 188

584 | Index

speed. *See also* sprinting speed *(continued)*
   velocity and 404
speed–endurance 119-120, 423-424, 424*t*, 433
speed of movement 212-213
speed skaters 12
speed–strength 53, 99, 100*f*, 347-348, 349*t*, 380
speed training
   cueing in 430-431
   density of 431
   description of 417-424
   discipline in 431
   duration of 431
   emphasis training model application to 435-436, 436*f*
   exercise order in 433
   fatigue in 433
   feedback in 431
   frequency of 431
   instruction in 430-431
   intensity of 432, 434
   motivation in 431
   multifactorial development in 430
   periodization models applied to 434-437
   periodized training plan for 437
   programming of 429-434
   quality of 429
   rest intervals in 433-434
   sequential training model application to 434, 434*f*, 437-438
   short-to-long method for 434
   specificity of 430
   technical precision in 429-430
   volume of 432-433
speed zones 273*t*
split snatch 61
sport. *See also* individual sports; team sports
   aerobic energy system use by 47*f*, 48*f*
   big data technological stack in 64, 65*f*
   biomotor abilities of 52-55, 53*f*, 54*f*, 55*f*
   classification of 51-52
   closed-skill 51-52
   competitive season length based on 133-134
   energetic profile of 12
   high-intensity interval training design based on 396-398, 397*f*
   machine learning algorithms in 64
   metabolic profiles of 48
   open-skill 51-52
   performance in 4, 4*f*, 93
   periodization model based on 125
   periodization plan for, psychological training integration into 71, 71*f*, 72*f*
   tactical aspects of 63
   technical models of 61
SPORT (acronym) 62-63

Sport and Exercise Nutrition Register 253, 254*f*
sporting form 89
sporting skills
   acyclic combined skills 52
   acyclic skills 52
   biomotor abilities 52-55, 53*f*, 54*f*
   classification of 52
   cyclic skills 52
   physical training needed for 56
sports drinks 244
sports form 58
sport-specific physical training (SSPT) 56-60, 57*f*, 58*f*, 131-132
spring–mass model (SMM) 414
sprint/sprinting
   acceleration in 405
   acceleration phase of 408*f*, 408-409, 414
   adenosine triphosphate affected by 405, 410
   all-out 392
   energy substrate storage in 410
   energy systems in 409, 423-424
   enzymatic activity in 410
   flight phase of 405
   importance of 403
   lactate dehydrogenase affected by 410
   maximal velocity 408*f*, 409, 417
   maximal velocity during 405
   muscle activation in 413
   neural fatigue effects on 414
   neuromuscular activation in 412
   nonsupport phase of 405
   phosphocreatine affected by 405, 410
   rate of force development and 415-416
   start phase of 407*f*, 407-408
   strength and 415
   stretch reflex in 413-414
   stretch-shortening cycle effects on 413
   strides in 405-406
   technical model of 405-409
sprinting speed. *See also* speed
   factors that affect 406
   importance of 403
   linear 407*f*, 407-409, 408*f*
   maximal 409
   rate of force development in 422
sprint interval training (SIT) 384-385
sprint performance 53, 404, 417*f*
sprint training
   adenosine triphosphate demands for 45-46
   annual training plan for 437, 437*f*
   assisted 418*t*, 418-419, 419*t*
   complementary training factors 123*t*
   description of 417
   emphasis training model application to 435-436, 436*f*
   energy systems for 39

   glycogen concentrations affected by 39
   intensity of 432, 432*t*
   periodized training plan for 437
   recommendations for 438*t*
   repeated 384, 395
   resisted 418*t*, 419*t*, 419-420
   rest intervals in 433-434
   volume load for 278-279
   volume of 432-433, 433*t*
squat snatch 61
staleness. *See* overtraining syndrome (OTS)
standard loading 92-93
starch 237
start phase, of sprint 407*f*, 407-408
static stretching 184, 189-190
step loaded mesocycles 156-157, 157*f*
step loading 94-96, 95*f*, 96*f*, 100
step taper 313-314, 314*f*
still rings cross 55-56
stimulating load 91
stimulus-fatigue-recovery adaptation theory 15. *See also* supercompensation
strain, training 279*t*, 279-280
strength. *See also* muscular strength
   as biomotor ability 52-55, 53*f*, 54*f*
   characteristics of 346-348
   continuum of 336, 337*f*
   endurance and 336*f*
   factors that affect 342-344
   maximal. *See* maximal strength
   motor unit rate coding and 342
   motor unit recruitment and 342
   motor unit synchronization and 342-343
   muscle fiber type and 343-344
   neuromuscular inhibition and 343
   performance and 337*f*
   periodization methods for 375-382
   protein timing effects on 246
   reactive 427
   relative 347
   speed and 336*f*
   speed–strength. *See* speed–strength
   stretch-shortening cycle 343
   supramaximal 348, 349*t*, 350-351
   training sessions that develop 188
strength–endurance
   definition of 351
   description of 53, 55, 347, 380
   resistance-training methods for 349*t*, 351-352
strength loading 99
strength–power potentiation complexes (SPPC) 188, 373-375
strength reserve 336, 337*f*
strength–speed 53, 348-350, 349*t*
strength training
   complementary training factors 123*t*

emphasis model for 380-382, 381f
force vectors 420-421
frequency of 363-364
generality of 420
intensity of 317
mesocycle for 439
methods of 354f
muscle fiber distribution in 347t
parallel model for 375-376
in periodized training plans 423
phase potentation in 99, 99f
relative intensity for 355f
sequential model for 376-380
training factor manipulations in 352f
transfer of training effects 420
variation and 420
strength zone 350
stress
  Acute Recovery and Stress Scale 292
  fatigue and 204-205, 205f
  in general adaptive syndrome 20, 21f
  in main competition phase 134-135
  psychological. *See* psychological stress
  recovery and 204-205, 205f, 215
  training 309
stressors 161, 220
stress response 21
stretching 184, 189-190
stretch reflex 413-414
stretch-shortening cycle (SSC) 17, 343, 409, 413, 429
stride length 406, 406f, 419, 423
stride rate 406, 406f
strides 405
structural exercises 363
structural proteins 238
structured cool-down 189
subclinical low energy availability 245t
substrates 35, 39-40
sucrose 237, 239t
summated microcycle 95, 378-379
supercompensation. *See also* overreaching
  catabolic phase of 17
  cycle of 16f
  definition of 15, 201
  diagram of 15, 16f, 202f
  fatigue in 15, 17
  history of 14-15
  onset of 207
  of performance capacity 96
  phase 1 (1 to 2 hours) 15-17, 16f
  phase 2 (2 to 48 hours) 15, 16f, 17-18
  phase 3 (36 to 72 hours) 15, 16f, 18
  phase 4 (3 to 7 days) 15, 16f, 18-19
  preparedness from 15
  training days for 194
  training load for 205, 207
  variations in 18
superelite athletes 70
supramaximal strength 348, 349t, 350-351

sweat 243
sympathetic overtraining 208-209, 209t
synchronization of motor units 342-343

T

tactical game plan
  construction of 63f, 63-64
  development of 63-67
  factors to consider for 64f
  implementation of 67, 69
  postcompetition analysis of 69
  systematic approach to 65, 66f
tactical metabolic training 60
tactical modeling 60
tactical skills 188
tactical training 63, 174
tactical training sessions 180
taper/tapering
  definition of 309
  delayed training effects and 310f
  description of 140, 307
  design of 310, 318
  duration of 310, 311f, 313, 317-318
  exponential 314
  factors that affect 313-318
  fast exponential 314
  as fatigue-management strategy 309, 311f
  goals of 309
  linear 314
  mathematical modeling of 318-321
  nonprogressive 313-314
  peaking after 308, 328
  performance effects of 311-313, 312f
  personalizing of 318
  preparedness and 311f
  progressive 314, 314f
  purpose of 307-308
  rationale of 309-310
  saw 314-315, 316f
  slow exponential 314
  step 313-314, 314f
  in strength–power training 308f
  team sport athletes 321-324
  for tournaments 322-324, 323t
  training frequency for 316-317
  training intensity for 317
  training load considerations in 309-310
  training volumes for 315-316
  two-phase 314, 315f
  types of 313f, 313-315
task mastery 70
team sports
  aerobic energy contributions 48f
  anaerobic energy contributions 48f
  annual training plans for 110, 139, 437, 438f
  block-emphasis model for 123
  competition in 324-325
  competition period in 328
  cortisol levels in 288

emphasis training model for 438-439, 439f
energy systems in 41
external load in 269
GPS technology in 85
heart rate monitoring in 85
high-intensity interval training 388, 394
individual sports versus 321
intensity in 85
main competition phase for 134
microcycles for 172f, 173f, 174
monitoring program for 296
parallel models for 125
peak in 135
peaking performance for 321-324
physical training in 55
precompetition phase for 134
preparation period for 131
sequential training models for 159
sleep patterns in 221
tactical metabolic training in 60
tactical plan for 64, 69
tactical training in 80
tapering in 321-324
technical training in 80
tournaments in 322-324, 323t
training loads in 76
training sessions for 178f, 178-179, 182
technical abilities, physical training requirements for 55-56
technical skills 188
technical training
  aims of 60-61
  deliberate practice 61
  learning technique. *See* learning technique
  in microcycle 174
  overload application to 62
  progression application to 62
  reversibility application to 62
  specificity application to 62
  technique in 60
  tedium in 62-63
  training load application to 62
  transfer of 62
  variation in 62-63
technical training sessions 180
techno-tactical training sessions 180
tedium 62-63
10-point peaking index 146, 146t
terminal velocity threshold 338, 358
testosterone 287-288
testosterone:cortisol (T:C) ratio 97-98, 215, 288-289
thermoneutral water immersion 226-227
thermotherapy 225-226
30-15 intermittent fitness test 390-392
3:1 loading paradigm 94, 95f, 100
three-peak microcycle 169, 171f
time-motion analysis 272-273

time-series analysis 299
torque 338
Total Quality Recovery (TQR) scale 292-293
Touretski, Gennadi 116
tournaments, peaking performance for 322-324, 323t
traffic-light systems 300, 305, 429f
training
  adaptation. *See* adaptation(s)
  aerobic. *See* aerobic training
  aftereffects 22, 23f
  agility. *See* agility training
  anaerobic. *See* anaerobic training
  bioenergetic specificity of 46-49, 48t
  cessation of 135
  classification of 55-71
  components of 4
  definition of 4
  density of 82, 194
  endurance. *See* endurance training
  energetic profile of sport matched with 12
  exercising versus 4
  exploitation of 4-6
  to failure 350-351, 357
  fluid requirements 243-244
  frequency of. *See* training frequency
  genetic ceiling affected by 4
  glucose uptake in 17
  intensity of. *See* training intensity
  intervals between 19f
  mobility 423
  monitoring of. *See* monitoring
  multilateral 111, 124
  in multiple sessions 10-11
  negative effect to 319
  nonspecific 13
  optimization of. *See* optimization of training
  performance and, transferability between 12
  periodization of. *See* periodization
  phase potentiation in 99, 99f
  physical. *See* physical training
  plyometric 60, 339f, 374, 423
  positive effect to 319
  preparedness affected by 24f
  protein supplementation after 252
  psychological. *See* psychological training
  recovery and 15, 207
  rehydration after 244
  repetition maximum 356-357
  resistance. *See* resistance training
  sequencing of 119
  speed. *See* speed training
  sport-specific 89
  sprint. *See* sprint training
  strength. *See* strength training
  technical. *See* technical training

velocity-based 338, 357-360, 359f, 360f
vertical integration of 79
volume of. *See* training volume
training age 14, 81, 191, 326
training blocks. *See also* mesocycles
  accumulation mesocycle 116-117
  definition of 115, 152
  realization mesocycle 116-118
  transmutation mesocycle 116-117
training day
  monitoring program integration into 300-301, 303f
  multiple-session 194-195, 364
  noncompetition 194-195
  single-session 194
  structuring of 178, 192-195
  training sessions in 182, 194-195
training effects
  acute 77
  cumulative 77
  delayed 77-78, 78f, 162, 207
  immediate 77
  interactions of 79f
  long-lasting delayed 115
  paradox 13
  residual 78f, 78-79
  transfer of 420
training factors
  complementary 122, 123f
  description of 55, 56f, 169f, 170f, 171f
  in mesocycles 159-160
  repetitions 352-354, 353t
  set 354
  volume 355
training frequency
  definition of 81, 363
  description of 7, 11
  performance gains and 18
  recovery time and 81-82
  resistance training 363-365
  for taper 316-317
  training load affected by 81-82
training history 14
training impulse (TRIMP) 285-286, 296
training intensity
  carbohydrate supplementation based on 249
  in competition period 133
  definition of 82
  description of 7
  energy systems for 38, 38t
  fluctuations in 88f
  in general preparation phase 131
  heart rate monitoring for 85-86
  manipulation of 10
  overtraining and 210f, 210-211
  percentage-based methods for determining 355-356
  perception of effort for quantifying of 280
  performance and 86

pyruvate in 29
quantification of 85
rating of perceived exertion for determining 360-361
repetition maximum training for determining 356-357
repetition maximum zones for determining 357
repetitions in reserve for determining 361
resistance training 84, 85t
substrates depleted by 17
for taper 317
training load affected by 82-86
training plan effects on 87, 88f
velocity-based training methods for determining 357-360, 359f, 360f
volume of training and, interaction between 87-89
zones 83t, 83-84, 169t
training load(s)
  adaptation to 6, 90-91, 113. *See also* adaptation(s)
  balance in 6
  in competition period 133, 328
  concentrated loading 96-99, 97f
  definition of 76-77, 268
  density of training effects on 82
  description of 75-76
  designing of 91-92, 92f
  detraining from 9, 9f, 91
  dose–response relationship in 6, 268, 351
  excessive 8, 8f, 20
  external. *See* external training load
  factors contributing to 79-86, 80f
  fatigue and 19, 22, 217
  flat loading 93-94, 94f, 100
  frequency of training and 81-82
  GPS measurements of 273t
  for hypertrophy 351
  increases in 7-8
  individualization of 6, 9, 90
  injury and 6, 8-9
  intensity of 7, 356f
  internal load. *See* internal training load
  involution effect from 9, 9f
  linear loading 93
  manipulation of 329-332
  in mesocycle 159-160
  in microcycles 165, 365f
  monotonous 8, 8f, 10, 89, 211
  overload from 7-8, 8f
  overreaching in 9-10
  overtraining and 20, 114, 170
  performance and 318-319
  performance capacity and 8f, 8-9, 9f
  periodization of 76, 89
  prescription of 281
  in pretaper training period 309
  priming exercise and 196f
  progression of 91-98

psychological stress and 14
recovery considerations 92
repetitions and 352, 353t
repetitions in reserve for determining 361
retaining 91
sequencing of 98-101, 99f, 100f
session rating of perceived exertion scale for determining 281-282, 282f
standard loading 92-93
step loading 94-96, 95f, 96f, 100
stimulating 91
stimuli for adaptation from 7
technical training application of 62
testosterone to cortisol ratio affected by 215
tolerance to 90, 113f
training factors and 159
training intensity effects on 82-86
training session classification based on 181, 181f
useless 9
variations in 10, 89-90, 356f
velocity-based training methods for 358
volume of training and 79-81, 81f
training monotony 279t, 279-280, 302
training objectives 107, 174
training plans
annual. *See* annual training plans
foundational importance of 127-128
goal of 106
history of 106
individualized 5-6
intensity of training affected by 87, 88f
microcycles in 110-111
monotonous 10
multiyear 109, 128f, 128-130, 147-148
periodized. *See* periodized training plans
preparedness in 88f
scientific principles used in 5
stimuli for adaptation from 7
volume of training affected by 87, 88f
training process(es)
designing of 4
evolution of 3
exploitive nature of 4-5
frequency of training in 81
goals of 4, 6, 109, 201
individualized nature of 6, 90
monitoring during 90, 109
objective of 9
optimization of 4, 6-7
performance improvements through 109
progressive overload in 9
schematic diagram of 76f
scientific disciplines related to 4-5, 5f
systems-model approach to 319
volume of training in 79-81

training programs
age and level of maturity considerations 13-14
anthropometric characteristics 14
for children 13-14
current psychological state considerations 14
current work capacity considerations 14
development of 109
dynamic correspondence principle in 12
fitness level considerations 14
individualization of 13-14
injury status considerations 14
neuromuscular adaptations affected by structure of 345
pre-session delivery of 182
repetitions in 352-354, 353t
sets in 354
speed development 417
training age considerations 14
training history considerations 14
training sessions
assessment 180
blueprint for 191-192
body of 186-188
combined 180
on competition days 195, 196f
construction of 182, 192
cool-down 189f, 189-190
defining of 181-182
definition of 177
digital delivery applications for 191
duration of 181, 190t, 190-191, 364
endurance development in 188
factors that affect 186
fatigue from 190-191
group 178f, 178-179
handouts in 182
individual 178f, 179
intensity of 434
introduction section of 182
load classification 181, 181f
loading phase of 186
long-duration 181, 190
in microcycles 164, 165f
mixed 179
moderate-duration 181, 190
multiple per day 194-195, 364
multitask 188
on noncompetition training days 194-195
organization of 178f, 178-179, 182-190, 183f, 184f, 185f, 187t, 189f
physical 180
priming 195
recovery 180
rest intervals in 19
short-duration 181
sleep patterns affected by 222
speed and agility development in 188

strength development in 188
structure of 188
tactical 180
task classification 179-180
technical 180
technical and tactical development and mastery in 188
techno-tactical 180
template for 192f, 193f
training load classification 181, 181f
training units in 191
types of 178f, 178-179
variations in 177-178
virtual 179
volume load of 433
volume of 432
warm-up. *See* warm-up
training status 191, 218
training stimulus
adaptation and, relationship between 7f, 8f
continuum of 6
as external load 76
lactate accumulation affected by 34
overtraining and 8, 8f, 18
variation of 10-12
training strain 279t, 279-280
training stress 309
Training Stress Score (TSS) 271-272, 272f
training theories
central concept of 3
description of 1
fitness–fatigue model 22-23, 23f
general adaptive syndrome 20f, 20-22, 21f
generalized 20-24
supercompensation. *See* supercompensation
training units 174, 177, 191
training volume
in active rest 136
for agility training 432
assessment of 80
athlete development and 80
concentrated loading criteria for 114
description of 7, 10-11, 17
fatigue associated with 87-89
fluctuations in 88f
increases in 80-81
intensity of training and, interaction between 87-89
in main competition phase 134-135
overtraining and 209-210
recovery considerations 81
repetitions 80, 355
resistance training 276-278, 277t
sets 355
for speed training 432
for sprint training 432-433, 433t
for taper 315-316
training load affected by 79-81, 81f
training plan effects on 87, 88f

trans fats 242-243
transition period
　active rest 136, 138
　annual training plan created in 148
　in bi-cycle annual training plans 143-144
　definition of 135
　detraining and 135-139, 137f
　passive rest 135-136
　seasons 138, 138f
transmutation mesocycle block 116-117, 153, 155t
travel
　in-travel considerations 219, 220f
　jet lag from 218-219, 219f
　posttravel considerations 220, 220f
　pretravel considerations 219, 220f
　recovery affected by 218-220
　time-zone differentials in 218-219
travel fatigue 218, 219f
trend analyses 298f, 298-299, 299f
tri-cycle annual training plans 140f, 144f, 144-145
triglycerides 242
troponin C 29
tumor necrosis factor alpha 289
two-factor theory. *See* fitness–fatigue model
two-peak microcycle 167, 170f, 171f
two-phase taper 314, 315f

U

undertraining 6, 6f, 9
undulating cluster set 370, 370t, 371f
University of Montreal Track Test (UM-TT) 386
unsaturated fats 242
upper-body priming exercises 196f
urea 38
U.S. Anti-Doping Agency 253
useless load 9

V

variation
　definition of 10
　overload and 10
　periodization and 10, 107
　planning of 109
　programming of 109
　qualitative 11f, 11-12
　quantitative 10-11
　strength training and 420
　in supercompensation cycle 18
　in technical training 62-63
　in training load 10, 89-90
variational training models 111-114, 112f
vegans 240
vegetarians 240
velocity
　definition of 404
　maximal 84, 405, 408f, 409, 416, 435
　of movement 212-213, 273
velocity-based training (VBT) 338, 357-360, 359f, 360f
Verkhoshansky, Yuri 115, 116f
vertical integration 79
vertical integration model 121-122, 435
vertical jump performance 213-214
vertical jump tests 274
video coach 179
virtual training sessions 179
volume load
　calculations 277t, 278t, 355, 432
　definition of 276
　for resistance training 276-278, 277t, 320f
　for sprint training 278-279
　for training monotony 279t, 279-280
　for training strain 279t, 279-280

W

warm-up
　activate and mobilize phase of 185f, 185-186, 187t
　active 182-183
　components of 184f, 184-186
　dynamic 184, 184f
　general 184, 184f
　goal of 184
　non-temperature-related effects of 183, 183f
　passive 182
　postactivation performance enhancement 183
　postactivation potentiation 183
　potentiate phase of 185f, 185-186, 187t
　psychological benefits of 183
　raise phase of 185f, 185-186, 187t
　specific 184, 184f
　static stretching in 184
　temperature-related effects of 183, 183f
water immersion
　cold-water 224-228, 230-231
　hot-water 225, 228
　hydrostatic pressure during 226-227
　thermoneutral 226-227
wave loaded cluster set 370, 370t, 371f
wave loading 367-368, 368f
wearables 293, 295, 419
weekly undulating microcycle 378
Weigert's law of supercompensation 14. *See also* supercompensation
weightlifting 277t, 339-340, 340f, 349, 358, 423
whey protein 242, 252
Wingate anaerobic cycle test 38
workload
　acute 297
　chronic 297
　in general preparation phase 131
　heart rate and 85
　for mesocycles 153
　in parallel models 113f
　recovery time and 82
workload accumulation 96
workouts. *See* training sessions
World Anti-Doping Agency 253
wort 237

Z

Zátopek, Emil 383-384
zone of optimization 6, 6f

ABOUT THE AUTHOR

G. Gregory Haff, PhD, CSCS,*D, FNSCA, is a professor of strength and conditioning and the course coordinator for the postgraduate degree in strength and conditioning at Edith Cowan University in Joondalup, Australia. He has published more than 240 articles, centering his research on performance effects in the areas of strength-training methodologies, performance testing, training theory, and nutritional supplementation.

Haff is a past president of the National Strength and Conditioning Association (NSCA) and a senior associate editor for the *Journal of Strength and Conditioning Research*. He was the United Kingdom Strength and Conditioning Association (UKSCA) Strength and Conditioning Coach of the Year for Education and Research and the 2011 NSCA William J. Kraemer Outstanding Sport Scientist Award winner. He is a certified strength and conditioning specialist with distinction (CSCS,*D), a UKSCA-accredited strength and conditioning coach (ASCC), and an accredited Australian Strength and Conditioning Association level 2 strength and conditioning coach.

Additionally, Haff is a national-level weightlifting coach in the United States and Australia. He serves as a consultant for numerous sporting bodies, including teams in the Australian Football League, Australian Rugby Union, Australian Basketball Association, and National Football League.

HUMAN KINETICS
CONTINUING EDUCATION

Now that you've read the book, complete the companion exam to **earn continuing education credit!**

Find your CE exam here:

US & International: US.HumanKinetics.com/collections/Continuing-Education
Canada: Canada.HumanKinetics.com/collections/Continuing-Education

Subscribe to our newsletters today!

US   Canada

Get exclusive offers and stay apprised of CE opportunities.